Mind and Cognition

MIND AND COGNITION

A Reader

William G. Lycan

Basil Blackwell

Basil Blackwell, Inc.
3 Cambridge Center
Cambridge, Massachusetts 02142, USA

Basil Blackwell Ltd
108 Cowley Road, Oxford, OX4 1JF, UK

Library of Congress Cataloging in Publication Data

Mind and cognition.
    Includes index.
    1. Mind and body. 2. Thought and thinking.
3. Cognitive science. I. Lycan, William G.
BF171.M55 1989   128'.2   88-7915
ISBN 0-631-16076-0
ISBN 0-631-16763-3 (pbk.)

British Library Cataloguing in Publication Data

A CIP catalogue record for this book is available from the British Library.

Typeset in 9½ on 11 pt Ehrhardt
by Photo·graphics, Honiton, Devon
Printed in Great Britain by Biddles Ltd., Guildford

Contents

Preface

In the past thirty years, the philosophy of mind has seen a massive shift of doctrine, of method, and of perspective. Characteristic of this shift is the unprecedented attention of philosophers of mind to science: not only to psychology and linguistics, but to computer science, evolutionary biology and neuroanatomy as well. As a result, the mind–body problem is now better understood than at any previous point in human history – so I would contend, and the contention is borne out by the contents of this anthology. That is not to claim consensus for any one solution to the mind–body problem, for (of course) none exists. It is to claim a fairish consensus on questions of what the going arguments do and do not show, what the live options are, and what is at stake.

The essays and excerpts collected here are themselves predominantly philosophical. I would rather have assembled a more eclectic gathering, to include works written by empirical scientists with no speculative parsnips to butter, but the presentation of a significant number of such pieces as an integrated whole would have required a book-length introductory survey. The reader will have to rely on my bibliographies and (better) on my authors' footnotes.

Even regarding philosophy alone, my choice of headings for the various Parts, and of the readings themselves, reflects my no doubt tendentious view of the field and of what has happened in the philosophy of mind since the 1960s. Others may see things differently, and I am sure others would have included different items in the bibliographies.

This volume's closest and most distinguished predecessor is Ned Block (ed.), *Readings in Philosophy of Psychology*, vols One and Two (Cambridge: Harvard University Press, 1980). I thank Block for his unselfish encouragement of my own project, and I urge every reader who has already purchased a copy of this anthology to buy Block's as well.

My greatest debts are to Stephan Chambers, of Basil Blackwell Ltd, who suggested this anthology and has supported my work unstintingly, to Kim Sterelny for valuable discussions on choice of contents, and of course to the authors, especially to those who have contributed new or substantially revised essays.

I have written a brief synoptic introduction to each of the Parts. Citations in those introductions refer to items in the "Further reading" lists at the end of each introduction.

Part   I

Ontology from Behaviorism to
Functionalism

Introduction

Machine Functionalism supposed that human brains may be described at each of three levels, the first two scientific and the third familiar and commonsensical. (1) Biologists would map out human neuroanatomy and provide neurophysiological descriptions of brain states. (2) Psychologists would (eventually) work out the machine program that was being realized by the lower-level neuroanatomy and would describe the same brain states in more abstract, computational terms. (3) Psychologists would also explain behavior, characterized in everyday terms, by reference to stimuli and to intervening mental states such as beliefs and desires, type-identifying the mental states with functional or computational states as they went. Such explanations would themselves presuppose nothing about neuroanatomy, since the relevant psychological/computational generalizations would hold regardless of what particular biochemistry might happen to be realizing the abstract program in question.

Machine Functionalism as described has more recently been challenged on each of a number of points, that together motivate a specifically teleological notion of "function" (Sober (this volume) speaks aptly of "putting the function back into Functionalism"):

(i) The Machine Functionalist still conceived psychological *explanation* in the Positivists' terms of subsumption of data under wider and wider universal generalizations. But Fodor (1968), Cummins (1983) and Dennett (this volume) have defended a competing picture of psychological explanation, according to which behavioral data are to be seen as manifestations of subjects' psychological capacities, and those capacities are to be explained by understanding the subjects as systems of interconnected components. Each component is a "homunculus," in that it is identified by reference to the function it performs, and the various homuncular components cooperate with each other in such a way as to produce overall behavioral responses to stimuli. The "homunculi" are themselves broken down into subcomponents whose functions and interactions are similarly used to explain the capacities of the subsystems they compose, and so again and again until the sub-sub- . . . components are seen to be neuroanatomical structures. (An automobile works – locomotes – by having a fuel reservoir, a fuel line, a carburetor, a combustion chamber, an ignition system, a

Behaviorism

In psychology, Behaviorism took primarily a methodological form: Psychological Behaviorists claimed (i) that psychology itself is a science for the prediction and control of behavior, (ii) that the only proper data or observational input for psychology are behavioral, specifically patterns of physical responses to physical stimuli, and (iii) that *inner* states and events, neurophysiological or mental, are not proper objects of psychological investigation – neurophysiological states and events are the business of biologists, and mental states and events, so far as they exist at all, are not to be mentioned unless operationalized nearly to death. Officially, the Psychological Behaviorists made no metaphysical claims; minds and mental entities might exist for all they knew, but this was not to be presumed in psychological experiment or theorizing. Psychological theorizing was to consist, *à la* Logical Positivism, of the subsuming of empirically established stimulus–response generalizations under broader stimulus–response generalizations.

In philosophy, Behaviorism did (naturally) take a metaphysical form: chiefly that of Analytical Behaviorism, the claim that mental ascriptions simply *mean* things about behavioral responses to environmental impingements. Thus, "Edmund is in pain" means, not anything about Edmund's putative inner life or any episode taking place within Edmund, but that Edmund either is actually behaving in a wincing-and-groaning way or is disposed so to behave (in that he would so behave were something not keeping him from so doing). "Edmund believes that broccoli will kill him" means just that if asked, Edmund will assent to that proposition, and if confronted by broccoli, Edmund will shun it, and so forth.

But it should be noted that a Behaviorist metaphysician need make no claim about the meanings of mental expressions. One might be a merely Reductive Behaviorist, and hold that although mental ascriptions do not *simply mean* things about behavioral responses to stimuli, they are ultimately (in reality) made true just by things about actual and counterfactual responses to stimuli. (On the difference between "analytic" reduction by linguistic meaning and "synthetic" reduction by *a posteriori* identification, see the next section of this introduction.) Or one might be an Eliminative Behaviorist, and hold that there are no mental states or events at all, but only behavioral responses to stimuli, mental ascriptions being uniformly false or meaningless.

Any Behaviorist will subscribe to what has come to be called the "Turing Test." In response to the perennially popular question "Can machines think?", Alan Turing (1964) replied that a better question is that of whether a sophisticated computer could ever pass a battery of (verbal) behavioral tests, to the extent of fooling a limited observer into thinking it is human and sentient; if a machine did pass such tests, then the putatively further question of whether the machine really *thought* would be idle at best, whatever metaphysical analysis one might attach to it. Barring Turing's tendentious limitation of the machine's behavior to verbal as opposed to nonverbal responses, any Behaviorist, psychological or philosophical, would agree that psychological differences cannot outrun behavioral test; organisms (including machines) whose actual and counterfactual behavior is just the same are psychologically just alike.

Philosophical Behaviorism adroitly avoided a number of nasty objections to

Cartesian Dualism (see Carnap 1932/33; Ryle 1949; Place, this volume; Smart 1959; Armstrong 1968, ch. 5; Campbell 1984), even besides solving the methodological problem of intersubjective verification: it dispensed with immaterial Cartesian egos and ghostly nonphysical events, writing them off as ontological excrescences. It disposed of Descartes's admitted problem of mind–body interaction, since it posited no immaterial, nonspatial causes of behavior. It raised no scientific mysteries concerning the intervention of Cartesian substances in physics or biology, since it countenanced no such intervention.

Yet some theorists were uneasy; they felt that in its total repudiation of the inner, Behaviorism was leaving out something real and important. When they voiced this worry, the Behaviorists often replied with mockery, assimilating the doubters to old-fashioned Dualists who believed in ghosts, ectoplasm, and/or the Easter Bunny. Behaviorism was the only (even halfway sensible) game in town. None the less, the doubters made several lasting points against it. First, anyone who is honest and not anaesthetized knows perfectly well that he/she experiences and can introspect actual inner mental episodes or occurrences, that are neither actually accompanied by characteristic behavior nor are merely static hypothetical facts of how he/she would behave if subjected to such-and-such a stimulation. Place (this volume) speaks of an "intractable residue" of conscious mental states that bear no clear relations to behavior of any particular sort; see also Armstrong (1968, ch. 5) and Campbell (1984). Second, contrary to the Turing Test, it seems perfectly possible for two people to differ psychologically despite total similarity of their actual and counterfactual behavior, as in a Lockean case of "inverted spectrum"; for that matter, a creature *might* exhibit all the appropriate stimulus–response relations and lack mentation entirely (Campbell 1984; Fodor and Block 1972; Block 1981; Kirk 1974). Third, the Analytical Behaviorist's behavioral analyses of mental ascriptions seem adequate only so long as one makes substantive assumptions about the rest of the subject's *mentality* (Chisholm 1957, ch. 11; Geach 1957, p. 8; Block 1981), and so are either circular or radically incomplete as analyses of the mental generally.

So matters stood in stalemate between Dualists, Behaviorists and doubters, until the mid-1950s, when Place (this volume) and Smart (1959) proposed a middle way, an irenic solution.

The Identity Theory

According to Place and Smart, contrary to the Behaviorists, at least some mental states and events are genuinely inner and genuinely episodic after all. They are not to be identified with outward behavior or even with hypothetical dispositions to behave. But, contrary to the Dualists, the episodic mental items are not ghostly or nonphysical either. Rather, they are neurophysiological. They are identical with states and events occurring in their owners' central nervous systems; more precisely, every mental state or event is numerically identical with some such neurophysiological state or event. To be in pain is to have one's (for example) c-fibers, or possibly a-fibers, firing; to believe that broccoli will kill you is to have one's B_{bk}-fibers firing, and so on.

By making the mental entirely physical, this Identity Theory of the mind shared the Behaviorist advantage of avoiding the nasty objections to Dualism; but it also brilliantly accommodated the inner and the episodic as the Behaviorists did not. For according to the Identity Theory, mental states and events actually occur in their owners' central nervous systems; hence they are *inner* in an even more literal sense than could be granted by Descartes. The Identity Theory also thoroughly vindicated the idea that organisms could differ mentally despite total behavioral similarity, since clearly organisms can differ neurophysiologically in mediating their outward stimulus–response regularities. And of course the connection between a belief or a desire and the usually accompanying behavior is defeasible by other current mental states, since the connection between a *B-* or *D-* neural state and its normal behavioral effect is defeasible by other psychologically characterizable interacting neural states. The Identity Theory was the ideal resolution of the Dualist/Behaviorist impasse.

Moreover, there was a direct deductive argument for the Identity Theory, hit upon independently by David Lewis (1972) and D. M. Armstrong (1968, this volume). Lewis and Armstrong maintained that mental terms were *defined* causally, in terms of mental items' typical causes and effects. For example, "pain" *means* a state that is typically brought about by physical damage and that typically causes withdrawal, favoring, complaint, desire for cessation, and so on. (Armstrong claimed to establish this by straightforward "conceptual analysis"; Lewis held that mental terms are the theoretical terms of a commonsensical "folk theory" (see Part VI below), and with the Positivists that all theoretical terms are implicitly defined by the theories in which they occur.) Now if by definition, pain is whatever state occupies a certain causal niche, and if, as is overwhelmingly likely, scientific research reveals that that particular niche is in fact occupied by such-and-such a neurophysiological state, it follows by the transitivity of identity that pain is that neurophysiological state; QED. Pain retains its conceptual connection to behavior, but also undergoes an empirical identification with an inner state of its owner. (An advanced if convolute elaboration of this already hybrid view is developed by Lewis (1980); for meticulous criticism, see Block (1978), Shoemaker (1981) and Tye (1983).)

Notice that although Armstrong and Lewis began their arguments with a claim about the meanings of mental terms, their Common-Sense Causal version of the Identity Theory itself was no such thing, any more than was the original Identity Theory of Place and Smart. Rather, all four philosophers relied on the idea that things or properties can sometimes be identified with "other" things or properties even when there is no synonymy of terms; there is such a thing as synthetic and *a posteriori* identity that is nonetheless genuine identity. While the identity of triangles with trilaterals holds simply in virtue of the meanings of the two terms and can be established by reason alone, without empirical investigation, the following identities are standard examples of the synthetic *a posteriori*, and were discovered empirically: clouds with masses of water droplets; water with H_2O; lightning with electrical discharge; the Morning Star with Venus; Mendelian genes with segments of DNA molecules; temperature (of a gas) with mean molecular kinetic energy. The Identity Theory was offered similarly, in a spirit of scientific speculation; one could not properly object that mental expressions do not mean anything about brains or neural firings.

So the Dualists were wrong in thinking that mental items are nonphysical but right in thinking them inner and episodic; the Behaviorists were right in their physicalism but wrong to repudiate inner mental episodes. Alas, this happy synthesis was too good to be true.

Machine Functionalism

In the mid-1960s Putnam (1960, this volume) and Fodor (1968) pointed out a presumptuous implication of the Identity Theory understood as a theory of "types" or *kinds* of mental items: that a mental state such as pain has *always and everywhere* the neurophysiological characterization initially assigned to it. For example, if the Identity Theorist identified pain itself with the firings of c-fibers, it followed that a creature of any species (earthly or science-fiction) could be in pain only if that creature *had* c-fibers and they were firing. But such a constraint on the biology of any being capable of feeling pain is both gratuitous and indefensible; why should we suppose that any organism must be made of the same chemical materials as we in order to have what can be accurately recognized as pain? The Identity Theorist had overreacted to the Behaviorists' difficulties and focused too narrowly on the specifics of biological humans' actual inner states, and in so doing they had fallen into species chauvinism.

Fodor and Putnam advocated the obvious correction: What was important was not its being c-fibers (*per se*) that were firing, but what the c-fiber firings were doing, what their firing contributed to the operation of the organism as a whole. The *role* of the c-fibers could have been performed by any mechanically suitable component; so long as that role was performed, the psychology of the containing organism would have been unaffected. Thus, to be in pain is not *per se* to have c-fibers that are firing, but merely to be in some state or other, of whatever biochemical description, that plays the same causal role as did the firings of c-fibers in the human beings we have investigated. We may continue to maintain that pain "tokens," individual instances of pain occurring in particular subjects at particular times, are strictly identical with particular neurophysiological states of those subjects at those times, viz., with the states that happen to be playing the appropriate roles; this is the thesis of "token identity" or "token physicalism." But pain itself, the kind, universal or "type," can be identified only with something more abstract: the causal or functional role that c-fiber firings share with their potential replacements or surrogates. Mental state-types are identified not with neurophysiological types but with more abstract functional roles, as specified by state-tokens' causal relations to the organism's sensory inputs, motor outputs, and other psychological states.

Putnam compared mental states to the functional or "logical" states of a computer: just as a computer program can be realized or instantiated by any of a number of physically different hardware configurations, so a psychological "program" can be realized by different organisms of various physiochemical composition, and that is why different physiological states of organisms of different species can realize one and the same mental state-type. Where an Identity Theorist's type-identification would take the form, "To be in mental state of type M is to be in the neurophysiological state of type N," Putnam's Machine Functionalism (as I shall call it) has it that to be in M is to be merely in some physiological state or other that plays role R in the relevant computer program (that is, the program that at a suitable level of abstraction mediates the creature's total outputs given total inputs and so serves as the creature's global psychology). The physiological state "plays role R" in that it stands in a set of relations to physical inputs, outputs and other inner states that matches one-to-one the abstract input/output/logical-state relations codified in the computer program.

The Functionalist, then, mobilizes three distinct levels of description but applies them all to the same fundamental reality. A physical state-token in someone's brain at a particular time has a neurophysiological description, but may also have a functional description relative to a machine program that the brain happens to be realizing, and it may further have a mental description if some mental state is correctly type-identified with the functional category it exemplifies. And so there is after all a sense in which "the mental" is distinct from "the physical": though there are no nonphysical substances or stuffs, and every mental token is itself entirely physical, mental characterization is not physical characterization, and the property of being a pain is not simply the property of being such-and-such a neural firing.

Cognitive Psychology

In a not accidentally similar vein, Psychological Behaviorism has almost entirely given way to "Cognitivism" in psychology. Cognitivism is roughly the view that (i) psychologists may and must advert to inner states and episodes in explaining behavior, so long as the states and episodes are construed throughout as physical, and (ii) human beings and other psychological organisms are best viewed as in some sense *information-processing* systems. As cognitive psychology sets the agenda, its questions take the form, "How does this organism receive information through its sense-organs, process the information, store it, and then mobilize it in such a way as to result in intelligent behavior?" During the 1960s, the cognitive psychologists' initially vague notion of "information processing" (inspired in large part by the popularity of "Information Theory" in regard to physical systems of communication) became the idea that organisms employ internal representations and perform computational operations on those representations; *cognition* became a matter of the rule-governed manipulation of representations much as it occurs in actual digital computers.

The working language of cognitive psychology is of course highly congenial to the Functionalist, for Cognitivism thinks of human beings as systems of interconnected functional components, interacting with each other in an efficient and productive way.

Artificial Intelligence and the computer model of the mind

Meanwhile, researchers in computer science have pursued fruitful research programs based on the idea of intelligent behavior as the output of skillful information-processing given input. Artificial Intelligence (AI) is, roughly, the project of getting computing machines to perform tasks that would usually be taken to demand human intelligence and judgment. Computers have achieved some modest success in proving theorems, guiding missiles, sorting mail, driving assembly-line robots, diagnosing illnesses, predicting weather and economic events, and the like. A computer *just is* a machine that receives, interprets, processes, stores, manipulates and uses information, and AI researchers think of it in just that way as they try to program intelligent behavior; an AI problem takes the form, "Given that the machine sees this as input, what must it already know and what must it accordingly do with that input in order to be able to . . . [recognize, identify, sort, put together, predict, tell us, etc.] . . .? And how, then, can we start it off knowing that and get it to do those things?" So we may reasonably attribute such success as AI has had to self-conscious reliance on the information-processing paradigm.

This encourages the aforementioned idea that *human* intelligence and cognition generally are matters of computational information-processing. Indeed, that idea has already filtered well down into the everyday speech of ordinary people, among whom computer jargon is fairly common. This tentative and crude coalescing of the notions *cognition, computation, information,* and *intelligence* raises two general questions, one in each of two directions. First, to what extent might computers approximate minds? Second, to what extent do minds approximate computers?

The first question breaks down into three, which differ sharply and importantly from each other. (i) What intelligent tasks will any computer ever be able to perform? (ii) Given that a computer performs interesting tasks X, Y and Z, does it do so *in the same way* that human beings do? (iii) Given that a computer performs X, Y and Z and that it does so in the same way humans do, does that show that it has psychological and mental properties, such as (real) intelligence, thought, consciousness, feeling, sensation, emotion, and the like? Subquestion (i) is one of engineering, (ii) is one of cognitive psychology, and (iii) is philosophical; theorists' answers will depend accordingly on their commitments in these respective areas. (See particularly part VIII below.) But for the record let us distinguish three different senses or grades of "AI": AI in the weakest sense is cautiously optimistic as regards (i); it says these engineering efforts are promising and should be funded. AI in a stronger sense says that the engineering efforts can well serve as modellings of human cognition, and that their successes can be taken as pointers toward the truth about human functional organization. AI in the strongest sense favors an affirmative answer to (iii) and some qualified respect for the Turing Test: it says that if a machine performs intelligently *and* does so on the basis of a sufficiently human-like information-processing etiology, then there is little reason to doubt that the machine has the relevant human qualities of mind and sensation. (AI in the strongest sense is fairly strong, but notice carefully that it does not presuppose affirmative answers to either (i) or (ii).)

The opposite issue, that of assimilating minds to computers, is very close to the philosophical matter of Functionalism. But here too there are importantly distinct subquestions, this time two: (i) Do human minds work in very like the way computers do as computers are currently designed and construed; for example, using flipflops grouped into banks and registers, with an assembly language collecting individual machine-code operations into subroutines and these subroutines being called by higher-level manipulations of real-world information according to programmed rules? (ii) Regardless of architecture, can human psychological capacities be entirely captured by a third-person, hardware-realizable design of *some* sort that could in principle be built in a laboratory? Subquestion (i) is very current (see Parts IV through VI below), but is not particularly philosophical. Subquestion (ii) is tantamount to the fate of Functionalism.

Chronic problems

Functionalism, cognitive psychology considered as a complete theory of human thought, and AI in the strongest sense all inherit some of the same problems that earlier beset Behaviorism and the Identity Theory. These remaining problems fall into two main categories, respectively headed, by philosophers, "qualia" and "intentionality."

The "quale" of a mental state or event is that state or event's *feel*, its introspectible "phenomenal character." Many philosophers have objected that neither Functionalist metaphysics nor cognitive psychology nor AI nor the computer model of the mind can explain, illuminate, acknowledge or even tolerate the notion of *what it feels like* to be in a mental state of such-and-such a sort. Yet, say these philosophers, the feels are quintessentially mental – it is the feels that make the mental states the mental states they are. Something, therefore, must be drastically wrong with Functionalism, cognitive psychology, AI in the strongest sense, and the computer model of the mind. Such "qualia"-based objections and responses to them will be the topic of Part VII below.

"Intentionality" is a feature common to most mental states and events, particularly the "propositional attitudes," those cognitive and conative states that are described in everyday language with the use of "that"-clauses. One believes *that broccoli is lethal*, desires *that visitors should wipe their feet*, hopes *that the Republican candidate will win*, etc. Other propositional attitudes include thoughts, intentions, rememberings, doubts, wishes, and wonderings.

A "that"-clause contains what is itself grammatically a sentence; intuitively that internal sentence expresses the "content" of the belief, desire, or other attitude in question. This is because propositional attitudes *represent* actual or possible states of affairs. That indeed is what makes them propositional attitudes, and accordingly they are described in terms of their respective representational contents.

The objects and states of affairs upon which our propositional attitudes are directed may actually obtain, in the real world. But equally they may not: beliefs are often false, desires can be frustrated, hopes may be dashed. The attitudes may also be about "things" that do not exist: Sherlock Holmes, the Easter Bunny, the free lunch. Franz Brentano raised the question of how any purely physical entity or state could have the property of being about or "directed upon" a nonexistent state of affairs or object; that is not the sort of feature that ordinary, purely physical objects can have. Many philosophers, including Chisholm (1957), have argued that no purely physical account of a system or organism, human or computer, could explain Brentano's property. That difficulty for Functionalism et al. will be addressed in Parts V and VI.

In alluding to sensory states and to mental states with intentional content, we have said nothing specifically about the emotions. Since the rejection of Behaviorism, theories of mind have tended not to be applied directly to the emotions; rather, the emotions have been generally thought to be conceptually analyzable as complexes of more central or "core" mental states, typically propositional attitudes such as belief and desire (and the intentionality of emotions has accordingly been traced back to that of attitudes). Armstrong (1968, ch. 8, sec. III) took essentially this line, as do Solomon (1977) and Gordon (1987). However, there is a nascent literature on Functionalism and the emotions; see Rey 1980 and some of the other papers collected in Rorty 1980. Some psychological literature on the topic is collected in Clark and Fiske 1982 and Scherer and Ekman 1984; the latter is especially useful to Functionalists.

It may be wondered whether materialist theories of the mind and/or functionalist theories in particular have any interesting implications for morality and ethics. Three materialists take this up explicitly: Smart (1963, ch. VIII), tries to exhibit a materialist basis for morals; Michael Levin (1979, ch. VII) addresses the specific charge that materialists cannot allow freedom of the will or whatever else may be necessary to make room for moral responsibility; Lycan (1985) explores some moral consequences of the computational view of the mind. A main purpose of Dennett 1978 is also to show why moral responsibility and the mental vernacular that supports it are possible despite Dennett's instrumentalist – sometimes fictionalist – treatment of the mental (see Part III of this volume).

FURTHER READING

Useful general works on theories of mind
Campbell, K. K. (1984) *Body and Mind* (2nd edn), University of Notre Dame Press.
Churchland, P. M. (1988) *Matter and Consciousness* (2nd edn), Bradford Books/MIT Press.

Both books contain very clear discussions of Dualism, Behaviorism, the Identity Theory and Functionalism, as well as bibliographies. Churchland's takes up some of the newer developments in "neurophilosophy" (see Part IV). See also McGinn, C. (1982) *The Character of Mind*, Oxford University Press; and Smith, P. and Jones, O. R. (1986) *The Philosophy of Mind*, Cambridge University Press.

Psychological Behaviorism
Skinner, B. F. (1933) *Science and Human Behavior*, Macmillan.
Chomsky, N. (1959) Review of B. F. Skinner's *Verbal Behavior*, *Language* 35, 26–58.
Behavioral and Brain Sciences 7, 4 (1984), a special issue on the "Canonical papers of B. F. Skinner." [See particularly Skinner's "Representations and misrepresentations." 655–65, his response to "Open peer commentary" on his article "Behaviorism at fifty."]

Analytical Behaviorism
Carnap, R. (1932/33) "Psychology in physical language," *Erkenntnis* 3, 107–42. [In the full text, Carnap considers possible objections at length.]
Hempel, C.G. (1949) "The logical analysis of psychology," in H. Feigl and W. Sellars (eds), *Readings in Philosophical Analysis*, Appleton Century Crofts.
Ryle, G. (1949) *The Concept of Mind*, Barnes and Noble.
Chisholm, R. M. (1957) *Perceiving*, Cornell University Press.
Geach, P. (1957) *Mental Acts*, Routledge & Kegan Paul.
Putnam, H. (1965) "Brains and behaviour," in R. J. Butler (ed.), *Analytical Philosophy, Part II*, Basil Blackwell.

The Turing Test

Turing, A. M. (1964) "Computing machinery and intelligence," reprinted in A. R. Anderson (ed.), *Minds and Machines*, Prentice-Hall.

Gunderson, K. (1985) *Mentality and Machines* (2nd edn), University of Minnesota Press.

Block, N. J. (1981) "Psychologism and Behaviorism," *Philosophical Review* 90, 5–43.

Rosenberg, J. F. (1982) "Conversation and intelligence," in B. de Gelder (ed.), *Knowledge and Representation*, Routledge & Kegan Paul.

Dennett, D. C. (1985) "Can machines think?", in M. Shafto (ed.), *How We Know*, Harper & Row.

The Identity Theory

Smart, J. J. C. (1959) "Sensations and brain processes," *Philosophical Review* 68, 141–56.

Feigl, H. (1967) *The "Mental" and the "Physical": The Essay and a Postscript*, University of Minnesota Press.

Presley, C. F. (ed.) (1967) *The Identity Theory of Mind*, University of Queensland Press.

Borst, C. V. (ed.), (1970) *The Mind/Brain Identity Theory*, Macmillan.

The Common-Sense Causal Theory

Armstrong, D. M. (1968) *A Materialist Theory of the Mind*, Routledge & Kegan Paul.

Armstrong, D. M. (1981) "Epistemological foundations for a materialist theory of the mind," reprinted in *The Nature of Mind and Other Essays*, Cornell University Press.

Lewis, D. (1972) "Psychophysical and theoretical identifications," *Australasian Journal of Philosophy* 50, 249–58.

Nagel, T. (1970) "Armstrong on the mind," *Philosophical Review* 79, 394–403.

Pappas, G. (1977) "Armstrong's Materialism," *Canadian Journal of Philosophy* 7, 569–92.

Block, N. J. (1978) "Troubles with Functionalism," in W. Savage (ed.), *Perception and Cognition: Minnesota Studies in the Philosophy of Science*, vol. IX, University of Minnesota Press. [N.b., Block's section on Lewis is included in neither the short version of his paper reprinted in this volume nor that reprinted in his own anthology, *Readings in Philosophy of Psychology, vol. One* (Harvard University Press, 1980).]

Lewis, D. (1980) "Mad pain and Martian pain," in N. Block (ed.), *Readings in Philosophy of Psychology, vol. One*, ibid.

Shoemaker, S. (1981) "Some varieties of Functionalism," *Philosophical Topics* 12, 93–119.

Tye, Michael (1983) "Functionalism and Type Physicalism," *Philosophical Studies* 44, 161–74.

Machine Functionalism

Putnam, H. (1960), "Minds and machines," in S. Hook (ed.), *Dimensions of Mind*, Collier Books.

Putnam, H. (1967) "The mental life of some machines," in H.-N. Castañeda (ed.), *Intentionality, Minds, and Perception*, Wayne State University Press.

Fodor, J. A. (1968) *Psychological Explanation*, Random House.

Kalke, W. (1969) "What is wrong with Fodor and Putnam's Functionalism?," *Noûs* 3, 83–94.

Rorty, R. (1972) "Functionalism, machines, and incorrigibility," *Journal of Philosophy* 69, 203–20.

Fodor, J. A., and Block, N. J. (1972) "What psychological states are not," *Philosophical Review* 81, 159–81.

Lycan, W. (1974) "Mental states and Putnam's Functionalist hypothesis," *Australasian Journal of Philosophy* 52, 48–62.

Cognitive Psychology

Johnson-Laird, P. N., and Wason, P. C. (1977) *Thinking: Readings in Cognitive Science*, Cambridge University Press.

Anderson, J.R . (1985) *Cognitive Psychology and its Implications* (2nd edn), W. H. Freeman.

Glass, A. L. and Holyoak, K. J. (1986) *Cognition* (2nd edn), Random House.

Artificial Intelligence and the computer model of the mind

Hofstadter, D. (1979) *Gödel, Escher, Bach: An Eternal Golden Braid*, Basic Books. [See also Hofstadter, D. and Dennett, D. C. (eds) (1981), *The Mind's I: Fantasies and Reflections on Self and Soul*, Basic Books.]

Ringle, M. (ed.) (1979) *Philosophical Perspectives in Artificial Intelligence*, Harvester Press.

Winston, P. H. (1984) *Artificial Intelligence* (2nd edn), Addison-Wesley.

Pylyshyn, Z. W. (1984) *Computation and Cognition: Toward a Foundation for Cognitive Science*, MIT Press.

Charniak, E. and McDermott, D. (1985) *Introduction to Artificial Intelligence*, Addison-Wesley.

Dennett, D. C. (1986) "The logical geography of computational approaches: a view from the East Pole," in M. Brand and R. M. Harnish (eds), *The Representation of Knowledge and Belief*, University of Arizona Press.

Johnson-Laird, P. (1988) *The Computer and the Mind*, Harvard University Press.

See also the works cited in the Introduction to Part VIII.

Emotions

Clark, M. S. and Fiske, S. (eds) (1982) *Affect and Cognition*, Lawrence Erlbaum Associates.

de Sousa, R. (1987) *The Rationality of Emotion*, Bradford Books/MIT Press.

Gordon, R. M. (1987) *The Structure of Emotions*, Cambridge University Press.

Rey, G. (1980) "Functionalism and the Emotions," in Rorty 1980.

Rorty, A. O. (ed.) (1980) *Explaining Emotions*, University of California Press.

Scherer, K. R. and Ekman, P. (eds) (1984) *Approaches to Emotion*, Lawrence Erlbaum Associates.

Solomon, R. (1977) *The Passions*, Doubleday.

Morality

Levin, M. (1979) *Metaphysics and the Mind–Body Problem*, Oxford University Press.

Lycan, W. (1985) "Abortion and the civil rights of machines," in N. T. Potter and M. Timmons (eds), *Morality and Universality*, D. Reidel.

Smart, J. J. C. (1963) *Philosophy and Scientific Realism*, Routledge & Kegan Paul.

1

Behaviorism

An excerpt from "Talking and Thinking," chapter 10 of *Behaviorism*

J. B. WATSON

The Behaviorist's View of Thought

The behaviorist advances the view that *what the psychologists have hitherto called thought is in short nothing but talking to ourselves.* The evidence for this view is admittedly largely theoretical but it is the one theory so far advanced which explains thought in terms of natural science. I wish here expressly to affirm that in developing this view I have never believed that the *laryngeal movements* . . . as such played the predominating role in thought. I admit that in my former presentations I have, in order to gain pedagogical simplicity, expressed myself in ways which can be so interpreted. We have all had the proofs before us time and again that the larynx can be removed without completely destroying a person's ability to think. Removal of the larynx does destroy articulate speech but it does not destroy whispered speech. Whispered speech (without articulation) depends upon muscular responses of the cheek, tongue, throat and chest – organization which, to be sure, has been built up with the use of the larynx, but which remains ready to function after the larynx has been removed. Anyone who has read my various presentations knows that I have tried everywhere to emphasize the enormous complexity of the musculature in the throat and chest. To claim that a mass of cartilage such as that composing the larynx is responsible for thought (internal speech) is like saying that the bone and cartilage that make up the elbow joint form the chief organ with which one plays tennis.

My theory does hold that the muscular habits learned in overt speech are responsible for implicit or internal speech (thought). It holds, too, that there are hundreds of muscular combinations with which one can say either aloud or to himself almost any word, so rich and so flexible is language organization and so varied are our overt speech habits. A good imitator, as you already know, can say the same phrases in dozens of different ways, in a bass voice, in a tenor voice, in a mezzo, in a soprano, in a loud whisper, in a soft whisper, as an English cockney would say them, as a broken-English-speaking Frenchman would say them, as a Southerner would say them, as a child, etc. The number and variety of habits we form in the speaking of almost every word is thus well nigh legion. We use speech, from infancy on, a thousand times to using our hands once. From this circumstance there grows up a complexity of organization which even the psychologist seemingly cannot grasp. Again, after our overt speech habits are formed, we are constantly talking to ourselves (thought). New combinations occur, new complexities arise, new substitutions take place – for example, where the shrug of the shoulders or the movement of any other bodily part becomes substituted for a word. Soon *any, and every* bodily response *may become a word substitute* . . .

The alternative sometimes advanced to this theory is that so-called central processes may take place in the brain so faintly that no neural impulse passes out over the motor nerve to the muscle, hence no response takes place in the muscles and glands. Even Lashley and his students, on account of their strong interest in the nervous system, seem to hold this view. Recently Agnes M. Thorson[1] has found that tongue movements are not universally present in internal speech. This, even if true, can have no bearing upon the present view. The tongue, while bearing very delicate receptors, is on the muscular side a bulk organ for rolling our food around. It plays a part in internal speech to be sure, but probably about the same part that the fist of the jazz cornet player plays when he thrusts it into the horn to modify the sound.

Some Positive Evidence for the Behaviorist's View

(1) Our main line of evidence comes from watching the child's behavior. The child talks incessantly when alone . . . At three he even plans the day aloud, as my own ear placed outside the keyhole of the nursery door has very often confirmed. Aloud he voices (may I use literary terms and not psychological ones?) his wishes, his hopes, his fears, his annoyances, his dissatisfactions with his nurse or his father. Soon society in the form of nurse and parents steps in. "Don't talk aloud – daddy and mother are not always talking to themselves." Soon the overt speech dies down to whispered speech and a good lip reader can still read what the child thinks of the world and of himself. Some individuals never even make this concession to society. When alone they talk aloud to themselves. A still larger number never go beyond even the whispering stage when alone. Watch people reading on the street car; peep through the keyhole some time when individuals not too highly socialized are just sitting and thinking. But the great majority of people pass on to the third stage under the influence of social pressure constantly exerted. "Quit whispering to yourself," and "Can't you even read without moving your lips?" and the like are constant mandates. Soon the process is forced to take

place behind the lips. Behind these walls you can call the biggest bully the worst name you can think of without even smiling. You can tell the female bore how terrible she really is and the next moment smile and overtly pay her a verbal compliment.

(2) I have collected considerable evidence that those deaf and dumb individuals who when talking use manual movements instead of words, use the same manual responses they employ in talking, in their own thinking. But even here society forces minimal movements so that evidence of overt responses is often hard to obtain. To Dr W. I. Thomas I am indebted for the following observation: Dr Samuel Gridley Howe, Superintendent of the Perkins Institute and Massachusetts Asylum for the Blind, taught the deaf, dumb, and blind Laura Bridgman a hand and finger language. He states (in one of the annual reports of the Institute) *that even in her dreams Laura talked to herself using the finger language with great rapidity.*

Possibly it always will be difficult to obtain an overwhelming mass of positive evidence for this view. The processes are faint and other processes such as swallowing, breathing, circulation, etc., are always going on and they will probably always obscure the more delicate internal speech activities. But there is no other theory at present advanced which is tenable – no other view in line with the known facts of physiology.

This throws all the burden of proof on any contrary hypothesis, such as that advanced by the imagists and by the psychological irradiationists. Naturally we are all interested in facts. If when they are obtained they make the present theory untenable, the behaviorist will give it up cheerfully. But the whole physiological conception of motor activity – that motor activity follows sensory stimulation – will have to be given up along with it.

When and How We Think

Before trying to answer the question "When do we think?", let me put a question to you. When do you act with your hands, legs, trunk, etc? You answer rightly, "Whenever action with hands and legs and trunk will help me escape from a situation to which I am not adjusted." The example I used in the last lecture . . . was walking to the icebox and eating when stomach contractions became intense; or pasting a piece of paper over a hole in the window shade to shut out the light. I would like to ask one other question, too. When do we *overtly* act with the laryngeal muscles – in other words, when do we talk and whisper aloud? The answer is: Whenever a situation demands it – whenever overt action with the voice will help us out of a situation which we cannot get out of otherwise. For example: I get upon a platform to lecture; I won't get my fifty dollars unless the words are forthcoming. I have broken through the ice and am in the water; I cannot get out unless I call aloud for help. Again, somebody asks me a question; politeness bids me return a civil answer.

This all seems fairly clear. Now let us go back to our original question – when do we think? And please bear in mind that thinking with us is subvocal talking. We think whenever by the subvocal use of our language organization we can escape from a situation to which we are not adjusted. Thousands of examples of such situations confront you almost daily. I will give you a rather dramatic one.

R's employer called him in one day and said, "I think you would become a much more stable member of this organization if you would get married. Will you do it? I want you to answer me one way or the other before you leave this room, because you either have to get married or I am going to fire you." R cannot talk aloud to himself. He would tell too much about his private affairs. If he did, he would probably get fired anyway! Manual action will not help him out. *He has to think it out and having thought it out he must speak aloud "yes" or "no"* – make the final overt response in a whole series of subvocal reactions. Not all situations which must be met by subvocal language responses are quite so severe or so dramatic. Daily you are asked such questions as, "Can you lunch with me next Thursday?" – "Would it be possible for you to take a trip to Chicago next week?" – "Could you lend me one hundred dollars until the first of the month?" – and the like.

In accordance with our theory of thinking we would like to suggest certain definitions and propositions.

The term "thinking" should cover all word behavior of whatever kind that goes on subvocally. You immediately say: "Well, you told us just awhile ago that there are people who think aloud and people who never get beyond the whispering stage." By definition this would not be thinking in the strict sense. We would have to say in such cases: He talks out his verbal problems aloud to himself or he whispers them aloud to himself. This does not mean that thinking is really different from the process of talking or whispering aloud to oneself. But since most people do really think according to the strict definition of the term, how many obviously different kinds of thinking must we assume in order to account for all the facts that we know about thinking – which facts we arrive at by watching the end result of thinking? And by end result we mean the final overtly spoken word (conclusion) of the individual, or the manual action that he performs after the process of thinking comes to an end. We believe that all forms of thinking can be brought under the following heads:

(1) The subvocal use of words which have been already completely habitized. For example, suppose I ask you the question, "What is the last word in the little prayer 'Now I lay me down to sleep'?" If the question has not been asked before, you merely run it off to yourself and then respond overtly with the word "take." No learning whatsoever is involved in thinking of this kind. You run through the old verbal habit just the way the accomplished musician runs through a familiar selection, or a child says a well memorized multiplication table aloud. *You are merely exercising implicitly a verbal function you have already acquired.*

(2) Thinking of a slightly different type goes on where fairly well organized implicit verbal processes are initiated by the situation or stimulus but are not so well or so recently exercised that they can function without some learning or relearning occurring. I can make this clear also by an example. Very few of you can give me offhand the result of subvocally multiplying 333 by 33, yet all of you are familiar with subvocal arithmetic. No new process or procedure is demanded, and with a few inefficient verbal movements (verbal fumbling) you can arrive at the correct answer. The organization for carrying out this operation is all there but it is a little rusty. It has to be practised before the operation can proceed smoothly. Two weeks of practice of three place numbers by two place numbers will enable you to give perfect answers almost immediately. We have in this type of thinking something similar to what we have in many manual activities. Nearly

everybody knows how to shuffle and deal cards. At the end of a long summer vacation we get pretty adept at it. If we happen to go a year or two without playing bridge and then take up the cards to shuffle and deal, the operation is a little rusty, must be practiced for a few days before we become adept again. Similarly in this kind of thinking, we are exercising a verbal function implicitly which we never completely acquired, or acquired so long ago that there has been some loss in retention.

(3) There is still another kind of thinking. Historically it has been called constructive thinking, planning, and the like. It always involves the same amount of learning that any first trial involves. The situation is new, or practically new to us – that is, it is as new as any situation can be to us. Before I give you an example of a new thinking situation, let me give you an example of a new manual situation. I first blindfold you and then hand you a mechanical puzzle consisting of three rings joined together. The problem is to get the three rings to come apart. No amount of thinking or "reasoning" or even talking aloud or whispering to yourself will bring the solution. In my last lecture I described your behavior in getting out of this situation. You would bring to bear all your previous manual organization upon the present problem. You would pull at the rings, turn them this way and that; finally in one combination of positions of the rings they would suddenly slip apart. Such a situation corresponds to one trial – the first one in a regular learning experiment.

In a similar way we are often placed in new thinking situations. We have to get out of them by following a similar procedure. I gave you an example a moment ago when I told you about the employer who asked his employee to get married. Here is another example.

Your friend comes to you and tells you that he is forming a new business. He asks you to leave your present splendid position and come into the new business as an equal partner. He is a responsible person; he has good financial backing. He makes the offer attractive. He urges the larger ultimate profits you will make. He enlarges upon the fact that you will be your own boss. He has to leave at once to see other people interested in the venture. He asks you to call him up and give him an answer in an hour. Will you think? Yes, you will, and you'll walk the floor too, and you will pull your hair, and you may even sweat and you will smoke. Follow out the process step by step: Your whole body is as busy as though you were cracking rock – but your laryngeal mechanisms are setting the pace – they are dominant.

Let me say once again for emphasis that the most interesting point in this kind of thinking is the fact that after such new thinking situations have been met or solved once, we usually do not have to face them again exactly in the same form. *Only the first trial of the learning process takes place.* But many of our manual situations are like this too. Suppose I start out to drive my car to Washington. I do not know much about the insides of a car. The car stops – something is wrong. I work and work and finally get it going. Fifty miles farther on something goes wrong again. Again I meet the situation. In real life we go from one difficult situation to another, but each situation is a little different from all the others (except where we are acquiring definite functions like typewriting or other acts of skill). We cannot plot the curves of our escapes from these situations as we can plot learning curves in the laboratory. Our daily thinking activity goes on in exactly the same way. Complicated verbal situations usually have to be thought out but once.

What evidence has the behaviorist that the complicated thinking such as we have just described goes on in terms of internal speech? I find that when I ask my subjects to think aloud they do so, *and in terms of words* (other bodily accessory movements do occur, of course). Their behavior in reacting in words is quite similar psychologically to the behavior of the rat in the maze. I cannot take the time to dwell very long upon this. You will remember that in the last lecture I told you that the rat started out from the entrance point slowly; that on the straightaways he ran rapidly; that he blundered into the blind alleys and often went back to the starting point, instead of going on towards food; that, after getting back to the starting point, he would turn and again start towards the food. Now put a question to your subject. Ask him to tell you what a certain object is to be used for (it must be new and strange to him, and complicated) and ask him to figure it out aloud. See if he does not wander about into every possible verbal blind alley, get lost, come back and ask you to start him off again, or to show him the object or to tell him again all you propose to tell him about it, until finally he arrives at the solution or else gives it up (the equivalent of the rat's giving up the problem of the maze and lying down in it and going to sleep).

I am sure that when you have tried this out for yourself you will be convinced that you have an accurate story of how your subject worked his problem out by word behavior. If then, you grant that *you have the whole story of thinking when he thinks aloud, why make a mystery out of it when he thinks to himself?*

You may object here and ask – how does the subject know when to stop thinking, when he has solved his problem? You may argue that that rat "knows" when it has solved its problem because it gets the food which makes the hunger contractions die down. How does a man know when a verbal problem is solved? The answer is equally simple. Why in our last lecture didn't our individual keep pasting pieces of paper over the hole in the shade when he had shut out the light? Because the *light was no longer present as a stimulus to keep him moving.* Just so in thinking situations; as long as there are elements in the situation (verbal) that keep stimulating the individual to further internal speech, the process keeps going. When he reaches a *verbal conclusion*, there is no further stimulus to thinking (equivalent of getting food). But the verbal conclusion, the Q.E.D., may not be reached at one sitting – he may get tired or bored. He goes to sleep and tackles it again the next day – if it has to be tackled.

How the 'new' comes into being. – One natural question often raised is: How do we ever get new verbal creations such as a poem or a brilliant essay? *The answer is that we get them by manipulating words, shifting them about until a new pattern is hit upon.* Since we are never twice in the same general situation when we begin to think, the word patterns will always be different. The elements are all old, that is the words that present themselves are just our standard vocabulary – it is only the arrangement that is different. Why can't you, who are not literary, write a poem or an essay? You can use all the words the literary man uses. It is not your trade, you do not deal in words, your word manipulation is poor; the literary man's is good. He has manipulated words under the influence of emotional and practical situations of one kind or another, as you have manipulated the keys of the typewriter or a group of statistics, or wood, brass and lead. It may help us to go to manual behavior again here. How do you suppose Patou builds a new gown? Has he any "picture in his mind" of what the gown is to look like when it is finished? He has not, or he would not waste his time making it up; he would make a rough sketch of it or he would tell his assistant how to make it. In starting upon his work of creation, remember that his organization about gowns is enormous. Everything in the mode is at his finger tips, as is everything that has been done in the past. He calls his model in, picks up a new piece of silk, throws it around her; he pulls it in here, he pulls it out there, makes it tight or loose at the waist, high or low, he makes the skirt short or long. He manipulates the material until it takes on the semblance of a dress. *He has to react to it as a new creation before manipulation stops.* Nothing exactly like it has ever been made before. His emotional reactions are aroused one way or another by the finished product. He may rip it off and start over again. On the other hand, he may smile and say, "Voilà, parfait!" In this case the model looks at herself in the mirror and smiles and says, "Merci, monsieur." The other assistants say, "Magnifique!" Behold, a Patou model has come into being! But suppose a rival couturier happens to be present and Patou hears him in an aside say, "Very pretty, but is it not a little like the one he made three years ago? Is it that Patou grows a little stale? Is he not becoming too old to keep up with this rapidly shifting world of fashion?" One can believe that Patou would tear off the creation and tramp it under foot. In this case manipulation would start again. Not until the new creation aroused admiration and commendation, both his own (an emotional reaction either verbalized or unverbalized) and others', would manipulation be complete (the equivalent of the rat's finding food).

The painter plies his trade in the same way, nor can the poet boast of any other method. Perhaps the latter has just read Keats, perhaps he is just back from a moonlight walk in the garden, perchance his beautiful fiancée has hinted just a little strongly that he has never sung her charms in sufficiently impassioned phrases. He goes to his room, the situation is set for him, the only way he can escape it is to do something and the only thing he can do is to manipulate words. The touch of the pencil starts the verbal activity just as the whistle of the referee at the football games releases a group of fighting, struggling men. Naturally words expressive of the romantic situation he is in soon flow – being in that situation he could not compose a funeral dirge nor a humorous poem. Again the situation he is in is slightly different from any other he was ever in before and therefore the pattern of his word creation will also be slightly new.[2]

Is There No Meaning in Acts

One of the chief criticisms directed against the behaviorist's position is that it is absolutely inadequate in its account of meaning. In our definitions may I point out that the logic of the critic is poor here? The theory must be judged on these premises. The premises of the behaviorist contain no propositions about meaning. It is an historical word borrowed from philosophy and introspective psychology. It has no scientific connotation. Go again, please, to your psychologists and philosophers.

Let me paraphrase their words – the meaning of the fragrant, yellow orange in front of me is an idea, but if at any time there happens to be an idea in my mind instead of a perception, the meaning of that idea is another idea, and so on *ad infinitum*. Mrs Eddy, even in her most ingenious verbal moments, could have constructed nothing more fitting to tantalize the earnest seeker after knowledge than the current explanations of meaning.

Here is the story as I see it, since the behaviorist in order to protect himself must give some kind of account of it. Let us take a simple case. Let us take the object "fire."

1 I am burnt by it at three years of age. For some time thereafter I run away from it. By a kindly process of unconditioning, my family get me over the complete negative response. Then new conditioning takes place.

2 I learn to approach the fire after coming in from the cold.

3 I learn to cook my fish and game upon it on my first hunting trip.

4 I learn that I can melt lead in it and that if I heat my iron red hot I can fashion it to suit my needs.

During the course of many years I become conditioned in a hundred ways to fire. In other words, depending upon the situation I am now in and the series of situations leading up to the present one, I may do one of a hundred things in the presence of fire. As a matter of fact, *I do but one at a time. Which one? The one which my previous organization and my present physiological state call forth.* I am hungry; the fire makes me start to cook bacon and fry eggs. On another occasion I go to the brook and get water to put out the fire after I am through camping. On another, I run down the street yelling "Fire!" I chase to the telephone and send for the fire department. On still another occasion when a forest fire hedges me about, I jump into the lake. On a cold day I stand in front of the fire and toast my whole body. Again, under the influence of some propagandist of murder, I pick up a burning brand and set fire to a whole village. *If you are willing to agree that 'meaning' is just a way of saying that out of all the ways the individual has of reacting to this object, at any one time he reacts in only one of these ways, then I find no quarrel with meaning.* While I have chosen my illustrations in the manual field, the same procedure holds good in the verbal field. In other words, when we understand the genesis of all forms of an individual's behavior, know the varieties of his organization, can arrange or manipulate the various situations that will call out one or another form of his organizaiton, then we no longer need such a term as meaning. Meaning is just one way of telling what the individual is doing.

So the behaviorist can turn the tables upon his critics. They cannot give any explanation of meaning. He can, but he does not believe the word is needed or that it is useful except as a literary expression.[3]

In this preliminary sketch of the function of language in our total organization, there are doubtless many things not clear to you. I have left out of the discussion two problems which we must take up in the next lecture. They are (1) What is the relation between verbal behavior and manual and visceral behavior? (2) Do we have to think always in terms of words?

NOTES

1   "The Relation of Tongue Movements to Internal Speech," *Journal of Experimental Psychology*, 1925. Her experiments are very inconclusive. Tongue movements were recorded by a compound system of delicate levers. Her setup could probably be depended upon for positive results, but the method was too inexact to serve as a basis for negative conclusions. No instrument less sensitive than the string galvanometer can be depended upon for negative results. Her saying that because she could find by the use of this method no correlation between tongue movements and internal speech, therefore "this leaves only the hypothesis that the activities are intra-neural, and do not necessarily involve complete motor expression at each stage of the process" – is in need of modification.

2   In most artists and in most critics of art there is little of that mastery of technique that comes from a lifetime of study with daily improvement as the goal. The artist draws around him an admiring group or a patron and stops improving at the adolescent level. Hence most artists are children – not intelligent at all. Most of the hokum comes from patrons who think they understand art. It is their all-admiring attitude toward even a budding artist that keeps the artists children. If the so-called 'high-brow' patrons and observers of art would only admit that they have no other basis for judging art than that it stirs up *visceral* (and at times manual and verbal) reactions, then we could not have criticized their pretensions. On this basis, good art for the child of five is one thing, good art for the Hottentot is another, good art for the sophisticated few in New York is still another.

   Still more hokum comes from the so-called art and dramatic critics. There really should be no art or dramatic critics. Our visceral reactions – the final touchstone of artistic judgments (at least of the so-called critics who are not artists themselves) – are our own. They are all we have left in the way of responses that have not been under the steam-roller process of society. From an emotional standpoint, my criticism of a picture, a poem, or the playing of a piece of music is as good as anybody else's. If I had to pass a critical judgment upon a work of art, a picture for example, I should do it experimentally. I should arrange to let crowds of people from all walks of life wander one at a time into a well-lighted room. I should have rival stimuli about, such as magazines, knick-knacks of one kind or another, two or three pictures on the wall, including the one I wanted to have judged. If an individual under observation spent time at this picture, if he showed some emotional reaction such as grief, joy, rage, then I should put him down as reacting positively to it. At the end of the day I should be able to say: "The so-called art critics will say your picture is terrible, the children will not look at it, the women are shocked by it, but the travelling salesmen chuckle with glee over it. It will be a failure if you exhibit it; I should advise you to send it to some sales manager and let him hang it over his desk." What I am trying to say is that there is a vast amount of charlatanism both in the making of art objects and in their so-called appreciation. Assuming that you are a real journeyman at the job – that is, you have passed your apprenticeship at the trade – whether you are recognized as a good artist or not depends largely upon whether you can get an admiring group around you, whether Mr and Mrs X have discovered you (and you may have been dead a hundred years or more before they do it) and made a hero of you.

3   Many of the introspectionists' terms should be similarly turned back upon them. For example, attention. The behaviorist, if he felt inclined, could "explain" attention and define it and use it, but he doesn't need the word. The introspectionist, even James, has to define it in terms of vitalism as an active process that selects this or that from other happenings. Such terms, of course, only slowly die out. Until they are dead someone will always be criticizing the behavioristic explanation for inadequacy.

An Excerpt from "Psychology in Physical Language"

RUDOLF CARNAP

2 The Forms of Psychological Sentences

The distinction between singular and general sentences is as important in psychology as in other sciences. A *singular psychological sentence*, e.g. "Mr. A was angry at noon yesterday" (an analogue of the physical sentence, "Yesterday at noon the temperature of the air in Vienna was 28 degrees centigrade"), is concerned with a particular person at a particular time. *General psychological sentences* have various forms, of which the following two are perhaps the most important. A sentence may describe a specific quality of a specific kind of event, e.g. "An experience of surprise always (or: always for Mr A, or: always for people of such and such a society) has such and such a structure." A physical analogy would be: "Chalk (or: chalk of such and such a sort) always is white." The second important form is that of universal-condition statements concerning sequences of events, that is, of causal laws. For instance, "When, under such and such circumstances, images of such and such a sort occur to a person (or: to Mr A, or: to anyone of such and such a society), an emotion of such and such a sort always (or: frequently, or: sometimes) is aroused." A physical analogy would be: "When a solid body is heated, it usually expands."

Research is primarily directed to the discovery of general sentences. These cannot, however, be established except by means of the so-called method of induction from the available singular sentences, i.e. by means of the construction of hypotheses.

Phenomenology claims to be able to establish universal synthetic sentences which have not been obtained through induction. These sentences about psychological qualities are, allegedly, known either *a priori* or on the basis of some single illustrative case. In our view, knowledge cannot be gained by such means. We need not, however, enter upon a discussion of this issue here, since even on the view of phenomenology itself, these sentences do not belong to the domain of psychology.

In physics it sometimes seems to be the case that a general law is established on the basis of some single event. For instance, if a physicist can determine a

This excerpt is reprinted from R. Carnap's "Psychology in Physical Language" first published in *Erkenntnis* 11 (1932–33).

certain physical constant, say, the heat-conductivity of a sample of some pure metal, in a single experiment, he will be convinced that, on other occasions, not only the sample examined but any similar sample of the same substance will, very probably, be characterizable by the same constant. But here too induction is applied. As a result of many previous observations the physicist is in possession of a universal sentence of a higher order which enables him in this case to follow an abbreviated method. This higher-order sentence reads roughly: "All (or: the following) physical constants of metals vary only slightly in time and from sample to sample."

The situation is analogous for certain conclusions drawn in psychology. If a psychologist has, as a result of some single experiment, determined that the simultaneous sounding of two specific notes is experienced as a dissonance by some specific person A, he infers (under favorable circumstances) the truth of the general sentence which states that the same experiment with A will, at other times, have the same result. Indeed, he will even venture – and rightly – to extend this result, with some probability, to pairs of tones with the same acoustic interval if the pitch is not too different from that of the first experiment. Here too the inference from a singular sentence to a general one is only apparent. Actually, a sentence inductively obtained from many observations is brought into service here, a sentence which, roughly, reads: "The reaction of any specific person as to the consonance or dissonance of a chord varies only very slightly with time, and only slightly on a not too large transposition of the chord." It thus remains the case that every general sentence is inductively established on the basis of a number of singular ones.

Finally, we must consider sentences about psycho-physical inter-relations, such as for instance, the connection between physical stimulus and perception. These are likewise arrived at through induction, in this case through induction in part from physical and in part from psychological singular sentences. The most important sentences of gestalt psychology belong also to this kind.

General sentences have the character of hypotheses in relation to concrete sentences, that is, the testing of a general sentence consists in testing the concrete sentences which are deducible from it. A general sentence has content insofar and only insofar as the concrete sentences deducible from it have content. Logical analysis must therefore primarily be directed towards the examination of the latter sort of sentence.

If A utters a singular psychological sentence such as "Yesterday morning B was happy," the epistemological situation differs according as A and B are or are not the same person. Consequently, we distinguish between sentences about *other minds* and sentences about *one's own mind*. As we shall presently see, this distinction cannot be made among the sentences of inter-subjective science. For the epistemological analysis of subjective, singular sentences it is, however, indispensable.

3   Sentences about Other Minds

The epistemological character of a singular sentence about other minds will now be clarified by means of an analogy with a sentence about a physical property, defined as a disposition to behave (or respond) in a specific manner under specific circumstances (or stimuli). To take an example: a substance is called "plastic" if, under the influence of deforming stresses of a specific sort and a specific magnitude, it undergoes a permanent change of shape, but remains intact.

We shall try to carry out this analogy by juxtaposing two examples. We shall be concerned with the epistemological situation of the example taken from psychology; the parallel example about the physical property is intended only to facilitate our understanding of the psychological sentence, and not to serve as a specimen of an argument from analogy. (For the sake of convenience, where the text would have been the same in both columns, it is written only once.)

A Sentence about a property of a physical substance.	*A Sentence about a condition of some other mind.*
Example: I assert the sentence P_1: "This wooden support is very firm."	Example: I assert the sentence P_1: "Mr. A is now excited."

There are two different ways in which sentence P_1 may be derived. We shall designate them as the "rational" and the "intuitive" methods. The *rational* method consists of inferring P_1 from some protocol sentence p_1 (or from several like it), more specifically, from a perception-sentence

about the shape and color of the wooden support.	about the behavior of A, e.g. about his facial expressions, his gestures, etc., or about physical effects of A's behavior, e.g. about characteristics of his handwriting.

In order to justify the conclusion, a major premise O is still required, namely the general sentence which asserts that

when I perceive a wooden support to be of this color and form, it (usually) turns out to be firm. (A sentence about the perceptual signs of firmness.)	when I perceive a person to have this facial expression and handwriting he (usually) turns out to be excited. (A sentence about the expressional or graphological signs of excitement.)

The content of P_1 does not coincide with that of p_1, but goes beyond it. This is evident from the fact that to infer P_1 from p_1 O is required. The cited relationship between P_1 and p_1 may also be seen in the fact that under certain circumstances, the inference from p_1 to P_1 may go astray. It may happen that, though p_1 occurs in a protocol, I am obliged, on the grounds of further protocols, to retract the established system sentence P_1. I would then say something like, "I made a mistake. The test has shown

that the support was not firm, even though it had such and such a form and color."	that A was not excited, even though his face had such and such an expression."

In practical matters the *intuitive* method is applied more frequently than this rational one, which presupposes theoretical knowledge and requires reflection. In accordance with the intuitive method, P_1 is obtained without the mediation of any other sentence from the identically sounding protocol sentence p_2.

"The support is firm."   "A is excited."

Consequently, one speaks in this case of *immediate perceptions*

of properties of substances, e.g., of the firmness of supports.	of other minds, e.g., of the excitement of A.

But in this case too the protocol sentence p_2 and the system sentence P_1 have different contents. The difference is generally not noted because, on the ordinary formulation, both sentences sound alike. Here too we can best clarify the difference by considering the possibility of error. It may happen that, though p_2 occurs in my protocol, I am obliged, on the basis of further protocols, to retract the established system sentence P_1. I would then say "I made a mistake. Further tests have shown

that the support was not firm, although I had the intuitive impression that it was."	that A was not excited, although I had the intuitive impression that he was."

[The difference between p_2 and P_1 is the same as that between the identically sounding sentences p and P_1: "A red marble is lying on this table," of an earlier example (see *Erkenntnis*, vol. II, p. 460 (The Unity of Science, p. 92)). The argument of that article shows that the inference of P_1 from p_2, if it is to be rigorous, also requires a major premise of general form, and that it is not in the least simple. In so far as ordinary usage, for convenience's sake, assigns to both sentences the same sequence of words, the inference is, in practice, simplified to the point of triviality.]

Our problem now is: *what does sentence P_1 mean?* Such a question can only be answered by the presentation of a sentence (or of several sentences) which has (or which conjointly have) the same content as P_1. The viewpoint which will here be defended is that P_1 has the same content as a sentence P_2 which asserts the existence of a physical structure characterized by the disposition to react in a specific manner to specific physical stimuli. In our example, P_2 asserts the existence of that physical structure (microstructure)

of the wooden support that is characterized by the fact that, under a slight load, the support undergoes no noticeable distortion, and, under heavier loads, is bent in such and such a manner, but does not break.	of Mr. A's body (especially of his central nervous system) that is characterized by a high pulse and rate of breathing, which, on the application of certain stimuli, may even be made higher, by vehement and factually unsatisfactory answers to questions, by the occurrence of agitated move-

ments on the application of certain stimuli, etc.

On my view, there is here again a thoroughgoing analogy between the examples from physics and from psychology. If, however, we were to question the experts concerning the examples from their respective fields, the majority of them nowadays would give us thoroughly non-analogous answers. The identity of the content of P_2

and of the content of the physical sentence P_1 would be agreed to as a matter of course by all physicists.	and of the content of the psychological sentence P_1 would be denied by almost all psychologists (the exceptions being the radical behaviorists).

The contrary view which is most frequently advocated by psychologists is that, "A sentence of the form of P_1 asserts the existence of a state of affairs not identical with the corresponding physical structure, but rather, only accompanied by it, or expressed by it. In our example:

P_1 states the support not only has the physical structure described by P_2, but that, besides, there exists in it a certain force, namely its *firmness*.	P_1 states that Mr. A not only has a body whose physical structure (at the time in question) is described by P_2, but that – since he is a *psychophysical being* – he has, besides, a consciousness, a certain power or entity, in which that excitement is to be found.
This firmness is not identical with the physical structure, but stands in some parallel relation to it in such a manner that the firmness exists when and only when a physical structure of the characterized sort exists.	This excitement cannot, consequently, be identical with the cited structure of the body, but stands in some parallel relation (or in some relation of interaction) to it in such a manner that the excitement exists when and only when (or at least, frequently when) a physical, bodily structure of the characterized sort exists.
Because of this parallelism one may consider the described reaction to certain stimuli – which is causally dependent upon that structure – to be an *expression* of firmness.	Because of this parallelism one may consider the described reaction to certain stimuli to be an *expression* of excitement.
Firmness is thus an occult property, an obscure power which stands behind physical structure, appears in it, but itself remains unknowable."	Excitement, or the consciousness of which it is an attribute, is thus an occult property, an obscure power which stands behind physical structure, appears in it, but itself remains unknowable."

This view falls into the error of a hypostatization as a result of which a remarkable duplication occurs: besides or behind a state of affairs whose existence is empirically determinable, another, *parallel* entity is assumed, whose existence is not determinable. (Note that we are here concerned with a sentence about other minds.) But – one may now object – is there not really at least one possibility of testing this claim, namely, by means of the protocol sentence p_2 about the intuitive impression of

the firmness of the support?   the excitement of A?

The objector will point out that this sentence, after all, occurs in the protocol along with the perception sentence p_1. May not then a system sentence whose content goes beyond that of P_2 be founded on p_2? This may be answered as follows. A sentence says no more than what is testable about it. If, now, the testing of P_1 consisted in the deduction of the protocol sentence p_2, these two sentences would have the same content. But we have already seen that this is impossible.

There is no other possibility of testing P_1 except by means of protocol sentences like p_1 or p_2. If, now, the content of P_1 goes beyond that of P_2, the component not shared by the two sentences is not testable, and is therefore meaningless. If one rejects the interpretation of P_1 in terms of P_2, P_1 becomes a metaphysical pseudo-sentence.

The various sciences today have reached very different stages in the process of their decontamination from metaphysics. Chiefly because of the efforts of Mach, Poincaré, and Einstein, physics is, by and large, practically free of metaphysics. In psychology, on the other hand, the work of arriving at a science which is to be free of metaphysics has hardly begun. The difference between the two sciences is most clearly seen in the different attitudes taken by experts in the two fields towards the position which we rejected as metaphysical and meaningless. In the case of the example from physics, most physicists would reject the position as anthropomorphic, or mythological, or metaphysical. They thereby reveal their anti-metaphysical orientation, which corresponds to our own. On the other hand, in the case of the example from psychology (though, perhaps, not when it is so crudely formulated), most psychologists would today consider the view we have been criticizing to be self-evident on intuitive grounds. In this one can see the metaphysical orientation of psychologists, to which ours is opposed.

2

The Identity Theory

Is Consciousness a Brain Process?

U. T. PLACE

The thesis that consciousness is a process in the brain is put forward as a reasonable scientific hypothesis, not to be dismissed on logical grounds alone. The conditions under which two sets of observations are treated as observations of the same process, rather than as observations of two independent correlated processes, are discussed. It is suggested that we can identify consciousness with a given pattern of brain activity, if we can explain the subject's introspective observations by reference to the brain processes with which they are correlated. It is argued that the problem of providing a physiological explanation of introspective observations is made to seem more difficult than it really is by the "phenomenological fallacy," the mistaken idea that descriptions of the appearances of things are descriptions of the actual state of affairs in a mysterious internal environment.

I Introduction

The view that there exists a separate class of events, mental events, which cannot be described in terms of the concepts employed by the physical sciences no longer commands the universal and unquestioning acceptance among philosophers and psychologists which it once did. Modern physicalism, however, unlike the materialism of the seventeenth and eighteenth centuries, is behavioristic. Consciousness on this view is either a special type of behavior, "sampling" or "running-back-and-forth" behavior as Tolman has it,[1] or a disposition to behave in a certain way, an itch, for example, being a temporary propensity to scratch. In the case of cognitive concepts like "knowing," "believing," "understanding," "remembering," and volitional concepts like "wanting" and "intending," there can be little doubt, I think, that an analysis in terms of dispositions to behave is

"Is Consciousness a brain process?" by U. T. Place was first published in the *British Journal of Psychology* (1956) pp. 44–50, and is reprinted here by kind permission of the author and the journal.

fundamentally sound.[2] On the other hand, there would seem to be an intractable residue of concepts clustering around the notions of consciousness, experience, sensation, and mental imagery, where some sort of inner process story is unavoidable.[3] It is possible, of course, that a satisfactory behavioristic account of this conceptual residuum will ultimately be found. For our present purposes, however, I shall assume that this cannot be done and that statements about pains and twinges, about how things look, sound, and feel, about things dreamed of or pictured in the mind's eye, are statements referring to events and processes which are in some sense private or internal to the individual of whom they are predicated. The question I wish to raise is whether in making this assumption we are inevitably committed to a dualist position in which sensations and mental images form a separate category of processes over and above the physical and physiological processes with which they are known to be correlated. I shall argue that an acceptance of inner processes does not entail dualism and that the thesis that consciousness is a process in the brain cannot be dismissed on logical grounds.

II The "Is" of definition and the "Is" of Composition

I want to stress from the outset that in defending the thesis that consciousness is a process in the brain, I am not trying to argue that when we describe our dreams, fantasies, and sensations we are talking about processes in our brains. That is, I am not claiming that statements about sensations and mental images are reducible to or analyzable into statements about brain processes, in the way in which "cognition statements" are analyzable into statements about behavior. To say that statements about consciousness are statements about brain processes is manifestly false. This is shown (a) by the fact that you can describe your sensations and mental imagery without knowing anything about your brain processes or even that such things exist, (b) by the fact that statements about one's consciousness and statements about one's brain processes are verified in entirely different ways, and (c) by the fact that there is nothing self-contradictory about the statement "X has a pain but there is nothing going on in his brain." What I do want to assert, however, is that the statement "Consciousness is a process in the brain," although not necessarily true, is not necessarily false. "Consciousness is a process in the brain" in my view is neither self-contradictory nor self-evident; it is a reasonable scientific hypothesis, in the way that the statement "Lightning is a motion of electric charges" is a reasonable scientific hypothesis.

The all but universally accepted view that an assertion of identity between consciousness and brain processes can be ruled out on logical grounds alone derives, I suspect, from a failure to distinguish between what we may call the "is" of definition and the "is" of composition. The distinction I have in mind here is the difference between the function of the word "is" in statements like "A square is an equilateral rectangle," "Red is a color," "To understand an instruction is to be able to act appropriately under the appropriate circumstances," and its function in statements like "His table is an old packing case," "Her hat is a bundle of straw tied together with string," "A cloud is a mass of water droplets or other particles in suspension." These two types of "is" statements have one thing in common. In both cases it makes sense to add the qualification "and nothing else." In this they differ from those statements in which the "is" is an "is" of predication; the statements "Toby is eighty years old and nothing else," "Her hat is red and nothing else," or "Giraffes are tall and nothing else," for example, are nonsense. This logical feature may be described by saying that in both cases both the grammatical subject and the grammatical predicate are expressions which provide an adequate characterization of the state of affairs to which they both refer.

In another respect, however, the two groups of statements are strikingly different. Statements like "A square is an equilateral rectangle" are necessary statements which are true by definition. Statements like "His table is an old packing-case," on the other hand, are contingent statements which have to be verified by observation. In the case of statements like "A square is an equilateral rectangle" or "Red is a color," there is a relationship between the meaning of the expression forming the grammatical predicate and the meaning of the expression forming the grammatical subject, such that whenever the subject expression is applicable the predicate must also be applicable. If you can describe something as red then you must also be able to describe it as colored. In the case of statements like "His table is an old packing-case," on the other hand, there is no such relationship between the meanings of the expressions "his table" and "old packing-case"; it merely so happens that in this case both expressions are applicable to and at the same time provide an adequate characterization of the same object. Those who contend that the statement "Consciousness is a brain process" is logically untenable, base their claim, I suspect, on the mistaken assumption that if the meanings of two statements or expressions are quite unconnected, they cannot both provide an adequate characterization of the same object or state of affairs: if something is a state of consciousness, it cannot be a brain process, since there is nothing self-contradictory in supposing that someone feels a pain when there is nothing happening inside his skull. By the same token we might be led to conclude that a table cannot be an old packing-case, since there is nothing self-contradictory in supposing that someone has a table, but is not in possession of an old packing-case.

III   The Logical Independence of Expressions and the Ontological Independence of Entities

There is, of course, an important difference between the table/packing-case and the consciousness/brain process case in that the statement "His table is an old packing-case" is a particular proposition which refers only to one particular case, whereas the statement "Consciousness is a process in the brain" is a general or universal proposition applying to all states of consciousness whatever. It is fairly clear, I think, that if we lived in a world in which all tables without exception were packing-cases, the concepts of "table" and "packing-case" in our language would not have their present logically independent status. In such a world a table would be a species of packing-case in much the same way that red is a species of color. It seems to be a rule of language that whenever a given variety of object or state of affairs has two characteristics or sets of characteristics, one of which is unique to the variety of object or state of affairs in question, the expression used to refer to the characteristic or set of characteristics which defines the variety of object or state of affairs in question will always entail the expression used to refer to the other characteristic or set of characteristics. If this rule admitted of no exception it would follow that any expression which is logically independent of another expression which uniquely characterizes a given variety of object or state of affairs must refer to a characteristic or set of characteristics which is not normally or necessarily associated with the object or state of affairs in question. It is because this rule applies almost universally, I suggest, that we are normally justified in arguing from the logical independence of two expressions to the ontological independence of the states of affairs to which they refer. This would explain both the undoubted force of the argument that consciousness and brain processes must be independent entities because the expressions used to refer to them are logically independent and, in general, the curious phenomenon whereby questions about the furniture of the universe are often fought and not infrequently decided merely on a point of logic.

The argument from the logical independence of two expressions to the ontological independence of the entities to which they refer breaks down in the case of brain processes and consciousness, I believe, because this is one of a relatively small number of cases where the rule stated above does not apply. These exceptions are to be found, I suggest, in those cases where the operations which have to be performed in order to verify the presence of the two sets of characteristics inhering in the object or state of affairs in question can seldom if ever be performed simultaneously. A good example here is the case of the cloud and the mass of droplets or other particles in suspension. A cloud is a large semi-transparent mass with a fleecy texture suspended in the atmosphere whose shape is subject to continual and kaleidoscopic change. When observed at close quarters, however, it is found to consist of a mass of tiny particles, usually water droplets, in continuous motion. On the basis of this second observation we conclude that a cloud is a mass of tiny particles and nothing else. But there is no logical connection in our language between a cloud and a mass of tiny particles; there is nothing self-contradictory in talking about a cloud which is not composed of tiny particles in suspension. There is no contradiction involved in supposing that clouds consist of a dense mass of fibrous tissue; indeed, such a consistency seems to be implied by many of the functions performed by clouds in fairy stories and mythology. It is clear from this that the terms "cloud" and "mass of tiny particles in suspension" mean quite different things. Yet we do not conclude from this that there must be two things, the mass of particles in suspension and the cloud. The reason for this, I suggest, is that although the characteristics of being a cloud and being a mass of tiny particles in suspension are invariably associated, we never make the observations necessary to verify the statement "That is a cloud" and those necessary to verify the statement "This is a mass of tiny particles in suspension" at one and the same time. We can observe the micro-structure of a cloud only when we are enveloped by it, a condition which effectively prevents us from observing those characteristics which from a distance lead us to describe it as a cloud. Indeed, so disparate are these two experiences that we use different words to describe them. That which is a cloud when we observe it from a distance becomes a fog or mist when we are enveloped by it.

IV   When Are Two Sets of Observations Observations of the Same Event?

The example of the cloud and the mass of tiny particles in suspension was chosen because it is one of the few cases of a general proposition involving what I have called the "is" of composition which does not involve us in scientific technicalities. It is useful because it brings out the connection between the ordinary everyday cases of the "is" of composition like the table/packing-case example and the more technical cases like "Lightning is a motion of electric charges" where the analogy with the consciousness/brain process case is most marked. The limitation of the cloud/tiny particles in suspension case is that it does not bring out sufficiently clearly the crucial problems of how the identity of the states of affairs referred to by the two expressions is established. In the cloud case the fact that something is a cloud and the fact that something is a mass of tiny particles in suspension are both verified by the normal processes of visual observation. It is arguable, moreover, that the identity of the entities referred to by the two expressions is established by the continuity between the two sets of observations as the observer moves towards or away from the cloud. In the case of brain processes and consciousness there is no such continuity between the two sets of observations involved. A closer introspective scrutiny will never reveal the passage of nerve impulses over a thousand synapses in the way that a closer scrutiny of a cloud will reveal a mass of tiny particles in suspension. The operations required to verify statements about consciousness and statements about brain processes are fundamentally different.

To find a parallel for this feature we must examine other cases where an identity is asserted between something whose occurrence is verified by the ordinary processes of observation and something whose occurrence is established by special procedures. For this purpose I have chosen the case where we say that lightning is a motion of electric charges. As in the case of consciousness, however closely we scrutinize the lightning we shall never be able to observe the electric charges, and just as the operations for determining the nature of one's state of consciousness are radically different from those involved in determining the nature of one's brain processes, so the operations for determining the occurrence of lightning are radically different from those involved in determining the occurrence of a motion of electric charges. What is it, therefore, that leads us to say that the two sets of observations are observations of the same event? It cannot be merely the fact that the two sets of observations are systematically correlated such that whenever there is lightning there is always a motion of electric charges. There are innumerable cases of such correlations where we have no temptation to say that the two sets of observations are observations of the same event. There is a systematic correlation, for example, between the movement of the tides and the stages of the moon, but this does not lead us to say that records of tidal levels are records of the moon's stages or vice versa. We speak rather of a causal connection between two independent events or processes.

The answer here seems to be that we treat the two sets of observations as observations of the same event in those cases where the technical scientific observations set in the context of the appropriate body of scientific theory provide an immediate explanation of the observations made by the man in the street. Thus we conclude that lightning is nothing more than a motion of electric charges, because we know that a motion of electric charges through the atmosphere, such as occurs when lightning is reported, gives rise to the type of visual stimulation which would lead an observer to report a flash of lightning. In the moon/tide case, on the other hand, there is no such direct causal connection between the stages of the moon and the observations made by the man who measures the height of the tide. The causal connection is between the moon and the tides, not between the moon and the measurement of the tides.

V   The Physiological Explanation of Introspection and the Phenomenological Fallacy

If this account is correct, it should follow that in order to establish the identity of consciousness and certain processes in the brain, it would be necessary to show that the introspective observations reported by the subject can be accounted for in terms of processes which are known to have occurred in his brain. In the light of this suggestion it is extremely interesting to find that when a physiologist, as distinct from a philosopher, finds it difficult to see how consciousness could be a process in the brain, what worries him is not any supposed self-contradiction involved in such an assumption, but the apparent impossibility of accounting for the reports given by the subject of his conscious processes in terms of the known properties of the central nervous system. Sir Charles Sherrington has posed the problem as follows:

> The chain of events stretching from the sun's radiation entering the eye to, on the one hand, the contraction of the pupillary muscles, and on the other, to the electrical disturbances in the brain-cortex are all straightforward steps in a sequence of physical "causation," such as, thanks to science, are intelligible. But in the second serial chain there follows on, or attends, the stage of brain-cortex reaction an event or set of events quite inexplicable to us, which both as to themselves and as to the causal tie between them and what preceded them science does not help us; a set of events seemingly incommensurable with any of the events leading up to it. The self "sees" the sun; it senses a two-dimensional disc of brightness, located in the "sky," this last a field of lesser brightness, and overhead shaped as a rather flattened dome, coping the self and a hundred other visual things as well. Of hint that this is within the head there is none. Vision is saturated with this strange property called "projection," the unargued inference that what it sees is at a "distance" from the seeing "self." Enough has been said to stress that in the sequence of events a step is reached where a physical situation in the brain leads to a psychical, which however contains no hint of the brain or any other bodily part ... The supposition has to be, it would seem, two continuous series of events, one physico-chemical, the other psychical, and at times interaction between them.[4]

Just as the physiologist is not likely to be impressed by the philosopher's contention that there is some self-contradiction involved in supposing consciousness to be a brain process, so the philosopher is unlikely to be impressed by the considerations which lead Sherrington to conclude that there are two sets of events, one physico-chemical, the other psychical. Sherrington's argument, for all its emotional appeal, depends on a fairly simply logical mistake, which is unfortunately all too frequently made by psychologists and physiologists and not infrequently in the past by the philosophers themselves. This logical mistake, which I shall refer to as the "phenomenological fallacy," is the mistake of supposing that when the subject describes his experience, when he describes how things look, sound, smell, taste, or feel to him, he is describing the literal properties of objects and events on a peculiar sort of internal cinema or television screen, usually referred to in the modern psychological literature as the "phenomenal field." If we assume, for example, that when a subject reports a green after-image he is asserting the occurrence inside himself of an object which is literally green, it is clear that we have on our hands an entity for which there is no place in the world of physics. In the case of the green after-image there is no green object in the subject's environment corresponding to the description that he gives. Nor is there anything green in his brain; certainly there is nothing which could have emerged when he reported the appearance of the green after-image. Brain processes are not the sort of things to which color concepts can be properly applied.

The phenomenological fallacy on which this argument is based depends on the mistaken assumption that because our ability to describe things in our environment depends on our consciousness of them, our descriptions of things are primarily descriptions of our conscious experience and only secondarily, indirectly, and inferentially descriptions of the objects and events in our environments. It is assumed that because we recognize things in our environment by their look, sound, smell, taste, and feel, we begin by describing their phenomenal properties, i.e. the properties of the looks, sounds, smells, tastes, and feels which they produce in us, and infer their real properties from their phenomenal properties. In fact, the reverse is the case. We begin by learning to recognize the real properties of things in our environment. We learn to recognize them, of course, by their look, sound, smell, taste, and feel; but this does not mean that we have to learn to describe the look, sound, smell, taste, and feel of things before we can describe the things themselves. Indeed, it is only after we have learned to describe the things in our environment that we learn to describe our consciousness of them. We describe our conscious experience not in terms of the mythological "phenomenal properties" which are supposed to inhere in the mythological "objects" in the mythological "phenomenal field," but by reference to the actual physical properties of the concrete physical objects, events, and processes which normally, though not perhaps in the present instance, give rise to the sort of conscious experience which we are trying to describe. In other words when we describe the after-image as green, we are not saying that there is something, the after-image, which is green; we are saying that we are having the sort of experience which we normally have when, and which we have learned to describe as, looking at a green patch of light.

Once we rid ourselves of the phenomenological fallacy we realize that the problem of explaining introspective observations in terms of brain processes is far from insuperable. We realize that there is nothing that the introspecting subject says about his conscious experiences which is inconsistent with anything the physiologist might want to say about the brain processes which cause him to describe the environment and his consciousness of that environment in the way he does. When the subject describes his experience by saying that a light which is in fact stationary appears to move, all the physiologist or physiological psychologist has to do in order to explain the subject's introspective observations is to show that the brain process which is causing the subject to describe his experience in this way is the sort of process which normally occurs when he is observing an actual moving object and which therefore normally causes him to report the movement of an object in his environment. Once the mechanism whereby the individual describes what is going on in his environment has been worked out, all that is required to explain the individual's capacity to make introspective observations is an explanation of his ability to discriminate between those cases where his normal habits of verbal descriptions are appropriate to the stimulus situation and those cases where they are not, and an explanation of how and why, in those cases where the appropriateness of his normal descriptive habits is in doubt, he learns to issue his ordinary descriptive protocols preceded by a qualificatory phrase like "it appears," "seems," "looks," "feels," etc.[5]

NOTES

1   E. C. Tolman, *Purposive Behaviour in Animals and Men* (Berkeley 1932).
2   L. Wittgenstein, *Philosophical Investigations* (Oxford 1953); G. Ryle, *The Concept of Mnd* (1949).
3   Place, "The Concept of Heed," *British Journal of Psychology* XLV (1954), 243–55.
4   Sir Charles Sherrington, *The Integrative Action of the Nervous System* (Cambridge 1947) pp. xx–xxi.
5   I am greatly indebted to my fellow-participants in a series of informal discussions on this topic which took place in the Department of Philosophy, University of Adelaide, in particular to Mr C. B. Martin for his persistent and searching criticism of my earlier attempts to defend the thesis that consciousness is a brain process, to Professor D. A. T. Gasking, of the University of Melbourne, for clarifying many of the logical issues involved, and to Professor J. J. C. Smart for moral support and encouragment in what often seemed a lost cause.

3

Early Causal and Functionalist Views

The Causal Theory of the Mind

D. M. ARMSTRONG

Is Philosophy Just Conceptual Analysis?

What can philosophy contribute to solving the problem of the relation to mind to body? Twenty years ago, many English-speaking philosophers would have answered: "Nothing beyond an analysis of the various mental *concepts*." If we seek knowledge of things, they thought, it is to science that we must turn. Philosophy can only cast light upon our concepts of those things.

This retreat from things to concepts was not undertaken lightly. Ever since the seventeenth century, the great intellectual fact of our culture has been the incredible expansion of knowledge both in the natural and in the rational sciences (mathematics, logic). Everyday life presents us with certain simple verities. But, it seems, through science and only through science can we build upon these verities, and with astonishing results.

The success of science created a crisis in philosophy. What was there for philosophy to do? Hume had already perceived the problem in some degree, and so surely did Kant, but it was not until the twentieth century, with the Vienna Circle and with Wittgenstein, that the difficulty began to weigh heavily. Wittgenstein took the view that philosophy could do no more than strive to undo the intellectual knots it itself had tied, so achieving intellectual release, and even a certain illumination, but no knowledge. A little later, and more optimistically, Ryle saw a positive, if reduced, role for philosophy in mapping the "logical geography" of our concepts: how they stood to each other and how they were to be analyzed.

On the whole, Ryle's view proved more popular than Wittgenstein's. After all, it

"The Causal Theory of the Mind" by D. M. Armstrong is reprinted from *The Nature of Mind and Other Essays*, Cornell University Press (1981), by kind permission of the author and publisher.

retained a special, if much reduced, realm for philosophy where she might still be queen. There was better hope of continued employment for members of the profession!

Since that time, however, philosophers in the "analytic" tradition have swung back from Wittgensteinian and even Rylean pessimism to a more traditional conception of the proper role and tasks of philosophy. Many analytic philosophers now would accept the view that the central task of philosophy is to give an account, or at least play a part in giving an account, of the most general nature of things and of man. (I would include myself among that many.)

Why has this swing back occurred? Has the old urge of the philosopher to determine the nature of things by *a priori* reasoning proved too strong? To use Freudian terms, are we simply witnessing a return of what philosophers had repressed? I think not. One consideration that has had great influence was the realization that those who thought that they were abandoning ontological and other substantive questions for a mere investigation of concepts were in fact smuggling in views on the substantive questions. They did not acknowledge that they held these views, but the views were there; and far worse from their standpoint, the views imposed a form upon their answers to the conceptual questions.

For instance, in *The Concept of Mind* (1949), Gilbert Ryle, although he denied that he was a Behaviorist, seemed to be upholding an account of man and his mind that was extremely close to Behaviorism. Furthermore, it seemed in many cases that it was this view of the mind–body problem that led him to his particular analyses of particular mental concepts, rather than the other way around. Faced with examples like this, it began to appear that, since philosophers could not help holding views on substantive matters, and the views could not help affecting their analyses of concepts, the views had better be held and discussed explicitly instead of appearing in a distorted, because unacknowledged, form.

The swing back by analytic philosophers to first-order questions was also due to the growth of a more sohpisticated understanding of the nature of scientific investigation. For a philosophical tradition that is oriented towards science, as, on the whole, Western philosophy is, the consideration of the *methods* of science must be an important topic. It was gradually realized that in the past scientific investigation had regularly been conceived in far too positivistic, sensationalistic and observationalistic a spirit. (The influence of Karl Popper has been of the greatest importance in this realization.) As the central role of speculation, theory and reasoning in scientific investigation began to be appreciated by more and more philosophers, the border-line between science and philosophy began to seem at least more fluid, and the hope arose again that philosophy might have something to contribute to first-order questions.

The philosopher has certain special skills. These include the stating and assessing of the worth of arguments, including the bringing to light and making explicit suppressed premises of arguments, the detection of ambiguities and inconsistencies, and, perhaps especially, the analysis of concepts. But, I contend, these special skills do not entail that the *objective* of philosophy is to do these things. They are rather the special *means* by which philosophy attempts to achieve further objectives. Ryle was wrong in taking the analysis of concepts to be the end of philosophy. Rather, the analysis of concepts is a means by which the philosopher makes his contribution to great general questions, not about concepts, but about things.

In the particular case of the mind–body problem, the propositions the philosopher arrives at need not be of a special nature. They perhaps might have been arrived at by the psychologist, the neuro-physiologist, the biochemist or others, and, indeed, may be suggested to the philosopher by the results achieved or programs proposed by those disciplines. But the way that the argument is marshalled by a philosopher will be a special way. Whether this special way has or has not any particular value in the search for truth is a matter to be decided in particular cases. There is no *a priori* reason for thinking that the special methods of philosophy will be able to make a contribution to the mind–body problem. But neither is there an *a priori* reason for assuming that the philosopher's contribution will be valueless.

The Concept of a Mental State

The philosophy of philosophy is perhaps a somewhat joyless and unrewarding subject for reflection. Let us now turn to the mind–body problem itself, hoping that what is to be said about this particular topic will confirm the general remarks about philosophy that have just been made.

If we consider the mind–body problem today, then it seems that we ought to take account of the following consideration. The present state of scientific knowledge makes it probable that we can give a purely physico-chemical account of man's body. It seems increasingly likely that the body and the brain of man are constituted and work according to exactly the same principles as those physical principles that govern other, non-organic, matter. The differences between a stone and a human body appear to lie solely in the extremely complex material set-up that is to be found in the living body and which is absent in the stone. Furthermore, there is rather strong evidence that it is the state of our brain that completely determines the state of our consciousness and our mental state generally.

All this is not beyond the realm of controversy, and it is easy to imagine evidence that would upset the picture. In particular, I think that it is just possible that evidence from psychical research might be forthcoming that a physico-chemical view of man's brain could not accommodate. But suppose that the physico-chemical view of the working of the brain is correct, as I take it to be. It will be very natural to conclude that mental states are not simply *determined* by corresponding states of the brain, but that they are actually *identical* with these brain-states, brain-states that involve nothing but physical properties.

The argument just outlined is quite a simple one, and it hardly demands philosophical skill to develop it or to appreciate its force! But although many contemporary thinkers would accept its conclusion, there are others, including many philosophers, who would not. To a great many thinkers it has seemed obvious *a priori* that mental states could not be physical states of the brain. Nobody would identify a number with a piece of rock: it is sufficiently obvious that the two entities fall under different categories. In the same way, it has been thought, a perception or a feeling of sorrow must be a different category of thing from an electro-chemical discharge in the central nervous system.

Here, it seems to me, is a question to which philosophers can expect to make a useful contribution. It is a question about mental concepts. Is our concept of a mental state such that it is an intelligible hypothesis that mental states are physical states of the brain? If the philosopher can show that it is an *intelligible* proposition (that is, a non-self-contradictory proposition) that mental states are physical states of the brain, then the scientific argument just given above can be taken at its face value as a strong reason for accepting the truth of the proposition.

My view is that the identification of mental states with physical states of the brain is a perfectly intelligible one, and that this becomes clear once we achieve a correct view of the analysis of the mental concepts. I admit that my analysis of the mental concepts was itself adopted because it permitted this identification, but such a procedure is commonplace in the construction of theories, and perfectly legitimate. In any case, whatever the motive for proposing the analysis, it is there to speak for itself, to be measured against competitors, and to be assessed as plausible or implausible independently of the identification it makes possible.

The problem of the identification may be put in a Kantian way: "How is it possible that mental states should be physical states of the brain?" The solution will take the form of proposing an *independently plausible* analysis of the concept of a mental state that will permit this identification. In this way, the philosopher makes the way smooth for a first-order doctrine, which, true or false, is a doctrine of the first importance: a purely physicalist view of man.

The analysis proposed may be called the Causal analysis of the mental concepts. According to this view, the concept of a mental state essentially involves, and is exhausted by, the concept of a state that is *apt to be the cause of certain effects or apt to be the effect of certain causes.*

An example of a causal concept is the concept of poison. The concept of poison is the concept of something that when introduced into an organism causes that organism to sicken and/or die.[1] This is but a rough analysis of the concept the structure of which is in fact somewhat more complex and subtle than this. If *A* pours molten lead down *B*'s throat, then he may cause *B* to die as a result, but he can hardly be said to have poisoned him. For a thing to be called a poison, it is necessary that it act in a certain *sort* of way: roughly, in a biological as opposed to a purely physical way. Again, a poison can be introduced into the system of an organism and that organism fail to die or even to sicken. This might occur if an antidote were administered promptly. Yet again, the poison may be present in insufficient quantities to do any damage. Other qualifications could be made.

But the essential point about the concept of poison is that it is the concept of *that, whatever it is, which produces certain effects.* This leaves open the possibility of the *scientific identification* of poisons, of discovering that a certain sort of substance, such as cyanide, is a poison, and discovering further what it is about the substance that makes it poisonous.

Poisons are accounted poisons in virtue of their active powers, but many sorts of thing are accounted the sorts of thing they are by virtue of their *passive* powers. Thus brittle objects are accounted brittle because of the disposition they have to break and shatter when sharply struck. This leaves open the possibility of discovering empirically what sorts of thing are brittle and what it is about them that makes them brittle.

Now *if* the concepts of the various sorts of mental state are concepts of that which is, in various sorts of way, apt for causing certain effects and apt for being the effect of certain causes, then it would be a quite unpuzzling thing if mental states should turn out to be physical states of the brain.

The concept of a mental state is the concept of something that is, characteristically, the cause of certain effects and the effect of certain causes. What sort of effects and what sort of causes? The effects caused by the mental state will be certain patterns of behavior of the person in that state. For instance, the desire for food is a state of a person or animal that characteristically brings about food-seeking and food-consuming behavior by that person or animal. The causes of mental states will be objects and events in the person's environment. For instance, a sensation of green is the characteristic effect in a person of the action upon his eyes of a nearby green surface.

The general pattern of analysis is at its most obvious and plausible in the case of *purposes*. If a man's purpose is to go to the kitchen to get something to eat, it is completely natural to conceive of this purpose as a cause within him that brings about, or tends to bring about, that particular line of conduct. It is, furthermore, notorious that we are unable to characterize purposes *except* in terms of that which they tend to bring about. How can we distinguish the purpose to go to the kitchen to get something to eat from another purpose to go to the bedroom to lie down? Only by the different outcomes that the two purposes tend to bring about. This fact was an encouragement to Behaviorism. It is still more plausibly explained by saying that the concept of purpose is a causal concept. The further hypothesis that the two purposes are, in their own nature, different physical patterns in, or physical states of, the central nervous system is then a natural (although, of course, not logically inevitable) supplement to the causal analysis.

Simple models have great value in trying to grasp complex conceptions, but they are ladders that may need to be kicked away after we have mounted up by their means. It is vital to realize that the mental concepts have a far more complex logical structure than simple causal notions such as the concept of poison. The fact should occasion no surprise. In the case of poisons, the effect of which they are the cause is a gross and obvious phenomenon and the level of causal explanation involved in simply calling a substance "a poison" is crude and simple. But in the case of mental states, their effects are all those complexities of behavior that mark off men and higher animals from the rest of the objects in the world. Furthermore, differences in such behavior are elaborately correlated with differences in the mental causes operating. So it is only to be expected that the causal patterns invoked by the mental concepts should be extremely complex and sophisticated.

In the case of the notion of a purpose, for instance, it is plausible to assert that it is the notion of a cause within which drives, or tends to drive, the man or animal through a series of actions to a certain end-state. But this is not the whole story. A purpose is only a purpose if it works to bring about behavioral effects *in a certain sort of way*. We may sum up this sort of way by saying that purposes are *information-sensitive* causes. By this is meant that purposes direct behavior by utilizing *perceptions* and *beliefs*, perceptions and beliefs about the agent's current situation and the way it develops, and beliefs about the way the world works. For instance, it is part of what it is to be a purpose to achieve X that this cause will cease to operate, will be "switched off," if the agent perceives or otherwise comes to believe that X has been achieved.

At this point, we observe that an account is being given of that special species of cause that is a purpose in terms of *further* mental items: perceptions and beliefs. This means that if we are to give a purely causal analysis even of the concept of a purpose we also will have to give a purely causal analysis of perceptions and beliefs. We may think of man's behavior as brought about by the joint operation of two sets of causes: first, his purposes and, second, his perceptions of and/or beliefs about the world. But since perceptions and beliefs are quite different sorts of thing from purposes, a Causal analysis must assign quite different causal *roles* to these different things in the bringing about of behavior.

I believe that this can be done by giving an account of perceptions and beliefs as *mappings* of the world. They are structures within us that model the world beyond the structure. This model is created in us by the world. Purposes may then be thought of as driving causes that utilize such mappings.

This is a mere thumb-nail, which requires much further development as well as qualification. One point that becomes clear when that development is given is that just as the concept of purpose cannot be elucidated without appealing to the concepts of perception and belief, so the latter cannot be elucidated without appealing to the concept of purpose. (This comes out, for instance, when we raise Hume's problem: what marks off beliefs from the mere entertaining of the same proposition? It seems that we can only mark off beliefs as those mappings in the light of which we are prepared to *act*, that is, which are potential servants of our purposes.) The logical dependence of purpose on perception and belief, and of perception and belief upon purpose, is not circularity in definition. What it shows is that the corresponding concepts *must be introduced together or not at all*. In itself, there is nothing very surprising in this. Correlative or mutually implicated concepts are common enough: for instance, the concepts of husband and wife or the concepts of soldier and army. No husbands without wives or wives without husbands. No soldiers without an army, no army without soldiers. But if the concepts of purpose, perception and belief are (i) correlative concepts and (ii) different species of purely causal concepts, then it is clear that they are far more complex in structure than a simple causal concept like poison. What falls under the mental concepts will be a complex and interlocking set of causal factors, which together are responsible for the "minded" behavior of men and the higher animals.

The working out of the Causal theory of the mental concepts thus turns out to be an extremely complex business. Indeed when it is merely baldly stated, the Causal theory is, to use the phrase of Imre Lakatos, a *research program* in conceptual analysis rather than a developed theory. I have tried to show that it is a hopeful program by attempting, at least in outline, a Causal analysis of all the main concepts in *A Materialist Theory of Mind* (1968); and I have supplemented the rather thin account given there of the concepts of belief, knowledge and inferring in *Belief, Truth and Knowledge* (1973).

Two examples of mental concepts where an especially complex and sophisticated type of Causal analysis is required are the notions of introspective awareness (one sense of the word "consciousness") and the having of mental imagery. Introspective awareness is analyzable as a mental state that is a "perception" of mental states. It is a mapping of the causal factors themselves. The having of mental imagery is a sort of mental state that cannot be elucidated in *directly* causal terms, but only by resemblance to the corresponding perceptions, which *are* explicated in terms of their causal role.

Two advantages of the Causal theory may now be mentioned. First, it has often been remarked by philosophers and others that the realm of mind is a shadowy one, and that the nature of mental states is singularly elusive and hard to grasp. This has given aid and comfort to Dualist or Cartesian theories of mind, according to which minds are quite different sorts of thing from material objects. But if the Causal analysis is correct, the facts admit of another explanation. What Dualist philosophers have grasped in a confused way is that our direct acquaintance with mind, which occurs in introspective awareness, is an acquaintance with something that we are aware of only as something that is causally linked, directly or indirectly, with behavior. In the case of our purposes and desires, for instance, we are often (though not invariably) introspectively aware of them. What we are aware of is the presence of factors within us that drive in a certain direction. We are not aware of the intrinsic nature of the factors. This emptiness or gap in our awareness is then interpreted by Dualists as immateriality. In fact, however, if the Causal analysis is correct, there is no warrant for this interpretation and, if the Physicalist identification of the nature of the causes is correct, the interpretation is actually false.

Second, the Causal analysis yields a still more spectacular verification. It shows promise of explaining a philosophically notorious feature of all or almost all mental states: their *intentionality*. This was the feature of mental states to which Brentano in particular drew attention, the fact that they may point towards certain objects or states of affairs, but that these objects and states of affairs need not exist. When a man strives, his striving has an objective, but that objective may never be achieved. When he believes, there is something he believes, but what he believes may not be the case. This capacity of mental states to "point" to what does not exist can seem very special. Brentano held that intentionality set the mind completely apart from matter.

Suppose, however, that we consider a concept like the concept of poison. Does it not provide us with a miniature and unsophisticated model for the intentionality of mental states? Poisons are substances apt to make organisms sicken and die when the poison is administered. So it may be said that this is what poisons "point" to. Nevertheless, poisons may fail of their effect. A poison does not fail to be a poison because an antidote neutralizes the customary effect of the poison.

May not the intentionality of mental states, therefore, be in principle a no more mysterious affair, although indefinitely more complex, than the death that lurks in the poison? As an intermediate case between poisons and mental states, consider the mechanisms involved in a homing rocket. Given a certain setting of its mechanism, the rocket may "point" towards a certain target in a way that is a simulacrum of the way in which purposes point towards their objectives. The mechanism will only bring the rocket to the target in "standard" circumstances: many factors can be conceived that would "defeat" the mechanism. For the mechanism to operate successfully, some device will be required by which the developing situation is "mapped" in the mechanism (i.e. what course the rocket is currently on, etc.). This mapping is an elementary analogue of perception, and so the course that is "mapped" in the mechanism may be thought of as a simulacrum of the perceptual intentional object. Through one circumstance or another (e.g. malfunction of the gyroscope) this mapping may be "incorrect."

It is no objection to this analogy that homing rockets are built by men with purposes, who deliberately stamp a crude model of their own purposes into the rocket. Homing rockets might have been natural products, and non-minded objects that operate in a similar but far more complex way are found in nature. The living cell is a case in point.

So the Causal analyses of the mental concepts show promise of explaining both the transparency and the intentionality of mental states. One problem quite frequently raised in connection with these analyses, however, is in what sense they can be called "analyses." The welter of complications in which the so-called analyses are involved make it sufficiently obvious that they do not consist of *synonymous translations* of statements in which mental terms figure. But, it has been objected, if synonymous translations of mental statements are unavailable, what precisely can be meant by speaking of "analyses of concepts"?

I am far from clear what should be said in reply to this objection. Clearly, however, it does depend upon taking all conceptual analyses as claims about the synonymy of sentences, and that seems to be too simple a view. Going back to the case of poison: it is surely not an empirical fact, to be learnt by experience, that poisons kill. It is at the center of our notion of what poisons are that they have the power to bring about this effect. If they did not do that, they would not be properly called "poisons." But although this seems obvious enough, it is extremely difficult to give exact translations of sentences containing the word "poison" into other sentences that do not contain the word or any synonym. Even in this simple case, it is not at all clear that the task can actually be accomplished.

For this reason, I think that sentence translation (with synonymy) is too strict a demand to make upon a purported conceptual analysis. What more relaxed demand can we make and still have a conceptual analysis? I do not know. One thing that we clearly need further light upon here is the concept of a concept, and how concepts are tied to language. I incline to the view that the connection between concepts and language is much less close than many philosophers have assumed. Concepts are linked primarily with belief and thought, and belief and thought, I think, have a great degree of logical independence of language, however close the empirical connection may be in many cases. If this is so, then an analysis of concepts, although of course conducted *in* words, may not be an investigation *into* words. (A compromise proposal: analysis of concepts might be an investigation into some sort of "deep structure" – to use the currently hallowed phrase – which underlies the use of certain words and sentences.) I wish I were able to take the topic further.

The Problem of the Secondary Qualities

No discussion of the Causal theory of the mental concepts is complete that does not say something about the *secondary qualities*. If we consider such mental states as purposes and intentions, their "transparency" is a rather conspicuous feature.

It is notorious that introspection cannot differentiate such states except in terms of their different objects. It is not so immediately obvious, however, that *perception* has this transparent character. Perception involves the experience of color and of visual extension; touch the experience of the whole obscure range of tactual properties, including tactual extension; hearing, taste and smell the experience of sounds, tastes and smells. These phenomenal qualities, it may be argued, endow different perceptions with different qualities. The lack of transparency is even more obvious in the case of bodily sensations. Pains, itches, tickles and tingles are mental states, even if mental states of no very high-grade sort, and they each seem to involve their own peculiar qualities. Again, associated with different emotions it is quite plausible to claim to discern special emotion qualities. If perception, bodily sensation and emotions involve qualities, then this seems to falsify a purely Causal analysis of these mental states. They are not mere "that whiches" known only by their causal role.

However, it is not at all clear how strong is the line of argument sketched in the previous paragraph. We distinguish between the intention and what is intended, and in just the same way we must distinguish between the perception and what is perceived. The intention is a mental state and so is the perception, but what is intended is not in general something mental and nor is what is perceived. What is intended may not come to pass, it is a merely intentional object, and the same may be said of what is perceived. Now in the case of the phenomenal qualities, it seems plausible to say that they are qualities not of the perception but rather of what is perceived. "Visual extension" is the shape, size, etc. that some object of visual perception is perceived to have (an object that need not exist). Color seems to be a quality of that object. And similarly for the other phenomenal qualities. Even in the case of the bodily sensations, the qualities associated with the sensations do not *appear* to be qualities of mental states but instead to be qualities of portions of our bodies: more or less fleeting qualities that qualify the place where the sensation is located. Only in the case of the emotions does it seem natural to place the quality on the mental rather than the object side: but then it is not so clear whether there really *are* peculiar qualities associated with the emotions. The different patterns of bodily sensations associated with the different emotions may be sufficient to do phenomenological justice to the emotions.

For these reasons, it is not certain whether the phenomenal qualities pose any threat to the Causal analysis of the mental concepts. But what a subset of these qualities quite certainly does pose a threat to, is the doctrine that the Causal analysis of the mental concepts is a step towards: Materialism or Physicalism.

The qualities of colour, sound, heat and cold, taste and smell together with the qualities that appear to be involved in bodily sensations and those that may be involved in the case of the emotions, are an embarrassment to the modern Materialist. He seeks to give an account of the world and of man purely in terms of *physical* properties, that is to say in terms of the properties that the physicist appeals to in his explanations of phenomena. The Materialist is not committed to the *current* set of properties to which the physicist appeals, but he is committed to whatever set of properties the physicist in the end will appeal to. It is clear that such properties as color, sound, taste and smell – the so-called "secondary qualities" – will never be properties to which the physicist will appeal.

It is, however, a plausible thesis that associated with different secondary qualities are properties that are respectable from a physicist's point of view. Physical surfaces *appear* to have color. They not merely appear to, but undoubtedly do, emit light-waves, and the different mixtures of lengths of wave emitted are linked with differences in color. In the same way, different sorts of sound are linked with different sorts of sound-wave and differences in heat with differences in the mean kinetic energy of the molecules composing the hot things. The Materialist's problem therefore would be very simply solved if the secondary qualities could be identified with these physically respectable properties. (The qualities associated with bodily sensations would be identified with different sorts of stimulation of bodily receptors. If there are unique qualities associated with the emotions, they would presumably be identified with some of the physical states of the brain linked with particular emotions.)

But now the Materialist philosopher faces a problem. Previously he asked: "How is it possible that mental states could be physical states of the brain?" This question was answered by the Causal theory of the mental concepts. Now he must ask: "How is it possible that secondary qualities could be purely physical properties of the objects they are qualities of?" A Causal analysis does not seem to be of any avail. To try to give an analysis of, say, the quality of being red in Causal terms would lead us to produce such analyses as "those properties of a physical surface, whatever they are, that characteristically produce *red sensations* in us." But this analysis simply shifts the problem unhelpfully from property of surface to property of sensation. Either the red sensations involve nothing but physically respectable properties or they involve something more. If they involve something more, Materialism fails. But if they are simply physical states of the brain, having nothing but physical properties, then the Materialist faces the problem: "How is it possible that red sensations should be physical states of the brain?" This question is no easier to answer than the original question about the redness of physical surfaces. (To give a Causal analysis of red sensations as the characteristic effects of the action of red surfaces is, of course, to move round in a circle.)

The great problem presented by the secondary qualities, such as redness, is that they are *unanalyzable*. They have certain relations of resemblance and so on to each other, so they cannot be said to be completely simple. But they are simple in the sense that they resist any analysis. You cannot give any complete account of the concept of redness without involving the notion of redness itself. This has seemed to be, and still seems to many philosophers to be, an absolute bar to identifying redness with, say, certain patterns of emission of light-waves.

But I am not so sure. I think it can be maintained that although the secondary qualities *appear* to be simple, they are not in fact simple. Perhaps their simplicity is *epistemological* only, not ontological, a matter of our awareness of them rather than the way they are. The best model I can give for the situation is the sort of phenomena made familiar to us by the *Gestalt* psychologists. It is possible to grasp that certain things or situations have a certain special property, but be unable to analyze that property. For instance, it may be possible to perceive that certain people are all alike in some way without being able to make it clear to oneself what the likeness is. We are aware that all these people have a certain likeness to each other, but are unable to define or specify that likeness. Later psychological research may achieve a specification of the likeness, a specification that may come as a complete surprise to us. Perhaps, therefore, the secondary qualities are in fact complex, and perhaps they are complex characteristics of a sort demanded by Materialism, but we are unable to grasp their complexity in perception.

There are two divergences between the model just suggested and the case of the secondary qualities. First, in the case of grasping the indefinable likeness of people, we are under no temptation to think that the likeness is a likeness in some simple quality. The likeness is indefinable, but we are vaguely aware that it is complex. Second, once research has determined the concrete nature of the likeness, our attention can be drawn to, and we can observe individually, the features that determine the likeness.

But although the model suggested and the case of the secondary qualities undoubtedly exhibit these differences, I do not think that they show that the secondary qualities cannot be identified with respectable physical characteristics of objects. Why should not a complex property appear to be simple? There would seem to be no contradiction in adding such a condition to the model. It has the consequence that perception of the secondary qualities involves an element of illusion, but the consequence involves no contradiction. It is true also that in the case of the secondary qualities the illusion cannot be overcome within perception: it is impossible to see a colored surface as a surface emitting certain light-waves. (Though one sometimes seems to *hear* a sound as a vibration of the air.) But while this means that the identification of color and light-waves is a purely *theoretical* one, it still seems to be a possible one. And if the identification is a possible one, we have general scientific reasons to think it a *plausible* one.

The doctrine of mental states and of the secondary qualities briefly presented in this paper seems to me to show promise of meeting many of the traditional philosophical objections to a Materialist or Physicalist account of the world. As I have emphasized, the philospher is not professionally competent to argue the positive case for Materialism. There he must rely upon the evidence presented by the scientist, particularly the physicist. But at least he may neutralize the objections to Materialism advanced by his fellow philosophers.

NOTE

1   "Any substance which, when introduced into or absorbed by a living organism, destroys life or injures health." (*Shorter Oxford Dictionary*, 3rd edn., rev., 1978.)

The Nature of Mental States

HILARY PUTNAM

The typical concerns of the Philosopher of Mind might be represented by three questions: (1) How do we know that other people have pains? (2) Are pains brain states? (3) What is the analysis of the concept *pain*? I do not wish to discuss questions (1) and (3) in this paper. I shall say something about question (2).[1]

"The Nature of Mental States" originally appeared as "Psychological Predicates" by Hilary Putnam in *Art, Mind and Religion*, edited by W. H. Capitan and D. D. Merrill. Published in 1967 by the University of Pittsburgh Press. Used by permission of the publisher.

I Identity Questions

"Is pain a brain state?" (Or, "Is the property of having a pain at time t a brain state?")[2] It is impossible to discuss this question sensibly without saying something about the peculiar rules which have grown up in the course of the development of "analytical philosophy" – rules which, far from leading to an end to all conceptual confusions, themselves represent considerable conceptual confusion. These rules – which are, of course, implicit rather than explicit in the practice of most analytical philosophers – are (1) that a statement of the form "being A is being B" (e.g., "being in pain is being in a certain brain state") can be *correct* only if it follows, in some sense, from the meaning of the terms A and B; and (2) that a statement of the form "being A is being B" can be philosophically *informative* only if it is in some sense reductive (e.g. "being in pain is having a certain unpleasant sensation" is not philosophically informative; "being in pain is having a certain behavior disposition" is, if true, philosophically informative). These rules are excellent rules if we still believe that the program of reductive analysis (in the style of the 1930s) can be carried out; if we don't, then they turn analytical philosophy into a mug's game, at least so far as "is" questions are concerned.

In this paper I shall use the term 'property' as a blanket term for such things as being in pain, being in a particular brain state, having a particular behavior disposition, and also for magnitudes such as temperature, etc. – i.e., for things which can naturally be represented by one-or-more-place predicates or functors. I shall use the term 'concept' for things which can be identified with synonymy-classes of expressions. Thus the concept *temperature* can be identified (I maintain) with the synonymy-class of the word 'temperature'.[3] (This is like saying that the number 2 can be identified with the class of all pairs. This is quite a different statement from the peculiar statement that 2 *is* the class of all pairs. I do not maintain that concepts *are* synonymy-classes, whatever that might mean, but that they can be identified with synonymy-classes, for the purpose of formalization of the relevant discourse.)

The question "What is the concept *temperature*?" is a very "funny" one. One might take it to mean "What is temperature? Please take my question as a conceptual one." In that case an answer might be (pretend for a moment 'heat' and 'temperature' are synonyms) "temperature is heat," or even "the concept of temperature is the same concept as the concept of heat." Or one might take it to mean "What are *concepts*, really? For example, what is "the concept of temperature'?" In that case heaven knows what an "answer" would be. (Perhaps it would be the statement that concepts *can be identified with* synonymy-classes.)

Of course, the question "What is the property temperature?" is also "funny." And one way of interpreting it is to take it as a question about the concept of temperature. But this is not the way a physicist would take it.

The effect of saying that the property P_1 can be identical with the property P_2 only if the terms P_1, P_2 are in some suitable sense "synonyms" is, to all intents and purposes, to collapse the two notions of "property" and "concept" into a single notion. The view that concepts (intensions) *are* the same as properties has been explicitly advocated by Carnap (e.g., in *Meaning and Necessity*). This seems an unfortunate view, since "temperature is mean molecular kinetic energy" appears to be a perfectly good example of a true statement of identity of properties, whereas "the concept of temperature is the same concept as the concept of mean molecular kinetic energy" is simply false.

Many philosophers believe that the statement "pain is a brain state" violates some rules or norms of English. But the arguments offered are hardly convincing. For example, if the fact that I can know that I am in pain without knowing that I am in brain state S shows that pain cannot be brain state S, then, by exactly the same argument, the fact that I can know that the stove is hot without knowing that the mean molecular kinetic energy is high (or even that molecules exist) shows that it is *false* that temperature is mean molecular kinetic energy, physics to the contrary. In fact, all that immediately follows from the fact that I can know that I am in pain without knowing that I am in brain state S is that the concept of pain is not the same concept as the concept of being in brain state S. But either pain, or the state of being in pain, or some pain, or some pain state, might still be brain state S. After all, the concept of temperature is not the same concept as the concept of mean molecular kinetic energy. But temperature is mean molecular kinetic energy.

Some philosophers maintain that both 'pain is a brain state' and 'pain states are brain states' are unintelligible. The answer is to explain to these philosophers, as well as we can, given the vagueness of all scientific methodology, what sorts of considerations lead one to make an empirical reduction (i.e. to say such things as "water is H_2O," light is electro-magnetic radiation," "temperature is mean molecular kinetic energy"). If, without giving reasons, he still maintains in the face of such examples that one cannot imagine parallel circumstances for the use of 'pains are brain states' (or, perhaps, 'pain states are brain states') one has grounds to regard him as perverse.

Some philosophers maintain that "P_1 is P_2" is something that can be true, when the 'is' involved is the 'is' of empirical reduction, only when the properties P_1 and P_2 are (a) associated with a spatio-temporal region; and (b) the region is one and the same in both cases. Thus "temperature is mean molecular kinetic energy" is an admissible empirical reduction, since the temperature and the molecular energy are associated with the same space-time region, but "having a pain in my arm is being in a brain state" is not, since the spatial regions involved are different.

This argument does not appear very strong. Surely no one is going to be deterred from saying that mirror images are light reflected from an object and then from the surface of a mirror by the fact that an image can be "located" three feet *behind* the mirror! (Moreover, one can always find *some* common property of the reductions one is willing to allow – e.g., temperature is mean molecular kinetic energy – which is not a property of some one identification one wishes to disallow. This is not very impressive unless one has an argument to show that the very purposes of such identification depend upon the common property in question.)

Again, other philosophers have contended that all the predictions that can be derived from the conjunction of neurophysiological laws with such statements as "pain states are such-and-such brain states" can equally well be derived from the conjunction of the same neurophysiological laws with "being in pain is correlated with such-and-such brain states," and hence (sic!) there can be no methodological grounds for saying that pains (or pain states) *are* brain states, as opposed to saying that they are *correlated* (invariantly) with brain states. This argument, too, would show that light is only correlated with electromagnetic radiation. The mistake is in ignoring the fact that, although the theories in question may indeed lead to the same predictions, they open and exclude different *questions*. "Light is invariantly correlated with electromagnetic radiation" would leave open the questions "What is the light then, if it isn't the same as the electromagnetic radiation?" and "What makes the light accompany the electromagnetic radiation?" – questions which are excluded by saying that the light *is* the electromagnetic radiation. Similarly, the purpose of saying that pains are brain states is precisely to exclude from empirical meaningfulness the questions "What is the pain, then, if it isn't the same as the brain state?" and "What makes the pain accompany the brain state?" If there are grounds to suggest that these questions represent, so to speak, the wrong way to look at the matter, then those grounds are grounds for a theoretical identification of pains with brain states.

If all arguments to the contrary are unconvincing, shall we then conclude that it is meaningful (and perhaps true) to say either that pains are brain states or that pain states are brain states?

1 It is perfectly meaningful (violates no "rule of English," involves no "extension of usage") to say "pains are brain states."
2 It is not meaningful (involves a "changing of meaning" or "an extension of usage," etc.) to say "pains are brain states."

My own position is not expressed by either (1) or (2). It seems to me that the notions "change of meaning" and "extension of usage" are simply so ill-defined that one cannot in fact say *either* (1) or (2). I see no reason to believe that either the linguist, or the man-on-the-street, or the philosopher possesses today a notion of "change of meaning" applicable to such cases as the one we have been discussing. The *job* for which the notion of change of meaning was developed in the history of the language was just a *much* cruder job than this one.

But, if we don't assert either (1) or (2) – in other words, if we regard the "change of meaning" issue as a pseudo-issue in this case – then how are to discuss the question with which we started? "Is pain a brain state?"

The answer is to allow statements of the form "pain is *A*," where 'pain' and '*A*' are in no sense synonyms, and to see whether any such statement can be found which might be acceptable on empirical and methodological grounds. This is what we shall now proceed to do.

II Is Pain a Brain State?

We shall discuss "Is pain a brain state?," then. And we have agreed to waive the "change of meaning" issue.

Since I am discussing not what the concept of pain comes to, but what pain is, in a sense of 'is' which requires empirical theory-construction (or, at least, empirical speculation). I shall not apologize for advancing an empirical hypothesis. Indeed, my strategy will be to argue that pain is *not* a brain state, not on *a priori* grounds, but on the grounds that another hypothesis is more plausible. The detailed development and verification of my hypothesis would be just as Utopian a task as the detailed development and verification of the brain-state hypothesis. But the putting-forward, not of detailed and scientifically "finished" hypotheses, but of schemata for hypotheses, has long been a function of philosophy. I shall, in short, argue that pain is not a brain state, in the sense of a physical-chemical state of the brain (or even the whole nervous system), but another *kind* of state entirely. I propose the hypothesis that pain, or the state of being in pain, is a functional state of a whole organism.

To explain this it is necessary to introduce some technical notions. In previous papers I have explained the notion of a Turing Machine and discussed the use of this notion as a model for an organism. The notion of a Probabilistic Automaton is defined similarly to a Turing Machine, except that the transitions between "states" are allowed to be with various probabilities rather than being "deterministic." (Of course, a Turing Machine is simply a special kind of Probabilistic Automaton, one with transition probabilities 0, 1.) I shall assume the notion of a Probabilistic Automaton has been generalized to allow for "sensory inputs" and "motor outputs" – that is, the Machine Table specifies, for every possible combination of a "state" and a complete set of "sensory inputs," an "instruction" which determines the probability of the next "state," and also the probabilities of the "motor outputs." (This replaces the idea of the Machine as printing on a tape.) I shall also assume that the physical realization of the sense organs responsible for the various inputs, and of the motor organs, is specified, but that the "states" and the "inputs" themselves are, as usual, specified only "implicitly" – i.e., by the set of transition probabilities given by the Machine Table.

Since an empirically given system can simultaneously be a "physical realization" of many different Probabilistic Automata, I introduce the notion of a *Description* of a system. A Description of S where S is a system, is any true statement to the effect that S possesses distinct states S_1, S_2 ..., S_n which are related to one another and to the motor outputs and sensory inputs by the transition probabilities given in such-and-such a Machine Table. The Machine Table mentioned in the Description will then be called the Functional Organization of S relative to that Description, and the S_i such that S is in state S_i at a given time will be called the Total State of S (at that time) relative to that Description. It should be noted that knowing the Total State of a system relative to a Description involves knowing a good deal about how the system is likely to "behave," given various combinations of sensory inputs, but does *not* involve knowing the physical realization of the S_i as, e.g., physical-chemical states of the brain. The S_i, to repeat, are specified only *implicitly* by the Description – i.e., specified *only* by the set of transition probabilities given in the Machine Table.

The hypothesis that "being in pain is a functional state of the organism" may now be spelled out more exactly as follows:

1 All organisms capable of feeling pain are Probabilistic Automata.
2 Every organism capable of feeling pain possesses at least one Description of

a certain kind (i.e., being capable of feeling pain *is* possessing an appropriate kind of Functional Organization.)

3 No organism capable of feeling pain possesses a decomposition into parts which separately possess Descriptions of the kind referred to in (2).

4 For every Description of the kind referred to in (2), there exists a subset of the sensory inputs such that an organism with that Description is in pain when and only when some of its sensory inputs are in that subset.

This hypothesis is admittedly vague, though surely no vaguer than the brain-state hypothesis in its present form. For example, one would like to know more about the kind of Functional Organization that an organism must have to be capable of feeling pain, and more about the marks that distinguish the subset of the sensory inputs referred to in (4). With respect to the first question, one can probably say that the Functional Organization must include something that resembles a "preference function," or at least a preference partial ordering, and something that resembles an "inductive logic" (i.e., the Machine must be able to "learn from experience"). (The meaning of these conditions, for Automata models, is discussed in my paper "The Mental Life of Some Machines") In addition, it seems natural to require that the Machine possess "pain sensors," i.e., sensory organs which normally signal damage to the Machine's body, or dangerous temperatures, pressures, etc., which transmit a special subset of the inputs, the subset referred to in (4). Finally, and with respect to the second question, we would want to require at least that the inputs in the distinguished subset have a high disvalue on the Machine's preference function or ordering (further conditions are discussed in "The Mental Life of Some Machines"). The purpose of condition (3) is to rule out such "organisms" (if they can count as such) as swarms of bees as single pain-feelers. The condition (1) is, obviously, redundant, and is only introduced for expository reasons. (It is, in fact, empty, since everything is a Probabilistic Automaton under *some* Description.)

I contend, in passing, that this hypothesis, in spite of its admitted vagueness, is far *less* vague than the "physical-chemical state" hypothesis is today, and far more susceptible to investigation of both a mathematical and an empirical kind. Indeed, to investigate this hypothesis is just to attempt to produce "mechanical" models of organisms – and isn't this, in a sense, just what psychology is about? The difficult step, of course, will be to pass from models of *specific* organisms to a *normal form* for the psychological description of organisms – for this is what is required to make (2) and (4) precise. But this too seems to be an inevitable part of the program of psychology.

I shall now compare the hypothesis just advanced with (a) the hypothesis that pain is a brain state, and (b) the hypothesis that pain is a behavior disposition.

III Functional State Versus Brain State

It may, perhaps, be asked if I am not somewhat unfair in taking the brain-state theorist to be talking about *physical-chemical* states of the brain. But (a) these are the only sorts of states ever mentioned by brain-state theorists. (b) The brain-state theorist usually mentions (with a certain pride, slightly reminiscent of the

Village Atheist) the incompatibility of his hypothesis with all forms of dualism and mentalism. This is natural if physical-chemical states of the brain are what is at issue. However, functional states of whole systems are something quite different. In particular, the functional-state hypothesis is *not* incompatible with dualism! Although it goes without saying that the hypothesis is "mechanistic" in its inspiration, it is a slightly remarkable fact that a system consisting of a body and a "soul," if such things there be, can perfectly well be a Probabilistic Automaton. (c) One argument advanced by Smart is that the brain-state theory assumes only "physical" properties, and Smart finds "non-physical" properties unintelligible. The Total States and the "inputs" defined above are, of course, neither mental nor physical *per se*, and I cannot imagine a functionalist advancing this argument. (d) If the brain-state theorist does mean (or at least allow) states other than physical-chemical states, then his hypothesis is completely empty, at least until he specifies *what* sort of "states" he *does* mean.

Taking the brain-state hypothesis in this way, then, what reasons are there to prefer the functional-state hypothesis over the brain-state hypothesis? Consider what the brain-state theorist has to do to make good his claims. He has to specify a physical-chemical state such that *any* organism (not just a mammal) is in pain if and only if (a) it possesses a brain of a suitable physical-chemical structure; and (b) its brain is in that physical-chemical state. This means that the physical-chemical state in question must be a possible state of a mammalian brain, a reptilian brain, a mollusc's brain (octopuses are mollusca, and certainly feel pain), etc. At the same time, it must *not* be a possible (physically possible) state of the brain of any physically possible creature that cannot feel pain. Even if such a state can be found, it must be nomologically certain that it will also be a state of the brain of any extra-terrestrial life that may be found that will be capable of feeling pain before we can even entertain the supposition that it may *be* pain.

It is not altogether impossible that such a state will be found. Even though octopus and mammal are examples of parallel (rather than sequential) evolution, for example, virtually identical structures (physically speaking) have evolved in the eye of the octopus and in the eye of the mammal, notwithstanding the fact that this organ has evolved from different kinds of cells in the two cases. Thus it is at least possible that parallel evolution, all over the universe, might *always* lead to *one and the same* physical "correlate" of pain. But this is certainly an ambitious hypothesis.

Finally, the hypothesis becomes still more ambitious when we realize that the brain-state theorist is not just saying that *pain* is a brain state; he is, of course, concerned to maintain that *every* psychological state is a brain state. Thus if we can find even one psychological predicate which can clearly be applied to both a mammal and an octopus (say "hungry"), but whose physical-chemical "correlate" is different in the two cases, the brain-state theory has collapsed. It seems to me overwhelmingly probable that we can do this. Granted, in such a case the brain-state theorist can save himself by *ad hoc* assumptions (e.g., defining the disjunction of two states to be a single "physical-chemical state"), but this does not have to be taken seriously.

Turning now to the considerations *for* the functional-state theory, let us begin with the fact that we identify organisms as in pain, or hungry, or angry, or in heat, etc., on the basis of their *behavior*. But it is a truism that similarities in the behavior of two systems are at least a reason to suspect similarities in the functional organization of the two systems, and a much *weaker* reason to suspect similarities in the actual physical details. Moreover, we expect the various psychological states – at least the basic ones, such as hunger, thirst, aggression, etc. – to have more or less similar "transition probabilities" (within wide and ill-defined limits, to be sure) with each other and with behavior in the case of different species, because this is an artifact of the way in which we identify these states. Thus, we would not count an animal as *thirsty* if its "unsatiated" behavior did not seem to be directed toward drinking and was not followed by "satiation for liquid." Thus any animal that we count as capable of these various states will at least *seem* to have a certain rough kind of functional organization. And, as already remarked, if the program of finding psychological laws that are not species-specific – i.e., of finding a normal form for psychological theories of different species – ever succeeds, then it will bring in its wake a delineation of the kind of functional organization that is necessary and sufficient for a given psychological state, as well as a precise definition of the notion "psychological state." In contrast, the brain-state theorist has to hope for the eventual development of neurophysiological laws that are species-independent, which seems much less reasonable than the hope that psychological laws (of a sufficiently general kind) may be species-independent, or, still weaker, that a species-independent *form* can be found in which psychological laws can be written.

IV   Functional State versus Behavior Disposition

The theory that being in pain is neither a brain state nor a functional state but a behavior disposition has one apparent advantage: it appears to agree with the way in which we verify that organisms are in pain. We do not in practice know anything about the brain state of an animal when we say that it is in pain; and we possess little if any knowledge of its functional organization, except in a crude intuitive way. In fact, however, this "advantage" is no advantage at all: for, although statements about how we verify that x is A may have a good deal to do with what the concept of being A comes to, they have precious little to do with what the property A is. To argue on the ground just mentioned that pain is neither a brain state nor a functional state is like arguing that heat is not mean molecular kinetic energy from the fact that ordinary people do not (they think) ascertain the mean molecular kinetic energy of something when they verify that it is hot or cold. It is not necessary that they should; what is necessary is that the marks that they take as indications of heat should in fact be explained by the mean molecular kinetic energy. And, similarly, it is necessary to our hypothesis that the marks that are taken as behavioral indications of pain should be explained by the fact that the organism is in a functional state of the appropriate kind, but not that speakers should *know* that this is so.

The difficulties with "behavior disposition" accounts are so well known that I shall do little more than recall them here. The difficulty – it appears to be more than "difficulty," in fact – of specifying the required behavior disposition except as "the disposition of X to behave as if X were in *pain*," is the chief one, of course. In contrast, we *can* specify the functional state with which we propose to identify pain, at least roughly, without using the notion of pain. Namely, the functional state we have in mind is the state of receiving sensory inputs which play a certain role in the Functional Organization of the organism. This role is characterized, at least partially, by the fact that the sense organs responsible for the inputs in question are organs whose function is to detect damage to the body, or dangerous extremes of temperature, pressure, etc., and by the fact that the "inputs" themselves, whatever their physical realization, represent a condition that the organism assigns a high disvalue to. As I stressed in "The Mental Life of Some Machines," this does *not* mean that the Machine will always *avoid* being in the condition in question ("pain"); it only means that the condition will be avoided unless not avoiding it is necessary to the attainment of some more highly valued goal. Since the behavior of the Machine (in this case, an organism) will depend not merely on the sensory inputs, but also on the Total State (i.e., on other values, beliefs, etc.), it seems hopeless to make any general statement about how an organism in such a condition *must* behave; but this does not mean that we must abandon hope of characterizing the condition. Indeed, we have just characterized it.[4]

Not only does the behavior-disposition theory seem hopelessly vague; if the "behavior" referred to is peripheral behavior, and the relevant stimuli are peripheral stimuli (e.g., we do not say anything about what the organism will do if its brain is operated upon), then the theory seems clearly false. For example, two animals with all motor nerves cut will have the same actual and potential "behavior" (viz., none to speak of); but if one has cut pain fibers and the other has uncut pain fibers, then one will feel pain and the other won't. Again, if one person has cut pain fibers, and another suppresses all pain responses deliberately due to some strong compulsion, then the actual and potential peripheral behavior may be the same, but one will feel pain and the other won't. (Some philosophers maintain that this last case is conceptually impossible, but the only evidence for this appears to be that *they* can't, or don't want to, conceive of it.)[5] If, instead of pain, we take some sensation the "bodily expression" of which is easier to suppress – say, a slight coolness in one's left little finger – the case becomes even clearer.

Finally, even if there *were* some behavior disposition invariantly correlated with pain (species-independently!), and specifiable without using the term 'pain,' it would still be more plausible to identify being in pain with some state whose presence *explains* this behavior disposition – the brain state or functional state – than with the behavior disposition itself. Such considerations of plausibility may be somewhat subjective; but if other things *were* equal (of course, they aren't) why shouldn't we allow considerations of plausibility to play the deciding role?

V Methodological Considerations

So far we have considered only what might be called the "empirical" reasons for saying that being in pain is a functional state, rather than a brain state or a behavior disposition; viz., that it seems more likely that the functional state we described is invariantly "correlated" with pain, species-independently, than that there is either a physical-chemical state of the brain (must an organism have a *brain* to feel pain? perhaps some ganglia will do) or a behavior disposition so correlated. If this is correct, then it follows that the identification we proposed is at least a candidate for consideration. What of methodological considerations? The methodological considerations are roughly similar in all cases of reduction, so no surprises need be expected here. First, identification of psychological states with functional states means that the laws of psychology can be derived from statements of the form "such-and-such organisms have such-and-such Descriptions" together with the identification statements ("being in pain is such-and-such a functional state," etc.). Secondly, the presence of the functional state (i.e., of inputs which play the role we have described in the Functional Organization of the organism) is not merely "correlated with" but actually explains the pain behavior on the part of the organism. Thirdly, the identification serves to exclude questions which (if a naturalistic view is correct) represent an altogether wrong way of looking at the matter, e.g., "What *is* pain if it isn't either the brain state or the functional state?" and "What causes the pain to be always accompanied by this sort of functional state?" In short, the identification is to be tentatively accepted as a theory which leads to both fruitful predictions and to fruitful *questions*, and which serves to discourage fruitless and empirically senseless questions, where by 'empirically senseless' I mean "senseless" not merely from the standpoint of verification, but from the standpoint of what there in fact *is*.

NOTES

1   I have discussed these and related topics in the following papers: "Minds and machines," in *Dimensions of Mind*, ed. Sidney Hook, New York, 1960, pp. 148–79; "Brains and behavior," in *Analytical Philosophy*, second series, ed. Ronald Butler, Oxford, 1965, pp. 1–20; and "The Mental Life of Some Machines," in *Intentionality, Minds, and Perception*, ed. Hector-Neri Castañeda, Detroit, 1967, pp. 177–200.

2   In this paper I wish to avoid the vexed question of the relation between *pains* and *pain states*. I only remark in passing that one common argument *against* identification of these two – viz., that a pain can be in one's arm but a state (of the organism) cannot be in one's arm – is easily seen to be fallacious.

3   There are some well-known remarks by Alonzo Church on this topic. Those remarks do not bear (as might at first be supposed) on the identification of concepts with synonymy-classes as such, but rather support the view that (in formal semantics) it is necessary to retain Frege's distinction between the normal and the "oblique" use of expressions. That is, even if we say that the concept of temperature *is* the synonymy-class of the word 'temperature', we must not thereby be led into the error of supposing that 'the concept of temperature' is synonymous with 'the synonymy-class of the word "temperature"' – for then 'the concept of temperature' and 'der Begriff der Temperatur' would not be synonymous, which they are. Rather, we must say that 'the concept of temperature' *refers* to the synonymy-class of the word 'temperature' (on this particular reconstruction); but that class is *identified* not as "the synonymy class to which such-and-such a word belongs," but in another way (e.g., as the synonymy-class whose members have such-and-such a characteristic use).

4   In the "Mental life of some machines" a further, and somewhat independent, characteristic of the pain inputs is discussed in terms of Automata models – namely the spontaneity of the inclination to withdraw the injured part, etc. This raises the question, which is discussed in that paper, of giving a functional analysis of the notion of a spontaneous inclination. Of course, still further characteristics come readily to mind – for example, that feelings of pain are (or seem to be) *located* in the parts of the body.

5   Cf. the discussion of "super-spartans" in "Brains and behavior."

Part II

Homuncular Functionalism and other Teleological Theories

Introduction

Machine Functionalism supposed that human brains may be described at each of three levels, the first two scientific and the third familiar and commonsensical. (1) Biologists would map out human neuroanatomy and provide neurophysiological descriptions of brain states. (2) Psychologists would (eventually) work out the machine program that was being realized by the lower-level neuroanatomy and would describe the same brain states in more abstract, computational terms. (3) Psychologists would also explain behavior, characterized in everyday terms, by reference to stimuli and to intervening mental states such as beliefs and desires, type-identifying the mental states with functional or computational states as they went. Such explanations would themselves presuppose nothing about neuroanatomy, since the relevant psychological/computational generalizations would hold regardless of what particular biochemistry might happen to be realizing the abstract program in question.

Machine Functionalism as described has more recently been challenged on each of a number of points, that together motivate a specifically teleological notion of "function" (Sober (this volume) speaks aptly of "putting the function back into Functionalism"):

(i) The Machine Functionalist still conceived psychological *explanation* in the Positivists' terms of subsumption of data under wider and wider universal generalizations. But Fodor (1968), Cummins (1983) and Dennett (this volume) have defended a competing picture of psychological explanation, according to which behavioral data are to be seen as manifestations of subjects' psychological capacities, and those capacities are to be explained by understanding the subjects as systems of interconnected components. Each component is a "homunculus," in that it is identified by reference to the function it performs, and the various homuncular components cooperate with each other in such a way as to produce overall behavioral responses to stimuli. The "homunculi" are themselves broken down into subcomponents whose functions and interactions are similarly used to explain the capacities of the subsystems they compose, and so again and again until the sub-sub- . . . components are seen to be neuroanatomical structures. (An automobile works – locomotes – by having a fuel reservoir, a fuel line, a carburetor, a combustion chamber, an ignition system, a transmission, and wheels that turn. If one wants to know how the carburetor works, one will be told what its parts are and how they work together to infuse oxygen into fuel; and so on.) Thus biologic and mechanical systems alike are hierarchically organized, on the principle of what computer scientists call "hierarchical control."

(ii) The Machine Functionalist treated functional "realization," the relation between an individual physical organism and the abstract program it was said to instantiate, as a simple matter of one-to-one correspondence between the organism's repertoire of physical stimuli, structural states and behavior, on the one hand, and the program's defining input/state/output function on the other. But this criterion of realization was seen to be too liberal; since virtually anything bears a one–one correlation of some sort to virtually anything else, "realization" in the sense of mere one–one correspondence is far too easily come by (Block (this volume), Lycan (1987, ch. 3)). Some theorists have proposed to remedy this defect by imposing a teleological requirement on realization: a physical state of an organism will count as realizing such-and-such a functional description only if the organism has genuine organic integrity and the state plays its functional role properly *for* the organism, in the teleological sense of "for" and in the teleological sense of "function." The state must do what it does as a matter of, so to speak, its biological purpose.

(iii) Machine Functionalism's two-levelled picture of human psychobiology is unbiological in the extreme. Neither living things nor even computers themselves are split into a purely "structural" level of biological/physiochemical description and any one "abstract" computational level of machine/psychological description. Rather, they are all hierarchically organized at many levels, each level "abstract" with respect to those beneath it but "structural" or concrete as it realizes those levels above it. The "functional"/"structural" or "software"/"hardware" distinction is entirely relative to one's chosen level of organization. This relativity has repercussions for Functionalist solutions to problems in the philosophy of mind (Lycan (1987, ch. 5)), and for current controversies surrounding the New Connectionism and neural modelling (see Part IV of this volume).

(iv) The teleologizing of functional realization has helped functionalists to rebut various objections based on the "qualia" or "feels" or experienced phenomenal characters of mental states (Lycan (1981), Sober (this volume)).

(v) Millikan (1984), Van Gulick (this volume), Fodor (1984, this volume), Dretske (this volume) and others have argued powerfully that teleology must enter into any adequate analysis of the intentionality or aboutness of mental states such as beliefs and desires, mentioned in the introduction to Part I above. According to the teleological theorists, a neurophysiological state should count as *a belief that broccoli will kill you*, and in particular as *about broccoli*, only if that state has the representing of broccoli as in some sense one of its psychobiological functions.

All this talk of teleology and biological function seems to presuppose that biological and other "structural" states of physical systems really have functions in the teleological sense. The latter claim is controversial to say the least. Some philosophers dismiss it as hilariously false, as a superstitious relict of primitive animism or Panglossian theism or at best the vitalism of the nineteenth century; others tolerate it but only as a useful metaphor; still others take teleological characterizations to be literally but only interest-relatively true, true *modulo* a convenient classificatory or interpretive scheme (Cummins (1975)). Only a few fairly recent writers (Wimsatt (1972), Wright (1973), Millikan (1984) and a few others) have taken teleological characterizations to be literally and categorically true. This may seem to embarrass teleologized Functionalist theories of mind.

Yes and no. Yes, because if a Homuncular and/or Teleological Functionalist type-identifies mental items with teleologically characterized items, and teleological characterizations are not literally true, then mental ascriptions cannot be literally true either. Equivalently, if people really do have mental states and events, on their own and not merely in virtue of anyone's superstitious or subjective interpretation of them, but their physical states do not have objectively teleological functions, then mental states cannot be type-identified with teleological states.

Fortunately for the Teleological Functionalist there is now a small but vigorous industry whose purpose is to explicate biological teleology in naturalistic terms, typically in terms of etiology. For example, a trait may be said to have the function of doing *F* in virtue of its having been selected for because it did *F*; a heart's function is to pump blood because hearts' pumping blood in the past has given them a selection advantage and so led to the survival of more animals with hearts. Actually, no simple etiological explication will do (Cummins (1975), Boorse (1976), Bigelow and Pargetter (1987)), but philosophers of biology have continued to refine the earlier accounts and to make them into adequate naturalistic analyses of genuine function.

It should be noted that the correctness of type-identifying mental items with teleological items does not strictly depend on the objectivity or even the truth of teleological descriptions. For corresponding to each metaphysical view of teleology, including deflationary and flatly derisive ones, there is a tenable view of mind. Just as teleology may be a matter of interest-relative interpretation, so, after all, may mental ascriptions be (see Part III of this volume). For that matter, just as teleology may be only metaphorical, fictional or illusory, so may mental ascriptions be; some philosophers now hold that mental ascriptions are in the end false (see Part IV). But we shall consider those possibilities in due course.

FURTHER READING

Homuncular Functionalism

Attneave, F. (1960) "In defense of homunculi," in W. Rosenblith (ed.), *Sensory Communication*, MIT Press.

Fodor, J. A. (1968) "The appeal to tacit knowledge in psychological explanation," *Journal of Philosophy* 65, 627–40.

Simon, H. (1969) "The architecture of complexity," in *The Sciences of the Artificial*, MIT Press.

Wimsatt, W. C. (1976) "Reductionism, levels of organization, and the mind–body problem," in G. Globus, G. Maxwell and I. Savodnik (eds), *Consciousness and the Brain*, Plenum.

Dennett, D. C. (1978) "Why you can't make a computer that feels pain," reprinted in *Brainstorms*, Bradford Books.

Haugeland, J. (1978) "The nature and plausibility of Cognitivism," *Behavioral and Brain Sciences* 1, 215–26.

Lycan, W. (1981) "Form, function, and feel," *Journal of Philosophy* 78, 24–50.

Cummins, R. (1983) *The Nature of Psychological Explanation*, Bradford Books/MIT Press.

Lycan, W. G. (1987) *Consciousness*, Bradford Books/MIT Press.

Teleological Functionalism

Dennett, D. C. (1969) *Content and Consciousness*, Routledge & Kegan Paul, chs. III and IV.

Fodor, J. A. (1984) "Semantics, Wisconsin Style," *Synthese* 59, 231–50.

Millikan, R. G. (1984) *Language, Thought, and Other Biological Categories*, Bradford Books/MIT Press.

Papineau, D. (1987) *Reality and Representation*, Basil Blackwell, ch. 4.

Dretske, F. (1988) *Explaining Behavior*, Bradford Books/MIT Press.

Naturalistic theories of teleology

Wimsatt, W. C. (1972) "Teleology and the logical structure of function statements," *Studies in History and Philosophy of Science* 3, 1–80.

Wright, L. (1973) "Functions," *Philosophical Review* 82, 139–68.

Cummins, R. (1975) "Functional analysis," *Journal of Philosophy* 72, 741–64.

Bennett, J. (1976) *Linguistic Behaviour*, Cambridge University Press, ch. 1.

Boorse, C. (1976) "Wright on functions," *Philosophical Review* 85, 70–86.

Bigelow, J. and Pargetter, R. (1987) "Functions," *Journal of Philosophy* 84, 181–96.

4

Homuncular Functionalism

Why the Law of Effect Will Not Go Away

DANIEL C. DENNETT

The poet Paul Valéry said: "It takes two to invent anything." He was not referring to collaborative partnerships between people but to a bifurcation in the individual inventor. "The one," he says, "makes up combinations; the other one chooses, recognizes what he wishes and what is important to him in the mass of the things which the former has imparted to him. What we call genius is much less the work of the first one than the readiness of the second one to grasp the value of what has been laid before him and to choose it."[1] This is a plausible claim. Why? Is it true? If it is, what kind of truth is it? An empirical generalization for which there is wide scale confirmation? Or a "conceptual truth" derivable from our concept of invention? Or something else?

Herbert Simon, in *The Sciences of the Artificial*, makes a related claim: "human problem solving, from the most blundering to the most insightful, involves nothing more than varying mixtures of trial and error and selectivity."[2] This claim is also plausible, I think, but less so. Simon presents it as if it were the conclusion of an inductive investigation, but *that*, I think, is not plausible at all. An extensive survey of human problem solving may have driven home this thesis to Simon, but its claim to our assent comes from a different quarter.

I want to show that these claims owe their plausibility to the fact that they are implications of an abstract principle whose "necessity" (such as it is) consists in this: we can know independently of empirical research in psychology that any adequate and complete psychological theory must exploit some version or other of the principle. The most familiar version of the principle I have in mind is the derided darling of the behaviorists: the Law of Effect. "The rough idea," Broadbent observes,[3] "that actions followed by reward are repeated, is one which is likely to occur to most intelligent people who think about possible explanations of behavior." This rough idea, refined, is the Law of Effect, and my claim is that

"Why the Law of Effect Will Not Go Away" by D. C. Dennett first appeared in the *Journal of the Theory of Social Behaviour* (1975), pp. 169–76, and is reprinted here by kind permission.

it is not just part of *a* possible explanation of behavior, but of *any* possible adequate explanation of behavior.

In order to establish this condition of adequacy for psychological theories, we must first be clear about the burden of psychology. Consider the way the rest of the social sciences depend on the more basic science of psychology. Economics, or at any rate classical economics, assumes at the outset an ontology of rational, self-interested agents, and then proposes to discover generalizations about how such agents, the "atoms" of economics, will behave in the market-place. This assumption of intelligence and self-interest in agents is not idle; it is needed to ground and explain the generalizations. Consider the law of supply and demand. There is no mystery about why the law holds as reliably as it does: *people are not fools*; they want as much as they can get, they know what they want and how much they want it, and they know enough to charge what the market will bear and buy as cheap as they can. If that didn't explain why the law of supply and demand works, we would be utterly baffled or incredulous on learning that it did. Political science, sociology, anthropology and social psychology are similarly content to *assume* capacities of discrimination, perception, reason and action based on reason, and then seek interesting generalizations about the exploitation of these capacities in particular circumstances. One way of alluding to this shared feature of these social sciences is to note that they are all *intentional*: they utilize the intentional or "mentalistic" or "cognitive" vocabulary – they speak of belief, desire, expectation, recognition, action, etc. – and they permit explanations to come to an end, at least on occasion, with the citation of a stretch of practical reasoning (usually drastically enthymematic): the voters elected the Democrat *because* they were working men and believed the Republican candidate to be anti-labor; the stock market dropped *because* investors believed other havens for their money were safer. These sciences leave to psychology the task of explaining *how there come to be* entities – organisms, human beings – that can be so usefully assumed to be self-interested, knowledgeable and rational. A fundamental task of psychology then is to explain intelligence. For the super-abstemious behaviorist who will not permit himself to speak even of intelligence (that being too "mentalistic" for him) we can say, with Hull, that a primary task of psychology "is to understand . . . why . . . behavior . . . is so generally adaptive, i.e., successful in the sense of reducing needs and facilitating survival . . ."[4] The account of intelligence required of psychology must not of course be question-begging. It must not explain intelligence in terms of intelligence, for instance by assigning responsibility for the existence of intelligence in creatures to the munificence of an intelligent Creator, or by putting clever homunculi at the control panels of the nervous system . . .[5] If that were the best psychology could do, then psychology could not do the job assigned it.

We already have a model of a theory that admirably discharges just this *sort* of burden in the Darwinian theory of evolution by natural selection, and as many commentators have pointed out, the Law of Effect is closely analogous to the principle of natural selection. The Law of Effect presumes there to be a "population" of stimulus–response pairs, more or less randomly or in any case arbitrarily mated, and from this large and varied pool, reinforcers *select* the well-designed, the adaptive, the fortuitously appropriate pairs in an entirely mechanical way: their recurrence is made more probable, while their maladaptive or merely neutral brethren suffer "extinction," not by being *killed* (all particular stimulus–response pairs come to swift ends), but by *failing to reproduce*. The analogy is very strong, very satisfying, and very familiar.

But there has been some misinterpretation of the nature of its appeal. Broadbent observes:

> The attraction both of natural selection and of the Law of Effect, to certain types of mind, is that they do not call on explanatory principles of a quite separate order from those used in the physical sciences. It is not surprising therefore that the Law of Effect had been seized on, not merely as a generalization which is true of animals under certain conditions, but also as a fundamental principle which would explain all adaptive behaviour.[6]

It is certainly true that these analogous principles appeal to physicalists or materialists because they are mechanistically explicable, but there is a more fundamental reason for favoring them: they both can provide clearly non-question-begging accounts of *explicanda* for which it is very hard to devise non-question-begging accounts. Darwin explains a world of final causes and teleological laws with a principle that is, to be sure, mechanistic but – more fundamentally – utterly independent of "meaning" or "purpose." It assumes a world that is *absurd* in the existentialist's sense of the term: not ludicrous but pointless, and this assumption is a necessary condition of any non-question-begging account of *purpose*. Whether we can imagine a *non*-mechanistic but also non-question-begging principle for explaining design in the biological world is doubtful; it is tempting to see the commitment to non-question-begging accounts here as tantamount to a commitment to mechanistic materialism, but the priority of these commitments is clear. It is not that one's prior prejudice in favour of materialism gives one reason to accept Darwin's principle because it is materialistic, but rather that one's prior acknowledgment of the constraint against begging the question gives one *reason to adopt materialism*, once one sees that Darwin's non-question-begging account of design or purpose in nature is materialistic. One argues: Darwin's materialistic theory may not be the only non-question-begging theory of these matters, but it is one such theory, and the only one we have found, which is quite a good reason for espousing materialism.

A precisely parallel argument might occur to the psychologist trying to decide whether to throw in with the behaviorists: theories based on the Law of Effect may not be the only psychological theories that do not beg the question of intelligence, but they *are* clearly non-question-begging in this regard, and their rivals are not, which is quite a good reason for joining the austere and demanding brotherhood of behaviorists. But all is not well in that camp, and has not been for some time. Contrary to the claims of the more optimistic apologists, the Law of Effect has not been knit into any theory with anything remotely like the proven power of the theory of natural selection. The Law of Effect has appeared in several guises since Thorndike introduced it as a principle of learning; most influentially, it assumed centrality in Hull's behaviorism as the "law of primary reinforcement" and in Skinner's as the "principle of operant conditioning,"[7] but the history of these attempts is the history of ever more sophisticated failures to get the Law of Effect to *do enough work*. It may account for a *lot* of learning, but it can't seem to account for it all. Why, then, not look for another fundamental principle of more power to explain the balance? It is not just mulishness or proprietary pride that has kept behaviorists from following this suggestion, but rather something like the conviction that the Law of Effect is not just *a* good idea, but the only possible good idea for this job. There is something right in this conviction, I want to maintain, but what is wrong in it has had an ironic result: allegiance to the Law of Effect in its behavioristic or peripheralistic versions has forced psychologists to beg small questions left and right in order to keep from begging the big question. One "saves" the Law of Effect from persistent counter-instances by the *ad hoc* postulation of reinforcers and stimulus histories for which one has not the slightest grounds except the demands of the theory. For instance, one postulates curiosity drives, the reduction of which is reinforcing, in order to explain "latent" learning, or presumes that when one exhibits an apparently novel bit of intelligent behavior, there *must have been* some "relevantly similar" responses in one's past for which one was reinforced. These strategies are not altogether bad; they parallel the evolutionist's speculative hypothetical ancestries of species, which are similarly made up out of whole cloth to begin with, but which differ usually in being clearly confirmable or disconfirmable. These criticisms of behaviorism are not new,[8] and not universally fair in application either. I am convinced, nevertheless, that no behaviorism, however sophisticated, can elude all versions of these familiar objections, but that is not a claim to be supported in short compass. It will be more constructive to turn to what I claim is right about the Law of Effect, and to suggest another way a version of it can be introduced to take up where behaviorism leaves off.

The first thing to note is that the Law of Effect and the principle of natural selection are not just analogs; they are designed to work together. There is a kind of intelligence, or pseudo-intelligence, for which the principle of natural selection itself provides the complete explanation, and that is the "intelligence" manifest in tropistic, "instinctual" behavior control. The environmental appropriateness, the biological and strategic wisdom, evident in bird's-nest-building, spider-web-making and less intricate "innate" behavioral dispositions is to be explained by the same principle that explains the well-designedness of the bird's wings or the spider's eyes. We are to understand that creatures so "wired" as to exhibit useful tropistic behavior in their environmental niches will have a survival advantage over creatures not so wired, and hence will gradually be selected by the vicissitudes of nature. Tropistic behavior is not plastic in the individual, however, and it is evident that solely tropistically controlled creatures would not be evolution's final solution to the needs-versus-environment problem. *If* creatures with some plasticity in their input–output relations were to appear, *some* of them might have an advantage over even the most sophisticated of their tropistic cousins. Which ones? Those that were able to distinguish good results of plasticity from bad, and preserve the good. The problem of selection reappears and points to its own solution: let some class of events in the organisms be genetically endowed with the capacity to increase the likelihood of the recurrence of behavior-controlling events upon which they act. Call them reinforcers. Some mutations, we can then speculate, appear with inappropriate reinforcers, others with neutral reinforcers, and a lucky few with appropriate reinforcers. Those lucky few survive, of course, and their progeny are endowed genetically with a capacity to *learn*, where learning is understood to be nothing more than a change (in the environmentally appropriate direction) in stimulus–response probability relations. The obviously adaptive positive reinforcers will be events normally caused by the presence of food or water, by sexual contact, and by bodily well-being, while the normal effects of injury and deprivation will be the obvious negative reinforcers, though there could be many more than these.[9]

The picture so far is of creatures well endowed by natural selection with tropistic *hard-wiring*, including the hard-wiring of some reinforcers. These reinforcers, in turn, permit the further selection and establishment of adaptive soft-wiring, such selection to be drawn from a pool of essentially arbitrary, *undesigned* temporary interconnections. Whenever a creature is fortunate enough to have one of its interconnections be followed by an environmental effect that in turn produces a reinforcer as "feedback", that interconnection will be favored. Skinner is quite explicit about all this. In *Science and Human Behavior* he notes that "The process of conditioning has survival value," but of course what he means is that the *capacity* to be conditioned has survival value. "Where inherited behavior leaves off, the inherited modifiability of the process of conditioning takes over."[10] So let us use the term "Skinnerian creatures" for all creatures that are susceptible to operant conditioning, all creatures whose learning can be explained by the Law of Effect. Skinnerian creatures clearly have it over merely tropistic creatures, but it seems that there are other creatures, e.g., at least ourselves and many other mammals, that have it over merely Skinnerian creatures.

The trouble, intuitively, with Skinnerian creatures is that they can learn only by actual behavioral trial and error in the environment. A useful bit of soft-wiring cannot get selected until it has had an opportunity to provoke some reinforcing feedback from the environment, and the problem seems to be that merely *potential*, as yet *unutilized* behavioral controls can *ex hypothesi* have no environmental effects which could lead to their being reinforced. And yet experience seems to show that we, and even monkeys, often think out and select an adaptive course of action without benefit of prior external feedback and reinforcement. Faced with this dilemma, we might indulge in a little wishful thinking: if only the Law of Effect could provide for the reinforcement of merely potential, unutilized bits of behavior control wiring! If only such unutilized controls could have some subtle effect on the environment (i.e., if only merely "thinking about the solution" could have some environmental effect) and if only the environment were benign enough to bounce back the appropriate feedback in response! But that, it seems, would be miraculous.

Not so. We can have all that and more by simply positing that creatures have *two* environments, the outer environment in which they live, and an "inner" environment they carry around with them. The inner environment is just to be conceived as an input–output box for providing feedback for events in the brain.[11] Now we can run just the same speculative argument on Skinnerian creatures that we earlier ran on tropistic creatures. Suppose there appear among the Skinnerian creatures of the world mutations that have inner environments of the sort just mentioned. Some, we can assume, will have maladaptive inner environments (the environments will make environmentally inappropriate behavior more likely); others will have neutral inner environments; but a lucky few will have inner environments that happen to reinforce, by and large, only adaptive *potential* behavioral controls. In a way we are turning the principle of natural selection on its head: we are talking of the evolution of (inner) environments to suit the organism, of environments that would have survival value in an organism. Mutations equipped with such benign inner environments would have a distinct survival advantage over merely Skinnerian creatures in any exiguous environment, since they could learn faster and *more safely* (for trial and error learning is not only tedious; it can be dangerous). The advantage provided by such a benign inner environment has been elegantly expressed in a phrase of Karl Popper's: it "permits our hypotheses to die in our stead."

The behaviorist, faced with the shortcomings of the Law of Effect, insisted that all we needed was more of the same (that only more of same could explain what had to be explained), and that is what we have given him. He was just construing "the same" too narrowly. The *peripheralism* of behaviorist versions of the Law of Effect turns out to be not so essential as they had thought. For instance, our talk of an inner *environment* is merely vestigial peripheralism; the inner environment is just an inner something that selects. Ultimately of course it is environmental effects that are the measure of adaptivity and the mainspring of learning, but the environment can delegate its selective function to something in the organism (just as death had earlier delegated its selective function to pain), and if this occurs, a more intelligent, flexible, organism is the result.

It might be asked if behaviorists haven't already, in fact long ago, taken this step to inner reinforcement or selection. I think the fairest answer is that some have and some have not, and even those that have have not been clear about what they are doing. On the one hand there are the neo-Skinnerians who have no qualms about talking about the operant conditioning that results in the subject who *imagines* courses of action followed by reinforcing results, and on the other hand you have the neo-Skinnerians that still rail against the use of such mentalistic terms as "imagine." Skinner himself falls into both camps, often within the compass of a single page.[12] "The skin," says Skinner, "is not that important as a boundary,"[13] but it is hard to believe he sees the implications of this observation. In any event it will be clearer here to suppose that behaviorists are "classical" peripheralists who do not envisage such a reapplication of the Law of Effect via an inner environment.

At this point it is important to ask whether this proposed principle of selection by inner environment hasn't smuggled in some incoherency or impossibility, for if it has not, we can argue that since our hypothesized mutations would clearly have the edge over merely Skinnerian creatures, there is no reason to believe that operant conditioning was evolution's final solution to the learning or intelligence problem, and we could then safely "predict" the appearance and establishment of such mutations. Here we are, we could add. We could then go on to ask how powerful our new principle was, and whether there was learning or intelligence *it* couldn't explain. And we could afford to be more open-minded about this question than the behaviorist was, since if we thought there *was* learning it couldn't handle, we would know where to look for yet a stronger principle: yet a *fourth* incarnation of our basic principle of natural selection (or, otherwise viewed, yet a *third* incarnation of our basic psychological principle of the Law of Effect). In fact we can already see just what it will be. Nothing requires the inner environment to be entirely genetically hard-wired. A more versatile capacity would be one in which the inner environment *itself* could evolve in the individual as a result of – for starters – operant conditioning. We not only learn; we learn better how to learn, and learn better how to learn better how to learn.[14]

So is there anything incoherent about the supposition of inner environments that can select adaptive features of *potential* behavior control systems (and favor their incorporation into *actual* behavior controls – for that is what reinforcement amounts to in this application)? Is anything miraculous or question-begging being assumed here? The notion of an inner environment was *introduced* in explicitly non-intentional language: the inner environment is simply any internal region that can affect and be affected by features of potential behavioral control systems. The benign and hence selected inner environments are simply those in which the result of these causal interactions is the increased conditional probability of the actualization of those potential controls that would be adaptive under the conditions in which they are probable. The way the notion is introduced is thus uncontaminated by covert appeal to intelligence, but it is still not obvious that an inner environment could "work."

What conditions must we put on features of bits of brain design to ensure that their selection by an optimally designed selector-mechanism will yield a better than chance improvement in ultimate performance? Since selection by inner environment is ultimately a mechanical sorting, which can key only on physical features of what is sorted, at the very least there would have to be a *normal* or *systematic* correlation between the physical event types selected and what we may call a *functional role* in some control program. A physically characterized type of wiring could not consist in the main of reliably adaptive tokens unless those tokens normally played a particular function.[15] This is the same condition, raised one level, that we find on operant conditioning: if physically characterized *response* classes do not produce a normally uniform environmental effect, reinforcement cannot be adaptive. So if and when this principle works, it works to establish high probabilities that particular appropriate functional roles will be filled at the appropriate times in control programs. Functional roles will be *discriminated*, and thereby control programs will become well designed.

It is hard to keep track of these purported functions and effects while speaking in the sterilized vocabulary of the behaviorist, but there is an easier way of talking: we can say that physical event tokens of a selected type have – in virtue of their normally playing a certain role in a well-designed functional organization – a *meaning* or *content*. We have many familiar examples of *adaptive potential behavior control elements*: accurate *maps* are adaptive potential behavior control elements, and so are true *beliefs*, warranted *expectations*, clear *concepts*, well-ordered *preferences*, sound *plans of action*, in short all the favorite tools of the cognitive psychologist. As Popper says, it is *hypotheses* – events or states endowed with an intentional characterization – that die in our stead. Is *cognitive* psychology then bound ultimately to versions of the Law of Effect? That it is, I hope to show by looking at artificial intelligence (AI) research.

AI program designers work backwards on the same task behaviorists work forwards on. We have just traced the behaviorists' cautious and self-denying efforts to build from mechanistic principles towards the levels of complexity at which it becomes apt and illuminating to speak in intentional terms about what they claim is going on. The AI researcher *starts* with an intentionally characterized problem (e.g., how can I get a computer to *understand* questions of English?), breaks it down into sub-problems that are also intentionally characterized (e.g., how do I get the computer to *recognize* questions, *distinguish* subjects from predicates, *ignore* irrelevant parsings?) and then breaks these problems down still further until finally he reaches problem or task descriptions that are obviously mechanistic. Here is a way of looking at the process. The AI programmer begins with an intentionally characterized problem, and thus frankly views the computer anthropomorphically: if he *solves* the problem he will say he has designed a computer that can understand questions in English. His first and highest level of design breaks the computer down into subsystems, each of which is given intentionally characterized tasks; he composes a flow chart of evaluators, rememberers, discriminators, overseers and the like. These are *homunculi* with a vengeance; the highest level design breaks the computer down into a committee or army of intelligent homunculi with purposes, information and strategies. Each homunculus in turn is analysed into *smaller* homunculi, but, more important, into *less clever* homunculi. When the level is reached where the homunculi are no more than adders and subtractors, by the time they need only the intelligence to pick the larger of two numbers when directed to, they have been reduced to functionaries "who can be replaced by a machine." The aid to comprehension of anthropomorphizing the elements just about lapses at this point, and a mechanistic view of the proceedings becomes workable and comprehensible. The AI programmer uses intentional language fearlessly because he *knows* that if he succeeds in getting his program to run, any questions he has been begging provisionally will have been paid back. The computer is more unforgiving than any human critic; if the program works then we can be certain that all homunculi have been discharged from the theory.[16]

Working backwards in this way has proved to be a remarkably fruitful research strategy, for powerful principles of design have been developed and tested, so it is interesting to note that the overall shape of AI models is strikingly similar to the organization proposed for our post-Skinnerian mutations, and the problems encountered echo the problems faced by the behaviorist. A ubiquitous strategy in AI programming is known as *generate-and-test*, and our opening quotation of Paul Valéry perfectly describes it. The problem solver (or inventor) is broken down at some point or points into a generator and a tester. The generator spews up candidates for solutions or elements of solutions to the problems, and the tester accepts or rejects them on the basis of stored criteria. Simon points out the analogy, once again, to natural selection (*The Sciences of the Artificial*, pp. 95–8).

The tester of a generate-and-test subroutine is none other than a part of the inner environment of our post-Skinnerian mutations, so if we want to know how well the principle of selection by inner environment can work, the answer is that it can work as well as generate-and-test methods can work in AI programs, which is hearteningly well.[17] Simon, as we saw at the outset, was prepared to go so far as to conclude that *all* "human problem solving, from the most blundering to the most insightful" can be captured in the net of generate-and-test programming: "varying mixtures of trial and error and selectivity." This claim is exactly analogous to the behaviorists' creed that the Law of Effect could explain all learning, and again we may ask whether this is short-sighted allegiance to an idea that is good, but not the only good idea. Generate-and-test programs can simulate, and hence account for (in one important sense)[18] a lot of problem-solving and invention; what grounds have we for supposing it is powerful enough to handle it all? The behaviorist was in no position to defend his creed, but the AI researcher is in better shape.

Some AI researchers have taken their task to be the *simulation* of particular cognitive capacities "found in nature," – even the capacities and styles of particular human individuals[19] – and such research is known as CS or "cognitive simulation" research, but others take their task to be, not simulation, but the construction of intelligent programs *by any means whatever*. The only constraint on design principles in AI thus viewed is that they should *work*, and hence any boundaries the AI programmer keeps running into are arguably boundaries that restrict *all possible* modes of intelligence and learning. Thus, if AI is truly the study of all possible modes of intelligence, and if generate-and-test is truly a necessary feature of AI learning programs, then generate-and-test is a necessary feature of all modes of learning, and hence a necessary principle in any adequate psychological theory.

Both premises in that argument need further support. The first premise was proposed on the grounds that AI's guiding principle is that *anything is permitted that works*, but isn't AI really more restrictive than that principle suggests? Isn't it really that AI is the investigation of all possible *mechanistically realizable* modes of intelligence? Doesn't AI's claim to cover all possible modes beg the question against the vitalist or dualist who is looking for a non-question-begging but also non-mechanistic psychology? The AI researcher is a mechanist, to be sure, but a mechanist-*malgré-lui*. He typically does not know or care what the hardware realizations of his designs will be, and often even relinquishes control and authorship of his programs at a point where they are still replete with intentionalistic constructions, still several levels away from machine language. He can do this because it is merely a clerical problem for compiler programs and the technicians that feed them to accomplish the ultimate "reduction" to a mechanistic level. The constraints of mechanism do not loom large for the AI researcher, for he is confident that any design he can state *clearly* can be mechanized. The operative constraint for him, then, is something like clarity, and in practice clarity is ensured for anything expressible in a programming language of some level. Anything thus expressible is clear; what about the converse? Is anything clear thus expressible? The AI programmer believes it, but it is not something subject to proof; it is, or boils down to, some version of Church's Thesis (e.g., anything computable is Turing-machine computable). But now we can see that the supposition that there might be a non-question-begging non-mechanistic psychology gets you nothing, unless accompanied by the supposition that Church's Thesis is false. For a non-question-begging psychology will be a psychology that makes no ultimate appeals to unexplained intelligence, and that condition can be reformulated as the condition that whatever functional parts a psychology breaks its subjects into, the smallest, or most fundamental, or least sophisticated parts must not be supposed to perform tasks or follow procedures requiring intelligence. That condition in turn is surely strong enough to ensure that any procedure admissible as an "ultimate" procedure in a psychological theory falls well within the intuitive boundaries of the "computable" or "effective" as these terms are presumed to be used in Church's Thesis. The intuitively computable functions mentioned in Church's Thesis are those that "any fool can do," while the admissible atomic functions of a psychological theory are those that "presuppose *no* intelligence." If Church's Thesis is correct, then the constraints of mechanism are no more severe than the constraint against begging the question in psychology, for any psychology that stipulated atomic tasks that were "too difficult" to fall under Church's Thesis would be a theory with undischarged homunculi.[20] So our first premise, that AI is the study of all possible modes of intelligence, is supported as much as it could be, which is *not quite* total support, in two regards. The first premise depends on two unprovable but very reasonable assumptions: that Church's Thesis is true, and that *there can be*, in principle, an adequate and complete psychology.

That leaves the second premise to defend: what reason is there to believe that generate-and-test is a necessary and not merely handy and ubiquitous feature of AI learning programs? First, it must be granted that many computer programs of great sophistication do not invoke any variety of generate-and-test. In these cases the correct or best steps to be taken by the computer are not selected but *given*; the program's procedures are completely designed and inflexible. These programs are the analogs of our merely tropistic creatures; their design is *fixed* by a prior design process. Sometimes there is a sequence of such programs, with the programmer making a series of changes in the program to improve its performance. Such genealogical developments do not so much represent problems solved as problems deferred, however, for the trick is to get the program to become self-designing, "to get the teacher out of the learner." As long as the programmer must, in effect, reach in and rewire the control system, the system is not *learning*. Learning can be viewed as *self-design*, and Simon suggests we "think of the design process as involving first the generation of alternatives and then the testing of these alternatives against a whole array of requirements and constraints" (*The Sciences of the Artificial*, p. 74). Of course he would suggest this, and we can follow his suggestion, but are there any alternatives? Is there any way of thinking (coherently) about the design process that is incompatible with (and more powerful than) thinking of it as an evolution wrought by generate-and-test? It seems not, and here is an argument supposed to show why. I suspect this argument could be made to appear more rigorous (while also, perhaps, being revealed to be entirely unoriginal) by recasting it into the technical vocabulary of some version of "information theory" or "theory of self-organizing systems." I would be interested to learn that this was so, but am content to let the argument, which is as intuitive as it is sketchy, rest on its own merits in the meantime.

We are viewing learning as ultimately a *process* of self-design. That process is for the purposes of this argument defined only by its *product*, and the product is a *new* design. That is, as a result of the process something comes to have a design it previously did not have. This new design "must come from somewhere." That is, it takes *information* to distinguish the new design from all other designs, and that information must come from somewhere – either all from outside the system, or all from inside, or a bit of both. If all from outside, then the system does not redesign itself; this is the case we just looked at, where the all-knowing programmer, who *has* the information, *imposes* the new design on the system from without. So the information must all come from inside, or from both inside and outside. Suppose it all comes from inside. Then either the information already exists inside or it is created inside. What I mean is this: either the new design *exists ready made* in the old design in the sense that its implementation at this time is already guaranteed by its old design, or the old design does not determine in this way what the new design will be. In the former case, the system has not really designed itself; it was designed all along to go into this phase at this time, and we must look to a prior design process to explain this. In the latter case, the new design is *underdetermined* by the old design. This is a feature shared with the one remaining possibility: that the information comes from both inside and outside. In both of these cases the new design is underdetermined by the old design by itself, and only in these cases is there "genuine" learning (as opposed to the merely "apparent" learning of the merely tropistic creature). In any such case of underdetermination, the new design is either underdetermined period – there is a truly random contribution here; nothing takes up all the slack left by the underdetermination of the old design – *or* the new design is determined by the combination of the old design and contributions (from either inside or outside or both) that are themselves *arbitrary*, that is, *undesigned* or *fortuitous*. But if the contribution of arbitrary elements is to yield a better than chance probability of the new design being an improvement over the old design, the old design must have the capacity to *reject* arbitrary contributions on the basis of design features – information – already present. In other words, there must be a *selection* from the fortuitous contributions, based on the old design. If the arbitrary or undesigned contribution comes from within, what we have is a non-deterministic automaton.[21] A non-deterministic automaton is one such that at some point or points its further operations must wait on the result of a procedure that is undetermined by its program and input. In other words, some tester must wait on some generator to produce a candidate for its inspection. If the undesigned contribution comes from the outside, the situation is much the same; the distinction between *input* and *random contribution* is just differently drawn. The automaton is now deterministic in that its next step is a determinate function of its program and its input, but what input it gets is a fortuitous matter. In either case the system can *protect itself* against merely fortuitous response to this merely fortuitous input only by *selecting* as a function of its old design from the fortuitous "stimulation" presented. Learning must tread the fine line between the idiocy of pre-programmed tropism on the one hand and the idiocy of an over-plastic domination by fortuitous impingements on the other. In short, every process of genuine learning (or invention, which is just a special sort of learning) must invoke, at at least one but probably many levels, the principle of generate-and-test.

The moral of this story is that cognitivist theoreticians of all stamps may proceed merrily and *fruitfully* with temporarily question-begging theoretical formulations, but if they expect AI to *pay their debts* some day (and if anything can, AI can), they must acknowledge that the *processes* invoked will inevitably bear the analogy to natural selection exemplified by the Law of Effect. The moral is *not*, of course, that behaviorism is the road to truth in psychology; even our hypothesized first-generation mutations of Skinnerian creatures were too intelligent for behaviorism to account for, and we have every reason to believe actual higher organisms are much more complicated than that. The only solace for the behaviorist in this account is that his theoretical paralysis has been suffered in a Good Cause; he has not begged the question, and if the high-flying cognitivists ever achieve his probity, it will only be by relying on principles fundamentally analogous to his.

This leaves open where these inevitable principles of selection will be invoked, and how often. Nothing requires generate-and-test formats to be simple and obviously mechanistic in any of their interesting realizations. On the contrary, *introspective* evidence, of a sort I will presently illustrate, seems to bear out the general claim that generate-and-test is a common and recognizable feature of human problem solving, at the same time that it establishes that the generators and testers with which we are *introspectively* familiar are themselves highly sophisticated – highly intelligent homunculi. As Simon points out, generate-and-test is not an efficient or powerful process unless the *generator* is endowed with a high degree of selectivity (so that it generates only the most likely or most plausible candidates in a circumstance), and since, as he says, "selectivity can always be equated with some kind of feedback of information from the environment" (p. 97), we must ask, of each sort and degree of selectivity in the generator, where *it* came from – is it learned or innate – and at the end of any successful answer to that question will be a generate-and-test process, either of natural selection if the selectivity is innate, or of some variety of learning, if it is not. A consequence of this is that we cannot tell by any simple inspection or introspection whether a particular stroke of genius we encounter is a bit of "genuine" invention at all – that is, whether the invention occurred just *now*, or is the result of much earlier processes of invention that are now playing out their effects. Did Einstein's genetic endowment guarantee his creativity, or did his genetic endowment together with his nurture, his stimulus history, guarantee his creativity or did he genuinely create (during his own thought processes), his great insights? I hope it is clear how little hinges on knowing the answer to this question.

At this point I am prepared to say that the first part of Valéry's claim stands vindicated: it takes two to invent anything: the one makes up combinations; the other one chooses. What of the second part of this claim: "What we call genius is much less the work of the first one than the readiness of the second one to grasp the value of what has been laid before him and to choose it"? We have seen a way in which this must be true, in the strained sense that the *ultimate* generators must contain an element of randomness or arbitrariness. "The original solution to a problem must lie in a category of luck."[22] But it does not seem that Valéry's second claim is true on any ordinary interpretation. For instance, it does not seem to be true of all *inter-personal* collaborations that the choosers are more the geniuses than their "idea-men" are. Some producers seldom offer poor suggestions; their choosers are virtual yes-men. Other producers are highly erratic in what they will propose, and require the censorship of severe and intelligent editors. There appears to be a trade-off here between, roughly, spontaneity or fertility of imagination on the one hand, and a critical eye on the other. A task of invention seems to require both, and it looks like a straightforwardly empirical question subject to continuous variation how much of each gets done by each collaborator.

Valéry seems to slight the contribution of the first, but perhaps that is just because he has in mind a collaboration at one end of the spectrum, where a relatively undiscriminating producer of combinations makes a lot of work for his editor. Of course, as said at the outset, Valéry is not talking about actual interpersonal collaboration, but of a bifurcation in the soul. He is perhaps thinking of his own case, which suggests that he is one of those who are *aware* of considering and rejecting many bad ideas. He does not credit *his* producer-homunculus with much genius, and is happy to identify with the *responsible* partner, the chooser. Mozart, it seems, was of the same type: "When I feel well and in a good humor, or when I am taking a drive or walking after a good meal, or in the night when I cannot sleep, thoughts crowd into my mind as easily as you would wish. Whence and how do they come? I do not know and *I have nothing to do with it*. Those which please me I keep in my head and hum them; at least others have told me that I do so."[23] In such cases the producer–chooser bifurcation lines up with the unconscious and conscious selves bifurcation. One is conscious only of the *products* of the producer, which one then consciously tests and chooses.

Poincaré, in a famous lecture of 1908, offers an "introspective" account of some mathematical inventing of his own that is more problematic: "One evening, contrary to my custom, I drank black coffee and could not sleep. Ideas rose in crowds; I felt them collide until pairs interlocked, so to speak, making a stable combination."[24] In this instance the chooser seems to have disappeared, but Poincaré has another, better interpretation of the incident. In this introspective experience he has been given a rare opportunity to glimpse the *processes* in the generator; what is normally accomplished out of sight of consciousness is witnessed on this occasion, and the ideas that form stable combinations are those few that would normally be presented to the conscious chooser for further evaluation. Poincaré supposes he has watched the selectivity within the generator at work. I am not a little sceptical about Poincaré's claimed *introspection* here (I think all introspection involves elements of rational reconstruction, and I smell a good deal of that in Poincaré's protocol), but I like his categories. In particular, Poincaré gives us, in his discussion of this experience, the key to another puzzling question.

For I have really had two burdens in this paper. The first, which I take to have discharged, is to explain why the Law of Effect is so popular in its various guises. The other is to explain why it is so *unpopular* in all its guises. There is no denying that the Law of Effect seems to be an affront to our self-esteem, and a lot of the resistance – even hatred – encountered by behaviorists is surely due to this. Poincaré puts his finger on it. He was, if anyone ever has been, a creative and original thinker, and yet his own analysis of how he accomplished his inventions seemed to deny him *responsibility* for them. He saw only two alternatives, both disheartening. One was that his unconscious self, the generator with whom he does not or cannot *identify* "is capable of discernment; it has tact, delicacy; it knows how to choose, to divine. What do I say? It knows better how to divine than the conscious self since it succeeds where that has failed. In a word, is not the subliminal self superior to the conscious self? I confess that, for my part, I should hate to accept this."[25] The other is that the generator is an automaton, an ultimately absurd, blind trier of all possibilities. That is of course no better a homunculus with whom to identify oneself. One does not want to be the generator, then. As Mozart says of his musical ideas: "Whence and how do they come? I do not know and I have nothing to do with it." Nor does one want to be just the tester, for then one's chances of being creative depend on the luck one has with one's collaborator, the generator. The fundamental passivity of the testing role leaves no room for the "creative self."[26] But we could not have hoped for any other outcome. If we are to have any adequate *analysis* of creativity, invention, intelligence, it must be one in which intelligence is analysed into something none of whose parts is intelligence, and at that level of analysis, of course, no "self" worth identifying with can survive. The mistake in this pessimism lies in confusing explaining with explaining away. Giving a non-question-begging account of *how* creatures are intelligent can hardly prove that they aren't intelligent. If we want to catch a glimpse of a creative self, we should look, for instance, at M. Poincaré, for *he* (and not any of his proper parts) was certainly a genius.

Finally, I cannot resist passing on a wonderful bit of incidental intelligence reported by Hadamard: the Latin verb *cogito* is derived, as St. Augustine tells us, from Latin words meaning *to shake together*, while the verb *intelligo* means *to select among*. The Romans, it seems, knew what they were talking about.

NOTES

1 Quoted by Jacques Hadamard, in *The Psychology of Inventing in the Mathematical Field* (Princeton University Press, 1949), p. 30.

2 Herbert Simon, *The Sciences of the Artificial* (MIT), p. 97.

3 D. E. Broadbent, *Behaviour* (University Paperbacks edn, 1961), p. 75.

4 Clark Hull, *Principles of Behavior* (1943), p. 19.

5 Cf. also B. F. Skinner, "Behaviorism at fifty," in T. W. Wann, ed., *Behaviorism and Phenomenology* (University of Chicago Press, 1969), p. 80.

6 Broadbent, ibid., p. 56.

7 Skinner explicitly identifies his principle with the Law of Effect in *Science and Human Behavior* (1953), p. 87.

8 Cf., e.g., Charles Taylor, *The Explanation of Behaviour* (1964); Chomsky's reviews of Skinner's *Verbal Behavior*, in *Language* (1959), and of *Beyond Freedom and Dignity*, in *New York Review of Books* (Dec. 30, 1971); Broadbent, *Behaviour*.

9 Cf. Skinner, *Science and Human Behavior*, p. 83. Skinner speaks of food and water *themselves* being the reinforcers, but commenting on this difference would entail entering the familiar and arid 'more peripheral than thou' controversy. A point of Skinner's that is always worth reiterating, though, is that negative reinforcers are not *punishments*; they are events the cessation of which is positively reinforcing, that is, their cessation *increases* the probability of recurrence of the behaviour followed by cessation.

10 *Science and Human Behavior*, p. 55.

11 This is not Simon's distinction between inner and outer environment in *The Sciences of the Artificial*, but a more restrictive notion. It also has *nothing whatever* to do with any distinction between the 'subjective' or 'phenomenal' world and the objective, public world.

12 See chapter 4 of my *Brainstorms* (1978) for detailed confirmation of this and similar vacillation in Skinner.

13 "Behaviorism at fifty", in Wann, ibid., p. 84.

14 At a glance it seems that ultimately we want one-shot learning to change the inner environment. In ordinary perspective, we want to account for the fact that if I am trying to solve a problem, *someone can tell me*, once, what won't work and I can take this lesson to heart immediately.

15 See Simon, ibid., p. 73, also pp. 90–2. He argues that *efficient* evolution of design also requires a hierarchical organization of design elements. My treatment of these issues is heavily indebted to Simon's illuminating and lucid account.

16 Cf. chapters 1 and 11 of *Brainstorms*. In *Content and Consciousness* I scorned theories that replaced the little man in the brain with a committee. This was a big mistake, for this is just

how one gets to "pay back" the "intelligence loans" of intentionalist theories. Several levels of homuncular discharge are pictured in the flow charts from Colby's *Artificial Paranoia* reproduced in *Brainstorms*.

17 Herbert Dreyfus would disagree – see *What Computers Can't Do: A Critique of Artificial Reason* (Harper & Row, 1973) – but Dreyfus has not succeeded in demonstrating any *a priori* limits to generate-and-test systems hierarchically organized, so his contribution to date is salutary scepticism, not refutation.

18 There is a tradition of overstating the import of successful AI or CS (cognitive simulation) programs (e.g., "programs are theories and successful programs are confirmed theories"). For the moment all we need accept is the minimal claim that a successful program proves a particular sort of capacity to be in principle mechanistically realizable and hence mechanistically explicable. Obviously much more can be inferred from successful programs, but it takes some detailed work to say what, where and why.

19 See, for instance, the computer-copy of a *particular* stockbroker in E. A. Feigenbaum and J. Feldman, eds, *Computers and Thought* (McGraw-Hill, 1964).

20 Note that this does *not* commit the AI researcher to the view that "men are Turing machines." The whole point of generate-and-test strategies in program design is to *permit* computers to *hit on* solutions to problems they cannot be *guaranteed* to solve either because we can prove there is no algorithm for getting the solution or because if there is an algorithm we don't know it or couldn't use it. Hence the utility of generate-and-test and heuristics in programming (see also chapter 13 of *Brainstorms*).

21 Gilbert Harman points out in *Thought* (Princeton, 1973), that non-deterministic automata can be physically deterministic (if what is random relative to the program is determined in the machine).

22 Arthur Koestler, in *The Act of Creation* (1964), p. 559, quotes the behaviorist E. R. Guthrie to this effect, but it is a misquotation, sad to say, for had Guthrie said what Koestler says he said, he would have said something true and important. Perhaps he did say it, but not on the page, or in the book, where Koestler says he said it.

23 Quoted in Hadamard, ibid., p. 16, italics added.

24 Quoted in Hadamard, ibid., p. 14.

25 Arthur Koestler, *The Act of Creation*, (ibid., Dell, 1964), p. 164.

26 This passivity is curiously evoked by Koestler in his account of "underground games" in *The Act of Creation*. It is a tell-tale sign of the inescapability of the principle of selectivity discussed here that Koestler, the arch-enemy of behaviorism, can do no better, when he sets himself the task of composing a rival account of creativity, than to accept the generate-and-test format and then endow the generator with frankly mysterious effects of uncoincidental coincidence.

The Continuity of Levels of Nature

WILLIAM G. LYCAN

Contemporary Functionalism in the philosophy of mind began with a distinction between *role* and *occupant*. As we have seen, the seductive comparison of people (or their brains) to computing machines drew our attention to the contrast between a machine's program (abstractly viewed) and the particular stuff of which the machine happens to be physically made, that *realizes* the program. It is the former, not the latter, that interests us *vis-à-vis* the interpretation, explanation,

"The Continuity of Levels of Nature by W. G. Lycan is excerpted from chapters 4 and 5 of *Consciousness* (Bradford Books/MIT Press 1987) by kind permission.

prediction, and exploitation of the machine's "behavior"; people build computers to run programs, and use whatever physical materials will best lend themselves to that task.

The distinction between "program" and "realizing-stuff," or more familiarly "software" and "hardware," lent itself happily back to the philosophy of mind when Putnam and Fodor exposed the chauvinistic implications of the Identity Theory. What "*c*-fibers" and the like are doing could have been done – this role could have been performed – by some physiochemically different structure. And sure enough, if the same role were performed, the same functions realized, by silicon- instead of carbon-based neurochemistry, or if our individual neurons were replaced piecemeal by electronic prostheses that did the same jobs, then intuitively our mentality would remain unaffected. What matters is function, not functionary; program, not realizing-stuff; software, not hardware; role, not occupant. Thus the birth of Functionalism, and the distinction between "functional" and "structural" states or properties of an organism.

Functionalism is the only positive doctrine in all of philosophy that I am prepared (if not licensed) to kill for.[1] And I see the "role"/"occupant" distinction (some say obsessively) as fundamental to metaphysics. But I maintain that the *implementation* of that distinction in recent philosophy of mind is both wrong and pernicious. And my purpose in this chapter is to attack the dichotomies of "software"/"hardware," "function"/"structure" in their usual philosophical forms, and to exhibit some of the substantive confusions and correct some of the mistakes that have flowed from them.

The hierarchy

Very generally put, my objection is that "software"/"hardware" talk encourages the idea of a bipartite Nature, divided into two levels, roughly the physiochemical and the (supervenient) "functional" or higher-organizational – as against reality, which is a multiple *hierarchy* of levels of nature, each level marked by nexus of nomic generalizations and supervenient on all those levels below it on the continuum.[2] See Nature as hierarchically organized in this way, and the "function"/"structure" distinction *goes relative*: something is a role as opposed to an occupant, a functional state as opposed to a realizer, or vice versa, only *modulo* a designated level of nature. Let me illustrate.

Physiology and microphysiology abound with examples: *Cells* – to take a rather conspicuously functional term(!) – are constituted of cooperating teams of smaller items including membrane, nucleus, mitochondria, and the like: these items are themselves *systems* of yet smaller, still cooperating constituents. For that matter, still lower levels of nature are numerous and markedly distinct: the chemical, the molecular, the atomic, the (traditional) subatomic, the microphysical. Levels are nexus of interesting lawlike generalizations, and are individuated according to the types of generalizations involved. But cells, to look back upward along the hierarchy, are grouped into tissues, which combine to form organs, which group themselves into organ systems, which cooperate – marvelously – to comprise whole organ*isms* such as human beings. Organisms, for that matter, collect themselves into organized (*organ-ized*) groups. And there is no clear difference of kind between what we ordinarily think of as single organisms and groups of organisms that function corporately in a markedly singleminded way – "group organisms" themselves, we might say.[3]

Corresponding to this bottom-up aggregative picture of the hierarchical organization of Nature is the familiar top–down explanatory strategy.[4] If we want to know how wastes and toxins are eliminated from the bodies of humans, we look for and find an *excretory system* interlocked with the digestive and circulatory systems. If we look at that system closely we find (not surprisingly) that it treats water-soluble and nonsoluble wastes differently. We find in particular a *kidney*, which works on soluble wastes in particular. If we probe the details further, proceeding downward through the hierarchy of levels, we find the kidney divided into renal cortex (a filter) and medulla (a collector). The cortex is composed mainly of nephrons. Each nephron has a glomerulus accessed by an afferent arteriole, and a contractile muscular cuff to control pressure (the pressure pushes water and solutes through the capillary walls into Bowman's Capsule, leaving blood cells and the larger blood proteins stuck behind). Reabsorption and so on are explained in cellular terms, e.g., by the special properties of the epithelial cells that line the nephron's long tubule; those special properties are in turn explained in terms of the physical chemistry of the cell membranes.

The brain is no exception to this hierarchical picture of the organism and its organs. *Neurons* are cells, comprised of *somata* containing a nucleus and protoplasm, and fibers attached to those somata, which fibers have rather dramatically isolable functions; and we are told even of smaller functional items such as the ionic pumps, which maintain high potassium concentration inside. Neurons themselves are grouped into nerve nets and other structures, such as columnar formations, which in turn combine to form larger, more clearly functional (though not so obviously modular) parts of the brain. The auditory system is a fair example. There is evidence that the auditory cortex displays two-dimensional columnar organization:[5] columns of variously specialized cells arranged along one axis respond selectively to frequencies indicated by incoming impulses from the auditory nerve, while columns roughly orthogonal to these somehow coordinate input from the one ear with input from the other. The particular sensitivities of the specialized cells is to be explained in turn by reference to ion transfer across cell membranes, and so on down. For its own part, the auditory cortex interacts with other higher-level agencies – the thalamus, the superior colliculus, and other cortical areas – which interactions are highly structured.

Thus do an aggregative ontology and a top–down epistemology of nature collaborate. The collaboration has been eloquently argued for the science of psychology in particular, by Attneave (1960), Fodor (1968), and Dennett (this volume). I shall develop the point at some length, following Lycan (1981a).

Homuncular Functionalism

Dennett (this volume, pp. 69–70) takes his cue from the methodology of certain AI research projects.[6]

> The AI researcher *starts* with an intentionally characterized problem (e.g., how can I get a computer to *understand* questions of English?), breaks it down into sub-problems that are also intentionally characterized (e.g., how do I get the computer to *recognize* questions, *distinguish* subjects from predicates, *ignore* irrelevant parsings?) and then breaks these problems down still further until finally he reaches problem or task descriptions that are obviously mechanistic.

Dennett extrapolates this methodological passage to the case of human psychology, and I take it to suggest that we view a *person* as a corporate entity that corporately performs many immensely complex functions – functions of the sort usually called mental or psychological. A psychologist who adopts Fodor's and Dennett's AI-inspired methodology will describe this person by means of a flow chart, which depicts the person's immediately sub-personal agencies and their many and various routes of access to each other that enable them to cooperate in carrying out the purposes of the containing "institution" or organism that that person is. Each of the immediately sub-personal agencies, represented by a "black box" on the original flow chart, is in turn describable by its own flow chart, that breaks *it* into further, sub-sub-personal agencies that cooperate to fulfill *its* purposes, and so on. On this view, the psychological capacities of a person and the various administrative units of a corporate organization stand in functional hierarchies of just the same type and in just the same sense.

To characterize the psychologists' quest in the way I have is to see them as first noting some intentionally or otherwise psychologically characterized abilities of the human subject at the level of data or phenomena, and positing – as theoretical entities – the homunculi or sub-personal agencies that are needed to explain the subject's having those abilities. Then the psychologists posit further, smaller homunculi in order to explain the previously posited molar behavior of the original homunculi, etc., etc. It is this feature of the Attneave/Fodor/Dennett model that ingeniously blocks the standard Rylean infinite-regress objection to homuncular theories in psychology.[7] We explain the successful activity of one homunculus, not by idly positing a second homunculus within it that successfully performs that activity, but by positing a *team* consisting of several smaller, individually less talented and more specialized homunculi – and detailing the ways in which the team members cooperate in order to produce their joint or corporate output.

Cognitive and perceptual psychologists have a reasonably good idea of the sorts of sub-personal agencies that will have to be assumed to be functioning within a human being in order for that human being to be able to perform the actions and other functions that it performs. Dennett (1978, ch. 9) mentions, at the immediately sub-personal level, a "print-out component" or speech center,[8] a "higher executive or *Control* component," a "short-term memory store or buffer memory," a "perceptual analysis component," and a "problem-solving component."

And Dennett (1978, ch. 11) examines, in some clinical detail, a multilevelled sub-personal structure that models the behavior that manifests human pain. "Behavior" here must be understood very richly, since Dennett scrupulously takes into account, not just the usual sorts of behavior that are common coin among philosophical Behaviorists and the apostles of commonsense psychology, but subtler phenomena as well: very small differences in our phenomenological descriptions of pain; infrequently remarked phenomena such as the felt time lag between our feeling that we have been burned and our feeling the deep pain of the burn; and (most interesting from the Homunctionalist point of view) the grandly varied effects of a number of different kinds of anesthetics and other drugs on a patient's live and retrospective reports concerning pain. Considerations of these various sorts serve the psychologists (and Dennett) as vivid pointers toward complexities in the relevant functional organization of the CNS, indicating the distinct black-box components at various levels of institutional organization that we must represent in our hierarchically arranged flow diagrams – the kinds of receptors, inhibitors, filters, damping mechanisms, triggers, and so on that we must posit – and the comparably various sorts of pathways that connect these components with each other and with the grosser functional components of their owners such as perceptual analyzers, information stores, and the speech center.

The homuncular approach, teleologically interpreted, has many advantages. I shall recount them when I have said a bit more about teleology. In the meantime, I put my cards on the table as regards the general form of a type-identification of the mental with the not-so-obviously mental: I propose to type-identify a mental state with the property of having such-and-such an institutionally characterized state of affairs obtaining in one (or more) of one's appropriate homunctional departments or subagencies. (The subagencies are those that would be depicted in the flow charts associated with their owners at various levels of institutional abstraction.) The same holds for mental events, processes, and properties. To be in pain of type T, we might say, is for one's sub- . . . sub-personal ϕ-er to be in a characteristic state $S_T(\phi)$, or for a characteristic activity $A_T(\phi)$ to be going on in one's ϕ-er.

Homunculi and teleology

It may be protested that the characterization "ϕ-er" and "$S_T(\phi)$" are themselves only implicitly defined by a teleological map of the organism, and that explications of them in turn would contain ultimately ineliminable references to other teleologically characterized agencies and states of the organism. This is plausible, but relatively harmless. Our job as philosophers of mind was to explicate the mental in a reductive (and noncircular) way, and this I am doing, by reducing mental characterization to homuncular institutional ones, which are teleological characterizations at various levels of functional abstraction. I am not additionally required to reduce the institutional characterizations to "nicer," more structural ones; if there were a reduction of institutional types to, say, physiological types, then on Homunctionalism the Identity Theory would be true. Institutional *types* (at any given hierarchical level of abstraction) are irreducible, though I assume throughout that institutional *tokens* are reducible in the sense of strict identity, all the way down to the subatomic level.

In fact, the irreducibility of institutional types makes for a mark in favor of Homunctionalism as a philosophical theory of the mental. As Donald Davidson and Wilfrid Sellars have both observed, an adequate theory of mind must, among its other tasks, explain the existence of the mind–body problem itself; this would involve explaining why the mental *seems* so different from the physical as to occasion Cartesianism in the naive, why it has historically proved so difficult even for the sophisticated to formulate a plausible reduction of the mental to the physical, and why our mental concepts as a family seem to comprise a "seamless whole," conceptually quite unrelated to the physiological or physical family.[9] Homunctionalism provides the rudiments of such explanations. The apparent irreducibility of the mental is the genuine irreducibility of institutional types to the less teleological.[10] The difficulty of outlining a tenable reduction of the mental even to the institutional is due to our ignorance of the organizational workings of the institution itself at a sufficiently low level of abstraction. Nor is the irreducibility of institutional types to more physiological types an embarrassment, so long as our system of institutional categories, our system of physiological categories, and our system of physical categories are just alternative groupings of the same tokens.

Some philosophers might find the Homunctionalist "reduction" very cold comfort. Certainly it would bore anyone who antecedently understands teleological characterizations of things *in terms of* mental items such as desires or intentions. Of course, as the foregoing discussion implies, I do not understand teleological talk in that way; rather, I am taking mental types to form a small subclass of teleological types occurring for the most part at a high level of functional abstraction. But if so, then how *do* I understand the teleological?

On this general issue I have little of my own to contribute. I hope, and am inclined to believe, that the teleological characterizations that Homunctionalism requires can be independently explained in evolutionary terms. This hope is considerably encouraged by the work of Karl Popper, William Wimsatt, Larry Wright, Karen Neander, and other philosophers of biology;[11] I cannot improve on their technical discussions. However, I do want to make one theoretical point, and then offer one example to back it up.

The theoretical point is that the teleologicalness of characterizations is a matter of degree: some characterizations of a thing are more teleological than others. One and the same space-time slice may be occupied by a collection of molecules, a piece of very hard stuff, a metal strip with an articulated flange, a mover of tumblers, a key, an unlocker of doors, an allower of entry to hotel rooms, a facilitator of adulterous liaisons, a destroyer of souls. Thus, we cannot split our theory of nature neatly into a well-behaved, purely mechanistic part and dubious, messy vitalistic part better ignored or done away with. And for this reason we cannot maintain that a reduction of the mental to the teleological is no gain in ontological tractability; highly teleological characterizations, unlike naive and explicated mental characterizations, have the virtue of shading off fairly smoothly into (more) brutely physical ones.[12]

Let me give one illustration pertinent to psychology. Consider an organism capable of *recognizing faces* (to take one of Dennett's nice examples of a programmable psychological capacity). There is plenty of point to the question of *how* the organism does its job; the creature might accomplish its face-recognizing by being built according to any number of entirely dissimilar functional plans. Suppose the particular plan it does use is as follows: It will accept the command to identify only when it is given as input a front view, right profile, or left profile. The executive routine will direct a *viewpoint locator* to look over the perceptual display, and the viewpoint locator will sort the input into one of the three possible orientation categories. The display will then be shown to the appropriate *analyzer*, which will produce as output a coding of the display's content. A *librarian* will check this coded formula against the stock of similarly coded visual reports already stored in the organism's memory; if it finds a match, it will look at the identification tag attached to the matching code formula and show the tag to the organism's *public relations officer*, who will give phonological instructions to the *motor subroutines* that will result in the organism's publicly and loudly pronouncing a name.

Knowing that this is the way in which our particular face-recognizer performs its job, we may want to ask for further details. We may want to know how the viewpoint locator works (is it a simple template?), or how the PR office is organized, or what kinds of sub-components the analyzer employs. Suppose the analyzer is found to consist of a *projector*, which imposes a grid on the visual display, and a scanner, which runs through the grid a square at a time and produces a binary code number. We may go on to ask how the scanner works, and be told that it consists mainly of a light meter that registers a certain degree of darkness at a square and reports "0" or "1" accordingly; we may ask how the light meter works and be told some things about photosensitive chemicals, etc., etc. Now at what point in this descent through the institutional hierarchy (from *recognizer* to *scanner* to *light meter* to *photosensitive substance*, and as much further down as one might care to go) does our characterization stop being teleological, period, and start being purely mechanical, period? I think it is clear that there is no such point, but rather a finely grained continuum connecting the abstract and highly teleological to the grittily concrete and only barely teleological. And this is why the mental can *seem* totally distinct and cut off from the physiochemical without *being*, ontologically, any such thing.[13]

A final word about my reliance on barely explicated teleology: I do not claim that barely explicated teleology is good or desirable. I do not like it at all, myself. My point is only that the mystery of the mental is *no greater than* the mystery of the heart, the kidney, the carburetor or the pocket calculator. And as an ontological point it is a very comforting one.[14]

Advantages of the teleological approach

The reader will not have failed to notice that I take *function* very seriously and literally: as honest-to-goodness natural teleology.[15] The policy of taking "function" teleologically has some key virtues: (i) As we have seen, a teleological understanding of "function" helps to account for the perceived *seamlessness* of the mental, the interlocking of mental notions in a way that has nothing visibly to do with chemical and physical concepts.[16] (ii) By imposing a teleological requirement on the notion of functional realization, we avoid all the standard counterexamples to Machine Functionalism, and, I would claim, to any other version of Functionalism; see below. (iii) A teleological functionalism also helps us to understand the nature of biological and psychological *laws*, particularly in the face of Davidsonian skepticism about the latter (Lycan 1981b; Cummins 1983). (iv) If teleological characterizations are themselves explicated in evolutionary terms, then our capacities for mental states themselves become more readily explicable by final cause; it is more obvious why we have pains, beliefs, desires, and so on.[17] (v) The teleological view affords the beginnings of an account of *intentionality* that avoids the standard difficulties for other naturalistic accounts and in particular allows brain states and events to have *false* intentional content. Causal and nomological theories of intentionality tend to falter on this last task (see Lycan 1989).

I have argued above that we need a notion of teleology that comes in degrees, or at least allows for degrees of teleologicalness of characterization, and that we already have such a notion, hard as it may be to explicate – recall the examples of the face-recognizer and the key. Philosophers may differ among themselves as to the correct analysis of this degree notion of teleology – for my own part, I tend to see the degrees as determined by amenability to explanation by final cause, where explanation "by final cause" is reconstrued in turn as a sort of evolutionary explanation (though some details of this remain to be worked out). But two main points are already clear: (i) At least for single organisms, degrees of teleologicalness of characterization correspond rather nicely to levels of nature.[18] And (ii) there is no single spot *either* on the continuum of teleologicalness or amid the various levels of nature where it is plainly natural to drive a decisive wedge, where descriptions of nature can be split neatly into a well-behaved, purely "structural," purely mechanistic mode and a more abstract and more dubious, intentional, and perhaps vitalistic mode – certainly not any spot that also corresponds to any intuitive distinction between the psychological and the merely chemical, for there is too much and too various biology in between.

My own panpsychist or at least panteleologic tendencies are showing now. Many tougher-minded philosophers will find them fanciful at best, and of course (in my lucid moments) I am prepared to admit that it is hard to see any use in regarding, say, *atomic*-level description as teleological to any degree;[19] certainly explanation-by-final-cause does not persist all the way down. *But:* unmistakably teleological characterization (description that is obviously teleological to some however small degree) persists *as far* down as could possibly be relevant to psychology (well below neuroanatomy, for example). And the *role/occupant* distinction extends much further down still. Thus the vaunted "function"/ "structure" distinction as ordinarily conceived by philosophers fails to get a grip on human psychology where it lives. . . .

Everything I have said so far may seem dull and obvious. I hope it does. I am trying to call attention to what I consider a home truth about the structure of the physical world, because I think neglect of this truth, inattention to the hierarchical nature of Nature, has led to significant errors about consciousness and qualia. In what remains I shall briefly discuss a few.

Block (1981, and this volume, chapter 16), Lycan (1987), and others have put forward various counterexample cases, designed to show that having a functional organization, however complex, is insufficient for hosting qualitative, phenomenally feely states; probably the best known and most discussed of these are Block's "homunculi-head" and "population of China" examples [see Part VII below – ed.]. If such counterexamples are to be rebutted, the Functionalist must exhibit some reasonable requirement that they fail to satisfy, despite their mimicking in one way or another the functional organization of a real sentient creature.

Homunctionalism teleologically understood does the trick with ease. For none of the systems imagined in the counterexamples is teleologically organized in anything like the right way; most are not even organisms at all (see Lycan 1987, chs 3 and 5).

Even if the puzzle cases fail to refute Homunctionalism, some problems of chauvinism and liberalism remain to be resolved. Whether or not Fodor and Block are right in suggesting that Putnam moved too far back toward Behaviorism in backing off from the Identity Theory, the Functionalist certainly bears the responsibility of finding a level of characterization of mental states that is neither so abstract or behavioristic as to rule out the possibility of inverted spectrum, etc., nor so specific and structural as to fall into chauvinism. Block himself goes on to argue that this problem is insoluble.

He raises the dilemma for the characterization of *inputs* and *outputs* in particular. Plainly, inputs and outputs cannot be characterized in human neural terms; this would chauvinistically preclude our awarding mental descriptions to machines, Martians, and other creatures who differ from us biologically, no matter what convincing credentials they might offer in defense of their sentience. On the other hand, inputs and outputs cannot be characterized in purely abstract terms (i.e., merely as "inputs" and "outputs"), since this will lead to the sort of ultraliberalism that Block has disparaged by means of his earlier examples and also by means of new ones, such as that of an economic system that has very complex inputs, outputs, and internal states but that certainly has no mental characteristics. Nor can we appeal to any particular sorts of interactions of the sentient being with its environment via inputs and outputs, since in a few cases (those of paralytics, brains *in vitro*, and the like) we want to award mental descriptions to objects that cannot succeed in interacting with their environments in any way. Block concludes,

Is there a description of inputs and outputs specific enough to avoid liberalism, yet general enough to avoid chauvinism? I doubt that there is.

Every proposal for a description of inputs and outputs I have seen or thought of is guilty of either liberalism or chauvinism. Though this paper has focused on liberalism, chauvinism is the more pervasive problem.

... *there will be no physical characterizations that apply to all mental systems' inputs and outputs.* Hence, any attempt to formulate a functional description with physical characterizations of inputs and outputs will inevitably either exclude some [possible] systems with mentality or include some systems without mentality.

... On the other hand, as you will recall, characterizing inputs and outputs simply *as* inputs and outputs is inevitably liberal. I, for one, do not see how functionalism can describe inputs and outputs without falling afoul of either liberalism or chauvinism, or abandoning the original project of characterizing mentality in nonmental terms. I do not claim that this is a conclusive argument against functionalism. Rather, like the functionalist argument against physicalism, it is perhaps best construed as a burden of proof argument. (pp. 464–5, this volume).

I am not sure how detailed a plan Block is demanding of the Functionalist here, though I have agreed that, on a mild-mannered understanding of "burden of proof," Block's challenge is one that the functionalist does bear the burden of meeting. The question is whether this burden is as prohibitively heavy as Block seems to assume. And there are at least three factors that I think lighten it considerably and give us some cause for optimism:

First, there is a line of argument that offers at least some slight positive reason or natural motivation for thinking that the dilemma of chauvinism and liberalism (either in regard to inputs and outputs or in regard to the inner states that the Functionalist identifies with our mental states) does admit a solution. It begins as a slippery-slope argument. Block has stated the dilemma very uncompromisingly, implying that one's only choices are (a) to characterize inputs and outputs physiologically and be a chauvinist, or (b) to characterize inputs and outputs "purely abstractly" and be a bleeding heart. But this brutal statement of the alternatives overlooks the fact . . . that functional abstraction is a matter of degree. Purely physiological characterization is an extreme, lying at the lower or "more structural" end of the spectrum; "purely abstract" characterization is the opposite extreme, lying at the higher or "more functional" end. Notice that . . . there are characterizations that are even *more* "structural" than physiological ones are, such as microphysical ones, relative to which physiological ones are "functional"; similarly, there are really more abstract characterizations than "input" and "output" themselves, such as "transfer," "motion," or even "occurrence." If it is true, as it seems to be, that "purely abstract" characterizations and physiological characterizations merely lie near the two ends of a continuum of functional abstraction, then it is reasonable to expect that there exists some intermediate level of abstraction that would yield characterizations that rules out the Bolivian economy, the Abnegonian Galaxy, the microbiology of the Everglades and their ilk, but would make room for human beings, molluscs, Martians, and brains *in vitro*. The truth lies (as it so often does) somewhere in between, and, depending on which aspect of which mental state interests one, not always at the same spot in between either. Wait and see what resources will be available at various intermediate levels.[20] . . .

Let us remember in addition (here is my second point in response to Block's challenge) that nothing forces us to assume that all the different kinds of mental states occur at the *same* level of functional abstraction. The intuitively "more behavioral" sorts of mental states, such as beliefs and desires and intentions, presumably occur at a relatively high level of abstraction, and this makes it easy for us to ascribe beliefs and desires and intentions to Martians whose overt behavior and very superficial psychology match ours; the same is true of highly "informational" mental activities such as remembering and (literal) computing. Intuitively, "less behavioral," more qualitative mental states probably occur at a much lower level of abstraction; sensings that have certain particular kinds of qualitative characters probably *are* quite specific to species (at least, we should not be very surprised to find out that this was so), and quite possibly our Martian's humanoid behavior *is* prompted by his having sensations (or possibly "schmensations") somewhat unlike ours, despite his superficial behavioral similarities to us.

I am not aware that anyone has ever explicitly defended Two-Levelism as such.[21] But Two-Levelism seems to be what lies directly behind such apparent dilemmas as Block's "problem of the inputs and the outputs."

Parallel considerations apply to the problem of intentionality. We think that a state of an organism is either an intentional state or not, period, and then we wonder what the functional or institutional locus of intentionality might be. I do not think intentionality can be a *purely* functional property at all, for reasons that are now familiar,[22] but insofar as it is, I think we would do well to admit that intentionality itself comes in degrees.[23] The "marks" of intentionality or aboutness are none too clear, but what does seem clear upon reflection is that there is an intermediate level of functional characterization that offers a *kind* of directedness-upon-a-possibly-nonexistent-object-or-type that nevertheless falls short of the rich, full-blooded intentionality exhibited by the human mind. At this intermediate level, we speak systems-theoretically of "detectors," "scanners," "filters," "inhibitors," and the like, meaning these terms quite literally but without actually imputing *thought* or what might be called "occurrent" aboutness. But I must leave the development of these observations for another occasion.[24]

Third, it might be profitable for us simply to stand by the "purely abstract" characterization of inputs and outputs, throwing the whole problem of chauvinism and liberalism back onto our characterization of internal states and events. There are so many possibilities, so many different levels of abstraction in the functional hierarchy as it applies to the brain (many of which overlap and cut across each other), that it seems quite reasonable to expect there to be, for each mental state-type, some middle way between chauvinism and liberalism – not necessarily the *same* middle way for each state-type. It is simply an error to think that all mental phenomena must be functionally located at the same level, or that any single mental state must be localized entirely at one level. Regarding the "more functional," *nearly* behavioristic mental states, perhaps we would not even mind admitting that an economic system or the population of China could have such states (say, dispositional beliefs), if it were to come to that. And possibly at the least functional end of the continuum there are even mental state-types of which the Identity Theory is true, though it is hard to think of any mental state that is as "qualitative" as that.

The foregoing remarks suggest a final additional response to Block's "absent qualia" arguments, one that I think is virtually conclusive. Earlier I characterized Block's intuitive disquiet over Functionalism as being a matter of feeling the incongruity between the relationalness of Functionalist explications and the homogeneous, primitively *monadic* qualitative characters of their explicanda; I gather that this incongruity seems to him absolute. Notice that evidently he has no similar objection to the Identity Theory; like any other materialist, he would simply charge the Identity Theorist with chauvinism and raise no further complaint. After all, one of the theory's main advantages was its ability to account for the possibility of inverted spectrum or other inner variation despite outward conformity. But if we also accept my claim that Homunctional characterizations and physiological characterizations of states of persons reflect merely different levels of abstraction within a surrounding functional hierarchy or continuum, then we can no longer distinguish the Functionalist from the Identity Theorist in any absolute way. "Neuron," for example, may be understood either as a physiological term (denoting a kind of human cell) or as a (teleo-) functional term (denoting a relayer of electrical charge); on *either* construal it stands for an instantiable – if you like, for a role being played by a group of more fundamental objects. Thus, *even the Identity Theorist is a Functionalist* – one who locates mental entities at a very low level of abstraction. The moral is that if Block does want to insist that Functionalist psychology is stymied by a principled incongruity of the sort I have mentioned and that a philosophy of mind that explicates mental items in terms of relational roles or instantiables cannot in principle accommodate the intractable monadicity of qualia, then one would have to make the same charge against the Identity Theorist as well, and this, I trust he feels no intuitive compulsion to do.[25] In fact, Block lets that Theory cop a plea of species chauvinism overall, and even allows that it is probably true of some mental properties (this volume, p. 460).

There is an idea, brought on by blind Two-Levelism, that Functionalism differs somehow *conceptually or structurally* from the Identity Theory, in such a way as to incur different sorts of objections. As I have said, the Identity Theory is just an empirically special case of Functionalism, one that (implausibly) locates all mental states at the same very low level of institutional abstraction – the neuroanatomical. Thus there should be no purely conceptual or philosophical objections that apply to Functionalism that do not apply to the Identity Theory or vice versa, even if one is empirically less reasonable than the other. Yet philosophers such as Block have claimed to see such objections. If my doctrine of the continuity of nature is right, something must be wrong here; for neuroanatomical terms are functional and so relational just as higher-organizational terms are, albeit at a lower level of abstraction. If there is a principled incongruity between relational characterization and the intrinsicness of phenomenal quality, and if that incongruity stymies Functionalism, then it should preclude the Identity Theory as well.[26]

Consider a second example of such an objection: Block further contends that Functionalism is unable to allow the possibility of "inverted spectrum" or other types of internally switched qualia unreflected even counterfactually in behavior – unable in a way that the Identity Theory is not, since the Identity Theory is *made to order* for representing cases of inverted qualia. But if my reflections on the continuity of levels of nature are right, something must be amiss here. And something is. Just as it is easy to imagine undetectably switched *neurophysiology* underlying inverted spectrum (see Lycan 1973), it is easy to imagine a switching of functional components more abstractly described (though doubtless there are limits to this, and quite possibly one could not ascend to a very much higher level of abstraction and keep the inversion behaviorally undetectable).

The truth of the matter is obscured by a pragmatic ambiguity in the notion of "inverted qualia," an ambiguity that I think has lent Block rhetorical aid even though it is far from subtle. To wit, there is a hidden parameter: "inverted" *with respect to what?* (Compare the correlative relation of *supervenience*: supervenient on what?) Traditionally, "inverted spectrum" has meant (color) qualia inverted with respect to actual and counterfactual input–output relations alone. Either from duty or by inclination, Analytical Behaviorists and Wittgensteinians denied the conceivability of *that* inversion, but most people's ordinary modal intuitions have favored it, and Identity and Functionalist theories alike have accommodated it with ease; it has never posed any threat to Functionalism. What would damage Functionalism is the conceivability of qualia inverted with respect to I–O relations *plus* internal functional organization. *This* inversion hypothesis is much stronger and more daring. Its possibility is controversial to say the least. Indeed, to assert it is simply to deny the truth of Functionalism – it is to say without argument that two organisms could differ in their qualitative states even though they were exactly alike in their entire global functional organization, *at whatever level of institutional abstraction is in question*. Of course there have been philosophers who have insisted without argument on the metaphysical possibility of organisms' differing in their qualitative states despite being *molecular* duplicates, for that matter, but such insistence has no intrinsic credibility even if the relevant theories of mind turn out in the end to be false. The possibility of spectrum inverted with respect to I–O relations alone is a well-entrenched and respectable though I suppose defeasible modal intuition; the possibility of spectrum inverted with respect to I–O relations *plus internal functional organization at however low a level of abstraction proponents feel it plausible to name* is anything but obvious and in conflict with some intuitively plausible supervenience theses.

(Some relationally minded theorists may find it natural to assume a certain *privileged* level of abstraction at the outset. For example, "*analytical* functionalists," or as I prefer to call them, commonsense relationalists, who hold that the *meanings of mental terms* are determined by the causal roles associated with those terms by common sense or "folk psychology," thereby deny themselves appeal to any level of functional organization lower than is accessible to common sense.[27] Folk psychology aside, the "High Church" computationalists[28] scorn appeal to human biology even within a purely *scientific* account of cognition and behavior, though their own chosen level of nature is none too clearly specified.[29] A theorist who cleaves to such a privileged level of organization may of course admit "inverted spectrum" relative to that chosen level, so long as he or she is willing to type-identify qualia with still lower-level items.[30]

Two alternative strategies

I have recommended one way of solving the problems of chauvinism and liberalism concerning qualia within a Functionalist ontology of the mental. There are alternative possible strategies. One alternative approach would be to bifurcate our view of the mental, by simply taking over the distinction between a mental state and its qualitative character, explicating the states in functional terms and the characters in rather broad physiological terms, tolerating the consequence that inverted spectrum or lesser interpersonal differences in qualia might be more prevalent than we think (viz., exactly as prevalent as are interpersonal physiological differences of comparable magnitude).[31]

Pain would present a useful test case for this second suggested way of accommodating qualia. An interesting and distinctive thing about pain is that (unlike most other mental states) it has both a strongly associated behavior pattern *and* vivid introspectible feely properties. This means, on the present proposal, that pain states may receive *multilevelled* analyses. For example (just to speculate a bit), we might end up wanting to classify any internal state of an organism that played pain's usual "gross" behavioral role (that of being caused by damage and producing withdrawal-*cum*-favoring) as being a pain, but to distinguish the feels of pains according to the states' physiological bases.[32] It would follow that, although mollusks and Martians have pains, their pains probably feel differently to them from the ways in which our pains feel to us. It would also follow that a state that feels like a pain state of mine might in a differently organized creature be a mental state of some kind other than pain; some philosophers may find this crassly counterintuitive.

Incidentally, the bifurcated view has become fairly popular in the past few years,[33] and is often expressed by saying that (e.g.) "pain itself is functional while its specific feel is neurophysiological." But the latter formulation again presupposes Two-Levelism. See the "functional"/"structural" distinction as level-relative, and the bifurcated theory collapses into a pointlessly specific version of the thesis (which I hope will become a truism) that mental states and their qualitative characters may well not be explicated in terms of the same level of nature (in particular, the locus of qualitative character may be lower in the hierarchy than that of the mental state generically considered). I emphatically agree with the latter thesis, as I have already indicated, but it is no competing *alternative* to Functionalism.

A third alternative approach suggests itself for the case of bodily sensations (though I doubt whether it could easily be applied to perceptual qualia). It is to suppose that feelings that seem phenomenally to be simple are actually complex and that the distinctive quale associated with a feeling of a certain type is really the coincidence or superimposition of a number of distinct, individually manageable homunctional features. I think this line, rather than that adumbrated in the foregoing paragraph, is the most plausible to take for the case of pain, because it is strongly suggested by the anesthesiological data collected and summarized by Dennett (1978, ch. 11). What these data seem to indicate is that chemically different anesthetics and analgesics disrupt subjects' normal "pain" subroutines at different functional junctures, eliciting from the subjects quite different verbal reports of their effects. Of a group of subjects suffering pain of roughly the same kind and intensity, one subgroup given drug *A* may report that the pain has diminished or gone away entirely, whereas a subgroup given drug *B* may report that although they know that the pain is still there, they cannot feel it; a subgroup given drug *C* may say that although they can still feel the pain just as intensely as ever, they do not *mind* any more; and so on. That some of these reports sound funny to us (they would be pooh-poohed as "unintelligible" by some Wittgensteinians) naturally reflects the fact that the subjects' normal inner workings are being disrupted, and their normal inner experience of pain being altered, by the drugs. What the drugs seem to be doing is *splitting off components* of the subjects' phenomenal experience of the pain, by splitting off component subsubroutines of its rather complicated functional basis. And if this is so, it follows that our phenomenal experience of pain *has* components – it is a complex, consisting (perhaps) of urges, desires, impulses, and beliefs, probably occurring at quite different levels of institutional abstraction. If these components can individually be split off from each other by drugs, then we may perform a

Gedankenexperiment in which we hypothetically take a suffering subject, split off one component of his pain by administering drug *A*, then split off another component by administering drug *B*, and repeat this process, eliciting reports as we go to keep track of how we are doing. It seems to me plausible to think that if we were to keep this up, disrupting one access pathway after another and eliminating the component urges, desires, and beliefs one by one, we would sooner or later succeed in eliminating the pain itself; it also seems that if we were to reverse the process – to begin restoring the pathways by withholding the various drugs one by one – the subject would necessarily come to feel the full-fledged pain again (provided his damaged tissues had not been repaired in the meantime). I believe this makes it reasonable to suppose that some (again) *multileveled* proper subsequence of the relevant complex of functional goings-on is both necessary and sufficient for the occurrence of the pain, contrary to the spirit of Block's antiliberalism.

I do not know how to make a conclusive choice among the three alternative approaches I have described, or what sorts of further evidence we might seek. I have run through some of the options only in order to show that the Homunctionalist has fairly rich resources that can be brought to bear both on the dilemma of chauvinism and liberalism and on the positive task of accounting for qualia. On the basis of these resources I believe we are entitled to conclude that Block's pessimism about qualia is unwarranted. . . .

If my continuity doctrine is obvious as stated, it has not been obvious enough to some of our leading philosophers of mind. I hope the foregoing demonstrations will also serve to make Homunctionalism all the more attractive as a theory of the mental.

NOTES

1 I believe just as firmly in some form of act-utilitarianism in ethics, but the sacred principle of utility itself forbids my even telling you this, much less committing (detectable) murders in its name.

2 This multileveled hierarchical structure was noted and eloquently presented by Herbert A. Simon (1969); I do not know if the idea predates him. William C. Wimsatt has also written brilliantly on it (1976).

Its application to psychology was first brought to my attention by Fodor (1968) and Dennett (this volume); see further references below.

3 I have in mind Lewis Thomas's (1974) discussion of insect societies and of the relation between human beings and their own mitochondria. The mereology of "organisms" is highly interest-relative. Note well, we must grant a pluralism of different reductive relations between levels of nature; consider also the entirely tenable notion of the corporation as person (Biro, 1981; French, 1984; Brooks, 1986).

4 For a rich exposition and defense of the strategy, see Cummins (1983). However, Richardson (1983) throws some fairly cold water.

5 For philosophically relevant discussion and references, see P. M. Churchland 1986, and P. S. Churchland 1986.

6 Dennett's main concern in the work containing the following passage is the explication of intentionality. That concern is not mine here; I am interested only in homuncular breakdown *per se*.

7   In fact, as David Armstrong has pointed out to me, the present maneuver blocks a number
    of typical infinite-regress arguments in the philosophy of mind, including Ryle's complaint
    against volitional theories of deciding. Dennett himself wields it against "Hume's problem"
    regarding self-understanding representations (1978, pp. 122ff.).

8   For an actual hands-on homuncular breakdown of the speech center, see figure 1, p. 262 of
    Lycan 1984.

9   For stout insistence on this, see Davidson 1970.

10 Thus, Smart's example of the logic of "nation" statements' being different from the logic of
    "citizen" statements may have been more apropos than he imagined.

11 Popper 1972; Wimsatt 1972; Wright 1973; Millikan 1984; Neander 1981, 1983. Neander's
    evolutionary explication is the best I know. It is criticized with effect by E. Prior in an
    unpublished note and by Pargetter and Bigelow (1987); the truth seems to me to lie
    somewhere in between.

    Jonathan Bennett (1976) offers a different naturalistic approach to teleology due to Ann
    Wilbur MacKenzie (1972) (and in discussion has urged me to switch).

12 Characterizations of the contents of our space-time slice may thus be arranged in a
    continuum, from the least teleological to the most (highly) teleological. This continuum
    corresponds fairly neatly to the hierarchy of functional instantiation or realization. The
    molecules jointly realize, or play the role of, the piece of metal; the piece of metal plays the
    role of the key; the key serves as our door-unlocker; and so on. The prevalence of
    functional hierarchies of this kind, I believe, is what encourages ontological reduction and
    the idea that "everything is ultimately a matter of physics." On the relations between
    teleology viewed from an evolutionary perspective, functional hierarchies, ontology, and the
    methodology of scientific reduction, see again Wimsatt 1976. I have also profited from
    reading Mellick 1973, and see Matthen and Levy 1984.

13 As Jerry Fodor has pointed out to me in discussion, there is one tolerably clear distinction
    that a Two-Leveler might have in mind and that is absolute: it is the distinction between
    objects whose proper parts are essential to them and objects whose parts are not. For
    example, a bicycle's or even a tree's parts are replaceable, while a water molecule's parts
    perhaps are not (one might argue either that if the molecule were to lose one of its hydrogen
    or oxygen atoms it would not be *that* molecule or that without the right sorts of atoms it
    would not be a water molecule at all). I agree that this distinction is genuine, and I expect it
    has some metaphysical importance. But it has no *psychological* importance. The level of
    chemistry is far too low in the institutional hierarchy to affect mentation; that is, if two
    neuroanatomies are just the same even though they are realized by different chemicals,
    psychology is the same.

14 Amelie Rorty has suggested to me the Aristotelian idea of explaining an organism's
    component functions (more exactly, of explaining its-functions'-constituting-its-thriving) by
    reference to the suitability of those functions for the material conditions of the organism's
    species. This idea fits well with the etiological account of function that I tend to favor.
    Given a relatively undifferentiated mass of "lower" biological material at a much earlier
    evolutionary stage, how would it clump together and articulate itself in order to face the
    world at large in a more robust and less vulnerable way? Its own "structural" or "material"
    nature would enforce some answers and suggest still others, and given selection pressures of
    various now retrodictable sorts it is no surprise that many or most of these answers have
    been realized. If "function" is understood in evolutionary terms, then, function itself gets
    explained in this way, in terms of the propensities of the organism's material substratum. I
    take that explanation to complement, rather than to compete with, "downward-causation"
    explanations based in higher levels of nature (of the sort Wimsatt talks about). In fact, we
    get a sort of pincer movement: selection pressure from much higher levels interacting with
    bottom-up pressure from the nature and propensities of the particular chemical constitution
    of the pre-existing neighborhood, the two pressures jointly molding what lies between. But

one might want to emphasize the bottom-up pressure at the expense of higher-level explanations. *In some sense* that emphasis has to be right, given supervenience of top on bottom, though it is tricky to work out all the different up–down interrelations there are.

Rorty points out (in correspondence) that full-scale multiple realizability must be distinguished from mere functional characterization of states of organisms, since detailed accounts of function tend to put strict requirements on realizing-stuff; there is a trade-off here. But I do not see that the Aristotelian bottom-up explanation strategy *per se* counts against multiple realizability. For the same functional answers or solutions might well be hit upon by chemically quite different bunches of primordial stuff. Rorty offers the example of *eating*: Computers do not eat, in any literal sense, and the earth does not ingest rain; multiple realizability fails even though the activity is functionally characterized. I want to make the same sort of rejoinder that I shall be making to an argument of Block's below: Of course computers and other (even biologic) entities do not eat; but there is an intermediate, more abstract characterization of eating itself – *holotropism* as it was called in my college biology classes – which excludes computers but includes lots of species biochemically quite different from ours; it has something to do with acquiring proteins very similar to one's own and physically homogenizing them and ingesting them and making them part of one without major rearrangement of amino acids or something of the sort – at any rate, it is a form of nourishment that is sharply distinguished from many other species' and is rather distinctive of our phylum or whatever. This point checks nicely with my usual idea of functional characterizations that hold for intermediate levels of nature and are neither too vague and general nor too chauvinistically species-bound.

15 Elliott Sober (this volume) praises this attitude as "putting the function back into functionalism"; cf. my remarks on p. 27 of Lycan 1981a, regarding Putnam and Fodor's pun on the word "function."

16 For details, see Lycan 1981b.

17 Why does pain hurt? Why could we not have a damage-signaling and repair-instigating system that was not uncomfortable? The answer is simple. Suppose I had just such a system, like the red warning light on my auto engine. Just as I habitually though irrationally ignore the warning light and vaguely hope it will go away, I would ignore a personal warning light if it did not intrinsically provide me with an urgent motive to do something about it.

18 Robert Van Gulick has presented me (in correspondence) with some meteorological and geological cases in which (apparent) degrees of teleologicalness do not follow levels of nature. Such cases are very much to the point, but I shall have to postpone going into them.

19 Ned Block, who violently disagrees with me on the present issues, once said (in conversation), "I'll give you *neurons* and *cells* and so on as functional, but when you come to *hydrogen* and *oxygen*, when you get right down to the level of *chemistry*, there's just nothing functional or teleological at all!" Oh, no? "Hydro-"*what*? "Oxy-"*what*? (The shot is a cheap one but immensely satisfying.)

20 "Wait till next year!" John Searle jeers in a different but very similar connection (1980). *Of course* wait till next year!

21 Save perhaps the "analytical functionalist," whose view I reject (see note 27).

22 Putnam 1975; Fodor 1980; Stich, this volume; Burge 1979; Lycan 1981c; . . .

23 This idea is anticipated in part by Dretske (1981). See also Van Gulick (this volume, 1982).

24 I would also observe that some current disputes within the cognitive science community are misconceived in the Two-Levelist way. For example, the "bottom-uppers" versus the "High-Church Computationalists" (see P. S Churchland, 1986, and Dennett, 1986) and the New Connectionists versus the same (see Bechtel, 1985). The New Connectionists in particular are a superb example of a biocomputational middle way. Somewhat in the same spirit is P. M. Churchland's (1986) "phase-space sandwich" model of sensorimotor coordination, based on Pellionisz and Llinas (1979, 1982); or rather, though *he* does not

William G. Lycan

always think it in a mediating way, I count it as another feasible middle way *within the spirit of a properly teleologized functionalism.*

25   Wilfrid Sellars does. But that is another story . . .; see chapter 8 of Lycan 1987.

26   Block does not himself stress the relational/monadic contrast, but offers his differential intuitions raw; so he may remain unmoved by my foregoing *ad hominem* and simply insist that having a neurochemistry roughly like ours is a necessary condition for experiencing qualia, relational or not. Yet, I wonder, how could a *philosopher* know *that?* Is it aglow with the Natural Light?

27   I am indebted to Sydney Shoemaker for useful correspondence on this point. For my own part, I cannot accept analytical functionalism, for two reasons: (i) I reject the alternatively conceptual-analysis or implicit-definition theory of meaning on which that theory rests. (See Armstrong 1968 and Lewis 1972 for its two most explicit versions and defenses, and Lycan 1981b, especially note 10, for my alternative view of the semantics of mental terms; also, for a similar view, see Jacoby 1985.) (ii) I doubt that common sense or "folk psychology" contains enough information about mental entities to characterize their natures as richly as would be needed to avoid counterexample. Clothespin models of folk psychology would be pretty easy to come by, without the massive complexity and teleological organization that would warrant an ascription of real mentality.

28   The term is due to Dennett (1986).

29   Here I follow some recent writers in supposing that there are really any High Church Computationalists; I am not sure that any actual Functionalist has ever self-consciously intended the view. It is usually ascribed to Zenon Pylyshyn and Jerry Fodor, on the basis of some of their remarks about multiple realizability. Perhaps Ned Block does really hold it, or he would not continue to resist my case against Two-Levelism as begun in my 1981a.

30   See particularly (again) Bechtel 1985, and the references made therein.

31   Block hints on p. 460 that he might not find this suggestion entirely uncongenial. And see note 33.

32   This move would take some of the sting out of what I take to be an anti-Functionalist argument in David Lewis 1980.

33   Block hinted at this view, as I have mentioned. I developed the suggestion in Lycan 1981a, pp. 47–8. It has also been picked up by Hilary Putnam (1981), Sydney Shoemaker (1981), Patricia Kitcher (1982), Terence Horgan (1984), and Gregory Sheridan (1986) among others (Shoemaker calls its "selective parochialism").

REFERENCES

Armstrong, D. M. (1968) *A Materialist Theory of the Mind*, Routledge & Kegan Paul.

Attneave, F. (1960) "In defense of homunculi," in W. Rosenblith (ed.), *Sensory Communication*, MIT Press.

Bechtel, P. W. (1985) "Contemporary connectionism: Are the new parallel distributed processing models cognitive or associationist?" *Behaviorism* 13, 53–61.

Bennett, J. (1976) *Linguistic Behaviour*, Cambridge University Press.

Bigelow, J. and Pargetter, R. (1987) "Functions," *Journal of Philosophy* 84, 181–96.

Biro, J. (1981) "Persons as corporate entities and corporations as persons," *Nature and System* 3, 173–80.

Block, N. J. (1981) "Psychologism and behaviorism," *Philosophical Review* 90, 5–43.

Brooks, D. H. M. (1986) "Group minds," *Australasian Journal of Philosophy* 64, 456–70.

Burge, T. (1979) "Individualism and the mental," in P. French, T. E. Uehling and H. Wettstein (eds), *Midwest Studies in Philosophy, vol. IV: Studies in Metaphysics*, University of Minnesota Press.

Churchland, P. M. (1986) "Some reductive strategies in cognitive neurobiology," *Mind* 95, 223–38.

Churchland, P. S. (1986) *Neurophilosophy*, Bradford Books/MIT Press.

Cummins, R. (1983) *The Nature of Psychological Explanation*, Bradford Books/MIT Press.

Davidson, D. (1970) "Mental events," in L. Foster and J. W. Swanson (eds), *Experience and Theory*, University of Massachusetts Press.

Dennett, D. C. (1978) *Brainstorms*, Bradford Books.

Dennett, D. C. (1986) "The logical geography of computational approaches: a view from the East Pole," in M. Brand and R. M. Harnish (eds), *The Representation of Knowledge and Belief*, University of Arizona Press.

Dretske, F. (1981) *Knowledge and the Flow of Information*, Bradford Books/MIT Press.

Fodor, J. A. (1968) "The appeal to tacit knowledge in psychological explanation," *Journal of Philosophy* 65, 627–40.

Fodor, J. A. (1980) "Methodological solipsism considered as a research strategy in cognitive psychology," *Behavioral and Brain Sciences* 3, 63–73.

French, P. (1984) *Collective and Corporate Responsibility*, Columbia University Press.

Horgan, T. (1984) "Functionalism, qualia, and the inverted spectrum," *Philosophy and Phenomenological Research* 44, 453–70.

Jacoby, H. (1985) "Eliminativism, meaning, and qualitative states," *Philosophical Studies* 47, 257–70.

Kitcher, P. (1982) "Two versions of the Identity Theory," *Erkenntnis* 17, 213–28.

Lewis, D. (1972) "Psychophysical and theoretical identifications," *Australasian Journal of Philosophy* 50, 249–58.

Lewis, D. (1980) "Mad pain and Martian pain," in N. Block (ed.), *Readings in Philosophy of Psychology*, vol. One, Harvard University Press.

Lycan, W. (1973) "Inverted spectrum," *Ratio* 15, 315–19.

Lycan, W. (1981a) "Form, function, and feel," *Journal of Philosophy* 78, 24–50.

Lycan, W. (1981b) "Psychological laws," *Philosophical Topics* 12, 9–38.

Lycan, W. (1981c) "Toward a homuncular theory of believing," *Cognition and Brain Theory* 4, 139–59.

Lycan, W. (1984) *Logical Form in Natural Language*, Bradford Books/MIT Press.

Lycan, W. (1987) *Consciousness*, Bradford Books/MIT Press.

Lycan, W. (1989) "Ideas of representation," in *Mind, Value, and Culture: Essays in Honor of E. M. Adams* (edited by D. Weissbord), Ridgeview Publishing.

MacKenzie, A. W. (1972) "An analysis of purposive behavior," Cornell University doctoral dissertation.

Matthen, M. and Levy, E. (1984) "Teleology, error, and the human immune system," *Journal of Philosophy* 81, 351–71.

Mellick, D. (1973) "Behavioral strata." Ohio State University doctoral dissertation.

Millikan, R. G. (1984) *Language, Thought, and Other Biological Categories*, Bradford Books/MIT Press.

Neander, K. (1981) "Teleology in biology." Unpublished Xerox.

Neander, K. (1983) "Abnormal psychobiology," La Trobe University doctoral dissertation.

Pellionisz, A. and Llinas, R. (1979) "Brain modelling by tensor network theory and computer simulation. The cerebellum: distributed processor for predictive coordination," *Neuroscience* 4, 323–48.

Pellionisz, A. and Llinas, R. (1982) "Space–time representation in the brain. The cerebellum as a predictive space–time metric tensor," *Neuroscience* 7, 2949–70.

Popper, K. (1972) "Of clouds and clocks: An approach to the problem of rationality and the freedom of Man," in *Objective Knowledge: An Evolutionary Approach*, Oxford University Press.

Putnam, H. (1975) "The meaning of 'meaning'," in K. Gunderson (ed.), *Minnesota Studies in the Philosophy of Science, vol. 7: Language, Mind and Knowledge*, University of Minnesota Press.

Putnam, H. (1981) *Reason, Truth and History*, Cambridge University Press.

Richardson, R. (1983) "Computational models of mind." Unpublished monograph.

Searle, J. (1980) "Minds, brains and programs," *Behavioral and Brain Sciences* 3, 417–24.

Sheridan, G. (1983) "Can there be moral subjects in a physicalistic universe?" *Philosophy and Phenomenological Research* 43, 425–48.

Sheridan, G. (1986) "Selective Parochialism and Shoemaker's Argument for Functionalism," typescript, Western Michigan University.

Shoemaker, S. (1981) "Some varieties of Functionalism," *Philosophical Topics* 12, 93–119.

Simon, H. (1969) "The architecture of complexity," in *The Sciences of the Artificial*, MIT Press.

Thomas, L. (1974 *Lives of a Cell*, Bantam Books.

Van Gulick, R. (1982) "Mental representation – a Functionalist view," *Pacific Philosophical Quarterly* 63, 3–20.

Wimsatt, W. C. (1972) "Teleology and the logical structure of function statements," *Studies in History and Philosophy of Science* 3, 1–80.

Wimsatt, W. C. (1976) "Reductionism, levels of organization, and the mind–body problem," in G. Globus, G. Maxwell and I. Savodnik (eds), *Consciousness and the Brain*, Plenum.

Wright, L. (1973) "Functions," *Philosophical Review* 82, 139–68.

5

Teleological Functionalism

Putting the Function Back into Functionalism

ELLIOTT SOBER

Functionalism got off on the wrong foot. The problem was that *function* is ambiguous, and the doctrine was developed with the wrong meaning in mind. A mathematical function is a mapping from some objects to others; each input has a unique output. For example, we may talk about the plus function, wherein a pair of numbers is mapped on to their sum. On the other hand, there is the teleological concept of function – as when we say that the function of the heart is to pump blood. Corresponding to the first concept, there arose in the philosophy of mind a view I will call Turing Machine Functionalism. Corresponding to the second is the view I will call Teleological Functionalism. Functionalism as a solution to the mind/body problem should have been developed as a form of Teleological Functionalism. Instead, Functionalism usually was understood to mean Turing Machine Functionalism.

As a result of this early mis-step, functionalism is thought to face a number of decisive objections. I will argue that these objections dissolve, once functionalism is understood teleologically. Not that this provides the mind/body problem with a solution, since the teleological idea has problems of its own. But if lessons are to be learned from the failure of theories, we must see what makes the best version of a theory fail.

Functionalism began as a reaction against the identity theory. Functionalism's negative insight was that psychological properties are not type-identical with physical properties. Psychological state types are multiply realizable (Putnam 1967; Block and Fodor 1972). But this claim about what psychological states are not had to be supplemented with some positive account of what the nature of psychological states is.

Functionalists found the beginning of a positive doctrine in their valve lifters and mouse traps (Fodor 1968). What makes a mouse trap a mouse trap is, roughly, that it plays a certain causal role. Given a free mouse as input, it produces a caught mouse as output. A particular functional state will bear certain cause and effect relationships to other states. Of course, the same is true of particular physical states; we can characterize what it is to be an acid in terms of the causal role that acidity plays (Lycan 1981). Functionalists hope to characterize psychological states in terms of their causal connections to behavior, to stimuli, and to other mental states. Only in so far as these provide substantive constraints on how psychological states are individuated does functionalism become a nontrivial doctrine.

Quite distinct from this teleological idea – that the mind is a functional device just as a mouse trap is a functional device – lurked another suggestive idea. This is the thought that the mind is a computer. Here the idea is that for an individual to have various cognitive capacities is for the individual to have access to certain computer programs. To perceive something or to come to hold a particular belief is then understood as the execution of a series of computations.

This still does not count as even a candidate solution for the mind/body problem. If mental states are to be individuated computationally, how is one to understand the concept of computation? It is here that the idea behind Turing Machine Functionalism made its appearance. A computer computes by instantiating a machine table, which is just a function from inputs to outputs. The state the machine occupies determines what the machine should output and what state the machine should go into next.

The principle for individuating machine tables is the principle for individuating any mathematical function. Roughly, it is simply the requirement of an abstract isomorphism. When I successively add 1 to itself fourteen times, I am executing the "same" program that the ocean executes when it adds another layer of sand to the beach each day for a fortnight.

This Turing Machine development of the idea of functionalism led to problems. Suppose we possess some psychological property P. Turing Machine functionalism would have it that any individual will possess P precisely when it is abstractly isomorphic with us. It is rather clear, however, that this suggestion is neither necessary nor sufficient.

The lack of sufficiency is illustrated by an idea discussed by Davis (1974), Dennett (1978a, 1978b) and Block (1978), among others. Suppose a large group of people is paid to behave in a way that is structurally isomorphic to the way my brain behaves when I think "I want an ice cream." When one neuron sends a signal to another, one hireling hits another over the head with a hammer. The group of people is structurally isomorphic with my brain, yet I have the belief, while the group (presumably) does not.

The fact that structural isomorphism is not necessary for possessing the same psychological state is a point made by Block and Fodor (1972). What defeated the identity theory was that two individuals can be in the same mental state even though they are in different physical states. In just the same way, it seems possible for two individuals to be in the same mental state even though they're in different computational states. Two computers can multiply 35 and 44 in very different ways. By analogy, two sentient beings might possess some of the same psychological properties even though their psychologies involve very different programs. The computer model of mind thereby suggests, surprisingly, that mental states are *not* to be identified with computational states.

Although these objections have seemed to be pretty decisive when applied to Turing Machine Functionalism, matters are different when Teleological Functionalism is considered instead. To see why, consider this analog to the mind/body problem: What is the relationship between the process of digestion and the physical processes of the body? What is the relationship between digestive states and properties and physical states and properties?

One possible suggestion is an identity theory: the processing of food does not consist in the operation of some immaterial substance on the food item. Rather, a perfectly down-to-earth physico-chemical process is all that is involved. This idea would be a step forward from the idea that food contains a mysterious spiritual substance which is extracted for use by the organism by recondite spiritual machinery. On the other hand, the identity theory has some obvious limitations. Multiple realizability is just as much a property of digestion as it is of perception and cogitation. Other species digest food via physico-chemical processes that differ markedly from those employed in our own species; in addition, it is not inconceivable that advanced computer automatons one day will forage for food and digest it, this being done in ways that will differ even more markedly from our own.

So the identity theory of digestion gives way to functionalism. How should this latter doctrine be formulated? The Turing Machine version falls prey to the same problems mentioned above in the mind/body problem. Just as a group of people can be paid to abstractly mimic my thought processes, a group can be hired to abstractly mimic my digestive processes. But the group that does this mimicking is no more digesting than it is thinking. A better approach is the teleological version of functionalism. Sameness of (teleological) function has nothing to do with sameness of abstract program. Two organisms can digest food in markedly different ways. There can be physical differences between their digestive processes, and there can be abstract differences between them too. For a system to engage in the process of digestion is for it to engage in a process that has a certain (teleological) function.

Another problem about functionalism, related to the one just described of group mimicry, is clarified by a teleological approach. Instead of having a group of people hired for an hour or a day to abstractly mimic the micro-processes in my brain (or gut), let's imagine that a quite different relationship obtains between this group entity and me. Here I have in mind Block's (1978) idea of homunculus heads. Suppose my brain is removed and replaced by a radio transmitter and receiver. The various different input channels leading into the brain now have their signals sent to a group of people. Each individual mimics the behavior of one of my neurons. Some of these individuals are hooked up directly to the radio transmitter in my head; others are hooked up only to other individuals in the group; and still others transmit signals back to the receiver in my body, which then relays signals to the rest of my body, causing behavior.

In this case, the group entity is not merely engaged in abstract and inconsequential mimicry. Rather, the group is functioning as my prosthetic brain (see also Lycan 1979). They are to my normal psychological functioning what a kidney machine might be to my normal kidney function. When I use a kidney machine, my blood gets cleaned. In the homunculus case, my hook-up to the group allows perception and cognition to proceed. The cases are parallel.

There is a puzzle here, which arises from taking seriously the idea that brains in vats can have mental states. Although my brain allows my body to interact in various ways with the environment, this connection of brain to body appears to be inessential for my brain to occupy psychological states. Even if we grant that belief is a wide psychological state (as urged by Putnam (1975)), so that the individuation of beliefs depends on facts about the environment, not just on the mind's internal states, the point still remains: it seems implausible to insist that a brain in a vat would have no mental states whatever.

Now if this is true for normal brains when they are detached from their containing bodies, it presumably also must be true for artificial brains. In the previous example, a group of people provided me with an artificial brain. Let us now sever the connection of this group with my body, and instead connect the group to a computer which sends and receives signals, much as a computer might send and receive signals when connected to a brain in a vat. In this case, the group of people is not functioning as a mental organ for any organism; it is just a cog in a simulation experiment. Do we still want to say that the group has mental states?

Intuition strongly suggests that brains in vats have mental states. Perhaps intuition is less single-minded about what one should say about prosthetic brains that are not connected (or are not connected "in the right way") to the sorts of containing systems for which brains normally perform functions. I do not see this as a difficulty for Teleological Functionalism. The same questions arise for other artificial organs – especially ones that we might call "control devices."

A healthy heart regulates its own contractions. A pacemaker is a device for performing the same function. Pacemakers, let us suppose, can be surgically implanted or kept external to the patient and made to do their work by radio hook-up. In addition, a group of people could abstractly mimic the workings of a pacemaker; they also could themselves *be* a pacemaker, if suitably connected to someone's heart. However, as in the case of the group of people that is disconnected from any organism for whom they might provide a prosthetic brain, it might be difficult to decide what one should say about a device which *could* perform a function but does not, in virtue of its lack of connection with the "normal" sort of containing system. Is a device that is physically indistinguishable from a pacemaker, which is hooked up to a computer, engaged in coronary regulation? Well, there is clearly no heart that it is regulating. On the other hand, there seems to be a sense in which the device is engaged in regulatory activity.

I'm not going to suggest a principled way to answer such puzzles. My hunch is that sufficiently bizarre examples deserve to be viewed with suspicion and not elevated into test cases for theories. However, I do want to urge that the difficulty that functionalism faces here in the mind/body problem is really a more general problem about function ascription, construed teleologically. The fact that this difficulty arises, and has the logical contours it does, supports, rather than disconfirms, Teleological Functionalism.

Another criticism that has been levelled against functionalism falls nicely into place when we substitute Teleological for Turing Machine Functionalism. This is Block's (1978) "problem of the inputs and the outputs." When functionalists describe the information processing procedures that you exploit when you form perceptual judgments, for example, they will characterize this set of procedures as a program, which has inputs and outputs. In the case of visual perception, we might want to describe the inputs physically in terms of patterns of light; the outputs might be described as the construction of a representation, which then may have effects on other representations and on behavior. Functionalism's negative insight, as Block has put it, is to avoid chauvinism. We shouldn't think that an organism with a mind must be just like us physically. But this lesson has relevance to how a functionalist should characterize inputs and outputs. There is no reason why perception or cogitation has to work via the kind of processing of light signals that we use in the case of vision, nor need perceptual representations be realized in the neuronal structures we happen to deploy. A functionalist should abstract away from such physical details.

How might this be done? If we abstract away from physical details too much, we will end up with a purely abstract specification of our own psychology, and we will be back to the problem of the group hired to engage in abstract mimicry. Block suspects that this problem is insoluble – a functionalist will either err on the side of chauvinism or on the side of liberalism, when it comes to determining the right description of the inputs and the outputs.

Teleological functionalism makes this problem look like it might be tractable. Again, let's consider digestion. We digest certain foods by way of certain physical processes. But digestion can and does proceed via other physical processes, and indeed, other organisms have diets markedly different from our own. Just as our perceptual contact with the world is mediated by some physical signals rather than others, so our energetic contact with the world is mediated by some tidbits rather than others. Perceiving and eating can be diverse in their mechanisms and diverse in what can serve as inputs. However, I do not see why this should spell doom for a functionalist theory of digestion. Despite the fact of multiple realizability, there seems to be something like a common core. Roughly speaking, it seems plausible to say that all digestion involves extracting energy from the environment. Although I have nothing substantive to say about what the function of the mind is, it is worth considering a (somewhat vague) answer to Block's question about inputs and outputs for the case of perception. Perception involves extracting information from the environment. Inputs are to be specified in terms of their information-bearing properties. Light-packets are inessential, as are retinas and neurons. These merely constitute one among many physical realizations of what we call the perceptual process. It is up to science to give a detailed account of the process of information flow. My point is that I can't see any *a priori* reason why theorizing at this level of abstraction should be impossible.

At the same time, we must be alive to the possibility that science may not deliver theoretical characterizations of some of the very abstract and general properties deployed in common sense psychology. Perhaps "perception" will turn out to be too broad a category to be worth theorizing about. If so, it would be wrong to criticize a functionalist psychology for failing to provide a functionalist theory of perception as a general category. Rather, what might be more realistic is that there be various functionalist theor*ies* about different sorts of perception. In any event, how things will turn out is not for armchair philosophy to say. I conclude that Block's problem of the inputs and the outputs is as tractable as it needs to be, once functionalism is construed teleologically.

Another problem for functionalism derives from applying Putnam's (1975) ideas about meaning to psychological states like belief. Twin Earth thought-experiments suggest that two individuals can be physically identical and yet have different beliefs. Your term "water" refers to H_2O, whereas your twin's term "water" refers to *XYZ*. If functionalism is understood as Turing Machine Functionalism, it looks like there can be no functionalist theory of belief. Your term "water" and your twin's term "water" have the same causal susceptibilities and powers. The presence of H_2O or *XYZ* under "normal" conditions will lead both of you to formulate the sentence "there is some water." And that sentence, when present in the "belief box," will lead to drinking, if you and your twin are thirsty.

This apparent failure of functionalism to deal with non-narrow psychological states like belief will not be bothersome to those, like Block (1978) and Fodor (1980), who think that psychology is about narrow states only. But for "pluralists" like myself (see Sober 1982), who hold that narrow and wide properties of the organism both have a role to play in psychology, it is a matter of concern that functionalism seems incapable of handling non-narrow states.

However, once again, matters change when Teleological Functionalism is considered. A simple fact about (teleological) functions is that what the function of something is depends on the kind of environment in which it is embedded (Wimsatt 1980). Two physically identical pieces of metal may have different functions, if they are placed in different machines. You have the concept of water; your twin has the concept of twin-water. How can the two of you have different concepts if you and your twin are physically identical? We might characterize the difference as a difference in function. Again, let me stress that I do not pretend to know what the function of any mental item is. But to illustrate the resources of Teleological Functionalism, I frame this conjecture: your term "water" has the function of representing water (= H_2O), whereas your twin's term functions to represent twin-water (= *XYZ*). A naturalistic theory of content faces the task of elaborating this bare suggestion; it remains to be seen how such a theory will fare. But as things now stand, I think that functionalism has nothing to fear from non-narrow psychological states.

The last objection to functionalism I will consider concerns qualia. It has been developed in various forms by Bradley (1964), Campbell (1970), and Block (1978), among others. The problem can be illustrated via the inverted spectrum problem. Suppose you and I are otherwise identical in our psychological characteristics, except that red things look green to you, while green things look red. I, on the other hand, am psychologically "normal." To me, green things look green and red things look red. When I look at a green thing (in normal lighting conditions, etc.), I go into state G, whereas you go into state R. When I look at a red thing, I go into state R, whereas you go into state G. The problem for functionalism is this: Although your state G (R) and my state R (G) are qualitatively different, they appear to be causally the same. You are caused to go into R (G) by exactly the same things that cause me to go into G (R). And the effects of my being in state R (G) are precisely the same as the effects of your being in state G (R). For example, looking at a fire engine produces state R in me and state G in you; and my being in state R causes me (if other psychological dispositions are right) to say "yes" to the question "Is that thing red?", which is exactly what your being in state *G* causes. So the states differ psychologically, even though they do not differ in terms of their causal (functional) role. Hence, functionalism cannot handle qualia.

Along with Block (1978), I will assume that "qualia realism" is true. There really could be a difference between your qualitative state and mine, even if this could not be detected in any of our outward behavior. My disagreement with Block concerns the issue of whether a qualia realist can be a functionalist.

To see why qualia realism need not be a problem for functionalism, consider the following parody of the above argument:

> Imagine two very different computer programs that both take pairs of numbers as inputs and output the product of those numbers. These two programs are interchangeable in any larger, containing computer. Hence, functionalism cannot characterize the difference between the two programs, since, by hypothesis, the two programs play identical causal roles.

The defect in this argument is that it fails to attend to what might be going on *inside* the programs. Although the two programs may be weakly equivalent, their internal processes may be functionally different.

Your qualia and mine differ, even though they appear to play the same causal roles. Does it follow that functionalism cannot capture the difference between greenish qualia in me and reddish qualia in you? No, this does not follow, for it may be the case that there is lots of structure lurking within that distinguishes the two. Perhaps we experience qualia as simples, but that does not mean that they are simples. For all we know, there may be lots of complexity that a functionalist theory may identify and thereby make out a different between your qualia and mine.

For this reason, I do not think we can conclude that functionalism cannot handle qualia. The sticking point is the assumption that qualia are simples. In spite of this, I think there is a lesson we can draw from the problem of qualia, one which does point to a real limitation in functionalism, even when that doctrine is given its strongest (teleological) formulation.

In any functionally organized system, whether it be the digestive system or the perceptual system, we should expect that there will be states or devices that are functionally equivalent. Not only is it true, as the functionalist realizes, that physically different states can be functionally equivalent. It also is the case that *psychologically different states can be identical in their psychological function.*

So my agreement with Block concerns a general point, rather than his specific conclusion about qualia. I see no compelling reason to think that functionalism cannot handle qualia. However, it would surprise me if every psychological difference corresponds to a functional difference. This would constitute a mark of the mental, in that it would place the mind in an entirely different category from our other functional systems, like digestion and respiration.

Upon discovering that two traits have identical biological functions, biologists do not conclude that there is no biological difference between them. The Javanese rhinoceros has two horns, but the Africa rhino has only one. There is absolutely no reason to think that there is any difference in function here. Does it follow that there is no biological difference between having two horns and having only one? Likewise, upon discovering that a certain trait simply has no biological function, why should we stipulate that it is not a biological trait at all? Gould and Lewontin (1979) say that the human chin has no function; is it thereby not a biological item?

Biology encompasses a great many things. One salient fact about biological function is this: where there is functional organization, there also will be artifacts of functional organization – items that have no function at all. When objects are unified into a system, each having their separate functions, there will be fallout; there will be traits of the system and of the objects involved which do not themselves have functions, but which are merely consequences – artifacts – of the functions that do exist. Since biology studies not just the fact of functional organization, but also the consequences of functional organization, biology will study artifacts.

Psychologists study the functional organization of the perceptual and cognitive systems. But as with any system of objects, the existence of function pretty much guarantees the existence of artifacts. If psychologists study the consequences of functional organization, they will end up studying traits that have no psychological function. They also will wish to distinguish between traits that are functionally equivalent.

So my view is that functionalism is a very bizarre doctrine, when taken as a claim about the identity conditions that attach to *every* psychological state. Functionalism seems to imagine that there is perfect economy – that every psychological state has its uniquely individuating psychological function. Following Gould and Lewontin (1979), I call this assumption *Panglossian*; recall Dr Pangloss in Voltaire's *Candide*, who claimed that everything has a function, which it executes optimally. Panglossian functionalism has the virtue of simplicity. But functional organization is more messy than this, perhaps necessarily so.

Since I have shamelessly plundered the concept of function in this essay, I should say a few words about how I have understood that shady idea. There is an extremely minimal interpretation of function, explicated by Cummins (1975), according to which everything has a function. The function of a part of a containing system is whatever that part does to contribute to the containing system's having whatever properties it has. The metaphor is that of the assembly line: the function of the components is whatever they do that allows the assembly line to do whatever it does. There is nothing wrong, on this view, with talking about the function of the heart's being to have a certain weight. The heart has a particular weight and thereby contributes to the body's being able to tip the scales at some, somewhat greater, weight. According to Cummins, there is nothing false about this ascription of function. It just doesn't strike us as very interesting. It will be clear that according to this analysis, there is no such thing as a thing's not having a function. Furthermore, any two devices with different effects of any kind will thereby have different functions. We can always find a function, and we can always find a difference in function.

I don't propose to argue that this analysis is false. However, within psychology, as in biology, we *do* want to be able to say that some items have no function, while other items have identical functions, even though there are obvious differences between them in their effects. What this means is that we must relativize our ascriptions of function to certain privileged states of the containing system. For example, if we want to say that the appendix has no function, we might put this point by saying that the appendix does not have a function as far as digestion is concerned. If we want to say that my red qualia and your green ones have the same function, this must mean that they have identical functions, as far as certain psychological processes are concerned.

Without such relativization and addition of detail, the claim that psychological states are functional states is incredibly trivial. Every psychological state has its causes and effects, and if we look carefully enough, we can always find a causal difference between any two different psychological states. Indeed, without relativization, functionalism is perfectly compatible with the identity theory, since physical states also can be individuated in terms of their causal connections (Lycan 1981). On the other hand, once functionalism is properly relativized, it becomes a suspect Panglossian doctrine. Not all biological states are individuated in terms of their biological functions. I expect no less of psychology.

Panglossian assumptions can be useful to a discipline, especially when the discipline is relatively young and theory is relatively undeveloped. The idea that every trait has a function and performs that function optimally has its uses in evolutionary theory, if only as a guide to asking questions (this is not to deny that the idea has been abused at times). But one sign that a functional theory has matured is that it is able to provide some independent source of evidence for whether a trait has a function and for whether two traits really are functionally equivalent.

In psychology and the philosophy of mind, Panglossian ideas arise in many contexts. I have explored just one of them here. Another that is worth mentioning is the status of the rationality assumption; many philosophers have held that ascribing beliefs to agents requires that they be viewed as rational. It has been held that this is not just a practical expedient but is an *a priori* requirement. My view is that it is a Panglossian simplification, useful but not inevitable for theorizing that has not sufficiently matured (Sober 1978, 1985).

As Panglossian assumptions steadily lose their grip in biology, a parallel problem in philosophy of biology becomes less interesting. What ever happened to vitalism and kindred theories about the relationship of biological states and properties to physical states and properties? It is a mistake to think that materialism (that is, a type/type identity theory) won the day. Functionalism's negative insight applies to biology no less than to psychology. Concepts like *fitness* and *predator* are not type-reducible to physical properties (Rosenberg 1978; Sober 1984b). I would suggest that we now have no adequate philosphical theory about the nature of biological states and properties as a category; I would add that this hyper-general question is not an interesting one in the first place. Progress in various areas of biology has removed the mystery that made the philosophical problem posed by vitalism seem so compelling. Separate biological theories circumscribe their own domains and characterize their own properties in a rather heterogeneous way. This biological analogy suggests that progress in the cognitive sciences, besides loosening the grip of Panglossian assumptions, will also change our perspective on some of the problems that functionalist ideas were invented to solve.

REFERENCES

Block, N. (1978) "Troubles with functionalism," in W. Savage (ed.), *Perception and Cognition: Issues in the Foundations of Psychology: Minnesota Studies in the Philosophy of Science*, vol. ix, University of Minnesota Press.

Block, N. and Fodor, J. (1972) "What psychological states are not." *Philosophical Review* 81, 159–82.

Bradley, M. (1964) "Critical notice of Smart's 'Philosophy and Scientific Realism,'" *Australasian Journal of Philosophy* 71, 262–83.

Campbell, K. (1970) *Body and Mind*, New York: Doubleday.

Cummins, R. (1975) "Functional analysis," *Journal of Philosophy* 72, 741–64. Reprinted in Sober 1984a.

Davis, L. (1974) "Functional definitions and how it feels to be in pain." Unpublished manuscript.

Dennett, D. (1978a) "Towards a cognitive theory of consciousness," in *Brainstorms*, Montgomery, Vt: Bradford Books.

Dennett, D. (1978b) "Why you can't make a computer that feels pain," in *Brainstorms*, Montgomery, Vt: Bradford Books.

Fodor, J. (1968) *Psychological Explanation*, New York: Random House.

Fodor, J. (1980) "Methodological solipsism as a research strategy in cognitive psychology," *Behavior and Brain Sciences* 3, 63–100.

Gould, S. and Lewontin, R. (1979), "The spandrels of San Marco and the Panglossian paradigm: A critique of the adaptationist programme," *Proceedings of the Royal Society of London* B 205, 581–98. Reprinted in Sober 1984a.

Lycan, W. (1979) "A new Lilliputian argument against machine functionalism," *Philosophical Studies* 35, 279–87.

Lycan, W. (1981) "Form, function, and feel," *Journal of Philosophy* 78, 24–50.

Putnam, H. (1967) "Psychological predicates," in W. Capitan and D. Merrills (eds), *Art, Mind, and Religion*, University of Pittsburgh Press.

Putnam, H. (1975) "The meaning of 'meaning'," in K. Gunderson (ed.), *Minnesota Studies in the Philosophy of Science*, vol. 7, University of Minnesota Press.

Rosenberg, A. (1978) "The supervenience of biological concepts," *Philosophy of Science* 45, 368–86. Reprinted in Sober 1984a.

Sober, E. (1978) "Psychologism," *Journal for the Theory of Social Behavior* 8, 165–91.

Sober, E. (1982) "Rational biology and naturalistic biology, *Behavior and Brain Sciences* 5, 300–2.

Sober, E. (1984a) *Conceptual Issues in Evolutionary Biology: An Anthology*, MIT Press.

Sober, E. (1984b) *The Nature of Selection: Evolutionary Theory in Philosophical Focus*, MIT Press.

Sober, E. (1985) "Panglossian functionalism and the philosophy of mind," *Synthese* 64, 165–93.

Wimsatt, W. (1980) "Teleology and the logical structure of function statements," *Studies in the History and Philosophy of Science* 3, 1–80.

6

Teleological Views of Intentionality

Functionalism, Information and Content
ROBERT VAN GULICK

Human beings are physical systems and thus in principle their activity can be described within the language of physical science. Yet it is clear that such descriptions will not suffice for every practical or explanatory purpose.[1] Among the theoretical perspectives which seem required for an adequate psychology of human action or behavior are those which describe human beings as acquiring information about their environment as well as storing, interrelating and using that information. Indeed, so large a role do such factors play in human behavior that many cognitive psychologists have adopted the notion of an *information processing system* as the dominant model in constructing theories of human psychological function.[2] However, despite the widespread popularity of the information processing approach, there is considerable theoretical unclarity about the notions of information and cognitive representation which are employed in formulating such theories. Various uses of the term 'information' drawn from computer science, communication theory, traditional psychology and common sense are often distinguished only inexactly, if at all.

Functionalism and content My intent below will be to provide an analytic, though nonrigorous,[3] treatment of the related concepts of information and content from a basically functionalist perspective, where functionalism is understood as the philosophic view that psychological states are type individuated by their distinctive role within a complex network of states mediating the perceptual conditions and behavior of organisms or systems.[4] States, including contentful states, are held to be of a given psychological type in virtue of their functional role within such a network. Thus the functionalist is obliged to explain how content is to be unpacked by reference to functional role.

"Functionalism, Information and Content" by R. Van Gulick in *Nature and System* 2 (1980), 139–62. Copyright © 1980 by Nature and System Inc.

The class of contentful states includes beliefs, desires, states of perceptual awareness in lower as well as higher animals, and at least some so-called "memory states" in digital computers. Roughly speaking, a contentful state is any state of a system whose adequate description requires a specification of its content. A particular belief state, for example, must be a state of believing that *p* or believing that *q*. Particular desires and intentions similarly require a specification of their content in order to be adequately characterized; we must say what is desired or intended and under what description.

The basic functionalist thesis is that psychological state types are to be characterized in terms of the functional roles which those states play in a structure of internal states, mediating stimulus inputs and behavioral outputs (leaving aside for now any further claims about the conceptual resources which will suffice to specify those roles.[5] Considerations of functional role are held to differentiate not only among general psychological state types such as beliefs, desires, and intentions, but also among subtypes such as *believing that p* and *believing that q*. A state has whatever content it does on the basis of its functional role.

Informational states   In accord with our primary interest in the concept of information, I will focus on those contentful states which can be thought of as informational states of their respective systems. Systems realize informational states in the relevant sense when they can be said to possess the information or to have stored it in a manner allowing them to make use of it. It is the idea of *information possession* which is crucial here. For while representations and symbols can be thought of as representing or encoding certain bits of information, it would make no sense to think of them as themselves possessing that information. The information is present in those representations to be retrieved by any person or system capable of interpreting them. But when we attribute to an agent the belief that *p* (a belief being a type of informational state), we clearly attribute to him also the ability to understand and utilize that information. The distinction corresponds to Dennett's between intelligent and nonintelligent information storage,[6] for the crucial feature with respect to both intelligent information storage and informational states is that the relevant information is information *for the system* storing it or being in that state. Our task is to say what functional role or relation to input and output a state must realize if it is to constitute a system's possessing information.

Input   Let us consider input relations first. Much contemporary psychological work on human and animal perception treats organic sensory structures as systems for extracting information from the physical stimuli impinging on the organism.[7] The processes are usually complex, involving first level transducers which convert physical stimuli in patterns of neural activity, followed by many levels of "analysis" performed on those neural patterns. In the retina, optic nerve, and cortex the pattern of neural firing is continually modified as it passes upward. The firing rates of neurons at upper levels are determined according to sometimes complex functions by the firing rates of neurons connecting to them from below. The firing of neurons from below has sometimes a facilitory and sometimes an inhibitory effect on neurons to which it inputs, but the details of these processes need not concern us here. What is relevant is that using this dual system of inhibition and excitement it is possible to build up structures, where neurons at the upper level are more and more selective in their response to features of the sensory stimuli. Thus using these so-called "perceptron" systems[8] we can construct sophisticated feature extractors or pattern recognition devices; for example, selectively firing cortical neurons which alter their firing rate only if a line of light is present on the retina, or a line of a certain width, or of a certain width, length and orientation.

Such perceptron systems are often spoken of as "extracting information" from the initial pattern of light falling on the retina. But in what sense can the firing of the relevant cortical neuron be thought of as recognition of the presence of a horizontal line or as the realization of an informational state whose content is that a horizontal line is present? 'Information' is being used here in a manner much as in communications theory, where we talk of the nonrandom covariance between the properties of two communicating systems.[9] In the visual perception system there is a nonrandom correlation between the presence or absence of various features in the initial stimuli and the firing of cortical neurons.

Given the correlations and its causal ties to the stimulus conditions, the firing of the relevant cortical neuron might seem to represent the presence of a horizontal line. But for whom or for what system does it represent such? The relevant system in this case must surely be the organism, but we are not justified in attributing to it the possession of information about the horizontal line purely on the basis of the sorts of input analysis described above.

Output   In order to possess that information, the organism must be able to *utilize* it. The possession of the information must make a difference in the organism's actual or counterfactual behavior. For the content of any given state is a matter not only of its relations to input but also of its relations to the outputs of the system of which it is a part. Unless the system is in some way disposed to act differentially with respect to the stimulus, or in consequence of the state occasioned by the stimulus, no sense could be made of the system's attaching any significance to that stimulus. There would be nothing about the system which would constitute its taking the stimulus to be of a certain sort. Thus we could assign no content to the supposed representational state. Such a system would be only a passive or nonintelligent storer of information. The point is not an epistemological one about our inability to assign or discover the contents of internal states in the absence of behavioral manifestations of those states, but rather a conceptual claim. For a state may well have content though it never in fact manifests itself in behavior. Its influence on the organism's behavior may remain purely potential in the absence of the appropriate circumstances for activating its effects. However, even in the case of such never activated structures, it is the difference which they *would* make to behavior which provides the basis for assigning them informational content.

Of course not all the influences which a system's states have on its behavior are relevant to determining what content, if any, those states realize for the system. There are many ways in which a system's inputs can alter its output which are not properly thought of as involving the acquisition of information. This point should emerge clearly if we consider two general classes of constraints which apply in relating behavior regulating role to content. The first consists of constraints which concern adaptivity and the specificity of a response's adaptive value. The others involve rationality and interstate relations.

Adaptivity   Speaking somewhat loosely, a system's states may be thought of as informational states or states of possessing information whenever the presence of those states leads to *adaptive modification* of the system's behavior; that is, modification which enhances the system's survival or the realization of its goals. To see a system as using information, we need not suppose that there is some separate store of information which it "consults" prior to acting to regulate its behavior. Rather in so far as structures within the system adaptively modify the behavioral responses of the system to changing environmental conditions, the very presence of those structures should be thought of as the possession of information by the system. For the likelihood that random behavioral changes occasioned by environmental conditions would be beneficial to the system is sufficiently low, that any structures which generally modify behavior in adaptive ways must be thought of as nonrandom and as constituting information possessed by the system about its environment. The point is put somewhat more strongly by the ethologist Konrad Lorenz when writing of organic adaptation. He argues:

> "Adaptation" is the process which molds the organism so that it fits its environment in a way achieving survival. .... Any molding of the organism to its environment is a process so akin to that of forming within organic structure an image of the environment that it is completely correct to speak of information concerning the environment being acquired by the organism.[10]

Specificity   This general characterization of information possession in terms of any adaptive structure is of course overly broad. It is at this point that considerations of specificity apply. The modifications of behavior brought about must be responsive to specific features of the changing environmental situation in order to justify the attribution of informational content to the structure. By running regularly a man may increase the strength of his legs, and the resultant increase in endurances and speed may well be considered adaptive. Yet we would not normally consider the organic changes in his musculature as the acquisition of information. What is missing in such a case is the development of structures regulating behavior which fit that behavior to the particular and specific circumstances of the environmental situation. We are in a strong position to attribute content to an internal state of a given system when the presence of that state is causally correlated with the presence of a particular environmental feature and the presence of the state modifies the behavior of the system in ways specifically adaptive to that particular environmental feature (for example, the cortical states of a frog which are excited only by small moving objects in its visual field and which produce "fly-catching" movements of its tongue). In very complex informational systems, the links between an informational state and adaptive behavior may be quite indirect. It may be difficult, for example, to locate any adaptive difference in behavior which connects with the average science student's true beliefs about the speed of light. But such cases can arise only within the context of a rich network of interconnected states. Specific adaptivity of response seems an essential element in the primary or basic cases of information possession.[11] Only where some states of a system have acquired content on such a basis can other states perhaps acquire content derivatively by relation to those states, without themselves having any specific adaptive consequences.[12]

Having introduced the notion of specific adaptivity, we cannot go further without discussing the idea of a system's *having goals* or being *goal directed*. Many philosophers and psychologists find such notions objectionably teleological, but properly understood their use need not involve us in any excessive metaphysical commitments. Moreover, there seems no hope of giving any satisfactory account of active information possession without using goal-based concepts. In as far as informational states have the contents that they do in virtue of the adaptive modifications of behavior which they bring about, we must be prepared to attribute goals and goal directedness to any system to which we wish to attribute informational states. For otherwise, the notion of adaptivity could have no application. A system could not have informational states in the interesting sense of actively possessing information unless that system also had goals whose achievement could be enhanced by the utilization of that information. Thus possessing information presupposes having goals. Moreover, a proper understanding of goal directed systems will show that the converse also holds; that is, any system which is goal directed in an interesting sense must also be a system possessing information, a system with informational states.

Goal directedness   To establish these connections, let us consider the generally plausible account of goal directedness offered by Ernest Nagel in his 1976 John Dewey lectures.[13] On Nagel's analysis which is fundamentally in keeping with general system theory, a goal-directed system is one which tends toward a fixed state, and whose behavior in tending toward that state is persistent and plastic in the face of disturbing influences but (causally) orthogonal to those disturbing forces. The conditions of persistence and plasticity build in the notion of variable response to changing environmental conditions and thus exclude as non-goal-directed any systems which uniformly proceed toward some equilibrium state in too simple a manner, exhibiting no substantial degree of correction or self regulation. Operationalizing or making more specific how one might measure variability or plasticity would be no easy matter, but the general notions are I hope sufficiently clear as is their applicability to the concept of goal directedness.

The requirement of orthogonality is needed to rule out cases where the character of the system's corrective responses are direct and simple causal consequences of the nature of the disturbing influences operating. Explaining the system's persistence in tending toward the fixed end state in such cases does not require appeal to any internal behavior regulating structures, but is a simple direct causal consequence of direct input/output relations. Here again there are difficulties in spelling out the constraint. How indirect must the link between disturbance and response be to count as orthogonal? And how might one measure directness? We surely cannot require that there be *no* causal link between disturbance and response without danger of depriving all physical systems of goal-directed status.[14] What is important is that the organizational structure of the system play an essential role in determining the behavioral response, and that *ceteris paribus* the more that response depends on the complex and systematic interaction of component structures within the system, the more basis there is for treating the behavior as goal directed. Still in many cases there will be an element of choice involved in our attribution of goal directedness, choices dependent on our explanatory aims and on the larger systematic context within which the structure or component we are describing occurs. If we understand what the causal determinants of that item's response to its environment are, the issue of whether or not to regard it as goal directed is not one of adding further causal factors or causal factors of a different sort to our story. It is rather a matter of choosing that descriptive framework which, consistent with the causal facts, meets our needs to explain and understand the item in question and its behavior. The teleological description might be apt in cases where we wish to explain why this structure rather than some other came to be (or to be perpetuated), by appeal to the selective advantage of the goals it secures. The teleological view may also bring out similarities between the item in question and other structures which emerge only when we depart from their causal details and consider them in terms of the goals toward which they can be seen as directed. In so far as characterizing any item X as of a given sort F is not a matter independent of taking it to be like or unlike other things (in some variety of respects), it may be necessary to exhibit those of X's similarities to other items which emerge only under a teleological description in order to achieve the sort of understanding of X which we aim at in a given situation. At the level of detailed causal structure X may bear little resemblance to Y and Z, though we may enhance our understanding of X if we recognize the affinities between X, Y, and Z considered teleologically. For example, they might all be seen to function as feedback devices regulating some growth process within their respective containing systems.

In consequence of this context dependence, we may find much better grounds to regard one of two very similar items as more goal directed than another, merely on the basis of its role within the system of which it is a component. We cannot restrict our attention to the component's input/output relations alone nor even to the causal determinants of its behavior. Of two structures acting similarly to achieve changes in the ionization balance internal and external to themselves, one may be more aptly thought of as goal directed, if its achieving such an effect can be seen to contribute to larger more clearly goal-directed behaviors in its containing system. Imagine perhaps that one structure is an isolated randomly occurring molecular structure and the other is a neural membrane of some vertebrate. In the latter case, we are more likely to derive explanatory value from describing the membrane in goal-directed terminology so as to fit its activity within the larger context of the organism's goal-directed processes. In doing so we do not attribute to its activity a different causal structure than that attributed to the isolated molecule, but rather focus attention on ways of relating the membrane and its behavior to other systematically related items.[15] The conditions which justify the description of some system as goal directed will not be independent of the pragmatic and explanatory context in which the description is to be used. This contextual dependence should emphasize that nothing said above is intended to provide a strict operational definition of what it is to be a goal-directed system.

Holism   Despite its somewhat open and pragmatic character, our basic account establishes important links between the notions of goal directedness and information possession. Modification of behavior which is specifically adaptive to changing environmental circumstances is a crucial element in both analyses. The sorts of internal structures which must be present regulating behavior to provide sufficient plasticity and orthogonality of behavior to justify the attribution of goal directedness to a system are of the same sort required to attribute the possession of information to the system. Just as possessing information presupposes the having of goals, so also no system could adapt its behavior in the ways required by our analysis of goal directedness without *ipso facto* possessing information. The two notions are analytically interdependent; indeed they might be thought of as merely two aspects of a single functional characteristic of complex systems, that of having structures which adaptively mold or fit the system to its environment and which manifest an understanding of that environment and its causal structure in their regulation of the system's behavior.[16] The existence of such conceptual connectons will come as no surprise to those sympathetic to the claims of mental holism, though the conceptual interdependence for which I have argued above seems both more intimate and more general in scope than in standard discussions of holism.[17] The oft alleged mutual interdependence of belief and desire can now be seen as merely a special case of a more general link between informational and goal-direction states. The considerations which so intimately tie belief and desire are not peculiar to any given theory of human or common-sense psychology, but would apply equally with respect to any psychological theory which employed the concepts of information or goal directedness in explaining behavior.

To adequately display the importance of holistic considerations in characterizing such systems, we must go on to discuss the second general class of constraints which apply to their functional organizations. For holistic interdependencies arise also within the fine-grained relations among large classes of particular contentful states, all of which may be of the same general state type. For example, the realization of a particular informational state will typically require the realization of a structure of other related informational states. If the state is a belief, it is clear that to have one belief, the believer must have many. And the beliefs which he has must be interconnected and interrelated in appropriate ways manifesting a rational order. Taking account of this holism requires us to expand our list of the constraints which must be honored in relating a state's content to its behavioral role by adding constraints which concern the nature and degree of the state's *interconnection or functional interaction* with other internal behavior regulating states, with special emphasis on connections of rationality.

Interconnection In considering constraints of interconnection it is important to distinguish between two sorts of reasons for attending to interstate relations in developing an account of content – one practical, the other more conceptual. As a practical matter, most of the systems to which we would wish to attribute informational states, are ones in which the behavior of the system can rarely if ever be explained by appeal to the influence of a single state acting in isolation. Rather it is characteristic of such systems that their behavior is the product of complex and multiple interactions involving many internal structures. Any adequate specification of the role which a given state or structure plays with respect to the system's behavior will have to be in terms of the partial contributions which that state makes to the determination of behavior in conjunction with a wide variety of internal state combinations. Thus as a practical matter, if we wish our account of content as a function of behavioral role to cover such systems, as we surely do, then we must be prepared to accommodate these interrelations. On the conceptual side, a stronger claim is suggested. For a high degree of interstate connection may be more than accidentally present in the actual systems of interest to us. Such rich connections among informational (or contentful) states may be necessary for possessing many sorts of information. If so, no system lacking such interstate connections within its functional organization could satisfy the conditions for possessing the relevant information.

To see how this might be so, we must note how the range of information which a system can possess is constrained by the character of its internal functional organization. In so far as content is understood as a function of functional role, relations among items of content must in some way be reflected in relations among functional structures. Now recognizing relations among items of content will be a pervasive and necessary feature of sophisticated information possessing systems. For given our sense of active information possession, a system cannot possess the information that a certain situation obtains or that some item satisfies a given description unless the system can in some sense "understand" what it would be for that situation to obtain or that description to apply. But achieving this understanding in most cases will require of the system that it 'recognize' how this particular fact links up with other facts. To understand what an individual fact comes to, the system will have to place it within a larger organized structure of facts (some analog of a theory). Thus in order to satisfy the conditions for possessing the one item of information, it must also realize in its functional organization the conditions for possessing those related items of content as well as reflecting their interrelations. The holism of the cognitive field at the level of content must be mirrored at the level of functional organization if content is as we suppose a function of functional organization. At some level of description, there must be an *isomorphism* between the logical and relational structure of the information possessed and the functional organization of states which constitutes the possession of that information.[18]

Unfortunately our use of isomorphism is likely to remain vague here, though it can perhaps be made a bit more specific by looking at its application in particular cases. Suppose for example that we wish our system to possess information about the relative volumes of a group of cylinders. The ordering of cylinders by relative volume will be transitive, and this transitivity should be reflected in our system's representation of those volumes. Now one need not suppose that the states of the system realizing the possession of information about the volumes of particular cylinders should themselves evidence some transitive *physical* ordering, far less an ordering in terms of relative volume. But the transitive ordering must somehow be embodied in the interactive relations between those states in virtue of which the behavior of the system is determined. The structure must be such that if the system is asked to select the member greater in volume from each of the three pairs of cylinders A and B, B and C, and C and A, it will not make any such intransitive selections as A, B, C, respectively. Thus the isomorphic relation which mirrors the transitive ordering of the cylinders' volumes may not be any simple physical relation, but rather a relation which emerges only at the level of the functional roles which the contentful states play in regulating the system's behavior. In such cases, the isomorphism between informational structure and functional structure can be established only when the functional organization is described in terms of its actual behavior regulating role. That the relevant isomorphism might be a mapping from a structure of informational items onto a structure of behavior regulating operations or procedures in no way undercuts the demand for some sort of 'mirroring' as an essential condition for possessing the relevant information. We must just avoid too narrow a conception of 'mirroring.'

The line of support for our conceptual claim should now be obvious. A system can actively possess information about a given fact only if it can understand that fact by placing it in a context. Thus to realize the initial informational state a system must also realize a structure of other interrelated states which constitute its possession of information about those related facts which form the necessary context for understanding the original fact. Holism is inescapable with respect to information possession, and the more sophisticated is the information possessed, the greater become the demands for functional interconnection.

If we remember that the relevant context of understanding for active information possession is a real world context and not a merely symbolic one, a second argument can be made for the necessity of interconnection by appeal to behavioral roles. The idea of information possession is essentially bound up with that of adaptive modification of behavior. However, with respect to many of the contents we might wish to use in specifying the information possessed by a system there is no simple or isolated set of behavioral routines or responses which would manifest its possession of just that information. The sorts of facts about a system's behavior which could count as its understanding and possessing such items of information would have to involve its realizing patterns of complex *conditional* response sensitive as well to a great many other environmental features or parameters. In such cases, then, the realization by any system of a functional structure which constituted its possession of the initial information would require its also realizing functional structures constituting the possession of a great deal of other information as well, information about those other factors.[19] Thus the argument from treating content as a function of behavioral role reaches the same holistic result as the argument from understanding. Indeed, the two are closely tied in so far as achieving greater understanding involves establishing more finely tuned adaptive behavior regulation.

Sententially specified content   This can be illustrated in an especially clear way by considering the special conditions which a system must satisfy to justify us in using the sentential mode to specify the contents of its informational states. By "sentential mode" or "sentential idiom" here I mean the use of *that*-clauses to specify content, as when we say of someone or something that it knows *that* or believes *that the door is open*. When we employ this method, we attribute to the system whose informational states we are specifying a degree of understanding very much like our own. We treat the informational state as the system's possession of the same sort of information which we would possess if we knew the declarative sentence portion of the *that*-clause to be true.[20] Thus possessing such information requires of a system that it realize a large network of richly and rationally interconnected states. The demands of holism are especially great when the sentential mode is to be employed.

Consider again our selectively firing cortical neuron which responds only to the presence on the retina of a horizontal line of light. We saw that to count the state of that neuron's firing as the recognition of a horizontal line's presence, that state would have to make an appropriate difference to the system's behavior, where "appropriate" was left to be spelled out in detail. In moving to the sentential mode of content specificiation we face increased requirements which must be met for a state to qualify as the recognition or awareness *that* a horizontal line is present. Here the appropriate behavior cannot be merely some limited set of responses which are apt given the line's presence. Rather we require of the system that it evidence the variety of differences in behavior which might result when a human possesses the equivalent belief. There will not be any easy or simple way to spell out the relevant behavior influencing role, since the number of effects which such recognition might have on the behavior of a human or other fully rational agent is virtually limitless and crucially dependent on the totality of his other psychological states.

A system's realizing a sentate informational state cannot be a matter of its realizing a state which merely produces some small repertoire of fixed adaptive behaviors. The behavioral role played by such a state will be considerably more abstract and involve the state's making a partial contribution to a great many different behavior regulating processes. The differences of response which the presence or absence of the given state produces in each of these many cases enables the system to exhibit an overall pattern of selective variation in its behavior which may be counted as its realizing the possession of the relevant abstract information.

Moreover, the possession of such information could be realized *only* via structures functioning in such relatively global ways. A system's possessing the information *that* X obtains, where X is some sententially specified state of affairs, could not be merely a matter of S's having a structure which causes it to act in certain ways *toward* X. Rather possessing such information will involve the system's acting in highly selective and differential ways toward a great many environmental features other than X, but in ways which can be seen as manifesting the information it possesses about X. That is, the system can understand and possess information about X's obtaining only in virtue of realizing structures modifying its behavior toward some Ys and Zs in ways which are selectively adaptive given X. These behaviors must be counted among the responses which S makes *with respect to* X, though not (directly) *toward* X.

Both types of behaviour are relevant to a state's content determining functional role, and in systems realizing sententially specified informational states it is often responses of the former sort which figure the largest in fixing content. If we wish to attribute to some system the possession of the information *that* the can before it contains blue paint or *that* five times seven equals thirty-five, we must suppose that the system realizes structures to utilize this information in a great many diverse applications. Thus a high degree of holistic interaction among functional states turns out to be an essential characteristic of any system which realizes contentful states of the abstract sort specified in the sentential mode. Holism, abstraction, and sentential content go naturally together. Thus the holism of common-sense psychology is not a peculiarity of that theory. The degree of interactive complexity among informational states which we find in the common-sense model will have to be a necessary feature of any system to which we might wish to attribute the sorts of contents specifiable by use of the sentential idiom. No system which was substantially less holistic in its system of possessing information could have states informationally equivalent to those of sententially specified systems. But of course it is not just the *degree* of interaction among states which matters, but also the *character* of that interaction. Not just any interconnections will suffice. For in addition to the richness of their interstate connections, sententially specified systems are distinguished by the degree to which those relations must satisfy what we may term the *constraints of rationality*.[21]

Rationality In so far as we wish to use the sentential idiom in characterizing the informational contents of a system's states, the contents which we attribute to that system must on the whole form a relatively consistent and coherent set. We cannot meaningfully attribute to a system a set of contents whose members are grossly incompatible in terms of their deductive or inductive relations. Nor can we suppose a system to have states with a particular set of sentential contents, C, while lacking any states whose contents correspond to the obvious inductive and deductive consequences of C.

We need not assume that a system's set of informational states satisfies the demands of strict closure under the consequence relation just as we do not expect human agents to be ideally rational or to draw all the consequences of their beliefs. Nonetheless, a certain minimal but hardly insignificant degree of rationality is built into the very notion of a sentential state. For a system cannot possess information in our sense about matters it cannot understand. At the level of sententially specified content, this entails that a person or system cannot believe or possess the information that a *particular proposition p obtains* unless it understands what the truth of p would amount to. Now such understanding will have to consist in large part of linking p with other propositions. For surely no system could be said to understand p while failing to connect p with any reasonable number of its deductive and inductive consequences.

Moreover, the rationality of the system must be reflected not only in the overall consistency and coherence of its set of contents *at a time*, but also in the procedures which govern the transitions in the system's set of states *over time*. The manner in which states are added to or deleted from the system's set should more often than not correspond to patterns of sound inference between the sententially characterized contents of those states.

The constraints of rationality are not merely methodological guides to be used in effectively employing the sentential mode of content specification. Rather, they are elements essential to viewing any system as realizing sentential states. As such they are a special case of the general requirement noted earlier for an information possessing system to mirror or preserve the relational structure of the information which it possesses. The notion of a set of propositions is essentially bound up with the logical relations among the members of that set. To possess the information that a given set of propositions obtains, a system must embody in the structure of its informational states the relations among those propositions. I do not wish to claim that to understand a given proposition, there is some well defined and explicit set of other propositions which the system must also understand and to which it must connect the original proposition. We surely must allow for individual differences, but that a system should be able to understand that a proposition *p* obtains while "recognizing" virtually none of *p*'s relations to other propositions is incoherent. Just as a sentence has meaning only within the context of a language, so too a state can have a content specified by a sententially generated *that*-clause only within the context of a network of rationally interconnected states. A grossly inconsistent set of sentences does not constitute a theory as it provides no coherent account of what it might be taken to describe. Similarly, one could not think of an informational system as realizing an overall set of contentful states with just the contents specified by such a set of inconsistent sentences. The set of sentences we use to specify the information possessed by a system must exhibit that minimal degree of rationality required to justify the use of the intentional idiom.

There are three elements present here which while differentiable must not be thought of as independent: the system's realizing a set of contentful or informational states, the interconnections or functional interactions between those states in regulating behavior, and the system's understanding of the relevant sorts of content. No one of these phenomena should be thought of as an independent element which comes about as a causal consequence of the others. Neither the interconnections between states nor the system's utilization of the information contained in those states should be thought of as a causal consequence of the system's understanding the relevant information. Rather its understanding *consists in* its having the structure of interactive relations among its states in regulating behavior which it does. It is also in virtue of those functional relations that the states have the contents that they do, but their content is not a *causal* consequence of those relations. Rather, that the system of states has the functional structure that it does and that the states have the contents that they do are one and the same state of affairs differently described; or perhaps the former could be said to constitute or realize the latter. Thus the two phenomena of a system's achieving understanding and its having contentful states turn out to be interdependent and mutually presupposing. Either both or neither will be present, and where they are present they will be so in virtue of the structure of interactive behavior regulating mechanisms which constitute their joint realization by the system.

Sentential and nonsentential content   Given the rough conditions that have been laid out for realizing sententially specified content, we can see that states justifying specification of their content in the sentential mode will be a limited subset of contentful states. While we often use the sentential idiom in attributing information to non-human animals, it seems that many such attributions are unjustified or justified only in so far as we are speaking loosely or metaphorically. The informational states which are the resultants of a frog's visual perception system, for example, cannot be literally described as states of recognizing *that there is a fly to the front*. We know that the frog is unable to discriminate between the presence of a moving fly and the presence of any roughly fly-sized moving object before it, no matter how unfly-like it might be in shape, color, or edibility.[22] The restricted range of input analysis clearly makes the use of the human concept of 'a fly' inappropriate in describing the information obtained by those processes. Might we describe the informational state as the frog's recognition *that a roughly half-inch sized object is moving to the front*? Again the answer must be negative, but not in this case due to the frog's limited abilities to discriminate among inputs. The deficiency lies rather in the limited nature of the differences which the frog's perceptual state can make to its behavior. The perceptual state will trigger the frog to thrust out its tongue and will spatially orient the tongue movements toward the location of the moving object. To the extent that this constitutes the whole of the behavioral influences produced by the presence of the relevant perceptual state, the sentential idiom is not at all appropriate. The state simply fails to interact in the requisite ways with other states to produce complex rational changes in the frog's behavior.

The sentential mode is also limited in its application to humans. For many of the informational states likely to be posited by a theory of human psychology will occur as components of networks not justifying the sentential idiom. An example might be the sort of information about the condition of local muscle fiber groups realized by brain structures regulating voluntary bodily movements.[23] Despite the highly specific character of the input or sensory analysis involved in such cases, it would be mistaken to specify the content of such a cortical state as an awareness *that* such-and-such fibers are fatigued to degree *n*, or *that* such-and-such muscle is bent at an angle of *x* degrees. The contents of those states simply do not enter into the sorts of inferential relations that these sentential characterizations would suggest. The information which is contained in these states of kinaesthetic afferentation is relatively isolated in the sorts of ways it affects behavior, notwithstanding the fineness of regulation it produces with respect to bodily movement. In so far as those neural structures realize an understanding of muscle activity and function, that understanding is opaquely embedded in movement-regulating processes and is not of an explicit sort which would allow for rich inferential connection.

The question of just how the content of such states ought to be specified so that we attribute to the state neither more nor less information than it actually contains is no simple problem once we recognize the impropriety of treating it as analogous to the informational content of our own familiar cognitive states, our conscious beliefs. Whatever methods we employ are likely to have some misleading implications, and caution will require us to keep a close watch on the overall structure of the relevant information systems in discussing the contents of their states.

Motivational states   Though our focus has been on informational states, the mutual interdependence of information possession and goal directedness should lead us to expect that the principal features of our account of content specification apply similarly to the contents of motivational or preference states. All the difficulties which confront us in attempting to specify what a given system *takes to obtain* will apply *mutatis mutandis* in specifying what it is the system *aims at* or is *directed toward bringing about*. For simple systems or organisms there is likely to be no natural language specification of the system's goals which characterizes them in a way reflecting the modesty of the system's psychological organization. It is no more appropriate to attribute to a frog a rich and exactly specified preference than it would be to attribute to it a similar belief or perceptual state. It would be wrong to attribute to a frog a preference or desire to ingest small moving objects of such-and-such shape and size, even where such a result is regularly achieved by the frog's behavior. In so far as we want our characterization of the frog's goals to reflect the overall structure of his psychological organization, we must describe those goals at a level of content specification consistent with the sort of awareness attributable to the frog and the sort of interaction present among its psychological states. Where a high level of rational interconnectedness is absent, neither goals nor informational content can be appropriately specified in the sentential mode.

Pragmatics and interest relativity Throughout our account, the general dependence of content on holistic interstate relations has provided the basis for distinguishing many degrees of content sophistication as well as degrees to which any system can be said to understand or be rational. Thus we need draw no sharp lines between those systems which are rational and those which are not. Moreover, attributions of content turn out to involve an element of choice dependent on our explanatory and practical interests. Specifications of content are not arbitrary and functional organization constrains content realization, but there is always discretion to use or forgo description in terms of content, as well as in how content is to be specified.

The way in which our choices in such cases depend pragmatically on our explanatory interests nicely turns our account of content and undertanding back on itself. Since possessing information about some item (or understanding it) is to have behavior-regulating mechanisms which allow one to deal with it in a way enhancing the realization of one's goals, what constitutes understanding or information will always be relative to one's goals or interests. Such interest relativity applied as well in those cases where it is information possessing systems themselves which are to be understood. What information we possess about such a system and in what ways we understand it will depend on how we are able to adaptively interact with it. Our understanding will be bound up with our goals and interests relative to it, and different descriptions will likely be appropriate for the various cases in which we wish to predict its behavior, experimentally investigate it, make sense of its actions, manipulate it, construct it, or communicate with it.

It is worth emphasizing this pragmatic element, since the adaptive interest-relative aspect of understanding tends to slip out of sight in considering our own informational states, while conversely the informational character of adaptivity tends to get hidden when we consider very simple systems. We might consider informational states as ordered on a continuum[24] according to the rough account of content sophistication developed above. To one extreme would fall such crude information as that possessed or "understood" by a chameleon about the color of its environment or the value of camouflage. At the other end would come such fully sentential states as the beliefs of a rational human agent, while intermediate would be states of the sort associated with the frog visual system and human fine muscle control. With cases of the one extreme, where adaptivity is a causally direct result of structure, speaking of the chameleon as acquiring information about the color of his surroundings or of the bird's wing and flight mechanisms as "understanding" or embodying the possession of information about the air, we may seem to strain the notion of understanding past its limit. But the prominence and directness of adaptivity in these cases should not blind us to the fact that the presence of such physically improbable structures constitutes the possession of phylogenetically acquired information about the environment.

As we move further along or up our ordering we do not move away from states linked to behavior. We move only away from states whose content lies in their connection with a single fixed behavior toward those whose content consists in their larger (or potentially infinite) number of links to behavior. As we move toward states with richer and more varied behavior influencing roles, the instrumentally adaptive character of their informational content tends to diffuse, but not diminish. In sophisticated systems, like ourselves, with fully sentential states, the interest-relative dependence of informational content on adaptive value is obscured by the wealth and diversity of interests involved. But one must not mistake cases of multiple use information possession for cases of a basically incoherent sort in which information is possessed in the absence of any even potential effects on goal-directed behavior.

Of course there is an enormous difference between the frog's understanding of its visual environment and a physicist's understanding of the principles of thermodynamics. But this should not lead us to draw a distinction between instrumental and noninstrumental (or purely theoretical) understanding; for given a functionalist analysis of content, understanding is necessarily bound up with instrumental function. The interesting contrast is rather between the sort of implicit understanding which is opaquely embedded in adaptive procedures and the explicit understanding and inferential richness characteristic of theoretical thinking (with many cases in between). It seems plausible to link explicitness and inferential connectedness; for we can view the progression from the frog to the physicist as a move toward systems which become "aware of" (understand or possess information about) the rationales which are implicit or embedded in their functional structures. Making the contents realized by such structures explicit and themselves the objects of understanding would be *ipso facto* to generalize their application and bring them within a wider inferential sphere.

In as far as this progression is toward forms of understanding which provide more open-ended possibilities for successful interaction with what is understood, its direction bears some resemblance to what Thomas Nagel has described as the "direction of objectivity."[25] The movement in each case is toward forms of understanding which abstract from the particular character of the direct causal dealings between the understanding system (or subject) S and its object. Coming to have a more objective understanding of x is to acquire a capacity for the sorts of indirect dealings with x that result from placing it within a larger inferential context. In so doing the system S realizes a greater understanding of x as an object playing a role in the world independently of S. Thus although the construction and use of theoretical representations is likely to be of great value in achieving such objective understanding, we can unpack the notion of objectivity and give an account of what it is to have objective understanding in purely functional terms.

Extending the functionalist account   Still, the absence from one functionalist account of any specific discussion of the role of theoretical and symbolic structures in achieving understanding should serve to underscore its status as only a preliminary account of content. It is intended to provide a general framework within which further issues about content may be addressed and elaborated. Thus it seems apt to close by considering how a few important issues about content, neglected above, might be handled in keeping with the main themes of our analysis. Three such areas of concern would be: giving some account of symbolic representation and representational content, the problem of self-conscious and self-understanding systems, and accommodating the social holism of content and meaning. Let us consider these three briefly and in turn.

Representations It is a virtue of the functionalist approach that it allows us to provide an account of contentful states and intelligent information-possessing systems without having to rely on talk of representations or representational content. Still it seems clear that representations and symbolic structures play so large a role in human understanding and information possession that one cannot hope to have a complete or adequate human psychology which fails to include an account of representations and their content.[26]

I suggest the following strategy. In keeping with the guiding ideal of functionalism, the notion of "being a representation" would be analyzed as specifying a functional category. Perhaps the functional class could be better specified as items which "are used as representations by some system *S*" or which "serve as representations for *S*." The content of any such item would depend on its use by or within the relevant system (focusing for present purposes on internally used representations). The notion of a *state*'s having content would be taken as analytically or theoretically more primitive than that of a *representation*'s having content, in that the idea of state content would be used in two ways to account for representational content.

First, representations and processes operating on representations can be understood as *underlying* or *realizing* a system's network of contentful states. That is, the description of the system's operations on representations would be at a lower level of abstraction, or nearer a hardware description than the contentful state description. The relevant system would satisfy the functional condition for possessing certain items of information about its environment on the basis of its internal structure of processes operating on representations. It is important to note that though the representation-based processes causally underlie or instantiate the system's contentful states, they do so only in virtue of realizing the necessary *functional* roles. As regards their own functional roles, the representations have whatever content they do only in virtue of the contentful states which they serve to realize within the system.

Moreover, the notion of state content must figure in a second respect; for not every causal structure which underlies a contentful state does so by functioning as a representation. The hope would be to mark off the special role played by representations by appeal to our theory of contentful states. In brief, representations might be classed as structures which not only underlie contentful states, but do so in virtue of themselves *being taken to have or understood to have content* by the very system within which they occur. The notion of a system's understanding certain features of its own structure or organization to have content would be explicated in terms of the system's having contentful states to that effect (that is, its bearing the appropriate causal functional relations to those features of itself). Of course, we cannot suppose that all of a system's contentful states are realized by representation based processes, if we are to avoid a vicious and infinite regress. But our functionalist theory can easily allow for some understanding which is simply embedded in processes.[27] Such processes could operate on representations and do so in a way which constitutes understanding those items as having content, without embodying that understanding itself in any representations. Though developing these suggestions in detail would be no simple matter, they offer the functionalist a basis for optimism.[28]

Self-consciousness and self-understanding   Our proposal for handling representations also suggests a strategy for developing a functionalist account of self-awareness or self-consciousness. The basic idea is to treat self-aware systems as realizing informational states about their own structure and functional organization.[29] The analysis of information possession would continue to be in terms of adaptive modification of behavior. A self-aware system's understanding of its own features would be a matter of its capacity for adaptive interaction with those features. We have often spoken above of the system's interaction with its environment, but of course the system itself can be a part of its environment, considered as the sphere of its adaptive activity. Moreover, self understanding need not be restricted to its structural features, but might include complex higher-order features of its functional organization as well.

As our discussion of internal representation use should suggest, a capacity for self-understanding may do more than simply allow a system to interact adaptively with itself as it does with other objects. Rather, a system's capacity for self-understanding may greatly enhance its ability to adaptively interact with other non-self portions of the world. Being able to use features of itself as representations of the external environment and being able to make explicit the rationales embedded in its behavioral procedures in a way which allows for their generalization would be just two of the many such possibilities. We also might consider a capacity for learning or self-design[30] as a form of functionally analyzable self-understanding. A system could be said to possess information about or understand the function of a given behavior-regulating mechanism insofar as it realized a set of internal procedures which modified that mechanism in a way enhancing its adaptive value on the basis of environmental feedback. Such understanding need not be explicit; indeed it might be opaquely embedded in the learning procedures. But where the resulting modifications are so apt to the mechanism's function, the procedures guiding that modification should be seen as constituting implicit understanding of that function.

It is unclear just how much can be gotten from our functional account of information possession by constructing systems which turn back on themselves iteratively and reiteratively. Especially lacking is a clear route which would lead us from such iterative structures to an account of the sort of self-consciousness which we associate with conscious human experience. No immediate solutions to different philosophic puzzles about the subjective and phenomenal features of conscious experience seem in the offing.[31] Still the basic functionalist strategy here presents a wealth of opportunities which have barely begun to be exploited.

The social holism of meaning and content   Indeed, the functionalist may be confronted with an embarrassment of programmatic riches. For complementary to the strategy of investigating self-conscious or inwardly turning informational systems is the equally promising project of considering information possession systems which are turned outward within a social context or community of interacting informational systems. Our basic functionalist account above focused on cases of isolated individual systems within well-defined nonsocial environments. While such a focus may have been heuristically justified, it clearly will not suffice for constructing an overall account of how social organisms, such as human beings, understand and possess information about their world. However, I believe it is possible to extend our functionalist account to accommodate the social dimension, while preserving its basic analysis of content and information. I hope to make this claim of extendability plausible by discussing in an admittedly quick and simple fashion three ways in which the introduction of the social context would make a difference to the functionalist analysis of content.

First, systems or organisms which live together in genuine communities would of necessity have to possess the ability to understand each other as systems which understand, possess information, and have goals. They would have to possess some *second-order* understanding; that is, they would need to realize contentful states concerned with the realization of contentful states by other systems. Not only would they have contentful states, but they would in some sense "understand" what it is to have contentful states. Of course, their understanding need not be at all like an explicit theoretical understanding of such matters. Indeed all the relevant understanding might be opaquely embedded in mechanisms which regulate the interactions among the members of the community. Given its adaptive value, the presence of a mechanism which puts a sparrow to flight in response to a 'warning call' cannot be regarded as a random fact. Rather it should be seen as constituting the possession of phylogenetically acquired information, part of which is an implicit understanding of other sparrows as perceivers capable of detecting or acquiring information about the presence of predators. Though human beings can understand each other as informational systems in a much more explicit and sophisticated way, the bird example should make clear that on our naturalistic and functionalist view of content, various forms of (at least implicit) second-order understanding are widely realized throughout the biological world.

The second feature of the social which the functionalist must accommodate is the existence of *socially constituted* objects of understanding. Societies bring into existence practices, institutions and states of affairs which could have no reality apart from the regularities of the social context (for example, pecking orders, law courts and ritual ceremonies). Moreover, the members of societies can and must realize informational and other contentful states about those socially constituted phenomena in order to participate in the behavioral regularities which do the constituting. It is this tail-biting aspect of social constitution which prevents us from treating such cases as differing from our standard cases of information possession only in their particular content. It is not like shifting from information about flies to information about sticks. For in the social case, the states of affairs which are taken to exist and about which information is possessed are dependent for their very existence on being recognized or taken to obtain by the members of the society. Thus in talking about content or information possession in such cases, we must complicate the simple picture presented above, in which content was analyzed in terms of causal functional relations obtaining between an informational system and an independently existing set of objects. Socially constituted phenomena do have a reality independent of their recognition by any *particular* informational system or society member, but it is clear that their dependence on the *collective* contentful states of the society's members will demand special attention in accommodating understanding and the possession of information about such phenomena within our functionalist account.

Moreover, reflection on the social cases reveals that in a less radical form such an interdependence between understanding and its objects is yet another form of pervasive holism that applies with respect to *all* contentful states. Such nonsocial objects as trees, rocks, and flies are not dependent upon recognition for their existence or character. But if we wish to specify the contentful states which a system has about such items, our choice of how to describe or classify them will not be independent of their relations to the system in question. Types of objects which might be classed together relative to one system which fails in any way to distinguish among them, might need to be described as of many different kinds relative to some other system. Thus in general our description of the objective component of the functional relations between a contentful system and its environment will not be independent of the character of the informational system or subjective element of the relation.

It is this sort of descriptive holism embracing the environment as well as the informational system which underlies familiar difficulties about specifying the inputs and outputs for human functional psychology. On the one hand, many classes of inputs such as red objects really only constitute a class on the basis of subjective facts; that is, facts about their functional equivalence in effecting the preceptual mechanisms of human subjects.[32] And on the other hand, such disparate outputs as nodding one's head, raising a hand, or uttering 'yes' get classed together only on the basis of all being taken as gestures of assent by the community of subjects. The human cases are not special in this regard but only make more evident the descriptive interdependence of subject and object which arises whenever we turn to specify the functional networks underlying contentful relations.

The third respect in which society makes a difference can be illustrated by again considering the example of the sparrow's warning call. In virtue of their coordinated collective behavior each member of the sparrow community gains perceptual or informational access to portions of its environment beyond the reach of its individual sensory organs.[33] Thus its position within a social group enhances each sparrow's ability to acquire information about nonsocial portions of the world. In analyzing information possession in terms of causal functional relations, we must acknowledge that the necessary connections will often be established only through the mediation of social structures.

Moreover, the social context can do more than merely extend the ability of its members to acquire information of a sort which they could acquire individually. Society can transform the nature of understanding in a more radical manner, such that the social group can be said to understand or possess information of a sort not possessed by any member of the group. Social insects provide clear examples of such more radically social information possession. There are good reasons for attributing to a *colony* of bees information not possessed by any of the individual bees. Collectively their behavior will result in the construction of a well-defined adaptive hive structure. Yet no bee possesses the information of how to build a hive. Rather such understanding is embedded in the mechanism which regulates each bee's behavior as a function of what other nearby bees are doing. That is, the individual bee's behavior is not under the control of feedback about the emerging overall structure of the hive. The behavior regulating mechanisms in each bee are under only local feedback control sensitive to its interaction with other nearby bees. Yet the end product of this activity is a completed hive. The presence of mechanisms within the individual bees which produce such a result cannot be treated as a random fact, but should be understood as constituting the possession by the bee colony as a whole of phylogenetically acquired information about how to build a hive. The shaping processes of natural selection in this case have operated at the social level, perpetuating the genetically based social structures which embody the possession of such understanding.

The dramatic character of social understanding in bees and other social insects should not blind us to the presence of similar phenomena in more sophisticated animal societies, including human culture and society. For if we keep our focus on the functional notion of information possession as a capacity for adaptive interaction with the environment, it should be clear that large organized human groups can successfully deal with the environment in ways which manifest an understanding of that environment not possessed by any of their members. It is important to note that in such cases collective action is required not merely to put into action or apply that understanding, but the very understanding itself may be irreducibly collective. Consider a large scientific research program which over time investigates some class of micro-phenomena. A great many specialists with diverse theoretical, computational, and experimental skills will need to collaborate and depend on one another's activities to advance the research effort. It is unreasonable and simply false to believe that each of these research team members has individual cognitive mastery of all the elements of the overall project. Indeed, there is likely to be no such team member. The thought that there *must* be some person who individually possesses all the information probably arises from overrating the understanding of those team members whose contribution to the program derives from their skill in manipulating the theoretical formalism rather than in using its experimental and equipmental analogs of sensory and effector mechanisms. Of course, the theoreticians will have some understanding of the experimental set ups, but it is only the entire organized and intercommunicating scientific group together with its technical devices which can actually carry out the successful dealings with the micro-phenomena in those ways which constitute the acquisition and possession of information. The ability of individual researchers to describe and discuss overall aspects of their research should not lead us to neglect the necessity in such contexts for a social division of epistemological labor.[34]

Despite the wealth of complications and further interdependencies we have encountered in considering the social context, I hope to have offered plausible suggestions for accommodating the social aspects of information possession within our functionalist framework. However, it should also be evident that it would be a very messy affair to construct for even a moderately sophisticated system an explicit account of content which would take us from a physical description of the system and its dealings with the environment to a specification of its informational and other contentful states. Most often we will rather be engaged in attributing a limited range of contentful states to some system of which we have some prior understanding on the basis of its dealing with an environment described in a manner already appropriate to that system's patterns of interacting with it. This is most evident when we deal with other humans whom we assume to be quite like us or with other natural organisms of whose biological nature and needs we are at least partially aware.

Adopting a functionalist approach to content carries no commitment to theoretical reductionism. The functionalist program does not aim to construct an account which would enable us to deduce every fact about a system's contentful states from a physical description of its causal relations to its environment. It does, however, offer a way to think about content which is naturalistic and metaphysically austere, allowing us to discern the continuities which fit facts about content within the natural and biological sphere. Thus it satisfies those of our desires for a unity of science which are reasonable, while providing us with basic guiding ideas to link information, understanding, and adaptive causal interaction in developing accounts of content for the particular systems and situations where we need them.

NOTES

I have benefited greatly from discussion of earlier versions of this paper with my colleagues at Rutgers University, especially Robert Matthews, Laverne Shelton, Sarah Stebbins, and Robert Weingard. My work was aided by a research leave granted by the Rutgers University FASP program.

1. The argument against the adequacy of physical description as a universal explanatory framework is made forcefully in Hilary Putnam, "Philosophy and our mental life," in Hilary Putnam, *Mind, Language, and Reality* (Cambridge, 1975), pp. 291–303.

2. For example, see P. Lindsay and D. Norman, *Human Information Processing* (Academic Press, 1972).

3. The account will be nonrigorous in that no attempt will be made to formulate strict necessary and sufficient conditions for key concepts. I do not take this to be a defect of the account. For, as discussed below, the applicability of those concepts appears to depend on pragmatic features of the given explanatory context.

4. The functionalist view is reflected in much contemporary work in the philosophy of mind. For some examples see D. C. Dennett, *Content and Consciousness* (Routledge & Kegan Paul, 1969); and "Intentional systems," *The Journal of Philosophy*, 1971, pp. 87–106; David Lewis, "An argument for the Identity Theory," *The Journal of Philosophy*, 1966, pp. 17–25; Gilbert Harman, *Thought* (Princeton University Press), pp. 34–53; and Hilary Putnam, ibid., pp. 429–40.

5. For some suggestions in this regard see Putnam, ibid., pp. 362–85, where a proposal in terms of Turing machine specification is offered; and D. K. Lewis, "Psychophysical and theoretical identifications," *Australasian Journal of Philosophy*, 1972, pp. 249–51, for an account in terms of common-sense causal relations. Criticisms may be found in N. Block and J. Fodor, "What psychological states are not," *Philosophical Review*, 1972, 159–81; and in N. Block, "Troubles with Functionalism," in W. Savage (ed.), *Minnesota Studies in the Philosophy of Science*, vol. IX, 1979 (University of Minnesota Press), pp. 261–325.

6. Dennett, "Intentional Systems."

7. Lindsay and Norman, ibid., pp. 58–114; and J. J. Gibson, *The Senses Considered as Perceptual Systems* (Houghton, 1966).

8. Detailed discussion of such structures, as well as of their limitations, can be found in M. Minsky and S. Pappert, *Perceptrons* (MIT Press), 1969).

9. See, for example, G. Raisbeck, *Information Theory* (MIT Press, 1963), pp. 4–12.

10. K. Lorenz, *Evolution and the Modification of Behavior* (University of Chicago Press, 1965), p. 8.

11. Clearly we can and do attribute to human agents informational states which are on the whole maladaptive. In some cases the maladaptiveness is due to the incorrectness of the state, though in others the state may be nonadaptive even though its content accords with the facts. My point above is that such cases are possible only within the context of a large number of interdependent contentful states, where our basic scheme for fixing the contents of those states accords in general with our principle that information possession produce adaptive behavior. For discussion of a related point concerning veridicality and belief attribution see D. C. Dennett, "Intentional systems," pp. 102–3.

12 Notorious difficulties surround the attempt to account for the meanings of theoretical statements by their relations to nontheoretical or observational statements. No such intent, positivistic or otherwise, is implied by my use of the term 'basic' here. As should be clear below, my view of content is thoroughly holistic rather than foundationalist. What is basic is the general connection between information and adaptivity, not a privileged set of cases where that connection is especially direct or atomistically isolable.

13. Ernest Nagel, "Teleology revisited," *The Journal of Philosophy*, 1977, pp. 261–301.

14. The difficulty here is that the causal influences and responses of a closed causal system will always be nonorthogonal under some sufficiently complex description of the system's causal structure. Thus the weight of the constraint must fall on the complexity and indirectness of a causal link, rather than on its total absence.

15. See also R. Cummins, "Functional analysis," *The Journal of Philosophy*, 1975, pp. 741–65.

16. There is thus more than a punning similarity between the teleological and non-teleological senses in which informational states (or psychological states in general) may be thought of as *functional* states. For the interdependence of information possession and goal directedness entails that it will not be possible to spell out the relevant *causal behavior determining roles* in virtue of which some feature (or state) functions to realize the possession of information, without also characterizing the system's states *vis-à-vis teleological* functions. Adaptivity is a teleological notion in so far as it requires us to attribute goals to the system being considered, and it is a state's causal role in determining adaptive behavior which is crucial to information possession. Thus with respect to information possessing systems the notion of a functional state as specified in terms of its contribution to behavior within a systematic context of interacting components of necessity merges with the notion of a functional state specified in terms of its adaptive value.

17. As in Donald Davidson, "Mental events," in L. Foster and J. W. Swanson (eds), *Experience and Theory* (Massachusetts, 1970); "Psychology as Philosophy," in S. C. Brown (ed.), *Philosophy and Psychology*, (Macmillan, 1974); and D. C. Dennett, "Intentional systems." A somewhat more general account of the interdependence is offered in H. P. Grice, "Method in philosophical psychology," *Proceedings and Addresses of the American Philosophical Association*, 1975, pp. 23–53.

18. For some interesting suggestions on a related point see Stephen Palmer, "Fundamental aspects of cognitive representation," in E. H. Rosch and B. B. Lloyd (eds), *Cognition and Categorization* (Erlbaum Press, 1978).

19. See also in this regard H. P. Grice, "Method in philosophical psychology."

20. This question of when it is appropriate to employ the sentential idiom in specifying content is related to the question raised by Dennett in "Intentional systems" of "What is involved in *treating something as* an intentional system?" However, I am here interested in the further question which Dennett declines to discuss there of "What is it for a system to *actually realize* the possession of sententially specified content, i.e. to *be* an intentional system?"

21. The coiner of this term is to my knowledge Donald Davidson ("Mental events"). My use, however, parallels his only in part. The main differences concern the emphasis placed here on rational connectedness as requisite for *understanding* and the use to which these constraints of rationality are put. I, unlike Davidson, am primarily concerned to distinguish the realization of sententially specified states from other forms of information possession.

Moreover, the constraints of rationality function above as constraints on sets of real state transitions, rather than as rules governing the reconstruction of an agent's psychological states from partial samples of his behavior. Understood in the manner described above the constraints seem of little value in support of Davidson's claims about the anomalous nature of the mental.

22. J. Y. Lettvin, H. R. Maturna, W. H. Pitts, and W. S. McCulloch, "What the frog's eye tells the frog's brain," *Proceedings of the IRE*, 1959, pp. 1940–51.

23. A. I. Luria, *The Working Brain* (Basic Books, 1973), especially pp. 35–8.

24. I use the term 'continuum' here primarily to suggest the density of the ordering and to emphasize that systems may vary by many subtle degrees in the nature and quality of the information which they possess. I do not wish to imply that there is a simple linear ordering of systems in terms of the sophistication of the contents which characterize their informational states. The construction of a general hierarchy of levels of constant specification would not be so simple a matter. For present purposes the rough judgments we can make distinguishing among substantially different levels of content specification should suffice.

25. T. Nagel, *Mortal Questions* (Cambridge University Press, 1978), p. 174. While the resonance between Nagel's remarks and the discussion above is suggestive, their apparent affinity should be regarded cautiously, given Nagel's strongly anti-functionalist bent.

26. For arguments to this effect see J. Fodor, *The Language of Thought*, ch. 2.

27. For discussion on procedural understanding see T. Winograd, "Formalism for knowledge," in *Thinking* (Cambridge University Press, 1977), pp. 62–71.

28. I make some attempt to carry this project a bit further in "Mental Representation: A Functionalist View," *Pacific Philosophical Quarterly*, 1982, pp. 3–20.

29. See D. C. Dennett's *Brainstorms*, pp. 149–73; and Grice's "Method in philosophical psychology."

30. The description of learning as self-design is Dennett's: *Brainstorms*, pp. 71–89.

31. T.. Nagel forcefully presents the case for difficulties in his essay "What is it like to be a bat?" in *Mortal Questions*, pp. 165–80.

32. To get a feel for just how complex and indirect is the relation between an object's light reflecting characteristics and its perceived color see E. H. Land, "The Retinex Theory of color vision," *Scientific American*, Dec. 1977, pp. 108–28.

33. This example and its use to illustrate the view of language as "the extension of the senses" is due to W. V. O. Quine and J. Ullian, *The Web of Belief* (Random House, 1970).

34. Such division of epistemological labor (there called linguistic labor) is discussed in H. Putnam, *Mind, Language, and Reality*, ch. 12, especially pp. 245–7.

Misrepresentation

FRED DRETSKE

Epistemology is concerned with knowledge: how do we manage to get things right? There is a deeper question: how do we manage to get things wrong? How is it possible for physical systems to *misrepresent* the state of their surroundings?

The problem is not how, for example, a diagram, *d*, can misrepresent the world, *w*. For if we have another system, *r*, already possessed of representational powers, *d* can be used as an expressive extension of *r*, thereby participating in *r*'s representational successes and failures. When this occurs, *d* can come to mean that *w* is *F* when, in fact, *w* is not *F*, but *d*'s meaning derives, ultimately, from *r*. A chart depicting unemployment patterns over the past ten years can misrepresent this condition, but the chart's capacity for misrepresentation is derived from its role as an expressive instrument for agents, speakers of the language, who already have this power.

No, the problem is, rather, one of a system's powers of representation in so far as these powers do not derive from the representational efforts of another source. Unless we have some clue to how this is possible, we do not have a clue how naturally evolving biological systems could have acquired the capacity for belief. For belief is, or so I shall assume, a *non-derived* representational capacity the exercise of which *can* yield a misrepresentation.

The capacity for misrepresentation is a part, perhaps only a small part, of the general problem of meaning or intentionality. Once we have meaning, we can, in our descriptions and explanations of human, animal, and perhaps even machine behaviour, lavish it on the systems we describe. Once we have intentionality, we can (to use Dennett's language) adopt the intentional stance.[1] But what (*besides* intentionality) gives us (and not, say, machines) the power to adopt this stance? Our ability to adopt this stance is an *expression*, not an analysis, of intentionality. The borrowed meaning of systems towards which we adopt appropriate attitudes tells us no more about the original capacity for misrepresentation than does a misplaced pin on a military map. What we are after, so to speak, is *nature*'s way of making a mistake, the place where the misrepresentational buck stops. Only when we understand this shall we understand how grey matter can misrepresent the weather for tomorrow's picnic.

I Natural signs

Naturally occurring signs mean something, and they do so without any assistance from us.[2] Water does not flow uphill; hence, a northerly flowing river means there is a downward gradient in that direction. Shadows to the east mean that the sun is in the west. A sudden force on the passengers in one direction means an acceleration of the train in the opposite direction. The power of these events or conditions to mean what they do is independent of the way we interpret them – or, indeed, of whether we interpret or recognize them at all. The dentist may *use* the X-ray to diagnose the condition of your upper right molar, but the dark shadows mean extensive decay has occurred whether or not he, or anyone else, appreciates this fact. Expanding metal indicates a rising temperature (and in this sense means that the temperature is rising) whether or not anyone, upon observing the former, comes to believe the latter. It meant that *before* intelligent organisms, capable of exploiting this fact (by building thermometers), inhabited the earth. If we are looking for the ultimate source of meaning, and with it an understanding of a system's power of misrepresentation, here, surely, is a promising place to begin.

Natural signs are indicators, more or less reliable indicators, and what they mean is what they indicate to be so. The power of a natural sign to mean something – for example, that Tommy has measles – is underwritten by certain objective constraints, certain lawful relations, between the sign (or the sign's having a certain property) and the condition that constitutes its meaning (Tommy's having measles). In most cases this relation is causal or lawful, one capable of supporting a counterfactual assertion to the effect that if the one condition had not obtained (if Tommy did not have measles), neither would the other (he would not have those red spots all over his face). Sometimes there are merely regularities, non-lawful but none the less pervasive, that help secure the connection between sign and significance. It is partly the fact, presumably not itself lawful, that animals (for example, squirrels or woodpeckers) do not regularly ring doorbells while foraging for food that makes the ringing bell *mean* that someone (i.e. some *person*) is at the door. If squirrels changed their habits (because, say, doorbells were made out of nuts), then a ringing doorbell would no longer mean what it now does. But as things *now* stand, we can (usually) say that the bell would not be ringing unless someone was at the door, that the bell indicates someone's presence at the door, and that, therefore, that is what it means. But this subjunctively expressed dependency between the ringing bell and someone's presence at the door is a reflection of a regularity which, though not conventional, is not fully lawful either. None the less, the doorbell retains its natural meaning as long as this regularity persists.

Beyond this I have nothing very systematic to say about what constitutes the natural meaning of an event or a condition.[3] I shall proceed with what I hope is a reasonably familiar notion, appealing (when necessary) to concrete examples. The project is to see how far one can go in understanding misrepresentation, the power of a condition (state, event, situation) r to mean (say, indicate) *falsely* that w is F (thereby misrepresenting w), in terms of a natural sign's meaning that w is F. Only when (or if) this project succeeds, or shows reasonable prospects of succeeding, will it, or might it, be necessary to look more carefully at what got smuggled in at the beginning.

Though natural meaning is a promising point of departure, it is hard to see how to get under way. Natural signs, though they mean something, though they can (in this sense) represent w (by indicating or meaning that w is F) are powerless to *misrepresent* anything. Either they do their job right or they don't do it at all. The spots on Tommy's face certainly can mean that he has measles, but they mean this *only* when he has measles. If he doesn't have measles, then the spots don't mean this. Perhaps all they mean is that Tommy has been eating too many sweets.

Grice expresses this point by saying that an occurrence (a tokening of some natural sign) means (in what he calls the natural sense of "meaning" – hereafter meaning$_n$) that P only if P.[4] He contrasts this sense of meaning with non-natural meaning where a sign can mean that P even though P is false. If we reserve the word 'meaning' (minus subscripts) for that species of meaning in which something can mean that w is F when w isn't F, the kind of meaning in which misrepresentation is possible, then meaning$_n$ seems a poorly qualified candidate for understanding meaning.

In speaking of signs and their natural meaning I should always be understood as referring to *particular* events, states or conditions: *this* track, *those* clouds, and *that* smoke. A sign type (for example, smoke) may be said to mean, in some natural sense, that there is fire even when every token of that type fails to mean$_n$ this (because, occasionally, there is no fire). But this type-associated meaning, whatever its proper analysis, does *not* help us understand misrepresentation unless the individual tokens of that type *have* the type-associated meaning, unless particular puffs of smoke mean$_n$ that there is fire when there is no fire. This, though, is not the case. A petrol gauge's registration of "empty" (this *type* of event) can signify an empty tank, but when the tank is not empty, no particular registration of "empty" by the gauge's pointer means$_n$ that the tank is empty. Hence, no particular registration of the gauge misrepresents the amount of gas in the tank (by meaning$_n$ that it is empty when it is not).

The inability of (particular) natural signs to misrepresent anything is sometimes obscured by the way we exploit them in manufactured devices. Interested as we may be in whether, and if so when, w becomes F, we concoct a device d whose various states are designed to function as natural signs of w's condition. Since this is how we use the device, we tend to say of some particular registration that d's being G (assuming this is the natural sign of w's being F) means that w is F even when, through malfunction or misuse, the system is failing to perform satisfactorily and w is not F. But this, clearly, is not what the particular pointer position means$_n$. This is what it is *supposed* to mean$_n$, what it was *designed* to mean$_n$, what (perhaps) tokens of type *normally* mean$_n$, but not what it *does* mean$_n$.

When there is a short circuit, the ring of the doorbell (regardless of what it was designed to indicate, regardless of what it normally indicates) does not indicate that the bellpush is being pressed. It still means$_n$ (indicates) that there is electric current flowing in the doorbell circuit (one of the things it always meant$_n$), but the latter no longer means$_n$ that the bellpush is being pressed. What the flow of current *now* means$_n$ – and this is surely how we would judge it if we could *see* the bellpush, *see that* it was *not* being pressed – is that the system is malfunctioning or that there is a short circuit somewhere in the wiring. The *statement*, "There is someone at the door," can mean that there is someone at the door even when no one is there, but the ringing doorbell cannot mean this when no one is there. Not, at least, if we are talking about meaning$_n$. If the bellpush is not being pressed, then we must look for something else for the ringing bell to mean$_n$. Often, we withdraw to some more proximal meaning$_n$, some condition or state of affairs in the normal chain of causal antecedents that *does* obtain (for example, the flow of current or the *cause* of the flow of current – for example, a short circuit) and designate it as the meaning$_n$ of the ringing bell.

2 Functional meaning

Granted, one may say, the doorbell's ringing cannot mean$_n$ that someone is at the door when no one is there; still, in some related sense of meaning, it means this whether or not anyone is there. If this is not natural meaning (meaning$_n$), it is a close cousin.

Whether it is a cousin or not, there certainly is a kind of meaning that attaches to systems, or components of systems, for which there are identifiable *functions*. Consider, once again, the fuel gauge. It has a function: to pass along information about the amount of petrol in the tank. When things are working properly, the position of the needle is a natural sign of the contents of the tank. Its pointing to the left means$_n$ that the tank is empty. Its pointing to the right means$_n$ that the tank is full. And so on for the intermediate positions. But things sometimes go wrong: connections work loose, the battery goes dead, wires break. The gauge begins to register "empty" when the tank is still full. When this happens there is a tendency to say that the gauge misrepresents the contents of the tank. It *says* the tank is empty when it is not. It *means* (not, of course means$_n$), but still means in *some* sense that the tank is empty.

When d's being G is, normally, a natural sign of w's being F, when this is what it normally means$_n$, then there is a sense in which it means this whether or not w is F *if it is the function of d to indicate the condition of w*. Let us call this kind of meaning *meaning$_f$* – the subscript indicating that this is a functionally derived meaning.

(M$_f$) d's being G means$_f$ that w is F = d's function is to indicate the condition of w, and the way it performs this function is, in part, by indicating that w is F by its (d's) being G

The position of the needle on the broken fuel gauge means$_f$ that the tank is empty because it is the gauge's function to indicate the amount of remaining fuel, and the way it performs this function is, in part, by indicating an empty tank when the gauge registers "empty".[5] And, for the same reason and in the same sense, the ringing doorbell says (i.e. means$_f$) that someone is at the door even when no one is there.

Whether or not M$_f$ represents any progress in our attempt to naturalize meaning (and thus understand a system's non-derivative power to misrepresent) depends on whether the functions in question can themselves be understood in some natural way. If these functions are (what I shall call) *assigned* functions, then meaning$_f$ is tainted with the purposes, intentions, and beliefs of those who assign the function from which meaning$_f$ derives its misrepresentational powers.[6] We shall not have tracked meaning, in so far as this involves the power of misrepresentation, to its original source. We shall merely have worked our way back, somewhat indirectly, to *our own* mysterious capacity for representation.

To understand what I mean by an *assigned* function, and the way *we* (our intentions, purposes and beliefs) are implicated in a system's having such a function, consider the following case. A sensitive spring-operated scale, calibrated in fractions of a gram, is designed and used to determine the weight of very small objects. Unknown to both designers and users, the instrument is a sensitive indicator of altitude. By registering a reduced weight for things as altitude increases (note: a thing's weight is a function of its height above sea level), the instrument *could* be used as a crude altimeter if the user attached a standard weight and noted the instrument's variable registration as altitude changed.

Suppose, now, that under normal use in the laboratory the instrument malfunctions and registers 0.98 g. for an object weighing 1 g. Is it misrepresenting the *weight* of the object? Is it misrepresenting the *altitude* of the object? What does the reading of 0.98 g mean? If we are talking about $meaning_n$, it clearly does not $mean_n$ that the object weighs 0.98 g. Nor does it $mean_n$, that the laboratory is 40,000 ft. above sea level. If we ask about $meaning_f$, though, it seems reasonable to say that the instrument's pointer says or indicates (i.e. $means_f$) that the object weighs 0.98 g. It is the function of this instrument to tell us what objects weigh, and it is telling us (incorrectly, as it turns out) that this object weighs 0.98 g.

But is the altitude being misrepresented? No. It should be noticed that the instrument cannot be misrepresenting *both* the altitude and the weight since a representation (or misrepresentation) of one presupposes a *fixity* (hence, *non*-representation) of the other.[7] Although the instrument *could* be used as an altimeter, it *is not* used that way. That is not its function. Its function is to register weight. That is the function we assign to it, the reason it was built and the explanation why it was built the way it was. Had our purposes been otherwise, it might have $meant_f$ something else. But they were not and it does not.

We sometimes change an instrument's assigned function. When we calibrate it, for example, we do not use it to measure what it is normally used to measure. Instead, we apply it to known quantities in order to use its indication as a (natural) sign of possible malfunction or inaccuracy in the instrument itself. In this case, a reading of 0.98 g. (for a weight *known* to be 1 g.) indicates that the spring has changed its characteristics, the pointer is bent, or some other component is out of adjustment. We get a new functional meaning because/our altered background knowledge (normally a result of different intentions and purposes) changes what the pointer's behaviour $means_n$. With *assigned* functions, the $meanings_f$ change as *our* purposes change.[8]

We sometimes use animals in the same way that we use instruments. Dogs have an acute sense of smell. Exploiting this fact, customs officers use dogs to detect concealed marijuana. When the dog wags it tail, barks, or does whatever it is trained to do when it smells marijuana, the dog's behaviour serves as a natural sign – a sign that the luggage contains marijuana. But this does not mean that the dog's behaviour (or the neural condition that triggers this behaviour) can misrepresent the contents of the luggage. The dog's behaviour may make the customs officer believe (falsely) that there is marijuana in the suitcase, but the dog's behaviour $means_f$ this only in a derived way. If the dog is particularly good at its job, barking only when there is marijuana present, we can say that its bark indicates (i.e. $means_n$) that there is marijuana present. Furthermore, it $means_n$ this whether or not anyone interprets it as $meaning_n$ this, whether or not we *use* this natural sign for our own investigative purposes. But when there is no marijuana present, when the dog barks at an innocent box of herbs, the bark does *not* $mean_n$ that there is marijuana present. Nor does it $mean_f$ this in any sense that is independent of *our* interpretative activities. We can, of course, say what the bark means *to us* (that there is marijuana in the suitcase), but this way of talking merely reveals our own involvement in the meaning assigned to the dog's behaviour. *We* assign this meaning because this is the information we are *interested* in obtaining, the information we *expect* to get by using the dog in this way, the information the dog was trained to deliver. But if we set aside our interests and purposes, then, *when there is no marijuana present*, there is *no* sense in which the dog's bark means that there is marijuana in the suitcase. The only kind of misrepresentation occurring here is of the derived kind we are familiar with in maps, instruments, and language.

Therefore, if M_f is to serve as a naturalized account of representation, where this is understood to include the power of *mis*representation, then the functions in question must be *natural* functions, functions a thing has which are independent of *our* interpretative intentions and purposes. What we are looking for are functions involving a system of natural signs that give these signs a content, and therefore a meaning (i.e. a meaning$_f$), that is not parasitic on the way *we* exploit them in our information-gathering activities, on the way we choose to interpret them.[9]

We need, then, some characterization of a system's natural functions. More particularly, since we are concerned with the function a system of natural signs might have, we are looking for what a sign is *supposed* to mean$_n$ where the "supposed to" is cashed out in terms of the function of that sign (or sign system) in the organism's *own* cognitive economy. We want to know how *the dog* represents the contents of the luggage – what (if anything) the smell of the box means$_f$ *to it*.

3 Needs

The obvious place to look for natural functions is in biological systems having a variety of organs, mechanisms, and processes that were developed (flourished, preserved) *because* they played a vital information-gathering role in the species' adaptation to its surroundings. An information-gathering function, essential in most cases to the satisfaction of a biological need, can only be successfully realized in a system capable of occupying states that serve as natural signs of external (and sometimes *other* internal) conditions. If that cluster of photoreceptors we call the retina is to perform its function (whatever, exactly, we take this function to be), the various states of these receptors must mean$_n$ something about the character and distribution of one's optical surroundings. Just what the various states of these receptors mean$_f$ will (in accordance with M_f) be determined by two things: (1) what it is the function of this receptor system to indicate, and (2) the meaning$_n$ of the various states that enable the system to perform this function.

To illustrate the way M_f is supposed to work it is convenient to consider simple organisms with obvious biological needs – some thing or condition without which they could not survive. I say this is convenient because this approach to the problem of misrepresentation has its most compelling application to cognitive mechanisms subserving some basic biological need. And the consideration of *primitive* systems gives us the added advantage of avoiding that kind of circularity in the analysis that would be incurred by appealing to those kinds of "needs" (for example, my need for a word processor) that are derived from desires (for example, my desire to produce faster, cleaner copy). We cannot bring desires in at this stage of the analysis since they already possess the kind of representational content that we are trying to understand.

Some marine bacteria have internal magnets (called magnetosomes) that function like compass needles, aligning themselves (and, as a result, the bacteria) parallel to the earth's magnetic field.[10] Since these magnetic lines incline downwards (towards geomagnetic north) in the northern hemisphere (upwards in the southern hemisphere), bacteria in the northern hemisphere, oriented by their internal magnetosomes, propel themselves towards geomagnetic north. The survival value of magnetotaxis (as this sensory mechanism is called) is not obvious, but it is reasonable to suppose that it functions so as to enable the bacteria to avoid surface water. Since these organisms are capable of living only in the absence of oxygen, movement towards geomagnetic north will take the bacteria away from oxygen-rich surface water and towards the comparatively oxygen-free sediment at the bottom. Southern-hemispheric bacteria have their magnetosomes reversed, allowing them to swim towards geomagnetic south with the same beneficial results. Transplant a southern bacterium in the North Atlantic and it will destroy itself – swimming upwards (towards magnetic south) into the toxic, oxygen-rich surface water.

If a bar magnet oriented in the opposite direction to the earth's magnetic field is held near these bacteria, they can be lured into a deadly environment. Although I shall return to the point in a moment (in order to question this line of reasoning), this appears to be a plausible instance of misrepresentation. Since, in the bacteria's normal habitat, the internal orientation of their magnetosomes means$_n$ that there is relatively little oxygen in *that* direction, and since the organism needs precisely this piece of information in order to survive, it seems reasonable to say that it is the function of this sensory mechanism to serve the satisfaction of this need, to deliver this piece of information, to indicate that oxygen-free water is in *that* direction. If this is what it is *supposed* to mean$_n$, this is what it means$_f$. Hence, in the presence of the bar magnet and in accordance with M_f, the organism's sensory state misrepresents the location of oxygen-free water.

This is not to say, of course, that bacteria have *beliefs*, beliefs to the effect that there is little or no oxygen in *that* direction. The capacity for misrepresentation is only *one* dimension of intentionality, only *one* of the properties that a representational system must have to qualify as a belief system. To qualify as a belief, a representational content must also exhibit (among other things) the familiar opacity characteristic of the propositional attitudes, and, unless embellished in some way, meaning$_f$ does not (yet) exhibit *this* level of intentionality. Our project, though, is more modest. We are looking for a naturalized form of misrepresentation and, if we do not yet have an account of false *belief*, we do, it seems, have a naturalized account of false *content*.

Apart from some terminological flourishes and a somewhat different way of structuring the problem, nothing I have said so far is particularly original. I have merely been retracing steps, some very significant steps, already taken by others. I am thinking especially of Stampe's seminal analysis of linguistic representation in which the (possibly false) content of a representation is identified with what would cause the representation to have the properties it has under conditions of well-functioning;[11] Enc's development of functional ideas to provide an account of the intentionality of cognitive states;[12] Fodor's application of teleological notions in supplying a semantics for his "language of thought";[13] and Millikan's powerful analysis of meaning in terms of the variety of proper functions a reproducible event (such as a sound or a gesture) might have.[14] I myself have tried to exploit (vaguely) functional ideas in my analysis of belief by defining a structure's semantic content in terms of the information it was developed to carry (hence, acquired the function of carrying).[15]

4 The indeterminacy of function

Though this approach to the problem of meaning – and, hence, misrepresentation – has been explored in some depth, there remain obstacles to regarding it as even a promising sketch, let alone a finished portrait, of nature's way of making a mistake.

There is, first, the question of how to understand a system's ability to misrepresent something for which it has no biological need. If *O* does not need (or need to avoid) *F*, it cannot (on the present account) be the *natural* function of any of *O*'s cognitive systems to alert it to the presence (absence, location, approach, identity) of *F*. And without this, there is no possibility of *mis*representing something *as F*. Some internal state could still mean$_n$ that an *F* was present (in the way the state of Rover's detector system means$_n$ that the luggage contains marijuana), but this internal state cannot mean$_f$ this. What we have so far is a way of understanding how an organism might misrepresent the presence of food, an obstacle, a predator, or a mate (something there is a biological need to secure or avoid[16]), but no way of understanding how *we* can misrepresent things as, say, can-openers, tennis-rackets, tulips, or the jack of diamonds. Even if we suppose our nervous systems sophisticated enough to indicate (under normal conditions) the presence of such things, it surely cannot be the *natural* function of these neural states to signal the presence – much less, specific kinds – of kitchen utensils, sporting equipment, flowers, and playing cards.

I think this is a formidable, but *not* an insuperable, difficulty. For it seems clear that a cognitive system might develop so as to service, and hence have the natural function of servicing, some biological need without its representational (*and* misrepresentational) efforts being confined to these needs. In order to identify its natural predator, an organism might develop detectors of color, shape, and movement of considerable discriminative power. Equipped, then, with this capacity for differentiating various colors, shapes, and movements, the organism acquires, as a fringe benefit so to speak, the ability to identify (and, hence, misidentify) things for which it has no biological need. The creature may have no need for green leaves, but its need for pink blossoms has led to the development of a cognitive system whose various states are capable, because of their need-related meaning$_f$, to mean$_f$ that there are green leaves present. Perhaps, though having no need for such things, it has developed a taste for them and hence a way of representing them with elements that already have a meaning$_f$.

There is, however, a more serious objection to this approach to the problem of misrepresentation. Consider, once again, the bacteria. It was said that it was the function of their magnetotactic system to indicate the whereabouts of oxygen-free environments. But why describe the function of this system in this way? Why not say that it is the function of this system to indicate the direction of geomagnetic north? Perhaps, to be even more modest, we should assign to this sensor the function of indicating the whereabouts (direction) of magnetic (not necessarily *geo*magnetic) north. This primitive sensory mechanism is, after all, functioning perfectly well when, under the bar magnet's influence, it leads its possessor into a toxic environment. *Something* is going wrong in this case, of course, but I see no reason to place the blame on the sensory mechanism, no reason to say it is not performing *its* function. One may as well complain that a fuel gauge is not performing its function when the petrol tank is filled with water (and the driver is consequently misled about the amount of *petrol* he has left). Under such abnormal circumstances, the instrument is performing its duties in a perfectly satisfactory way – i.e., indicating the amount of liquid in the tank. What has gone wrong is something for which the instrument itself is not responsible: namely, a breakdown in the normal correlations (between the quantity of liquid in the tank and the quantity of petrol in the tank) that make the gauge serviceable as a *fuel* gauge, that allow it (when conditions are normal) to mean$_n$ that there is petrol in the tank. Similarly, there is nothing wrong with one's perceptual system when one consults a slow-running clock and is, as a result, misled about the time of day. It is the function of one's eyes to tell one what *the clock says*; it is the function of *the clock* to say what the time is. Getting things right about what you need to know is often a *shared* responsibility. You have to get G right and G has to get F right. Hence, even if it is F that you need, or need to know about, the function of the perceptual system may be only to inform you of G.

If we think about the bacterium's sensory system in this way, then *its* function is to align the organism with the prevailing magnetic field. It is, so to speak, the job of magnetic north to be the direction of oxygen-free water. By transplanting a northern bacterium in the southern hemisphere we can make things go awry, but *not* because a hemispheric transplant undergoes *sensory* disorientation. No, the magnetotactic system functions as it is supposed to function, as it was (presumably) evolved to function. The most that might be claimed is that there is some *cognitive* slip (the bacterium mistakenly "infers" from its sensory condition that *that* is the direction of oxygen-free water). This sort of reply, however, begs the question by presupposing that the creature *already* has the conceptual or representational capacity to represent something *as* the direction of oxygen-free water. Our question is *whether* the organism has this capacity and, if so, where it comes from.[17]

Northern bacteria, it is true, have no need to live in northerly climes *qua* northerly climes. So to describe the function of the bacterium's detectors in terms of the role they play in identifying geomagnetic north is not to describe them in ways that reveal *how* this function is related to the satisfaction of its needs. But we do not have to describe the function of a mechanism in terms of its possessor's ultimate biological needs.[18] It is the function of the heart to circulate the blood. Just *why* the blood needs to be circulated may be a mystery.

So the sticky question is: *given* that a system needs F, and *given* that mechanism M enables the organism to detect, identify or recognize F, *how* does the mechanism carry out this function? Does it do so by representing *nearby Fs as nearby Fs* or does it, perhaps, represent them merely *as nearby Gs*, trusting to nature (the correlation between F and G) for the satisfaction of its needs? To describe a cognitive mechanism as an F-detector (and, therefore, as a mechanism that plays a vital role in the satisfaction of an organism's needs) is not *yet* to tell the functional story by means of which this mechanism does its job. All we know when we know that O needs F and that m enables O to detect F is that M *either*

$means_f$ that F is present *or* it $means_r$ that G is present where G is, in O's natural surroundings, a natural sign of F's presence (where G $means_n$ F).[19] If I need vitamin C, my perceptual–cognitive system should not automatically be credited with the capacity for recognizing objects *as* containing vitamin C (as $meaning_f$ that they contain vitamin C) just because it supplies me with the information required to satisfy this need. Representing things as oranges and lemons will do quite nicely.

The problem we face is the problem of accounting for the misrepresentational capacities of a system *without* doing so by artificially *inflating* the natural functions of such a system. We need some *principled* way of saying what the natural function of a mechanism is, what its various states not only $mean_n$, but what they $mean_f$. It sounds a bit far-fetched (to my ear at least) to describe the bacteria's sensory mechanism as indicating, and having the function of indicating, the whereabouts of oxygen. For this makes it sound as though it is not performing its function under deceptive conditions (for example, in the presence of a bar magnet). This is, after all, a *magneto*tactic, not a *chemo*tactic, sensor. But if we choose to describe the function of this sensor in this more modest way, we no longer have an example of a system with misrepresentational powers. A northern bacterium (transplanted in the southern hemisphere) will not be misrepresenting anything when, under the guidance of its magnetotactic sensor, it moves upwards (towards geomagnetic north) into the lethal surface water. The alignment of its magnetosomes will $mean_n$ what it has always $meant_n$, what it is its function to $mean_n$, what it is supposed to $mean_n$: namely, that *that* is the direction of magnetic north. The disaster can be blamed on the abnormal surroundings. Nor can we salvage some residual misrepresentational capacity by supposing that the bacterium, under the influence of a bar magnet, at least misrepresents the direction of geomagnetic north. For, once again, the same problem emerges: why suppose it is the function of this mechanism to indicate the direction of *geo*magnetic north rather than, simply, the direction of the surrounding magnetic field? If we describe the function only in the latter way, it becomes impossible to fool the organism, impossible to make it misrepresent anything. For its internal states only $mean_f$ that the magnetic field is pointing in *that* direction and (like a compass) this is always accurate.

5 Functional determination

For the purpose of clarifying issues, I have confined the discussion to simple organisms with primitive representational capacities. It is not surprising, then, to find no clear and unambiguous capacity for misrepresentation at this level. For this power – and, presumably, the dependent capacity for belief – requires a certain threshold of complexity in the information-processing capabilities of a system. Somewhere between the single cell and man we cross that threshold. It is the purpose of this final section to describe the character of this threshold, to describe the *kind* of complexity responsible for the misrepresentational capabilities of higher organisms.

Suppose an organism (unlike our bacterium) has *two* ways of detecting the presence of some toxic substance F. This may be because the organism is equipped with two sense modalities, each (in their different way) sensitive to F (or some modally specific natural sign of F), or because a single sense modality exploits different external signs (or symptoms) of F. As an example of the latter, consider the way we might identify oak trees visually by either one of two ways: by the distinctive leaf pattern (in the summer) or by the characteristic texture and pattern of the bark (in winter). We have, then, two internal states or conditions, I_1 and I_2, each produced by a different chain of antecedent events, that are natural signs of the presence of F. Each means$_n$ that F is present. Suppose, furthermore, that, having a need to escape from the toxic F, these internal states are harnessed to a third state, call it R, which triggers or releases a pattern of avoidance

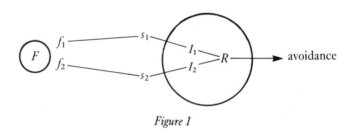

Figure 1

behaviour. Figure 1 assembles the relevant facts. R, of course, is also a natural sign of F. Under normal circumstances, R does not occur unless F is present. f_1 and f_2 are properties typical of normal Fs. s_1 and s_2 are proximal stimuli.

If, now, we present the system with some ersatz F (analogous to the bar magnet with the bacteria), something exhibiting *some* of the properties of the real f (say f_1), we trigger a chain of events (s_1, I_1, R and avoidance) that normally occurs, and is really only appropriate, in the presence of F. If we look at the internal state R and ask what it means$_f$ under these deceptive conditions, we find ourselves unable to say (as we could in the case of the bacteria) that it means$_f$ anything short of (i.e. more proximal than) F itself. Even though s_1 (by means of I_1) is triggering the occurrence of R, R does not mean$_n$ (hence, cannot mean$_f$) that s_1 (or f_1) is occurring. R is analogous to a light bulb connected to switches wired in parallel *either* of whose closure will turn the light on. When the bulb lights up, it does not mean$_n$ that switch no. 1 is closed even when it is this switch's closure that causes the light to go on. It does not mean$_n$ this, because there is no regular correlation between the bulb lighting up and switch no. 1 being closed (50 per cent of the time it is switch no. 2).

If we think of the detection system described above as having the function of enabling the organism to detect F, then the multiplicity of ways of detecting F has the consequence that certain internal states (for example, R) can indicate (hence mean$_f$) that F is present without indicating anything about the intermediate conditions (i.e. f_1 or s_1) that "tell" it that F is present. Our problem with the bacteria was to find a way of having the orientation of its magnetosomes mean$_f$ that oxygen-free water was in a certain direction without *arbitrarily* dismissing the possibility of its meaning$_f$ that the magnetic field was aligned in that direction. We can now see that, with the multiple resources described in figure 1, this possibility can be *non*-arbitrarily dismissed. R *cannot* mean$_f$ that f_1 or s_1 is occurring, because it *does not*, even under optimal conditions, mean$_n$ this. We can therefore claim to have found a non-derivative case of misrepresentation (i.e., R's meaning$_f$ that F is present when it is not) which cannot be dismissed by redescribing what R means$_f$ so as to eliminate the appearance of misrepresentation. The threatened inflation of possible meanings$_f$, arising from the variety of ways a system's natural function might be described, has been blocked.

Still, it will be said, we *need not* accept this as a case of genuine misrepresentation *if* we are prepared to recognize that R has a *disjunctive* meaning$_n$. The lighting up of the bulb (connected to switches wired in parallel) does not mean$_n$ that any particular switch is on, but it does indicate that *one* of the switches is on. Similarly, it may be said, even though it is the function of the mechanism having R as its terminal state to alert the organism to the presence of F, it does so by R's indicating, and having the function of indicating, the occurrence of a certain disjunctive condition – namely, that either f_1 or f_2 (or s_1 or s_2). Our hypothetical organism mistakenly withdraws from F, *not* because it misrepresents the ersatz F as F, but because what it correctly indicates (i.e. that the ersatz F is either f_1 or f_2) is no longer correlated in the normal way with something's being F.

No matter how versatile a detection system we might design, no matter how many routes of informational access we might give an organism, the possibility will always exist of describing its function (and therefore the meaning$_f$ of its various states) as the detection of some highly disjunctive property of the proximal input. At least, this will always be possible *if* we have a determinate set of disjuncts to which we can retreat.

Suppose, however, that we have a system capable of some form of associative learning. Suppose, in other words, that through repeated exposures to *cs* (a conditioned stimulus) in the presence of F, a change takes place. R (and, hence, avoidance behaviour) can now be triggered by the occurrence of *cs* alone. Furthermore, it becomes clear that there is virtually no limit to the kind of stimulus that can acquire this "displaced" effectiveness in triggering R and subsequent avoidance behaviour. Almost any *s* can become a *cs*, thereby assuming "control" over R, by functioning (in the "experience" of the organism) as a sign of F.

We now have a cognitive mechanism that not only transforms a variety of different sensory inputs (the s_i) into *one* output-determining state (R), but is capable of modifying the character of this many–one mapping over time. If we restrict ourselves to the sensory inputs (the s_i of figure 1), R means$_n$ one thing at t_1 (for example, that either s_1 or s_2), something else at t_2 (for example, that either s_1 or s_2 or, through learning, cs_3), and something still different at a later time. Just *what* R means$_n$ will depend on the individual's learning history – on *what* s_i became cs_i *for it*. There is no *time-invariant* meaning$_n$ for R; hence, nothing that, through time, could be its function to indicate. In terms of the s_i that produce R, R can have no time-invariant meaning$_f$.

Of course, throughout this process, R continues to indicate the presence of F. It does so because, by hypothesis, any new s_i to which R becomes conditioned is a natural sign of F. Learning is a process in which stimuli that indicate the presence of F are, in their turn, indicated by some relevant internal state of the organism (R in this case). Therefore, if we are to think of these cognitive mechanisms as having a time-invariant function at all (something that is implied by their continued – indeed, as a result of learning, more efficient – servicing of the associated need), then we *must* think of their function, not as indicating the nature of the proximal (even distal) conditions that trigger positive responses (the s_i and f_i), but as indicating the condition (F) for which these diverse stimuli are signs. The mechanism just described has, then, as its natural function, the indication of the presence of F. Hence, the occurrence of R means$_f$ that F is present. It does not mean$_f$ that s_1 or s_2 or ... s_x obtains, even though, at any given stage of development, it will mean$_n$ this for some definite value of x.

A system at this level of complexity, having not only multiple channels of access to what it needs to know about, but the resources for expanding its information-gathering resources, possesses, I submit, a genuine power of misrepresentation. When there is a breakdown in the normal chain of natural signs, when, say, cs_7 occurs (a learned sign of F) under circumstances in which it does not mean$_n$ that F is present (in the way that the broken clock does not mean$_n$ that it is 3.30 a.m.), R still means$_f$ (though not, of course, means$_n$) that F is present. It means$_f$ this because that is what it is *supposed* to mean$_n$, what it is its natural function to mean$_n$, and there is available no other condition it can mean$_f$.[20]

NOTES

1 D. C. Dennett, "Intentional systems," *Journal of Philosophy* 68 (1971), 87–106, reprinted in *Brainstorms* (Montgomery, Vt, 1978).

2 This needs some qualification, but it will do for the moment. What a natural sign means often does depend on us, on what we *know* about relevant alternative possibilities or on how we *use* an associated device. But if we don't know anything, or if the sign occurs in the operation of a device having no normal use, the sign still means something – just not, specifically, what we say it means under epistemically (or functionally) richer conditions. I return to this point in n. 8 below.

3 I give a fuller account of it in F. Dretske, *Knowledge and the Flow of Information* (MIT Press, 1981), chs 1 and 2.

4 P. Grice, "Meaning," *Philosophical Review* 66 (1957), 377–88.

5 I hope it is clear, that I am not here concerned with the word "empty" (or the letter "E") that might appear on the gauge. This symbol means empty whatever the gauge is doing, but this is purely conventional. I am concerned with what the pointer's position means$_n$ *whatever* we choose to print on the face of the instrument.

6 L. Wright calls these "conscious" functions; see his "Functions," *Philosophical Review* 82.2 (1973), 142.

7 A doorbell, for example, cannot mean$_n$ *both* that there is someone at the door *and* that there is a short circuit.

8 It isn't the change of purpose *alone* that changes what something means$_n$ (hence, means$_f$). It is the fact that this change in use is accompanied by altered background knowledge, and meaning$_n$ changes as background knowledge changes. If, for example, A depends on both B and C, a changing A can mean$_n$ that C is changing *if* we know that B is constant. If we know that C is constant, it can mean$_n$ that B is changing. If we know nothing, it only means that either B or C is changing. Natural meaning is relative in this sense, but derelativizing it (by ignoring what we know and how we use a device) does not eliminate natural meaning. It merely makes *less determinate* what things mean$_n$. For a fuller discussion of this point, see ch. 3 in Dretske, *Knowledge and the Flow of Information*.

9 I think much of our talk about the representational capacities of computers is of this assigned, hence derived, kind. It tells us nothing about the intrinsic power of a machine to

represent or misrepresent anything. Hence, nothing about the cognitive character of its internal states. R. Cummins, I think, gets it exactly right by distinguishing *cognition (a version of *assigned* meaning) from genuine cognition. See his *Psychological Explanation* (MIT Press, 1983).

10 My source for this example is R. P. Blakemore and R. B. Frankel, "Magnetic navigation in bacteria," *Scientific American* 245. 6 (Dec. 1981).

11 D. Stampe, "Toward a causal theory of linguistic representation," in P. French, T. Uehling and H. Wettstein (eds), *Midwest Studies in Philosophy*, vol. 2 (University of Minnesota Press, 1977).

12 B. Enc, "Intentional states of mechanical devices," *Mind* 91 (Apr. 1982), 362. Enc identified the content of a functional state with the (construction of the) properties of the event to which the system has the function of responding.

13 J. Fodor, "Psychosemantics, or where do truth conditions come from?" Manuscript.

14 R. Millikan, *Language, Thought and other Biological Categories* (MIT Press, 1984).

15 Dretske, *Knowledge and the Flow of Information*, part 3.

16 Something for which there is, in Dennett's (earlier) language, an "appropriate efferent continuation": see his *Content and Consciousness* (London, 1969).

17 Fodor (in a circulated draft of "Why paramecia don't have mental representations") distinguishes organisms for which a representational theory of mind is not appropriate (paramecia, for example) and ones for which it is (us, for example) in terms of the latter's ability to respond to non-nomic stimulus properties (properties that are not transducer-detectable). We, but not paramecia, are capable of representing something as, say, a crumpled shirt, and *being a crumpled shirt*, is not a projectible property. In this article, Fodor is not concerned with the question of *where* we get this extraordinary representational power from (he suggests it requires inferential capacities). He is concerned only with offering it as a way of distinguishing us from a variety of other perceptual and quasi-cognitive systems.

I agree with Fodor about the importance and relevance of this distinction, but my present concern is to understand *how* a system could acquire the power to represent something in this way. The power to represent something *as* a crumpled shirt (where this implies the correlative ability to misrepresent it as such) is certainly not innate.

18 Enc, "Intentional states of mechanical devices," p. 168, says that a photoreceptor in the fruit-fly has the function of enabling the fly to reach humid spots (in virtue of the correlation between dark spots and humid spots). I have no objection to describing things in this way. But the question remains: *how* does it perform this function? We can answer this question without supposing that there is any mechanism of the fly whose function it is to indicate the degree of humidity. The sensory mechanism can perform this funciton if there is merely something to indicate the luminosity – i.e. a photoreceptor. *That* will enable the fly to reach humid spots. Likewise, the bacteria's magnetotactic sense *enables* (and, let us say, has the *function* of enabling) the bacteria to avoid oxygen-rich water. But the way it does it (it may be argued) is by having a sensor that indicates, and has the function of indicating, the direction of the magnetic field.

19 In Fodor's way of putting the point (in "Psychosemantics"), this is merely a way of saying that his identification of the semantics of *M* (some mental representation) with entry conditions (relative to a set of normalcy conditions) still leaves some slack. We can say that the entry condition is the absence (presence) of oxygen *or* a specific orientation of the magnetic field. Appeal to the selectional history of this mechanism won't decide *which* is the right specification of entry conditions – hence, won't tell us whether the bacteria are capable of *mis*representing anything. Fodor, I think, realizes this residual indeterminacy and makes the suggestive remark (n. 9) that this problem is an analog of the problems of specifying the perceptual object for theories of perception.

20 I am grateful to Berent Enc, Dennis Stampe, and Jerry Fodor for their helpful criticisms, both constructive and destructive, of earlier drafts of this essay.

Part III

Instrumentalism

Introduction

The Identity Theorists and the Functionalists (Machine or Teleological) joined common sense and current cognitive psychology in understanding mental states and events both as *internal to human subjects* and as *causes*. Beliefs and desires in particular are thought to be caused by perceptual or other cognitive events and as in turn conspiring from within to cause behavior. If Armstrong's or Lewis's theory of mind is correct, this idea is not only commonsensical but a conceptual truth; if Functionalism is correct, it is at least a metaphysical fact.

In rallying to the inner-causal story, as we saw in the Introduction to Part I, the Identity Theorists and Functionalists broke with the Behaviorists, for Behaviorists did not think of mental items as entities, as inner, or as causes in any stronger sense than the bare hypothetical. Behaviorists either dispensed with the mentalistic idiom altogether, or paraphrased mental ascriptions in terms of putative responses to hypothetical stimuli. More recently, other philosophers have followed them in rejecting the idea of beliefs and desires as inner causes and in construing them in a more purely operational or instrumental fashion. Daniel Dennett, notoriously, denies that beliefs and desires are causally active inner states of people, and maintains instead that belief- and desire-ascriptions are merely calculational devices that happen to have predictive usefulness for a reason he goes on to explain. Such ascriptions are often objectively true, but not in virtue of describing inner mechanisms.

Thus Dennett is an *instrumentalist* about propositional attitudes such as belief and desire. (An "instrumentalist" about *X*s is a theorist who claims that although sentences about "*X*s" are often true, they do not really describe entities of a special kind, but only serve to systematize more familiar phenomena. For example, we are all instrumentalists about "the average American homeowner," who is white, male, and the father of exactly 1.9 children.) To ascribe a "belief" or a "desire" is not to describe some segment of physical reality, Dennett, says, but is more like moving a group of beads in an abacus.

In his collected works on "the intentional stance" (1978, 1987), Dennett offers basically five grounds for his rejection of the commonsensical inner-cause thesis. (i) He thinks it quite unlikely that any science will ever turn up any distinctive inner-causal mechanism that would be shared by all the possible subjects that had a particular belief. (ii) He offers numerous objections to "language-of-thought psychology," currently the most popular inner-cause theory. (iii) He compares the belief/desire interpretation of human beings to that of lower animals, chess-playing computers, and even lightning-rods, arguing that (a) in their case we have no reason to think of belief- and desire-ascriptions as other than mere calculational/predictive devices and (b) we have no more reason for the case of humans to think of belief- and desire-ascriptions as other than that. (iv) Dennett argues from the verification conditions of belief- and desire-ascriptions – basically a matter of extrapolating rationally from what a subject *ought* to believe and want in his/her circumstances – and then he boldly just identifies the truth-makers of those ascriptions with their verification-conditions, challenging inner-cause theorists to show why instrumentalism does not accommodate all the actual evidence. (v) He argues that in any case if a purely normative assumption (the "rationality assumption") is required for the licensing of an ascription, then the ascription cannot itself be a purely factual description of a plain state of affairs.

Stich (this volume, this Part) explores and criticizes Dennett's instrumentalism at length (perhaps oddly, Stich (this volume, Part VI) goes on to defend a view nearly as deprecating as Dennett's, though clearly distinct from it). Dennett (this volume, this Part) responds to Stich, bringing out more clearly the force of the "rationality assumption" assumption. Other critics of Dennett are listed in the bibliography.

A close cousin of Dennett's view, in that it focuses on the rationality assumption, is Donald Davidson's (1970) "Anomalous Monism." Unlike Dennett's instrumentalism it endorses token physicalism and grants (indeed insists) that individual mental tokens are causes, but it rejects on similarly epistemological grounds the possibility of any interesting naturalistic type-reduction of the propositional attitudes.

FURTHER READING

Other Instrumentalist Works

Dray, W. H. (1963) "The historical explanation of action reconsidered," in S. Hook (ed.), *Philosophy and History*, New York University Press.

Dennett, D. C. (1978) *Brainstorms*, Bradford Books, Part I.

Dennett, D. C. (1987) *The Intentional Stance*, Bradford Books/MIT Press.

Critics of Instrumentalism

Churchland, P. M. (1970) "The logical character of action explanations," *Philosophical Review* 79, 214–36.

Richardson, R. (1980) "Intentional Realism or Intentional Instrumentalism?" *Cognition and Brain Theory* 3, 125–35.

Bechtel, P. W. (1985) "Realism, reason, and the intentional stance," *Cognitive Science* 9, 473–97.

Fodor, J. A. (1981) "Three cheers for propositional attitudes," in *Representations*, Bradford Books/MIT Press.

Lycan, W. (1988) "Dennett's Instrumentalism," *Behavioral and Brain Sciences*, 11, 518–19. [And other contributions to the "Open peer commentary" in that issue on Dennett's précis of *The Intentional Stance*.]

Peacocke, C. (1983) *Sense and Content*, Oxford University Press, ch. 8.

Anomalous Monism

Davidson, D. (1970) "Mental events," in L. Foster and J. W. Swanson (eds), *Experience and Theory*, University of Massachusetts Press.

Lycan, W. (1981) "Psychological laws," *Philsophical Topics* 12, 9–38.

Van Gulick, R. (1980) "Rationality and the anomalous nature of the mental," *Philosophy Research Archives* 7, 1404.

Johnston, M., "Why having a mind matters," and Kim, J., "Psychophysical laws," in E. LePore and B. McLaughlin (eds), *Actions and Events: Perspectives on the Philosophy of Donald Davidson*, Basil Blackwell, 1985.

7

An Instrumentalist Theory

True Believers: The Intentional Strategy and Why it Works

DANIEL C. DENNETT

Death speaks

There was a merchant in Baghdad who sent his servant to market to buy provisions and in a little while the servant came back, white and trembling, and said, Master, just now when I was in the market-place I was jostled by a woman in the crowd and when I turned I saw it was Death that jostled me. She looked at me and made a threatening gesture; now, lend me your horse, and I will ride away from the city and avoid my fate. I will go to Samarra and there Death will not find me. The merchant lent him his horse, and the servant mounted it, and he dug his spurs in its flanks and as fast as the horse could gallop he went. Then the merchant went down to the market-place and he saw me standing in the crowd, and he came to me and said, why did you make a threatening gesture to my servant when you saw him this morning? That was not a threatening gesture, I said, it was only a start of surprise. I was astonished to see him in Baghdad, for I had an appointment with him tonight in Samarra.

W. Somerset Maugham

In the social sciences, talk about *belief* is ubiquitous. Since social scientists are typically self-conscious about their methods, there is also a lot of talk about *talk about belief*. And since belief is a genuinely curious and perplexing phenomenon, showing many different faces to the world, there is abundant controversy. Sometimes belief attribution appears to be a dark, risky, and imponderable business – especially when exotic, and more particularly religious or superstitious, beliefs are in the limelight. These are not the only troublesome cases; we also court argument and scepticism when we attribute beliefs to non-human animals, or to infants, or to computers or robots. Or when the beliefs we feel constrained to attribute to an apparently healthy, adult member of our own society are contradictory, or even just wildly false. A biologist colleague of mine was once called on the telephone by a man in a bar who wanted him to settle a bet. The man asked: "Are rabbits birds?" "No" said the biologist. "Damn!" said the man as he hung up. Now could he *really* have believed that rabbits were birds? Could anyone really and truly be attributed that belief? Perhaps, but it would take a bit of a story to bring us to accept it.

In all of these cases belief attribution appears beset with subjectivity, infected with cultural relativism, prone to "indeterminacy of radical translation" – clearly an enterprise demanding special talents: the art of phenomenological analysis, hermeneutics, empathy, *Verstehen*, and all that. On other occasions, normal occasions, when familiar beliefs are the topic, belief attribution looks as easy as speaking prose, and as objective and reliable as counting beans in a dish. Particularly when these straightforward cases are before us, it is quite plausible to suppose that *in principle* (if not yet in practice) it would be possible to confirm these simple, objective belief attributions by *finding something inside the believer's head* – by finding the beliefs themselves, in effect. "Look," someone might say, "You either believe there's milk in the fridge or you don't believe there's milk in the fridge" (you might have no opinion, in the latter case). But if you do believe this, that's a perfectly objective fact about you, and it must come down in the end to your brain's being in some particular physical state. If we knew more about physiological psychology we could in principle determine the facts about your brain state, and thereby determine whether or not you believe there is milk in the fridge, even if you were determined to be silent, or disingenuous on the topic. In principle, on this view physiological psychology could trump the results – or non-results – of any "black box" method in the social sciences that divines beliefs (and other mental features) by behavioral, cultural, social, historical, *external* criteria.

These differing reflections congeal into two opposing views on the nature of belief attribution, and hence on the nature of belief. The latter, a variety of *realism*, likens the question of whether a person has a particular belief to the question of whether a person is infected with a particular virus – a perfectly objective internal matter of fact about which an observer can often make educated guesses of great reliability. The former, which we could call *interpretationism* if we absolutely had to give it a name, likens the question of whether a person has a particular belief to the question of whether a person is immoral, or has style, or talent, or would make a good wife. Faced with such questions, we preface our answers with "Well, it all depends on what you're interested in," or make some similar acknowledgment of the relativity of the issue. "It's a matter of interpretation," we say. These two opposing views, so baldly stated, do not fairly represent any serious theorists' positions, but they do express views that are typically seen as mutually exclusive and exhaustive; the theorist must be friendly with one and only one of these themes.

I think this is a mistake. My thesis will be that while belief is a perfectly objective phenomenon (that apparently makes me a realist), it can be discerned only from the point of view of one who adopts a certain *predictive strategy*, and its existence can be confirmed only by an assessment of the success of that strategy (that apparently makes me an interpretationist).

First I will describe the strategy, which I call the intentional strategy, or adopting the intentional stance. To a first approximation, the intentional strategy consists of treating the object whose behavior you want to predict as a rational agent with beliefs and desires and other mental states exhibiting what Brentano and others call *intentionality*. The strategy has often been described before, but I shall try to put this very familiar material in a new light, by showing *how* it works, and by showing *how well* it works.

Then I will argue that any object – or as I shall say, any *system* – whose behavior is well predicted by this strategy is in the fullest sense of the word a believer. *What it is* to be a true believer is to be an *intentional system*, a system whose behavior is reliably and voluminously predictable via the intentional strategy. I have argued for this position before,[1] and my arguments have so far garnered few converts and many presumed counterexamples. I shall try again here, harder, and shall also deal with several compelling objections.

The intentional strategy and how it works

There are many strategies, some good, some bad. Here is a strategy, for instance, for predicting the future behavior of a person: determine the date and hour of the person's birth, and then feed this modest datum into one or another astrological algorithm for generating predictions of the person's prospects. This strategy is deplorably popular. Its popularity is deplorable only because we have such good reasons for believing that *it does not work*.[2] When astrological predictions come true this is sheer luck, or the result of such vagueness or ambiguity in the prophecy that almost any eventuality can be construed to confirm it. But suppose the astrological strategy did in fact work well on some people. We could call those people *astrological systems* – systems whose behavior was, as a matter of fact, predictable by the astrological strategy. If there were such people, such astrological systems, we would be more interested than most of us in fact are in *how the astrological strategy works* – that is, we would be interested in the rules, principles, or methods of astrology. We could find out how the strategy works by asking astrologers, reading their books, and observing them in action. But we would also be curious about *why* it worked. We might find that astrologers had no useful opinions about this latter question – they either had no theory of why it worked, or their theories were pure hokum. Having a good strategy is one thing; knowing why it works is another.

So far as we know, however, the class of astrological systems is empty, so the astrological strategy is of interest only as a social curiosity. Other strategies have better credentials. Consider the physical strategy, or physical stance: if you want to predict the behavior of a system, determine its physical constitution (perhaps all the way down to the micro-physical level) and the physical nature of the impingements upon it, and use your knowledge of the laws of physics to predict the outcome for any input. This is the grand and impractical strategy of Laplace for predicting the entire future of everything in the universe, but it has more modest, local, actually usable versions. The chemist or physicist in the laboratory can use this strategy to predict the behavior of exotic materials, but equally the cook in the kitchen can predict the effect of leaving the pot on the burner too long. The strategy is not always practically available, but that it will always work *in principle* is a dogma of the physical sciences. (I ignore the minor complications raised by the sub-atomic indeterminacies of quantum physics.)

Sometimes, in any event, it is more effective to switch from the physical stance to what I call the design stance, where one ignores the actual (possibly messy) details of the physical constitution of an object, and, on the assumption that it has a certain design, predicts that it will behave *as it is designed to behave* under various circumstances. For instance, most users of computers have not the foggiest idea what physical principles are responsible for the computer's highly reliable, and hence predictable, behavior. But if they have a good idea of what the computer is designed to do (a description of its operation at any one of the many possible levels of abstraction), they can predict its behavior with great accuracy and reliability, subject to disconfirmation only in cases of physical malfunction. Less dramatically, almost anyone can predict when an alarm clock will sound on the basis of the most casual inspection of its exterior. One does not know or care to know whether it is spring wound, battery driven, sunlight powered, made of brass wheels and jewel bearings or silicon chips – one just assumes that it is designed so that the alarm will sound when it is set to sound, and it is set to sound where it appears to be set to sound, and the clock will keep on running until that time and beyond, and is designed to run more or less accurately, and so forth. For more accurate and detailed design stance predictions of the alarm clock, one must descend to a less abstract level of description of its design; for instance, to the level at which gears are described, but their material is not specified.

Only the designed behavior of a system is predictable from the design stance, of course. If you want to predict the behavior of an alarm clock when it is pumped full of liquid helium, revert to the physical stance. Not just artifacts, but also many biological objects (plants and animals, kidneys and hearts, stamens and pistils) behave in ways that can be predicted from the design stance. They are not just physical systems but designed systems.

Sometimes even the design stance is practically inaccessible, and then there is yet another stance or strategy one can adopt: the intentional stance. Here is how it works: first you decide to treat the object whose behavior is to be predicted as a rational agent; then you figure out what beliefs that agent ought to have, given its place in the world and its purpose. Then you figure out what desires it ought to have, on the same considerations, and finally you predict that this rational agent will act to further its goals in the light of its beliefs. A little practical reasoning from the chosen set of beliefs and desires will in many – but not all – instances yield a decision about what the agent ought to do; that is what you predict the agent *will* do.

The strategy becomes clearer with a little elaboration. Consider first how we go about populating each other's heads with beliefs. A few truisms: sheltered people tend to be ignorant; if you expose someone to something he comes to know all about it. In general, it seems, we come to believe all the truths about the parts of the world around us we are put in a position to learn about. *Exposure* to *x*, that is, sensory confrontation with *x* over some suitable period of time, is the *normally sufficient* condition for knowing (or having true beliefs) about *x*. As we say, we come to *know all about* the things around us. Such exposure is only *normally* sufficient for knowledge, but this is not the large escape hatch it might appear; our threshold for accepting abnormal ignorance in the face of exposure is quite high. "I didn't know the gun was loaded," said by one who was observed to be present, sighted, and awake during the loading, meets with a variety of utter scepticism that only the most outlandish supporting tale could overwhelm.

Of course we do not come to learn or remember all the truths our sensory histories avail us. In spite of the phrase 'know all about', what we come to know, normally, are only all the *relevant* truths our sensory histories avail us. I do not typically come to know the ratio of spectacle-wearing people to trousered people in a room I inhabit, though if this interested me, it would be readily learnable. It is not just that some facts about my environment are below my thresholds of discrimination or beyond the integration and holding-power of my memory (such as the height in inches of all the people present), but that many perfectly detectable, graspable, memorable facts are of no interest to me, and hence do not come to be believed by me. So one rule for attributing beliefs in the intentional strategy is this: attribute as beliefs all the truths relevant to the system's interests (or desires) that the system's experience to date has made available. This rule leads to attributing somewhat too much – since we all are somewhat forgetful, even of important things. It also fails to capture the false beliefs we are all known to have. But the attribution of false belief, *any* false belief, requires a special genealogy, which will be seen to consist in the main in true beliefs. Two paradigm cases: S believes (falsely) that *p*, because S believes (truly) that Jones told him that *p*, that Jones is pretty clever, that Jones did not intend to deceive him, . . . etc. Second case: S believes (falsely) that there is a snake on the barstool, because S believes (truly) that he seems to see a snake on the barstool, is himself sitting in a bar not a yard from the barstool he sees, and so forth. The falsehood has to start somewhere; the seed may be sown in hallucination, illusion, a normal variety of simple misperception, memory deterioration, or deliberate fraud, for instance, but the false beliefs that are reaped grow in a culture medium of true beliefs.

Then there are the arcane and sophisticated beliefs, true and false, that are so often at the focus of attention in discussions of belief attribution. They do not arise directly, goodness knows, from exposure to mundane things and events, but their attribution requires tracing out a lineage of mainly good argument or reasoning from the bulk of beliefs already attributed. An implication of the intentional strategy, then, is that true believers mainly believe truths. If anyone could devise an agreed-upon method of individuating and counting beliefs (which I doubt very much), we would see that all but the smallest portion (say, less than 10 per cent) of a person's beliefs were attributable under our first rule.[3]

Note that this rule is a derived rule, an elaboration and further specification of the fundamental rule: attribute those beliefs the system *ought to have*. Note also that the rule interacts with the attribution of desires. How do we attribute the desires (preferences, goals, interests) on whose basis we will shape the list of beliefs? We attribute the desires the system *ought to have*. That is the fundamental rule. It dictates, on a first pass, that we attribute the familiar list of highest, or most basic, desires to people: survival, absence of pain, food, comfort, procreation, entertainment. Citing any one of these desires typically terminates the "Why?"

game of reason giving. One is not supposed to need an ulterior motive for desiring comfort or pleasure or the prolongation of one's existence. Derived rules of desire attribution interact with belief attributions. Trivially, we have the rule: attribute desires for those things a system believes to be good for it. Somewhat more informatively, attribute desires for those things a system believes to be best means to other ends it desires. The attribution of bizarre and detrimental desires thus requires, like the attribution of false beliefs, special stories.

The interaction between belief and desire becomes trickier when we consider what desires we attribute on the basis of verbal behavior. The capacity to *express* desires in language opens the floodgates of desire attribution. "I want a two-egg mushroom omelette, some French bread and butter, and a half bottle of lightly chilled white Burgundy." How could one begin to attribute a desire for anything so specific in the absence of such verbal declaration? How, indeed, could a creature come to *contract* such a specific desire without the aid of language? Languages *enables* us to formulate highly specific desires, but it also *forces* us on occasion to commit ourselves to desires altogether more stringent in their conditions of satisfaction than anything we would otherwise have any reason to endeavour to satisfy. Since in order to get what you want you often have to say what you want, and since you often cannot say what you want without saying something more specific than you antecedently mean, you often end up giving others evidence – the very best of evidence, your unextorted word – that you desire things or states of affairs far more particular than would satisfy you – or better, than would have satisfied you, for once you have declared, being a man of your word, you acquire an interest in satisfying exactly the desire you declared and no other.

"I'd like some baked beans, please."

"Yes sir. How many?"

You might well object to having such a specification of desire demanded of you, but in fact we are all socialized to accede to similar requirements in daily life – to the point of not noticing it, and certainly not feeling oppressed by it. I dwell on this because it has a parallel in the realm of belief, where our linguistic environment is forever forcing us to give – or concede – precise verbal expression to convictions that lack the hard edges verbalization endows them with.[4] By concentrating on the *results* of this social force, while ignoring its distorting effect, one can easily be misled into thinking that it is *obvious* that beliefs and desires are rather like *sentences stored in the head*. Being language-using creatures, it is inevitable that we should often come to believe that some particular, actually formulated, spelled and punctuated sentence *is true*, and that on other occasions we should come to want such a sentence to *come true*, but these are special cases of belief and desire, and as such may not be reliable models for the whole domain.

That is enough, on this occasion, about the principles of belief and desire attribution to be found in the intentional strategy. What about the rationality one attributes to an intentional system? One starts with the ideal of perfect rationality and revises downwards as circumstances dictate. That is, one starts with the assumption that people believe all the implications of their beliefs, and believe no contradictory pairs of beliefs. This does not create a practical problem of clutter (infinitely many implications, for instance), for one is interested only in ensuring that the system one is predicting is rational enough to get to the particular implications that are relevant to its behavioural predicament of the moment. Instances of irrationality, or of finitely powerful capacities of inference, raise particularly knotty problems of interpretation, which I will set aside on this occasion.[5]

For I want to turn from the description of the strategy to the question of its use. Do people actually use this strategy? Yes, all the time. There may someday be other strategies for attributing belief and desire and for predicting behavior, but this is the only one we all know now. And when does it work? It works with people almost all the time. Why would it *not* be a good idea to allow individual Oxford colleges to create and grant academic degrees whenever they saw fit? The answer is a long story, but very easy to generate. And there would be widespread agreement about the major points. We have no difficulty thinking of the reasons people would then have for acting in such ways as to give others reasons for acting in such ways as to give others reasons for . . . creating a circumstance we would not want. Our use of the intentional strategy is so habitual and effortless that the role it plays in shaping our expectations about people is easily overlooked. The strategy also works on most other mammals most of the time. For instance, you can use it to design better traps to catch those mammals, by reasoning about what the creature knows or believes about various things, what it prefers, what it wants to avoid. The strategy works on birds, and on fish, and on reptiles, and on insects and spiders, and even on such lowly and unenterprising creatures as clams (once a clam believes there is danger about, it will not relax its grip on its closed shell until it is convinced that the danger has passed). It also works on some artifacts: the chess-playing computer will not take your knight because it knows that there is a line of ensuing play that would lead to losing its rook, and it does not want that to happen. More modestly, the thermostat will turn off the boiler as soon as it comes to believe the room has reached the desired temperature.

The strategy even works for plants. In a locale with late spring storms you should plant apple varieties that are particularly *cautious* about *concluding* that it is spring – which is when they *want* to blossom, of course. It even works for such inanimate and apparently undesigned phenomena as lightning. An electrician once explained to me how he worked out how to protect my underground water pump from lightning damage: lightning, he said, always wants to find the best way to ground but sometimes it gets tricked into taking second-best paths. You can protect the pump by making another, better path more *obvious* to the lightning.

True believers as intentional systems

Now clearly this is a motley assortment of "serious" belief attributions, dubious belief attributions, pedagogically useful metaphors, *façons de parler*, and perhaps worse: outright frauds. The next task would seem to be distinguishing those intentional systems that *really* have beliefs and desires from those we may find it handy to treat *as if* they had beliefs and desires. But that would be a Sisyphean labour, or else would be terminated by fiat. A better understanding of the phenomenon of belief begins with the observation that even in the worst of these cases, even when we are surest that the strategy works *for the wrong reasons*, it is nevertheless true that it does work, at least a little bit. This is an interesting fact, which distinguishes this class of objects, the class of *intentional systems*, from the class of objects for which the strategy never works. But is this so? Does our definition of an intentional system exclude any objects at all? For instance, it seems the lectern in this lecture room can be construed as an intentional system, fully rational, and believing that it is currently located at the centre of the civilized world (as some of you may also think); and desiring above all else to remain at that centre. What should such a rational agent so equipped with belief and desire do? Stay put, clearly, which is just what the lectern does. I predict the lectern's behavior, accurately, from the intentional stance, so is it an intentional system? If it is, anything at all is.

What should disqualify the lectern? For one thing, the strategy does not recommend itself in this case, for we get no predictive power from it that we did not antecedently have. We already knew what the lectern was going to do – namely nothing – and tailored the beliefs and desires to fit in a quite unprincipled way. In the case of people, or animals, or computers, however, the situation is different. In these cases often the only strategy that is at all practical is the intentional strategy; it gives us predictive power we can get by no other method. But, it will be urged, this is no difference in nature, but merely a difference that reflects upon our limited capacities as scientists. The Laplacean omniscient physicist could predict the behavior of a computer – or of a live human body, assuming it to be ultimately governed by the laws of physics – without any need for the risky, short-cut methods of either the design or intentional strategies. For people of limited mechanical aptitude, the intentional interpretation of a simple thermostat is a handy and largely innocuous crutch, but the engineers among us can quite fully grasp its internal operation without the aid of this anthropomorphizing. It may be true that the cleverest engineers find it practically impossible to maintain a clear conception of more complex systems, such as a time-sharing computer system or remote-controlled space probe, without lapsing into an intentional stance (and viewing these devices as asking and telling, trying and avoiding, wanting and believing), but this is just a more advanced case of human epistemic frailty. We would not want to classify these artifacts with the true believers – ourselves – on such variable and parochial grounds, would we? Would it not be intolerable to hold that some artifact, or creature, or person was a believer from the point of view of one observer, but not a believer at all from the point of view of another, cleverer observer? That would be a particularly radical version of interpretationism, and some have thought I espoused it in urging that belief be viewed in terms of the success of the intentional strategy. I must confess that my presentation of the view has sometimes invited that reading, but I now want to discourage it. The decision to adopt the intentional stance is free, but the facts about the success or failure of the stance, were one to adopt it, are perfectly objective.

Once the intentional strategy is in place, it is an extraordinarily powerful tool in prediction – a fact that is largely concealed by our typical concentration on the cases in which it yields dubious or unreliable results. Consider, for instance, predicting moves in a chess game. What makes chess an interesting game, one can see, is the *un*predictability of one's opponent's moves, except in those cases where moves are "forced" – where there is *clearly* one best move – typically the least of the available evils. But this unpredictability is put in context when one recognizes that in the typical chess situation there are very many perfectly legal and hence available moves, but only a few – perhaps half a dozen – with anything to be said for them, and hence only a few high probability moves according to the intentional strategy. Even where the intentional strategy fails to distinguish a single move with a highest probability, it can dramatically reduce the number of live options.

The same feature is apparent when the intentional strategy is applied to "real world" cases. It is notoriously unable to predict the exact purchase and sell decisions of stock traders, for instance, or the exact sequence of words a politician will utter when making a scheduled speech, but one's confidence can be very high indeed about slightly less specific predictions: that the particular trader *will not buy utilities today*, or that the politician *will side with the unions against his party*, for example. This inability to predict fine-grained descriptions of actions, looked at another way, is a source of strength for the intentional strategy, for it is this neutrality with regard to details of implementation that permits one to exploit the intentional strategy in complex cases, for instance, in *chaining predictions*.[6] Suppose the US Secretary of State were to announce he was a paid agent of the KGB. What an unparalleled event! How unpredictable its consequences! Yet in fact we can predict dozens of not terribly interesting but perfectly salient consequences, and consequences of consequences. The President would confer with the rest of the Cabinet, which would support his decision to relieve the Secretary of State of his duties pending the results of various investigations, psychiatric and political, and all this would be reported at a news conference to people who would write stories that would be commented upon in editorials that would be read by people who would write letters to the editors, and so forth. None of that is daring prognostication, but note that it describes an arc of causation in space-time that could not be predicted under *any* description by any imaginable practical extension of physics or biology.

The power of the intentional strategy can be seen even more sharply with the aid of an objection first raised by Robert Nozick some years ago. Suppose, he suggested, some beings of vastly superior intelligence – from Mars, let us say – were to descend upon us, and suppose that we were to them as simple thermostats are to clever engineers. Suppose, that is that they did not *need* the intentional stance – or even the design stance – to predict our behavior in all its detail. They can be supposed to be Laplacean super-physicists, capable of comprehending the activity on Wall Street, for instance, at the micro-physical level. Where we see brokers and buildings and sell orders and bids, they see vast congeries of sub-atomic particles milling about – and they are such good physicists that they can predict days in advance what ink marks will appear each day on the paper tape labelled 'Closing Dow Jones Industrial Average'. They can predict the individual behaviors of all the various moving bodies they observe without ever treating any of them as intentional systems. Would we be right then to say that from *their* point of view we really were not believers at all (any more than a simple thermostat is)? If so, then our status as believers is nothing objective, but rather something in the eye of the beholder – provided the beholder shares our intellectual limitations.

Our imagined Martians might be able to predict the future of the human race by Laplacean methods, but if they did not also see us as intentional systems, they would be *missing something* perfectly objective: the *patterns* in human behavior that are describable from the intentional stance, and only from that stance, and which support generalizations and predictions. Take a particular instance in which the Martians observe a stock broker deciding to place an order for 500 shares of General Motors. They predict the exact motions of his fingers as he dials the phone, and the exact vibrations of his vocal cords as he intones his order. But if the Martians do not see that indefinitely many *different* patterns of finger motions and vocal cord vibrations – even the motions of indefinitely many different individuals – could have been substituted for the actual particulars without perturbing the subsequent operation of the market, then they have failed to see a real pattern in the world they are observing. Just as there are indefinitely many ways of *being a spark plug* – and one has not understood what an internal combustion engine is unless one realizes that a variety of different devices can be screwed into these sockets without affecting the performance of the engine – so there are indefinitely many ways of *ordering 500 shares of General Motors*, and there are societal sockets in which one of these ways will produce just about the same effect as any other. There are also societal pivot points, as it were, where which way people go depends on whether they *believe that p*, or *desire A*, and does not depend on any of the other infinitely many ways they may be alike or different.

Suppose, pursuing our Martian fantasy a little further, that one of the Martians were to engage in a predicting contest with an Earthling. The Earthling and the Martian observe (and observe each other observing) a particular bit of local physical transaction. From the Earthling's point of view, this is what is observed. The telephone rings in Mrs Gardner's kitchen. She answers, and this is what she says: "Oh, hello dear. You're coming home early? Within the hour? And bringing the boss to dinner? Pick up a bottle of wine on the way home, then, and drive carefully." On the basis of this observation, our Earthling predicts that a large metallic vehicle with rubber tyres will come to a stop in the drive within one hour, disgorging two human beings one of whom will be holding a paper bag containing a bottle containing an alcoholic fluid. The prediction is a bit risky, perhaps, but a good bet on all counts. The Martian makes the same prediction, but has to avail himself of much more information about an extraordinary number of interactions of which, so far as he can tell, the Earthling is entirely ignorant. For instance, the deceleration of the vehicle at intersection *A*, five miles from the house, without which there would have been a collision with another vehicle – whose collision course had been laboriously calculated over some hundreds of meters by the Martian. The Earthling's performance would look like magic! How did the Earthling know that the human being who got out of the car and got the bottle in the shop would get back in? The coming true of the Earthling's prediction, after all the vagaries, intersections, and branches in the paths charted by the Martian, would seem to anyone bereft of the intentional strategy as marvellous and inexplicable as the fatalistic inevitability of the appointment in Samarra. Fatalists – for instance, astrologers – believe that there is a pattern in human affairs that is inexorable, that will impose itself *come what may*, that is, no matter how the victims scheme and second-guess, no matter how they twist and turn in their chains. These fatalists are wrong, but they are *almost* right. There *are* patterns in human affairs that impose themselves, not quite inexorably but with great vigor, absorbing physical perturbations and variations that might as well be considered random; these are the patterns that we characterize in terms of the beliefs, desires, and intentions of rational agents.

No doubt you will have noticed, and been distracted by, a serious flaw in our thought-experiment: the Martian is presumed to treat his Earthling opponent as an intelligent being like himself, with whom communication is possible, a being with whom one can make a wager, against whom one can compete. In short, a being with beliefs (such as the belief he expressed in his prediction) and desires (such as the desire to win the prediction contest). So if the Martian sees the pattern in one Earthling, how can he fail to see it in the others? As a bit of narrative, our example could be strengthened by supposing that our Earthling cleverly learned Martian (which is transmitted by X-ray modulation) and disguised himself as a Martian, counting on the species-chauvinism of these otherwise brilliant aliens to permit him to pass as an intentional system while not giving away the secret of his fellow human beings. This addition might get us over a bad twist in the tale, but might obscure the moral to be drawn: namely, the unavoidability of the intentional stance with regard to oneself and one's fellow intelligent beings. This unavoidability is itself interest relative; it is perfectly possible to adopt a physical stance, for instance, with regard to an intelligent being, oneself included, but not to the exclusion of maintaining at the same time an intentional stance with regard to oneself at a minimum, and one's fellows *if* one intends, for instance, to learn what they know (a point that has been powerfully made by Stuart Hampshire in a number of writings). We can perhaps suppose our super-intelligent Martians fail to recognize *us* as intentional systems, but we cannot suppose them to lack the requisite concepts.[7] If they observe, theorize, predict, communicate, they view *themselves* as intentional systems.[8] Where there are intelligent beings the patterns must be there to be described, whether or not we care to see them.

It is important to recognize the objective reality of the intentional patterns discernible in the activities of intelligent creatures, but also important to recognize the incompleteness and imperfections in the patterns. The objective fact is that the intentional strategy *works as well as it does*, which is not perfectly. No one is perfectly rational, perfectly unforgetful, all-observant, or invulnerable to fatigue, malfunction, or design imperfection. This leads inevitably to circumstances beyond the power of the intentional strategy to describe, in much the same way that physical damage to an artifact, such as a telephone or an automobile, may render it indescribable by the normal design terminology for that artifact. How do you draw the schematic wiring diagram of an audio amplifier that has been partially melted, or how do you characterize the program state of a malfunctioning computer? In cases of even the mildest and most familiar cognitive pathology – where people seem to hold contradictory beliefs, or to be deceiving themselves, for instance – the canons of interpretation of the intentional strategy fail to yield clear, stable verdicts about which beliefs and desires to attribute to a person.

Now a *strong* realist position on beliefs and desires would claim that in these cases the person in question really does have some particular beliefs and desires which the intentional strategy, as I have described it, is simply unable to divine. On the milder sort of realism I am advocating, there is no fact of the matter of exactly which beliefs and desires a person has in these degenerate cases, but this is not a surrender to relativism or subjectivism, for *when* and *why* there is no fact of the matter is itself a matter of objective fact. On this view one can even acknowledge the *interest relativity* of belief attributions, and grant that given the different interests of different cultures, for instance, the beliefs and desires one culture would attribute to a member might be quite different from the beliefs and desires another culture would attribute to that very same person. But supposing that were so in a particular case, there would be the further facts about *how well* each of the rival intentional strategies worked for predicting the behavior of that person. We can be sure in advance that no intentional interpretation of an individual will work to perfection, and it may be that two rival schemes are about equally good, and better than any others we can devise. That this is the case is itself something about which there can be a fact of the matter. The objective presence of one pattern (with whatever imperfections) does not rule out the objective presence of another pattern (with whatever imperfections).

The bogey of radically different interpretations with equal warrant from the intentional strategy is theoretically important – one might better say metaphysically important – but practically negligible once one restricts one's attention to the largest and most complex intentional systems we know: human beings.[9]

Until now I have been stressing our kinship to clams and thermostats, in order to emphasize a view of the logical status of belief attribution, but the time has come to acknowledge the obvious differences, and say what can be made of them. The perverse claim remains: *all there is* to being a true believer is being a system whose behavior is reliably predictable via the intentional strategy, and hence *all there is* to really and truly believing that *p* (for any proposition *p*) is being an intentional system for which *p* occurs as a belief in the best (most predictive) interpretation. But once we turn our attention to the truly interesting and versatile intentional systems, we see that this apparently shallow and instrumentalistic criterion of belief puts a severe constraint on the internal constitution of a genuine believer, and thus yields a robust version of belief after all.

Consider the lowly thermostat, as degenerate a case of an intentional system as could conceivably hold our attention for more than a moment. Going along with the gag we might agree to grant it the capacity for about half a dozen different beliefs and fewer desires – it can believe the room is too cold or too hot, that the boiler is on or off, and that if it wants the room warmer it should turn on the boiler, and so forth. But surely this is imputing too much to the thermostat; it has no concept of heat or of a boiler, for instance. So suppose we *de-interpret* its beliefs and desires: it can believe the *A* is too *F* or *G*, and if it wants the *A* to be more *F* it should do *K*, and so forth. After all, by attaching the thermostatic control mechanism to different input and output devices, it could be made to regulate the amount of water in a tank, or the speed of a train, for instance. Its attachment to a heat-sensitive "transducer" and a boiler is too impoverished a link to the world to grant any rich semantics to its belief-like states.

But suppose we then enrich these modes of attachment. Suppose we give it more than one way of learning about the temperature, for instance. We give it an eye of sorts that can distinguish huddled, shivering occupants of the room, and an ear so that it can be told how cold it is. We give it some facts about geography so that it can conclude that it is probably in a cold place if it learns that its spatio-temporal location is Winnipeg in December. Of course giving it a visual system that is multi-purpose and general – not a mere shivering-object detector – will require vast complications of its inner structure. Suppose we also give our system more behavioral versatility: it chooses the boiler fuel, purchases it from the cheapest and most reliable dealer, checks the weatherstripping and so forth. This adds another dimension of internal complexity; it gives individual belief-like states *more to do*, in effect, by providing more and different occasions for their derivation or deduction from other states, and by providing more and different occasions for them to serve as premises for further reasoning. The cumulative effect of enriching these connections between the device and the world in which it resides is to enrich the semantics of its dummy predicates, *F* and *G* and the rest. The more of this we add, the less amenable our device becomes to serving as the control structure of anything other than a room temperature maintenance system. A more formal way of saying this is that the class of indistinguishably satisfactory models of the formal system embodied in its internal states gets smaller and smaller as we add such complexities; the more we add, the richer or more demanding or specific the semantics of the system, until eventually we reach systems for which a *unique* semantic interpretation is *practically* (but never *in principle*) dictated.[10] At that point we say this device (or animal, or person) has beliefs *about heat*, and *about this very room*, and so forth, not only because of the system's *actual* location in, and operations on, the world, but because we cannot imagine another niche in which it could be placed *where it would work*.

Our original simple thermostat had a state we called a belief about a particular boiler, to the effect that it was on or off. Why about *that* boiler? Well, what *other* boiler would you want to say it was about? The belief is about the boiler because it is *fastened* to the boiler.[11] Given the actual, if minimal, causal link to the world that happened to be in effect, we could endow a state of the device with *meaning* (of a sort) and *truth conditions*, but it was altogether too easy to substitute a different minimal link and completely change the meaning (in this impoverished sense) of that internal state. But as systems become perceptually richer and behaviorally more versatile, it becomes harder and harder to make substitutions in the actual links of the system to the world without changing the organization of the system itself. If you change its environment, it will *notice*, in effect, and make a change in its internal state in response. There comes to be a two-way constraint of growing specificity between the device and the environment. Fix the device in any one state and it demands a *very* specific environment in which to operate properly (you can no longer switch it easily from regulating temperature to regulating speed or anything else); but at the same time, if you do not *fix* the state it is in, but just plonk it down in a changed environment, its sensory attachments will be sensitive and discriminative enough to respond appropriately to the change, driving the system into a new state, in which it will operate effectively in the new environment. There is a familiar way of alluding to this tight relationship that can exist between the organization of a system and its environment: you say that the organism continuously *mirrors* the environment, or that there is a *representation* of the environment in – or implicit in – the organization of the system.

It is not that we attribute (or should attribute) beliefs and desires only to things in which we find internal representations, but rather that when we discover some object for which the intentional strategy works, we endeavour to interpret some of its internal states or processes as internal representations. What makes some internal feature of a thing a representation could only be its role in regulating the behavior of an intentional system. Now the reason for stressing our kinship with the thermostat should be clear. There is no magic moment in the transition from a single thermostat to a system that *really* has an internal representation of the world around it. The thermostat has a minimally demanding representation of the world, fancier thermostats have more demanding representations of the world, fancier robots for helping around the house would have still more demanding representations of the world. Finally you reach us. We are so multifariously and intricately connected to the world that almost no substitution is possible – though it is clearly imaginable in a thought-experiment. Hilary Putnam imagines the planet Twin Earth, which is just like Earth right down to the scuff marks on the shoes of the Twin Earth replica of your neighbour, but which differs from Earth in some property that is entirely beneath the thresholds of your capacities to discriminate. (What they call water on Twin Earth has a different chemical analysis.) Were *you* to be whisked instantaneously to Twin Earth and exchanged for your Twin Earth replica, you would never be the wiser – just like the simple control system that cannot tell whether it is regulating temperature, speed, or volume of water in a tank. It is easy to devise radically different Twin Earths for something as simple and sensorily deprived as a thermostat, but your internal organization puts a much more stringent demand on substitution. Your Twin Earth and Earth must be virtual replicas or you will change state dramatically on arrival.

So which boiler are *your* beliefs about, when you believe the boiler is on? Why, the boiler in your cellar (rather than its twin on Twin Earth, for instance). What *other* boiler would your beliefs be about? The *completion* of the semantic interpretation of your beliefs, fixing the *referents* of your beliefs, requires, as in the case of the thermostat, facts about your actual embedding in the world. The principles, and problems, of interpretation that we discover when we attribute beliefs to people are the *same* principles and problems we discover when we look at the ludicrous, but blessedly simple, problem of attributing beliefs to a thermostat. The differences are of degree, but nevertheless of such great degree that understanding the internal organization of a simple intentional system gives one very little basis for understanding the internal organization of a complex intentional system, such as a human being.

Why does the intentional strategy work?

When we turn to the question of *why* the intentional strategy works as well as it does, we find that the question is ambiguous, admitting of two very different sorts of answers. If the intentional system is a simple thermostat, one answer is simply this: the intentional strategy works because the thermostat is well designed; it was designed to be a system that could be easily and reliably comprehended and manipulated from this stance. That is true, but not very informative, if what we are after are the actual features of its design that explain its performance. Fortunately, however, in the case of a simple thermostat those features are easily discovered and understood, so the other answer to our *why* question, which is really an answer about *how the machinery works*, is readily available.

If the intentional system in question is a person, there is also an ambiguity in our question. The first answer to the question of why the intentional strategy works is that evolution has designed human beings to be rational, to believe what they ought to believe and want what they ought to want. The fact that we are products of a long and demanding evolutionary process guarantees that using the intentional strategy on us is a safe bet. This answer has the virtues of truth and brevity, and on this occasion the additional virtue of being an answer Herbert Spencer would applaud, but it is also strikingly uninformative. The more difficult version of the question asks, in effect, how the machinery which Nature has provided us works. And we cannot yet give a good answer to that question. We just do not know. We do know how the *strategy* works, and we know the easy answer to the question of why it works, but knowing these does not help us much with the hard answer.

It is not that there is any dearth of doctrine, however. A Skinnerian behaviorist, for instance, would say that the strategy works because its imputations of beliefs and desires are shorthand, in effect, for as yet unimaginably complex descriptions of the effects of prior histories of response and reinforcement. To say that someone wants some ice cream is to say that in the past the ingestion of ice cream has been reinforced in him by the results, creating a propensity under certain background conditions (also too complex to describe) to engage in ice-cream-acquiring behavior. In the absence of detailed knowledge of those historical facts we can nevertheless make shrewd guesses on inductive grounds; these guesses are embodied in our intentional stance claims. Even if all this were true, it would tell us very little about the way such propensities were regulated by the internal machinery.

A currently more popular explanation is that the account of how the strategy works and the account of how the mechanism works will (roughly) *coincide*: for each predictively attributable belief, there will be a functionally salient internal state of the machinery, decomposable into functional parts in just about the same way the sentence expressing the belief is decomposable into parts – that is, words or terms. The inferences we attribute to rational creatures will be mirrored by physical, causal processes in the hardware; the *logical* form of the propositions believed will be copied in the *structural* form of the states in correspondence with them. This is the hypothesis that there is a *language of thought* coded in our brains, and our brains will eventually be understood as symbol manipulating systems in at least rough analogy with computers. Many different versions of this view are currently being explored, in the new research program called cognitive science, and provided one allows great latitude for attenuation of the basic, bold claim, I think some version of it will prove correct.

But I do not believe that this is *obvious*. Those who think that it is obvious, or inevitable, that such a theory will prove true (and there are many who do), are confusing two different empirical claims. The first is that intentional stance description yields an objective, real pattern in the world – the pattern our imaginary Martians missed. This is an empirical claim, but one that is confirmed beyond skepticism. The second is that this real pattern is *produced* by another real pattern roughly isomorphic to it within the brains of intelligent creatures. Doubting the existence of the second real pattern is not doubting the existence of the first. There *are* reasons for believing in the second pattern, but they are not overwhelming. The best simple account I can give of the reasons is as follows. As we ascend the scale of complexity from simple thermostat, through sophisticated robot, to human being, we discover that our efforts to design systems with the requisite behavior increasingly run foul of the problem of *combinatorial explosion*. Increasing some parameter by, say, 10 per cent – 10 per cent more inputs, or more degrees of freedom in the behavior to be controlled, or more words to be recognized, or whatever – tends to increase the internal complexity of the system being designed by orders of magnitude. Things get out of hand very fast and, for instance, can lead to computer programs that will swamp the largest, fastest machines. Now somehow the brain has solved the problem of combinatorial explosion. It is a gigantic network of billions of cells, but still finite, compact, reliable, and swift, and capable of learning new behaviors, vocabularies, theories, almost without limit. Some elegant, *generative*, indefinitely extendable principles of representation must be responsible. We have only one model of such a representation system: a human language. So the argument for a language of thought comes down to this: what else could it be? We have so far been unable to imagine any plausible alternative in any detail. That is a good enough reason, I think, for recommending as a matter of scientific tactics that we pursue the hypothesis in its various forms as far as we can.[12] But we will engage in that exploration more circumspectly, and fruitfully, if we bear in mind that its inevitable rightness is far from assured. One does not well understand even a true empirical hypothesis so long as one is under the misapprehension that it is necessarily true.[13]

NOTES

1. "Intentional systems," *Journal of Philosophy* (1971). "Conditions of personhood, in *The Identities of Persons* (ed. A. Rorty), University of California Press (1975). Both reprinted in *Brainstorms*, Montgomery Vt, Bradford (1978). "Three kinds of intentional psychology," in *Mind, Psychology and Reductionism* (ed. R. A. Healey), Cambridge University Press (1981).

2. *Pace* Paul Feyerabend, whose latest book, *Science in a Free Society*, New Left Books, London (1978), is heroically open-minded about astrology.

3. The idea that most of anyone's beliefs *must* be true seems obvious to some people. Support for the idea can be found in works by Quine, Putnam, Shoemaker, Davidson, and myself. Other people find the idea equally incredible – so probably each side is calling a different phenomenon belief. Once one makes the distinction between belief and opinion (in my technical sense – see "How to change your mind," in *Brainstorms*, ch. 16), according to which opinions are linguistically infected, relatively sophisticated cognitive states – *roughly*, states of betting on the truth of a particular, formulated sentence, one can see the near triviality of the claim that most beliefs are true. A few reflections on peripheral matters should bring it out. Consider Democritus, who had a systematic, all-embracing, but (let us say, for the sake of argument) entirely false physics. He had things *all wrong*, though his views held together and had a sort of systematic utility. But even if every *claim* that scholarship permits us to attribute to Democritus (either explicit or implicit in his writings) is false, these represent a vanishingly small fraction of his *beliefs*, which include both the vast numbers of humdrum standing beliefs he must have had (about which house he lived in, what to look for in a good pair of sandals, and so forth), and also those occasional beliefs that came and went by the millions as his perceptual experience changed.

   But, it may be urged, this isolation of his humdrum beliefs from his science relies on an insupportable distinction between truths of observation and truths of theory; all Democritus's beliefs are theory-laden, and since his theory is false, they are false. The reply is as follows: Granted that all observation beliefs are theory laden, why should we choose Democritus's *explicit*, sophisticated theory (couched in his *opinions*) as the theory with which to burden his quotidian observations? Note that the least theoretical compatriot of Democritus also had myriads of theory-laden observation beliefs – and was, in one sense, none the wiser for it. Why should we not suppose their observations are laden with the same theory? If Democritus forgot his theory, or changed his mind, his observational beliefs would be *largely* untouched. To the extent that his sophisticated theory played a discernible role in his routine behavior and expectations and so forth, it would be quite appropriate to couch his humdrum beliefs in terms of the sophisticated theory, but this will not yield a *mainly false* catalog of beliefs, since so few of his beliefs will be affected. (The effect of theory on observation is nevertheless often underrated. See Paul Churchland, *Scientific Realism and the Plasticity of Mind*, Cambridge University Press (1979), for dramatic and convincing examples of the tight relationship that can sometimes exist between theory and experience.) (The discussion in this note was distilled from a useful conversation with Paul and Patricia Churchland and Michael Stack.)

4. See my *Content and Consciousness*, Routledge & Kegan Paul, London (1969), pp. 184–5, and "How to change your mind," in *Brainstorms*.

5. See *Brainstorms*, and "Three kinds of intentional psychology." See also C. Cherniak, "Minimal Rationality," *Mind*, (1981), and my response to Stephen Stich's "Headaches," in *Philosophical Books* (1980).

6. See "On giving libertarians what they say they want," in *Brainstorms*.

7. A member of the audience in Oxford pointed out that if the Martian included the Earthling in his physical stance purview (a possibility I had not explicitly excluded), he would not be surprised by the Earthling's prediction. He would indeed have predicted exactly the pattern of X-ray modulations produced by the Earthling speaking Martian. True, but as the Martian wrote down the results of his calculations, his prediction of the Earthling's prediction would appear, word by Martian word, as on a Ouija board, and what would be baffling to the Martian was how this chunk of mechanism, the Earthling predictor dressed up like a Martian, was able to yield this *true* sentence of Martian when it was so informationally isolated from the events the Martian needed to know of in order to make his own prediction about the arriving automobile.

8. Might there not be intelligent beings who had no use for communicating, predicting, observing . . .? There might be marvellous, nifty, invulnerable entities lacking these modes of action, but I cannot see what would lead us to call them *intelligent*.

9. John McCarthy's analogy to cryptography nicely makes this point. The larger the corpus of cipher text, the less chance there is of dual, systematically unrelated decipherings. For a very useful discussion of the principles and presuppositions of the intentional stance applied to machines – explicitly including thermostats – see McCarthy's "Ascribing mental qualities to machines," in *Philosophical Perspectives on Artificial Intelligence* (ed. Martin Ringle), Humanities Press (1979).

10. Patrick Hayes explores this application of Tarskian model theory to the semantics of mental representation in "The naive physics manifesto" in *Expert Systems in the Micro-Electronic Age* (ed. D. Michie) Edinburgh University Press.

11. This idea is the ancestor in effect of the species of different ideas lumped together under the rubric of *de re* belief, If one builds from this idea towards its scions one can see better the difficulties with them, and how to repair them.

12. The fact that all *language of thought* models of mental representation so far proposed fall victim to combinatorial explosion in one way or another should temper one's enthusiasm for engaging in what Fodor aptly calls "the only game in town."

13. This paper was written during a Fellowship at the Center for Advanced Study in the Behavioral Sciences. I am grateful for financial support provided by the National Endowment

for the Humanities, the National Science Foundation (BNS 78-24671), and the Alfred P. Sloan Foundation.

Dennett on Intentional Systems

STEPHEN P. STICH

During the last dozen years, Daniel Dennett has been elaborating an interconnected – and increasingly influential – set of views in the philosophy of mind, the philosophy of psychology, and those parts of moral philosophy that deal with the notions of freedom, responsibility and personhood. The central unifying theme running through Dennett's writings on each of these topics is his concept of an *intentional system*. He invokes the concept to "legitimize" mentalistic predicates (*Brainstorms*, p. xvii),[1] to explain the theoretical strategy of cognitive psychology and artificial intelligence, and, ultimately, to attempt a reconciliation between "our vision of ourselves as responsible, free, rational agents, and our vision of ourselves as complex parts of the physical world of science" (*BS*, p. x). My goal in this paper is to raise some doubts about the "intentional coin" (*BS*, p. xviii) with which Dennett proposes to purchase his moral and "mental treasures." Since I aim to offer a critique of Dennett's views, it is inevitable that much of what I say will be negative in tone. But this tone should not be misconstrued. It is my view that Dennett's theories are of great importance and will shape discussion in the philosophy of mind for decades to come. Moreover, I think that much of what Dennett says is close to being true. If we reconstruct his notion of an intentional system to eliminate its instrumentalism and its unfortunate infatuation with idealized rationality, we can use the result to give a better account of common-sense mentalistic notions, and also to give a clearer and more tenable account of the strategy of cognitive science. Toward the end of this paper I will sketch the outlines of such a "de-rationalized" cousin to Dennett's idea of an intentional system.

I

In explaining the idea of an intentional system, Dennett's recurrent illustration is the chess-playing computer. There are, he urges, three quite different stances we might "adopt in trying to predict and explain its behavior" (*BS*, p. 237).

> First there is the *design stance*. If one knows exactly how the computer's program has been designed . . . one can predict the computer's designed response to any move

"Dennett on Intentional Systems," by Stephen P. Stich first appeared in *Philosophical Topics* 12 (1981) pp. 39–62, and is reprinted by kind permission.

one makes. One's prediction will come true provided only that the computer performs as designed, that is, without breakdown. . . . The essential feature of the design stance is that we make predictions solely from knowledge or assumptions about the system's design, often without making any examination of the innards of the particular object.

Second, there is what we may call the *physical stance*. From this stance our predictions are based on the actual state of the particular system, and are worked out by applying whatever knowledge we have of the laws of nature. . . . One seldom adopts the physical stance in dealing with a computer just because the number of critical variables in the physical constitution of a computer would overwhelm the most prodigious human calculator. . . . Attempting to give a physical account or prediction of the chess playing computer would be a pointless and herculean labor, but it would work in principle. One could predict the response it would make in a chess game by tracing out the effects of the input energies all the way through the computer until once more type was pressed against paper and a response was printed.

There is a third stance one can adopt toward a system, and that is the *intentional stance*. This tends to be the most appropriate when the system one is dealing with is too complex to be dealt with effectively from the other stances. In the case of a chess playing computer one adopts this stance when one tries to predict its response to one's move by figuring out what a good or reasonable response would be, given the information the computer has about the situation. Here one assumes not just the absence of malfunction but the rationality of the design or programming as well.

Whenever one can successfully adopt the intentional stance toward an object, I call that object an *intentional* system. The success of the stance is of course a matter settled pragmatically, without reference to whether the object *really* has beliefs, intentions, and so forth; so whether or not any computer can be conscious, or have thoughts or desires, some computers undeniably *are* intentional systems, for they are systems whose behavior can be predicted, and most efficiently predicted, by adopting the intentional stance towards them. (*BS*, pp. 237–8; for a largely identical passage, cf. *BS*, pp. 4–7.)

So *any* object will count as an intentional system if we can usefully predict its behavior by assuming that it will behave *rationally*. And what is it to behave rationally? Here, Dennett suggests, the full answer must ultimately be provided by a new sort of theory, *intentional–system theory*, which will provide us with a *normative* account of rationality. This new theory "is envisaged as a close kin of – and overlapping with – such already existing disciplines as epistemic logic, decision theory and game theory, which are all similarly abstract, normative and couched in intentional language" (*TK*, p. 19). Of course, we already have some "rough and ready principles" of rationality which we can and do press into service pending a more detailed normative theory:

1 A system's beliefs are those it *ought to have*, given its perceptual capacities, its epistemic needs, and its biography. Thus in general, its beliefs are both true and relevant to its life. . . .

2 A system's desires are those it ought to have, given its biological needs and the most practicable means of satisfying them. Thus [naturally evolved] intentional systems desire survival and procreation, and hence desire food, security, health, sex, wealth, power, influence, and so forth, and also

whatever local arrangements tend (in their eyes – given their beliefs) to further these ends in appropriate measure. . . .

3   A system's behavior will consist of those acts that *it would be rational* for an agent with those beliefs and desires to perform. (*TK*, pp. 8–9)

Obviously these three principles are very rough and ready indeed. However, we also have a wealth of more detailed common-sense principles that anchor our intuitive notion of rationality. Some of these, in turn, are systematized and improved upon by existing theories in logic, evolutionary biology and decision theory. But though the intentional–system theorist can count on some help from these more developed disciplines, he still has a great deal of work to do. Neither singly nor severally do these disciplines tell us what beliefs a given organism or system ought to have, what desires it ought to have, or how it should act, given the beliefs and desires it has. Dennett has no illusions on the point. He portrays intentional-system theory – the general normative theory of rationality – as a discipline in its infancy. When the course of our argument requires some substantive premises about what it would be rational for a system to believe or do, we can follow Dennett's lead and let our common-sense intuitions be our guide.

I have been stressing the role of a normative theory of rationality in Dennett's account of the intentional stance. But there is a second, equally important, component in his view. According to Dennett, when we describe an organism or an artifact as an intentional system, we are making no commitments about the internal physical workings of the system. *Nor are we saying anything about the design or program of the system.* Just as a single program or design description is compatible with indefinitely many physical realizations, so too a single intentional description is compatible with indefinitely many different programs or design descriptions. To view an object as an intentional system we must attribute to it a substantial range of beliefs and desires – the beliefs and desires it would be rational for such an object to have, given its nature and history. However, we need not assume that the beliefs and desires attributed correspond in any systematic way to internal states characterized either physically or functionally. Dennett makes the point vividly with the example of two robots each designed to be identical to a given person, Mary, when viewed from the intentional stance. The first robot, Ruth, "has internal processes which 'model' Mary's as closely as you like" (*BS*, p. 105). It is functionally identical to Mary, though the two may be quite different physically. Since Mary and Ruth share a common design or program, they will behave identically. Thus any beliefs and desires we attribute to Mary we may attribute also to Ruth, and the attributions will be equally useful in predicting their behavior. The second robot, Sally, has a program which is input–output equivalent to Ruth's, though it uses a quite different computational strategy. "Sally may not be a very good psychological model of Mary," since "Sally's response delays, errors and the like may not match Mary's." But at the level of common-sense descriptions of actions, all three will behave alike. ". . . the ascription of all Mary's beliefs and desires (etc.) to Sally will be just as predictive as their ascription to Ruth so far as prediction of action goes" (*BS*, p. 105). So when we adopt the intentional stance, Mary, Ruth and Sally are indistinguishable.

Dennett, then, is a self-professed instrumentalist about the beliefs and desires we ascribe to an object when we adopt the intentional stance toward it. "... the beliefs and other intentions of an intentional system need [not] be *represented* 'within' the system in any way for us to get a purchase on predicting its behavior by ascribing such intentions to it" (*BS*, p. 277). Rather, these "putative ... states" can be relegated "to the role of idealized fictions in an action-predicting, action-explaining calculus" (*BS*, p. 30). For Dennett, the belief and desire states of an intentional system are not what Reichenbach calls "illata – posited theoretical entities." Rather they are "abstracta – calculation bound entities or logical constructs" (*TK*, p. 13). Their status is analogous to the lines in a parallelogram of forces (*TK*, p. 20). Of course, it is conceivable that some objects which are usefully treated as intentional systems really do have internal states that correspond to the beliefs and desires ascribed to them in an intentional characterization. As some writers have suggested, there might be functionally distinct neural belief and desire stores where each belief and desire is inscribed in an appropriate neural code. Dennett, however, thinks this is not likely to be true for people, animals and other familiar intentional systems.[2] Be this as it may, the important point in the present context is that when we describe an object in intentional-system terms, we are quite explicitly *not* making any commitment about its workings, beyond the minimal claim that whatever the mechanism causally responsible for the behavior may be, it must be the sort of mechanism which will produce behavior generally predictable by assuming the intentional stance.

This completes my sketch of Dennett's notion of intentional systems. Let us now consider what Dennett wants to do with the notion. The principal project Dennett has in mind for intentional systems is "legitimizing" (*BS*, p. xvii), or providing a sort of "conceptual reduction" (*TK*, p. 30) of various notions in common-sense or folk psychology. The sort of legitimizing Dennett has in mind is explained by analogy with Church's Thesis. Church proposed that the informal, intuitive mathematical concept of an "effective" procedure be identified with the formal notion of a recursive (or Turing-machine computable) function. The proposal "is not provable, since it hinges on the intuitive and unformalizable notion of an effective procedure, but it is generally accepted, and it provides a very useful reduction of a fuzzy-but-useful mathematical notion to a crisply defined notion of apparently equal scope and greater power" (*BS*, p. xviii; cf. also *TK*, p. 30). It is Dennett's hope to provide the same sort of legitimization of the notions of folk psychology by showing how these notions can be characterized in terms of the notions of intentional-system theory. "... the claim that every mental phenomenon alluded to in folk psychology is *intentional-system-characteriz-able* would, if true, provide a reduction of the mental as ordinarily understood – a domain whose boundaries are at best fixed by mutual acknowledgement and shared intuition – to a clearly defined domain of entities, whose principles of organization are familiar, relatively formal and systematic, and entirely general" (*TK*, pp. 30–1).

All this sounds reasonable enough – an exciting project, if Dennett can pull it off. The effort looks even more intriguing when we note how broadly Dennett intends to cast his net. It is his aim to show not only that such "program receptive" (*BS*, p. 29) features of mentality as belief and desire are intentional-system-characterizable, but also that "program resistant features of mentality" like pain, dreams, mental images, and even free will are "captured in the net of intentional systems" (*BS*, p. xviii). But a dark cloud looms on the horizon, one that will continue to plague us. In much of his work Dennett exhibits an exasperating tendency to make bold, flamboyant, fascinating claims in one breath, only to take them back, or seem to, in the next. Thus, scarcely a page after proclaiming his intention to show that a broad range of common-sense mental phenomena are intentional-system-characterizable and thus legitimized, Dennett proclaims himself to be an eliminative materialist concerning these very same phenomena. Beliefs, desires, pains, mental images, experiences – as these are ordinarily understood – "are not good theoretical entities, however well entrenched" (*BS*, p. xx) the terms 'belief,' 'pain,' etc. may be in the habits of thought of our society. So "we legislate the putative items right out of existence" (*BS*, p. xx). How are we to make sense of this apparent contradiction?

There is, I think, a plausible – and uncontradictory – interpretation of what Dennett is up to. The problem he is grappling with is that the fit between our intuitive folk-psychological notions and the intentional-system characterizations he provides for them is just not as comfortable as the fit between the intuitive notion of effective mathematical procedure and the formal notion of Turing computability. Our folk-psychological concepts, "like folk productions generally," are complex, messy, variegated and in danger of incoherence (*TK*, p. 16). By contrast, notions characterized in terms of intentional-system theory are – it is to be hoped – coherent, sharply drawn and constructed with a self-conscious eye for their subsequent incorporation into science (*TK*, p. 6). The intentional-system analysans are intended to be improvements on their analysanda. What they give us is not an "anthropological" (*TK*, p. 6) portrait of our folk notions (warts and all), but rather an improved version of "the parts of folk psychology worth caring about" (*TK*, p. 30). So Dennett is an eliminative materialist about mental phenomena alluded to in warts-and-all folk psychology; what are intentional-system-characterizable are not the notions of folk psychology, but rather related successor concepts which capture all that's worth caring about.

But now what are we to make of the claim that the intentional system *Ersätze* capture all that's worth caring about in folk psychology: What *is* worth caring about? Dennett concedes that an "anthropological" study of unreconstructed folk notions which includes "whatever folk actually include in their theory, however misguided, incoherent, gratuitous some of it may be," (*TK*, p. 6) would be a perfectly legitimate endeavor. Folk theory may be myth, "but it is a myth we live in, so it is an 'important' phenomenon in nature" (*TK*, p. 6).[3] However, Dennett does not share the anthropologist's (or the cognitive simulator's) interest in the idiosyncrasies and contradictions embedded in our folk notions. What is of interest to him, he strongly suggests, is "the proto-scientific quest": "an attempt to prepare folk theory for subsequent incorporation into or reduction to the rest of science," eliminating "all that is false or ill-founded" (*TK*, p. 6). If matters stopped there, we could parse Dennett's "all that's worth caring about" as "all that's worth caring about for the purposes of science." But matters do not stop there. To see why, we will have to take a detour to survey another central theme in Dennett's thinking.

As we have noted, a basic goal of Dennett's theory is to reconcile "our vision of ourselves as responsible, free, rational agents, and our vision of ourselves as complex parts of the physical world of science" (*BS*, p. x). The conflict that threatens between these two visions is a perennial philosophical preoccupation:

> the validity of our conceptual scheme of moral agents having dignity, freedom and responsibility stands or falls on the question: can men ever be truly said to have beliefs, desires, intentions? If they can, there is at least some hope of retaining a notion of the dignity of man; if they cannot, if men never can be said truly to want or believe, then surely they never can be said truly to act responsibly, or to have a conception of justice, or to know the difference between right and wrong. (*BS*, pp. 63–4)

Yet many psychologists, most notoriously Skinner, have denied that people have beliefs, desires and other mental states.[4] This threat to our view of ourselves as moral agents does not arise only from rabid behaviorism. Dennett sees it lurking also in certain recently fashionable philosophical theories about the nature of mental states. Consider, for example, the type–type identity theory which holds that every mental-state type is to be identified with a physical-state type – a brain state characterized in physico-chemical terms. What if it should turn out that there simply is *no* physical-state type that is shared by all beings to whom we commonly attribute the belief that snow is white? If we hang on to the type–type identity theory, then this very plausible empirical finding would seem to entail that there is no such mental state as believing that snow is white. Much the same result threatens from those versions of functionalism which hold that "each mental type is identifiable as a functional type in the language of Turing machine description" (*BS*, p. xvi). For "there is really no more reason to believe you and I 'have the same program' in *any* relaxed and abstract sense, considering the differences in our nature and nurture, than that our brains have identical physico-chemical descriptions" (*BS*, p. xvi). So if we adhere to functionalism, a plausible result in cognitive psychology – the discovery that people do not have the same programs – threatens to establish that people do not have beliefs at all.[5]

We can now see one of the principal virtues of Dennett's instrumentalism about intentional systems. Since describing an object as an intentional system entails nothing whatever about either the physico-chemical nature or the functional design of the mechanism that causes the object's behavior, neither neurophysiology nor "sub-personal cognitive psychology" (which studies the functional organization or program of the organism) could possibly show that the object was not an intentional system. Thus if beliefs and desires (or some respectable *Ersätze*) can be characterized in terms of intentional-system theory, we need have no fear that advances in psychology or brain science might establish that people do not really have beliefs and desires. So the viability of our "conceptual scheme of moral agents" is sustained, in this quarter at least.[6]

Now, finally, it is clear how Dennett's preoccupation with moral themes bears on his eliminative materialism. Recall that Dennett proposes to trade our ungainly folk-psychological notions for concepts characterized in terms of intentional systems. The claim is not that the new concepts are identical with the old, but that they are *better*. They are clearer, more systematic, free from the incoherence lurking in folk notions, *and they capture everything in folk psychology that is worth caring about*. One of the things worth caring about, for Dennett, is the suitability of the clarified notions for incorporation into science. However, if he is to succeed in insulating our moral world-view from the threat posed by scientific psychology, then there is obviously something else Dennett must count as worth caring about. The new concepts built from intentional-system notions must be as serviceable as the older folk notions in sustaining our vision of ourselves as persons.

II

In this section I want to examine just how well Dennett's intentional system *Ersätze* mirror the notions of folk psychology. My focus will be on the "program receptive" notions of belief and desire, concepts which should be easiest to purchase "with intentional coin," and my claim will be that the fit between our common-sense notions and Dennett's proffered replacements is a very poor one.[7] Of course, Dennett does not maintain that the fit is perfect, only that intentional-system theory preserves "the parts of folk psychology worth caring about" (*TK*, p. 30). This is the doctrine I am concerned to challenge. On my view, the move to an intentional-system-characterized notion of belief would leave us unable to say a great deal that we wish to say about ourselves and our fellows. Moreover, the losses will be important ones. If we accept Dennett's trade, we will have no coherent way to describe our cognitive shortcomings nor the process by which we may learn to overcome them. Equally unwelcome, the thriving scientific study of the strengths and weaknesses of human reasoning would wither and die, its hypotheses ruled literally incoherent. What is more, the instrumentalism of Dennett's intentional-system notions seems to fly in the face of some deeply rooted intuitions about responsibility and moral agency. Throughout most of what follows, I will cleave to the fiction that we already have a tolerably well worked out normative theory of rationality, or could readily build one, though in the closing pages I will offer some skeptical thoughts about how likely this fiction is.

I begin with the problems posed by irrationality. An intentional system, recall, is an ideally rational system; it believes, wants and does just what it ought to, as stipulated by a normative theory of rationality. People, by contrast, are not ideally rational, and therein lies a devastating problem for Dennett. If we were to adopt his suggestion and trade up to the intentional-system notions of belief and desire (hereafter IS belief and IS desire), then we simply would not be able to say all those things we need to say about ourselves and our fellows when we deal with each other's idiosyncrasies, shortcomings, and cognitive growth.

Consider belief. Presumably no system *ought* to hold contradictory beliefs, and all systems *ought* to believe all the logical truths, along with all the logical consequences of what they believe (cf. *BS*, pp. 11, 20, 44; *TK*, p. 11). But people depart from this ideal in a variety of ways. We generally fail to believe *all* logical consequences of our beliefs – sometimes because the reasoning required would be difficult, and sometimes because we simply fail to take account of one or more of our beliefs. Suppose, for example, that an astronaut set the controls incorrectly and has sent his craft into a perilous spin. One possible explanation of his mistake would be that the on-board computer was down, and he had to hand-calculate the setting for the controls. He made a mistake in the calculation, and thus came to have a mistaken belief about what the setting should be. Another possibility is that, although he knew the craft was in the gravitational field of a nearby asteroid – indeed he could see it through the window – he simply forgot to take this into account in figuring out where the control should be set. There is nothing in the least paradoxical about these explanations. We offer similar explanations all the time in explaining our own actions and those of other people. Indeed, since these explanations are so intimately bound up with our notions of excuse and blame, quick-wittedness, absent-mindedness and a host of others, it boggles the mind to try imagining how we would get on with each other if we resolved to renounce them. But if, following Dennett, we agree to swap the folk notion of belief for the intentional-system notion, then renounce them we must. It simply makes no sense to attribute inferential failings or inconsistent beliefs to an ideally rational system.

Our intuitive grasp on the notion of rational desire is rather more tenuous than our grasp on the analogous notion for belief. Still, there seem to be many cases in which we want to ascribe desires to people which are not rational on any plausible reading of that term. Jones is a successful writer, in good health, with many friends and admirers. But he says he wants to die, and ultimately takes his own life. Smith has a dreadful allergy to chocolate, and he knows it. One taste and he is condemned to a week of painful, debilitating hives. But he *really* wants that chocolate bar at the checkout counter. After staring at it for a minute, he buys it and gobbles it down. Brown collects spiders. They are of no economic value, and he doesn't even think they are very pretty. But it is his hobby. He wants to add to his collection a specimen of a species found only in the desert. So, despite his dislike of hot weather, he arranges to spend his vacation spider hunting in Nevada. By my lights, both Jones's desire and Smith's are simply irrational. As for Brown, "irrational" seems much too strong. Yet it is certainly implausible to say that he *ought* to want that spider. So, on Dennett's account, it is not a rational desire. But idealized intentional systems have all and only the desires they ought to have. Thus if we trade the common-sense notion of want for Dennett's IS want, we simply will not be able to say that Brown wants the spider or that Jones wants to die.

The existence of examples like the ones I have been sketching is not news to Dennett. From his earliest paper on intentional systems to his most recent, he has struggled with analogous cases. Unfortunately, however, he is far from clear on what he proposes to do about them. As I read him, there are two quite different lines that he proposes; I will call them the *hard line* and the *soft line*. Neither is carefully spelled out in Dennett's writings, and he often seems to endorse both within a single paper. Once they have been sharply stated, I think it will be clear that neither line is tenable.

The hard line

The hard line sticks firmly with the idealized notion of an intentional system and tries to minimize the importance of the gap between IS beliefs and IS desires and their folk-psychological namesakes. The basic ploy here is to suggest that when folk psychology ascribes contradictory beliefs to people or when it insists that a person does not believe some of the consequences of his beliefs, folk psychology undermines its own usefulness and threatens to lapse into incoherence. When this happens, we are forced back to the design stance or the physical stance:

> The presumption of rationality is so strongly entrenched in our inference habits that when our predictions [based on the assumption] prove false, we at first cast about for adjustments in the information possession conditions (he must not have heard, he must not know English, he must not have seen *x*, . . .) or goal weightings, before questioning the rationality of the system as a whole. In extreme cases personalities may prove to be so unpredictable from the intentional stance that we abandon it, and if we have accumulated a lot of evidence in the meanwhile about the nature of response patterns in the individual, we may find that a species of design stance can be effectively adopted. This is the fundamentally different attitude we occasionally adopt toward the insane. (*BS*, pp. 9–10)

Here, surely, Dennett is *just wrong* about what we do when predictions based on idealized rationality prove false. When a neighborhood boy gives me the wrong change from my purchase at his lemonade stand, I do not assume that he believes quarters are only worth 23 cents, nor that he wants to cheat me out of the 2 cents I am due. My *first* assumption is that he is not yet very good at doing sums in his head. Similarly, when a subject working on one of Wason and Johnson-Laird's deceptively difficult reasoning tasks gets the wrong answer, we are not likely to assume that he didn't understand the instructions, nor that he didn't want to get the right answer. Our *first* assumption is that he blew it; he made a mistake in reasoning.[8] What misleads Dennett here is that he is focusing on cases of counter-intuitive or unfamiliar cognitive failings. When someone seems to have made a mistake we can't readily imagine ourselves ever making, we do indeed begin to wonder whether he might perhaps have some unanticipated beliefs and desires. Or if a person seems to be making enormous numbers of mistakes and ending up with a substantial hoard of bizarre beliefs, we grow increasingly reluctant to ascribe beliefs and desires to him at all. Perhaps we count him among the insane. These facts will assume some importance later on. But they are of little use to the hard-line defense of intentional systems. For it is in the diverse domain of more or less familiar inferential shortcomings that common sense most readily and usefully portrays people as departing from an idealized standard of rationality.

Dennett frequently suggests that we cannot coherently describe a person whose beliefs depart from the idealized standard:

> Conflict arises . . . when a person falls short of perfect rationality, and avows beliefs that either are strongly disconfirmed by the available empirical evidence or are self-contradictory or contradict other avowals he has made. If we lean on the myth that a man is perfectly rational, we must find his avowals less than authoritative: "You *can't* mean – understand – what you're saying!"; if we lean on his right as a speaking intentional system to have his word accepted, we grant him an irrational set of beliefs. Neither position provides a stable resting place, for, as we saw earlier, *intentional explanation and prediction cannot be accommodated either to breakdown or to less than optimal design, so there is no coherent intentional description of such an impasse. (BS,* 20; last emphasis added)[9]

In the paper from which the quote is taken, Dennett uses 'intentional description,' 'intentional explanation' and the like for both common-sense belief-desire accounts and idealized intentional system accounts. The ambiguity this engenders is crucial in evaluating his claim. On the idealized intentional systems reading it is a tautology that "there is no coherent intentional description of such an impasse." But on the common-sense reading it is simply false. There is nothing at all incoherent about a (common-sense) intentional description of a man who has miscalculated the balance in his checking account!

The fact that folk psychology often comfortably and unproblematically views people as departing from the standard of full rationality often looms large in cases where questions of morality and responsibility are salient. Consider the case of Oscar, the engineer. It is his job to review planned operations at the factory and halt those that might lead to explosion. But one day there is an explosion and, bureaucracy being what it is, three years later Oscar is called before a board of inquiry. Why didn't he halt the hazardous operation? It looks bad for Oscar, since an independent expert has testified that the data Oscar had logically entail a certain equation, and it is a commonplace amongst competent safety engineers that the equation is a sure sign of trouble. But Oscar has an impressive defense. Granted the data he had entails the equation, and granted any competent engineer would know that the equation is a sign of trouble. But at the time of the accident neither Oscar nor anyone else knew that the data logically entailed the equation. It was only six months after the accident that Professor Brain at Cambridge proved a fundamental theorem needed to show that the data entail the equation. Without knowledge of the theorem, neither Oscar nor anyone else could be expected to believe that the data entail the equation.

At several places Dennett cites Quine as a fellow defender of the view that the ascription of inconsistent beliefs is problematic.

> To echo a theme I have long cherished in Quine's work, all the evidence –
> behavioral *and internal* – we acquire for the correctness of one of these ascriptions is
> not only evidence against the other, but the best sort of evidence. (*R*, p. 74)

However, Dennett misconstrues Quine's point. What Quine urges is not that *any* inconsistency is evidence of bad translation (or bad belief ascription), but rather that *obvious* inconsistency is a sign that something has gone wrong. For Quine, unlike Dennett, sees translation (and belief ascription) as a matter of putting ourselves in our subject's shoes. And the self we put in those shoes, we are too well aware, departs in many ways from the standard of optimal rationality. The point can be made vividly by contrasting Oscar, our safety engineer, with Otto, a lesser functionary. Otto is charged with the responsibility of memorizing a list of contingency plans: if the red light flashes, order the building evacuated; if the warning light goes on, turn the big blue valve; if the buzzer sounds, alert the manager. Now suppose that while he is on duty the red light flashes but Otto fails to order an evacuation. There is a strong prima-facie case that Otto is to be held responsible for the consequences. Either he failed to see the light (he was asleep or not paying due attention), or he did not memorize the contingency plans as he was obligated to, or he has some sinister motive. But, and this is the crucial point, it will be no excuse for Otto to claim that he had memorized the plan, saw the light, and was paying attention, but it just never occurred to him to order the evacuation. It is in these cases of apparently blatant or "incomprehensible" irrationality that we hunt first for hidden motives or beliefs. For, absent these, the subject must be judged irrational in a way we cannot imagine ourselves being irrational; and it is this sort of irrationality that threatens the application of our common-sense notions of belief and desire.

In Dennett's writings there are frequent hints of a second strategy for defending the hard line, a strategy which relies on an evolutionary argument. He cheerfully concedes that he has "left [his] claim about the relation between rationality and evolutionary considerations so open-ended that it is hard to argue against efficiently" (*R*, p. 73). Still, I think it is important to try wringing some arguments out of Dennett's vague meditations on this topic. As I read him, Dennett is exploring a pair of ideas for showing that the gap between IS notions and folk notions is much smaller than some have feared. If he can show this, the hard line will have been vindicated.

The first idea is suggested by a passage (*BS*, pp. 8–9) in which Dennett asks whether we could adopt the intentional stance toward exotic creatures encountered on an alien planet. His answer is that we could, provided "we have reason to suppose that a process of natural selection has been in effect . . ." (*BS*, p. 8). The argument seems to be that natural selection favors true beliefs, and thus will favor cognitive processes which generally yield true beliefs in the organism's natural environment. So if an organism is the product of natural selection, we can safely assume that most of its beliefs will be true, and most of its belief-forming strategies will be rational. Departures from the normative standard required by the intentional stance will be few and far between.

For two quite different reasons, this argument is untenable. First, it is simply not the case that natural selection favors true beliefs over false ones. What natural selection does favor is beliefs which yield selective advantage. And there are many environmental circumstances in which false beliefs will be more useful than true ones. In these circumstances, natural selection ought to favor cognitive processes which yield suitable false beliefs and disfavor processes which yield true beliefs. Moreover, even when having true beliefs is optimal, natural selection may often favor a process that yields false beliefs most of the time, but which has a high probability of yielding true beliefs when it counts. Thus, for example, in an environment with a wide variety of suitable foods, an organism may do very well if it radically overgeneralizes about what is inedible. If eating a certain food caused illness on a single occasion, the organism would immediately come to believe (falsely, let us assume) that all passingly similar foods are poisonous as well. When it comes to food poisoning, *better safe than sorry* is a policy that recommends itself to natural selection.[10]

The second fault in the argument I am attributing to Dennett is a subtle but enormously important one. As stated, the argument slips almost unnoticeably from the claim that natural selection favors cognitive processes which yield true beliefs in the natural environment to the claim that natural selection favors *rational* belief-forming strategies. But, even if the first claim were true, the second would not follow. There are many circumstances in which inferential strategies which from a normative standpoint are patently invalid will nonetheless generally yield the right answer. The social-psychology literature is rich with illustrations of inferential strategies which stand subjects in good stead ordinarily but which subjects readily overextend, with unhappy results.[11]

So long as we recognize a distinction between a normative theory of inference or decision making and a set of inferential practices which (in the right environment) generally get the right (or selectively useful) answer, it will be clear that the two need not, and generally do not, coincide. However, in a number of places Dennett seems to be suggesting that there really *is* no distinction here, that by "normative theory of inference and decision" he simply *means* "practices favored by natural selection." This move is at the core of the second idea I see in Dennett for using evolutionary notions to buttress the hard line (Cf. *R*, pp. 73–4.) And buttress it would! For it would then become *tautologous* that naturally evolved creatures are intentional systems, believing, wanting and doing what they ought, save when they are malfunctioning. Yet Dennett will have to pay a heavy price for turning the hard line into a tautology. For if *this* is what he means by "normative theory of belief and decision," then such established theories as deductive and inductive logic, decision theory and game theory are of no help in assessing what an organism "ought to believe." Natural selection, as we have already noted, sometimes smiles upon cognitive processes that depart substantially from the canons of logic and decision theory. So these established theories and our guesses about how to extend them will be of no help in assessing what an intentional system should believe, desire or do. Instead, to predict from the intentional stance we should need a detailed study of the organism's physiology, its ecological environment and its history. But predicting from the intentional stance, characterized in *this* way, is surely not to be recommended when we "doubt the practicality of prediction from the design or physical stance" (*BS*, p. 8). Nor, obviously, does *this* intentional stance promise to yield belief and desire attributions that are all but co-extensive with those made in common sense.

This is all I shall have to say by way of meeting the hard line head on. I think it is fair to conclude that the hard line simply cannot be maintained. The differences separating the IS notions of belief and desire from their common-sense counterparts are anything but insubstantial. Before turning to Dennett's soft line, we should note a further unwelcome consequence of rejecting folk psychology in favor of intentional-system theory. During the last decade, cognitive psychologists have become increasingly interested in studying the strengths and foibles of human reasoning. There is a substantial and growing literature aimed at uncovering predictable departures from normative standards of reasoning and decision making, almost all of it implicitly or explicitly cast in the idiom of folk psychology.[12] Were we to replace folk notions with their intentional-system analogs, we should have to conclude that all of this work lining the boundaries of human rationality is simply incoherent. For, as Dennett notes, "the presuppositions of intentional explanation . . . put prediction of *lapses* in principle beyond its scope . . ." (*BS*, p. 246).[13]

The soft line

In contrast with the hard line, which tries to minimize the size or importance of the difference between folk and IS notions, the soft line acknowledges a substantial and significant divergence. To deal with the problems this gap creates, the soft line proposes some fiddling with the idealized notion of an intentional system. The basic idea is that once we have an idealized theory of intentional systems in hand, we can study an array of variations on the idealized theme. We can construct theories about "imperfect intentional systems" (the term is mine, not Dennett's) which have specified deficiences in memory, reasoning power, etc. And we can attempt to determine empirically which imperfect intentional system best predicts the behavior of a particular subject or species. Rather than assuming the intentional stance toward an organism or person, we may assume one of a range of "imperfect intentional stances," from which it will make sense to ascribe a less than fully rational set of beliefs and desires. From these various stances we can give intentional descriptions of our cognitive shortcomings and elaborate an empirical science which maps the inferential strengths and weaknesses of humans and other creatures. We can also legitimize our folk-psychological descriptions of ourselves – protecting "personhood from the march of science" (*R*, p. 75) – by appeal to the imperfect-intentional-system theory which best predicts our actual behavior. But *genuine* intentional-system theory (*sans phrase*) would have a definite pride of place among these theories of imperfect intentional systems. For all of the latter would be variations on the basic IS framework.

Dennett, with his disconcerting penchant for working both sides of the street, never flatly endorses the soft line, though it is clear that he has pondered something like it:

> Consider a set *T* of transformations that take beliefs into beliefs. The problem is to determine the set T_S for each intentional system *S*, so that if we know that *S* believes *p*, we will be able to determine other things that *S* believes by seeing what the transformations of *p* are for T_S. If *S* were ideally rational, every valid transformation would be in T_S; *S* would believe every logical consequence of every belief (and, ideally, *S* would have no false beliefs). Now we know that no actual intentional system will be ideally rational; so we must suppose any actual system will have a *T* with less in it. But we also know that, to qualify as an intentional system at all, *S* must have a *T* with some integrity; *T* cannot be empty. (*BS*, p. 21)

In the next few sentences, however, Dennett expresses qualms about the soft line:

> What rationale could we have, however, for fixing some set between the extremes and calling it *the* set for belief (for *S*, for earthlings, for ten-year-old-girls)? This is another way of asking whether we could replace Hintikka's normative theory of belief with an empirical theory of belief, and, if so, what evidence we would use. "Actually," one is tempted to say, "people do believe contradictions on occasion, as their utterances demonstrate; so any adequate logic of belief or analysis of the concept of belief must accommodate this fact." But any attempt to *legitimize* human fallibility in a theory of belief by fixing a permissible level of error would be like adding one more

rule to chess: an Official Tolerance Rule to the effect that any game of chess containing no more than k moves that are illegal relative to the other rules of the game is a legal game of chess. (*BS*, p. 21)

In a more recent paper, Dennett sounds more enthusiastic about the soft line:

> *Of course* we don't all sit in the dark in our studies like mad Leibnizians rationalistically excogitating behavioral predictions from pure, idealized concepts of our neighbors, nor do we derive all our readiness to attribute desires to a careful generation of them from the ultimate goal of survival. . . . Rationalistic generation of attributions is augmented and even corrected on occasion by empirical generalizations about belief and desire that guide our attributions and are learned more or less inductively. . . . I grant the existence of all this naturalistic generalization, and its role in the normal calculation of folk psychologists – i.e., all of us. . . . *I would insist, however, that all this empirically obtained lore is laid over a fundamental generative and normative framework that has the features I have described.* (*TK*, pp. 14–15, last emphasis added)

Whatever Dennett's considered view may be, I think the soft line is clearly preferable to the hard line. Indeed, the soft line is similar to a view that I have myself defended.[14] As a way of focusing in on my misgivings about the soft line, let me quickly sketch my own view and note how it differs from the view I am trying to foist on Dennett. Mine is an effort squarely situated in what Dennett calls "the anthropological quest" (*TK*, p. 6). I want to describe as accurately as possible just what we are up to when we engage in the "folk practice" of ascribing beliefs to one another and dealing with one another partly on the basis of these ascriptions. My theory is an elaboration on Quine's observation that in ascribing beliefs to others "we project ourselves into what, from his remarks and other indications, we imagine the speaker's state of mind to have been, and then we say what, in our language, is natural and relevant for us in the state thus feigned" (*Word and Object*, p. 219). As I see it, when we say *S believes that p* we are saying that *S* is in a certain sort of functionally characterized psychological state, viz., a "belief state." The role of the "content sentence", *p*, is to specify *which* belief state it is. If we imagine that we ourselves were now to utter *p* in earnest, the belief we are attributing to *S* is one *similar* (along specified dimensions) to the belief which would cause our own imagined assertion. One of the dimensions of similarity that figures in belief ascription is the pattern of inference that the belief states in question enter into. When the network of potential inferences surrounding a subject's belief state differs substantially from the network surrounding our own belief that *p*, we are reluctant to count the subject's belief as a belief *that p*. Thus we will not have any comfortable way of ascribing content to the belief states of a subject whose inferential network is markedly different from ours. Since we take ourselves to approximate rationality, this explains the fact, noted by Dennett, that intentional description falters in the face of egregious irrationality. It also explains the fact, missed by Dennett, that familiar irrationality – the sort we know ourselves to be guilty of – poses no problem for folk psychology.

A full elaboration of my theory would be a long story, out of place here. What is important for our present purposes is to note the differences between my account and what I have been calling Dennett's soft line. These differences are two. First, my story does not portray folk psychology as an *instrumentalist* theory. Belief states are *functional* states which can and do play a role in the causation of behavior. Thus folk psychology is not immune from the advance of science. If it turns out that the human brain does not have the sort of functional organization assumed in our folk theory, then there are no such things as beliefs and desires. Second, the notion of idealized rationality plays *no role at all* in my account. In ascribing content to belief states, we measure others not against an idealized standard but against ourselves. It is in virtue of this Protagorean parochialism that the exotic and the insane fall outside the reach of intentional explanation.

So much for the difference between my view and Dennett's. Why should mine be preferred? There are two answers. First, I think it is simply wrong that we ordinarily conceive of beliefs and desires in instrumentalist terms – as abstracta rather than illata. It is, however, no easy task to take aim at Dennett's instrumentalism, since the target refuses to stay still. Consider:

Folk psychology is *instrumentalistic* . . . Beliefs and desires of folk psychology . . . are abstracta. (*TK*, p. 13)

It is not particularly to the point to argue against me that folk psychology is *in fact* committed to beliefs and desires as distinguishable, causally interacting *illata*; what must be shown is that it ought to be. The latter claim I will deal with in due course. The former claim I *could* concede without embarrassment to my overall project, but I do not concede it, for it seems to me that the evidence is quite strong that our ordinary notion of belief has next to nothing of the concrete in it. (*TK*, p. 15)

The *ordinary* notion of belief no doubt does place beliefs somewhere midway between being *illata* and being *abstracta*. (*TK*, p. 16)

In arguing for his sometimes instrumentalism Dennett conjures the sad tale of Pierre, shot dead by Jacques in Trafalgar Square. Jacques

is apprehended on the spot by Sherlock; Tom reads about it in the *Times* and Boris learns of it in *Pravda*. Now Jacques, Sherlock, Tom and Boris have had remarkably different experiences – to say nothing of their earlier biographies and future prospects – but there is one thing they share: they all believe that a Frenchman has committed a murder in Trafalgar Square. They did not all *say* this, not even "to themselves"; *that proposition* did not, we can suppose, "occur to" any of them, and even if it had, it would have had entirely different import for Jacques, Sherlock, Tom and Boris. (*TK*, p. 15)

Dennett's point is that while all four men believe that a Frenchman committed a murder in Trafalgar Square, their histories, interests and relations to the deed are so different that they could hardly be thought to share a single, functionally characterizable state. This is quite right, but it does not force us to view beliefs as abstracta. For if, as my theory insists, there is a *similarity* claim embedded in belief ascriptions, then we should expect these ascriptions to be both vague and sensitive to pragmatic context. For Jacques and Boris both to believe that a Frenchman committed a murder in Trafalgar Square, they need not be in the very same functional state, but only in states that are sufficiently similar for the communicative purposes at hand.

As Dennett notes, one need not be crucially concerned with what "folk psychology is in fact committed to." Since he aims to replace folk psychology with intentional-system notions, it would suffice to show that the instrumentalism of these latter notions is no disadvantage. But here again I am skeptical. It is my hunch that our concept of ourselves as moral agents simply will not sit comfortably with the view that beliefs and desires are mere computational conveniences that correspond in no interesting way to what goes on inside the head. I cannot offer much of an argument for my hunch, though I am encouraged by the fact that Dennett seems to share the intuition lying behind it:

> Stich accurately diagnoses and describes the strategic role I envisage for the concept of an intentional system, permitting the claim that human beings are genuine believers and desirers to survive almost any imaginable discoveries in cognitive and physiological psychology, thus making our status as moral agents well nigh invulnerable to scientific disconfirmation. Not 'in principle' invulnerable, for in a science-fiction mood we can imagine startling discoveries (e.g., some 'people' are organic puppets remotely controlled by Martians) that would upset any particular home truths about believers and moral agenthood you like. . . . (*R*, p. 73)

Now if our concept of moral agenthood were really compatible with the intentional-system construal of beliefs and desires, it is hard to see why the imagined discovery about Martians should be in the least unsettling. For, controlled by Martians or not, organic puppets are still intentional systems in perfectly good standing. So long as their behavior is usefully predictable from the intentional stance, the transceivers inside their heads sanction no skepticism about whether they really have IS beliefs and IS desires. But Dennett is right, of course. We would not count his organic puppets as believers or moral agents. The reason, I submit, is that the morally relevant concept of belief is not an instrumentalistic concept.

The second reason for preferring my line to Dennett's soft line is that the idea of a *normative* theory of beliefs and desires, which is central to Dennett's view, plays no role in mine. And this notion, I would urge, is one we are best rid of. Recall that from the outset we have been relying on rough and ready intuitions about what an organism ought to believe, desire and do, and assuming that these intuitions could be elaborated and systematized into a theory. But I am inclined to think that this assumption is mistaken. Rather, it would appear that the intuitions Dennett exploits are underlain by a variety of different ideas about what an organism ought to believe or desire, ideas which as often as not pull in quite different directions. Sometimes it is an evolutionary story which motivates the intuition that a belief or desire is the one a well-designed intentional system should have. At other times intuitions are guided by appeal to logic or decision theory. But as we have seen, the evolutionary account of what an organism ought to believe and desire just will not do for Dennett, since it presupposes an abundance of information about the ecological niche and physiological workings of the organism. Nor is there any serious prospect of elaborating logic and decision theory into a suitably general account of what an organism ought to believe and desire. Indeed, apart from a few special cases, I think our intuitions about what an organism ought to believe and desire are simply nonexistent. The problem is not merely that we lack a worked-out normative theory of belief and desire; it runs much deeper. For in general we have no idea what such a normative theory would be telling us. We do not really know what it *means* to say that an organism *ought to have* a given belief or desire. Consider some examples:

Ought Descartes to have believed his theory of vortices?
Ought Nixon to have believed that he would not be impeached?
Ought William James to have believed in the existence of a personal God?
Should all people have perfect memories, retaining for life all beliefs save those for which they later acquire negative evidence?

In each of these cases our grasp of what the question is supposed to *mean* is at best tenuous. The prospects of a *general theory* capable of answering all of them in a motivated way are surely very dim. Worse still, the general theory of intentional systems that Dennett would have us work toward must tell us not only what *people* in various situations ought to believe, but also what other animals ought to believe. Ought the frog to believe that there is an insect flying off to the right? Or merely that there is some food there? Or perhaps should it only have a conditional belief: if it flicks its tongue in a certain way, something yummy will end up in its mouth? Suppose the fly is of a species that causes frogs acute indigestion. Ought the frog to believe this? Does it make a difference how many fellow frogs he has seen come to grief after munching on similar bugs? A normative theory of desire is, if anything, more problematic. Should I want to father as many offspring as possible? Should the frog?

To the extent that these questions are obscure, the notion of a normative theory of belief and desire is obscure. And that obscurity in turn infects much of what Dennett says about intentional systems and the intentional stance. Perhaps Dennett can dispel some of the mystery. But in the interim I am inclined to think that the normatively appropriate attitude is the skepticism I urged in my opening paragraph.[15]

NOTES

1 References to Dennett's writings will be identified in parentheses in the text. I will use the following abbreviations:
   BS = Daniel Dennett, *Brainstorms* (Montgomery, Vt: Bradford Books, 1978).
   TK = Daniel Dennett, "Three kinds of intentional psychology," in *Reduction, Time, and Reality* (ed. R. A. Healey), Cambridge University Press, 1981.
   R = Daniel Dennett, "Reply to Professor Stich," *Philosophical Books*, 21, 2 (April, 1980).
   TB = Daniel Dennett, "True believers: The intentional strategy and why it works," reprinted in this volume above.
2 For his arguments on this point, cf. "Brain writing and mind reading," (*BS*, pp. 39–50) and "A cure for the common code," (*BS*, pp. 90–108).
3 This "anthropological quest," when pursued systematically is the business of the cognitive simulator. Cf., for example, Roger Shank and Robert Abelson, *Scripts, Plans, Goals and Understanding* (Hillsdale, NJ: Lawrence Erlbaum Associates, 1977); also Aaron Sloman, *The Computer Revolution in Philosophy* (Atlantic Highlands, NJ: Humanities Press, 1978), ch. 4.
4 Skinner often muddies the waters by claiming to offer "translations" of common-sense

mentalistic terms into the language of behaviorism. But, as Dennett and others have noted, (*BS*, pp. 53–70) these "translations" generally utterly fail to capture the meaning or even the extension of the common-sense term being "translated."

5   For an elaboration of the point, cf. Thomas Nagel, "Armstrong on the mind," *Philosophical Review*, 79 (1970), pp. 394–403.

6   An entirely parallel strategy works for those other common-sense mental phenomena which Dennett takes to be essential to our concept of ourselves as persons – e.g., consciousness (*BS*, p. 269). If we can give an acceptable intentional system *Ersatz* for the folk-psychological notion of consciousness, we need have no fear that advances in science will threaten our personhood by showing that the notion of consciousness is otiose in the causal explanation of our behavior.

7   For some qualms about Dennett's treatment of "program resistant" features of mentality like pains, see my "Headaches," *Philosophical Books*, April 1980.

8   Cf. P. C. Wason and P. N. Johnson-Laird, *The Psychology of Human Reasoning: Structure and Content* (London: Batsford, 1972).

9   For parallel passages, cf. *TB*, p. 19; *R*, p. 74; *BS*, p. 22.

10 For a detailed discussion of some examples and further references, cf. H. A. Lewis, "The argument from evolution," *Proceedings of the Aristotelian Society*, Supplementary vol. LIII, 1979; also my "Could man be an irrational animal?" *Synthese* 64 (1985), 115–35.

11 Cf. Richard Nisbett and Lee Ross, *Human Inference* (Englewood Cliffs, NJ: Prentice-Hall, 1980).

12 E.g., Nisbett and Ross, ibid., and Wason and Johnson-Laird, ibid., along with the many studies cited in these books.

13 Dennett appends the following footnote to the quoted sentence: "In practice we predict lapses at the intentional level ('You watch! He'll forget all about your knight after you move the queen') on the basis of loose-jointed inductive hypotheses about individual or widespread human frailties. These hypotheses are expressed in intentional terms, but if they were given rigorous support, they would in the process be recast as predictions from the design or physical stance" (*BS*, p. 246). So the scientific study of intentionally described inferential shortcomings can aspire to no more than "loose-jointed hypotheses" in need of recasting. But cf. *TK*, pp. 11–12, where Dennett pulls in his horns a bit.

14 In "On the ascription of content," in A. Woodfield (ed.), *Thought and Object* (Oxford University Press, 1982).

15 I have learned a good deal from the helpful comments of Bo Dahlbom, Robert Cummins, Philip Pettit and Robert Richardson.

Making Sense of Ourselves

DANIEL C. DENNETT

Stich has (again[1]) given a lively, sympathetic, and generally accurate account of my view and once again he disagrees, this time with more detailed objections and counterproposals. My proposed refinement of the folk notion of belief (via the concept of an *intentional system*) would, he claims, "leave us unable to say a great deal that we now wish to say about ourselves." For this to be an objection, he

"Making Sense of Ourselves" by D. C. Dennett first appeared in *Philosophical Topics* 12 (1981), pp. 63–81, and is reprinted here by permission.

must mean it would leave us unable to say a great deal we *rightly* want to say – because it is true, presumably. We must see what truths, then, he supposes are placed out of reach by my account. Many of them lie, he says, in the realm of facts about our cognitive shortcomings, which can be given no coherent description according to my account: "if we trade up to the intentional-system notions of belief and desire ... then we simply would not be able to say all those things we need to say about ourselves and our fellows when we deal with each other's idiosyncrasies, shortcomings, and cognitive growth" (this volume, p. 173). He gives several examples. Among them are the forgetful astronaut, the boy at the lemonade stand who gives the wrong change, and the man who has miscalculated the balance in his checking account. These three are cases of simple, unmysterious cognitive failure – cases of people *making mistakes* – and Stich claims that my view cannot accommodate them. One thing that is striking about all three cases is that in spite of Stich's summary expression of his objection, these are *not* cases of "familiar irrationality" or cases of "inferential failings" at all. They are not cases of what we would *ordinarily* call irrationality, and since there are quite compelling cases of what we *would* ordinarily call irrationality (and since Stich knows them and indeed cites some of the best documented cases[2]), it is worth asking why he cites instead these cases of miscalculation as proof against my view. I shall address this question shortly, but first I should grant that these are in any case examples of suboptimal behavior of the sort my view is not supposed to be able to handle.

I hold that such errors, as either *malfunctions* or the outcomes of *misdesign*, are unpredictable from the intentional stance, a claim with which Stich might agree, but I go on to claim that there will inevitably be an instability or problematic point in the mere *description* of such lapses at the intentional system level – at the level at which it is the agent's beliefs and desires that are attributed. And here it seems at first that Stich must be right. For although we seldom if ever suppose we can *predict* people's particular mistakes from our ordinary folk-psychological perspective, there seems to be nothing more straightforward than the folk-psychological *description* of such familiar cases. This presumably is part of the reason why Stich chose these cases: they are so uncontroversial.

Let's look more closely, though, at one of the cases, adding more detail. The boy's sign says "LEMONADE – 12 cents a glass." I hand him a quarter, he gives me a glass of lemonade and then a dime and a penny change. He's made a mistake. Now what can we *expect* from him when we point out his error to him? That he will exhibit surprise, blush, smite his forehead, apologize, and give me two cents. Why do we expect him to exhibit surprise? Because we attribute to him the belief that he's given me the right change – he'll be surprised to learn that he hasn't.[3] Why do we expect him to blush? Because we attribute to him the desire not to cheat (or be seen to cheat) his customers. Why do we expect him to smite his forehead or give some other acknowledgment of his lapse? Because we attribute to him not only the belief that 25 - 12 = 13, but also the belief that that's obvious, and the belief that no one his age should make any mistakes about it. While we can't predict his particular error – though we might have made an actuarial prediction that he'd probably make some such error before the day was out – we can pick up the skein of our intentional interpretation once he has made his mistake and predict his further reactions and activities with no more than the usual attendant risk. At first glance then it seems that belief attribution in this instance is as easy, predictive and stable as it ever is.

But now look yet more closely. The boy has made a mistake all right, but *exactly which mistake?* This all depends, of course, on how we tell the tale – there are many different possibilities. But no matter which story we tell, we will uncover a problem. For instance, we might plausibly suppose that so far as all our evidence to date goes, the boy believes:

1 that he has given me the right change
2 that I gave him a quarter
3 that his lemonade costs 12 cents
4 that a quarter is 25 cents
5 that a dime is 10 cents
6 that a penny is 1 cent
7 that he gave me a dime and a penny change
8 that $25 - 12 = 13$
9 that $10 + 1 = 11$
10 that $11 \neq 13$

Only (1) is a false belief, but how can he be said to believe *that* if he believes all the others? It surely is not plausible to claim that he has *mis-inferred* (1) from any of the others, directly or indirectly. That is, we would not be inclined to attribute to him the inference of (1) directly from (7) and – what? Perhaps he would infer

11 that he gave me 11 cents change

from (9) and (7) – he *ought to*, after all – but *it would not make sense* to suppose he *inferred* (1) from (11) unless he were under the misapprehension

12 that 11 cents is the right change from a quarter.

We would expect him to believe *that* if he believed

13 that $25 - 12 = 11$

and while we *might* have told the tale so that the boy simply had this false belief – and *didn't* believe (8) – (we can imagine, for instance, that he thought that's what his father told him when he asked), this would yield us a case that was not at all a plausible case of either irrationality or even miscalculation, but just a case of a perfectly rational thinker with a single false belief (which then generates other false beliefs such as (1)). Stich rightly does not want to consider such a case, for of course I do acknowledge the possibility of mere false belief, when special stories can be told about its acquisition. If we then attribute (13) *while retaining* (8) we get a blatant and bizarre case of irrationality: someone believing simultaneously that $25 - 12 = 13$, $25 - 12 = 11$ and $13 \neq 11$. This is not what we had supposed at all, but so strange that we are bound to find the conjoined attributions frankly incredible. Something has to give. If we say, as Stich proposes, that the boy "is not yet very good at doing sums in his head" what is the implication? That he doesn't *really* believe the inconsistent triad, that he *sort* of understands arithmetical notions well enough to have the cited beliefs? That is, if we say what Stich says and *also* attribute the inconsistent beliefs, we still have the problem of brute irrationality too stark to countenance; if we take Stich's observation to temper or withdraw the attribution, then Stich is agreeing with me: even the simplest and most familiar errors require us to resort to scare-quotes or other *caveats* about the literal truth of the total set of attributions.

There is something obtuse, of course, about the quest exhibited above for a total belief-set surrounding the error. The demand that we find an inference – even a *mis*-inference – to the false belief (1) is the demand that we find a practice or tendency with something like a rationale, an exercise of which has led in this instance to (1). No mere succession in time or even regular causation is enough in itself to count as an inference. For instance, were we to learn that the boy was led directly from his belief (6) that a penny is 1 cent to his belief (2) that I gave him a quarter, then no matter how habitual and ineluctable the passage in him from (6) to (2), we wouldn't call it *inference*.[4] Inferences are passages of thought for which there is a reason, but people don't make mistakes for reasons. Demanding reasons (as opposed to "mere" causes) for mistakes generates spurious edifices of belief, as we have just seen in (11–13), but simply acquiescing in the attribution of reasonless belief is no better. It is not as if *nothing* led the boy to believe (1); it is not as if that belief was utterly baseless. We do not suppose, for instance, that he would have believed (1) had his hand been empty, or filled with quarters, or had I given him a dollar or a credit card. He does somehow base his mistaken belief on a distorted or confused or mistaken perception of what he is handing me, what I have handed him, and the appropriate relationships between them.

The boy is basically on top of the situation, and is no mere change-giving robot; nevertheless, we must descend from the level of beliefs and desires to some other level of theory to describe his mistake, since no account in terms of his beliefs and desires will make sense completely. At some point our account will have to cope with the sheer senselessness of the transition in any error.

My perhaps tendentious examination of a single example hardly constitutes an argument for my general claim that this will always be the outcome. It is presented as a challenge: try for yourself to tell the total belief story that surrounds such a simple error and see if you do not discover just the quandary I have illustrated.

Mistakes of the sort exhibited in this example are slips in good procedures, not manifestations of an allegiance to a bad procedure or principle. The partial confirmation of our inescapable working hypothesis that the boy is fundamentally rational is his blushing acknowledgement of his error. He doesn't defend his action once it is brought to his attention, but willingly corrects his error. This is in striking contrast to the behavior of agents in the putative cases of genuine irrationality cited by Stich. In these instances, people not only persist in their "errors," but stubbornly defend their practice – and find defenders among philosophers as well.[5] It is at least *not obvious* that there are any cases of systematically irrational behavior or thinking. The cases that have been proposed are all controversial, which is just what my view predicts; no such thing as a cut-and-dried or obvious case of "familiar irrationality." This is not to say that we are always rational, but that when we are not, the cases defy description in ordinary terms of belief and desire. There is no mystery about why this should be so. An intentional interpretation of an agent is an exercise that attempts to *make sense* of the agent's acts, and when acts occur that make no sense, they cannot be straightforwardly interpreted in sense-making terms. Something must give: we allow that the agent either only "sort of" believes this or that, or believes this or that "for all practical purposes," or believes some falsehood which creates a context in which what had appeared to be irrational turns out to be rational after all. (See, e.g., Cohen's suggestions, op. cit, n. 5). These particular fall-back positions are themselves subject to the usual tests on belief attribution, so merely finding a fall-back position is not confirming it. If it is disconfirmed, the search goes on for another saving interpretation. If there is no *saving* interpretation – if the person in question is irrational – no interpretation at all will be settled on.

The same retreat from the abyss is found in the simple cases of miscalculation and error of which Stich reminds us, but with a few added wrinkles worth noting. In the case of the lemonade seller, we might excuse ourselves from further attempts to sort out his beliefs by just granting that while he knew (and thus believed)[6] all the right facts, he "just forgot" or "overlooked" a few of them temporarily – until we reminded him of them. This has the appearance of being a modest little psychological hypothesis: something roughly to the effect that although something or other was stored safe and sound inside the agent's head where it belonged, its address was temporarily misplaced. Some such story may well in the end by supported within a confirmed and detailed psychological theory,[7] but it is important to note that at the present time we make these hypotheses *simply* on the basis of our abhorrence of the vacuum of contradiction.

For instance, consider absentmindedness – a well-named affliction, it seems. At breakfast I am reminded that I am playing tennis with Paul instead of having lunch today. At 12.45 I find myself polishing off dessert when Paul, in tennis gear, appears at my side and jolts me into recollection. "It completely slipped my mind!" I aver, blushing at my own absentmindedness. But why do I say *that*? Is it because, as I recall, not a single conscious thought about my tennis date passed through my head after breakfast? That might be true, but perhaps no conscious thought that I was going to lunch today occurred to me in the interim either, and yet here I am, finishing my lunch. Perhaps if I *had* thought consciously about going to lunch as usual, that very thought would have reminded me that I wasn't, in fact. And in any case, even if I remember now that it *did* once occur to me in mid-morning that I was to play tennis today – to no avail, evidently – I will still say it subsequently slipped my mind.

Why, indeed, am I eager to *insist* that it completely slipped my mind? To assure Paul that I haven't stood him up on purpose? Perhaps, but that should be obvious enough not to need saying, and if my eagerness is a matter of not wanting to insult him, I am not entirely succeeding, since it is not at all flattering to be so utterly forgotten. I think a primary motive for my assertion is just to banish the possibility that otherwise would arise: I am starkly irrational; I believe both that I am playing tennis at lunch and that I am free to go to lunch as usual. I cannot act on both beliefs at once; whichever I act on, I declare the other to have slipped my mind. Not on any introspective evidence (for I may, after all, have *repeatedly* thought of the matter in the relevant interim period), but on *general principles*. It does not matter how close to noon I have reflected on my tennis date; if I end up having lunch as usual the tennis date *must have* slipped my mind at the last minute.

There is no direct relationship between one's conscious thoughts and the occasions when we will say something has slipped one's mind. Suppose someone asks me to have lunch today and I reply that I can't: I have another appointment then, but for the life of me I can't recall what it is – it will come to me later. Here although in one regard my tennis date has slipped my mind, in another it has not, since my belief that I am playing tennis, while not (momentarily) consciously retrievable, is yet doing some work for me: it is keeping me from making the conflicting appointment. I hop in my car and I get to the intersection: left takes me home for lunch; right takes me to the tennis court; I turn right this time without benefit of an accompanying conscious thought to the effect that I am playing tennis today at lunchtime. It has not slipped my mind, though; had it slipped my mind, I would no doubt have turned left.[8] It is even possible to have something slip one's mind while one is thinking of it consciously! "Be careful of this pan," I say, "it is very hot" – reaching out and burning myself on the very pan I am warning about. The height of absentmindedness, no doubt, but possible. We would no doubt say something like "You didn't think what you were saying!" – which doesn't mean that the words issued from my mouth as from a zombie, but that if I had believed – *really* believed – what I was saying, I *couldn't* have done what I did. If I can in this manner not think what I am saying, I could also in about as rare a case not think what I was thinking. I could think "careful of that hot pan" *to myself*, while ignoring the advice.

There is some temptation to say that in such a case, while I knew full well that the pan was hot, I just forgot for a moment. Perhaps we want to acknowledge this sort of forgetting, but note that it is not at all the forgetting we suppose to occur when we say I have forgotten the telephone number of the taxicab company I called two weeks ago, or forgotten the date of Hume's birth. In those cases we presume the information is gone for good. Reminders and hints won't help me recall. When I say "I completely forgot our tennis date," I don't at all mean I completely forgot it – as would be evidenced if on Paul's arrival in tennis gear I was blankly baffled by his presence, denying any recollection of having made the date.

Some other familiar locutions of folk psychology are in the same family: 'notice', 'overlook', 'ignore', and even 'conclude.' One's initial impression is that these terms are applied by us to our own cases on the basis of direct introspection. That is, we classify various conscious acts of our own as concludings, noticings, and the like – but what about ignorings and overlookings? Do we find ourselves doing these things? Only retrospectively, and in a self-justificatory or self-critical mood: "I ignored the development of the pawns on the queen side" says the chess player, "because it was so clear that the important development involved the knights on the king side." Had he lost the game, he would have said "I simply overlooked the development of the pawns on the queen side, since I was under the misapprehension that the king side attack was my only problem."

Suppose someone asks, "Did you *notice* the way Joe was evading your questions yesterday?" I might answer, "yes," even though I certainly did not *think any conscious thoughts* at the time (that I can recall) about the way Joe was evading my questions; if I can nevertheless see that my reactions to him (as I recall them) took appropriate account of his evasiveness, I will (justly) aver that I did notice. Since I did the appropriate thing in the circumstances, I must have noticed, mustn't I?

In order just now for you to get the gist of my tale of absentmindedness, you had to conclude from my remark about "polishing off dessert" that I had just finished a lunch and missed my tennis date. And surely you did so conclude, but did you *consciously* conclude? Did anything remotely like "Hmm, he must have had lunch . . ." run through your head? Probably not. It is no more likely that the boy selling lemonade consciously thought that the eleven cents in his hand was the right change. "Well, if he didn't *consciously* think it, he unconsciously thought it; we must posit an unconscious controlling thought to that effect to explain, or ground, or *be* (!) his belief that he is giving the right change."

It is tempting to suppose that when we retreat from the abyss of irrationality and find a different level of explanation on which to flesh out our description of errors (or, for that matter, of entirely felicitous passages of thought), the arena we properly arrive at is the folk-psychological arena of thinkings, concludings, forgettings, and the like – not mere abstract mental *states* like belief, but concrete and clockable episodes or activities or processes that can be modeled by psychological model-builders and measured and tested quite directly in experiments. But as the examples just discussed *suggest* (though they do not by any means *prove*), we would be unwise to model our serious, academic psychology too closely on these putative illata of folk theory. We postulate all these apparent activities and mental processes *in order to make sense* of the behavior we observe – in order, in fact, to make as much sense as possible of the behavior, especially when the behavior we observe is our own. Philosophers of mind used to go out of their way to insist that one's access to one's own case in such matters is quite unlike one's access to others', but as we learn more about various forms of psycho-pathology and even the foibles of apparently normal people,[9] it becomes more plausible to suppose that although there are still some small corners of unchallenged privilege, some matters about which our authority is invincible, each of us is in most regards a sort of inveterate auto-psychologist, effortlessly *inventing* intentional interpretations of our own actions in an inseparable mix of confabulation, retrospective self-justification and (on occasion, no doubt) good theorizing. The striking cases of confabulation by subjects under hypnosis or suffering from various well-documented brain disorderse (Korsakoff's syndrome, split brains, various "agnosias") raise the prospect that such virtuoso displays of utterly unsupported self-interpretation are not manifestations of a skill suddenly learned in response to trauma, but of a normal way of life unmasked.[10]

As creatures of our own attempts to make sense of ourselves, the putative mental activities of folk theory are hardly a neutral field of events and processes to which we can resort for explanations when the normative demands of intentional system theory run afoul of a bit of irrationality. Nor can we suppose their counterparts in a developed cognitive psychology, or even their "realizations" in wetware of the brain, will fare better. Stich holds out the vision of an entirely norm-free, naturalized psychology that can *settle* the indeterminacies of intentional system theory by appeal, ultimately, to the presence or absence of real, functionally salient, causally potent states and events that can be identified and *ascribed content independently of the problematic canons of ideal rationality my view requires.* What did the lemonade seller *really believe?* Or what, in any event, was the *exact content* of the sequence of states and events that figure in the cognitivistic description of his error? Stich supposes we will be able, in principle, to say, even in cases where my method comes up empty-handed. I claim, on the contrary, that just as the interpretation of a bit of *outer,* public communication – a spoken or written utterance in natural language, for instance – *depends on* the interpretation of the utterer's beliefs and desires, so the interpretation of a bit of *inner,* sub-personal cognitivistic machinery must inevitably depend on exactly the same thing: the whole person's beliefs and desires. Stich's method of content ascription depends on mine, and is not an alternative, independent method.

Suppose we find a mechanism in Jones that reliably produces an utterance of 'It is raining' whenever Jones is queried on the topic and it is raining in Jones' epistemically accessible vicinity. It also produces 'yes' in response to 'Is it raining?' on those occasions. Have we discovered Jones' belief that it is raining? That is, more circumspectly, have we found the mechanism that "subserves" this belief in Jones' cognitive apparatus? Maybe – it all depends on whether or not Jones believes that it is raining when (and only when) this mechanism is "on." That is, perhaps we have discovered a weird and senseless mechanism (like the "assent-inducing tumor" I imagined in "Brain writing and mind reading," *Brainstorms,* p. 44) that deserves no intentional interpretation at all – or at any rate not this one: that it is the belief that it is raining. We need a standard against which to judge our intentionalistic labels for the illata of sub-personal cognitive theory; what we must use for this standard is the system of abstracta that fixes belief and desire by a sort of hermeneutical process that tells the best, most rational, story that can be told. If we find that Jones passes the right tests – he demonstrates that he really understands what the supposition that it is raining means, for instance – we may find confirmation of our hypothesis that we have uncovered the mechanistic realization of his beliefs. But where we find such fallings-short, such imperfect and inappropriate proclivities and inactivities, we will *thereby* diminish our grounds for ascribing belief content to mechanisms we find.

It is unlikely, I have said, that the illata we eventually favor in academic psychology will resemble the putative illata of folk theory enough to tempt us to identify them. But whatever illata we find, we will interpret them and assign content to them by the light of our holistic attribution to the agent of beliefs and desires. We may not find structures in the agent that can be made to line up belief-by-belief with our intentional system catalog of beliefs for the agent. On Stich's view, and on Fodor's, we would be constrained to interpret this outcome – which all grant is possible – as the discovery that *there were no such things as beliefs after all.* Folk psychology was just false. On my view we would instead interpret this discovery – and a very likely one it is – as the discovery that the concrete systems of representations whereby brains realize intentional systems are simply not *sentential* in character.[11]

Of course sometimes there are sentences in our heads, which is hardly surprising, considering that we are language-using creatures. These sentences, though, are as much in need of interpretation via determination of our beliefs and desires as are the public sentences we utter. Suppose the words occur to me (just "in my head"): 'Now is the time for violent revolution!' – did I thereby *think* the thought with the content that now is the time for violent revolution? It all depends, doesn't it? On what? On what I happened to believe and desire and intend when I internally uttered those words "to myself." Similarly, if "cerebroscopes" show that while the boy was handing me my change he was internally accompanying his transaction with the conscious or subconscious expression in his natural language or in Mentalese: 'this is the right change,' that would not settle the correct interpretation of that bit of internal language and hence would not settle the intentional interpretation of his act. And since he has made a mistake, there is no unqualified catalog of his intentional states and acts of the moment.

So I stick to my guns: even for the everyday cases of error Stich presents, the problems of belief-interpretation encountered by my view *really are there* in the folk-psychological practice, although they often lurk behind our confabulations and excuses. Nor will they go away for Stich's proposed alternative theory of content ascription. This is *not* to say that such phenomena cannot be given any coherent description. Of course they can be coherently described from either the design stance or the physical stance – a point on which Stich and I agree. So I do not discover any truths of folk theory I must regretfully forswear.

In thus resisting Stich's objections, and keeping rationality at the foundation of belief and desire attribution, am I taking what Stich calls the *hard line*, or the *soft line?* The hard line, according to Stich, insists that intentional system theory's idealizing assumption of rationality is actually to be found in the folk practice from which intentional system theory is derived. The soft line "proposes some fiddling with the idealized notion of an intentional system" to bring it more in line with folk practice, which does not really (Stich insists) invoke considerations of rationality at all. These distinct lines are Stich's inventions, born of his frustration in the attempt to make sense of my expression of my view, which is both hard and soft – that is to say, flexible. The *flexible line* insists both that the assumption of rationality is to be found in the folk practice and that what rationality is is not what it appears to be to some theorists – so the idealization will require some "fiddling." What, then, do I say of the ideal of rationality exploited self-consciously by the intentional system strategist and as second nature by the rest of the folk?

Here Stich finds me faced with a dilemma. If I identify rationality with *logical consistency and deductive closure* (and the other dictates of the formal normative systems such as game theory and the calculus of probability) I am embarrassed by absurdities. Deductive closure, for instance, is just too strong a condition, as Stich's case of Oscar the engineer witnesses.[12] If, flying to the other extreme, I identify rationality with *whatever it is that evolution has provided us*, I either lapse into uninformative tautology or fly in the face of obvious counterexamples: cases of evolved manifest irrationality. What then do I say rationality is? I don't say.

Stich is right; for ten years I have hedged and hinted and entertained claims that I have later qualified or retracted. I didn't know what to say, and could see problems everywhere I turned. With that *mea culpa* behind me, I will now take the offensive, however, and give what I think are good reasons for cautiously resisting the demand for a declaration on the nature of rationality while still insisting that an assumption of rationality plays the crucial role I have seen for it.

First, a few words on what rationality is *not*. It is not deductive closure. In a passage Stich quotes from "Intentional Systems" I present the suggestion that "If S were ideally rational . . . S would believe every logical consequence of every belief (and ideally, S would have no false beliefs)" and I make a similar remark in "True believers." That is, after all, the logically guaranteed resting point of the universally applicable, indefinitely extendable demand that one believe the "obvious" consequences of one's genuine, fully understood beliefs. But Stich's example of Oscar nicely reveals what is wrong with letting sheer entailment expand a rational agent's beliefs, and as Lawrence Powers shows in his important article "Knowledge by deduction"[13] there is work to be done by a theory of knowledge *acquisition* by deduction: one *comes* to know (and believe) what one *didn't* already know (or believe) by deducing propositions from premises already believed – a familiar and "obvious" idea, but one that requires the very careful exposition and defense Powers gives it. And it is important to note that in the course of making his case for what we might call implication-insulated cognitive states, Powers must advert to neologism and caveat: we must talk about what our agent "pseudo-believes" and "pseudo-knows" (pp. 360 ff). It puts one in mind, in fact, of Stich's own useful neologism for belief-like states lacking the logical fecundity of beliefs: "sub-doxastic states."[14]

Nor is rationality perfect logical consistency, although the *discovery* of a contradiction between propositions one is inclined to assent to is always, of course, an occasion for sounding the epistemic alarm.[15] Inconsistency, when discovered, is of course to be eliminated one way or another, but making the rooting out of inconsistency the pre-eminent goal of a cognizer would lead to swamping the cognitive system in bookkeeping and search operations to the exclusion of all other modes of activity.[16] Now how can I talk this way about inconsistency, given my account of the conditions for correct belief attribution? Who said anything about inconsistency of *beliefs*? When one enters the domain of considerations about the wise design of cognitive structures and operations, one has left belief proper behind, and is discussing, in effect, structurally identified features with more-or-less apt intentionalistic labels (see "Three kinds of intentional psychology", and *Brainstorms*, pp. 26–7).

If I thus do not identify rationality with consistency and deductive closure, when then could be my standard? If I turn to evolutionary considerations, Stich suggests, "such established theories as deductive and inductive logic, decision theory and game theory" will be "of no help in assessing what an organism 'ought to believe'." This is just not true. The theorist who relinquishes the claim that these formalisms are the final *benchmark* of rationality can still turn to them for help, can still exploit them in the course of criticizing (on grounds of irrationality) and reformulating strategies, designs, interpretations. The analogy is imperfect, but just as one may seek help from a good dictionary, or a good grammar book, in supporting one's criticism of someone's spelling, word choice, or grammar, so may one appeal to the defeasible authority of, say, decision theory in objecting to someone's strategic formulation. One can also reject as wrong – or irrational – the advice one gets from a dictionary, a grammar, a logic, or any other normative theory, however well established.[17]

What of the evolutionary considerations? I am careful *not* to define rationality in terms of what evolution has given us – so I avoid outright tautology. Nevertheless, the relation I claim holds between rationality and evolution is more powerful than Stich will grant. I claim, as he notes, that if an organism is the product of natural selection we can assume that *most* of its beliefs will be true, and *most* of its belief-forming strategies will be rational. Stich disagrees: "it is simply not the case that natural selection favors true beliefs over false ones," because all natural selection favors is beliefs "that yield selective advantage" and "there are many environmental circumstances in which false beliefs will be more useful than true ones." I do not think it is *obvious* that it is *ever* advantageous to be designed to arrive at false beliefs about the world, but I have claimed that there are describable circumstances – rare circumstances – where it can happen, so I agree with Stich on this point: "*better safe than sorry* is a policy that recommends itself to natural selection," Stich says, echoing my claim in "Three kinds of intentional psychology" – "Erring on the side of prudence is a well recognized good strategy, and so Nature can be expected to have valued it on occasions when it came up" (p. 45n).

But does this go any way at all toward rebutting my claim that natural selection guarantees that *most* of an organism's beliefs will be true, *most* of its strategies rational? I think not. Moreover, even if a strategy is, as I grant it very well may be, a "patently invalid" strategy that works most of the time in the contexts it is invoked – does this show it is an *irrational* strategy? Only if one is still clinging to the ideals of Intro Logic for one's model of rationality. It is not even that there are no "established" academic canons of rationality in opposition to the logicians' to which one might appeal. Herbert Simon is duly famous for maintaining that *it is rational* in many instances to *satisfice* – e.g., to leap to possibly "invalid" conclusions when the costs of further calculation probably outweigh the costs of getting the wrong answer. I think he is right, so I for one would not tie rationality to any canons that prohibited such practices. Stich declares:

> So long as we recognize a distinction between a normative theory of inference or decision-making and a set of inferential practices which (in the right environment) generally get the right (or selectively useful) answer, it will be clear that the two need not, and generally do not, coincide. (this volume, p. 178)

This is a puzzling claim, for there are normative theories for different purposes, including the purposes of "generally getting the right answer." If one views these as at odds with one another, one makes a mistake. Deductive logic might be held to advise that in the face of uncertainty or lack of information one should simply *sight tight and infer nothing* – bad advice for a creature in a busy world, but fine advice if avoiding falsehood *at all costs* is the goal. It is better to recognize the various uses to which such strategies can be put, and let rationality consist in part of a good sense of when to rely on what. (It is also useful to remind ourselves that only a tiny fraction of all the "rational animals" that have ever lived have ever availed themselves self-consciously of *any* of the formal techniques of the normative theories that have been proposed.)

The concept of rationality is indeed a slippery concept. We agree, it seems, that a system would be improperly called irrational if although its *normal, designed* operation were impeccable (by the standards of the relevant norms), it suffered occasional *malfunctions*. But of course a system that was particularly delicate, particularly prone to uncorrected malfunctions, would hardly be a well-designed sysetem; a system that was foolproof or failsafe would in this regard be better. But which would be better – which would be more rational – all things considered: a very slow but virtually failsafe system, or a very fast but only 90 per cent malfunction-free system? It depends on the application, and there are even normative canons for evaluating such choices in some circumstances.

I want to use "rational" as a general-purpose term of cognitive approval – which requires maintaining only conditional and revisable allegiances between rationality, so considered, and the proposed (or even universally acclaimed) methods of getting ahead, cognitively, in the world. I take this usage of the term to be quite standard, and I take *appeals* to rationality by proponents of cognitive disciplines or practices to require this understanding of the notion. What, for instance, could Anderson and Belnap be appealing to, what could they be assuming about their audience, when they recommend their account of entailment over its rivals, if not to an assumably shared rationality which is such that it is an *open question* which formal system best captures it?[18] Or consider this commentary on the discovery that a compartmentalized memory is a necessary condition for effective cognition in a complex, time-pressured world:

> We can now appreciate both the costs and the benefits of this strategy; *prima facie*, the resulting behavior can be characterized as departures from rationality, but on the assumption that exhaustive memory search is not feasible, such memory organization is advisable overall, despite its costs. Correspondingly, a person's action may seem irrational when considered in isolation, but it may be rational when it is more broadly considered as part of the worthwhile price of good memory management.[19]

The claim is that it is rational to be inconsistent sometimes, not the pseudo-paradoxical claim that it is rational sometimes to be irrational. As the example shows, the concept of rationality is systematically pre-theoretical. One may, then, decline to *identify* rationality with the features of any formal system or the outcome of any process and still make appeals to the concept, and assertions about appeals to it (such as mine), without thereby shirking a duty of explicitness.

When one leans on our pre-theoretical concept of rationality, one relies on our shared intuitions – when they *are* shared, of course – about what makes sense. What else, in the end, could one rely on? What else would it be *rational* to rely on? When considering what we *ought to do*, our reflections lead us eventually to a consideration of what we *in fact do*; this is inescapable, for a catalog of our considered intuitive judgments on what we ought to do is both a compendium of what we *do* think, and a shining example (by our lights – what else?) of how we *ought* to think.[20]

Now it will appear that I am backing into Stich's own view, the view that when we attribute beliefs and other intentional states to others, we do this by comparing them *to ourselves*, by projecting ourselves into their states of mind. One doesn't ask: "what ought this creature believe?" but "what would *I* believe if I were in its place?" (I have suggested to Stich that he call his view *ideological solipsism*, but he apparently feels this would court confusion with some other doctrine.) Stich contrasts his view with mine and claims that "the notion of idealized rationality plays *no role at all*" (Stich's emphasis) in his account. "In ascribing content to belief states we measure others not against an idealized standard but against ourselves." But for the reasons just given, measuring "against ourselves" *is* measuring against an idealized standard.

Now Stich at one point observes that "since we take ourselves to approximate rationality, this explains the fact, noted by Dennett, that intentional description falters in the face of egregious irrationality." He must grant, then, that since we take ourselves to approximate rationality, it is also true that the results of his method and my method will coincide very closely. He, asking "what would I do if ...?" and I, asking "what ought he to do ...?" will typically arrive at the same account, since Stich will typically suppose that he would do what he ought to do, and I would typically suppose that what he ought to do is what I would do if I were in his shoes. If the methods were actually extensionally equivalent, one might well wonder about the point of the quarrel, but is there not room for the two methods to diverge in special cases? Let us see.

Can it be like this? Stich, cognizant of his lamentable and embarrassing tendency to affirm the consequent, imputes this same tendency to those whose beliefs and desires he is trying to fathom. He does this instead of supposing they might be free from his own particular foible, but guilty of others. Unlikely story. Here is a better one. Having learned about "cognitive dissonance," Stich is now prepared to find both in himself and in others the resolution of cognitive dissonance in the favoring a self-justifying belief over a less comfortable belief better supported by the evidence. This is a fine example of the sort of empirical discovery that can be used to tune the intentional stance, by suggesting hypotheses to be tested by the attributer, but how would Stich say it had anything to do with *ourselves*, and how would this discovery be put into effective use independently of the idealizing assumption? For, first, is it not going to be an empirical question whether all people respond to cognitive dissonance as we do? If Stich builds this (apparently) sub-optimal proclivity into his very method of attribution, he forgoes the possibility of discovering varieties of believers happily immune to this pathology.

Moreover, consider how such an assumption of sub-optimality would get used in an actual case. Jones has just spent three months of hard work building an addition to his house; it looks terrible. Something must be done to resolve the uncomfortable cognitive dissonance. Count on Jones to slide into some belief that will save the situation. But which one? He might come to believe that the point of the project, really, was to learn all about carpentry by the relatively inexpensive expedient of building a cheap addition. Or he might come to believe that the bold thrust of the addition is just the touch that distinguishes his otherwise hackneyed if "tasteful" house from the run of the neighborhood houses. Or, ... for many possible variations. But which of these is actually believed will be determined by seeing what he says and does, and then asking: what beliefs and desires would make those acts rational? And whatever delusion is embraced, it must be – and *will* be – carefully surrounded by plausible supporting material, generatable on the counterfactual assumption that the delusion is an entirely rationally held belief. Given what we already know about Jones, we might be able to predict which comforting delusion would be most attractive and efficient for him – that is, which would most easily cohere with the rest of the fabric of his beliefs. So even in a case of cognitive dissonance, where the beliefs we attribute are not optimal by anyone's lights, the test of rational coherence is the preponderant measure of our attributions.

I do not see how my method and Stich's can be shown to yield different results, but I also do not see that they could not. I am not clear enough about just what Stich is asserting. An interesting idea which is lurking in Stich's view is that when we interpret others we do so not so much by *theorizing* about them as by *using ourselves as analog computers* that produce a result. Wanting to know more about *your* frame of mind, I somehow put myself in it, or as close to being in it as I can muster, and see what I thereupon think (want, do . . .).[21] There is much that is puzzling about such an idea. How can it work *without* being a kind of theorizing in the end? For the state I put myself in is not belief, but make-believe belief. If I make believe I am a suspension bridge and wonder what I will do when the wind blows, what "comes to me" in my make-believe state depends on how sophisticated my knowledge is of the physics and engineering of suspension bridges. Why should my making believe I have your beliefs be any different? In both cases, knowledge of the imitated object is needed to drive the make-believe "simulation," and the knowledge must be organized into something rather like a theory. Moreover, establishing that we do somehow arrive at our interpretations of others by something like simulation and self-observation would not by itself show that the guiding question of our effort is "what would I believe?" *as opposed to* "what ought he to believe?" A wary attributer might exhibit the difference by using the trick of empathy or make-believe to *generate* a candidate set of attributions to test against his "theory" of the other before settling on them. Note that the issue is far from clear even in the case of imagined *self*-attribution. What would your state of mind be if you were told you had three weeks to live? How do you think about this? In a variety of ways, probably; you do a bit of simulation and see what you'd say, think, and so on, and you also reflect on what kind of a person you think you are – so you can conclude that a person *like that* would believe – ought to believe – or want such-and-such.

Stich's paper raises many more problems well worth a response from me, but the deadline for this issue of *Philosophical Topics* mercifully intervenes at this point. I close with one final rejoinder. Stich seems to embarrass me in closing with a series of rhetorical questions about what a frog *ought to believe* – for I have made my determination of what a frog *does* believe hinge on such questions. I grant that such questions are only problematically answerable under even the best conditions,[22] but view that as no embarrassment. I respond with a rhetorical question of my own: does Stich suppose that the exact content of what a frog does in fact believe is any more likely of determination?

NOTES

1 See Stephen Stich's review of *Brainstorms*; "Headaches," *Philosophical Books*, April, 1980, and my reply, ibid.
2 Wason and Johnson-Laird, and Nisbett and Ross (see Stich's notes 8 and 11). See also S. Stich and R. Nisbett, "Justification and the psychology of human reasoning" in *Philosophy of Science*, 1980, vol. 47, no. 2, pp. 188–202.

3   See J. Weizenfeld "Surprise and intentional content," presented at the 3rd Annual meeting of the Society for Philosophy and Psychology, Pittsburgh, March 1977.

4   Cf. Jerry Fodor, "Computation and reduction" in C. W. Savage (ed.), *Perception and Cognition: Issues in the Foundations of Psychology*, 1978, pp. 229–60.

5   E.g., L. Jonathan Cohen, "Can human irrationality be experimentally demonstrated?", *Behavioral and Brain Sciences* 4 (1981), pp. 317–31.

6   I will continue to fly in the face of the examples raised by Vendler et al., about the differences between the objects of knowledge and the objects of belief until I can see that this imprecision is *dangerous*. Perhaps I will be shown this tomorrow, but I haven't been shown it yet.

7   See C. Cherniak, "Rationality and the structure of human memory" (Tufts University Cognitive Science Working Papers WP13, June 1980).

8   Cf. Ryle, "A puzzling element in the notion of thinking" (1958), a British Academy Lecture reprinted in P. F. Strawson (ed.), *Studies in the Philosophy of Thought and Action*, 1968, Oxford University Press.

9   See, especially R. Nisbett and T. DeC. Wilson, "Telling more than we can know: verbal reports on mental processes," *Psychological Review*, 1977.

10 Michael Gazzaniga and J. E. Ledoux advocate a position along these lines in *The Integrated Mind* (New York: Plenum Press, 1978). For graphic accounts of confabulations in victims of brain disorders, see also Howard Gardner, *The Shattered Mind: The Person After Brain Damage*, Knopf, New York, 1975.

11 See my "Beyond belief," in Andrew Woodfield (ed.), *Thought and Object*, Oxford University Press, 1982.

12 Cf. also Jerry Fodor, "Three cheers for propositional attitudes," in *Representations*, Bradford Book, 1981.

13 *Philosophical Review*, July 1978, pp. 337–71.

14 "Belief and sub-doxastic states," *Philosophy of Science*, December 1978, pp. 499–518.

15 See R. de Sousa, "How to give a piece of your mind; or the logic of belief and assent," *Reviews of Metaphysics*, September 1971, pp. 52–79.

16 See C. Cherniak, "Rationality and the structure of human memory," ibid., and Howard Darmstadter, "Consistency of belief," *Journal of Philosophy*, May 20, 1971, pp. 301–10. The point has often been made in different contexts by Marvin Minsky as well.

17 See, e.g., L. Jonathan Cohen, ibid., and for a dissenting view, see S. Stich and R. Nisbett, "Justification and the psychology of human reasoning," *Philosophy of Science*, June, 1980, pp. 188–202.

18 A. R. Anderson and N. Belnap, *Entailment: The Logic of Relevance and Necessity*, Princeton University Press, 1974.

19 Cherniak, ibid., p. 23.

20 "Thus, what and how we do think is evidence for the principles of rationality, what and how we ought to think. This itself is a methodological principle of rationality; call it the *Factunorm Principle*. We are (implicitly) accepting the Factunorm Principle whenever we try to determine what or how we ought to think. For we must, in that very attempt, think. And unless we can think that what and how we do think there is correct – and thus is evidence for what and how we ought to think – we cannot determine what or how we ought to think." R. Wertheimer, "Philosophy on humanity," in R. L. Perkins (ed.), *Abortion: Pro and Con*, Schenkman, 1974, pp. 110–11. See also Nelson Goodman, *Fact, Fiction, and Forecast*, 2nd edition, Bobbs-Merrill, 1965, p. 63.

21 Adam Morton's book *Frames of Mind* (Oxford University Press, 1980) has much to say on this topic which I have not yet had an opportunity to digest. Hence my tentative and sketchy remarks on this occasion.

22 Cf. Dennett, *Content and Consciousness*, Routledge & Kegan Paul, 1969, pp. 83–5.

Part IV

Eliminativism and Neurophilosophy

Introduction

We saw that Dennett's instrumentalism broke fairly radically with common sense and with philosophical tradition in denying that propositional attitudes such as belief and desire are real inner causal states of people. But Dennett concedes – indeed urgently insists – that belief- and desire-ascriptions are true, and objectively true, nonetheless. Other philosophers have taken a less conciliatory, still more radically uncommonsensical view: that mental ascriptions are not true after all, but are simply *false*. Common sense is just mistaken in supposing that people believe and desire things, and perhaps in supposing that people have sensations and feelings, disconcerting as that nihilistic claim may seem.

Following standard usage, let us call the nihilistic claim "Eliminative Materialism," or "Eliminativism" for short. It is important to note a customary if unexpected alliance between the Eliminativist and the token physicalist: the Eliminativist, the Identity Theorist and the Functionalist all agree that mental items are, *if anything*, real inner causal states of people. They disagree only on the empirical question of whether any real neurophysiological states of people do in fact answer to the commonsensical mental categories of "folk psychology." Eliminativists praise Identity Theorists and Functionalists for their forthright willingness to step up and take their empirical shot. Both Eliminativists and token physicalists scorn the Instrumentalist's sleazy evasion. (But Eliminativists agree with Instrumentalists that Functionalism is a pipe dream, and Functionalists agree with Instrumentalists that mental ascriptions are often true and obviously so. The three views form an Eternal Triangle of a not uncommon sort.)

Paul Feyerabend (this volume) was the first to argue openly that the mental categories of folk psychology simply fail to capture anything in physical reality and that everyday mental ascriptions are therefore false. (Rorty (1965) took a notoriously Eliminativist line also, but following Wilfrid Sellars tried to soften its nihilism; Lycan and Pappas (1972) argued that the softening served only to collapse Rorty's position into incoherence.) Feyerabend attracted no great following, presumably because of his view's outrageous flouting of common sense. But Eliminativism was resurrected by Paul Churchland (this volume) and others, and defended in more detail.

Churchland argues mainly from the poverty of "folk psychology"; he claims that historically, when other primitive theories such as alchemy have done as badly on scientific grounds as folk psychology has, they have been abandoned and rightly so. Patricia Churchland (1986, this volume (with Terrence Sejnowski)) emphasizes the comparative scientific reality and causal efficacy of neuroanatomical mechanisms: given the scientific excellence of neurophysiological explanation and the contrasting diffuseness and type-irreducibility of folk psychology, why should we suppose even for a minute, much less automatically, that the platitudes of folk psychology express truths?

Patricia Churchland's intense interest in neuroanatomy and her distrust of the categories of folk psychology are matched within a recent sector of the AI community, in an equally intense upsurge of "neural modelling." In particular, what is called the "New Connectionism" or Parallel Distributed Processing ("PDP" for short; McClelland et al. 1986) is highly current as an AI research program that diverges from the standard deployment of "rules and representations" (see Part V of this volume) and from the idea of linear or monotonic theorem-proving from a pre-loaded data base. PDP employs (in practice, only simulates) an array of "units," each unit connected by ligatures to other units and each having an "activation potential" that is directly affected by the potentials of adjoining units; the obvious, and intended, allusion is to the brain's neural nets. Some units are designated as inputs, others as outputs; the rest are "hidden," and mysteriously regulate output given input according to various algorithms. A major focus of PDP research is on *learning over time*; connectionist networks are good at learning pattern-recognition tasks, notably when their activation algorithms work by back-propagation of error.

"Connectionism" as described is an engineering approach within AI. But the term has caught on among both psychologists and philosophers, and is now often used neologistically, as naming (a) a psychological theory, roughly that such-and-such behavioral capacities are explained by connectionist architecture actually realized in organisms' brains, or (b) a philosophical contention reminiscent of Ryle, roughly that intelligent human capacities, thinking and rationality are somehow holistically emergent from connectionist architecture in the brain rather than being a matter of the manipulation of internal beliefs or other representations according to rules.

Some philosophers take connectionism in one or another of its several senses to refute or at least embarrass the idea that human cognition is a matter of hosting internal representational states such as beliefs and desires. But, logically speaking, connectionism seems entirely compatible with representationalism (Bechtel, this volume; Smolensky 1988), and arguably it is *an instance of* representationalism (Fodor and Pylyshyn in *Cognition* (1988)). The matter needs considerable further examination.

FURTHER READING

Classical eliminativism

Feyerabend, P. (1963) "Materialism and the mind–body problem," *Review of Metaphysics* 17, 49–67.

Quine, W. V. (1966) "On mental entities," reprinted in *The Ways of Paradox and Other Essays*, Random House.

Rorty, R. (1965) "Mind–body identity, privacy, and categories," *Review of Metaphysics* 19, 24–54.

Lycan, W., and Pappas, G. (1972) "What is eliminative materialism?" *Australasian Journal of Philosophy* 50, 149–59.

Current eliminativism

Dennett, D. C. (1982) "How to study consciousness empirically, or: Nothing comes to mind," *Synthese* 53, 159–80.

Bricke, J. (1984) "Dennett's eliminative arguments," *Philosophical Studies* 45, 413–30.

Churchland, P. S. (1986) *Neurophilosophy*, Bradford Books/MIT Press, section 9.6.

[See also the defenses of "folk psychology" cited in the Introduction to Part VI.]

Connectionism

McClelland, J., Rumelhart, D. and the PDP Research Group (eds) (1986) *Parallel Distributed Processing: Explorations in the Microstructure of Cognition*, Bradford Books/MIT Press.

Smolensky, P. (1988) "On the proper treatment of connectionism," *Behavioral and Brain Sciences* 11, 1–23.

[Accompanied by multifarious "Open Peer Commentary."]

Cognition (1988) vol. 28: special issue on connectionism. Reissued as S. Pinker and J. Mehler (eds), *Connections and Symbols*, MIT Press, 1988.

[Especially Fodor and Pylyshyn, "Connectionism and cognitive architecture: A critical analysis," 3–71.]

Horgan, T. and Tienson, J. (eds) (1988) *Spindel Conference 1987: Connectionism and the Philosophy of Mind. Southern Journal of Philosophy*, Supplement to vol. 26.

8

Classical Eliminativism

Mental Events and the Brain

PAUL K. FEYERABEND

Shaffer's note[1] and the preceding discussion to which it refers show very clearly the dilemma of any identity hypothesis concerning mental events and brain processes. Such hypotheses are usually put forth by physiologically inclined thinkers who want also to be empiricists. Being physiologically inclined, they want to assert the *material* character of mental processes. Being empiricists, they want their assertion to be a testable statement about *mental* processes. They try to combine the two tendencies in an empirical statement of the form:

X is a mental process of kind A $\equiv$ X is a central process of kind α (H)

But this hypothesis backfires. It not only implies, as it is intended to imply, that mental events have physical features; it also seems to imply (if read from the right to the left) that some physical events, viz. central processes, have non-physical features. It thereby replaces a dualism of events by a dualism of features. Moreover, this consequence seems to be the result of the way in which the physiologist has *formulated* his thesis. Even if he is a convinced monist he seems to be forced, by the very content of his thesis of monism, to acknowledge the correctness of a *dualistic* point of view.

For a dualist this predicament is proof of the untenability of monism. But surely he is too rash in drawing this conclusion! H implies dualism. Hence, dualism will be true *provided* H is true. However, if *monism* is correct, then H is false: there are then *no* mental processes in the usual (non-materialistic) sense. This shows that the discussion of the content of H regarded as an empirical hypothesis is not at all sufficient for deciding the issue between monism and dualism. It also shows *that the monist misstates his case when defending* H.

The proper procedure for him to adopt is to develop his theory without any recourse to existent terminology. If he wants to use H at all, he ought to use it for

"Mental Events and the Brain" by P. K. Feyerabend first appeared in *The Journal of Philosophy* 60 (1963), pp. 295–96, and is reprinted by kind permission.

redefining "mental process" (if he intends to perpetuate ancient terminology, that is). The empirical character of his theory is not endangered thereby. After all, a physiological theory of epilepsy does not become an empty tautology on account of the fact that it does not make use of the phrase – or of the notion – "possessed by the devil," "devil" here occurring in its *theological* sense. There are enough independent predictions available, many more predictions in fact than the mentalist could ever provide – or would even be willing to provide (think only of the tremendous field of the physiology of perception).

However, so it is usually objected, unless a connection is established with previous language, we do not know what we are talking about, and we are therefore not able to formulate our observational results. This objection assumes that the terms of a general point of view and of a corresponding language can obtain meaning only by being related to the terms of some other point of view that is familiar and known by all. Now if that is indeed the case, then how did the latter point of view and the latter language ever obtain its familiarity? And if it could obtain its familiarity without help "from outside," as it obviously did, then there is no reason to assume that a different point of view cannot do equally well. (Besides, we learn the ordinary idiom when we are small children; is it assumed that a grown-up physiologist will be incapable of doing what a small child does quite well?) Moreover, observational results always have to be formulated with respect to a certain background of theory (with respect to a certain language-game, to use more fashionable terminology). There is no reason why physiology should not by itself be capable of forming such a background. We have to conclude, then, that the reasonableness – and the success – of a purely physiological approach to human beings is not at all dependent on the outcome of an analysis of H.

"Bridge-laws" such as H play a most important role within the current theory of explanation and reduction. If our comments above are correct, then it follows that these theories are inadequate as measures of the success of theory construction.

NOTE

1 "Mental events and the brain," *Journal of Philosophy* 60 (1963), 160–6.

9

Current Eliminativism

Eliminative Materialism and the Propositional Attitudes

PAUL M. CHURCHLAND

Eliminative materialism is the thesis that our common-sense conception of psychological phenomena constitutes a radically false theory, a theory so fundamentally defective that both the principles and the ontology of that theory will eventually be displaced, rather than smoothly reduced, by completed neuroscience. Our mutual understanding and even our introspection may then be reconstituted within the conceptual framework of completed neuroscience, a theory we may expect to be more powerful by far than the common-sense psychology it displaces, and more substantially integrated within physical science generally. My purpose in this paper is to explore these projections, especially as they bear on (1) the principal elements of common-sense psychology: the propositional attitudes (beliefs, desires, etc.), and (2) the conception of rationality in which these elements figure.

This focus represents a change in the fortunes of materialism. Twenty years ago, emotions, qualia, and "raw feels" were held to be the principal stumbling blocks for the materialist program. With these barriers dissolving,[1] the locus of opposition has shifted. Now it is the realm of the intentional, the realm of the propositional attitude, that is most commonly held up as being both irreducible to and ineliminable in favor of anything from within a materialist framework. Whether and why this is so, we must examine.

Such an examination will make little sense, however, unless it is first appreciated that the relevant network of common-sense concepts does indeed constitute an empirical theory, with all the functions, virtues, *and perils* entailed by that status. I shall therefore begin with a brief sketch of this view and a summary rehearsal of its rationale. The resistance it encounters still surprises me. After all, common sense has yielded up many theories. Recall the view that space has a preferred

"Eliminative Materialism and Propositional Attitudes" by P. M. Churchland first appeared in *The Journal of Philosophy* 78 (1981), pp. 67–90, and is reprinted by kind permission of the author and journal.

direction in which all things fall; that weight is an intrinsic feature of a body; that a force-free moving object will promptly return to rest; that the sphere of the heavens turns daily; and so on. These examples are clear, perhaps, but people seem willing to concede a theoretical component within common sense only if (1) the theory and the common sense involved are safely located in antiquity, and (2) the relevant theory is now so clearly false that its speculative nature is inescapable. Theories are indeed easier to discern under these circumstances. But the vision of hindsight is always 20/20. Let us aspire to some foresight for a change.

I   Why folk psychology is a theory

Seeing our common-sense conceptual framework for mental phenomena as a theory brings a simple and unifying organization to most of the major topics in the philosophy of mind, including the explanation and prediction of behavior, the semantics of mental predicates, action theory, the other-minds problem, the intentionality of mental states, the nature of introspection, and the mind–body problem. Any view that can pull this lot together deserves careful consideration.

Let us begin with the explanation of human (and animal) behavior. The fact is that the average person is able to explain, and even predict, the behavior of other persons with a facility and success that is remarkable. Such explanations and predictions standardly make reference to the desires, beliefs, fears, intentions, perceptions, and so forth, to which the agents are presumed subject. But explanations presuppose laws – rough and ready ones, at least – that connect the explanatory conditions with the behavior explained. The same is true for the making of predictions, and for the justification of subjunctive and counterfactual conditionals concerning behavior. Reassuringly, a rich network of common-sense laws can indeed be reconstructed from this quotidean commerce of explanation and anticipation; its principles are familiar homilies; and their sundry functions are transparent. Each of us understands others, as well as we do, because we share a tacit command of an integrated body of lore concerning the lawlike relations holding among external circumstances, internal states, and overt behavior. Given its nature and functions, this body of lore may quite aptly be called "folk psychology."[2]

This approach entails that the semantics of the terms in our familiar mentalistic vocabulary is to be understood in the same manner as the semantics of theoretical terms generally: the meaning of any theoretical term is fixed or constituted by the network of laws in which it figures. (This position is quite distinct from logical behaviorism. We deny that the relevant laws are analytic, and it is the lawlike connections generally that carry the semantic weight, not just the connections with overt behavior. But this view does account for what little plausibility logical behaviorism did enjoy.)

More importantly, the recognition that folk psychology is a theory provides a simple and decisive solution to an old skeptical problem, the problem of other minds. The problematic conviction that another individual is the subject of certain mental states is not inferred deductively from his behavior, nor is it inferred by inductive analogy from the perilously isolated instance of one's own case. Rather, that conviction is a singular *explanatory hypothesis* of a perfectly straightforward kind. Its function, in conjunction with the background laws of folk psychology, is to provide explanations/predictions/understanding of the individual's continuing behavior, and it is credible to the degree that it is successful in this regard over competing hypotheses. In the main, such hypotheses are successful, and so the belief that others enjoy the internal states comprehended by folk psychology is a reasonable belief.

Knowledge of other minds thus has no essential dependence on knowledge of one's own mind. Applying the principles of our folk psychology to our behavior, a Martian could justly ascribe to us the familiar run of mental states, even though his own psychology were very different from ours. He would not, therefore, be "generalizing from his own case."

As well, introspective judgments about one's own case turn out not to have any special status or integrity anyway. On the present view, an introspective judgment is just an instance of an acquired habit of conceptual response to one's internal states, and the integrity of any particular response is always contingent on the integrity of the acquired conceptual framework (theory) in which the response is framed. Accordingly, one's *introspective* certainty that one's mind is the seat of beliefs and desires may be as badly misplaced as was the classical man's *visual* certainty that the star-flecked sphere of the heavens turns daily.

Another conundrum is the intentionality of mental states. The "propositional attitudes," as Russell called them, form the systematic core of folk psychology; and their uniqueness and anomalous logical properties have inspired some to see here a fundamental contrast with anything that mere physical phenomena might conceivably display. The key to this matter lies again in the theoretical nature of folk psychology. The intentionality of mental states here emerges not as a mystery of nature, but as a structural feature of the concepts of folk psychology. Ironically, those same structural features reveal the very close affinity that folk psychology bears to theories in the physical sciences. Let me try to explain.

Consider the large variety of what might be called "numerical attitudes" appearing in the conceptual framework of physical science: '. . . has a mass$_{kg}$ of n', '. . . has a velocity of n', '. . . has a temperature$_K$ of n', and so forth. These expressions are predicate-forming expressions: when one substitutes a singular term for a number into the place held by 'n', a determinate predicate results. More interestingly, the relations between the various "numerical attitudes" that result are precisely the relations between the numbers "contained" in those attitudes. More interesting still, the argument place that takes the singular terms for numbers is open to quantification. All this permits the expression of generalizations concerning the lawlike relations that hold between the various numerical attitudes in nature. Such laws involve quantification over numbers, and they exploit the mathematical relations holding in that domain. Thus, for example,

(1) $(x)(f)(m)[((x \text{ has a mass of } m)$ & $(x \text{ suffers a net force of } f))$
$\supset (x \text{ accelerates at } f/m)]$

Consider now the large variety of propositional attitudes:
'. . . believes that p', '. . . desires that p', '. . . fears that p',
'. . . is happy that p', etc. These expressions are predicate-forming expressions also. When one substitutes a singular term for a proposition into the place held by

'*p*', a determinate predicate results, e.g., '. . . believes that Tom is tall.' (Sentences do not generally function as singular terms, but it is difficult to escape the idea that when a sentence occurs in the place held by '*p*', it is there functioning as or like a singular term. On this, more below.) More interestingly, the relations between the resulting propositional attitudes are characteristically the relations that hold between the propositions "contained" in them, relations such as entailment, equivalence, and mutual inconsistency. More interesting still, the argument place that takes the singular terms for propositions is open to quantification. All this permits the expression of generalizations concerning the lawlike relations that hold among propositional attitudes. Such laws involve quantification over propositions, and they exploit various relations holding in that domain. Thus, for example,

(2) $(x)(p)[(x \text{ fears that } p) \supset (x \text{ desires that } \sim p)]$

(3) $(x)(p)[(x \text{ hopes that } p) \ \& \ (x \text{ discovers that } p)$
$$\supset (x \text{ is pleased that } p)]$$

(4) $(x)(p)(q)[((x \text{ believes that } p) \ \& \ (x \text{ believes that (if } p \text{ then } q)))$
$$\supset (\text{barring confusion, distraction, etc., } x \text{ believes that } q)]$$

(5) $(x)(p)(q)[((x \text{ desires that } p) \ \& \ (x \text{ believes that (if } q \text{ then } p))$
$$\& \ (x \text{ is able to bring it about that } q))$$
$$\supset (\text{barring conflicting desires or preferred strategies,}$$
$$x \text{ brings it about that } q)]^3$$

Not only is folk psychology a theory, it is so *obviously* a theory that it must be held a major mystery why it has taken until the last half of the twentieth century for philosophers to realize it. The structural features of folk psychology parallel perfectly those of mathematical physics; the only difference lies in the respective domain of abstract entities they exploit – numbers in the case of physics, and propositions in the case of psychology.

Finally, the realization that folk psychology is a theory puts a new light on the mind–body problem. The issue becomes a matter of how the ontology of one theory (folk psychology) is, or is not, going to be related to the ontology of another theory (completed neuroscience); and the major philosophical positions on the mind–body problem emerge as so many different anticipations of what future research will reveal about the intertheoretic status and integrity of folk psychology.

The identity theorist optimistically expects that folk psychology will be smoothly *reduced* by completed neuroscience, and its ontology preserved by dint of transtheoretic identities. The dualist expects that it will prove *ir*reducible to completed neuroscience, by dint of being a nonredundant description of an autonomous, nonphysical domain of natural phenomena. The functionalist also expects that it will prove irreducible, but on the quite different grounds that the internal economy characterized by folk psycholgy is not, in the last analysis, a law-governed economy of natural states, but an abstract organization of functional states, an organization instantiable in a variety of quite different material substrates. It is therefore irreducible to the principles peculiar to any of them.

Finally, the eliminative materialist is also pessimistic about the prospects for reduction, but his reason is that folk psychology is a radically inadequate account of our internal activities, too confused and too defective to win survival through intertheoretic reduction. On his view it will simply be displaced by a better theory of those activities.

Which of these fates is the real destiny of folk psychology, we shall attempt to divine presently. For now, the point to keep in mind is that we shall be exploring the fate of a theory, a systematic, corrigible, speculative *theory*.

II   Why folk psychology might (really) be false

Given that folk psychology is an empirical theory, it is at least an abstract possibility that its principles are radically false and that its ontology is an illusion. With the exception of eliminative materialism, however, none of the major positions takes this possibility seriously. None of them doubts the basic integrity or truth of folk psychology (hereafter, "FP"), and all of them anticipate a future in which its laws and categories are conserved. This conservatism is not without some foundation. After all, FP does enjoy a substantial amount of explanatory and predictive success. And what better grounds than this for confidence in the integrity of its categories?

What better grounds indeed? Even so, the presumption in FP's favor is spurious, born of innocence and tunnel vision. A more searching examination reveals a different picture. First, we must reckon not only with FP's successes, but with its explanatory failures, and with their extent and seriousness. Second, we must consider the long-term history of FP, its growth, fertility, and current promise of future development. And third, we must consider what sorts of theories are *likely* to be true of the etiology of our behavior, given what else we have learned about ourselves in recent history. That is, we must evaluate FP with regard to its coherence and continuity with fertile and well-established theories in adjacent and overlapping domains – with evolutionary theory, biology, and neuroscience, for example – because active coherence with the rest of what we presume to know is perhaps the final measure of any hypothesis.

A serious inventory of this sort reveals a very troubled situation, one which would evoke open skepticism in the case of any theory less familiar and dear to us. Let me sketch some relevant detail. When one centers one's attention not on what FP can explain, but on what it cannot explain or fails even to address, one discovers that there is a very great deal. As examples of central and important mental phenomena that remain largely or wholly mysterious within the framework of FP, consider the nature and dynamics of mental illness, the faculty of creative imagination, or the ground of intelligence differences between individuals. Consider our utter ignorance of the nature and psychological functions of sleep, that curious state in which a third of one's life is spent. Reflect on the common ability to catch an outfield fly ball on the run, or hit a moving car with a snowball. Consider the internal construction of a 3-D visual image from subtle differences in the 2-D array of stimulations in our respective retinas. Consider the rich variety of perceptual illusions, visual and otherwise. Or consider the miracle of memory, with its lightning capacity for relevant retrieval. On these and many other mental phenomena, FP sheds negligible light.

One particularly outstanding mystery is the nature of the learning process itself, especially where it involves large-scale conceptual change, and especially as it appears in its pre-linguistic or entirely nonlinguistic form (as in infants and animals), which is by far the most common form in nature. FP is faced with special difficulties here, since its conception of learning as the manipulation and storage of propositional attitudes founders on the fact that how to formulate, manipulate, and store a rich fabric of propositional attitudes is itself something that is learned, and is only one among many acquired cognitive skills. FP would thus appear constitutionally incapable of even addressing this most basic of mysteries.[4]

Failures on such a large scale do not (yet) show that FP is a false theory, but they do move that prospect well into the range of real possibility, and they do show decisively that FP is *at best* a highly superficial theory, a partial and unpenetrating gloss on a deeper and more complex reality. Having reached this opinion, we may be forgiven for exploring the possibility that FP provides a positively misleading sketch of our internal kinematics and dynamics, one whose success is owed more to selective application and forced interpretation on our part than to genuine theoretical insight on FP's part.

A look at the history of FP does little to allay such fears, once raised. The story is one of retreat, infertility, and decadence. The presumed domain of FP used to be much larger than it is now. In primitive cultures, the behavior of most of the elements of nature were understood in intentional terms. The wind could know anger, the moon jealousy, the river generosity, the sea fury, and so forth. These were not metaphors. Sacrifices were made and auguries undertaken to placate or divine the changing passions of the gods. Despite its sterility, this animistic approach to nature has dominated our history, and it is only in the last two or three thousand years that we have restricted FP's literal application to the domain of the higher animals.

Even in this preferred domain, however, both the content and the success of FP have not advanced sensibly in two or three thousand years. The FP of the Greeks is essentially the FP we use today, and we are negligibly better at explaining human behavior in its terms than was Sophocles. This is a very long period of stagnation and infertility for any theory to display, especially when faced with such an enormous backlog of anomalies and mysteries in its own explanatory domain. Perfect theories, perhaps, have no need to evolve. But FP is profoundly imperfect. Its failure to develop its resources and extend its range of success is therefore darkly curious, and one must query the integrity of its basic categories. To use Imre Lakatos's terms, FP is a stagnant or degenerating research program, and has been for millennia.

Explanatory success to date is of course not the only dimension in which a theory can display virtue or promise. A troubled or stagnant theory may merit patience and solicitude on other grounds; for example, on grounds that it is the only theory or theoretical approach that fits well with other theories about adjacent subject matters, or the only one that promises to reduce to or be explained by some established background theory whose domain encompasses the domain of the theory at issue. In sum, it may rate credence because it holds promise of theoretical integration. How does FP rate in this dimension?

It is just here, perhaps, that FP fares poorest of all. If we approach *Homo sapiens* from the perspective of natural history and the physical sciences, we can tell a coherent story of his constitution, development, and behavioral capacities which encompasses particle physics, atomic and molecular theory, organic chemistry, evolutionary theory, biology, physiology, and materialistic neuroscience. That story, though still radically incomplete, is already extremely powerful, outperforming FP at many points even in its own domain. And it is deliberately and self-consciously coherent with the rest of our developing world picture. In short, the greatest theoretical synthesis in the history of the human race is currently in our hands, and parts of it already provide searching descriptions and explanations of human sensory input, neural activity, and motor control.

But FP is no part of this growing synthesis. Its intentional categories stand magnificently alone, without visible prospect of reduction to that larger corpus. A successful reduction cannot be ruled out, in my view, but FP's explanatory impotence and long stagnation inspire little faith that its categories will find themselves neatly reflected in the framework of neuroscience. On the contrary, one is reminded of how alchemy must have looked as elemental chemistry was taking form, how Aristotelean cosmology must have looked as classical mechanics was being articulated, or how the vitalist conception of life must have looked as organic chemistry marched forward.

In sketching a fair summary of this situation, we must make a special effort to abstract from the fact that FP is a central part of our current *lebenswelt*, and serves as the principal vehicle of our interpersonal commerce. For these facts provide FP with a conceptual inertia that goes far beyond its purely theoretical virtues. Restricting ourselves to this latter dimension, what we must say is that FP suffers explanatory failures on an epic scale, that it has been stagnant for at least twenty-five centuries, and that its categories appear (so far) to be incommensurable with or orthogonal to the categories of the background physical science whose long-term claim to explain human behavior seems undeniable. Any theory that meets this description must be allowed a serious candidate for outright elimination.

We can of course insist on no stronger conclusion at this stage. Nor is it my concern to do so. We are here exploring a possibility, and the facts demand no more, and no less, than it be taken seriously. The distinguishing feature of the eliminative materialist is that he takes it very seriously indeed.

III   Arguments against elimination

Thus the basic rationale of eliminative materialism: FP is a theory, and quite probably a false one; let us attempt, therefore to transcend it.

The rationale is clear and simple, but many find it uncompelling. It will be objected that FP is not, strictly speaking, an *empirical* theory; that it is not false, or at least not refutable by empirical considerations; and that it ought not or cannot be transcended in the fashion of a defunct empirical theory. In what follows we shall examine these objections as they flow from the most popular and best-founded of the competing positions in the philosophy of mind: functionalism.

An antipathy toward eliminative materialism arises from two distinct threads running through contemporary functionalism. The first thread concerns the *normative* character of FP, or at least of that central core of FP which treats of the propositional attitudes. FP, some will say, is a characterization of an ideal, or at least praiseworthy mode of internal activity. It outlines not only what it is to have and process beliefs and desires, but also (and inevitably) what it is to be rational in their administration. The ideal laid down by FP may be imperfectly achieved by empirical humans, but this does not impugn FP as a normative characterization. Nor need such failures seriously impugn FP even as a descriptive characterization, for it remains true that our activities can be both usefully and accurately understood as rational *except for* the occasional lapse due to noise, interference, or other breakdown, which defects empirical research may eventually unravel. Accordingly, though neuroscience may usefully augment it, FP has no pressing need to be displaced, even as a descriptive theory; nor could it be replaced, *qua* normative characterization, by any descriptive theory of neural mechanisms, since rationality is defined over propositional attitudes like beliefs and desires. FP, therefore, is here to stay.

Daniel Dennett has defended a view along these lines.[5] And the view just outlined gives voice to a theme of the property dualists as well. Karl Popper and Joseph Margolis both cite the normative nature of mental and linguistic activity as a bar to their penetration or elimination by any descriptive/materialist theory.[6] I hope to deflate the appeal of such moves below.

The second thread concerns the *abstract* nature of FP. The central claim of functionalism is that the principles of FP characterize our internal states in a fashion that makes no reference to their intrinsic nature or physical constitution. Rather, they are characterized in terms of the network of causal relations they bear to one another, and to sensory circumstances and overt behavior. Given its abstract specification, that internal economy may therefore be realized in a nomically heterogeneous variety of physical systems. All of them may differ, even radically, in their physical constitution, and yet at another level, they will all share the same nature. This view, says Fodor, "is compatible with very strong claims about the ineliminability of mental language from behavioral theories."[7] Given the real possibility of multiple instantiations in heterogeneous physical substrates, we cannot eliminate the functional characterization in favor of any theory peculiar to one such substrate. That would preclude our being able to describe the (abstract) organization that any one instantiation shares with all the other. A functional characterization of our internal states is therefore here to stay.

This second theme, like the first, assigns a faintly stipulative character to FP, as if the onus were on the empirical systems to instantiate faithfully the organization that FP specifies, instead of the onus being on FP to describe faithfully the internal activities of a naturally distinct class of empirical systems. This impression is enhanced by the standard examples used to illustrate the claims of functionalism – mousetraps, valve-lifters, arithmetical calculators, computers, robots, and the like. These are artifacts, constructed to fill a preconceived bill. In such cases, a failure of fit between the physical system and the relevant functional characterization impugns only the former, not the latter. The functional characterization is thus removed from empirical criticism in a way that is most unlike the case of an empirical theory. One prominent functionalist – Hilary Putnam – has argued outright that FP is not a corrigible theory at all.[8] Plainly, if FP is construed on these models, as regularly it is, the question of its empirical integrity is unlikely ever to pose itself, let alone receive a critical answer.

Although fair to some functionalists, the preceding is not entirely fair to Fodor.

On his view the aim of psychology is to find the *best* functional characterization of ourselves, and what that is remains an empirical question. As well, his argument for the ineliminability of mental vocabulary from psychology does not pick out current FP in particular as ineliminable. It need claim only that *some* abstract functional characterization must be retained, some articulation or refinement of FP perhaps.

His estimate of eliminative materialism remains low, however. First, it is plain that Fodor thinks there is nothing fundamentally or interestingly wrong with FP. On the contrary, FP's central conception of cognitive activity – as consisting in the manipulation of propositional attitudes – turns up as the central element in Fodor's own theory on the nature of thought (*The Language of Thought*, ibid.). And second, there remains the point that, whatever tidying up FP may or may not require, it cannot be displaced by any naturalistic theory of our physical substrate, since it is the abstract functional features of his internal states that make a person, not the chemistry of his substrate.

All of this is appealing. But almost none of it, I think, is right. Functionalism has too long enjoyed its reputation as a daring and *avant garde* position. It needs to be revealed for the short-sighted and reactionary position it is.

IV   The conservative nature of functionalism

A valuable perspective on functionalism can be gained from the following story. To begin with, recall the alchemists' theory of inanimate matter. We have here a long and variegated tradition, of course, not a single theory, but our purposes will be served by a gloss.

The alchemists conceived the "inanimate" as entirely continuous with animated matter, in that the sensible and behavioral properties of the various substances are owed to the ensoulment of baser matter by various spirits or essences. These nonmaterial aspects were held to undergo development, just as we find growth and development in the various souls of plants, animals, and humans. The alchemist's peculiar skill lay in knowing how to seed, nourish, and bring to maturity the desired spirits enmattered in the appropriate combinations.

On one orthodoxy, the four fundamental spirits (for "inanimate" matter) were named "mercury," "sulphur," "yellow arsenic," and "sal ammoniac." Each of these spirits was held responsible for a rough but characteristic syndrome of sensible, combinatorial, and causal properties. The spirit mercury, for example, was held responsible for certain features typical of metallic substances – their shininess, liquefiability, and so forth. Sulphur was held responsible for certain residual features typical of metals, and for those displayed by the ores from which running metal could be distilled. Any given metallic substance was a critical orchestration principally of these two spirits. A similar story held for the other two spirits, and among the four of them a certain domain of physical features and transformations was rendered intelligible and controllable.

The degree of control was always limited, of course. Or better, such prediction and control as the alchemists possessed was owed more to the manipulative lore acquired as an apprentice to a master, than to any genuine insight specified by the theory. The theory followed, more than it dictated, practice. But the theory did supply some rhyme to the practice, and in the absence of a developed alternative it was sufficiently compelling to sustain a long and stubborn tradition. The tradition had become faded and fragmented by the time the elemental chemistry of Lavoisier and Dalton arose to replace it for good. But let us suppose that it had hung on a little longer – perhaps because the four-spirit orthodoxy had become a thumb-worn part of everyman's common sense – and let us examine the nature of the conflict between the two theories and some possible avenues of resolution.

No doubt the simplest line of resolution, and the one which historically took place, is outright displacement. The dualistic interpretation of the four essences – as immaterial spirits – will appear both feckless and unnecessary given the power of the corpuscularian taxonomy of atomic chemistry. And a reduction of the old taxonomy to the new will appear impossible, given the extent to which the comparatively toothless old theory cross-classifies things relative to the new. Elimination would thus appear the only alternative – *unless* some cunning and determined defender of the alchemical vision has the wit to suggest the following defense.

Being "ensouled by mercury," or "sulphur," or either of the other two so-called spirits, is actually a *functional* state. The first, for example, is defined by the disposition to reflect light, to liquefy under heat, to unite with other matter in the same state, and so forth. And each of these four states is related to the others, in that the syndrome for each varies as a function of which of the other three states is also instantiated in the same substrate. Thus, the level of description comprehended by the alchemical vocabulary is abstract: various material substances, suitably "ensouled," can display the features of a metal, for example, or even of gold specifically. For it is the total syndrome of occurrent and causal properties which matters, not the corpuscularian details of the substrate. Alchemy, it is concluded, comprehends a level of organization in reality distinct from and irreducible to the organization found at the level of corpuscularian chemistry.

This view might have had considerable appeal. After all, it spares alchemists the burden of defending immaterial souls that come and go; it frees them from having to meet the very strong demands of a naturalistic reduction; and it spares them the shock and confusion of outright elimination. Alchemical theory emerges as basically all right! Nor need they appear too obviously stubborn or dogmatic in this. Alchemy as it stands, they concede, may need substantial tidying up, and experience must be our guide. But we need not fear its naturalistic displacement, they remind us, since it is the particular orchestration of the syndromes of occurrent and causal properties which makes a piece of matter gold, not the idiosyncratic details of its corpuscularian substrate. A further circumstance would have made this claim even more plausible. For the fact is, the alchemists *did* know how to make gold, in this relevantly weakened sense of 'gold', and they could so so in a variety of ways. Their "gold" was never as perfect, alas, as the "gold" nurtured in nature's womb, but what mortal can expect to match the skills of nature herself?

What this story shows is that it is at least possible for the constellation of moves, claims, and defenses characteristic of functionalism to constitute an outrage against reason and truth, and to do so with a plausibility that is frightening. Alchemy is a terrible theory, well-deserving of its complete elimination, and the defense of it just explored is reactionary, obfuscatory, retrograde, and wrong. But in historical context, that defense might have seemed wholly sensible, even to reasonable people.

The alchemical example is a deliberately transparent case of what might well be called "the functionalist strategem," and other cases are easy to imagine. A cracking good defense of the phlogiston theory of combustion can also be constructed along these lines. Construe being highly phlogisticated and being dephlogisticated as functional states defined by certain syndromes of causal dispositions; point to the great variety of natural substrates capable of combustion and calxification; claim an irreducible functional integrity for what has proved to lack any natural integrity; and bury the remaining defects under a pledge to contrive improvements. A similar recipe will provide new life for the four humors of medieval medicine, for the vital essence or archeus of pre-modern biology, and so forth.

If its application in these other cases is any guide, the functionalist strategem is a smokescreen for the preservation of error and confusion. Whence derives our assurance that in contemporary journals the same charade is not being played out on behalf of FP? The parallel with the case of alchemy is in all other respects distressingly complete, right down to the parallel between the search for artificial gold and the search for artificial intelligence!

Let me not be misunderstood on this last point. Both aims are worthy aims: thanks to nuclear physics, artificial (but real) gold is finally within our means, if only in submicroscopic quantities; and artificial (but real) intelligence eventually will be. But just as the careful orchestration of superficial syndromes was the wrong way to produce genuine gold, so may the careful orchestration of superficial syndromes be the wrong way to produce genuine intelligence. Just as with gold, what may be required is that our science penetrate to the underlying *natural* kind that gives rise to the total syndrome directly.

In summary, when confronted with the explanatory impotence, stagnant history, and systematic isolation of the intentional idioms of FP, it is not an adequate or responsive defense to insist that those idioms are abstract, functional, and irreducible in character. For one thing, this same defense could have been mounted with comparable plausibility no matter *what* haywire network of internal states our folklore had ascribed to us. And for another, the defense assumes essentially what is at issue: it assumes that it is the intentional idioms of FP, plus or minus a bit, that express the *important* features shared by all cognitive systems. But they may not. Certainly it is wrong to assume that they do, and then argue against the possibility of a materialistic displacement on grounds that it must describe matters at a level that is different from the important level. This just begs the question in favor of the older framework.

Finally, it is very important to point out that eliminative materialism is strictly *consistent* with the claim that the essence of a cognitive system resides in the abstract functional organization of its internal states. The eliminative materialist is not committed to the idea that the correct account of cognition *must* be a naturalistic account, though he may be forgiven for exploring the possibility. What he does hold is that the correct account of cognition, whether functionalistic or naturalistic, will bear about as much resemblance to FP as modern chemistry bears to four-spirit alchemy.

Let us now try to deal with the argument, against eliminative materialism, from the normative dimension of FP. This can be dealt with rather swiftly, I believe.

First, the fact that the regularities ascribed by the intentional core of FP are predicated on certain logical relations among propositions is not by itself grounds for claiming anything essentially normative about FP. To draw a relevant parallel, the fact that the regularities ascribed by the classical gas law are predicated on arithmetical relations between numbers does not imply anything essentially normative about the classical gas law. And logical relations between propositions are as much an objective matter of abstract fact as are arithmetical relations between numbers. In this respect, the law

(4) $(x)(p)(q)[(x$ believes that $p)$ & $(x$ believes that (if p then $q)))$
$\supset$ (barring confusion, distraction, etc., x believes that $q)]$

is entirely on a par with the classical gas law

(6) $(x)(P)(V)(\mu)[((x$ has a pressure $P)$ & $(x$ has a volume $V)$
& $(x$ has a quantity $\mu)) \supset$ (barring very high pressure or density,
x has a temperature of $PV/\mu R)]$

A normative dimension enters only because we happen to *value* most of the patterns ascribed by FP. But we do not value all of them. Consider

(7) $(x)(p)[((x$ desires with all his heart that $p)$ & $(x$ learns that $\sim p))$
$\supset$ (barring unusual strength of character, x is shattered that $\sim p)]$

Moreover, and as with normative convictions generally, fresh insight may motivate major changes in what we value.

Second, the laws of FP ascribe to us only a very minimal and truncated rationality, not an ideal rationality as some have suggested. The rationality characterized by the set of all FP laws falls well short of an ideal rationality. This is not surprising. We have no clear or finished conception of ideal rationality anyway; certainly the ordinary man does not. Accordingly, it is just not plausible to suppose that the explanatory failures from which FP suffers are owed primarily to human failure to live up to the ideal standard it provides. Quite to the contrary, the conception of rationality it provides appears limping and superficial, especially when compared with the dialectical complexity of our scientific history, or with the ratiocinative virtuosity displayed by any child.

Third, even if our current conception of rationality – and more generally, of cognitive virtue – is largely constituted within the sentential/propositional framework of FP, there is no guarantee that this framework is adequate to the deeper and more accurate account of cognitive virtue which is clearly needed. Even if we concede the categorial integrity of FP, at least as applied to language-using humans, it remains far from clear that the basic parameters of intellectual virtue are to be found at the categorial level comprehended by the propositional attitudes. After all, language use is something that is learned, by a brain already capable of vigorous cognitive activity; language use is acquired as only one among a great variety of learned manipulative skills; and it is mastered by a brain that evolution has shaped for a great many functions, language using being only the very latest and perhaps the least of them. Against the background of these facts, language use appears as an extremely peripheral activity, as a species specific mode of social interaction which is mastered thanks to the versatility and power of a more basic mode of activity. Why accept, then, a theory of cognitive activity that models its elements on the elements of human language? And why assume that the fundamental parameters of intellectual virtue are or can be defined over the elements at this superficial level?

A serious advance in our appreciation of cognitive virtue would thus seem to *require* that we go beyond FP, that we transcend the poverty of FP's conception of rationality by transcending its propositional kinematics entirely, by developing a deeper and more general kinematics of cognitive activity, and by distinguishing within this new framework which of the kinematically possible modes of activity are to be valued and encouraged (as more efficient, reliable, productive, or whatever). Eliminative materialism thus does not imply the end of our normative concerns. It implies only that they will have to be reconstituted at a more revealing level of understanding, the level that a matured neuroscience will provide.

What a theoretically informed future might hold in store for us, we shall now turn to explore. Not because we can foresee matters with any special clarity, but because it is important to try to break the grip on our imagination held by the propositional kinematics of FP. As far as the present section is concerned, we may summarize our conclusions as follows. FP is nothing more and nothing less than a culturally entrenched theory of how we and the higher animals work. It has no special features that make it empirically invulnerable, no unique functions that make it irreplaceable, no special status of any kind whatsoever. We shall turn a skeptical ear then, to any special pleading on its behalf.

V   Beyond folk psychology

What might the elimination of FP actually involve – not just the comparatively straightforward idioms for sensation, but the entire apparatus of propositional attitudes? That depends heavily on what neuroscience might discover, and on our determination to capitalize on it. Here follow three scenarios in which the operative conception of cognitive activity is progressively divorced from the forms and categories that characterize natural language. If the reader will indulge the lack of actual substance, I shall try to sketch some plausible form.

First suppose that research into the structure and activity of the brain, both fine-grained and global, finally does yield a new kinematics and correlative dynamics for what is now thought of as cognitive activity. The theory is uniform for all terrestrial brains, not just human brains, and it makes suitable conceptual contact with both evolutionary biology and non-equilibrium thermodynamics. It ascribes to us, at any given time, a set or configuration of complex states, which are specified within the theory as figurative "solids" within a four- or five-dimensional phase space. The laws of the theory govern the interaction, motion, and transformation of these "solid" states within that space, and also their relations to whatever sensory and motor transducers the system possesses. As with celestial mechanics, the exact specification of the "solids" involved and the exhaustive accounting of all dynamically relevant adjacent "solids" is not practically possible, for many reasons, but here also it turns out that the obvious approximations we fall back on yield excellent explanations/predictions of internal change and external behavior, at least in the short term. Regarding long-term activity, the theory provides powerful and unified accounts of the learning process, the nature of mental illness, and variations in character and intelligence across the animal kingdom as well as across individual humans.

Moreover, it provides a straightforward account of "knowledge," as traditionally conceived. According to the new theory, any declarative sentence to which a speaker would give confident assent is merely a one-dimensional *projection* – through the compound lens of Wernicke's and Broca's areas onto the idiosyncratic surface of the speaker's language – a one-dimensional projection of a four- or five-dimensional "solid" that is an element in his true kinematical state. (Recall the shadows on the wall of Plato's cave.) Being projections of that inner reality, such sentences do carry significant information regarding it and are thus fit to function as elements in a communication system. On the other hand, being *sub*dimensional projections, they reflect but a narrow part of the reality projected. They are therefore *un*fit to represent the deeper reality in all its kinematically, dynamically, and even normatively relevant respects. That is to say, a system of propositional attitudes, such as FP, must inevitably fail to capture what is going on here, though it may reflect just enough superficial structure to sustain an alchemylike tradition among folk who lack any better theory. From the perspective of the newer theory, however, it is plain that there simply are no law-governed states of the kind FP postulates. The real laws governing our internal activities are defined over different and much more complex kinematical states and configurations, as are the normative criteria for a developmental integrity and intellectual virtue.

A theoretical outcome of the kind just described may fairly be counted as a case of elimination of one theoretical ontology in favor of another, but the success here imagined for systematic neuroscience need not have any sensible effect on common practice. Old ways die hard, and in the absence of some practical necessity, they may not die at all. Even so, it is not inconceivable that some segment of the population, or all of it, should become intimately familiar with the vocabulary required to characterize our kinematical states, learn the laws governing their interactions and behavioral projections, acquire a facility in their first-person ascription, and displace the use of FP altogether, even in the marketplace. The demise of FP's ontology would then be complete.

We may now explore a second and rather more radical possibility. Everyone is familiar with Chomsky's thesis that the human mind or brain contains innately and uniquely the abstract structures for learning and using specifically human natural languages. A competing hypothesis is that our brain does indeed contain innate structures, but that those structurse have as their original and still primary function the organization of perceptual experience, the administration of linguistic categories being an acquired and additional function for which evolution has only incidentally suited them.[9] This hypothesis has the advantage of not requiring the evolutionary saltation that Chomsky's view would seem to require, and there are other advantages as well. But these matters need not concern us here. Suppose, for our purposes, that this competing view is true, and consider the following story.

Research into the neural structures that fund the organization and processing of perceptual information reveals that they are capable of administering a great variety of complex tasks, some of them showing a complexity far in excess of that shown by natural language. Natural languages, it turns out, exploit only a very elementary portion of the available machinery, the bulk of which serves far more complex activities beyond the ken of the propositional conceptions of FP. The detailed unraveling of what that machinery is and of the capacities it has makes it plain that a form of language far more sophisticated than "natural" language, though decidedly "alien" in its syntactic and semantic structures, could also be learned and used by our innate systems. Such a novel system of communication, it is quickly realized, could raise the efficiency of information exchange between brains by an order of magnitude, and would enhance epistemic evaluation by a comparable amount, since it would reflect the underlying structure of our cognitive activities in greater detail than does natural language.

Guided by our new understanding of those internal structures, we manage to construct a new system of verbal communication entirely distinct from natural language, with a new and more powerful combinatorial grammar over novel elements forming novel combinations with exotic properties. The compounded strings of this alternative system – call them "übersätze" – are not evaluated as true or false, nor are the relations between them remotely analogous to the relations of entailment, etc., that hold between sentences. They display a different organization and manifest different virtues.

Once constructed, this "language" proves to be learnable; it has the the power projected; and in two generations it has swept the planet. Everyone uses the new system. The syntactic forms and semantic categories of so-called "natural" language disappear entirely. And with them disappear the propositional attitudes of FP, displaced by a more revealing scheme in which (of course) "übersatzenal attitudes" play the leading role. FP again suffers elimination.

This second story, note, illustrates a theme with endless variations. There are possible as many different "folk psychologies" as there are possible differently structured communication systems to serve as models for them.

A third and even stranger possibility can be outlined as follows. We know that there is considerable lateralization of function between the two cerebral hemispheres, and that the two hemispheres make use of the information they get from each other by way of the great cerebral commissure – the corpus callosum – a giant cable of neurons connecting them. Patients whose commissure has been surgically severed display a variety of behavioral deficits that indicate a loss of access by one hemisphere to information it used to get from the other. However, in people with callosal agenesis (a congenital defect in which the connecting cable is simply absent), there is little or no behavioral deficit, suggesting that the two hemispheres have learned to exploit the information carried in other less direct pathways connecting them through the subcortical regions. This suggests that, even in the normal case, a developing hemisphere *learns* to make use of the information the cerebral commissure deposits at its doorstep. What we have then, in the case of a normal human, is two physically distinct cognitive systems (both capable of independent function) responding in a systematic and learned fashion to exchanged information. And what is especially interesting about this case is the sheer amount of information exchanged. The cable of the commissure consists of ≈ 200 million neurons,[10] and even if we assume that each of these fibres is capable of one of only two possible states each second (a most conservative estimate), we are looking at a channel whose information capacity is $> 2 \times 10^8$ binary bits/second. Compare this to the < 500 bits/second capacity of spoken English.

Now, if two distinct hemispheres can learn to communicate on so impressive a scale, why shouldn't two distinct brains learn to do it also? This would require an artificial "commissure" of some kind, but let us suppose that we can fashion a workable transducer for implantation at some site in the brain that research reveals to be suitable, a transducer to convert a symphony of neural activity into (say) microwaves radiated from an aerial in the forehead, and to perform the reverse function of converting received microwaves back into neural activation. Connecting it up need not be an insuperable problem. We simply trick the normal processes of dendritic arborization into growing their own myriad connections with the active microsurface of the transducer.

Once the channel is opened between two or more people, they can learn (*learn*) to exchange information and coordinate their behavior with the same intimacy and virtuosity displayed by your own cerebral hemispheres. Think what this might do for hockey teams, and ballet companies, and research teams! If the entire population were thus fitted out, spoken language of any kind might well disappear completely, a victim of the "why crawl when you can fly?" principle. Libraries become filled not with books, but with long recordings of exemplary bouts of neural activity. These constitute a growing cultural heritage, an evolving "Third World," to use Karl Popper's terms. But they do not consist of sentences or arguments.

How will such people understand and conceive of other individuals? To this question I can only answer, "In roughly the same fashion that your right hemisphere 'understands' and 'conceives of' your left hemisphere – intimately and efficiently, but not propositionally!"

These speculations, I hope, will evoke the required sense of untapped possibilities, and I shall in any case bring them to a close here. Their function is to make some inroads into the aura of inconceivability that commonly surrounds the idea that we might reject FP. The felt conceptual strain even finds expression in an argument to the effect that the thesis of eliminative materialism is incoherent since it denies the very conditions presupposed by the assumption that it is meaningful. I shall close with a brief discussion of this very popular move.

As I have received it, the reductio proceeds by pointing out that the statement of eliminative materialism is just a meaningless string of marks or noises, unless that string is the expression of a certain *belief*, and a certain *intention* to communicate, and a *knowledge* of the grammar of the language, and so forth. But if the statement of eliminative materialism is true, then there are no such states to express. The statement at issue would then be a meaningless string of marks or noises. It would therefore *not* be true. Therefore it is not true. Q.E.D.

The difficulty with any nonformal reductio is that the conclusion against the initial assumption is always no better than the material assumptions invoked to reach the incoherent conclusion. In this case the additional assumptions involve a certain theory of meaning, one that presupposes the integrity of FP. But formally speaking, one can as well infer, from the incoherent result, that this theory of meaning is what must be rejected. Given the independent critique of FP leveled earlier, this would even seem the preferred option. But in any case, one cannot simply assume that particular theory of meaning without begging the question at issue, namely, the integrity of FP.

The question-begging nature of this move is most graphically illustrated by the following analog, which I owe to Patricia Churchland.[11] The issue here, placed in the seventeenth century, is whether there exists such a substance as *vital spirit*. At the time, this substance was held, without significant awareness of real alternatives, to be that which distinguished the animate from the inanimate. Given the monopoly enjoyed by this conception, given the degree to which it was integrated with many of our other conceptions, and given the magnitude of the revisions any serious alternative conception would require, the following refutation of any anti-vitalist claim would be found instantly plausible.

> The anti-vitalist says that there is no such thing as vital spirit. But this claim is self-refuting. The speaker can expect to be taken seriously only if his claim cannot. For if the claim is true, then the speaker does not have vital spirit and must be *dead*. But if he is dead, then his statement is a meaningless string of noises, devoid of reason and truth.

The question-begging nature of this argument does not, I assume, require elaboration. To those moved by the earlier argument, I commend the parallel for examination.

The thesis of this paper may be summarized as follows. The propositional attitudes of folk psychology do not constitute an unbreachable barrier to the advancing tide of neuroscience. On the contrary, the principled displacement of folk psychology is not only richly possible, it represents one of the most intriguing theoretical displacements we can currently imagine.

NOTES

An earlier draft of this paper was presented at the University of Ottawa, and to the *Brain, Mind, and Person* colloquium at SUNY, Oswego. My thanks for the suggestions and criticisms that have informed the present version.

1 See Paul Feyerabend, "Materialism and mind–body problem," *Review of Metaphysics* XVII.I, 65 (September 1963), 49–66; Richard Rorty, "Mind–body identity, privacy, and categories," *Journal of Metaphysics*, XIX.I, 73 (September 1965), 24–54; and my *Scientific Realism and the Plasticity of Mind* (New York: Cambridge, 1979).

2 We shall examine a handful of these laws presently. For a more comprehensive sampling of the laws of folk psychology; see my *Scientific Realism and the Plasticity of Mind*, ibid., ch. 4. For a detailed examination of the folk principles that underwrite action explanations in particular, see my "The logical character of action explanations," *Philosophical Review* LXXIX, 2 (April 1970), 214–36.

3 Staying within an objectual interpretation of the quantifiers, perhaps the simplest way to make systematic sense of expressions like $\ulcorner x$ believes that $p \urcorner$ and closed sentences formed therefrom is just to construe whatever occurs in the nested position held by 'p', 'q', etc. as there having the function of a singular term. Accordingly, the standard connectives, as they

occur between terms in that nested position, must be construed as there functioning as operators that form compound singular terms from other singular terms, and not as sentence operators. The compound singular terms so formed denote the appropriate compound propositions. Substitutional quantification will of course underwrite a different interpretation, and there are other approaches as well. Especially appealing is the prosentential approach of Dorothy Grover, Joseph Camp, and Nuel Belnap, "A prosentential theory of truth," *Philosophical Studies* XXVII, 2 (February 1975), 73–125. But the resolution of these issues is not vital to the present discussion.

4　A possible response here is to insist that the cognitive activity of animals and infants is linguaformal in its elements, structures, and processing right from birth. J. A. Fodor, in *The Language of Thought* (New York: Crowell 1975), has erected a positive theory of thought on the assumption that the innate forms of cognitive activity have precisely the form here denied. For a critique of Fodor's view, see Patricia Churchland, "Fodor on Language Learning," *Synthese* XXXVIII, 1 (May 1978), 149–59.

5　Most explicitly in "Three kinds of intentional psychology," in R. A. Healy (ed.), *Reduction, Time and Reality*, Cambridge University Press, 1981, but this theme of Dennett's goes all the way back to his "Intentional systems," *Journal of Philosophy*, LXVIII, 4 (Feb. 25, 1971), 87–106; reprinted in his *Brainstorms* (Montgomery, Vt.: Bradford Books, 1978).

6　Popper, *Objective Knowledge* (New York: Oxford, 1972); with J. Eccles, *The Self and Its Brain* (New York: Springer Verlag, 1978). Margolis, *Persons and Minds* (Boston: Reidel, 1978).

7　*Psychological Explanation* (New York: Random House, 1968), p. 116.

8　"Robots: Machines or artificially created life?", *Journal of Philosophy*, LXI, 21 (Nov. 12, 1964): 668–91, pp. 675, 681 ff.

9　Richard Gregory defends such a view in "The Grammar of Vision," *Listener* LXXXIII, 2133 (February 1970), 242–6; reprinted in his *Concepts and Mechanisms of Perception* (London: Duckworth, 1975), pp. 622–9.

10　M. S. Gazzaniga and J. E. LeDoux, *The Integrated Mind* (New York: Plenum Press, 1975).

11　"Is determinism self-refuting?", *Mind* 90 (1981), 99–101.

10

Neurophilosophy and Connectionism

Neural Representation and Neural Computation

PATRICIA SMITH CHURCHLAND and TERRENCE J. SEJNOWSKI

The types of representation and the styles of computation in the brain appear to be very different from the symbolic expressions and logical inferences that are used in sentence-logic models of cognition. In this paper we explore the consequences that brain-style processing may have on theories of cognition. Connectionist models are used as examples to illustrate neural representation and computation in the pronouncing of English text and in the extracting of shape parameters from shaded images. Levels of analysis are not independent in connectionist models, and the dependencies between levels provide an opportunity to co-evolve theories at all levels. This is a radical departure from the a priori, introspection-based strategy that has characterized most previous work in epistemology.

1 How do we represent the world?

The central epistemological question, from Plato on, is this: *How is representation of a world by a self possible?* So far as we can tell, there is a reality existing external to ourselves, and it appears that we do come to represent that reality, and sometimes even to know how its initial appearance to our senses differs from how it actually is. How is this accomplished, and how is knowledge possible? How is science itself possible?

The dominant philosophical tradition has been to try to resolve the epistemological puzzles by invoking mainly intuition and logic to figure out such things as the organization of knowledge, the nature of the "mirroring" of the outer world by the inner world, and the roles of reason and inference in the generation of

"Neural Representation and Neural computation" by P. S. Churchland and T. J. Sejnowski. From *Neural Connections, Mental Computations*, edited by L. Nadel, L. Cooper, P. Culicover and R. M. Harnish, MIT Press (1989), by kind permission of the publisher.

internal models of reality. Epistemology thus pursued was the product of "pure reason," not of empirical investigation, and thus epistemological theories were believed to delimit the necessary conditions, the absolute foundations, and the incontrovertible presuppositions of human knowledge. For this a priori task – a task of reflective understanding and pure reason – empirical observations by psychologists and neurobiologists are typically considered irrelevant, or at least incapable of effecting any significant correction of the a priori conclusions. Plato, Descartes, and Kant are some of the major historical figures in that tradition; some contemporary figures are Chisholm (1966), Strawson (1966), Davidson (1974), and McGinn (1982). It is safe to say that most philosophers still espouse the a priori strategy to some nontrivial extent.

In a recent departure from this venerable tradition of a priori philosophy, some philosophers have argued that epistemology itself must be informed by the psychological and neurobiological data that bear upon how in fact we represent and model the world. First articulated in a systematic and powerful way by Quine (1960),[1] this new "naturalism" has begun to seem more in keeping with evolutionary and biological science and to promise more testable and less speculative answers.

If, as it seems, acquiring knowledge is an essentially biological phenomenon, in the straightforward sense that it is something our brains do, then there is no reason to expect that brains should have evolved to have a priori knowledge of the true nature of things: not of fire, not of light, not of the heart and the blood, and certainly not of knowledge or of its own microstructure and microfunction. There are, undoubtedly, innate dispositions to behave in certain ways, to believe certain things, and to organize data in certain ways, but innateness is no guarantee of truth, and it is the truth that a priori reflections are presumed to reveal. Innate beliefs and cognitive structure cannot be assumed to be either optimal or true, because all evolution "cares" about is that the internal models enable the species to survive. Satisficing is good enough. It is left for science to care about the truth (or perhaps empirical adequacy), and the theories science generates may well show the inadequacies of our innately specified models of external reality. Even more dramatically, they may show the inadequacy of our model of our internal reality – of the nature of our selves.

The a priori insights of the Great Philosophers should be understood, therefore, not as The Absolute Truth about how the mind-brain must be, but as articulations of the *assumptions* that live deep in our collective *conception* of ourselves. As assumptions, however, they may be misconceived and empirically unsound, or at least they may be open to revision in the light of scientific progress. The possibility of such revision does not entail that the assumptions are ludicrous or useless. On the contrary, they may well be very important elements in the theoretical scaffolding as neurobiology and psychology inch their way toward empirically adequate theories of mind-brain function. The methodological point is that in science we cannot proceed with no theoretical framework, so even intuitive folk theory is better than nothing as the scientific enterprise gets underway.

In addition to asking how the self can know about the external reality, Kant asked: How is representation of a *self* by a knowing self possible? One of his important ideas was that the nature of the internal world of the self is no more unmediated or *given* than is knowledge of the external world of physical objects in space and time. A modern version of this insight says: Just as the inner thoughts and experiences may represent but not *resemble* the outer reality, so the inner thoughts may represent but not resemble the inner reality of which they are the representation. This idea, taken with Quine's naturalism, implies that if we want to know how we represent the world – the external world of colored, moving objects, and the internal world of thoughts, consciousness, motives, and dreams – the scientific approach is likely to be the most rewarding. Inner knowledge, like outer knowledge, is conceptually and theoretically mediated – it is the result of complex information processing. Whether our intuitive understanding of the nature of our inner world is at all adequate is an empirical question, not an a priori one.

If empirical results are relevant to our understanding of how the mind-brain represents, it is also entirely possible that scientific progress on this frontier will be as revolutionary as it has been in astronomy, physics, chemistry, biology, and geology. With this observation comes the recognition that it may reconfigure our current assumptions about knowledge, consciousness, representations, and the self at least as much as Copernicus and Darwin reconfigured our dearest assumptions about the nature of the universe and our place in it. Our intuitive assumptions, and even what seems phenomenologically obvious, may be misconceived and may thus undergo reconfiguration as new theory emerges from psychology and neurobiology.

Philosophers – and sometimes psychologists, and occasionally even neuroscientists – generally make one of two responses to the naturalists' conception of the status of our self-understanding:

[1] Philosophy is an a priori discipline, and the fundamental conceptual truths about the nature of the mind, of knowledge, of reason, etc. will come only from a priori investigations. In this way, philosophy sets the bounds for science – indeed, the bounds of sense, as Strawson (1966) would put it. In a more extreme vein, some existentialist philosophers would claim that the naturalistic approach is itself symptomatic of a civilizational neurosis: the infatuation with science. On this view, the scientific approach to human nature is deeply irrational. Mandt (1986, p. 274) describes the existentialist criticism as follows: "That scientific modes of thought have become paradigmatic indicates the degree to which traditional modes of human life and experience have disintegrated, plunging civilization into a nihilistic abyss."

[2] Even if a naturalistic approach is useful for some aspects of the nature of knowledge and representation, the neurosciences in particular are largely irrelevant to the enterprise. Neuroscience may be fascinating enough in its own right, but for a variety of reasons it is irrelevant to answering the questions we care about concerning cognition, representation, intelligent behavior, learning, consciousness, and so forth. Psychology and linguistics might actually be useful in informing us about such matters, but neurobiology is just off the book.

2 Why is neurobiology dismissed as irrelevant to understanding how the mind works?

2.1 *The traditional problem*

In its traditional guise, the mind–body problem can be stated thus: Are mental phenomena (experiences, beliefs, desires, etc.) actually phenomena of the physical brain? Dualists have answered No to this question. On the dualist's view, mental phenomena inhere in a special, nonphysical substance: the mind (also referred to as the soul or the spirit). The mind, on the dualist's theory, is the ghost in the machine; it is composed not of physical material obeying physical laws but of soul-stuff, or "spooky" stuff, and it operates according to principles unique to spooky stuff.

The most renowned of the substance dualists are Plato and Descartes, and, more recently, J. C. Eccles (1977) and Richard Swinburne (1986). Because dualists believe the mind to be a wholly separate kind of stuff or entity, they expect that it can be understood only in its own terms. At most, neuroscience can shed light on the *interaction* between mind and body, but not on the nature of the mind itself. Dualists consequently see psychology as essentially independent of neurobiology, which, after all, is devoted to finding out how the *physical* stuff of the nervous system works. It might be thought a bonus of dualism that it implies that to understand the mind we do not have to know much about the brain.

Materialism answers the mind–body question (Are mental states actually states of the physical brain?) in the affirmative. The predominant arguments for materialism draw upon the spectacular failure of dualism to cohere with the rest of ongoing science. And as physics, molecular biology, evolutionary biology, and neuroscience have progressed, this failure has become more rather than less marked. In short, the weight of empirical evidence is against the existence of special soul-stuff (spooky stuff). (For a more thorough discussion of the failures of substance dualism, see P. S. Churchland 1986.) Proponents of materialism include Hobbes (in the seventeenth century), B. F. Skinner (1957, 1976), J. J. C. Smart (1959), W. V. O. Quine (1960), D. C. Dennett (1978), and P. M. Churchland (1988).

Despite the general commitment to materialism, there are significant differences among materialists in addressing the central question of how best to explain psychological states. Strict behaviorists, such as Skinner, thought that explanations would take the form of stimulus–response profiles *exclusively*. Supporting this empirical hypothesis with a philosophical theory, philosophical behaviorists claimed that the mental terminology itself could be analyzed into sheerly physicalistic language about dispositions to behave. (For discussion, see P. M. Churchland 1988). Curiously, perhaps, the behaviorists (both empirical and philosophical) share with the dualists the conviction that it is not necessary to understand the workings of the brain in order to explain intelligent behavior. On the behaviorists' research ideology, again we have a bonus: In order to explain behavior, *we do not have to know anything about the brain*.

In contrast to behaviorism, identity theorists (Smart 1959; Enc 1983) claimed that mental states, such as visual perceptions, pains, beliefs, and drives, were in fact identical to states of the brain, though it would of course be up to neuroscience to discover precisely what brain states were in fact identical to what mental states. On the research ideology advocated by these materialists, explanation of behavior will have to refer to inner representations and hence to what the brain is doing.

2.2   The contemporary problem: theory dualism

Many philosophers who are materialists to the extent that they doubt the existence of soul-stuff nonetheless believe that psychology ought to be essentially autonomous from neuroscience, and that neuroscience will not contribute significantly to our understanding of perception, language use, thinking, problem solving, and (more generally) cognition. Thus, the mind–body problem in its contemporary guise is this: Can we get a *unified* science of the mind-brain? Will psychological theory reduce to neuroscience?

A widespread view (which we call theory dualism) answers No to the above question. Typically, three sorts of reasons are offered:

(a)   *Neuroscience is too hard.* The brain is too complex; there are too many neurons and too many connections, and it is a hopeless task to suppose we can ever understand complex higher functions in terms of the dynamics and organization of neurons.

(b)   *The argument from multiple instantiability.* Psychological states are functional states and, as such, can be implemented (instantiated) in diverse machines (Putnam 1967; Fodor 1975; Pylyshyn 1984). Therefore, no particular psychological state, such as believing that the earth is round or that $2 + 2 = 4$, can be identified with exactly this or that machine state. So no functional (cognitive) process can be reduced to the behavior of particular neuronal systems.

(c)   *Psychological states have intentionality.* That is, they are identified in terms of their semantic content; they are "about" other things; they represent things; they have logical relations to one another. We can think about objects in their absence, and even of nonexistent objects. For example, if someone has the belief that Mars is warmer than Venus, then that psychological state is specified as the state it is in terms of the sentence "Mars is warmer than Venus", which has a specific meaning (its content) and which is logically related to other sentences. It is a belief *about* Mars and Venus, but it is not caused by Mars or Venus. Someone might have this belief because he was told, or because he deduced it from other things he knew. In cognitive generalizations states are related semantically and logically, whereas in neurobiological generalizations states can only be *causally* related. Neurobiological explanations cannot be sensitive to the logical relations between the contents of cognitive states, or to meaning or "aboutness." They respond only to *causal* properties. Neurobiology, therefore, cannot do justice to cognition, and thus no reduction is possible.

2.3 *What is wrong with theory dualism?*

In opposition to theory dualists, reductionists think we ought to strive for an integration of psychological and neurobiological theory. Obviously, a crucial element in the discussion concerns what is meant by "reduction"; hence, part of what must first be achieved is a proper account of what sort of business inter-theoretic reduction is.

Roughly, the account is this: Reductions are *explanations* of phenomena described by one theory in terms of the phenomena described by a more basic theory. Reductions typically involve the co-evolution of theories over time, and as they co-evolve one theory is normally revised, corrected, and modified by its co-evolutionary cohort theory at the other level. This revisionary interaction can, and usually does, go both ways: from the more basic to the less basic theory and vice versa. It is important to emphasize the modification to theories as they co-evolve, because sometimes the modification is radical and entails massive reconfiguration of the very categories used to describe the phenomena. In such an event, the very data to be explained may come to be redescribed under pressure from the evolving theories. Examples of categories that have undergone varying degrees of revision, from the minor to the radical, include impetus, caloric, gene, neuron, electricity, instinct, life, and very recently, excitability (in neurons) (Schaffner 1976; P. M. Churchland 1979; Hooker 1981).

Because reductionism is frequently misunderstood, it is necessary to be explicit about what is *not* meant. First, seeking reductions of macro-level theory to micro level does not imply that one must first know everything about the elements of the micro theory before research at the macro level can be usefully undertaken. Quite the reverse is advocated – research should proceed at all levels of the system, and co-evolution of theory may enhance progress at all levels. Data from one level *constrain* theorizing at that level and at other levels. Additionally, the reduction of theories does *not* mean that the reduced phenomena somehow disappear or are discredited. The theory of optics was reduced to the theory of electromagnetic radiation, but light itself did not disappear, not did it become disreputable to study light at the macro level. Nor was the reduced theory cast out as useless or discredited; on the contrary, it was and continues to be useful for addressing phenomena at a higher level of description. As for the phenomenon, it is what it is, and it continues to be whatever it is as theories are reduced or abandoned. Whether a category is ultimately rejected or revised depends on its scientific integrity, and that is, of course, determined empirically. (For more detail on inter-theoretic reduction, see P. S. Churchland 1986.)

Given this brief account of reduction as a backdrop, an outline of how the reductionist answers the theory dualist goes as follows:

(a) Neuroscience *is* hard, but with many new techniques now available, an impressive body of data is available to constrain our theories, and a lot of data are very suggestive as to how neural networks function. (See Sejnowski and Churchland, in press.) We have begun to see the shape of neurobiological answers to functional questions, such as how information is stored, how networks learn, and how networks of neurons represent.

(b) High-level states are multiply instantiable. So what? If, in any given species, we can show that particular functional states are identical to specific neuronal configurations (for example, that being in REM sleep is having a specified neuronal state, or that one type of learning involves changing synaptic weights according to a Hebb rule), that will be sufficient to declare a reduction relative to that domain (Richardson 1979; Enc 1983; P. S. Churchland 1986; section 3 below). Very pure philosophers who cannot bring themselves to call these perfectly respectable domain-relative explanations "reductions" are really just digging in on who gets to use the word. Moreover, it should be emphasized that the explanation of high-level cognitive phenomena will not be achieved directly in terms of phenomena at the lowest level of nervous-system organization, such as synapses and individual neurons. Rather, the explanation will refer to properties at higher structural levels, such as networks or systems. Functional properties of networks and systems will be explained by reference to properties at the next level down, and so on. What we envision is a chain of explanations linking higher to next-lower levels, and so on down the ladder of structural levels. (See Sejnowski and Churchland, in press.) Aspects of individual variation at the synaptic and cellular levels are probably invisible at the systems level, where similarity of larger-scale emergent properties, such as position in a high-dimensional parameter space, is critical in identifying similarity of information-processing function (Sejnowski et al. 1988). A theory of how states in a nervous system represent or model the world will need to be set in the context of the evolution and development of nervous systems, and will try to explain the interactive role of neural states in the ongoing neuro-cognitive economy of the system. Nervous systems do not represent all aspects of the physical environment; they selectively represent information a species needs, given its environmental niche and its way of life. Nervous systems are programmed to respond to certain selected features, and within limits they learn other features through experience by encountering examples and generalizing. Cognitive neuroscience is now beginning to understand how this is done (Livingstone 1988; Goldman-Rakic 1988; Kelso et al. 1986). Although the task is difficult, it now seems reasonable to assume that the "aboutness" or "meaningfulness" of representational states is not a spooky relation but a neurobiological relation. As we come to understand more about the dynamical properties of networks, we may ultimately be able to generate a theory of how human language is learned and represented by our sort of nervous system, and thence to explain language-dependent kinds of meaning. Because this answer is highly cryptic and because intentionality has often seemed forever beyond the reach of neurobiology, the next section will focus on intentionality: the theory dualist's motivation, and the reductionist's strategy.

3 Levels, intentionality, and the sentence-logic model of the mind

3.1 Sentential attitudes and the computer metaphor

Two deep and interrelated assumptions concerning the nature of cognition drive the third anti-reductionist argument:

[1] Cognition essentially involves representations and computations. Representations are, in general, symbolic structures, and computations are, in general, rules (such as rules of logic) for manipulating those symbolic structures.

[2] A good model for understanding mind-brain functions is the computer – that is, a machine based on the same logical foundations as a Turing machine and on the von Neumann architecture for a digital computer. Such machines are ideally suited for the manipulation of symbols according to rules. The computer metaphor suggests that the mind-brain, at the information-processing level, can be understood as a kind of digital computer, the problem for cognitive psychology is to determine the program that our brains run.

The motivating vision here is that cognition is to be modeled largely on language and logical reasoning; having a thought is, functionally speaking, having a sentence in the head, and thinking is, functionally speaking, doing logic, or at least running on procedures very like logic. Put thus baldly, it may seem faintly ridiculous, but the theory is supported quite plausibly by the observation that beliefs, thoughts, hopes, desires, and so forth are essential in the explanation of cognition, and that such states are irreducibly semantic because they are identified in virtue of their content sentences. That is, such states are always and essentially beliefs that *p*, thoughts that *p*, or desires that *p*, where for "*p*" we substitute the appropriate sentence, such as "Nixon was a Russian spy" or "Custard is made with milk". Such cognitive states – the so-called sentential attitudes – are the states they are in virtue of the sentences that specify what they are about. Moreover, a content sentence stands in specific logical and semantic relations to other sentences. The state transitions are determined by semantic and logical relations between the content sentences, not by casual relations among states neurobiologically described. Thus, cognitive states have *meaning* (that is, content, or intentionality), and it might be argued that it is precisely in virtue of their meaningfulness that they play the role in cognition that they do.

The fundamental conception is, accordingly, well and truly rooted in folk psychology, the body of concepts and everyday lore by means of which we routinely explain one another's behavior by invoking sentential attitudes (Stich 1983; P. M. Churchland 1988) – for example, Smith paid for the vase because he believed that his son had dropped it and he feared that the store owner would be angry. In these sorts of intentional explanations, the basic unit of representation is the sentence, and state transitions are accomplished through the following of rules: deductive inference, inductive inference, and assorted other rules.

Extending the framework of folk psychology to get an encompassing account of cognition in general, this approach takes it that thinking, problem solving, language use, perception, and so forth will be understood as we determine the sequence of sentences corresponding to the steps in a given information-processing task; that is, as we understand the mechanics of sentence crunching. According to this research paradigm, known as sententialism, it is the task of cognitive science to figure out what programs the brain runs, and neuroscience can then check these top-down hypotheses against the wetware to see if they are generally possible. (See especially Fodor 1975, 1981; Pylyshyn 1984.)

3.2   Is cognition mainly symbol manipulation in the language of thought?

Although this view concerning the nature of cognition and the research strategy for studying the cognition may be appealing (where much of the appeal is derived from the comfortable place found for folk psychology), it suffers from major defects. Many of these defects have been discussed in detail by Anderson and Hinton (1981) by P. S. Churchland (1986), and in various chapters of McClelland and Rumelhart (1986). A summary will call them to mind:

[1] Many cognitive tasks, such as visual recognition and answering simple true-or-false questions, can be accomplished in about half a second. Given what we know about conduction velocities and synaptic delays in neurons, this allows about 5 milliseconds per computational step, which means that there is time for only about 100 steps. For a sequential program run on a conventional computer, 100 steps is not going to get us remotely close to task completion. Feldman and Ballard (1982) call this the hundred-step rule.

[2] Anatomically and physiologically, the brain is a parallel system, not a sequential von Neumann machine. The neural architecture is highly interconnected. Neurons such as Purkinje cells may have upwards of 80,000 input connections, and neurons in cerebral cortex can have upwards of 10,000 output connections (Anderson and Hinton 1981; Pellionisz and Llinas 1982; Sejnowski 1986).

[3] However information is stored in nervous systems, it appears to be radically unlike information storage in a digital computer, where storage and processing are separated and items are stored in memory according to addressable *locations*. In nervous systems, information seems to be stored in the connections between the same neurons that process the information. There does not appear to be a distinct storage location for each piece of stored information, and information is content addressable rather than location addressable. Information storage is probably at least somewhat distributed rather than punctuate, since memories tend to be degraded with damage to the system rather than selectively wiped out one by one.

[4] A task may fall gracefully to one architecture and not to another. Certain kinds of tasks, such as numerical calculation, fall gracefully to a von Neumann architecture, but others, such as learning or associative memory, do not. Things we humans find effortless (such as facial recognition and visual perception) are tasks which artificial intelligence has great difficulty

simulating on a von Neumann architecture, whereas things we find "effortful" (such as simple proofs in the propositional calculus or mathematic calculations) are straightforward for a digital computer (Anderson and Hinton 1981; Rumelhart, Hinton and McClelland 1986). This suggests that the computational style of nervous systems may be very unlike that suited to von Neumann architectures.

[5] The hardware/software analogy fails for many reasons, the most prominent of which are that nervous systems are plastic and that neurons continually change as we grow and learn. Related, perhaps, is the observation that nervous systems degrade gracefully and are relatively fault tolerant. A von Neumann machine is rigid and fault intolerant, and a breakdown of one tiny component disrupts the machine's performance.

[6] The analogy between levels of description in a conventional computer (such as the hardware/software distinction) and levels of explanation in nervous systems may well be profoundly misleading. Exactly how many levels of organization we need to postulate in order to understand nervous-system function is an empirical question, and it may turn out that there are many levels between the molecular and the behavioral. In nervous systems we may already discern as distinct descriptive levels the molecule, the membrane, the cell, the circuit, networks, maps, brain systems, and several levels of behavior (from the reflexive to the highest levels of cognition). Other levels may come to be described as more is discovered about the nature of nervous systems. As is discussed below, the properties at one level may constrain the kind of properties realizable at another level.

[7] Nonverbal animals and infraverbal humans present a major problem for the sentence-logic theory of cognition: How is their cognition accomplished? On the sentence-logic theory of cognition, either their cognition resembles the human variety (and hence involves symbol manipulation according to rules, and a language of thought replete with a substantial conceptual repertoire) or their cognitive processes are entirely different from the usual human ones. Neither alternative is remotely credible. The first lacks any evidence. At best, its defense is circular; it helps to save the theory. The second alternative entails a radical discontinuity in evolution – sufficiently radical that language-of-thought cognition is a bolt from the blue. This implies that evolutionary biology and developmental neurobiology are mistaken in some fundamental respects. Since neither alternative can be taken seriously, the hypothesis itself has diminished credibility.

If cognition, then, is *not*, in general, to be understood on the sentence-logical model, the pressing questions then are these: How *does* the brain represent? How do nervous systems model the external world of objects in motion and the internal world of the nervous system itself? And when representations do stand in semantic and logical relations to one another, how is this achieved by neural networks? How is the semantic and logical structure of language – as we both comprehend and speak – represented in the brain? According to the rejected model, we postulate an internal organization – a language of thought – with the very same structure and organization as language. But if that model is rejected, what do we replace it with?

These are, of course, *the* central questions, and getting answers will not be easy. But the difficulty should not make the language-of-thought hypothesis more appealing. In certain respects, the current scientific state of a general theory of representation is analogous to the science of embryology in the nineteenth century. The development of highly structured, complex, fully formed organisms from eggs and sperm is a profoundly amazing thing. Faced with this mystery, some scientists concluded that the only way to explain the emergence of a fully structured organism at birth was to join the ancients in assuming that the structure was already there. Hence the homuncular theory of reproduction, which claimed that a miniature but complete human already exists in the sperm and merely expands during its tenure in the womb.

We now know that there *is* structure in the sperm (and the egg) – not in the form of a miniature, fully structured organism, but mainly in the form of DNA – a molecule that looks not at *all* like a fully formed human. Thus, the structure of the cause does not resemble the structure of the effect. Accordingly, the homuncular theorists were right in supposing that the highly structured neonate does not come from *nothing*, but they were wrong in looking for a structural resemblance between cause and effect. It was, of course, terribly hard to imagine the nature of the structural organization that enables development yet in no way resembles the final product. Only through molecular biology and detailed work in embryology have we begun to understand how one kind of structure can, through intermediate mechanisms, yield another, very different kind of structure.

The parallel with cognitive neurobiology is this: The neuronal processes underlying cognition have a structure of some kind, but almost certainly it will not, in general, look anything like the semantic/logic structure visible in overt language. The organizational principles of nervous systems are what permit highly complex, structured patterns of behavior, for it is certain that the behavioral structure does not emerge magically from neuronal chaos. As things stand, it is very hard to imagine what those organizational principles could look like, and, just as in genetics and embryology, we can find answers only by framing hypotheses and doing experiments.

Instead of starting from the old sentence-logic model, we model information processing in terms of *the trajectory of a complex nonlinear dynamical system in a very high-dimensional space*. This structure does not resemble sentences arrayed in logical sequences, but it is potentially rich enough and complex enough to yield behavior capable of supporting semantic and logical relationships. We shall now explore what representing looks like in a particular class of nonlinear dynamical systems called connectionist models.

4   Representation in connectionist models

As the name implies, a connectionist model is characterized by connections and differential strengths of connections between processing units. Processing units are meant to be rather like neurons, and communicate with one another by signals (such as firing rate) that are numerical rather than symbolic. Connectionist models are designed to perform a task by specifying the architecture: the number of units, their arrangement in layers and columns, the patterns of connectivity,

Neurons as Processors

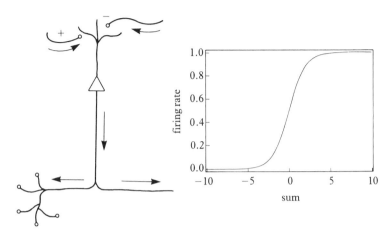

Figure 1   Left: Schematic model of a neuron-like processing unit that receives synapse-like inputs from other processing units. Right: Nonlinear sigmoid-shaped transformation between summed inputs and the output "firing rate" of a processing unit. The output is a continuous value between 0 and 1.

and the weight or strength of each connection (figures 1 and 2). These models have close ties with the computational level on which the task is specified, and with the implementation level on which the task is physically instantiated (Marr 1982). This species of network models should properly be considered a class of algorithms specified at various levels of organization – in some cases at the small-circuit level, in other cases at the system level. Both the task description and the neural embodiment are, however, crucially important in constraining the class of networks that will be explored. On the one hand the networks have to be powerful enough to match human performance of the computational tasks, and on the other hand they have to be built from the available materials. In the case of the brain, that means neurons and synapses; in the case of network models, that means neuron-like processing units and synapse-like weights.

Digital computers are used to simulate neural networks, and the network models that can be simulated on current machines are tiny in comparison with the number of synapses and neurons in the mammalian brain. The networks that have been constructed should be understood, therefore, as small parts of a more complex processing system whose general configuration has not yet been worked out, rather than as simulations of a whole system. To avoid misunderstanding, it should be emphasized that connectionist models cannot yet support a full cognitive system. To begin to reach that goal will require both a computing technology capable of supporting more detailed simulations and a more complete specification of the nervous system.

Granting these limitations, we may none the less be able to catch a glimpse of

Feedforward Network

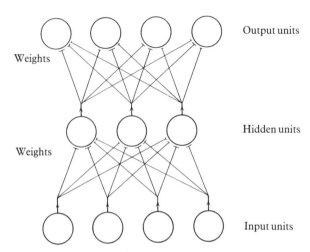

Figure 2 Schematic model of a three-layered network. Each input unit makes connections with each of the hidden units on the middle layer, which in turn projects to each of the output units. This is feedforward architecture in which information provided as an input vector flows through the network, one layer at a time, to produce an output vector. More complex architectures allow feedback connections from an upper to a lower layer and lateral interactions between units within a layer.

what representations might look like within the parallel-style architecture of the brain by taking a look inside a connectionist network. The place to look is in the dynamics of the system; that is, in the patterns of activity generated by the system of interconnected units. This approach has its roots in the work of previous generations of researchers – primarily the Gestalt school of psychology and D. O. Hebb (1949), who developed many ideas about learning and representation in neural assemblies. Only recently, however, has sufficient computer power been available to explore the consequences of these ideas by direct simulation, since the dynamics of massively parallel nonlinear networks is highly computation intensive. Parallel-network models are now being used to explore many different aspects of perception and cognition (McClelland and Rumelhart 1986; Feldman and Ballard 1982; *Cognitive Science*, special issue, vol. 9, 1985) but in this chapter we shall focus on two representative examples. The first is NETtalk, perhaps the most complex network model yet constructed, which learns to convert English text to speech sounds (Sejnowski and Rosenberg 1987, 1988). The second is a network model that computes surface curvatures of an object from its gray-level input image. NETtalk wil be used primarily to illustrate two things: how a network can learn to perform a very complex task without symbols and without rules to manipulate symbols, and the differences between local and distributed representations.

Connectionist models can be applied on a large scale to model whole brain systems or, on a smaller scale, to model particular brain circuits. NETtalk is on a large scale, since the problem of pronunciation is constrained mainly by the abstract cognitive considerations and since its solution in the brain must involve a number of systems, including the visual system, the motor-articulatory system, and the language areas. The second example is more directly related to smaller brain circuits used in visual processing; the representational organization achieved by the network model can be related to the known representational organization in visual cortex.

In the models reviewed here, the processing units sum the inputs from connections with other processing units, each input weighted by the strength of the connection. The output of each processing unit is a real number that is a nonlinear function of the linearly summed inputs. The output is small when the inputs are below threshold, and it increases rapidly as the total input becomes more positive. Roughly, the activity level can be considered the sum of the postsynaptic potentials in a neuron, and the output can be considered its firing rate (figure 1).

4.1 Speech processing: text to speech

In the simplest NETtalk system[2] there are three layers of processing units. The first level receives as input letters in a word: the final layer yields the elementary sounds, or phonemes (table 1); and an intervening layer of "hidden units," which is fully connected with the input and output layers, performs the transformation of letters to sounds (figure 3). On the input layer, there is *local representation* with respect to letters because single units are used to represent single letters of the alphabet. Notice, however, that the representation could be construed as *distributed* with respect to *words*, inasmuch as each word is represented as a pattern of activity among the input units. Similarly, each phoneme is represented by a pattern of activity among the output units, and phonemic representation is therefore distributed. But each output unit is coded for a particular *distinctive feature* of the speech sound, such as whether the phoneme was voiced, and consequently each unit is local with respect to distinctive features.

NETtalk has 309 processing units and 18 629 connection strengths (weights) that must be specified. The network does not have any initial or built-in organization for processing the input or (more exactly) mapping letters on to sounds. All the structure emerges during the training period. The values of the weights are determined by using the "back-propagation" learning algorithm developed by Rumelhart, Hinton and Williams (1986). (For a review of network learning algorithms, see Hinton 1988 and Sejnowski 1988.) The strategy exploits the calculated error between the *actual* values of the processing units in the output layer and the *desired* values, which is provided by a training signal. The resulting error signal is propagated from the output layer backward to the input layer and used to adjust each weight in the network. The network learns, as the weights are changed, to minimize the mean squared error over the training set of words. Thus, the system can be characterized as following a path in weight space (the space of all possible weights) until it finds a minimum (figure 4). The important point to be illustrated, therefore, is this: The network processes information by nonlinear dynamics, not by manipulating symbols and accessing rules. It learns by

Table I   Symbols for phonemes used in NETtalk.

Symbol	Phoneme	Symbol	Phoneme
/a/	father	/D/	this
/b/	bet	/E/	bet
/c/	bought	/G/	sing
/d/	debt	/I/	bit
/e/	bake	/J/	gin
/f/	fin	/K/	sexual
/g/	guess	/L/	bottle
/h/	head	/M/	absym
/i/	Pete	/N/	button
/k/	Ken	/O/	boy
/l/	let	/Q/	quest
/m/	met	/R/	bird
/n/	net	/S/	shin
/o/	boat	/T/	thin
/p/	pet	/U/	book
/r/	red	/W/	bout
/s/	sit	/X/	excess
/t/	test	/Y/	cute
/u/	lute	/Z/	leisure
/v/	vest	/@/	bat
/w/	wet	/!/	Nazi
/x/	about	/#/	examine
/y/	yet	/*/	one
/z/	zoo	/|/	logic
/A/	bite	/^/	but
/C/	chin		

gradient descent in a complex interactive system, not by generating new rules (Hinton and Sejnowski 1986).

The issue that we want to focus on next is the structural organization that is "discovered" by the network, in virtue of which it succeeds in converting letters to phonemes and manages to pronounce, with few errors, the many irregularities of English. If there are no rules in the network, how is the transformation accomplished? Since a trained network can generalize quite well to new words, some knowledge about the pattern of English pronunciation must be contained inside the network. Although a representational organization was imposed on the input and output layers, the network had to create new, internal representations in the hidden layer of processing units. How did the network organize its "knowledge"? To be more accurate: How did the equivalence class of networks organize its knowledge? (Each time the network was started from a random set of weights, a different network was generated.)

The answers were not immediately available, because a network does not leave an explanation of its travels through weight space, nor does it provide a decoding scheme when it reaches a resting place. Even so, some progress was made by

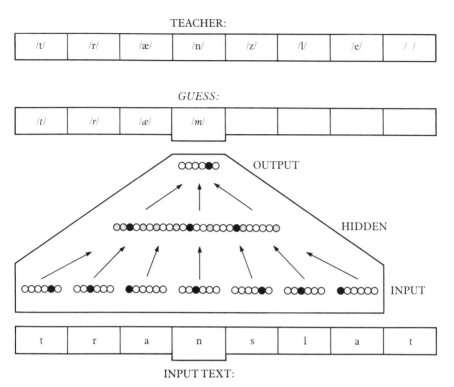

TEACHER:

| /t/ | /r/ | /æ/ | /n/ | /z/ | /l/ | /e/ | / / |

GUESS:

| /t/ | /r/ | /æ/ | /m/ | | | | |

OUTPUT

HIDDEN

INPUT

| t | r | a | n | s | l | a | t |

INPUT TEXT:

Figure 3 Schematic drawing of the NETtalk network architecture. A window of letters in an English text is fed to an array of 203 input units arranged in 7 groups of 29 units each. Information from these units is transformed by an intermediate layer of 80 hidden units to produce a pattern of activity in 26 output units. The connections in the network are specified by a total of 18 629 weight parameters (including a variable threshold for each unit). During the training, information about the desired output provided by the Teacher is compared with the actual output of the network, and the weights in the network are changed slightly so as to reduce the error.

measuring the activity pattern among the hidden units for specific inputs. In a sense, this test mimics at the modeling level what neurophysiologists do at the cellular level when they record the activity of a single neuron to try to find the effective stimulus that makes it respond. NETtalk is a fortunate "preparation," inasmuch as the number of processing units is relatively small, and it is possible to determine the activity patterns of all the units for all possible input patterns. These measurements, despite the relatively small network, did create a staggering amount of data, and then the puzzle was this: How does one find the order in all these data?

For each set of input letters, there is a pattern of activity among the hidden units (figure 5). The first step in the analysis of the activity of the hidden units was to compute the average level of activity for each letter-to-sound correspon-

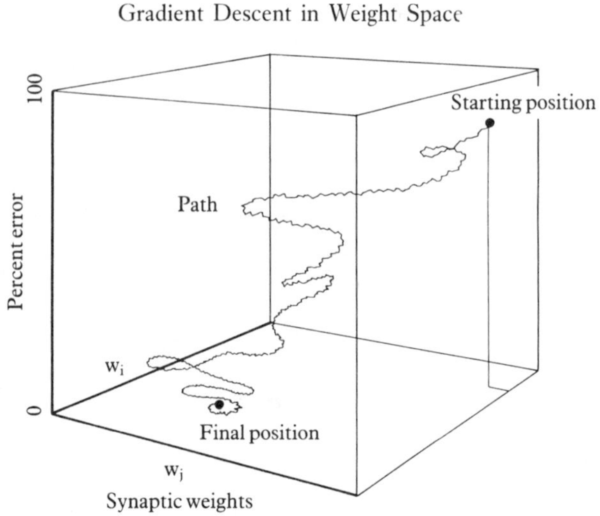

Gradient Descent in Weight Space

Figure 4   Schematic drawing of a path followed in weight space as the network finds a minimum of the average error over the set of training patterns. Only two weights out of many thousands are shown. The learning algorithm only ensures convergence to a local minimum, which is often a good solution. Typically, many sets of weights are good solutions, so the network is likely to find one of them from a random starting position in weight space. The learning time can be reduced by starting the network near a good solution; for example, the pattern of connections can be limited to a geometry that reduces the number of variable weights that must be searched by gradient descent.

dence. For example, all words with the letter c in the middle position yielding the hard-c sound /k/ were presented to the network, and the average level of activity was calculated. Typically, about 15 of the 80 hidden units were very highly activated, and the rest of the hidden units had little or no activity. This procedure was repeated for each of the 79 letter-to-sound correspondences. The result was 79 vectors, each vector pointing in a different direction in the 80-dimensional space of average hidden-unit activities. The next step was to explore the relationship among the vectors in this space by cluster analysis. It is useful to conceive of each vector as the internal code that is used to represent a specific letter-to-sound correspondence; consequently, those vectors that clustered close together would have similar codes.

Remarkably, all the vectors for vowel sounds clustered together, indicating that they were represented in the network by patterns of activity in units that were distinct from those representing the consonants (which were themselves clustered together). (See figure 6.) Within the vowels, all the letter-to-sound corespondences that used the letter a were clustered together, as were the vectors of e, i, o, and u and the relevant instances of y. This was a very robust organizational scheme that occurred in all the networks that were analyzed, differences in starting weights

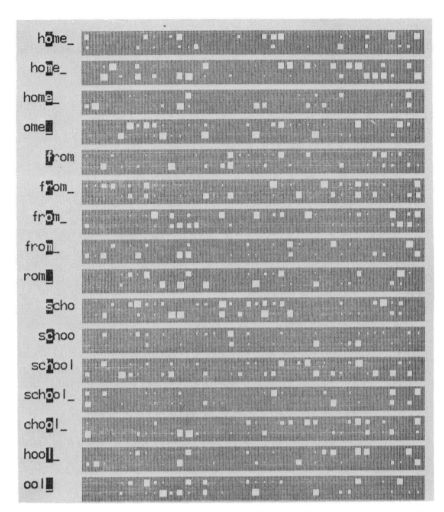

Figure 5 Levels of activation in the layer of hidden units for a variety of words. The input string in the window of seven letters is shown to the left, with the target letter emphasized. The output from the network is the phoneme that corresponds to the target letter. The transformation is accomplished by 80 hidden units, whose activity levels are shown to the right in two rows of 40 units each. The area of each white square is proportional to the activity level. Most units have little or no activity for a given input, but a few are highly activated.

notwithstanding. The coding scheme for consonants was more variable from network to network, but as a general rule the clustering was based more on similarities in sounds than on letters. Thus, the labial stops /p/ and /b/ were very close together in the space of hidden-unit activities, as were all the letter-to-sound corespondences that result in the hard-c sound /k/.

Other statistical techniques, such as factor analysis and multidimensional scaling, are also being applied to the network, and activity patterns from individual inputs, rather than averages over classes, are also being studied (Rosenberg 1988). These statistical techniques are providing us with a detailed description of the representation for single inputs as well as classes or input–output pairs.

Several aspects of NETtalk's organization should be emphasized:

[1] The representational organization visible in the trained-up network is not programmed or coded into the network; it is found by the network. In a sense it "programs" itself, by virtue of being connected in the manner described and having weights changed by experience according to the learning algorithm. The dynamical properties of this sort of system are such that the network will settle into the displayed organization.

[2] The network's representation for letter-to-sound correspondences is neither local nor completely distributed; it is somewhere in between. The point is, each unit participates in more than one correspondence, and so the representation is not local, but since it does not participate in all correspondences, the representation is not completely distributed either.

[3] The representation is a property of the collection of hidden units, and does not resemble sentence-logic organization.

[4] The organization is structured, which suggests that emergent subordinate and superordinate relations might be a general principle of network organization that could be used as input for other networks assigned other tasks if NETtalk were embedded in a larger system of networks.

[5] General properties of the hierarchical organization of letter-to-sound correspondences emerged only at the level of groups of units. This organization was invariant across all the networks created from the same sample of English words, even where the processing units in distinct networks had specialized for a different aspect of the problem.

[6] Different networks created by starting from different initial conditions all achieved about the same level of performance, but the detailed response properties of the individual units in the networks differed greatly. Nonetheless, all the networks had similar functional clusterings for letter-to-sound correspondence (figure 6). This suggests that single neurons code information relative to other neurons in small groups or assemblies (Hebb 1949).

The representational organization in NETtalk may illustrtae important principles concerning network computation and representation, but what do they tell us about neural representations? Some of the principles uncovered might be generally applicable to a wide class of tasks, but it would be surprising if the details of the model bore any significant resemblance to the way reading skills are represented in the human nervous system. NETtalk is more of a demonstration of certain network capacities and properties than a faithful model of some subsystem of the brain, and it may be a long time before data concerning the human neurobiology of reading become available. Nevertheless, the same network techniques that were used to explore the language domain can be applied to problems in other domains, such as vision, where much more is known about the anatomy and the physiology.

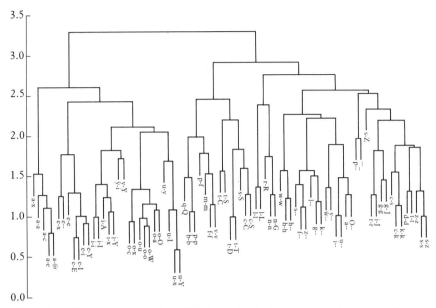

Figure 6   Hierarchical clustering of hidden units for letter-to-sound correspondences. The vectors of average hidden unit activity for each correspondence ('l-p' for letter l and phoneme p) were successively merging from right to left in the binary tree. The scale at the top indicates the Euclidean distance between the clusters. (From Sejnowski and Rosenberg 1987.)

4.2   Visual processing: computing surface curvature from shaded images

The general constraints from brain architecture touched on in section 3 should be supplemented, wherever possible, by more detailed constraints from brain physiology and anatomy. Building models of real neural networks is a difficult task, however, because essential knowledge about the style of computation in the brain is not yet available (Sejnowski 1986). Not only is the fine detail (such as the connectivity patterns in neurons in cerebral cortex) not known, but even global-level knowledge specifying the flow of information through different parts of the brain during normal function is limited. Even if more neurophysiological and neuroanatomical detail were available, current computing technology would put rather severe limits on how much detail could be captured in a simulation. Nevertheless, the same type of network model used in NETtalk could be useful in understanding how information is coded within small networks confined to cortical columns. The processing units in this model will be identified with neurons in the visual cortex.

Ever since Hubel and Wiesel (1962) first reported that single neurons in the cat visual cortex respond better to oriented bars of light and to dark/light edges than to spots of light, it has been generally assumed, or at least widely hoped, that the function of these neurons is to detect boundaries of objects in the world. In general, the inference from a cell's response profile to its function in the wider information-processing economy is intuitively very plausible, and if we are to have any hope of understanding neural representations we need to start in an area – such as visual cortex – where it is possible to build on an impressive body of existing data. The trouble is, however, that many functions are consistent with the particular response properties of a neuronal population. That a cell responds optimally to an oriented bar of light is compatible with its having lots of functions other than detecting object boundaries, though the hypothesis that it serves to detect boundaries does tend to remain intuitively compelling. To see that our intuitions might really mislead us as we try to infer function from response profiles, it would be useful if we could demonstrate this point concretely. In what follows we shall show how the same response properties could in fact serve in the processing of visual information about the regions of a surface between boundaries rather than about the boundaries themselves.

Boundaries of objects are relatively rare in images, yet the preponderance of cells in visual cortex respond preferentially to oriented bars and slits. If we assume that all those cells are detecting boundaries, then it is puzzling that there should be so many cells whose sole function is to detect boundaries when there are not many boundaries to detect. It would, therefore, seem wasteful if, of all the neurons with oriented fields, only a small fraction carried useful information about a particular image. Within their boundaries, most objects have shaded or textured surfaces that will partially activate these neurons. The problem, accordingly, is this: Can the information contained in a population of partially activated cortical neurons be used to compute useful information about the three-dimensional surfaces between the boundaries of objects in the image?

One of the primary properties of a surface is its curvature. Some surfaces, such as the top of a table, are flat, and have no intrinsic curvature. Other surfaces, such as cylinders and spheres, are curved, and around each point on a surface the degree of curvature can be characterized by the direction along the surface of maximum and minimum curvature. It can be shown that these directions are always at right angles to each other, and the values are called the *principle curvatures* (Hilbert and Cohn-Vossen 1952). The principal curvatures and the orientation of the axes provide a complete description of the local curvature.

One problem with extracting the principal curvatures from an image is that the gray-level shading depends on many factors, such as the direction of illumination, the reflectance of the surface, and the orientation of the surface relative to the viewer. Somehow our visual system is able to separate these variables and to extract information about the shape of an object independent of these other variables. Pentland (1984) has shown that a significant amount of information about the curvature of a surface is available locally. Can a network model be constructed that can extract this information from shaded images?

Until recently it was not obvious how to begin to construct such a network, but network learning algorithms (see above) provide us with a powerful method for creating a network by giving it examples of the task at hand. The learning algorithm is being used in this instance simply as a design tool to see whether some network can be found that performs the task. Many examples of simple surfaces (elliptic paraboloids) were generated and presented to the network. A set of weights was indeed found with this procedure that, independent of the direction of illumination, extracted the principal curvatures of three-dimensional surfaces and the direction of maximum curvature from shaded images (Lehky and Sejnowski 1987).

The input to the network is from an array of on-center and off-center receptive fields similar to those of cells in the lateral geniculate nucleus. The output layer is a population of units that conjointly represent the curvatures and the broadly tuned direction of maximum curvature. The units of the intermediate layer, which are needed to perform the transformation, have oriented receptive fields, similar to those of simple cells in the visual cortex of cats and monkeys that respond optimally to oriented bars and edges (figure 7). It is important to emphasize that these properties of the hidden units were not put into the network directly but emerged during training. The system "chose" these properties because they are useful in performing a particular task. Interestingly, the output units, which were required to code information about the principal curvatures and principal orientations of surfaces, had properties, when probed with bars of light, that were similar to those of a class of complex cells that are end-stopped (Lehky and Sejnowski 1988). The surprising thing, given the plasuible receptive-field-to-function inference rule, is that the function of the units in the network is not to detect boundary contours, but to extract curvature information from shaded images.

What the shape-from-shading network demonstrates is that we cannot directly infer function from receptive field properties. In the trained-up network, the hidden units represent an intermediate transformation for a computational task quite different from the one that has been customarily ascribed to simple cells in visual cortex – they are used to determine shape from shading, not to detect boundaries. It turns out, however, that the hidden units have *receptive fields similar to those of simple cells in visual cortex.* Therefore, bars and edges as receptive-field properties do not necessarily mean that the cell's function is to detect bars and edges in objects; it might be to detect curvature and shape, as it is in the network model, or perhaps some other surface property such as texture. The general implication is that there is no way of determining the function of each hidden unit in the network simply by "recording" the receptive-field properties of the unit. This, in turn, implies that, despite its intuitive plausibility, the receptive-field-to-function inference rule is untenable.

The function of a unit is revealed only when its *outputs* – its "projective field" (Lehky and Sejnowski 1988) – are also examined. It is the projective field of a unit that provides the additional information needed to interpret the unit's computational role in the network. In the network model the projective field could be examined directly, but in real neural networks it can only be inferred indirectly by examining the next stage of processing. Whether or not curvature is directly represented in visual cortex, for example, can be tested by designing experiments with images of curved surfaces.

4.3   Next-generation networks

NETtalk and the shape-from-shading network are important examples because they yield clues to how the nervous system can embody models of various domains of the world. Parallel-network modeling is still in a pioneering stage of

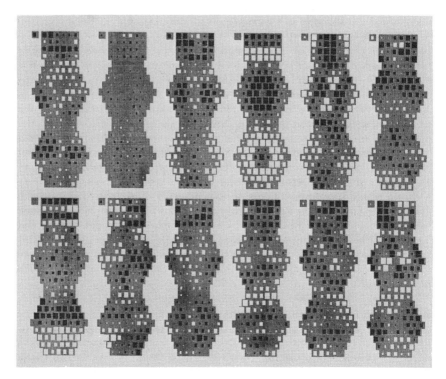

Figure 7　　Hinton diagram showing the connection strengths in a network that computes the principal curvatures and direction of minimum curvature from shaded images in a small patch of the visual field corresponding roughly to the area represented in a cortical column. There are 12 hidden units which receive connections from the 122 inputs and project to each of the 23 output units. The diagram shows each of the connection strengths to and from the hidden units. Each weight is represented by one square, the area of which is proportional to the magnitude of the weight. The color is white if the weight is excitatory and black if it is inhibitory. The inputs are two hexagonal arrays of 61 processing units each. Each input unit has a concentric on-center (top) or off-surround (bottom) receptive field similar to those of principal cells in the lateral geniculate nucleus. The output consists of 24 units that conjointly represent the direction of maximum curvature (six columns) and principal curvature (four rows: two for each principal curvature). Each of the 12 hidden units is represented in the diagram in a way that reveals all the connections to and from the unit. Within each of the 12 gray background regions, the weights from the inputs are shown on the bottom and the weights to the output layer are shown above. To the left of each hidden unit, the lone square gives the threshold of the unit, which was also allowed to vary. Note that there emerged two different types of hidden units as revealed by the "projective field." The six units in the bottom row and the fourth and fifth from the left in the top row were mainly responsible for providing information about the direction of minimum curvature, while others were responsible for computing the signs and magnitudes of the two principal curvatures. The curvature-selective units could be further classified as convexity detectors (top row, third from left) or elongation filters (top row, second and sixth from left).

development. There are bound to be many snags and hitches, and many problems yet undreamt of will have to be solved. At this stage, the representational structure of networks has not yet been explored in detail, nor is it known how well the performance of network models will scale with the number of neurons and the difficulty of the task. (That is, will representations and computations in a cortical column with 200 000 neurons be similar to those in a model network comprising only a few hundred processing units?)

Moreover, taken literally as a model of functioning neurons, back-propagation is biologically implausible, inasmuch as error signals cannot literally be propagated back down the very same axon the signal came up. Taken as a *systems-level* algorithm, however, back-propagation may have a realization using feedback projections that do map on to neural hardware. Even squarely facing these cautionary considerations, the important thing is that something with this sort of character at least lets us see what representational structure – good, meaty, usable structure – could *look like* in a neuronal network.

Temporal chaining of sequences of representations is probably a prominent feature of many kinds of behavior, and it may turn out to be particularly important for language acquisition and use. It is conceivable that structured sequences – long, temporally extended sequences – are the elements of an abstract sort of neural state space that enable humans to use language. Sereno (1986) has suggested something along these lines, pointing out that DNA, as a spatially extended sequence of nucleotides, allows for encoding; by analogy, one may envision that the development of mechanisms for generating temporally extended sequences of neuronal (abstract) structures may allow for a kind of structured behavior (that is, language) that short sequences do not allow for. (See also MacKay 1987; Dehaene et al. 1987.)

One promising strategy will be to try first to unscramble the more fundamental kinds of representing accomplished by nervous systems, shelving until later the problem of complex representations such as linguistic representations. To solve such problems, the solutions discovered for simpler representations may be crucial. At the most basic level, there appears to be an isomorphism between cell responses and external events (for example, cells in visual cortex responding to bars of light moving in a specific direction). At higher levels the receptive-field properties change (Allman et al. 1985; Andersen 1987), and it may be that the lower-level isomorphism gives way to more complicated and dynamic network effects. Motivation, planning, and other factors may, at this level, have roles in how a representation is generated. At still higher levels, still other principles may be operative. Once we understand the nature of representing in early sensory processing, as we have indeed begun to do, and go on to address the nature of representations at more and more abstract levels, we may finally be able to address how learning a language yields another kind of representation, and how symbols can be represented in neural networks. Whatever the basic principles of language representation, they are not likely to be utterly unrelated to the way or ways that the nervous system generates visual representations or auditory representations, or represents spatial maps and motor planning. (On semantic relations in connectionist models, see Hinton 1981, 1986.)

5   Dogmas and dreams: George Boole, Ramon y Cajal, David Marr

The connectionist models discussed are valuable for the glimpse of representational and computational space that they provide, for it is exactly such glimpses that free us from the bonds of the intuitive conceptions of representations as language-like and computation as logic-like. They thus free us from what Hofstadter (1982) called the *Boolean Dream*, where all cognition is symbol-manipulation according to the rules of logic.

Equally important, they also free us from what we call the *Neurobiologists' Dream* (perhaps, with all due respect, it might be called Cajal's Dream), which is really the faith that the answers we seek will be manifest once the fine-grain details of each neuron (its morphology, physiology, and connections) are revealed – these models also teach the tremendously important lesson that *system properties are not accessible at the single-unit level*. In a system, what we need to know is how the elements in large sets of elements interact over time. Until we have new physiological techniques for supplying data of that sort, building network models is a method of first resort.

To be really useful, a model must be biologically constrained. However, exactly which biological properties are crucial to a model's utility and which can be safely ignored until later are matters that can be decided only by hunches until a mature theory is in place. Such "bottom-up" constraints are crucial, since computational space is immensely vast – too vast for us to be lucky enough to light on the correct theory simply from the engineering bench. Moreover, the brain's solutions to the problems of vision, motor control, and so forth may be far more powerful, more beautiful, and even more simple than what we engineer into existence. This is the point of Orgel's Second Rule: Nature is more ingenious than we are. And we stand to miss all that power and ingenuity unless we attend to neurobiological plausibility. The point is, *evolution has already done it*, so why not learn how that stupendous machine, our brain, actually works?

This observation allows us to awake from *Marr's Dream* of three levels of explanation: the computational level of abstract problem analysis, the level of the algorithm, and the level of physical implementation of the computation. In Marr's view, a higher level was independent of the levels below it, and hence computational problems could be analyzed independent of an understanding of the algorithm that executes the computation, and the algorithmic problem could be solved independent of an understanding of the physical implementation. Marr's assessment of the relations between levels has been re-evaluated, and the dependence of higher levels on lower levels has come to be recognized.

The matter of the interdependence of levels marks a major conceptual difference between Marr and the current generation of connectionists. Network models are not independent of either the computational level or the implementational level; they depend in important ways on constraints from all levels of analysis. Network models show how knowledge of brain architecture can contribute to the devising of likely and powerful algorithms that can be efficiently implemented in the architecture of the nervous system and may alter even how we construe the computational problems.

On the heels of the insight that the use of constraints from higher up and lower down matters tremendously, the notion that there are basically *three* levels of analysis also begins to look questionable. If we examine more closely how the three levels of analysis are meant to map on to the organization of the nervous system, the answer is far from straightforward.

To begin with, the idea that there is essentially one single implementational level is an oversimplification. Depending on the fineness of grain, research techniques reveal structural organization at many strata: the biochemical level; then the levels of the membrane, the single cell, and the circuit; and perhaps yet other levels, such as brain subsystems, brain systems, brain maps, and the whole central nervous system. But notice that at each structurally specified stratum we can raise the functional question: What does it contribute to the wider, functional business of the brain?

This range of structural organization implies, therefore, that the oversimplification with respect to implementation has a companion oversimplification with respect to computational descriptions. And indeed, on reflection it does seem most unlikely that a single type of computational description can do justice to the computational niche of diverse structural organization. On the contrary, one would expect distinct task descriptions corresponding to distinct structural levels. But if there is a ramifying of task specifications to match the ramified structural organization, this diversity will probably be reflected in the ramification of the *algorithms* that characterize how a task is accomplished. And this, in turn, means that the notion of *the* algorithmic levels is as oversimplified as the notion of *the* implementation level.

Similar algorithms were used to specify the network models in NETtalk and the shape-from-shading network, but they have a quite different status in these two examples. On this perspective of the levels of organization, NETtalk is a network relevant to the *systems* level, whereas the shape-from-shading network is relevant to the *circuit* level. Since the networks are meant to reflect principles at entirely different levels of organization, their implementations will also be at different scales in the nervous system. Other computational principles may be found to apply to the single cell or to neural maps.

Once we look at them closely, Marr's three *levels of analysis* and the brain's *levels of organization* do not appear to mesh in a very useful or satisfying manner. So poor is the fit that it may be doubted whether levels of analysis, *as conceived by Marr*, have much methodological significance. Accordingly, in light of the flaws with the notion of *independence*, and in light of the flaws with the *tripartite* character of the conception of levels, it seems that Marr's dream, inspiring though it was for a time, must be left behind.

The vision that inspires network modeling is essentially and inescapably interdisciplinary. Unless we explicitly theorize above the level of the single cell, we will never find the key to the order and the systematicity hidden in the blinding minutiae of the neuropil. Unless our theorizing is geared to mesh with the neurobiological data, we risk wasting our time exploring some impossibly remote, if temporarily fashionable, corner of computational space. Additionally, without the constraints from psychology, ethology, and linguistics to specify more exactly the parameters of the large-scale capacities of nervous systems, our conception of the functions for which we need explanation will be so woolly and tangled as to effectively smother progress. Consequently, cross-disciplinary research, combining constraints from psychology, neurology, neurophysiology, linguistics, and computer modeling, is the best hope for the co-evolution that could ultimately yield a unified, integrated science of the mind-brain. It has to be admitted, however, that this vision is itself a dream. From within the dream, we cannot yet reliably discern what are the flaws that will impede progress, what crucial elements are missing, or at which points the vague if tantalizing hunches might be replaced by palpable results.

NOTES

1   An earlier exploration of these ideas is to be found in Kenneth Craik's book *The Nature of Explanation* (Cambridge University Press, 1943).
2   NETtalk networks can differ in how input letters and output phonemes are represented, and in the number and arrangement of hidden units.

REFERENCES

Allman, J., Miezin, F., and McGuinness E. (1985) "Stimulus specific responses from beyond the classic receptive field." *Annual Review of Neuroscience* 8: 407–30.
Andersen, R. A. (1987) "The role of posterior parietal cortex in spatial perception and visual-motor integration." In *Handbook of Physiology – The Nervous System V*, ed. V. B. Mountcastle, F. Plum and S. R. Geiger.
Anderson, J. A. and Hinton, G. E. (1981) "Models of information processing in the brain." In Hinton and Anderson 1981.
Chisholm, R. M. (1966) *Theory of Knowledge*. Englewood Cliffs, N.J.: Prentice-Hall.
Churchland, P. M. (1979) *Scientific Realism and the Plasticity of Mind*. Cambridge University Press.
Churchland, P. M. (1988) *Matter and Consciousness* (revised edition). Cambridge, Mass.: MIT Press.
Churchland, P. S. (1986) *Neurophilosophy: Toward a Unified Science of the Mind-Brain*. Cambridge, Mass.: MIT Press.
Davidson, D. (1974) "On the very idea of a conceptual scheme." *Proceedings and Addresses of the American Philosophical Association* 47: 5–20.
Dehaene, S., Changeux, J.-P., and Nadal, J.-P. (1987) "Neural networks that learn temporal sequences by selection." *Proceedings of the National Academy of Sciences* 84: 2727–31.
Dennett, D. C. (1978) *Brainstorms: Philosophical Essays on Mind and Psychology*. Cambridge, Mass.: MIT Press.
Eccles, J. C. (1977) Part II of K. Popper, *The Self and Its Brain*. Berlin: Springer-Verlag.
Enc, B. (1983) "In defense of the identity theory." *Journal of Philosophy* 80: 279–98.
Feldman, J. A., and Ballard, F. H. (1982) "Connectionist models and their properties." *Cognitive Science* 6: 205–54.
Fodor, J. A. (1975) *The Language of Thought*. New York: Crowell. (Paperback edition: Cambridge, Mass.: MIT Press, 1979.)
Fodor, J. A. (1981) *Representations*. Cambridge, Mass.: MIT Press.
Goldman-Rakic, P. S. (1987) "Circuitry of primate prefrontal cortex and regulation of behavior by representational memory." In *Handbook of Physiology – The Nervous System V*, ed. V. B. Mountcastle, F. Plum and S. R. Geiger.
Hebb, D. O. (1949) *Organization of Behavior*. New York: Wiley.
Hilbert, J. and Cohn-Vossen, S. (1952) *Geometry and the Imagination*. New York: Chelsea.

Hinton, G. E. (1981) "Implementing semantic networks in parallel hardware." In Hinton and Anderson 1981.

Hinton, G. E. (1986) "Learning distributed representations of concepts." In *Proceedings of the Eighth Annual Conference of the Cognitive Science Society*. Hillsdale, NJ: Erlbaum.

Hinton, G. E. (1988) "Connectionist learning procedures." *Artificial Intelligence*, in press.

Hinton, E. E. and Anderson, J. A. (eds) (1981) *Parallel Models of Associative Memory*. Hillsdale, NJ: Erlbaum.

Hinton, G. E. and Sejnowski, T. J. (1986) "Learning and relearning in Boltzmann machines." In McClelland and Rumelhart 1986.

Hofstadter, D R. (1982) "Artificial intelligence: Subcognition as computation." *Technical Report No. 132*, Computer Science Department, Indiana University.

Hooker, C. A. (1981) "Toward a general theory of reduction. Part I: Historical and scientific setting. Part II: Identity in reduction. Part III: Cross-categorical reduction." *Dialogue* 20: 38–59, 201–36, 496–529.

Hubel, D. H. and Wiesel, T. N. (1962) "Receptive fields, binocular interaction and functional architecture in cat's visual cortex." *Journal of Physiology* 160: 106–54.

Kelso, S. R., Ganong, A. H. and Brown, T. H. (1986) "Hebbian synapses in hippocampus." *Proceedings of National Academy of Sciences* 83: 5326–30.

Lehky, S. and Sejnowski, T. J. (1987) "Extracting 3-D curvatures from images using a neural model." *Society for Neuroscience Abstracts* 13: 1451.

Lehky, S. and Sejnowski, T. J. (1988) "Neural network model for the representation of surface curvature from images of shaded surfaces." In *Organizing Principles of Sensory Processing*, ed. J. Lund, Oxford University Press.

Livingstone, M. S. (1988) "Art, illusion, and the visual system." *Scientific American* 258: 78–85.

McClelland, J. L. and Rumelhart, D. E. (1986) *Parallel Distributed Processing: Explorations in the Microstructure of Cognition*. Cambridge, Mass.: MIT Press.

McGinn, C. (1982) *The Character of Mind*. Oxford University Press.

MacKay, D. (1987) *The Organization and Perception of Action*. Berlin: Springer-Verlag.

Mandt, A. J. (1986) "The triumph of philosophical pluralism? Notes on the transformation of academic philosophy." *Proceedings and Addresses of the American Philosophical Association* 60: 265–77.

Marr, D. (1982) *Vision*. San Francisco: Freeman.

Pellionisz, A. and Llinas, R. (1982) "Space-time representation in the brain. The cerebellum as a predictive space-time metric tensor." *Neuroscience* 7: 2249–70.

Pentland, A. P. (1984) "Local shading analysis." *IEEE Transactions: Pattern Analysis and Machine Intelligence* 6: 170–87.

Putnam, H. (1967) "The nature of mental states." In *Arts, Mind and Religion*, ed. W. H. Capitan and D. D. Merrill (University of Pittsburgh Press). Reprinted in H. Putnam, *Mind, Language, and Reality: Philosophical Papers*, vol. 2 (Cambridge University Press, 1975).

Pylyshyn, Z. (1984) *Computation and Cognition*. Cambridge, Mass.: MIT Press.

Quine, W. V. O. (1960) *Word and Object*. Cambridge, Mass.: MIT Press.

Richardson, R. (1979) "Functionalism and reductionism." *Philosophy of Science* 46: 533–58.

Rosenberg, C. R. (1988) Ph.D. thesis, Princeton University.

Rumelhart, D. E., Hinton, G. E. and McClelland, J. L. (1986) "A general framework for parallel distributed processing." In McClelland and Rumelhart 1986.

Rumelhart, D. E., Hinton, G. E. and Williams, R. J. (1986) "Learning internal representations by error propagation." In McClelland and Rumelhart 1986.

Schaffner, K. F. (1976) "Reductionism in biology: Prospects and problems." In *PSA Proceedings 1974*, ed. R. S. Cohen, C. A. Hooker, A. C. Michalos and J. W. Van Evra. Dordrecht: Reidel.

Sejnowski, T. J. (1986) "Open questions about computation in cerebral cortex." In McClelland and Rumelhart 1986.

Sejnowski, T. J. (1988) "Neural network learning algorithms." In *Neural Computers*, ed. R. Eckmiller and C. von der Malsberg, Berlin: Springer-Verlag.

Sejnowski, T. J. and Churchland, P. S. In press. "Brain and cognition." In *Foundations of Cognitive Science*, ed. M. I. Posner, Cambridge, Mass.: MIT Press.

Sejnowski, T. J. and Rosenberg, C. R. (1987) "Parallel networks that learn to pronounce English text." *Complex Systems* I: 145–68.

Sejnowski, T. J. and Rosenberg, C. R. (1988) "Learning and representation in connectionist models." In *Perspective in Memory Research and Training*, ed. M. Gazzaniga, Cambridge, Mass.: MIT Press.

Sejnowski, T.J., Koch, C. and Churchland, P. S. (1988) "Computational neuroscience." *Science*, 241, pp. 1299–1306.

Sereno, M. (1986) "A program for the neurobiology of mind." *Inquiry* 29; 217–40.

Skinner, B. F. (1957) *Verbal Behavior*. New York: Appleton-Century-Crofts.

Skinner, B. F. (1976) *About Behaviorism*. New York: Knopf.

Smart, J. J. C. (1959) "Sensations and brain processes." *Philosophical Review* 68: 141–56.

Stich, S. P. (1983) *From Folk Psychology to Cognitive Science: The Case Against Belief*. Cambridge, Mass.: MIT Press.

Strawson, P. F. (1966) *The Bounds of Sense: An Essay on Kant's Critique of Pure Reason*. London: Methuen.

Swinburne, R. (1986) *The Evolution of the Soul*. Oxford University Press.

Connectionism and the Philosophy of Mind: An Overview

WILLIAM BECHTEL

Connectionism has recently attracted much interest in cognitive science because it seems to promise an alternative to the now traditional rule-based approaches to modeling cognition. Philosophers have also begun to take note of connectionism. My objective in this paper is to provide a brief introduction to some of the philosophical issues generated by connectionism. I will not in this paper be defending connectionism *per se*, although I would not be undertaking a mission such as this if I did not think connectionism could offer some important contributions to our understanding of mind and mental phenomena. My goal is rather to generate and focus further discussion. Thus, in each section of this paper I will pose and briefly discuss one or more questions. In discussing these questions I will indicate some answers that I find attractive, but I will not attempt to advance definitive arguments for them on this occasion.

"Connectionism and the Philosophy of Mind" by W. Bechtel first appeared in *The Southern Journal of Philosophy* Vol. XXVI, Supplement, pp. 17–41, and is reprinted by kind permission.

The basic character of connectionist models of cognition

Connectionist approaches to studying cognition begin with a different conception of the mechanism underlying cognition than the traditional computer model that has guided much thinking about cognition in recent decades. The alternative model is *inspired* by our understanding of brain. Although the connectionist model attempts to incorporate important features of the brain's architecture, connectionism does not advance a detailed account of neural processes. Rather, it proposes a model of the kind of processing involved in cognition. In a subsequent section I will discuss further how connectionist models relate to neural models. In this section, I will present the connectionist model abstractly in the manner employed by the connectionists themselves.

The basic components of the connectionist architecture are simple *units* which, like neurons, are, at any given time, *activated* to some degree. Typically, this activation consists in possessing an electrical charge. These units, again like neurons, are *connected* (these connections can be of varying strengths) to other units so that, depending on their own activations, they can act to increase (excite) or decrease (inhibit) the activations of these other units. Additionally, in some connectionist systems, these connection strengths can be altered as a result of activity in the system so that the effect of one unit on another can change over time.

While this sketch covers the basic components of a connectionist system, there are a number of different ways a connectionist system can actually be set up, depending on the way a variety of parameters are set. One parameter fixes the permissible activation levels of the units: the units can be restricted to a small number of discrete states (e.g., on and off), or they can be allowed to vary over a specified range (e.g., 0 to 1). Another parameter governs how the activation of a unit is altered as a result of its previous states and the inputs it receives from other units. For example, a decay function can be included so that, without new activation, the activation of a unit drops, and a threshold can be employed such that a unit is not activated unless the inputs exceed a certain quantity. A third parameter determines the output of a given unit. The output could be proportional to its own activation, or it could be governed by a threshold value. Finally, there are a variety of learning rules that can be employed to adjust the connection strengths on a given pathway. Two of the most widely employed are a Hebbian rule (which strengthens or weakens a pathway depending on whether the two units are alike or different in their level of activation) and the delta rule, which increases or decreases the strengths of each input pathway so as to increase the fit between the target value and the current value of the unit. (For further details on the possible configurations of connectionist systems, see Rumelhart, Hinton and McClelland 1986).

The basic processing system is an ensemble of such connected units. The activity of such an ensemble begins when an initial pattern of activation is supplied to some or all of the units. This pattern can be viewed as a problem given to the ensemble. Processing ends when the system has settled into a *stable state* (e.g., one where the passing of activations through connections does not lead units to change their activation strengths). This settling occurs in accordance with thermodynamic principles: units change their activations as a result of their inputs and thereby alter their outputs, until the system settles into a state of highest entropy. The overall stable pattern, or the values on certain of the units when a stable pattern has been achieved, represents the system's answer to the problem.

In construing such a system as problem solving, we are supplying an *interpretation* to the activity of the system. In general, connectionists have employed two different types of interpretive schemes. In a *localized* interpretive scheme each unit represents some object or property. In Rumelhart and McClelland's system for word recognition, for instance, each unit represents a hypothesis about a feature, letter, or word that might be present. The degree of activation of the unit represents the degree of confidence that the corresponding item is part of the input.[1]

The alternative interpretive scheme is a *distributed* one where an interpretation is assigned to a pattern of activation over an ensemble of units. The activities of individual units may themselves have some symbolic role (e.g., representing features of an object to be recognized) but it is the overall pattern that is of primary interest, not the particular features. What makes this approach particularly interesting is that the same network can possess the capacity to settle into different activation patterns given different inputs. When one pattern is realized the others are only latently present in the sense that they could be activated with appropriate inputs. It is much more difficult for humans to follow activity in systems developed using distributed representations, but there are a variety of properties that make such systems highly attractive, such as the ability of related representations to activate units in common (which can then be interpreted as representing features of the overall objects represented by the patterns). (See Hinton et al. 1986.)

While, for the most part, philosophers will not be engaged in the actual design of connectionist networks, there are some fundamental philosophical issues concerning their design. One concerns the principles which govern their operation and in terms of which we explain their capacities.

1 Are there fundamental design principles in terms of which we can *explain* the behavior of connectionist systems? Or is the behavior of connectionist systems simply emergent (in a strong case)?

Some theorists have foreseen the prospect that we might build connectionist systems that simulate human cognitive performance but not be able to explain this behavior in a mechanistic fashion. The mechanistic approach to explanation is widely accepted in many disciplines where scientists have tried to explain the behavior of complex sysetems by *decomposing* them into components and then showing how the behavior of the system arises from the behavior of the components. In this mechanistic view, each component is viewed as making a discrete kind of contribution to the behavior of the whole system.[2] In connectionist programs, the contributions of the components are minimized and the behavior of the system results more from the interaction of components than the behavior of the components themselves. While there are a few disciplines (e.g., thermodynamics) where explanatory models have been developed in which little explanatory function is assigned to the components and mathematical theories have been developed to show how the behavior of ensembles produces the higher-level effects, such explanations are often dissatisfying. But a potential consequence of the development of connectionist models is that in psychology we may also need to forgo the mechanistic, decompositional approach, and accept mathematical, statistical explanations of the emergence at a higher level of a phenomenon which is not built up piecemeal from operations at the next lower level.[3]

A related issue concerns the principles researchers employ in interpreting connectionist systems:

2 Is the assignment of cognitive, intentional interpretations to activities in connectionist networks grounded on any fundamental principles?

One possibility is that researchers assign a cognitive, intentional interpretation to a connectionist network simply because the system behaves in a manner that allows it to perform the task. For example, we treat a system as recognizing a word because so interpreted, its behavior is appropriate. This is how Dennett (1978) views the attribution of intentional characterizations to any system, ourselves included, and what accounts for the instrumentalistic character of Dennett's account of intentionality. To many people, however, this is a deeply disturbing result. For them, it is a fundamental characteristic of our mental states that they are really *about* things, that is, they bear what Searle (1980) refers to as "intrinsic intentionality." If there is nothing in the actual character of states in connectionist systems that undergirds our intentional attributions then some critics will see connectionist systems as failing to account for a basic characteristic of cognitive states. Searle makes the same objection to traditional computational accounts of mental functions such as those captured in traditional AI programs, but in at least Fodor's (1975) version of the computational theory, the syntactic operations of the program are supposed to mirror the semantics. Thus, the internal processing of the states is viewed as mirroring the kinds of semantically interpreted inferences we take the system to be making (e.g., if the system infers that it will thunder because there has been lightning, the internal processes will include an inference from the symbol we interpret as the proposition "there has been lightning" to the proposition "there will be thunder"). Connectionism rejects this sort of sentence processing model, and as a result, may seem to provide an even less well-motivated account of whatever semantic interpretation we give to the system.

There is, though, another perspective from which we might judge connectionist systems as actually faring better than traditional cognitive models with respect to intentionality. One of the objections Dreyfus (1979) raises to traditional AI programs is that they try to represent explicitly all information the system is to use. In addition to potentially rendering the endeavor of AI impossible, this attempt may also explain why such systems seem to lack intrinsic intentionality. The system's behavior is totally determined by its internal representations and hence it is not closely linked to the external objects which these representations are supposedly about. A connectionist system, however, does not rely on internal representations as its processing units. It produces internal representations as *responses* to its inputs and it is possible to develop systems that adjust the weights of their connections in such a way as to develop their own system for categorizing inputs (see Rumelhart and Zipser 1985).[4] Moreover, it does not need to represent all relevant aspects of its environment in order to perform its cognitive operations. It must simply be able to respond to those features of the environment in the appropriate manner. This combination of tuning itself to its environment and not operating totally in terms of syntactically encoded representations may make it more reasonable to take the activities of connectionist systems as genuinely being *about* things in their environment, and hence enjoying a more intrinsic intentionality than traditional cognitive models.[5] This, however, only sketches a way in which we might motivate intentional interpretations of connectionist systems, and the potential for accounting for intentionality in these systems needs further investigation (see Bechtel 1985a).

Contrasts between connectionist and rule-based accounts of cognition

Advocates of connectionist approaches often present connectionism as an alternative to and potential replacement for the now more traditional approach to explaining cognition which supposes that cognitive systems manipulate representations in accord with rules. If connectionism really is an alternative, then it will help if we can clarify precisely how the two approaches differ.

The rules-and-representations model of cognition is one that became prominent in cognitive science as a result of both Chomskian accounts of language (according to which linguistically proper structures could be generated by application of recursive sets of rules to other linguistic structures) and the attempts to simulate cognition on the digital computer. Central to the use of the computer to simulate human cognitive performance was the assumption that both the mind and the computer are what Newell (1980) refers to as "physical symbol systems." The idea is that symbols are physically encoded in data structures which can be manipulated according to specified rules. While these rules may be directly embodied in the physics of the system (as they are in a pocket calculator), they are more typically themselves encoded in data structures, so that some elements in a data structure govern the manipulation of other components.

A basic issue arises as to how connectionist models differ from rule-based models. Since representations and rules for manipulating them are the key elements in rule-based accounts, let us examine whether there are analogs to them in connectionist models. On first appearance, connectionist systems seem to be quite unlike rule-based systems. There are no fixed representations upon which operations are performed in connectionist systems. Instead, there are activated units. which function to increase or decrease the activations of other units until a stable configuration is achieved. Yet, appearances may be deceiving. The appearance of difference may be more a product of the grain or analysis we adopt with respect to the two systems. In connectionist systems we are considering activities within a single ensemble and the tasks\ we view such an ensemble as performing typically are basic cognitive operations (e.g., recognizing and classifying a given input). But a connectionist system that is to simulate interesting cognitive activity will require use of numerous ensembles and it may be necessary to use some ensembles to store the contents of others or to control the processing of others. When we consider ways in which collections of ensembles may be invoked to perform larger-scale cognitive tasks, we may find it much more natural to describe the activity as rule-based processing of representations.

In order to clarify the differences, if there are such, between connectionist and rule-based models, we need to look more carefully at the concepts of *representations* and *rules* for processing them. Focusing first on representation, we can ask:

3 Do representations as employed in connectionist systems differ from the representations employed in rule-based systems.[6]

Fodor and Pylyshyn (1988), in their critique of connectionism, argue that connectionists are representationalists since they supply semantic interpretations either to units (in localist interpretations) or to patterns of activation (in distributed interpretations). Is this sufficient to equate the representations used in the two systems? There remain some differences to consider. In a localized interpretation of a connectionist system, the units which are assigned representational functions are constantly present, but are turned on or off by other activity in the system. This is different from the way representations are usually handled in rule-based systems, but it is not clear how fundamental this difference is. There may be a greater difference in the case of distributed systems where it is a pattern over an ensemble of units that serves as a representation. In such systems, when a pattern is not present in the system, it is not stored, as in traditional cognitive models. Such patterns are not retrieved from memory, but are reconstructed on appropriate occasions. There are differences here, but these differences may be only matters of implementation and not such as to constitute a fundamental difference between the two types of systems. The more fundamental question is whether the representations in a connectionist system are capable of performing the same basic functions as representations in rule-based systems. This is a vexed issue, which I can only pose, not try to answer here.

There may be greater hope to contrast the two types of systems when we focus on the principles governing the operations in them. Rule-based systems operate by having specifically articulated rules direct manipulation of representations. A major objective of connectionist theorists has been to see if we cannot do away with rules by having all activity controlled by the connections that determine how activations are passed between units.[7] But this forces us to consider the question:

4 What, precisely, are the differences (if any) between the rules that govern processing in rule-based systems and the sets of connections which govern processing in connectionist systems? Are connections the functional equivalents of rules?

There is one sense in which connections do serve the same function as rules: They serve to transform the system from one representational state to another. The relation between sets of connections and rules is brought out even more clearly in what are called "programmable connection systems" where activity in one ensemble of units sets the connections in another ensemble, thereby determining its processing capacities (McClelland 1986). Again, the issue of distinguishing clearly the two types of systems is vexed and I cannot resolve it here.

The attempt to differentiate connectionist from rule-based systems is made more difficult by the fact that current connectionist systems are not built directly out of hardware. Rather, they are simulated by traditional computers, where programs (consisting of rule statements) are written to determine how connectionist systems will behave. Hence, we must ask the further question:

5 Does the use of rule-based von Neumann computers to simulate connectionist systems indicate a basic similarity between connectionist systems and rule-based systems?[8]

The issue seems rather tricky. Some of those who have accepted the rule-based model of cognition have maintained that if we program a computer to perform the same symbol manipulations as a human being, we will have produced a real thinking entity. In a simulation of a connectionist system in a traditional computer, the computer calculates the equations governing the changes of activations of units in a connection system, and thereby determines what will be the activation strengths of all the units in a connectionist system. If the traditional computer can simulate the connectionist system, how can we maintain that the two are fundamentally different?

This way of collapsing the distinction between connectionist and rule-based systems, however, seems inadequate. The simulation of the connectionist machine in a rule-based computer is comparable to the simulation of a hurricane in a computer. In both cases what the computer does is to determine what would be the result of the causal processes that occur without actually going through those causal operations. On this view, the rule-based computer simulating the connectionist system does not instantiate the important causal properties of the connectionist system, but only tells us the result of the causal interactions in the system.

Competition between connectionist and rule-based approaches to cognition

Although it is not clear that, in response to questions 3 and 4 above, we can draw a sharp distinction between connectionist and rule-based systems, advocates of each kind of system advance relatively clear exemplars of the type of system they espouse and argue for the virtues of their type of model. Let us assume that the two types of systems are fundamentally different and turn to the question:

6 What criteria should we employ to evaluate whether connectionist or rule-based accounts give more adequate accounts of human cognitive processes?

This task would be easy if there were cognitive tasks which humans could perform which one, but not the other of these two types of systems could perform. Then we would have fairly strong reasons for favoring the system that could perform the tasks which humans could perform. The initial response of many rule-based theorists to connectionist models was to claim that this was the situation that actually accrued. They maintained that there are processes like recursion which humans can perform but which connectionist systems cannot and hence connectionist systems are inadequate (Fodor and Pylyshyn 1988, and Pinker and Prince 1988, raise objections of this sort). This sort of outcome in which one side will show that their system can do things the other cannot is unlikely. This type of debate between rule-based and network-type models has a history that predates the current popularity of connectionism. Early generations of connectionist type models (e.g., the network models of Selfridge 1955, and Rosenblatt 1962) were rejected as it became clear that there were limitations to the types of models then being considered. Minsky and Papert (1969) established some important theorems showing these limitations. Current connectionists, however, have tried to show how some of these limitations can be overcome (Rumelhart and McClelland, 1986). In the early 1970s there were disputes in cognitive psychology over the relative virtues of a somewhat different type of network models, semantic networks (see, e.g., Quillan 1968), and feature set models as tools for representing concepts. Smith et al. (1974) argued that their feature set model had properties that distinguished it from network models. Hollan (1975), however, challenged this distinction by showing how the model of Smith et al. was isomorphic to a network model. Rips et al. (1975) basically accepted Hollan's claim, but then advanced a different view of the distinction to which I will turn below. At this point, though, it seems plausible to assume that any task that can be performed by connectionist models can be accomplished through the rule-based models and vice versa.

The alternative view of the distinction Rips et al. advance is that "the choice of one type of representation rather than another can lead to substantive processing differences between theories, even though the representations themselves are isomorphic at some level" (p. 156). The same consideration may apply to the current dispute over connectionism. While connectionist and rule-based models may each be able to replicate the overall performance of the other, they may differ in the way they perform the task and these differences may reveal which type of model offers a better simulation of human cognition. This is, in fact, the approach many connectionists advance when they argue that their models work in ways that are more like humans than traditional rule-based models.

Connectionists argue, for example, that their models are much more biologically realistic than rule-based models. For example, they point to what is sometimes referred to as the 100 step principle (Feldman and Ballard 1982). Given that individual neuronal processes take on the order of a few milliseconds and that many basic cognitive tasks are performed in a matter of a few hundred milliseconds, they argue that the mind/brain cannot go through more than approximately 100 serial steps. Most contemporary AI programs for carrying out these tasks, however, require many more than 100 steps, whereas connectionist machines can settle on answers well within the 100 step limit.

Connectionists also point to a number of performance features of connectionist systems which they claim show the superiority of connectionist models for human cognition. For example, it is a natural feature of a connectionist system involved in pattern recognition to be able to respond to deformed inputs or new inputs that are not precisely like those for which it has been designed or to which it has been trained to respond. It will respond to the altered input in the way it would respond to that of its previous inputs to which it most closely corresponds and it will do so without being provided special instructions telling it how to treat this new input. Moreover, the performance of a connectionist system degrades smoothly when part of the system is destroyed or when it is overloaded. For example, if some units in a connectionist system are destroyed, the system may still respond to inputs by settling into approximately the same stable states.

Put in this way, however, the connectionist argument is likely to encounter the same difficulty as the claim that one type of system can perform tasks which the other cannot. Advocates of rule-based processing models can satisfy both these biological and processing considerations. One reason, for example, that rule-based AI models seem to violate the biological constraint on the number of processing steps is that they are designed for serial processing computers. But many contemporary cognitive theories (e.g., Anderson's ACT* model) employ production system designs, and production systems would very naturally be implemented in parallel architectures. Doing so will dramatically reduce the number of sequential steps that seem to be needed for rule-based simulations of cognitive processes. Moreover, Allen Newell (1987), while adopting a rule-based approach, also invokes considerations of processing time. He uses the information about processing time as a guide to the character of the architecture and contends that his candidate architecture for a unified theory of cognition, SOAR, satisfies the data about time constraints on mental processes.

Advocates of rule-based processing can also accommodate the processing data that is advanced on behalf of connectionist models. There already exist rule-based categorization models that handle deformed or incomplete input. These systems take in information on a variety of features and employ algorithms which determine what category the object is most likely to be in on the basis of that information. To devise rule-based systems that degrade naturally, it will be necessary to build in partial redundancy to the processing procedures such systems employ. But this is not fundamentally incompatible with the idea of a rule-based model.

Behavioral data about what the two types of systems can do or about their manner of performance may be insufficient to answer question 6. The only remedy would seem to be to find some direct way of determining how the human mind works. Already within the rule-processing approach theorists like Pylyshyn (1984) have argued that we must examine the basic architecture of the mind in order to compare a cognitive simulation to a human being. He claimed that only in terms of knowledge of this architecture could we determine whether the simulation performed the same set of operations.[9] If there were a way of identifying this architecture, then we might be able to settle whether the basic operations of the human mind are those of connectionist systems or those of rule-based systems.

How, though, are we to identify the architecture of the human mind? Pylyshyn's criteria for identifying the architecture (relative reaction times for different tasks and cognitive penetrability) are behavioral and encounter the problem that we may be able to simulate with one architecture the performance of the other just as we can compile or interpret one architecture into another in computers. Moreover, his criterion of cognitive penetrability may already introduce a bias toward seeking a rule processing system since Pylyshyn seems to be focusing on penetrability of propositional sorts of information.

If it becomes so difficult to determine whether connectionist or rule-based theorists have the right account of our cognitive architecture, it may seem that the conflict between them is far less interesting than it has seemed to many. Connectionist at first seemed to offer a real contrast to rule-based processing accounts, but what I have been suggesting, both in this section and the previous one, is that the differences between the two accounts may be difficult to identify. But perhaps I am looking at the conflict in the wrong way. I have viewed it as a conflict between competing theoretical hypotheses, and I have questioned how we can determine which is right. A potentially more fruitful way to approach the matter is as a conflict between two different sets of tools for building cognitive models. Here there is a fundamental difference between the two approaches. Different tasks become easier or harder to perform depending on which kind of system we adopt. Classical reasoning tasks are easier to model if we adopt a rule-based model since most models of reasoning, stemming from work in logic, are rule-based. On the other hand, there are quite different kinds of tasks, such as pattern recognition, which seem easier to handle in connectionist frameworks.

What this suggests is that we should think of the conflict not in terms of which model provides a correct account of the human cognitive system but by asking which provides a more useful framework for developing cognitive theories. In this way, we turn the conflict into one about strategies of theory development, and we can pose a new question:

7   What are the relative advantages of developing cognitive theories within a connectionist versus a rule-processing framework?

From this perspective, the question of what it is easy to model in a particular type of system becomes salient and the fact that we could perform many of the same processes in the competing type of system becomes far less important. The fact that a certain kind of operation is easy to perform in a particular type of system may lead those employing that type of system to take greater note of that cognitive operation than those that are difficult to realize in their system. From this perspective, the widespread introduction of connectionist models can be seen as a truly important event in cognitive science, for it may lead us to take note of different sorts of cognitive phenomena. In particular, it may lead us to look beyond language processing and reasoning tasks (which seemed to lend themselves to treatment in rule-based models) to other cognitive activities, such as pattern recognition, which have proven more difficult to handle in rule-based models. To pursue this approach, let us consider pattern recognition, which has become the paradigm task studied by connectionists.

The importance of pattern recognition in human cognition

The settling of a connectionist system into different stable states depending on the inputs it received made it natural to view such systems as performing pattern recognition or categorization. Since systems which can change their connection strengths change their response patterns over time, it became natural to view these systems as learning to classify inputs. Accordingly, researchers have investigated a variety of learning procedures for such systems. As a result, connectionist systems have been designed which learn to categorize input patterns and, after this learning, proceed to categorize new inputs on the basis of similarity to previously learned patterns. (In saying that these systems judge on the basis of similarity connectionists, of course, are not saying that connectionist systems can determine objective similarity and solve the sorts of problems regarding similarity that have been discussed in the philosophical literature. The similarity judgments of those systems is determined by the strengths of the connections in the system. Our license to speak of these systems as judging similarity depends upon the fact that they classify together patterns that we also take to be similar.) It is through their ability to make such similarity judgments that the connectionist systems demonstrate their capacity to generalize to new inputs and respond appropriately to deformed input.

The ease of performing pattern recognition tasks in connectionist systems raises an interesting question:

8   How important a cognitive task is pattern recognition?

It has been the general view of researchers in cognitive science that pattern recognition is an important, but subordinate cognitive activity. One context where pattern recognition has been important has been in work on machine vision, where the challenge is to get machines to be able to recognize objects via sensory inputs. This is clearly a skill that machines will require before they can interact with things in the world (e.g., as intelligent robots). But it has not been easy to develop rule-based processing systems with good pattern recognition abilities, in part because such recognition requires the machine to be able to deal with an enormous number of contextual cues, whose relevance may differ from context to context. For many purposes, however, it has been possible to overlook the problem since we can encode the information symbolically in the system and then focus directly on higher level processing that employs that information. The ability to circumvent the task of recognizing sensory inputs has given the impression that pattern recognition may only be a subordinate cognitive function that can be overlooked while addressing other cognitive tasks.

In recent years, though, there has developed a relatively large psychological literature on concepts and categorization. Categorization is a task comparable to pattern recognition in that it requires the ability to recognize similar items so as to classify them together. Within the rule-based framework it is natural to think of categorization being governed by rules that specify what characteristics something must have to belong to a category. The psychologist Eleanor Rosch (1975) challenged this perspective by arguing that categories have a prototype structure: some exemplars (e.g., robin) are judged to be better examples of the category (e.g., bird) than others (e.g., duck). This suggested that categories are not characterized in terms of necessary and sufficient conditions. Rosch herself did not make the prototype theory into a theory of how categories are mentally represented (see Rosch 1978), but other psychologists have. Although the adoption of a prototype theory of categories undercuts the idea that categorization is based upon simple rules specifying necessary and sufficient conditions, most psychologists who have tried to develop an account of mental representation to accommodate the prototype data still use a rule approach according to which subjects would judge the similarity of an object to a prototype on a variety of features and then apply rules to determine whether the object belonged to the category (for a review of this literature, see Smith and Medin 1981). There is good reason to think that this kind of process could be performed naturally by a connectionist system. As we have already noted, judging similarity is a basic capacity of connectionist model. A connectionist pattern recognition device will classify a new input pattern with the closest match of previous input patterns without requiring a specially stipulated rule. So a Roschian prototype theory of categorization might be readily and naturally implemented in a connectionist system and avoid some of the difficulties that have confronted attempts to devise rule-based categorization processes.

To those who have celebrated rule-based processing in cognitive science, though, categorization tasks may seem no more central than vision tasks (this despite the evidence that how we categorize things may critically influence how we think and reason about them). The real cognitive work, they might maintain, begins once the information is represented in the proper symbolic form or code. However, once we view these tasks as pattern recognition tasks, we may also see how pattern recognition may also figure in more central cognitive processing. Probably the most widely accepted view of higher cognitive activities like problem solving (a view due to the contributions of theorists like Simon, Newell, and Anderson) is that skilled performance in these activities depends on acquiring appropriate rules. Often these rules are thought to be learned in a fairly conscious manner, but then are made automatic so that the skilled performer can generally apply them without explicit conscious thought. Dreyfus and Dreyfus (1986), however, have argued that such rule learning only leads to competent performance in a domain. They maintain that expert performance depends upon being able to recognize a situation as being like certain previous ones and then responding to it in similar ways. One of the examples they consider is chess playing, an activity much studied by theorists who adopt a rule-based approach. Dreyfus and Dreyfus contend that what distinguishes expert from competent chess players is not additional rule-based knowledge but a better developed ability to recognize how a current situation resembles ones previously encountered.[10] If Dreyfus and Dreyfus are right, pattern recognition may figure in even what seemed to be exemplars of high-level reasoning tasks that seemed to require rule-based reasoning. Given the ease of performing pattern recognition and comparison in a connectionist system, this would suggest that it might be worth exploiting this capacity of connectionist systems to see how much can be accomplished through pattern recognition without invoking rule-based reasoning processes.

What I have tried to do in this section is indicate some respects in which pattern recognition might be an important cognitive capacity. There are some other areas where this capacity may also be important. For example, through a pattern recognition process, a connectionist system can activate patterns associated with previous similar experiences. This provides a suggestive way of approaching the task of modeling content-addressable memory. This is a form of memory that is characteristic of humans, but hard to achieve in classical architectures. We may also find a role for pattern recognition in activities that have served as exemplars of rule-processing activities such as syntax processing. We may discover that using pattern recognition systems we could devise systems that could subserve language comprehension and production without invoking complex linguistic rules. These are, of course, only suggestions, and it remains to be seen how much connectionist systems can accomplish through pattern recognition processes that do not invoke rules. It should also be recalled that in all likelihood it will prove possible to design rule-based systems that can perform the same pattern recognition tasks. The relative ease of carrying them out in connectionist systems, though, suggests that we should exploit such systems to determine how much of cognition relies on pattern recognition and does not *require* rule-based processing. If connectionist systems serve to direct our attention to such other cognitive activities as pattern recognition, which have not been focal in recent, rule-based cognitive science, they will have served an important heuristic function regardless of the final outcome of the debate over whether humans are really connectionist or rule-based processing systems.

Possible reconciliation of connectionist and rule-and-representation models

Although connectionist and rule-based theorists often view themselves as competitors, I have emphasized in the last section that the two kinds of systems are naturally good at quite different types of activity. Since reasoning has often been viewed as a matter of following rules such as those articulated in systems of natural deduction, it has been relatively easy to design rule-based systems to perform complex reasoning tasks. On the other hand, connectionist systems have proven to be good at such things as pattern recognition and motor control and offer the potential for content-addressable memory. This should lead us to ask:

9 Is it possible to integrate connectionist and rule-based models so as to acquire the benefits of both in a single cognitive model?

Since connectionists view themselves as revolutionaries struggling to overcome the domination of the more traditional rule-based approach, it is not surprising that they would want to push the new approach to its limits to see just how far they can proceed with it alone. But in fact most of the work on connectionism has pursued tasks that terminate with a specific response by a system—for example, the system may identify the particular pattern with which it is confronted and then wait for its next input. But in typical human cognition the recognition of a pattern is not the end of the process. It may provide the basis for other kinds of activity. When I recognize my cat, I might consider whether I had left any food out for her or given her medicine to her today, or I might be prompted to say something to her.

There are two ways we might envisage the completion of a pattern recognition task in a connectionist system as leading to other cognitive processing. The particular pattern that is activated might spread its activation to other modules with which it is connected in a form of spreading activation. Or the recognition of a pattern might trigger further processing in which rules are applied. For example, if the pattern recognition process idientified my chairperson, that might also serve to satisfy the antecedent of the currently activated rule "If I see my chairperson, ask about my travel allowance" and so fire the production.

Advocates of both approaches have allowed some room for rapprochement. Connectionists like Rumelhart and McClelland characterize their own program as one addressed to the microstructures of cognition and this seems to allow for the possibility that more traditional cognitive models might characterize the macrostructure. Rumelhart, Smolensky, McClelland and Hinton (1986) have even tried to show how certain features of traditional rule-based cognitive systems, such as the use of schemes and frames, can be realized in connectionist systems. Touretsky (1986) has shown how to implement traditional LISP operations in a connectionist system.

On the other side, rule-based theorists such as Fodor and Pylyshyn (1988) are willing to consider the possibility that in humans rule-based processing is implemented in something like a connectionist system. What this would involve, presumably, is having the formal inference principles of a rule-based system mapped on to states of a connectionist network. Fodor and Pylyshyn, however, distinguish sharply between the mode of implementation and the actual cognitive architecture. The architecture, they maintain, must be a rule-processing system which employs (1) a combinatorial syntax and semantics, and (2) structure sensitive processes. They argue for these requirements on the architecture by describing several features of cognition which they maintain require such processes: (a) the productivity of though (i.e., we can build up complex propositions by recursive processes), (b) the systematicity of cognitive representations (which is revealed by the fact that anyone who can think that John loves Mary is also able to think that Mary loves John), and (c) the compositionality of representations (i.e., a component of a mental representation makes approximately the same semantic contribution to all mental representations in which it appears). Fodor and Pylyshyn maintain, however, not only that these features of cognition require a rule-processing system but also that all cognitive or psychological activity takes place within that architecture. The features of the system in which the architecture is implemented are *mere* matters of implementation, and so not a matter for the psychologist.

Even if we provisionally accept Fodor and Pylyshyn's claim that some features of cognition require a rule-processing type system, we can still question their negative conclusion about connectionism by asking:

10 If a rule-processing system is implemented in a connectionist system, could that have implications for the cognitive aspects of the rule-based processing system?

If in fact the human rule-processing system is implemented in a connectionist type system and this provides the system with certain capacities like pattern recognition, concept learning, and content-addressable memory, then it would seem that the mode of implementation has cognitive significance. The issue is not merely a matter of implementation but of central importance to the character of cognitive inquiry. Fodor and Pylyshyn seem to assume that investigations at lower levels, such as those at which rule-processing is implemented, do not have consequences for investigations at higher levels. They characterize psychological inquiry as basically autonomous.[11] But in other disciplines autonomy assumptions have not proven viable. For example, knowledge of structure of physical membranes has been critical for determining the form of biochemical theories and vice versa. Moreover, researchers have sometimes found it critical to bring in approaches from other disciplines (e.g., cytology) to solve problems (e.g., oxidative phosphorylation) that were thought to fall solely within the purview of one discipline (e.g., biochemistry). (For further discussion of the problems confronting the kinds of autonomy claims advanced by Fodor and Pylyshyn, see Bechtel 1988a.) It is far from clear that implementation studies will not similarly contribute material relevant for explaining some aspects of cognitive processing within rule-based systems.

To suggest a more fruitful way of integrating rule-processing and connectionist models, I will return briefly to the topic of concepts and categorization. Concepts are a likely candidate for the units of rule-based cognitive processing. Earlier I touched upon the possibility that categorization into concepts might be implemented in a connectionist system to take advantage of the ability of such systems to recognize similarities and associate examples with prototypes. There is a further advantage to doing so. Generally, even within a Roschian perspective on concepts, concepts are taken to be relatively stable. Thus, they seem like the atoms of thought–not divisible or modifiable in themsleves. But Barsalou (1987, in press) has produced significant evidence for variability in our concepts. One of Rosch's measures to demonstrate the character of concepts was to ask subjects to rank the prototypicality of different members of a category. She claimd to find evidence of high between-subject correlations in such rankings. Barsalou, however, showed that her statistical measure is flawed and that when a more appropriate statistical measure is used, between-subject correlations of prototypicality judgments drop to approximately 0.4. Moreover, he found that even intrasubjectively, prototypicality judgments change measurably over a time interval of one month, with correlations of only 0.8.

From these results Barsalou draws the inference that concepts might not be stored in long-term memory as fixed units, but might be "constructed on the fly" as needed for particular reasoning tasks. It is somewhat difficult to make sense of this view within a rule-based account of cognition, since concepts would seem to be the atoms of such systems, but much easier to make sense of it from a connectionist perspective where what exist in long-term memory are only connections. These enable the subject to produce representations that play the role of concepts and may be used in solving problems for which even rules might be invoked, but the concepts need not be fixed, atomic structures as they are in most rule-based accounts. Thus, implementing concepts in a connectionist system might allow us to explain in a straightforward manner some characteristics of concepts that might otherwise be difficult to explain. In addition, a significant advantage of using connectionist systems to represent concepts is that we could invoke the learning capacities of connectionist system to explain how new primitive concepts are learned, a phenomenon which a rule-processing theorist like Fodor (1980) denies is possible (see Bechtel 1985b).

I have here only sketched in broad outline how connectionist and rule-based accounts might be integated. The basic idea is that states in connectionist systems might serve as the representations (including representations of rules) of a rule-based processing system. The advantage of such an arrangement is that some of the desirable features of connectionist systems can be utilized by the rule-processing system, and not themselves have to be performed through the invocation of rules. (I develop this sketch in a bit more detail in Bechtel 1988b.) Clearly there are many technical problems to be solved before such an integrated system will be available, but it seems at least possible that one might be developed.

Relation of connectionist models to neuroscience accounts of cognition

Another philosophical issue raised by connectionism concerns the relation of connectionist theories to other theories. On the one hand, there is a question about the relation of connectionist models to those of neuroscience and, on the other, a question about the relation of connectionist models to folk psychology. Both of these questions raise the issue of whether connectionism is in some way a "reductionist" program. I shall take these topics up in turn in these last two sections.   I noted at the outset that connectionist models are neurally inspired. The degree of activation of units can be seen as comparable to the firing rate of neurons, and the passing of activations to other units is comparable to the passing of signals between neurons. But is is also clear that connectionist models are not themselves neural models since connectionists do not try to take into account all the details of neural systems, and connectionists are not, by and large, interested in making their models into more realistic neural ones. So we need to address the question:

11 If connectionist models are not themselves neural models, what are they models of? How do the components of connectionist models relate to the components of the brain?

Those who advocate rule-based models have a natural way of addressing the comparable question about their models: the rule-based accounts specify processes that are realized by more basic processes performed in the computer or the brain. They are accounts of real causal processes, but processes that take place at a higher level than the activities of individual neurons or even neural assemblies. But such an answer on behalf of connectionists would seem less motivated. The activities in connectionist models seem to be so like those in neural networks that it seems most natural to treat them as models of processing in those very networks.

Another way connectionists can address this issue is by maintaining that their models are abstract models of the neural processing system. As such, they overlook some of the details of real neural systems so as to characterize the features of a general class of systems (Smolensky 1988). An analysis at such a level of abstraction in fact makes a great deal of sense when the point is to show how a certain kind of process that previously seemed miraculous might actually be carried out by a system like the brain. It proves that mechanisms of a certain kind can do certain kinds of things. Morever, such an approach can also guide the search for understanding at the neural level. One problem neuroscience has faced is figuring out how the activities of neurons could be performing cognitive functions. Connectionist models show how they might figure in such activities, and thus prepare the way for further research to determine in detail how neural systems perform these functions.

It seems reasonable at the current time to think of connectionist models as abstract accounts of the neural system. But if this is right, then connectionist models are accounts of neural activity, not of higher levels of activity in the brain. They simply ignore some of the details of this activity. Moreover, it would seem that a plausible goal in the future would be to develop ever more accurate accounts of how neural systems actually do operate and not to maintain a distinction between connectionist theories and neural theories. The difference between neural models and connectionist models would seem to dissolve into a pragmatic difference–at this juncture in the development of our understanding of the brain and cognition it is useful to consider a broad class of connectionist models, whereas as the program develops it will be more crucial to develop accounts that are more neurally accurate. This is, however, to reduce the distinction between connectionist models and neural models, which seems to be important at least to some connectionists.

This view of connectionism I have just presented may seem to give it a prominent place in a reductionist program. If connectionist models do succeed in accounting for the full range of cognitive phenomena, it would seem proper to see them as showing how to reduce traditional cognitive theorizing to neural-level theorizing. There is, however a different perspective we might take. The distinction between cognitive research (whether connectionist or rule-based) and neural research might better be viewed more as a matter of the kinds of questions researchers ask and the concepts and research tools they employ to answer them, than as a matter of the level of organization in nature at which the research occurred (see also Abrahamsen 1987 for a discussion of relations between research disciplines that would accommodate this view). Moreover, even if some of the basic cognitive operations are performed in simple connectionist networks, some will involve the higher level interactions between these networks and their integration. As was suggested in the previous section, this is where rule-based processes might figure. The higher-level activities might be characterized in neuroscience terms, but it will also prove important to characterize them in more cognitive terms. What might emerge as a result of connectionist perspectives is a repudation of the view that there is one unique level for cognitive theorizing but rather a view according to which cognitive theorizing (as well as neural theorizing) occurs at a variety of levels, some of which are lower than the symbolic level of traditional cognitive theorizing.

Relation of connectionist models to folk psychology

When philosophers have considered mental activities, they have often focused on folk psychology. This is a perspective from which we view people as having beliefs and desires and interpret them as behaving on the basis of these beliefs and desires. A major concern of philosophers is how folk psychology fares in the wake of the development of experimental inquiries in psychology and neuroscience. In folk psychology we characterize people as reasoning from their beliefs and desires to determine what to do and such folk psychology is one source of the view that cognition is a rule-based process. In so far as rule-based models of cognition employ the model of logical reasoning that figures in folk psychological accounts and use that structure as a basis for a scientific psychology, they preserve the validity of folk psychology. On the other hand, if connectionists are right in their strong claims that the mind is not a rule-based system, they may seem to undercut the legitimacy of folk psychology as well as rule-based cognitive psychology. This possibility is emphasized by Eliminative Materialists like Patricia and Paul Churchland, who view connectionist and related accounts of how the brain actually performs cognitive taks as showing the need to reject folk psychology in much the way we have learned to reject folk physics and folk medicine (see P.S. Churchland 1986; P.M. Churchland 1986). A final question concerning connectionism is thus posed:

12 If connectionist models are correct, does that show that we need to eliminate folk psychology? Or is there still a place for folk psychology?

The Churchlands have maintained that psychology (including especially folk psychology) must reduce to our best theories of how the mind/brain works, or be eliminated. By reduction they seem to have in mind a reduction in the philosophical sense wherein the terms of folk psychology would be identified with terms from our scientific account of the mind/brain and then theoretical accounts of folk psychology would be derived from those of our new mind/brain theory. They doubt the likelihood of such a reduction and therefore call for the elimination of folk psychology. On the other hand, the Churchlands consider connectionist models as potentially correct accounts of the operation of the mind/brain and thus as potential replacements for folk psychology. For now I will accept both the denial of reduction and the claim that connectionism may provide a basically correct account of how the mind/brain works. What I will question is whether we need to accept the choice of either reducing folk psychology to connectionist theories or eliminating it.

Let me briefly sketch an alternative perspective. Although some supporters of rule-based accounts of cognition have seen folk psychology as a prototype of a rule-based model of how the mind actually works, that may misrepresent the function of folk psychology. Folk psychology may better be understood as an account of people rather than of their internal mental processes. People have beliefs and desires, but these may not be internal states of people. Folk psychology may give us a way of characterizing people *vis-à-vis* their environment, but it may not be the case that people internally represent all aspects of their environment. Their internal states may enable them to behave appropriately given certain aspects of their environment to them, but there may be no internal state that itself constitutes that knowledge (Bechtel 1985a).

If this is correct, then the failure of folk psychology to reduce to connectionism does not undercut the viability of folk psychology. We may continue to view folk psychology as providing a description of the behaving subject, specifying the information it has about its environment and its goals for action. As such, folk psychology (or some revised version of it) still has an important role to play. One of the dangers to which experimental theorizing has sometimes succumbed is developing theoretical models to account for behavior (like ability to memorize nonsense words) which can be elicited in laboratories, but does not play an important role when organisms pursue their ordinary life. Folk psychology gives us one perspective on what information people have about their world and the kinds of cognitive activities they perform in it. It is not the only way to gain such a perspective. Ecological approaches to psychology that emphasize real-life activity of cognitive agents are another (see Neisser 1975, 1982). My claim is only that some such perspective which characterizes people and the information they have about their environment plays a critical role for those developing any internal processing account – connectionist or rule-based. Hence, this perspective is not eliminated by internal processing accounts. To the contrary, a successful internal processing account will explain what makes it possible for someone, when confronted with an actual environment, to satisfy the descriptions of folk psychology or ecological psychology. (See further Bechtel and Abrahamsen, 1990).

Conclusions

My goal in this paper has been to indicate some of the philosophical problems to which connectionism gives rise. I have noted twelve such questions, covering such issues as how connectionist models are developed, how they can be tested against rival rule-based models, how they might be integrated with rule-based accounts, and how they relate to neuroscience theories and folk psychological accounts. The rise of connectionism constitutes a major event in the development of cognitive science, and I hope it is clear that it also poses a number of questions that are ripe for philosophical examination.

NOTES

The manuscript of this paper was prepared while I was a visiting fellow at the Center for Philosophy of Science at the University of Pittsburgh. I am most grateful to the Center for its hospitality and to Georgia State University for providing me a leave of absence. Adele Abrahamsen, Larry Barsalou, David Blumenfeld, C. Grant Luckhardt, Marek Lugowski, Ulric Neisser, and Robert McCauley have each provided me with valuable comments for which I am thankful.

1   For discussion of a variety of other connectionist simulations using this localized interpretation scheme, see Fahlman 1979; Feldman and Ballard 1982; Rumelhart and Norman 1982; and Cottrell and Small 1983.

2   In Bechtel and Richardson (in preparation), we analyze how this decompositional view of nature underlies the research in a variety of disciplines of the life sciences and the kinds of research tools scientists have invoked in trying to develop explanations built on this assumption. The program of homuncular functionalism in philosophy of mind (Dennett 1978; Lycan 1981) represents this sort of approach to scientific explanation, for the homunculi posited each perform a significant task which is needed in order to carry out the overall activity of the system.

3   Kauffman (1986) has proposed a model of genetic regulatory systems which, like

connectionist models, construes the stability of genetic systems as an emergent phenomenon, not something performed by particular genetic units.

4 By noting this as a feature of connectionist systems, I do not mean to imply that it cannot be found in more traditional cognitive models (e.g., Anderson 1983). This, however, is a feature that arises naturally in connectionist systems and requires complex rule sets in rule-based systems.

5 Neisser (personal communication) suggests that what is important for intrinsic intentionality is that the system extract the right invariants (information patterns in the sensory medium specifying features of the environment) from its sensory contact with the world. While we will be able to assess whether a system is capable of such pick-up of information only when we have a full-scale system that inhabits and functions in an environment, I see no reason why connectionist devices could not subserve this extraction function.

6 Dan Lloyd first directed me to the importance of this question.

7 Connectionists do speak of the procedures for changing connection strengths as "learning rules." But these are quite different from the sorts of rules that figure in rule-based systems. Learning rules are simply mathematical specifications of how connection strengths will change as a result of activity in the system. They are not explicitly stored rules which are formally applied to previous representations so as to create new ones.

8 This question was initially posed to me by Max Coltheart.

9 With traditional computer systems this idea of an architecture which specified the primitive operations is generally relative. While the machine language of a particular system ultimately specifies what primitive operations can be used in the system, most programming is done in higher level languages that are either compiled or interpreted directly, or via intermediate languages, into the machine language. But Pylyshyn maintains that things are not so relative in the case of the human being. There is a basic architecture that is privileged and once we identify it, we will be able to compare the operations performed in a machine simulation with those performed in us.

10 Of course, we do not always do in the new situation precisely what we did in a similar previous situation. There are at least two situations in which we may depart from the pattern. First, if the action taken in the previous instance did not have satisfactory consequences, then we may elect not to try it again. Or if we have time to be reflective, we might contemplate how we should adjust our previous response either to deal with circumstances that distinguish the current situations from the previous one or to improve upon previous performance. These might be situations where we might want to consider rules (e.g., never do A in situation B), but it is also possible that we might employ a great deal more pattern matching. For example, by activating the previous pattern we might also activate an associated recollection of the previous negative consequences of the response we tried. And one thing we might do in trying to adjust or improve on a previous response is to activate other related patterns and compare the responses we had associated with those patterns to the primary one we have just activated for the current circumstance.

11 In fact, all Fodor and Pylyshyn actually maintain is that psychology has "autonomously stateable principles." But it is far from clear what this means. It could mean that we can discover the principles of psychology through psychological investigations alone. This would seem to be the implication required to justify the denial of any capacity of connectionism to force changes in cognitive theorizing. But it could also mean that once discovered, the principles of psychology could be stated solely in psychological terms. This is more plausible, but as I discuss below, it too may be false.

REFERENCES

Abrahamsen, A. A. (1987) "Bridging boundaries versus breaking boundaries: Psycholinguistics in perspective," *Synthese* 72, 355–88.

Anderson, J. R. (1983) *The Architecture of Cognition*. Cambridge: Harvard University Press.

Barsalou, L. W. (1987) "The instability of graded structure: Implications for the nature of concepts," in U. Neissser (ed.), *Concepts Reconsidered: The Ecological and Intellectual Bases of Categories*. Cambridge: Cambridge University Press.

Barsalou, L. W. (in press) "Intra-concept similarity and its implications for inter-concept similarity. In S. Vosniadou and A. Ortony (eds), *Similarity and Analogy*. Cambridge: Cambridge University Press.

Bechtel, W. (1985a) "Realism, instrumentalism, and the intentional stance," *Cognitive Science*, 9, 265–92.

Bechtel, W. (1985b) "Are the new parallel distributed processing models of cognition cognitivist or associationist?" *Behaviorism*, 13, 53–61.

Bechtel, W. (1986) "What happens to accounts of the mind–brain relation if we forgo an architecture of rules and representations?" In A. Fine and P. Machamer (eds), *PSA 1986* (159–71). East Lansing, MI: Philosophy of Science Association.

Bechtel, W. (1988a) *Philosophy of Science: An Overview for Cognitive Science*. Hillsdale, NJ: Lawrence Erlbaum Associates.

Bechtel, W. (1988b) "Connectionism and rules-and-representations systems: Are they compatible?" *Philosophical Psychology*, 15–16.

Bechtel W. and Abrahamsen, A. A. (forthcoming) *Connectionism and the Mind: An Introduction to Parallel Processing in Networks*, Basil Blackwell.

Bechtel, W. and Richardson, R. C. (in preparation) *A Model of Theory Development: Localization as a Scientific Research Strategy*.

Churchland, P. M. (1986) "Some reductive strategies in neurobiology," *Mind*, 95, 279–309.

Churchland, P. S. (1986) *Neurophilosophy: Toward a Unified Science of the Mind-Brain*. Cambridge: MIT Press/Bradford Books.

Cottrell, G. W. and Small, S. L. (1983) "A connectionist scheme for modelling word sense disambiguation," *Cognition and Brain Theory*, 6, 89–120.

Dennett, D. C. (1978) *Brainstorms*. Cambridge, MA: MIT Press/Bradford Books.

Dreyfus, H. L. (1979) *What Computers Can't Do: The Limits of Artificial Intelligence*. New York: Harper & Row.

Dreyfus, H. L. and Dreyfus, Stuart, E. (1986) *Mind over Machine. The Power of Human Intuition and Expertise in the Era of the Computer*. New York: The Free Press.

Fahlman, S. A. (1979) *NETL. A System for Representing and Using Real Knowledge*. Cambridge: MIT Press.

Feldman, J. A. and Ballard, D. H. (1982) "Connectionist models and their properties," *Cognitive Science* 6, 205–54.

Fodor, J. A. (1975) *The Language of Thought*. New York: Crowell.

Fodor, J. A. (1980) *Representations*. Cambridge: MIT Press (Bradford Books).

Fodor, J. A. and Pylyshyn, Z. W. (1988) "Connectionism and cognitive architecture: A critical analysis," *Cognition*, 28, 3–71.

Hinton, G. E., McClelland, J. L. and Rumelhart, D. E. (1986) "Distributed representations," in Rumelhart and McClelland 1986, 77–109.

Hollan, J. D. (1975) "Features and semantic memory: Set theoretic or network models?" *Psychological Review*, 82, 154–5.

Kauffman, S. A. (1986) "A framework to think about evolving genetic regulatory systems," in W. Bechtel (ed.), *Integrating Scientific Disciplines*. Dordrecht: Martinus Nijhoff.

Lycan, W. G. (1981) "Form, function, and feel," *The Journal of Philosophy*, 78, 24–49.

McClelland, J. L. (1986) "The programmable blackboard model of reading," in McClelland and Rumelhart 1986, 122–69.

McClelland, J. L. and Rumelhart, D. E. (1981) "An interactive activation model of context effects in letter perception. Part I, An account of basic findings," *Psychological Review*, 88, 375–407.

McClelland, J. L., Rumelhart, D. E. and the PDP Research Group (1986) *Parallel Distributed Processing: Explorations in the Microstructures of Cognition. Volume 2: Psychological and Biological Models*. Cambridge MA: MIT Press.

Minsky, A. and Papert, S. (1969) *Perceptions*. Cambridge MA: MIT Press.

Newell, A. (1980) "Physical symbol system," *Cognitive Science*, 4, 135–83.

Newell, A. (1987) "Unified theories of cognition." The William James Lectures, Harvard University and repeated at Carnegie Mellon University.

Neisser, U. (1975) *Cognition and Reality: Principles and Implications of Cognitive Psychology*. San Francisco: Freeman.

Neisser, U. (1982) *Memory Observed*. San Francisco: Freeman.

Pinker, S. and Prince, A. (1988) "On language and connectionism: Analysis of a parallel distributed processing model of language acquisition," *Cognition*, 28, 73–193.

Pylyshyn, Z. W. (1984) *Computation and Cognition. Toward a Foundation for Cognitive Science*. Cambridge: MIT Press (Bradford Books).

Quillan, M. R. (1968) "Semantic memory," in M. Minsky (ed.), *Semantic Information Processing* (227–70). Cambridge, MA: MIT Press.

Rips, L. J., Smith, E. E. and Shoben, E. J. (1975) "Set-theoretic and network models reconsidered: A comment on Hollan's "Features and semantic memory." *Psychological Review*, 82, 156–57.

Rosch, E. H. (1975) "Cognitive Representations of semantic categories," *Journal of Experimental Psychology: General*: 104, 192–233.

Rosch, E. H. (1978) "Principles of categorization," in E. H. Rosch and B. B. Lloyd, *Cognition and Categorization* (24–48). Hillsdale, NJ: Erlbaum.

Rosenblatt, F. (1962) *Principles of Neurodynamics*. New York: Spartan.

Rumelhart, D. E., Hinton, G. and McClelland, J. L. (1986) "A general framework for parallel distributed processing," in Rumelhart and McClelland 1986, 45–76.

Rumelhart, D. E., McClelland, J. L. and the PDP Research Group (1986) *Explorations in the Microstructure of Cognition. Volume I: Foundations*. Cambridge: MIT Press (Bradford Books).

Rumelhart, D. E. and Norman, D. A. (1982) "Simulating a skilled typist: A study of skilled cognitive–motor performance," *Cognitive Science*, 6, 1–36.

Rumelhart, D. E. Smolensky, P., McClelland, J. L. and Hinton, G. E. (1986) "Schemata and sequential thought processes in PDP models," in McClelland and Rumelhart 1986.

Rumelhart, D. E. and Zipser, D. (1985) "Feature discovery by competitive learning," *Cognitive Science*, 9, 75–112.

Searle, J. (1980) "Minds, brains, and programs," *Behavioral and Brain Sciences*, 3, 417–24.

Selfridge, O. (1955) "Pattern recognition in modern computers," *Proceedings of the Western Joint Computer Conference*.

Smith, E. E., Shoben, E. J. and Rips, L. J. (1974) "Structure and process in semantic memory: A featural model for semantic decisions," *Psychological Review*, 81, 214–41.

Smith, E. E. and Medin, D. L. (1981) *Categories and Concepts*. Cambridge, MA: Harvard University Press.

Smolensky, P. (1988) "On the proper treatment of connectionism," *Behavioral and Brain Sciences*, 11, 1–23.

Touretsky, D. S. (1986) "BoltzCONS: Reconciling connectionism with the recursive nature of stacks and trees," *Proceedings of the Eighth Annual Conference of the Cognitive Science Society*. Hillsdale, NJ: Lawrence Erlbaum Associates.

Part V

The "Language of Thought" Hypothesis

Introduction

In the introductions to previous parts we have alluded to the intentionality, aboutness or representational character of beliefs and desires, their "directedness upon objects." "Brentano's Problem," as Field (1978) calls it, is to explain how a purely physical system or organism can be in states having such features.

A key point to note is that intentional or representational features are *semantical* features: beliefs are *true*, or false; they *entail* or imply other beliefs; they are (it seems) composed of concepts and depend for their truth on a match between their internal structures and the way the world is; in particular their "aboutness" is very naturally regarded as a matter of mental *referring*. Some philosophers, most notably Sellars (1963), Fodor (1975, 1981, this volume) and Field (1978), have taken this semanticity of beliefs as a strong clue to the nature of intentionality itself, suggesting that beliefs and thoughts have their intentionality in virtue of properties they share with other semantically characterized items, the sentences of public natural languages.

Sellars argued (against the Behaviorists) that people's intentional states are indeed inner and are indeed representations. They are physical states of the central nervous system. None the less (*contra* Brentano) they are physical states *that have semantical properties*. They have those properties in virtue of the functional roles they play in their owners' behavioral economies, closely analogous to the inferential roles that corresponding linguistic tokens play in public, entirely physical language-games. To put the thesis slightly more formally: for a subject S to think or "occurrently believe" that P is for there to be a state of S's central nervous system that bears the semantic content that P; the state bears that content in much the same sense and in much the same way that a sentence of English or another natural language means that P. Let us call this the Representational Theory of thinking.

It is tempting to gloss the Representational Theory by speaking of a "language of thought," and its leading proponents have given in to that temptation. Fodor argues that representation and the inferential manipulation of representations require a medium of representation, no less in human subjects than in computers. Computers employ machine languages of various kinds; it is reasonable to posit one or more human "machine languages" in which human thought and cognition take place. On the other hand, there are obvious disanalogies between private thought and public speech, so if we are to take Representationalism seriously we must specify, in at least a preliminary way, what similarities are being claimed.

On the Representationalist's behalf, let us say that physically realized thoughts and mental representations are "linguistic" in the following sense: (i) They are composed of parts and are syntactically structured; (ii) their atomic parts refer to or denote things and properties in the world; (iii) their meanings as wholes are determined by the semantical properties of their atomic parts together with the grammatical rules that have generated their overall syntactic structures; (iv) they have truth-conditions, and accordingly truth-values determined by the way the world is; (v) they bear logical relations of entailment or implication to each other. Thus, according to the Representational Theory: human beings have systems of physical states that serve as the elements of a lexicon or vocabulary, and human beings (somehow) physically realize rules that combine strings of those elements into configurations having the complex representational contents that common sense associates with the propositional attitudes. And that is why thoughts and beliefs are true or false just as English sentences are, though a "language of thought" (Mentalese, or Brainese) may differ sharply in its grammar from any natural language.

The arguments for the Representational Theory take a number of impressively different forms (most recently, Fodor 1981, 1987; Lycan 1981; Devitt and Sterelny 1987). Though they are formidable, the theory has also come in for a good deal of criticism in recent years, and there too the arguments take a number of impressively different forms. Some leading objections are these:

1 Chisholm (1972) and others have pointed out that the meanings of natural-language sentences are conventional, and so depend on the beliefs and intentions of human speakers. Beliefs and intentions are propositional attitudes. How, then, without circularity or regress, can attitude content be explicated in terms of meaning in the public-linguistic sense?

2 Dennett (1978) argues on several grounds that the idea of "sentences in the head," implemented as inscriptions scrawled in brain chalk upon a brain blackboard, is fanciful, not to say grotesque. (Though his target seems to be a stronger and more outlandish version of Representationalism than the one sketched above.)

3 Churchland and Churchland (this volume) contend that the "language of thought" idea is distinctly *unbiological*. When one recalls that human beings are card-carrying members of the animal kingdom and that we have evolved in the usual way by natural selection, our linguistic abilities, and our cognitive functions on any highly linguisticized account of them, seem to be an evolutionary afterthought at best, and a tiny fragment of the psychology that actually gets us around in the world. P. S. Churchland (1986) and P. M. Churchland (1986) compellingly depict a brain that works by connectionist networking (see the introduction to Part IV above) and by physically hard-wired coordinate transformation, not by digital-computer-like inferential computation over syntactically structured sentences or logical formulas.

4 While public language is (again) conventional in each of several ways, there is obviously nothing social or conventional about the workings of the brain. The "reference" of the alleged language-of-thought's vocabulary items must be natural. The English word "dog" is an arbitrary vocable socially

attached by the English-speaking community to dogs, but the Mentalese word for "dog" must somehow be naturally connected to dogs, without human intervention. That is a bit hard to swallow.

5 Fodor himself (1975) argues, with reservations but without shame, that if the "language of thought" story is correct so far, then Mentalese concepts must also be *innate* in a very strong sense: every normal child must naturally and at a very early age develop every concept to which he or she can ever afterward attach a public word of a natural language. (But Devitt and Sterelny (1987) safely block this outrageous implication.)

6 If thoughts and beliefs can be about Margaret Thatcher or about Santa Claus because the neurophysiological states that realize them somehow semantically refer to Margaret Thatcher or Santa Claus, and if the neurophysiological states do their semantical referring in virtue of some physical, functional or otherwise naturalistic property they have, what is that property? We may imagine that our thoughts of Thatcher stand in some historical relation to Thatcher herself, but our thoughts of Santa Claus do not stand in any historical relation to Santa Claus himself, for he does not exist. Nor, in trying to say what it is in virtue of which some neurophysiological state "refers to" anything, may we invoke unexplicated propositional attitudes or representational content, and that proves to be a biting constraint.

The attempt to find any naturalistic property or relation with which noncircularly to identify "mental reference" has come to be called the problem of "psychosemantics," following Fodor (this volume). It admits of (so far) two basic lines of approach, reconcilable though entirely distinct in origin.

The first is the "Causal–Historical" approach, in the spirit of Kripke (1972) and Putnam (1975), according to which a mental/brain item M refers to a thing X just in case X figures appropriately in M's etiology. Practitioners of this approach cash the word "appropriately" in any number of hopeful ways; any successful way will have to account for reference to *nonexistent* things, no small task in itself and multiply hard given that one may not, on pain of circularity, invoke unexplicated propositional-attitude contents.

The second approach to psychosemantics is the teleological, already mentioned in the introduction to Part II. Its main hurdle is to secure full generality: human mental states can be about anything, but so far as the external world is concerned, no individual brain state can have more than a few psychobiological functions at a time; how can neurophysiological states be about anything but food, shelter, predators and opposite-sexed conspecifics? Fodor (this volume) was the first teleological theorist to solve that problem – however inadequately, and however quickly he repudiated the details of that solution (in a book (1987) of the sardonically identical title).

The problem of psychosemantics is further exacerbated by a resounding discovery of Hilary Putnam's, later exploded by Fodor into an enormous and very fruitful literature that goes under the label of "methodological solipsism." Putnam and Fodor's thesis will be taken up in the introduction to Part VI below.

FURTHER READING

For the standard works on intentionality and "Brentano's Problem" previous to the 1970s, see A. Marras (ed.) (1972) *Intentionality, Mind, and Language*, University of Illinois Press.

Defending the "language of thought"

Sellars, W. (1963) *Science, Perception and Reality*, Routledge & Kegan Paul.
Sellars, W. (1981) "Mental events," *Philosophical Studies* 39, 325–45.
"The Rosenthal–Sellars Correspondence on Intentionality," published in Marras 1972, ibid.
Harman, G. (1973) *Thought*, Princeton University Press.
Rosenberg, J. F. (1974) *Linguistic Representation*, D. Reidel.
Fodor, J. A. (1975) *The Language of Thought*, Harvester Press.
Fodor, J. A. (1981) *Representations*, Bradford Books/MIT Press.
Field, H. (1978) "Mental representation," *Erkenntnis* 13, 9–61.
Lycan, W. (1981) "Toward a homuncular theory of believing," *Cognition and Brain Theory* 4, 139–59; reprinted with revisions in his *Judgement and Justification*, Cambridge University Press, 1988.

Attacking the "language of thought"

Chisholm, R. M. (1972) Contributions to "The Chisholm–Sellars Correspondence on Intentionality," reprinted in Marras 1972, ibid.
Marras, A. (1973) "On Sellars' linguistic theory of conceptual activity," *Canadian Journal of Philosophy* 2, 471–83.
Dennett, D. C. (1978) "Brain writing and mind reading" and "A cure for the common code", both reprinted in *Brainstorms*, Bradford Books.
Harman, G. (1978) "Is there mental representation?", in *Minnesota Studies in the Philosophy of Science, vol. IX*, University of Minnesota Press. [Second thoughts.]
Churchland, P. S. (1980) "Language, thought, and information processing," *Noûs* 14, 147–70.
Loar, B. (1983) "Must beliefs be sentences?," in P. Asquith and T. Nickles (eds), *Proceedings of the PSA, 1982*, East Lansing, Michigan. [There are replies by Fodor and Harman.]
Churchland, P. M. (1986) "Some reductive strategies in neurobiology," *Mind* 95, 279–309.
Churchland, P. S. (1986) *Neurophilosophy*, Bradford Books / MIT Press.
Schiffer, S. (1987) *Remnants of Meaning*, Bradford Books / MIT Press.

Developing psychosemantics

Kripke, S. (1972) "Naming and necessity," in D. Davidson and G. Harman (eds), *Semantics of Natural Language*, D. Reidel.
Putnam, H. (1975) "The meaning of 'meaning'," in K. Gunderson (ed.), *Minnesota Studies in the Philosophy of Science, Vol. 7: Language, Mind and Knowledge*, (University of Minnesota Press. [The Kripke and Putnam essays propose a causal-historical account of public linguistic meaning, but the account has been extrapolated by others to cover the "language of thought" as well.]
Loar, Brian (1981) *Mind and Meaning*, Cambridge University Press.
Sterelny, K. (1983) "Mental representation: What language is Brainese?" *Philosophical Studies* 43, 365–82.
Stalnaker, R. (1984) *Inquiry*, Bradford Books / MIT Press.
Fodor, J. A. (1987) *Psychosemantics*, Bradford Books/ MIT Press. [To be sharply distinguished from, because it repudiates, the paper "Psychosemantics" that appears in this volume.]

Fodor, J. A. (1986) "Why Paramecia don't have mental representations," in P. French, T. E. Uehling and H. Weinstein (eds), *Midwest Studies in Philosophy X: Studies in the Philosophy of Mind*, University of Minnesota Press.

Devitt, M., and Sterelny, K. (1987) *Language and Reality*, Bradford Books / MIT Press.

Dretske, F. (1988) *Explaining Behavior*, Bradford Books / MIT Press.

11

Defending the "Language of Thought"

Why There Still Has to Be a Language of Thought

JERRY A. FODOR

"But why", Aunty asks with perceptible asperity, "does it have to be a *language?*" Aunty speaks with the voice of the Establishment, and her intransigence is something awful. She is, however, prepared to make certain concessions in the present case. First, she concedes that there are beliefs and desires and that there is a matter of fact about their intentional contents; there's a matter of fact, that is to say, about which proposition the intentional object of a belief or a desire is. Second, Aunty accepts the coherence of physicalism. It may be that believing and desiring will prove to be states of the brain, and if they do that's OK with Aunty. Third, she is prepared to concede that beliefs and desires have causal roles and that overt behavior is typically the effect of complex interactions among these mental causes. (That Aunty was raised as a strict behaviorist goes without saying. But she hasn't been quite the same since the sixties. Which of us has?) In short, Aunty recognizes that psychological explanations need to postulate a network of causally related intentional states. "But why," she asks with perceptible asperity, "does it have to be a *language?*" Or, to put it more succinctly than Aunty often does, what – over and above mere Intentional Realism – does the Language of Thought Hypothesis buy? That is what this discussion is about.[1]

A prior question: What – over and above mere Intentional Realism – does the language of Thought Hypothesis *claim?* Here, I think, the situation is reasonably clear. To begin with, LOT wants to construe propositional-attitude tokens as relations to symbol tokens. According to standard formulations, to believe that *P* is to bear a certain relation to a token of a symbol which means that *P*. (It is generally assumed that tokens of the symbols in question are neural objects, but this assumption won't be urgent in the present discussion.) Now, symbols have

"Why There Still Has to Be a Language of Thought" first appeared in *Psychosemantics* by J. A. Fodor, published by Bradford Books/MIT Press, 1987, pp. 135–67. Copyright © Bradford Books/MIT Press. Reprinted by permission of the publisher.

intentional contents and their tokens are physical in all the known cases. And – *qua* physical – symbol tokens are the right sorts of things to exhibit causal roles. So there doesn't seem to be anything that LOT wants to claim *so far* that Aunty needs to feel uptight about. What, then, exactly is the issue?

Here's a way to put it. Practically everybody thinks that the *objects* of intentional states are in some way complex: for example, that what you believe when you believe that John is late for dinner is something composite whose elements are – as it might be – the concept of John and the concept of being late for dinner (or – as it might be – John himself and the property of being late for dinner). And, similarly, what you believe when you believe that *P* & *Q* is also something composite, whose elements are – as it might be – the proposition that *P* and the proposition that *Q*.

But the (putative) complexity of the *intentional object* of a mental state does not, of course, entail the complexity of the mental state itself. It's here that LOT ventures beyond mere Intentional Realism, and it's here that Aunty proposes to get off the bus. LOT claims that *mental states – and not just their propositional objects – typically have constituent structure.* So far as I can see, this is the *only* real difference between LOT and the sorts of Intentional Realism that even Aunty admits to be respectable. So a defense of LOT has to be an argument that believing and desiring are typically structured states.

Consider a schematic formulation of LOT that's owing to Stephen Schiffer. There is, in your head, a certain mechanism, an *intention box.* To make the exposition easier, I'll assume that every intention is the intention to make some proposition true. So then, here's how it goes in your head, according to this version of LOT, when you intend to make it true that *P*. What you do is, you put into the intention box a token of a mental symbol that *means* that *P*. And what the box does is, it churns and gurgles and computes and causes and the outcome is that you behave in a way that (*ceteris paribus*) makes it true that *P*.   So, for example, suppose I intend to raise my left hand (I intend to make true the proposition that I raise my left hand). Then what I do is, I put in my intention box a token of a mental symbol that means 'I raise my left hand.' And then, after suitable churning and gurgling and computing and causing, my left hand goes up. (Or it doesn't, in which case the *ceteris paribus* condition must somehow not have been satisfied.) Much the same story would go for my intending to become the next king of France, only in that case the gurgling and churning would continue appreciably longer.

Now, it's important to see that although this is *going* to be a Language of Thought story, it's not a Language of Thought story yet. For so far all we have is what Intentional Realists qua Intentional Realists (including Aunty qua Aunty) are prepared to admit: viz., that there are mental states that have associated intentional objects (for example, the state of having a symbol that means, 'I raise my left hand' in my intention box) and that these mental states that have associated intentional objects also have causal roles (for example, my being in one of these states causes my left hand to rise). What makes the story a Language of Thought story, and not just an Intentional Realist story, is the idea that these mental states that have content also have syntactic structure – constituent structure in particular – that's appropriate to the content that they have. For example, it's compatible with the story I told above that what I put in the intention box when I intend to raise my left hand is a *rock*; so long as it's a rock that's semantically evaluable. Whereas according to the LOT story, what I put in the intention box has to be something like a *sentence*; in the present case, it has to be a formula which contains, inter alia, an expression that denotes me and an expression that denotes my left hand.

Similarly, on the merely Intentional Realist story, what I put in the intention box when I intend to make it true that I raise my left hand and hop on my right foot might also be a rock (though not, of course, the same rock, since the intention to raise one's left hand is not the same as the intention to raise one's left hand and hop on one's right foot). Whereas according to the LOT story, if I intend to raise my left hand and hop on my right foot, I must put into the intention box a formula which contains, *inter alia*, a subexpression that means *I raise my left hand* and a subexpression that means *I hop on my right foot*.

So then, according to the LOT story, these semantically evaluable formulas that get put into intention boxes typically contain semantically evaluable subformulas as constituents; moreover, they can *share* the constituents that they contain, since, presumably, the subexpression that denotes 'foot' in 'I raise my left foot' is a token of the same type as the subexpression that denotes 'foot' in 'I raise my right foot.' (Similarly, *mutatis mutandis*, the '*P*' that expresses the proposition *P* in the formula '*P*' is a token of the same type as the '*P*' that expresses the proposition *P* in the formula '*P & O*'.) If we wanted to be slightly more precise, we could say that the LOT story amounts to the claims that (1) (some) mental formulas have mental formulas as parts; and (2) the parts are 'transportable': the same parts can appear in *lots* of mental formulas.

It's important to see – indeed, it generates the issue that this discussion is about – that Intentional Realism doesn't logically require the LOT story; it's no sort of *necessary* truth that only formulas – only things that have syntactic structure – are semantically evaluable. No doubt it's puzzling how a rock (or the state of having a rock in your intention box) could have a propositional object; but then, it's no less puzzling how a formula (or the state of having a formula in your intention box) could have a propositional object. It is, in fact, approximately equally puzzling how *anything* could have a propositional object, which is to say that it's puzzling how Intentional Realism could be true. For better or for worse, however, Aunty and I are both assuming that Intentional Realism *is* true. The question we're arguing about isn't, then, whether mental states have a semantics. Roughly, it's whether they have a syntax. Or, if you prefer, it's whether they have a *combinatorial* semantics: the kind of semantics in which there are (relatively) complex expressions whose content is determined, in some regular way, by the content of their (relatively) simple parts.

So here, to recapitulate, is what the argument is about: Everybody thinks that mental states have intentional objects; everybody thinks that the intentional objects of mental states are characteristically complex – in effect, that propositions have parts; everybody thinks that mental states have causal roles; and, for present purposes at least, everybody is a functionalist, which is to say that we all hold that mental states are individuated, at least in part, by reference to their causal powers. (This is, of course, implicit in the talk about 'intention boxes' and the like: To be – metaphorically speaking – in the state of having such-and-such a rock in your intention box is just to be – literally speaking – in a state that is the normal cause of certain sorts of effects and/or the normal effect of certain sorts of causes.) What's at issue, however, is the internal structure of these functionally individuated states. Aunty thinks they have none; only the *intentional objects* of mental states are complex. I think they constitute a language; roughly, the syntactic structure of mental states mirrors the semantic relations among their intentional objects. If it seems to you that this dispute among Intentional Realists is just a domestic squabble, I agree with you. But so was the Trojan War.

In fact, the significance of the issue comes out quite clearly when Aunty turns her hand to cognitive architecture; specifically to the question 'What sorts of relations among mental states should a psychological theory recognize?' It is quite natural, given Aunty's philosophical views, for her to think of the mind as a sort of directed graph; the nodes correspond to semantically evaluable mental states, and the paths correspond to the causal connections among these states. To intend, for example, that $P \, \& \, Q$ is to be in a state that has a certain pattern of (dispositional) causal relations to the state of intending that P and to the state of intending that Q. (E.g., being in the first state is normally causally sufficient for being in the second and third.) We could diagram this relation in the familiar way illustrated in figure 1.

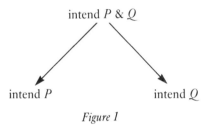

intend $P \, \& \, Q$

intend P intend Q

Figure 1

NB: in this sort of architecture, the relation between – as it might be – intending that $P \, \& \, Q$ and intending that P is a matter of *connectivity* rather than *constituency*. You can see this instantly when you compare what's involved in intending that $P \, \& \, Q$ on the LOT story. On the LOT story, intending that $P \, \& \, Q$ requires having a sentence in your intention box – or, if you like, in a register or on a tape – one of whose parts is a token of the very same type that's in the intention box when you intend that P, and another of whose parts is a token of the very same type that's in the intention box when you intend that Q.

So, it turns out that the philosophical disagreement about whether there's a Language of Thought corresponds quite closely to the disagreement, current among cognitive scientists, about the appropriate architecture for mental models. If propositional attitudes have internal structure, then we need to acknowledge constituency – as well as causal connectivity – as a fundamental relation among mental states. Analogously, arguments that suggest that mental states have constituent structure *ipso facto* favor Turing/Von Neumann architectures, which can compute in a language whose formulas have transportable parts, as against associative networks, which by definition cannot. It turns out that dear Aunty is, of all things, a New Connectionist Groupie. If she's in trouble, so are they, and for much the same reasons.[2]

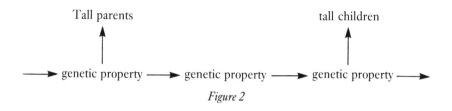

Figure 2

In what follows I propose to sketch three reasons for believing that cognitive states – and not just their intentional objects – typically have constituent structure. I don't suppose that these arguments are knockdown; but I do think that, taken together, they ought to convince any Aunty who hasn't a *parti pris*.

First, however, I'd better 'fess up to a metaphysical prejudice that all three arguments assume. I don't believe that there are intentional mechanisms. That is, I don't believe that contents per se determine causal roles. In consequence, it's got to be possible to tell the whole story about mental causation (the whole story about the implementation of the generalizations that belief/desire psychologies articulate) *without referring to the intentional properties of the mental states that such generalizations subsume.* Suppose, in particular, that there is something about their causal roles that requires token mental states to be complex. Then I'm assuming that it does *not* suffice to satisfy this requirement that these mental states should have *complex intentional objects.*

This is not, by the way, any sort of epiphenomenalism; or if it is, it's patently a harmless sort. There are plenty of cases in the respectable sciences where a law connects a pair of properties, but where the properties that the law connects *don't figure in the story about how the law is implemented.* So, for example, it's a law, more or less, that tall parents have tall children. And there's a pretty neat story about the mechanisms that implement that law. But the property of *being tall* doesn't figure in the story about the implementation; all that figures in that story is *genetic* properties. You got something that looks like figure 2, where the arrows indicate routes of causation.

The moral is that even though it's true that psychological laws generally pick out the mental states that they apply to by specifying the intentional contents of the states, it *doesn't* follow that intentional properties figure in psychological mechanisms.[3] And while I'm prepared to sign on for counterfactual-supporting intentional generalizations, I balk at intentional causation. There are two reasons I can offer to sustain this prejudice (though I suspect that the prejudice goes deeper than the reasons). One of them is technical and the other is metaphysical.

Technical reason: If thoughts have their causal roles in virtue of their contents *per se*, then two thoughts with identical contents ought to be identical in their causal roles. And we know that this is wrong; we know that causal roles *slice things thinner* than contents do. The thought that P, for example, has the same content as the thought that $\sim \sim P$ on any notion of content that I can imagine defending; but the effects of entertaining these thoughts are nevertheless not guaranteed to be the same. Take a mental life in which the thought that $P \ \& \ (P \rightarrow Q)$ immediately and spontaneously gives rise to the thought that Q; there is *no* guarantee that the thought that $\sim \sim P \,\&\, (P{\to}Q)$ immediately and spontaneously gives rise to the thought that Q in that mental life.

Metaphysical reason: It looks as though intentional properties essentially involve relations between mental states and *merely possible* contingencies. For example, it's plausible that for a thought to have the content THAT SNOW IS BLACK is for that thought to be related, in a certain way, to the possible (but nonactual) state of affairs in which snow is black; viz., it's for the thought to be true just in case that state of affairs obtains. Correspondingly, what distinguishes the content of the thought that snow is black from the content of the thought that grass is blue is differences among the truth values that these thoughts have in possible but nonactual worlds.

Now, the following metaphysical principle strikes me as plausible: the causal powers of a thing are not affected by its relations to merely possible entities; only relations to *actual* entities affect causal powers. It is, for example, a determinant of my causal powers that I am standing on the brink of a high cliff. But it is *not* a determinant of my causal powers that I am standing on the brink of a possible-but-nonactual high cliff; I can't throw myself off one of *those*, however hard I try.[4]

Well, if this metaphysical principle is right, and if it's right that intentional properties essentially involve relations to nonactual objects, then it would follow that intentional properties are not per se determinants of causal powers, hence that there are no intentional mechanisms. I admit, however, that that is a fair number of ifs to hang an intuition on.

OK, now for the arguments that mental states, and not just their intentional objects are structured entities.

1 A methodological argument

I don't, generally speaking, much like methodological arguments; who wants to win by a TKO? But in the present case, it seems to me that Aunty is being a little unreasonable even by her own lights. Here is a plausible rule of nondemonstrative inference that I take her to be at risk of breaking:

> Principle P: Suppose there is a kind of event c1 of which the normal effect is a kind of event e1; and a kind of event c2 of which the normal effect is a kind of event e2; and a kind of event c3 of which the normal effect is a complex event e1 $\&$ e2. Viz.:
> c1→e1
> c2→e2
> c3→e1 & e2
> Then, ceteris paribus, it is reasonable to infer that c3 is a complex event whose constituents include c1 and c2.

So, for example, suppose there is a kind of event of which the normal effect is a bang and a kind of event of which the normal effect is a stink, and a kind of event of which the normal effect is that kind of a bang and that kind of a stink. Then, according to P, it is ceteris paribus reasonable to infer that the third kind of event consists (inter alia) of the co-occurrence of events of the first two kinds.

You may think that this rule is arbitrary, but I think that it isn't; P is just a special case of a general principle which untendentiously requires us to prefer theories that *minimize accidents*. For, if the etiology of events that are e1 and e2 does not somehow include the etiology of events that are e1 but not e2, then it must be that there are *two* ways of producing e1 events; and the convergence of these (*ex hypothesi*) distinct etiologies upon events of type e1 is, thus far, unexplained. (It won't do, of course, to reply that the convergence of two etiologies is only a very *little* accident. For in principle, the embarrassment *iterates*. Thus, you can imagine a kind of event c4, of which the normal effect is a complex event e1 & e6 & e7; and a kind of event c5, of which the normal effect is a complex event e1 & e10 & e12 . . . etc. And now, if P is flouted, we'll have to tolerate a *four*-way accident. That is, barring P – and all else being equal – we'll have to allow that theories which postulate four kinds of causal histories for e1 events are just as good as theories which postulate only one kind of causal history for e1 events. It is, to put it mildly, hard to square this with the idea that we value our theories for the generalizations they articulate.)

Well, the moral seems clear enough. Let c1 be intending to raise your left hand, and e1 be raising your left hand; let c2 be intending to hop on your right foot, and e2 be hopping on your right foot; let c3 be intending to raise your left hand and hop on your right foot, and e3 be raising your left hand and hopping on your right foot. Then the choices are: *either* we respect P and hold that events of the c3 type are complexes which have events of type c1 as constituents, *or* we flout P and posit two etiologies for e1 events, the convergence of these etiologies being, thus far, accidental. I repeat that what's at issue here is the complexity of mental events and not merely the complexity of the propositions that are their intentional objects. P is a principle that constrains etiological inferences, and – according to the prejudice previously confessed to – the intentional properties of mental states are *ipso facto not* etiological.

But we're not home yet. There's a way out that Aunty has devised; she is, for all her faults, a devious old dear. Aunty could accept P but deny that (for example) raising your left hand counts as *the same sort of* event on occasions when you *just* raise your left hand as it does on occasions when you raise your left hand while you hop on your right foot. In effect, Aunty can avoid admitting that *intentions* have constituent structure if she's prepared to deny that *behavior* has constituent structure. A principle like P, which governs the assignment of etiologies to complex events, will be vacuously satisfied in psychology if no behaviors are going to count as complex.   But Aunty's back is to the wall; she is, for once, constrained by vulgar fact. Behavior does – very often – exhibit constituent structure, and that it does is vital to its explanation, at least as far as anybody knows. Verbal behavior is the paradigm, of course; everything in linguistics, from phonetics to semantics, depends on the fact that verbal forms are put together from recurrent elements; that, for example, [oon] occurs in both 'Moon' and 'June'. But it's not just verbal behavior for whose segmental analysis we have pretty conclusive evidence; indeed, it's not just *human* behavior. It turns out, for one example in a plethora, that bird song is a tidy system of recurrent phrases; we lose 'syntactic' generalizations of some elegance if we refuse to so describe it.

To put the point quite generally, psychologists have a use for the distinction between segmented behaviors and what they call "synergisms." (Synergisms are cases where what appear to be behavioral elements are in fact 'fused' to one another, so that the whole business functions as a unit; as when a well-practiced pianist plays a fluent arpeggio.) Since it's empirically quite clear that not all behavior is synergistic, it follows that Aunty may not, in aid of her philosophical prejudices, simply help herself to the contrary assumption.

Now we *are* at home. If, as a matter of fact, behavior is often segmented, then principle P requires us to prefer the theory that the causes of behavior are complex over the theory that they aren't, all else being equal. And all else *is* equal to the best of my knowledge. For if Aunty has any *positive* evidence against the LOT story, she has been keeping it very quiet. Which wouldn't be at all like Aunty, I assure you.[5]

Argument 2   Psychological processes (why Aunty can't have them for free)

In the cognitive sciences mental symbols are the rage. Psycholinguists in particular, often talk in ways that make Aunty simply livid. For example, they say things like this: "When you understand an utterance of a sentence, what you do is construct a *mental representation* [*sic*; emphasis mine] of the sentence that is being uttered. To a first approximation, such a representation is a parsing tree; and this parsing tree specifies the constituent structure of the sentence you're hearing, together with the categories to which its constituents belong. Parsing trees are constructed left to right, bottom to top, with restricted look ahead . . ." and so forth, depending on the details of the psycholinguist's story. Much the same sort of examples could be culled from the theory of vision (where mental operations are routinely identified with transformations of structural descriptions of scenes) or, indeed, from any other area of recent perceptual psychology.

Philosophical attention is hereby directed to the logical form of such theories. They certainly look to be quantifying over a specified class of mental objects: in the present case, over parsing trees. The usual apparatus of ontological commitment – existential quantifiers, bound variables, and such – is abundantly in evidence. So you might think that Aunty would argue like this: "When I was a girl, ontology was thought to be an a priori science; but now I'm told that view is out of fashion. If, therefore, psychologists say that there are mental representations, then I suppose that there probably are. I therefore subscribe to the Language of Thought hypothesis." That is not, however, the way that Aunty actually does argue. Far from it.

Instead, Aunty regards Cognitive Science in much the same light as Sodom, Gomorrah, and Los Angeles. If there is one thing that Aunty believes in in her bones, it is the ontological promiscuity of psychologists. So in the present case, although psycholinguists may *talk as though* they were professionally committed to mental representations, Aunty takes that to be *loose* talk. Strictly speaking, she explains, the offending passages can be translated out with no loss to the explanatory/predictive power of psychological theories. Thus, an ontologically profligate psycholinguist may speak of perceptual processes that construct a parsing tree; say, one that represents a certain utterance as consisting of a noun

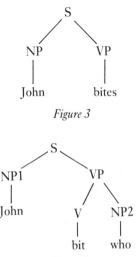

Figure 3

Figure 4

phrase followed by a verb phrase, as in figure 3.

But Aunty recognizes no such processes and quantifies over no such trees. What she admits instead are (1) the utterance under perceptual analysis (the 'distal' utterance, as I'll henceforth call it) and (2) a mental process which eventuates in the distal utterance being *heard as* consisting of a noun phrase followed by a verb phrase. Notice that this ontologically purified account, though it recognizes mental states with their intentional contents, does not recognize mental representations. Indeed, the point of the proposal is precisely to emphasize as live for Intentional Realists the option of postulating representational mental states and then crying halt. If the translations go through, then the facts which psychologists take to argue for mental representations don't actually do so; and if those facts don't, then maybe nothing does.

Well, but *do* the translations go through? On my view, the answer is that some do and others don't, and that the ones that don't make the case for a Language of Thought. This will take some sorting out.

Mental representations do two jobs in theories that employ them. First, they provide a canonical notation for specifying the intentional contents of mental states. But second, mental symbols constitute domains over which *mental processes* are defined. If you think of a mental process – extensionally, as it were – as a sequence of mental states each specified with reference to its intentional content, then mental representations provide a mechanism for the construction of these sequences; they allow you to get, in a mechanical way, from one such state to the next *by performing operations on the representations*.

Suppose, for example, that this is how it goes with English wh- questions: Such sentences have two constituent structures, one in which the questioned phrase is in the object position, as per figure 4, and one in which the questioned phrase is in the subject position, as per figure 5. And suppose that the psycholinguistic

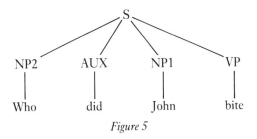

Figure 5

story is that the perceptual analysis of utterances of such sentences requires the assignment of these constituent structures in, as it might be, reverse order. Well, Aunty can tell *that* story *without* postulating mental representations; *a fortiori* without postulating mental representations that have constituent structure. She does so by talking about *the intentional contents of the hearer's mental states* rather than the mental representations he constructs. "The hearer," Aunty says, "starts out by representing the distal utterance as having 'John' in the subject position and a questioned NP in the object position; and he ends up by representing the distal utterance as having these NPs in the reverse configuration. Thus we see that when it's *properly* construed, claims about 'perceiving as' are all that talk about mental representation ever really comes to." Says Aunty.

But in saying this, it seems to me that Aunty goes too fast. For what *doesn't* paraphrase out this way is the idea that the hearer gets from one of these representational states to the other *by moving a piece of the parsing tree* (e.g., by moving the piece that represents 'who' as a constituent of the type NP2). This untranslated part of the story isn't, notice, about what intentional contents the hearer entertains or the order in which he entertains them. Rather, it's about the mechanisms that mediate the transitions among his intentional states. Roughly, the story says that the mechanism of mental state transitions is *computational*; and if the story's true, then (a) there must *be* parsing trees to define the computations over, and (b) these parsing trees need to have a kind of structure that will sustain talk of moving part of a tree while leaving the rest of it alone. In effect, they need to have constituent structure.

I must now report a quirk of Aunty's that I do not fully understand: she refuses to take seriously the ontological commitments of computational theories of mental processes. This is all the more puzzling because Aunty is usually content to play by the following rule: given a well-evidenced empirical theory, either you endorse the entities that it's committed to or you find a paraphrase that preserves the theory while dispensing with the commitments. Aunty holds that this is simply good deportment for a philosopher; and I, for once, agree with her completely. So, as we've seen, Aunty has a proposal for deontologizing the computational story about which state understanding a sentence is: she proposes to translate talk about trees in the head into talk about hearing utterances under descriptions, and that seems to be all right as far as it goes. But it doesn't go far enough, because the ontological commitments of psychological theories are inherited not just from their account of mental states but also from their account of mental processes and the computational account of mental processes would appear to be *ineliminably* committed to mental representations construed as structured objects.

The moral, I suppose, is that if Aunty won't bite the bullet, she will have to pay the piper. As things stand now, the cost of not having a Language of Thought is not having a theory of thinking. It's a striking fact about the philosophy of mind that we've indulged for the last fifty years or so that it's been quite content to pony up this price. Thus, while an eighteenth-century Empiricist – Hume, say – took it for granted that a theory of cognitive *processes* (specifically, Associationism) would have to be the cornerstone of psychology, modern philosophers – like Wittgenstein and Ryle and Gibson and Aunty – *have* no theory of thought to speak of. I do think this is appalling; how can you seriously hope for a good account of belief if you have no account of belief *fixation*? But I don't think it's entirely surprising. Modern philosophers who haven't been overt behaviorists have quite generally been covert behaviorists. And while a behaviorist can recognize mental states – which he identifies with behavioral dispositions – he has literally no use for cognitive processes such as causal trains of thought. The last thing a behaviorist wants is mental causes ontologically distinct from their behavioral effects.

It may be that Aunty has not quite outgrown the behaviorist legacy of her early training (it's painfully obvious that Wittgenstein, Ryle, and Gibson never did). Anyhow, if you ask her what she's prepared to recognize in place of computational mental processes, she unblushingly replies (I quote): "Unknown Neurological Mechanisms." (I think she may have gotten that from John Searle, whose theory of thinking it closely resembles.) If you then ask her whether it's not sort of unreasonable to prefer no psychology of thought to a computational psychology of thought, she affects a glacial silence. Ah well, there's nothing can be done with Aunty when she stands upon her dignity and strikes an Anglo-Saxon attitude – except to try a different line of argument.

Argument 3   Productivity and systematicity

The classical argument that mental states are complex adverts to the productivity of the attitudes. There is a (potentially) infinite set of – for example – belief-state types, each with its distinctive intentional object and its distinctive causal role. This is immediately explicable on the assumption that belief states have combinatorial structure; that they are somehow built up out of elements and that the intentional object and causal role of each such state depends on what elements it contains and how they are put together. The LOT story is, of course, a paradigm of this sort of explanation, since it takes believing to involve a relation to a syntactically structured object for which a compositional semantics is assumed.

There is, however, a notorious problem with productivity arguments. The facts of mortality being what they are, not more than a finite part of any mental capacity ever actually gets exploited. So it requires idealization to secure the crucial premise that mental capacities really *are* productive. It is, for example, quite possible to deny the *productivity* of thought even while admitting that people are forever thinking new things. You can imagine a story – vaguely Gibsonian in spirit – according to which cognitive capacity involves a sort of 'tuning' of the brain. What happens, on this view, is that you have whatever experiences engender such capacities, and the experiences have Unknown Neurological Effects (these Unknown Neurological Effects being mediated, it goes without saying, by the corresponding Unknown Neurological Mechanisms), and the upshot is that you come to have a very large – but finite – number of, as it were, *independent* mental dispositions. E.g., the disposition to think that the cat is on the mat on some occasions; and the disposition to think that 3 is prime on other occasions; and the disposition to think that secondary qualities are epiphenomenal on other occasions . . . and so forth. New occasions might thus provoke novel thoughts; and yet the capacity to think wouldn't have to be productive. In principle it could turn out, after a lot of thinking, that your experience catches up with your cognitive capacities so that you actually succeed in thinking everything that you are able to. It's no good saying that you take this consequence to be absurd; I agree with you, but Aunty doesn't.

In short, it needs productivity to establish that thoughts have combinatorial structure, and it needs idealization to establish productivity; so it's open to Somebody who doesn't want to admit productivity (because, for example, She doesn't like LOT) simply to refuse to idealize. This is, no doubt, an empirical issue in the very long run. Scientific idealization is demonstrably appropriate if it eventually leads to theories that are independently well confirmed. But vindication in the very long run is a species of cold comfort; perhaps there's a way to get the goodness out of productivity arguments *without* relying on idealizations that are plausibly viewed as tendentious.

Here's how I propose to argue:

a   There's a certain property that linguistic capacities have in virtue of the fact that natural languages have a combinatorial semantics.
b   Thought has this property too.
c   So thought too must have a combinatorial semantics.

Aunty, reading over my shoulder, remarks that this has the form of affirmation of the consequent. So be it; one man's affirmation of the consequent is another man's inference to the best explanation.

The property of linguistic capacities that I have in mind is one that inheres in the ability to understand and produce sentences. That ability is – as I shall say – *systematic*: by which I mean that the ability to produce/understand some of the sentences is *intrinsically* connected to the ability to produce/understand many of the others. You can see the force of this if you compare learning a language the way we really do learn them with learning a language by memorizing an enormous phrase book. The present point isn't that phrase books are finite and can therefore exhaustively describe only nonproductive languages; that's true, but I've sworn off productivity arguments for the duration of this discussion, as explained above. The point that I'm now pushing is that you can learn *any part* of a phrase book *without learning the rest*. Hence, on the phrase book model, it would be perfectly possible to learn that uttering the form of words 'Granny's cat is on Uncle Arthur's mat' is the way to say that Granny's cat is on Uncle Arthur's mat, and yet have no idea how to say that it's raining (or, for that matter, how to say that Uncle Arthur's cat is on Granny's mat). I pause to rub this point in. I know –

to a first approximation – how to say 'Who does his mother love very much?' in Korean; viz., *ki-iy emma-ka nuku-lil mewu saranna-ci?* But since I did get this from a phrase book, it helps me not at all with saying anything else in Korean. In fact, I don't know how to say anthing else in Korean; I have just shot my bolt.

Perhaps it's self-evident that the phrase book story must be wrong about language acquisition because a speaker's knowledge of his native language is never like that. You don't, for example, find native speakers who know how to say in English that John loves Mary but don't know how to say in English that Mary loves John. If you did find someone in such a fix, you'd take that as presumptive evidence that he's not a native English speaker but some sort of a tourist. (This is one important reason why it is so misleading to speak of the block/slab game that Wittgenstein describes in paragraph 2 of the *Investigations* as a "complete primitive language"; to think of languages that way is precisely to miss the systematicity of linguistic capacities – to say nothing of their productivity.)

Notice, by the way, that systematicity (again like productivity) is a property of sentences but not of words. The phrase book model really *does* fit what it's like to learn the *vocabulary* of English, since when you learn English vocabulary you acquire a lot of basically *independent* dispositions. So you might perfectly well learn that using the form of words 'cat' is the way to refer to cats and yet have no idea that using the form of words 'deciduous conifer' is the way to refer to deciduous conifers. My linguist friends tell me that there are languages – unlike English – in which the lexicon, as well as the syntax, is productive. It's candy from babies to predict that a native speaker's mastery of the vocabulary of such a language is always systematic. Productivity and systematicity run together; if you postulate mechanisms adequate to account for the one, then – assuming you're prepared to idealize – you get the other automatically.

What sort of mechanisms? Well, the alternative to the phrase book story about acquisition depends on the idea, more or less standard in the field since Frege, that the sentences of a natural language have a combinatorial semantics (and, *mutatis mutandis*, that the lexicon does in languages where the lexicon is productive). On this view, learning a language is learning a perfectly general procedure for determining the meaning of a sentence from a specification of its syntactic structure together with the meanings of its lexical elements. Linguistic capacities *can't help but* be systematic on this account, because, give or take a bit, the very same combinatorial mechanisms that determine the meaning of any of the sentences determine the meaning of all of the rest.

Notice two things:

First, you can make these points about the systematicity of language without idealizing to astronomical computational capacities. *Productivity* is involved with our ability to understand sentences that are a billion trillion zillion words long. But *systematicity* involves facts that are much nearer home: such facts as the one we mentioned above, that no native speaker comes to understand the form of words 'John loves Mary' except as he *also* comes to understand the form of words 'Mary loves John.' In so far as there are 'theory neutral' data to constrain our speculations about language, this surely ought to count as one of them.

Second, if the systematicity of linguistic capacities turns on sentences having a combinatorial semantics, the fact that sentences have a combinatorial semantics turns on their having constituent structure. You can't construct the meaning of an object out of the meanings of its constituents unless it *has* constituents. The sentences of English wouldn't have a combinatorial semantics if they weren't made out of recurrent words and phrases.

OK, so here's the argument: linguistic capacities are systematic, and that's because sentences have constituent structure. But cognitive capacities are systematic too, and that must be because *thoughts* have constituent structure. But if thoughts have constituent structure, then LOT is true. So I win and Aunty loses. Goody!

I take it that what needs defending here is the idea that cognitive capacities are systematic, *not* the idea that the systematicity of cognitive capacities implies the combinatorial structure of thoughts. I get the second claim for free for want of an alternative account. So then, how do we know that cognitive capacities are systematic?

A fast argument is that cognitive capacities must be *at least* as systematic as linguistic capacities, since the function of language is to express thought. To understand a sentence is to grasp the thought that its utterance standardly conveys; so it wouldn't be possible that everyone who understands the sentence 'John loves Mary' also understands the sentence 'Mary loves John' if it weren't that everyone who can *think the thought* that John loves Mary can also think the thought that Mary loves John. You can't have it that language expresses thought *and* that language is systematic unless you also have it that thought is as systematic as language is.

And that is quite sufficiently systematic to embarrass Aunty. For, of course, the systematicity of thought does *not* follow from what Aunty is prepared to concede: viz., from mere Intentional Realism. If having the thought that John loves Mary is just being in one Unknown But Semantically Evaluable Neurological Condition, and having the thought that Mary loves John is just being in another Unknown But Semantically Evaluable Neurological Condition, then it is – to put it mildly – not obvious why God couldn't have made a creature that's capable of being in one of these Semantically Evaluable Neurological conditions but not in the other, hence a creature that's capable of thinking one of these thoughts but not the other. But if it's compatible with Intentional Realism that God could have made such a creature, then Intentional Realism doesn't explain the systematicity of thought; as we've seen, Intentional Realism is exhausted by the claim that there *are* Semantically Evaluable Neurological Conditions.

To put it in a nutshell, what you need to explain the systematicity of thought appears to be Intentional Realism *plus* LOT. LOT says that having a thought is being related to a structured array of representations; and, presumably, to have the thought that John loves Mary is *ipso facto* to have access to the same representations, and the same representational structures, that you need to have the thought that Mary loves John. So *of course* anybody who is in a position to have one of these thoughts is *ipso facto* in a position to have the other. LOT explains the systematicity of thought; mere Intentional Realism doesn't (and neither, for *exactly* the same reasons, does Connectionism). Thus I refute Aunty and her friends!

Four remarks to tidy up:

First: This argument takes it for granted that systematicity is *at least sometimes* a contingent feature of thought; that there are *at least some cases* in which it is logically possible for a creature to be able to entertain one but not the other of two content-related propositions.

I want to remain neutral, however, on the question whether systematicity is *always* a contingent feature of thought. For example, a philosopher who is committed to a strong 'inferential role' theory of the individuation of the logical concepts might hold that you can't, in principle, think the thought that (*P* or *Q*) unless you are able to think the thought that *P*. (The argument might be that the ability to infer (*P* or *Q*) from *P* is *constitutive of having* the concept of disjunction.) If this claim is right, then – to that extent – you don't need LOT to explain the systematicity of thoughts which contain the concept OR; it simply *follows from* the fact that you can think that (*P* or *Q*) that you can also think that *P*.

Aunty is, of course, at liberty to try to explain *all* the facts about the systematicity of thought in this sort of way. I wish her joy of it. It seems to me perfectly clear that there could be creatures whose mental capacities constitute a proper subset of our own; creatures whose mental lives – viewed from our perspective – appear to contain gaps. If inferential role semantics denies this, then so much the worse for inferential role semantics.

Second: It is, as always, essential not to confuse the properties of the attitudes with the properties of their objects. I suppose that it *is* necessarily true that the *propositions* are 'systematic'; i.e., that if there is the proposition that John loves Mary, then there is also the proposition that Mary loves John. But that necessity is no use to Aunty, since it doesn't explain the systematicity of our capacity to *grasp* the propositions. What LOT explains – and, to repeat, mere Intentional Realism does not – is a piece of our empirical psychology: the *de facto*, contingent connection between our ability to think one thought and our ability to think another.

Third: Many of Aunty's best friends hold that there is something very special about language; that it is only when we come to explaining linguistic capacities that we need the theoretical apparatus that LOT provides. But in fact, we can kick the ladder away: we don't need the systematicity of language to argue for the systematicity of thought. All we need is that it is on the one hand true, and on the other hand not a *necessary* truth, that whoever is able to think that John loves Mary is *ipso facto* able to think that Mary loves John.

Of course, Aunty has the option of arguing the *empirical* hypothesis that thought is systematic only for creatures that speak a language. But think what it would mean for this to be so. It would have to be quite usual to find, for example, animals capable of learning to respond selectively to a situation such that *a R b*, but quite unable to learn to respond selectively to a situation such that *b R a* (so that you could teach the beast to choose the picture with the square larger than the triangle, but you couldn't for the life of you teach it to choose the picture with the triangle larger than the square). I am not into rats and pigeons, but I once had a course in Comp Psych, and I'm prepared to assure you that animal minds aren't, in general, like that.

It may be partly a matter of taste whether you take it that the minds of animals are *productive*; but it's about as empirical as anything can be whether they are systematic. And – by and large – they are.

Fourth: Just a little systematicity of thought will do to make things hard for Aunty, since, as previously remarked, mere Intentional Realism is compatible with there being no systematicity of thought at all. And this is just as well, because although we can be sure that thought is somewhat systematic, we can't perhaps, be sure of just how systematic it is. The point is that if we are unable to think the thought that P, then I suppose we must also be unable to think the thought that we are unable to think the thought that P. So it's at least arguable that to the extent that our cognitive capacities are *not* systematic, the fact that they aren't is bound to escape our attention. No doubt this opens up some rather spooky epistemic possibilities; but, as I say, it doesn't matter for the polemical purposes at hand. The fact that there are *any* contingent connections between our capacities for entertaining propositions is remarkable when rightly considered. I know of no account of this fact that isn't tantamount to LOT. And neither does Aunty.

So we've found at least three reasons for preferring LOT to mere Intentional Realism, and three reasons ought to be enough for anybody's Aunty. But is there any general moral to discern? Maybe there's this one:

If you look at the mind from what has recently become the philosopher's favorite point of view, it's the semantic evaluability of mental states that looms large. What's puzzling about the mind is that anything *physical* could have satisfaction conditions, and the polemics that center around Intentional Realism are the ones that this puzzle generates. On the other hand, if you look at the mind from the cognitive psychologist's viewpoint, the main problems are the ones about mental processes. What puzzles psychologists is belief fixation – and, more generally, the contingent, causal relations that hold among states of mind. The characteristic doctrines of modern cognitive psychology (including, notably, the idea that mental processes are computational) are thus largely motivated by problems about mental causation. Not surprisingly, given this divergence of main concerns, it looks to philosophers as though the computational theory of mind is mostly responsive to technical worries about mechanism and implementation; and it looks to psychologists as though Intentional Realism is mostly responsive to metaphysical and ontological worries about the place of content in the natural order. So, deep down, what philosophers and psychologists really want to say to one another is, "Why do you care so much about *that?*"

Now as Uncle Hegel used to enjoy pointing out, the trouble with perspectives is that they are, by definition, *partial* points of view; the Real problems are appreciated only when, in the course of the development of the World Spirit, the limits of perspective come to be transcended. Or, to put it less technically, it helps to be able to see the whole elephant. In the present case, I think the whole elephant looks like this: The key to the nature of cognition is that mental processes preserve semantic properties of mental states; trains of thought, for example, are generally truth preserving, so if you start your thinking with true assumptions you will generally arrive at conclusions that are also true. The central problem about the cognitive mind is to understand how this is so. And my point is that neither the metaphysical concerns that motivate Intentional Realists nor the problems about implementation that motivate cognitive psychologists suffice to frame this issue. To see this issue, you have to look at the problems about content and the problems about process *at the same time*. Thus far has the World Spirit progressed.

If Aunty's said it once, she's said it a hundred times: Children should play nicely together and respect each other's points of view. I do think Aunty's right about that.

NOTES

1 Aunty's not the only one who'd like to know; much the same question has been raised by Noam Chomsky, John Searle, Brian Loar, David Israel, Jon Barwise and John Perry, and Tyler Burge, to name just a few. Aunty and I are grateful to all of the above for conversations which led to the present reflections. Also to Ned Block for characteristically perceptive comments on an earlier draft.

2 Do not be misled by the fact that the *node labels* in associative networks are composed of transportable constituents; the labels play no part in the theory. Cf. Fodor in press where this point is made twelve thousand eight hundred and fifteen times.

By the way, it isn't the *associative* part of 'associative network' that's at issue here. Classical Associationists – Hume, say – held that mental representations have transportable constituents and, I suppose, a combinatorial semantics: the mental image of a house contains, as proper parts, mental images of proper parts of houses. Hume is therefore on my side of the argument as against Aunty and the New Connectionists. The heart of the issue – to repeat the text – is whether you need *both* constituency *and* connectivity as basic relations among the semantically evaluated mental objects, or whether you can make do with connectivity alone.

3 In *From Folk Psychology to Cognitive Science*, Stich wrings his hands a lot about how I could hold that the counterfactual-supporting generalizations of psychology are uniformly intentional *and also hold* the 'solipsistic' principle that mental operations are computational (viz., formal/ syntactic). "How is it possible for Fodor to have it both ways, for him to urge *both* that cognitive generalizations apply to mental states in virtue of their content' and that 'only *non-* semantic properties of mental representations can figure in determining which mental operations apply to them'?" (p. 188).

But there's no contradiction. The vocabulary required to articulate the characteristic laws of a special science is – almost invariably – different from the vocabulary required to articulate the mechanisms by which these laws are sustained, the theory of the mechanisms being pitched – to put it crudely – one level down. So the typical *laws* of psychology are intentional, and the typical *operations* of psychological mechanisms are computational, and everything's fine except that Stich has missed a distinction.

4 Notice – by contrast – that relations to nonactual entities can perfectly well be *constitutive of* causal powers: the solubility of this salt consists in such facts as that if there *were* water here, the salt would dissolve in it. The point in the text, then, is that though relations to nonactual objects can figure in the analysis of a causal power, they can't be among its causal determinants. Nothing – causal powers included – can be an effect of a merely possible cause. (I'm grateful to Georges Rey for helping me to get this sorted out.)

5 It remains open to Aunty to argue in the following relatively subtle sort of way: "All right, so principle P requires that the causes of complex behaviors should themselves be complex. But that still doesn't show that there's a Language of Thought, because the required complex causal objects could be the *propositional attitude states themselves* rather than the (putative) formulas of this (putative) mental language. *Believing that P & Q is itself a complex state* of which the simple parts are the state of believing that *P* and the state of believing that *Q*." In effect, Aunty could try conceding that propositional attitudes are *complex* but denying that they are, in the relevant respect, *relational*.

This, however, will not do. Believing that *P* is *not* a constituent of, for example, believing that *P* or *Q* (or of believing that if *P* then *Q*. . .etc.); for it is perfectly possible to believe that *P* or *Q* (or that if *P* then *Q*) and not to believe that *P*. For similar reasons the required notion of constituency can't be defined over the *causal roles* of the attitudes, either. Thus, the causal role of believing that *P* is not a constituent of the causal role of believing that *P* or *Q* since, for example, the effects of believing that it will snow in August are categorically different from – and are not included among – the effects of believing that either it will snow in August or it won't.

See Fodor 1981 *circa* p. 30, and Fodor (1983) where these sorts of observations are parlayed into yet another argument for LOT. (I do wish that Aunty would read my stuff occasionally!)

REFERENCES

Fodor, J. A. (in press) "Information and association," *Notre Dame Journal of Formal Logic*.

Fodor, J. A. (1981) *Representations*, Bradford Books/MIT Press.

Fodor, J. A. (1983) "Reply to Brian Loar's 'Must beliefs be sentences?'," in P. Asquith and T. Nickles (eds), *Proceedings of the Philosophy of Science Association for 1982*, East Lansing, Michigan.

Stich, S. P. (1983) *From Folk Psychology to Cognitive Science*, Bradford Books/MIT Press.

12

Attacking the "Language of Thought"

Stalking the Wild Epistemic Engine

PAUL M. CHURCHLAND and PATRICIA SMITH CHURCHLAND

Introduction

In some manner, devolving from Evolution's blind trials and blunders, densely crowded packets of excitable cells inevitably come to represent the world. The conglomeration which is the human brain standardly evolves an awesomely complex world-representation in short order and on the basis of scanty input. Less distinguished beasts such as slugs and sloths are presumed to have world-representations which are less rich, or anyhow, different. It is perhaps salutory here to bear in mind that some animals have sensory detectors where we are stony blind. Pigeons have tiny ferro-magnets for detecting the earth's magnetic field; rattlesnakes have infra-red detectors; electric fish have organs which discern small variations in electric fields, and so on (Bullock et al. 1977). It is remarkable also that in the human case the world-representation evolves, and it evolves not only during the lifetime of one human brain, but across the life-spans of collections of brains. But *how* can a brain be a world-representer? How can brains change so that some of their changes consist in learning about the world? How are representations used by a brain such that the output yields purposive and intelligent behavior?

Broadly speaking, research on the question of how the mind-brain works follows one of two methodological colors. The first is in substantial degree part of the rationalist tradition, emphasizing the linguistic and rule-following aspect of cognition, and is now prominently represented by cognitive/computational psychology, or by a substantial movement within that field (see especially Fodor

"Stalking the Wild Epistemic Engine" by P. M. Churchland and P. S. Churchland is reprinted by permission of the authors and of the editor of *Nous*, Vol. 17 (1983); pp. 5–18.

1975, 1978a, 1980; Pylyshyn 1980). The second is naturalistic in character, and is part of the tradition containing such thinkers as de la Mettrie, Darwin, Helmholtz and Hebb, and is the guiding framework for most neuroscientists and physiological psychologists. On closer inspection, the distinction fuzzes and smears at border spots, but the general contrasts are distinct enough. Which approach, if any, will succeed in treeing answers is an empirical question, and in recent work (see Churchland, P. M. 1979, 1980, 1981, 1981; Churchland, P. S. 1980a, 1980b, 1982) we have argued that the odds favor the naturalistic approach. In this we turn to semantic questions, and confess at the outset to some trepidation. For one thing, semantics is a tar-baby. It is difficult to handle without becoming horribly stuck, and worse, once stuck, it is difficult to avoid the conviction that one is embraced by a verity. Additionally, the bounds of the paper exact brevity of presentation, and there are places where we have had to be ruthlessly synoptic.

Unadorned, the gist of the paper is twofold. The first and more familiar point is that computational psychology should seek a wider conception of cognitive processes than is embodied in a sentential/rationalistic model. The second point, however is our main concern. We argue that, because computational psychology is quite properly methodologically solipsistic (we will explain what this means shortly), it cannot provide, and should not be expected to provide, a theory of how a representational system *hooks up to the world*. In so far, it cannot explain how the representing creature survives and flourishes in the environment the creature is struggling to represent. To make good this deficit, we probe the possibilities for a naturalistic strategy. But first, a few remarks are needed on the contrast between naturalistic and non-naturalistic approaches.

Simplifying to the very bone, the dominant hypotheses of the rationalist version of computational psychology are as follows.

(a) The paradigm of the information-bearing or representational state is the propositional attitude, where the object of the attitude (its content) is a sentence.
(b) In cognitive activity, the transitions between representational states are a function of the logical relations holding between the *contents* of those states.
(c) Such representations, and the transitions between them, can thus be modeled or realized in a computer. (Dennett 1978; Fodor 1975; Haugeland 1981; Pylyshyn 1980.)

Church's Thesis says that whatever is computable is Turing computable. Assuming, with some safety, that what the mind-brain does is computable, then it can in principle be simulated by a computer. So what needs to be done is to figure out the program that mimics what cognitive organisms do. Fortunately, goes the rationale (and here is where we start to disagree), the essentially correct basis for devising that program can be found in the propositional attitudes of folk psychology. Extensions and innovations are to be expected, but folk psychological characterizations of the nature of representational structures are fundamentally correct. This is providential, since it means that part of the theory sought is already in hand, and moreover the work can be done without so much as opening a skull and implanting an electrode, and no one has to feed the animals and clean the cages. For those who are squeamish about looking nature in her occasionally noisome face, this assurance of remoteness comes as a relief.

A different strategy inspires the naturalist. The naturalist is moved by two large-scale intellectual visions: the evolution of complex nervous systems from simpler nervous systems, and secondly, the displacement of primitive theories, and their ontologies, by more encompassing and more powerful theories. Enthusiasm for the computational strategy is gutted by the observation that folk theories about the way one or other part of the universe works have typically lost out in the competition for explanatory space. They have, in the light of new theories, been revealed as misdirected, narrow, animistic, and misconceived in varying degrees – despite their having passed as uncontestable truths of common sense for eons. The history of science is littered with the dry bones of folk theory. Even as folk theories of the nature of fire, of the sky, of matter, of heat, of light, of space, of life, of numbers, of weather and climate, of birth and death and disease – even as these folk theories have succumbed to the sharper tooth and fleeter foot of modern biology, chemistry, physics, etc., so it would not be surprising to find folk psychology primitve and inadequate in competition with newer theories of how the mind-brain works. We do not say folk psychology *must* be as inadequate as, say, alchemy, but only that it would be astonishing if it alone amongst folk theories happened to be good enough to survive. A far, far more complex and devious object of wonder than heat or light, the brain is unlikely to have been adequately groped by folk theory in the misty dawn of emerging verbalization (Churchland P. M. 1981).

In loosening the grip of the bonds of common sense psychology, the naturalist suggests we view ourselves as epistemic engines (Churchland, P. M. 1979). Call an epistemic engine any device that exploits a flow of environmental energy, and the information it already contains, to produce more information, and to guide movement. So far as natural (wild) epistemic engines are concerned, survival depends on a fit between the information contained and the world it inhabits. For example, a simple bottom creature who has sensory neurons which happen to be responsive to changes in magnetic field will not benefit from such responses unless the changes are related to its feeding, fleeing, fighting or reproducing. The choice of the word 'engine' is more apt than might be supposed, since its original meaning is 'naive intelligence' or 'mother wit,' and is the source of 'ingenuity.' The planet abounds with a wondrous profusion of epistemic engines; building nests and bowers, peeling bark, dipping for termites, hunting wildebeests, and boosting themselves off the planet altogether. The human brain is but one result of Evolution's blind maunderings, and like other creatures with a nervous system, we too are epistemic engines. Accordingly, cast within the naturalist's framework, the problem consists in figuring out how epistemic engines work.

In considering the problem, the naturalists suggest we dethrone language as the model for the structure and dynamics of representational activity generally. Representations – information-bearing structures – did not emerge of a sudden with the evolution of verbally competent animals. As Sellars (1980) remarks, "the generic concept of a representation admits of many gradations between primitive systems and the sophisticated systems on which philosophers tend to concentrate" (p. 15). Whatever information-bearing structures humans enjoy, such structures have evolved from simpler structures, and such structures are part of a *system* of information-bearing structures and structure-manipulating processes. If we want to understand how epistemic engines work, we might have to understand simpler systems first, and that means we cannot avoid penetrating the skull, implanting electrodes, and looking nature full in the face.

The formality condition: epistemic engines are syntactic engines

The central insight of computational psychology is that intentional and purposive behavior is the outcome of mental states and operations, where a mental state is characterized as standing in a relation to a representation, and where mental operations are defined over representations. Computers are formal machines, in the sense that they operate on symbols in virtue of the form of the symbol, not in virtue of how the symbol may be interpreted. As Fodor (1980) puts it:

> Formal operations are the ones that are specified without reference to the semantic properties of representations, as, e.g., truth, reference, or meaning.

The basic point can be put in the following way: the machine goes from one state to another because it is caused to do so. If the machine treats two tokens differently, it will be because they have a formal difference in virtue of which the machine can discriminate them, and if they are formally indistinguishable, then the machine cannot distinguish them either.

The *formality condition* says that cognitive states are type-distinct only if the representations which constitute their objects are formally distinct. Fodor (1980) has argued that computational psychology should honor the formality condition. This yields the position known as *methodological solipsism*: the causal explanation of cognitive processes must proceed without reference to whatever semantic properties our cognitive states may or may not have. So far as cognitive activity is concerned, semantics enters the picture inessentially, and only in so far as it has a purely syntactic image.

The question spawned by this methodological point is this: what *is* the semantics which has a syntactic image (i.e. syntactic stand-ins for semantic features)? The question is more approachable and familiar if put this way: what criteria of ascribing content to mental states specify content which has a syntactic image, and what criteria fail to specify content?

P. M. Churchland (1979) and Stich (1981) have made the observation that ascription of beliefs and desires (and propositional attitudes generally) to others is fundamentally akin to translation. Stich has developed the point, showing that when I ascribe the belief that *p* to Trudeau, this is to be analyzed roughly as saying that Trudeau has a mental state which is like the one I would be in were I to sincerely say this: *p*. Without tarrying over the niceties, notice that the ascription is a *similarity* judgment, and that it makes ineliminable reference to oneself and *to one's own representational system*. In that respect, such ascriptions are observer relative. Deepening his analysis, Stich has then convincingly argued that like similarity judgments in other domains, these similarity judgments (e.g. belief ascriptions) vary as a function of *which* criteria are used, and that a hodge-podge of criteria jockey for position. Depending on purpose, context, and sundry other considerations, one criterion may be preferred to another, and application of different critiera may well give conflicting desciptions of what Trudeau believes. Sometimes sameness of natural-kind-reference is made to count (cf. Putnam 1975), sometimes it is not. Sometimes conceptual role counts more, sometimes ideological similarity counts, sometimes linguistic practice figures in (see Burge 1979), sometimes social practice takes precedence over conceptual role and so on (see Stich 1981, 1983).

The question raised earlier can now be asked again: if computational psychology is to abide by the formality condition, which way of ascribing content will specify content which has a syntactic stand-in? Evidently the criterion which counts beliefs as different if the references are different will not do. Stich's own view, and we concur, is that the best choice will be the criterion which specifies similarity in terms of functional role (which he calls 'narrow causal role,' and is close enough to 'conceptual role'). The point here is this: if what is wanted in computational psychology are generalizations describing routes from input to output, and the only semantic features relevant are features the machine can detect, then the semantic content of representations must be fixed by their conceptual role, by their narrow causal role, because that is what co-varies with differences in a representation's intrinsic formal structure. This kind of content we call *translational content*, since similarity of conceptual role is what faithful translation attempts to capture. Thus, when I ascribe to Trudeau the belief that dopamine is a neurotransmitter, I am saying that Trudeau stands in the belief-relation to a representation that plays the same inferential/causal/functional role in his representational system that "Dopamine is a neurotransmitter" (or its internal analog) plays in *my* representational system (see Sellars 1981). A translational mapping has been postulated between Trudeau and me. Notice that the relation is not between Trudeau's representations and some part of *the world*, but between Trudeau's representational system and *my representational system*.

Already it will be evident that a computational psychology which confines its semantics to conceptual role semantics will depart from folk psychology in certain minor ways. That is surely inevitable and part of what progress here requires. It is also important to mention that Stich argues that for a scientific psychology, even translational content is too much semantics, and that the ʒemantics will have to be laundered out altogether. His worry here stems from the fact that the description of content is observer-relative. He finds this troublesome because for one thing, to the extent that another organism's representational system diverges from mine, I cannot ascribe content (translational content is what we are confined to now) to the other's representations. If the generalizations of cognitive psychology require specification of content, then the generalizations will be incapable of reaching cases where content specification is uncertain. Most obviously this happens in the case of pre-verbal children, humans from different cultures, humans with brain damage, and as well, the entire animal kingdom. Such a psychology threatens to be a psychology of Me-and-My-Friends, and chartered provincialism is a methodological *faux pas*. Hence Stich's (1983) attempt to see if computational psychology can define operations over uninterpreted syntactic objects.

We are convinced that computational psychology should honor the formality condition. Moreover, P. M. Churchland (1980) has argued that methodological solipsism can be derived from entirely naturalistic assumptions. The brain is evidently a syntactic engine, for a neuron cannot know the distant causal ancestry or the distant causal destiny of its input and outputs. An activated neuron causes a creature to withdraw into its shell not because such activation represents the presence of a predator – though it may indeed represent this – but because that neuron is connected to the withdrawal muscles, and because its activation is of the kind that causes them to contract. The 'semantic' content of the state, if any, is causally irrelevant. What does adherence to the formality condition signify for the research program of computational psychology? It means, for one thing, that questions about how mental states hook up to the world are questions it simply shelves as not within its proper province. On the one hand this is fine, but on the other it means that a completed computational psychology is nonetheless a radically *incomplete* theory of how humans work. For if it has nothing whatsoever to say about how representational systems represent features in the world, it has left out a crucial part of the theory. It is like a genetic theory which tells us how genes produce phenotypic traits, but which throws up its hands on the matter of the relation between the traits and the world the organism inhabits.

Permit us to milk the point briefly. Organisms are syntactic engines. Yet via the nervous system an organism exhibits behavior suited to its surroundings. For example, honey bees remove dead bees from the hive, a herring gull chick pecks its mother's bill for food, a person drinks polio vaccine. Now even if computational psychology did dope out the internal cognitive program, it would still seem miraculous that a person's being in a certain state, syntactically described as say, I-P38, is followed by his drinking polio vaccine, rather than by his moving his rook or by his firing his bazooka or what have you (see also Fodor 1978b). The point is that *it seems* that brains do what they do in virtue of the referents of their assorted states, inasmuch as there is a stupendously good fit between representational systems and the world. Of course if I should specify the content of Trudeau's state by saying he intends to drink polio vaccine, I am specifying the *translational content*; I am saying his representational system is like mine, and his hooks up to the world the way mine does, *whatever way that is*. And that is no *theory* of the way representational systems hook up to the world.

Perhaps this can all be avoided by saying that mind–brain states have intrinsic of-ness or original intentionality or ultimate aboutness, call it what you will. To some it may seem a plain, observable fact that epistemic engines – fancy ones anyhow – operate on states with intrinsic of-ness. It may even be conjectured that this is what makes mental states mental. The suggestion, to the extent that it makes sense, is unappealing. For one thing, it gives up just when things get particularly exciting. And it is a bit like explaining the nature of life by citing 'original vitality,' or the nature of neuronal responsiveness by citing 'original excitability,' and, in so far, it is a way of trumping up a virtue out of being stumped. Moreover, the exasperating thing about 'plain facts' is that they often turn out to be neither plain nor factual. Intrinsic of-ness is an illusion, like intrinsic up-ness or intrinsic down-ness.

Another possibility here will be to base a theory of how representations hook up to the world on the idea that the content of a subject's mental state is linked to truth conditions for the content sentence. The analysis of 'Jones knows the meaning of *p*' in terms of 'Jones knows what conditions could make *p* true' is the basis. While there is more to be said here, our simple response is that this strategy will not work because it connects internal aspects of Jones's representational system

– namely *his taking* (believing, etc.) the meaning to be thus and such with *his taking* the truth conditions to be thus and such – and hence does not clear the fence and tell us anything whatever about how representational systems hook up to the world.

A more promising suggestion addresses the *causal* relations that hold between representations and states of the world. For example, it may be that a specific representation R_1 occurs in a creature's 'perceptual belief-register' only when something in its environment is F. We could thus ascribe "$(\exists x) (Fx)$" as R_1's propositional content. Other representations may be similarly keyed to other aspects of the environment, and we can thus ascribe content to each of them. This would constitute the first stage of a theory which would then go on to develop a wider account of how representations less tightly keyed to the environment acquire content (see, e.g., Stampe 1972; Dretske 1981).

For perceptually-sensitive representations, one can indeed ascribe propositional content in this way, and on the basis of real causal connections with the world. We call content thus ascribed *calibrational content* since this procedure is just another instance of calibrating an instrument of measurement or detection. The states of living creatures do indeed carry systematic information about the environment, in virtue of their law-governed connections with it.

Our enthusiasm for this approach to how representations hook up to the world must be dimmed, however, by three serious problems. First, it is very difficult to see how to make the jump from ascribing content to representations at the sensory periphery to assigning content to the dominant mass of representations not so conveniently tied to aspects of the environment.

Second, and more important, even for perceptual representations, the contents assigned in this way are not identical with their more familiar translation contents. These two kinds of content can and often do diverge radically. A Neanderthal's representation might have the calibrational content, "The wind is producing atmospheric resonances," but have the translational content, "The Storm god is howling at us." An Aristotelean's representation might have the calibrational content, "The planet beneath me has a non-zero angular momentum," but have the translational content, "The crystal sphere above me is turning." A Puritan's representation might have the calibrational content, "She is epileptic," but have the translational content, "She is possessed by Satan." In general, calibrational contents do nothing to reflect how the representing creature happens to conceive of things. This approach fails to explicate how our familiar *translational* contents hook up with the world.

Third, and equally important, the dynamic or functional properties of a representation, within one's overall cognitive economy, are not determined by its calibrational content, but by its 'formal' or 'structural' properties. An account of how a representational system hooks up to the world should make some contact with the system's behavior over time, but calibrational content is dynamically irrelevant. This is just the thesis of methodological solipsism showing itself again.

In sum, a causal approach must disappoint some of our original expectations regarding a general account of how epistemic, representing creatures 'hook up' to the world. But we should not despair immediately. Perhaps it is those original expectations that need schooling. Perhaps we should not expect that all epistemic creatures must have representations that are somehow like sentences, and that a satisfactory account of the important hook-ups must address the relation between singular terms and things, the relation between predicates and properties, and the relation between sentences and states of affairs. Perhaps we should not expect this even for ourselves. Let us explore the problem without making these assumptions.

Neuroscience: calibrational and computational.

In its bones, neuroscience is also solipsistic; it must honor the formality condition. How then does neuroscience expect to deal with the question of how representational systems hook up to the world? For if it sees the brain as syntactic, then it does seem miraculous that a sequence of events in a herring gull's brain results in its asking for food, or a sequence in a bee's brain results in its taking a particular flight path to nectar-heavy blossoms.

In the case of such animals as bees and slugs, we confidently expect to be able to defrock the mystery by giving evolutionary/neurobiological/neuroethological explanations. The idea is to treat the organism's nervous system as something which evolution calibrates (i.e. as something which, by random mutation and on random selection, is tuned to measure, via the excitable cells, certain features in the environment). When responses involved in measuring such features happen to be linked to motor responses relevant to survival, then the probability is enhanced that the organism's genes will be passed on. Bees are 'calibrated,' by natural selection, to detect oleic acid, and are tuned to produce a motor sequence which results in their lugging its source (dead bees) out of the hive. Herring gull chicks are calibrated to detect small red spots on moving objects (this picks out their mother's bill), and are tuned to peck at them, which results in their being fed. The neuronal story of how this works is not beyond us, and for simple creatures ascription of calibrational content to states of their humble nervous system is well underway.

What then of complex organisms such as humans? The story which defrocks the miracle in the case of the bees and the herring gull is relatively simple, in that their behavior is essentially fixed-action-pattern stuff. The story which defrocks the miracle in the case of persons will be much harder to ferret out. For here the enigma ramifies because these organisms are spectacular learners. Seemingly, they learn about the world, though in the syntactic spirit one would say, roughly, that their syntactic organization is fancied up with the end result that they do new things, where some of those things enhance their survival chances. The miracle now is how the syntactic engine ends up as advantageously tuned as it is. How is it that the fancy organisms "make hypotheses die in their stead"? And learn to become increasingly proficient at doing so? How is it that a syntactic engine evolved so that certain of its states seem to have intentionality? How can a person come to have an I-P38 state such that this state typically causes it to drink polio vaccine? Not, evidently, in virtue of evolution's *directly* selecting for a match between P-38 states and drinking polio vaccine but rather, one guesses, in virtue of evolution's selecting 'learner–planner rigmaroles.' If the person acquires new concepts, that is, of course, a syntactical affair, but what is the causal story in virtue of which it can invent concepts which surpass the old when what is on the receiving end of the predictions are events in the world? The miracle is that the organism has become so 'well-tuned' that it seems to have *an evolving world-picture*, rather as though the organism has tricked up an analog of the evolutionary process itself.

Here then the job for neurobiology and neuroethology is Herculean, but the bets are that the story for complex organisms will build on the more basic story of calibrational semantics for simpler organisms, following the steps of evolution itself. The backbone of what we are calling *calibrational content* is the observation that there are reliable, regular, standardized relations obtaining between specific neural responses on the one hand, and *types* of states in the world. The notion exploits the fact that specific neural responses are regularly caused by types of state in the organism's normal environment. Inching closer to a working definition, we suggest the following:

A state S of a system O contains the calibrational content P if and only if O would not be in S unless P, with some high degree of probability n/m.

For example, normally the receptor cells of the rattlesnake's pit organ respond only if there is a warm object within half a metre or so of the pit. That is, with very high probability, the receptors are not excited unless there is a warm object in the vicinity. The probability is less than 1 because receptors might be caused to respond by oddball things, such as an ethologist's injecting a drug into the pit, or by malfunction, as when the tired old receptors of a senescent rattlesnake fire spontaneously. In any case, these occurences are rare. Crudely formalized, we can say, where x ranges over the relevant receptor cells and y ranges over objects in the environment:

1   (x) (Excited $[x]{\to}$(Prob $(\exists y)$ (Warm$[y]$)=0.98).

Moreover, given the snake's environment, there is a decent probability, let us say, 0.7, that the warm object is warm-blooded prey, such as a rabbit, mouse, etc. The probability is less than 1 because the pit receptors can be excited by something warm which is not the customary comestible – like a sun-heated rock, or a smoldering ember. The probability will vary with night and day, being higher at night, and of course it will plummet if the snake is put in an ethologist's laboratory filled with light bulbs and kettles. But assume his standard environment. Then we can crudely formalize the relation between warmth and food:

2   (x) (Warm$[x]{\to}$(Prob(Food$[x]$))=0.7).

Accordingly, the excitation of receptors is a moderately reliable indicator of the presence of food; $0.7 \times 0.98 = 0.686$. In a primitive infrared engine, an excited cell may be a sign for warm blooded prey often enough that it can rely on that simple connection to guide its motor response. In fact of course evolution cranks up the probability as it stumbles on better correlations between neural responses and food, but some of the fine tuning of responses will not be at the sensory periphery, but will be deeper in the neural network. The rattlesnake is eminently better tuned than the simple infrared engine. Information from the pit organ is sent to the optic tectum in a two-stage relay, and in the tectum there is integration of visual and infrared information. Some tectal cells, for example, respond with a brief high-frequency burst of impulses only when there is a *small, moving, warm* object nearby, where the visual system provides the movement data, and the infrared system provides the temperature data. In particular, these cells do not respond to hot rocks (Newman and Hartline 1982). These cells represent small, moving, warm objects – their excited state contains calibrational content to the effect that there are small, moving warm objects nearby. Of these deeper cells, we might now say, again crudely:

3 (x) Excited$[x] \supset$ Prob $(\exists y)$ (Small$[y]$ & Moving$[y]$ & Warm$[y]$)=0.98))

where x ranges over the relevant tectal cells, and y ranges over objects. Now in the rattlesnake's environment, the probability is, say 0.97, that small, moving warm objects are mice, so we can say with high probability (0.98 x 0.97 = 0.95) that the relevant cells would not be excited unless there were mice in the snake's vicinity. Excitation of these cells represents the presence of mice nearby.

The 'computations' executed by the preceding system are of course trivial, and yet the story provides us with a useful conception of the snake's representational attunement to certain aspects of its environment, a conception which helps explain how the snake survives and flourishes. And none of the story ascribes representations with a sentence-like syntax, or talks about the reference of terms or the meaning of predicates.

But what of more talented creatures, creatures whose computational activities are more broadly directed and more intricately constituted? In particular, what of creatures in whom *learning* is a major element in their progressive attunement to the environment? In such cases, are we not forced to postulate an entire *system* of representations, manipulable by the creature? It seems that we are. But here we must resist our parochial impulses concerning the structure of such a system. In the first place, *such a system need not and almost certainly will not be monolithic or uniform at all.* More likely, we possess an integrated hierarchy of quite different computational/representational systems, facing very different problems and pursuing quite different strategies of solution. Why should we expect the representational systems used by the visual system, the auditory system, the proprioceptive system, and the motor system all to be the same? Even the cytoarchitecture of the relevant brain areas is different for each of these cognitive sub-systems.

Will *some* sub-system of this functional mosaic display the familiar structures of human language? In humans, presumably yes, though other species need not possess it. And even in humans it may play a relatively minor role in our overall cognitive activities, serving a mainly social function. The bulk of cognition may take place in other sub-systems, and follow principles inapplicable in the linguistic domain. What those other representational systems are, and how they are knit together to form human cognition, these are empirical questions, begging empirical answers. Lesion studies from neurology are one source of answers: the accidental destruction of isolated brain areas leaves people with isolated and often very curious cognitive deficits. The direct examination of active neural networks is another, though here animal studies must dominate. The computer simulation of proposed representational systems will also be invaluable, if it is neurophysiologically guided, since computers will allow us to defeat the problems of sheer functional complexity in the systems we discover. Research is well-established in all three of these areas, and it wants only our attention.

Our conclusion is that computational psychology cannot afford to embrace a principle of categorical aloofness from or methodological disdain for neuroscience, for at least two reasons. First, if we want to know how cognitive creatures hook up to the world they inhabit, neuroscience holds out the best hope for an enlightening account. And second, even if we restrict our concern to the brain's abstract computational activities, empirical neuroscience will provide authoritative data on just what those activities are, and on their many varieties. In particular, neuroscience holds out the best hope for understanding the individual evolutionary process we call *learning*, since the elements of variation, and the mechanisms of selection, whatever they are, are there under the skull, awaiting our exploration. A truly informed story of how the human cognitive system hooks up to the world must await their discovery and examination.

NOTE

This research was supported by a grant from the Social Sciences and Humanities and Research Council of Canada, no. 410-81-0182.

REFERENCES

Bullock, T. H., Orkand, R. and Grinnel, A. (1977) *Introduction to Nervous Systems*, San Francisco; W. H. Freeman.

Burge, Tyler (1979) "Individualism and the mental," in P. A. French, T. E. Uehling and H. K. Wettstein (eds). *Midwest Studies in Philosophy, Vol IV*, Minneapolis: University of Minnesota Press.

Churchland, Paul M. (1979) *Scientific Realism and the Plasticity of Mind* Cambridge: Cambridge University Press.

Churchland, Paul M. (1980) "In defense of naturalism," *Behavioral and Brain Sciences* 3: 74–5.

Churchland, Paul M. (1981) "Eliminative materialism and the propositional attitudes," *Journal of Philosophy* 78: 67–90.

Churchland, Paul M. (1982) "Is *Thinker* a natural kind?," *Dialogue* 21: 223–38.

Churchland, Patricia S. (1980a) "A perspective on mind-brain research," *Journal of Philosophy*, 77: 185–207.

Churchland, Patricia S. (1980b) "Neuroscience and psychology: Should the labor be divided" *Behavioral and Brain Sciences* 3: 133.

Churchland, Patricia S. (1982) "Mind-brain reduction: New light from philosophy of science," *Neuroscience* 7: 1041–7.

Dennett, Daniel (1978) "Artificial Intelligence as philosophy and as psychology," *Brainstorms*, Cambridge, MA: MIT Press/Bradford.

Dennett, Daniel (1981) "Three kinds of intentional psychology," in R. Healey (ed.), *Reduction, Time and Reality*. Cambridge: Cambridge University Press: 37–61.

Dretske, Fred I. (1981) *Knowledge and the Flow of Information*, Cambridge, MA: MIT Press/Bradford.

Fodor, Jerry A. (1975) *The Language of Thought*, New York: Thomas Y. Crowell.

Fodor, Jerry A. (1978a) "Computation and Reduction," C. Wade Savage (ed.), *Minnesota Studies in the Philosophy of Science Vol. 9*, Minneapolis: University of Minnesota Press; reprinted in his *Representations*, Cambridge, MA: MIT Press/Bradford; 146–74.

Fodor, Jerry A. (1978b) "Tom Swift and his procedural grandmother," *Cognition*; reprinted in his *Representations*, Cambridge, MA: MIT Press/Bradford, 1981: 204–24.

Fodor, Jerry A. (1980) "Methodological solipsism considered as a research strategy in cognitive psychology," *Behavioral and Brain Sciences* 3; reprinted in his *Representations*, Cambridge, MA: MIT Press/Bradford 1981: 225–53.

Haugeland, John (1981) "Semantic engines: An introduction to mind design," *Mind Design*, Cambridge, MA: MIT Press/Bradford: 1–34.

Newman, Eric A. and Hartline, Peter H. (1982) "The infrared 'Vision' of snakes," *Scientific American* 246: 116–27.

Putnam, Hilary (1975) "The meaning of 'meaning'," in Keith Gunderson (ed.), *Minnesota Studies in the Philosophy of Science*, Vol. 7, Minneapolis: University of Minnesota Press: 131–93.

Pellionisz, A. and Llinas, R. (1979) "Brain modeling by tensor network theory and computer simulation: distributed processor for predictive coordination," *Neuroscience* 4: 323–48.

Pylyshyn, Zenon (1980) "Computation and cognition: Issues in the foundations of cognitive science," *Behavioral and Brain Sciences* 3: 111–32.

Sellars, Wilfrid (1980) "Behaviorism, language, and meaning," *Pacific Philosophical Quarterly* 61: 3–25.

Sellars, Wilfrid (1981) "Mental events," *Philosophical Studies* 39: 325–45.

Stampe, Dennis W. (1972) "Toward a causal theory of linguistic representation", in French, Uehling and Wettstein (eds), *Midwest Studies in Philosophy Vol. 2*, Minneapolis: University of Minnesota Press: 82–102.

Stich, Stephen P. (1981) "On the ascription of content," in Andrew Woodfield (ed.), *Thought and Object*, Oxford: Clarendon Press: 153–206.

Stich, Stephen P. (1983) *Folk Psychology and Cognitive Science: The Case Against Belief*, Cambridge, MA: MIT Press/Bradford.

13

Psychosemantics

Psychosemantics or: Where Do Truth Conditions Come From?
JERRY A. FODOR

Introduction

Let's pretend. Let's pretend that the Representational Theory of Mind is true. Here is how you do so: Imagine that there is an internal representational system in which we think, a sort of language of thought. To say that we think in this language is to say at least the following:

(a) Token mental states crucially involved in thinking (especially such token propositional attitudes as believing that P) are to be viewed as relations between organisms and token mental representations. (If you don't like pretending that, you can pretend that such organism-to-mental symbol relations are nomologically necessary and sufficient for the tokening of propositional attitudes. That is, it doesn't matter, for the issues to be discussed, whether RTM is taken to be an *identity* thesis.)

(b) Mental processes (reasoning, for example, and other species of rational fixation of belief) are to be viewed as sequences of operations upon

Only reluctantly has Professor Fodor allowed this paper to be published, for he now thinks the view it defends is hopelessly and viciously wrong. (For his own *previously* published criticisms of the view, see *Psychosemantics* (Bradford Books / MIT Press, 1987), pp. 105–6, and "A theory of content," in a volume of his recent essays forthcoming from MIT Press.) The paper is included in this volume because (a) the editor thinks it offers what is currently the best worked-out version of a Darwinian–teleological psychosemantics; (b) the paper has drawn published commentary and criticism besides Fodor's own (for example, Barry Loewer, "From information to intentionality," *Synthese* 70 (1987), 287–317); and (c) the editor and others believe the view to be considerably more promising than Fodor now grants. In any case, sincere thanks are due to Fodor for his willingness to let the paper see print at last.

formulae belonging to this internal language. Specifically, they're to be viewed as sequences of *computational* operations: ones that apply to internal representations in virtue of formal – that is, nonsemantic – properties of the representations.

That may be a pipe dream, but it's the picture of the mind that emerges from the cognitive science of the last twenty years or so and it is, I think, the closest thing to a serious cognitive psychology that we've got. No doubt, some of the central notions are obscure, but it would be perverse to deny that RTM has provided the theoretical framework within which some quite successful and revealing empirical research has been carried out. In which case, one might argue, the best strategy is to accept the framework, warts and all, and hope that the obscurities will be resolved by that 'further research' the Federal support of which we all so ardently desire.

There is, however, a class of problems about this framework that is both crucial and, in a certain sense, self-insulating. These are problems about the semantic properties of mental representations. I propose to discuss some of them in this paper.

Why are these problems crucial? Perhaps the most interesting property of RTM, at least from a philosopher's point of view, is that it purports to account for the intentionality of mental states (that is, for such facts as that beliefs are typically about things, and that they are typically true [or false] in virtue of their correspondence to matters of fact). The strategy of RTM is to view the intentional properties of mental states as inherited from the semantic properties of the mental representations which, according to principle (a), are implicated in their tokening. Many philosophers find the prospect of this sort of reduction attractive because, on the one hand, they are convinced by antibehaviorist arguments that a workable empirical psychology is probably going to have to postulate intentional states with some abandon; and, on the other hand, they are repulsed by the idea that intentionality is a *fundamental* property of mental states (or, indeed, of anthing else – talk about your ontological danglers!). My point, however, is that anybody who jibs at intentionality as an irreducible property of the mental is likely to be equally distressed by semanticity as an irreducible property of the symbolic. The explanation of intentionality by reference to internal representations looks like a serious intellectual advance only if there is some prospect of a correspondingly serious theory about what bestows semantic properties upon mental symbols. Quine has – rightly – warned us against so positioning one's account of mind with respect to one's account of meaning that all they do is one another's wash.

The point, moreover, is not merely that we *may* have trouble finding a way out of Quine's circle. One of the deeper sources of philosophical skepticism about the whole RTM enterprise is the sense that some semantic problems about mental representations derive precisely from the assumption that principle (a) is true. This worry is worth considering.

Proponents of RTM have sometimes offered the following in lieu of a theory of the semanticity of mental symbols. "Look," they say, "we know that there *are* such things as symbols, and we know that symbols do have semantic properties. For example, the English noun 'talcum powder' is a symbol and designates the stuff, talcum powder. Moreover, the English sentence 'Talcum powder tastes nasty' is a symbol and has a certain truth conditon: viz., is true iff talcum powder tastes nasty. In short, there *are* semantic facts of the sort to which RTM is committed. Agreed, *somebody* has the problem of saying what such facts amount to; what it is for something to be a symbol or (equivalently for our purposes) what it is for a symbol to have the semantic properties that it does. But why should RTM be saddled with the job? Why not, for purposes of developing a cognitive theory, simply take the general notion of a symbol as given and get on with putting together a psychology elaborated around the notion of *mental* symbolism? It is, surely, a part of tactical wisdom in research not to worry other people's worries. Symbols *qua* symbols are for semioticists *qua* semioticists."

There is, however, a serious objection to this tactic of evasion: namely, that the defense of RTM may well require us to view mental symbols as *sui generis*. If this is so, then we cannot assume that the semanticity of mental symbols is merely a special case of a phenomenon to be explained by a semiotic theory of symbolhood-at-large. The difficulty is this: it's not at all implausible that, for all cases of *non*mental representation (such as words and sentences of natural languages, formulae of ALGOL, smoke signals, hieroglyphs, numerals, gestures, bill boards, pictures, or what have you), the semanticity of the symbol is to be explained, at least in part, by reference to the psychological states of people who produce or interpret it. So, for example, consider the fact that tokens of 'talcum powder tastes nasty' are true iff talcum powder tastes nasty. It may well be that the best story we can tell about that fact adverts essentially to certain communicative intentions of speaker/hearers of English. I don't offer anything like a detailed account of how this story might go. Perhaps it would implicate the speaker's intention that the token he produces should be *taken* to be true iff talcum powder tastes nasty; or perhaps what's crucial is the speaker's intention to adhere to a system of conventions, shared by members of his language community, which have among their deductive consequences that tokens of 'talcum powder tastes nasty' are true iff talcum powder tastes nasty. Though the details are disputed, some such account can be pieced together from the insights of philosophers like Grice, Schiffer, Lewis and Harnish, among others.

As I say, I'm not claiming that this sort of account is right about the semanticity of natural language symbols; only that it very well might be and that, moreover, it might be a special case of a quite general story about symbols: viz., that the semantic properties of symbols *always* trace back to some fact or other about the propositional attitudes of their users. Even images arguably work this way. Somebody, or so we're told, sat for the Statue of Liberty. But the Statue of Liberty is not a portrait of its sitter; indeed, it's not a portrait at all. What it is, is: a representation of Liberty holding aloft the torch of freedom. And what makes it that is, surely, closely connected to the fact (perhaps it is identical to the fact) that a representation of Liberty holding aloft the . . . etc., is what the sculptor *intended* it to be. Resemblance won't do it, and neither will causal connections unless they run *via* the intentions of an agent. The appeal to propositional attitudes appears to be essential in explaining why the representation represents what it does.

This is all supposed to be getting to a point, albeit a reasonably familiar one: there is one kind of symbol whose semanticity is *not*, in point of principle, to be traced to the psychological states of agents, and that sort of symbol is a mental representation. The reason is, of course, that RTM wants to use the notion of a mental symbol as part of the explanatory apparatus for a theory of the intentionality of mental states:[1] according to RTM, mental states are intentional in virtue of the semantic properties of mental representations. So it had better not also be that mental representations have semantic properties in virtue of the intentionality of mental states.

So, RTM can't just take the notion of mental symbolism for granted, secure in the faith that somebody will someday arrive at an account of symbolism in general of which mental representation can then be treated as a special case. On the contrary, in so far as it is plausible that the semantic rests on the mental in the *general* case, RTM is in trouble since RTM entails that there is at least one sort of symbol for which that doctrine is not true. RTM thus requires an account of mental symbols that does *not* appeal to propositional attitudes as the source of their semanticity. If it can't produce one, cash on the barrelhead, it had at least better provide some reason for thinking that such an account could be produced in principle.

I said that the problem of accounting for the semanticity of mental representations is both crucial and, in a certain sense, self-insulating. The former remark having been elucidated, I'll close this part of the discussion with a word about the latter.

Tokens of symbols are physical particulars in good standing. I suppose this to be true, *inter alia*, of tokens of mental representations which are, presumably, neural objects. Now, *qua* physical particulars, token symbols may be assumed to have a host of *non*semantic properties, and these we may take to be – at least for present purposes – relatively unproblematical. The point is this: it is very characteristic of current versions of RTM – indeed, it is one of the few respects in which they differ significantly from classical formulations of the doctrine – to be explicit in requiring that only *non*semantic properties of mental representations can figure in determining which mental operations apply to them. I shan't go on about this since it is a point that I have discussed at length elsewhere (Fodor 1981, chapter 9). But I take it to be part and parcel of the idea that mental processes are computational, and I take the idea that mental processes are computational to be among the central tenets of cognitive science.

The upshot is that one can do quite a lot of cognitive science without raising foundational – or, indeed, any – issues about the semanticity of mental representations. In a certain sense, you can do the whole theory of mental processes without raising such issues, what with mental operations being computational and mental processes being causal sequences of mental operations (see (b) above). That is, in fact, pretty much what has happened in the cognitive science literature (though the situation has been considerably unilluminated by a widespread failure to distinguish issues of logical syntax from semantic issues strictly so called; in consequence of this confusion, many cognitive scientists have imagined themselves to be doing semantics when, in fact, they weren't).

So, then, on the one hand, it is essential to the integrity of RTM that some insight be generated into the semanticity of mental representations; and, on the other hand, we can't simply assume that 'further research' – at least of the sort that cognitive scientists have heretofore pursued – is likely to generate any. And, on the third hand (as it were), the issue is critical because there is some positive reason to fear that, in seeking to derive the intentionality of propositional attitudes from the semanticity of mental symbols, RTM may have gotten the order of explanation backwards.

So much by way of an introduction.

Semantic assumptions

What I want to do in this paper is to sketch a (roughly teleological) account of the semanticity of mental representations. The sketch is reasonably explicit. In particular, it says what it is for S to be the truth condition of M, where M is a mental representation and S is the actual-or-possible state of affairs in virtue of which M has its truth value.[2] This account will meet the crucial condition that the explication of the semantic relation does not appeal to intentional notions. Yet it might be argued that the account is incomplete since 'S is the truth conditon of M' is the *only* semantic context discussed, and I provide no argument that the semanticity of mental representations consists exhaustively in their possession of truth conditions. This bears some discussion.

It seems reasonably clear that symbols with the same truth conditions may nevertheless differ in their semantic properties (where this means: may be nonsynonymous.) The very fact that makes 'The Morning Star is bright' true makes 'The Evening Star is bright' true too. I do not take this sort of problem lightly. It does seem to me to suggest very strongly that purely truth-conditional analyses are probably too coarse-grained to reconstruct the semantic properties either of linguistic or of mental symbols.[3] I am nevertheless going to take the issues about truth conditions to be central for the following reasons: it seems likely that an account of the semanticity of mental representations must *at least* make clear the nature of their relation to their truth conditions; and it is not beyond reason to hope that, given an account of that relation, the rest of the work can be done by appeal to notions like 'inferential role.' I am mostly whistling in the dark, but the following seems not *too* implausible. It is constitutive of the nonsynonymy of 'The Morning Star is bright' and 'The Evening Star is bright' that you get from them to, say, '. . . a star which rises in the morning . . .' by relevantly different inferential routes. 'Relevantly' is, of course, the blank check; and, of course, I don't know how to cash it.

Anyhow, for want of better, I'm tentatively endorsing what is coming to be called a "two factor" account of the semanticity of mental representations (see, for example, Field 1977, Loar 1981 and McGinn 1982). According to such accounts, a sufficient condition for identity of semantic properties is identity of truth conditions *and of inferential role*, and all theory-relevant semantic properties of mental representations are to be explained by appeal to one or other or both of these factors. Now, according to RTM, inferences are transformations of mental representations, so the 'inferential role' of a mental symbol is presumably some sort of logical construct out of facts about the mental operations that do (or would under suitable idealization) apply to it. Since, however, mental operations are supposed to apply solely in virtue of syntactic features of mental symbols (form as frozen function) it is quite compatible with the two-factor idea to suppose that *the only symbol-to-world* relations that affect the semanticity of mental representations are the relations they bear to states of affairs that determine their truth value.[4]

What all this comes to is that I'm assuming that the canonical form of the problem about the semanticity of mental representations is this: what is it that relates a mental representation to the state of affairs that satisfies its truth condition? But what kind of question is that?

One way to understand what kind of question it is is to see something of what would *not* count as a relevant answer. So, suppose somebody said: "What relates a mental representation M to the state of affairs S which is its truth condition is simply that S is the state of affairs which, if it obtains, *makes M true*. Or, to put it in a slightly more metaphysical sounding way, S is the truth condition of M just in case M corresponds to the world if and only if it is the case that S." I hope it is intuitively obvious that this is *not* the sort of answer that we want; anyhow, it's worth a moment's reflection to get some sense of why it's not.

One point is that we don't want semantic notions (like truth or correspondence) to appear in the account of '. . . is the truth condition of . . .' any more than we want intentional notions to appear there. But that objection is superficial. Imagine that we have a truth theory for the system of mental representations; that is, a function from mental symbols on to actual-or-possible states of affairs satisfying the condition that each symbol is true iff the state of affairs it is paired with obtains. We could now consider this function in extension and say: what relates a mental representation to its truth condition is that the latter is the image of the former under this mapping. This formula contains no objectionable occurrences of semantic or intentional notions, so why won't it do?

The problem is that there are too many ways of mapping symbols on to the world (too many ways in which symbols can 'correspond to' states of affairs); and although – as we may suppose – there is only one pairing whose extension is the (ordered) pairs of symbols and their truth conditions, there is nothing about the notion of correspondence *as such* which distinguishes this pairing from the others. Consider an arbitrary mapping of symbols on to states of affairs, one which does *not* pair each symbol with its truth condition. Even so, this pairing defines *a* kind of symbol–world correspondence. We could call this kind of correspondence (not 'truth' but) 'shmuth'. And we could say that T is a shmuth-theory for mental representations if it defines a mapping coextensive with this pairing. So, if somebody wanted to know what the relations between a mental symbol and its shmuth condition amounts to, we could say 'it's the fact that the shmuth condition is the image of the symbol under the mapping that a shmuth theory defines;' just the sort of thing that we said about the *truth* conditon. To which one wants to reply that there is something *special* about the sort of symbol–world correspondence that truth definitions specify; something that shmuth correspondence doesn't have; something in virtue of which facts about their truth conditions illuminate the functioning of symbols in a way that facts about their shmuth conditions do not. Well, yes; but what could the mystery ingredient be?

What this question calls for is not a semantic theory as formal semanticists understand that notion, but a 'theory of meaning' in an older and looser sense of the phrase. Here, for example, is a kind of answer that *is* relevant (and would be decisive except, alas, that it is false). One could say, more or less in the spirit of Hume, that what relates a mental representation to its truth condition is that the former *pictures* the latter. What makes this the right sort of answer is that, by assumption, *it distinguishes the sort of correspondence that a truth theory specifies for mental representations from every other mapping of mental representations on to the world.* This is because, again by assumption, mental representations picture *only* their truth conditions; they don't, for example, picture their shmuth conditions. Not even if, as it happens, the truth condition of a mental representation is satisfied iff its shmuth condition is satisfied. Suppose that M is a mental symbol such that a truth theory maps it on to snow's being white and a shmuth theory maps it on to grass's being green. What distinguishes the former mapping is that (still by assumption) M *pictures* snow's being white and does not picture grass's being green (for example, M is a picture of white snow and not a picture of green grass.)

I have already remarked (see n. 2) that the following inference scheme is plausibly invalid: *S is the truth condition of M; S iff R; R is the truth condition of M.* We do not want it to turn out that grass's being green is the truth condition for 'snow is white' even though it's true that 'grass is green' and 'snow is white' are materially equivalent. (See Davidson 1967; Reeves 1974; Fodor, J. D. 1977, pp. 36–7). Now, one of the things that a theory of meaning does for you is to make clear why such inferences don't go through. It does this precisely by showing what it is in virtue of which S is the truth conditon of M; that is, by elucidating a relation that holds between S and M, but does not hold between R and M, even where 'S iff R' is true. As, for example, that M is a picture of S and not a picture of R.

Well, we all know what's wrong with *Hume's* theory of meaning; it's precisely that there is no way of defining 'pictures' (or 'resembles', or any of that group of notions) which makes it come out that mental representations do picture only their truth conditions. This is largely independent of the much mooted question whether mental representations (some or all of them) are 'iconic' rather than 'discursive'. Even if you suppose that the thought that John is tall is a picture that shows John as tall, you are stuck with the fact that any such picture would also show him in lots of other ways (as having a head, for example). But John's having a head is not the state of affairs that renders true the thought that John is tall.

None of this is contentious any more; I suppose that nobody now thinks that picturing could be what relates mental representations to their truth conditions. I raise the issue only to make clear a respect in which Hume was luckier with his version of RTM than we are with ours. He had an answer (albeit not ultimately a good one) to a question at which we merely gawp: what makes S the truth condition of M?

We can now summarize the semantic assumptions that will inform the rest of the discussion. Two sorts of questions must be answerable about any collection of objects that one proposes to treat as symbols; *a fortiori* about the (presumably neurological) objects which function as mental representations. These are:

(c) what semantic properties do the symbols have; and
(d) in virtue of what do the symbols have their semantic properties.

Questions of the first sort are answered by providing a formal semantics. I assume, in the case of mental representations, that their semanticity consists in their possession of truth conditions, hence that a formal semantics for mental representations would take the form of a truth theory.

Questions of the second sort are answered by providing a theory of meaning. In the present case, a theory of meaning must explicate the relation between a mental symbol and a state of affairs in virtue of which the latter is what determines the truth value of the former. Specimen answers to this sort of question include: "it's the fact that (the user of the symbol intends that it should be true if and only if the truth condition is satisfied)," or "it's the fact that (the symbol pictures the world as the world would look if the truth condition were satisfied)," or, for that matter, "it's the fact that (the production of the symbol is a discriminated response to a stimulus which consists of the truth condition's being satisfied)"; etc. There may be *some* symbols for which one or other of these answers is right. But I take it as clear that none of them can be right for mental representations. So what, in the case of mental representation, is the answer going to be?

Psychological assumptions

Fundamentally, a theory of meaning (in the sense in which I'm using the phrase) consists in the claim that a certain relation is coextensive with the relation that a truth theory specifies. So, Hume's theory of meaning consisted in the claim that the relation *M pictures S* is coextensive with the relation *S is the truth condition of M*; Skinner's theory of meaning consisted in the claim that the relation *S is the discriminative stimulus of M* is coextensive with the relation *S is the truth condition of M*; and so forth. The theory of meaning I'm about to propose will also be that sort of thing. That is, I'm going to characterize a relation between a state of affairs S and a mental symbol M which, I'll claim, is the relation in virtue of which the former is the truth condition of the latter. Since this relation is going to be defined by reference to presumed functional and teleological properties of cognitive systems, my account of it (like, for that matter, Hume's and Skinner's) is going to rest heavily on assumptions about what sort of psychology is actually true; specifically, about what cognitive mechanisms there are and what functions they perform. I'm afraid that some of these assumptions may strike you as quite mad. Ah, well.

To begin with, I'm going to assume something which, given the RTM framework, should *not* seem particularly tendentious (the wild stuff comes later). I'll take it for granted that we are going to get a computational psychology of belief. A computational psychology of belief is a theory which specifies a certain relation (call it R*)[5] and a system of mental representations (call them Ms) such that:

(e) O believes S iff (there is mental representation M such that (1) S is the truth condition of M and (2) O bears R* to M).[6]

So – still on the convenient assumption that the language of thought is English – instances of (e) would include: 'O believes that it's raining iff there is a mental representation M such that (1) that it is raining is the truth condition of M; and (2) O bears R* to M.' The idea is that, given the semantics of English, it would turn out that the left-hand side of this biconditional would be true when and only when O bears R* to 'it's raining' (or to one of its synonyms).

There are a number of points to be made about this. First off, this characterization assumes, in the spirit of RTM, that the belief relation is to be unpacked by reference to explicitly semantic notions like 'is the truth condition of.' According to RTM, belief is a computational relation *to a semantically interpreted symbol*. Computational psychological theories do not *explicate* symbol-to-world relations; they merely presuppose them. It follows, of course, that we can't, on pain of cirularity, appeal to the belief relation in our analysis of the semanticity of mental representations.

On the other hand, we can, if we wish, allow ourselves to appeal to R*. That is because RTM assumes that the relations between organisms and formulae, in terms of which theories of pscyhological states are elaborated, must be computational (viz., formal; viz., characterizable exhaustively by reference to nonsemantic properties of the formulae). Of course, someone might doubt that there *is* any purely computational relation between organisms and formulae such that the former believe what the latter express in virtue of the fact that the purely computational relation obtains. For example, someone might hold that there is a bedrock relation of *apprehending a proposition* such that an organism believes what a formula expresses only if it apprehends a proposition in a certain way (assentively, say). I don't think that it would be at all silly to hold this; it's not, after all, as though anybody were now in a position to offer anything like a remotely satsifactory computational alternative. However, if you do think that R* can't be a computational relation, then you *ipso facto* think that RTM must be false. And we are pretending that RTM is true.

The next point is that although, *qua* computational relation, R* can't, as it were, know about the semantic properties of mental representation, it must nevertheless be so specified as to *respect* those properties. The line of argument that leads to this conclusion is familiar from the writings of Dennett, Davidson and others. Roughly, it's a condition on entertaining a belief that one be disposed to draw the appropriate inferences; and which inferences it is that one is disposed to draw partially determines which belief it is that one is entertaining. Seen from the point of view of a computational psychology, this means that some of the computations that R* specifies will have to interrelate formulae whose *semantic* properties are appropriate to the premises and conclusions of arguments (inductive, deductive, plausible or whatever). Suppose that an organism bears R* to M_1 and suppose it's a fact that its doing so is causally sufficient for its coming to bear R* to M_2. Moreover, suppose that the causal situation is that bearing R* to M_1 normally results in bearing it to M_2 practically instantly; the former state is, as it were, the efficient cause of the latter. Then one would want to avoid attributing the truth condition *it's raining* to M_1 and the truth condition *it's not raining* to M_2; or, at least, one would want to avoid having that sort of thing happen very often. To that extent, at least, the formulation of R* constrains the assignment of truth conditions to mental representations and vice versa.

I'm putting this very loosely because it's by no means clear precisely what this sort of constraint amounts to. Nobody knows how much inferential incoherence the concept of belief can tolerate before, as one used to say, the cookie crumbles. Moreover, there is good reason to suppose that the answer to this sort of question may be very messy; for example, that it may have to be relativized to types of organisms (see Cherniak 1986). I raise this whole unpleasant issue only in aid of a negative point: I take it that there is *no* way in which the specification of R* could *uniquely* constrain the assignment of truth conditions to mental representations. That is, I take it that however much complexity R* acknowledges in the computational operations it postulates, there will always be more than one possibility for assigning semantic properties to the mental symbols over which R* is defined. Call each such assignment an 'interpretation' of the system of mental representations and processes. Then, to return to a sort of point we were making in the previous section, the problem for a theory of meaning is to make clear what it is that chooses the *right* interpretation from among all the rest; what distinguishes the truth condition of a mental representation from other states of affairs that it could be mapped on to consonant with viewing the mental life of the organism as coherent over all.

Well, as the reader will no doubt have anticipated, I propose to use 'O bears R* to M' as a clause in the characterization of 'M has the truth condition S' (though – given the preceding paragraph – it should be clear that I'll need a lot of other stuff as well). By way of making the situation graphic, I'm going to borrow a heuristic from Steve Schiffer. Pretend that every organism that has beliefs at all has a box in its head. This box is capable of containing token mental representations. One can imagine (though this plays no essential role in the story) that the box is marked 'yes'. The contents of the yes-box are determined by the following principle: for each mental representation M, O bears R* to M (and hence believes what M expresses) iff a token of M is in the yes-box.

The property of being a yes-box is, by stipulation, a functional property. In particular, I assume that every yes-box is connected with an elaborate mechanism of wheels, pulleys, relays and so forth, such that putting a mental representation token in the box has a correspondingly elaborate variety of causal consequences, both for the behaviour of the organism and for the distribution of other such tokens. Moreover, which causal consequences you get from putting a given token into the box depends, again elaborately, on (nonsemantic) properties of the tokens. (Maybe it depends on their weight, or their shape, or their electrical conductivity). Anyhow, for each M_i the consequence of putting M_i-tokens into the yes-box must include whatever R* says has to be the case in order that O believes what M_i expresses.

There are, I suppose, respects in which this story could be improved. For example, we have ignored the productivity of beliefs, and that would need rectifying if we were to start getting serious. Perhaps we would want to distinguish a finite set of "core beliefs" (see Dennett 1975) from the presumably infinite set of beliefs that the organism holds only dispositionally. Only for the former would a token M's being in the yes-box be necessary and sufficient for O bearing R* to that M. For non-core beliefs, R* would be defined in terms of some sort of closure principles whose details I do not wish even to contemplate.

All that can, however, be left to the psychologists. For, given the nature of computational analysis, we are assured that any specification of R* that satisfied functionalist ground rules will be just an elaboration of the yes-box theory; an elaboration tending – so one would hope – in the direction of increased empirical plausibility. In what follows, I will work with 'an M-token is in the yes-box' rather than 'O bears R* to M,' the former notion having a force and vivacity which the latter somehow lacks.

We are getting close to where the assumptions turn tendentious; before we get there, however, there is room for one more tame one. I take it that we can recognize a number of psychological mechanisms which, *de facto*, bring it about that tokens of mental representations get into the yes-box (that O bears R* to a variety of Ms). The yes-box is itself one of those mechanisms since we may suppose it to be so constructed that putting some tokens in directly eventuates in other tokens being in too. (This is, perhaps, what the model offers by way of reconstructing the notion of 'immediate inference' (or 'direct association' in case there is anyone around who still prefers the older idiom)).

Anyhow, the yes-box is surely not the only mechanism whose activities determine which tokens are in the yes-box. Presumably there are perceptual mechanisms at work too, and memory mechanisms and inferential mechanisms, and generally, whatever the right psychology says is involved in the fixation of belief. I want a cover term for the collection of psychological mechanisms whose operations affect the contents of the yes-box. I'll call it the '*de facto*' cognitive system.

I want to emphasize that there are no teleological assumptions built into this characterization of the *de facto* cognitive system. I haven't said, for example, that what these mechanisms *are for* is to put stuff into the yes-box; I've just said that they do, in fact, put stuff in there. So, for example, if there are mechanisms of forgetting (including nonrational mechanisms like mechanical trace decay as a function of time), then since they partially determine what's in the yes-box, they're part of the *de facto* cognitive system too.

I am, however, about to make some teleological assumptions. Now. The first is that there are psychological mechanisms – by definition, a subset of the *de facto* cognitive system – whose function *is* to put tokens into the yes-box. I shall call the collection of these mechanisms 'the cognitive system' *tout court*. I don't suppose that the mechanisms of trace decay are among them since I don't suppose that trace decay has any function at all. It just happens. But I do suppose that, say, the perceptual mechanisms are part of the cognitive system, as are the rest of the mechanisms that subserve the *rational* fixation of belief. It is very important for the rest of my story that this teleological claim – and a considerably stronger one that I'm about to make – should actually be true. Perhaps, therefore, I'd better say something about my attitude towards teleological claims in general.

To begin with, I take it that teleological contexts (like 'the function of . . . is to bring it about that ——') are typically non-truth-functional. The arguments here are well known. Consider, for example, such truths as that *a function of the heart is to bring it about that the blood circulates*. And suppose that, *de facto*, all and only hearts that succeed in circulating the blood make a sort of wooshing sound as the stuff goes through. It would still be an open question whether making the sound is one of the functions of the heart: one of the things that the heart does such that a heart that failed to do that would thereby fail to function normally. Suppose that it is not; then we have: 'the function of the heart is to bring it about that the blood circulates' and 'the blood circulates iff there is the right sort of wooshing sound' as both true, but 'the function of the heart is to bring it about that there is the right sort of wooshing sound' as false. In short, teleological contexts are intensional in at least the sense of being non-truth-functional. But I take it that the exploitation of teleological notions is nevertheless within the ground rules of the project we have in hand. I promised you an account of 'S is the truth condition of M' that appealed to no intentional contexts, but I didn't promise to eschew intensional ones.

In fact, to let what's left of the cat out of the bag, it should now be clear what the overall strategy of this paper is going to be. It's old news that teleology is about as close as you can get to inten*t*ionality without logically presupposing an agent. (In fact, in the kind of teleology where there *is* an agent – as in *pencils are for writing* – elements of function and intention get all mixed together. I suppose that what makes it true that pencils are for writing is that they are intended for that use by the pencil makers.) Now, I'm strongly inclined to believe that Grice and Co. are right in thinking that intentionality is at the heart of quite a lot of semantic phenomena; in particular, that the intentionality of propositional attitudes is the source of the semanticity of words, sentences and suchlike natural language expressions. However, as we've seen, we can't tell Grice's sort of story about the language of thought on pain of generating circularities in RTM. So, I'm proposing to do the next best thing: to inherit the semanticity of mental representations – in particular, their possession of truth conditions – from something about the teleology of cognitive systems. Still more particularly, such facts as that *S is the truth condition of M* are not transparent for S (see n. 2) is going to be explained by appeal to the fact that 'the function of . . . is bringing it about that ——' is not transparent for ——.

Finally, I take it that the truth (/falsity) of teleological ascriptions has something to do with the truth (/falsity) of corresponding counterfactuals, with different counterfactuals being relevant in different cases. It is, indeed, the connection of teleological truths with counterfactual ones that I presume accounts for the intensionality of the former. In insisting on there being teleological facts I'm not, therefore, insisting upon there being *irreducible* teleological facts. It's OK with me if the truth of the relevant counterfactuals is all there is to the truth of a teleological claim. On the other hand, I don't know which counterfactuals are the ones to pick on to back up ascriptions of functions to cognitive systems. I'll assume, for heuristic and expository purposes, that they are facts about natural selection; facts of the type *selection wouldn't have applied in the way it did but that* . . . I dislike vulgarized Darwinism intensely, but I'm forced to descend to it for want of anything better.

I had better be very explicit about what is going on here. I'm going to specify a certain (nonsemantic) property P such that, or so I'll claim, its' precisely because a mental representation has P that it has the truth conditions it does. Now, P is a property that mental representations have in virtue of facts about the teleology of cognitive systems; mental representations have P because the cognitive systems of organisms have certain normal functions. These normal functions are, I suppose, themselves to be specified by rehearsing certain counterfactuals; for the cognitive system of an organism to be functioning normally is for it to be true of that system that it *would* do such-and-such if it *were* the case that so-and-so (for some by-no-means-necessarily-finite list of such-and-suches and so-and-sos). So far, then, all that the account of the semanticity of mental representations cares about, strictly speaking, is that there be certain truths about the normal functioning of cognitive systems. So far, the account of the semanticity of mental representations does *not* care about whether Darwinism is true, or whether cognitive systems are, as a matter of fact, products of natural selection. It would, for example, be satisfied by organisms assembled (not by natural selection but) in somebody's garage, so long as these organisms have cognitive systems and their cognitive systems have the appropriate normal functions. Where the Darwinian stuff does come in is: I have to say *what the normal function of a cognitive apparatus is*, and I have to *give some reasons to suppose that the cognitive apparatus of organisms does have the normal function that I say that it does*. The Darwinian story is convenient to both of these purposes. It seems plausible that, in the case of evolved organisms, facts about normal functioning come down to some or other facts about patterns of selection; roughly, that the normal function of an evolved system is that function in virtue of which it has selectional advantage. But, again, the story I'll tell about the truth conditions of mental representations doesn't require (that is, doesn't *entail*) that Darwinism be true or that cognitive systems be evolved; it requires only that there be the facts about the normal functioning of cognitive systems that I say there are.

Summary: I assume that there are teleological facts. I assume that they are probably reducible. I assume that teleological contexts are intensional in virtue of their connection with counterfactual contexts. I assume that there is a system of cognitive mechanisms whose function is to put token mental representations in the yes-box.

But, of course, not just any old token mental representation, and not just on any old occasion. If, for example, the cognitive system was shaped by selection pressures, they must have been pressures that preferred Ms to be placed in the yes-box other than at random. (After all, to be in the yes-box is to have an organism bear R* to you. And which Ms an organisms bears R* to affects – vitally – its behavior and its eventual viability.) If, however, not at random then, presumably, under some constraints.

Call such constraints 'entry conditions'. Then: the entry condition for a mental representation M is that state of affairs such that, when functioning normally, (the cognitive system brings it about that M is in the yes-box) iff (the entry condition is satisfied). *Entry condition* will be a basic construct in what follows. I have a number of things to say about it.

(f) The entry condition for a mental symbol could be practically *anything* so long as it's what has to be satisfied for the normally functioning cognitive system to bring it about that tokens of that symbol are in the yes-box. For example, if you are a frog your cognitive system might so function as to place a certain sort of token in your yes-box iff a fly is in your visual field (see Lettvin et al. 1959); or it might so function as to place a certain type of token in your yes-box iff your auditory system is stimulated by the call of a conspecific (Capranica 1976).

I want to emphasize, in particular, that there is no requirement that entry conditions be specified in terms of (for example) retinal arrays, vibratory patterns of the tympanic membrane, or, in general, any other transducer states. Entry conditions are typically constraints on the way that *the world is*. This should be immediately evident from the consideration that entry conditions are defined in terms of the teleology of the cognitive systems (they are, for example, the conditions that these systems respect when they're doing *what they were selected to do)*; and the primary function of cognitive systems is, surely, to bring about coherent relations between the propositional attitudes of an organism *and the states of its environment.* So, for example, *why* does a light go on in a frog's head when a conspecific croaks? Well, because there are (cognitive) mechanisms which throw the light switch just in case a certain array of acoustic energy impinges upon the frog's auditory transducers. But why are there those mechanisms? In virtue of what do they have their selectional advantage? *In virtue of their ability to correlate the mental states of the frog with the presence of a croaking conspecific.* What, then, is it for the cognitive system of the frog to be functioning normally in this respect? It's for the frog's yes-box to contain a 'hello, there's a grunting conspecific' token iff there's a grunting conspecific on the scene. And what, then, is the entry condition for grunting-conspecific tokens? It's, again, that there be a grunting conspecific there. NB, it's *not* that the frog's tympanic membrane (if that's what frogs have) be appropriately stimulated; though, of course, the usual causal chain connects the frog with conspecific grunts via such stimulations.

"All very well," you may say; "but, even if teleological considerations suggest that the entry condition for a mental representation will often be something *external* to the organism, there is still the question *which* external thing we ought to take it to be. Between the conspecific's grunt and the depositing of M in the yes-box there intrudes a long causal chain. Which of its links are we to take as the entry condition for the neural response?" The next considerations are supposed to throw light on this issue.

(g) The entry condition associated with a given mental symbol is likely to have two quite different sorts of components: those that are specific to that symbol, and those which reflect one or other aspect of, as it were, the mechanics of the various cognitive systems. Consider, to stick to relatively primitive examples, the frog *qua* fly-catcher.[7] Presumably the entry condition in question is something like this: there's a fly dancing around; the fly and its surround are illuminated by light whose intensity, frequency, contrast gradient, and God knows what all else, fall within certain critical ranges; light reflected from the fly strikes the surface of the frog's eye for a period of time not less than ————; the visual angle of the light so reflected is not less than ————; and so forth. (I don't know how to fill in the blanks, but no doubt they can be filled in in principle. Visual psychophysics is in precisely that line of business.)

My point is that, quite clearly, some of these clauses in the entry condition of the 'there's a fly' symbol are inherited from perfectly general features of the frog's mechanism of visual perception. We'd have essentially the same clauses in the entry conditions for 'there's a lily-pad,' 'there's a worm,' or whatever other symbols get into the frog's yes-box as a result of the activities of its visual apparatus.[8] From here on, I shall adopt a terminology according to which those clauses of entry conditions which reflect *general* demands that the cognitive mechanisms make upon situations in respect of which they function are "conditions of epistemic appropriateness." The entry conditions strictly so-called will thus be constraints associated with the tokening of *particular* mental symbols.

We can now put these considerations together with the ones rehearsed under heading (f). To wit: to find the entry condition of a mental representation M, you first find out what state of affairs would be required to bring it about that M is in the yes-box when the cognitive apparatus is functioning normally. You then, in effect, employ the method of differences to factor out the contribution of the epistemic appropriateness conditions, leaving only those conditions on being in the yes-box that are specific to M. This residuum is, by stipulation, the entry condition for M.[9]

> (h) The entry condition for a mental symbol may be arbitrarily complex. If there are, as it were, many entry conditions for a certain symbol, take their disjunction.

Given all this, we can think of the cognitive apparatus as realizing a certain function; viz., a function from entry conditions (considered as actual-or-possible states of affairs) onto mental representation types. Under this mapping, each mental symbol M gets correlated with the state of affairs S such that: (given the satisfaction of relevant epistemic appropriateness conditions) *it is constitutive of the normal function of the cognitive system that it puts a token of M into the yes-box iff S obtains.* Let's call this the 'entry condition function' for a system of mental representations. I assume that, if we knew all there is to know about the teleology of the frog's visual system, and about the epistemic appropriateness conditions implied by the structure of its visual apparatus, it would turn out that the image of one of the frog's mental symbols under the entry condition function for its language of thought is: that there be a fly dancing about.

I can now say what my theory of meaning comes to; it's that the entry condition function for a system of mental representations is coextensive with its truth definition. That is, for each mental representation M, S is the truth condition of M iff S is the entry condition for M. Or rather, something stronger: what *makes* S the truth condition for M – the precise fact in virtue of which S counts as the truth condition for M – is that S is the entry condition for M. A truth definition for a language of thought is thus simply a specification of the input/output function for an (appropriately idealized) cognitive system. Or, what with identity being symmetrical, you could equally put it that a cognitive system is simply a mechanism whose (appropriately idealized) input/output function is a truth definition for the representational system that it employs.

There are very serious reasons for thinking that this theory of meaning cannot be true. I'm about to consider some of them at length. First, however, I want to try to convince you that it is at least plausible prima facie that truth conditions should be the sorts of things that I have claimed they are – however ludicrous that idea may turn out to be on closer examination.

Consider once again the frog. And, by the way of clearing out some philosophical cobwebs, imagine that you are Capranaca, or Lettvin, or some other highly skilled neuropsychologist, and that you've set yourself the task of figuring out what the neural spikes you've been picking up represent. (If this isn't the sort of thing that investigating semantic properties of mental representations comes down to in practice, I can't imagine what would be.) Well, what would you do? I suppose you'd do just what Lettvin and Capranica did: *you'd try to find entry conditions.*[10] This means (1) you would look for a state of affairs such that bringing it about is necessary and sufficient for the occurrence of the spike given that the organism's visual apparatus is intact and that the relation of the organism to that state of affairs is epistemically appropriate to the visual fixation of belief; and (2) you would ask yourself whether making the assumption that that state of affairs *is* the truth condition of the spike lets you tell a reasonable story about the behavioral (etc.) consequences of the neuron's firing.[11] Well, in the present case it's the fly dancing around that makes the neuron go off, and the behavioral consequences of the firing include the activation of various capture-and-feeding reflexes, such as that the animal orients, the tongue goes out, etc. All of this is about what you'd expect if, on the one hand, the semantic content of the firing is that there's a fly there and, on the other, the frog's mental life is coherent in the way that Dennett, Davidson and the rest tell us that a kosher mental life has to be.

So now you've shown that the entry condition for the firing is that there's a fly dancing around. Suppose that you're committed (say, on philosophical grounds) to the view that neural spikes are the sorts of things that have truth conditions. (Remember, we're pretending to believe that RTM is true). My case for the prima facie plausibility of the identification of truth conditions with entry conditions rests on the fact that I can't think of a plausible answer to the following rhetorical question: What on earth more would you have to do to show that the spike is true if there's a fly there?

I propose to leave it there because there is more serious work at hand. Someone might want to say this: "Never mind whether your story is plausible prima facie; there are objections so serious as to be, on second thought, overriding." My program for the rest of this paper is to show that these objections are, perhaps, not quite so decisive as they may seem. Then, at the end, I'll do a little moralizing about theories of meaning at large.

I can think of two sorts of objection to the identification of truth conditions with entry conditions: one that it is absurdly too strong, and the other that it is empty. I'll take these worries in order.

The apparent absurdity of the theory is that it does sort of imply that, under normal conditions, everybody is omniscient; and I have noticed, in informal discussion, that eyebrows tend to get raised about this. Whence this implication? Well, if S is the *entry* condition for M then, under normal conditions, a token of M is in the yes-box iff it's the case that S. And if S is also the *truth* condition for M, then it follows that M is in the yes-box iff it's truth condition is satisfied. But, on the one hand, if M's truth condition is satisfied, then M is true; and, on the other, our functional psychology assures us that M's being in the yes-box is necessary and sufficient for O's believing what M expresses. So, putting all this together, we have it that O believes M iff M is true; which is *almost* to say that O is omniscient. There is, however, a popular prejudice to the contrary based, apparently, upon the observation that some people believe some things that are false and that nobody believes everything that is true.

Observation, bah humbug! I propose to argue that, in the relevant sense, everybody *is* almost omniscient; so the conclusion of the *reductio* should simply be embraced.

To begin with, let's have that 'almost' out. To be omniscient is to believe all and only the true propositions. But we have no guarantee that, for every true proposition, there is a symbol in O's language of thought that can express it. For this reason, the sort of omniscience I claim we have is quite compatible with the doctrine that I have elsewhere called 'epistemic boundedness'; viz., that there may well be things which, given the nature of our psychological constitution, we cannot come to know (see Fodor 1983). On the present assumptions, these would include true propositions which our mental symbols cannot express. Such restrictions may perfectly well be severe, as is at once apparent when we think about species other than our own. For example, for all I know, *there's a fly* and *there's a grunting conspecific* are the *only* propositions that a frog can grasp. that would be quite compatible with the frog being omniscient, as it were, modulo the expressive power of its system of mental representations.

Anyhow, I'm not really committed to claiming that we are omniscient even in the limited sense that tolerates epistemic boundedness. What I'm committed to is just that we (and, by the way, any other organism that has beliefs) are omniscient *in the teleologically relevant circumstances*, where these include the satisfaction of all pertinent conditions of epistemic appropriateness. To put it vulgarly, I'm committed to: "Rub our nose in the fact that P and (if we can think that P) we'll come to believe that P." But, of course, for indefinitely many states of affairs which our mental symbols are capable of representing, our noses are never so rubbed – the appropriateness conditions are never satisfied – and about these states of affairs we may form erroneous beliefs or no beliefs at all. In short, in the sense of 'normal functioning' in which it implies that we believe what M expresses iff what M expresses is true, it is perfectly possible that the normal function of the cognitive system is one that it never performs.[12]

Another way of putting the point is that what I'm committed to isn't almost-omniscience but rather a certain sort of account of error, ignorance and other such epistemic lapses. What I'm claiming (in company, by the way, with a venerable tradition of Platonists) is that error and ignorance are, in a certain sense, *accidents*. That is, they're to be explained otherwise than by reference to those properties of the cognitive apparatus in virtue of which it performs its function. The most usual of these 'accidents' is, of course, the failure of epistemic appropriateness conditions in virtue of facts about the causal/spatio-temporal situation of the organism. ("I couldn't see it from here," "I'm not old enough to have met him," "it was dark out," "I was asleep at the time," "nobody told me, so how could I have known?") It seems to me that *any* theory of belief fixation is going to have to attribute quite a lot of ignorance to this kind of failure to satisfy conditions of epistemic appropriateness. Very often we don't have a belief that we otherwise would have had because we are simply not in the right place at the right time for acquiring it. Why can't we *see* which foot Caesar put down first when he got to the other side of the Rubicon? Not because our visual systems aren't working right; not because we can't think: *Caesar put his left (/right) foot down first*; but simply because, *de facto*, we are not spatially–temporally situated in respect of the event in the kind of way that visual perception demands. It is the aggregate of boring, geographical facts of this sort that explains why we can't tell (and hence don't know) which foot . . . etc. Compare God, Whose omniscience is, according to the present view, largely implicit in His omnipresence.

I don't, of course, mean to suggest that the failure of appropriateness conditions is the only sort of 'accident' that serves to bound our epistemic performance. There are also psychological accidents reflecting, at it were, mechanical limitations of the cognitive mechanisms of belief fixation. ("It was too complicated for me to figure out," "I can't think that fast (/see that far), " "I'm terrible at remembering facts," "I can't judge distances," "I always forget names," "I was too scared to notice (/too bored to care).") These latter involve lapses attributable to the mechanisms of fixation of belief, but not to those properties in virtue of which selectional advantage accrues to these mechanisms; not to their *functional* properties in the teleological sense of that notion. Failures to see clearly are failures of the visual system to do what it's supposed to do; correct the failures and one *sees better*. Hence glasses.

In short, there are anyhow three sorts of conditions that need to be attended to in accounting for why a given mental symbol does (or doesn't) turn up in the yes-box: whether the entry conditions on the symbol are satisfied; whether the cognitive apparatus of the organism is functioning normally in respect of the state of affairs which satisfies the entry conditions; and whether the organism is appropriately situated in respect of that state of affairs. Intuitively, these correspond to: constraints on the state of the world, constraints on the state of the organism, and constraints on the (causal) relation between the organism and the object of belief. The omniscience claim is in force only when all three sorts of constraints are simultaneously satisfied.

What that claim comes down to, I think, is just that failures of omniscience are not design failures of the cognitive apparatus; rather, they're to be explained by reference to facts that are, from the teleological point of view, relatively extrinsic and uninteresting.

What makes this claim not just a stipulation about what should be called accidental is the possibility that lapses are, as it were, built into the cognitive apparatus; that its *modus operandi* favors the fixation of false beliefs (or the failure to fix true ones) even when the circumstances are epistemically optimal. To see how this sort of question can be other than just terminological, consider a doctrine that is, in its logic, quite close to 'we are omniscient-except-for-accident'; viz., that we are *immortal*-except-for-accident. This last is a respectable scientific hypothesis, and it is *not* refuted by the casual observation that quite a lot of people are dead.

There is a scientific issue about whether aging and death are intrinsic to our construction. One picture – the optimistic one – has it that we die only because we age, and we age only because of the pile-up of random errors in mechanisms like protein synthesis. Of course, this picture is doubly idealized; not only does it abstract from superficial contingencies (like being hit by a brick or falling into the Charles), but also what it considers to be mere errors are, from another point of view, thermodynamic necessities. The 'optimistic view' holds no comfort to anybody who actually wants to live forever.

Nevertheless, there is clearly an empirical issue as between the idea that mortality is, in this sense, accidental and the idea that we are, as it were, designed to die. There are, in fact, some famous data which make the latter sort of story seem quite likely to be true (see, for example, Williams 1966 [also Alexander 1987 – ed.]); they provide a crux for evolutionary theories that stress individual survival (as opposed to the transmission of the genome) as the state of affairs that natural selection propagates.

Similarly in our case; one can at least imagine data which would bear on the question whether truth is what the cognitive mechanisms are built to register. For example, as Steve Stich likes to point out, there are cases which do make it seem (first blush) that the cognitive mechanisms aim at something else. The logic of such examples is well worth considering.

Simple ones come from the ethological literature. Many animals are extremely conservative in the identification of their species' predator. Stimulus configurations that only remotely resemble the predator will release avoidance responses (so that some birds that are hunted by hawks exhibit escape behavior when you merely flutter a black cloth at them (see Tinbergen 1969)). One way to look at this is to say that the animal simply doesn't care about "false positives"; it's quite happy to have lots of *false* beliefs of the type *there's a predator* so long as (given the satisfaction of appropriateness conditions) it also has all the *true* beliefs of that type. In such cases, you might argue, one can't assume that the cognitive apparatus is designed to delivery *only* truths. *A fortiori*, one can't assume that it tends towards omniscience in the limit.

Such considerations are, however, by no means decisive since one has the usual trade-off between belief and utility to play with. You *can* describe the animal as prepared to tolerate false beliefs, but you can also describe it as sometimes prepared to act on beliefs to which it assigns very low probabilities. Not, 'there's a predator, so I'd better duck,' but 'that just might be a predator and I'm taking no chances.' And anyhow, these are the wrong sorts of cases for adjudicating the claims presently at issue. Flight responses and the like are, after all, necessarily relatively hectic affairs. The point of the exercise, in such behaviors, is to avoid getting eaten, and this interest is not best served by waiting around until the data become apodictic. What is interesting – indeed, what is crucial – from the point of view of the omniscience story, is to consider what one wants to say about the animal's propositional attitudes *as the quality of the data available to it improves.*

So, imagine, by way of thought experiment, that we can contrive to calm the panicky bird. Instead of letting it beetle off as soon as the black cloth is seen to flutter, we persuade it to contemplate its situation in a more impartial and deliberative frame of mind. "Look bird," we say, "it's just a dumb old black cloth, see?" (Bird does whatever is required to satisfy conditions of epistemic appropriateness: bird examines cloth from various points of view: bird sniffs, tastes, listens to, otherwise communes with cloth; bird's beak is, literally and metaphorically, rubbed in it.) And *then* the bird beetles off. At this point we're inclined to think that we do know which story about the bird's beliefs we ought to tell. What we're now inclined to say is: the bird thinks it's a black-fluttery thing all right; that is, the bird thinks something true. But we were wrong in supposing that the bird flees because it thinks that this black fluttery thing is or may be a hawk. In particular, we've misdescribed the eliciting stimulus for the bird's escape response. It's not *predators* the response is attached to, it's *black fluttery things*. There is still, of course, an explanation of the bird's behavior in terms of facts about the appearance of its predator: a conservative evolutionary strategy produces hawk-avoidance by attaching flight responses to whatever looks like hawks. Epistemologically speaking, we let the bird off the hook and blame the false positives on Mother Nature. And we do this *by retranslating a mental representation*; by reading what's in the yes-box as, say, 'it's black and fluttery so be gone,' rather than, say, 'it's a hawk, so beetle off.'

The point of all this is that a kind of principle of charity governs our belief ascriptions; something like: *so ascribe beliefs that, as the organism's evidence that P becomes arbitrarily transparent, the likelihood that the organism believes that P approaches arbitrarily close to unity* (The transparency of the evidence being largely a matter of the degree to which relevant conditions of epistemic appropriateness are satisfied). This is to say that we assign beliefs to organisms in such a fashion as to preserve the principle of omniscience in-the-limit. As we have seen, that is just what the identification of entry conditions with truth conditions requires.[13]

Well, but what about the possibility that the identification of entry conditions with truth conditions is *empty*? This argument could be made in a couple of different ways. You could say either (1) that claims for the coextension of entry conditions and truth conditions amount to mere stipulations, or (2) that the enterprise is undermined by the failure to provide a non-question-begging definition of 'cognitive system.' I want to consider both these objections.

To see what's bothering the first objector, it's important to grasp a difference between the evidential situation for claims about the semantic properties of mental representations, on the one hand, and of (for example) natural language symbols on the other hand. Let's consider, for one last time, the frog.

The Pseudo-Capranica establishes that the entry condition for a certain spike-type is a conspecific grunt and *goes on* to claim that that is also its truth condition. The operative bit is 'goes on.' Clearly, what is intended is an *empirical claim*. The picture is: there is a state of affairs which is the spike's entry condition, and there is a state of affairs which is the spike's truth condition and Lo!, I have discovered them to be one and the same state of affairs. Now, what the objector alleges is this: that sort of reasoning is fine when you can, at least in principle, tell whether something is the truth condition of a symbol *independently of telling whether it is the entry condition*. That, however, in the present case we cannot do. So the appearance of empirical discovery – the appearance of having *found out* what the truth condition is *by finding out* what the entry condition is – that's mere show.

Notice that this problem does not arise, in this way, for truth theories of natural languages. This is because, in the latter cases, there is some antecedent notion of truth-condition-of-a-symbol which the theory claims to reconstruct. That is, we know antecedent to theory construction such facts as that 'it's raining' is true iff it's raining. What a truth theory for English claims is at least that it gets all these intuitively given pairings right, and that claim is empirically testable. Compare the frog's spike, about the semantic properties of which we know, prior to the discovery of its entry condition, damn all.[14]

This sounds like a serious objection, but actually it's frivolous. True, a truth theory for mental representations is not tested by comparing its predictions with antecedently available intuitions about the truth conditions of mental symbols. But we have another body of empirical data which will do equally well. Remember that we have assumed a psychological theory which, for each value of M, fills in

the schema *O believes that S iff (S is the truth condition of M and O bears R* to M)*.
Of course, S is a free parameter from the point of view of this sort of theory
since, on the one hand, the psychology we've imagined is restricted to the
explication of computational relations and, on the other hand, the relation
between a symbol and its truth condition is *not* computational. In effect, what the
psychology does is to define R*, thereby predicting the beliefs of an organism
given a specification of the truth conditions of its mental representations.

Now, I do take it that there are facts of the matter about what O believes, and
that some of these are available, as data, antecedent to testing theories about the
truth conditions of mental symbols.[15] Here, then, is how you generate and test
empirical predictions from claims about the truth conditions of mental
representations (and, more generally, from the claim that their truth conditions
are identical to their entry conditions).

1 Find the entry condition for M; call it 'E'.
2 Substitute a specification of E for each occurrence of 'S' in the biconditional:
   O believes that S iff (S is the truth condition of M and O bears R* to M).
3 Bring it about (say, experimentally) that O bears R* to M.
4 Find out whether the left-hand side of the biconditional is true. The truth
   of the left-hand side is evidence *for* the identification of the entry condition
   with the truth condition; the falsity of the left-hand side is evidence against.
   If, in general, we get true left-hand sides whenever our confidence that
   we've located the entry condition is considerable and our functional account
   of R* is well confirmed, then we have good empirical evidence for the
   theory of meaning that identifies entry conditions with truth conditions.

Finally, let's consider the objection that the introduction of 'cognitive system'
(hence of 'normal functioning of the cognitive system'; hence, of 'entry condition')
was question-begging. I think this might actually be true.

Remember that I distinguished teleologically between the '*de facto*' and the '*tout
court*' cognitive system; the former included whatever mechanisms get stuff into or
out of the yes-box (hence such mechanisms of forgetting as trace decay, assuming
that trace decay *is* a mechanism of forgetting). The latter included only such
mechanisms as *function* to affect the contents of the yes-box.[16] Now, suppose, as
seems reasonable enough, that there is some psychological phenomenon as
repression. Clearly, if repression exists, it affects what's in the yes-box. Repression
leads you to forget things, and hence (given RTM) partially determines which
mental representations you bear R* to. Moreover, we might suppose, it's the
function of the repression-system to bring it about that you forget things. Maybe
organisms which repress (selectively, of course) are at competitive advantage. The
more you think about it, the more plausible that seems.

But, now, we clearly don't want to define 'entry condition' in terms of the
normal functioning of a cognitive system which includes repression mechanisms.
For, it's no accident that *that* cognitive system doesn't mediate omniscience. By
assumption, for some truths it's actually *designed* not to put Ms that express them
into the yes-box. However, as you will remember, it is precisely the assumption
that failures of omniscience are accidental that identification of truth conditions
with entry conditions depends upon. Selection for repression is to the omniscience

assumption what selection for lethal genes is to the immortality assumption: Very Bad News.

One way out would, of course, be simply to stipulate that repression mechanisms don't belong to the cognitive system. To which, however, the objector replies, correctly, that the analysis of 'truth condition' is now circular. On the one hand, whether something is an entry condition depends on what one is prepared to take to be a cognitive mechanism and, on the other hand, what counts as a cognitive mechanism depends upon what one is prepared to take as an entry condition. I think that the gist of this objection is probably right: there may well be no way of identifying cognitive mechanisms (in the intended sense) other than that they are the mechanisms which, when functioning normally, establish entry conditions that can be identified with truth conditions. No way, that is, except by enumeration.

But what's wrong with enumeration? After all, the project is not to *analyze* 'S is the truth condition of M'. If that had been the project, we would have had considerable inductive grounds for giving up at the onset. Analyses are what close out of town; surely it is the lesson of modern philosophy that interesting ideas don't get analyzed. No, the point was rather to show *how it is possible* that mental symbols should have truth conditions even though, since there are no agents who employ them, their semanticity cannot trace back to the intentionality of anybody's propositional attitudes. And this we have done. It is possible for mental representations to have truth conditions because – or so we hypothesize – each organism that has beliefs also has mechanisms which serve to place token representations in the yes-box under certain sorts of constraints. *Which* sorts of constraints? Why, those observed by, for example, such mechanisms as . . . (lots of enumeration here). And what's so interesting about those constraints? Just the fact that states of affairs that satisfy the constraints can be identified with the truth conditions of mental representations in a way that, given a specification of R*, leads to empirically plausible assignments of contents to propositional attitudes. If that's circular, it's just the normal circularity of scientific theory construction.

I promised to end with a little moralizing. Ever since Kant, philosophers have been interested in the idea that there is an internal connection between issues about meaning and issues about the fixation of belief. Verificationism is one offshoot of this idea, as are 'procedural semantics' and many other aberrations of theory. Despite which it turns out according to the present account that there is *something* to this intuition after all. For, if what I've been saying is right, the assignment of truth conditions to mental symbols is relativized to the functioning of the apparatus that effects the fixation of belief. In particular, it turns out that the fact that your belief has the semantic content that it does is determined by the fact that you hold the belief in the circumstances that you do; or, at least, that you *would* hold it under certain circumstances given normal functioning of the cognitive apparatus.

In a certain sense, you couldn't have a stronger form of verificationism. After all, a verificationist says that the meaning of a symbol is a construct out of the conditions under which it is asserted; and that's what I say too (only read 'mental representation' for 'symbol', 'truth conditions' for 'meaning', and 'being in the yes-box' for 'being asserted'.).

But what I find agreeable about my kind of verificationism – as opposed to any other kinds that I have heard of – is this. Traditional verificationism was supposed to have all sorts of strange and wonderful consequences: as that metaphysical concepts have no content, and that there are no such things as electrons, and that tables and chairs are made out of sense data, and that logical truths are analytic, and Lord knows what else. The way you get these surprising results is by first identifying meaning with conditions of assertion *and then placing very severe* (and, so far as I can see, quite unjustifiable) *constraints on what can count as a condition of assertion*; as, for example, that conditions of assertion have to be specifiable in terms of observables, or of sense data, or of properties of middle-sized objects . . . and so forth.

Whereas, on the present account, what corresponds to a condition of assertion (viz., an entry condition) can be, as I remarked, *just anything*. What can satisfy an entry condition is any state of affairs to which a cognitive apparatus can respond selectively; and that state of affairs can be very big, or very small, or very far away, or impossible to find out about except very indirectly, or even impossible to find out about at all, so long as the reason that you can't find out about it is only the *de facto* impossibility of satisfying the relevant appropriateness conditions. Why, a state of affairs could satisfy an entry condition EVEN IF IT WASN'T MADE OUT OF SENSE-DATA.

Here's the moral. It's perfectly OK to be a verificationist as long as, while you're doing so, you cleave absolutely to the correspondence theory of truth. What you get when you do that is a kind of verificationism which (except for its usefulness in legitimizing RTM), has, so far as I can tell, *no interesting consequences at all*. Philosophy of this kind – to borrow a phrase from a fellow verificationist – leaves everything *exactly as it was*. Which is, of course, quite a strong argument in its favor.[17]

NOTES

1 I want to distinguish between intentionality – which is, by stipulation, a property of *mental* states – and intensionality (roughly, aboutness) which is a property of symbols as well. Both of these terms need to be distinguished from homophones which refer specifically to psychological states of intending something, on the one hand, and to a galaxy of logical properties of certain sentential contexts, on the other hand.

2 On the simplifying assumption that the language of thought is morphosyntactically like English, substitution instances of this schema would include 'that it be raining is the truth condition of "it's raining"' and so forth. In general, it's intended that S be the state of affairs such that: if M is true, it's true because it's the case that S, and if M is false, it's false because it's not the case that S.

The "true because" talk is in honor of the sentiment – widespread but hard to explicate – that the relation between a symbol and the state of affairs that satisfies its truth condition is somehow closer than what holds between the symbol and arbitrary states of affairs that obtain if the symbol is true. That is: I'm sympathetic to the view that, in so far as the semanticity of a representation consists in its having truth conditions, 'S is the truth condition of M' should be opaque to substitution of materially equivalent expressions in the position occupied by 'S'. Some of this will presently come out in the wash.

3 I take it for granted that if a theory is unable to capture the semantic distinctions that can be expressed in English, it must be inadequate to capture the semantic distinctions that can be expressed by mental symbols. This follows from the view that the semanticity of linguistic

symbols derives (via the communicative intentions of speaker/hearers) from the semanticity of mental ones.

4 I am reading the relation between a symbol and whatever determines its truth value as paradigmatically a symbol-to-world relation; the truth-conditional approach to semantics presupposes a correspondence theory of truth. For this reason, and others that will become apparent, I have considerable doubt about the application of this apparatus to explaining the semanticity of such symbols as express necessary truths of logic and mathematics. On the one hand, it's unclear what truth-as-correspondence would mean for such symbols and, on the other, the problem of distinguishing coextensivity from synonymy seems especially intractable when the coextensions are necessary. Since I simply don't know what to do about necessary truths, I propose to restrict the present discussion to symbols which have their truth values contingently.

5 R* is, of course, quite a different relation from the symbol-to-world relation that theories of meaning explicate. R* is a relation between an organism and a mental representation in virtue of which the former believes what the latter expresses. Theories of meaning, by contrast, characterize a relation between (say) an organism, a state of affairs, and a mental representation, in virtue of which the representation has the semantic properties that it does.

6 This is putting it very roughly, and things get complicated (in ways which, for present purposes, I do not wish to care about) if one tries to be more precise. The best thing is to take (e) to be a schema which is required to be true under appropriate simultaneous substitutions of: the name of an organism for 'O'; and an English sentence for each occurrence of 'S'.

7 One thing that makes this sort of case primitive – and useful – is that it's likely that the frog's 'there's a fly' neurons light up *only* via the activity of its visual system; I suppose the frog never lights them up by, for example, deducing the presence of a fly from premises previously entertained. (Whereas for us, by contrast, there are typically several different cognitive systems, including inferential mechanisms, which can eventuate in a given type of mental symbol being tokened in the yes-box.) This makes the frog's case easier to think about than ours, but it alters nothing fundamental.

8 The reader will have noticed that I'm making the expository assumption that the frog's language of thought is morphosyntactically English too. That assumption is as useful in talking about the frog's mental processes as it is in talking about ours, and not much less plausible.

   I don't, of course, seriously suppose that the frog has a mental symbol that means exactly what 'there's a fly' means in English; nor, indeed, that we have any a priori right to suppose that the content of the frog's thought is expressible by *any* symbol that we can understand. "If lions could talk . . ." Ditto frogs.

9 Not very surprisingly, the problem of specifying which among the causal conditions for M being in the yes-box counts as its entry condition is closely related to the problem of specifying which link in the causal chain leading to the formation of a perceptual belief counts as the object of perception. I expect the rough treatment suggested in the text could be much improved by integration with the perceptual literature.

10 That really *is* what they did only, strictly speaking, they did it the other way around. That is, they started with what, given the ethology of the organism, seemed to be a plausible candidate entry condition – the croak of a conspecific, the presence of food on the wing – and then they looked for a neural event type whose tokening was specific to the satisfaction of that condition.

11 Notice that this second condition is built into the notion of an entry condition. S is the entry condition of M only if S eventuates in tokens of M being in the yes-box, hence in the organism being in the belief relation to whatever it is that M expresses. It follows that S is the entry condition only if it eventuates in whatever behavioral consequences R* entails for an organism that has M in its yes-box.

12 "Aha", you say, "if the cognitive system never in fact functions in respect of tokens of a type, how could selection pressures have determined how it *would* function if the appropriateness conditions *were* satisfied?" Answer: once selection has shaped a cognitive (or any other) mechanism, there are indefinitely many counterfactuals that will be true in virtue of the structure of that mechanism. Suppose that selection pressures favor organisms that can add. Then, *inter alia*, they favor organisms that can add 27 and 54. That can be true even though no organism ever did add 27 and 54, so that cases of doing the sum played no role in the etiology of the mechanisms that perform it. It is a serious misunderstanding of evolutionary theory to suppose that the explanation of a capacity by reference to selectional advantage presupposes that *that very capacity* has sometimes been exercised in the evolutionary history of the organism.

13 Stronger forms of the principle of charity have, of course, been proposed by a number of philosophers; but I doubt that any such are warranted. Nor am I prepared to grant the popular inference from 'charity operates in the ascription of content to beliefs' to 'belief ascription is heuristic, instrumental, or otherwise unfacticious.' In my view, what the exercise of charity comes to is this: our (implicit) propositional attitude psychology involves us in (equally implicit) teleological assumptions about the cognitive mechanisms; that is, that they're designed to fix beliefs that are true. We can (and do) defend the teleology by appropriately redescribing threatening data (see the example in the text). But, of course, such strategies are typical of the deployment of theories *wherever* they are elaborately textured and highly valued. In this respect, psychology would seem to be on much the same footing as physics.

14 In fact, there's an important respect in which this consideration cuts two ways. It is tempting to suppose that one can refute the main contention of this paper just by insisting on the possibility that a formula which expresses *that P* should be in the yes-box even though the organism's cognitive system is functioning normally and its evidence is, overwhelmingly, *that not P*. But, of course, the claim that this *is* possible is merely question-begging barring some alternative, nonepistemic account of what it is for a mental representation to express *that P*. In particular, we can't support such claims by appeal to our intuitions about what a mental representation means because, simply, we have no such intuitions. The polemical situation in defending (or attacking) theories of meaning for mental representations is thus quite different from what we're accustomed to from arguments about meaning theories for natural languages. New ball game.

15 I'm not taking it to be *self-evident* that there are such facts available. Someone could deny that there are propositional attitudes, or that there is any possibility of finding out which propositional attitudes an organism has. However, the whole issue about mental representations arose primarily in the context of the evaluation of RTM, which is explicitly a theory about the beliefs of organisms. If you think there are no such things as beliefs, or that facts about beliefs are inaccessible in principle, you are unlikely to be worried about how to save RTM; and, conversely, if you are interested in saving RTM, you are likely to be willing to concede that there are facts about beliefs to which RTM is responsible. (Also: if you want to deny that there are matters of fact about propositional attitudes in *this* context, you'd better not do so on the grounds that one can't make sense of such notions as 'content of a belief.' That sort of move, made here, is just question-begging.)

16 I also said that the cognitive system *tout court* is the mechanism of *rational* fixation of belief, but that surely *was* question-begging since the rationality of an operation involves its respecting semantic properties of the symbols it applies to; and, of course, it's the notion 'semantic property of a mental symbol' that we're trying to reconstruct.

17 A note for real verificationists. I suppose that a verificationist version of RTM would think of mental representations as being of two sorts: *data symbols* and *all the others*. The semantic properties of the data symbols are determined by reference to causal properties of the perceptual mechanisms. The semantic properties of all the others are determined by logical

construction out of the data symbols. So, for example, a classic form of verificationism might be reconstructed as follows: data symbols are ones whose entry conditions can be exhaustively characterized by reference to the normal performance of the sensory apparatus. (For example, the 'that's red' symbol is the one such that the normal functioning of the sensory apparatus is such that the symbol is in the yes-box iff the causally efficacious distal stimulus is red.) All the other mental symbols are abbreviations of ones of which the nonlogical vocabulary consists exhaustively of data symbols. Notice that this theory is a special case of the one in the text; it's the special case where symbol–world relations are mediated solely by the sensory component of the cognitive system. Notice, too, that the appropriate omniscience conditions are in force: for this account to work, it must be that normal sensory systems deliver the right output given that they are appropriately exposed to the appropriate stimulation.

Evidently, the more of this sort of reductionism there is, the easier it is to make my sort of theory work. Alas, I think in fact that there are almost *no* examples where the semantic properties of symbols are established by these sorts of means, so the interest of the case is merely theoretical. Roughly, the situation is this; it is relatively easy to see how to assign truth conditions to mental symbols in either of two limiting cases: in God's case (because God is omniscient by independent assumption), and in the verificationist's case (because, for a verificationist, all symbol–world relations are mediated by perceptual mechanisms). If the conditions that make these limiting cases soluble are artificial, what we must now do is gradually nibble away at them.

REFERENCES

Alexander, R. (1987) *The Biology of Moral Systems*, Aldine de Gruyter.

Capranica, R. R. (1976) *Frog Neurobiology: A Handbook*, Springer-Verlag.

Cherniak, C. (1986) *Minimal Rationality*, Bradford Books / MIT Press.

Davidson, D. (1967) "Truth and meaning," *Synthese* 17, 304–23.

Dennett, D. C. (1975) "Brain writing and mind reading," in K. Gunderson (ed.), *Minnesota Studies in the Philosophy of Science, Vol. 7: Language, Mind and Knowledge*, University of Minnesota Press.

Field, H. (1977) "Logic, meaning and conceptual role," *Journal of Philosophy* 74, 379–409.

Fodor, J. A. (1980) "Methodological solipsism considered as a research strategy in cognitive psychology," *Behavioral and Brain Sciences* 3, 63–73.

Fodor, J. A. (1981) *Representations*, Bradford Books / MIT Press.

Fodor, J. A. (1983) *The Modularity of Mind*, Bradford Books / MIT Press.

Fodor, J. D. (1977) *Semantics: Theories of Meaning in Generative Grammar*, Crowell.

Lettvin, J. Y. et al. (1959) "What the frog's eye tells the frog's brain," *Proceedings of the Institute of Radio Engineers*, 1940–51.

Loar, B. (1981) *Mind and Meaning*, Cambridge University Press.

McGinn, C. (1982) "The structure of content," in A. Woodfield (ed.), *Thought and Object*, Oxford University Press.

Putnam, H. (1975) "The meaning of 'meaning'," in K. Gunderson (ed.), *Minnesota Studies in the Philosophy of Science. Vol. 7: Language, Mind and Knowledge*, University of Minnesota Press.

Reeves, A. (1974) "On truth and meaning," *Noûs* 8, 343–59.

Tinbergen, N. (1969) *The Study of Instinct*, Oxford: Clarendon Press.

Williams, G. C. (1966) *Adaptation and Natural Selection*, Princeton University Press.

Part VI

The Status of "Folk Psychology"

Introduction

In Part IV above we were introduced to the somewhat strange idea that mental terms and mental entities themselves are at risk. Sellars, Feyerabend and Quine in the 1960s first urged the "theory" theory, as Morton (1980) calls it; that is, the idea that mental terms are the theoretical terms of a folk science. After an understandable period of incredulity, the "theory" theory became widely accepted. But the "theory" theory leads in a disconcerting direction: if the only reason we have for accepting the existence of mental entities is the utility and presumed truth of folk psychology, and if folk psychology should turn out to be largely *false* or seriously infirm in some other way, as scientific theories and especially folk theories often do, then presumably some version of Eliminativism is correct.

We have already looked (in Part IV above) at some Eliminativist arguments. In this part we shall turn to a special issue regarding propositional attitude content, the issue of "methodological solipsism" in Putnam's (1975) phrase, and examine its consequences for the probity of folk psychology.

Methodological solipsism

Suppose for the sake of argument that we attribute representational content to the internal states of computers – as in real life we do, however, anthropomorphically. A computer sometimes thinks this or wants that; at the very least, it computes this or computes that: the GNP of Monaco, the outcome of the coming Presidential election, the balance of our checking account or whatever.

Now, to take a key example of Jerry Fodor's (1980): it is quite possible that two computers, programmed by entirely different users for entirely different purposes, should happen to run physically in parallel. They might go through precisely the same sequence of electrical currents and flipflop settings and yet have their outputs interpreted differently by their respective users, especially if what they write to their screens is all in numerical form. One of them would naturally and correctly be described as figuring out the GNP of Monaco, while the other would just as naturally and correctly be described as figuring out the batting averages of New York Yankees then and now. The point, plain enough when we think about it, is simply that *what* a machine is computing is not fully determined by the physical or even the abstract-functional operations that are going on entirely inside the machine. What the machine is computing depends to some extent on something outside the machine itself – users' intentions, causal-historical chains (see Part V above), teleology, interpretation by observers, or just the convenience of the beholder.

The point is not particularly surprising. But Putnam (1975) drew a broader conclusion that was developed to startling effect by Fodor (1980) and by Stich (this volume, this part): as it is with computers, so it is with humans. The representational content of a human subject's propositional attitudes is underdetermined by even the total state of that subject's head. Putnam's "Twin Earth" and indexical examples show that, surprising at it may seem, two human beings could be molecule-for-molecule alike and still differ in their beliefs and desires, depending on various factors in their spatial and historical environments. Philosophers now distinguish between "narrow" properties, those that are determined by a subject's intrinsic physical composition, and "wide" properties, those that are not so determined.

The fact that attitude contents are "wide" raises serious problems about the vaunted role of propositional attitudes in the explaining of behavior, and attendant questions for psychology (Fodor 1980; Stich, this volume, this part). But for our purposes in this part, the main question is this: if the representational content of a propositional attitude depends on factors outside the physical boundary of its owner's skin, what are those factors, and more importantly, can we still suppose that the attitude contents are genuine properties of the owner/subject? The spectre of Elimination reappears; perhaps it is not really, objectively true of people that they believe this or desire that.

The question of what the environmental factors actually are is just the question of psychosemantics again (Part V above). But what about the ontological status of people's beliefs and desires themselves? There are several different possibilities.

1   The external semantical interpretation of an organism's internal physical/ functional states is entirely up for grabs: any interpretation that suits anyone's convenience is good enough, and if two interpreters' interpretations conflict, neither is correct to the exclusion of the other. (Schiffer (1981) discusses this possibility sympathetically, and construes Quine's famous doctrine of the "indeterminacy of translation" as getting at this position.) If we fall in with this view, we can hardly call it a hard fact that a subject believes one thing rather than another.

2   The semantical interpretation of beliefs is not up for grabs; it is at least loosely determined by various contextual factors, and some interpretations are correct while others are just wrong. But the contextual factors in question are intolerably vague and messy and social and interest-infested – quite unsuitable for incorporation into any genuine science. To ascribe the belief that P to someone is no more scientific, explanatory or useful than is calling something "nice." (2) is the position of Stich (1983, this volume, this part).

3   The semantical interpretation of beliefs is loosely determined by various contextual factors, and some interpretations are correct while others are just wrong, and this is what it is for the subject to believe one thing rather than another. Some complex causal–historical and/or teleological feature of the subject's environment (cf. the introduction to Part V) makes it objectively

true that the subject believes so-and-so rather than such-and-such, whether or not the feature is scientifically interesting or well-behaved. (Lycan (1981) staunchly defends this view.)

4 There is nothing messy, interest-relative etc. about the contextual factors in question, even though they extend outside the skin boundary. They are a matter of *simple* nomological or teleological fact. This position is endorsed by "indicator" semanticists among others (Dretske, Stampe, Stalnaker).

The first position, (1), is essentially an Eliminative view, and certainly flouts the folk-psychological thesis that propositional attitudes *qua* propositional attitudes are real causal constituents of the world; (2) allows that attitude ascriptions may be true (however interest-infested), and consequently that people do believe one thing rather than another, but still rejects the folk-psychological view that the attitudes genuinely cause behavior; (3) and (4) are entirely compatible with folk psychology; (1) and (2) differ from each other, it seems, only in degree, so the real issue so far is that of whether (2) or (3) is more plausible.

There is a further and deeper issue. Even if we grant that (2), or (1), is true, why should we care about "wide" properties at all? What explanatory need do they fulfil? Fodor (this volume, this part) tries to answer that deeper question; Devitt (this volume) investigates further.

FURTHER READING

"Methodological solipsism"

Putnam, H. (1975) "The meaning of 'meaning'," in K. Gunderson (ed.), *Minnesota Studies in the Philosophy of Science, Vol. 7: Language, Mind and Knowledge*, University of Minnesota Press.

Fodor, J. A. (1980) "Methodological solipsism considered as a research strategy in cognitive psychology," *Behavioral and Brain Sciences* 3, 63–73, as well as the Open Peer Commentaries on Fodor's article in the same issue and Elliott Sober's later commentary in vol. 5 (1982), 300–2.

Burge, T. (1979) "Individualism and the mental," in P. French, T. E. Uehling and H. Wettstein (eds), *Midwest Studies in Philosophy IV: Studies in Metaphysics*, University of Minnesota Press.

Stich, S. (1983) *From Folk Psychology to Cognitive Science: The Case Against Belief*, Bradford Books/ MIT Press. [Excerpt reprinted in this volume.]

Reverberations of the "narrow"/"wide" distinction

Lycan, W. (1981) "Toward a homuncular theory of believing," *Cognition and Brain Theory* 4, 139–59.

Schiffer, S. (1981) "Truth and the theory of content," in H. Parret and J. Bouveresse (eds), *Meaning and Understanding*, Walter de Gruyter.

Dennett, D. C. (1982) "Beyond belief," in A. Woodfield (ed.), *Thought and Object*, Oxford University Press.

McGinn, C. (1982) "The structure of content," in A. Woodfield (ed.), *Thought and Object*.

Putnam, H. (1983) "Computational psychology and interpretation theory," reprinted in *Realism and Reason: Philosophical Papers*, vol. 3, Cambridge University Press; and most recently (1988) in *Representation and Reality*, Bradford Books / MIT Press.

Owens, J. (1983) "Functionalism and propositional attitudes," *Noûs* 17, 529–49.

Burge, T. (1986) "Individualism and psychology," *Philosophical Review* 95, 3–45.

Fodor, J. A. (1987) *Psychosemantics*, Bradfords Books / MIT Press.

Baker, L. R. (1988) *Saving Belief*, Princeton University Press.
Block, N. J. (1986) "Advertisement for a semantics for psychology," in P. French, T. E. Uehling, and H. Wettstein (eds), *Midwest Studies in Philosophy X*, University of Minnesota Press.

Attacking folk psychology
Churchland, P. M. (1979) *Scientific Realism and the Plasticity of Mind*, Cambridge University Press.
Churchland, P. S. (1986) *Neurophilosophy*, Bradford Books / MIT Press.

Defending folk psychology
Morton, A. (1980) *Frames of Mind*, Oxford University Press. [Not a defense of folk psychology *qua* empirical theory; Morton christens and criticizes the "theory" theory of folk psychology.]
von Eckardt, B. (1984) "Cognitive psychology and principled skepticism," *Journal of Philosophy* 81, 67–88.
Kitcher, P. (1984) "In defense of intentional psychology," *Journal of Philosophy* 81, 89–106.

14

Attacking "Folk Psychology"

Autonomous Psychology and the Belief–Desire Thesis

STEPHEN P. STICH

A venerable view, still very much alive, holds that human action is to be explained at least in part in terms of beliefs and desires. Those who advocate the view expect that the psychological theory which explains human behavior will invoke the concepts of belief and desire in a substantive way. I will call this expectation *the belief–desire thesis*. Though there would surely be a quibble or a caveat here and there, the thesis would be endorsed by an exceptionally heterogeneous collection of psychologists and philosophers ranging from Freud and Hume, to Thomas Szasz and Richard Brandt. Indeed, a number of philosophers have contended that the thesis, or something like it, is embedded in our ordinary, workaday concept of action.[1] If they are right, and I think they are, then in so far as we use the concept of action we are *all* committed to the belief–desire thesis. My purpose in this paper is to explore the tension between the belief–desire thesis and a widely held assumption about the nature of explanatory psychological theories, an assumption that serves as a fundamental regulative principle for much of contemporary psychological theorizing. This assumption, which for want of a better term I will call the *principle of psychological autonomy*, will be the focus of the first of the sections below. In the second section I will elaborate a bit on how the belief–desire thesis is to be interpreted, and try to extract from it a principle that will serve as a premise in the argument to follow. In the third section I will set out an argument to the effect that large numbers of belief–desire explanations of action, indeed perhaps the bulk of such explanations, are incompatible with the principle of autonomy. Finally, in the last section, I will fend off a possible objection to my argument. In the process, I will try to make clear just why the argument works and what price we should have to pay if we were resolved to avoid its consequences.

"Autonomous Psychology and the Belief–Desire Thesis" by S. P. Stich first appeared in *Monist* 61 (1978), pp. 573–91, and is reprinted by kind permission.

I The principle of psychological autonomy

Perhaps the most vivid way of explaining the principle I have in mind is by invoking a type of science fiction example that has cropped up with some frequency in recent philosophical literature. Imagine that technology were available which would enable us to duplicate people. That is, we can build living human beings who are atom for atom and molecule for molecule replicas of some given human being.[2] Now suppose that we have before us a human being (or, for that matter, any sort of animal) and his exact replica. What the principle of autonomy claims is that these two humans will be psychologically identical, that any psychological property instantiated by one of these subjects will also be instantiated by the other.

Actually, a bit of hedging is needed to mark the boundaries of this claim to psychological identity. First, let me note that the organisms claimed to be psychologically identical include any pair of organisms, existing at the same time or at different times, who happen to be atom for atom replicas of each other. Moreover, it is inessential that one organism should have been built to be a replica of the other. Even if the replication is entirely accidental, the two organisms will still be psychologically identical.

A caveat of another sort is needed to clarify just what I mean by calling two organisms "psychologically identical." For consider the following objection: "The original organism and his replica do not share *all* of their psychological properties. The original may, for example, remember seeing the Watergate hearings on television, but the replica remembers no such thing. He may think he remembers it, or have an identical "memory trace", but if he was not created until long after the Watergate hearings, then he did not see the hearings on television, and thus he could not remember seeing them." The point being urged by my imagined critic is a reasonable one. There are many sorts of properties plausibly labeled "psychological" that might be instantiated by a person and not by his replica. Remembering that *p* is one example, knowing that *p* and seeing that *p* are others. These properties have a sort of "hybrid" character. They seem to be analyzable into a "purely psychological" property (like seeming to remember that *p*, or believing that *p*) along with one or more non-psychological properties and relations (like *p* being true, or the memory trace being caused in a certain way by the fact that *p*). But to insist that "hybrid" psychological properties are not psychological properties at all would be at best a rather high handed attempt at stipulative definition. Still, there is something a bit odd about these hybrid psychological properties, a fact which reflects itself in the intuitive distinction between "hybrids" and their underlying "purely psychological" components. What is odd about the hybrids, I think, is that we do not expect them to play any role in an explanatory psychological theory. Rather, we expect a psychological theory which aims at explaining behavior to invoke only the "purely psychological" properties which are shared by a subject and its replicas. Thus, for example, we are inclined to insist it is Jones's *belief* that there is no greatest prime number that plays a role in the explanation of his answering the exam question. He may, in fact, have *known* that there is no greatest prime number. But even if he did not know it, if, for example, the source of his information had himself only been guessing, Jones's behavior would have been unaffected. What knowledge adds to belief is psychologically irrelevant. Similarly the difference between really remembering that p and merely seeming to remember that p makes no diffference to the subject's behavior. In claiming that physical replicas are psychologically identical, the principle of psychological autonomy is to be understood as restricting itself to the properties that can play a role in explanatory psychological theory. Indeed, the principle is best viewed as a claim about what sorts of properties and relations may play a role in explanatory psychological theory. If the principle is to be observed, then the only properties and relations that may legitimately play a role in explanatory psychological theories are the properties and relations that a subject and its replica will share.

There is another way to explain the principle of psychological autonomy that does not appeal to the fanciful idea of a replica. . . . Jaegwon Kim has explicated and explored the notion of one class of properties *supervening* upon another class of properties.[3] Suppose S and W are two classes of properties, and that S# and W# are the sets of all properties constructible from the properties in S and W respectively. Then, following Kim, we will say that the family S of properties supervenes on the family W of properties (with respect to a domain D of objects) just in case, necessarily, any two objects in D which share all properties in W# will also share all properties in S#. A bit less formally, one class of properties supervenes on another if the presence or absence of properties in the former class is completely determined by the presence or absence of properties in the latter.[4] Now the principle of psychological autonomy states that the properties and relations to be invoked in an explanatory psychological theory must be supervenient upon the *current, internal physical* properties and relations of organisms (i.e., just those properties that an organism shares with all of its replicas).

Perhaps the best way to focus more sharply on what the autonomy principle states is to look at what it rules out. First, of course, if explanatory psychological properties and relations must supervene on *physical* properties, then at least some forms of dualism are false. The dualist who claims that there are psychological (or mental) properties which are not nomologically correlated with physical properties, but which nonetheless must be invoked in an explanation of the organism's behavior, is denying that explanatory psychological states supervene upon physical states. However, the autonomy principle is not inimical to all forms of dualism. Those dualists, for example, who hold that mental and physical properties are nomologically correlated need have no quarrel with the doctrine of autonomy. However, the principle of autonomy is significantly stronger than the mere insistence that psychological states supervene on physical states.[5] For autonomy requires in addition that certain physical properties and relations are psychologically irrelevant in the sense that organisms which differ *only* with respect to those properties and relations are psychologically identical.[6] In specifying that only "current" physical properties are psychologically relevant, the autonomy principle decrees irrelevant all those properties that deal with the history of the organism, both past and future. It is entirely possible, for example, for two organisms to have quite different physical histories and yet, at a specific pair of moments, to be replicas of one another. But this sort of difference, according to the autonomy principle, can make no difference from the point of view of explanatory psychology. Thus remembering that p (as contrasted with having a memory trace that p)

cannot be an explanatory psychological state. For the difference between a person who remembers that p and a person who only seems to remember that p is not dependent on their current physical state, but only on the history of these states. Similarly, in specifying that only *internal* properties and relations are relevant to explanatory psychological properties, the autonomy principle decrees that relations between an organism and its external environment are irrelevant to its current (explanatory) psychological state. The restriction also entails that properties and relations of external objects cannot be relevant to the organism's current (explanatory) psychological state. Thus neither my seeing that Jones is falling nor my knowing that Ouagadougou is the capital of Upper Volta can play a role in an explanatory psychological theory, since the former depends in part on my relation to Jones, and the latter depends in part on the relation between Ouagadougou and Upper Volta.

Before we leave our discussion of the principle of psychological autonomy, let us reflect briefly on the status of the principle. On Kim's view, the belief that one set of properties supervenes on another "is largely, and often, a combination of metaphysical convictions and methodological considerations."[7] The description seems particularly apt for the principle of psychological autonomy. The autonomy principle serves a sort of regulative role in modern psychology, directing us to restrict the concepts we invoke in our explanatory theories in a very special way. When we act in accordance with the regulative stipulation of the principle we are giving witness to the tacit conviction that the best explanation of behavior will include a theory invoking properties supervenient upon the organism's current, internal physical state.[8] As Kim urges, this conviction is supported in part by the past success of theories which cleave to the principle's restrictions, and in part by some very fundamental metaphysical convictions. I think there is much to be learned in trying to pick apart the various metaphysical views that support the autonomy principle, for some of them have implications in areas quite removed from psychology. But that is a project for a different paper.

II   The belief–desire thesis

The belief–desire thesis maintains that human action is to be explained, at least in part, in terms of beliefs and desires. To sharpen the thesis we need to say more about the intended sense of *explain*, and more about what it would be to explain action *in terms of beliefs and desires*. But before trying to pin down either of these notions, it will be useful to set out an example of the sort of informal belief–desire explanations that we commonly offer for our own actions and the actions of others.

> Jones is watching television; from time to time he looks nervously at a lottery ticket grasped firmly in his hand. Suddenly he jumps up and rushes toward the phone. Why? It was because the TV announcer has just announced the winning lottery number, and it is the number on Jones's ticket. Jones believes that he has won the lottery. He also believes that to collect his winnings he must contact the lottery commission promptly. And, needless to say, he very much wants to collect his winnings.

Many theorists acknowledge that explanations like the one offered of Jones rushing toward the phone are often true (albeit incomplete) explanations of action. But this concession alone does not commit the theorist to the belief–desire thesis as I will interpret it here. There is considerable controversy over how we are to understand the 'because' in "Jones rushed for the phone because he believed he had won the lottery and he wanted . . ." Some writers are inclined to read the 'because' literally, as claiming that Jones's belief and his desire were the *causes* (or among the causes) of his action. Others offer a variety of non-causal accounts of the relation between beliefs and desires on the one hand and actions on the other.[9] However, it is the former, "literal," reading that is required by the belief–desire thesis as I am construing it.

To say that Jones's belief that he had won the lottery was among the causes of his rushing toward the phone is to say of one specific event that it had among its causes one specific state. There is much debate over how such "singular causal statements" are to be analyzed. Some philosophers hold that for a state or event S to be among the causes of an event E, there must be a law which somehow relates S and E. Other philosophers propose other accounts. Even among those who agree that singular causal statements must be subsumed by a law, there is debate over how this notion of subsumption is to be understood. At the heart of this controversy is the issue of how much difference there can be between the properties invoked in the law and those invoked in the description of the event if the event is to be an instance of the law.[10] Given our current purposes, there is no need to take a stand on this quite general metaphysical issue. But we will have to take a stand on a special case of the relation between beliefs, desires, and the psychological laws that subsume them. The belief–desire thesis, as I am viewing it, takes seriously the idea of developing a psychological theory couched in terms of beliefs and desires. Thus, in addition to holding that Jones's action was caused by his belief that he had won the lottery and his desire to collect his winnings, it also holds that this singular causal statement is true in virtue of being subsumed by laws which specify nomological relations among beliefs, desires and action.[11]

There is one further point that needs to be made about my construal of the belief-desire thesis. If the thesis is right, then action is to be explained at least in part by appeal to laws detailing how beliefs, desires and other psychological states effect action. But how are we to recognize such laws? It is, after all, plainly not enough for a theory simply to invoke the terms 'belief' and 'desire' in its laws. If it were, then it would be possible to convert any theory into a belief–desire theory by the simple expedient of replacing a pair of its theoretical terms with the terms 'belief' and 'desire'. The point I am laboring is that the belief–desire thesis must be construed as the claim that psychological theory will be couched in terms of beliefs and desires *as we ordinarily conceive of them*. Thus to spell out the belief–desire thesis in detail would require that we explicate our intuitive concepts of belief and desire. Fortunately, we need not embark on that project here.[12] To fuel the arguments I will develop in the following section, I will need only a single, intuitively plausible, premise about beliefs.

As a backdrop for the premise that I need, let me introduce some handy terminology. I believe that Ouagadougou is the capital of Upper Volta, and if you share my interest in atlases then it is likely that you have the same belief. Of course, there is also a perfectly coherent sense in which your belief is not the same as mine, since you could come to believe that Bobo Dioulasso is the capital of Upper Volta, while my belief remains unchanged. The point here is the obvious one that beliefs, like sentences, admit of a type–token distinction. I am inclined to view belief tokens as states of a person. And I take a state to be the instantiation of a property by an object during a time interval. Two belief states (or belief tokens) are of the same type if they are instantiations of the same property and they are of different types if they are instantiations of different properties.[13] In the example at hand, the property that both you and I instantiate is *believing that Ouagadougou is the capital of Upper Volta.*

Now the premise I need for my argument concerns the identity conditions for belief properties. Cast in its most intuitive form, the premise is simply that if a particular belief of yours is true and a particular belief of mine is false, then they are not the same belief. A bit more precisely: If a belief token of one subject differs in truth value from a belief token of another subject, then the tokens are not of the same type. Given our recent account of belief states, this is equivalent to a sufficient condition for the non-identity of belief properties: If an instantiation of belief property p_1 differs in truth value from an instantiation of belief property p_2 then p_1 and p_2 are different properties. This premise hardly constitutes an analysis of our notion of sameness of belief, since we surely do not hold belief tokens to be of the same type if they merely have the same truth value. But no matter. There is no need here to explicate our intuitive notion of belief identity in any detail. What the premise does provide is a necessary condition on any state counting as a belief. If a pair of states can be type identical (i.e., can be instantiations of the same property) while differing in truth value, then the states are not beliefs as we ordinarily conceive of them.

Before putting my premise to work, it might be helpful to note how the premise can be derived from a quite traditional philosophical account of the nature of beliefs. According to this account, belief is a relation between a person and a proposition. Two persons have the same belief (instantiate the same belief property) if they are belief-related to the same proposition. And, finally, propositions are taken to be the vehicles of truth, so propositions with different truth values cannot be identical. Given this account of belief, it follows straightforwardly that belief tokens differing in truth value differ in type. But the entailment is not mutual, so those who, like me, have some suspicions about the account of belief as a relation between a person and a proposition are free to explore other acounts of belief without abandoning the intuitively sanctioned premise that differences in truth value entail difference in belief.

III   The tension between autonomy and the belief–desire thesis

In this section I want to argue that a certain tension exists between the principle of psychological autonomy and the belief–desire thesis. The tension is not, strictly speaking a logical incompatibility. Rather, there is an incompatibility between the autonomy principle and some assumptions that are naturally and all but universally shared by advocates of the belief–desire thesis. The additional assumptions are that singular causal statements like the ones extractable from our little story about Jones and the lottery ticket are often true. Moreover, they are true because they are subsumed by laws which invoke the very properties which are invoked in the characterization of the beliefs and desires. A bit less abstractly, what I am assuming is that statements like "Jones's belief that he had won the lottery was among the causes of his rushing toward the phone" are often true; and that they are true in virtue of being subsumed by laws invoking properties like *believing that he had just won the lottery*. The burden of my argument is that if we accept the principle of autonomy, then these assumptions must be rejected. More specifically, I will argue that if the autonomy principle is accepted then there are large numbers of belief properties that cannot play a role in an explanatory psychological theory. My strategy will be to examine four different cases, each representative of a large class. In each case we will consider a pair of subjects who, according to the autonomy principle, instantiate all the same explanatory psychological properties, but who have different beliefs. So if we accept the principle of psychological autonomy, then it follows that the belief properties our subjects instantiate cannot be explanatory psychological properties. After running through the examples, I will reflect briefly on the implications of the argument for the belief–desire thesis.

Case 1: Self-referential beliefs[14]

Suppose, as we did earlier, that we have the technology for creating atom for atom replicas of people. Suppose, further, that a replica for me has just been created. I believe that I have tasted a bottle of Chateau d'Yquem, 1962. Were you to ask me whether I had ever tasted a d'Yquem, 1962, I would likely reply, "Yes, I have." An advocate of the belief–desire thesis would urge, plausibly enough, that my belief is among the causes of my utterance. Now if you were to ask my replica whether he had ever tasted a d'Yquem, 1962, he would likely also reply, "Yes, I have." And surely a belief–desire theorist will also count my replica's belief among the causes of *his* utterance. But the belief which is a cause of my replica's utterance must be of a different type from the one which is a cause of my utterance. For his belief is false; he has just been created and has never tasted a d'Yquem, nor any other wine. So by the premise we set out in section II, the belief property he instantiates is different from the one I instantiate. Yet since we are replicas, the autonomy principle entails that we share all our explanatory psychological properties. It follows that the property of believing that I have tasted a Chateau d'Yquem, 1962, cannot be one which plays a role in an explanatory psychological theory. In an obvious way, the example can be generalized to almost all beliefs about oneself. If we adhere to the principle of autonomy, then beliefs about ourselves can play no role in the explanation of our behavior.

Case 2: Beliefs about one's spatial and temporal location

Imagine, to vary the science fiction example, that cryogenics, the art of freezing people, has been perfected to the point at which a person can be frozen, stored, then defrosted, and at the end of the ordeal be atom for atom identical with the way he was at the beginning of the freezing process. Now suppose that I submit myself to cryogenic preservation this afternoon, and, after being frozen, I am transported to Iceland where I am stored for a century or two, then defrosted. I now believe that it is the twentieth century and that there are many strawberry farms nearby. It would be easy enough to tell stories which would incline the belief–desire theorists to say that each of these beliefs is serving as a cause of my actions. I will leave the details to the reader's imagination. On being defrosted, however, I would presumably still believe that it is the twentieth century and that there are many strawberry farms nearby. Since my current beliefs are both true and my future beliefs both false, they are not belief tokens of the same type, and do not instantiate the same belief property. But by hypothesis, I am, on defrosting, a replica of my current self. Thus the explanatory psychological properties that I instantiate cannot have changed. So the belief property I instantiate when I now believe that it is the twentieth century cannot play any role in an explanatory psychological theory. As in the previous case, the example generalizes to a large number of other beliefs involving a subject's temporal and spatial location.

Case 3: Beliefs about other people

In several papers Hilary Putnam has made interesting use of the following fanciful hypothesis.[15] Suppose that in some distant corner of the universe there is a planet very much like our own. Indeed, it is so much like our own that there is a person there who is my doppelganger. He is atom for atom identical with me and has led an entirely parallel life history. Like me, my doppelganger teaches in a philosophy department, and like me has heard a number of lectures on the subject of proper names delivered by a man called 'Saul Kripke'. However, his planet is not a complete physical replica of mine. For the philosopher called 'Saul Kripke' on that planet, though strikingly similar to the one called by the same name on our planet, was actually born in a state they call 'South Dakota', which is to the north of a state they call 'Nebraska'. By contrast, our Saul Kripke was born in Nebraska – our Nebraska, of course, not theirs. But for reasons which need not be gone into here, many people on this distant planet, including my doppelganger, hold a belief which they express by saying 'Saul Kripke was born in Nebraska'. Now I also hold a belief which I express by saying 'Saul Kripke was born in Nebraska'. However, the belief I express with those words is very different from the belief my doppelganger expresses using the same words, so different, in fact, that his belief is false while mine is true. Yet since we are doppelgangers the autonomy principle dictates that we instantiate all the same explanatory psychological properties. Thus the belief property I instantiate in virtue of believing that Saul Kripke was born in Nebraska cannot be a property invoked in an explanatory psychological theory.

Case 4: Natural kind predicates

In Putnam's doppelganger planet stories, a crucial difference between our planet and the distant one is that on our planet the substance which we call 'water', which fills our lakes, etc. is in fact H_2O, while on the other planet the substance they call 'water' which fills their lakes, etc. is in fact some complex chemical whose chemical formula we may abbreviate XYZ. Now imagine that we are in the year 1700, and that some ancestor of mine hears a story from a source he takes to be beyond reproach to the effect that when lizards are dipped in water, they dissolve. The story, let us further suppose, is false, a fact which my ancestor might discover to his dismay when attempting to dissolve a lizard. For the belief–desire theorist, the unsuccessful attempt has as one of its causes the belief that lizards dissolve in water. Now suppose that my ancestor has a doppelganger on the far off planet who is told an identical sounding story by an equally trustworthy racanteur. However, as it happens that story is true, for there are lizards that do dissolve in XYZ, though none will dissolve in H_2O. The pattern should by now be familiar. My ancestor's belief is false, his doppelganger's is true. Thus the belief tokens instantiate different belief properties. But since *ex hypothesi* the people holding the beliefs are physically identical, the belief properties they instantiate cannot function in an explanatory psychological theory.[16]

This completes my presentation of cases. Obviously, the sorts of examples we have looked at are not the only ones susceptible to the sort of arguments I have been using. But let us now reflect for a moment on just what these arguments show. To begin, we should note that they do *not* show the belief–desire thesis is false. The thesis, as I have construed it here, holds that there are psychological laws which invoke various belief and desire properties and which have a substantive role to play in the explanation of behavior. Nothing we have said here would suffice to show that there are no such laws. At best, what we have shown is that, if we accept the principle of psychological autonomy, then a large class of belief properties cannot be invoked in an explanatory psychological theory. This, in turn, entails that many intuitively sanctioned singular causal statements which specify a belief as a cause of an action cannot be straightforwardly subsumed by a law. And it is just here, I think, that our argument may serve to undermine the belief–desire thesis. For the plausibility of the thesis rests, in large measure, on the plausibility of these singular causal statements. Indeed, I think the belief–desire thesis can be profitably viewed as the speculation that these intuitively sanctioned singular causal statements can be cashed out in a serious psychological theory couched in terms of beliefs and desires. In showing that large numbers of these singular causal statements cannot be cashed out in this way, we make the speculation embodied in the belief–desire thesis appear idle and unmotivated. In the section that follows, I will consider a way in which an advocate of the belief–desire thesis might try to deflect the impact of our arguments, and indicate the burden that this escape route imposes on the belief–desire theorist.

IV A way out and its costs

Perhaps the most tempting way to contain the damage done by the arguments of the previous section is to grant the conclusions while denying their relevance to the belief–desire thesis. I imagine a critic's objection going something like this: "Granted, if we accept the autonomy principle, then certain belief properties cannot be used in explanatory theories. But this does nothing to diminish the plausibility of the belief–desire thesis, because the properties you have shown incompatible with autonomy are the *wrong kind* of belief properties. All of the examples you consider are cases of *de re* beliefs, none of them are *de dicto* beliefs. But those theorists who take seriously the idea of constructing a belief–desire psychological theory have in mind a theory invoking *de dicto* beliefs and desires.

De re beliefs are a sort of hybrid; a person has a *de re* belief if he has a suitable underlying *de dicto* belief, *and* if he is related to specific objects in a certain way. But it is only the underlying *de dicto* belief that will play a role in psychological explanation. Thus your arguments do not cast any serious doubt on the belief–desire thesis."[17]

Before assessing this attempt to protect the belief–desire thesis, a few remarks on the *de dicto/de re* distinction are in order. In the recent philosophical discussion of *de re* and *de dicto* beliefs, the focus has been on the logical relations among various sorts of belief attributions. Writers concerned with the issue have generally invoked a substitution criterion to mark the boundary between *de dicto* and *de re* belief attributions. Roughly, a belief attribution of the form

S believes that *p*

is *de re* if any name or other referring expression within *p* can be replaced with a co-designating term without risk of change of truth value; otherwise the attribution is *de dicto*.[18]

But now given this way of drawing the *de re/de dicto* distinction, my imagined critic is simply wrong in suggesting that all of the examples used in my arguments are cases of *de re* belief. Indeed, just the opposite is true; I intend all of the belief attribution in my examples to be understood in the *de dicto* sense, and all my arguments work quite as well when they are read in this way. Thus, for example, in Case 3 I attribute to myself the belief that Saul Kripke was born in Nebraska. But I intend this to be understood in such a way that

Stich believes 'ϕ' was born in Nebraska

might well be false if 'ϕ' were replaced by a term which, quite unbeknownst to me, in fact denotes Saul Kripke.

There is, however, another way the critic could press his attack that sidesteps my rejoinder. Recently, a number of writers have challenged the substitutional account of the *de dicto/de re* distinction. The basic idea underlying their challenge is that the term '*de re*' should be used for all belief attributions which intend to ascribe a "real" relation of some sort between the believer and the object of his belief. The notion of a real relation is contrasted with the sort of relation that obtains between a person and an object when the object happens to satisfy some description that the person has in mind.[19] Burge, for example, holds that "a *de dicto* belief is a belief in which the believer is related only to a completely expressed proposition (*dictum*)," in contrast to a *de re* belief which is "a belief whose correct ascription places the believer in an appropriate, *nonconceptual*, *contextual* relation to the objects the belief is about."[20] Thus, if Brown believes that the most prosperous Oriental rug dealer in Los Angeles is an Armenian, and if he believes it simply because he believes all prosperous Oriental rug dealers are Armenian, but has no idea who the man may be, then his belief is *de dicto*. By contrast, if Brown is an intimate of the gentleman, he may have the *de re* belief that the most prosperous Oriental rug dealer in Los Angeles is an Armenian. The sentence

Brown believes that the most prosperous Oriental rug dealer in Los Angeles is an Armenian.

is thus ambiguous, since it may be used either in the *de re* sense to assert that Brown and the rug dealer stand in some "appropriate, nonconceptual, contextual relation" or in the *de dicto* sense which asserts merely that Brown endorses the proposition that the most prosperous rug dealer in Los Angeles (whoever he may be) is an Armenian.

The problem with the substitutional account of the *de dicto/de re* distinction is that it classifies as *de dicto* many belief attributions which impute a "real" relation between the believer and the object of his belief. In many belief attributions the names or definite descriptions that occur in the content sentence do a sort of double duty. First, they serve the function commonly served by names and descriptions; they indicate (or refer to) an object, in this case the object to which the believer is said to be related. The names or descriptions in the content sentence *also* may serve to indicate how the believer conceives of the object, or how he might characterize it. When a name or description serving both roles is replaced by a codesignating expression which does *not* indicate how the believer conceives of the object, then the altered attribution (interpreted in the "double duty" sense) will be false. Thus the substitutional account classifies the original attribution as *de dicto*, despite its imputation of a "real" relation between believer and object.[21]

Now if the *de dicto/de re* distinction is drawn by classifying as *de re* all those belief attributions which impute a "real" relation between believer and object, then the critic conjured in the first paragraph of this section is likely right in his contention that all of my arguments invoke examples of *de re* beliefs. Indeed, the strategy of my arguments is to cite an example of a *de re* (i.e., "real relation") belief, then construct a second example in which the second believer is a physical replica of the first, but has no "real relation" to the object of the first believer's belief. However, to grant this much is not to grant that the critic has succeeded in blunting the point of my arguments.

Let me begin my rejoinder with a fussy point. The critic's contentions were two: first, that my examples all invoked *de re* belief properties; second, that *de re* belief properties are hybrids and are analyzable into *de dicto* belief properties. The fussy point is that even if both the critic's contentions are granted, the critic would not quite have met my arguments head on. The missing premise is that *de dicto* belief properties (construed now according to the "real relation" criterion) are in fact compatible with the principle of psychological autonomy. This premise may be true, but the notion of a "real" relation, on which the current account of *de dicto* belief properties depends, is sufficiently obscure that it is hard to tell. Fortunately, there is a simple way to finesse the problem. Let us introduce the term *autonomous beliefs* for those beliefs that a subject must share with all his replicas; and let us use the term *non-autonomous* for those beliefs which a subject need not share with his replica.[22] More generally, we can call any property which an organism must share with its replicas an *autonomous property*. We can now reconstrue the critic's claims as follows:

1 All the examples considered in section III invoke non-autonomous belief properties.

2 Non-autonomous belief properties are hybrids, analyzable into an underlying autonomous belief property (which can play a role in psychological explanation) plus some further relation(s) between the believer and the object of his belief.

On the first point I naturally have no quarrel, since a principal purpose of this paper is to show that a large class of belief properties are non-autonomous. On the second claim, however, I would balk, for I am skeptical that the proposed analysis can in fact be carried off. I must hasten to add that I know of *no argument* sufficient to show that the analysis is impossible. But, of course, my critic has no argument either. Behind my skepticism is the fact that no such analysis has ever been carried off. Moreover, the required analysis is considerably more demanding than the analysis of *de re* belief in terms of *de dicto* belief, when the distinction between the two is drawn by the substitutional criterion. For the class of autonomous beliefs is significantly smaller than the class of *de dicto* beliefs (characterized substitutionally).[23] And the most impressive attempts to reduce *de re* beliefs to *de dicto* plainly will not be of much help for the analysis my critic proposes.[24] But enough, I have already conceded that I cannot prove my critic's project is impossible. What I do hope to have established is that the critic's burden is the burden of the belief–desire theorist. If the reduction of non-autonomous beliefs to autonomous beliefs cannot be carried off, then there is small prospect that a psychological theory couched in terms of beliefs and desires will succeed in explaining any substantial part of human behavior.

A final point. It might be argued that, however difficult the analysis of non-autonomous beliefs to autonomous ones may be, it must be possible to carry it off. For, the argument continues, a subject's non-autonomous beliefs are determined in part by the autonomous psychological properties he instantiates and in part by his various relations to the objects of the world. Were either of these components suitably altered, the subject's non-autonomous beliefs would be altered as well. And since non-autonomous beliefs are jointly determined by autonomous psychological properties and by other relations, there must be some analysis, however complex, which specifies how this joint determination works. Now this last claim is not one I would want to challenge. I am quite prepared to grant that non-autonomous beliefs admit of some analysis in terms of autonomous psychological properties plus other relations. But what seems much more doubtful to me is that the autonomous properties invoked in the analysis would be *belief properties*. To see the reasons for my doubt, let us reflect on the picture suggested by the examples in section III. In each case we had a pair of subjects who shared all their autonomous properties though their non-autonomous beliefs differed in truth value. The difference in truth value, in turn, was rooted in a difference in reference; the beliefs were simply about different persons, places or times. In short, the beliefs represented different states of affairs. If the non-autonomous belief properties of these examples are to be analyzed into autonomous psychological properties plus various historical or external relations, then it is plausible to suppose that the autonomous psychological properties do not determine a truth value, an appropriate reference or a represented state of affairs.

So the state of exhibiting one (or more) of these autonomous properties itself has no truth value, is not referential, and does not represent anything. And this, I would urge, is more than enough reason to say that it is not a belief at all. None of this amounts to an *argument* that non-autonomous beliefs are not analyzable into autonomous ones. Those who seek such an analyis are still free to maintain that there will be at least one autonomous belief among the autonomous properties in the analysans of each non-autonomous belief property. But in the absence of an argument for this claim, I think few will find it particularly plausible. The ball is in the belief–desire theorist's court.[25,26]

APPENDIX

A bit more needs to be said about the premise urged at the end of section II. The premise, it will be recalled, was this:

> If a belief token of one subject differs in truth value from a belief token of another subject, then the tokens are not of the same type.

A number of helpful critics have pointed out to me that we actually have a variety of intuitively sanctioned ways to decide when two belief tokens are of the same type. Moreover, some of these patently violate my premise. Thus, for example, if Jones and Smith each believes that he will win the next presidential election, there would be no intuitive oddness to the claim that Jones and Smith have the same belief. Though, of course, if Jones's belief is true, Smith's belief is false. It would be equally natural in this case to say that Jones and Smith have different beliefs. So I cannot rest my premise on our intuitive judgments; the intuitions will not bear the weight.

I think the best way of defending the premise is to make clear how it is related to a certain view (actually a category of views) about what beliefs are. The views I have in mind all share two features in common:

(i) they take belief to be a relation between a believer and a type of abstract object;

(ii) they take the abstract objects to be representational – that is, the abstract objects are taken to picture the world as being a certain way, or to claim that some state of affairs obtains. Thus the object, along with the actual state of the believer's world, determines a truth value.

For example, certain theorists take belief to be a relation between a person and a proposition; a proposition, in turn, determines a truth value for every possible world – truth for those worlds in which it is true and falsity for those worlds in which it is false. A person's belief is true if the proposition is true in his or her world. Rather more old fashioned is the theory which holds belief to be a relation between a person and an image or a mental picture. The belief is true if and only if the mental picture correctly depicts the believer's world.

Now on views such as these which take belief to be a relation between a person and an abstract object, the most natural way of determining when a pair of belief tokens are of the same type is by appeal to the abstract objects. A pair of subjects' belief tokens are of the same type when the subjects are related to the same abstract object. Thus when subjects are in the same possible world, their belief tokens are of the same type only if they are identical in truth value. And this, in effect, was the premise advanced in section II. The thesis of this paper is best taken to be that the principle of psychological autonomy is in conflict with the belief–desire thesis, *when beliefs are construed as in (i) and (ii)*. Let me add a final observation. A number of theorists have taken belief to be a relation between a person and a sentence or sentence-like object. For example, in *The Language of Thought* (Crowell, 1975) Jerry Fodor holds that belief is a relation between a person and a sentence in "the language of thought." It is interesting to ask whether a theory like Fodor's is at odds with the principle of psychological autonomy. The answer, I think, turns on whether the sentences in the language of thought are taken to have truth values, and whether their referring expressions are taken to determine a referent in a given world, independent of the head in which they happen to be inscribed. If sentences in the language of thought are taken to be analogous to Quine's eternal sentences, true or false in a given world regardless of who utters them or where they may be inscribed, then Fodor's view will satisfy (i) and (ii) and will run head on into the principle of psychological autonomy. For Fodor, I suspect, this would be argument enough to show that the sentences in the language of thought are not eternal.

NOTES

1 The clearest and most detailed elaboration of this view that I know of is to be found in Goldman 1970. The view is also argued in Brandt and Kim 1963, and in Davidson 1963. However, Davidson does not advocate the belief-desire thesis as it will be construed below (cf. n. 11).

2 Cf. Putnam 1973 and 1975.

3 Kim 1978.

4 Kim's account of supervenience is intentionally non-committal on the sort of necessity invoked in the definition. Different notions of necessity will yield different, though parallel, concepts of supervenience.

5 This weaker principle is discussed at some length in Kim 1977.

6 Note, however, that physical properties that are irrelevant in this sense may nonetheless be *causally* related to those physical properties upon which psychological properties supervene. Thus they may be "psychologically relevant" in the sense that they may play a role in the explanation of how the organism comes to have some psychological property.

7 Kim 1978.

8 It has been my experience that psychologists who agree on little else readily endorse the autonomy principle. Indeed, I have yet to find a psychologist who did not take the principle to be obviously true. Some of these same psychologists also favored the sort of belief–desire explanations of action that I will later argue are at odds with the autonomy principle. None, however, was aware of the incompatibility, and a number of them vigorously resisted the contention that the incompatibility is there.

9 For a critique of these views, cf. Goldman 1970, chapter 3; Alston 1967b.

10 For discussion of these matters, see Kim 1973. Kim defends the view that the property invoked in the description must be identical with the one invoked in the law. For a much more liberal view see Davidson 1967.

11 Thus Davidson is not an advocate of the belief–desire thesis as I am construing it. For on

his view, though beliefs and desires may be among the causes of actions, the general laws supporting the causal claims are not themselves couched in terms of beliefs and desires (cf. Davidson 1970). But Davidson's view, though not without interest, is plainly idiosyncratic. Generally, philosophers who hold that beliefs and desires are among the causes of behavior also think that there are psychological laws to be found (most likely probabilistic ones) which are stated in terms of beliefs and desires. Cf., for example, Hempel 1965, pp. 463–87; Alston 1967a and 1967b; Goldman 1970, chapters 3 and 4.

We should also note that much of recent psychology can be viewed as a quest for psychological laws couched in terms of beliefs and/or desires. There is, for example, an enormous and varied literature on problem solving (cf. Newell and Simon 1972) and on informal inference (cf. Nisbett and Ross 1980) which explores the mechanisms and environmental determinants of belief formation. Also, much of the literature on motivation is concerned with uncovering the laws governing the formation and strength of desires (cf. Atkinson 1964).

12 For an attempt to explicate our informal concepts of belief and desire in some detail, see Stich (1983).

13 For more on this way of viewing states and events, cf. Kim 1969 and 1976. I think that most everything I say in this paper can be said as well, though not as briefly, without presupposing this account of states and events.

14 The examples in Case 1 and Case 2, along with my thinking on these matters, have been influenced by a pair of important papers by Castañeda 1966 and 1967.

15 Putnam 1973 and 1975.

16 We should note that this example and others invoking natural kind words work only if the extension of my ancestor's word 'water' is different from the extension of the word 'water' as used by my ancestor's doppelganger. I am inclined to agree with Putnam that the extensions are different. But the matter is controversial. For some support of Putnam's view, see Kripke 1972 and Teller 1977; for an opposing view cf. Zemach 1976. Incidentally, one critic has expressed doubt that my doppelganger and I could be physically identical if the stuff called 'water' on the far off planet is actually XYZ. Those who find the point troubling are urged to construct a parallel example using kinds of material not generally occurring within people.

17 The idea that *de dicto* beliefs are psychologically more basic is widespread. For a particularly clear example, see Armstrong 1973, pp. 25–31. Of the various attempts to analyze *de re* beliefs in terms of *de dicto* beliefs, perhaps the best known are to be found in Kaplan 1968 and Chisholm 1976.

18 The substitutional account of the *de re/de dicto* distinction has a curious consequence that has been little noted. Though most belief sentences of the form

S believes that Fa

can be used to make either *de re or de dicto* attributions, the substitutional account entails that some can only be used to make *de re* attributions. Consider, for example.

(i) Quine believes that the Queen of England is a turtle.

The claim of course, is false. Indeed, it is *so* false that it could not be used to make a *de dicto* belief attribution. For in all likelihood, there is *no* name or definite description ɸ denoting Elizabeth II such that

Quine believes that ɸ is a turtle

is true. Thus 'Quine believes that the Queen of England is a turtle' is false and cannot be turned into a truth by the replacement of 'the Queen of England' by a codesignating expression. So on the substitutional account, this sentence can be used to make only *de re* attributions. A parallel problem besets Quine's well known substitutional account of a *purely referential position* (Quine 1960, pp. 142 ff.). In (i), the position occupied by 'the Queen of England' can only be regarded as purely referential.

19 For more on the distinction between "real" relations and mere "satisfaction" relations, cf. Kim 1977.

20 Burge 1977, pp. 345 and 346; last emphasis added.

21 For more on this "double duty" view of the role of names and descriptions in content sentences, see Loar 1972.

22 Of course when the notion of a "real relation" has been suitably sharpened it might well turn out that the autonomous/non-autonomous distinction coincides with the "real relation" version of the *de dicto/de re* distinction.

23 For example, when I say, "I believe that Kripke was born in Nebraska," I am attributing to myself a belief which is substitutionally *de dicto*, but not autonomous.

24 Kaplan's strategy, for example, will be of no help, since his analysans are, for the most part, non-autonomous substitutionally *de dicto* belief sentences. Cf. Kaplan 1968 and Burge 1977, pp. 350 ff.

25 I am indebted to Robert Cummins, Jaegwon Kim, William Alston and John Bennett for their helpful comments on the topics discussed in this paper.

26 After completing this paper, I was delighted to discover a very similar view in Perry 1979. Fodor 1980 defends a version of the principle of psychological autonomy.

REFERENCES

Alston, W. P. (1967a) "Motives and motivation," *The Encyclopedia of Philosophy*, New York.

Alston, W. P. (1967b) "Wants, actions and causal explanations," in H. N. Castañeda (ed.) *Intentionality, Minds and Perception*, Detroit.

Armstrong, D. M. (1973) *Belief, Truth and Knowledge*, Cambridge.

Atkinson, J. W. (1964) *An Introduction to Motivation*, New York.

Brandt, R. B. and Kim, Jaegwon (1963) "Wants as explanations of actions," *Journal of Philosophy* LX 425–35.

Burge, T. (1977) "Belief de re," *Journal of Philosophy* LXXIV, 338–62.

Castañeda, H. N. (1966). "'He': A study in the logic of self-consciousness," *Ratio*, 8, 130–57.

Castañeda, H. N. (1967) "Indicators and quasi-indicators," *American Philosophical Quarterly* 4, 85–100.

Chisholm, R. (1976) *Person and Object*, LaSalle Ill.

Davidson, D. (1963) "Actions, reasons and causes," *Journal of Philosophy* LX, 685–700.

Davidson, D. (1967) "Causal relations," *Journal of Philosophy* LXIV, 691–703.

Davidson, D. (1970) "Mental events," in L. Foster and J. W. Swanson (eds), *Experience and Theory* Amherst, 1970.

Fodor, J. (1980) "Methodological solipsism considered as a research strategy in cognitive psychology," *Behavioral and Brain Sciences* 3, 63–73.

Goldman, A. (1970) *A Theory of Human Action*, Englewood Cliffs.

Hempel, C. G. (1965) *Aspects of Scientific Explanation*, New York.

Kaplan, D. (1968) "Quantifying in," *Synthese*, 19, 178–214.

Kim, J. (1969) "Events and their descriptions: Some considerations," in N. Rescher et al. (eds), *Essays in Honor of C. G. Hempel*, Dordrecht, Holland.

Kim, J. (1973) "Causation, nomic subsumption and the concept of event," *Journal of Philosophy*, LXX, 217–36.

Kim, J. (1976) "Events as property-exemplifications," in M. Brand and D. Walton (eds), *Action Theory*, Dordrecht, Holland.

Kim, J. (1977) "Perception and reference without causality," *Journal of Philosophy*, 74, 606–20.

Kim, J. (1978) "Supervenience and nomological incommensurables." *American Philosophical Quarterly* 15, 2, 149–56.

Kripke, S. (1972) "Naming and necessity," in D. Davidson and G. Harman (eds), *Semantics and Natural Language*, Dordrecht, Holland.

Loar, B. (1972) "Reference and propositional attitudes," *Philosophical Review*, LXXX, 43–62.

Newell, A. and Simon, H. A. (1972) *Human Problem Solving*, Englewood Cliffs.

Nisbett, R. and Ross, L. (1980) *Human Inference: Strategies and Shortcomings of Social Judgment*, Prentice-Hall.

Perry, J. (1979) "The problem of the essential indexical," *Noûs*, 13, 3–21.

Putnam, H. (1973). "Meaning and reference," *Journal of Philosophy* LXX, 699–711.

Putnam, H. (1975) "The meaning of 'meaning'," in K. Gunderson (ed.), *Language, Mind and Knowledge*, Minneapolis.

Quine, W. V. O. (1960) *Word and Object*, Cambridge.

Stich, S. (1983) *From Folk Psychology to Cognitive Science*, Bradford Books / MIT Press.

Teller, P. (1977) "Indicative introduction," *Philosophical Studies* 31, 173–95.

Zemach, E. (1976) "Putnam's theory on the reference of substance terms," *Journal of Philosophy* LXXXIII, 116–27.

An excerpt from "The Syntactic Theory of Mind," chapter 8 of *From Folk Psychology to Cognitive Science*

STEPHEN P. STICH

[In his book, Professor Stich defends the "Syntactic Theory of the Mind" ("STM" for short) against both a strong and a weak version of the Representational Theory of the Mind ("RTM"). Strong RTM maintains (Stich 1983, p. 129) "that 'serious cognitive psychology' is founded on the hope that the empirical generalizations of commonsense psychology can be systematized and made rigorous . . . [and] that the generalizations of commonsense psychology, and thus also the generalizations of cognitive science, will 'advert to the contents of mental states'." (According to Strong RTM, the generalizations of cognitive science will hold *in virtue of* the contents of psychological states.) STM denies that content (if any) will have aught to do with the generalizations of cognitive science; rather they will be stated purely in terms of the psychological states' inner "syntax" and causal profiles. Weak RTM joins STM in dropping the requirement that contents drive the generalizations, but insists in dissent that the psychological states *have* content and that their contents track their causal profiles fairly well.(WGL)]

2 The advantages of STM theories

It is my contention that STM theories are a better choice for the cognitive theorist than those theories whose generalizations appeal to content, since syntactic theories can do justice to all of the generalizations capturable by quantifying over content sentences while avoiding the limitations that the folk language of content imposes. Thus STM theories can capture generalizations which are beyond the reach of theories in the Strong RTM mold. Strong RTM theories take belief and other folk constructs seriously by generalizing over the content sentences that are used in ascribing folk psychological states. And a subject's belief counts as the belief *that p* if it is content-similar to the belief that would underlie *our own* normal assertion of '*p*'. Content-similarity, in turn, resolves into causal-pattern similarity, ideological similarity, reference similarity, and perhaps some others. Now, to put the matter most simply, *the virtue of STM theories is that they eliminate the middleman*. The mental states postulated by an STM theory are not characterized by their content sentences but, rather, by the syntactic objects to which they are mapped. These can be selected by the theorist with an eye to giving the simplest and most powerful account of the causal links among stimuli, mental states, and behavior and without any concern for similarities or dissimilarities between the subject and the theorist. By eliminating the middleman, STM theories are able to characterize the cognitive states of a subject in terms appropriate to the subject rather than in terms that force a comparison between the subject and ourselves. And this eliminates the central problem of Strong RTM theories, since there is no risk of generalizations being lost when subjects are so different from us that folk psychology is at a loss to describe them. Further, by eliminating the appeal to various dimensions of *similarity* much of the vagueness that plagues content-based cognitive theories is eliminated as well.

Let me pin down these points by working through a few examples. . . . [At this point Stich revisits several of the cases that he used in his chapter 7 to embarrass RTM.(WGL)]

3 Methodological solipsism and the autonomy principle

Let me summarize where the argument . . . has taken us thus far. The question at hand is whether the notion of belief and related folk psychological notions will find a comfortable home in cognitive science. One view that urges an affirmative answer is the Strong Representational Theory of the Mind, which sees a mature cognitive science postulating representational states and adverting to content in its generalizations. However, in chapter 7 we assembled a number of arguments aimed at showing that the cognitive scientist is ill advised to adopt the Strong RTM paradigm. The cost in vagueness and in missed generalizations is very high. In this chapter I have been arguing that there is a better alternative available. The Syntactic Theory of the Mind, by avoiding any appeal to content in cognitive generalizations, sidesteps the difficulties that beset the strong RTM. In this section I want to buttress the case in favor of the STM as an alternative to the

Strong RTM by developing a pair of arguments. Each of these arguments works by defending a principle about what psychological theories should be like. The principles, *methodological solipsism* and the *principle of autonomy*, are very closely related, and each clearly entails that cognitive psychology should not aspire to couch its generalizations in terms of content. The arguments in favor of the principles are very different, however, both in their strategy and in their plausibility. Though neither argument pretends to be apodictic, I am inclined to think that the argument to be developed for the autonomy principle is significantly more persuasive than the argument for methodological solipsism. But perhaps this is because the former argument is mine. The latter is due to Jerry Fodor. I include it here not because I think it adds much weight to the case for the STM and against the Strong RTM, but because it has been so widely discussed that no consideration of these matters can ignore it. Let me begin with methodological solipsism.

The term 'methodological solipsism' was originally introduced by Putnam (1975) to characterize a view he wished to disparage. On Putnam's account, there is a distinction between "psychological states in the wide sense" and "psychological states in the narrow sense" (p. 137). Psychological states in the narrow sense do not presuppose "the existence of any individual other than the subject to whom the state is ascribed" (p. 136). Psychological states in the wide sense do presuppose the existence of some other object or individual. Pain might be a natural example of a narrow psychological state, while being jealous of Henry is a prima facie example of a psychological state in the wide sense, since it entails the existence of Henry. (Strictly speaking, of course, it is not the state that entails Henry's existence; rather, the statement that the state obtains entails the statement that Henry exists.) The doctrine of methodological solipsism holds that psychology ought to be concerned exclusively with psychological states in the narrow sense. It is the burden of Putnam's argument that methodological solipsism is untenable since it excludes from psychology such states as knowing the meaning of a term.

Fodor, by contrast, urges that we adopt methodological solipsism as a research strategy in cognitive psychology. However, in Fodor's hands, the notion of methodological solipsism undergoes important elaboration. His central thesis is that mental states and processes, or at least those that cognitive psychology ought to concern itself with, are "computational" (1980a, p. 226). "Computational processes are both *symbolic* and *formal*. They are symbolic because they are defined over representations, and they are formal because they apply to representations in virtue of (roughly) their *syntax*" (p. 226). Further, "what makes syntactic operations a species of formal operations is that being syntactic is a way of *not* being semantic. Formal operations are the ones which are specified without reference to such semantic properties of representations as truth, reference and meaning" (p. 227). Finally, it would appear that for Fodor, methodological solipsism is simply the doctrine that *cognitive psychology ought to restrict itself to postulating formal operations on mental states*. It ought not to postulate processes which apply to mental states in virtue of their semantic properties. Fodor is quite forthright in conceding that the doctrine of methodological solipsism is less than precise, since he can provide neither a criterion nor a complete enumeration of what is to count as a semantic property.

As should be clear, methodological solipsism is thoroughly congenial to the

Syntactic Theory of the Mind. It also entails the rejection of the Strong RTM. For on any plausible account of what counts as semantic, the theorist who couches his generalizations (his account of mental processes) in terms of the *content sentences* used to characterize mental states is surely postulating mental operations whose specification requires reference to semantic properties of these states. The case is clearest, I suppose, for reference, which is a semantic notion *par excellence*. Since reference similarity is one of the features determining the propriety of a content sentence, any mental operation whose specification turns on the content sentences appropriate to the states involved will run afoul of the methodological solipsist's scruples. By contrast, cognitive theories in the STM mold are paradigm cases of the sort of theory a methodological solipsist would endorse. So it would appear that a sound argument for methodological solipsism would provide us with another reason to prefer the STM over the Strong RTM.

For our purposes the essential part of Fodor's argument is his defense of the formality condition which requires that semantic properties of mental states play no role in the specification of psychological generalizations. Unfortunately, what Fodor says on this topic is none too perspicuous. As I read him, he argues as follows. First, if a mental state has semantic properties, these are presumably fixed by one or more "organism/environment relations" (p. 244). Second, those psychologists who would flout the formality condition and reject methodological solipsism (Fodor calls them "naturalists") "propose to make science out of the organism/environment relations which (presumably) fix semantic properties" (p. 244). Third, to do this the naturalist "would have to define generalizations over mental states on the one hand and environmental entities on the other" (p. 249). But, fourth, to define such generalizations, the naturalist must have some "canonical way of referring to the latter," and this way must make the generalizations "law-instantiating" (p. 249) when the environmental entities are so described. Put in another way, the characterization of the objects on the environmental side of organism/environment interaction must be "projectable" characterizations (p. 250), which "express nomologically necessary properties" (p. 249) of the objects. As Fodor sees it, however, this last point is the kicker. For, fifth, to get such projectable or law-instantiating characterizations we must wait for appropriate developments in the science that studies that object. If the object is salt, then the appropriate projectable characterization, viz. 'NaCl', will be "available only *after* we've done our chemistry" (p. 249). But since the objects on the environment side might be anything we can think about or refer to, we will not have appropriate characterizations for these objects until all of the nonpsychological sciences have done their work. "The theory which characterizes the objects of thought is the theory of *everything*: it's all of science. Hence. . .naturalistic psychologists will inherit the Earth, but only after everybody else is finished with it." (p. 248) We ought not to attempt a naturalistic psychology, Fodor concludes, because the attempt must wait on all of the other sciences to provide projectable characterizations of the environmental objects interacting with the organism. "No doubt it's all right to have a research strategy that says 'wait awhile'. But who wants to wait *forever*?" (p. 248).

Though I would happily endorse the principle of methodological solipsism, I am a bit wary about the reasoning that supports it. If I have reconstructed Fodor's argument correctly, then there are two places in which I suspect it is open to attack. The first is step three, which claims that to "make science" out of those organism/environment relations which determine reference amounts to seeking *nomological generalizations* linking environmental entities and mental states. This is surely *one* way in which a science concerned with reference-fixing relations might proceed, and as Fodor points out it has typically been what psychologists of a naturalistic bent have sought (1980b, p. 102). But, as best I can see, there is no necessity for those who would make science of the organism/environment interactions which underlie reference to do so by seeking causal laws. There are, after all, many quite respectable scientific domains, from descriptive botany, ethology, and paleobiology to anthropology and linguistics, in which the quest for nomological generalizations plays a relatively minor role. Focusing on the case at hand, it is certainly true, as the second step of Fodor's argument suggests, that if a psychologist couches his cognitive generalizations in terms of the content sentences appropriate to various states, then his theory will in one way or another *involve* those organism/environment relations which contribute to determining the propriety of content sentences. But without further argument, it is not at all clear that the psychologist who pursues the Strong RTM strategy must seek *nomological generalizations about* those reference and content determining organism/ environment relations.

The second spot where I fear Fodor's argument is vulnerable is step five, which claims that appropriate projectable characterizations of the objects on the environment side of organism/environment interactions will be forthcoming only from the sciences that study these objects. There is a strong suggestion in Fodor's essay that physics and chemistry are the appropriate sciences to look to for natural kinds like salt and water, and he expresses some puzzlement about "which science does uncles and umbrellas and undertakers" (p. 103). Now perhaps Fodor has better antennae than I do for these delicate matters, but without further argument I am not convinced that such commonsense predicates as 'salt', 'uncle', and 'undertaker' are not perfectly respectable candidates for incorporation in nomological generalizations. They are, no doubt, not the ideal projectable predicates to be used in the generalizations of physics and chemistry. But those of us who take the special sciences seriously have come to expect that the classificatory schemes invoked in those sciences will cut across the classificatory grain imposed by physics. Physics and chemistry, presumably, will have no generalizations invoking 'uncle' or 'umbrella', but anthropology and economics might well find these terms rather more useful. Ironically, Fodor himself has been an eloquent defender of the scientific respectability of classificatory schemes which do not reduce smoothly to those of the physical sciences (see Fodor 1974).

Despite all this, I am a bit reluctant simply to dismiss Fodor's argument for methodological solipsism. Perhaps the argument can be fleshed out in a way which makes clear why the cognitive psychologist who would use folk psychological notions must seek the sorts of generalizations required by step three. And perhaps something more can be said to establish that workaday predicates like 'salt' and 'umbrella' are not suitable for formulating organism/environment generalizations. But absent these elaborations, I am not inclined to rest much weight on the argument.

Let me turn, now, to the principle of autonomy. The basic idea of the principle is that the states and processes that ought to be of concern to the psychologist are those that supervene on the current, internal, physical state of the organism. (One class of states and processes supevenes on another when, roughly speaking, the presence or absence of states and processes in the first class is completely determined by the presence or absence of states and processes in the second. For a less rough-and-ready account of supervenience, see Kim 1978, 1982.) What this amounts to is the claim that any differences between organisms which do not manifest themselves as differences in their current, internal, physical states ought to be ignored by a psychological theory. If we respect the autonomy principle, then the fact that a pair of organisms have different histories or that they are in significantly different environments will be irrelevant to a psychological theory except in so far as these differences make a difference to the organism's current, internal, physical state. Or, to put the matter the other way around, historical and environmental facts will be psychologically relevant only when they influence an organism's current, internal, physical state. So if a feature of the organism's history or environment might have been different without affecting the organism's current, internal, physical state, then that historical or environmental feature must play no role in the psychologist's theory.

Like methodological solipsism, the autonomy principle is incompatible with the explanatory strategy urged in the Strong RTM. The autonomy principle prohibits generalizations couched in terms of the content sentences that characterize mental states, since the propriety of a content sentence in characterizing a mental state is in part determined by reference similarity. Reference in turn is determined in part by the distant causal histories of a subject's term or concept and in part by the socio-linguistic environment in which the subject is embedded. But neither of these factors need leave their trace on the current, internal, physical state of the organism. Thus it is possible for a pair of subjects to differ in the reference of some term they use even though there is no corresponding difference in their current, internal, physical state. The formality condition urged by the methodological solipsist directly prohibits generalizations which turn on semantic properties of the states to which they apply. The principle of pyschological autonomy accomplishes much the same goal by barring appeal to those external historical and environmental factors on which semantic properties like reference in part depend.

In Stich (1978, this volume, this part) I offered no argument in defense of the autonomy principle, since it seemed to have substantial intuitive plausibility. But in subsequent discussion it has become clear that the intuitive appeal of the autonomy principle begins to pale when people see just what it entails about the use of folk psychological notions in scientific psychology. So plainly some argument is in order. I think the best defense of the autonomy principle begins with what might be called the *replacement argument*. Suppose that someone were to succeed in building an exact physical replica of me – a living human body whose current internal physical states at a given moment were identical to mine at that moment. And suppose further that while fast asleep I am kidnapped and replaced by the replica. It would appear that if the crime were properly concealed, no one (apart from the kidnappers and myself) would be the wiser. For the replica, being an exact physical copy, would behave just as I would in all circumstances. Even the replica himself would not suspect that he was an imposter. But now, the argument continues, since psychology is the science which aspires to explain behavior, any states or processes or properties which are not shared by Stich and his identically behaving replica must surely be irrelevant to psychology.

I think there is an important kernel of truth in the replacement argument. But as it stands, it plainly will not do. The problem is that in many circumstances my replica and I do not (indeed could not) behave in the same way, at least not as our behavior would ordinarily be described. An example will serve to make the point. One of my possessions is an old clunker of a car. If you were to offer me $1000 for it, I would delightedly sell it to you on the spot. But suppose that just prior to your offer I had been kidnapped and my replica sent out into the world in my place. Being quite unaware of the switch you offer the $1000 to my replica, and he agrees to the sale with the same sincere delight that I would exhibit. When it comes down to actually transferring ownership, however, my replica's behavior and mine diverge. He signs all the appropriate documents just as I would, and the signatures would convince a handwriting expert. None the less, my replica does not sell you the old clunker. He can't, since he does not own it. I do. So it would appear to be just plain false that my replica and I would behave identically. I would sell you the car, and he wouldn't.

Now I think the right move to make in response to this objection is to grant the point. If we are willing to countenance the full range of commonsense descriptions of behavior, then it is false that a person and his replica will always behave identically. However, we should not expect a psychological theory to predict or explain behavior under any and every description countenanced by common sense. To see this more clearly, an analogy with chemistry is useful. It may be quite true that boiling a bottle of Chateau Lafitte causes a substantial reduction in its market value. But this is nothing that we expect chemistry alone to explain. Rather, we expect chemistry to explain the effects of boiling described in an appropriately delimited, proprietary chemical vocabulary. Moreover, there is not likely to be any antecendently obvious specification of the range of descriptions appropriate in chemical explananda. Elaborating or delimiting the language in which explananda are to be described is one aspect and often quite a fundamental aspect of theory construction in science (Shapere 1982). To explain why boiling causes a decline in the market value of Chateau Lafitte we will have to supplement the chemical explanation of the effects of boiling with facts about the way chemical changes affect the sensory qualities of a wine and facts about the relation between sensory qualities and the market value of rare Bordeaux wines. The situation is similar in psychology. We cannot expect that a scientific psychology will explain behavioral events under all imaginable descriptions. Rather the psychologist must select or formulate an appropriate descriptive language for his explananda. And the formulation of such a vocabulary will be a fundamental part of psychological theory construction.[1]

Now where does this leave the autonomy principle? Well, the replacement argument maintained that an organism and its replica would behave identically and should be regarded as psychologically identical. But we then granted that an organism and its replica will not behave identically on some characterizations of behavior. Let me introduce the term *autonomous behavioral description* for any description of behavior which satisfies the following condition: if it applies to an organism in a given setting, then it would also apply to any replica of the organism in that setting. It would appear, then, that the issue before us reduces to the question of whether autonomous behavioral descriptions include all those that a psychologist will find useful in constructing systematic explanations of behavior. If the answer is affirmative, then the replacement argument leads to the desired conclusion, since replicas will behave identically in identical settings, when the behavior is described in the psychologists' proprietary behavioral–descriptive language. So let us ask whether there is any reason to think that autonomous behavioral descriptions include all those that a psychologist will find useful.

In thinking about this question it is helpful to reflect on the analogy between organisms and industrial robots. Both robots and organisms are complex, largely internally controlled systems which interact with their environments in systematic ways. Unless one is tempted by dualism, it is plausible to think that theories explaining the behavior of various sorts of robots and theories explaining the behavior of various sorts of organisms will be at least roughly analogous. So let us ask whether we would expect a theory of "robot psychology" to attempt explanations of robot behavior under non-autonomous descriptions. As a beginning, we should note that there are many ways in which the doings of a robot might be described in non-autonomous language. For example, a given robot on the production line at General Motors might, on a certain occasion, successfully perform its millionth weld. Although 'performing its millionth weld' might be a correct description of what the robot does, it is clearly not an autonomous description. If, just prior to performing the weld, the robot in question had been replaced by a brand new replica robot, the replica would have performed a qualitatively identical weld. But it would be successfully performing its first weld, not its millionth. In performing a weld, a robot might also be falsifying Professor Hubert's prediction that no robot would ever perform a million welds, and simultaneously fulfilling a provision in the contract between General Motors and the robot's manufacturer. But again, neither of these descriptions of the robot's behavior is autonomous. It seems obvious that if we seek systematic generalizations to explain the robot's behavior, we should not expect our generalizations to explain the robot's behavior under *these* descriptions. The descriptions under which we expect a theory of robot behavior to explain that behavior are autonomous descriptions.

This is not to suggest that there is anything mysterious about the fact that the older robot performed its millionth weld, or that it falsified Professor Hubert's prediction, or that it fulfilled the contract. What it does suggest is that these facts and the descriptions which recount them are best viewed as logical or conceptual hybrids. To successfully perform its one millionth weld, a device must successfully perform a weld *and* it must have previously performed 999,999 other welds. The first element in this conjunct describes the behavior autonomously; it is just the sort of fact that we expect a theory of robot behavior to explain. The second element is a historical fact, and it is not at all what we expect a theory of robot behavior to explain. An analogous account can be given of the fact that the robot fulfilled a provision of the contract. Here again we have a conceptual hybrid, with one element being the occurrence of an autonomously described behavioral event and the other being the existence of a contract containing certain provisions about what the robot will or must do. If we are seeking a set of generalizations to explain robot behavior, it would be perverse to expect them to explain the latter fact or the hybrid into which it enters.

The view suggested by these examples is that all non-autonomous descriptions of robot behavior are conceptually complex hybrids. An explanation of the behavior they describe would naturally divide into two parts, the first being a theory of "robot psychology" which explains autonomously described behavioral events and the second being a heterogeneous collection of considerations from history, law, or what have you which collectively explain why the autonomously described event *counts* also as an event falling under the non-autonomous description. Now if the analogy between robots and organisms is a good one – and I think it is – it suggests that we should seek a parallel pattern of explanation in real psychology (as contrasted with "robot psychology"). We should expect to have our theory aim at explaining behavioral events autonomously described. Non-autonomous descriptions of behavioral events should be viewed as conceptually complex, resolvable into an autonomous component and a potpourri of other factors which explain why the autonomously described event *counts* as satisfying the non-autonomous description. Of course the other factors that enter into the analysis of non-autonomous behavioral descriptions will be rather richer and more complex when the subjects of our theory are people instead of animals or industrial robots. They may include the history of the individual in question, the history of the terms he uses, the linguistic, social, legal, and ritual practices that obtain in the society of which he is a part, and perhaps many other factors as well. So if our analogy is a good one, it is plausible to conclude that the descriptions of behavior that a psychological theory should use in its explananda will be autonomous descriptions. This is just the conclusion we needed to make a go of the replacement argument and thus to support the principle of autonomy.

On the view I have been urging, non-autonomous commonsense descriptions of behavior are typically conceptual hybrids. Sometimes there will be a readily available commonsense description of the autonomous component of a non-autonomous act. But this need not always be the case. It may be that substantial work needs to be done in forging appropriate autonomous behavioral descriptions for use in scientific psychology (see Alston 1974). But this should come as no surprise, for, as we remarked earlier, the formulation of an appropriate terminology for describing the explananda is often an essential step in the growth of a new science. Note by the way, that there is no reason to expect that the autonomous behavior-descriptive terminology ultimately found to be most useful will be a purely physical description of movements of the sort that behaviorists sought but never found.

In evolving hybrid non-autonomous behavioral descriptions, common sense produces behavioral descriptions that are more fine grained than those that would be available if we restricted ourselves to autonomous descriptions. There is nothing unreasonable about this, since often enough our practical concerns demand some more fine grained description of behavior. But if I am right, then these practical concerns lead to a taxonomy of behavior which is ill suited to a systematic science aimed at explaining behavior. Folk psychology has followed the commonsense strategy by evolving a set of hybrid descriptions for *mental states* which build in various historical, contextual, and comparative features of the organism. Thus . . . the folk notion of believing that *p* is an amalgam of historical, contextual, ideological, and perhaps other considerations. No doubt this way of slicing the mental pie proved itself to be efficient and useful in the day-to-day business of dealing with other people. Had it not, it surely would not have survived. The thrust of the autonomy principle, however, is that by building historical, contextual, and ideological features into mental state descriptions, folk psychology has taxonomized states too narrowly, drawing distinctions which are unnecessary and cumbersome when we are seeking a systematic causal explanation of behavior. To believe that *p* is to be in an autonomous functional state *and* to have a certain history, context, and ideological relation to the ascriber. These further factors can surely be studied by various disciplines. But they have no place in a science aimed at explaining behavior. By slicing the pie too finely, they impede the formulation of those generalizations which apply equally to an organism and its replica.

The Strong RTM would have us couch our cognitive generalizations in the hybrid language of content ascription. The Syntactic Theory of the Mind, on the other hand, requires purely formal generalizations which ignore those historical and environmental factors that may distinguish an organism from its replica in the eyes of folk psychology. If the argument for the autonomy principle is persuasive, then the STM strategy is the one to be preferred.

NOTES

1 Fodor gets this point just exactly right:

> It's worth emphasizing that the sense of "behavior" *is proprietary*, and that is pretty much what you would expect. Not every true description of an act can be such that a theory of the mental causation of behavior will explain the act under that description. ... You can't have explanations of everything under every description, and it's a question for empirical determination which descriptions of behavior reveal its systematicity vis-à-vis its causes. (Fodor 1980a, pp. 330–1; cf. Shapere 1982)

Wilkes makes essentially the same point:

> Every science must devise a taxonomy of the events that fall within its domain of discourse, and hence has to devise a descriptive vocabulary of observational and theoretical predicates. Since events can be variously described, not every description of an action or a capacity for action will be a description in the domain of psychology. (Wilkes 1981, p. 150)

REFERENCES

Alston, W. P. (1974) "Conceptual prolegomena to a psychological theory of intentional action," in S. C. Brown (ed.), *Philosophy of Psychology*, Harper & Row.
Fodor, J. A. (1974) "Special sciences," *Synthese* 28, 97–115.
Fodor, J. A. (1980a) "Methodological solipsism considered as a research strategy in cognitive psychology," *Behavioral and Brain Sciences* 3, 63–73. Reprinted in *Representations* (Bradford Books / MIT Press, 1981); page references are to the latter.
Fodor, J. A. (1980b) "Methodological solipsism: Replies to commentators," *Behavioral and Brain Sciences* 3, 99–108.

Kim, J. (1978) "Supervenience and nomological incommensurables," *American Philosophical Quarterly* 15, 149–56.

Kim, J. (1982) "Psychological supervenience," *Philosophical Studies* 41, 51–70.

Putnam, H. (1975) "The meaning of 'meaning'," in K. Gunderson (ed.), *Minnesota Studies in the Philosophy of Science, vol. 7: Language, Mind and Knowledge*, University of Minnesota Press.

Shapere, D. (1982) "The concept of observation in science and philosophy," *Philosophy of Science* 49, 485–525.

Stich, S. P. (1983) *From Folk Psychology to Cognitive Science*, Bradford Books / MIT Press.

Wilkes, K. (1981) "Functionalism, psychology and the philosophy of mind," *Philosophical Topics* 12, 147–67.

A Narrow Representational Theory of the Mind

MICHAEL DEVITT

1 Introduction

Cognitive science contains two sharply different lines of thought about thought. We might call them "the Folk Line" and "the Revisionist Line".

The general inspiration for the Folk Line is folk theory or, less pretentiously, folk opinion about the mind. More particularly, the inspiration is the folk view that people have thoughts with rich representational and semantic properties; in particular, people have mental states with truth-conditional content. Cognitive psychology must explain the interaction of thoughts with each other and the world by laws that advert to these semantic properties: psychology must be "wide."[1] Many who have joined in the debate follow the Folk Line. I suspect that many others do also. In my view, it has been most persuasively argued by Tyler Burge (1986).

The general inspiration for the Revisionist Line is the functionalist theory of the mind. More particularly, the inspiration is the arguments for "methodological solipsism" and autonomous psychology, and the analogy between the mind and a computer. Revisionists frequently hold that cognitive psychology must explain the interaction of mental states with each other and the world by laws that advert only to formal or syntactic properties, not to truth-conditional ones. They hold sometimes that the semantics for psychology must be functional-(conceptual-)role semantics; psychology must be "narrow."[2]

It might seem appropriate for the Revisionists to take their disagreement with the Folk further: mental states do not have truth-conditional contents at all. For,

"A Narrow Representational Theory of the Mind" by M. Devitt is printed here by kind permission of the author.

if we do not need those contents for psychology, there seems no principled reason for supposing that mental states have them. Some Revisionists have taken this position, or at least toyed with it. Some have suggested that there are nonpsychological reasons for believing in truth conditions. Finally, some have simply assumed that mental states have truth conditions without confronting the question of why we should think they have.

My main concern is not with these variations but rather with the Revisionist Line on psychology. However, I will make some passing remarks that bear on them.

Stephen Stich's "Syntactic Theory of the Mind" ("STM"; see Stich (this volume, this part)) seems to be a clear example of the Revisionist Line:

> cognitive states. . .can be systematically mapped to abstract syntactic objects in such a way that causal interactions among cognitive states, as well as causal links with stimuli and behavioral events, can be described in terms of the syntactic properties and relations of the abstract objects to which the cognitive states are mapped. (1983, p. 149)

> The substantive and empirically exacting part of the theory consists in a set of generalizations which detail causal interactions among stimuli, B- and D-states [STM analogues of beliefs and desires], and behavioral events by appeal to the syntactic structure of the wffs to which they are mapped. (1983, p. 154)

A similar view has been urged by Hartry Field (1978, pp. 100–2) and Stephen Schiffer (1981, pp. 214–15).

It is natural to take many writings of Jerry Fodor and Zenon Pylyshyn as powerful defences of the Revisionist Line. Fodor urges the "formality condition" which is definitive of "the computational theory of the mind" ("CTM"):

> mental processes have access only to formal (nonsemantic) properties of the mental representations over which they are defined (1980a, p. 63).

Pylyshyn endorses this condition (1980a, pp. 111–15; 1980b, pp. 158–61). He believes that "cognition *is* a type of computation" (1984, p. xiii). Since CTM is about mental processes, it seems to be about the lawlike generalizations of psychology: it seems to agree with Stich that these laws may advert only to syntactic properties. CTM has been taken this way by friend and foe alike.[3] However, this is not the way Fodor and Pylyshyn take it. They think that psychological laws will advert to full truth-conditional contents. This leads Stich to accuse Fodor of trying to "have it both ways" (1983, p. 188): the intentional talk of folk psychology on the one hand, and the formality condition on the other. Fodor thinks that he can have it both ways because CTM is concerned with a different level from that of the laws: the level of their implementation (1987, pp. 139–40, 166n). CTM certainly does suggest a claim about a level of physical implementation, as we shall see (section 2). However, it is largely concerned with a psychological level, which Fodor thinks of as between the physical and the folk-psychological. I think that this *is* an attempt to have it both ways, but I shall not argue that here.[4] My interest is in CTM construed as a doctrine like STM that is

revisionist about the laws of psychology; an example of the Revisionist Line.
I think that there is a great deal of confusion in the debate between the Folk
and the Revisionist. When properly understood, methodological solipsism and the
computer analogy do support a position that diverges from the Folk Line.
However, the position may not be revisionist or eliminativist at all, and if it is, it is
not disturbingly so. As a result, it is not open to the criticisms that Burge and
others have aimed at the Revisionist Line. My diagnosis of most of the confusion
and error in this debate is: too little attention to inputs (stimuli) and outputs
(behavior).

I shall briefly describe a theory of the mind that ascribes a meaning or content
to mental states that is not truth-conditional and hence is less than the Folk Line
requires (section 4). However, the meaning is proto-truth-conditional and so is
more than the Revisionist Line usually seems to allow. What is crucial about this
meaning for my argument is that it goes beyond syntax: it includes links to
sensory inputs. Whilst acknowledging the force of methodological solipsism and
the computer analogy (section 3), I shall argue that we need to ascribe this much
meaning for psychology (section 5). I shall then argue that this much meaning is
sufficient for psychology (section 6).

The theory is a narrow representational theory of the mind, a narrow RTM.
There have been signs of it elsewhere.[5] However, it has not been adquately
distinguished from others, and hence its significance for the debate between
Revisionist and Folk has not been brought out.

2 'Syntactic' and 'Formal'

What precisely is the Revisionist Line? Much of the confusion in the debate
comes from the absence of a clear answer to this question. I have described the
Line as the view that psychology adverts only to the formal or syntactic properties
of a representation; or, that it adverts only to the narrow properties of a
functional-(conceptual-)role semantics not the wide ones of a truth-conditional
semantics. Sometimes the properties needed for psychology are described as
"nonsemantic" (for example by Fodor above). Sometimes psychology is said to
treat representations as "meaningless" (Field 1978, p. 101) or "uninterpreted"
(Schiffer 1981, pp. 214–15). These various descriptions reflect a jumble of
different ideas that are best kept distinct.

I want to define a Revisionist doctrine using the term 'syntactic'. I am anxious
to diminish the confusion and so I shall start by trying to be very clear about what
I mean by that term. I think that my meaning is the standard one – outside this
debate at least – and hence that the doctrines I define are appropriate ways to
understand the most frequent statements of the Revisionist Line.

'Syntactic' is often treated in this debate as if it were a near-synonym of
'formal'. This is appropriate enough given the use of 'formal' in logic. However, it
is worth noting that there is an ordinary use of 'formal' which would make the
treatment quite inappropriate.

In this ordinary sense, formal properties are fairly "brute-physical" ones that
are *intrinsic* to a symbol; for example, the shape of a letter, the pattern of on–off
switches in a computer, or the array of neurons in the brain. If 'formal' had the

brute-physical sense in statements of CTM,[6] then there would be a straightforward way to understand CTM as concerned with a different level from folk psychology, a level of the physical realization of psychological states (cf. section 1 above). CTM would then be a physicalist doctrine (a false one if the arguments of this paper are sound). However, it would not be concerned with a psychological level, which is contrary to what Fodor and Pylyshyn claim for it and to the way it has been universally taken.

'Syntax' refers to properties that are quite different from the above brute-physical ones. It refers to properties a symbol has in virtue of its role in relation to other symbols in the language. These properties are the ones that bear on the construction of some symbols out of others. They are studied in the field known as "Syntax" (Chomsky 1957, p. 11). They are functional and *extrinsic* to the symbol.[7] Being a name, [8] being a one-place predicate, and being a sentence, are examples of such properties.[9]

I shall bring out my meaning of 'syntactic' by likening it to the logicians' technical use of 'formal'. This use arises from the notions of a *formal language* and a *formal system*. It is very different from the above "ordinary" use.

A *formal system* is like a game in which tokens are manipulated according to rules, in order to see what configurations can be obtained. (Haugeland 1985, p. 48)

Chess is a good example of such a system. In a realization of the system, a token of any type – for example, a pawn or a bishop – is, of course, a physical entity of a certain form in the above ordinary sense. It is usually important that tokens of each type differ in their brute-physical properties from those of any other type but, beyond that, it does not matter what form the tokens have in the ordinary sense. So far as the system is concerned, all that matters about a token is its role in the system. To be a token of a particular type is simply to be covered in a certain way by the rules. So a pawn is a pawn, however it is physically realized, because it plays the role of a pawn in the game. It is common to call types or properties, like *being a pawn*, "formal." Such properties abstract from the brute-physical properties of any realization of the system; that is, from the formal properties in the earlier ordinary sense. They are functional, structural, or relational properties. Note finally that nothing outside the system has any bearing on these properties. In particular, meaning is irrelevant to them.

The contrast between this sort of formal property and the earlier sort might be brought out as follows. Properties of the earlier sort characterize the "shape" of *an object*; they are intrinsic to the object. Properties of the present sort characterize the "shape" of *a structure of objects*; they are intrinsic to the structure but not to any object.

Some formal systems are or contain languages. Such a language consists of a set of basic symbols classified into various types – for example names, variables, one-place predicates, a conjunction symbol – together with *formation* rules for combining symbols of various types to form other symbols (such as sentences). The system containing the language also includes *transformation* rules for moving from some symbols to others as in an inference. Properties like *being a name* are just like *being a pawn*: they are functional. They are properties that a token has not in virtue of its brute-physical make-up but in virtue of its role in the system. So what matters to *being a conjunction symbol* is not whether a token looks like '&' or '.', but that it is governed by certain rules. Such properties of tokens in a formal language are also commonly called "formal".[10] And, of course, any meaning a token may have is irrelevant to its having one of these properties.[11]

It is important to note a feature of this sort of system that distinguishes it from chess: it is concerned with sameness and difference of types *within the basic types*. Thus it matters to the transformation rules not only whether a token is a name but also whether it is a token of the *same name* type as, or of a *different name* type from, another token. Consider, for example, the transformation rule *modus ponens*, which we might express:

Given both a conditional and its antecedent, derive its consequent.

What is meant by "its antecedent"? It means, of course, a token of the same type as that of the token that is the antecedent of the conditional. But it means this not merely in the sense that the token must also be a sentence. The token has to be a token of the *same* sentence type as the token antecedent; that is, it has to have the same structure and have tokens of the same name type, predicate type, etc., occupying that structure. For example, if the conditional is a token of 'Fa→Fb', then what is referred to by 'its antecedent' is a token of 'Fa'. So *relations of sameness and difference* of sentence type, name type, predicate type, etc., are also formal relations of the system. However – and this is especially important in what follows – the *properties of being a certain* sentence type, *being a certain* name type, *being a certain* predicate type, etc., are not formal properties, because such properties play no role in the system.

Of course, a token may *be* of a certain sentence type, name type, etc.; for example, it may be of the name type that refers to Reagan. But this property is irrelevant to the system and so is not a formal property. Word meaning is semantic not formal. A token may also be of a certain shape type; for example, it may be shaped like 'a'. But this property is relevant only to the realization of the system and so is not a formal property in this technical sense; it is a formal property in the ordinary sense.

The formal properties of symbols in a formal language, in the technical sense, are clearly just like the earlier-described syntactic properties of symbols in a natural language; and formal relations are just like syntactic relations. Indeed, formal properties and relations are often called "syntactic", most notably by Carnap (1937).[12] These are the properties and relations I shall be referring to by 'syntactic'.

In sum, a symbol has its syntactic properties and relations solely in virtue of its relations to others in a system of symbols; it has them solely in virtue of the system's *internal* relations.

3 Arguments for the Revisionist Line

I take it that my remarks about 'syntactic' and 'formal' are standard and hence that there is nothing eccentric about my use of 'syntactic'. So it is appropriate to take the many statements of Revisionism using 'syntactic' and 'formal' to be aptly captured by the following doctrine (with 'syntactic' understood as above):

SYNTACTIC PSYCHOLOGY: The laws of mental processes advert only to the syntactic properties of representations.

Further, I think that it is because Revisionism has been understood as SYNTACTIC PSYCHOLOGY that it has seemed so *excitingly* radical to its proponents and so *dangerously* radical to its opponents.

Do the arguments offered for Revisionism support SYNTACTIC PSYCHOLOGY? These arguments are familiar and so I shall be brief in my description of them.

The argument from the computer analogy It is argued that we should take the computer analogy seriously and so see thought processes as computational. Now computational processes are defined syntactically; they are "syntactic operations over symbolic expressions" (Pylyshyn 1980a, p. 113); they are "both *symbolic* and *formal*" (Fodor 1980a, p. 64). So we should see thought processes as defined syntactically. A typical example of a law that satisfies this requirement might be one for *modus ponens* inferences:

Whenever a person believes both a conditional and its antecedent, she tends to infer its consequent.

This law is, of course, reminiscent of the rule *modus ponens* for a formal system discussed in the last section. We saw then that all the properties and relations adverted to in such rules are syntactic.

This may seem to be an argument for SYNTACTIC PSYCHOLOGY. However, it is an argument only if we overlook a vital distinction: the distinction between thought processes and mental processes in general. The mental processes that concern (cognitive) psychology come in three sorts, as our initial quotes from Stich brought out (Section 1):

(i)   processes from thoughts to thoughts;
(ii) processes from sensory inputs to thoughts;
(iii) processes from thoughts to behavioral outputs.

What I have been calling "thought processes" are mental processes of sort (i): inferential processes. Computation is indeed a good analogy for those and so provides a good reason for taking them as syntactic. But since the literature provides no reason to believe that a computer's input and output processes are analogous to (ii) and (iii), we have been given no reason to believe that (ii) and (iii) are syntactic. The argument from the computer analogy supports not SYNTACTIC PSYCHOLOGY but rather the much more modest

SYNTACTIC THOUGHT PROCESSES: The laws of thought processes advert only to the syntactic properties of representations.

The argument has no bearing on whether the laws of mental processes in general have to advert to semantic properties or contents.

Not only is there no argument for the more extensive computer analogy required to support SYNTACTIC PSYCHOLOGY, that analogy seems very unlikely. The problem is that computers do not have transducers anything like those of humans and do not produce behavior in anything like the way humans do. Computers move from symbolic input via symbolic manipulation (computation) to symbolic output. Humans, in contrast, move from largely nonsymbolic sensory stimulation via symbolic manipulation (thinking) to largely nonsymbolic action. Any interpretation a computer's symbols have, *we* give them. However, it is plausible to suppose that a human's symbols have a particular interpretation in virtue of their perceptual causes, whatever we theorists may do or think about them. Furthermore, it is because of those links to sensory input that a symbol has its distinctive role in causing action. I shall be arguing for this later (section 5).

Participants in the debate about the mind are strangely uninterested in the distinction between thought processes and mental processes in general. The problem is not that they are unaware of the distinction: typically discussions will start with what amounts to an acknowledgement of the distinction – as, for example, in the quotes from Stich. The problem is that from then on all processes except thought processes tend to be ignored. Thought processes are treated as if they were representative of them all. Fodor is particularly striking in this respect. He begins his discussion of CTM by distinguishing the three sorts of process (1987, p. 12). Yet a few pages later, in a passage important enough to be displayed, he describes "the nature of mental processes" in a way that applies only to thought processes.[13] Despite this, there is every sign that he takes CTM to cover all mental processes (see, for example, 1987, p. 139).[14]

The argument from methodological solipsism and psychological autonomy In psychology, we are concerned to explain why, given stimuli at her sense organs, a person evinced certain behavior. Only something that is entirely supervenient on what is inside her skin – on her intrinsic internal physical states, particularly her brain – could play the required explanatory role between peripheral input and output. Environmental causes of her stimuli and effects of her behavior are beside the psychological point. The person and all her physical, even functional, duplicates must be psychologically the same, whatever their environments. Mental states must be individuated according to their role within the individual, without regard to their relations to an environment. All of this counts against the Folk view that a thought's property of having a wide meaning, or truth conditions, is relevant to psychology. For that property is *not* supervenient on what is inside the person's skin. It *does* depend on relations to the environment because it depends on referential links. And Putnam's Twin-Earth discussion has brought out that duplicates may *not* share wide meanings; that is the point of the slogan, "meanings just ain't in the head" (1975, p. 227).[15] Psychology should advert only to meanings that are determined by what is in the head, or, at least, inside the skin; it should advert only to narrow meaning.

This argument is open to question, as we shall see (section 6). For the moment, assume that it is good. Then it establishes that truth-conditional properties are irrelevant to psychology. The point to be made now is that the argument does *not* establish SYNTACTIC PSYCHOLOGY. Let us take for granted that syntactic properties are relevant to psychology. The argument does not establish that *only* syntactic properties are relevant. To establish that we need the further premise that there are no other non-truth-conditional properties that are relevant.

To my knowledge, *no argument for this premise has ever been given.* I shall argue that the premise is false (section 5).

Similarly, the argument from methodological solipsism does not establish that only "nonsemantic" properties are relevant, nor that representations are "meaningless" or "uninterpreted" so far as psychology is concerned, unless 'nonsemantic', 'meaningless', and 'uninterpreted', simply *mean* non-truth-conditional. I am as enthusiastic as anyone about truth-conditional semantics, but surely the question whether it is the *right* semantics is an empirical one, not something to be settled by definition.

Though the Revisionist Line is most frequently urged using 'syntactic' and 'formal' it is sometimes urged, often in the same breath, as a case for functional-(conceptual-)role, or narrow meaning (or content), in psychology.[16] Yet this version of the Line is very different from SYNTACTIC PSYCHOLOGY as we shall see (section 4). Briefly, syntax involves only the relations between representations, whereas functional-role meaning also involves the relations between representations and stimuli. Syntactic roles are not the only functional roles that go into narrow meaning.

In so far as the argument from methodological solipsism is good, I think that it does support the case for functional-role semantics.[17] The narrow RTM I shall be urging proposes such a semantics for psychology. For proto-truth-conditional meaning is a type of functional-role meaning and does supervene on what is inside the skin; so it is a type of narrow meaning.

Now it may be that when Revisionists talk of "syntactic" or "formal" properties, they mean to refer to some sort of narrow meaning (or content). This is certainly suggested sometimes by the company the talk keeps. If this is what is meant, my only objection to the talk is that it is very misleading, for reasons to be brought out (section 4). However, understood in this way, Revisionism does not seem nearly so radical. Indeed, I shall argue that the proper form of it is hardly radical at all (section 6).

In sum, the argument from the computer analogy establishes SYNTACTIC THOUGHT PROCESSES but not SYNTACTIC PSYCHOLOGY. The argument from methodological solipsism may establish the irrelevance of truth-conditional properties to psychology but it does not establish that only syntactic ones are relevant. So it does not establish SYNTACTIC PSYCHOLOGY either. I shall argue that SYNTACTIC PSYCHOLOGY is false (section 5).

4   Narrow psychology

According to the narrow RTM that I shall urge, the meaning (or content) that must be ascribed for the purposes of psychology can be abstracted from wide truth-conditional meaning. So first I need to consider the nature of that meaning. In so doing, I will draw on the semantics described and (partly) explained in *Language and Reality*.[18] However, many of the details of that semantics are irrelevant to our present concerns.

The initial idea is that the core of the meaning of a sentence – whether a public one or a mental sentence in thought – is its property of having certain truth conditions. We need to explain that property. The most plausible explanation is in terms of the syntactic structure of the sentence and the referential properties of its parts. We must then explain syntax and reference. Syntax is a matter of functional role (section 2). But how are we to explain reference? I think that three sorts of theory are possible and that very likely each sort has some application.

Description theories are one sort. They were once popular, for proper names but are more plausible for terms like 'bachelor' and 'pediatrician'. According to a description theory, the reference of a term is determined by the reference of certain other terms with which it is associated by speakers. Though such a theory may well be true of some terms it could not be true of all terms, for it is *essentially incomplete* as an explanation of reference. It explains the reference of one term by appealing to the reference of others. How then is the reference of those other terms to be explained? Perhaps, we can use description theories again. This process cannot, however, go on for ever: there must be some terms whose referential properties are not parasitic on those of others. Otherwise, language as a whole is cut loose from the world. Description theories pass the referential buck. But the buck must stop somewhere.

In the light of Twin Earth and Putnam's slogan, it seems plausible to suppose that the referential buck stops with terms covered by "pure-causal" theories of reference. Pure-causal theories seem to be suggested for natural-kind terms and names by Putnam (1975), Saul Kripke (1980), and Keith Donnellan (1972). According to such a theory, the reference of a term is determined by direct causal links to external reality.

The third sort of theory of reference is a mixture of the other two, a "descriptive-causal" theory. In my view, it is the most plausible theory for proper names and natural-kind terms. According to it, the reference of a term is determined partly by direct causal links to external reality and partly by the reference of certain other terms with which it is associated by speakers.

How does word meaning relate to reference? For Frege a word's *meaning* was (roughly) a "mode of presentation" of its referent (1952, p. 57). I think Frege was right about that but not about the nature of the mode. We should identify a word's meaning with the sort of mechanism that, according to our theories of reference, explains its reference.[19] This mechanism may include descriptive associations. It must include causal links to reality, for the reference of any term is determined either by its own direct causal links, or by those of terms on which it referentially depends.

The truth-conditional meaning explained in this way is clearly wide, for it partly depends on causal links that are "outside the skin." If we abstract from those outside links, we are left with "proto-truth-conditional" meaning. This meaning is narrow in that it is entirely supervenient on the intrinsic inner states of the thinker. It is the inner, functional-role *part* of wide meaning. It is what I shall mean in future by "narrow meaning."

Narrow meaning (or content) is very rich. Not only does it include all the functional roles that determine the syntactic structure of sentences, but also the inner functional roles that partly determine the reference of words.[20] The latter roles are what is left of wide word meaning when the extra-cranial links are subtracted. The roles constitute narrow word meanings. Those meanings are functions taking external causes of peripheral stimuli as arguments to yield wide (referential) meanings as values.[21] *Narrow word meaning is (mostly) not a matter of syntax.* That is crucial to distinguishing my narrow RTM from SYNTACTIC PSYCHOLOGY.

Consider a term that is covered by a pure-causal theory. Its reference depends on its direct causal link to external reality. If we abstract from the part of that link that is external to the subject, we are left with the functional-role connections between peripheral stimuli and the term. This inner link is not negligible; it is the inner processing that must take place if a representation is to take referential advantage of the causal action of the world on the subject. The link, together with the term's syntactic category, determines the term's narrow meaning.

A pure-causal term's narrow meaning involves much more than its syntactic properties. Terms have their syntactic properties solely in virtue of their relations to other terms *within* the symbol system (section 2). Pure-causal terms have their narrow semantic properties largely in virtue of their relations to stimuli, which are *outside* the system. It is in virtue of these relations to stimuli that a token has the non-syntactic property of *being a certain* term type within a syntactic category. Thus, consider the terms 'echidna' and 'platypus', which are clearly in the same category, and suppose that they are pure-causal terms (which I doubt). There is a relation of difference between them that is syntactic (section 2). However, what makes something an 'echidna' token, and not a 'platypus' token, is that it is linked to echidna-ish stimuli. That is what gives the term the narrow meaning of 'echidna' in particular. These links to stimuli are not in any way syntactic.

The same applies to part of the narrow meaning of a descriptive-causal term. For that part of its meaning is determined in the same way as the meaning of a pure-causal term. The other part of its narrow meaning depends on associations with other terms just as does all of the narrow meaning of a term covered by a description theory. At first sight, these meanings may seem to be syntactic. For the association of a term with other terms is plausibly seen as a syntactic relation. However, that association is only the first step in determining the term's reference. It simply passes the referential buck to the other terms. If the buck is to stop, the explanation must ultimately be of terms relying for their reference, fully or partly, on direct causal links to external reality. These links, as I have just noted, are not syntactic. So to the extent that the narrow meaning of a descriptive, or descriptive-causal, term is dependent on these links, that link is not syntactic.

Every part of the narrow meaning of every term involves functional-role links between the term and peripheral stimuli. Narrow word meaning is largely determined by relations that are not syntactic.

The theory I have been sketching differs from almost all others in not being holist. It is not holist in two respects. (i) It does not subscribe to the main tenet of holism: the meaning of any term depends on the meaning of every term. According to description and descriptive-causal theories, the meaning of a term does depend on others, but not on all others. This departure from holism requires an argument. I shall not give the argument, because the departure has no significance for this paper. I make the departure only because I think that the main tenet is, despite its popularity, implausible, underargued, and destructive of cognitive psychology.

(ii) The theory is not holist about the links between language and the world, and language and stimuli. The meanings of pure-causal and descriptive-causal terms depend immediately on causal links to particular parts of reality via particular stimuli. This aspect of a term's meaning, narrow and wide, is almost entirely independent of the meaning of any other term and so yields a striking departure from holism. I think that this departure is significant to this paper. However, I shall not argue for it because the contrary view is wildly implausible and, so far as I know, completely unsupported. For the contrary view is that the world contributes unselectively to meaning, so that echidna sightings have no more to do with the meaning of 'echidna' than with the meanings of 'oyster', 'elephant', 'telephone', 'pediatrician', and 'Alpha Centauri'.[22]

In sum, a truth-conditional theory of wide meaning (or content) must include an explanation of a sentence's property of having certain truth conditions. This explanation will justify the ascription of a narrow functional-role meaning (or content) to the sentence: we simply abstract from the extra-cranial links referred to in the explanation. Narrow sentence meaning depends on narrow word meaning, and that is mostly not a matter of syntax.

The narrow RTM that I urge claims that narrow meaning is all that is required for psychology (I take narrow meaning, and also wide meaning, to include syntactic properties on the ground that syntactic properties partly constitute them):

NARROW PSYCHOLOGY: The laws of mental processes advert only to the narrow semantic properties of representations.

This doctrine, unlike SYNTACTIC PSYCHOLOGY, allows psychological laws to advert to narrow word meanings as well as the syntactic properties of sentences.

The contrast between this doctrine and the Folk Line can be brought out neatly by the following statement of that Line:

WIDE PSYCHOLOGY: The laws of mental processes advert to the wide semantic properties of representations.

In the last section I indicated that Revisionists sometimes seem to have a doctrine like NARROW PSYCHOLOGY in mind in their talk of "syntactic" and "formal" properties. If so, their talk shows a Humpty-Dumptyish contempt for the conventions of language (and even Humpty Dumpty *told us* what he meant by 'glory'). Narrow word meanings cannot be captured syntactically, in any ordinary sense of that term. Nor are they like the formal properties of symbols in a formal system.[23] However, in so far as Revisionists are urging NARROW PSYCHOLOGY, I have no quarrel with them.

This section began with a semantics that ascribes truth-conditional contents to sentences, yet it ends by claiming that we do not need such contents for psychology. In introducing the Revisionist Line (section 1), I pointed out that such a claim raises a question: what *do* we need those contents for? This question is not so pressing for NARROW PSYCHOLOGY as for SYNTACTIC PSYCHOLOGY, because the former unlike the latter comes so close to truth-conditional content (as Hartry Field has pointed out to me).[24] Nevertheless, it would be nice to have an answer to the question. I think we have. We need truth-conditional content for *linguistics*.[25] Folk are interested in sentences not only to explain behavior but also to learn about the world (Field 1972, pp. 370–1). What properties do sentences have that make them thus interesting? They have truth-conditional content (Devitt and Sterelny 1987, pp. 169–71).

5 The necessity of narrow meaning

I shall argue for NARROW PSYCHOLOGY in two steps. First, in this section, I shall argue that psychological laws must advert to narrow semantic properties *at least*. This is an argument against SYNTACTIC PSYCHOLOGY. In the next section, I shall argue that psychological laws must advert to narrow semantic properties at *most*. This is an argument against WIDE PSYCHOLOGY.

It is important to see that the disagreement with SYNTACTIC PSYCHOLOGY is not a boring verbal one over whether we should *call* the further properties that may be required for psychology "semantic," "meanings," or "contents." I do so, because I can see no reason for not doing so, but nothing hinges on that. The disagreement is over whether the further properties are required, whatever they are called.

Psychology seeks laws covering the three types of mental processes:

(i)   processes from thoughts to thoughts;
(ii) processes from sensory inputs to thoughts;
(iii) processes from thoughts to behavioral outputs.

According to SYNTACTIC PSYCHOLOGY, all these laws advert only to syntactic properties. I agree about the laws for (i), and so I agree with SYNTACTIC THOUGHT PROCESSES. I disagree about the laws for (ii) and (iii).

SYNTACTIC PSYCHOLOGY differs from SYNTACTIC THOUGHT PROCESSES in being too sweeping: it covers mental processes that are not thought processes. It differs from NARROW PSYCHOLOGY in being too restrictive about psychological laws: it does not allow them to advert to narrow meanings.

Laws for (ii) have to explain the fact that a particular sensory stimulus affects some thoughts and not others; for example, it may lead to certain beliefs being formed and others dropped, but leave the vast majority of beliefs unchanged. Suppose that the stimulus is the sight of Ron riding and that the only effect of this is the formation of the belief 'F*a*'. How could that formation possibly be explained if we follow SYNTACTIC PSYCHOLOGY and ascribe to 'F*a*' only syntactic properties like being a one-place predicate, and syntactic relations like being different from 'F*b*', 'G*a*', 'G*b*', etc.? Why should the stimulus lead to 'F*a*' rather than any of these other beliefs, each of which is also a one-place predication and different from the others? A stimulus has a distinctive role in thought formation (which is not to say, of course, that a stimulus is ever sufficient – irrespective of other thoughts – for the formation of a thought). Syntax alone cannot explain that distinctive role.

WIDE PSYCHOLOGY has an explanation. Mental sentences don't have just syntax, they have wide meaning. 'F*a*' means that Ron is riding, whereas, say, 'F*b*' means that Maggie is riding, 'G*a*' means that Ron is kicking, and 'G*b*' means that Maggie is kicking. With the help of these properties of the mental sentences, we have some hope of finding the required laws. These laws will build on the idea that experience of Ron tends to affect thoughts that refer to Ron and not Maggie; that experience of riding tends to affect thoughts that refer to riding not kicking; and so on.

According to NARROW PSYCHOLOGY, we do not need this recourse to wide meaning to get our laws. However, we do need a recourse to the narrow part of this meaning. Talk of the syntax of the mental sentences is quite inadequate because syntax does not include links to sensory stimuli. By adverting to the links of 'Ron' and 'riding' to stimuli, we can hope to find laws about the roles of those sorts of stimuli in affecting thoughts containing the terms.[26]

A similar story holds for laws for (iii). These must explain the fact that a thought led to certain behavior and not others. Suppose that the behavior is the opening of a gate in the path of the mounted Ron, and that the belief that led to this is 'F*a*'. How could the role of this belief possibly be explained if we ascribe to it only syntactic properties? Why should that belief lead to this behavior rather than clearing Maggie's vicinity of kickable objects, or whatever? A thought has a distinctive role in producing behavior (which is not to say, of course, that a thought is ever sufficient – irrespective of other thoughts – for a piece of behavior.) Syntax alone cannot explain that distinctive role.

WIDE PSYCHOLOGY'S explanation is that 'F*a*' means that Ron is riding and not, for example, that Maggie is kicking. We have some hope then of finding laws that build on the idea that thoughts about Ron tend to lead to behavior that affects Ron and not Maggie; that thoughts about riding tend to lead to behavior that affects riding and not kicking. NARROW PSYCHOLOGY does not go that far. The narrow meaning of each term in a mental sentence includes links to certain sorts of stimuli. As a result, we can hope to find laws about the role of thoughts containing the term in bringing about certain sorts of behavior.

It may be objected that this criticism of SYNTACTIC PSYCHOLOGY rests on an unargued assumption that laws for (ii) and (iii) must advert to the *composition* of mental sentences; briefly, it assumes that the laws must be compositional. For it assumes that the way to supply what SYNTACTIC PSYCHOLOGY is alleged to miss is to include the links of *words* to stimuli. So differences between beliefs are to be explained partly in terms of syntax and partly in terms of word meaning. Yet if the laws for (ii) and (iii) need advert only to the input and output links of mental sentences *as a whole*, then it is not obvious that SYNTACTIC PSYCHOLOGY misses anything.

In discussing an objection by Patricia Churchland, Stich gives the following examples (1983, pp. 178–9) of the sorts of laws for (ii) and (iii) that his STM might contemplate:[27]

(12) For all subjects S, when an elephant comes into view, S will typically come to have a sequence of symbols, E, in his B-store.

(14) For all subjects S, if S has D-state R (i.e., if S has the sequence of symbols R in his D-store), and if S has no stronger incompatible D-states, then S will raise his arm.

So the response to my criticism might be that the only laws for (ii) and (iii) that we need are along these lines. Yet these do not advert to the composition of symbol sequences, nor indeed to any semantic property of the sequences.

(12) and (14) are certainly not the only laws that we *need*; they are not at the right theoretical level. This is indicated by the fact that psychology would require indefinitely many such laws to cope with the indefinitely many possible stimuli for, and behavioral outcomes of, beliefs. At best, (12) and (14) are low-level laws that are *applications* of higher level laws for (ii) and (iii) that we need.

Aside from that, the import of these laws is unclear. How are the symbol sequences E and R to be specified? They can't be specified by their "shape" (specified formally, in the ordinary sense; section 2), for that would take us outside psychology. (Futher, any shape can realize any symbol.) Merely specifying the syntactic properties and relations of the sequences will not do. For example, it will not be sufficient to say only that E has the syntactic properties and relations of 'There is an elephant in front of me'. Those properties and relations are insufficient to distinguish E appropriately from many other symbol sequences brought about by quite different stimuli; for example, the sequence T referred to in

(12)* For all subjects S, when a tiger is on top of S, S will typically come to have a sequence of symbols, T, in his B-store.

The differences between E and T are psychologically very significant, for E and T will lead to quite different behavior. We must say what the differences are. Very likely they have identical syntactic structures. They will still, of course, differ syntactically: they are different sentence types. But this difference clearly won't explain the differences in what E and T dispose S to do. For that we need to say what sentence type E is and what one T is; we need accounts of their natures. And those natures are not a matter of syntax (section 2). Could we not say simply that E is linked to the elephant input and T to the tiger input? So (12) and (12)* are explanatory of the very natures of E and T. I think that this is what we would have to say.

If we do say this we are abandoning the strict letter of SYNTACTIC PSYCHOLOGY, because we are assigning nonsyntactic properties to mental sentences for psychological purposes. On my usage, these properties constituted by links to input are meanings or contents of the mental states. So (12) determines that E as a whole has a certain meaning.

Despite this, if we could find the laws of which (12) and (14) are applications, and those laws were adequate for our theoretical purposes, then SYNTACTIC PSYCHOLOGY would seem only a little bit wrong. A desperately crude attempt at the law for (12) might be as follows:[28]

For all subjects S, sequences of symbols Q, input types I, if the meaning of Q depends on I and S is presented with instance of I, then S will typically come to have Q in his B-store.

The meanings of sentences adverted to in this law are nothing more than are explained in the applications of the law. The meanings are not, as it were, something additional to the applications. So they might seem hardly worth mentioning. It is only when we see that laws for (ii) and (iii) have to advert to the meanings of parts of the sentences, meanings explained to a degree independently of the applications, that we see how badly wrong SYNTACTIC PSYCHOLOGY is. To see this we must show that the laws are compositional.

Note first that *according to* SYNTACTIC PSYCHOLOGY laws for (i) are compositional: they advert to the syntactic structure of thoughts. There is something paradoxical about the view that the "meaning" that accrues to a thought in virtue of its syntax is compositional, but that what accrues to it in virtue of its links to stimuli is not. There is something paradoxical about the view that laws for (i) are compositional, but laws for (ii) and (iii) are not. This apparent paradox indicates which way we should go.

Consider laws for (iii). The distinctive potential role of each thought in producing behavior must depend on the thought's causal relation to particular sorts of stimuli. E's role differs from T's because it is linked to elephantish stimuli not tigerish ones. This example suggest the following simple account of the dependency on stimuli: a thought linked to a certain sort of stimulus tends to produce a certain sort of behavior. This account is far too simple. Such a mental state would be a mere input–output function of the sort dear to behaviorist hearts. There would be no basis for ascribing even a syntax to it and no point in calling it a thought at all. A thought is something that *interacts with other thoughts* in inferences. Its causal relation to stimuli – hence its distinctive potential for behavior – must be partly via its relation to other thoughts in its history. But how can a thought pass on to another a link to stimuli? It cannot pass on all its links. That would lead to the following: belief B1 is linked to input I1; B2 to I2; B3 is inferred from B1 and B2 and so is linked to I1 and I2. Yet consider this example:

All police officers are corrupt

Dee Dee is a police officer

So, Dee Dee is corrupt.

The distinctive role of the belief that Dee Dee is corrupt is determined by the links of *parts of* each premise to stimuli. The links of each premise to police officers is beside the point. In some cases, a belief that plays a role in an inference contributes no stimulus to the distinctive role of the conclusion:

All A are B

All B are C

All C are D

So, all A are D

It seems clear that thoughts pass on their links to stimuli *at the level of their terms*.

I take it then that in considering what beliefs are likely to cause what behavior – laws for (iii) – we have to advert to the links of the terms in the beliefs to stimuli. These laws must be compositional.

The case for the compositionality of laws for (ii) is harder. These laws cover noninferential belief formations. My picture is as follows. Each term in a mental sentence, either directly, or indirectly via its association with other terms, has links to certain sorts of stimuli as part of its meaning. The way the term is linked depends on which theory of reference covers it (section 4). The link will be direct if it is a pure-causal term. It will be partly direct, and partly indirect via its association with other terms, if it is a descriptive-causal term. It will be entirely indirect if it is a descriptive term. For terms that are causal or descriptive-causal, and thus have direct links to stimuli, we can hope to find laws about the roles of those sorts of stimuli in affecting thoughts containing those sorts of term. The laws will capture the idea that stimulus from Ron tends to affect beliefs containing a term with a certain sort of narrow meaning; and stimulus from someone riding tends to affect beliefs containing a term with another sort of meaning. So the laws will capture the idea that the combination of stimuli provided by Ron riding will tend to produce the narrow belief that we would ordinarily describe widely as the belief that Ron is riding.

A desperately crude example of what we might hope for as a law for (ii) is as follows:

> For all subjects S, names N, descriptive-causal one-place predicates P, input types I1 and I2, if the meaning of N depends on I1 and that of P on I2, and S is presented with instances of I1 and I2 together, then S will typically come to stand in the believing relation to a sentence with N as subject and P as predicate.

This is the compositional alternative to the earlier similarly crude noncompositional law.

A difficulty in producing a more convincing rejection of the possibility of noncompositional laws for (ii) is that the same causal interactions that have a role in belief formation are likely to be having a role in determining the meaning of a term. Perhaps the strongest case for the compositionality of laws for (ii) comes from the fact that they have to be unified with the compositional laws for (i) and (iii).

Stich, in his response to Churchland, is comforted by his doubts that there are any satisfactory laws for (ii) and (iii) to be found (above the level of (12) and (14) perhaps). His doubts arise from his prediction that the laws will collapse into vacuity; the terms to which they will apply will be defined as the ones to which they apply (1983, pp. 180–1). But there is no more danger of vacuity here than anywhere in science. Our theory of tigers does not become vacuous because, in some sense, tigers are "defined" as what the theory applies to. In any case, if we cannot find satisfactory laws, that would not save SYNTACTIC PSYCHOLOGY. Rather, it would destroy cognitive psychology altogether.

I conclude my case against SYNTACTIC PSYCHOLOGY by considering some remarks of Pylyshyn. He gives the example of Mary running out of a smoke-filled building. Why did she run out? WIDE PSYCHOLOGY has an answer, central to which is the attribution to Mary of the belief that the building is on fire. She might have come by this belief in various ways: by hearing the utterance, "the building is on fire"; by hearing the fire alarm; by smelling smoke; indeed, by experiencing any event interpretable (given the appropriate beliefs) as entailing that the building is on fire. Pylyshyn argues against Stich's STM that leaving Mary's mental sentences

as uninterpreted formal symbols begs the question of why these particular expressions should arise under what would seem (in the absence of interpretation) like a very strange collection of diverse circumstances, as well as the question of why these symbols should lead to building-evacuation behavior as opposed to something else. (1980b, p. 161)

Pylshyn's second question about building-evacuation behavior is just the same as mine about laws for (iii). His first question about belief formation is different but related to mine about laws for (ii).

Stich's response to Pylyshyn is striking. He dismisses Pylyshyn's attempted answers as vacuous, but *makes no attempt to offer nonvacuous answers himself* (1983, p. 176). Yet Pylyshyn's questions are very good ones that demand answers. What I have been arguing is that it is impossible for SYNTACTIC PSYCHOLOGY to provide answers.

We are a very long way from having plausible candidate laws for (ii) and (iii), as the crudity of the laws proposed above indicates. So we cannot expect anyone to provide detailed answers to Pylyshyn's questions. Pylyshyn thinks that the answers must be sought by appealing to the truth-conditional interpretations of the symbols. I think that we achieve the desired level of generality by appealing to less.

I have already indicated how NARROW PSYCHOLOGY offers the hope that we can arrive at laws for (iii) by making use of the links to stimuli that partly constitute word meaning. Such laws would answer Pylyshyn's second question. Consider now Pylyshyn's first question about the several paths to the one thought. Laws for (ii) alone might go a long way to answer this. To take a crude example, suppose that the meaning of 'fire' is tied to both the sight of flames and the smell of smoke. Then we might hope for laws predicting beliefs involving 'fire', sometimes the same belief, from the sight of flames and from the smell of smoke. But, of course, the variety of paths becomes much richer when we take account of the fact that a thought can be inferred from other thoughts. The meaning of any term in those other thoughts is also linked to certain stimuli. We can then hope for laws for (ii) explaining the formation of one of these thoughts following stimuli. With the help of laws for (i), we can explain how that thought joined with others to lead by inference to the original thought. Thus we open up the possibility of indefinitely many paths from stimuli to the one thought.

In sum, we need narrow meaning, at least, to have a hope of coming up with the laws for (ii) and (iii). We need it also to answer Pylyshyn's questions. SYNTACTIC PSYCHOLOGY is not only unargued (section 3) but also false.

6 The sufficiency of narrow meaning

We have completed the first step of my argument for NARROW PSYCHOLOGY: psychology needs narrow meaning *at least*. The next step is to argue that psychology needs narrow meaning *at most*. This conclusion differs from WIDE PSYCHOLOGY. It may also differ from folk psychology. However, I doubt this and so doubt that NARROW PSYCHOLOGY is revisionist or eliminativist. And if it is, it is not disturbingly so. So, part of my aim in arguing for NARROW PSYCHOLOGY is to make it seem moderate.

WIDE PSYCHOLOGY holds that psychological laws must advert to wide semantic properties. The argument against this has already been given: the argument from methodological solipsism and psychological autonomy (section 3). The key to this argument is the claim that the states we need to posit for psychological explanation must supervene on the intrinsic internal physical states of the organism; roughly, on the brain. Burge points out that many seem to think that this claim is implied by the following principles:

> events in the external world causally affect the mental events of a subject only by affecting the subject's bodily surfaces; . . . nothing (not excluding mental events) causally affects behavior except by affecting (causing or being a causal antecedent of causes of) local states of the subject's body. (1986, p. 15)

Yet the claim does not follow from these principles of local causation. For these principles are quite compatible with mental states being *individuated* in terms of their relations to the environment (pp. 16–17). States that are so individuated do not supervene on the brain alone: they partly supervene on the brain's external relations.

Burge gives some nice examples of relational individuation: continents in geology; lungs in biology. Indeed, relational individuation serves many explanatory purposes. It pervades the social sciences: someone is a capitalist in virtue of her economic relations. Think also of the parts of a car: something is an accelerator partly in virtue of its relations to the engine. Closer to home, think of syntactic properties: something is a conjunction symbol in virtue of its role within a language (section 2). In general, relational individuation is to be found wherever functional/structural explanations are appropriate. Such explanations do not go against principles of local causation like those above.

So I agree with Burge's objection. What then is left of the argument from methodological solipsism? Though the argument may often appear to rest on the mistaken inference above, I do not think that it really does. It is possible to draw boundaries anywhere and to look for explanations of the characteristics and peripheral behavior of the bounded entity or system in terms of what goes on within the boundary. I think that underlying the argument is the strong conviction that a scientifically appropriate boundary for explaining the behavior of an organism is its skin. It is by stopping at that point that we shall get the appropriate laws. I share this conviction.

Of course, if the argument against WIDE PSYCHOLOGY is understood in this way, it does not look very conclusive: the proof of the pudding seems to lie very much in the eating. But such is life.

Opposition to WIDE PSYCHOLOGY usually raises objections that start from the following questions:

1 How is narrow content to be ascribed in a psychological explanation?
2 How is behavior to be described so that it is open to psychological explanation?

Question (2) is particularly pressing given what I have just conceded to Burge. If behavior is described in ways that refer to things outside the skin, as it is by the folk, then it will have to be explained by mental states that refer to such things also.[29] The appropriate boundary for psychology will not be the skin. It is convenient to set these questions aside for a moment.

I shall try to support the above-mentioned conviction by describing NARROW PSYCHOLOGY in more detail. I shall be particularly concerned to show how little, if at all, NARROW PSYCHOLOGY is revisionist. I see this as strong support for NARROW PSYCHOLOGY, for conservatism is a theoretical virtue.[30]

Cognitive psychology seems to be concerned with mental states that purport to represent a world which is external to the mind and toward which the organisms's behavior is directed. It is of the essence of those mental states – thoughts – that they do purport to represent a world. The Revisionist Line has usually seemed to deny this, and SYNTACTIC PSYCHOLOGY certainly does deny it. This is an important factor in making Revisionism seem so implausible to many. However, NARROW PSYCHOLOGY does not deny the importance of representation. It simply claims that psychology does not care *which* entities the organism, as a result of its external links to the environment, is actually representing; indeed, it does not care whether there really are such entities. What matters is only how the world seems from the point of view of the organism. The nature of a mental state is indeed "outward-looking". It just does not matter to psychology which world, if any, the state actually "sees".

WIDE PSYCHOLOGY is inspired by folk psychology. Yet it is not *obvious* that the latter is WIDE. The main reason for concluding that it *is* WIDE is that ordinary ascription of thought, which is the folk way of explaining behavior, always seems to take account of reference. So it is part of the truth conditions of an ascription, whether it is construed transparently or opaquely, that the thinker's representation refers to the objects and properties picked out by the content sentence of the ascription. In brief, the folk taxonomize thoughts widely. This reason is rather far from sufficient for the conclusion.

The first problem is that though an ordinary thought ascription may be a psychological *explanation*, it is not a psychological *law*. And WIDE PSYCHOLOGY is about laws. It is hard to be confident where folk stand on psychological laws, for they seem not to talk or think much about them.

The second problem is that it is unclear how much of the ascribed content the folk take to be psychological. Folk ascribe thoughts not only for psychological purposes but also to learn about the world (section 4). This dual purpose raises the possibility that the folk do not regard all the content they ascribe as relevant to the explanation of behavior. Futher, an explanation of behavior is always of an organism in a particular natural and social context. Perhaps the folk find it convenient to bring some of these contextual features into the explanation even though they do not regard them as *psychologically* relevant; they might be regarded as sociologically relevant, for example. So, thought ascriptions may be several-ways hybrid. To discover which parts the folk think are psychological, we would need to know which parts fall under folk psychological laws. That brings us back to the first problem. In sum, the folk taxonomy of thoughts is not merely psychological. And there is no simple way to read off folk psychology from the nature of thought ascriptions.

In so far as we have any evidence of the nature of folk psychological laws – which is not very far – I suggest that it favours the view that the folk are for

NARROW rather than for WIDE PSYCHOLOGY.

Consider thoughts involving demonstratives and pronouns (briefly, "demonstratives"). Suppose that Raelene reaches for her gun. To explain this behavior we ascribe to her the belief that that is a man with a knife who means her no good. This ascription seems to require that Raelene have a thought about the man indicated, and so seems to be wide. What law do folk think the explanation comes under? If the folk have any law in mind, it is unlikely that the law is wide, so far as the demonstrative is concerned. Thus, suppose Gail reaches for her gun in a similar situation to Raelene, but one involving a different man. To explain Gail's behavior, we ascribe to her the belief that that is a man with a knife who means her no good. Then surely the folk would regard this belief as the same as Raelene's for the purpose of psychological explanation (thus using a narrow taxonomy for beliefs instead of the above-noted transparent and opaque taxonomies exemplified in thought ascriptions). They would think that even the lowest level laws that cover Raelene's belief will also cover Gail's; the different references of 'that' are psychologically irrelevant. The laws will be concerned only with the functional-role properties of 'that' which remain constant as the external links of the organism to the environment change; in that respect, the laws will be narrow. Indeed, if Raelene and Gail were alike in the other relevant respects, the folk would think that the explanations of their behaviors were the same.

In sum, if folk have psychological laws for demonstrative thoughts, it is likely that the laws, so far as the demonstratives are concerned, are narrow. In any case, I take it as obvious that the law should be thus narrow. Where does WIDE PSYCHOLOGY stand on this? It would be uncharitable to suppose that it disagrees. When people urge the importance of wide meaning to psychology, we should not suppose that they intend to include demonstratives. They do not think that the laws for these advert to the extra-cranial links, varying from context to context, that determine a demonstrative's reference.

The folk, WIDE and NARROW PSYCHOLOGY may agree on demonstratives, but they do not on proper names. Suppose that the Englishmen Jeremy and Nigel have functionally identical thoughts about different Australian philosophers called 'Bruce'. To avoid assuming that the two philosophers look alike, let us suppose that Jeremy and Nigel have not met the philosophers but have gained their names by reference borrowing. According to NAROW PSYCHOLOGY, the lowest level psychological laws covering Jeremy's thought will also cover Nigel's. For the laws will advert only to the narrow meanings they share. According to WIDE PSYCHOLOGY, in contrast, the lowest level laws for Jeremy and Nigel must differ because the laws advert to wide meanings that depend on reference and the thoughts of Jeremy and Nigel differ in reference. Where do the folk stand? Once again it is hard to say. However, the evidence surely shows them leaning toward NARROW PSYCHOLOGY, because it seems as if they would count Jeremy's and Nigel's beliefs the same for the purposes of explaining and predicting relevant behavior (a narrow taxonomy again); for example, in explaining or predicting their remarks about "Bruce" whilst having cocktails; or their actions when finally meeting an Australian philosopher called 'Bruce'.

Whatever the case with the folk, the claim that the reference of 'Bruce' is irrelevant to psychological explanation is very plausible.

We have gone quite a way in our discussion of NARROW PSYCHOLOGY and revisionism – we have covered the many parts of thought involving demonstratives and names – without resorting to fantasies about Twin Earth or brains in a vat. There is nothing fantastic about Raelene, Gail, Jeremy and Nigel.[31] However, if we want to go further, covering natural-kind terms for example, we have to resort to these fantasies. For these terms do not, as a matter of ordinary fact, normally vary in reference with changes in context without concomitant changes in their inner functional role. We need the fantasies to show that reference is irrelevant to their psychological role. Whether this conclusion is contrary to folk wisdom is again unclear, for in so far as the folk have constructed psychological laws they have not been worried about fantasies. What would they say if we were to worry them? My guess is that they would come down on the side of NARROW PSYCHOLOGY.

It is common to argue against wide meaning in psychology by noting that we want the one explanation to cover all functional duplicates; to cover, for example, Oscar, Twin Oscar, and brain-in-the-vat Oscar. This may seem a rather uninteresting demand since there probably are no functional duplicates. However, what we really want is that the explanation should cover all organisms that are functionally alike *in the respects relevant to the explanation*. Thus, Raelene and Gail may be relevantly alike in the above situation even though otherwise quite different. Similarly, Jeremy and Nigel.

On the matter of laws, I have suggested that there may be nothing revisionist about NARROW PSYCHOLOGY at all. If I am wrong about this, and the folk are committed to wide psychological laws, I hope to have shown that the revisionism of NARROW PSYCHOLOGY is not in any way shocking: the folk would be only a little bit wrong.

On the matter of explanations, NARROW PSYCHOLOGY claims that, for the purposes of psychology, these need not advert to the referential properties of thoughts. This does not mean that the folk are wrong to advert to these properties in their thought ascriptions. There is more to life than psychology. There is nothing wrong with hybrid ascriptions.

It is time to return to the two questions we set aside that are prompted by opposition to WIDE PSYCHOLOGY. The first was:

1 How is narrow content to be ascribed in a psychological explanation?

Behind this question usually lies an objection along the following lines. "Our language is truth-conditional. So we are unable to express any narrow contents in our language. If we cannot express them, we cannot ascribe them. So narrow contents are indescribable and useless for explaining behavior." Despite its apparent popularity, this objection has little force, in my view.

As it stands, the objection must be faulty. A scientific proposal should not be rejected on the ground that we do not already have the linguistic resources to put it into effect. Consider, for example, such a response to Einstein's proposal of the Theory of Relativity. Language must adapt to science, not constrain it. If there is any force to the objection it is this: the linguistic changes required by the proposal for psychology are so radical as to cast grave doubt on the wisdom of the proposal.

The changes are not radical. We already have linguistic devices for ascribing wide content; for example.

Raelene believes that that is a man with a knife who means her no good.

This ascription makes the referential properties of each part of the appropriate thought relevant to the truth of the ascription. If we want to ascribe only narrow content – the content relevant to psychology – we need to bracket off the links outside the skin that go into determining those referential properties. This we can easily do. Let '*' be such a bracketing device, exemplified in the following ascription:

Raelene believes* that that is a man with a knife who means her no good.

The '*' indicates that only the narrow meaning of the content clause is relevant to the ascription. It is not obvious that we also need to be able to *express* narrow content, but if we do, the same device will serve.

A protest can be expected "We don't understand these *ascriptions." I think we understand them as well, or as badly, as we understand ordinary ascriptions.

If I am right in my earlier claim that the folk sometimes use a narrow taxonomy of thoughts, they have *already* caught on to the idea that *ascriptions rest on. In any case, it would be easy to *teach someone to use* *ascriptions with the help of ideas like those mentioned in this discussion. Thus, it is easy to grasp that the truth of the *ascription to Raelene does not depend on her representing the particular person picked out by the speaker's 'that'; we are abstracting from that. It is sufficient that she be representing someone demonstratively; or even that it be for her as if she is. In this respect, we already understand or could easily come to understand *ascriptions.

In another respect, we understand *ascriptions badly: we do not have a *worked out semantic theory* of them. But in this respect, we are no better off with ordinary ascriptions.[32] And it is a feature of this proposal that any theory we have of ordinary ascriptions is *ipso facto* a theory of *ascriptions. For the latter ascribe what the former do minus a bit.

*Ascriptions are necessary if we want our explanation to be strictly and solely psychological; an explanation falling under the laws of psychology. But, as I have pointed out, there is no harm in not being so strict, particularly in the market place; hybrid explanations are OK. So there is nothing wrong in continuing to explain behavior in a folk-theoretic way, making reference to wide content.

The other question we set aside was as follows:

2 How is behavior to be described so that it is open to psychological explanation?

Behind this question usually lies an objection along the following lines.

Opponents of WIDE PSYCHOLOGY seem to have in mind that behavior should be construed as mere bodily movement. "But this construal has almost no relevance to psychology as it is actually practiced." Psychology attempts to explain *actions*, which are behaviors intentionally described. For example (Burge 1986, p. 11): "she picked up the apple, pointed to the square block, tracked the moving ball, smiled at the familiar face, took the money instead of the risk."

This objection raises a deep point, not just for the Revisionist Line on thought but for the functionalist theory of the mind in general. Ned Block has pointed out that "functionalism . . . has typically insisted that characterizations of mental states should contain descriptions of inputs and outputs in *physical* language" (1978, pp. 263–4). At least it has insisted on the descriptions being nonmental. The motivation for this is clear: to reduce the mental to something nonmental. Block criticizes this approach on the ground that it is chauvinistic (pp. 314–17). There is a deeper problem with it. What psychological laws explain is not behavior described as neural impulses, as mere bodily movements, or as any other brute-physical event. These descriptions are at the wrong level, the level of psychological *implementation*. The level that yields the interesting generalizations of psychology requires that the behavior be treated as an action.[33] This goes against the demands of old-fashioned reductionism, but so much the worse for that reductionism. Functionalism often seems not to have fully grasped its own message about explanatory levels.

The laws linking thoughts to input and outputs must advert to certain properties of thoughts, inputs, and outputs. I have argued that the appropriate properties for thoughts are not merely syntactic (section 5). The present point is that the ones appropriate for outputs are not brute-physical.

According to NARROW PSYCHOLOGY, just as we do not need wide-semantic properties for thoughts, we do not need fully intentional ones for output: "proto-intentional" ones will do. To bring behavioral outputs under psychological laws, the outputs must be seen as goal-directed and as actions. However, we can see them in this way whilst abstracting from the particular contexts that are referred to in intentional descriptions and that are effected by actions. For example, the saga of Raelene may end with an action that we would ordinarily describe as "her shooting that man". But for strictly psychological purposes, it does not matter that it was that particular man that she shot. Our language does not have a way of setting aside that fact, but we can easily introduce one using '*' again.[34] And, once again, there is no harm in not being so strict: in giving a description that makes the behavior open to a hybrid explanation, part psychological and part sociological.[35]

7 Conclusions

The Revisionist Line about psychology frequently urges a doctrine that is most naturally understood as

SYNTACTIC PSYCHOLOGY: The laws of mental processes advert only to the syntactic properties of representations.

This doctrine is not supported by any of the arguments offered for Revisionism. The argument from the computer analogy supports a doctrine that is only about thought processes:

SYNTACTIC THOUGHT PROCESSES: The laws of thought processes advert only to the syntactic properties of representations.

This doctrine does not cover the processes linking inputs to thoughts, and thoughts to outputs. The argument from methodological solipsism, modified to take account of Burge's criticisms, goes against

WIDE PSYCHOLOGY: The laws of mental processes advert to the wide semantic properties of representations,

but it does not support SYNTACTIC PSYCHOLOGY. Rather, it supports

NARROW PSYCHOLOGY: The laws of mental processes advert only to the narrow semantic properties of representations.

This doctrine allows psychology to advert to narrow word meanings, which are (mostly) not syntactic.

I argue that we need to advert to narrow meanings, at least, in the laws linking inputs to thoughts, and thoughts to output. SYNTACTIC PSYCHOLOGY is not only not supported by argument, it is false.

I complete my argument for NARROW PSYCHOLOGY by adding to the above case against WIDE PSYCHOLOGY: psychology needs narrow meaning at most. Though WIDE PSYCHOLOGY is encouraged by folk psychological explanations, I argue that it is unlikely that folk psychology is WIDE. For WIDE PSYCHOLOGY is about laws, not explanations, and the little evidence we have suggests that the folk lean toward narrow laws. Even if they don't, the revisionism of NARROW PSYCHOLOGY should not be disturbing. It does not pose serious problems for the description of content and behavior.

The narrow meaning I urge is obtained from wide truth-conditional meaning by abstracting from referential links that lie outside the skin. Though wide meaning is not needed for psychology, I claim that it is needed for linguistics. One semantic theory will do for psychology and linguistics.

NOTES

1 On the terminology, 'wide' and 'narrow', see Putnam 1975 pp. 220–2; Field 1978, pp. 102–4.

2 I shall not be taking account of the extreme eliminativism of Paul and Patricia Churchland (1983).

3 For example, Baker 1986: p. 41; Demopoulos 1980; Kitcher 1985 p. 89; LePore and Loewer 1986, pp. 598–9; McGinn 1982, p. 208; Schiffer 1981, pp. 214–15; Stich 1980, p. 97.

4 But see my in press c.

5 White 1982; Kitcher 1985, p. 87; Devitt 1984a, pp. 81–3. 100–1, 1984b, pp. 387, 395–6; Devitt and Sterelny 1987, p. 166. The idea started for me with my reaction (1981, pp. 156–7) to Hartry Field's conceptual-role semantics (1977).

6 There are some passages in Fodor that seem to suggest this sense; 1980a, p. 64, 1980b, p. 106. See also the following comments, with which Fodor largely agrees: Haugeland 1980, pp. 81–2; Rey 1980, p. 91. But see below.

7 This is the deep truth in the structuralist tradition in linguistics. For the deep falsehood, particularly in the French version, see Devitt and Sterelny 1987, ch. 13.

8 I do not mean to suggest that properties like being a name may not *also* be semantic.

9 Mostly, it seems clear that Fodor has in mind a functional sense for both 'formal' and

'syntactic'; 1985, p. 93, 1987, pp. 18–19, 156n. In comments on Fodor 1980a, Loar distinguishes the two senses and takes Fodor to intend the functional one; 1980, p. 90. See also Pylyshyn 1980a, pp. 111–15. Some write as if they are uninterested in the distinction: Baker 1986, p. 27; Block 1986, p. 616.

10 This usage relates to that of 'logical form'. To say that these properties are formal is not, of course, to make a claim about what 'name' and 'conjunction symbol' "ordinarily mean"; doubtless their ordinary meaning is partly semantic. It is to say what they mean in discussing a formal language.

11 For more on the matter of the last three paragraphs, see e.g. Haugeland 1978, pp. 5–10, 21–2, 1985, pp. 4, 50–2, 58–63, 100–3.

12 It is natural to think of syntactic properties as a sub-class of formal properties (in the senses specified): they are the formal properties of *symbols* (but not, say, of pawns). However, Haugeland extends 'syntactic' to cover all formal properties (1985, p. 100).

13 "Mental processes are causal sequences of tokenings of mental representations" (1987, p. 17).

14 For another example of a swift move from mental processes to thought processes, see Block 1986, p. 628.

15 Searle (1983) argues against Putnam that meanings are in the head. See Devitt in press a for a response.

16 For example, Field 1978, pp. 100–1; Fodor 1980b, p. 102; Stich 1983, pp. 190–1. See also Baker, a critic of Revisionism; 1986, p. 27.

17 Of the usual solipistic sort. Harman urges a nonsolipsistic functional-role semantics: 1982, 1983.

18 Devitt and Sterelny 1987. See also Devitt 1981.

19 This view of word meaning goes against the theory of "direct reference", which is often associated with the causal theory of reference. I have, in effect, argued against this association repeatedly, to no apparent avail: e.g. 1980, and 1985, pp. 222–3. I am trying again; in press b.

20 In this respect my narrow meaning differs from the functional-role factor proposed by "two-factor" theorists. Those theorists tend to treat this factor as if it were unrelated to the truth-conditional factor; see, e.g., McGinn 1982, pp. 211, 230; Loar 1982, p. 280–2, 1983, p. 629.

21 Note that narrow word meanings do not determine *reference* to the peripheral stimuli, because the words do not refer to the stimuli (cf. McDermott 1986). The *theory* of the word's reference to *external reality* refers to the stimuli.

22 Do holists believe the contrary view? According to Fiona Cowie (1987), it is very difficult to tell because the holists typically do not address the issue (a striking example of inattention to inputs). However, they usually write *as if* they believed the view. My approach to holism, reflected in these two paragraphs, owes a lot to Cowie.

23 A Revisionist's claim to have meant by 'only syntactic properties', *only syntactic properties, or narrow semantic properties needed to explain behavior*, might be compared with a vegetable grower's claim to have meant by 'only natural fertilizers', *only natural fertilizers, or artificial fertilizers needed to keep vegetables alive*.

24 So I worried too much about the question in *Realism and Truth* (1984a, chapter 6).

25 This goes against the common view that linguistics is part of psychology: Devitt and Sterelny in press.

26 McDermott also emphasizes that the laws require that there be some semantically significant link between thoughts and stimuli, but he wrongly thinks that this entails that the thoughts be about stimuli (1986, pp. 281–3).

27 Though it seems that Stich even has doubts about laws along these lines: 1983, p. 180.

28 For a suggestion along these lines, see Field 1978, p. 102.

29 Fodor confronts a difficulty like this in an interesting argument against Burge. Fodor argues

that we should not individuate a mental state in terms of its relations to an environment because those relations are irrelevant to its *causal powers* (1987, pp. 33–4). The difficulty is that the individuation of causal powers depends on the individuation of their output. So if behavior is individuated relationally, mental states will be too (pp. 34–8). Fodor's solution to this difficulty is to insist that causal powers are always individuated nonrelationally; hence those of mental states are; hence behavior is (pp. 38–42). This not only begs the question against Burge, it seems quite wrong; think, for example, of the causal powers of a capitalist.

30   Despite this, I think that Burge goes a bit too far in his sermon against philosophical revisionism in general, and the imposition of philosophically motivated methodological constraints on psychology in particular (1986, pp. 17–22). Burge gives insufficient weight to the critical and unifying concerns that are proper to philosophy.

31   Given my earlier remarks about how thoughts are taxonomized, I must then disagree with Fodor (who is agreeing with Burge) when he says: "the differences between the way that [commonsense and psychologically appropriate] taxonomies carve things up only show in funny cases" like Twin-Earth fantasies (1987, p. 159n). Any taxonomy of thoughts that takes account of reference differs rather extensively from the one appropriate for psychology. And most, though I think not all, ordinary taxonomies do take account of reference.

32   My own best attempt at a theory is 1984b.

33   .On this see Fodor 1987, pp. 8–10. Later, Fodor nicely mocks the tendency of functionalists to brush this problem under the carpet: "Since I am very busy just now, please do not ask me what 'inputs' and 'outputs' are" (p. 68). Interestingly enough, even Stich finds "no reason to expect" that "a purely physical description of movements" (1983, p. 169) will be the sort we want for psychology.

34   Both Fodor (1987, pp. 36–44) and Stich (1983, pp. 166–70) think that many folk-psychological descriptions of behavior are unsuitable for psychology. However, Stich seems to think that *some* ordinary descriptions – for example, 'successfully performing a weld' (p. 168) – are suitable. Fodor does not think this, but neither does emphasize the consequence: that the taxonomy of behavior for psychology will require a new linguistic device.

35   This paper grew from one called "The need for truth" which I gave at the following places in the period December 1986 to January 1987: University of Maryland; University of Connecticut; University of Vermont; University of Cincinnati; Northwestern University; University of California, San Diego. Earlier versions were part of a seminar I gave to faculty and students at the University of Sydney from July to October 1987. The paper has benefitted from all these experiences. I am indebted also to at least the following for comments: John Bacon, John Bigelow, Ned Block, Fiona Cowie, Hartry Field, Jerry Fodor, Denise Gamble, Bill Lycan, Joseph Tolliver, Kim Sterelny, and Stephen Stich.

REFERENCES

Asquith, P. D. and Nickles, T. (eds) (1983) *PSA 1982*, vol. 2. East Lansing, MI: Philosophy of Science Association.

Baker, Lynne Rudder (1986) "Just what do we have in mind?", in French, Uehling and Wettstein (eds) 1986, pp. 25–48.

Block, Ned (1978) "Troubles with Functionalism", in Savage (ed.) (1978), pp. 261–325; reprinted in Block (1981a), pp. 268–305, and, in part, in this volume.

Block, Ned (ed.) (1981a) *Readings in Philosophy of Psychology* vol. 1. Cambridge, MA: Harvard University Press.

Block, Ned (ed.) (1981b) *Readings in Philosophy of Psychology*, vol. 2. Cambridge, MA: Harvard University Press.

Block, Ned (1986) "Advertisement for a semantics for psychology", in French, Uehling and Wettstein (eds) (1986), pp. 615–78.

Burge, Tyler (1986) "Individualism and psychology", *Philosophical Review* 95, 3–45.

Carnap, Rudolf (1937) *The Logical Syntax of Language*. New York: Harcourt, Brace.

Chomsky, Noam (1957) *Syntactic Structures*. The Hague: Mouton & Co.

Churchland, Patricia S. and Churchland, Paul M. (1983) "Stalking the wild epistemic engine", *Noûs* 17, 5–20. Reprinted in this volume.

Cowie, Fiona (1987) "Meaning holism". Unpublished BA Thesis, University of Sydney.

Davidson, Donald and Harman, Gilbert (eds) (1972) *Semantics of Natural Language*. Dordrecht: Reidel.

Demopoulos, William (1980) "A remark on the completeness of the computational model of mind", *Behavioral and Brain Sciences* 3, 135.

Devitt, Michael (1980) 'Brian Loar on singular terms', *Philosophical Studies* 37, 271–80.

Devitt, Michael (1981) *Designation*. New York: Columbia University Press.

Devitt, Michael (1984a) *Realism and Truth*. Oxford: Basil Blackwell; Princeton: Princeton University Press.

Devitt, Michael (1984b) "Thoughts and their ascription" in P. A. French, T. E. Uehling Jr and H. K. Wettstein (eds) *Midwest Studies in Philosophy, Volume IX: Causation and Causal Theories*. Minneapolis: University of Minnesota Press, pp. 385–420.

Devitt, Michael (1985) "Critical notice of *The Varieties of Reference*, Gareth Evans", *Australasian Journal of Philosophy* 63, 216–32.

Devitt, Michael (in press a) "Meanings just ain't in the head", in George Boolos (ed.), *Method, Reason and language: Essays in Honor of Hilary Putnam*. Cambridge: Cambridge University Press.

Devitt, Michael (in press b) "Against direct reference", in French, Uehling and Wettstein (eds), *Midwest Studies in Philosophy, Volume XIV: Contemporary Perspectives in the Philosophy of Language II*. Notre Dame: University of Notre Dame Press.

Devitt, Michael (in press c) "Why Fodor can't have it both ways", in Barry Loewer and Georges Rey (eds), *Meaning in Mind: Fodor and His Critics*, Cambridge, MA: MIT Press.

Devitt, Michael and Sterelny, Kim (1987) *Language and Reality: An Introduction to the Philosophy of Language*. Oxford: Basil Backwell.

Devitt, Michael and Sterelny, Kim (in press) "What's wrong with 'the Right View'" in J. E. Tomberlin (ed.), *Philosophical Perspectives, Volume III: Philosophy of Mind and Action Theory*.

Donnellan, Keith (1972) "Proper names and identifying descriptions", in Davidson and Harman (eds) (1972), pp. 356–79.

Field, Hartry (1972) "Tarski's theory of truth", *Journal of Philosophy* 69, 347–75.

Field, Hartry (1977) "Logic, meaning, and conceptual role", *Journal of Philosophy* 74, 379–409.

Field, Hartry (1978) "Mental representation", *Erkenntnis* 13, 9–61; Reprinted with Postscript in Block (1981b), pp. 78–114 (page references are to Block).

Fodor, Jerry A. (1980a) "Methodological solipsism considered as a research strategy in cognitive psychology", *Behavioral and Brain Sciences* 3, 63–73.

Fodor, Jerry A. (1980b) "Methodological solipsism: replies to commentators", *Behavioral and Brain Sciences* 3, 99–109.

Fodor, Jerry A. (1985) "Fodor's guide to mental representation: the intelligent auntie's vademecum", *Mind* 94, 76–100.

Fodor, Jerry A. (1987) *Psychosemantics: The Problem of Meaning in the Philosophy of Mind*. Cambridge, MA: MIT Press.

Frege, Gottlob (1952) *Translations from the Philosophical Writings of Gottlob Frege*, Peter Geach and Max Black (eds). Oxford: Basil Blackwell.

French, Peter A., Uehling, Theodore E. Jr. and Wettstein, Howard K. (eds) (1986) *Midwest Studies in Philosophy, Volume X: Studies in the Philosophy of Mind*. Minneapolis: University of Minnesota Press.

Harman, Gilbert (1982) "Conceptual role semantics", *Notre Dame Journal of Formal Logic* 28, 242–56.

Harman, Gilbert (1983) "Beliefs and concepts: comments on Brian Loar", in Asquith and Nickles (eds) (1983).

Haugeland, John (1978) "The nature and plausibility of cognitivism", *Behavioral and Brain Sciences* 1, 215–26; reprinted in Haugeland (ed.) (1981) pp. 243–81 (page references are to Haugeland 1981).

Haugeland, John (1980) "Formality and naturalism", *Behavioral and Brain Sciences* 3, 81–2.

Haugeland, John (ed.) (1981) *Mind Design: Philosophy, Psychology, Artificial Intelligence.* Cambridge, MA: MIT Press.

Haugeland, John (1985) *Artificial Intelligence: The Very Idea.* Cambridge, MA: MIT Press.

Kitcher, Patricia (1985) "Narrow taxonomy and wide functionalism", *Philosophy of Science* 52, 78–97.

Kripke, Saul (1980) *Naming and Necessity.* Cambridge, MA: Harvard University Press. [A corrected version of an article of the same name (plus an appendix) in Davidson and Harman 1972, together with a new preface.]

LePore, Ernest and Loewer, Barry (1986) "Solipsistic semantics", in French, Uehling and Wettstein (eds) (1986), pp. 595–614.

Loar, Brian (1980) "Syntax, functional semantics, and referential semantics" *Behavioral and Brain Sciences* 3, 89–90.

Loar, Brian (1982) "Conceptual role and truth-conditions", *Notre Dame Journal of Formal Logic* 23, 272–83.

Loar, Brian (1983) "Must beliefs be sentences?", in Asquith and Nickles (eds) (1983), pp. 627–43.

McDermott, Michael (1986) "Narrow content", *Australasian Journal of Philosophy* 64, 277–88.

McGinn, Colin (1982) "The structure of content", in Woodfield (ed.) (1982), pp. 207–58.

Putnam, Hilary (1975) *Mind, Language and Reality: Philosophical Papers*, vol. 2. Cambridge: Cambridge University Press.

Pylyshyn, Z. (1980a) "Computation and cognition: issues in the foundations of cognitive science", *Behavioral and Brain Sciences* 3, 111–32.

Pylyshyn, Z. (1980b) "Cognitive representation and the process–architecture distinction", *Behavioral and Brain Sciences* 3, 154–69.

Pylyshyn, Z. (1984) *Computation and cognition.* Cambridge, MA: Bradford Books/MIT Press.

Rey, Georges (1980) "The formal and the opaque", *Behavioral and Brain Sciences* 3, 90–2.

Savage, C. Wade (1978) *Minnesota Studies in the Philosophy of Science, Volume IX: Perception and Cognition: Issues in the Foundations of Psychology.* Minneapolis: University of Minnesota Press.

Schiffer, Stephen (1981) "Truth and the theory of content", in Herman Parret and Jacques Bouveresse (eds), *Meaning and Understanding.* Berlin: Walter de Gruyter, pp. 204–22.

Searle, John R. (1983) *Intentionality: An Essay in the Philosophy of Mind.* Cambridge: Cambridge University Press.

Stich, Stephen P. (1980) "Paying the price for methodological solipsism", *Behavioral and Brain Sciences* 3, 97–8.

Stich, Stephen P. (1983) *From Folk Psychology to Cognitive Science: The Case Against Belief.* Cambridge, MA: MIT Press.

White, Stephen L. (1982) "Partial character and the language of thought", *Pacific Philosophical Quarterly* 63, 347–65.

Woodfield, A. (ed.) (1982) *Thought and Object.* Oxford: Clarendon Press.

15

Defending "Folk Psychology"

Folk Psychology is Here to Stay

TERENCE HORGAN AND JAMES WOODWARD

Folk psychology is a network of principles which constitutes a sort of common-sense theory about how to explain human behavior. These principles provide a central role to certain propositional attitudes, particularly beliefs and desires. The theory asserts, for example, that if someone desires that p, and this desire is not overridden by other desires, and he believes that an action of kind K will bring it about that p, and he believes that such an action is within his power, and he does not believe that some other kind of action is within his power and is a preferable way to bring it about that p, then *ceteris paribus*, the desire and the beliefs will cause him to perform an action of kind K. The theory is largely functional, in that the states it postulates are characterized primarily in terms of their causal relations to each other, to perception and other environmental stimuli, and to behavior.

Folk psychology (henceforth FP) is deeply ingrained in our common-sense conception of ourselves as persons. Whatever else a person is, he is supposed to be a rational (at least largely rational) *agent* – that is, a creature whose behavior is systematically caused by, and explainable in terms of, his beliefs, desires, and related propositional attitudes. The wholesale rejection of FP, therefore, would entail a drastic revision of our conceptual scheme. This fact seems to us to constitute a good prima facie reason for not discarding FP too quickly in the face of apparent difficulties.

Recently, however, FP has come under fire from two quarters. Paul Churchland (1981) has argued that since FP has been with us for at least twenty-five centuries, and thus is not the product of any deliberate and self-conscious attempt to develop a psychological theory which coheres with the account of *Homo sapiens* which the natural sciences provide, there is little reason to suppose that FP is true, or that humans undergo beliefs, desires, and the like. And Stephen Stich (1983) has argued that current work in cognitive science suggests

"Folk Psychology is Here to Stay" by T. Horgan and J. Woodward first appeared in *The Philosophical Review*, XCIV, No. 2 (April 1985), and is reprinted by kind permission of the authors and the journal.

that no events or states posited by a mature cognitive psychology will be identifiable as the events and states posited by FP; Stich maintains that if this turns out to be the case, then it will show that FP is radically false, and that humans simply do not undergo such mental states as beliefs and desires.

In this paper we shall argue that neither Churchland nor Stich has provided convincing reasons for doubting the integrity of FP. Much of our discussion will be devoted to showing that they each employ an implausibly stringent conception of how FP would have to mesh with lower-level theories in order to be compatible with them. We do not deny the possibility that FP will fail to be compatible with more comprehensive theories; this would happen, for instance, if the correct theoretical psychology turned out to be a version of radical Skinnerian behaviorism. But we maintain that there is no good reason to suppose that it will *actually* happen.

Before proceeding, several preliminaries. First, we shall use the rubric 'event' in a broad sense, to include not only token changes, but also token states and token processes. Thus, non-momentary folk-psychological token states will count as mental events, in our terminology.

Second, we shall take FP to consist of two components: a set of *theoretical principles*, and an *existential thesis*. Many or all of the theoretical principles may be expected to have the general form exemplified by the example in our opening paragraph; that is, they are universal closures of conditional formulas.[1] As such they do not carry any existential import, since they might all be vacuously true. The existential thesis of FP, on the other hand, is the assertion that generally our everyday folk-psychological descriptions of people are true, and that humans generally do undergo the folk-psychological events that we commonly attribute to them. We take it that Churchland and Stich are arguing primarily against the existential thesis of FP; i.e., they are claiming that our everyday folk-psychological ascriptions are radically false, and that there simply do not exist such things as beliefs, desires, and the rest. Thus their argument, as we understand it, leaves open the possibility that the theoretical principles of FP are true but merely vacuously so.

Third, we are not necessarily claiming that FP is fully correct in every respect, or that there is no room to correct or improve FP on the basis of new developments in cognitive science or neuroscience. Rather, we are claiming that FP's theoretical principles are *by and large* correct, and that everyday folk-psychological ascriptions are often true.

Fourth, we want to dissociate ourselves from our currently influential strategy for insulating FP from potential scientific falsification – viz., the instrumentalism of Daniel Dennett (1978, 1981). He says, of beliefs and desires, that these "putative . . . states" can be relegated "to the role of idealized fictions in an action-predicting, action-explaining calculus" (1978, p. 30). They are not what Reichenbach calls "illata – posited theoretical entities"; instead, he maintains, they are "abstracta – calculation-bound entities or logical constructs" (1981, p. 13), whose status is analogous to components in a parallelogram of forces (1981, p. 20). In short, he evidently holds that they are instrumentalistic fictions, and hence that they are compatible with virtually anything we might discover in cognitive science or neuroscience. We reject Dennett's instrumentalism. We maintain that FP, in addition to providing a useful framework for prediction, also provides genuine *causal explanations*. Although an instrumentalistic attitude toward the intentional idioms of FP is compatible with the mere predictive use of these idioms, it simply is not compatible with their explanatory use, or with talk of beliefs and desires as causes. Accordingly, FP requires a defense more vigorous than Dennett's instrumentalism.

I

Churchland's (1981) argument against the compatibility of FP and neuroscience rests on three considerations. First "FP suffers explanatory failures on an epic scale" (p. 76). Second, "it has been stagnant for at least twenty-five centuries" (p. 76). And third, "its intentional categories stand magnificently alone, without any visible prospect of reduction" to neuroscience (p. 75). Irreducibility is the main consideration, and it is allegedly reinforced by the other two points: "A successful reduction cannot be ruled out, in my view, but FP's explanatory impotence and long stagnation inspire little faith that its categories will find themselves neatly reflected in the framework of neuroscience" (p. 75).

Let us consider each of Churchland's three points in turn. In elaboration of the first point, he writes:

> As examples of central and important mental phenomena that remain largely or wholly mysterious within the framework of FP, consider the nature and dynamics of mental illness, the faculty of creative imagination. . .the nature and psychological functions of sleep . . . the common ability to catch an outfield fly ball on the run . . . the internal construction of a 3-D visual image. . .the rich variety of perceptual illusions. . .the miracle of memory . . . the nature of the learning process itself . . . (p. 73)

There are at least two important respects in which this passage is misleading. First, while FP itself may have little to say about the matters Churchland mentions, theories based on concepts deriving from FP have a good deal to say about them. For example, cognitive psychologists have developed extensive and detailed theories about visual perception, memory, and learning that employ concepts recognizably like the folk-psychological concepts of belief, desire, judgment, etc.[2] The versions of attribution theory and cognitive dissonance theory considered below in connection with Stich are important cases of theories of this kind. That all such theories are unexplanatory is most implausible, and in any case requires detailed empirical argument of a sort Churchland does not provide.

Secondly, Churchland's argument seems to impose the a priori demand that any successful psychological theory account for a certain pre-established range of phenomena, and do so in a unified way. Arguments of this general type deserve to be treated with skepticism and caution. The history of science is full of examples in which our pre-theoretical expectations about which phenomena it is reasonable to expect a theory to account for or group together have turned out to be quite misleading. For example, the demand was frequently imposed on early optical theories that they account for facts which we would now recognize as having to do with the physiology or psychology of vision; this had a deleterious effect on early optical theorizing. Similar examples can readily be found in the history of chemistry. [3]

The general point is that reasonable judgments about which phenomena a theory of some general type should be expected to account for require considerable theoretical knowledge; when our theoretical knowledge is relatively primitive, as it is with regard to many psychological phenomena, such judgments can go seriously astray. There is no good reason, a priori, to expect that a theory like FP, designed primarily to explain common human actions in terms of beliefs, desires, and the like, should also account for phenomena having to do with visual perception, sleep, or complicated muscular coordination. The truth about the latter phenomena may simply be very different from the truth about the former.

What about Churchland's second argument, viz., that FP has remained stagnant for centuries? To begin with, it seems to us at least arguable that FP has indeed changed in significant and empirically progressive ways over the centuries, rather than stagnating. For example, it is a plausible conjecture that Europeans in the eighteenth or nineteenth centuries were much more likely to explain human behavior in terms of character types with enduring personality traits than twentieth century Europeans, who often appeal instead to "situational" factors. (Certainly this difference is dramatically evident in eighteenth and twentieth century literature; contrast, say, Jane Austen and John Barth.)[4] Another example of empirically progressive change, perhaps, is the greater willingness, in contemporary culture, to appeal to unconscious beliefs and motivations.

Another reason to question the "empirical unprogressiveness" argument is that cognitive psychological theories employing belief-like and desire-like events have led to a number of novel and surprising predictions, which have been borne out by experiment. (We discuss some pertinent examples below. For other striking cases the reader is referred to Nisbett and Ross (1980).) Yet Churchland seems to argue as though the (alleged) empirical unprogressiveness of FP is a good reason for taking any theory modeled on FP to be false.[5] This is rather like arguing that any sophisticated physical theory employing central forces must be false on the grounds that the ordinary person's notions of pushing and pulling have been empirically unprogressive.

Furthermore, the standard of "empirical progressiveness" is not very useful in assessing a theory like FP anyway. The typical user of FP is interested in applying a pre-existing theory to make particular causal judgments about particular instances of human behavior, not in formulating new causal generalizations. He is a consumer of causal generalizations, not an inventor of them. In this respect he resembles the historian, the detective, or the person who makes ordinary singular causal judgments about inanimate objects. It is not appropriate, we submit, to assess these activities using a standard explicitly designed to assess theories that aim at formulating novel causal generalizations.

This point emerges clearly when one realizes that much of the implicit theory behind many ordinary (but non-psychological) particular causal judgments has presumably changed very slowly, if at all, over the past thousand years. Both we and our ancestors judge that the impact of the rock caused the shattering of the pot, that the lack of water caused the camel to die, that a very sharp blow on the head caused A's death, that heat causes water to boil, etc. None of these judgments are part of a (swiftly) empirically progressive theory, yet it seems ludicrous to conclude (on those grounds alone) that they are probably false. A similar point can be made about much (although by no means all) of the implicit causal theory employed by historians. These examples serve to remind us that not all folk theorizing is now regarded as radically false.

This brings us to Churchland's third, and most fundamental, argument for the alleged incommensurability of FP with neuroscience: viz., the likely irreducibility of the former to the latter. An ideal intertheoretic reduction, as he describes it, has two main features:

> First, it provides us with a set of rules – "correspondence rules" or "bridge laws," as the standard vernacular has it – which effect a mapping of the terms of the old theory (T_o) onto a subset of the expressions of the new or reducing theory (T_n). These rules guide the application of those selected expressions of T_n in the following way: we are free to make singular applications of those expressions in all those cases where we normally make singular applications of their correspondence-rule doppelgangers in T_o. . . .
>
> Second, and equally important, a successful reduction ideally has the outcome that, under the term mapping effected by the correspondence rules, the central principles of T_o (those of semantic and systematic importance) are mapped onto general sentences of T_n that are *theorems* of T_n. (1979, p. 81)

We certainly agree that an ideal, or approximately ideal, reduction of FP to natural science would be *one* way of salvaging FP. And we also agree that such a reduction – indeed, even a species-specific reduction – is an unlikely prospect, given that FP is at least twenty-five centuries old and hence obviously was not formulated with an eye toward smooth term-by-term absorption into twentieth-century science. (A non-species-specific reduction is even less likely, because if FP is true of humans then it can equally well be true of Martians whose physico-chemical composition is vastly different from our own – so different that there are no theoretically interesting physical descriptions that can subsume both the physico-chemical properties which "realize" FP in humans and the corresponding physico-chemical properties in Martians.)

But even if FP cannot be reduced to lower-level theories, and even if lower-level theories can themselves provide a marvelous account of the nature and behavior of *Homo sapiens*, it simply does not follow that FP is radically false, or that humans do not undergo the intentional events it posits. Churchland's eliminative materialism is not the only viable naturalistic alternative to reductive materialism. Another important alternative is the non-reductive, non-eliminative materialism of Donald Davidson (1970, 1973, 1974).

Davidson advocates a thesis which asserts that every concrete mental event is identical to some concrete neurological event, but which does not assert (indeed, denies) that there are systematic bridge laws linking mental event-*types*, or properties, with neurological event-types. He calls this view *anomalous monism*; it is a form of monism because it posits psychophysical identities, and it is "anomalous" because it rejects reductive bridge laws (or reductive type–type identities).[6]

The availability of anomalous monism as an alternative to reductive materialism makes it clear that even if FP is not reducible to neuroscience, nevertheless the token mental events posited by FP might well exist, and might well bear all the causal relations to each other, to sensation, and to behavior which FP says they do.

Churchland never mentions Davidson's version of the identity theory – a very odd fact, given its enormous influence and its obvious relevance to his argument. Instead he argues directly from the premise that FP probably is not reducible to neuroscience to the conclusion that FP probably is false. So his argument is fallacious, in light of token–token identity theory as an alternative possible account of the relation between FP and neuroscience. He is just mistaken to assume that FP must be reducible to neuroscience in order to be compatible with it.

II

Let us now consider Stich's reasons for claiming that FP probably will not prove compatible with a developed cognitive science (henceforth CS). Unlike Churchland, Stich does not assume that FP must be reducible to more comprehensive lower-level theories in order to be compatible with them. We shall say more presently about the way he thinks FP must fit with these theories.

Stich offers two arguments against the compatibility of FP and CS; we shall examine these in this section and the next. The first argument purports to show that the overall causal organization of the cognitive system probably does not conform with the causal organization which FP ascribes to it. The argument runs as follows. Events which satisfy a given sortal predicate of the form ". . .is a belief that p" are supposed to have typical behavioral effects of both verbal and non-verbal kinds. On the verbal side, the events in this class are ones which typically cause the subject, under appropriate elicitation conditions, to utter an assertion that p. On the non-verbal side, these events are ones which, in combination with a subject's other beliefs, desires, and the like, typically cause the subject to perform those actions which FP says are appropriate to the combination of that belief with those other propositional attitudes. But recent experimental evidence suggests, according to Stich, that the psychological events which control non-verbal behavior are essentially independent of those which control verbal behavior – and hence that the cognitive system simply does not contain events which, taken singly, occupy the causal role which FP assigns to beliefs. If these experimental results prove generalizable, and if CS subsequently develops in the direction of positing separate, largely independent, cognitive subsystems for the control of verbal and non-verbal behavior respectively, then we will be forced to conclude, argues Stich, that there are no such things as beliefs.

One of his central empirical examples is a study in attribution theory, performed by Storms and Nisbett (1970). He describes its first phase this way:

> Storms and Nisbett. . .asked insomniac subjects to record the time they went to bed and the time they finally fell asleep. After several days of record keeping, one group of subjects (the "arousal" group) was given a placebo pill to take fifteen minutes before going to bed. They were told that the pill would produce rapid heart rate, breathing irregularities, bodily warmth and alertness, which are just the typical symptoms of insomnia. A second group of subjects (the "relaxation" group) was told that the pills would produce the opposite symptoms: lowered heart rate, breathing

rate, body temperature and alertness. Attribution theory predicts that the arousal group subjects would get to sleep *faster* on the nights they took the pills, because they would attribute their symptoms to the pills rather than to the emotionally laden thoughts that were running through their minds. It also predicts that subjects in the relaxation group will take *longer* to get to sleep. Since their symptoms persist despite having taken a pill intended to relieve the symptoms, they will infer that their emotionally laden thoughts must be particularly disturbing to them. And this belief will upset them further, making it all that much harder to get to sleep. Remarkably enough, both of these predictions were borne out. Arousal group subjects got to sleep 28 percent faster on the nights they took the pill, while relaxation subjects took 42 percent longer to get to sleep. (Stich 1983, p. 232)

What Stich finds particularly significant is the second phase of this study. After the completion of the initial insomnia experiments, the members of the arousal group were informed that they had gotten to sleep more quickly after taking the pill, and the members of the relaxation group were informed that they had taken longer to fall asleep. They were asked *why* this happened, and Nisbett and Wilson report the following pattern of responses:

> Arousal subjects typically replied that they usually found it easier to get to sleep later in the week, or that they had taken an exam that had worried them but had done well on it and could now relax, or that problems with a roommate or girlfriend seemed on their way to resolution. Relaxation subjects were able to find similar sorts of reasons to explain their increased sleeplessness. When subjects were asked if they had thought about the pills at all before getting to sleep, they almost uniformly insisted that after taking the pills they had completely forgotten about them. When asked if it had occurred to them that the pill might be producing (or counteracting) the arousal symptoms, they reiterated their insistence that they had not thought about the pills at all after taking them. Finally, the experimental hypothesis and the postulated attribution process were described in detail. Subjects showed no recognition of the hypothesized process and...made little pretense of believing that *any* of the subjects could have gone through such processes. (Nisbett and Wilson, 1977, p. 238)

It is very likely, given the data from the first phase of the study, that the cognitive mechanisms which controlled the subjects' verbal responses in the second phase were largely distinct from the cognitive mechanisms which influenced their actual sleep patterns. And in numerous other studies in the literature of attribution theory and cognitive dissonance theory, the data support a similar conclusion: the mechanisms which control an initial piece of non-verbal behavior are largely distinct from the mechanisms which control the subject's subsequent verbal accounts of the reasons for that behavior.[7]

Stich, if we understand his argument correctly, draws three further conclusions. (1) In cases of the sort described, there is no cogent and consistent way to ascribe beliefs and desires; for FP typically attributes both verbal and non-verbal behavioral effects to particular beliefs and desires, but in these cases the cognitive causes of the non-verbal behavior are distinct from the cognitive causes of the verbal behavior, and hence neither kind of cause can comfortably be identified with a belief or desire. (2) It is likely that *in general* our verbal behavior is controlled by cognitive mechanisms different from those that control our non-verbal behavior; for the Storms–Nisbett pattern emerges in a broad range of studies in attribution theory and dissonance theory. From (1) and (2) he concludes: (3) It is likely that FP is radically false; that is, that humans do not undergo beliefs and desires.

We do not dispute the contention that in a surprising number of cases, as revealed by studies in attribution theory and dissonance theory, the mental states and processes which cause an initial item of non-verbal behavior are distinct from the states and processes which cause a subject's subsequent remarks about the etiology of that behavior. But we deny that either (1) or (2) is warranted by this contention. And without (1) or (2), of course the argument for (3) collapses.

Consider (1). Is there really a problem in consistently ascribing beliefs, desires, and other folk-psychological states in light of the phenomena described in the Storms–Nisbett study, for instance? No. For we can appeal to *unconscious* beliefs, desires, and inferences. Although FP asserts that beliefs and desires *normally* give rise to their own verbal expression under appropriate elicitation conditions, it does not assert this about unconscious beliefs and desires. On the contrary, part of what it means to say that a mental event is unconscious is that it lacks the usual sorts of direct causal influence over verbal behavior. Thus we have available the following natural and plausible folk-psychological account of the subjects' behavior in the Storms–Nisbett study; their initial non-verbal behavior was caused by unconscious beliefs and inferences, whereas their subsequent verbal behavior was caused by distinct, conscious, beliefs about the likely causes of their initial non-verbal behavior. In short, FP does not break down in such cases, because one has the option – the natural and plausible option – of positing unconscious folk-psychological causes.

There is a temptation, we realize, to identify FP with "what common sense would say," and to take the fact that the Storms–Nisbett results confute our common-sense expectations as automatically falsifying some component of FP. But this temptation should be resisted. Common sense would not postulate the relevant unconscious beliefs and desires. But once we *do* postulate them, perhaps on the basis of rather subtle non-verbal behavioral evidence, FP seems to yield the *correct* predictions about how the subjects will perform in Storms and Nisbett's study.

Indeed, as we understand the views of psychologists like Storms, Nisbett, and Wilson who cite such studies as evidence that verbal and non-verbal behavior often are under separate cognitive controls, this appeal to unconscious folk-psychological causes is precisely the theoretical move *they* are making concerning such cases. Attribution theory and cognitive dissonance theory give center stage to folk-psychological notions like desire and belief. Accordingly, the dual control thesis is nothing other than the folk-psychological thesis just stated: it is the claim that unconscious beliefs and inferences cause the subjects' initial non-verbal behavior, whereas distinct conscious beliefs (which constitute hypotheses about the causes of their original behavior) cause their subsequent verbal behavior.[8] Notice how Stich himself, in the above-quoted passage, describes the first phase of the Storms–Nisbett study. "Attribution theory," he says, "predicts that subjects in the relaxation group will *infer* that their emotionally laden thoughts must be particularly disturbing to them. And this *belief* will upset them further..."

(emphasis ours). Now Stich may have in mind a way of reinterpreting these claims so that the notions of belief and inference they employ are very different from the FP-notions, but in the absence of such a reinterpretation, his contention that beliefs and belief-generating mechanisms cannot be cogently ascribed to subjects like those of Storms and Nisbett is quite unfounded.

Our construal of the dual-control thesis assumes, of course, that it makes sense to speak of beliefs and other mental events as unconscious. But Storms, Nisbett, and Wilson claim quite explicitly that there can be non-verbal behavioral criteria which warrant the ascription of beliefs and other mental events even when a subject's verbal behavior appears inconsistent with the existence of such events.[9]

It may well be that the appeal to these criteria – and to unconscious beliefs and inferences generally – constitutes an extension and partial modification of traditional FP; but even if it does, this is hardly a wholesale rejection of folk-psychological notions. On the contrary, the very naturalness of the appeal to unconscious folk-psychological causes reflects the fact that the overall causal architecture posited by FP remains largely intact even when we introduce the conscious/unconscious distinction.

So conclusion (1) should be rejected. This means that even if (2) were accepted, FP would not necessarily be undermined. But conclusion (2) should be rejected in any case. From the fact that unconscious mental mechanisms control our non-verbal behavior in a surprising number of cases, one may not reasonably infer that *in general* our verbal and non-verbal behavior are under separate cognitive control. The findings of attribution theory and dissonance theory, although they do caution us against excessive confidence in our ability to know ourselves, fall far short of establishing such a sweeping conclusion. In this connection it is useful to examine the remarks of Timothy Wilson (unpublished), a leading advocate of the idea of "dual cognitive control" over verbal and non-verbal behavior respectively. Stich makes much of Wilson's position, which he construes as the radical thesis that our own statements concerning the mental events that cause our non-verbal behavior are virtually *never* caused by those mental events themselves. But this is a mistaken interpretation, in our judgment. Wilson articulates his proposal this way:

> In essence the argument is that there are two mental systems: One which mediates behavior (especially unregulated behavior), is largely nonconscious, and is perhaps, the older of the two systems in evolutionary terms. The other, perhaps newer system, is largely conscious, and its function is to attempt to verbalize, explain, and communicate mental states. As argued earlier, people often have direct access to their mental states, and in these cases the verbal system can make direct and accurate reports. When there is limited access, however, the verbal system makes inferences about what these processes and states might be. (pp. 18–19)

It seems clear from this passage that Wilson is not suggesting that *in general* our utterances about our mental events are generated by cognitive events other than those mental events themselves. Rather, he is acknowledging that people often have direct conscious access to the mental causes of their behavior, and that at such times these states typically cause accurate reports about themselves. Only where access is limited, where the events are not conscious, are our subsequent utterances caused by inferences about likely mental causes rather than by the mental events themselves.[10]

Wilson goes on to suggest that it will typically be events that are results of considerable processing which will be relatively inaccessible to the agent, and that "more immediate states" (such as precognitive states) may be much more accessible (p. 39). Moreover, there are many cases which do seem to involve complex processing in which people exhibit integrated verbal and non-verbal behavior in a way that seems difficult to understand if the systems controlling verbal and non-verbal behavior are entirely independent. Consider engaging in some complicated task while explaining to someone else what you are doing – as in working logic problems on the blackboard as one lectures. It is hard to see how such an integrated performance is possible if the actor has no access to the beliefs which cause the non-verbal portion of his behavior (other than via after-the-fact inferences).

We conclude, then, that neither conclusion (1) nor conclusion (2) is warranted by the kinds of psychological studies Stich cites, and hence that his "dual-control" argument against FP is not successful.

III

The "dual-control" argument does not presuppose any particular conception of how FP must be related to CS in order for the two theories to be compatible. Stich's second argument for the incompatibility of FP and CS, however, does rest upon such a conception. In particular, he requires that beliefs, desires, and the like should be identical with "naturally isolable" parts of the cognitive system; he calls this the *modularity* principle.

Stich does not attempt to make this principle precise, but instead leaves the notion of natural isolability at the intuitive level. Accordingly, we too shall use this notion without explication; we think the points we shall make are applicable under any reasonable construal.

Stich argues that FP probably fails to satisfy the modularity principle *vis-à-vis* CS, and hence that there probably are no such events as beliefs, desires, and the like. He focuses on recent trends within CS concerning the modeling of human memory. Some early models of memory organization, he points out, postulate a distinct sentence or sentence-like structure for each memory. These models are clearly modular, he says, because the distinct sentence-like structures can be identified with separate beliefs. Another sort of model, motivated largely by the desire to explain how poeple are able to locate information relevant to a given task at hand, treats memory as a complex network of nodes and labeled links, with the nodes representing concepts and the links representing various sorts of relations among concepts. Stich regards network models as "still quite far over to the modular end of the spectrum," however, because in a network model it is generally unproblematic to isolate the part of the network which would play the causal role characteristic of a given belief (1983, p. 239).

But in recent years, he points out, several leading theorists have become quite skeptical about highly modular models, largely because such models do not seem capable of handling the enormous amount of non-deductive inference which is involved in language use and comprehension. Citing Minsky (1981) as an example, Stich writes:

> In a . . . recent paper Minsky elaborates what he calls a "Society of Mind" view in which the mechanisms of thought are divided into many separate "specialists that communicate only sparsely" (p. 95). On the picture Minsky suggests, none of the distinct units or parts of the mental model "have meanings in themselves" (p. 100) and thus none can be identified with individual beliefs, desires, etc. Modularity – I borrow the term from Minsky – is violated in a radical way since meaning or content emerges only from "great webs of structure" (p. 100) and no natural part of the system can be correlated with "explicit" or verbally expressible beliefs. (1983, p. 241)

If Minsky's "Society of Mind" view is the direction that CS will take in the future, then presumably modularity will indeed be violated in a radical way.

We are quite prepared to acknowledge that CS may well become dramatically non-modular, and hence that the modularity principle may well end up being refuted empirically.[11] Indeed, if one considers the relation between FP and neuroscience – or even the relation between CS and neuroscience, for that matter – one would expect modularity to be violated in an even more dramatic way. There are tens of billions of neurons in the human central nervous system, and thousands of billions of synaptic junctures; so if the "naturally isolable" events of neuroscience are events like neuron firings and inter-synaptic transfers of electrical energy, then it is entirely likely that the naturally isolable events of both FP and CS will involve "great webs of structure" neurally – that is, great conglomerations of naturally isolable neural events.

So if modularity is really needed in order for FP-events to exist and to enter into causal relations, then the failure of modularity would indeed spell big trouble for the proffered compatibility of FP with lower-level theories. In fact, it also would spell big trouble for the proffered compatibility of *cognitive science* with lower-level theories like neuroscience; thus Stich's style of argument appears to prove more than he, as an advocate of CS, would like it to prove! And indeed, the demand for modularity even spells big trouble for the compatibility of *neuroscience* with physics-chemistry; for, if the natural-kind predicates of physics-chemistry are predicates like ". . . is an electron" and ". . . is a hydrogen atom," then it is most unlikely that entities falling under neuroscientific natural-kind terms like ". . . is a neuron" will also fall under physico-chemical natural kind terms. Rather, neurons and neuron firings are entities which, from the physico-chemical point of view, involve "great webs of structure."

We point out these generalizations of Stich's argument because we think they make clear the enormous implausibility of the modularity principle as an inter-theoretic compatibility condition. Surely objects like neurons, or events like neuron firings, don't have to be "naturally isolable" from the perspective of fundamental physics-chemistry in order to be compatible with it; rather, it is enough that they be fully decomposable into naturally isolable *parts*. Similarly, cognitive-psychological events don't have to be naturally isolable from the perspective of neuroscience in order to be compatible with it; again, it is enough that these events are decomposable into naturally-isolable parts.[12]

The situation is exactly the same, we submit, for folk-psychological events in relation to the events of CS. Perhaps Minsky is right, and the role of a belief (say) is typically played by a vast, highly gerrymandered, conglomeration of CS-events. This doesn't show that the belief doesn't exist. On the contrary, all it shows is that the belief is an enormously *complex* event, consisting of numerous CS-events as parts.[13] After all, we expect those CS-events, in turn, to consist of numerous neurological events as parts; and we expect those neurological events, in their turn, to consist of numerous physico-chemical events as parts.

Stich never attempts to justify the modularity principle as a compatibility condition, just as Churchland never attempts to justify the demand for reducibility. Thus Stich's modularity argument suffers the same defect as Churchland's reducibility argument: viz., it rests upon an unsubstantiated, and implausibly strong, conception of how FP must mesh with more comprehensive lower-level theories in order to be compatible with them. (It is important to note, incidentally, that even though Stich does not demand reducibility, still in a certain way his notion of inter-theoretic fit is actually *stronger* than Churchland's notion. For, even a reductionist need not require that entities falling under higher-level natural-kind sortals should be naturally isolable from the lower-level perspective. A reductionist does require that there should be biconditional bridge laws correlating the higher-level sortals with open sentences of the lower-level theory, but these lower-level open sentences can be quite complex, rather than being (say) simple natural-kind sortal predicates.)

Although Stich offers no explicit rationale for the modularity principle, perhaps he is influenced by the following line of thought:

> The propositional attitudes of FP involve a relation between a cognizer and a sentence-like "internal representation" (Fodor 1975, 1978; Field 1978; Lycan 1981). If FP is true, then part of the task of CS is to explain the nature of these internal representations. But CS cannot do this unless internal representations fall under its natural-kind predicates, or at any rate are *somehow* "naturally isolable" within the cognitive system. And if Minsky's "Society of Mind" approach is the direction CS will take in the future, then this requirement will not be met. Hence if the events of FP do not obey the modularity principle *vis-à-vis* CS, then FP must be radically false.

One reason we have for rejecting this line of reasoning is that we doubt whether propositional attitudes really involve internal representations – or whether they have "objects" at all (cf. note 1). Furthermore, if Minsky's approach did become the general trend in CS, then presumably this fact too would tend to undermine the claim that sentence-like representations are involved in the propositional attitudes – just as his appraoch already tends to undermine the claim that such representations are involved in the non-deductive inference that underlies the use and comprehension of language.

Moreover, even if the internal-representation view is correct, and even if part of the task of CS is to give an account of these representations, approaches like Minsky's would not necessarily render CS incapable of accomplishing this task. For it might turn out that the "atoms" of CS are the components of Minsky's Society of Minds, and that CS also posits complex, sentence-like "molecules" constructed from these "atoms." The molecules might be *very* complex, and highly gerrymandered. If so, then they won't count as naturally isolable components of the cognitive system when that system is viewed from the atomic perspective; however, they *will* count as naturally isolable from the higher, molecular perspective. (We think it more likely, however, that if the "Society of Minds" approach proves generalizable within CS, then the result will be a widespread rejection of the mental-representation view of propositional attitudes – a view which, as we said, we think is mistaken anyway.)

Another way one might try to defend the modularity principle is by appeal to Davidsonian considerations involving the role of laws in causality. One might argue (i) that FP contains no strict laws, but only so-called "heteronomic" generalizations (Davidson 1970, 1974); (ii) that two events are related as cause and effect only if they have descriptions which instantiate a strict law (Davidson 1967); and (iii) that event-descriptions which instantiate a strict law of a given theory must pick out events that are naturally isolable from the perspective of that theory. From these three claims, plus the assumption that folk-psychological events enter into causal relations, the modularity principle seems to follow.[14]

But suppose an event c causes an event e, where c and e both are naturally isolable from the perspective of FP. Suppose that c is fully decomposable into events which respectively satisfy the sortal predicates $F_1 \ldots F_m$ of an underlying homonomic theory T, and hence that these component-events all are naturally isolable from the perspective of T; suppose also that these events jointly satisfy a (possibly quite complex) description D_1 of T which specifies their structural interconnection. Likewise, suppose that e is fully decomposable into events which respectively satisfy the sortal predicates $G_1 \ldots G_n$ of T, and hence that these components events all are naturally isolable from the perspective of T; suppose also that these component events jointly satisfy a description D_2 of T which specifies their structural interconnection. Now even if c and e do not have natural-kind descriptions under which they themselves instantiate a strict law of T, nevertheless the strict laws of T might jointly entail an assertion of the following form:

For any event x, if x is fully decomposable into events $x_1 \ldots x_m$ such that $D_1(x_1 \ldots x_m)$ and $F_1(x_1)$, $F_2(x_2)$, and $\ldots F_m(x_m)$, then x will be followed by an event y that is fully decomposable into events $y_1 \ldots y_n$ such that $D_2(y_1 \ldots y_n)$ and $G_1(y_1)$, $G_2(y_2)$, and $\ldots$ and $G_n(y_n)$.

We see no reason why the causal relation between c and e cannot rest upon a regularity of this form. One either can call such regularities strict laws, in which case claim (iii) above will be false; or else one can reserve the term 'strict law' for the relatively simple nomic postulates of a homonomic theory, rather than the set of logical consequences of those postulates – in which case claim (ii) above will be false. Either way, the Davidson-inspired argument for the modularity principle has a false premise. (Incidentally, we do not mean to attribute the argument to Davidson himself, since we doubt whether he would accept claim (iii).)

IV

We have been arguing that FP-events might well be identical with arbitrarily complex, highly gerrymandered, CS-events which themselves are not naturally-isolable relative to CS, but instead are fully decomposable into *parts* which have this feature. Of course, if FP-events really do exist, then they will have to accord with the causal architecture of FP; that is, they will have to be causally related to each other, to sensation, and to behavior in the ways that FP says they are. Indeed, as functionalists in philosophy of mind have so often stressed, the causal or functional principles of FP are crucial to the very individuation of FP-events; what makes a given event count (say) as a token belief-that-p is, to a considerable extent, the fact that it occupies the causal role which FP assigns to tokens of that belief-type.[15]

So if our non-modular picture of the relation between FP and CS is to be plausible, it is essential that complex, gerrymandered events can properly be considered causes, even if they involve "great webs of structure" relative to lower-level theory. While a detailed discussion must be beyond the scope of this paper, a brief consideration of the causal status of complex events will help to clarify our argument.

Let us say that an event e *minimally* causes an event f just in case e causes f and no proper part of e causes f. We want to advance two claims about minimal causation, each of which will receive some support below. First, even if an event e is a genuine cause of an event f, nevertheless f also might be caused by some event which is a proper part of e; thus e might be a genuine cause of f without being a minimal cause of f. Second, if e causes not only f but also some other event g, then it might be that the part of e which minimally causes f is different from the part of e which minimally causes g.[16]

These two facts are important because they make it relatively easy for events to exist which satisfy the causal principles of FP. If FP attributes both the event f and the event g to a single cause e at time t, and in fact there are distinct (though perhaps partially overlapping) events e_1 and e_2 such that e_1 minimally causes f (at t) and e_2 minimally causes g (at t), this does not necessarily falsify FP. For, e might well have both e_1 and e_2 as *parts*; indeed, it might well have as parts all those events which minimally cause (at t) one or another of the various events which FP says are effects (at t) of e. As long as this complex event is itself the effect of whatever prior events FP says are e's causes, the event will be (identical with) e.

The upshot is that FP could very easily turn out to be true, even if modularity is dramatically violated. Not only can FP-events be complex and highly gerrymandered, with numerous naturally-isolable CS-events as parts, but any given FP-event e can cause its effects in a conglomerative manner, with different effects having different parts of e as their respective minimal causes.[17]

V

Perhaps it will be objected that our analysis is too permissive; that unless we adopt Stich's modularity condition, over and above the requirement that FP-events conform to the causal architecture which FP assigns to them, we impose no non-trivial constraints on the truth conditions of upper-level causal claims; that is, we allow such claims to come out true regardless of the character of the theory that underlies them. We shall conclude by considering this objection.

It is clear that some underlying theories are inconsistent with the truth of some upper-level causal claims. For example, if the world is anything like the way our current chemistry and physics describe it, then possession by the devil cannot be a cause of any psychological disorders, and loss of phlogiston cannot be a cause of the chemical changes undergone by metals when they oxidize. To consider a case which is closer to home, it seems clear that if we are Skinnerian creatures – that is, creatures whose behavior is fully described and explained by the basic principles of Skinnerian psychology – then folk-psychological claims postulating beliefs, desires, and the like as among the causes of our behavior cannot be true.

The worry under consideration is that our non-modular approach to inter-theoretic compatibility is so liberal that it would allow claims of the above sort to come out true even though they seem clearly inconsistent with underlying theory. We shall argue that this worry is ill-founded.

It will be helpful to distinguish two different conceptions or expectations regarding the epistemic role of a radical failure of fit or integration between an upper-level theory and an underlying theory. On the first conception one thinks of this failure of fit as an important epistemic route to the falsity of the upper-level theory, where that falsity may not be obvious otherwise. The idea.is that even if direct evidence at the upper level does not clearly point to the falsity of an upper-level theory (and indeed may even seem to support this theory), none the less we can detect the falsity of the upper-level theory by noting its failure to fit in some appropriate way with some underlying theory which we have strong reason to believe is true. Clearly, both Stich and Churchland argue in accordance with this conception.

We find more plausible an importantly different conception of the epistemic significance of failure of fit between an upper-level and a lower-level theory. We do not deny, of course, that lower-level theories can be incompatible with upper-level theories. We do doubt, however, whether it is common or typical that one can know that an upper-level theory is false only by noting its failure to fit with a true underlying theory. More typically, when an upper-level theory is false there is direct evidence for this fact, independently of the failure of fit. The incompatibility arises not because of a failure of modularity, but rather because there simply are no events – either simple or complex – which have all the features which the upper-level theory attributes to the events it posits. Crudely put, the idea is that while various theories of juvenile delinquency or learning behavior can be inconsistent with neurophysiological theories or with physical theories, the former are *likely* to be confirmable or discomfirmable by the sorts of evidence available to sociologists and psychologists. It will be rare for a theory to be supported by a very wide range of evidence available to the sociologist or the psychologist and yet turn out to be radically false (because its ontology fails to mesh properly with that of some underlying theory). So our conception suggests a greater epistemological autonomy for upper-level disciplines like psychology than does a conception of inter-theoretic compatibility which incorporates a modularity condition.

We have emphasized this epistemological point because it bears directly on worries about the permissiveness of our non-modular conception. While our approach is by no means trivial in the sense that it allows every upper-level theory to be compatible with every underlying theory, it is permissive and deflationary in that, at least for a wide variety of cases, considerations of fit will not play the sort of independent normative role which they would play under a modularity requirement.

With this in mind, let us return to the examples with which we began this section. Consider first the case of possession by the devil. Like other causally explanatory notions, the notion of possession by the devil is to be understood, in large measure, in terms of the role it plays in a network of causal relations. Possession by the devil causes or may cause various kinds of pathological behavior. Such effects may be diminished or eliminated by the use of appropriate religious ceremonies (for example, prayers or exorcism). When behavior is due to possession by the devil, there is no reason to suppose that it will be affected by other forms of treatment (drugs, nutritional changes, psychotherapy, etc.). The state of possession is itself the effect of the activities of a being who has many other extraordinary powers.

Now if an event of possession by the devil (call it d) is to be a cause of a certain bit of behavior (for example, jabbering incoherently), then d must, on our analysis, be identifiable with some event (call it e) describable in terms of the predicates of our underlying theory; and it must be the case that, given this identification, at least most of the other causal generalizations in which d is held to figure, according to the theory of devil-possession, should come out true. (Although our conception of inter-theoretic fit countenances failures of modularity, it does insist that the identifications we make preserve the "causal architecture" of the upper-level theory.) We submit that no matter how large and complex one makes the event e with which one proposes to identify d, and no matter how willing one may be to regard proper parts of e as causally efficacious, there is simply *no* plausible candidate· for e which, given our present physical and chemical theory, will make the network of causal claims associated with possession by the devil come out mainly true. That is, there is simply no event e, however complex, which is linked by law to various forms of behavior associated with possession, which is inefficacious in producing such behavior when exorcism is used, which is shown by law to be produced by an agency having the properties of the devil, and so forth.

This example illustrates the general epistemological claim made above. In effect, we have argued that causal claims about possession by the devil are false not because of sophisticated considerations having to do with modularity (or with "smoothness of reduction"), but because the causal architecture associated with possession by the devil is radically mistaken; nothing stands in the network of causal relations with various other events in the way that possession by the devil is supposed to. We can see this immediately by noting that the falsity of claims attributing causal efficacy to devil-possession is, so to speak, directly discoverable without considerations having to do with chemistry, physics, or biology. If one were to run suitably controlled experiments, then presumably one would quickly discover that exorcism does not affect devil-possession type behavior, that certain other therapies do, and so forth.[18]

A similar set of observations seems relevant in connection with the allegation that our approach would permit causal claims about beliefs to be true even if we are Skinnerian creatures. FP asserts that beliefs, desires, and other propositional attitudes are related to one another in many and various ways, over and above their causal relations to sensation and behavior. Skinnerian theory, on the other hand, denies that we need to postulate such richly interacting internal events in order to explain behavior, and it also denies that such events exist at all. Rather, the Skinnerian claims that the causal chains leading from environmental "stimulus" to behavioral "response" are largely isolated from one another, rather like the various parallel non-interacting communication-channels in a fiber-optics communications line; thus, whatever internal events are involved in any particular stimulus–response pairing will not bear very many significant causal relations to the internal events that are involved in other stimulus–response pairings; that is, the Skinnerian claims that as a matter of empirical fact, the generalizations linking stimuli and behavior are so simple and straightforward that they are incompatible with the existence of internal events which interact in the rich way which folk-psychological events are supposed to interact with one another. So if the Skinnerian is right, then there simply are no internal events, in humans or in other organisms, which bear all the causal relations to sensation, to behavior, and to one another which FP assigns to beliefs, desires, and the like. Thus our non-modular conception of inter-theoretic fit would indeed be violated if humans should turn out to be mere Skinnerian creatures. Accordingly, this conception is not unduly permissive after all.

This example also illustrates the epistemological claims made above. It is satisfaction of the "causal architecture" of FP, by some set of (possibly complex) events in the central nervous system, which is crucial to the truth of FP. Hence if we are Skinnerian creatures, so that the causal architecture assumed by FP is not instantiated in us by any events either simple or complex, then presumably this fact will show up at the level of a relatively coarse-grained analysis of our molar behavior. Simulus–response laws that are incompatible with the causal architecture of FP will be discoverable, and will be usable to explain and predict the full range of human behavior. Hence it will not be the case the FP seems to be largely true, according to the best available coarse-grained evidence, and yet turns out to be false merely because of failure to fit properly with some underlying theory.

The upshot, then, is that our approach seems exactly as permissive as it should be, and this fact speaks in its favor; by contrast, a modular conception of inter-theoretic fit seems excessively strict, since it is unmotivated and it denies higher-level theories an adequate degree of epistemological autonomy. So, given (i) the notable failure, to date, of behaviorist-inspired psychology's efforts to unearth stimulus–response laws which are applicable to human behavior generally and which undercut the causal architecture of FP, (ii) the fact that folk-psychological notions seem to lie at the very heart of cognitivist theories like attribution theory and cognitive dissonance theory, and (iii) the fact that FP serves us very well in the everyday explanation and prediction of behavior, it seems very hard to deny that in all probability, folk psychology is here to stay.[19,20,21]

1 Actually, we regard the example in the first paragraph as a schema which yields a whole range of instances when various sentences are substituted for the letter 'p' and various sortal predicates are substituted for the dummy phrase 'of kind K.' (The word 'someone', though, functions as a quantificational term; under appropriate regimentation, it would go over into a

universal quantifier whose scope is the whole schema.) We prefer to think of predicates of the form "...believes that p" as what Quine (1970) calls *attitudinatives* – i.e., complex one-place predicates constructed by appending a predicate-forming operator ('believes that') to a sentence. On this view, propositional attitudes have no "objects," since they are not relational states. For further discussion see Horgan 1989.

2 For visual perception, see e.g. Gregory (1970).

3 For example, eighteenth-century chemical theories attempted to explain such properties of metals as their shininess and ductility by appeal to the same factors which were also thought to explain the compound-forming behavior of metals. Chemical theories such as Lavosier's focused just on compounds, and orginally were criticized for their failure to provide also a unified explanation of metallic shininess and ductility.

4 For some striking evidence that situational theories are more empirically adequate, and hence that this change has been a progressive one, see Nisbett and Ross (1980).

5 Thus his critical remarks on Fodor (1975), and in general on cognitive psychological theories that take information to be stored in sentential form; cf. Churchland (1981, pp. 78 ff).

6 In order to elevate anomalous monism into a full-fledged version of materialism, one must add to it an account of the metaphysical status of mental state-types (properties) *vis-à-vis* physico-chemical state-types. The appropriate doctrine, we think, is one also propounded by Davidson (1970, 1974): viz., that mental properties are *supervenient* upon physical ones. Several philosophers recently have developed this idea, arguing that materialism should incorporate some sort of supervenience thesis. Cf. Kim (1978, 1982); Haugeland (1982); Horgan (1981b, 1982b); and Lewis (1983). Also see the papers collected in the Spindel issue of *The Southern Journal of Philosophy*, 22, 1984.

7 For surveys of the relevant literature, see Nisbett and Wilson 1977, and Wilson (unpublished).

8 At any rate, this is what the dual-control thesis amounts to as regards the Storms–Nisbett study. Other kinds of mental events besides beliefs and inferences might sometimes be involved too.

9 See, for instance, Wilson (unpublished), pp. 7 ff.

10 Still, one can understand why Stich would be led to attribute the radical dual-control thesis to Wilson, even though Wilson evidently does not actually hold this view. Stich quotes from what evidently was an earlier version of the above-quoted passage, wherein Wilson said that the function of the verbal system "is to attempt to verbalize, explain and communicate what is occurring in the unconscious system." Admittedly, this earlier wording suggests that in verbalizing our mental states we *never* have conscious access to those states. But the present passage, with its explicit acknowledgment of frequent conscious access, evidently cancels this suggestion, along with any implicit commitment to the radical dual-control thesis.

11 Although we think it quite possible that CS will become non-modular at its most fundamental levels, we also believe that certain higher-level branches of theoretical pscyhology probably not only will remain modular, but will continue to employ the concepts of FP itself. Attribution theory is a case in point. (By a "higher-level" psychological theory we mean one which posits events that are wholes whose parts are the events posited by "lower-level" psychological theories. More on this below.)

12 It is worth noting another respect in which Stich's (and Churchland's) arguments seem to lead to sweeping and implausibly strong conclusions. Much formal theory in the social sciences involves ascribing to individual actors states which are recognizably like, or recognizably descended from, the FP notions of belief and desire. Within economic and game theory, for example, individual actors are thought of as having indifference curves, utility schedules, or preference orderings over various possible outcomes, and beliefs about the subjective probabilities of these outcomes. Within economic theories of voting or political party behavior, similar assumptions are made. Even among theorists of voting behavior who reject the "economic" approach, typically there are appeals to voters' beliefs

and attitudes to explain behavior. (See, for example, Campbell et al 1960.) Clearly, if Stich's modularity requirement and Churchland's smoothness of reduction requirement are not satisfied by the FP notions of belief and desire, then they are unlikely to be satisfied by the notions of utility, degree of belief, and so forth employed by such theories. Thus Stich and Churchland seem to have produced general arguments which, if cogent, would show – quite independently of any detailed empirical investigation of the actual behavior of markets, voters, etc. – that all these theories must be false, at least on their most natural interpretation.

13 A complex event of the relevant kind might be a mereological sum, or *fusion*, of simpler events; alternatively, it might be an entity distinct from this event-fusion. We shall take no stand on this matter here. (The issue is closely related to the question whether an entity like a ship is identical with the fusion of its physical parts, or is instead an entity distinct from this fusion, with different intra-world and trans-world identity conditions.) To our knowledge, the most explicit and well-developed theory of parts and wholes for events is that of Thompson (1977); event-fusions are the only kinds of complex events she explicitly countenances.

14 This Davidsonian argument was suggested to us by Stich himself, in conversation.

15 But as the famous case of Twin Earth (Putnam 1975) seems to show, an event's causal role is not the only factor relevant to its folk-psychological individuation. Our doppelgangers on Twin Earth don't undergo tokens of the type *believing that water is good to drink*, even though they do undergo events that are functionally indistinguishable from our own token beliefs that water is good to drink. The trouble is that the stuff they call "water" isn't water at all. Cf. Burge 1979.

16 While a full defense of these claims must be beyond the scope of this paper, we think they are required for the truth of many causal statements in contexts where highly developed and precise formal theories are not available. Consider the claims (a) that application of a certain fertilizer causes plants to increase in mean height, and also causes them to increase in leaf width; (b) that following a certain study routine R causes an increase in SAT verbal scores, and also causes an increase in SAT mathematical scores; or (c) that certain child-rearing practices cause an increase in the incidence of juvenile delinquency in certain populations. There is an enormous literature detailing complex and ingenious statistical techniques for testing such claims. (Fisher 1935 is an early classic, inspired largely by problems connected with testing claims like (a); and many books on "causal modeling," like Blalock 1971, discuss procedures that are relevant to (b) and (c).) These techniques might well establish that the three claims are true. Yet the cases described in (a), (b), and (c) can easily fail to be minimal causes; the fertilizer will commonly be a mixture, containing compounds which are inert, or which have other effects on the plant besides those mentioned in (a); and it seems implausible to suppose that every feature or detail of study routine R or child rearing practice C is causally necessary for the above effects. (Typically, we have no practical way of determining what the minimal causes in such cases are.) Thus (a) can be true even though the fertilizer is a mixture of several distinct compounds, one of which causes increase in height (but not increase in leaf width) while the other causes increase in leaf width (but not height). Similarly, (b) can be true even though different aspects of study routine R are responsible for the increases in math and in verbal scores. (See Thomson (1977) for further defense of the claim that genuine causes don't have to be minimal causes.)

17 The point about conglomerative causation is also relevant to Stich's dual-control argument against FP. Even if verbal and non-verbal behavior should turn out to have largely separate minimal causes, FP could be true anyway; for, FP-events might be complexes of the minimal causes, and these complex events might be genuine causes (albeit non-minimal causes) of both the verbal and the non-verbal behavior. (We should stress, however, that we are *not* claiming that if the dual-control thesis is true, then whenever a subject is in some state B of his non-verbal behavioral system and some state V of his verbal system, it will

always be possible, consistently with FP, to ascribe to him some single folk-psychological cause of both his verbal and non-verbal behavior. Whether this will be possible depends upon the specific states V and B and upon the behavior they cause. In the Storms–Wilson insomnia experiment, for example, the state B (subjects' attribution of their symptoms to pills) which causes the arousal group to fall asleep is not merely distinct from the state V which causes their verbal behavior (denial that the above attribution had anything to do with their falling asleep); but in addition, these two states cannot, consistently with the causal principles embodied in FP, be treated as components of some single belief.)

18 Of course, it might be that some cases of exorcism appear to be efficacious, but this is only because they involve certain features which are also cited by other, more secular, theories (e.g., reassuring the "possessed" person, giving him attention, etc.). Establishing this can require ingenuity in experimental design, but poses no problem in principle. It is just false that we could never obtain direct experimental evidence (distinct from considerations of modularity or failure of fit) that would make it rational to reject the claim that exorcism is efficacious in itself, by virtue of dislodging the devil.

19 Although we have assumed throughout that folk-psychological events are complex events consisting of lower-level events as their parts, we want to acknowledge that it may be possible to defend the compatibility of FP and CS without this assumption. Jaegwon Kim (1966, 1969, 1973) holds that an event is an entity consisting in the instantiation of a property by an object at a time, and that mental events consist in the instantiation of mental properties by individuals at times. Under this approach, it is unclear whether lower-level events can sensibly be treated as parts of FP-events. Nevertheless, an advocate of Kim's theory of events still might be able to argue that FP-events exist and bear all the causal relations to one another that FP says they do. For he might be able to argue that these events are supervenient upon groups of lower-level events, and that supervenience transmits causal efficacy. Cf. Kim 1979, 1982, 1984.

20 Throughout this paper we have assumed, as is usual, that if everyday folk-psychological statements are indeed true, then there really exist folk-psychological mental events – that is, token desires, token beliefs, and so forth. In fact, however, one of us (Horgan) thinks there are good reasons for denying the existence of events in general; cf. Horgan 1978, 1981a, 1982a. Horgan also thinks that if physico-chemical events exist, then normally there will be numerous classes of physico-chemical events from within someone's head which jointly meet all the causal conditions which would qualify a given class for identification with the class consisting of that person's folk-psychological mental events; and he takes this to indicate that even if physico-chemical events exist, and even if garden-variety folk-psychological statements (including statements about mental causation) are often true, nevertheless there really are no such entities as mental events; cf. Horgan and Tye 1985. We believe that the essential points of the present paper can be reformulated in a way which does not require the existence of mental events (even if physico-chemical events are assumed to exist), and also in a way which does not require the existence of any events at all. But our objective here has been the more limited one of defending FP within the framework of the ontology of events which is widely taken for granted in contemporary philosophy of mind.

21 We thank Stephen Stich, William Tolhurst, and Michael Tye for helpful comments on an earlier version of this paper.

REFERENCES

Blalock, H. (ed.) (1971) *Causal Models in the Social Sciences*, New York, Aldine,

Burge, T. (1979) "Individualism and the mental," in P. French, T. Uehling, and H. Wettstein (eds), *Midwest Studies in Philosophy*, vol. 4, *Studies in Epistemology*, Minneapolis, University of Minnesota Press.

Campbell, A., Converse, P., Miller, W. and Stokes, D. (1960) *The American Voter*, New York, John Wiley & Sons.

Churchland, P. (1979) *Scientific Realism and the Plasticity of Mind*, New York, Cambridge University Press.

Churchland, P. (1981) "Eliminative materialism and propositional attitudes," *Journal of Philosophy*, 78.

Davidson, D. (1967) "Causal relations," *Journal of Philosophy*, 64.

Davidson, D. (1970) "Mental events," in L. Foster and J. Swanson (eds), *Experience and Theory*, London, Duckworth.

Davidson, D. (1973). "The material mind," in P. Suppes et al. (eds), *Logic, Methodology, and the Philosophy of Science*, vol. 4, Amsterdam, North-Holland.

Davidson, D. (1974) "Psychology as philosophy," in S. C. Brown (ed.), *Philosophy of Psychology* New York, Harper & Row.

Dennett, D. (1978) *Brainstorms*, Cambridge, MA, Bradford.

Dennett, D. (1981) "Three kinds of intentional psychology," in R. Healey (ed.), *Reduction, Time, and Identity*, New York, Cambridge University Press.

Field, H. (1978) "Mental representation," *Erkenntnis*, 13.

Fisher, R. (1935) *The Design of Experiments*, Edinburgh, Oliver and Boyd.

Fodor, J. (1975) *The Language of Thought*, New York, Thomas Y. Crowell.

Fodor, J. (1978) "Propositional attitudes," *The Monist*, 61.

Gregory, R. (1970) *The Intelligent Eye*, New York, McGraw-Hill.

Haugeland, J. (1982) "Weak supervenience," *American Philosophical Quarterly*, 19.

Horgan, T. (1978) "The case against events," *Philosophical Review*, 87.

Horgan, T. (1981a) "Action theory without actions," *Mind*, 90.

Horgan, T. (1981b) "Token physicalism, supervenience, and the generality of physics," *Synthese*, 34.

Horgan, T. (1982a) "Substitutivity and the causal connective," *Philosophical Studies*, 42.

Horgan, T. (1982b) "Supervenience and microphysics," *Pacific Philosophical Quarterly*, 63

Horgan, T. (1989) "Attitudinatives," *Linguistics and Philosophy* 12, 133–65.

Horgan, T. and Tye, M. (1985) "Against the token identity theory," in E. LePore and B. McLaughlin (eds), *Essays on Actions and Events*, Basil Blackwell.

Kim, J. (1966) "On the psycho-physical identity theory," *American Philosophical Quarterly*, 3.

Kim, J. (1969) "Events and their descriptions: Some considerations," in N. Rescher et al. (eds), *Essays in Honor of Carl G. Hempel*, Dordrecht, Reidel.

Kim, J. (1973) "Causation, nomic subsumption, and the concept of event," *Journal of Philosophy*, 70.

Kim, J. (1978) "Supervenience and nomological incommensurables," *American Philosophical Quarterly*, 15.

Kim, J. (1979) "Causality, identity, and supervenience in the mind–body problem," *Midwest Studies in Philosophy*, 4.

Kim, J. (1982) "Psychophysical supervenience," *Philosophical Studies*, 41.

Kim, J. (1984) "Supervenience and supervenient causation," *Southern Journal of Philosophy*, 22.

Lewis, D. (1983) "New work for a theory of universals," *Australasian Journal of Philosophy*, 61.

Lycan, W. (1981) "Toward a homuncular theory of believing," *Cognition and Brain Theory*, 4.

Minsky, M. (1981) "K-Lines: A theory of memory," in D. Norman (ed.), *Perspectives on Cognitive Science*, Norwood, NJ, Ablex.

Nisbett, R., and Ross, L. (1980) *Human Inference: Strategies and Shortcomings of Social Judgment*, Englewood Cliffs, NJ, Prentice-Hall.

Nisbett, R. and Wilson, T. (1977) "Telling more than we can know: Verbal reports on mental processes," *Psychological Review*, 84.

Putnam, H. (1975) "The Meaning of 'Meaning'," in K. Gunderson (ed.), *Language, Mind, and*

Knowledge, Minnesota Studies in the Philosophy of Science, 7, Minneapolis, University of Minnesota Press.

Quine, W. V. O. (1970) *Philosophy of Logic*, Englewood Cliffs, NJ, Prentice-Hall.

Stich, S. (1983) *From Folk Psychology to Cognitive Science: The Case Against Belief*, Cambridge, MA, Bradford.

Storms, M. and Nisbett, R. (1970) "Insomnia and the attribution process," *Journal of Personality and Social Psychology*, 2.

Thomson, J. (1977) *Acts and Other Events*, Ithaca, Cornell.

Wilson, T. (unpublished) "Strangers to ourselves: The origins and accuracy of beliefs about one's own mental states."

Banish DisContent

JERRY A. FODOR

It is a curiosity of the philosophical temperament, this passion for radical solutions. Do you feel a little twinge in your epistemology? Absolute scepticism is the thing to try. Has the logic of confirmation got you down? Probably physics is a fiction. Worried about individuating objects? Don't let anything in but sets. Nobody has yet suggested that the way out of the Liar paradox is to give up talking, but I expect it's only a matter of time. Apparently the rule is: if aspirin doesn't work, try cutting off your head.

The latest of these cures for which there is no adequate disease is the suggestion that – largely on account of some semantic puzzles about content – psychological theory should dispense with the attribution of propositional attitudes. In my view, this is a *grotesque* proposal; both because we can't do without propositional attitude psychology and because it's far from clear that the semantic problems are as bad as they are alleged to be. The plan of this paper is to look very briefly at the first of these considerations and rather extensively at the second.

1   Why we can't do without propositional attitude psychology

We can't do without propositional attitude psychology because, on the one hand, propositional attitude psychology works and, on the other hand, nothing else does. Propositional attitude psychology works so well that the mechanism is practically invisible. It is like those mythical Rolls Royce cars whose engines are sealed when they leave the factory; only it's better because it's not mythical. Someone I don't know telephones me at my office in Cambridge from – as it might be – Arizona. "Would you like to lecture here next Tuesday?" are the words that he utters. "Yes, thank you. I'll be at your airport on the 3.00 p.m. flight" are the words that I reply.[1] That's *all* that happens, but it's more than enough; the rest of the burden is routinely taken up by theory. And the theory works so well that, several days later (or weeks later, or months later, or years later; you can vary the example to taste) and several thousand miles away, there I am at the airport, and there he is to meet me. Or if I don't turn up, it's less likely that the theory has failed than that something went wrong with the airline and the aeroplane is late. For these sorts of purposes, people are more predictable mechanisms than jets.

The point is that the theory from which we get this extraordinary predictive power is just good old commonsense propositional attitude psychology. That's what tells us, for example, how to infer people's intentions from the sounds they make (if someone utters the form of words "I'll be at your airport on the 3.00 p.m. flight" then, with enormously high probability, he intends to be at your airport on the 3.00 p.m. flight) and how to infer people's behavior from their intentions (if someone intends to be at your airport on the 3.00 p.m. flight then, with enormously high probability, he will produce behavior of a sort which will eventuate in his arriving at that place at that time barring mechanical failure). And all this works not just with people whose psychology you know intimately: your closest friends, say, or the spouse of your bosom. It works with absolute strangers: people you wouldn't know if you bumped into them. And it works not just in laboratory conditions – where you can control the interacting variables – but also, indeed pre-eminently, in field conditions where *all* you know about the sources of variance is what commonsense psychology tells you about them. Remarkable. If we could do that well with predicting the weather, no one would ever get his feet wet. Yet the etiology of the weather is surely child's play compared with the causes of behavior.

Physics, by the way, doesn't begin to complete: though we can, by exploiting our knowledge of their psychology, routinely bring off these extraordinary predictions of the *behavior* of "intentional systems," there is no way – practically speaking – that we can hope to predict their *trajectories*. If you think of me as two hundred pounds (less in the jogging season) of peripatetic philosopher whose itinerary you've just been informed of, there are long odds you can predict where I'll be at 3.00 p.m. on Tuesday. Whereas, if you think of me as an equivalent mass of hydrocarbons which just produced a couple of seconds of local acoustic perturbation, nothing useful follows from any physical science we now have or can ever reasonably expect.

To be sure, that's just *commonsense* propositional attitude psychology; and it's mostly *implicit* commonsense propositional attitude psychology to boot. It might still be that, for scientific purposes, something other – something better – is required. After all, what we want in science is insight and explanation, not just prediction and control. It is now widely said that propositional attitude psychology is seen to be a "stagnant" theory when viewed in the light of these desiderata. By contrast, what is not stagnant, what is said to be making scientific progress, is computational psychology, in which appeals to the attitudes are dispensed with. (See, for example, Stich 1983.)

I am, I suppose, as good a friend of computational psychology as the next chap;

especially if the next chap is a philosopher. But that view of the current scene in cognitive science strikes me as a gross distortion. For, one can say in a phrase what it is that computational psychology has been proving so successful at: viz. *the vindication of generalizations about propositional attitudes*; specifically, of the more or less commonsense sort of generalizations about propositional attitudes illustrated a paragraph or so above. Thus, for example, we've got fragments of a theory of perception, and it makes clear how a computational system could regularly come to believe that P in causal consequence of its being visibly the case that P. Analogously, we've got fragments of a theory of language, and what it does is to make clear how, in a computational system, the intention to communicate the belief that P could eventuate, causally, in the production of an utterance that means that P. Or again, we've got fragments of a theory of memory; it explains how a computational system could come to believe that it was once the case that P in causal consequence of the fact that it was once the case that P. And so forth. The mental processes that such computational theories acknowledge are, no doubt, in some sense "purely syntactic"; at a minimum, they're supposed to be specifiable without recourse to intentional idiom. But the generalizations that such theories account for are intentional down to their boots. Accordingly, computational theories of mental process don't replace the commonsense story about propositional attitudes and their behavioural effects. Rather, what a computational theory does is to make clear the mechanism of intentional causation; to show how it is (nomologically) possible that purely computational – indeed, purely physical – systems should act out of their beliefs and desires.

I don't suppose that all that comes to much; I just wanted to remind you that – given standard principles of Scientific Realism – there is an enormous prima facie case for taking commonsense propositional attitude psychology to be more or less true. No doubt this case is less than literally conclusive. In principle, somebody might find overwhelming reason for rejecting intentional psychology; so overwhelming that rejecting intentional psychology would be rational even if we had no idea at all what to replace it with. (As, indeed, we don't.) But *overwhelming* reason is surely what rationality would require. If the sky opened up and God told us that there aren't any propositional attitudes, then I suppose that we would have to believe Him. But it's not clear that a great deal less than that would do.

Having thus made clear where the burden of proof resides, let's look at the semantic puzzles about content.

2   Puzzles about content: Twin-Earth

Is there anybody who *hasn't* heard? There's this place, you see, that's just like here except that they've got XYZ where we've got H_2O. In this place, there's someone who's just like me down to and including his neurological microstructure. The intuition that we're invited to have is that, in virtue of the hydrochemical facts and in spite of the neurological ones, the form of words "water is wet" means something different in his mouth than it does in mine. And, similarly, the content of the thought that Twin-Me has when he thinks (*in re* XYZ, as one might say) that water is wet is different from the content of the thought that I have when I think that water is wet *in re* H_2O.

Suppose these intuitions are reliable; what follows? Well, on the one hand, my Twin and I are identical in physical constitution but, on the other hand, our thoughts have different truth conditions (that is, what makes *his* 'water'-thoughts true is the facts about XYZ, whereas what makes my water-thoughts true is the facts about H_2O). So, it looks as though we have to say either (a) that thoughts don't have their truth conditions essentially (that is, that two tokens of the *same* thought can have *different* truth conditions), or (b) that type-identity of thoughts doesn't supervene upon biochemical type-identity of their thinkers.

That, then, is the "Twin-Earth Problem." Except that so far it isn't a problem; it's just a handful of intuitions together with a commentary on some immediate implications of accepting them. If that were all there is, the right response would surely be "So what?" What connects the intuitions and implications with the proposal that we give up on propositional attitude psychology is a certain *Diagnosis*. And, while a lot has been written about the intuitions and their implications, the Diagnosis has gone largely unexamined.

Here's the Diagnosis: "Look, on *anybody's* story, the notion of content (or 'intention') has got to be a little problematic. For one thing, it is proprietary to the information sciences, and *soi-disant* 'emergents' ought, at a minimum, to bear the burden of proof. At the very minimum, if you're going to have contents, you owe us some sort of account of their individuation.

"Now, prior to the Twin-Earth problem, there *was* some sort of account of their individuation; you could say, to a first approximation, that identity of intention depends on identity of extension. No doubt that story leaked a bit: thoughts about the Morning Star look to be different in content from the corresponding thoughts about the Evening Star, even though their truth conditions are arguably the same. But at least one could hold firmly to this: 'No difference in extension without some difference in intention.' Conversely, it was a test for identity of intention that the extensions came out to be the same. And that was the best test; it was the one source of evidence about intentional identity that seemed surely reliable. Compare the notorious wobbliness of intuitions about synonymy, analyticity and the like.

"But now we see that after all it's not true that difference of extension implies difference of intention. Your Twin's 'water'-thoughts and your own are intentionally identical – assuming supervenience – but extensionally distinct. So unclear are we now about what intentional identity comes to – hence about what identity of propositional attitudes comes to – that we can't even assume that if two thoughts are intentionally identical they will be true and false together. The fact is, as we now see, we have no idea at all of what criteria of individuation for propositional attitudes might be like; hence we have no idea at all what counts as evidence for identity of propositional attitudes. (Given which, by the way, it is hardly surprising that propositional attitude psychology so rarely proves to be disconfirmed; once you abandon the extensional constraints, ascriptions of propositional attitudes are arbitrarily available for being gerrymandered.)

"*To summarize*: Inferences from difference of extension to difference of content used to bear almost all the weight of propositional attitude attribution. That was, however, a frail reed and now it has broken. The Twin-Earth problem is a problem *because it breaks the connection between extensional identity and intentional identity.*"[2]

Now, the Twin-Earth intuitions are fascinating, and if you care about the semantics of kind-terms you will, no doubt, do well to attend to them. But, as I've taken pains to emphasize, you need the Diagnosis to connect the Twin-Earth intuitions to the issues about belief/desire psychology, and – fortunately for friends of propositional attitudes – the Diagnosis rests on a quite trivial mistake: THE TWIN-EARTH EXAMPLES DON'T BREAK THE CONNECTION BETWEEN INTENTION AND EXTENSION; THEY JUST RELATIVIZE IT TO CONTEXT.

Suppose that what you used to think, prior to Twin-Earth, is that intentions are something like functions from thoughts to truth conditions. Presumably, a truth condition would then be a function from worlds to truth values; condition TC takes world W on to the value T iff TC is satisfied in W. For example, in virtue of its intention, the thought that it's raining has the truth condition *that it's raining* and is thus true in every world in which it's raining and false in every other world.

I hasten to emphasize that if you don't – or didn't – like that story, it's quite all right for you to choose some other; my point is going to be that if you liked that *kind* of story before Twin-Earth, you're perfectly free to go on liking it now. For, even if all the intuitions about Twin-Earth are right, and even if they have the implications that they are said to have, extensional identity still constrains intentional identity because *intentions still determine extensions* (relative to a context). If you like, intentions are functions from *contexts* and thoughts on to truth conditions.

What, if anything, does that mean? Well, there is presumably something about the relation between Twin-Earth and Twin-Me in virtue of which his 'water'-thoughts are about XYZ even though mine are not. Call this condition that's satisfied by {Twin-Me, Twin Earth} condition C (because it determines a Context). Similarly, there must be something about the relation between me and Earth in virtue of which my water-thoughts are about H_2O even though my Twin's 'water'-thoughts aren't. Call this condition that is satisfied by {me, Earth} condition C'. We don't know what sorts of things C and C' constrain, but causal relations of some kind are the current best bet and, anyhow, it doesn't matter much for the purposes at hand. Because we *do* know this: short of a miracle, it must be possible to satisfy C without satisfying C' and vice versa. How do we know that? Well, because short of a miracle, the following must be true: if an organism shares the neurophysical constitution of my Twin *and satisfies C*, it follows that its thoughts and my Twin's thoughts share their truth conditions. In particular, the following counterfactual is true: in a world where I am in my Twin's context, given the neurophysical identity between us, my 'water'-thoughts are about XYZ iff his are.[3]

But now we have an extensional identity criterion for intentions: two intentions are identical only if they effect the same mapping of contexts on to truth conditions. Specifically, your thought is intentionally identical to mine only if in every context in which your thought has truth conditions TC mine has truth condition TC and vice versa.[4] It is worth noting that, by this criterion, my Twin's 'water'-thoughts are intentionally identical to my water-thoughts; they have the same intentional content even though, since their contexts are *de facto* different, they differ in truth conditons. In effect, what we have here is an extensional criterion for what is sometimes called "narrow" content. (The "broad content" of a thought, by contrast, is what you can semantically evaluate; it's what you get when you specify a narrow content *and fix a context*. This makes the notion of narrow content the more basic of the two; which is just what sensible people have always supposed it to be.)

We can now see why we ought to reject both of the following two suggestions found in Putnam 1975: That we consider the extension of a term (/concept) to be an independent component of the (to use Putnam's terminology) "vector" that is the meaning of the term; and that we make do, in our psychology, with stereotypes *instead of* intentions. The first proposal is redundant since, given a context, intentions determine extensions; and we have – so far at least – no reason for supposing that there aren't intentions. The second proposal is unacceptable because, unlike intentions, stereotypes *don't* determine extensions *even* given a context. And, as the Diagnosis rightly says, we need an extension-determiner as a component of the meaning vector because we rely on "different extension→different intentions" for the individuation of concepts.

There are, no doubt, serious objections to the line that I've been pushing. For example, "different extension→different intention" gives us only a necessary condition on intentional identity where what we really want is a biconditional. And if we try to parley what we've got into what we want, we run into the familiar troubles about thoughts that are extensionally identical but intentionally distinct. So, for example, it looks like – on the biconditional version – the thought that $2+2=4$ would come out to have the same intention as the thought that $3+3=6$. Not good.

However, these are just the old-fashioned, pre-Twin-Earth objections to the reduction of intentional identity to extensional identity, so they needn't concern us here. The main point to bear in mind is that if "different extension→different intention" substantively constrains the attribution of propositional attitudes, then so too does this same principle when it is relativized to context. So, if the worry about propositional attitudes is that Twin-Earth shows that extensions don't constrain intentions, the right thing to do about Twin-Earth is to STOP WORRYING.

Which is not, alas, to say that there is *nothing* to worry about.

First worry: It is one thing to have a (for example, extensional) criterion for the intentional identity of thoughts (which, indeed, we do); it is quite another to be able to say what the intention of a thought is (which, indeed, we can't). What, for example, is the intention of the thought – or, as we might as well say, what is the *thought* – such that when I have that thought its truth condition is that HO_2 is wet and when my Twin has it its truth condition is that XYZ is wet? Or, to put it another way (to put it, in fact, the old way) what is the *concept* WATER assuming that the concept WATER is not the concept H_2O?

I don't know the answer to this question, but I know how to find out: find out what (the word) "water" means. Perhaps "water" means something like "the local, transparent, potable, dolphin-torn, gong-tormented . . . , etc. stuff one sails on." If that is so, then the intention of my thought that water is wet (and of my Twin's thought that "water" is wet) is that the local transparent, potable, dolphin-torn, gong-tormented . . . , etc. stuff one sails on is wet. My water-thoughts are about H_2O because H_2O is the local transparent, potable . . . , etc. stuff in the context in which my water-thoughts transpire (and similarly, *mutatis mutandis*, for XYZ in the context of my Twin's 'water'-thoughts). This would mean that a kind concept is some sort of implicit description after all, and it does leave one wondering just which description the concept WATER is. Just as it always used to.

But why does this question have to have an answer? Why, that is, does there have to be a way of expressing the intention of "water" in English – or in Tw-English, for that matter – except as the intention of "water"? Does English have to have more than one way of expressing every intention that it can express at all? Does every word (concept) that has an intention have to have a definition? (There is, of course, a way of expressing the intention of "water" in, say, French: "water" *veut dire l'eau*. But if you're worried about what the intention of "water" could be – what it could be that picks out H_2O in the context Earth and XYZ in the context Twin-Earth – I don't suppose you will find this consideration comforting.)

I think this is all rather puzzling, but notice that it's a sort of puzzle that one has to face regardless of one's views about the Twin-Earth problem. So, for example, suppose you think that Twin-Earth shows that intention doesn't determine extension and/or that intention doesn't supervene upon neurophysiology. Still – and quite aside from all that – there's the following question: When my Twin says "water is wet" what does what he says mean? Not presumably, that water is wet since, on the present assumptions, there is no reason to identify the intention of "water $_{TW}$" (viz., of the Tw-English vocable that is pronounced like our word "water") with the intention of "water." And not that XYZ is wet since my Twin will presumably take "water is XYZ" to say something informative; something, indeed, which he might wish to deny. And not, for sure, that H_2O is wet since there isn't any H_2O on Twin-Earth, and my Twin has never so much as heard of the stuff. It looks like either "water $_{TW}$' means water (that is, has the same intention that "water" does) or its meaning is inexpressible in English. The moral seems to be: there is going to be a problem about saying what "water" and "water $_{TW}$" mean whatever view you take of the Twin-Earth problem. Or, to put it another way: the real problem is to figure out what "water" means. You tell me what "water" means and I'll bet that "water $_{TW}$" means that too.

Second worry: Since intentional identity supervenes upon neurophysical identity, and since – given a context – there is no difference of extension without a difference of intention, it follows that the corresponding thoughts of neurophysically identical intentional systems in the same context are coextensive. Good. But, as I remarked above (see note 3) you can have intentional (hence extensional) identity of thoughts without neurophysical identity of their thinkers. This suggests the following question: how much (and what kinds of) similarity between thinkers does the intentional identity of their thoughts require? This is, notice, a question one had better be able to answer if there is going to be a scientifically interesting propositional attitude psychology. For, generally speaking, the creatures that the generalizations of such a theory would have to subsume would not be anything like neurophysically identical; at a minimum they would differ as much as you and I differ from each other (at a maximum, they might differ as much as you and I differ from a silicon chip).

"What sorts of differences does intentional identity tolerate?" is the general form of the so-called "collateral information" problem; and whereas I think that the Twin-Earth problem is, for the reasons I've set forth, something of a red herring, the collateral information problem is really very nasty and I don't know how to fix it; not, at least, in any detail. The next section is devoted to poking at the collateral information problem in the hope that something will come loose.

3 Puzzles about content: Collateral information

Suppose Psmith (a neighbour, not a Twin) shares with me the belief that water is wet. And suppose we share all our other beliefs about water as well, except that he believes, and I do not, that cats like to drink water. This supposition looks to be OK; I mean, if it is possible that two people should have all their beliefs about water in common, it is also possible that two people should have all their beliefs about water in common except for the belief that water is something that cats like. On the other hand, the following is perhaps not OK: Psmith and I share all our beliefs about water except that he believes that water is animate and I do not. Here one feels inclined to say that if somebody really believes that water is animate, then he has a different concept of water and hence cannot, *strictu dictu*, be said to share one's belief that water is wet. In the first case, one feels inclined to say, having the belief that cats like (/don't like) water is *merely collateral* to having the concept WATER; whereas in the second case, one feels inclined to say, the belief that water is (in)animate *partially determines* the identity of the WATER concept that one has; sharing the concept WATER doesn't survive disagreement about things like that.

The philosophical point, however, is that it doesn't make the slightest bit of difference what one feels inclined to say about the examples. What is wanted is a principled way of drawing the distinction. Unless we have that, we have no way of determining identity and difference of intentional content in any case that falls short of a Twin case; in any case that falls short of neurophysical identity, that is.

This, of course, is just Quine psychologized. Quine puts it that you can't distinguish between theory and language. Putnam, drawing out the implications for computational pscyhology, puts it that you can't distinguish between concept and collateral information. In either case, the putative moral is the same: individual symbols (including mental representations) "are meaningful in the sense of making a systematic contribution to the functioning of the whole language; they don't have 'meanings', in the form of isolable objects, properties or processes, which are associated with them individually and which determine individual assertability conditions" (Putnam 1984, p. 1). But if mental representations don't have meanings, beliefs don't have contents. And if beliefs don't have contents, there are no beliefs.

Preliminary comment: The present problem arises whether or not you think there is a defensible notion of *narrow* mental content; that is, whether or not it is possible to preserve the intuition that my water-thoughts are somehow intentionally identical to my Twin's. You might, for example, take the view: "save the truth conditions and cognitive science be damned; there is no kind of belief content that supervenes on the neurophysical identify of believers." Even so, one must decide whether someone who believes that water is animate can have beliefs about water. If, as Quine and Putnam suppose, such questions aren't rationally resolvable, then the broad propositional attitudes go along with the narrow ones.

That would be all right with Putnam, of course; what he's stalking is the idea – which, by the way, he sometimes seems to suppose was invented at MIT – that an organism's behavior should be explained by reference to its propositional attitudes. Putnam sees that belief/desire explanations presuppose some such notion as content, and it is precisely the explication of content that considerations of semantic holism are supposed to preclude. Putnam is cheerful in face of this conclusion; but, for the reasons set out at the beginning, this insouciance strikes me as unwarranted.

At this point, I want to float a diagnosis of my own. As far as I can tell, the arguments for semantic holism invariably presuppose some form of "functional role" theory of meaning. If this diagnosis is correct, it comes down to a choice between the idea that behaviours are effects of beliefs and desires and the idea that meanings are constructs out of the functional roles of symbols; in which case, it seems to me that we ought to scrap the latter notion. For nothing that we believe about meaning is as likely to be true as most of what we believe about propositional attitudes. The rest of this paper will consist of variations on this theme.[5]

I take it that the argument from functional role semantics to semantic holism goes approximately as follows. First premise: Individual symbols "are meaningful in the sense of making a systematic contribution to the functioning of the whole language." Second premise: there is no principled distinction between aspects of a symbol's function that determine its meaning and aspects of its function that do not. Conclusion: Two symbols that differ in function at all must therefore differ in meaning at least to some extent. Similarly, *mutatis mutandis*, for concepts.

So if Psmith and I disagree at all in our beliefs, there is *ipso facto* some difference in the concepts that are the constituents of those beliefs. In face of this, we can say that nobody ever has the same concepts as anybody else, hence that the concepts "concept" and "conceptual identity" are unfit for serious scientific purposes; or we can say that the question when concepts are shared must be answered by fiat, hence again that the concepts "concept" and "conceptual identity" are unfit for serious scientific purposes. In either case, QED. We're not, in short, intended to infer from the identification of meanings with functional roles that there might be some way of saying which distinctions among roles correspond to distinctions among meanings. On the contrary, the idea is that because there is no principled way of individuating functional roles, there can be no principled way of individuating meanings either.

Now, in my view, both premises of the Quine/Putnam argument are false. But while the second premise is only false *strictu dictu*, I'm inclined to think that the first is false, root and branch. So let's start with it.

Neither Quine, nor Putnam, nor – to my knowledge – anybody else, has provided serious arguments for the identification of meaning with functional role, and I suspect that the main argument is simply a lack of alternatives.[6] This suggests a tactic for dealing with meaning holism arguments; namely, don't grant the theory of meaning that they presuppose.

It's not, after all, as though functional role theory offers a particularly plausible reconstruction of meaning. On the contrary, there is lots to be said against it; for example:

1 it invites meaning holism and hence scepticism about meaning. Thereby tending to refute itself.
2 it underestimates the inertia of content. By the inertia of content, I mean the fact that concepts can be shared by organisms whose overall psychological organizations differ in quite radical respects. So, for example, intuition strongly suggests that the concept WATER can be shared by me and Blind Me. Landau and Gleitman have some lovely data which suggest that a great many spatial concepts can be shared by me and Blind Me too; see Landau and Gleitman (1985). This sort of fact looks to present serious problems for functional role theories of concept individuation. For example, the *causal* roles that their concepts of water enter into must surely be very different for an organism like Blind Me, which never infers the presence of water from what it sees, than for an organism like me, that makes such inferences routinely. Yet the *functional* roles of their concepts will have to be the same if identity of functional roles is necessary for concept identity.

   The obvious reply is that the properties of causal relations that make for sameness and difference of functional role are very abstract indeed. Well, maybe; but there is an alternative proposal that seems a lot less strained. Namely that if Blind Me can share my concept of water, that's not because we both have mental representations with identical abstract causal roles; rather, it's because we both have mental representattions that are appropriately connected (causally, say) to water.
3 prima facie, functional role semantics is question-begging if functional role is taken to include referential role and hopeless if it's not.

I take it that the first half of the dilemma in 3 is patent. It is all right to speak informally of the inferential role of a concept as determining its functional role. But, *strictu dictu* for purposes of semantic theory, all one has at hand is the causal role of mental representations *syntactically individuated*. Assume more than that and the theory is going to take for granted precisely what most needs doing: namely, the reconstruction of the semantical notions in a vocabulary that is neither semantical nor intentional.[7]

The other half of the dilemma, however, is that if functional role is a syntactic notion, it's awfully hard to see how the functional role of a representation could determine what it means. There are widely publicized considerations which suggest that you can't get semantical properties out of symbols just by piling up their syntactical ones.

To summarize: once you have functional role semantics you are well on your way to meaning holism (and hence scepticism about the contents of propositional attitudes). For, their functional roles – unlike, notice, their causal attachments to the world – aren't, even in principle, things tht symbols can have severally. But who says you have to buy functional role semantics? Looked at the other way: if there is nothing serious against mental content except meaning holism, and if meaning holism is plausible only if functional role semantics is assumed, then all

that the enthusiast for mental content need do to shift the burden of argument is
to show that alternatives to functional role semantics are not out of the question.
(My friend Ned Block says that one shouldn't be interested in shifting the burden
of argument; one should be interested in *truth*. From each according to his ability
is what I say.)

So now I want to try to shift the burden of argument. I've thought a lot about
how to organize this discussion, and decided on balance not to. I shall simply set
out, in no particular order, some questions that come up if one thinks about a
theory that is Realist about content but does not take the notion of functional role
as fundamental in semantics. I should say that the line here is in broad agreement
with the semantical and ontological views of Barwise and Perry (1983) and with
the suggestions of Dretske (1981) and Stampe (1977). I don't know that any of
them have advertised their views as antidotes to semantic holism of the Quine/
Putnam variety, but that is what I'm now about to do.

Questions and answers

We begin with an easy question. (Discussion of the hard questions is postponed
indefinitely.)

Q1: Functionalism in the philosophy of mind teaches that believing that such-
and-such is a functional state; for, it argues, since dualism and type physicalism
are false, functionalism is all that's left, and whatever is all that's left must be true
(see, for example, Fodor 1968, where this line of argument is pursued
interminably). But functional states are *ipso facto* individuated by their functional
roles, are they not? So how can you be a Functionalist in philosophy of mind and
not be a functional role theorist in semantics?

A1: The (usually tacit) assumption that Functionalism in philosophy of mind
somehow comforts – or even implies – functional role semantics is responsible
for no end of confusion. In fact, the best you can get from Functionalism is that
what makes something a belief is its functional role. Functionalism does *not*
certify that functional role makes a belief the belief that *P*.

This is important for the following reason. Imagine a quite crude semantic
theory which holds that it is *being caused by water* that makes something a water-
belief. It might be objected to such a theory that there are many things that are
caused by water that are not water-beliefs: mudslides, hydroelectric power and
the growth of strawberries are examples that suggest themselves. But this objection
is frivolous. Mudslides, hydroelectric power and the growth of strawberries do not
have the functional roles which (if Functionalism is true) it is essential for beliefs
to have; *a fortiori* they are not beliefs; *a fortiori* they are not water-beliefs. The
interesting proposal is that, given that something *does* have whatever functional
properties beliefs have to have, what makes it a *water*-belief is the character of its
causal attachment to water.

Q2: If only attachment to the world counts for something being a water-belief,
then people could have all sorts of crazy beliefs that are, nevertheless, water-
beliefs; they could believe that water is *animate*, for example.

A2: Alchemists had the following crazy belief: they believed that mercury is alive
and grows from seeds. Contrary to what functional role theory implies, we have

no doubt, in practice, about the content of their belief. What they had was the crazy belief that mercury is alive and grows from seeds. Functional role semantics systematically underestimates the inertia of content; see above.

Q3: You say that nobody bothers to argue for functional role semantics; but that is surely untrue. Consider: it's important to have a semantic theory that slices mental states thin enough; a theory that allows us to distinguish beliefs about the Morning Star from beliefs about the Evening Star, beliefs about closed triangulars from beliefs about closed trilaterals, and so forth. But since the Morning Star *is* the Evening Star (since all closed triangulars are closed trilaterals and vice versa) a theory that makes content out of "relations to the world" can't slice the mental states thin enough to distinguish thoughts that are in fact distinct. In short, there must be something more to the content of mental states than their extensions, and what could this something more be if it isn't functional role? Even friends of mental content frequently find this sort of argument persuasive, hence "two factor" theories of representation: a more or less causal factor gets the representations attached to the world, and a functional role factor distinguishes between representations that are extensionally equivalent but nonsynonymous. What, to put this in the form of a question, is wrong with that?

A3: What is wrong with that is that it leads to meaning holism, a doctrine without which we have decided that we can do. Anyhow, the thinness of slice argument, though interesting, isn't conclusive. Consider the trinagular/trilateral case: one could take the view that the property of being a closed triangle is simply different from the property of being a closed trilateral. On this view, the corresponding concepts differ in content because they express different properties. The way to slice mental contents thin enough is by postulating thin enough properties.

Q4: That seems to me to be a question-begging sort of semantic theory; it says what a symbol means by taking for granted what the symbol denotes; and denotation is itself a semantic relation.

A4: We need a theory of what it is for a (mental) symbol to have the extension it does (a theory of Contexts, to use the vocabulary introduced above). Here is a first approximation to such a theory: A symbol S denotes an entity D just in case under certain sorts of circumstances, tokenings of S are causally contingent upon D. (Which sorts of circumstances count depends, *inter alia*, on the ontological status of D. In the case where D is a property, for example, S denotes D just in case, under the appropriate circumstances, the instantiation of D brings about the tokening of S.) Skinner was roughly right after all – except, of course, for the learning theory and the behaviorism.

By the way, this sort of theory of denotation is far more plausible for mental representations than for the expressions of a natural langauge since the tokenings of the latter – but not, presumably, of the former – are contingent upon the motivations, linguistic competences and communicative intentions of the speaker who utters them; in fact, on a whole range of "pragmatic" variables. Thus, for example: suppose Psmith notices that Mary's hair is on fire – and hence, perforce, thinks: "Mary's hair is on fire" (thereby tokening the Mentalese expression whose truth condition is that Mary's hair is on fire). Whether Psmith then *says* "Mary's hair is on fire" (thereby tokening the English expression whose truth condition is that Mary's hair is on fire) depends, *inter alia*, on whether he thinks that Mary (or some other suitably situated auditor) would be interested to know that Mary's hair is on fire. (See Grice 1975) for an indication of how complex these sorts of pragmatic considerations can become.) In short, the causal chain that connects the tokenings of mental representations to events which satisfy their truth conditions is typically shorter than (indeed, is typically a proper part of) the causal chain that connects the tokenings of English sentences to events which satisfy their truth conditions. That is the principal reason why it is mental representations, not English sentences, that are the natural candidates for being the primitive bearers of semantic properties.

Q5, Q6, Q7, Q8: I hardly know where to begin. Let's go back to the thinness of slice problem. First worry: Heaven only knows how you are supposing properties to be individuated; but with the best intentions in the world, it's not obvious that the property of being the Morning Star is distinct from the property of being the Evening Star; and I simply do not believe that the property of being Cicero is distinct from the property of being Tully. So (Q5, Q6) how are you going to distinguish the belief that the Morning Star is wet from the belief that the Evening Star is wet? Or the belief that Tully was wet from the belief that Cicero was wet? Still worse, you have a fatness of slice problem to worry about too. It's plausible that the property of being water is the property of being H_2O. So (Q7) how are you going to keep the thought that water is wet distinct from the thought that H_2O is if you hold – as you appear to do – that identity of denotation makes identity of intention?

And finally, property Realism as a solution to the thinness of slice problem sits badly with a causal theory of denotation; since every tokening of closed trilaterality is going to be a tokening of closed triangularity (Q8) doesn't every causal chain that traces back to the one *ipso facto* trace back to the other? Note that counterfactuals won't pull this apart; no causal chain *could* trace back to a tokening of one property without tracing back to a tokening of the other because "all closed triangles are closed trilaterals and vice versa" is necessary.

A5: On the other hand, I didn't say I had a working semantic theory. It is well to emphasize about here that nobody – functional role theorists definitely included – has a working semantic theory. I'm arguing the narrow case that a more-or-less denotational theory isn't *known* to be out of the question. Well, it isn't.

In fact, I porpose to argue a narrower case still: to get meaning holism out of functional role semantics, you need to assume that just *any* aspect of functional role can be a determinant of the semantic properties of a representation (this is, in effect, the second premise of the Quine/Putnam argument reconstructed above). For, if some aspect of functional role is a priori irrelevant to meaning, then representations which differ in that respect may nevertheless be semantically equivalent; and meaning holism is the doctrine that you can't have a principled notion of semantic equivalence for representations whose functional roles differ at all. So the present suggestion is that extension plus a *little* functional role might do to determine meaning. We'll see how this works as we look at the examples.

To begin with, if you take "the Morning Star" and "the Evening Star" as *descriptions* it seems reasonable to say that they express different properties and that that's why the belief that the Morning Star is wet differs in content from the belief that the Evening Star is wet. The hard problem is what to say about the reading which takes these expressions to be *names*. So Q5 reduces to Q6.

A6: The problem about names is, as just remarked, a hard problem; even if there is a property of being Tully – which property the word "Tully" expresses – it is not plausibly distinct from the property of being Cicero. But the expressions "Cicero" and "Tully" can't be semantically equivalent since, as Frege pointed out, the thought that Cicero is Tully is informative.

The obvious suggestion is that "Cicero" means something like "the person called 'Cicero'" whereas "Tully" means something like "the person called 'Tully'". Or, to put this more in the present terms, the obvious suggestion is that "is Tully"(/"is Cicero") expresses a certain linguistic property, viz. the property of being called "Tuly"(/"Cicero"). But, as Kripke has insisted, the obvious suggestion won't work; though it explains how "Cicero is Tully" could be informative, it implies that "Cicero was called 'Cicero'" is a necessary truth. Which, in fact, it isn't. So now what?

The path of wisdom would be to repeat that this is a hard problem, emphasizing that it is hard for *everybody*. For, even if you propose to pull "Cicero" and "Tully" apart by reference to their functional roles – and quite aside from the holism issues about which bits of their functional roles count for their meanings – you're still left with the question that nobody can answer: what *do* "Cicero" and "Tully" mean if, on the one hand, they're not synonyms and, on the other, they don't mean anything linguistic?

The course of wisdom, as I say, would be to shut up and leave this alone. Still, how about this: "Cicero" and "Tully" are synonymous but differ in presupposition (slightly like "and" and "but"; more like the demonstratives "he" and "she." The present doctrine is that proper names are, as it were, "dedicated" demonstratives: your name is a demonstrative pronoun that you get to keep for your very own). "Cicero was wet" says, in effect, HE WAS WET and presupposes that he was called "Cicero." "Tully was wet" says that HE WAS WET too, but it presupposes that he was called "Tully." That is, "Cicero was wet" and "Tully was wet" differ in semantic value because the former is not-true unless the relevant Roman has the (linguistic) property of being called "Cicero," whereas the latter is not-true unless that same Roman has the (different) linguistic property of being called "Tully." "Cicero is Tully" is informative because, although it doesn't *say* that the guy who was called "Cicero" was called "Tully," it carried the information that he was (see Dretske 1981; Barwise and Perry 1983). "Cicero was called 'Cicero'" fails to be necessary because, uttered in a world in which Cicero was called "Psmith" it would be (not false but) not-true.[8]

If that won't work, perhaps something else will.

A7: I think the way to fix the fatness of slice problem is to let in a moderate, restricted and well-behaved amount of functional role. The point about the formulas "water" vs "H_2O" is that, though they – presumably – express the same property, the second is a complex, built out of expressions which themselves denote hydrogen and oxygen. I do want to let into meaning – over and above denotation – those implications which accrue to an expression in virtue of its compositional semantics; that is, in virtue of its relations to such other expressions as occur as its morpho-syntactic constituents. This is to say that the distinction between the concept WATER and the concept H_2O is that you can have the former but not the latter even if you lack the concepts HYDROGEN and OXYGEN.

The point to emphasize is that letting in that much functional role does not, in and of itself, raise the collateral information problem. True, having the concept

H_2O requires more than just having a concept that denotes water; it requires that you know about hydrogen and oxygen. But it doesn't, thus far, open the flood gates. It doesn't, for example, constrain your views about what cats like to drink since neither "cat" nor "drink" is a morpho-syntactic constituent of "H_2O."

A8: Much the same point applies. Tokenings of the concept CLOSED TRIANGULAR trace back to triangles via tokenings of the concept ANGLE; whereas tokenings of the concept CLOSED TRILATERAL trace back to triangles via tokenings of the concept SIDE. Notice that though not even counterfactuals can pull closed triangulars apart from closed trilaterals, there is no problem about pulling apart ANGLES and SIDES *tout court*: lots of figures have more of the one than they do of the other, for example. (This suggests that you couldn't have nonsynonymous but logically equivalent primitive expressions; that if two representations are logically equivalent but non synonymous, at least one of them must be complex. Is that true?)

Q9: What are you going to do about "bachelor" and "unmarried man", surely these *do* express the same concept even though one is built out of constituents that don't appear in the other? Are you going to say that somebody could have the concept BACHELOR but not have the concept MARRIED MAN?

A9: I'm going to say that there are some cases of word-to-phrase synonymy; cases where a word happens to express the same concept that a phrase does. Word-to-phrase synonymy is a linguistic accident; one which, in fact, almost never occurs. It would be a waste of effort to worry about it.

Q10: On reflection, I am inclined to doubt that your proposal has even the virtue claimed for it: that it does, in fact, avoid meaning holism. For, after all, you're prepared to admit that the causal route from things happening in the world to the tokening of a mental symbol may sometimes run via tokenings of other concepts (cf. TRILATERAL and SIDE). So it turns out that world–symbol connections are like functional roles after all: symbols have their attachments to the world en bloc. Don't we, then, have the holism problem all over again?

A10: This mistakes the spirit of the proposal, which is that, fundamentally, what matters for denotation is the covariation of symbol tokens with denotation tokens. In particular, the inferential route that effects the covariation usually doesn't matter. The exceptions acknowledged to this principle are, from this point of view, merely technical. They involve *only* cases in which the semantic value of an expression is determined by the semantic values of its morpho-syntactic constituents.

Let me tell you – by way of making the spirit of the proposal clear – a story about what was wrong with verificationism. Verificationism was the idea that the meaning of an expression could be identified with whatever route connects the use of the expression with its denotation. So, for example, there's something that connects our use of the word "star" with stars: a causal chain that starts with light leaving stars, passsing – maybe – through telescopes, falling on our retinas, and eventuating, finally, in utterances of "star." The verificationist idea was that it's that sort of thing that constitutes the meaning of "star."

Now, there is something right about this: namely, that tokenings of the verification procedures for "star" have stars on one end and "stars" on the other; when they work, verification procedures connect terms with their denotations.

On the other hand, there is also something wrong with it. Namely that verification procedures connect terms with their denotations in too many ways. Think of the routes via which stars can determine tokenings of "star": via telescopes; via just looking; via looking at reflections in a puddle; via inference from astronomical theory; via inference from astrological theory; via inference from what somebody happened to say, via paintings of stars in a museum, via just thinking about stars. . ., etc. The point is: these different routes do not determine different semantic values for "star." The moral is that *the route doesn't matter (much)*; what determines that "star" means star is *that* the two are connected, not *how* the two are connected. *It's the covariance that counts.*

Similarly for concepts of course. It may be that my concept of water is, from time to time, connected to water via my concept of cat; (I believe that water is what cats like; I find that my cat likes this; I infer that this is water). But that's not what makes my concept of water a water-concept. What makes it a water-concept is that its tokenings covary with water tokenings under appropriate circumstances. It doesn't matter (much) by what route the covariance may be achieved; we get meaning by quantifying over the routes from a symbol to its denotation.

Q11: Covariation is no help. At best – and barring accidents – my beliefs about stars will covary with star tokenings *only when they are true*. Other times they'll covary with fireflies. If you really think that covariation "under certain circumstances" makes meaning, you must have in mind circumstances that are frequently – not to say typically – counterfactual. You wouldn't, by any chance, like to say something about what these circumstances are?

A11: No. The collateral information problem isn't real, but it's the reflection of a problem that is. The real problem is: what sorts of covariations establish denotation? That not every causal route from the world to a symbol establishes a semantically relevant covariation is patent; even if the wind regularly traces "wind" in the sand, these "wind"-tokenings don't denote the wind (or anything else). And, as you say – as Plato said, for that matter – there is a worry about how symbols(/beliefs) can be false. These are hard problems; but at least they're the *right* problems.

Q12: How about properties? You rely a lot on distinctness of properties for coping with thinness of slice arguments. Would you like to give us some idea about how you suppose properties to be individuated?

A12: No. Everybody has a problem of individuation to face. I don't know how to individuate properties; functional role theorists don't know how to individuate functional roles. It is none the less a substantive issue whether this problem should be faced in the semantics or in the ontology. I am assuming that it should be faced in the ontology.

Q13: What about necessary connections? If functional roles don't determine meanings, how do you account for the necessity of the relation between, say, being a father and being male?

A13: Everybody has a problem about necessary conections. It is none the less a substantive issue whether this problem should be faced in the semantics or in the metaphysics. I am assuming that it should be faced in the metaphysics. There is a lot that we do not know about necessary connections, but of one thing I am practically certain: for the most part, they aren't linguistic.

I concede, of course, that having the concept FATHER involves, *inter alia*, having a concept that denotes a property that is necessarily connected with the property of being male; hence that believing that Psmith is a father is believing something that entails that Psmith is male. What I deny is that having the concept requires acknowledging the entailment. On the contrary; all it requires is having a concept whose tokenings covary, in the right way, with tokenings of fatherhood.

Q14:

> Imagine that there is a country somewhere on earth called Ruritania. In this country. . .there are small differences between the dialects which are spoken in the north and in the south. One of these differences is that the word "grug" means silver in the northern dialect and aluminium in the southern dialect. Imagine two children, Oscar and Elmer. . .alike in genetic constitution and environment as you please, except that Oscar grows up in the south of Ruritania and Elmer grows up in the north of Ruritania. Imagine that in the north. . .pots and pans are normally made of silver, whereas in the south [they]. . .are normally made of aluminium. So [both] childen grow up knowing that pots and pans are normally made of "grug". . .But if the word "grug" and the mental representations that stand behind the word. . .have the same content at [the initial] stage, *when do they come to differ in content?* By the time Oscar and Elmer have become adults, have learned foreign languages, and so on, they certainly will not have the same conception of grug. Oscar will know that "grug" is the metal called "aluminium" in English. . .and Elmer will know that the metal called "grug" in his part of Ruritania is the metal called "silver" in English. Each of them will know many facts which serve to distinguish silver from aluminium and "grug" in the south Ruritanian sense from "grug" in the North Ruritanian sense. . .Moreover this change. . .is *continuous*. (Putnam 1983)

What about Oscar and Elmer, then?

A14: The difference in extension between Elmer and Oscar's use of "grug" doesn't, in and of itself, betoken a difference in the intentional content of their mental states; when they start out – when, intuitively speaking, they have the same beliefs about "grug" – theirs is just a Twin-Earth case; different extensions because of the difference in contexts; but the *same* intentions because there's the same mapping from contexts on to truth conditions realized in each of their heads. As they get older, the patterns of covariation change; for, whereas at first tokenings of "grug" would covary with either aluminium or silver for both children, by the end only silver can control "grug" for Elmer and only aluminium can control "grug" for Oscar. *Just* when the change happens depends on which counterfactuals have to be true for there to be the right sort of covariance – the semantically relevant sort – between tokenings of "grug" and tokenings of the metal that it denotes. There is, however, no reason to suppose that this question presents a *principled* difficulty; or that its application in the Oscar/Elmer case is of any special theoretical interest.

The controlling consideration, as usual is this: intentions differ only when they are different functions from contexts to truth conditions. We will know how to apply that principle when we have a theory that tells us what it is about an organism and a context that determines how the organism's intentional states are semantically evaluated in that context (for example, what truth conditions its beliefs have in that context). When we have the theory, we will be able to say exactly when Oscar and Elmer's mental states began to differ in intention; or there will be something wrong with the theory.

Q15: Are you quite finished now?
A15: Yes, thank you, I believe I am.

NOTES

For useful discussions of earlier drafts of this work, I'm especially indebted to Ned Block, Tyler Burge, David Israel, and Ron McClamrock.

1 *So* invisible is the mechanism that one may overlook such facts as that even the notion of a word belongs to commonsense intentional psychology and not to acoustics (say) or to physics.

2 Cf. Putnam (1989, p. 148): "Once we decide to put the reference . . . aside . . . far from making it easier for ourselves to decide whether the representations are synonymous, we have made it impossible. In fact, the first approximation we have to a principle for deciding whether words have the same meaning or not in actual translation practice is to look at the extensions. 'Factoring out' differences in extension will only make a principled decision on when there has been a change in meaning totally impossible." I'm not, however, claiming that Putnam actually endorses the Diagnosis I sketched in the text; I'm not sure whether he thinks that the Twin-Earth cases show that intentional Realists have to "factor out the extension" from the individuation conditions on meanings. Such passages as the one I've quoted make it seem as though he does, but I can't find a place where he straight-out says it. My claim, in any event, is that without the Diagnosis, it's unclear that Twin-Earth considerations have any bearing at all on the facticity of propositional attitude ascriptions.

3 Given shared context, the neurophysical identity of thinkers is, of course, sufficient but not necessary for the intentional identity of their thoughts. This is a matter we will return to.

4 This condition has to be applied with some care when the thoughts are truly indexical (as some thoughts no doubt are). Thus specifying the context which – together with its intentions – determines the truth condition of the thought that I am bored includes specifying the thinker of that thought.

Somewhat similarly, "visiting cases" suggest that Context must be four dimensional: what state of affairs makes your thought true or false probably depends on your history as well as your current surround.

This is all much in the spirit of David Kaplan – or, at least, I hope it is – though, patently, he is not to be blamed for any of it.

5 Putnam says, in "Meaning holism," that whereas Frege taught us that the unit of meaning can't be smaller than a sentence. Quine took the case a step further, showing us that it can't be smaller than a theory. The present reading is that Quine thereby effected a *reductio ad absurdum*, demonstrating that there must be something wrong with the idea that what you believe determines what you mean.

6 It may be that semantic holism, which is a dubious doctrine of sceptical import, gets some reflected glamour from *epistemic* holism, a much more plausible doctrine, and one to which Realists about propositional attitudes – or about anything else – may perfectly well accede. Roughly, epistemic holism is the view that whole theories are the unit of *confirmation*; by contrast, semantic holism is the view that whole theories are the unit of *meaning*. There is no obvious reason why the former doctrine should be taken to imply the latter, though Quine and Putnam are famous for having sponsored both. (On the other hand, one *can* infer a holistic account of meaning from a holistic account of confirmation if like Quine and sometimes Putnam you happen to be a verificationist. For a verificationist, the meaning of an expression is identified with the means of its confirmation, so if the latter is holistic it follows that the former must be too. That is a very good argument against being a verificationist, in case another such happens to be required.)

7 This is not, by the way, particularly a problem about the semantics of *mental* representations: the corresponding point holds for functional role theories of the meaning of expressions in English. So, if you really think that the meaning of a word is a construct out of its use, and if

you want this doctrine not to be question-begging, then you had better have a nonsemantical and nonintentional notion of the individuation of uses. This is one – not the only – reason why Wittgensteinians have to be behaviorists; it would be no good individuating uses by reference to, say, actions since action is itself an intentional notion.

8 We – in this world – can, of course, say truly that Cicero is not called "Cicero" in a world in which Cicero is called "Psmith." That is, the presupposition of our use of "Cicero" to refer to Cicero in some possible world is that Cicero is called "Cicero" here in our world.

REFERENCES

Barwise, J. and Perry, J. (1983) *Situations and Attitudes*, Cambridge MA: MIT Press.
Dretske, F. (1981) "Knowledge and the flow of information", Cambridge, MA: MIT Press.
Fodor, J. (1968) *Psychological Explanation*, New York: Random House.
Fodor, J. (1982) "Cognitive science and the Twin-Earth problem", *Notre Dame Journal of Formal Logic*, 23: 98–118.
Grice, H. P. (1975) "Logic and conversation" in P. Cole and J. L. Morgan (eds), *Syntax and Semantics*, vol. 3. New York: Seminar Press.
Landau, B. and Gleitman, L. (1985) *Language and Experience: Evidence from the Blind Child*, Cambridge, MA: Harvard University Press.
Putnam, H. (1975) "The meaning of 'meaning'," in *Mind, Language and Reality: Philosophical Papers*, vol. II, Cambridge: Cambridge University Press.
Putnam, H. (1983) "Computational psychology and interpretation theory", in *Realism and Reason: Philosophical Papers*, vol. III, Cambridge: Cambridge University Press.
Putnam, H. (1984) "Meaning holism", unpublished, Harvard University.
Stampe, D. (1977) "Towards a causal theory of linguistic representation", *Midwest Studies in Philosophy*, 2: 42–63.
Stich, S. (1983) *From Folk Psychology to Cognitive Science*, Cambridge, MA: MIT Press.

Part VII

Consciousness, "Qualia" and Subjectivity

Introduction

"The" problem of consciousness or qualia is familiar. Indeed it is so familiar that we tend to overlook the most important thing about it: that its name is Legion, for it is many. There is no *single* problem of consciousness; there are at least the following eight quite distinct objections that have been brought against Functionalism and (in some cases) against materialism generally.

1 Early critics of the Identity Theory argued that our immediate mental access to qualia militates against their being features of any purely neurophysiological item.
2 Saul Kripke (1972) made ingenious use of modal distinctions against type or even token identity, arguing that unless mental items are necessarily identical with neurophysiological ones, which they are not, they cannot be identical with them at all. Kripke's close reasoning has attracted considerable critical attention.
3 As we saw in the introduction to Part II, philosophers such as Block (this volume) have urged various counterexample cases against various materialist views – examples which seem to satisfy all the right materialist conditions but which lack mentality or one of its crucial aspects.
4 Farrell (1950), Gunderson (1970, 1974) and Nagel (1974) have worried over first-person/third-person asymmetries and the perspectivalness or subjective point-of-view-iness of consciousness.
5 Nagel (1974) and Jackson (this volume) argue for the existence of a special, intrinsically perspectival kind of *fact*, the fact of "what it is like" to have a mental experience of such-and-such a kind, which intractably and in principle cannot be captured or explained by physical science.
6 Jackson (1977) and others have defended the claim that in consciousness we are presented with mental individuals that themselves bear phenomenal, qualitative properties. For example, when a red flash bulb goes off in your face, your visual field exhibits a green blotch, an "after-image," a *thing* that is really green and has a fairly definite shape and exists for a few seconds before disappearing. If there are such things, they are entirely different from anything physical to be found in the brain of a (healthy) human subject. Belief in such "phenomenal individuals" as genuinely green after-images has been unpopular among philosophers for some years, but it can

be powerfully motivated (besides Jackson, see Lycan (1987b)).

7 A number of philosophers, most notably Sellars (1963), have stressed the ultra-smoothness, homogeneity or grainlessness of phenomenal feels, and contended for this reason that those feels cannot peacefully be dissolved into a metaphysic of little brute particles and their erratic motion through the void.

8 If human beings are functionally (even teleologically) organized systems of physical components and nothing more, then their "behavior" is only the mechanical, physically determined outcome of physical inputs and internal energy transformations. The inputs were themselves only the physical impacts of environmental causes, which causes were themselves the results of events completely external to us. We are merely automata. (It is no accident that Putnam's original inspiration was the Turing Machine.) But we know from the inside that this is false. Our conscious choices and our deliberate actions are entirely up to us; they feel entirely free. If I simply wish to raise my hand, then nothing can stop me from doing so unless quite externally and by making news (for example, a madman suddenly pinning me to the floor or a Phantom Jet hurtling through the wall of the building).

This is a formidable array of objections, and each is plausible on its face. Materialists and particularly Functionalists must respond in turn and in detail. Needless to say, materialists have responded at length; I list some of the most powerful replies in the Further Reading below.

FURTHER READING

Kripke's modal argument

Kripke, S. (1972) "Naming and necessity," in D. Davidson and G. Harman (eds), *Semantics of Natural Language*, D. Reidel.

Levin, M. (1975) "Kripke's argument against the identity thesis," *Journal of Philosophy* 72, 149–67.

Hill, C. S. (1981) "Why Cartesian intuitions are compatible with the identity thesis," *Philosophy and Phenomenological Research* 42, 254–65.

Leplin, J. (1979) "Theoretical explanation and the mind–body problem," *Philosophia* 8, 673–88.

Sher, G. (1977) "Kripke, Cartesian intuitions, and materialism," *Canadian Journal of Philosophy* 7, 227–38.

Levine, J. (1983) "Materialism and qualia: The explanatory gap," *Pacific Philosophical Quarterly* 64, 354–61.

Lycan, W. (1987a) *Consciousness*, Bradford Books / MIT Press, ch. 2.

Puzzle cases

Shoemaker, S. (1975) "Functionalism and qualia," *Philosophical Studies* 27, 291–315.

Kirk, R. (1974) "Zombies *v.* Materialists," *Aristotelian Society Supplementary Volume* 48, 135–52.

Searle, J. (1980) "Minds, brains and programs," *Behavioral and Brain Sciences* 3, 417–24.
    [Officially about intentionality rather than qualia, but is easily adapted.]

Churchland, P. M. and Churchland, P. S. (1981) "Functionalism, qualia, and intentionality," *Philosophical Topics* 12, 121–45.

Davis, L. (1982) "Functionalism and absent qualia," *Philosophical Studies* 41, 231–49.

Subjectivity and/or "perspectival facts"

Farrell, B. (1950) "Experience," *Mind* 50, 170–98.

Gunderson, K. (1970) "Asymmetries and mind–body perplexities," in M. Radner and S. Winokur (eds), *Minnesota Studies in the Philosophy of Science*, vol. IV, University of Minnesota Press.

McGinn, C. (1983) *The Subjective View*, Oxford University Press.

McMullen, C. (1985) "'Knowing what it's like' and the essential indexical," *Philosophical Studies* 48, 211–34.

Nagel, T. (1974) "What is it like to be a bat?," *Philosophical Review* 83, 435–50.

Rosenthal, D. (1983) "Reductionism and knowledge," in L. S. Cauman et al. (eds), *How Many Questions?* Hackett Publishing.

Churchland, P. M. (1985) "Reduction, qualia, and the direct introspection of brain states," *Journal of Philosophy* 82, 8–28.

Tye, M. (1986) "The subjective character of experience," *Mind* 95, 1–17.

Lycan, W. (1990) "What is the 'subjectivity' of the mental?" in J. Tomberlin (ed.), *Philosophical Perspectives*, vol. 4, Ridgeview Publishing.

Phenomenal individuals

Jackson F. (1977) *Perception*, Cambridge University Press.

Lycan, W. (1987b) "Phenomenal objects: A backhanded defense," in J. Tomberlin (ed.), *Philosophical Perspectives, 1: Metaphysics*, Ridgeview Publishing.

Homogeneity or grainlessness

Gunderson, K. (1974) "The texture of mentality," in R. Bambrough (ed.), *Wisdom – Twelve Essays*, Oxford University Press.

Sellars, W. (1963) *Science, Perception, and Reality*, Routledge & Kegan Paul.

Green, M. (1979) "The grain objection," *Philosophy of Science*, 46, 559–89.

Richardson, R. and Muilenburg, G. (1982) "Sellars and sense impressions," *Erkenntnis* 17, 171–212.

Freedom of the will

Levin, M. (1979) *Metaphysics and the Mind–Body Problem*, Oxford University Press, ch. VII.

Dennett, D. C. (1984) *Elbow Room*, Bradford Books / MIT Press.

Lycan, W. (1987) *Consciousness*, Bradford Books / MIT Press, ch. 9.

16

"Qualia"-Based Objections to Functionalism

An excerpt from "Troubles with Functionalism"
NED BLOCK

1.0 Functionalism, behaviorism, and physicalism

The functionalist view of the nature of the mind is now widely accepted.[1] Like behaviorism and physicalism, functionalism seeks to answer the question "What are mental states?" I shall be concerned with identity thesis formulations of functionalism. They say, for example, that pain is a functional state, just as identity thesis formulations of physicalism say that pain is a physical state.

I shall begin by describing functionalism, and sketching the functionalist critique of behaviorism and physicalism. Then I shall argue that the troubles ascribed by functionalism to behaviorism and physicalism infect functionalism as well.

One characterization of functionalism that is probably vague enough to be acceptable to most functionalists is: each type of mental state is a state consisting of a disposition to act in certain ways *and to have certain mental states*, given certain sensory inputs and certain mental states. So put, functionalism can be seen as a new incarnation of behaviorism. Behaviorism identifies mental states with dispositions to act in certain ways in certain input situations. But as critics have pointed out (Chisholm 1957; Geach 1957; Putnam 1963), desire for goal G cannot be identified with, say, the disposition to do A in input circumstances in which A leads to G, since, after all, the agent might not *know* that A leads to G and thus might not be disposed to do A. Functionalism replaces behaviorism's

"Troubles with Functionalism" by N. Block first appeared in *Perception and Cognition: Minnesota Studies in the Philosophy of Science, Vol IX*, edited by W. Savage. Copyright © 1978 by the University of Minnesota Press. Reprinted with revisions by permission of the publisher and the author.

"sensory inputs" with "sensory inputs and mental states"; and functionalism replaces behaviorism's "dispositions to act" with "dispositions to act and have certain mental states." Functionalists want to individuate mental states causally, and since mental states have mental causes and effects as well as sensory causes and behavioral effects, functionalists individuate mental states partly in terms of causal relations to other mental states. One consequence of this difference between functionalism and behaviorism is that there are possible organisms that according to behaviorism, have mental states but, according to functionalism, do not have mental states.

So, necessary conditions for mentality that are postulated by functionalism are in one respect stronger than those postulated by behaviorism. According to behaviorism, it is necessary and sufficient for desiring that G that a system be characterized by a certain set (perhaps infinite) of input–output relations; that is, according to behaviorism, a system desires that G just in case a certain set of conditionals of the form "It will emit O given I" are true of it. According to functionalism, however, a system might have these input–output relations, yet not desire that G; for according to functionalism, whether a system desires that G depends on whether it has internal states which have certain causal relations to other internal states (and to inputs and outputs). Since behaviorism makes no such "internal state" requirement, there are possible systems of which behaviorism affirms and functionalism denies that they have mental states.[2] One way of stating this is that, according to functionalism, behaviorism is guilty of *liberalism* – ascribing mental properties to things that do not in fact have them.

Despite the difference just sketched between functionalism and behaviorism, functionalists and behaviorists need not be far apart in spirit.[3] Shoemaker (1975), for example, says, "On one construal of it, functionalism in the philosophy of mind is the doctrine that mental, or psychological, terms are, in principle, eliminable in a certain way" (pp.306–7). Functionalists have tended to treat the mental-state terms in a functional characterization of a mental state quite differently from the input and output terms. Thus in the simplest Turing-machine version of the theory (Putnam 1967; Block and Fodor 1972), mental states are identified with the total Turing-machine states, which are themselves *implicitly* defined by a machine table that *explicitly* mentions inputs and outputs, described nonmentalistically.

In Lewis's version of functionalism, mental-state terms are defined by means of a modification of Ramsey's method, in a way that eliminates essential use of mental terminology from the definitions but does not eliminate input and output terminology. That is, 'pain' is defined as synonymous with a definite description containing input and output terms but no mental terminology (see Lewis 1972).

Furthermore, functionalism in both its machine and nonmachine versions has typically insisted that characterizations of mental states should contain descriptions of inputs and outputs in *physical* language. Armstrong (1968), for example, says,

We may distinguish between 'physical behaviour', which refers to any merely physical action or passion of the body, and 'behaviour proper' which implies relationship to mind. ...Now, if in our formula ["state of the person apt for bringing about a certain sort of behaviour"] 'behaviour' were to mean 'behaviour proper', then we would be giving an account of mental concepts in terms of a concept that already presupposes mentality, which would be circular. So it is clear that in our formula, 'behaviour' must mean 'physical behaviour'. (p.84).

Therefore, functionalism can be said to "tack down" mental states only at the periphery – that is, through physical, or at least nonmental, specification of inputs and outputs. One major thesis of this article is that, because of this feature, functionalism fails to avoid the sort of problem for which it rightly condemns behaviorism. Functionalism, too, is guilty of liberalism, for much the same reasons as behaviorism. Unlike behaviorism, however, functionalism can naturally be altered to avoid liberalism – but only at the cost of falling into an equally ignominious failing.

The failing I speak of is the one that functionalism shows *physicalism* to be guilty of. By 'physicalism', I mean the doctrine that pain, for example, is identical to a physical (or physiological) state.[4] As many philosophers have argued (notably Fodor 1965; Putnam 1966; see also Block and Fodor 1972), if functionalism is true, physicalism is probably false. The point is at its clearest with regard to Turing-machine versions of functionalism. Any given abstract Turing machine can be realized by a wide variety of physical devices; indeed, it is plausible that, given any putative correspondence between a Turing-machine state and a configurational physical (or physiological) state, there will be a possible realization of the Turing machine that will provide a counterexample to that correspondence. (See Kalke 1969; Gendron 1971; and Mucciolo 1974, for unconvincing arguments to the contrary; see also Kim 1972.) Therefore, if pain is a functional state, it cannot, for example, be a brain state, because creatures without brains can realize the same Turing machine as creatures with brains.

I must emphasize that the functionalist argument against physicalism does not appeal merely to the fact that one abstract Turing machine can be realized by systems of different *material composition* (wood, metal, glass, etc.). To argue this way would be like arguing that temperature cannot be a microphysical magnitude because the same temperature can be had by objects with *different* microphysical structures (Kim 1972). Objects with different microphysical structures, such as objects made of wood, metal, glass, etc. can have many interesting microphysical properties in common, such a molecular kinetic energy of the same average value. Rather, the functionalist argument against physicalism is that it is difficult to see how there *could be* a nontrivial first-order (see note 4) physical property in common to all and only the possible physical realizations of a given Turing-machine state. Try to think of a remotely plausible candidate! At the very least, the onus is on those who think such physical properties are conceivable to show us how to conceive of one.

One way of expressing this point is that, according to functionalism, physicalism is a *chauvinist* theory: it withholds mental properties from systems that in fact have them. In saying mental states are brain states, for example, physicalists unfairly exclude those poor brainless creatures who none the less have minds.

A second major point of this paper is that the very argument which functionalism uses to condemn physicalism can be applied equally well against functionalism; indeed, any version of functionalism that avoids liberalism falls, like physicalism, into chauvinism.

This article has three parts. The first argues that functionalism is guilty of

Table 1

	S_1	S_2	
nickel input	Emit no output Go to S_2	Emit a Coke Go to S_1	
dime input	Emit a Coke Stay in S_1	Emit a Coke and a nickel Go to S_1	

liberalism, the second that one way of modifying functionalism to avoid liberalism is to tie it more closely to empirical psychology, and the third that no version of functionalism can avoid both liberalism and chauvinism.

1.1 More about what functionalism is

One way of providing some order to the bewildering variety of functionalist theories is to distinguish between those that are couched in terms of a Turing machine and those that are not.

A Turing-machine table lists a finite set of machine-table states, $S_1 \ldots S_n$; inputs, $I_1 \ldots I_m$; and outputs, $O_1 \ldots O_p$. The table specifies a set of conditionals of the form: if the machine is in state S_i and receives input I_j, it emits output O_k and goes into state S_l. That is, given any state and input, the table specifies an output and in next state. Any system with a set of inputs, outputs, and states related in the way specified by the table is described by the table and is a realization of the abstract automaton specified by the table.

To have the power for computing any recursive function, a Turing machine must be able to control its input in certain ways. In standard formulations, the output of a Turing machine is regarded as having two components. It prints a symbol on a tape, then moves the tape, thus bringing a new symbol into the view of the input reader. For the Turing machine to have full power, the tape must be infinite in at least one direction and movable in both directions. If the machine has no control over the tape, it is a "finite transducer," a rather limited Turing machine. Finite transducers need not be regarded as having tape at all. Those who believe that machine functionalism is true must suppose that just what power automaton we are is a substantive empirical question. If we are "full power" Turing machines, the environment must constitute part of the tape. . . .

One very simple version of machine functionalism (Block and Fodor 1972) states that each system having mental states is described by at least one Turing-machine table of a specifiable sort and that each type of mental state of the system is identical to one of the machine-table states. Consider, for example, the Turing machine described in table 1 (cf. Nelson 1975). One can get a crude picture of the simple version of machine functionalism by considering the claim that S_1 = dime-desire, and S_2 = nickel-desire. Of course, no functionalist would claim that a Coke machine desires anything. Rather, the simple version of machine functionalism described above makes an analogous claim with respect to a much more complex hypothetical machine table. Notice that machine functionalism specifies inputs and outputs explicitly, internal states implicitly (Putnam (1967, p. 434) says: "The S_i, to repeat, are specified only *implicitly* by the description, i.e., specified *only* by the set of transition probabilities given in the machine table"). To be described by this machine table, a device must accept nickels and dimes as inputs and dispense nickels and Cokes as outputs. But the states S_1 and S_2 can have virtually any natures (even nonphysical natures), so long as those natures connect the states to each other and to the inputs and outputs specified in the machine table. All we are told about S_1 and S_2 are these relations; thus machine functionalism can be said to reduce mentality to input–output structures. This example should suggest the force of the functionalist argument against physicalism. Try to think of a first-order (see note 4) physical property that can be shared by all (and only) realizations of this machine table!

One can also categorize functionalists in terms of whether they regard functional identities as part of a priori psychology or empirical psychology.... The a priori functionalists (such as Smart, Armstrong, Lewis, Shoemaker) are the heirs of the logical behaviorists. They tend to regard functional analyses as analyses of the meanings of mental terms, whereas the empirical functionalists (such as Fodor, Putnam, Harman) regard functional analyses as substantive scientific hypotheses. In what follows, I shall refer to the former view as 'Functionalism' and the latter as 'Psychofunctionalism'. (I shall use 'functionalism' with a lowercase 'f' as neutral between Functionalism and Psychofunctionalism. When distinguishing between Functionalism and Psychofunctionalism, I shall always use capitals.)

Functionalism and Psychofunctionalism and the difference between them can be made clearer in terms of the notion of the Ramsey sentence of a psychological theory. Mental-state terms that appear in a psychological theory can be defined in various ways by means of the Ramsey sentence of the theory ... All functional state identity theories ... can be understood as defining a set of functional states ... by means of the Ramsey sentence of a psychological theory – with one functional state corresponding to each mental state. The functional state corresponding to pain will be called the 'Ramsey functional correlate' of pain, with respect to the psychological theory. In terms of the notion of a Ramsey functional correlate with respect to a theory, the distinction between Functionalism and Psychofunctionalism can be defined as follows: Functionalism identifies mental state S with S's Ramsey functional correlate with respect to a *common-sense* psychological theory; Psychofunctionalism identifies S with S's Ramsey functional correlate with respect to a *scientific* psychological theory.

This difference between Functionalism and Psychofunctionalism gives rise to a difference in specifying inputs and outputs. Functionalists are restricted to specification of inputs and outputs that are plausibly part of common-sense knowledge; Psychofunctionalists are under no such restriction. Although both groups insist on physical – or at least nonmental – specification on inputs and outputs, Functionalists require externally observable classifications (such as inputs characterized in terms of objects present in the vicinity of the organism, outputs in terms of movements of body parts). Psychofunctionalists, on the other hand, have the option to specify inputs and outputs in terms of internal parameters, such as signals in input and output neurons....

Let T be a psychological theory of either common-sense or scientific psychology.

T may contain generalizations of the form: anyone who is in state w and receives input x emits output y, and goes into state z. Let us write T as

$$T(S_1 \ldots S_n, I_1 \ldots I_k, O_1 \ldots O_m)$$

where the Ss are mental states, the Is are inputs, and the Os are outputs. The 'S's are to be understood as mental state *constants* such as 'pain', not variables, and likewise for the 'I's and 'O's. Thus, one could also write T as

T(pain . . . , light of 400 nanometers entering left eye . . . , left big toe moves 1 centimeter left . . .)

To get the Ramsey sentence of T, replace the mental state terms – *but not the input and output terms* – by variables, and prefix an existential quantifier for each variable:

$$\exists F_1 \ldots \exists F_n T(F_1 \ldots F_n$$
$$I_1 \ldots I_k, O_1 \ldots O_m)$$

If 'F_{17}' is the variable that replaced the word 'pain' when the Ramsey sentence was formed, then we can define pain as follows in terms of the Ramsey sentence:

$$x \text{ is in pain} \Leftrightarrow \exists F_1 \ldots \exists F_n$$
$$T[(F_1 \ldots F_n, I_1 \ldots I_k, O_1 \ldots O_m) \ \& \ x \text{ has } F_{17}]$$

The Ramsey functional correlate of pain is the property expressed by the predicate on the right hand side of this biconditional. Notice that this predicate contains input and output constants, but no mental constants since the mental constants were replaced by variables. The Ramsey functional correlate for pain is defined in terms of inputs and outputs, but not in mental terms.

For example, let T be the theory that pain is caused by skin damage and causes worry and the emission of "ouch", and worry, in turn, causes brow wrinkling. Then the Ramsey definition would be:

x is in pain ⇔ There are 2 states (properties), the first of which is caused by skin damage and causes both the emission of "ouch" and the second state, and the second state causes brow wrinkling, and x is in the first state.

The Ramsey functional correlate of pain with respect to this "theory" is the property of being in a state that is caused by skin damage and causes the emission of "ouch" and another state that in turn causes brow wrinkling. (Note that the words 'pain' and 'worry' have been replaced by variables, but the input and output terms remain.)

The Ramsey functional correlate of a state S is a state that has much in common with S. Specifically, S and its Ramsey functional correlate share the structural properties specified by the theory T. But, there are two reasons why it is natural to suppose that S and its Ramsey functional correlate will be distinct. First, the Ramsey functional correlate of S with respect to T can "include" at most those aspects of S that are captured by T; any aspects not captured by T will be left out. Second, the Ramsey functional correlate may even leave out some of what T does capture, for the Ramsey definition does not contain the "theoretical" vocabulary of T. The example theory of the last paragraph is true only of pain-feeling organisms – but trivially, in virtue of its use of the word 'pain'. However, the predicate that expresses the Ramsey functional correlate does not contain this word (since it was replaced by a variable), and so can be true of things that don't feel pain. It would be easy to make a simple machine that has some artificial skin, a brow, a tape-recorded "ouch", and two states that satisfy the mentioned causal relations, but no pain.

The bold hypothesis of functionalism is that for *some* psychological theory, this natural supposition that a state and its Ramsey functional correlate are distinct is false. Functionalism says that there is a theory such that pain, for example, *is* its Ramsey functional correlate with respect to that theory.

One final preliminary point: I have given the misleading impression that functionalism identifies *all* mental states with functional states. Such a version of functionalism is obviously far too strong. Let X be a newly created cell-for-cell duplicate of you (which, of course, is functionally equivalent to you). Perhaps you remember being bar-mitzvahed. But X does not remember being bar-mitzvahed, since X never was bar-mitzvahed. Indeed, something can be functionally equivalent to you but fail to know what you know, or [verb], what you [verb], for a wide variety of "success" verbs. Worse still, if Putnam (1975b) is right in saying that "meanings are not in the head," systems functionally equivalent to you may, for similar reasons, fail to have many of your other propositional attitudes. Suppose you believe water is wet. According to plausible arguments advanced by Putnam and Kripke, a condition for the possibility of your believing water is wet is a certain kind of causal connection between you and water. Your "twin" on Twin Earth, who is connected in a similar way to XYZ rather than H_2O would not believe water is wet.

If functionalism is to be defended, it must be construed as applying only to a subclass of mental states, those "narrow" mental states such that truth conditions for their application are in some sense "within the person." But even assuming that a notion of narrowness of psychological state can be satisfactorily formulated, the interest of functionalism may be diminished by this restriction. I mention this problem only to set it aside.

I shall take functionalism to be a doctrine about all "narrow" mental states.

1.2   Homunculi-headed robots

In this section I shall describe a class of devices that are prima facie embarrassments for all versions of functionalism in that they indicate functionalism is guilty of liberalism – classifying systems that lack mentality as having mentality.

Consider the simple version of machine functionalism already described. It says that each system having mental states is described by at least one Turing-machine table of a certain kind, and each mental state of the system is identical to one of the machine-table states specified by the machine table. I shall consider inputs and outputs to be specified by descriptions of neural impulses in sense organs and motor-output neurons. This assumption should not be regarded as restricting what will be said to Psychofunctionalism rather than Functionalism. As already mentioned, every version of functionalism assumes *some* specification of inputs and outputs. A Functionalist specification would do as well for the purposes of what follows.

Imagine a body externally like a human body, say yours, but internally quite different. The neurons from sensory organs are connected to a bank of lights in a hollow cavity in the head. A set of buttons connects to the motor-output neurons. Inside the cavity resides a group of little men. Each has a very simple task: to implement a "square" of an adequate machine table that describes you. On one wall is a bulletin board on which is posted a state card; that is, a card that bears a symbol designating one of the states specified in the machine table. Here is what the little men do: Suppose the posted card has a 'G' on it. This alerts the little men who implement G squares – 'G-men' they call themselves. Suppose the light representing input I_{17} goes on. One of the G-men has the following as his sole task: when the card reads 'G' and the I_{17} light goes on, he presses output button O_{191} and changes the state card to 'M'. This G-man is called upon to exercise his task only rarely. In spite of the low level of intelligence required of each little man, the system as a whole manages to simulate you because the functional organization they have been trained to realize is yours. A Turing machine can be represented as a finite set of quadruples (or quintuples, if the output is divided into two parts): current state, current input; next state, next output. Each little man has the task corresponding to a single quadruple. Through the efforts of the little men, the system realizes the same (reasonably adequate) machine table as you do and is thus functionally equivalent to you.[5]

I shall describe a version of the homunculi-headed simulation, which has more chance of being nomologically possible. How many homunculi are required? Perhaps a billion are enough.

Suppose we convert the government of China to functionalism, and we convince its officials . . . to realize a human mind for an hour. We provide each of the billion people in China (I chose China because it has a billion inhabitants) with a specially designed two-way radio that connects them in the appropriate way to other persons and to the artificial body mentioned in the previous example. We replace each of the little men with a citizen of China plus his or her radio. Instead of a bulletin board, we arrange to have letters displayed on a series of satellites placed so that they can be seen from anywhere in China.

The system of a billion people communicating with one another plus satellites plays the role of an external "brain" connected to the artifical body by radio. There is nothing absurd about a person being connected to his brain by radio. Perhaps the day will come when our brains will be periodically removed for cleaning and repairs. Imagine that this is done initially by treating neurons attaching the brain to the body with a chemical that allows them to stretch like rubber bands, thereby assuring that no brain–body connections are disrupted. Soon clever businessmen discover that they can attract more customers by replacing the stretched neurons with radio links so that brains can be cleaned without inconveniencing the customer by immobilizing his body.

It is not at all obvious that the China-body system is physically impossible. It could be functionally equivalent to you for a short time, say an hour.

"But," you may object, "how could something be functionally equivalent to me for *an hour?* Doesn't my functional organization determine, say, how I would react to doing nothing for a week but reading the *Reader's Digest?*" Remember that a machine table specifies a set of conditionals of the form: if the machine is in S_i and receives input I_j, it emits output O_k and goes into S_l. These conditionals are to be understood *subjunctively*. What gives a system a functional organization at a time is not just what it *does* at that time, but also the counterfactuals true of it at that time: what it *would* have done (and what its state transitions would have been) had it had a different input or been in a different state. If it is true of a system at time t that it *would* obey a given machine table no matter which of the states it is in and no matter which of the inputs it receives, then the system is described at t by the machine table (and realizes at t the abstract automaton specified by the table), even if it exists for only an instant. For the hour the Chinese system is "on," it *does* have a set of inputs, outputs, and states of which such subjunctive conditionals are true. This is what makes any computer realize the abstract automaton that it realizes.

Of course, there are signals the system would respond to that you would not respond to – for example, massive radio interference or a flood of the Yangtze River. Such events might cause a malfunction, scotching the simulation, just as a bomb in a computer can make it fail to realize the machine table it was built to realize. But just as the computer *without* the bomb *can* realize the machine table, the system consisting of the people and artificial body can realize the machine table so long as there are no catastrophic interferences, such as floods, etc.

"But," someone may object, "there is a difference between a bomb in a computer and a bomb in the Chinese system, for in the case of the latter (unlike the former), inputs as specified in the machine table can be the cause of the malfunction. Unusual neural activity in the sense organs of residents of Chungking Province caused by a bomb or by a flood of the Yangtze can cause the system to go haywire."

Reply: The person who says what system he or she is talking about gets to say what signals count as inputs and outputs. I count as inputs and outputs only neural activity in the artificial body connected by radio to the people of China. Neural signals in the people of Chungking count no more as inputs to this system than input tape jammed by a saboteur between the relay contacts in the innards of a computer counts as an input to the computer.

Of course, the object consisting of the people of China + the artificial body has *other* Turing-machine descriptions under which neural signals in the inhabitants of Chungking *would* count as inputs. Such a new system (that is, the object under such a new Turing-machine description) would not be functionally equivalent to you. Likewise, any commercial computer can be redescribed in a way that allows tape jammed into its innards to count as inputs. In describing an object as a Turing machine, one draws a line between the inside and the outside. (If we count only neural impulses as inputs and outputs, we draw that line inside the body; if we count only peripheral stimulations as inputs, . . . we draw that line at the skin.) In describing the Chinese system as a Turing machine, I have drawn the line in such a way that it satisfies a certain type of functional description – one that you *also* satisfy, and one that, according to functionalism, justifies attributions of mentality. Functionalism does not claim that every mental system has a machine table of a sort that justifies attributions of mentality with respect to *every* specification of inputs and outputs, but rather, only with respect to *some* specification.

Objection: The Chinese system would work too slowly. The kind of events and processes with which we normally have contact would pass by far too quickly for the system to detect them. Thus, we would be unable to converse with it, play bridge with it, etc.

Reply: It is hard to see why the system's time scale should matter. . . . Is it really contradictory or nonsensical to suppose we could meet a race of intelligent beings with whom we could communicate only by devices such as time-lapse photography? When we observe these creatures, they seem almost inanimate. But when we view the time-lapse movies, we see them conversing with one another. Indeed, we find they are saying that the only way they can make any sense of us is by viewing movies greatly slowed down. To take time scale as all important seems crudely behavioristic. . . .

What makes the homunculi-headed system (count the two systems as variants of a single system) just described a prima facie counterexample to (machine) functionalism is that there is prima facie doubt whether it has any mental states at all – especially whether it has what philosophers have variously called "qualitative states," "raw feels," or "immediate phenomenological qualities." (You ask: What is it that philosophers have called qualitative states? I answer, only half in jest: As Louis Armstrong said when asked what jazz is, "If you got to ask, you ain't never gonna get to know.") In Nagel's terms (1974), there is a prima facie doubt whether there is anything which it is like to be the homunculi-headed system.[6] . . .

1.3 Putnam's proposal

One way functionalists can try to deal with the problem posed by the homunculi-headed counterexamples is by the *ad hoc* device of stipulating them away. For example, a functionalist might stipulate that two systems cannot be functionally equivalent if one contains parts with functional organizations characteristic of sentient beings and the other does not. In his article hypothesizing that pain is a functional state, Putnam stipulated that "no organism capable of feeling pain possesses a decomposition into parts which separately possess Descriptions" (as the sort of Turing machine which can be in the functional state Putnam identifies with pain). The purpose of this condition is "to rule out such 'organisms' (if they count as such) as swarms of bees as single pain feelers" (Putnam 1967, pp. 434–5).

One way of filling out Putnam's requirement would be: a pain-feeling organism cannot possess a decomposition into parts *all* of which have a functional organization characteristic of sentient beings. But this would not rule out my homunculi-headed example, since it has nonsentient parts, such as the mechanical body and sense organs. It will not do to go to the opposite extreme and require that *no* proper parts be sentient. Otherwise pregnant women and people with sentient parasites will fail to count as pain-feeling organisms. What seems to be important to examples like the homunculi-headed simulation I have described is that the sentient beings *play a crucial role* in giving the thing its functional organization. This suggests a version of Putnam's proposal which requires that a pain-feeling organism has a certain functional organization and that it has no parts which (1) themselves possess that sort of functional organization and also (2) play a crucial role in giving the whole system its functional organization.

Although this proposal involves the vague notion "crucial role," it is precise enough for us to see it will not do. Suppose there is a part of the universe that contains matter quite different from ours, matter that is infinitely divisible. In this part of the universe, there are intelligent creatures of many sizes, even humanlike creatures much smaller than our elementary particles. In an intergalactic expedition, these people discover the existence of our type of matter. For reasons known only to them, they decide to devote the next few hundred years to creating out of *their* matter substances with the chemical and physical characteristics (except at the subelementary particle level) of *our* elements. They build hordes of space ships of different varieties about the sizes of our electrons, protons, and other elementary particles, and fly the ships in such a way as to mimic the behavior of these elementary particles. The ships also contain generators to produce the type of radiation elementary particles give off. Each ship has a staff of experts on the nature of our elementary particles. They do this so as to produce huge (by our standards) masses of substances with the chemical and physical characteristics of oxygen, carbon, etc. Shortly after they accomplish this, you go off on an expedition to that part of the universe, and discover the "oxygen," "carbon," etc. Unaware of its real nature, you set up a colony, using these "elements" to grow plants for food, provide "air" to breathe, etc. Since one's molecules are constantly being exchanged with the environment, you and other colonizers come (in a period of a few years) to be composed mainly of the "matter" made of the tiny people in space ships. Would you be any less capable of feeling pain, thinking, etc. just because the matter of which you are composed contains (and depends on for its characteristics) beings who themselves have a functional organization characteristic of sentient creatures? I think not. The basic electrochemical mechanisms by which the synapse operates are now fairly well understood. As far as is known, changes that do not affect these electrochemical mechanisms do not affect the operation of the brain, and do not affect mentality. The electrochemical mechanisms in your synapses would be unaffected by the change in your matter.[7]

It is interesting to compare the elementary-particle-people example with the homunculi-headed examples the chapter started with. A natural first guess about the source of our intuition that the initially described homunculi-headed simulations lack mentality is that they have *too much* internal mental structure. The little men may be sometimes bored, sometimes excited. We may even imagine that they deliberate about the best way to realize the given functional organization and make changes intended to give them more leisure time. But the example of the elementary-particle people just described suggests this first guess is wrong. What seems important is *how* the mentality of the parts contributes to the functioning of the whole.

There is one very noticeable difference between the elementary-particle-people example and the earlier homunculus examples. In the former, the change in you as you become homunculus-infested is not one that makes any difference to your psychological processing (that is, information processing) or neurological processing but only to your microphysics. No techniques proper to human psychology or neurophysiology would reveal any difference in you. However, the homunculi-headed simulations described in the beginning of the paper are not things to which neurophysiological theories true of us apply, and *if they are construed as Functional* (rather than Psychofunctional) simulations, they need not be things to which psychological (information-processing) theories true of us apply. This difference suggest that our intuitions are in part controlled by the not unreasonable view that our mental states depend on our having the psychology and/or neurophysiology we have. So something that differs markedly from us in both regards (recall that it is a Functional rather than Psychofunctional simulation) should not be assumed to have mentality just on the ground that it has been designed to be Functionally equivalent to us.

1.4   Is the prima facie doubt merely prima facie?

The Absent Qualia Argument rested on an appeal to the intuition that the homunculi-headed simulations lacked mentality or at least qualia. I said that this intuition gave rise to prima facie doubt that functionalism is true. But intuitions unsupported by principled argument are hardly to be considered bedrock. Indeed, intuitions incompatible with well-supported theory (such as the pre-Copernican intuition that the earth does not move) thankfully soon disappear. Even fields like linguistics whose data consist mainly in intuitions often reject such intuitions as that the following sentences are ungrammatical (on theoretical grounds):

The horse raced past the barn fell.
The boy the girl the cat bit scratched died.

These sentences are in fact grammatical though hard to process.[8]

Appeal to intuitions when judging possession of mentality, however, is *especially* suspicious. *No* physical mechanism seems very intuitively plausible as a seat of qualia, least of all a *brain*. Is a hunk of quivering gray stuff more intuitively appropriate as a seat of qualia than a covey of little men? If not, perhaps there is a prima facie doubt about the qualia of brain-headed systems too?

However, there is a very important difference between brain-headed and homunculi-headed systems. Since we know that *we are brain-headed systems*, and that *we* have qualia, we know that brain-headed systems can have qualia. So even though we have no theory of qualia which explains how this is *possible*, we have overwhelming reason to disregard whatever prima facie doubt there is about the qualia of brain-headed systems. Of course, this makes my argument partly *empirical* – it depends on knowledge of what makes us tick. But since this is knowledge we in fact possess, dependence on this knowledge should not be regarded as a defect.[9]

There is another difference between us meat-heads and the homunculi-heads: they are systems designed to mimic us, but we are not designed to mimic anything (here I rely on another empirical fact). This fact forestalls any attempt to argue on the basis of an inference to the best explanation for the qualia of homunculi-heads. The best explanation of the homunculi-heads' screams and winces is not their pains, but that they were designed to mimic our screams and winces.

Some people seem to feel that the complex and subtle behavior of the homunculi-heads (behavior just as complex and subtle – even as "sensitive" to features of the environment, human and nonhuman, as your behavior) is itself sufficient reason to disregard the prima facie doubt that homunculi-heads have qualia. But this is just crude behaviorism. . . .

My case against Functionalism depends on the following principle: if a doctrine has an absurd conclusion which there is no independent reason to believe, and if there is no way of explaining away the absurdity or showing it to be misleading or irrelevant, and if there is no good reason to believe the doctrine that leads to the absurdity in the first place, then don't accept the doctrine. I claim that there is no independent reason to believe in the mentality of the homunculi-head, and I know of no way of explaining away the absurdity of the conclusion that it has mentality (though of course, my argument is vulnerable to the introduction of such an explanation). The issue, then, is whether there is any good reason to believe Functionalism. One argument for Functionalism is that it is the best solution available to the mind–body problem. I think this is a bad form of argument, but since I also think that Psychofunctionalism is preferable to Functionalism (for reasons to be mentioned below), I'll postpone consideration of this form of argument to the discussion of Psychofunctionalism.

The only other argument for Functionalism that I know of is that Functional identities can be shown to be true on the basis of analyses of the meanings of mental terminology. According to this argument, Functional identities are to be justified in the way one might try to justify the claim that the state of being a bachelor is identical to the state of being an unmarried man. A similar argument appeals to commonsense platitudes about mental states instead of truths of meaning. Lewis says that functional characterizations of mental states are in the province of "common sense psychology – folk science, rather than professional science" (Lewis 1972, p. 250). (See also Shoemaker 1975, and Armstrong 1968. Armstrong equivocates on the analyticity issue. See Armstrong 1968, pp. 84–5, and p. 90). And he goes on to insist that Functional characterizations should "include only platitudes which are common knowledge among us – everyone knows them, everyone knows that everyone else knows them, and so on" (Lewis 1972, p. 256). I shall talk mainly about the "platitude" version of the argument. The analyticity version is vulnerable to essentially the same considerations, as well as Quinean doubts about analyticity. . . .

I am willing to concede, for the sake of argument, that it is possible to define any given mental state term in terms of platitudes concerning other mental state terms, input terms, and output terms. But this does not commit me to the type of definition of mental terms in which all mental terminology has been eliminated via Ramsification or some other device. It is simply a fallacy to suppose that if each mental term is definable in terms of the others (plus inputs and outputs), then each mental term is definable nonmentalistically. To see this, consider the example given earlier. Indeed, let's simplify matters by ignoring the inputs and outputs. Let's define pain as the cause of worry, and worry as the effect of pain. Even a person so benighted as to accept this needn't accept a definition of pain as *the cause of something,* or a definition of worry as *the effect of something.* Lewis claims that it is analytic that pain is the occupant of a certain causal role. Even if he is right about a causal role, specified in part mentalistically, one cannot conclude that it is analytic that pain is the occupant of any causal role, nonmentalistically specified.

I don't see any decent argument for Functionalism based on platitudes or analyticity. Further, the conception of Functionalism as based on platitudes leads to trouble with cases that platitudes have nothing to say about. Recall the example of brains being removed for cleaning and rejuvenation, the connections between one's brain and one's body being maintained by radio while one goes about one's business. The process takes a few days and when it is completed, the brain is reinserted in the body. Occasionally it may happen that a person's body is destroyed by an accident while the brain is being cleaned and rejuvenated. If hooked up to input sense organs (but not output organs) such a brain would exhibit *none* of the usual platitudinous connections between behavior and clusters of inputs and mental states. If, as seems plausible, such a brain could have almost all the same (narrow) mental states as we have (and since such a state of affairs could become typical), Functionalism is wrong.

It is instructive to compare the way Psychofunctionalism attempts to handle brains in bottles. According to Psychofunctionalism, what is to count as a system's inputs and outputs is an empirical question. Counting neural impulses as inputs and outputs would avoid the problems just sketched, since the brains in bottles and paralytics could have the right neural impulses even without bodily movements. Objection: There could be paralysis that affects the nervous system, and thus affects the neural impulses, so the problem which arises for Functionalism arises for Psychofunctionalism as well. Reply: Nervous system diseases can actually *change mentality*: for example they can render victims incapable of having pain. So it might actually be true that a widespread nervous system disease that caused intermittent paralysis rendered people incapable of certain mental states.

According to plausible versions of Psychofunctionalism, the job of deciding what neural processes should count as inputs and outputs is in part a matter of deciding *what malfunctions count as changes in mentality and what malfunctions count as changes in peripheral input and output connections* Psychofunctionalism has a resource that Functionalism does not have, since Psychofunctionalism allows us to *adjust the line we draw between the inside and the outside of the organism so as to avoid problems of the sort discussed.* All versions of Functionalism go wrong in attempting to draw this line on the basis of only common-sense knowledge; "analyticity" versions of Functionalism go especially wrong in attempting to draw the line a priori.

2.0 Psychofunctionalism

In criticizing Functionalism, I appealed to the following principle: if a doctrine has an absurd conclusion which there is no independent reason to believe, and if there is no way of explaining away the absurdity or showing it it to be misleading or irrelevant, and if there is no good reason to believe the doctrine that leads to the absurdity in the first place, then don't accept the doctrine. I said that there was no independent reason to believe that the homunculi-headed Functional simulation has any mental states. However, there *is* an independent reason to believe that the homunculi-headed *Psycho*functional simulation has mental states, namely that a Psychofunctional simulation of you would be Psychofunctionally equivalent to you, so any psychological theory true of you would be true of it too. What better reason could there be to attribute to it whatever mental states are in the domain of psychology?

This point shows that any Psychofunctional simulation of you shares your *non*qualitative mental states. However, in the next section I shall argue that there is nonetheless some doubt that it shares your qualitative mental states.

2.1   Are qualia Psychofunctional states?

I began this paper by describing a homunculi-headed device and claiming there is prima facie doubt about whether it has any mental states at all, especially whether it has qualitative mental states like pains, itches, and sensations of red. The special doubt about qualia can perhaps be explicated by thinking about *inverted* qualia rather than *absent* qualia. It makes sense, or seems to make sense, to suppose that objects we both call green look to me the way objects we both call red look to you. It seems that we could be functionally equivalent even though the sensation fire hydrants evoke in you is qualitatively the same as the sensation grass evokes in me. Imagine an inverting lens which when placed in the eye of a subject results in exclamations like "Red things now look the way green things used to look, and vice versa." Imagine further, a pair of identical twins one of whom has the lenses inserted at birth. The twins grow up normally, and at age 21 are functionally equivalent. This situation offers at least some evidence that each's spectrum is inverted relative to the other's. (See Shoemaker 1975, note 17, for a convincing description of intrapersonal spectrum inversion.) However, it is very hard to see how to make sense of the analog of spectrum inversion with respect to nonqualitative states. Imagine a pair of persons one of whom believes that p is true and that q is false while the other believes that q is true and that p is false. Could these persons be functionally equivalent? It is hard to see how they could.[10] Indeed, it is hard to see how two persons could have only this difference in beliefs and yet there be no possible circumstance in which this belief difference would reveal itself in different behavior. Qualia seem to be supervenient on functional organization in a way that beliefs are not . . .

There is another reason to firmly distingush between qualitative and nonqualitative mental states in talking about functionalist theories: Psychofunctionalism avoids Functionalism's problems with nonqualitative states – for example propositional attitudes like beliefs and desires. But Psychofunctionalism may be no more able to handle qualitative states than is Functionalism. The reason is that qualia may well not be in the domain of psychology.

To see this let us try to imagine what a homunculi-headed realization of human psychology would be like. Current psychological theorizing seems directed toward the description of information-flow relations among psychological mechanisms. The aim seems to be to decompose such mechanisms into psychologically primitive mechanisms, "black boxes" whose internal structure is in the domain of physiology rather than in the domain of psychology. (See Fodor 1968, Dennett 1975, and Cummins 1975; interesting objections are raised in Nagel 1969). For example, a near-primitive mechanism might be one that matches two items in a representational system and determines if they are tokens of the same type. Or the primitive mechanisms might be like those in a digital computer – for example, they might be (a) *add 1 to a given register*, and (b) *subtract 1 from a given register, or if the register contains 0, go to the nth (indicated) instruction.* (These operations can be combined to accomplish any digital computer operation; see Minsky 1967, p. 206). Consider a computer whose machine-language code contains only two instructions corresponding to (a) and (b). If you ask how it multiplies or solves differential equations or makes up payrolls, you can be answered by being shown a program couched in terms of the two machine-language instructions. But if you ask how it adds 1 to a given register, the appropriate answer is given by a wiring diagram, not a program. The machine is hard-wired to add 1. When the instruction corresponding to (a) appears in a certain register, the contents of another register "automatically" change in a certain way. The computational structure of a computer is determined by a set of primitive operations and the ways nonprimitive operations are built up from them. Thus it does not matter to the computational structure of the computer whether the primitive mechanisms are realized by tube circuits, transistor circuits, or relays. Likewise, it does not matter to the psychology of a mental system whether its primitive mechanisms are realized by one or another neurological mechanism. Call a system a "realization of human psychology" if every psychological theory true of us is true of it. Consider a realization of human psychology whose primitive psychological operations are accomplished by little men, in the manner of the homunculi-headed simulations discussed. So, perhaps one little man produces items from a list, one by one, another compares these items with other representations to determine whether they match, etc.

Now there is good reason for supposing this system has some mental states. Propositional attitudes are an example. Perhaps psychological theory will identify remembering that P with having "stored" a sentencelike object which expresses the proposition that P (Fodor 1975). Then if one of the little men has put a certain sentencelike object in "storage," we may have reason for regarding the system as remembering that P. But unless having qualia is just a matter of having certain information processing (at best a controversial proposal) there is no such theoretical reason for regarding the system as having qualia. In short, there is perhaps as much doubt about the qualia of this homunculi-headed system as there was about the qualia of the homunculi-headed Functional simulation discussed early in the paper.

But the system we are discussing is *ex hypothesi* something of which any true psychological theory is true. *So any doubt that it has qualia is a doubt that qualia are in the domain of psychology.*

It may be objected: "The kind of psychology you have in mind is *cognitive* psychology, that is, psychology of thought processes; and it is no wonder that qualia are not in the domain of *cognitive* psychology!" But I *do not* have cognitive psychology in mind and if it sounds that way, this is easily explained: nothing we know about the psychological processes underlying our conscious mental life has anything to do with qualia. What passes for the "psychology" of sensation or pain, for example, is (a) physiology, (b) psychophysics (that is, the study of the mathematical functions relating stimulus variables and sensation variables; for example, the intensity of sound as a function of the amplitude of the sound waves), or (c) a grab bag of descriptive studies (see Melzack 1973, ch. 2). Of these, only psychophysics could be construed as being about qualia *per se*. And it is obvious that psychophysics touches only the *functional* aspect of sensation, not its qualitative character. Psychophysical experiments done on you would have the same results if done on any system Psychofunctionally equivalent to you, even if it had inverted or absent qualia. If experimental results would be unchanged whether or not the experimental subjects have inverted or absent qualia, they can hardly be expected to cast light on the nature of qualia.

Indeed, on the basis of the kind of conceptual apparatus now available in psychology, I do not see how psychology in anything like its present incarnation *could* explain qualia. We cannot now conceive how psychology could explain qualia, though we *can* conceive how psychology could explain believing, desiring, hoping, etc. (see Fodor 1975). That something is currently inconceivable is not a good reason to think it is impossible. Concepts could be developed tomorrow that would make what is now inconceivable conceivable. But all we have to go on is what we know, and on the basis of what we have to go on, it looks as if qualia are not in the domain of psychology. . . .

It is no objection to the suggestion that qualia are not psychological entities that qualia are the very paradigm of something in the domain of psychology. As has often been pointed out, it is in part an empirical question what is in the domain of any particular branch of science. The liquidity of water turns out not to be explainable by chemistry, but rather by subatomic physics. Branches of science have at any given time a set of phenomena they seek to explain. But it can be discovered that some phenomenon which seemed central to a branch of science is actually in the purview of a different branch. . . .

The Absent Qualia Argument exploits the possibility that the Functional or Psychofunctional state Functionalists or Psychofunctionalists would want to identify with pain can occur without any quale occurring. It also seems to be conceivable that the latter occur without the former. Indeed, there are facts that lend plausibility to this view. After frontal lobotomies, patients typically report that they still have pains, though the pains no longer bother them (Melzack 1973, p. 95). These patients show all the "sensory" signs of pain (such as recognizing pin pricks as sharp), but they often have little or no desire to avoid "painful" stimuli.

One view suggested by these observations is that each pain is actually a *composite* state whose components are a quale and a Functional or Psychofunctional state.[11] Or what amounts to much the same idea, each pain is a quale playing a certain Functional or Psychofunctional role. If this view is right, it helps to explain how people can have believed such different theories of the nature of pain and other sensations; they have emphasized one component at the expense of the other. Proponents of behaviorism and functionalism have had one component in mind; proponents of private ostensive definition have had the other in mind. Both approaches err in trying to give one account of something that has two components of quite different natures.

3.0   Chauvinism vs. liberalism

It is natural to understand the psychological theories Psychofunctionalism adverts to as theories of *human* psychology. On Psychofunctionalism, so understood, it is impossible for a system to have beliefs desires, etc., except in so far as psychological theories true of us are true of it. Psychofunctionalism (so understood) stipulates that Psychofunctional equivalence to us is necessary for mentality.

But even if Psychofunctional equivalence to us is a condition on our *recognition of mentality*, what reason is there to think it is a condition on mentality itself? Could there not be a wide variety of possible psychological processes that can underlie mentality, of which we instantiate only one type? Suppose we meet Martians and find that they are roughly Functionally (but not Psychofunctionally) equivalent to us. When we get to know Martians, we find them about as different from us as humans we know. We develop extensive cultural and commercial intercourse with them. We study each other's science and philosophy journals, go to each other's movies, read each other's novels, etc. Then Martian and Earthian psychologists compare notes, only to find that in underlying psychology, Martians and Earthians are very different. They soon agree that the difference can be described as follows. Think of humans and Martians as if they were products of conscious design. In any such design project, there will be various options. Some capacities can be built in (innate), others learned. The brain can be designed to accomplish tasks using as much memory capacity as necessary in order to minimize use of computation capacity; or, on the other hand, the designer could choose to conserve memory space and rely mainly on computation capacity. Inferences can be accomplished by systems which use a few axioms and many rules of inference, or, on the other hand, few rules and many axioms. Now imagine that what Martian and Earthian psychologists find when they compare notes is that Martians and Earthians differ as if they were the end products of maximally different design choices (compatible with rough Functional equivalence in adults). Should we reject our assumption that Martians can enjoy our films, believe their own apparent scientific results, etc.? Should they "reject" their "assumption" that we "enjoy" their novels, "learn" from their textbooks, etc.? Perhaps I have not provided enough information to answer this question. After all, there may be many ways of filling in the description of the Martian–human differences in which it would be reasonable to suppose there simply is no fact of the matter, or even to suppose that the Martians do not deserve mental ascriptions. But surely there are many ways of filling in the description of the Martian–Earthian difference I sketched on which it would be perfectly clear that even if Martians behave differently from us on subtle psychologcical experiments, they none the less think, desire, enjoy, etc. To suppose otherwise would be crude human chauvinism. (Remember theories are chauvinist in so far as they falsely *deny* that systems have mental properties and liberal in so far as they falsely *attribute* mental properties.) . . .

An obvious suggestion of a way out of this difficulty is to identify mental states with Psychofunctional states, taking the domain of psychology to include *all creatures with mentality*, including Martians. The suggeston is that we define "Psychofunctionalism" in terms of "universal" or "cross-system" psychology, rather than the human psychology I assumed earlier. Universal psychology however, is a suspect enterprise. For how are we to decide what systems should be included in the *domain* of universal psychology? One possible way of deciding what systems have mentality, and are thus in the domain of universal psychology would be to use some *other* developed theory of mentality such as, behaviorism or

Functionalism. But such a procedure would be at least as ill-justified as the other theory used. Further, if Psychofunctionalism must presuppose some other theory of mind, we might just as well accept the other theory of mind instead.

Perhaps universal psychology will avoid this "domain" problem in the same way other branches of science avoid it or seek to avoid it. Other branches of science start with tentative domains based on intuitive and prescientific versions of the concepts the sciences are supposed to explicate. They then attempt to develop natural kinds in a way which allows the .formulations of lawlike generalizations which apply to all or most of the entities in the prescientific domains. In the case of many branches of science – including biological and social sciences such as genetics and linguistics – the prescientific domain turned out to be suitable for the articulation of lawlike generalizations.

Now it may be that we shall be able to develop universal psychology in much the same way we develop Earthian psychology. We decide on an intuitive and prescientific basis what creatures to include in its domain, and work to develop natural kinds of psychological theory which apply to all or at least most of them. Perhaps the study of a wide range of organisms found on different worlds will one day lead to theories that determine truth conditions for the attribution of mental states like belief, desire, etc., applicable to systems which are pretheoretically quite different from us. Indeed, such cross-world psychology will no doubt require a whole new range of mentalistic concepts. Perhaps there will be families of concepts corresponding to belief, desire etc.; that is, a family of belief-like concepts, desire-like concepts, etc. If so, the universal psychology we develop shall, no doubt, be somewhat dependent on which new organisms we discover first. Even if universal psychology is in fact possible, however, there will certainly be many possible organisms whose mental status is indeterminate.

On the other hand, it may be that universal psychology is *not* possible. Perhaps life in the universe is such that we shall simply have no basis for reasonable decisions about what systems are in the domain of psychology and what systems are not.

If universal psychology *is* possible, the problem I have been raising vanishes. Universal-Psychofunctionalism avoids the liberalism of functionalism and the chauvinism of human-Psychofunctionalism. But the question of whether universal psychology is possible is surely one which we have no way of answering now.

Here is a summary of the argument so far:

1 Functionalism has the bizarre consequence that a homunculi-headed simulation of you has qualia. This puts the burden of proof on the Functionalist to give us some reason for believing his doctrine. However, the one argument for Functionalism in the literature is no good, and so Functionalism shows no sign of meeting the burden of proof.

2 Psychofunctional simulations of us share whatever states are in the domain of psychology, so the Psychofunctional homunculi-head does not cast doubt on Psychofunctional theories of cognitive states, but only on Psychofunctionalist theories of qualia, there being a doubt as to whether qualia are in the domain of psychology.

3 Psychofunctionalist theories of mental states that are in the domain of psychology, however, are hopelessly chauvinist.

So one version of functionalism has problems with liberalism, the other has problems with chauvinism. As to qualia, if they are in the domain of psychology, then Psychofunctionalism with respect to qualia is just as chauvinist as Psychofunctionalism with respect to belief. On the other hand, if qualia are not in the domain of psychology, the Psychofunctionalist homunculi-head can be used against Psychofunctionalism with respect to qualia. For the only thing that shields Psychofunctionalism with respect to mental state S from the homunculi-head argument is that if you have S, then any Psychofunctional simulation of you must have S, because the correct theory of S applies to it just as well as to you.

3.1 The problem of the inputs and the outputs

I have been supposing all along (as Psychofunctionalists often do – see Putnam 1967) that inputs and outputs can be specified by neural impulse descriptions. But this is a chauvinist claim, since it precludes organisms without neurons (such as machines) from having functional descriptions. How can one avoid chauvinism with respect to specification of inputs and outputs? One way would be to characterize the inputs and outputs *only as* inputs and outputs. So the functional description of a person might list outputs by number: output$_1$, output$_2$, . . . Then a system could be functionally equivalent to you if it had a set of states, inputs, and outputs causally related to one another in the way yours are, no matter what the states, inputs, and outputs were like. Indeed, though this approach violates the demand of some functionalists that inputs and outputs be physically specified, other functionalists – those who insist only that input and output descriptions be *nonmental* – may have had something like this in mind. This version of functionalism does not "tack down" functional descriptions at the periphery with relatively specific decriptions of inputs and outputs: rather, this version of functionalism treats inputs and outputs just as all versions of functionalism treat internal states. That is, this version specifies states, inputs, and outputs only by requiring that they *be* states, inputs, and outputs.

The trouble with this version of functionalism is that it is wildly liberal. Economic systems have inputs and outputs, such as influx and outflux of credits and debits. And economic systems also have a rich variety of internal states, such as having a rate of increase of GNP equal to double the Prime Rate. It does not seem impossible that a wealthy sheik could gain control of the economy of a small country, for example Bolivia, and manipulate its financial system to make it functionally equivalent to a person, for example himself. If this seems implausible, remember that the economic states, inputs, and outputs designated by the sheik to correspond to his mental states, inputs, and outputs need not be "natural" economic magnitudes. Our hypothetical sheik could pick *any* economic magnitudes at all – for example, the fifth time derivative of the balance of payments. His only constraint is that the magnitudes he picks be economic, that their having such-and-such values be inputs, outputs, and states, and that he be able to set up a financial structure which can be made to fit the intended formal mold. The mapping from psychological magnitudes to economic magnitudes could be as bizarre as the sheik requires.

This version of functionalism is far too liberal and must therefore be rejected. If there are any fixed points when discussing the mind–body problem, one of them is that the economy of Bolivia could not have mental states, no matter how it is distorted by powerful hobbyists. Obviously, we must be more specific in our descriptions of inputs and outputs. The question is: is there a description of inputs and outputs specific enough to avoid liberalism, yet general enough to avoid chauvinism? I doubt that there is.

Every proposal for a description of inputs and ouputs I have seen or thought of is guilty of either liberalism or chauvinism. Though this paper has concentrated on liberalism, chauvinism is the more pervasive problem. Consider standard Functional and Psychofunctional descriptions. Funtionalists tend to specify inputs and outputs in the manner of behaviorists: outputs in terms of movements of arms and legs, sound emitted and the like; inputs in terms of light and sound falling on the eyes and ears.... Such descriptions are blatantly *species-specific*. Humans have arms and legs, but snakes do not – and whether or not snakes have mentality, one can easily imagine snake-like creatures that do. Indeed, one can imagine creatures with all manner of input–output devices, for example creatures that communicate and manipulate by emitting strong magnetic fields. Of course, one could formulate Functional descriptions for each such species, and somewhere in disjunctive heaven there is a disjunctive description which will handle all species that ever actually exist in the universe (the description may be infinitely long). But even an appeal to such suspicious entities as infinite disjunctions will not bail out Functionalism, since even the amended view will not tell us what there is in common to pain-feeling organisms in virtue of which they all have pain. And it will not allow the ascription of pain to some hypothetical (but nonexistent) pain-feeling creatures. Further, these are just the grounds on which functionalists typically acerbically reject the disjunctive theories sometimes advanced by desperate physicalists. If functionalists suddenly smile on wildly disjunctive states to save themselves from chauvinism they will have no way of defending themselves from physicalism.

Standard Psychofunctional descriptions of inputs and outputs are also species-specific (for example in terms of neural activity) and hence chauvinist as well.

The chauvinism of standard input–output descriptions is not hard to explain. The variety of possible intelligent life is enormous. Given any fairly specific descriptions of inputs and outputs, any high-school-age science-fiction buff will be able to describe a sapient sentient being whose inputs and outputs fail to satisfy that description.

I shall argue that *any physical description* of inputs and outputs (recall that many functionalists have insisted on physical descriptions) yields a version of functionalism that is inevitably chauvinist or liberal. Imagine yourself so badly burned in a fire that your optimal way of communicating with the outside world is via modulations of your EEG pattern in Morse Code. You find that thinking an exciting thought produces a pattern that your audience agrees to interpret as a dot, and a dull thought produces a "dash". Indeed, this fantasy is not so far from reality. According to a recent newspaper article (*Boston Globe*, 21 March 1976), "at UCLA scientists are working on the use of EEG to control machines.... A subject puts electrodes on his scalp, and thinks an object through a maze." The "reverse" process is also presumably possible: others communicating with you in Morse Code by producing bursts of electrical activity that affect your brain (for example causing a long or short afterimage). Alternatively, if the cerebroscopes that philosophers often fancy become a reality, your thoughts will be readable directly from your brain. Again, the reverse process also seems possible. In these cases, *the brain itself becomes an essential part of one's input and output devices.* This possibility has embarrassing consequences for functionalists. You will recall that functionalists pointed out that physicalism is false because a single mental state can be realized by an indefinitely large variety of physical states that have no necessary and sufficient physical characterization. But if this functionalist point against physicalism is right *the same point applies to inputs and outputs,* since the physical realization of mental states can serve as an essential part of the input and output devices. That is, on any sense of 'physical' in which the functionalist criticism of physicalism is correct, *there will be no physical characterization that applies to all and only mental systems' inputs and outputs.* Hence, any attempt to formulate a functional description with physical characterizations of inputs and outputs will inevitably either exclude some systems with mentality or include some systems without mentality. Hence, . . . *functionalists cannot avoid both chauvinism and liberalism.*

So physical specifications of inputs and outputs will not do. Moreover, mental or "action" terminology (such as "punching the offending person") cannot be used either, since to use such specifications of inputs or outputs would be to give up the functionalist program of characterizing mentality in nonmental terms. On the other hand, as you will recall, characterizing inputs and outputs simply *as* inputs and outputs is inevitably liberal. I, for one, do not see how there can be a vocabulary for describing inputs and outputs that avoids both liberalism and chauvinism. I do not claim that this is a conclusive argument against functionalism. Rather, like the functionalist argument against physicalism, it is best construed as a burden-of-proof argument. The functionalist says to the physicalist: "It is very hard to see how there could be a single physical characterization of the internal states of all and only creatures with mentality." I say to the functionalist: "It is very hard to see how there could be a single physical characterization of the inputs and outputs of all and only creatures with mentality." In both cases, enough has been said to make it the responsibility of those who think there could be such characterizations to sketch how they could be possible.[12]

NOTES

1   See Fodor 1965; Lewis 1972; Putnam 1966, 1967, 1970, 1975a; Armstrong 1968; Locke 1968; perhaps Sellars 1968; perhaps Dennett 1969, 1978b; Nelson 1969, 1975 (but see also Nelson 1976); Pitcher 1971; Smart 1971; Block and Fodor 1972; Harman 1973; Grice 1975; Shoemaker 1975; Wiggins 1975.

2   The converse is also true.

3   Indeed, if one defines 'behaviorism' as the view that mental terms can be defined in nonmental terms, then functionalism *is* a version of behaviorism. . . .

4   State type, not state token. Throughout the paper I shall mean by 'physicalism' the doctrine that says each distinct type of mental state is identical to a distinct type of physical state; for example, pain (the universal) is a physical state. Token physicalism, on the other hand, is the (weaker) doctrine that each particular datable pain is a state of some physical type or other. Functionalism shows that type physicalism is false, but it does not show that token physicalism is false.

    By 'physicalism', I mean *first-order* physicalism, the doctrine that, e.g., the property of being in pain is a first-order (in the Russell–Whitehead sense) physical property. (A first-order property is one whose definition does not require quantification over properties; a second-order property is one whose definition requires quantification over first-order properties – and not other properties.) The claim that being in pain is a second-order physical property is actually a (physicalist) form of functionalism. See Putnam 1970.

5   The basic idea for this example derives from Putnam (1967). I am indebted to many conversations with Hartry Field on the topic. Putnam's attempt to defend functionalism from the problem posed by such examples is discussed in section 1.3 of this paper.

6   Shoemaker (1975) argues (in reply to Block and Fodor 1972) that absent qualia are logically impossible; that is, that it is logically impossible that two systems be in the same functional state yet one's state have and the other's state lack qualitative content. . . .

7   Since there is a difference between the role of the little people in producing your functional organization in the situation just described and the role of the homunculi in the homunculi-headed simulations this paper began with, presumably Putnam's condition could be reformulated to rule out the latter without ruling out the former. But this would be a most *ad hoc* maneuver.

8   Compare the first sentence with 'The fish eaten in Boston stank.' The reason it is hard to process is that 'raced' is naturally read as active rather than passive. See Fodor et al., 1974, p. 360. For a discussion of why the second sentence is grammatical, see Fodor and Garrett 1967; Bever 1970; and Fodor et al., 1974.

9   We often fail to be able to conceive of how something is possible because we lack the relevant theoretical concepts. For example, before the discovery of the mechanism of genetic duplication, Haldane argued persuasively that no conceivable physical mechanism could do the job. He was right. But instead of urging that scientists should develop ideas that would allow us to conceive of such a physical mechanism, he concluded that a *non*physical mechanism was involved. (I owe the example to Richard Boyd.)

10   Suppose a man who has good color vision mistakenly uses 'red' to denote green and 'green' to denote red. That is, he simply confuses the two words. Since his confusion is purely linguistic, though he says of a green thing that it is red, he does not *believe* that it is red, any more than a foreigner who has confused 'ashcan' with 'sandwich' believes people eat ashcans for lunch. Let us say that the person who has confused 'red' and 'green' in this way is a victim of Word Switching.

     Now consider a different ailment: having red/green inverting lenses placed in your eyes without your knowledge. Let us say a victim of this ailment is a victim of Stimulus Switching. Like the victim of Word Switching, the victim of Stimulus Switching applies 'red' to green things and vice versa. But the victim of Stimulus Switching *does* have false color beliefs. If you show him a green patch he says *and believes* that it is red.

     Now suppose that a victim of Stimulus witching suddenly becomes a victim of Word Switching as well. (Suppose as well that he is a lifelong resident of a remote Arctic village, and has no standing beliefs to the effect that grass is green, fire hydrants are red, and so forth.) He speaks normally, applying 'green' to green patches and 'red' to red patches. Indeed, he is functionally normal. But his *beliefs* are just as abnormal as they were before he became a victim of Word Switching. Before he confused the words 'red' and 'green', he applied 'red' to a green patch, and mistakenly believed the patch to be red. Now he (correctly) says 'red', but his belief is still wrong.

     So two people can be functionally the same, yet have incompatible beliefs. Hence, the inverted qualia problem infects belief as well as qualia (though presumably only qualitative belief). This fact should be of concern not only to those who hold functional state identity theories of belief, but also to those who are attracted by Harman-style accounts of meaning as functional role. Our double victim – of Word and Stimulus Switching – is a counter-example to such accounts. For his word 'green' plays the normal role in his reasoning and inference, yet since in saying of something that it "is green," he expresses his belief that it is *red*, he uses 'green' with an abnormal meaning. I am indebted to Sylvain Bromberger for discussion of this issue.

11 The quale might be identified with a physico-chemical state. This view would comport with a suggestion Hilary Putnam made in the late 1960s in his philosophy of mind seminar. See also ch. 5 of Gunderson 1971.

12 I am indebted to Sylvain Bromberger, Hartry Field, Jerry Fodor, David Hills, Paul Horwich, Bill Lycan, Georges Rey, and David Rosenthal for their detailed comments on one or another earlier draft of this paper. Beginning in the fall of 1975, parts of earlier versions were read at Tufts University, Princeton University, the University of North Carolina at Greensboro, and the State University of New York at Binghamton.

REFERENCES

Armstrong, D. (1968) *A materialist theory of mind*. London: Routledge & Kegan Paul.

Bever, T. (1970) "The cognitive basis for linguistic structures", in J. R. Hayes (ed.), *Cognition and the Development of Language*. New York: Wiley.

Block, N. (1980) "Are absent qualia impossible?" *Philosophical Review*, 89(2).

Block, N. and Fodor, J. (1972) "What psychological states are not", *Philosophical Review*, 81, 159–81.

Chisholm, Roderick (1957) *Perceiving*. Ithaca: Cornell University Press.

Cummins, R. (1975) "Functional analysis", *Journal of Philosophy*, 72, 741–64.

Davidson, D. (1970) "Mental events", in L. Swanson and J. W. Foster (eds), *Experience and Theory*. Amherst: University of Massachusetts Press.

Dennett, D. (1969) *Content and Consciousness*. London: Routledge & Kegan Paul. 1969.

Dennett, D. (1975) "Why the law of effect won't go away", *Journal for the Theory of Social Behavior*, 5, 169–87.

Dennett, D. (1978a) "Why a computer can't feel pain," *Synthese*, 38, 3.

Dennett, D. (1978b) *Brainstorms*, Montgomery, Vt.: Bradford.

Feldman, F. (1973) "Kripke's argument against materialism", *Philosophical Studies*, 416–19.

Fodor, J. (1965) "Explanations in psychology", in M. Black (ed.), *Philosophy in Ameria*. London: Routledge & Kegan Paul.

Fodor, J. (1968) "The appeal to tacit knowledge in psychological explanation", *Journal of Philosophy*, 65, 627–40.

Fodor, J. (1974) "Special sciences", *Synthese*, 28, 97–115.

Fodor, J. (1975) *The Language of Thought*. New York: Crowell.

Fodor, J., Bever, T. and Garrett, M. (1974) *The Psychology of Language*. New York: McGraw-Hill.

Fodor, J. and Garrett, M. (1967) "Some syntactic determinants of sentential complexity", *Perception and Psychophysics*, 2, 289–96.

Geach, P. (1957) *Mental Acts*. London: Routledge & Kegan Paul.

Gendron, B. (1971) "On the relation of neurological and psychological theories: A critique of the hardware thesis", in R. C. Buck and R. S. Cohen (eds), *Boston Studies in the Philosophy of Science VIII*. Dordrecht: Reidel.

Grice, H. P. (1975) "Method in philosophical psychology (from the banal to the bizarre)", *Proceedings and Addresses of the American Philosophical Association*.

Gunderson, K. (1971) *Mentality and Machines*. Garden City: Doubleday Anchor.

Harman, G. (1973) *Thought*. Princeton: Princeton University Press.

Hempel, C. (1970) "Reduction: Ontological and linguistic facets", in S. Morgenbesser, P. Suppes and M. White (eds), *Essays in Honor of Ernest Nagel*. New York: St. Martins Press.

Kalke, W. (1969) "What is wrong with Fodor and Putnam's functionalism?" *Noûs*, 3, 83–93.

Kim, J. (1972) "Phenomenal properties, psychophysical laws, and the identity theory", *The Monist*, 56(2), 177–92.

Lewis, D. (1972) "Psychophysical and theoretical identifications", *Australasian Journal of Philosophy*, 50(3), 249–58.

Locke, D. (1968) *Myself and Others*. Oxford: Oxford University Press.

Melzack, R. (1973) *The Puzzle of Pain*. New York: Basic Books.

Minsky, M. (1967) *Computation*. Englewood Cliffs NJ: Prentice-Hall.

Mucciolo, L. F. (1974) "The identity thesis and neuropsychology", *Noûs*, 8, 327–42.

Nagel, T. (1969) "The boundaries of inner space", *Journal of Philosophy*, 66, 452–8.

Nagel, T. (1970) "Armstrong on the mind", *Philosophical Review*, 79, 394–403.

Nagel, T. (1972) Review of Dennett's *Content and Consciousness*, *Journal of Philosophy*. 50, 220–34.

Nagel, T. (1974) "What is it like to be a bat?" *Philosophical Review*, 83, 435–50.

Nelson, R. J. (1969) "Behaviorism is false", *Journal of Philosophy*, 66, 417–52.

Nelson, R. J. (1975) "Behaviorism, finite automata and stimulus response theory", *Theory and Decision*, 6, 249–67.

Nelson, R. J. (1976) "Mechanism, functionalism, and the identity theory", *Journal of Philosophy*, 73, 365–86.

Oppenheim, P. and Putnam, H. (1958) "Unity of science as a working hypothesis", In H. Feigl, M. Scriven and G. Maxwell (eds), *Minnesota Studies in the Philosophy of Science II*. Minneapolis: University of Minnesota Press.

Pitcher, G. (1971) *A Theory of Perception*. Princeton: Princeton University Press.

Putnam, H. (1963) "Brains and behavior"; reprinted as are all Putnam's articles referred to here (except "On properties") in *Mind, Language and Reality: Philosophical Papers*, vol. 2. London: Cambridge University Press, 1975.

Putnam, H. (1966) "The mental life of some machines".

Putnam, H. (1967) "The nature of mental states" (originally published under the title "Psychological Predicates").

Putnam, H. (1970) "On properties", in *Mathematics, Matter and Method: Philosophical Papers*, vol. 1. London: Cambridge University Press.

Putnam, H. (1975a) "Philosophy and our mental life".

Putnam, H. (1975b) "The meaning of 'meaning'."

Rorty, R. (1972) "Functionalism, machines and incorrigibility," *Journal of Philosophy*, 69, 203–20.

Scriven, M. (1966) *Primary Philosophy*. New York: McGraw-Hill.

Sellars, W. (1956) "Empiricism and the philosophy of mind", in H. Feigl and M. Scriven (eds), *Minnesota Studies in Philosophy of Science I*. Minneapolis: University of Minnesota Press.

Sellars, W. (1968) *Science and Metaphysics* (ch. 6). London: Routledge & Kegan Paul.

Shoemaker, S. (1975) "Functionalism and qualia", *Philosophical Studies*, 27, 271–315.

Shoemaker, S. (1976) "Embodiment and behavior", in A. Rorty (ed.), *The Identities of Persons*. Berkeley: University of California Press.

Shallice, T. (1972) "Dual functions of consciousness", *Psychological Review*, 79, 383–93.

Smart, J. J. C. (1971) "Reports of immediate experience", *Synthese*, 22, 346–59.

Wiggins, D. (1975) "Identity, designation, essentialism, and physicalism", *Philosophia*, 5, 1–30.

Epiphenomenal Qualia

FRANK JACKSON

It is undeniable that the physical, chemical and biological sciences have provided a great deal of information about the world we live in and about ourselves. I will use the label 'physical information' for this kind of information, and also for information that automatically comes along with it. For example, if a medical scientist tells me enough about the processes that go on in my nervous system, and about how they relate to happenings in the world around me, to what has happened in the past and is likely to happen in the future, to what happens to other similar and dissimilar organisms, and the like, he or she tells me – if I am clever enough to fit it together appropriately – about what is often called the functional role of those states in me (and in organisms in general in similar cases). This information, and its kin, I also label 'physical'.

I do not mean these sketchy remarks to constitute a definition of 'physical information', and of the correlative notions of physical property, process, and so on, but to indicate what I have in mind here. It is well known that there are problems with giving a precise definition of these notions, and so of the thesis of Physicalism that all (correct) information is physical information.[1] But – unlike some – I take the question of definition to cut across the central problems I want to discuss in this paper.

I am what is sometimes known as a "qualia freak." I think that there are certain features of the bodily sensations especially, but also of certain perceptual experiences, which no amount of purely physical information includes. Tell me everything physical there is to tell about what is going on in a living brain, the kind of states, their functional role, their relation to what goes on at other times and in other brains, and so on and so forth, and be I as clever as can be in fitting it all together, you won't have told me about the hurtfulness of pains, the itchiness of itches, pangs of jealousy, or about the characteristic experience of tasting a lemon, smelling a rose, hearing a loud noise or seeing the sky.

There are many qualia freaks, and some of them say that their rejection of Physicalism is an unargued intuition.[2] I think that they are being unfair to themselves. They have the following argument. Nothing you could tell of a physical sort captures the smell of a rose, for instance. Therefore, Physicalism is false. By our lights this is a perfectly good argument. It is obviously not to the point to question its validity, and the premise is intuitively obviously true both to them and to me.

I must, however, admit that it is weak from a polemical point of view. There are, unfortunately for us, many who do not find the premise intuitively obvious. The task then is to present an argument whose premises are obvious to all, or at least to as many as possible. This I try to do in section I with what I will call "the Knowledge argument." In section II I contrast the Knowledge argument with the modal argument and in section III with the "What is it like to be" argument. In

"Epiphenomenal Qualia" by F. Jackson first appeared in *Philosophical Quarterly* 32 (1982), pp. 127–36, and is reprinted here by kind permission.

section IV I tackle the question of the causal role of qualia. The major factor in stopping people from admitting qualia is the belief that they would have to be given a causal role with respect to the physical world and especially the brain;[3] and it is hard to do this without sounding like someone who believes in fairies. I seek in section IV to turn this objection by arguing that the view that qualia are epiphenomenal is a perfectly possible one.

I The Knowledge argument for qualia

People vary considerably in their ability to discriminate colors. Suppose that in an experiment to catalog this variation Fred is discovered. Fred has better color vision than anyone else on record; he makes every discrimination that anyone has ever made, and moreover he makes one that we cannot even begin to make. Show him a batch of ripe tomatoes and he sorts them into two roughly equal groups and does so with complete consistency. That is, if you blindfold him, shuffle the tomatoes up, and then remove the blindfold and ask him to sort them out again, he sorts them into exactly the same two groups.

We ask Fred how he does it. He explains that all ripe tomatoes do not look the same color to him, and in fact that this is true of a great many objects that we classify together as red. He sees two colors where we see one, and he has in consequence developed for his own use two words 'red$_1$' and 'red$_2$' to mark the difference. Perhaps he tells us that he has often tried to teach the difference between red$_1$ and red$_2$ to his friends but has got nowhere and has concluded that the rest of the world is red$_1$–red$_2$ color-blind – or perhaps he has had partial success with his children; it doesn't matter. In any case he explains to us that it would be quite wrong to think that because 'red' appears in both 'red$_1$' and 'red$_2$' that the two colors are shades of the one color. He only uses the common term 'red' to fit more easily into our restricted usage. To him red$_1$ and red$_2$ are as different from each other and all the other colors as yellow is from blue. And his discriminatory behavior bears this out: he sorts red$_1$ from red$_2$ tomatoes with the greatest of ease in a wide variety of viewing circumstances. Moreover, an investigation of the physiological basis of Fred's exceptional ability reveals that Fred's optical system is able to separate out two groups of wavelengths in the red spectrum as sharply as we are able to sort out yellow from blue.[4]

I think that we should admit that Fred can see, really see, at least one more color than we can; red$_1$ is a different color from red$_2$. We are to Fred as a totally red–green color-blind person is to us. H. G. Wells' story "The country of the blind" is about a sighted person in a totally blind community.[5] This person never manages to convince them that he can see, that he has an extra sense. They ridicule this sense as quite inconceivable, and treat his capacity to avoid falling into ditches, to win fights and so on as precisely that capacity and nothing more. We would be making their mistake if we refused to allow that Fred can see one more color than we can.

What kind of experience does Fred have when he sees red$_1$ and red$_2$? What is the new color or colors like? We would dearly like to know but do not; and it seems that no amount of physical information about Fred's brain and optical system tells us. We find out perhaps that Fred's cones respond differentially to certain light waves in the red section of the spectrum that make no difference to ours (or perhaps he has an extra cone) and that this leads in Fred to a wider range of those brain states responsible for visual discriminatory behavior. But none of this tells us what we really want to know about his color experience. There is something about it we don't know. But we know, we may suppose, everything about Fred's body, his behavior and dispositions to behavior and about his internal physiology, and everything about his history and relation to others that can be given in physical accounts of persons. We have all the physical information. Therefore, knowing all this is *not* knowing everything about Fred. It follows that Physicalism leaves something out.

To reinforce this conclusion, imagine that as a result of our investigations into the internal workings of Fred we find out how to make everyone's physiology like Fred's in the relevant respects; or perhaps Fred donates his body to science and on his death we are able to transplant his optical system into someone else – again the fine detail doesn't matter. The important point is that such a happening would create enormous interest. People would say "At last we will know what it is like to see the extra color, at last we will know how Fred has differed from us in the way he has struggled to tell us about for so long." Then it cannot be that we knew all along all about Fred. But *ex hypothesi* we did know all along everything about Fred that features in the physicalist scheme; hence the physicalist scheme leaves something out.

Put it this way. *After* the operation, we will know *more* about Fred and especially about his color experiences. But beforehand we had all the physical information we could desire about his body and brain, and indeed everything that has ever featured in physicalist accounts of mind and consciousness. Hence there is more to know than all that. Hence Physicalism is incomplete.

Fred and the new color(s) are of course essentially rhetorical devices. The same point can be made with normal people and familiar colors. Mary is a brilliant scientist who is, for whatever reason, forced to investigate the world from a black and white room *via* a black and white television monitor. She specializes in the neurophysiology of vision and acquires, let us suppose, all the physical information there is to obtain about what goes on when we see ripe tomatoes, or the sky, and use terms like 'red', 'blue', and so on. She discovers, for example, just which wavelength combinations from the sky stimulate the retina, and exactly how this produces *via* the central nervous system the contraction of the vocal chords and expulsion of air from the lungs that results in the uttering of the sentence 'The sky is blue'. (It can hardly be denied that it is in principle possible to obtain all this physical information from black and white television, otherwise the Open University would *of necessity* need to use color television.)

What will happen when Mary is released from her black and white room or is given a color television monitor? Will she *learn* anything or not? It seems just obvious that she will learn something about the world and our visual experience of it. But then it is inescapable that her previous knowledge was incomplete. But she had *all* the physical information. *Ergo* there is more to have than that, and Physicalism is false.

Clearly the same style of Knowledge argument could be deployed for taste, hearing, the bodily sensations and generally speaking for the various mental states which are said to have (as it is variously put) raw feels, phenomenal features or qualia. The conclusion in each case is that the qualia are left out of the physicalist story. And the polemical strength of the Knowledge argument is that it is so hard to deny the central claim that one can have all the physical information without having all the information there is to have.

II The Modal Argument

By the Modal argument I mean an argument of the following style.[6] Sceptics about other minds are not making a mistake in deductive logic, whatever else may be wrong with their position. No amount of physical information about another *logically entails* that he or she is conscious or feels anything at all. Consequently there is a possible world with organisms exactly like us in every physical respect (and remember that includes functional states, physical history, et al.) but which differ from us profoundly in that they have no conscious mental life at all. But then what is it that we have and they lack? Not anything physical *ex hypothesi*. In all physical regards we and they are exactly alike. Consequently there is more to us than the purely physical. Thus Physicalism is false.[7]

It is sometimes objected that the Modal argument misconceives Physicalism on the ground that that doctrine is advanced as a *contingent* truth.[8] But to say this is only to say that physicalists restrict their claim to *some* possible worlds, including especially ours; and the Modal argument is only directed against this lesser claim. If we in *our* world, let alone beings in any others, have features additional to those of our physical replicas in other possible worlds, then we have non-physical features or qualia.

The trouble rather with the modal argument is that it rests on a disputable modal intuition. Disputable because it is disputed. Some sincerely deny that there can be physical replicas of us in other possible worlds which nevertheless lack consciousness. Moreover, at least one person who once had the intuition now has doubts.[9]

Head-counting may seem a poor approach to a discussion of the modal argument. But frequently we can do no better when modal intuitions are in question, and remember our initial goal was to find the argument with the greatest polemical utility.

Of course, *qua* protagonists of the Knowledge argument we may well accept the modal intuition in question; but this will be a *consequence* of our already having an argument to the conclusion that qualia are left out of the physicalist story, not our ground for that conclusion. Moreover, the matter is complicated by the possibility that the connection between matters physical and qualia is like that sometimes held to obtain between esthetic qualities and natural ones. Two possible worlds which agree in all "natural" respects (including the experiences of sentient creatures) must agree in all esthetic qualities also, but it is plausibly held that the esthetic qualities cannot be reduced to the natural.

III The "What is it like to be" argument

In "What is it like to be a bat?" Thomas Nagel argues that no amount of physical information can tell us what it is like to be a bat, and indeed that we, human beings, cannot imagine what it is like to be a bat.[10] His reason is that what this is like can only be understood from a bat's point of view, which is not our point of view and is not something capturable in physical terms which are essentially terms understandable equally from many points of view.

It is important to distinguish this argument from the Knowledge argument. When I complained that all the physical knowledge about Fred was not enough to tell us what his special color experience was like, I was not complaining that we weren't finding out what it is like to *be* Fred. I was complaining that there is something *about* his experience, a property of it, of which we were left ignorant. And if and when we come to know what this property is we still will not know what it is like to *be* Fred, but we will know more *about* him. No amount of knowledge about Fred, be it physical or not, amounts to knowledge "from the inside" considering Fred. We are not Fred. There is thus a whole set of items of knowledge expressed by forms of words like 'that is *I myself* who is . . .' which Fred has and we simply cannot have because we are not him.[11]

When Fred sees the color he alone can see, one thing he knows is the way his experience of it differs from his experience of seeing red and so on; *another* is that he himself is seeing it. Physicalist and qualia freaks alike should acknowledge that no amount of information of whatever kind that *others* have *about* Fred amounts to knowledge of the second. My complaint though concerned the first and was that the special quality of his experience is certainly a fact about it, and one which Physicalism leaves out because no amount of physical information told us what it is.

Nagel speaks as if the problem he is raising is one of extrapolating from knowledge of one experience to another, of imagining what an unfamiliar experience would be like on the basis of familiar ones. In terms of Hume's example, from knowledge of some shades of blue we can work out what it would be like to see other shades of blue. Nagel argues that the trouble with bats et al. is that they are too unlike us. It is hard to see an objection to Physicalism here. Physicalism makes no special claims about the imaginative or extrapolative powers of human beings, and it is hard to see why it need do so.[12]

Anyway, our Knowledge argument makes no assumptions on this point. If Physicalism were true, enough physical information about Fred would obviate any need to extrapolate or to perform special feats of imagination or understanding in order to know all about his special color experience. *The information would already be in our possession.* But it clearly isn't. That was the nub of the argument.

IV The bogey of epiphenomenalism

Is there any really *good* reason for refusing to countenance the idea that qualia are causally impotent with respect to the physical world? I will argue for the answer no, but in doing this I will say nothing about two views associated with the classical epiphenomenalist position. The first is that mental *states* are inefficacious with respect to the physical world. All I will be concerned to defend is that it is possible to hold that certain *properties* of certain mental states, namely those I've called qualia, are such that their possession or absence makes no difference to the physical world. The second is that the mental is *totally* causally inefficacious. For all I will say it may be that you have to hold that the instantiation of *qualia* makes a difference to *other mental states* though not to anything physical. Indeed general considerations to do with how you could come to be aware of the instantiation of qualia suggest such a position.[13]

Three reasons are standardly given for holding that a quale like the hurtfulness of a pain must be causally efficacious in the physical world, and so, for instance, that its instantiation must sometimes make a difference to what happens in the brain. None, I will argue, has any real force. (I am much indebted to Alec Hyslop and John Lucas for convincing me of this.)

(i) It is supposed to be just obvious that the hurtfulness of pain is partly responsible for the subject seeking to avoid pain, saying 'It hurts' and so on. But, to reverse Hume, anything can fail to cause anything. No matter how often *B* follows *A*, and no matter how initially obvious the causality of the connection seems, the hypothesis that *A* causes *B* can be overturned by an over-arching theory which shows the two as distinct effects of a common underlying causal process.

To the untutored the image on the screen of Lee Marvin's fist moving from left to right immediately followed by the image of John Wayne's head moving in the same general direction looks as causal as anything.[14] And of course throughout countless Westerns images similar to the first are followed by images similar to the second. All this counts for precisely nothing when we know the over-arching theory concerning how the relevant images are both effects of an underlying causal process involving the projector and the film. The epiphenomenalist can say exactly the same about the connection between, for example, hurtfulness and behavior. It is simply a consequence of the fact that certain happenings in the brain cause both.

(ii) The second objection relates to Darwin's Theory of Evolution. According to natural selection the traits that evolve over time are those conducive to physical survival. We may assume that qualia evolved over time – we have them, the earliest forms of life do not – and so we should expect qualia to be conducive to survival. The objection is that they could hardly help us to survive if they do nothing to the physical world.

The appeal of this argument is undeniable, but there is a good reply to it. Polar bears have particularly thick, warm coats. The Theory of Evolution explains this (we suppose) by pointing out that having a thick warm coat is conducive to survival in the Arctic. But having a thick coat goes along with having a heavy coat, and having a heavy coat is *not* conducive to survival. It slows the animal down.

Does this mean that we have refuted Darwin because we have found an evolved trait – having a heavy coat – which is not conducive to survival? Clearly not. Having a heavy coat is an unavoidable concomitant of having a warm coat (in the context, modern insulation was not available), and the advantages for survival of having a warm coat outweighed the disadvantages of having a heavy one. The point is that all we can extract from Darwin's theory is that we should expect any evolved characteristic to be *either* conducive to survival *or* a by-product of one that is so conducive. The epiphenomenalist holds that qualia fall into the latter category. They are a by-product of certain brain processes that are highly conducive to survival.

(iii) The third objection is based on a point about how we come to know about other minds. We know about other minds by knowing about other behavior, at least in part. The nature of the inference is a matter of some controversy, but it is not a matter of controversy that it proceeds from behavior. That is why we think that stones do not feel and dogs do feel. But, runs the objection, how can a person's behavior provide any reason for believing he has qualia like mine, or indeed any qualia at all, unless this behavior can be regarded as the *outcome* of the qualia. Man Friday's footprint was evidence of Man Friday because footprints are causal outcomes of feet attached to people. And an epiphenomenalist cannot regard behavior, or indeed anything physical, as an outcome of qualia.

But consider my reading in *The Times* that Spurs won. This provides excellent evidence that The *Telegraph* has also reported that Spurs won, despite the fact that (I trust) the *Telegraph* does not get the results from *The Times*. They each send their own reporters to the game. The *Telegraph*'s report is in no sense an outcome of *The Times*', but the latter provides good evidence for the former nevertheless.

The reasoning involved can be reconstructed thus. I read in *The Times* that Spurs won. This gives me reason to think that Spurs won because I know that Spurs' winning is the most likely candidate to be what caused the report in *The Times*. But I also know that Spurs' winning would have had many effects, including almost certain a report in the *Telegraph*.

I am arguing from one effect back to its cause and out again to another effect. The fact that neither effect causes the other is irrelevant. Now the epiphenomenalist allows that qualia are effects of what goes on in the brain. Qualia cause nothing physical but are caused by something physical. Hence the epiphenomenalist can argue from the behavior of others to the qualia of others by arguing from the behavior of others back to its causes in the brains of others and out again to their qualia.

You may well feel for one reason or another that this is a more dubious chain of reasoning than its model in the case of newspaper reports. You are right. The problem of other minds is a major philosophical problem, the problem of other newspaper reports is not. But there is no special problem for Epiphenomenalism as opposed to, say, Interactionism here.

There is a very understandable response to the three replies I have just made. "All right, there is no knockdown refutation of the existence of epiphenomenal qualia. But the fact remains that they are an excrescence. They *do* nothing, they *explain* nothing, they serve merely to soothe the intuitions of dualists, and it is left a total mystery how they fit into the world view of science. In short we do not and cannot understand the how and why of them."

This is perfectly true; but is no objection to qualia, for it rests on an overly optimistic view of the human animal, and its powers. We are the products of Evolution. We understand and sense what we need to understand and sense in order to survive. Epiphenomenal qualia are totally irrelevant to survival. At no stage of our evolution did natural selection favor those who could make sense of how they are caused and the laws governing them, or in fact why they exist at all. And that is why we can't.

It is not sufficiently appreciated that Physicalism is an extremely optimistic view of our powers. If it is true, we have, in very broad outline admittedly, a grasp of our place in the scheme of things. Certain matters of sheer complexity defeat us – there are an awful lot of neurons – but in principle we have it all. But consider the antecedent probability that everything in the Universe be of a kind that is relevant in some way or other to the survival of *Homo sapiens*. It is very low surely. But then one must admit that it is very likely that there is a part of the whole scheme of things, maybe a big part, which no amount of evolution will ever bring us near to knowledge about or understanding of. For the simple reason that such knowledge and understanding is irrelevant to survival.

Physicalists typically emphasize that we are a part of nature on their view, which is fair enough. But if we are a part of nature, we are as nature has left us after however many years of evolution it is, and each step in that evolutionary progression has been a matter of chance constrained just by the need to preserve or increase survival value. The wonder is that we understand as much as we do, and there is no wonder that there should be matters which fall quite outside our comprehension. Perhaps exacty how epiphenomenal qualia fit into the scheme of things is one such.

This may seem an unduly pessimistic view of our capacity to articulate a truly comprehensive picture of our world and our place in it. But suppose we discovered living on the bottom of the deepest oceans a sort of sea slug which manifested intelligence. Perhaps survival in the conditions required rational powers. Despite their intelligence, these sea slugs have only a very restricted conception of the world by comparison with ours, the explanation for this being the nature of their immediate environment. Nevertheless they have developed sciences which work surprisingly well in these restricted terms. They also have philosophers, called slugists. Some call themselves tough-minded slugists, others confess to being soft-minded slugists.

The tough-minded slugists hold that the restricted terms (or ones pretty like them which may be introduced as their sciences progress) suffice in principle to describe everything without remainder. These tough-minded slugists admit in moments of weakness to a feeling that their theory leaves something out. They resist this feeling and their opponents, the soft-minded slugists, by pointing out – absolutely correctly – that no slugist has ever succeeded in spelling out how this mysterious residue fits into the highly successful view that their sciences have and are developing of how their world works.

Our sea slugs don't exist, but they might. And there might also exist super beings which stand to us as we stand to these slugs. We cannot adopt the perspective of these super beings, because we are not them, but the possibility of such a perspective is, I think, an antidote to excessive optimism.[15].

NOTES

1 See, e.g., D. H. Mellor, "Materialism and phenomenal qualities," *Aristotelian Society Supp. Vol.* 47 (1973), 107–19; and J. W. Cornman, *Materialism and Sensations*, New Haven and London, 1971.

2 Particularly in discussion, but see, e.g., Keith Campbell, *Metaphysics*, Belmont, 1976, p. 67.

3 See, e.g., D. C. Dennett, "Current issues in the philosophy of mind," *American Philosophical Quarterly* 15 (1978), 249–61.

4 Put this, and similar specifications below, in terms of Land's theory if you prefer. See, e.g., Edwin H. Land, "Experiments in color vision," *Scientific American* 200 (5 May 1959), 84–99.

5 H. G. Wells, *The Country of the Blind and Other Stories*, London, n.d.

6 See, e.g., Keith Campbell, *Body and Mind*, New York, 1970; and Robert Kirk, "Sentience and behavior," *Mind* 83 (1974), 43–60.

7 I have presented the argument in an inter-world rather than the more usual intra-world fashion to avoid inessential complications to do with supervenience, causal anomalies and the like.

8 See, e.g., W. G. Lycan, "A new Lilliputian argument against machine functionalism," *Philosophical Studies* 35 (1979), 279–87, p. 280; and Don Locke, "Zombies, schizophrenics and purely physical objects," *Mind* 85 (1976), 97–9.

9 See R. Kirk, "From physical explicability to full-blooded materialism," *Philosophical Quarterly* 29 (1979), 229–37. See also the arguments against the modal intuition in, e.g., Sydney Shoemaker, "Functionalism and qualia," *Philosophical Studies* 27 (1975), 291–315.

10 *Philosophical Review* 83 (1974), 435–50. Two things need to be said about this article. One is that, despite my dissociations to come, I am much indebted to it. The other is that the emphasis changes through the article, and by the end Nagel is objecting not so much to Physicalism as to all extant theories of mind for ignoring points of view, including those that admit (irreducible) qualia.

11 Knowledge *de se* in the terms of David Lewis, "Attitudes de dicto and de se," *Philosophical Review* 88 (1979), 513–43.

12 See Laurence Nemirow's comments on "What it is . . ." in his review of T. Nagel *Mortal Quesitons* in *Philosophical Review* 89 (1980), 473–7. I am indebted here in particular to a discussion with David Lewis.

13 See my review of K. Campbell, *Body and Mind*, in *Australasian Journal of Philosophy* 50 (1972), 77–80.

14 Cf. Jean Piaget, "The child's conception of physical causality," reprinted in *The Essential Piaget*, London, 1977.

14. I am indebted to Robert Pargetter for a number of comments and, despite his dissent, to section IV of Paul E. Meehl's "The complete autocerebroscopist," in Paul Feyerabend and Grover Maxwell (eds), *Mind, Matter and Method*, Minneapolis, 1966.

17

Functionalist Responses

Could Love Be Like a Heatwave?
Physicalism and the Subjective Character of
Experience

JANET LEVIN

In his well-known paper, 'What is it like to be a bat?', Thomas Nagel argues that no purely "objective" description of the world – that is, no description equally accessible to observers, regardless of their point of view – could give us knowledge of what it is like to be a bat. Such knowledge, he argues, is available only to those who, unlike· ourselves, are capable of having the experiences of bats. Therefore, he concludes, there are facts about the subjective character of experience, such as what it is like to be a bat, that no physicalist, functionalist, or otherwise "objective" theory of mental states could adequately describe.[1]

Frank Jackson, in his paper 'Epiphenomenal qualia' (reprinted in this volume), argues similarly, choosing an example that is closer to home. Jackson argues that Mary, a brilliant physicist and neuropsychologist who has grown up and pursued her career in a black-and-white environment, would clearly gain some knowledge about color and color experience upon first viewing the world outside: she would come to know what it is like to see colors. Therefore, he concludes, "it is inescapable that her previous knowledge was incomplete. But she had *all* the physical information. Ergo there is more to have than that, and Physicalism is false."[2]

It has been objected, however, that both arguments depend upon an equivocation. For the premises to be plausible, "knowledge of what it is like to be a bat" or "knowledge of what it is like to see colors" must be understood as a kind of *practical* knowledge or ability:[3] in Nagel's case, the ability to imaginatively project oneself into another's point of view; in Jackson's, an ability that is not so clearly defined. But the lack of such an ability, it is argued, is not the same as a

"Could Love be Like a Heatwave? Physicalism and the Subjective Character of Experience" by J. Levin first appeared in *Philosophical Studies*, Vol. 49, No. 2, 1986, pp. 245–61. Copyright © 1986/1985 by D. Reidel Publishing Company. Reprinted by permission.

gap in one's *theoretical* knowledge, or knowledge of the facts. Further, there does not seem to be any important tie between these two sorts of knowledge, as it is hard to see why even the most comprehensive description of mental states should be expected to provide one with the practical abilities in question.[4]

Thus, though sufficient experience of the sort had by bats may be required for knowing what it is like to be one, it does not follow that this experience is the only source of any theoretical knowledge about bats. And though Mary may not know what it is like to see colors without actually having seen them, it does not follow that she is missing any theoretical knowledge about colors or color experience. Thus it does not follow that there are facts about experience that no objective theory can describe.

It is clear, then, that Nagel's and Jackson's arguments are open to objection. None the less, these arguments have been extremely influential, as there are intuitively compelling grounds for the view that without the capacity for a certain sort of experience, one cannot have knowledge of certain simple and straightforward facts about experiences of that kind.

First of all, it would be perverse to claim that bare experience can provide us *only* with various practical abilities, and never with theoretical knowledge.[5] By being shown an unfamiliar color, I acquire information about its similarities and compatibilities with other colors, and its effects on other of our mental states: surely I seem to be acquiring certain facts about that color and the visual experience of it.

Second, it is not implausible to think that experience is the *only* source of at least some of these facts. It would be unfair, of course, to expect Nagel or Jackson to specify these facts in any detail, as this would fail to take seriously their claim that they cannot be objectively described. However, this view has had a long and impressive history, beginning with the Empiricists' contention that one cannot have "ideas" of colors, sounds, smells, and tastes (and thus the materials for theoretical knowledge about them) without first having the corresponding impressions. And though Empiricism has been widely rejected as a general theory of concept-acquisition, here, in accounting for our knowledge of mental states, is where it seems to become common sense: how *does* one convey the taste of pineapple to someone who has not yet tried it, and does that first taste not dramatically increase, if not fully constitute, the knowledge of what the taste of pineapple is?

Finally, there seem to be important cognitive differences between ourselves and those incapable of sharing our experiences. It would seem extremely natural to explain this by appeal to differences in our knowledge of the facts about experience: indeed, what other explanation could there be?

Thus Nagel's and Jackson's arguments, whatever their flaws, serve as reminders of the claim that one needs to have had experiences of a specific sort to have access to all the facts about mental states. Clearly, this is something that a physicalist must deny, as physicalism requires that the world and everything in it be describable in the objective vocabulary of science. Consequently, there is still a burden upon the physicalist, even after the Nagel–Jackson argument has been challenged, to dispel the plausibilty of this claim.

My aim in this paper is to do just that. My view is that this claim derives its plausibility from an argument which, though similar to Jackson's and Nagel's, ·is considerably harder to refute. This argument has two premises: The first is that if one lacks certain experiences, one will lack a certain *recognitional* or *discriminative ability* – an ability to know that one is in a particular state without making inferences, or consulting instruments, but simply by applying one's concept of that mental state to the experiences at hand. Let us call this kind of recognitional or discriminative ability "direct." The second premise is that this capacity to recognize or discriminate among mental states is required for having full and complete factual knowledge of them. This argument has been explicitly advanced by Richard Warner, in a recent paper that argues for the Nagel–Jackson conclusion.[6] It is also implicit in classical discussions of the relation between experience and theoretical knowledge, such as the Molyneux question addressed by Locke and Berkeley. And it seems to improve upon the formulation, while retaining the spirit, of Nagel's and Jackson's arguments themselves.

Indeed, these premises, at least on first glance, appear to be quite plausible. The first seems intuitively obvious: surely Mary would not be able to immediately identify her visual experiences as being of red or of green, if she were presented with a simple patch of each color in her black-and-white room. And surely it is hard to see how we would be able to accurately identify the perceptual experiences of bats if we somehow became able to have them, no matter how much objective information we had acquired about bats.

What about the second premise? On the Empiricists' theory of concept-formation, of course, it would have been completely uncontroversial: if concepts, or "ideas," are nothing but "faint copies" of the experiences themselves, then one ought to be able to match one's current experience, feature by feature, with the copy stored in memory. Even without Empiricism, however, this premise has appeal. After all, if one knows *all* the facts about some mental state, including the way it feels, it seems that one could not fail to identify it, without evidence or instruments, upon presentation. This argument appears to be lurking in Jackson's paper, and it is made explicitly by Warner in his. If they are correct, then the possession of this recognitional or discriminative capacity, unlike Nagel's imaginative ability, seems to be essentially tied to one's knowledge of the facts.[7]

I will argue, however, that though this argument is more compelling than Jackson's or Nagel's, it too relies upon an equivocation. More specifically, I will argue that there is an ambiguity in the notion of "direct recognitional capacity" as it is used in both the contemporary and classical versions of this argument, and that neither reading can make both premises true. The source of this ambiguity, I will suggest, is the failure to distinguish between having a concept and having the wherewithal to apply it. Once this distinction is made, however, it will be clear that it is the latter ability, and that alone, which objective descriptions may not be able to supply to a person who has not had sufficient experiences of the type described. It will also be clear that this ability is not needed for full and complete knowledge of the facts about these experiences.

The problem with this argument against physicalism, then, is not that it equivocates between knowledge as "having an ability" and knowledge as "being in relation to the facts," but that it equivocates between two sorts of abilities, only one of which is required for having knowledge of all the facts in question. This distinction, I will argue, has been overlooked because of an implicit acceptance of an overly Empiricistic view of the acquisition and individuation of concepts. Once this distinction is made, however, the physicalist will be able to give an account of what differentiates our knowledge of color experiences from Mary's, and our knowlege of alien experiences from that of the creatures who have them, and say why these differences make no difference to our knowledge of the facts. Further, this distinction will provide the physicalist with the tools to describe and explain the important, if not essential, contribution made by the experience of mental states to one's knowledge of the facts about them.

II

In examining the notion of a direct recognitional capacity, I would first like to consider its role in a classical Empiricist conjecture, namely, Molyneux's question of whether a "man born blind and then made to see" could determine, by sight alone, which of two objects was a sphere and which a cube. By starting with the Empiricists, it will be easier to see how far our current views about the relation of sense-experience to knowledge have come.

Molyneux's answer, endorsed by Locke and Berkeley, was that the man born blind would fail this discriminative test. For Molyneux, this failure would have been proof that the "ideas" of visible shape and contour could not be acquired by touch, or reasoning, or anything short of visual experience itself. Thus a person who had never seen a cube or sphere would be missing certain facts about cubes and spheres. Nagel's and Jackson's concern in such a case, of course, would be somewhat different: their question would be whether the blind man could discriminate between his *visual experiences* of cubes and spheres, and thus whether he knew all the facts about *those experiences*. But it is easy to see how the issues raised in one case will be relevant to the other, as a negative answer to Molyneux's question assures a negative answer to Nagel's and Jackson's.[8] What is important is that Molyneux, quite explicitly, took a person's recognitional or discriminative capacities to provide the definitive test of his knowledge of the facts.

But what exactly was this test to be? As Locke reported it in the *Essay*, Molyneux specified merely that "the sphere and cube [be] placed on a table, and the blind man made to see,'" and asked "whether by his sight, before he touched them, he could now distinguish and tell which is the globe, which the cube?"[9] Let us assume that Molyneux's blind man had to give his answer not only before touching the cube and the sphere, or for that matter anything else, but before seeing the ostensive identification of any item whatsoever. And suppose, as Molyneux predicted, that the man born blind failed the recognitional test. What would this have shown about his theoretical knowledge?

For the Empiricists, this failure would have been good evidence that the man born blind was lacking the ideas of the visual properties of cubes and spheres: if he had had "faint copies" of these properties in mind, he should have been able to match them to the items he could currently see. But on any other view of concept-formation, it is not clear why this lack of recognitional ability, by itself, should indicate a conceptual gap. To make the example relevant to the questions that concern us here, let us imagine a man born blind with the omniscience attributed to Mary, Jackson's neuropsychologist who had never seen color. That is, suppose that he had mastered all the facts about 3-dimensional figures and visual experiences that could be stated in the "objective" vocabularies of geometry and psychology, including the judgments made by sighted people about the similarities and differences among their visual experiences. Presumably, this theoretically sophisticated blind man would be able to correctly answer any questions about cubes, spheres and the visual experiences of them.

Further, suppose that, after being shown a few examples of *other* geometrical figures and being told that they were examples of their kind, he was able to go on and correctly identify the cube and sphere. In this case, it is even more plausible to think that the blind man's initial lack of recognition showed no gap in his knowledge of the facts. The accuracy of his answers and of his subsequent identifications of novel geometric shapes could be evidence that what he was missing was not a set of facts or concepts, but the ability to apply to his new experiences the concepts that he already had. Even the strictest nativist, after all, would agree that the full-fledged use of one's innate ideas requires some "ostensive" sessions with the environment, some lessons in how these concepts are to be applied. The question of their innateness, in such cases, is traditionally decided by how easily the individual, after learning to apply these concepts, could go on to identify new experiences of that sort. Similarly if the man born blind, after his lesson, was able to discriminate cube from sphere at first sight before he touched them, he may be taken to have the necessary concepts, and thus the materials for theoretical knowledge, of the visual experiences of cubes and spheres. But if so, then on this understanding of "direct recognitional capacity," the man born blind, plausibly, could be regarded as knowing all the facts about the visual experiences of cubes and spheres without having the relevant recognitional capacities. That is, on an understanding of "direct recognitional capacity" that makes the first premise of our argument plausible, the second premise appears to be false.

However, Molyneux's specifications for the thought-experiment permit another interpretation, namely, that in cases such as this, the recognitional capacities of the man born blind *would* be sufficiently "direct": after all, given a minimal number of lessons of the sort detailed above, he would be able to identify the cube and sphere, by his sight, without having touched them, just as Molyneux required. On this understanding of "direct recognitional capacity," it is more plausible to use recognitional capacities as a test for theoretical knowledge; if the man born blind fails *this* test of recognition, it may well seem that he was lacking something conceptual that only the relevant visual experience could provide. But unfortunately for the argument linking experience and factual knowledge, if the blind man could *pass* this test, then he would have the relevant recognitional capacities without having had the corresponding experiences. That is, on an undertanding of "direct recognitional capacity" that makes the second premise plausible, the first premise appears false.

But is it plausible to think that the man born blind could pass this weaker recognitional test? Intuitively, this conjecture seems plausible indeed. By hypothesis, he would have learned all there is to know about the geometry of 3-dimensional objects and the similarities and differences in the way they strike visually acute perceivers when viewed in normal light. It seems that he would be able to reflect upon his knowledge, and the features of of his new experiences, and make the proper judgment.

Indeed, there is even some empirical confirmation of this hypothesis, as Molyneux's problem is no longer just a thought-experiment. The results of such questions put to congenitally blind people whose eyesight has recently been restored are mixed: some can immmediately distinguish cubes from spheres, and some cannot. There are all sorts of variables, of course, whose precise effects are unknown; for example, it is unclear whether there are differences in the way the visual system adapts to given differences in operative procedure and in the nature of the blindness itself. Yet R. L. Gregory reports a trend that is of interest. In observations of the Molyneux problem put to congenitally blind people upon regaining their sight, "some did see well almost immediately, particularly those who were intelligent and active, and who had received a good education while blind."[10] So the view that having comprehensive theoretical knowledge can make for recognitional capacities has at least a bit of empirical support.

However, there are two problems with this scenario that could defuse my argument. First is the worry that, even if the man born blind could discriminate the cube from the sphere upon first viewing, his discrimination would not be sufficiently direct. After all, he has had, presumably, extensive tactile contact with cubes and spheres and other 3-dimensional objects while blind. Also, presumably, he has a reasonably good memory of how things feel. Thus, even if he were merely *shown* an arc and angle, and were not permitted to touch them, it could be argued that he identifies the cube and sphere *by inference*: having made the initial correlation between the look of the sample objects and his memory of how they felt, he is able to use his knowledge of the similarities and differences among tactile experiences (and among visual experiences) to make the proper call. If inference is responsible for his recognitional capacities, however, then our version of Molyneux's man born blind cannot be a counterexample to the claim that recognitional capacities depend upon prior experiences of a particular sort.

There is no definitive argument that I can give against this worry: it is possible for the man born blind to be using inference, rather than merely learning how to apply his concepts, and in such a case his discriminations would not be sufficiently direct. This worry, however, may be assuaged if we move to a different case.

It is best to make this move because of yet another problem with the Molyneux conjecture. The perceptual experiences of spheres and cubes appear to be structurally complex, unlike the rawer feels of perceived colors, tastes and bodily sensations such as pain. It may seem that there are intrinsic structural features that are common to visual and tactile experiences of spheres and cubes – abstract features such as continuity and discontinuity in contour – that may permit one to distinguish them visually without prior visual experience of them.[11] In other words, Locke, Berkeley, and Molyneux were just plain wrong: the ideas of spheres and cubes afforded by sight and touch are not completely heterogeneous after all. The case envisioned by Molyneux, both for the Empiricists and their contemporary successors, is just a bad example.

III

However, I think the same issues can be raised for cases involving the recognition of "purer" bodily sensations and perceptions. Thus I would like to move to an example, proposed in a 1986 paper by Richard Warner, in support of the claim that neither physicalism nor functionalism can capture all the facts about the experience of pain.

In his paper, Warner has us imagine an omniscient Alpha Centaurian who until this time, like all members of his kind, had been incapable of experiencing unpleasant sensations. Just for the experience, however, he contrives an apparatus that would modify his nervous system enough to allow him to feel the sensation – pain – that a stomach cramp normally produces in us. Suppose that the experiment works, and the machine indeed produces in him the new sensation of pain. But suppose also that, as an unforeseen consequence, the machine induces in him another as yet unexperienced sensation, the sensation of nausea. Warner claims that the Alpha Centaurian would not be able to determine, without consulting instruments or making inferences, which state was pain and which was nausea, no matter how much knowledge he had gleaned about the physical and functional structure of human beings. Thus, he concludes, physicalism and functionalism have left out certain facts about how pain feels.

Now, pain is a "feel" as raw as any, and there is no obvious isomorphism between pains and any other sort of human (or presumably Alpha Centaurian) bodily sensation. This case, then, would seem purer than Molyneux's for appraising the question of whether the experientially deficient have access to all the facts. However, the same sorts of tensions and ambiguities in the notion of direct recognitional capacities arise here, too. For consider: Given my description of the case so far, it is hard to see why the Alpha Centaurian would not be able to make the appropriate discrimination. If there is a functional distinction between pain and nausea, the Alpha Centaurian would have learned it.[12] And surely there is such a difference: nausea, but not stomach cramping, produces an intense desire to avoid food and to vomit, and to believe that the state was caused by food.[13] Thus, it seems, the Alpha Centaurian would be able to reflect upon the differences in beliefs and desires that each state produces in him and make the proper call.

Moreover, unlike the case of Molyneux's man born blind, it would be hard to argue that this identification was not sufficiently direct.[14] It might be thought that the Alpha Centaurian's reflections upon the relations among pain, nausea, and other mental states involved inference, or the gathering of evidence, rather than the simple application of concepts to the experiences at hand. This argument, however, would beg the question against the objective theorists. By hypothesis, information about these relational or otherwise objective properties of pain and nausea constitutes the Alpha Centaurian's concepts of those mental states, and the question was whether the possession of concepts of that sort was sufficient to give him the relevant recognitional capacities. For the insufficiency of these concepts to be a *conclusion* drawn from the Alpha Centaurian's lack of a recognitional ability, the lack of this recognitional ability must be established in some other way. Further, the claim is independently implausible: even we, as sophisticated pain feelers, must sometimes take time, and engage in reflection, to unravel one type of painful experience from another if they occur together, especially for the first time. If this involves inference, then our own abilities to discriminate among our experiences would not be sufficiently direct. Thus, it looks as if this is a case in which recognition can occur without prior experiences of the relevant sort.

However, this case, like Molyneux's, may be just another bad example. It may be wondered, that is, why this case should impress Nagel and Jackson, as their claim was that objective theories cannot provide one with all the facts about experiences that are *significantly* different from one's own. Pain and nausea, though distinctive in their unpleasantness, may be too close to the prior experiences of the Alpha Centaurian to illustrate their point. For consider: To distinguish pain from nausea in the way I described, the Alpha Centaurian must be able to distinguish between a state of his stomach due to the ingestion of food, and a state of his stomach that results from strenuous exercise. However, the Alpha Centaurian may be able to do this only because he had experienced certain sensations – a pleasant fullness after dinner, perhaps, or the mild exhilaration of a good abdominal stretch – which, though not unpleasant, were in other ways similar to pain and nausea.

But what if the Alpha Centaurian had never had *any* sensations in his stomach or abdominal area, and had acquired his concepts of food-related and exercise-related bodily states in some other way? In this case, the sensations of pain and nausea would be *radically* different from any he had ever felt, different enough, presumably, to make Nagel's and Jackson's point. In this case, moreover, it is indeed unlikely that the Alpha Centaurian could "directly" discriminate between them.

However, as in the Molyneux case, it is not clear that the Nagel–Jackson conclusion would follow, as it is not clear why the Alpha Centaurian's failure should show a gap in his knowledge of the facts about pain and nausea. The Alpha Centaurian, after all, would be able to answer all the questions about pain and nausea that he answered, correctly, in the previous case. And if after feeling some kinds of pain, he was able to go on and identify others upon first presentation, we could conclude that, like Molyneux's man born blind, what the Alpha Centaurian is missing is merely an ability to *apply* certain of his concepts, and not those concepts themselves. Thus, as in the Molyneux case, in the sense of "direct recognitional ability" in which it is plausible to think that recognition is required for factual knowledge, it is implausible to think it is contingent upon experiences of some specific sort and vice versa.

It is clear, then, what can be said along these lines about Mary's knowledge of color experience and our knowledge of the perceptual experiences of bats. In Mary's case, the failure to immediately identify red and green upon first being shown any colors at all may be taken to show a deficiency in her ability to apply color concepts to her experience, and not a deficiency in those concepts themselves. As in the case of the Alpha Centaurian, or Molyneux's man born blind, Mary will have the relevant color concepts as long as she has sufficient information about the structure of that perceptual field, the similarities and differences among the experiences in it, and the "constitutive" truths about it, such as "Nothing can look red all over and green all over at the same time." Evidence of her mastery of this information may be acquired by close questioning about these features of color experience, and eventually, by seeing how quickly she can go on to correctly identify other colors, or other shades of the same colors, after witnessing the ostensive identification of a representative few.

The situation is somewhat different, however, for our knowledge about the perceptual experiences of bats. In this case, we are not only lacking the wherewithal to apply our concepts of sonar perception to our experiences, but we lack sufficient information about sonar perception even to come close to having adequate concepts of experiences in that perceptual field. If the only way to acquire these concepts was to have a specific set of experiences, then Nagel's conclusion would stand. But there is no reason to think that this is so. It is true that one must have *some* experiences in order to have concepts, and thus the materials for theoretical knowledge. However, all sorts of experiences can provide the conceptual wherewithal for understanding what it is for experiences to be similar and different from one another along various dimensions – what it is for them to differ in intensity, compatibility, and cause and effect. That is why, contrary to both Locke and Nagel, it *could* be helpful for a blind person to be told that red is like the sound of a trumpet (or a prepubescent that love is like a heatwave). It will be helpful as long as he is told what pink and orange and green are like as well.[15]

At the end of 'What is it like to be a bat', Nagel encourages the development of an "objective phenomenology," an enterprise devoted to the objective description of just these sorts of relations among experiences of the types we cannot have.[16] He goes on, however, to deny that this information could give us all the facts about the experiences of bats. My suspicion, however, is that these more exotic cases seem more intractable because we now know quite little about the relevant dimensions of alien experiences, and even less about how these experiences are to be ordered along those dimensions. Our current lack of knowledge may indeed be due to a gap in our objective theories, but there is no reason to think that it cannot be overcome by acquiring more information of a perfectly objective sort.

IV

So far, I have argued that the failure to identify one's mental states immediately, upon first presentation, may be due to a gap in one's knowledge *or in one's ability to apply certain concepts*. I have also argued that though this ability, perhaps, could be acquired only through the experience of the mental states in question, its lack is by no means indicative of a gap in one's factual knowledge about mental states.

One might wonder, however, whether this account suffices to shift the burden of proof back to Nagel and Jackson. First, it may seem that it would be difficult, if not impossible, to draw a distinction between having the concept of a mental state, and having the ability to apply it to one's own experience. That is, it may seem that the only alternative to the Empiricists' theory of concepts as "faint copies" is a theory which identifies having the concept of red or pain with having the ability to directly classify one's experiences as experiences of red or pain. However, the concepts of mental states may be identified with certain capacities or dispositions without assuming that they are capacities to classify experiences, under all circumstances, in any particular way. This assumption would be a vestige of Empiricism and not an alternative to it, as it would ignore the other ways in which differences among these concepts could be manifested, namely, by the differences in the roles they play in reasoning, inference, and judgment. Such differences insure that there is a fact of the matter about whether a person who is unable to discriminate red from green upon first presentation really does have the concept of red. Moreover, these differences will be manifested, eventually, in the person's classificatory behavior: once the person has witnessed the ostensive identification of enough experiences of this sort, if he has the appropriate concepts, he will be able to directly identify new ones of that kind.

Because of this last contention, it may seem that I am committed none the less to a necessary connection between recognitional capacities and factual knowledge. After all, I have affirmed that a person with complete factual knowledge of a certain type of mental state would be able to directly identify new instances given sufficient "priming" with experiences of that type. However, this sort of connection would not threaten the physicalist, as it is just not clear how many samples from some particular experiential field are required for a person to apply his knowledge of those mental states to the experiences themselves. Thus, a failure to "go on" in some particular case will not be definitive evidence of a theoretical gap.

To be sure, I have suggested that neither Mary nor the man born blind would require much experiential priming to go on to identify new experiences, and I acknowledge that this prediction gives important support to my claim that they have the relevant concepts. However, what makes it plausible that each could quickly develop the relevant recognitional capacities is that two conditions hold: first, the experiences in each field can be individuated by an objective description,[17] and second, the dimensions along which they are individuated are perceptually salient for human beings.

Indeed, it would seem as if the continuing recognitional failure of *any* experientially primed, objectively "omniscient" subject may be traced to the failure of one of these two conditions. If the second condition did not hold in some situation, however, it is hard to see why the subject's recognitional failure should indicate any factual deficiency, and thereby any difficulty for physicalism. On the other hand, if the first condition did not hold, then the subject's lack of recognition would surely indicate a conceptual gap. But if a physicalistic theory is unable to distinguish, objectively, among mental states that are, intuitively, distinct,[18] then it has fallen short of its own requirements for an adequate theory of mental states. The Nagel–Jackson argument, however, was designed to show that even if a theory can give an objective individuation of mental states that conforms to our intuitions, there will still be facts about those mental states that it leaves out, namely, what it is like to have them. Thus, the only cases in which a person's recognitional failure would threaten a physicalistic theory of mental states are ones in which the Nagel–Jackson argument would be beside the point.

V

But why, then, does the connection between having a concept of a mental state and having the appropriate recognitional capacities seem so invulnerable? And why does it seem that there must be something extra that experience contributes to our factual knowledge about mental states?

I do not want to deny that there is indeed a tight connection between knowledge and recognitional capacities in the case of concepts such as seeing red or feeling pain. However, this connection is not necessary. Its importance, rather, is in large part *epistemic*. A person, in exercising the relevant recognitional capacities, provides a reliable *demonstration* of this mastery of the concepts in question: these recognitional capacities provide evidence, perhaps the *best* evidence, that knowledge, rather than guesswork or ill-absorbed platitude, is at hand.

As it happens, of course, the inability to recognize or discriminate among items of a certain type most often shows a gap in one's knowledge of them. But this is not peculiar to our knowledge of mental states. In general, we would doubt the competence of any alleged expert on dogs who could not distinguish collies from cocker spaniels, or the expertise of any physicist unable to reliably identify the track of an electron in a bubble chamber. It is true that in these cases we would not always require recognitional capacities for knowledge: we would presumably grant knowledge of dogs or electrons to a theoretically sophisticated man born blind even if he could not identify them immediately upon first being made to see. But this is not because our knowledge of mental states is knowledge of a special kind of entity, or knowledge of a special, subjective, sort.

Rather, our concepts of dog and electron are tied to a rich and varied network of other concepts by numerous logical and inductive connections. Thus, even if a person lacks the specific recognitional capacities associated with their use, there are other obvious, if more roundabout, ways to determine that they have been mastered. This is less so, however, for concepts such as pain and looking red. Because they have fewer internal connections, we rely almost exclusively upon recognitional capacities as evidence of a person's mastery of them. Thus, it becomes tempting to think that the relevant recognitional capacities are necessary for the theoretical knowledge of mental states.

This temptation can be avoided, however, by acknowledging that the differences between the number of internal connections among experiental concepts and others is merely a matter of degree. Thus, contrary to the Empiricists, recognitional capacities will not constitute the only evidence for the mastery of concepts of this sort. To be sure, in persons who have never had a particular type of experience, the lack of recognitional capacities is usually good evidence of a gap in their theoretical knowledge. For example, contrast our theoretically sophisticated man born blind with another reported by Richard Gregory who, upon recovery, expressed great surprise that the quarter moon looked like a crescent rather than a wedge of pie.[19] Here, the lack of recognition is a clear indication that something conceptual was amiss. But the cases of the sophisticated man born blind, the omniscient Alpha Centaurian, and Jackson's neuropsychologist Mary were designed to give the protagonists all possible objective knowledge of the experiences they have never had. If this objective knowledge is sufficient to individuate the experiences in question from others of that kind, and if a person has mastered that knowledge, then there is no reason to treat any recognitional failures that occur upon first having the experiences in question any more seriously than the failures of the dog-expert or physicist.

But even if this is acknowledged, it may seem as if there is a special *contribution* that experience makes to knowledge, a contribution that is unattainable in any other way. If so, then is there not some bit of knowledge that a congenitally blind person or a person who cannot feel pain must lack about the experiences they have not had?

Here again, I want to stress that there is, indeed, a tremendous contribution that having an experience makes to having knowledge. What makes it special, however, is not that the experience contributes a chunk of knowledge that could not be gleaned in any other way, but that it contributes such knowledge as it does so *efficiently*. The function of experience here is primarily causal and evidential: it is not likely that one will have gleaned knowledge about the causes, effects, and similarity relations holding of a particular experiential state unless one has actually *had* it. Further, having had the experience (and having one's inferential capacities intact) provides the closest thing to a guarantee that one has picked up all there is to know. It provides not only the best possible evidence that one knows all there is to know about x's, but also the best method for acquiring this knowledge. It is not necessary, however, especially if one sets out, as did Mary, the Alpha Centaurian, and the man born blind, to laboriously absorb all that a full and complete scientific description of a particular phenomenon can provide.

Moreover, the special effectiveness of the contribution to the knowledge of x that is provided by having the experience of x is not restricted to knowledge of mental phenomena. Consider the admonition of parent to child that "you don't know what being a parent *is*!" Think of the many times children are told that they do not yet *understand* family, or responsibility, or death. One's claims to knowledge about all sorts of things, that is, are often suspect unless one has actually experienced the phenomena in question. But they are not irreversibly suspect, and can be bolstered by questions that are both careful and comprehensive.

What all these examples show is that we expect there to be a connection between experience and knowledge in many of our ordinary epistemic judgments; this expectation is by no means confined to our knowledge of mental states. Thus, the appeal to a special necessary connection between experience and knowledge of mental states ignores the generality of this phenomenon. More important, however, it takes this phenomenon too seriously: our unreflective expectations about the previous experiences of a person who has knowledge, as I have argued, have little to do with whether these experiences are necessary for knowledge of that sort. Thus, they provide no threat to physicalism, or any other objective theory of mental states.

To be sure, it is not hard to see why reductionist theses in the philosophy of mind raise suspicion, as they have often ignored the complexity of our mental lives. In this case, however, the suspicion leads to unwarranted fears about Procrusteans under the bed: it is not the insufficiencies of objectivity, but the vestiges of Empiricism, that suggest that these theories may be inadequate for expressing all the truth about experience that there is.

ACKNOWLEDGMENT

I wish to thank Michael Friedman, Barbara Herman, Tamara Horowitz, and Thomas Ricketts for helpful comments on earlier versions of this paper. I am indebted to Brain Loar and, especially, Richard Warner, for helpful comments and criticisms as well as for many stimulating discussions of these issues. I thank the Sloan Foundation and the Cognitive Science Program at the University of Pennsylvania for providing resources which enabled me to complete this work.

NOTES

1 "What is it like to be a bat?" reprinted in *Mortal Questions*, Cambridge, 1979, p. 166.
2 "Epiphenomenal qualia," p. 130. By "physicalism," Jackson means any version of the psycho-physical identity thesis *or* functionalism.
3 Laurence Nemirow makes this point in his review of *Mortal Questions* (Philosophical Review, July 1980). This account has also been given by Stephen Schiffer and Brian Loar.
4 This point has been made against Nagel by Frank Jackson himself, in "Epiphenomenal qualia," *Philosophical Quarterly*, 1982, and reprinted in this voluime.
5 See, for example, Brian Loar, in "Skepticism about phenomenal qualities" (forthcoming). I am indebted to Loar for discussion of these points.
6 See Richard Warner, "A challenge to physicalism," *Australasian Journal of Philosophy* 64, 1986, 249–65. My discussion of these issues owes much to Warner's formulation and defense of this argument.
7 I am indebted to Richard Warner for discussion of these points. His paper, in my view, provides the clearest and most compelling argument for such a premise.
8 I will not consider cases in which, because of some optical illusion, the cube *looks* spherical and vice versa.
9 II.ix.8.
10 See R. L. Gregory, *Eye and Brain*, 2nd edn, McGraw-Hill, p. 193.
11 This did not worry Berkeley, who claimed in his *New Theory of Vision* that we still would not know what continuity *looked like*, but it may give us some pause.
12 If not, there are troubles for functionalism independently of this argument.
13 Even rats believe this: if nausea is induced in them even hours after they have ingested a particularly salient food, they will avoid that food for days.
14 Warner's notion here is "non-evidential" knowledge: knowledge acquired without inference, and that needs no evidential backing to be justified.
15 I am indebted to Lila Gleitman and Barbara Landau for discussion of these points.
16 pp. 178–80.
17 This may not in fact be true, given the "inverted spectrum" problem for functionalism. If not, however, objective theories may have problems independently of this argument.
18 And here one may think, again, of functionalism.
19 Gregory, *Eye and Brain*, pp. 195–6.

Physicalism and the Cognitive Role of Acquaintance

LAURENCE NEMIROW

I Some theories of the cognitive role of acquaintance

In a classical essay on the mind–body problem, Herbert Feigl briefly raises a perplexing problem for physicalism in the philosophy of mind, the view that a

"Physicalism and the Cognitive Role of Acquaintance" by L. Nemirow is printed here for the first time, by kind permission of the author.

physical theory of nature can fully describe mental activity.[1] The problem is to fit the epistemology of experience into a physicalist frame of reference, and to capture, within the framework of physical science, the cognitive role of direct acquaintance with experience.

The physicalist framework, according to Feigl, is essentially *objective*, in that creatures with diverse sensory systems can formulate and test a physical hypothesis. In theory, no particular sensory organs are crucial to the capacity to advance physical science. Even a congenitally deaf-blind person "could in principle construct and confirm a complete system of the natural sciences ..."[2] Feigl pictures the method of science as the "triangulation of entities in logical space" grounded on types of sensory input none of which is, by itself, indispensable to the formulation and testing of the hypothesis.[3]

By contrast, the most remarkable information about a sensory experience appears to be *subjective* – accessible only to those who can employ a sensory organ of the same type as the one that produces the experience. As Feigl observes, the "philosophically intriguing problems" regarding direct acquaintance with experience "are best expressed by asking, e.g., 'What is it that the blind man cannot know concerning color qualities?'"[4] The problem for physicalism is to account for the salient knowledge of visual experience that a scientist without eyes could not infer.

Feigl attacks the problem by denying the premise that there is such knowledge. According to him, a blind person must lack only acquaintance with the experience of sight and knowledge by acquaintance of it. Although acquaintance is not knowledge (because "mere having or living through is not knowledge in any sense"), knowledge by acquaintance "is propositional, and does make truth claims."[5] Someone might know by acquaintance that he is seeing a bright color, for example. But that knowledge, Feigl observes, could be inferred by a blind psychologist, incapable of experiencing color, who examines the behavior and anatomy of the subject of experience.

Feigl underestimates the difficulty. Even if we grant that a congenitally blind psychologist might triangulate the experience of sight, thus confirming that it occurs and discerning all of its physiological aspects, he would not thereby learn what the experience of seeing is *like*. Knowledge of what seeing is like cannot be inferred from nonvisual sensory input.

Nor could Feigl plausibly assert that "knowledge of what an experience is like" amounts to mere acquaintance and thus fails to stand for genuine knowledge. Such an assertion would fail to account for our use of the vocabulary of knowledge in talking about what an experience is like. We speak of "knowing" what an experience is like, as well as "realizing," "discovering," "learning," "remembering" and "forgetting" what an experience is like, and in so doing we describe a common yet elusive kind of knowledge. Plainly, there is knowlege of what it's like to see that can be learned, remembered and forgotten, but it eludes those who are uninitiated to the experience of sight.

Knowledge of what an experience is like signifies genuine knowledge that does not yield to the method of triangulation. Some opponents of physicalism rely on this fact to show that physical science can never completely explain experience.

In what I shall call the "subjective qualities hypothesis," Thomas Nagel analyzes knowing what an experience is like as an act of appreciating its *subjective qualities* – qualities, that is, the attributions of which express subjective information, as defined above.[6] According to him, information about subjective qualities may be understood only from the "point of view of the experiencer." For Nagel, this means that a person must imagine an experience in order to understand its subjective quality.[7] Such understanding, he contends, evades creatures whose sensory apparatus is so unlike that of the experiencer that they cannot imagine from his point of view. Nagel thus concludes that physicalism is false, for he agrees with Feigl that physical science presupposes no particular sensory capacities.[8]

Frank Jackson engages a less burdened account of the argument against physicalism, which is referred to below as the "knowledge argument."[9] Declining to demarcate the class of physical properties (hence dispensing with the notion of objectivity), and making no attempt to explain what is peculiarly nonphysical about the mental (thus avoiding the concept of subjectivity), he merely observes that no amount of physical theorizing will convey to the uninitiated what it's like to see in color. Hypothetical neurophysiologists who could make observations only in black and white would learn less about the world than if they could learn what seeing in color is like. Yet no physical understanding would elude them by reason of their optical disability. So it must follow that physical science cannot describe the way things are mentally.

Nagel and Jackson are right to disagree with Feigl, but their own accounts of the cognitive role of acquaintance are nevertheless flawed. Contrary to Feigl, what the blind cannot know about seeing escapes scientific triangulation. But Nagel and Jackson too quickly conclude that what the blind cannot know is physically indescribable goings-on. That conclusion, I shall argue, is based on three familiar philosophical errors. The first mistake is to confound distinct types of knowledge by treating an ability as propositional knowledge. A second mistake is to confuse grammar and logic by assuming that a grammatical singular term must function as a referring term. The third mistake – and, arguably, the philosophically deep mistake – is to mischaracterize imagining, by equating the act of imagining the experience of a quality with the act of intellectually apprehending the quality itself.

II   The ability equation

The knowledge argument rests on a shaky inference. From the premise that knowing what it's like escapes physical theorizing, the inference is made that there is information about what it's like that escapes physical science. In short, it is assumed that knowledge of what it's like must be knowledge of the way things are. But that assumption ignores the fact that the vocabulary of knowledge also applies to abilities.[10]

As Nagel's own theory provides, however, knowing what it's like essentially correlates with knowing how to imagine. Ask Harry if he knows what seeing chartreuse is like. If he takes you seriously, he may make an effort to imagine the sight of chartreuse. If he believes that he can imagine seeing chartreuse, he will affirm that he knows what seeing chartreuse is like; otherwise, he will deny that he knows it. It would be nonsense for Harry to insist that he can easily visualize chartreuse, but does not know what seeing it is like, or to maintain that he knows just what it's like, but cannot visualize it. (Throughout this paper, I use the expressions "visualizing a color" and "imagining the sight of a color" interchangeably. Visualizing is not identical to imagining, but visualizing is the special type of imagining that one must be able to perform in order to know what seeing a color is like.)

The correlation stated above suggests an equation: Knowing what it's like may be identified with knowing how to imagine.

The more seriously we take this ability equation, the easier it becomes to resist the knowledge argument. The latter assumes that science cannot convey what it's like to see red. The premise is uncontentious, for science does not seek to instill imaginative abilities. But the knowledge argument concludes that physical science cannot describe certain information about seeing red. The inference is invalid because it presumes that knowing what it's like is propositional knowledge rather than an ability.

The ability equation is confirmed by its explanatory power. It accounts for several facts that, considered together, threaten to undermine physicalism. First, the equation explains why it is appropriate to use the vocabulary of knowledge in discussing what an experience is like. It may be appropriate to speak of "discovering," "knowing," "remembering," "forgetting" what an experience is like because such expressions are used to speak about abilities.

Moreover, the ability equation obviates the need to attribute subjectivity to experience on the ground that knowing what it's like belongs only to those who are able to imagine having the experience (only to those who, as Nagel puts it, can "adopt the experiencer's point of view"). The ability equation avoids having to explain the correlation by transforming it into an equation, and thus circumvents the subjective qualities hypothesis.

The ability equation further explains the linguistic inexpressibility of knowing what it's like. It is a perennial philosophical puzzle that the congenitally blind cannot be told what seeing red is like. Opponents of physicalism may explain the puzzle by referring to inexpressble qualities of experience. But a more elegant explanation is that knowing what it's like is a linguistically inexpressible ability, like the ability to wiggle your ears or the ability to ride a bicycle.

But more must be said. After all, many kinds of knowing how can be expressed verbally. A complete resolution of the puzzle, then, will require a description of the conditions of inexpressibility, together with a demonstration that knowing what it's like satisfies the conditions.

How are abilities communicated? As R. M. Hare tells us, "knowing how to do something is normally communicated, *where it can be communicated at all*, by means of imperative sentences, as can be seen by looking at a cookery book."[11] Putting it schematically, we tell someone how to do A by telling him to do B, where the expression "B" is within the student's repertoire. A description of an action may be said to fall within a person's repertoire provided (i) the person has the ability to perform the action as described, and (ii) the person understands the description: that is, he understands that he can act so as to satisfy it.

Specifically, the ability to imagine a color (that is, knowing what the color is like) may be communicated to someone who has within his repertoire a description of an action by which visualizing can be accomplished. Normally, the ability to visualize a color can be exercised only by the performance of one of three mental actions:

1 Directly visualizing the color itself.
2 Remembering a visual experience of the color.
3 Visualizing or remembering similar colors and interpolating. (This third way of visualizing is, of course, Hume's way.)

It is only contingently true that this list is exhaustive. Someone with an abnormal imaginative capacity might provide a counterexample: Perhaps he could visualize green by banging his head against a wall, or by remembering a humiliating experience. But for most of us, the only activities that amount to visualizing a given color are the activities on the list. Consequently, we may tell those who are able to visualize or remember similar colors that they can imagine by visualizing or remembering and interpolating; and we may instruct others to refresh their recollection by remembering previous experiences of the color. As for those who are unable to follow any of these instructions, imagining is expressible only as such. These uninitiated, therefore, cannot be told what it's like to see green.

This account generalizes to all cases of knowing what its's like. It is generally, albeit contingently, true that imagining an experience may be accomplished only by (1) imagining the experience itself, (2) remembering previous experiences, or (3) imagining or remembering similar experiences and interpolating. So the ability to imagine an experience is describable only *as* imagining for those who cannot do (2) or (3). Those people might be able to imagine, and imagining might be expressible to them as such. But they cannot be told how if they do not already know. Accordingly, the uninitiated cannot be told what it's like.

In sum, the advantages of the ability equation are these: Forgoing nonphysical aspects of experience,[12] it renders the knowledge argument invalid. It also explains the pertinence of the vocabulary of knowledge, the essential connection between knowing what it's like and imaginative capacities, and the inexpressibility of knowing what it's like.

III The ability analysis

The ability equation prompts an ability analysis. The expression "x knows how to visualize red" either should replace or can be used to paraphrase "x knows what the experience of seeing red is like." This analysis demystifies the subexpression "what the experience of seeing red is like." On a naive reading, the subexpression is a name for a quality of experience. The latter must be subjective (in Nagel's terms) because only those who are able to visualize red can understand what seeing red is like. Under the analysis, however, the subexpression is a "pseudo-singular term" – an expression that has the grammatical form of a singular term, but, on analysis, does not even purport to refer. Like some other pseudo-singular terms (such as the term "sake" in the sentence, "she did it for her country's sake") the term "what it's like" is syncategoramatic; in other words, it is not separately analyzed.

Although the ability analysis palpably parses the meaning of the phrase "knowing what it's like," those who generally doubt the meaningfulness of synonymy may view the analysis as a possible linguistic reform that would preserve the explanatory power of the phrase while eliminating the use of a misleading singular term. In any event, the analysis should forestall the temptation to treat the expression "what it's like" as a referring expression in virtue of its grammatical form.[13]

IV   The cognitive role of imagining: some metaphysical apprehensions

A polemically successful answer to the subjective qualities hypothesis and the knowledge argument must explain the intuitive appeal of the contention that what it's like is irreducibly nonphysical information about experience. The following points together may help accomplish that task:

(i)   Knowing what an experience is like is the same as knowing how to imagine having the experience.

(ii) It is intuitively appealing, albeit incorrect, to analyze the act of imagining an experience of an instance of a certain universal as the intellectual apprehension of the universal itself.

Sentence (i), of course, repeats the ability equation, elaborated in the earlier parts of this paper. Sentence (ii) expresses a familiar point that underlies several classical discussions of universals.[14]

Sentence (ii) incorporates the thesis of Berkeley and Hume that the imagination represents particulars rather than apprehends universals. To visualize red, for example, is to apprehend neither the quality of being red nor the quality of seeing red; it is only to represent particular perceptions of a particular shade of red. Similarly, to imagine pain is not intellectually to apprehend the quality of being in pain; it is to represent a particular painful experience. "For myself, I find indeed I have a faculty of imagining, or representing to myself, the idea of those *particular* things I have perceived . . ."[15]

Berkeley and Hume dispelled the philosophical clouds surrounding imaginative representation.[16] Quite obviously, however, an intuitive fog persists. Imagining pain just seems to reveal its painful nature.

The persistent illusion that imagination grants direct access to universals may be explained by what gives imagining its functional utility. We can begin to understand imagination functionally by considering its role in our reasoning, both propositional and practical. Berkeley illuminated that role when he wrote: "[A]n idea which, considered in itself, is particular, becomes general by being made to represent or stand for all other particular ideas of the same sort."[17]

Successfully visualizing a color, for example, engenders the ability to compare the color to other colors. So visualizing a color permits us to draw conclusions (or reason propositionally) about other colors as if we were seeing the imagined color. (I might conclude that the color I am imagining is a deeper shade of purple than the color I am witnessing.) Imagining seeing a color thus functionally represents seeing the color in our propositional reasoning about colors.

So too, successfully imagining a pain of a certain intensity enables us to consider what we would accept as compensation for agreeing to undergo pain of the same degree of intensity. By imagining pain we are able to draw conclusions (or reason practically) about whether to avoid impending pain as if we were experiencing ongoing pain. (I might conclude that the pain that I imagine the dentist would inflict upon me is not worth the intended benefits of a trip to the dentist.) Imagining pain thus functionally represents actual pain in our reasoning about future pain. Part of the functional utility of imagining, then, is that it engenders abilities to reason about experiences, both propositionally and practically, as if we were having an experience of the sort imagined.

We can explain the role of imagining in reasoning by invoking a notion of triangulation, although one that differs from Feigl's concept of triangulation. A key difference is the direction of the inferences in each case. For Feigl, triangulation in physical science involves inferences from sensory experiences, no one of which is critical, to an hypothesis of physical events. Such patterns of inference account for the capacity of scientific inquiry to reach objective generalizations. In reasoning from what an experience is like, a person begins by imagining particular experiences, and draws specific inferences about actual or future sensory experiences, none of which is itself critical to the function of the imagination. Such lines of inference in turn begin to account for the general utilities of imagining that cause imagining to appear to grant direct access to the essential qualities of experience.

Sentences (i) and (ii) together produce the conclusion that knowing what it's like to be in pain is an ability that is appealingly analyzed as the ability to apprehend a universal. If we were to treat what is appealing as fact, Nagel's theory of subjective qualities would follow. We would attribute a special understanding of what pain *is* only to those who know what it's *like*.

V   Objections and replies

One objection to the ability equation is that knowing how to imagine is too sophisticated an ability to attribute to everyone (or thing) who may know what it's like. For such an ability is, for all we know, well beyond the capabilities of creatures to whom we may on occasion attribute knowledge of what an experience is like – creatures such as cats and infants. But anything that is true of mature persons by reason of knowing what an experience is like should also be true of cats and infants who know what it's like – a point that apparently refutes the ability· equation.

Rather than providing counterexamples to the ability equation, however, these hard cases suggest only that there are auxiliary concepts of "what it's like" that are triggered by nonparadigmatic applications of the phrase, and which would often be inapposite to use when speaking of mature persons.

If we say of a cat that it knows what the smell of abalone is like, for example, we might mean merely that, exposed to the smell, it will come running to its dish. The proposition apparently does not imply that the cat knows how to imagine the smell.

To apply the mature concept of knowing what the smell of abalone is like to a person, however, is not to assume any such behavioral correlation. Such an attribution directly describes what a person knows how to do in the privacy of his own mind, not how he would behave when exposed to the smell.

Similarly, we might say of an infant that he knows what a certain taste is like, without intending to imply that the infant knows how to imagine the taste. We may mean only that he can recognize the taste. On the other hand, when we use the mature concept of knowing what a taste is like, we mean more than that. We additionally attribute the ability to imagine. Someone might appropriately claim, "I can recognize the taste of chestnuts, I feel sure, but I have forgotten just what the taste is like." Similarly, no one is surprised to forget how to imagine a certain melody (what it's like to hear the melody), while remembering how to recognize the melody; or to forget what someone's face is like (what it's like to see his face), without forgetting how to recognize the face.

Someone might question the recognition examples by asking what the ability to imagine amounts to over and above the ability to recognize. As explained in the previous section of this paper, the ability to imagine is, at least in part, an ability to reason propositionally and practically as if one were having an experience of the sort imagined. The recognition examples suggest also that the ability to imagine produces certain other practical abilities that do not ordinarily fall under the rubric of practical reasoning. For example, if Beth can recognize but not imagine a melody, then she cannot imagine variations on it either. But if Beth can imagine the melody, not only can she imagine variations on it (assuming she has some modest musical talent), she can also ascertain whether one note of the melody is higher or lower than the next. Further, she can tap its beat or hum the tune. And she might even try to imagine hearing the notes in reverse order. But Beth could perform none of these tasks if she could only recognize without imagining. Similarly, if Frank can vividly imagine what the burglar looks like, then he can describe his looks so that a police artist might render a likeness. But if he could only recognize without imagining, he would be unable to describe in any detail how the burglar looks.

In any event, as the examples of sophisticated attributions of knowing what it's like show, such attributions do ascribe imaginative abilities, while the auxiliary concepts of knowing what it's like, such as conditioned response or recognitional ability do not.[18]

A second objection to the ability equation relies on the concept of *successful* imagining. Successful imagining, so the objection goes, presupposes subjective qualities (or qualities the attribution of which may be understood only by those with the right sensory capacities) for this reason: the ability successfully to imagine is the ability to entertain a truly representative state; but representation is a relationship between imagined and imagining states based on the similarity of their subjective qualities.

The crucial point in this objection is unmotivated. Assume for argument's sake, both that imagining constitutes mental representation, and that the relationship of representation holds between imagined and imagining states just in case they are similar with respect to certain qualities. What argument demonstrates that those qualities are subjective? The case had better not be that knowledge of what those qualities are like depends on acquaintance. That would merely repeat the knowledge argument, which the ability equation renders invalid. To be sure, an understanding of imaginative representation might require acquaintance with it; but such understanding itself consists of imaginative abilities rather than knowledge that may be summarized propositionally.

VI Final remarks

The principal importance of acquaintance in cognition is the production of sophisticated imaginative abilities that give rise to an elaborate network of other abilities, including abilities to reason, both propositionally and practically, and to behave as if the person doing the imagining were having an experience of the sort imagined. These imaginative abilities are of such importance cognitively that they may properly be characterized as constituting a deep understanding of experience. Thus it does justice to the cognitive significance of acquaintance to equate knowlege of what an experience is like with the ability to imagine.

ACKNOWLEDGMENT

I am deeply grateful to David Lewis for his support, and to Joanne Kadish for discussion and for detailed comments on earlier drafts.

NOTES

1   Feigl, *The 'Mental' and the 'Physical'*, Minneapolis: University of Minnesota, 1967, especially pp. 66–9.
2   Ibid., p. 66.
3   Ibid., pp. 66–8.
4   Ibid., p. 68.
5   Ibid.
6   See "What is it like to be bat?", *Philosophical Review* 84 (1974), pp. 435–50; reprinted in Nagel, *Mortal Questions*, Cambridge: Cambridge University Press, 1979, pp. 165–81. (All page references are to *Mortal Questions*.)
7   Nagel equates the act of taking up the experiencer's point of view with the act of imagining having the experience many times throughout "What is it like to be a bat?" See, for example, p. 178.
8   Ibid., p. 172.
9   Frank Jackson, "Epiphenomenal qualia," *Philosophical Quarterly* 32 (1982), pp. 127–36. For a less sympathetic presentation of the argument against physicalism based on what the blind cannot know, see section IV of Paul E. Meehl, "The compleat autocerebroscopist," in Paul Feyerabend and Grover Maxwell (eds), *Mind, Matter and Method*, Minneapolis: U. of Min.. Press, 1966.
10 See Gilbert Ryle, *The Concept of Mind*, New York: Barnes & Noble, 1949, pp. 27–32.
11 R. M. Hare, *Practical Inferences*, Berkeley: University of California Press, 1972, p. 3. (Emphasis added.)
12 It should be considered an advantage of an explanatory hypothesis if it facilitates physicalist reduction. Such a contribution is praiseworthy from the point of view of advancing systematization, which is an important criterion of theory selection. See Oppenhéim and Kemeny, "On reduction," *Philosophical Studies* 7 (1956), pp. 9–16.
13 Frank Jackson and David Lewis have observed that the ability analysis may be read either as

countenancing, or as not countenancing, an inference from "Sam knows how to imagine seeing chartreuse" to "Sam knows that he knows how to imagine seeing chartreuse." The analysandum shares the same ambiguity, which is excellent confirmation of the analysis.

14 Berkeley, *A Treatise Concerning The Principles of Human Knowledge*, especially the Introduction; and Hume, *A Treatise of Human Nature*, part I, section VII.

15 *A Treatise Concerning the Principles of Human Knowledge*, paragraph 10 of the Introduction. (Emphasis added.)

16 I find the Berkeley–Hume argument, so construed, to be compelling, but I do not believe that there is a knockdown refutation of the view that the imagination apprehends universals. My own prejudice is based on a preference for explanatory simplicity. See note 12.

17 *A Treatise Concerning the Principles of Human Knowledge*, paragraph 12 of the Introduction.

18 A phrase of the form "knowing what it's like to be a ——" expresses the sophisticated concept of knowing what it's like because it entails complex imaginative capabilities rather than any characteristic recognitional or conditioned responses. Assuming that cats do not know how to imagine (which is consistent with, but not necessarily entailed by, auxiliary attributions to cats of knowing what it's like), it would follow that a cat does not know what it's like to be a cat. Or, more to the point, there is no knowledge of what it's like to be a cat.

What Experience Teaches

DAVID LEWIS

Experience the best teacher

They say that experience is the best teacher, and the classroom is no substitute for Real Life. There's truth to this. If you want to know what some new and different experience is like, you can learn it by going out and really *having* that experience. You can't learn it by being told about the experience, however thorough your lessons may be.

Does this prove much of anything about the metaphysics of mind and the limits of science? I think not.

Example: Skunks and Vegemite. I have smelled skunks, so I know what it's like to smell skunks. But skunks live only in some parts of the world, so you may never have smelled a skunk. If you haven't smelled a skunk, then you don't know what it's like. You never will, unless someday you smell a skunk for yourself. On the other hand, you may have tasted Vegemite, that famous Australian substance; and I never have. So you may know what it's like to taste Vegemite. I don't, and

This paper was collected in *Proceedings of the Russellian Society*, University of Sydney, 1988, and appears here by permission of the volume's editor, J. Copley-Coltheart.

unless I taste Vegemite (what, and spoil a good example!), I never will. It won't help at all to take lessons on the chemical composition of skunk scent or Vegemite, the physiology of the nostrils or the taste-buds, and the neurophysiology of the sensory nerves and the brain.

Example: The Captive Scientist.[1] Mary, a brilliant scientist, has lived from birth in a cell where everything is black or white. (Even she herself is painted all over.) She views the world on black-and-white television. By television she reads books, she joins in discussion, she watches the results of experiments done under her direction. In this way she becomes the world's leading expert on color and color vision and the brain states produced by exposure to colors. But she doesn't know what it's like to see color. And she never will, unless she escapes from her cell.

Example: The Bat.[2] The bat is an alien creature, with a sonar sense quite unlike any sense of ours. We can never have the experiences of a bat; because we could not become bat-like enough to have those experiences and still be ourselves. We will never know what it's like to be a bat. Not even if we come to know all the facts there are about the bat's behavior and behavioral dispositions, about the bat's physical structure and processes, about the bat's functional organization. Not even if we come to know all the same sort of physical facts about all the other bats, or about other creatures, or about ourselves. Not even if we come to possess all physical facts whatever. Not even if we become able to recognize all the mathematical and logical implications of all these facts, no matter how complicated and how far beyond the reach of finite deduction.

Experience is the best teacher, in this sense: having an experience is the best way or perhaps the only way, of coming to know what that experience is like. No amount of scientific information about the stimuli that produce that experience and the process that goes on in you when you have that experience will enable you to know what it's like to have the experience.

. . . but not necessarily

Having an experience is surely one good way, and surely the only practical way, of coming to know what that experience is like. Can we say, flatly, that it is the only *possible* way? Probably not. There is a change that takes place in you when you have the experience and thereby come to know what it's like. Perhaps the exact same change could in principle be produced in you by precise neurosurgery, very far beyond the limits of present-day technique. Or it could possibly be produced in you by magic. If we ignore the laws of nature, which are after all contingent, then there is no necessary connection between cause and effect: anything could cause anything. For instance, the casting of a spell could do to you exactly what your first smell of skunk would do. We might quibble about whether a state produced in this artificial fashion would deserve the *name* "knowing what it's like to smell a skunk," but we can imagine that so far as what goes on within you is concerned, it would differ not at all.[3]

Just as we can imagine that a spell might produce the same change as a smell, so likewise we can imagine that science lessons might cause that same change. Even that is possible, in the broadest sense of the word. If we ignored all we know about how the world really works, we could not say what might happen to someone if he were taught about the chemistry of scent and the physiology of the nose. There might have been a causal mechanism that transforms science lessons into whatever it is that experience gives us. But there isn't. It is not an absolutely necessary truth that experience is the best teacher about what a new experience is like. It's a contingent truth. But we have good reason to think it's true.

We have good reason to think that something of this kind is true, anyway, but less reason to be sure exactly what. Maybe some way of giving the lessons that hasn't yet been invented, and some way of taking them in that hasn't yet been practiced, could give us a big surprise. Consider sight-reading: a trained musician can read the score and know what it would be like to hear the music. If I'd never heard that some people can sight-read, I would never have thought it humanly possible. Of course the moral is that new music isn't altogether new – the big new experience is a rearrangement of lots of little old experiences. It just might turn out the same for new smells and tastes *vis-à-vis* old ones; or even for color vision *vis-à-vis* black and white;[4] or even for sonar sense experience *vis-à-vis* the sort we enjoy. The thing we can say with some confidence is that we have no faculty for knowing on the basis of mere science lessons what some *new enough* experience would be like. But how new is "new enough"? – There, we just might be in for surprises.

Three ways to miss the point

The First Way. A literalist might see the phrase "know what it's like" and take that to mean: "know what it resembles." Then he might ask: what's so hard about that? Why can't you just be told which experiences resemble one another? You needn't have had the experiences – all you need, to be taught your lessons, is some way of referring to them. You could be told: the smell of skunk somewhat resembles the smell of burning rubber. I have been told: the taste of Vegemite somewhat resembles that of Marmite. Black-and-white Mary might know more than most of us about the resemblances among color-experiences. She might know which ones are spontaneously called "similar" by subjects who have them; which gradual changes from one to another tend to escape notice; which ones get conflated with which in memory; which ones involve roughly the same neurons firing in similar rhythms; and so forth. We could even know what the bat's sonar experiences resemble just by knowing that they do not at all resemble any experiences of humans, but do resemble – as it might be – certain experiences that occur in certain fish. This misses the point. *Pace* the literalist, "know what it's like" does not mean "know what it resembles." The most that's true is that knowing what it resembles *may* help you to know what it's like. If you are taught that experience A resembles B and C closely, D less, E not at all, that will help you know what A is like – *if* you know already what B and C and D and E are like. Otherwise, it helps you not at all. I don't know any better what it's like to taste Vegemite when I'm told that it tastes like Marmite, because I don't know what Marmite tastes like either. (Nor do I know any better what Marmite tastes like for being told it tastes like Vegemite.) Maybe Mary knows enough to triangulate each color experience exactly in a network of resemblances, or in many networks of resemblance in different respects, while never knowing what any node of any network is like. Maybe we could do the same for bat experiences. But no amount of information about resemblances, just by itself, does anything to help us know what an experience is like.

The Second Way. In so far as I don't know what it would be like to drive a steam locomotive fast on a cold, stormy night, part of my problem is just that I don't know what experiences I would have. The firebox puts out a lot of heat, especially when the fireman opens the door to throw on more coal; on the other hand, the cab is drafty and gives poor protection from the weather. Would I be too hot or too cold? Or both by turns? Or would it be chilled face and scorched legs? If I knew the answers to such questions, I'd know much better what it would be like to drive the locomotive. So maybe "know what it's like" just means "know what experiences one has." Then again: what's the problem? Why can't you just be told what experiences you would have if, say, you tasted Vegemite? Again, you needn't have had the experiences – all you need, to be taught your lessons, is some way of referring to them. We have ways to refer to experiences we haven't had. We can refer to them in terms of their causes: the experience one has upon tasting Vegemite, the experience one has upon tasting a substance of such-and-such chemical composition. Or we can refer to them in terms of their effects: the experience that just caused Fred to say "Yeeuch!" Or we can refer to them in terms of the physical states of the nervous system that mediate between those causes and effects: the experience one has when one's nerves are firing in such-and-such pattern. (According to some materialists, I myself for one, this means the experience which is identical with such-and-such firing pattern. According to other materialists it means the experience which is realized by such-and-such firing pattern. According to many dualists, it means the experience which is merely the lawful companion of such-and-such firing pattern. But whichever it is, we get a way of referring to the experience.) Black-and-white Mary is in a position to refer to color-experiences in all these ways. Therefore you should have no problem in telling her exactly what experiences one has upon seeing the colors. Or rather, your only problem is that you'd be telling her what she knows very well already! In general, to know what is the X is to know that the X is the Y, where it's not too obvious that the X is the Y. (Just knowing that the X is the X won't do, of course, because it is too obvious.) If Mary knows that the experience of seeing green is the experience associated with such-and-such pattern of nerve firings, then she knows the right sort of unobvious identity. So she knows what experience one has upon seeing green.

(Sometimes it's suggested that you need a "rigid designator": you know what is the X by knowing that the X is the Y only if "the Y" is a term whose referent does not depend on any contingent matter of fact. In the first place, this suggestion is false. You can know who is the man on the balcony by knowing that the man on the balcony is the Prime Minister even if neither "the Prime Minister" nor any other phrase available to you rigidly designates the man who is, in fact, the Prime

Minister. In the second place, according to one version of Materialism (the one I accept) a description of the form "the state of having nerves firing in such-and-such a pattern" *is* a rigid designator, and what it designates is in fact an experience; and according to another version of Materialism, a description of the form "having some or other state which occupies so-and-so functional role" is a rigid designator of an experience. So even if the false suggestion were granted, still it hasn't been shown, without begging the question against Materialism, that Mary could not know what experience one has upon seeing red.)

Since Mary *does* know what experiences she would have if she saw the colors, but she *doesn't* know what it would be like to see the colors, we'd better conclude that "know what it's like" does not after all mean "know what experiences one has." The locomotive example was misleading. Yes, by learning what experiences the driver would have, I can know what driving the locomotive would be like; but only because I already know what those experiences are like. (It matters that I know what they're like under the appropriate descriptions – as it might be, the description "chilled face and scorched legs." This is something we'll return to later.) Mary may know as well as I do that when the driver leans out into the storm to watch the signals, he will have the experience of seeing sometimes green lights and sometimes red. She knows better than I what experiences he has when signals come into view. She can give many more unobviously equivalent descriptions of those experiences than I can. But knowing what color-experiences the driver has won't help Mary to know what his job is like. It will help me.

The Third Way. Until Mary sees green, here is one thing she will never know: she will never know that she is seeing green. The reason why is just that until she sees green, it will never be true that she is seeing green. Some knowledge is irreducibly egocentric, or *de se*.[5] It is not just knowledge about what goes on in the world; it is knowledge of who and when in the world one is. Knowledge of what goes on in the world will be true alike for all who live in that world;. whereas egocentric knowledge may be true for one and false for another, or true for one at one time and false for the same one at another time. Maybe Mary knows in advance, as she plots her escape, that 9 a.m. on the 13th of May, 1997, is the moment when someone previously confined in a black-and-white cell sees color for the first time. But until that moment comes, she will never know that she herself is then seeing color – because she isn't. What isn't true isn't knowledge. This goes as much for egocentric knowledge as for the rest. So only those of whom an egocentric proposition is true can know it, and only at times when it is true of them can they know it. That one is then seeing color is an egocentric proposition. So we've found a proposition which Mary can never know until she sees color – which, as it happens, is the very moment when she will first know what it's like to see color! Have we discovered the reason why experience is the best teacher? And not contingently after all, but as a necessary consequence of the logic of egocentric knowledge?

No; we have two separate phenomena here, and only some bewitchment about the "first-person perspective" could make us miss the difference. In the first place, Mary will probably go on knowing what it's like to see green after she stops knowing the egocentric proposition that she's then seeing green. Since what isn't true isn't known she must stop knowing that proposition the moment she stops seeing green. (Does that only mean that we should have taken a different egocentric proposition: that one *has* seen green? No; for in that case Mary could go on knowing the proposition even after she forgets what it's like to see green, as might happen if she were soon recaptured.) In the second place, Mary might come to know what it's like to see green even if she didn't know the egocentric proposition. She might not have known in advance that her escape route would take her across a green meadow, and it might take her a little while to recognize grass by its shape. So at first she might know only that she was seeing some colors or other, and thereby finding out what some color-experiences or other were like, without being able to put a name either to the colors or to the experiences. She would then know what it was like to see green, though not under that description, indeed not under any description more useful than "the color-experience I'm having now"; but she would not know the egocentric proposition that she is then seeing green, since she wouldn't know which color she was seeing. In the third place, the gaining of egocentric knowledge may have prerequisites that have nothing to do with experience. Just as Mary can't know she's seeing green until she *does* see green, she can't know she's turning 50 until she *does* turn 50. But – I hope! – turning 50 does not involve some special experience. In short, though indeed one can gain egocentric knowledge that one is in some situation only when one is in it, that is not the same as finding out what an experience is like only when one has that experience.

We've just rejected two suggestions that don't work separately, and we may note that they don't work any better when put together. One knows what is the X by knowing that the X is the Y, where the identity is not too obvious; and "the Y" might be an egocentric description. So knowledge that the X is the Y might be irreducibly egocentric knowledge, therefore knowledge that cannot be had until it is true of one that the X is the Y. So one way of knowing what is the X will remain unavailable until it comes true of one that the X is the Y. One way that I could gain an unobvious identity concerning the taste of Vegemite would be for it to come true that the taste of Vegemite was the taste I was having at that very moment– and that would come true at the very moment I tasted Vegemite and found out what it was like! Is this why experience is the best teacher? – No; cases of gaining an unobvious egocentric identity are a dime a dozen, and most of them do not result in finding out what an experience is like. Suppose I plan ahead that I will finally break down and taste Vegemite next Thursday noon. Then on Wednesday noon, if I watch the clock, I first gain the unobvious egocentric knowledge that the taste of Vegemite is the taste I shall be having in exactly 24 hours, and thereby I have a new way of knowing what is the taste of Vegemite. But on Wednesday noon I don't yet know what it's like. Another example: from time to time I find myself next to a Vegemite-taster. On those occasions, and only those, I know what is the taste of Vegemite by knowing that it is the taste being had by the person next to me. But on no such occasion has it ever yet happened that I knew what it was like to taste Vegemite.

The Hypothesis of Phenomenal Information

No amount of the physical information that black-and-white Mary gathers could help her know what it was like to see colors; no amount of the physical information that we might gather about bats could help us know what it's like to have their experiences; and likewise in other cases. There is a natural and tempting explanation of why physical information does not help. That is the hypothesis that besides physical information there is an irreducibly different kind of information to be had: *phenomenal information*. The two are independent. Two possible cases might be exactly alike physically, yet differ phenomenally. When we get physical information we narrow down the physical possibilities, and perhaps we narrow them down all the way to one, but we leave open a range of phenomenal possibilities. When we have an experience, on the other hand, we acquire phenomenal information; possibilities previously open are eliminated; and that is what it is to learn what the experience is like.

(Analogy. Suppose the question concerned the location of a point within a certain region of the *x-y* plane. We might be told that its *x*-coordinate lies in certain intervals, and outside certain others. We might even get enough of this information to fix the *x*-coordinate exactly. But no amount of *x*-information would tell us anything about the *y*-coordinate; any amount of *x*-information leaves open all the *y*-possibilities. But when at last we make a *y*-measurement, we acquire a new kind of information; possibilities previously open are eliminated; and that is how we learn where the point is in the *y*-direction.)

What might the subject matter of phenomenal information be? *If* the Hypothesis of Phenomenal Information is true, then you have an easy answer: it is information about experience. More specifically, it is information about a certain part or aspect or feature of experience. But if the Hypothesis is false, then there is still experience (complete with all its parts and aspects and features) and yet no information about experience is phenomenal information. So it cannot be said in a neutral way, without presupposing the Hypothesis, that information about experience is phenomenal information. For if the Hypothesis is false and Materialism is true, it may be that all the information there is about experience is physical information, and can very well be presented in lessons for the inexperienced.

It makes no difference to put some fashionable new phrase in place of "experience." If instead of "experience" you say "raw feel" (or just "feeling"), or "way it feels," or "what it's like," then I submit that you mean nothing different. Is there anything it's like to be this robot? Does this robot have experiences? – I can tell no difference between the new question and the old. Does sunburn feel the same way to you that it does to me? Do we have the same raw feel? Do we have the same experience when sunburned? – Again, same question. "Know the feeling," "know what it's like" – interchangeable. (Except that the former may hint at an alternative to the Hypothesis of Phenomenal Information.) So if the friend of phenomenal information says that its subject matter is raw feels, or ways to feel, or what it's like, then I respond just as I do if he says that the subject matter is experience. Maybe so, *if* the Hypothesis of Phenomenal Information is true; but if the Hypothesis is false and Materialism is true, nevertheless there is still information about raw feels, ways to feel or what it's like; but in that case it is physical information and can be conveyed in lessons.

We might get a candidate for the subject matter of phenomenal information that is not just experience renamed, but is still tendentious. For instance, we might be told that phenomenal information concerns the intrinsic character of experience. A friend of phenomenal information might indeed believe that it reveals certain special, non-physical intrinsic properties of experience. He might even believe that it reveals the existence of some special non-physical thing or process, *all* of whose intrinsic properties are non-physical. But he is by no means alone in saying that experience has an intrinsic character. Plenty of us materialists say so too. We say that a certain color-experience is whatever state occupies a certain functional role. So if the occupant of that role (universally, or in the case of humans, or in the case of certain humans) is a certain pattern of neural firing, then that pattern of firing *is* the experience (in the case in question). Therefore the intrinsic character of the experience is the intrinsic character of the firing pattern. For instance, a frequency of firing is part of the intrinsic character of the experience. If we materialists are right about what experience is, then black-and-white Mary knows all about the intrinsic character of color-experience; whereas most people who know what color-experience is like remain totally ignorant about its intrinsic character.[6]

To say that phenomenal information concerns "qualia" would be tendentious in much the same way. For how was this notion introduced? Often thus. We are told to imagine someone who, when he sees red things, has just the sort of experiences that we have when we see green things, and vice versa; and we are told to call this a case of "inverted qualia". And then we are told to imagine someone queerer still, who sees red and responds to it appropriately, and indeed has entirely the same functional organization of inner states as we do and yet has no experiences at all; and we are told to call this a case of "absent qualia". Now a friend of phenomenal information might well think that these deficiencies have something to do with the non-physical subject matter of phenomenal information. But others can understand them otherwise. Some materialists will reject the cases outright, but others, and I for one, will make sense of them as best we can. Maybe the point is that the states that occupy the roles of experiences, and therefore *are* the experiences, in normal people are inverted or absent in victims of inverted or absent qualia. (This presupposes, what might be false, that most people are enough alike). Experience of red – the state that occupies that role in normal people – occurs also in the victim of "inverted qualia," but in him it occupies the role of experience of green; whereas the state that occupies in him the role of experience of red is the state that occupies in normal people the role of experience of green. Experience of red and of green – that is, the occupants of those roles for normal people – do not occur at all in the victim of "absent qualia"; the occupants of those roles for him are states that don't occur at all in the normal. Thus we make good sense of inverted and absent qualia; but in such a way that "qualia" is just the word for role-occupying states taken *per se* rather than *qua* occupants of roles. Qualia, so understood, could not be the subject matter of phenomenal information. Mary knows all about them. We who have them mostly don't.[7]

It is best to rest content with an unhelpful name and a *via negativa*. Stipulate that "the phenomenal aspect of the world" is to name whatever is the subject matter of phenomenal information, if there is any such thing; the phenomenal aspect, if such there be, is that which we can become informed about by having new experiences but never by taking lessons. Having said this, it will be safe to say that information about the phenomenal aspect of the world can only be phenomenal information. But all we really know, after thus closing the circle, is that phenomenal information is supposed to reveal the presence of some sort of non-physical things or processes within experience, or else it is supposed to reveal that certain physical things or processes within experience have some sort of non-physical properties.

The Knowledge Argument

If we invoke the Hypothesis of Phenomenal Information to explain why no amount of physical information suffices to teach us what a new experience is like, then we have a powerful argument to refute any materialist theory of the mind. Frank Jackson (see note 1) calls it the "Knowledge Argument." Arguments against one materialist theory or another are never very conclusive. It is always possible to adjust the details. But the Knowledge Argument, if it worked, would directly refute the bare minimum that is common to *all* materialist theories.

It goes as follows. First in a simplified form; afterward we'll do it properly. Minimal Materialism is a supervenience thesis: no difference without physical difference. That is: any two possibilities that are just alike physically are just alike *simpliciter*. If two possibilities are just alike physically, then no physical information can eliminate one but not both of them. If two possibilities are just alike *simpliciter* (if that is possible) then no information whatsoever can eliminate one but not both of them. So if there is a kind of information – namely, phenomenal information – that can eliminate possibilites that any amount of physical information leaves open, then there must be possibilities that are just alike physically, but not just alike *simpliciter*. That is just what minimal Materialism denies.

(Analogy. If two possible locations in our region agree in their x-coordinate, then no amount of x-information can eliminate one but not both. If, *per impossibile*, two possible locations agreed in all their coordinates, then no information whatsoever could eliminate one but not both. So if there is a kind of information – namely, y-information – that can eliminate locations that any amount of x-information leaves open, then there must be locations in the region that agree in their x-coordinate but not in all their coordinates.)

Now to remove the simplification. What we saw so far was the Knowledge Argument against Materialism taken as a necessary truth, applying unrestrictedly to all possible worlds. But we materialists usually think that Materialism is a contingent truth. We grant that there are spooky possible worlds where Materialism is false, but we insist that our actual world isn't one of them. If so, then there might after all be two possibilities that are alike physically but not alike *simpliciter*, but one or both of the two would have to be possibilities where Materialism was false. Spooky worlds could differ with respect to their spooks without differing physically. Our minimal Materialism must be a *restricted* supervenience thesis: within a certain class of worlds, which includes our actual world, there is no difference without physical difference. Within that class, any two possibilities just alike physically are just alike *simpliciter*. But what delineates the relevant class? (It is trivial that our world belongs to *some* class wherein there is no difference without physical difference. That will be so however spooky our world may be. The unit class of our world is one such class, for instance. And so is any class that contains our world, and contains no two physical duplicates.) I think the relevant class should consist of the worlds that have nothing wholly alien to this world. The inhabitants of such a non-alien world could be made from the inhabitants of ours, so to speak, by a process of division and recombination. That will make no wholly different kinds of things, and no wholly different fundamental properties of things.[8] Our restricted materialist supervenience thesis should go as follows: throughout the non-alien worlds, there is no difference without physical difference.

If the Hypothesis of Phenomenal Information be granted, then the Knowledge Argument refutes this restricted supervenience nearly as decisively as it refutes the unrestricted version. Consider a possibility that is eliminated by phenomenal information, but not by any amount of physical information. There are two cases. Maybe this possibility has nothing that is alien to our world. In that case the argument goes as before: actuality and the eliminated possibility are just alike physically, they are not just alike *simpliciter*; furthermore, both of them fall within the restriction to non-alien worlds, so we have a counterexample even to restricted supervenience. Or maybe instead the eliminated possibility does have something X which is alien to this world – an alien kind of thing, or maybe an alien fundamental property of non-alien things. Then the phenomenal information gained by having a new experience has revealed something negative: at least in part, it is the information that X is *not* present. How can that be? If there is such a thing as phenomenal information, presumably what it reveals is positive: the presence of something hitherto unknown. Not, of course, something alien from actuality itself; but something alien from actuality as it is inadequately represented by the inexperienced and by the materialists. If Mary learns something when she finds out what it's like to see the colors, presumably she learns that there's *more* to the world than she knew before – not *less*. It's easy to think that phenomenal information might eliminate possibilities that are impoverished by comparison with actuality, but that would make a counterexample to the restricted supervenience thesis. To eliminate possibilities without making a counterexample, phenomenal information would have to eliminate possibilities less impoverished than actuality. And how can phenomenal information do that? Compare ordinary perceptual information. Maybe Jean-Paul can just *see* that Pierre is absent from the café, at least if it's a small café. But how can he just see that Pierre is absent from Paris, let alone from the whole of actuality?

(Is there a third case? What if the eliminated possibility is in one respect richer than actuality, in another respect poorer? Suppose the eliminated possibility has X, which is alien from actuality, but also it lacks Y. Then phenomenal information might eliminate it by revealing the actual presence of Y, without having to reveal the actual absence of X – But then I say there ought to be a third possibility, one with neither X nor Y, poorer and in no respect richer than actuality, and again without any physical difference from actuality. For why should taking away X automatically restore Y? Why can't they vary independently?[9] But this third possibility differs *simpliciter* from actuality without differing physically. Further, it has nothing alien from actuality. So we regain a counterexample to the restricted supervenience thesis.)

The Knowledge Argument works. There is no way to grant the Hypothesis of Phenomenal Information and still uphold Materialism. Therefore I deny the Hypothesis. I cannot refute it outright. But later I shall argue, first, that it is more peculiar, and therefore less tempting, that it may at first seem; and, second, that we are not forced to accept it, since an alternative hypothesis does justice to the way experience best teaches us what it's like.

Three more ways to miss the point

The Hypothesis of Phenomenal Information characterizes information in terms of eliminated possibilities. But there are other conceptions of "information." Therefore the Hypothesis has look-alikes: hypotheses which say that experience produces "information" which could not be gained otherwise, but do not characterize this "information" in terms of eliminated possibilities. These look-alikes do not work as premises for the Knowledge Argument. They do not say that phenomenal information eliminates possibilities that differ, but do not differ physically, from uneliminated possibilities. The look-alike hypotheses of phenomenal "information" are consistent with Materialism, and may very well be true. But they don't make the Knowledge Argument go away. Whatever harmless look-alikes may or may not be true, and whatever conception may or may not deserve the name "information," the only way to save Materialism is fix our attention squarely on the genuine Hypothesis of Phenomenal Information, and deny it. To avert our eyes, and attend to something else, is no substitute for that denial.

Might a look-alike help at least to this extent: by giving us something true that well might have been confused with the genuine Hypothesis, thereby explaining how we might have believed the Hypothesis although it was false? I think not. Each of the look-alikes turns out to imply not only that experience can give us "information" that no amount of lessons can give, but also that lessons in Russian can give us "information" that no amount of lessons in English can give (and vice versa). I doubt that any friend of phenomenal information ever thought that the special role of experience in teaching what it's like was on a par with the special role of Russian! I will have to say before I'm done that phenomenal information is an illusion, but I think I must look elsewhere for a credible hypothesis about what sort of illusion it might be.

The Fourth Way. If a hidden camera takes photographs of a room, the film ends up bearing traces of what went on in the room. The traces are distinctive: that is, the details of the traces depend on the details of what went on, and if what went on had been different in any of many ways, the traces would have been correspondingly different. So we can say that the traces bear information, and that he who has the film has the information. That might be said because the traces, plus the way they depend on what went on, suffice to eliminate possibilities; but instead we might say "information" and just mean "distinctive traces." If so, it's certainly true that new experience imparts "information" unlike any that can be gained from lessons. Experience and lessons leave different kinds of traces. That is so whether or not the experience eliminates possibilities that the lessons leave open. It is equally true, of course, that lessons in Russian leave traces unlike any that are left by lessons in English, regardless of whether the lessons cover the same ground and eliminate the same possibilities.

The Fifth Way. When we speak of transmission of "information," we often mean transmission of text. Repositories of "information," such as libraries, are storehouses of text. Whether the text is empty verbiage or highly informative is beside the point. Maybe we too contain information by being storehouses of text. Maybe there is a language of thought, and maybe the way we believe things is to store sentences of this language in some special way, or in some special part of our brains. In that case, we could say that storing away a new sentence was storing away a new piece of "information," whether or not that new piece eliminated any possibilities not already eliminated by the sentences stored previously. Maybe, also, the language of thought is not fixed once and for all, but can gain new words. Maybe, for instance, it borrows words from public language. And maybe, when one has a new experience, that causes one's language of thought to gain a new word which denotes that experience – a word which could not have been added to the language by any other means. If all this is so, then when Mary sees colors, her language of thought gains new words, allowing her to store away new sentences and thereby gain "information." All this about the language of thought, the storing of sentences, and the gaining of words is speculation. But it is plausible speculation, even if no longer the only game in town. If it is all true, then we have another look-alike hypothesis of phenomenal "information." When Mary gains new words and stores new sentences, that is "information" that she never had before, regardless of whether it eliminates any possibilities that she had not eliminated already.

But again, the special role of experience turns out to be on a par with the special role of Russian. If the language of thought picks up new words by borrowing from public language, then lessons in Russian add new words, and result in the storing of new sentences, and thereby impart "information" that never could have been had from lessons in English. (You might say that the new Russian words are mere synonyms of old words, or at least old phrases, that were there already; and synonyms don't count. But no reason has been given why the new inner words created by experience may not also be synonyms of old phrases, perhaps of long descriptions in the language of neurophysiology.)

The Sixth Way. A philosopher who is skeptical about possibility, as so many are, may wish to replace possibilities themselves with linguistic ersatz possibilities: maximal consistent sets of sentences. And he may be content to take "consistent" in a narrowly logical sense, so that a set with "Fred is married" and "Fred is a bachelor" may count as consistent, and only an overt contradiction like "Fred is married" and "Fred is not married" will be ruled out.[10] The ersatz possibilities might also be taken as sets of sentences of the language of thought, if the philosopher believes in it. Then if someone's language of thought gains new words, whether as a result of new experience or as a result of being taught in Russian, the ersatz possibilities become richer and more numerous. The sets of sentences that were maximal before are no longer maximal after new words are added. So when Mary sees colors and her language of thought gains new words, there are new ersatz possibilities; and she can straightway eliminate some of them. Suppose she knows beforehand that she is about to see green, and that the experience of seeing green is associated with neural firing pattern F. So when she sees green and gains the new word G for her experience, then straightway there are new, enriched ersatz possibilities with sentences saying that she has G without F, and straightway she knows enough to eliminate these ersatz possibilities. (Even if she does not know beforehand what she is about to see, straightway she can eliminate at least those of her new-found ersatz possibilities with sentences denying that she then has G.) Just as we can characterize information in terms of elimination of possibilities, so we can characterize ersatz "information" in terms of elimination of ersatz "possibilities." So here we have the closest look-alike hypothesis of all, provided that language-of-thoughtism is true. But we still do not have the genuine Hypothesis of Phenomenal Information, since the eliminated ersatz possibility of G without F may not have been a genuine possibility at all. It may have been like the ersatz possibility of married bachelors.

Curiouser and curiouser

The Hypothesis of Phenomenal Information is more peculiar than it may at first seem. For one thing, because it is opposed to more than just Materialism. Some of you may have welcomed the Knowledge Argument because you thought all along that physical information was inadequate to explain the phenomena of mind. You may have been convinced all along that the mind could do things that no physical system could do: bend spoons, invent new jokes, demonstrate the consistency of arithmetic, reduce the wave packet, or what have you. You may have been convinced that the full causal story of how the deeds of mind are accomplished involves the causal interactions not only of material bodies but also of astral bodies; not only the vibrations of the electromagnetic field but also the good or bad vibes of the psionic field; not only protoplasm but ectoplasm. I doubt it, but never mind. It's irrelevant to our topic. The Knowledge Argument is targeted against you no less than it is against Materialism itself.

Let *parapsychology* be the science of all the non-physical things, properties, causal processes, laws of nature, and so forth that may be required to explain the things we do. Let us suppose that we learn ever so much parapsychology. It will make no difference. Black-and-white Mary may study all the parapsychology as well as all the psychophysics of color vision, but she still won't know what it's like. Lessons on the aura of Vegemite will do no more for us than lessons on its chemical composition. And so it goes. Our intuitive starting point wasn't just that *physics* lessons couldn't help the inexperienced to know what it's like. It was that *lessons* couldn't help. If there is such a thing as phenomenal information, it isn't just independent of physical information. It's independent of every sort of information that could be served up in lessons for the inexperienced. For it is supposed to eliminate possibilities that any amount of lessons leave open.

Therefore phenomenal information is not just parapsychological information, if such there be. It's something very much stranger.

The genuine Hypothesis of Phenomenal Information, as distinguished from its look-alikes, treats information in terms of the elimination of possibilities. When we lack information, several alternative possibilities are open, when we get the information some of the alternatives are excluded. But a second peculiar thing about phenomenal information is that it resists this treatment. (So does logical or mathematical "information." However, phenomenal information cannot be logical or mathematical, because lessons in logic and mathematics no more teach us what a new experience is like than lessons in physics or parapsychology do.) When someone doesn't know what it's like to have an experience, where are the alternative open possibilities? I cannot present to myself in thought a range of alternative possibilities about what it might be like to taste Vegemite. That is because I cannot imagine either what it *is* like to taste Vegemite, or any alternative way that it *might* be like but in fact isn't. (I could perfectly well imagine that Vegemite tastes just like peanut butter, or something else familiar to me, but let's suppose I've been told authoritatively that this isn't so.) I can't even pose the question that phenomenal information is supposed to answer: is it this way or that? It seems that the alternative possibilities must be unthinkable beforehand; and afterward too, except for the one that turns out to be actualized. I don't say there's anything altogether impossible about a range of unthinkable alternatives; only something peculiar. But it's peculiar enough to suggest that we may somehow have gone astray.

From phenomenal to epiphenomenal

A third peculiar thing about phenomenal information is that it is strangely isolated from all other sorts of information; and this is so regardless of whether the mind works on physical or parapsychological principles. The phenomenal aspect of the world has nothing to do with explaining why people seemingly talk about the phenomenal aspect of the world. For instance, it plays no part in explaining the movements of the pens of philosophers writing treatises about phenomenal information and the way experience has provided them with it.

When Mary gets out of her black-and-white cell, her jaw drops. She says "At last! So this is what it's like to see colors!" Afterward she does things she couldn't do before, such as recognizing a new sample of the first color she ever saw. She may also do other things she didn't do before: unfortunate things, like writing about phenomenal information and the poverty of Materialism. One might think she said what she said and did what she did because she came to know what it's like to see colors. Not so, if the Hypothesis of Phenomenal Information is right. For suppose the phenomenal aspect of the world had been otherwise, so that she gained different phenomenal information. Or suppose the phenomenal aspect of the world had been absent altogether, as we materialists think it is. Would that have made the slightest difference to what she did or said then or later? I think not. Making a difference to what she does or says means, at least in part, making a difference to the motions of the particles of which she is composed. (Or better: making a difference to the spatiotemporal shape of the wave-function of those particles. But let that pass.) For how could she do or say anything different, if none of her particles moved any differently? But if something non-physical sometimes makes a difference to the motions of physical particles, then physics as we know it is wrong. Not just silent, not just incomplete – wrong. Either the particles are caused to change their motion without benefit of any force, or else there is some extra force that works very differently from the usual four. To believe in the phenomenal aspect of the world, but deny that it is epiphenomenal, is to bet against the truth of physics. Given the success of physics hitherto, and even with due allowance for the foundational ailments of quantum mechanics, such betting is rash! A friend of the phenomenal aspect would be safer to join Jackson in defense of *epiphenomenal* qualia.

But there is more to the case than just an empirical bet in favor of physics. Suppose there is a phenomenal aspect of the world, and suppose it does make some difference to the motions of Mary's jaw or the noises out of her mouth. Then we can describe the phenomenal aspect, if we know enough, in terms of its physical effects. It is that on which physical phenomena depend in such-and-such way. This descriptive handle will enable us to give lessons on it to the inexperienced. But in so far as we can give lessons on it, what we have is just parapsychology. That whereof we cannot learn except by having the experience still eludes us. I do not argue that *everything* about the alleged distinctive subject matter of phenomenal information must be epiphenomenal. Part of it may be parapsychological instead. But I insist that *some* aspect of it must be epiphenomenal.

Suppose that the Hypothesis of Phenomenal Information is true and suppose that V_1 and V_2 are all of the maximally specific phenomenal possibilities concerning what it's like to taste Vegemite; anyone who tastes Vegemite will find out which one obtains, and no one else can. And suppose that P_1 and P_2 are all the maximally specific physical possibilities. (Of course we really need far more than two Ps, and maybe a friend of phenomenal information would want more than two Vs, but absurdly small numbers will do for an example.) Then we have four alternative hypotheses about the causal independence or dependence of the Ps on the Vs. Each one can be expressed as a pair of counterfactual conditionals. Two hypotheses are patterns of dependence.

K_1: if V_1 then P_1, if V_2 then P_2
K_2: if V_1 then P_2, if V_2 then P_1

The other two are patterns of independence.

K_3: if V_1 then P_1, if V_2 then P_1
K_4: if V_1 then P_2, if V_2 then P_2

These dependency hypotheses are, I take it, contingent propositions. They are made true, if they are, by some contingent feature of the world, though it's indeed a vexed question what sort of feature it is.[11] Now we have eight joint possibilities.

$K_1V_1P_1$	$K_3V_1P_1$	$K_3V_2P_1$	$K_2V_2P_1$
$K_2V_1P_2$	$K_4V_1P_2$	$K_4V_2P_2$	$K_1V_2P_2$

Between the four on the top row and the four on the bottom row, there is the physical difference between P_1 and P_2. Between the four on the left and the four on the right, there is the phenomenal difference between V_1 and V_2. And between the four on the edges and the four in the middle there is a parapsychological difference. It is the difference between dependence and independence of the physical on the phenomenal; between efficacy and epiphenomenalism, so far as this one example is concerned. There's nothing ineffable about that. Whether or not you've tasted Vegemite, and whether or not you can conceive of the alleged difference between V_1 and V_2, you can still be told whether the physical difference between P_1 and P_2 does or doesn't depend on some part of the phenomenal aspect of the world.

Lessons can teach the inexperienced which parapsychological possibility obtains, dependence or independence. Let it be dependence: we have either K_1 or K_2. For if we had independence, then already we would have found our epiphenomenal difference: namely, the difference between V_1 and V_2. And lessons can teach the inexperienced which of the two physical possibilities obtains. Without loss of generality let it be P_1. Now two of our original eight joint possibilities remain open: $K_1V_1P_1$ and $K_2V_2P_1$. The difference between those is not at all physical, and not at all parapsychological: it's P_1, and it's dependence, in both cases. The difference is entirely phenomenal. And also it is entirely epiphenomenal. Nothing physical, and nothing parapsychological, depends on the difference between $K_1V_1P_1$ and $K_2V_2P_1$. We have the same sort of pattern of dependence either way; it's just that the phenomenal possibilities have been swapped. Whether it's independence or whether it's dependence, therefore, we have found an epiphenomenal part of the phenomenal aspect of the world. It is the residue left behind when we remove the parapsychological part.

Suppose that someday I taste Vegemite, and hold forth about how I know at last what it's like. The sound of my holding forth is a physical effect, part of the realized physical possibility P_1. This physical effect is exactly the same whether it's part of the joint possibility $K_1V_1P_1$ or part of its alternative $K_2V_2P_1$. It may be caused by V_1 in accordance with K_1, or it may instead be caused by V_2 in accordance with K_2, but it's the same either way. So it does not occur because we have K_1V_1 rather than K_2V_2, or vice versa. The alleged difference between these two possibilities does nothing to explain the alleged physical manifestation of my finding out which one of them is realized. It is in that way that the difference is epiphenomenal. That makes it very queer, and repugnant to good sense.

The Ability Hypothesis

So the Hypothesis of Phenomenal Information turns out to be very peculiar indeed. It would be nice, and not only for materialists, if we could reject it. For materialists, it is essential to reject it. And we can. There is an alternative hypothesis about what it is to learn what an experience is like: the *Ability Hypothesis*. Laurence Nemirow summarizes it thus:

> some modes of understanding consist, not in the grasping of facts, but in the acquisition of abilities. . . . As for understanding an experience, we may construe that as an ability to place oneself, at will, in a state representative of the experience. I

understand the experience of seeing red if I can at will visualize red. Now it is perfectly clear why there must be a special connection between the ability to place oneself in a state representative of a given experience and the point of view of experiencer: exercising the ability just *is* what we call "adopting the point of view of experiencer." ... We can, then, come to terms with the subjectivity of our understanding of experience without positing subjective facts as the objects of our understanding. This account explains, incidentally, the linguistic incommunicability of our subjective understanding of experience (a phenomenon which might seem to support the hypothesis of subjective facts). The latter is explained as a special case of the linguistic incommunicability of abilities to place oneself at will in a given state, such as the state of having lowered blood pressure, and the state of having wiggling ears.[12]

If you have a new experience, you gain abilities to remember and to imagine. After you taste Vegemite, and you learn what it's like, you can afterward remember the experience you had. By remembering how it once was, you can afterward imagine such an experience. Indeed, even if you eventually forget the occasion itself, you will very likely retain your ability to imagine such an experience.

Further, you gain an ability to recognize the same experience if it comes again. If you taste Vegemite on another day, you will probably know that you have met the taste once before. And if, while tasting Vegemite, you know that it is Vegemite you are tasting, then you will be able to put the name to the experience if you have it again. Or if you are told nothing at the time, but later you somehow know that it is Vegemite that you are then remembering or imagining tasting, again you can put the name to the experience, or to the memory, or to the experience of imagining, if it comes again. Here, the ability you gain is an ability to gain information if given other information. Nevertheless, the information gained is not phenomenal, and the ability to gain information is not the same thing as information itself.

Earlier, I mentioned "knowing what an experience is like under a description." Now I can say that what I meant by this was having the ability to remember or imagine an experience while also knowing the egocentric proposition that what one is then imagining is the experience of such-and-such description. One might well know what an experience is like under one description, but not under another. One might even know what some experience is like, but not under any description whatever – unless it be some rather trivial description like "that queer taste that I'm imagining right now." That is what would happen if you slipped a dab of Vegemite into my food without telling me what it was: afterward, I would know what it was like to taste Vegemite, but not under that description, and not under any other non-trivial description. It might be suggested that "knowing what it's like to taste Vegemite" really means what I'd call "knowing what it's like to taste Vegemite under the description 'tasting Vegemite'"; and if so, knowing what it's like would involve both ability and information. I disagree. For surely it would make sense to say: "I know this experience well, I've long known what it's like, but only today have I found out that it's the experience of tasting Vegemite." But this verbal question is unimportant. For the information involved in knowing what it's like under a description, and allegedly involved in knowing what it's like, is anyhow not the queer phenomenal information that needs rejecting.

(Is there a problem here for the friend of phenomenal information? Suppose he says that knowing what it's like to taste Vegemite means knowing that the taste of Vegemite has a certain "phenomenal character." This requires putting the name to the taste, so clearly it corresponds to our notion of knowing what it's like to taste Vegemite under the description "tasting Vegemite." But we also have our notion of knowing what it's like *simpliciter*, and what can he offer that corresponds to that? Perhaps he should answer by appeal to a trivial description, as follows: knowing what it's like *simpliciter* means knowing what it's like under the trivial description "taste I'm imagining now," and that means knowing that the taste one is imagining now has a certain phenomenal character.)

As well as gaining the ability to remember and imagine the experience you had, you also gain the ability to imagine related experiences that you never had. After tasting Vegemite, you might for instance become able to imagine tasting Vegemite ice cream. By performing imaginative experiments, you can predict with some confidence what you would do in circumstances that have never arisen – whether you'd ask for a second helping of Vegemite ice cream, for example.

These abilities to remember and imagine and recognize are abilities you cannot gain (unless by super-neurosurgery, or by magic) except by tasting Vegemite and learning what it's like. You can't get them by taking lessons on the physics or the parapsychology of the experience, or even by taking comprehensive lessons that cover the whole of physics and parapsychology. The Ability Hypothesis says that knowing what an experience is like just *is* the possession of these abilities to remember, imagine, and recognize. It isn't the possession of any kind of information, ordinary or peculiar. It isn't knowing that certain possibilities aren't actualized. It isn't knowing-that. It's knowing-how. Therefore it should be no surprise that lessons won't teach you what an experience is like. Lessons impart information; ability is something else. Knowledge-that does not automatically provide know-how.

There are parallel cases. Some know how to wiggle their ears; others don't. If you can't do it, no amount of information will help. Some know how to eat with chopsticks, others don't. Information will help up to a point – for instance, if your trouble is that you hold one chopstick in each hand – but no amount of information, by itself, will bring you to a very high level of know-how. Some know how to recognize a C-38 lcoomotive by sight, others don't. If you don't, it won't much help if you memorize a detailed geometrical description of its shape, even though that does all the eliminating of possibilities that there is to be done. (Conversely, knowing the shape by sight doesn't enable you to write down the geometrical description.) Information very often contributes to know-how, but often it doesn't contribute enough. That's why music students have to practice.

Know-how is ability. But of course some aspects of ability are in no sense knowledge: strength, sufficient funds. Other aspects of ability are, purely and simply, a matter of information. If you want to know how to open the combination lock on the bank vault, information is all you need. It remains that there are aspects of ability that do *not* consist simply of possession of information, and that we *do* call knowledge. The Ability Hypothesis holds that knowing what an experience is like is that sort of knowledge.

If the Ability Hypothesis is the correct analysis of knowing what an experience is like, then phenomenal information is an illusion. We ought to explain that illusion. It would be feeble, I think, just to say that we're fooled by the ambiguity of the word "know": we confuse ability with information because we confuse knowledge in the sense of knowing-how with knowledge in the sense of knowing-that. There may be two senses of the word "know," but they are well and truly entangled. They mark the two pure endpoints of a range of mixed cases. The usual thing is that we gain information and ability together. If so, it should be no surprise if we apply to pure cases of gaining ability, or to pure cases of gaining information, the same word "know" that we apply to all the mixed cases.

Along with information and ability, acquaintance is a third element of the mixture. If Lloyd George died too soon, there's a sense in which Father never can know him. Information won't do it, even if Father is a most thorough biographer and the archives are very complete. (And the trouble isn't that there's some very special information about someone that you can only get by being in his presence.) Know-how won't do it either, no matter how good Father may be at imagining Lloyd George, seemingly remembering him, and recognizing him. (Father may be able to recognize Lloyd George even if there's no longer any Lloyd George to recognize – if *per impossibile* he did turn up, Father could tell it was him.) Again, what we have is not just a third separate sense of "know." Meeting someone, gaining a lot of information about him that would be hard to gain otherwise, and gaining abilities regarding him usually go together. The pure cases are exceptions.

A friend of phenomenal information will agree, of course, that when we learn what an experience is like, we gain abilities to remember, imagine, and recognize. But he will say that it is because we gain phenomenal information that we gain the abilities. He might even say the same about other cases of gaining know-how: you can recognize the C-38 when you have phenomenal information about what it's like to see that shape, you can eat with chopsticks or wiggle your ears when you gain phenomenal information about the experience of doing so, and so on. What should friends of the Ability Hypothesis make of this? Is he offering a conjecture, which we must reject, about the causal origin of abilities? I think not. He thinks, as we do, that experiences leave distinctive traces in people, and that these traces enable us to do things. Likewise being taught to recognize a C-38 or to eat with chopsticks, or whatever happens on first wiggling the ears, leave traces that enable us to do things afterward. That much is common ground. He also interprets these enabling traces as representations that bear information about their causes. (If the same traces had been caused in some deviant way they might perhaps have carried misinformation.) We might even be able to accept that too. The time for us to quarrel comes only when he says that these traces represent special phenomenal facts, facts which cannot be represented in any other way, and therefore which cannot be taught in physics lessons or even in parapsychology lessons. That is the part, and the *only* part, which we must reject. But that is no part of his psychological story about how we gain abilities. It is just a gratuitous metaphysical gloss on that story.

We say that learning what an experience is like means gaining certain abilities. If the causal basis for those abilities turns out also to be a special kind of representation of some sort of information, so be it. We need only deny that it represents a special kind of information about a special subject matter. Apart from that it's up for grabs what, if anything, it may represent. The details of stimuli: the chemical composition of Vegemite, reflectances of surfaces, the motions of well-handled chopsticks or of ears? The details of inner states produced by those stimuli: patterns of firings of nerves? We could agree to either, so long as we did not confuse 'having information' represented in this special way with having the same information in the form of knowledge or belief. Or we could disagree. Treating the ability-conferring trace as a representation is optional. What's essential is that when we learn what an experience is like by having it, we gain abilities to remember, imagine, and recognize.

ACKNOWLEDGMENT

Part of this paper derives from a lecture at LaTrobe University in 1981. I thank LaTrobe for support in 1981, Harvard University for support under a Santayana Fellowship in 1988, and Frank Jackson for very helpful discussion.

NOTES

1 See Frank Jackson, "Epiphenomenal qualia," *Philosophical Quarterly* 32 (1982), pp. 127–36, and reprinted in this volume; "What Mary didn't know," *Journal of Philosophy* 83 (1986), pp. 291–5.
2 See B. A. Farrell, "Experience," *Mind* 59 (1950), pp. 170–98; and Thomas Nagel, "What is it like to be a bat?" *Philosophical Review* 83 (1974), pp. 435–50, also in Thomas Nagel, *Mortal Questions* (Cambridge: Cambridge University Press, 1979).
3 See Peter Unger, "On experience and the development of the understanding," *American Philosophical Quarterly* 3 (1966), pp. 1–9.
4 For such speculation, see Paul M. Churchland, "Reduction, qualia, and the direct introspection of brain states," *Journal of Philosophy* 82 (1985), pp. 8–28.
5 See my "Attitudes *de dicto* and *de se*," *Philosophical Review* 88 (1979), pp. 513–43, also in my *Philosophical Papers*, vol. I (New York: Oxford University Press, 1983); and Roderick Chisholm, *The First Person: An Essay on Reference and Intentionality* (Minneapolis: University of Minnesota Press, 1981).
6 See Gilbert Harman, "The intrinsic quality of experience," *Philosophical Perspectives* 4 (1990).
7 See Ned Block and Jerry A. Fodor, "What psychological states are not," *Philosophical Review* 81 (1972), pp. 159–81, also in Ned Block (ed.), *Readings in Philosophy of Psychology*, vol. I (Cambridge, MA: Harvard University Press, 1980); and my "Mad pain and Martian pain", in *Readings in Philosophy of Psychology*, vol. I, and in my *Philosophical Papers*, vol. I.
8 See my "New work for a theory of universals," *Australasian Journal of Philosophy* 61 (1983), pp. 343–77, especially pp. 361–4. For a different view about how to state minimal Materialism, see Terence Horgan, "Supervenience and microphysics," *Pacific Philosophical Quarterly* 63 (1982), pp 29–43. .
9 On recombination of possibilities, see my *On the Plurality of Worlds* (Oxford: Blackwell, 1986), pp. 87–92. The present argument may call for a principle that also allows recombination of properties; I now think that would not necessarily require treating properties as non-spatiotemporal parts of their instances. On recombination of properties, see also D. M. Armstrong, *A Combinatorial Theory of Possibility* (Cambridge: Cambridge University Press 1989).
10 See *On the Plurality of Worlds*, pp. 142–65, on linguistic ersatz possibilities.
11 On dependency hypotheses, see my "Causal decision theory," *Australasian Journal of Philosophy* 59 (1981), pp. 5–30, reprinted in my *Philosophical Papers*, vol. II (New York: Oxford University Press, 1986).

12 Laurence Nemirow, review of Nagel's *Mortal Questions*, *Philosophical Review* 89 (1980), pp.
    475–6. For a fuller statement, see Nemirow, "Physicalism and the cognitive role of acquaintance,"
    in this volume; and *Functionalism and the Subjective Quality of Experience* (doctoral dissertation,
    Stanford, 1979). See also Michael Tye, "The subjective qualities of experience," *Mind* 95
    (1986), pp. 1–17.
        I should record a disagreement with Nemirow on one very small point. We agree that the
    phrase "what experience E is like" does not denote some "subjective quality" of E, something
    which supposedly would be part of the subject matter of the phenomenal information gained
    by having E. But whereas I have taken the phrase to denote E itself, Nemirow takes it to be
    a syncategorematic part of the expression "know what experience E is like". See "Physicalism
    and the cognitive role of acquaintance" section III.

Quining Qualia

DANIEL C. DENNETT

1 Corralling the quicksilver

"Qualia" is an unfamilar term for something that could not be more familiar to
each of us: the *ways things seem to us*. As is so often the case with philosophical
jargon, it is easier to give examples than to give a definition of the term. Look at a
glass of milk at sunset; *the way it looks to you* – the particular, personal, subjective
visual quality of the glass of milk is the *quale* of your visual experience at the
moment. The *way the milk tastes to you then* is another, gustatory, *quale*, and *how it
sounds to you* as you swallow is an auditory *quale*. These various "properties of
conscious experience" are prime examples of *qualia*. Nothing, it seems, could you
know more intimately than your own qualia; let the entire universe be some vast
illusion, some mere figment of Descartes's evil demon, and yet what the figment
is *made of* (for you) will be the *qualia* of your hallucinatory experiences. Descartes
claimed to doubt everything that could be doubted, but he never doubted that his
conscious experiences had qualia, the properties by which he knew or apprehended
them.

The verb "to quine" is even more esoteric. It comes from *The Philosophical
Lexicon* (Dennett 1978c, 8th edn 1987), a satirical dictionary of eponyms: "quine,
v. To deny resolutely the existence or importance of something real or significant."
At first blush it would be hard to imagine a more quixotic quest than trying to
convince people that there are no such properties as qualia; hence the ironic title
of this chapter. But I am not kidding.

"Quining Qualia" by D. C. Dennett, first appeared in *Consciousness in Contemporary Science*,
edited by A. Marcel and E. Bisiach (Oxford: Oxford University Press) and is reprinted by kind
permission.

My goal is subversive. I am out to overthrow an idea that, in one form or another, is "obvious" to most people – to scientists, philosophers, lay people. My quarry is frustratingly elusive; no sooner does it retreat in the face of one argument than "it" reappears, apparently innocent of all charges, in a new guise.

Which idea of qualia am I trying to extirpate? Everything real has properties, and since I don't deny the reality of conscious experience, I grant that conscious experience has properties. I grant moreover that each person's states of consciousness have properties in virtue of which those states have the experiential content that they do. That is to say, whenever someone experiences something as being one way rather than another, this is true in virtue of some property of something happening in them at the time, but these properties are so unlike the properties traditionally imputed to consciousness that it would be grossly misleading to call any of them the long-sought qualia. Qualia are supposed to be *special* properties, in some hard-to-define way. My claim – which can only come into focus as we proceed – is that conscious experience has *no* properties that are special in *any* of the ways qualia have been supposed to be special.

The standard reaction to this claim is the complacent acknowledgment that while some people may indeed have succumbed to one confusion or fanaticism or another, one's own appeal to a modest, innocent notion of properties of subjective experience is surely safe. It is just that presumption of innocence I want to overthrow. I want to shift the burden of proof, so that anyone who wants to appeal to private, subjective properties has to prove first that in so doing they are *not* making a mistake. This status of *guilty until proven innocent* is neither unprecedented nor indefensible (so long as we restrict ourselves to concepts). Today, no biologist would dream of supposing that it was quite all right to appeal to some innocent concept of *élan vital*. Of course one *could* use the term to mean something in good standing; one could use *élan vital* as one's name for DNA, for instance, but this would be foolish nomenclature, considering the deserved suspicion with which the term is nowadays burdened. I want to make it just as uncomfortable for anyone to talk of qualia – or "raw feels" or "phenomenal properties" or "subjective and intrinsic properties" or "the qualitative character" of experience – with the standard presumption that they, and everyone else, knows what on earth they are talking about.[1]

What are qualia, *exactly*? This obstreperous query is dismissed by one author ("only half in jest") by invoking Louis Armstrong's legendary reply when asked what jazz was: "If you got to ask, you ain't never gonna get to know." (Block 1978 p. 281). This amusing tactic perfectly illustrates the presumption that is my target. If I succeed in my task, this move, which passes muster in most circles today, will look as quaint and insupportable as a jocular appeal to the ludicrousness of a living thing – a living thing, mind you! – doubting the existence of *élan vital*.

My claim, then, is not just that the various technical or theoretical concepts of qualia are vague or equivocal, but that the source concept, the "pretheoretical" notion of which the former are presumed to be refinements, is so thoroughly confused that even if we undertook to salvage some "lowest common denominator" from the theoreticians' proposals, any acceptable version would have to be so radically unlike the ill-formed notions that are commonly appealed to that it would be tactically obtuse – not to say Pickwickian – to cling to the term. Far better, tactically, to declare that there simply are no qualia at all.[2]

Rigorous arguments only work on well-defined materials, and since my goal is to destroy our faith in the pretheoretical or "intuitive" concept, the right tools for my task are intuition pumps, not formal arguments. What follows is a series of fifteen intuition pumps, posed in a sequence designed to flush out – and then flush away – the offending intuitions. In section 2, I will use the first two intuition pumps to focus attention on the traditional notion. It will be the burden of the rest of the paper to convince you that these two pumps, for all their effectiveness, mislead us and should be discarded. In section 3, the next four intuition pumps create and refine a "paradox" lurking in the tradition. This is not a formal paradox, but only a very powerful argument pitted against some almost irresistibly attractive ideas. In section 4, six more intuition pumps are arrayed in order to dissipate the attractiveness of those ideas, and section 5 drives this point home by showing how hapless those ideas prove to be when confronted with some real cases of anomalous experience. This will leave something of a vacuum, and in the final section three more intuition pumps are used to introduce and motivate some suitable replacements for the banished notions.

2   The special properties of qualia

Intuition pump #1: watching you eat cauliflower. I see you tucking eagerly into a helping of steaming cauliflower, the merest whiff of which makes me faintly nauseated, and I find myself wondering how you could possibly relish *that taste*, and then it occurs to me that to you, cauliflower probably tastes (must taste?) different. A plausible hypothesis, it seems, especially since I know that the very same food often tastes different to me at different times. For instance, my first sip of breakfast orange juice tastes much sweeter than my second sip if I interpose a bit of pancakes and maple syrup, but after a swallow or two of coffee, the orange juice goes back to tasting (roughly? exactly?) the way it did the first sip. Surely we want to say (or think about) such things, and surely we are not wildly wrong when we do, so . . . surely it is quite OK to talk of *the way the juice tastes to Dennett at time t*, and ask whether it is just the same as or different from *the way the juice tastes to Dennett at time t'* or *the way the juice tastes to Jones at time t*.

This "conclusion" seems innocent, but right here we have already made the big mistake. The final step presumes that we can isolate the qualia from everything else that is going on – at least in principle or for the sake of argument. What counts as *the way the juice tastes to x* can be distinguished, one supposes, from what is a mere accompaniment, contributory cause, or by-product of this "central" way. One dimly imagines taking such cases and stripping them down gradually to the essentials, leaving their common residuum, the way things look, sound, feel, taste, smell to various individuals at various times, independently of how those individuals are stimulated or non-perceptually affected, and independently of how they are subsequently disposed to behave or believe. The mistake is not in supposing that we can in practice ever or always perform this act of purification with certainty, but the more fundamental mistake of supposing that there is such a residual property to take seriously, however uncertain our actual attempts at isolation of instances might be.

The examples that seduce us are abundant in every modality. I cannot imagine, will never know, could never know, it seems, how Bach sounded to Glenn Gould. (I can barely recover in my memory the way Bach sounded to me when I was a child.) And I cannot know, it seems, what it is like to be a bat (Nagel 1974), or whether you see what I see, colorwise, when we look up at a clear "blue" sky. The homely cases convince us of the reality of these special properties – those subjective tastes, looks, aromas, sounds – that we then apparently isolate for definition by this philosophical distillation.

The specialness of these properties is hard to pin down, but can be seen at work in *intuition pump #2: the wine-tasting machine*. Could Gallo Brothers replace their human wine tasters with a machine? A computer-based "expert system" for quality control and classification is probably within the bounds of existing technology. We now know enough about the relevant chemistry to make the transducers that would replace taste buds and olfactory organs (delicate color vision would perhaps be more problematic), and we can imagine using the output of such transducers as the raw material – the "sense data" in effect – for elaborate evaluations, descriptions, classifications. Pour the sample in the funnel and, in a few minutes or hours, the system would type out a chemical assay, along with commentary: "a flamboyant and velvety Pinot, though lacking in stamina" – or words to such effect. Such a machine might well perform better than human wine tasters on all reasonable tests of accuracy and consistency the winemakers could devise,[3] but *surely* no matter how "sensitive" and "discriminating" such a system becomes, it will never have, and enjoy, what *we* do when we taste a wine: the qualia of conscious experience! Whatever informational, dispositional, functional properties its internal states have, none of them will be special in the way qualia are. If you share that intuition, you believe that there are qualia in the sense I am targeting for demolition.

What is special about qualia? Traditional analyses suggest some fascinating second-order properties of these properties. First, since one *cannot say* to another, no matter how eloquent one is and no matter how cooperative and imaginative one's audience is, exactly what way one is currently seeing, tasting, smelling and so forth, qualia are *ineffable* – in fact the paradigm cases of ineffable items. According to tradition, at least part of the reason why qualia are ineffable is that they are *intrinsic* properties – which seems to imply *inter alia* that they are somehow atomic and unanalyzable. Since they are "simple" or "homogeneous" there is nothing to get hold of when trying to describe such a property to one unacquainted with the particular instance in question.

Moreover, verbal comparisons are not the only cross-checks ruled out. *Any* objective, physiological or "merely behavioral" test – such as those passed by the imaginary wine-tasting system – would of necessity miss the target (one can plausibly argue), so all interpersonal comparisons of these ways-of-appearing are (apparently) systematically impossible. In other words, qualia are essentially *private* properties. And, finally, since they *are* properties of *my experiences* (they're not chopped liver, and they're not properties of, say, my cerebral blood flow – or haven't you been paying attention?), qualia are essentially directly accessible to the consciousness of their experiencer (whatever that means) or qualia are properties of one's experience with which one is intimately or directly acquainted (whatever that means) or "immediate phenomenological qualities" (Block 1978) (whatever that means). They are, after all, the very properties the appreciation of which permits us to identify our conscious states. So, to summarize the tradition, qualia are supposed to be properties of a subject's mental states that are

1 ineffable
2 intrinsic
3 private
4 directly or immediately apprehensible in consciousness

Thus are qualia introduced onto the philosophical stage. They have seemd to be very significant properties to some theorists because they have seemed to provide an insurmountable and unavoidable stumbling block to functionalism, or more broadly, to materialism, or more broadly still, to any purely "third-person" objective viewpoint or approach to the world (Nagel 1986). Theorists of the contrary persuasion have patiently and ingeniously knocked down all the arguments, and said most of the right things, but they have made a tactical error, I am claiming, of saying in one way or another: "We theorists can handle *those qualia* you talk about just fine; we will show that you are just slightly in error about the nature of qualia." What they ought to have said is: "What qualia?"

My challenge strikes some theorists as outrageous or misguided because they think they have a much blander and hence less vulnerable notion of qualia to begin with. They think I am setting up and knocking down a strawman, and ask, in effect: "Who said qualia are ineffable, intrinsic, private, directly apprehensible ways things seem to one?" Since my suggested fourfold essence of qualia may strike many readers as tendentious, it may be instructive to consider, briefly, an apparently milder alternative: qualia are simply "the qualitative or phenomenal features of sense experience[s], in virtue of having which they resemble and differ from each other, qualitatively, in the ways they do" (Shoemaker 1982, p. 367). Surely I do not mean to deny *those* features!

I reply: it all depends on what "qualitative or phenomenal" comes to. Shoemaker contrasts *qualitative* similarity and difference with "intentional" similarity and difference – similarity and difference of the properties an experience represents or is "of". That is clear enough, but what then of "phenomenal"? Among the non-intentional (and hence qualitative?) properties of my visual states are their physiological properties. Might these very properties be the qualia Shoemaker speaks of? It is supposed to be obvious, I take it, that these sorts of features are ruled out, because they are not "accessible to introspection" (Shoemaker, private correspondence). These are features of my visual *state*, perhaps, but not of my visual *experience*. They are not *phenomenal* properties.

But then another non-intentional similarity some of my visual states share is that they tend to make me think about going to bed. I think this feature of them *is* accessible to introspection – on any ordinary, pretheoretical construal. Is that a phenomenal property or not? The term "phenomenal" means nothing obvious and untendentious to me, and looks suspiciously like a gesture in the direction leading back to ineffable, private, directly apprehensible ways things seem to one.[4]

I suspect, in fact, that many are unwilling to take my radical challenge seriously largely because they want so much for qualia to be acknowledged. Qualia seem to many people to be the last ditch defense of the inwardness and elusiveness of our minds, a bulwark against creeping mechanism. They are sure there must be *some* sound path from the homely cases to the redoubtable category of the philosophers, since otherwise their last bastion of specialness will be stormed by science.

This special status for these presumed properties has a long and eminent tradition. I believe it was Einstein who once advised us that science could not give us the *taste* of the soup. Could such a wise man have been wrong? Yes, if he is taken to have been trying to remind us of the qualia that hide forever from objective science in the subjective inner sancta of our minds. There are no such things. Another wise man said so – Wittgenstein (1958, esp. pp. 91–100). Actually, what he said was:

> The thing in the box has no place in the language-game at all; not even as a *something*; for the box might even be empty. – No, one can "divide through" by the thing in the box; it cancels out, whatever it is. (p. 100)

and then he went on to hedge his bets by saying "It is not a *something*, but not a *nothing* either! The conclusion was only that a nothing would serve just as well as a something about which nothing could be said" (p. 102). Both Einstein's and Wittgenstein's remarks are endlessly amenable to exegesis, but rather than undertaking to referee this War of the Titans, I choose to take what may well be a more radical stand than Wittgenstein's.[5] Qualia are not even "something about which nothing can be said"; "qualia" is a philosophers' term which fosters[6] nothing but confusion, and refers in the end to no properties or features at all.

3   The traditional paradox regained

Qualia have not always been in good odor among philosophers. Although many have thought, along with Descartes and Locke, that it made sense to talk about private, ineffable properties of minds, others have argued that this is strictly nonsense – however naturally it trips off the tongue. It is worth recalling how qualia were presumably rehabilitated as properties to be taken seriously in the wake of Wittgensteinian and verificationist attacks on them as pseudo-hypotheses. The original version of *intuition pump #3: the inverted spectrum* (Locke 1690: II, xxxii, 15) is a speculation about two people: how do I know that you and I see the same subjective color when we look at something? Since we both learned color words by being shown public colored objects, our verbal behavior will match *even if we experience entirely different subjective colors* The intuition that this hypothesis is systematically unconfirmable (and undisconfirmable, of course) has always been quite robust, but some people have always been tempted to think technology could (in principle) bridge the gap.

Suppose, in *intuition pump #4: the Brainstorm machine*, there were some neuroscientific apparatus that fits on your head and feeds your visual experience into my brain (as in the movie, *Brainstorm*, which is not to be confused with the book, *Brainstorms*). With eyes closed I accurately report everything you are looking at, except that I marvel at how the sky is yellow, the grass red, and so forth. Would this not confirm, empirically, that our qualia were different? But suppose the technician then pulls the plug on the connecting cable, inverts it 180 degrees and reinserts it in the socket. Now I report the sky is blue, the grass green, and so forth. Which is the "right" orientation of the plug? Designing and building such a device would require that its "fidelity" be tuned or calibrated by the normalization of the two subjects' reports – so we would be right back at our evidential starting point. The moral of this intuition pump is that no intersubjective comparison of qualia is possible, even with perfect technology.

So matters stood until someone dreamt up the presumably improved version of the thought experiment: the *intra*personal inverted spectrum. The idea seems to have occurred to several people independently (Gert 1965; Putnam 1965; Taylor 1966; Shoemaker 1969, 1975; Lycan 1973). Probably Block and Fodor (1972) have it in mind when they say "It seems to us that the standard verificationist counterarguments against the view that the 'inverted spectrum' hypothesis is conceptually incoherent are not persuasive" (p. 172). In this version, *intuition pump #5: the neurosurgical prank*, the experiences to be compared are all in one mind. You wake up one morning to find that the grass has turned red, the sky yellow, and so forth. No one else notices any color anomalies in the world, so the problem must be in you. You are entitled, it seems, to conclude that you have undergone visual color qualia inversion (and we later discover, if you like, just how the evil neurophysiologists tampered with your neurons to accomplish this).

Here it seems at first – and indeed for quite a while – that qualia are acceptable properties after all, because propositions about them can be justifiably asserted, empirically verified and even explained. After all, in the imagined case, we can tell a tale in which we confirm a detailed neurophysiological account of the precise etiology of the dramatic change you undergo. It is tempting to suppose, then, that neurophysiological evidence, incorporated into a robust and ramifying theory, would have all the resolving power we could ever need for determining whether or not someone's qualia have actually shifted.

But this is a mistake. It will take some patient exploration to reveal the mistake in depth, but the conclusion can be reached – if not secured – quickly with the help of *intuition pump #6: alternative neurosurgery*. There are (at least) two different ways the evil neurosurgeon might create the inversion effect described in intuition pump #5:

I   Invert one of the "early" qualia-producing channels, e.g. in the optic nerve, so that all relevant neural events "downstream" are the "opposite" of their original and normal values. *Ex hypothesi* this inverts your qualia.

II   Leave all those early pathways intact and simply invert certain memory-access links – whatever it is that accomplishes your tacit (and even unconscious!) comparison of today's hues with those of yore. *Ex hypothesi* this does *not* invert your qualia at all, but just your memory-anchored dispositions to react to them.

On waking up and finding your visual world highly anomalous, you should exclaim "Egad! *Something* has happened! Either my qualia have been inverted or my memory-linked qualia-reactions have been inverted. I wonder which!"

The intrapersonal inverted spectrum thought experiment was widely supposed to be an improvement, since it moved the needed comparison into one subject's head. But now we can see that this is an illusion, since the link to earlier experiences, the link via memory, is analogous to the imaginary cable that might link two subjects in the original version.

This point is routinely – one might say traditionally – missed by the constructors of "intrasubjective inverted spectrum" thought experiments, who suppose that the subject's *noticing the difference* – surely a vivid experience of discovery by the subject – would have to be an instance of (directly? incorrigibly?) recognizing the difference *as a shift in qualia*. But as my example shows, we could achieve the same startling effect in a subject without tampering with his presumed qualia at all. Since *ex hypothesi* the two different surgical invasions can produce exactly the same introspective effects while only one operation inverts the qualia, nothing in the subject's experience can favor one of the hypotheses over the other. So unless he seeks outside help, the state of his own qualia must be as unknowable to him as the state of anyone else's qualia. Hardly the privileged access or immediate acquaintance or direct apprehension the friends of qualia had supposed "phenomenal features" to enjoy!

The outcome of this series of thought experiments is an intensification of the "verificationist" argument against qualia. *If* there are qualia, they are even less accessible to our ken than we had thought. Not only are the classical intersubjective comparisons impossible (as the Brainstorm machine shows), but we cannot tell in our own cases whether our qualia have been inverted – at least not by introspection. It is surely tempting at this point – especially to non-philosophers – to decide that this paradoxical result must be an artifact of some philosophical misanalysis or other, the sort of thing that might well happen if you took a perfectly good pretheoretical notion – our everyday notion of qualia – and illicitly stretched it beyond the breaking point. The philosophers have made a mess; let them clean it up; meanwhile we others can get back to work, relying as always on our sober and unmetaphysical acquaintance with qualia.

Overcoming this ubiquitous temptation is the task of the next section, which will seek to establish the unsalvageable incoherence of the hunches that lead to the paradox by looking more closely at their sources and their motivation.

4 Making mistakes about qualia

The idea that people might be mistaken about their own qualia is at the heart of the ongoing confusion, and must be explored in more detail, and with somewhat more realistic examples, if we are to see the delicate role it plays.

Intuition pump #7: Chase and Sanborn. Once upon a time there were two coffee tasters, Mr Chase and Mr Sanborn, who worked for Maxwell House.[7] Along with half a dozen other coffee tasters, their job was to ensure that the taste of Maxwell House stayed constant, year after year. One day, about six years after Mr Chase had come to work for Maxwell House, he confessed to Mr Sanborn:

> I hate to admit it, but I'm not enjoying this work any more. When I came to Maxwell House six years ago, I thought Maxwell House coffee was the best-tasting coffee in the world. I was proud to have a share in the responsibility for preserving that flavor over the years. And we've done our job well; the coffee tastes just the same today as it tasted when I arrived. But, you know, I no longer like it! My tastes have changed. I've become a more sophisticated coffee drinker. I no longer like *that taste* at all.

Sanborn greeted this revelation with considerable interest. "It's funny you should mention it," he replied, "for something rather similar has happened to me." He went on:

> When I arrived here, shortly before you did, I, like you, thought Maxwell House coffee was tops in flavor. And now I, like you, really don't care for the coffee we're making. But *my* tastes haven't changed; my . . . *tasters* have changed. That is, I think something has gone wrong with my taste buds or some other part of my taste-analyzing perceptual machinery. Maxwell House coffee doesn't taste to me the way it used to taste; if only it did, I'd still love it, for I still think *that taste* is the best taste in coffee. Now I'm not saying we haven't done our job well. You other tasters all agree that the taste is the same, and I must admit that on a day-to-day basis I can detect no change either. So it must be my problem alone. I guess I'm no longer cut out for this work.

Chase and Sanborn are alike in one way at least: they both used to like Maxwell House coffee, and now neither likes it. But they claim to be different in another way. Maxwell House tastes to Chase just the way it always did, but not so for Sanborn. But can we take their protestations at face value? Must we? Might one or both of them simply be wrong? Might their predicaments be importantly the same and their apparent disagreement more a difference in manner of expression than in experiential or psychological state? Since both of them make claims that depend on the reliability of their memories, is there any way to check on this reliability?

My reason for introducing two characters in the example is not to set up an interpersonal comparison between how the coffee tastes to Chase and how it tastes to Sanborn, but just to exhibit, side-by-side, two poles between which cases of intrapersonal experiential shift can wander. Such cases of intrapersonal experiential shift, and the possibility of adaptation to them, or interference with memory in them, have often been discussed in the literature on qualia, but without sufficient attention to the details, in my opinion. Let us look at Chase first. Falling in for the nonce with the received manner of speaking, it appears at first that there are the following possibilities:

(a) Chase's coffee-taste-qualia have stayed constant, while his reactive attitudes to those qualia, devolving on his canons of aesthetic judgment, etc., have shifted – which is what he seems, in his informal, casual way, to be asserting.

(b) Chase is simply wrong about the constancy of his qualia; they have shifted gradually and imperceptibly over the years, while his standards of taste haven't budged – in spite of his delusions about having become more sophisticated. He is in the state Sanborn claims to be in, but just lacks Sanborn's self-knowledge.

(c) Chase is in some predicament intermediate between (a) and (b); his qualia have shifted some *and* his standards of judgment have also slipped.

Sanborn's case seems amenable to three counterpart versions:

(a) Sanborn is right; his qualia have shifted, due to some sort of derangement in his perceptal machinery, but his standards have indeed remained constant.

(b) Sanborn's standards have shifted unbeknownst to him. He is thus misremembering his past experiences, in what we might call a nostalgia effect. Think of the familiar experience of returning to some object from your childhood (a classroom desk, a tree-house) and finding it much smaller than you remember it to have been. Presumably as you grew larger your internal standard for what was large grew with you somehow, but your memories (which are stored as fractions or multiples of that standard) didn't compensate, and hence when you consult your memory, it returns a distorted judgment. Sanborn's nostalgia-tinged memory of good old Maxwell House is similarly distorted. (There are obviously many different ways this impressionistic sketch of a memory mechanism could be implemented, and there is considerable experimental work in cognitive psychology that suggests how different hypotheses about such mechanisms could be tested.)

(c) As before, Sanborn's state is some combination of (a) and (b).

I think that everyone writing about qualia today would agree that there are all these possibilities for Chase and Sanborn. I know of no one these days who is tempted to defend the high line on infallibility or incorrigibility that would declare that alternative (a) is – and must be – the truth in each case, since people just cannot be wrong about such private, subjective matters.[8]

Since quandaries are about to arise, however, it might be wise to review in outline why the attractiveness of the infallibilist position is only superficial, so it won't recover its erstwhile allure when the going gets tough. First, in the wake of Wittgenstein (1958) and Malcolm (1956, 1959) we have seen that one way to buy such infallibility is to acquiesce in the complete evaporation of content (Dennet 1976). "Imagine someone saying: 'But I know how tall I am!' and laying his hand on top of his head to prove it." (Wittgenstein 1958, p. 96) By diminishing one's claim until there is nothing left to be right or wrong about, one can achieve a certain empty invincibility, but that will not do in this case. One of the things we want Chase to be right about (if he is right) is that he is not in Sanborn's predicament, so if the claim is to be viewed as infalliable, it can hardly be because it declines to assert anything.

There is a strong temptation, I have found, to respond to my claims in this paper more or less as follows: "But after all is said and done, there is still something I know in a special way: I know *how it is with me right now*." But if absolutely nothing follows from this presumed knowledge – nothing, for instance, that would shed any light on the different psychological claims that might be true of Chase or Sanborn – what is the point of asserting that one has it? Perhaps people just want to reaffirm their sense of proprietorship over their own conscious states.

The infallibilist line on qualia treats them as properties of one's experience one cannot in principle misdiscover, and this is a mysterious doctrine (at least as mysterious as papal infallibility) unless we shift the emphasis a little and treat qualia as *logical constructs* out of subjects' qualia-judgments: a subject's experience has the quale *F* if and only if the subject judges his experience to have quale *F*. We can then treat such judgings as constitutive acts, in effect, bringing the quale into existence by the same sort of license as novelists have to determine the hair color of their characters by fiat. We do not ask how Dostoevski knows that Raskolnikov's hair is light brown.

There is a limited use for such interpretations of subjects' protocols, I have argued (Dennett 1978a; 1979, esp. pp. 109–10; 1982), but they will not help the defenders of qualia here. Logical constructs out of judgments must be viewed as akin to theorists' fictions, and the friends of qualia want the existence of a particular quale in any particular case to be an empirical fact in good standing, not a theorists's useful interpretive fiction, else it will not loom as a challenge to functionalism or materialism or third-person, objective science.

It seems easy enough, then, to dream up empirical tests that would tend to confirm Chase and Sanborn's different tales, but if passing such tests could support their authority (that is to say, their reliability), failing the tests would have to undermine it. The price you pay for the possibility of empirically confirming your assertions is the outside chance of being discredited. The friends of qualia are prepared, today, to pay that price, but perhaps only because they haven't reckoned how the bargain they have struck will subvert the concept they want to defend.

Consider how we could shed light on the question of where the truth lies in the particular cases of Chase and Sanborn, even if we might not be able to settle the matter definitively. It is obvious that there might be telling objective support for one extreme version or another of their stories. Thus if Chase is unable to reidentify coffees, teas, and wines in blind tastings in which only minutes intervene between first and second sips, his claim to *know* that Maxwell House tastes just the same to him now as it did six years ago will be seriously undercut. Alternatively, if he does excellently in blind tastings, and exhibits considerable knowledge about the canons of coffee style (if such there be), his claim to have become a more sophisticated taster will be supported. Exploitation of the standard principles of inductive testing – basically Mill's method of differences – can go a long way toward indicating what sort of change has occurred in Chase or Sanborn – a change near the brute perceptual processing end of the spectrum or a change near the ultimate reactive judgment end of the spectrum. And as Shoemaker (1982) and others have noted, physiological measures, suitably interpreted in some larger theoretical framework, could also weight the scales in favor of one extreme or the other. For instance, the well-studied phenomenon of induced illusory boundaries (see figure 1) has often been claimed to be a particularly "cognitive" illusion, dependent on "top down" processes, and hence, presumably, near the reactive judgment end of the spectrum, but recent experimental work (Von der Heydt et al. 1984) has revealed that "edge detector" neurons *relatively* low in the visual pathways – in area 18 of the visual cortex – are as responsive to illusory edges as to real light–dark boundaries on the retina, suggesting (but not quite proving, since these might somehow still be "descending effects") that illusory contours are not imposed from on high, but generated quite early in visual processing. One can imagine discovering a similarly "early" anomaly in the pathways leading from taste buds to judgment in Sanborn, for instance, tending

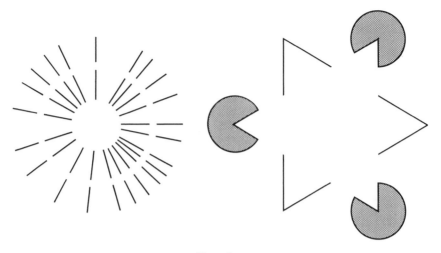

Figure 1

to confirm his claim that he has suffered some change in his basic perceptual – as opposed to judgmental – machinery.

But let us not overestimate the resolving power of such empirical testing. The space in each case between the two poles represented by possibility (a) and possibility (b) would be occupied by phenomena that were the product, somehow, of two factors in varying proportion: roughly, dispositions to generate or produce qualia and dispositions to react to the qualia once they are produced. (That is how our intuitive picture of qualia would envisage it.) Qualia are supposed to affect our action or behavior only via the intermediary of our judgments about them, so any behavioral test, such as a discrimination or memory test, since it takes acts based on judgments as its primary data, can give us direct evidence only about the *resultant* of our two factors. In extreme cases we can have indirect evidence to suggest that one factor has varied a great deal, the other factor hardly at all, and we can test the hypothesis further by checking the relative sensitivity of the subject to variations in the conditions that presumably alter the two component factors. But such indirect testing cannot be expected to resolve the issue when the effects are relatively small – when, for instance, our rival hypotheses are Chase's preferred hypothesis (a) and the minor variant to the effect that his qualia have shifted *a little* and his standards *less than he thinks*. This will be true even when we include in our data any unintended or unconscious behavioral effects, for their import will be ambiguous (Would a longer response latency in Chase today be indicative of a process of "attempted qualia renormalization" or "extended aesthetic evaluation"?)

The limited evidential power of neurophysiology comes out particularly clearly if we imagine a case of adaptation. Suppose, in *intuition pump #8: the gradual post-operative recovery*, that we have somehow "surgically inverted" Chase's taste bud connections in the standard imaginary way: post-operatively, sugar tastes salty, salt tastes sour, etc. But suppose further – and this is as realistic a supposition as its denial – that Chase has subsequently compensated – as revealed by his behavior. He now *says* that the sugary substance we place on his tongue is sweet, and no longer favors gravy on his ice cream. Let us suppose the compensation is so thorough that on all behavioral and verbal tests his performance is indistinguishable from that of normal subjects – and from his own pre-surgical performance.

If all the internal compensatory adjustment has been accomplished early in the process – intuitively, pre-qualia – then his qualia today are restored to just as they were (relative to external sources of stimulation) before the surgery. If on the other hand some or all of the internal compensatory adjustment is post-qualia, then his qualia have not been renormalized *even if he thinks they have*. But the physiological facts will not in themselves shed any light on where in the stream of physiological process twixt tasting and telling to draw the line at which the putative qualia appear as properties of that phase of the process. The qualia are the "immediate or phenomenal" properties, of course, but this description will not serve to locate the right phase in the physiological stream, for, echoing intuition pump #6, there will always be at least two possible ways of interpreting the neurophysiological theory, however it comes out. Suppose our physiological theory tells us (in as much detail as you like) that the compensatory effect in him has been achieved by an *adjustment in the memory-accessing process* that is required for our victim to compare today's hues to those of yore. There are *still* two stories that might be told:

I Chase's current qualia are still abnormal, but thanks to the revision in his memory-accessing process, he has in effect adjusted his memories of how things used to taste, so he no longer notices any anomaly.

II The memory-comparison step occurs just prior to the qualia phase in taste perception; thanks to the revision, it now *yields* the same old qualia for the same stimulation.

In (I) the qualia contribute to the input, in effect, to the memory-comparator. In (II) they are part of the output of the memory-comparator. These seem to be two substantially different hypotheses, but the physiological evidence, no matter how well developed, will not tell us on which side of memory to put the qualia. Chase's introspective evidence will not settle the issue between (I) and (II) either, since *ex hypothesi* those stories are not reliably distinguishable by him. Remember that it was in order to confirm or disconfirm Chase's opinion that we turned to the neurophysiological evidence in the first place. We can hardly use his opinion in the end to settle the matter between our rival neurophysiological theories. Chase may think that he thinks his experiences are the same as before *because* they really are (and he remembers accurately how it used to be), but he must admit that he has no introspective resources for distinguishing that possibility from alternative (I), on which he thinks things are as they used to be *because* his memory of how they used to be has been distorted by his new compensatory habits.

Faced with their subject's systematic neutrality, the physiologists may have their own reasons for preferring (I) to (II) or vice versa, for they may have *appropriated* the term "qualia" to their own theoretical ends, to denote some family of detectable properties that strike them as playing an important role in their neurophysiological theory of perceptual recognition and memory. Chase or Sanborn might complain – in the company of more than a few philosophical spokesmen – that these properties the neurophysiologists choose to call "qualia" are not the qualia they are speaking of. The scientists' retort is: "If we cannot distinguish (I) from (II), we certainly cannot support either of your claims. If you want our support, you must relinquish your concept of qualia."

What is striking about this is not just that the empirical methods would fall short of distinguishing what seem to be such different claims about qualia, but that they would fall short *in spite of being better evidence than the subject's own introspective convictions.* For the subject's own judgments, like the behaviors or actions that express them, are the resultant of our two postulated factors, and cannot discern the component proportions any better than external behavioral tests can. Indeed, a subject's "introspective" convictions will generally be *worse* evidence than what outside observers can gather. For if our subject is – as most are – a "naive subject," unacquainted with statistical data about his own case or similar cases, his immediate, frank judgments are, evidentially, like any naive observer's perceptual judgments about factors in the outside world. Chase's intuitive judgments about his qualia constancy are no better off, epistemically, than his intuitive judgments about, say, lighting intensity constancy or room temperature constancy – or his own body temperature constancy. Moving to a condition inside his body does not change the intimacy of the epistemic relation in any special way. Is Chase running a fever or just feeling feverish? Unless he has taken steps to calibrate and cross-check his own performance, his opinion that his fever-perception apparatus is undisturbed is no better than a hunch. Similarly, Chase may have a strongly held opinion about the degree to which his taste-perceiving apparatus has maintained its integrity, and the degree to which his judgment has evolved through sophistication, but pending the results of the sort of laborious third-person testing just imagined, he would be a fool to claim to know – especially to know directly or immediately – that his was a pure case (a), closer to (a) than to (b), or a case near (b).

He is on quite firm ground, epistemically, when he reports that *the relation* between his coffee-sipping activity and his judging activity has changed. Recall that this is the factor that Chase and Sanborn have in common: they used to like Maxwell House; now they don't. But unless he carries out on himself the sorts of tests others might carry out on him, his convictions about what has stayed constant (or nearly so) and what has shifted *must be sheer guessing.*

But then qualia – supposing for the time being that we know what we are talking about – must lose one of their "essential" second-order properties: far from being directly or immediately apprehensible properties of our experience, they are properties whose changes or constancies are either entirely beyond our ken, or inferrable (at best) from "third-peson" examinations of our behavioral and physiological reaction patterns (if Chase and Sanborn acquiesce in the neurophysiologists' sense of the term). On this view, Chase and Sanborn should be viewed not as introspectors capable of a privileged view of these properties, but as autopsychologists, theorists whose convictions about the properties of their own nervous systems are based not only on their "immediate" or current experiential convictions, but also on their appreciation of the import of events they remember from the recent past.

There are, as we shall see, good reasons for neurophysiologists and other "objective, third-person" theorists to single out such a class of properties to study. But they are not qualia, for the simple reason that one's epistemic relation to them is *exactly* the same as one's epistemic relation to such external, but readily – if fallibly – detectable, properties as room temperature or weight. The idea that one should consult an outside expert, and perform elaborate behavioral tests on oneself in order to confirm what qualia one had, surely takes us too far away from our original idea of qualia as properties with which we have a particularly intimate acquaintance.

So perhaps we have taken a wrong turning. The doctrine that led to this embarrassing result was the doctrine that sharply distinguished qualia from their (normal) effects on reactions. Consider Chase again. He claims that coffee tastes "just the same" as it always did, but he admits – nay insists – that his reaction to "that taste" is not what it used to be. That is, he pretends to be able to divorce his apprehension (or recollection) of the quale – the taste, in ordinary parlance – from his different reactions to the taste. But this apprehension or recollection is itself a reaction to the presumed quale, so some sleight-of-hand is being perpetrated – innocently no doubt – by Chase. So suppose instead that Chase had insisted that precisely *because* his reaction was now different, the taste had changed for him. (When he told his wife his original tale, she said "Don't be silly! Once you add the dislike you change the experience!" – and the more he thought about it, the more he decided she was right.)

Intuition pump #9: the experienced beer drinker. It is familiarly said that beer, for example, is an acquired taste; one gradually trains oneself – or just comes – to enjoy that flavor. What flavor? The flavor of the first sip? No one could like *that* flavor, an experienced beer drinker might retort:

> Beer tastes different to the experienced beer drinker. If beer went on tasting to me the way the first sip tasted, I would never have gone on drinking beer! Or to put the same point the other way around, if my first sip of beer had tasted to me the way my most recent sip just tasted, I would never have had to acquire the taste in the first place! I would have loved the first sip as much as the one I just enjoyed.

If we let this speech pass, we must admit that beer is *not* an acquired taste. No one comes to enjoy *the way the first sip tasted*. Instead, prolonged beer drinking leads people to experience a taste they enjoy, but precisely their enjoying the taste guarantees that it is not the taste they first experienced.[9]

But this conclusion, if it is accepted, wreaks havoc of a different sort with the traditional philosophical view of qualia. For if it is admitted that one's attitudes towards, or reactions to, experiences are in any way and in any degree constitutive of their experiential qualities, so that a change in reactivity *amounts to* or *guarantees* a change in the property, then those properties, those "qualitative or phenomenal features," cease to be "intrinsic" properties, and in fact become paradigmatically extrinsic, relational properties.

Properties that "seem intrinsic" at first often turn out on more careful analysis to be relational. Bennett (1965) is the author of *intuition pump #10: the world-wide eugenics experiment*. He draws our attention to phenol-thio-urea, a substance which tastes very bitter to three-fourths of humanity, and as tasteless as water to the rest. Is it bitter? Since the reactivity to phenol-thio-urea is genetically transmitted, we could make it paradigmatically bitter by performing a large-scale breeding experiment: prevent the people to whom it is tasteless from breeding, and in a few generations phenol would be as bitter as anything to be found in the world. But we could also (in principle!) perform the contrary feat of mass "eugenics"' and thereby make phenol paradigmatically tasteless – as tasteless as water – without ever touching phenol. Clearly, public bitterness or tastelessness is not an intrinsic property of phenol-thio-urea but a relational property, since the property is changed by a change in the reference class of normal detectors.

The public versions of perceptual "qualia" all *seem* intrinsic, in spite of their relationality. They are not alone. Think of the "felt value"' of a dollar (or whatever your native currency is). "How much is that in *real* money?" the American tourist is reputed to have asked, hoping to translate a foreign price onto the scale of "intrinsic value" he keeps in his head. As Elster (1985) claims, "there is a tendency to overlook the implicitly relational character of certain monadic predicates." Walzer (1985) points out that ". . . a ten-dollar bill might seem to have a life of its own as a thing of value, but, as Elster suggests, its value implicitly depends on 'other people who are prepared to accept money as payment for goods.'" But even as one concedes this, there is still a tendency to reserve something subjective, felt value, as an "intrinsic" property of that ten-dollar bill. But as we now see, such intrinsic properties cannot be properties to which a subject's access is in any way privileged.

Which way should Chase go? Should he take his wife's advice and declare that since he can't stand the coffee any more, it no longer tastes the same to him (it used to taste good and now it tastes bad)? Or should he say that really, in a certain sense, it does taste the way it always did or at least it sort of does – when you subtract the fact that it tastes so bad now, of course?

We have now reached the heart of my case. The fact is that we have to ask Chase which way he wants to go, and there really are two drastically different alternatives available to him *if we force the issue*. Which way would *you* go? Which concept of qualia did you "always have in the back of your mind," guiding your imagination as you thought about theories? If you acknowledge that the answer is not obvious, and especially if you complain that this forced choice drives apart two aspects that you had supposed united in your pretheoretic concept, you support my contention that there is no secure foundation in ordinary "folk psychology" for a concept of qualia. We *normally* think in a confused and potentially incoherent way when we think about the ways things seem to us.

When Chase thinks of "that taste" he thinks equivocally or vaguely. He harkens back in memory to earlier experiences but need not try – or be able – to settle whether he is including any or all of his reactions or excluding them from what he intends by "that taste." His state then and his state now are different – *that* he can avow with confidence – but he has no "immediate" resources for making a finer distinction, nor any need to do so.[10]

This suggests that qualia are no more essential to the professional vocabulary of the phenomenologist (or professional coffee taster) than to the vocabulary of the physiologist (Dennett 1978b). To see this, consider again the example of my dislike of cauliflower. Imagine now, in *intuition pump #11: the cauliflower cure*, that someone offers me a pill to cure my loathing for cauliflower. He promises that after I swallow this pill cauliflower will taste exactly the same to me as it always has, but I will like that taste! "Hang on," I might reply. "I think you may have just contradicted yourself." But in any event I take the pill and it works. I become an instant cauliflower-appreciater, but if I am asked which of the two possible effects (Chase-type or Sanborn-type) the pill has had on me, I will be puzzled, and will find nothing *in my experience* to shed light on the question. Of course I recognize that the taste is (sort of) the same – the pill hasn't made cauliflower taste like chocolate cake, after all – but at the same time my experience is so different now that I resist saying that cauliflower tastes the way it used to taste. There is in any event no reason to be cowed into supposing that my cauliflower experiences have some intrinsic properties behind, or in addition to, their various dispositional, reaction-provoking properties.

"But in principle there has to be a right answer to the question of how it is, intrinsically, with you now, even if you are unable to say with any confidence!" Why? Would one say the same about all other properties of experience? Consider *intuition pump #12: visual field inversion created by wearing inverting spectacles*, a phenomenon which has been empirically studied for years. (G. M. Stratton published the pioneering work in 1896, and J. J. Gibson and Ivo Kohler were among the principal investigators. For an introductory account, see Gregory 1977.) After wearing inverting spectacles for several days subjects make an astonishingly successful adaptation. Suppose we pressed on them this question: "Does your adaptation consist in your re-inverting your visual field, or in your turning the rest of your mind upside-down in a host of compensations?" If they demur, may we insist that there has to be a right answer, even if they cannot say with any confidence which it is? Such an insistence would lead directly to a new version of the old inverted spectrum thought experiment: "How do I know whether some people see things upside-down (but are perfectly used to it), while others see things right-side-up?"

Only a very naive view of visual perception could sustain the idea that one's visual field has a property of right-side-upness or upside-downness *independent of one's dispositions to react to it* – "intrinsic right-side-upness" we could call it. (See my discussion of the properties of the "images" processed by the robot SHAKEY, in Dennett 1982.) So not all properties of conscious experience invite or require treatment as "intrinsic"' properties. Is there something distinguishing about a certain subclass of properties (the "qualitative or phenomenal" subclass, presumably) that forces us to treat them – unlike subjective right-side-upness – as intrinsic properties? If not, such properties have no role to play, in either physiological theories of experience, or in introspective theories.

Some may be inclined to argue this way: I can definitely imagine the experience of "spectrum inversion" from the inside; after all I have actually experienced temporary effects of the same type, such as the "taste displacement" effect of the maple syrup on the orange juice. What is imaginable, or actual, is possible. Therefore spectrum inversion or displacement (in all sensory modalities) is possible. But such phenomena just *are* the inversion or displacement of qualia, or intrinsic subjective properties. Therefore there must be qualia: intrinsic subjective properties.

This is fallacious. What one imagines and what one says one imagines may be two different things. To imagine visual field inversion, of the sort Stratton and Kohler's subjects experienced, is not necessarily to imagine the absolute inversion of a visual field (even if that is what it "feels like" to the subjects). Less obviously, imagining – as vividly as you like – a case of subjective color-perception displacement is not necessarily imagining what that phenomenon is typically called by philosophers: an inverted or displaced spectrum *of qualia*. In so far as that term carries the problematic implications scouted here, there is no support for its use arising simply from the vividness or naturalness of the imagined possibility.

If there are no such properties as qualia, does that mean that "spectrum inversion" is impossible? Yes and no. Spectrum inversion as classically debated is impossible, but something like it is perfectly possible – something that is as like "qualia inversion" as visual field inversion is like the impossible *absolute* visual image inversion we just dismissed.

5   Some puzzling real cases

It is not enough to withhold our theoretical allegiances until the sunny day when the philosophers complete the tricky task of purifying the everyday concept of qualia. Unless we take active steps to shed this source concept, and replace it with better ideas, it will continue to cripple our imaginations and systematically distort our attempts to understand the phenomena already encountered.

What we find, if we look at the actual phenomena of anomalies of color perception, for instance, amply bears out our suspicions about the inadequacy of the traditional notion of qualia. Several varieties of *cerebral achromatopsia* (brain based impairment of color vision) have been reported, and while there remains much that is unsettled about their analysis, there is little doubt that the philosophical thought experiments have underestimated or overlooked the possibilities for counter-intuitive collections of symptoms, as a few very brief excerpts from case histories will reveal.

> Objects to the right of the vertical meridian appeared to be of normal hue, while to the left they were perceived only in shades of gray, though without distortions of form. . . . He was unable to recognize or name any color in any portion of the left field of either eye, including bright reds, blues, greens and yellows. As soon as any portion of the colored object crossed the vertical meridian, he was able to instantly recognize and accurately name its color. (Damasio et al. 1980).

This patient would seem at first to be unproblematically describable as suffering a shift or loss of color qualia in the left hemifield, but there is a problem of interpretation here, brought about by another case:

> The patient failed in all tasks in which he was required to match the seen color with its spoken name. Thus, the patient failed to give the names of colors and failed to

choose a color in response to its name. By contrast, he succeeded on all tasks where the matching was either purely verbal or purely nonverbal. Thus, he could give verbally the names of colors corresponding to named objects and vice versa. He could match seen colors to each other and to pictures of objects and could sort colors without error. (Geschwind and Fusillo 1966)

This second patient was quite unaware of any deficit. He "never replied with a simple 'I don't know' to the demand for naming a color" (Geschwind and Fusillo 1966, p. 140). There is a striking contrast between these two patients; both have impaired ability to name the colors of things in at least part of their visual field, but whereas the former is acutely aware of his deficit, the latter is not. Does this difference make all the difference about qualia? If so, what on earth should we say about this third patient?

His other main complaint was that "everything looked black or grey" and this caused him some difficulty in everyday life. . . . He had considerable difficulty recognizing and naming colours. He would, for example, usually describe bright red objects as either red or black, bright green objects as either green, blue or black, and bright blue objects as black. The difficulty appeared to be perceptual and he would make remarks suggesting this; for example when shown a bright red object he said "a dirty smudgy red, not as red as you would normally see red." Colours of lesser saturation or brightness were described in such terms as "grey" "off-white" or "black," but if told to guess at the colour, he would be correct on about 50 per cent of occasions, being notably less successful with blues and greens than reds. (Meadows 1974)

This man's awareness of his deficit is problematic to say the least. It contrasts rather sharply with yet another case:

One morning in November 1977, upon awakening, she noted that although she was able to see details of objects and people, colors appeared "drained out" and "not true." She had no other complaint . . . her vision was good, 20/20 in each eye . . . The difficulty in color perception persisted, and she had to seek the advice of her husband to choose what to wear. Eight weeks later she noted that she could no longer recognize the faces of her husband and daughter . . . [So in] addition to achromatopsia, the patient had prosopagnosia, but her linguistic and cognitive performances were otherwise unaffected. The patient was able to tell her story cogently and to have remarkable insight about her defects. (Damasio et al. 1980).

As Meadows notes, "Some patients thus complain that their vision for colours is defective while others have no spontaneous complaint but show striking abnormalities on testing."

What should one say in these cases? When no complaint is volunteered but the patient shows an impairment in color vision, is this a sign that his qualia are unaffected? ("His capacities to discriminate are terribly impaired, but luckily for him, his inner life is untouched by this merely public loss!") We could line up the qualia this way, but equally we could claim that the patient has simply not noticed the perhaps gradual draining away or inversion or merging of his qualia revealed by his poor performance. ("So slowly did his inner life lose its complexity and variety that he never noticed how impoverished it had become!") What if our last patient described her complaint just as she did above, but performed normally on testing? One hypothesis would be that her qualia had indeed, as she suggested, become washed out. Another would be that in the light of her sterling performance on the color discrimination tests, her qualia were fine; she was suffering from some hysterical or depressive anomaly, a sort of color-vision hypochondria that makes her complain about a loss of color perception. Or perhaps one could claim that her qualia were untouched; her disorder was purely verbal: an anomalous understanding of the words she uses to describe her experience. (Other startlingly specific color-*word* disorders have been reported in the literature.)

The traditional concept leads us to overlook genuine possibilities. Once we have learned of the curious deficit reported by Geschwind and Fusillo, for instance, we realize that our first patient was never tested to see if he could still sort colors seen on the left or pass other non-naming, non-verbal color-blindness tests. Those tests are by no means superfluous. Perhaps he would have passsed them; perhaps, *in spite of what he says* his qualia are as intact for the left field as for the right! – if we take the capacity to pass such tests as "criterial." Perhaps his problem is "purely verbal." If your reaction to this hypothesis is that this is impossible, that must mean you are making his verbal, reporting behavior sovereign in settling the issue – but then you must rule out a priori the possibility of the condition I described as color-vision hypochondria.

There is no prospect of *finding* the answers to these brain-teasers in our everyday usage or the intuitions it arouses, but it is of course open to the philosopher to *create* an edifice of theory defending a particular set of interlocking proposals. The problem is that although normally a certain family of stimulus and bodily conditions yields a certain family of effects, any particular effect can be disconnected, and our intuitions do not tell us which effects are "essential" to quale identity or qualia constancy (cf. Dennett 1978a, ch. 11). It seems fairly obvious to me that none of the real problems of interpretation that face us in these curious cases is advanced by any analysis of how the concept of *qualia* is to be applied – unless we wish to propose a novel, technical sense for which the traditional term might be appropriated. But that would be at least a tactical error: the intuitions that surround and *purport* to anchor the current understanding of the term are revealed to be in utter disarray when confronted with these cases.

My informal sampling shows that some philosophers have strong opinions about each case and how it should be described in terms of qualia, but they find they are in strident (and ultimately comic) disagreement with other philosophers about how these "obvious'" descriptions should go. Other philosophers discover they really don't know what to say – not because there aren't enough facts presented in the descriptions of the cases, but because it begins to dawn on them that they haven't really known what they were talking about over the years.

6 Filling the vacuum

If qualia are such a bad idea, why have they seemed to be such a good idea? Why does it seem as if there are these intrinsic, ineffable, private, "qualitative" properties in our experience? A review of the presumptive second-order properties of the properties of our conscious experiences will permit us to diagnose their attractiveness and find suitable substitutes. (For a similar exercise see Kitcher 1979).

Consider "intrinsic" first. It is far from clear what an intrinsic property would be. Although the term has had a certain vogue in philosophy, and often seems to secure an important contrast, there has never been an accepted definition of the second-order property of intrinsicality. If even such a brilliant theory-monger as David Lewis can try and fail, by his own admission, to define the extrinsic/intrinsic distinction coherently, we can begin to wonder if the concept deserves our further attention after all. In fact Lewis (1983) begins his survey of versions of the distinction by listing as one option: "We could Quine the lot, give over the entire family as unintelligible and dispensable," but he dismisses the suggestion immediately: "That would be absurd" (p. 197). In the end, however, his effort to salvage the accounts of Chisholm (1976) and Kim (1982) are stymied, and he conjectures that "if we still want to break in we had best try another window" (p. 200).

Even if we are as loath as Lewis is to abandon the distinction, shouldn't we be suspicious of the following curious fact? If challenged to explain the idea of an intrinsic property to a neophyte, many people would hit on the following sort of example: consider Tom's ball; it has many properties, such as its being made of rubber from India, its belonging to Tom, its having spent the last week in the closet, and its redness. All but the last of these are clearly *relational* or *extrinsic* properties of the ball. Its redness, however, is an intrinsic property. Except this isn't so. Ever since Boyle and Locke we have known better. Redness – public redness – is a quintessentially relational property, as many thought experiments about "secondary qualities" show. (One of the first was Berkeley's (1713) pail of lukewarm water, and one of the best is Bennett's (1965) phenol-thio-urea.) The seductive step, on learning that public redness (like public bitterness, etc.) is a relational property after all, is to cling to intrinsicality (*"something* has to be intrinsic!") and move it into the subject's head. It is often thought, in fact, that if we take a Lockean, relational position on objective bitterness, redness, etc., we *must* complete our account of the relations in question by appeal to non-relational, intrinsic properties. If what it is to be objectively bitter is to produce a certain effect in the members of the class of normal observers, we must be able to specify that effect, and distinguish it from the effect produced by objective sourness and so forth.

What else could distinguish this effect but some intrinsic property? Why not another relational or extrinsic property? The relational treatment of monetary value does not require, for its completion, the supposition of items of intrinsic value (value independent of the valuers' dispositions to react behaviorally). The claim that certain perceptual properties are different is, in the absence of any supporting argument, just question-begging. It will not do to say that it is just obvious that they are intrinsic. It may have seemed obvious to some, but the considerations raised by Chase's quandary show that it is far from obvious that any intrinsic property (whatever that comes to) could play the role of anchor for the Lockean relational treatment of the public perceptual properties.

Why not give up intrinsicality as a second-order property altogether, at least pending resolution of the disarray of philosophical opinion about what intrinsicality might be? Until such time the insistence that qualia are the intrinsic properties of experience is an empty gesture at best; no one could claim that it provides a clear, coherent, understood prerequisite for theory.[11]

What, then, of ineffability? Why does it seem that our conscious experiences have ineffable properties? Because they do have *practically* ineffable properties. Suppose, in *intuition pump #13: the osprey cry*, that I have never heard the cry of an osprey, even in a recording, but know roughly, from reading my bird books, what to listen for: "a series of short, sharp, cheeping whistles, *cheep cheep* or *chewk chewk*, etc; sounds annoyed" (Peterson 1947) (or words to that effect or better). The verbal decription gives me a partial confinement of the logical space of possible bird cries. On its basis I can rule out many bird calls I have heard or might hear, but there is still a broad range of discriminable-by-me possibilities within which the actuality lies hidden from me like a needle in a haystack.

Then one day, armed with both my verbal description and my binoculars, I identify an osprey visually, and then hear its cry. So *that's* what it sounds like, I say to myself, ostending – it seems – a particular mental complex of intrinsic, ineffable qualia. I dub the complex "S" (*pace* Wittgenstein), rehearse it in short term memory, check it against the bird book descriptions, and see that while the verbal descriptions are true, accurate and even poetically evocative – I decide I could not do better with a thousand words – they still fall short of *capturing* the qualia-complex I have called *S*. In fact, that is why I need the neologism "*S*" to refer directly to the ineffable property I cannot pick out by description. My perceptual experience has pinpointed for me the location of the osprey cry in the logical space of possibilities in a way verbal description could not.

But tempting as this view of matters is, it is overstated. First of all, it is obvious that from a single experience of this sort I don't – can't – know how to generalize to other osprey calls. Would a cry that differed only in being half an octave higher also be an osprey call? That is an empirical, ornithological question for which my experience provides scant evidence. But moreover – and this is a psychological, not ornithological, matter – I don't and can't know, from a single such experience, which physical variations and constancies in stimuli would produce an indistinguishable experience in me. Nor can I know whether I would react the same (have the same experience) if I were presented with what was, by all physical measures, a re-stimulation identical to the first. I cannot know the modulating effect, if any, of variations in my body (or psyche).

This inscrutability of projection is surely one of the sources of plausibility for Wittgenstein's skepticism regarding the possibility of a private language.

> Wittgenstein emphasizes that ostensive definitions are always in principle capable of being misunderstood, even the ostensive definition of a color word such as "sepia". How someone understands the word is exhibited in the way someone goes on, "the use that he makes of the word defined". One may go on in the right way given a purely minimal explanation, while on the other hand one may go on in another way no matter how many clarifications are added, since these too can be misunderstood ... (Kripke 1982, p. 83; see also pp. 40–6).

But what is inscrutable in a single glance, and somewhat ambiguous after limited testing, can come to be justifiably seen as the deliverance of a highly specific, reliable, and projectible property-detector, once it has been field-tested under a suitably wide variety of circumstances.

In other words, when first I hear the osprey cry, I may have identified a property-detector in myself, but I have no idea (yet) what property my new-found property-detector detects. It might seem then that I know nothing new at all – that my novel experience has not improved my epistemic predicament in the slightest. But of course this is not so. I may not be able to describe the property or identify it relative to any readily usable public landmarks (yet), but I am acquainted with it in a modest way: I can refer to the property I detected: it is the property I detected in *that* event. My experience of the osprey cry has given me a new way of thinking about osprey cries (an unavoidably inflated way of saying something very simple) which is practically ineffable both because it has (as yet for me) an untested profile in response to perceptual circumstances, and because it is – as the poverty of the bird-book description attests – such a highly informative way of thinking: a deliverance of an informationally very sensitive portion of my nervous system.

In this instance I mean information in the formal information theory sense of the term. Consider (*intuition pump #14: the Jello box*) the old spy trick, most famously encountered in the case of Julius and Ethel Rosenberg, of impróving on a password system by tearing something in two (a Jello box, in the Rosenberg's case), and giving half to each of the two parties who must be careful about identifying each other. Why does it work? Because tearing the paper in two produces an edge of such informational complexity that it would be virtually impossible to reproduce by deliberate construction. (Cutting the Jello box with straight edge and razor would entirely defeat the purpose.) The particular jagged edge of one piece becomes a *practically* unique pattern-recognition device for its mate; it is an apparatus for detecting the shape property M, where M is uniquely instantiated by its mate. It is of the essence of the trick that we cannot replace our dummy predicate "M" with a longer, more complex, but accurate and exhaustive description of the property, for if we could, we could use the description as a recipe or feasible algorithm for producing another instance of M or another M detector. The only *readily available* way of saying what property M is is just to point to our M-detector and say that M is the shape property detected by this thing here.

And that is just what we do when we seem to ostend, with the mental finger of inter intention, a quale or qualia-complex in our experience. We refer to a property – a public property of uncharted boundaries – via reference to our personal and idiosyncratic capacity to respond to it. That idiosyncrasy is the extent of our privacy. If I wonder whether your blue is my blue, your middle-C is my middle-C, I can coherently be wondering whether our discrimination profiles over a wide variation in conditions will be approximately the same. And they may not be; people experience the world quite differently. But that is empirically discoverable by all the usual objective testing procedures.[12]

Peter Bieri has pointed out to me that there is a natural way of exploiting Dretske's (1981) sense of information in a reformulation of my first three second-order properties of qualia: intrinsicality, ineffability, and privacy. (There are problems with Dretske's attempt to harness information theory in this way – see my discussion in "Evolution, error and intentionality" (Dennett 1987) – but they are not relevant to this point.) We could speak of what Bieri would call "phenomenal information properties" of psychological events. Consider the information – what Dretske would call the *natural meaning* – that a type of internal perceptual event might carry. That it carries that information is an objective (and hence, in a loose sense, intrinsic) matter since it is independent of what information (if any) the subject *takes* the event type to carry. Exactly what information is carried is (practically) ineffable, for the reasons just given. And it is private in the sense just given: proprietary and potentially idiosyncratic.

Consider how Bieri's proposed "phenomenal information properties" (let's call them *pips*) would apply in the case of Chase and Sanborn. Both Chase and Sanborn ought to wonder whether their pips have changed. Chase's speech shows that he is under the impression that his pips are unchanged (under normal circumstances – all bets are off if he has just eaten horseradish). He believes that the same objective things in the world – in particular, chemically identical caffeine-rich fluids – give rise to his particular types of taste-experiences now as six years ago.

Sanborn is under the impression that his pips are different. He thinks his objective property-detectors are deranged. He no longer has confidence that their deliverances today inform him of what they did six years ago. And what, exactly, did they inform him of then? If Sanborn were an ordinary person, we would not expect him to have an explicit answer, since most of us treat our taste-detectors as mere M-detectors, detecting whatever-it-is that they detect. (There are good reasons for this, analyzed by Akins 1987.) But professional coffee-tasters are probaby different. They probably have some pretty good idea of what kind of chemical-analysis transduction machinery they have in their mouths and nervous systems.

So far, so good. We could reinterpret Chase and Sanborn's speeches as hypotheses about the constancies or changes in the outputs of their perceptual information-processing apparatus, and just the sort of empirical testing we imagined before would tend to confirm or disconfirm their opinions thus interpreted. But what would justify calling such an information-bearing property "phenomenal"?

Such a pip has, as the testimony of Chase and Sanborn reveals, the power to provoke in Chase and Sanborn acts of (apparent) re-identification or recognition. This power is of course a Lockean, dispositional property on a par with the power of bitter things to provoke a certain reaction in people. It is this power alone, however it might be realized in the brain, that gives Chase and Sanborn "access" to the deliverances of their individual property-detectors.

We may "point inwardly" to one of the deliverances of our idiosyncratic, proprietary property-detectors, but when we do, what are we pointing *at*? What does that deliverance itself *consist of*? Or what are its consciously apprehensible properties, if not just our banished friends the qualia? We must be careful here, for if we invoke an inner perceptual process in which we observe the deliverance with some inner eye and thereby discern its properties, we will be stepping back into the frying pan of the view according to which qualia are just ordinary properties of our inner states.

But nothing requires us to make such an invocation. We don't have to know how we identify or re-identify or gain access to such internal response types in order to be able so to identify them. This is a point that was forcefully made by the pioneer functionalists and materialists, and has never been rebutted (Farrell 1950; Smart 1959). The properties of the "thing experienced" are not to be confused with the properties of the event that realizes the experiencing. To put the matter vividly, the physical difference between someone's imagining a purple cow and imagining a green cow *might* be nothing more than the presence or absence of a particular zero or one in one of the brain's "registers." Such a brute physical presence is all that it would take to anchor the sorts of dispositional differences between imagining a purple cow and imagining a green cow that could then flow, causally, from that "intrinsic" fact. (I doubt that this is what the friends of qualia have had in mind when they have insisted that qualia are intrinsic properties.)

Moreover, it is our very inability to expand on, or modify, these brute dispositions so to identify or recognize such states that creates the doctrinal illusion of "homogeneity" or "atomicity to analysis" or "grainlessness" that characterizes the qualia of philosophical tradition.

This putative grainlessness, I hypothesize, is nothing but a sort of functional invariability: it is close kin to what Pylyshyn (1980, 1984) calls *cognitive impenetrability*. Moreover, this functional invariability or impenetrability is not absolute but itself plastic over time. Just as on the efferent side of the nervous system, *basic actions* – in the sense of Danto (1963, 1965) and others (see Goldman 1970) – have been discovered to be variable, and subject under training to decomposition (one can learn with the help of "biofeedback" to will the firing of a particular motor neuron "directly"), so what counts for an individual as the simple or atomic properties of experienced items is subject to variation with training.[13]

Consider the results of "educating" the palate of a wine taster, or "ear training" for musicians. What had been "atomic" or "unanalyzable" becomes noticeably compound and describable; pairs that had been indistinguishable become distinguishable, and when this happens we say *the experience changes*. A swift and striking example of this is illustrated in *intuition pump #15: the guitar string*. Pluck the bass or low E string open, and listen carefully to the sound. Does it have describable parts or is it one and whole and ineffably guitarish? Many will opt for the latter way of talking. Now pluck the open string again and carefully bring a finger down lightly over the octave fret to create a high "harmonic." Suddenly a *new* sound is heard: "purer" somehow and of course an octave higher. Some people insist that this is an entirely novel sound, while others will describe the experience by saying "the bottom fell out of the note" – leaving just the top. But then on a third open plucking one can hear, with surprising distinctness, the harmonic overtone that was isolated in the second plucking. The homogeneity and ineffability of the first experience is gone, replaced by a duality as "directly apprehensible" and clearly describable as that of any chord.

The difference in experience is striking, but the complexity apprehended on the third plucking was *there* all along (being responded to or discriminated). After all, it was by the complex pattern of overtones that you were able to recognize the sound as that of a guitar rather than a lute or harpsichord. In other words, although the subjective experience has changed dramatically, the *pip* hasn't changed; you are still responding, as before, to a complex property so highly informative that it practically defies verbal description.

There is nothing to stop further refinement of one's capacity to describe this heretofore ineffable complexity. At any time, of course, there is one's current horizon of distinguishability – and that horizon is what sets, if anything does, what we should call the primary or atomic properties of what one consciously experiences (Farrell 1950). But it would be a mistake to transform the fact that inevitably there is a limit to our capacity to describe things we experience into the supposition that there are absolutely indescribable properties in our experience.

So when we look one last time at our original characterization of qualia, as ineffable, intrinsic, private, directly apprehensible properties of experience, we find that there is nothing to fill the bill. In their place are relatively or practically ineffable public properties we can refer to indirectly via reference to our private property-detectors – private only in the sense of idiosyncratic. And in so far as we wish to cling to our subjective authority about the occurrence within us of states of certain types or with certain properties, we can have some authority – not infallibility or incorrigibility, but something better than sheer guessing – but only if we restrict ourselves to relational, extrinsic properties like the power of certain internal states of ours to provoke acts of apparent re-identification. So contrary to what seems obvious at first blush, there simply are no qualia at all.[14]

NOTES

1 A representative sample of the most recent literature on qualia would include Block 1980; Shoemaker 1981, 1982; Davis 1982; White 1985; Armstrong and Malcolm 1984; Churchland 1985; and Conee 1985.

2 The difference between "eliminative materialism" – of which my position on qualia is an instance – and a "reductive" materialism that takes on the burden of identifying the problematic item in terms of the foundational materialistic theory is thus often best seen not so much as a doctrinal issue as a tactical issue: how might we most gracefully or effectively enlighten the confused in this instance? See my discussion of "fatigues" in the Introduction to *Brainstorms* (Dennett 1978a), and earlier, my discussion of what the enlightened ought to say about the metaphysical status of *sakes* and *voices* in *Content and Consciousness* (Dennett 1969), ch. 1.

3 The plausibility of this concession depends less on a high regard for the technology than on a proper skepticism about human powers, now documented in a fascinating study by Lehrer (1983).

4 Shoemaker (1984) seems to be moving reluctantly towards agreement with this conclusion: "So unless we can find some grounds on which we can deny the possibility of the sort of situation envisaged . . . we must apparently choose between rejecting the functionalist account of qualitative similarity and rejecting the standard conception of qualia.

   I would prefer not to have to make this choice; but if I am forced to make it, I reject the standard conception of qualia" (p. 356).

5 Shoemaker (1982) attributes a view to Wittgenstein (acknowledging that "it is none too clear" that this is actually what Wittgenstein held) which is very close to the view I defend here. But to Shoemaker, "it would seem offhand that Wittgenstein was mistaken" (p. 360), a claim Shoemaker supports with a far from offhand thought experiment – which Shoemaker misanalyzes if the present paper is correct. (There is no good reason, contrary to Shoemaker's declaration, to believe that his subject's *experience* is systematically different from what it was before the inversion.) Smart (1959) expresses guarded and partial approval

of Wittgenstein's hard line, but cannot see his way clear to as uncompromising an eliminativism as I maintain here.

6　In 1979, I read an earlier version of this paper in Oxford, with a commentary by John Foster, who defended qualia to the last breath, which was: "qualia should not be quined but fostered!" Symmetry demands, of course, the following definition for the eighth edition of *The Philosophical Lexicon*: "foster, *v.* To acclaim resolutely the existence or importance of something chimerical or insignificant."

7　This example first appeared in print in my "Reflections on Smullyan" in *The Mind's I* (Hofstadter and Dennett 1981), p. 427–8.

8　Kripke (1982) comes close, when he asks rhetorically "Do I not know, directly, and *with a fair degree of certainty* [emphasis added], that I mean plus [by the function I call "plus"]?" (p. 40) Kripke does not tell us what is implied by "a fair degree of certainty," but presumably he means by this remark to declare his allegiance to what Millikan (1984) attacks under the name of "meaning rationalism."

9　We can save the traditional claim by ignoring presumably private or subjective qualia and talking always of public tastes – such as the public taste of Maxwell House coffee that both Chase and Sanborn agree has remained constant. Individuals can be said to acquire a taste for such a public taste.

10　"I am not so wild as to deny that my sensation of red today is like my sensation of red yesterday. I only say that the similarity can *consist* only in the physiological force behind consciousness – which leads me to say, I recognize this feeling the same as the former one, and so does not consist in a community of sensation." (C. S Peirce, *Collected Works*, vol. V, p. 172, fn. 2).

11　A heroic (and, to me, baffling) refusal to abandon intrinsicality is Wilfrid Sellars's contemplation over the years of his famous pink ice cube, which leads him to postulate a revolution in microphysics, restoring objective "absolute sensory processes" in the face of Boyle and Locke and almost everybody since them. See Sellars (1981) and my commentary (Dennett 1981).

12　Stich (1983) discusses the implications for psychological theory of incommensurability problems that can arise from such differences in discrimination profiles. See esp chs. 4 and 5.

13　See Churchland 1979, esp. ch 2, for supporting observations on the variability of perceptual properties, and for novel arguments against the use of "intrinsic properties" as determiners of the meaning of perceptual predicates. See also Churchland 1985 for further arguments and observations in support of the position sketched here.

14　The first version of this paper was presented at University College London, in November 1978, and in various revisions at a dozen other universities in 1979 and 1980. It was never published, but was circulated widely as Tufts University Cognitive Science Working Paper #7, December 1979. A second version was presented at the Universities of Adelaide and Sydney in 1984, and in 1985 to psychology department colloquia at Harvard and Brown under the title "Properties of conscious experience." The second version was the basis for my presentation at the workshop on consciousness in modern science, Villa Olmo, Como, Italy, April 1985, and circulated in preprint in 1985, again under the title "Quining qualia." The present version, the fourth, is a substantial revision, thanks to the helpful comments of many peope, including Kathleen Akins, Ned Block, Alan Cowey, Sydney Shoemaker, Peter Bieri, William Lycan, Paul Churchland, Gilbert Harman and the participants at Villa Olmo.

REFERENCES

Akins, K. (1987) *Information and Organisms: Or, Why Nature Doesn't Build Epistemic Engines*, Ph.D. dissertation, Univ. of Michigan Dept of Philosophy.

Armstrong, D. and Malcolm, N. (eds) (1984) *Consciousness and Causality*. Oxford: Basil Blackwell.

Bennett, J. (1965) "Substance, reality and primary qualities," *American Philosophical Quarterly* 2, 1–17.

Berkeley, G. (1713) *Three Dialogues between Hylas and Philonous*.

Block, N. (1978) "Troubles with Functionalism," in W. Savage (ed.) *Perception and Cognition: Minnesota Studies in the Philosophy of Science, Vol. IX* Minneapolis: University of Minnesota Press.

Block, N. (1980) "Are absent qualia impossible?," *Philosophical Review* 89, 257.

Block, N. and Fodor J. (1972) "What psychological states are not," *Philosophical Review* 81, 159–81.

Chisholm, R. (1976) *Person and Object*. La Salle, Illinois: Open Court Press.

Churchland, P. M. (1979) *Scientific Realism and the Plasticity of Mind*. Cambridge, MA: Cambridge University Press.

Churchland, P. M. (1985) "Reduction, qualia and the direct inspection of brain states," *Journal of Philosophy*, LXXXII, 8–28.

Conee, E. (1985) "The possibility of absent qualia," *Philosophical Review* 94, 345–66.

Damasio, A. et al. (1980) "Central Achromatopsia: Behavioral, anatomic, and physiological aspects," *Neurology* 30, 1064–71.

Danto, A. (1963) "What we can do," *Journal of Philosophy*, LX, 435–45.

Danto, A. (1965) "Basic actions," *American Philosophical Quarterly*, 141–8.

Davis, L. (1982) "Functionalism and absent qualia," *Philosophical Studies* 41, 231–51.

Dennett, D. C. (1969) *Content and Consciousness*. London: Routledge & Kegan Paul.

Dennett, D. C. (1976) "Are dreams experiences?," *Philosophical Review* 85, 151–71. (Reprinted in Dennett 1978a.)

Dennett, D. C. (1978a) *Brainstorms*. Bradford Books/MIT Press.

Dennett, D C. (1978b) "Two approaches to mental images," in Dennett 1978a.

Dennett, D. C. (1978c) *The Philosophical Lexicon* (privately printed, available from the American Philosophical Association, University of Delaware), 8th edn.

Dennett, D. C. (1979) "On the absence of phenomenology," in D. F. Gustafson and B. L. Tapscott (eds) *Body, Mind, and Method* (Festschrift for Virgil Aldrich). Dordrecht: Reidel, pp. 93–114.

Dennett, D. C. (1981) "Wondering where the yellow went," *Monist* 64, 102–8.

Dennett, D. C. (1982) "How to study human consciousness empirically: Or nothing comes to mind," *Synthese* 53, 159–80.

Dennett, D. C. (1987) *The Intentional Stance*. Cambridge MA: Bradford/MIT.

Dretske, F. (1981) *Knowledge and the Flow of Information*. Cambridge MA: Bradford/MIT.

Elster, J. (1985) *Making Sense of Marx*. Cambridge, England: Cambridge University Press.

Farrell, B. A. (1950) "Experience," *Mind* 59, 170–98.

Gert, B. (1965) "Imagination and verifiability," *Philosophical Studies* 16, 44–7.

Geschwind, N. and Fusillo, M. (1966) "Color-naming defects in association with alexia," *Archives of neurology* 15, 137–46.

Goldman, A. (1970) *A Theory of Human Action*. Englewood Cliffs, NJ: Prentice Hall.

Gregory, R. (1977) *Eye and Brain*, 3rd edn. London: Weidenfeld & Nicolson.

Hofstadter, D. and Dennett, D. C. (1981) *The Mind's I: Fantasies and Reflections on Mind and Soul*. New York: Basic Books.

Kim, J. (1982) "Psychophysical supervenience," *Philosophical Studies* 41, 51–70.

Kitcher, P. (1979) "Phenomenal qualities," *American Philosophical Quarterly* 16, 123–9.

Kripke, S. (1982) *Wittgenstein on Rules and Private Language*. Cambridge, MA: Harvard University Press.

Lehrer, A. (1983) *Wine and Conversation*. Bloomington, Indiana: Univ. of Indiana Press.

Lewis, D. (1983) "Extrinsic properties," *Philosophical Studies* 44, 197–200.

Locke, J. (1690) *An Essay Concerning Human Understanding* (A. C. Fraser edition). New York: Dover, 1959.

Lycan, W. (1973) "Inverted spectrum," *Ratio* XV, 315–19.

Malcolm, N. (1956) "Dreaming and skepticism," *Philosophical Review* 64, 14–37.

Malcolm, N. (1959) *Dreaming*. London: Routledge & Kegan Paul.

Meadows, J. C. (1974) "Disturbed perception of colours associated with localized cerebral lesions," *Brain* 97, 615–32.

Millikan, R. (1984) *Language, Thought and Other Biological Categories.* Cambridge, MA: Bradford/MIT.

Nagel, T. (1974) "What is it like to be a bat?," *Philosophical Review* 83, 435–51.

Nagel, T. (1986) *The View from Nowhere.* Oxford: Oxford University Press.

Peirce, C. (1931–58) C. Hartshorne and P. Weiss (eds), *Collected Works.* Cambridge MA: Harvard University Press.

Peterson, R. T. (1947) *A Field Guide to the Birds,* Boston: Houghton Mifflin.

Putnam, H. (1965) "Brains and behavior," in J. Butler (ed.) *Analytical Philosophy* (second series). Oxford: Basil Blackwell.

Pylyshyn, Z. (1980) "Computation and cognition: Issues in the foundation of cognitive science," *Behavioral and Brain Sciences* 3, 111–32.

Pylyshyn, Z (1984) *Computation and Cognition: Toward a Foundation for Cognitive Scienec.* Cambridge, MA: Bradford/MIT Press.

Sellars, W. (1981) "Foundations for a metaphysics of pure process" (the Carus Lectures), *Monist,* 64, 3–90.

Shoemaker, S. (1969) "Time without change," *Journal of Philosophy* 66, 363–81.

Shoemaker, S. (1975) "Functionalism and qualia," *Philosophical Studies* 27, 291–315.

Shoemaker, S. (1981) "Absent qualia are impossible – A Reply to Block," *Philosophical Review* 90, 581–99.

Shoemaker, S. (1982) "The inverted spectrum," *Journal of Philosophy* 79, 357–81.

Shoemaker, S. (1984) "Postscript (1983)," in *Identity, Cause, and Mind.* Cambridge, England: Cambridge Univ. Press, pp. 351–7.

Smart, J. J. C. (1959) "Sensations and brain processes," *Philosophical Review* 68, 141–56. (Reprinted in Chappell 1962).

Stich, S. (1983) *From Folk Psychology to Cognitive Science: The Case Against Belief.* Cambridge, MA: Bradford/MIT.

Taylor, D. M. (1966) "The incommunicability of content," *Mind* 75, 527–41.

Von der Heydt, R., Peterhans, E. and Baumgartner, G. (1984) "Illusory contours and cortical neuron response," *Science* 224, 1260–2.

Walzer, M. (1985) "What's left of Marx," *New York Review of Books,* Nov. 21, pp. 43–6.

White, S. (1985) "Professor Shoemaker and so-called 'qualia' of experience," *Philosophical Studies* 47, 369–83.

Wittgenstein, L. (1958) G. E. M. Anscombe (ed.), *Philosophical Investigations.* Oxford: Basil Blackwell.

Part VIII

Special Topics

Introduction

In this part we shall briefly visit four issues in cognitive science. Each is pressing, each is volatile, and each has significant philosophical implications.

1 Perception and physical theory

Colors seem to us to be simple, visible properties of physical objects. If it is not the standard yellow, a pencil is grey, black, brown, blue, or whatever. Moreover, the pencil is that color even in the dark or under strange lighting conditions, even if it does not look that color; common sense applies the appearance/reality distinction to colors. But physics seems to tell us that ordinary macroscopic physical objects are not really colored at all, much less really as opposed to apparently colored, for they consist solely of tiny colorless particles whizzing at odd angles through almost entirely empty space. Perhaps for an object to be "colored" is just for it to cause certain sensations in us perceivers, or perhaps the whole idea of color is as mistaken as the Eliminativists claim mental ascriptions are. Hardin (this volume) contributes an introduction to the issue; Campbell (this volume) examines a possible line of response based on one current and attractive physical theory of color.

2 The imagery issue

Most of us see pictures in our minds. At least, if asked, we can form mental images of one thing and another. So it seems that even if the "language of thought" hypothesis is correct for the case of ordinary propositional attitudes, there is a style of mental representation that is pictorial or iconic rather than propositional or sentential. This possibility has given rise to an enormous literature; Block (this volume, below) and Sterelny (this volume) try to sort out that literature and adjudicate the question of imagery and pictorial representation as they might figure in cognitive science.

3   Language and innateness

Since the 1950s, Zellig Harris (1951), Noam Chomsky (1957, 1959, 1965) and their followers have argued against the Behaviorists that human linguistic capacities are governed and explained by abstract functional rules realized in brain hardware. Since even a five-year-old's linguistic "competence" is infinite, in that the child would be able to understand any number of indefinitely long and novel utterances, the child must somehow mobilize rules of grammar that parse the sentences she hears into the semantically significant parts of speech from which they are composed. This claim of grammatical compositionality is now a truism of theoretical linguistics.

But a considerably stronger claim has also been pushed by Chomsky and other linguists: that much of human language is both *species-wide* and *innate*. According to Chomsky (1965, 1966, 1975, this volume) and Lightfoot (1982, this volume), all normal human beings are born not only with the capacity to learn language, but with a language *faculty* prewired in our brains and dedicated to that purpose; Lightfoot speaks of a "linguistic genotype." We are genetically programmed to develop an "initial state" called "universal grammar" (UG). UG is a device that takes an infant's environmental input and turns it into knowledge of a particular natural language such as English or Japanese. Now, since natural languages seem to differ greatly from each other in grammar as well as (obviously) in vocabulary, one would assume that any putative UG would have little to it, and little to do by way of enforcing species-wide linguistic commonalities. But Chomsky and Lightfoot argue that in fact UG imposes strong constraints on the structure of any possible human language, and that natural languages differ only fairly superficially, in (of course) their actual vocabularies and in a few grammatical "switch" or parameter settings imposed by empirical, environmental influence. Only the vocabulary items and the switch settings are *learned* by the child, for UG has already grown in naturally, like teeth.

That a general capacity or even faculty for language-speaking should be innate is no surprise. Children all over the world develop languages, like teeth, relentlessly and at much the same age, irrespective of wide climatic and cultural differences. Moreover, there is plenty of psycholinguistic and neurological evidence of localization of some linguistic functions within the brain (see the references collected in chapter 12 of Akmajian et al. 1984). What is startling about Chomsky's and Lightfoot's innateness thesis is their claim that the children develop, not just some language or other, but everywhere *much the same* language so far as grammar is concerned. That is, of course, an empirical claim and a daring one, so impressive evidence is needed.

The principal type of argument brought to bear (though hardly the only type) is based on "the poverty of the stimulus." When we think of children learning to talk, we tend to think of them as *pupils* being instructed by their parents and teachers; at least, we think of them as bombarded by linguistic data and as forming generalizations regarding grammaticality. Recent research shows, however, that few of the sorts of linguisitic data to which children are exposed have any significant effect on the children's linguistic development. For example, "negative data" in the form of *correction* by a mentor has negligible effect. Children also largely ignore "degenerate data" – irregular or locally incorrect usage – even on the part of immigrant parents. According to Lightfoot, the child "needs access only to simple, robust expressions." Thus, the infinite and highly structured linguistic competence of a five-year-old is absurdly underdetermined by the only environmental stimuli that actually affect learning; all else, in particular most of grammar, must therefore be innate.

Chomskyan innatism is not without its critics. Chomsky has carried on a running debate with Putnam (1967, 1980), who argues that no special "language acquisition device" need be posited, for the facts can be as well explained by reference to the same *general* learning principles that govern the acquisition of all other cognitive skills.

4 The prospects for Artificial Intelligence

If functionalism is true, it seems to follow (see the introductions to Parts I and II above) that any system or organism that (genuinely) realizes such-and-such a program or flow chart would have mental states like ours. Thus, if we can build a machine to certain functional specifications, we can artificially create a thinking, feeling machine. Some theorists welcome this consequence warmly, and look forward to the day. Others find the prospect grotesque and preposterous on its face, a reduction of Functionalism to absurdity. So one must confront the question of optimism or pessimism regarding AI. (But recall our distinctions in the introduction to Part I, between weak, stronger and strongest versions of "AI.") Haugeland (this volume) offers a partial prognosis for weak and stronger AI; other views are considered in the works in the list of Further Reading below.

FURTHER READING

A good overview is provided by Stillings et al. (1987) *Cognitive Science: An Introduction*, Bradford Books / MIT Press.

Perception and Physical Theory
Campbell, K. (1969) 'Colours', in R. Brown and C. D. Rollins (eds), *Contemporary Philosophy in Australia*. Humanities Press.
Armstrong, D. M. (1969) 'Colour realism and the argument from microscopes', in R. Brown and C. D. Rollins (eds), *Contemporary Philosophy in Australia*.
Hurvich, L. M. (1981) *Color Vision*, Sinauer Associates, Inc.
Nassau, K. (1983) *The Physics and Chemistry of Color*, John Wiley and Sons.
Hilbert, D. (1987) *Color and Color Perception: A Study in Anthropocentric Realism*, Center for the Study of Language and Information.
Hardin, C. L. (1988) *Color for Philosophers*, Hackett Publishing Company.

The Imagery Issue
Block, N. (ed.) (1981) *Imagery*, Bradford Books / MIT Press.
Shepard, R. N. and Cooper, L. A. (1982) *Mental Images and their Transformations*, Bradford Books / MIT Press.

Language and Innateness
Harris, Z. (1951) *Methods in Structural Linguistics*, University of Chicago Press.
Chomsky, N. (1957) *Syntactic Structures*, Mouton.
Chomsky, N. (1959) "A Review of B. F. Skinner's *Verbal Behavior,*" *Language* 35 (1959), 26–58.
Chomsky, N. (1965) *Aspects of the Theory of Syntax*, MIT Press.
Chomsky, N. (1966) *Cartesian Linguistics*, Harper and Row.
Chomsky, N. (1975) *Reflections on Language*, Pantheon.
Putnam, H. (1967) 'The "Innateness Hypothesis" and explanatory models in linguistics', *Synthese* 17, 12–22.
Putnam, H. (1981) "What Is Innate and Why," in Block, N. (ed.), *Readings in Philosophy of Psychology, Volume Two*, Harvard University Press.
Stich, S. (ed.) (1975) *Innate Ideas*, University of California Press.
Piattelli-Palmarini, M. (ed.) (1980) *Language and Learning: The Debate Between Jean Piaget and Noam Chomsky*, Harvard University Press.
Lightfoot, D. (1982) *The Language Lottery*, MIT Press.
Akmajian, A., Demers, R. A., and Harnish, R. M. (1984) *Linguistics: An Introduction to Language and Communication*, Second Edition, MIT Press.

The prospects for Artificial Intelligence
Anderson, A. R. (ed.) (1964) *Minds and Machines*, Prentice-Hall.
Ringle, M. (1979) *Philosophical Perspectives in Artificial Intelligence*, Harvester Press.
Haugeland, J. (ed.) (1981) *Mind Design*, Bradford Books / MIT Press.
Haugeland, J. (1985) *Artificial Intelligence: The Very Idea*, Bradford Books/MIT Press.

18

Perception and Physical Theory

Color and Illusion

C. L. HARDIN

Imagine the following experiment. Before you is a spinning disk, illuminated by an ordinary incandescent lamp. If most people are asked what color they see on the face of the disk, they will unhesitatingly reply that they see a bluish green. But you, ever the skeptical and cagey philosopher, may hesitate, not because what you see doesn't look bluish green, for it very plainly does, but because you suspect a trick. And, indeed, this proves to be a trick of sorts. When the wheel is made to turn very slowly you see a half-black, half-white disk, with a slot through which a red lamp flashes. You saw no red at all before, and you can discern no bluish green now. The bluish green color the disk looked to have was entirely the color of an after-image, one that appeared to be the color of the surface of a physical object rather than the color of a free-floating patch. This particular after-image phenomenon is called Bidwell's ghost, after the early twentieth century psychologist who first discovered it.[1] When you view Bidwell's ghost, it is always open to you to deny that you are seeing bluish green, on the ground that after-images are not physical objects and only physical objects can have colors. But it is then fair to ask you what color you do see. Red? Gray? No color at all? None of these answers is intuitively very appealing.

If you are like most philosophers, you will nevertheless be inclined to say that Bidwell's ghost is a color illusion, and that when the disk is rapidly spinning, you don't see its true colors. But just what is a color illusion? Isn't it a failure of correspondence between the color that an object seems to have and the color that it does have? If it is, to characterize an object's apparent possession of a color as illusory is to presume that one knows what counts as the object's true color. In ordinary practice this presumption seems natural enough. But it is in fact quite difficult to justify in a principled fashion, especially if you happen to be a physicalist.

"Color and Illusion" by C. L. Hardin is printed here for the first time, by kind permission of the author.

I shall argue that the facts about chromatic phenomena[2] make it very hard to construe colors as properties of physical objects or processes outside the body of the perceiver. I shall consider three attempts at a physicalistic reduction of colors: to wavelengths of light as Armstrong[3] would have it; to the dispositions of objects appropriately to affect normal observers under standard conditions, a thesis defended by Smart[4] and Lewis;[5] and to spectral reflectances, as proposed by Averill[6] and Hilbert.[7] We shall have reason to suppose that all such reductions will fail, and thus to question the legitimacy of the conception of a color illusion.

We normally see color because light of certain wavelengths strikes the retina and excites the photoreceptors that dwell there. They in turn hyperpolarize, generating small electrochemical signals in other cells. The photoreceptors that are relevant to color vision are called *cones*. There are three types of cones, each sensitive to a particular range of the visible spectrum. They are often misleadingly labeled the blue, green and red cones. Let us call them instead the shortwave, middlewave and longwave cones. Their sensitivity curves are rather broad and overlap substantially. When a cone absorbs a photon of light of a particular wavelength, it generates a voltage, and the character of this voltage is independent of the wavelength of the photon that the receptor absorbed. Subsequent cells in the visual processing chain can only "know" that a receptor of a particular type has been excited, but they cannot "know" the wavelength of the photon that has caused it to become excited. Information about wavelength can only be gleaned by cells that are able to compare the outputs of cones of different types that are in the same retinal region. So chromatic information about the light in a particular retinal region that is conveyed to higher visual cells takes the form of the ratios of excitations of the three cones types in that region. The vast amount of wavelength information in the optical array that strikes a small retinal region is reduced to a three-termed cone excitation ratio right at the beginning of the visual processing chain. This is a massive information loss, and it has important consequences. In particular, any two stimuli of the same intensity that produce the same cone excitation ratios will be regarded as equivalent by the chromatic visual system. This is one of the most fundamental facts about color vision, since it means that for most perceptible light stimuli, there exist indefinitely many other stimuli, each with a physically distinct wavelength composition, that will evoke precisely the same perceived color. Color vision stimuli that are perceptually equivalent but physically inequivalent are known as *metamers*.

The existence of metamers might be expected to make trouble for a purported reduction of colors to combinations of wavelengths of light. The difficulty arises conspicuously in the case of white. It is often said that white is a combination of light of all colors. But this seems odd on the fact of it. Although orange looks reddish as well as yellowish, and purple looks both reddish and bluish, white, far from looking reddish and greenish and yellowish and bluish, looks to have no chromatic colors in it at all. Had he the opportunity to do it all over again, the biblical Joseph would have doubtless preferred his coat of many colors to have been white.

You may reply that this misrepresents the intention of the specification of white, which is not to advance the claim that white is a combination of all other perceived colors, but to assert that perceptions of white are produced by light of all the visible wavelengths put together in the appropriate amounts. Now it is true that light that we call white is most often composed in this fashion, but it is also true that a white light can be generated from the superposition of as few as two monochromatic light sources, and there are infinitely many distinct pairs of such monochromatic sources. Furthermore, one can superimpose as many of these pairs as one likes, and still get light that looks white. On the other hand, each of these white-looking lights has, as we shall see, color-rendering properties that are different from the rest. Which of these, according to the account of color that identifies colors with wavelengths of light, is "real" white, and which is just "apparent" white? And by virtue of what principles does one make such choices?

Let us consider another example. It might seem plausible to identify "pure" yellow with a spectral wavelength that most people see as "pure" yellow – about 577 nm (a *nanometer* is a billionth of a meter) – and to suppose that anything that is yellow is such in virtue of sending light to the eye containing a component of 577 nm light. But what are we to say of a spot of light that has just two components: monochromatic 540 nm light (that most people see as green) and monochromatic 670 nm light (that most people see as red)? Such a spot will not only appear yellow, but will exactly match the appearance of a monochromatic yellow, although the one stimulus consists entirely of 577 nm light, whereas the other hasn't a trace of 577 nm light.

The reason that both stimuli look yellow is that they produce the same ratios of excitations in the three cone types. To find out what *looks* yellows, we obviously must attend to the operating characteristics of human visual systems. But the physicalist who would reduce real colors to wavelengths of light should be able to pick out the *real* colors on the basis of physical considerations alone.

Such physical considerations seem to fail entirely to give us a conceptual grip on the phenomenon of colored shadows, first described in detail by Count Rumford in 1794.[8] One may illustrate colored shadows in a variety of ways, but a simple and striking way to do it is to arrange two slide projectors so that the light that they project falls on the same area of the screen. First turn them on separately. Let one projector carry a slide that consists of a piece of green celluloid on which is fixed a cross made of two strips of tape. The image that it projects is of a black cross on a green field. Let the second projector carry only the empty frame of a slide, so that it casts a rectangle of incandescent projector light on the screen. What will happen when the two images are superimposed? To the black cross and the green field, the second projector adds only some broadband, approximately white, light. According to the wavelength theorist, you should see nothing particularly remarkable, only a grayish cross on a somewhat washed-out green field. What you will in fact see is quite different: the cross will look bright pink. If you were to bring in a spectrophotometer, it would tell you that the spectrum of light reflected from the area of the screen on which the cross appears is only that which is characteristic of ordinary projector light, and not that which would have been there had you produced the effect by means of a red filter.

"Ah, but this is just another illusion," the wavelength theorist might reply. "What I am concerned to do is to give an account of the real colors of things, not a theory of the colors things seem to have in demonstrations of bizarre effects." Very well. But any theory of color that is to be of any interest must go beyond a set of raw stipulations to the effect that such-and-such wavelength combinations are to count as red, and that so-and-so wavelengths are to be cyan, and so on. Their proponents always claim that materialist theories of color fit into a scientific picture of the world (often The Scientific Picture of the World), so any such theory of color should provide the framework for a scientific theory of the color qualities that we see. At the very least, we can demand of a theory of color that it satisfactorily represent what is going on when we see red and brown and white and black in ordinary life. But in fact, a proper account of our everyday experience of black and brown requires an appeal to one of the fundamental phenomena – namely, simultaneous contrast – that is involved in colored shadows, so this so-called "illusion" is not as far removed from ordinary experience as one might have supposed.

Simultaneous contrast is ubiquitous and easily illustrated. The principle involved is, roughly speaking, that a large area of color tends to induce its complementary color into a neighboring area. Thus, an area of red makes adjacent areas look greener, blue makes a nearby region look more yellow, white induces black, and so on. The effect is rooted in the physiology of the visual system. The biological details are at least roughly understood and quite interesting, but they need not detain us now. The pink that appears on the cross in our colored shadow experiment is, roughly, the complement of the green in the field, and is induced by it.

Simultaneous contrast is consciously manipulated by painters, often to great effect. Delacroix once said "Give me mud, let me surround it as I think fit, and it shall be the radiant flesh of Venus." For examples of simultaneous contrast we do not strictly require either mud or the radiant flesh of Venus. Some experimentation with pieces of colored paper will soon persuade you that two squares cut from the same piece of colored paper can look very different from one another when placed on backgrounds that differ from each other in color.

With certain choices of background, the phenomenon is so strong that often people need to be specially persuaded that the specimen areas will indeed look the same when seen in isolation. When confronted with an effective example of simultaneous contrast, you can undo the effect by using a viewing tube or other device to replace the inducing surround by a neutral one. (It is well to bear in mind that what is "neutral" depends upon the color in question; there is no such thing as a universal neutral surround). It is easy to construct a tolerably useful viewing tube. Just roll up a piece of paper, preferably dark gray, into a tube and peer at the patch you wish to inspect, rolling the paper tightly enough to shut out the view of the ambient light and the surrounding regions. In the colored shadow experiment, if you look at the pink cross through a viewing tube, its pinkness disappears.

Now what does simultaneous contrast have to do with the everyday perception of black and brown? The answer, in brief, is that both blackness and brownness are always the products of simultaneous contrast. Nakedly stated, this seems implausible. But let us examine some of the evidence for it. Take black first. We are commonly told that black is the absence of light, a visual nullity. But in truth, what we see in the absence of visual stimulation is not black, but a dark gray; the blackest blacks arise as a result of contrast. You can see this for yourself by entering at night an unilluminated room containing a collection of objects that, by good light, range from white through the grays to black. Equip yourself with a lamp that is controlled by a dimmer. Go into the darkened room, slowly turn up the dimmer, and look at the contents. Notice that when you look at them under conditions of very dim light, the gray range is tightly compressed, with little visible lightness difference between the lightest and darkest objects. But as the light increases, the gray range expands in both directions: not only do the whites look whiter, the blacks look blacker. An increase in the total amount of light has increased blackness.

Another, more painful, way of seeing this is to watch some daytime television. Before you turn on the set, notice that the screen is, by daylight, a middle gray. Turn on the set, find a clear picture, and stand far enough away from it to minimize most of the remaining visual noise. Look for a good black, and mentally compare its lightness with the middle gray of the turned-off screen. (If you are sufficiently sinful to have two television sets, the comparison could be direct.) The black is obviously darker than the gray. But since television pictures are produced by generating light, not by subtracting it, the blackening of that area of the screen must be the result of contrast.

Browns are, for most people, a distinctive set of colors, as differentiated in character from reds and yellows as reds and yellows are diffentiated from each other. But in fact, browns are simply blackened oranges and yellows, and their characteristic (or, to use the technical term, "dominant") wavelengths are the same as those of most orange and yellow objects. The spectral profile of a chocolate bar closely resembles that of an orange, but, under the same lighting conditions, the light reflected from the chocolate bar is of much lower intensity. The characteristic difference in appearance between the two depends entirely upon their perceived relationships to the ambient light.

To see this, you can first project an orange spot on a darkened screen, and then, using a second projector, surround the orange spot with bright projector light. The slides may be prepared in the following way. First, use a paper punch to cut a round hole in a piece of stiff paper, glue a piece of orange celluloid onto the paper, and cut the paper and its attached celluloid so that it will fit inside an empty slide frame. This gives you a projectable orange spot. The second slide, the one that is responsible for the bright surround and blackened center, is produced by gluing onto a piece of transparent celluloid the round piece of paper that was made when you cut out the hole with the punch when you were making the first slide. On the screen, line up the projected (orange) hole with the projected (shadow) disk, and try the experiment. The whiteness of the surround induces blackness into the orange, transforming it into a brown. Here, as before, the action of simultaneous contrast may be undone by the judicious use of a viewing tube. You might also like to use a viewing tube to examine a chocolate bar, or other brown object, in a bright light. It will lose its brownness, and look like a dim orange or yellow. In performing such experiments it is best to use a tube with a blackened interior, and to avoid looking at portions of the surface that contain highlights.

So to write off simultaneous contrast as something that need not enter into one's fundamental theory of colors is also to write off the possibility of giving a proper account of the nature of black and brown. This seems unacceptable, unless one is prepared to think of black and brown as "illusory" rather than as "real" colors.

We also ought to demand that a minimally adequate theory of color lend itself to an account of the elementary laws of color mixing. For example, since orange is visibly yellow-red (notice that it could not *fail* to be yellow-red), it has a red component and a yellow component. Furthermore, when color-normal observers look at *monochromatic* spectral light of 590 nm, they see orange. But how can this be on a wavelength theory that maintains that red *is* light of a wavelength of, say, 650 nm, and yellow *is* light of a wavelength of 577 nm? And what of the basic and simple relationships about the relations that colors bear to each other? How is it that we can see reddish blues – the purples – but no reddish greens? One will search the writings of wavelength theorists in vain to find persuasive answers to any of these questions. We might be tolerant of such shortcomings if nobody else had an explanation for color mixing and color compatibilities and incompatibilities – in short, if there were no such discipline as color science. In truth, visual scientists know a great deal about all of these matters. But they do not encumber themselves with the supposition that chromatic phenomena can be accounted for without an essential reference to eyes and brains.

Most philosophers are, indeed, not very sympathetic to a program such as wavelength reductionism. They are aware that a wide variety of distinct physical circumstances can be responsible for producing a given color appearance, and that because of the peculiarities of human perceptual mechanisms, the relationship between external physical conditions and what we see is not a simple one. "No matter," say they, "how physically diverse and, indeed, gerrymandered the class of red things may be, what makes them red is that they are disposed to look red to normal observers under standard conditions." According to the adherents of this position, colors are, to use Locke's term, *powers* of objects to cause us to be in particular perceptual states under particular circumstances. The perceptual states are not themselves to be thought of as colors or as being colored, but, rather, as signs or indices of certain dispositions in physical objects. The human perceptual apparatus is to be regarded as a stalking-horse to pick out and classify physical powers that are of interest to us and to creatures constituted like us, although those powers would not have been picked out or thought to form natural classes on the basis of purely physical considerations.

This way of approaching the problem has much to commend it. For a variety of purposes, the practitioners of that branch of color science known as colorimetry employ a statistically defined Standard Observer whose "receptoral" sensitivities are used in combination with various standard illuminants and viewing conditions to sort objects into classes according to such technical parameters as purity and dominant wavelength. In turn, these parameters are correlated with perceptual variables like saturation and hue. But unlike some philosophers, color scientists are well aware that, for example, hue is a quite different property from dominant wavelength, and that the correlation between the two is only approximate and is well-defined only under certain carefully specified standard viewing conditions.

Furthermore, the standard viewing conditions to be employed will depend upon the purpose for which the measurement is being taken. There is, in color science, no set of conditions for determining the "true" or "real" colors of objects. As we shall now see, if they are construed non-pragmatically and in more than a rough-and-ready sense, the notions of "normal observer" and "standard condition" are philosophers' fictions.

Let's look more closely into these matters by returning to the centrally important phenomenon of metamerism. We have previously considered the metameric matches of spots of light. The conception can be extended to reflective surfaces. The wavelength distribution that strikes the eye depends upon the spectral characteristics of both the illumination and the surface that reflects it to the eye. A change in the spectral characteristics of either illumination or surface will often make a difference in what we see. If two spectrally distinct surfaces visually match under a given illuminant for a given observer, the surfaces are said to be metamers for that illuminant and that observer. But we must expect that since the two samples are spectrally different, that difference will be made visually apparent under some illuminant or other. It is not difficult in our age of synthetic colorants to find two color samples that are, for most people, a good match in daylight but when shifted to another illuminant – one or another variety of artificial light – fail to match. Furthermore, when we use first one, then another, illuminant to see a piece of white paper, the illuminants may look to be very similar or even identical, but they may give dramatically different results when they illuminate various pieces of chromatically colored paper.

These effects are well known to people who pay attention to colors. Many people know that it is advisable to see whether the coat and trousers that look so handsome together in the store are equally pleasing when taken into the natural light of the street. Photographers learn to their sorrow that a film that yields a proper color balance when used out of doors gives pictures with a markedly yellow tinge when the same subject is photographed under incandescent light.

It is perfectly true that if you saw the subject of such photographs, first in natural light, then in incandescent light, you would not be aware of such a profound shift in hue. In fact, you might not notice any difference at all if you weren't looking for it. The perceived colors of objects tend to remain relatively stable over a wide variety of changes in illumination. This is partly due to the fact that most people don't attend to relatively small color differences and possess poor color memories for even relatively large differences. But it is also because the eye, unlike a camera's film, adapts automatically to the character of the illuminant and, in large measure, successfully discounts illumination changes. We are more sensitive to the relationships of the colors in a scene than we are to their absolute values. A piece of white paper in shadow looks to us to be lighter than a piece of coal in sunlight, even though the coal sends more light to the eye than the paper does.

This stability across variations in ambient lighting has been called color constancy, and it has frequently been noted, theorized about, and its completeness exaggerated, especially by Land and his followers.[9] Although the phenomenon is robust, constancy is far from complete, even under the range of natural lighting conditions. Inconstancy becomes a very vexing problem with artificial colorants and illuminants, and color technologists wrestle with problems of metamerism every day. For instance, restorers of old paintings are often unable to replicate the original colorants. They create an excellent visual match with the old paint under the illumination of the workshop, only to find that when it is exhibited under the illumination of the gallery, the restoration is plainly visible. So even though adaptation may preserve color appearances for the most part, a change in illuminants that transforms a metameric match into a mismatch – especially a gross mismatch – will always be noticeable.

Let us now see what problems metamerism poses for a theory that would assign colors to objects on the basis of normal observers and standard conditions. First of all, consider two colorants that match metamerically under the standard illuminant. Because the match is metameric, the colorants will have different spectral characteristics and will thus fail to match under some other illuminant. Instead of saying that the two colorants have the same color because they match under the standard illuminant, shouldn't we say that they can't be the same color because under the other illuminant they look different to normal observers?

Although this objection certainly has some force, it is open to the proponent of the normal-observer and standard-condition thesis to stick by her guns, and insist that it is the comparison of samples under the standard illuminant that must decide the issue. But it is now necessary for her to specify the standard illuminant. Two frequently employed standards are sunlight and north daylight. But although some philosophers seem to be unaware of the fact, the spectral characteristics of the two are not the same. So we must expect – and it is in fact the case – that there will be colorants that will match under the one illuminant but not under the other. Then which illuminant is to be the standard? Are there any principled philosophical grounds – as opposed to the pragmatic considerations of color technologists – for choosing one over the other? And shall we let our illuminant have energy outside the visible range and take fluorescence into account, or use a band-limited source so as to exclude it?

There is much more to specifying a set of standard conditions than the choice of illuminant. What are we to do about simultaneous contrast? For many purposes, it makes sense to require that the sample be seen through a viewing tube or other aperture with a "neutral" surround. What counts as "neutral" will depend upon the sample itself, since dark surrounds will brighten light colors, and light surrounds will darken dark colors. There are no all-purpose neutral surrounds, just compromises of various degrees of utility. On the other hand, to insist on using an aperture for all determinations is to forbear categorizing objects as black or brown, since, as we have already seen, these are essentially contrast colors.

The next decision that must be made in assigning standard conditions concerns the angular size of the sample with respect to the eye of the observer. Both a ten-degree standard and a two-degree standard are in use in colorimetric practice. They don't give exactly the same results, and there is no agreed-upon recipe for converting from the one to the other. Color technologists will choose to use the one or the other, depending upon the purpose for which the measurement is to be made, but it never occurs to them to choose one rather than the other because it enables them to determine the "true" colors of material samples. Are we to conclude that color technologists lack a healthy sense of reality? Or do they understand something about standard conditions that philosophers don't?

Then there is the matter of the illuminant–sample–observer viewing angle. The colors we see from all manner of materials depend upon viewing angles, not only because some surfaces are glossy, but because much of the world's color is due to such physical mechanisms as scattering, refraction, interference and polarization, and these are typically angle-dependent. The colors of rainbows, oil films, and iridescent beetles are obvious examples. There are many others. For instance, crumple a piece of transparent cellophane and sandwich it between two sheets of polaroid material. Hold the sandwich up to a strong light, rotate one piece of the polaroid material relative to the other, and enjoy the spectacle of shifting colors. Many objects have transmission colors, which may be quite different from their reflection colors and may interact with them in surprising ways: gold is a notable example. Some objects are translucent, and there do not at the moment exist standards for determining their color characteristics. Then there are fluorescent objects, and self-luminous objects and the like. What are the standard conditions for viewing the colors of stars and bioluminescent fish? North daylight and six inches away?[10]

Still more might be said about viewing conditions, but we must cease beating this moribund horse. However, we should devote a moment to examining the remaining term of the equation, the "normal" observer. About six per cent of all males and a much smaller proportion of females are color deficient; doubtless some of the readers of the present volume fall into this category. Color-deficient people can make some visual discriminations that so-called "color normals" can't, a capability used by the military to penetrate camouflage that confuses color normals. Nevertheless, we, the majority, choose not to let them be the arbiters of the colors of things; we reserve this privilege for ourselves.

I have previously referred to the Standard Observer that is used in colorimetric determinations. The Standard Observer (also known as the Average Observer) is actually a standardized set of color matching curves that are based on average values obtained from the color matches made by fifty or so normal – that is, non-color-deficient – observers. The utility of having a standard observer so defined is scarcely to be doubted, but the fact remains that this is only an average taken over a range of people who vary significantly from each other in their visual performance. Indeed, the color matches made by the standard observer would not be fully acceptable to 90 per cent of the population, especially if they got more persnickity about the matches than they do in most everyday situations.

You might like to get an intuitive idea of the magnitude of the variation in color perception among normal observers. To do this, it will be helpful to look at a printed hue circle, such as may be found in textbooks on color for students of painting. Notice that all of the hues in the circle look to be either red, or yellow, or blue, or green, or some perceptual combination of two of them. Thus orange is a perceptual mixture of yellow and red, and turquoise is a perceptual mixture of blue and green. Now observe that some of the hues are more elementary than others. For instance, you can locate a red that is neither yellowish nor bluish, but you cannot find a purple that is neither reddish nor bluish; indeed a hue that was not reddish or not bluish could, for this reason alone, not count as purple. Visual scientists refer to hues such as purple and orange as *binary* hues, and to a non-binary hue such as the red that is neither yellowish nor bluish as a *unique* hue. It is easy to see that there are exactly four unique hues: there is a unique red, a unique yellow, a unique green, and a unique blue.

Do color-normal observers see unique hues at the same wavelength locations in the spectrum? Experimental investigations show that they do not. For example, Hurvich and Jameson[11] did a study on the spectral location of unique green, a hue that is neither yellowish nor bluish. Under carefully controlled conditions, any individual observer can consistently locate his or her unique green on a spectrum with an error of plus or minus three nanometers. But the average settings for 50 normal observers spanned a range of almost *thirty* nanometers, from 490 nm to 520 nm. Most people will see this range of greens as consisting of several distinguishable hues, ranging from a bluish green at one end to a yellowish green at the other. If your library has the *Munsell Book of Color*, you can get some idea of the perceptual breadth of the range. Look at the medium Value, high Chroma color chips in the Hue sequence from 5 Blue-Green to 2.5 Green.

The moral that we can draw from this is that the variability between normal observers is distinctly larger than the accuracy with which any of them can make hue distinctions. Equally large variability holds for the other perceptual dimensions of color. It should not be surprising, then, that just as metameric matches vary with the spectrum of the illumination, they vary from one observer to the next under the same conditions of observation. We may conclude that she who would fix the colors of the surfaces of objects by appealing to the perceptions of a normal observer under standard conditions is obliged not only to specify which normal observer and which set of standard conditions she has in mind, but is also obliged to give us a set of principles that will justify her choices. Needless to say, the philosophical literature contains neither the specifications nor the justifications.

We must now consider the third of the theories we had set out to investigate. This theory maintains that the colors of the surfaces of physical objects are to be identified with the spectral reflectances of such surfaces. Because of the mechanisms of approximate color constancy, reflectance is a physically measurable (though of course non-fundamental) feature of objects that, under ordinary conditions, correlates better with what we see than does the wavelength of the light that strikes the eye. This is because color vision has evolved so that animals can distinguish reflectances from each other without being confused by illuminance changes. Furthermore, reflectance is what is typically picked out by the phrase 'physical color' when that is used by color scientists to refer to an attribute of the surfaces of objects. It is a consequence of the reflectance theory that if objects have distinct spectral reflectances, they must be accounted distinct colors, even though they may not look distinct under any but the most special and bizarre illuminants. So, for the reflectivists, a metameric color match is a match of apparent colors, but not a match of real ones. Therefore, the problems that metamerism poses for the normal-observer, standard-condition theory are not problems for the reflectance theory.

However, there are two tasks that remain to be carried out by the reflectivist before he can claim that his is an adequate theory of color. The first of them is to extend the theory to cover chromatic physical phenomena that do not depend upon the reflection of light. There are many of these, and their number has increased rapidly with the advent of technology. Holograms and color television are obvious examples. The extension of the theory to encompass some of these phenomena will be relatively easy, but rather more difficult in others. For instance, there is more than one basic way to produce color television pictures. One of them, not commercially successful because of ineradicable problems of low saturation and flicker, has the interesting property that it permits the reception of color pictures on "black-and-white" television sets! The picture to be transmitted must be first be encoded by a device, the Butterfield encoder,[12] whose effect depends upon the ability of suitably sequenced achromatic pulses to stimulate differentially the color-perception mechanisms in the eye. The same principle is employed on a spinning wheel or top often sold as a novelty item. Psychologists know it as the "Benham disk."[13] The wheel has only a black-and-white pattern on it, but as it spins, you will, if you look at it closely and under a bright incandescent light, see rings of various desaturated colors, the hues of which depend upon the speed and direction of the rotation of the disk. If its inventor had succeeded in circumventing the limitations of the process, the Butterfield encoder might have become the industry standard. Would one then have been so easily tempted to regard these as "illusory" colors?

Let's suppose, though, that the reflectivist has successfully extended his account to cover the wide range of the physical causes of color perceptions. Has he thereby given us a theory of color? Surely he has not until he has told us about red, and green, and yellow, and blue. These, after all, are what most of us have in mind when we think about colors. By avoiding the problems of metamerism as well as other products of the workings of our visual systems, the reflectivist has no resources within his theory for collecting reflectances into the hue classes that we find in experience. We recall that metamerism comes about because our chromatic information consists entirely of the excitation ratios of three cone types. This trivariant chromatic information is transformed into fourfold hue perception in consequence of the way that the outputs of the cones are subsequently summed and differenced to generate two chromatic channels. One chromatic channel carries information that is registered by the brain as redness or greenness, but not both at once, and the other carries information that is registered by the brain as yellowness or blueness, but not both at once. The four unique hues along with their binary perceptual mixtures arise from this post-receptoral processing, as does the mutual exclusion of color complements. (This is why there are reddish yellows – the oranges – but no reddish greens.) This fourfold color structure has no counterpart in physical structures outside the organism, and any attempt to assign reflectances to fourfold color classes will inevitably appeal to normal observers and standard conditions, with inevitable arbitrariness. But beyond all of that, the colors that we actually see depend upon many more factors than relative spectral reflectance, such as the intensity with which the receptors are stimulated, what is going on in surrounding receptors at the moment, and what went on in the receptors during the previous milliseconds.

Let's look for a moment at just one of these factors, the effect of the intensity of light upon hue. Take an ordinary incandescent bulb and hold it next to a white wall. Since the wall looks white, it ought to reflect pretty faithfully the spectrum of any light that is incident upon it. When it is illuminated by the bulb, the light that the wall reflects will have the same wavelength make-up of the light that comes to your eye directly from the bulb, although the reflected light will be significantly less intense. A piece of red celluloid placed between your eyes and the bulb will serve as a transmission filter that will reduce the intensity of light from both sources. Its wavelength selectivity will be exactly the same for both the direct and the reflected light. Now if hue were to depend only upon the spectrum of the light, the light from the wall should have the same hue as the light that comes directly from the filament of the bulb. But as you will see when you try the experiment, the light from the filament is significantly more yellowish than the light reflected from the wall, although a spectrophotometer would show that the spectral profile is the same for both. Visual scientists explain the effect – a shifting of hues toward yellows and blues as light levels are increased – as a consequence of an increase in sensitivity of the yellow–blue channel relative to the red–green channel as the intensity of the light increases.

So the redness, greeness, yellowness and blueness we see when we look at the surfaces of objects depend upon quite a few more variables than just their wavelength profile. The reflectivist theory, like the wavelength theory, suffers from an irremediable underdetermination: too many of the mechanisms essential to the production of the colors that we see lie within the bodies of perceivers.

This should not be an unwelcome conclusion, even to physicalists. Why should chromatic phenomena not depend essentially upon processes that take place within the confines of the head? The stuffings of the head are, after all, material, and the whole process of color perception is physical, determinate, and lawlike from beginning to end. Physical objects need not have colors of their own, in some special, elitist manner, in order to look colored. The world need contain only objects and "looks," and sometimes just the looks will do. In a spirit of chromatic democracy, we should be willing to embrace Bidwell's ghost, for its origins are not supernatural, but only out of the ordinary. It is no more, but also no less, illusory than all the rest of the world's colors.

NOTES

1 Bidwell, S., "On negative after-images and their relation to certain other visual phenomena," *Proceedings of the Royal Society of London B* 68 (1901), 262–9.
2 An excellent source for these facts about color and color vision is L. M. Hurvich, *Color Vision*, Sunderland, MA: Sinauer Associates, 1981. Many of the chromatic phenomena likely to be of interest to philosophers are discussed in C. L. Hardin, *Color for Philosophers*, Indianapolis and Cambridge: Hackett Publishing Company, 1988.
3 Armstrong, D. M., *A Materialist Theory of the Mind*, London: Routledge & Kegan Paul, 1968.
4 Smart, J. J., "On some criticisms of a physicalistic theory of colors," in C.- Y. Cheng (ed), *Philosophical Aspects of the Mind–Body Problem*, pp. 54–63. Honolulu: University of Hawaii Press, 1975.
5 David Lewis's view is described in Smart, ibid.
6 Averill, E. W., "Color and the anthropocentric problem." *Journal of Philosophy* 82, 6 (1982), 281–303.
7 Hilbert, D., *Color and Color Perception: A Study in Anthropocentric Realism*. Chicago: University of Chicago Press, 1987.
8 Thompson, B. (Count Rumford), *Philosophical Papers*, Vol. 1. London: Cadell and Davies, 1802.
9 For a brief discussion of the advantages and difficulties of Edwin Land's retinex theory of color vision, see the appendix to Hardin, *Color for Philosophers*.
10 Cf. J. L. Austin, *Sense and Sensibilia*. Oxford: Oxford University Press, 1962.

11   Hurvich, L. M., Jameson, D. and Cohen, J. D., "The experimental determination of unique green in the spectrum." *Perceptual Psychology* 4 (1968), 65–8.

12   Butterfield, J. F., "Subjective (induced) color television." *Society of Motion Picture and Television Engineers Journal* 77 (1968), 1025–8.

13   Cf. C. E. Benham, "Notes." *Nature* (Lond.) 51 (1894), 113–14.

The Implications of Land's Theory of Color Vision

KEITH CAMPBELL

1 The situation prior to Land's contribution

There are two critical areas of difficulty for any metaphysical materialism in the philosophy of mind; the interpretation of intentionality, and the reduction of secondary qualities. In the first instance at least, a theory of color vision is, of course, a contribution to the debate over secondary qualities. Dr E. H. Land, of the Polaroid Corporation and instant photography, has made proposals which amount to a new theory of the whole process of seeing in color.[1] His accomplishment can be summarized, I believe, very briefly: hitherto, the colors have been in a worse position, so far as the prospects of a satisfactory reduction are concerned, than other secondary qualities. If Land is fundamentally right, colors are in the same condition, no worse (and no better) than sounds, smells, and perceived warmth.

Colors were formerly in a worse position than, for example, sounds, because strenuous efforts had failed to find a single physical reality corresponding to each of the different colors. By great misfortune, investigations of the physical basis of color began with the celebrated Newtonian prismatic resolution of sunlight into its spectrum. With the development of the wave theory of light, the association of distinctive spectral colors with their own distinctive wavelength was inevitable. The subsequent discovery of emission spectra for the different elements, consisting of narrow bands of emission at particular wavelengths, each of a characteristic hue, further consolidated the view that color is, more or less, directly, a matter of wavelength.

Indeed, this view became so entrenched that many philosophers still believe it. It is, however, false.

"The Implications of Land's Theory of Color Vision" by K. Campbell first appeared in *Logic, Methodology and Philosophy of Science VI. Proceedings of the Sixth International Congress of Logic, Methodology and Philosophy of Science, Hanover 1979*, pp 541–52. Copyright © 1982 by North-Holland Publishing Company and PWN – Polish Scientific Publishers.

If the light coming from any surface is concentrated in a narrow waveband, then that surface will indeed have one distinctive color under a wide variety of observational circumstances. Such surfaces are, however, very exceptional. The great majority of colored surfaces are selective reflectors of incident light. They reflect to some degree across at least a considerable segment of the visible spectrum. The great majority of illuminants providing the incident light contain at least some light at all visible wavelengths. Selective reflection of such light sends to the eye light with a component at most, if not all, the wavelengths to which the eye is sensitive.

Ordinarily, two surfaces which look different in color send to the eye light containing different proportions of the various visible wavelengths. The *flux* at a given wavelength is the amount of energy (the intensity) in that wavelength's light. Total energy across a range of wavelengths can be arrived at by integration. Different amounts of energy at the various wavelengths will yield different flux profiles for light of different compositions. Under conditions in which two surfaces receiving the same incident illumination look different in color, they will be found to be sending different fluxes to the observer. Hence flux became a natural candidate for the physical basis of color.

One great stumbling block to flux theories of color lay in the discovery that not only do surfaces of differing colors deliver different fluxes to the observer, but so do many surfaces between which normal human color vision does not distinguish.

Even if we put to one side anomalous or unusual cases, such as the colors produced by spinning a white disc with a black spiral on it, or colors in after-images, or colors seen on a thin oil film, there remains a wide range of fluxes, emanating from normal selective reflectors, associated with any given specific color. Worse, no unifying formula could be found to fit all and only these various fluxes belonging to one specific color. The attempt to identify flux as the physical correlate of color did not succeed. The search for a physical basis in flux proves to be a long wavelength herring.

With hindsight, we should have suspected this. The colors we see objects as having do not vary even under quite a wide range of variations in the local illumination, from indoor to outdoor, or noon to evening, or sunlight to overcast, which alter the flux leaving their surfaces.

2 Land's negative achievement

A major part of Land's contribtion to the problem lies in a series of experiments demonstrating the independence of color and flux, and so explaining why no unifying flux formulae for the different colors are forthcoming.

Land set up experiments in which the flux reaching the eye could be known with precision. He did this by using as illuminant a set of three narrow waveband projectors, one each in the long, middle, and short wavelength ranges of the visible spectrum (a red, a green, and a blue).

Many sets of three such light sources, combined in varying proportions, and sometimes diluted with white, can replicate any color discernible by normal humans – such sets of lights are known as sets of *additive primaries*. Color television sets reproduce color by a mosaic array of additive primaries.

Since a set of additive primaries matches the whole visible spectrum in the richness of its color-producing powers, use of such a set in place of whole-spectrum illuminants seems an acceptable simplification.

In Land's experiments, the three illuminators light up large square arrays of patches of many different colors, arranged so that each patch is surrounded by several differently colored ones. The arrays are nicknamed "color Mondrians": two identical color Mondrians are illuminated by two identical sets of narrow-band projectors.

On one color Mondrian a white patch is selected. The intensity of light it reflects to the eyes at each of the three incident wavelengths (the flux) is measured. On the second color Mondrian another patch, say a green one, is chosen. The intensity of light from the second set of projectors is now adjusted so that the flux from the green patch matches, wavelength for wavelength, that from the original white patch.

Under these circumstances, despite identity of flux, the white looks white and the green looks green. The two patches are viewed simultaneously, so no rapid adaptation phenomenon nor any trick of memory is involved.

Moreover, the projectors can be further adjusted so that a red or a blue patch, keeping its red or blue appearance, can send the same flux to the eye as the original white and green. Land goes so far as to claim that *any* color on his Mondrian can be made to send the original flux to the observer.

In short, the same light, entering eyes in the same condition, can give rise to impressions of color from seemingly anywhere on the color wheel. One could scarcely ask for a more convincing display of the independence of color and flux.

One could, however, ask for some indication of what, if not flux, constitutes the physical basis of color. For color vision is not capricious. Non-collusive agreement over color qualities and color changes is copious and subtle. Intersubjective coincidence in judgment calls for an objective reality underpinning it.

3   Land's positive experiments

In a second series of experiments Land takes up the positive task of identifying the real physical correlate for color. Here simplified color Mondrians, with only 17 color patches, are used in conjunction with the *Munsell Book of Color*, which contains over 1000 standard color "chips" for use in matching tests. The strategy is admirable: take a group of color Mondrian patches, and adjust the illuminators till each sends the same flux to the eye. Match each in turn with a Munsell chip, which, although indistinguishable in color from one of the Mondrian patches, will in fact be sending the eye a quite different flux.

The original negative conclusion, that flux is neither common to all surfaces of the same color, nor peculiar to surfaces of that color only, is reinforced.

The matching pairs, Mondrian patch and Munsell chip, are the objects of study. Some physical feature which both share, but which no other non-matching surface possesses, will be a good candidate for the physical basis we seek, common and peculiar to surfaces of each specific color considered in turn.

4   The theory built on these experiments

At any given wavelength, a surface will reflect some incident light and absorb some. The proportion reflected at given wavelength is the *reflectance* at that wavelength. Colored surfaces, as contrasted with white, grey or black ones, have different reflectances at different points on the spectrum, which is why they are described as selective reflectors.

In the Mondrian–Munsell matching experiments, both the intensity of incident illumination and intensity of reflected light are known for each of the three projected wavelengths. From this the reflectance at those wavelengths is determined.

Land is able to show that the reflectances of matching surfaces match, while the reflectances of differently colored surfaces do not match.

To be precise, he shows this for the three wavelengths at which his projectors illuminate the scene. It requires a further step to check that reflectances match or are otherwise equivalent right across the spectrum. So far as I know, this further step has not yet been taken. But there is at this point no reason to think that it would prove recalcitrant.

A match in reflectance is a match in how a surface modifies light in reflecting it. This modification is plainly a different matter from its product, the composition of the light coming to an observer. A match in reflectance is different from a match in consequent flux.

Provided they receive the same illumination, surfaces with the same reflectance will of course send to the eye the same flux. When experimenters controlled illumination, they created the situation in which matching reflectance coincides with matching flux at the eye. Controlling the illumination in experiments on color vision, an apparently obvious desideratum, thus ironically misled by appearing to cement a link between color and flux.

Constant illumination not only gives flux a misleading constancy. It diverts attention from the striking phenomenon of color constancy under varying illumination.

Under varying illumination reflected flux varies but reflectance does not. Within wide limits, nor does color. This is the key fact upon which Land proposes to build.

5   The mechanisms involved in color vision

Apart from the supersensitive rods, which generate the monochrome field of various greys with which we are familiar from experience of the world in twilight, there are in the eye three cone systems each responding over a part of the visible spectrum, each reaching peak sensitivity at a different wavelength. There is no doubt a connection between the existence of three cone systems and the need for exactly three well-chosen illuminators to serve as additive primaries for normal ("trichromatic") perceivers.

According to Land, the primary determination which visual receptor systems make concerns how light a surface is. Lightness is a familiar quantity; white surfaces have it in high degree, various greys in diminishing amount, and blacks practically not at all. Lightness is a feature belonging to appearance; lightness values are established by getting observers to judge a surface's position relative to black and white. Such judgments correspond closely to the relative reflectance of the surface in question. Although we cannot isolate and stimulate cone systems individually, Land holds that each of the cone systems makes its own independent judgement of lightness. Each surface we see is, so to speak, seen three times over, on three different, though overlapping, wavebands. And on each of those wavebands, the human visual system establishes how light the surface is. The result is a triple of lightness judgments over long-, middle-, and short-wave segments of the visible spectrum. These lightness values are the appearances to observers of reflectance values in the surface which is being seen.

Each surface has a reflectance at every wavelength, and this can be integrated across the range to which each cone system is sensitive. This yields a triplet of reflectances, which constitute the physical basis of color. The reflectances give rise to a triplet of lightnesses, which constitute the observational basis of color. To every discernible color corresponds a unique triplet of lightnesses. That is the essence of Land's doctrine.

Three lightness values means three dimensions of variation, so the colors can all be located on a Color Cube, with each color's unique lightness triple serving as a uniquely locating set of coordinates. Black, darkest on all three cone systems, is at the origin, white at the opposite vertex, the greys along the diagonal representing equal lightness on each system. The other colors are dispersed through the space of the cube.

6 Determining reflectance triples

But now the problem to be faced is this: the information on which color vision works must all be contained in the light reaching the observer. However, reflectance, and hence how light things look, consists in the relationship between illumination and reflected flux. How can reflectance be judged without knowledge of the composition and strength of the illumination?

Land's approach to this problem is by way of *comparison* of flux coming from different surfaces at the same time. Hence his use of polychrome color Mondrians. Take one cone system, say the short-wave sensitive one. Under illumination uniform in the range to which that system responds, different surfaces in the visual field will send different fluxes to an observer. This will enable a rank order of lightnesses to be established. The absolute levels of flux from lightest and darkest areas, and hence the range of lightness values, will also be available.

Where the range of lightnesses is wide, the lightest surface will be highly reflective over the short-wave band, and the ratios other, darker, surfaces bear to the lightest will be closely related to their reflectances.

I think less favourable cases will involve comparisons not only within one cone system, but between different systems.

A narrow range of lightness at flux values which are rather high in the context of the total illumination can be produced in two ways; either by a set of surfaces all of which reflect strongly at the short end of the spectrum, or by an illumination whose composition is skewed towards the short end. The result in either case is that everything has a bluish cast. The effect can be produced in the first way by painting everything blue, or in the second way by using a blue plastic lamp shade.

Comparisons of flux values between different cone systems can likewise establish lightness values for a narrow range all located at the darker end.

Thus lightness triples can be established for the three cone systems, and by their means we can get to reflectance triples, and so to colors.

7   The virtues of this theory

If Land is right, every variation in color can be correlated with a specific physical variation. In principle, the color which a surface will have in any specified illumination can be calculated and predicted in advance. Color will be in the same position as sound, or felt temperature, or, if stereo-chemical theory is on the right track, smell.

So far as I can see, Land's doctrine can accommodate most of the color variation phenomena, such as change of color on very close approach, or under a microscope, or in the distance, or through haze, or tinted glass. These are all cases where a non-standard relationship between flux leaving a surface and flux entering the eye can affect judgment on flux and hence judgment on reflectance. With objects in shadow, the darker shift arises from non-standard illumination.

Every theory of color needs a comfortable machinery to accommodate our dual way of ascribing colors. On one use colors are standing phenomena, changed only by intrinsic change in the object, such as a leaf undergoes in autumn or a motor car at the spray-painters. Standing colors remain the same through changes in illumination or other extrinsic circumstances. Hills do not change from blue to green on closer approach, nor does water go pink in the dawn.

On another use, color terms pick out just the occurrent hue of the present moment, and colored spotlights in the theatre are said to transform the colors of skin, clothing and sets.

There are two correct answers to Locke's question about porphyry in the dark, one for the standing, one for the transitory, color.

Land's theory provides the required machinery for dealing with this double use. In the object, *reflectance* triples provide an objective basis for an intrinsic standing color – just which one will be determined by the apparent color in standard noon-day conditions.

In experience, the *lightness* triples are subject to variation even when reflectance is not altered, by change in distance, illumination, and state of observer. Lightness triples provide the basis for transitory colors.

The theory is attractive in another way too. Colors apparently play a negligible role in causal chains in the inanimate realm. Notoriously, in offering physical explanations we have little occasion to invoke the colors of objects. In Stout's phrase, colors seem not to belong to the executive order of nature. This has been one source of subjectivism about colors.

But here we have the materials for an objectivist account of the situation: if colors are integrated reflectances across three overlapping segments clustered in the middle of the total electromagnetic spectrum, then they are, from the inanimate point of view, such highly arbitrary and idiosyncratic properties that it is no wonder the particular colors we are familiar with are manifest only in transactions with humans, rhesus monkeys, and machines specially built to replicate just their particular mode of sensitivity to photons.

Another virtue of the theory is its properly empirical character. It claims that a certain quite specific mode of processing flux inputs at the eye is performed somewhere in the retina–optic-nerve–cortex complex. Just where is not yet specified – hence Land's use of the term "retinex" to cover the proposed location of the processing activity.

A computer program has made good progress towards reproducing the flux-comparison processing which the theory requires. If there are neural functions which constitute the integrating and comparing activities involved, it is, in principle, possible to identify them. If on the other hand the nervous system is not capable of performing the required tasks, it is in principle possible to establish that. This is as it should be.

In this connection, it is noteworthy that independent work by Dr A. L. Gilchrist confirms the importance to vision of contrasts at edges in the visual field.[2] These are crucial to interpretation, and can enable judgments about illumination to be made, which is plainly a bonus in the business of determining reflectance.

8   Its problems

There are, however, some unresolved problems in the theory. As it stands, it is organised to account only for colored *reflecting* surfaces. It needs further elaboration to cope with visual fields containing both emitters and reflectors. For, of course, a light source has a color, and so presumably a set of lightness values, but these lightness values are not determined by its reflectance at all. Is a light source identified, perhaps, by its exceptionally high flux values, then treated by considering relativities between the three cone systems as if they were produced by reflection under white light?

Further, there are difficulties with visual fields which are not variegated and polychromatic. Land discusses the spot-in-the-void, a single small source of narrow band light on a black ground. How can its lightness triple be determined, where no comparisons are available for fixing relative lightnesses? According to Land, comparisons between the three cone systems suffice. The three systems respond differently, and the relationship between these responses is nearly invariant with changes in intensity of the light source.

But the cone systems are responding to flux, and lightness is supposed to relate not to flux but to reflectance. The same relative responses, on the three systems, can be produced by many different reflectances under different illuminations. If the spot were not an emitter but a reflector, how could we tell that it is a very narrowly selective reflector without knowledge of the illumination? A *reflecting* spot in a void does not provide enough information for a Land-type determination of color. I see no basis on which arriving at the lightness triple for emitters of light should be significantly easier.

The position is not better, indeed is potentially worse, with a monochrome field sending light of all wavelengths to the eye, such as a cloudless summer sky viewed while lying on your back, or a color card brought right up to your nose. I do not know how lightnesses can be established in these conditions.

9 Prospects for a materialist reduction of color vision

Let us accept that Land's work lays at least the foundations for a satisfactory theory of color vision. Do colors now cease to be an embarrassment for materialist theories of the mind?

No, they do not. As already mentioned, colors move into a position comparable to the other secondary qualities: sounds, smells, tastes, felt warmths. But from a materialist perspective, that is not a particularly satisfactory position.

We must here face once more the old issue of qualia. It seems such an arbitrary and contingent matter that sundry lightness triples should appear as scarlet, yellow or ultramarine. To which the natural reply is: well the lightness triples must look like *something*, why shouldn't they been seen as colors? Why shouldn't the colors be no more than ways in which lightness triples are seen, hence intentional characters no more troublesome to materialism than intentionality itself?

I cannot regard that as a satisfactory reply. Contrast the case of color with that of the true-blue primary qualities. Take position, or shape, or size, or orientation. Each of these physical characters is perceived, visually, through the occurrence of position, shape, size, or orientation in the visual field. The perceptual character through which each of these primary qualities is perceived is that very quality itself. Likewise for changes in these primary qualities. Change of position – movement .– is perceived through movement in the visual field. The· growth, deformation, and rotation of bodies can be seen thanks to growth, deformation, and rotation in the visual field. There is no gulf between the physical fact and its appearance.

But how different are the colors! What natural link could lead us to expect particular lightness triples to present themselves as emerald, indigo, or rose? Or that changes in lightness triples would be manifest as a kaleidoscope?

To highlight the distinction between color and reflectance, consider selective fatigue. If you sit for a while in a room full of long-wavelength light, the long-wavelength cone system will get fatigued relative to the other two systems, and will respond less than normal to further stimulation. If you now step outside and look around, the visual system will react as if there were a systematic decline in relative long wavelength lightness values. The effect is comparable to that of adding to daylight an additional middle- and short-wave illuminant. The scene will appear as if bathed in mixed blue and green; that is, cyan auxiliary light. Colors will shift systematically. Reds will go dark. Yellows will go greenish. Magentas will go blue. Whites and greys will drift to cyan.

Now so far as we can tell, it could perfectly well have happened that humans evolved with a long-wave cone system more weakly sensitive than the others. If that had happened, standard conditions would have yielded us these experiences of color which are now obtainable only under selective fatigue. In that case, while reflectances would have remained the same, colors would have been systematically transformed. This possibility shows that in the absence of a particular mode of sensibility which we humans have there is nothing peculiarly or intrinsically *red* about a certain reflectance triple. The connection between reflectance triples and the color experiences to which they give rise is looser and more contingent than in the case of size, shape, or solidity, for which no comparable systematic transformation seems possible.

If colors resist identification with the appropriate physical characteristics of physical surfaces, perhaps seeing the colors can be identified with the corresponding physiological processes in the "retinex" system?

Two sorts of considerations suggest otherwise. First, the mutual independence of the three lightness judgments over the three ranges is of the essence of Land's theory, and this makes a lightness triple analogous to a musical chord. But unlike the musical case, the experience of scarlet contains no independent elements which nature or training could enable us to distingish as its three components.

It could be urged in reply that in the perception of color, lightness values are held separate and compared with one another at an early processing stage, from which only a single, summary, resultant response emerges into consciousness.

This does not, in my view, dispose of the difficulty entirely. It accounts for the absence of any chord-like structure in the colors, but leaves us in the dark as to how seeing scarlet, for example, could be doing a complex set of transformations on lightness inputs which we have no reason to suppose are themselves inherently color experiences. The experience of seeing scarlet has none of the characteristics which experiences of abstracting, comparing, and combining typically have. And *they* on the other hand, are diaphanous. Hue is one feature they most conspicuously lack.

The second sort of ground for resisting a physiological identification for color vision is structural.

Changes in lightness and changes in color are not isomorphic. Equal lightness differences are by no means tied to equal color differences. On the color cube, adjacent places in some regions have colors much more different than equally adjacent places elsewhere. Reds and greens furnish perhaps the most striking example. A strong red and an equally vivid green may differ only in a small change in lightness in the middle wavelength range. Comparable changes in other contexts result in no more than a slight change in hue.

This is not, so far, a decisive point. It may be argued that survival adaptation has built in exaggerations at certain points, so that we habitually mistake certain degrees of color difference. Perhaps in that case the color cube will teach us to mend our ways and lead us to admit that reds and greens are really close to one another.

It may be argued that when we sit down to test the question, we will find that we can discriminate as many different shades between two initially very alike blues, adjacent on a "coarse-texture" color cube, as we can discriminate intermediates between the red and the green adjacent on the coarse-texture cube. Such a result would reveal a sort of color-distance illusion phenomenon.

I rest no confidence in these lines of reply. For to some degree color experience is essentially diverse. The visual field gets some of its quality from being a field of color contrasts and color likenesses. There could be a monochrome world. But whatever its color, it would not be *that* color unless it would differ in color, to just such-and-such a degree, from other possible ones. Reds cannot stay reds while somehow becoming, or seeming to become, more like greens.

Qualia will not go away. They belong to mental life on its experiencing side, and resist reduction. They suggest the experiencing mind's existence is in some measure independent of its material base.

NOTES

1 An account accessible to laymen is to be found in *Scientific American* 237, no. 6, Dec. 1977.
2 *Scientific American* 240, no. 3, March 1979, pp. 88ff.

19

The Imagery Issue

Mental Pictures and Cognitive Science

NED BLOCK

Cognitive scientists have made some amazing claims about mental images. We are told that people *rotate* mental images, and at measurable speeds. Three-dimensional shapes were rotated in one experiment at 60 degrees per second, while letters of the alphabet have been clocked at 800 degrees per second. We are told that mental images can be scanned, just as are scenes and pictures – and again at measurable speeds. Smaller mental images are supposed to be harder to see than larger ones, and when mental images are made larger, they eventually overflow. Further, what they overflow *from* has a determinable shape – roughly elliptical. There's more. Images subtend a determinate visual angle, which, at the point of overflow, is described as the angle of vision of the mind's eye (roughly 20 degrees, as it happens).[1]

Such claims are part of a viewpoint according to which mental images represent in the manner of pictures. It is very natural to think that such claims are confused or nonsensical. One of my purposes here is a limited defense of this supposedly confused doctrine, especially against its chief cognitive science rival. But this paper has another quite distinct topic: the concept of representation in general (not just pictorial representation) as it functions in cognitive science. I put the two together by arguing that it *matters* to cognitive science whether it has to encompass pictorial representations as well as the standard strings of zeros and ones (and similar language-like or descriptive representations). If cognitive science must postulate pictorial representations in the head, then cognitive science may be in serious trouble, for much of what it hopes to explain will probably be in the domain of a different discipline: neurophysiology.

It will be useful for those who know nothing of the experiments that motivate the picture-in-the-head view for me to sketch a few of them. Readers who are familiar with these experiments can skip the next three paragraphs.

"Mental Pictures and Cognitive Science" by N. Block first appeared in *Philosophical Review* 93 (1983), pp. 499–542, and is reprinted here by kind permission.

Block figure rotation

The three pairs of block figures in figure 1 are from an experiment by Shepard and Metzler.[2] Your task is to look at pair A and say whether the objects pictured are congruent or not. Do the same for B, and then for C. The two drawings in A are the same except that they are pasted on the page in different orientations. In B we have two-dimensional projections of objects that differ not by a rotation in the plane of the page as in A, but rather by a rotation out of the page (that is, around an axis in the page). In C, the figures are noncongruent mirror images. Subjects in this experiment were presented with 1600 such pairs and asked to pull one lever if the objects were congruent, and another if not. Result: the greater the angular separation of the congruent figures, the longer it took subjects to respond. Indeed, the time to respond was a *linear* function of angle of separation, independently of whether the rotation was in the plane of the page or perpendicular to it. (So if this experiment suggests pictures in the head, they will have to be 3-D pictures.) Subjects reported imagining one object rotated so as to be superimposable on the other. This experiment is often taken to indicate that people can rotate mental images, and at measurable speed. Metzler later chose a group of these subjects whose rotation speeds were relatively constant (not variable), and calculated their individual speeds. Then she gave subjects single figures (not pairs), and asked them to start rotating in a clockwise direction. Next she presented *rotated* versions of the original stimulus ("probes") in accordance with calculations based on the subject's known speed. For example, if the subject rotated at 50 degrees per second, she might present a 50-degree rotated figure after one second, or a 100-degree rotated figure after two seconds, or a 75-degree rotated figure after 1.5 seconds. Subjects were instructed to say whether the original figure (whose image they had been asked to rotate) and the "flashed" rotated figure were congruent or not. What she found was that the time it took subjects to respond (to congruent probes) was always about the same, independently of the angular separation of the first and second figure. That is, whether she presented a 50-degree rotated figure after one second or a 100-degree rotated figure after two seconds made no difference to response time. And the response times were short – about the same as the shortest response times of the Shepard and Metzler experiment just described. This is interpreted as indicating that she *caught* their rotated images at *just the right point* with her probe.[3]

Map scanning

Subjects studied the map in figure 2 until they could draw it, getting the seven locations marked by red dots (Xs in figure 2) approximately right. In one of the experiments done by Kosslyn and his colleagues, subjects were asked to "zoom in" on one of the objects on the map, say the well, until that object "filled their entire image."[4] They were told that they would soon hear the name of another

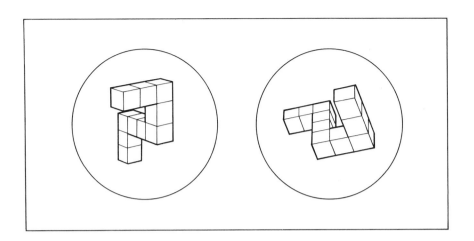

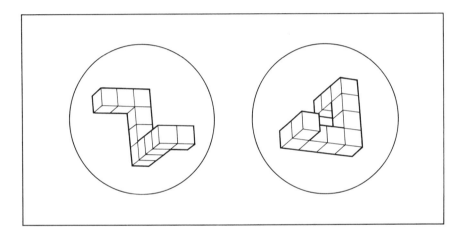

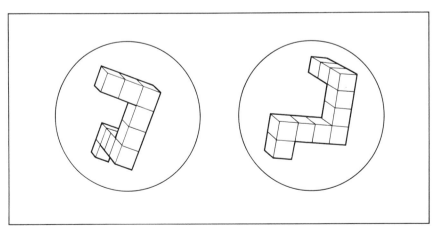

Figure 1 This figure was reprinted with the permission of *Science*, 171, no. 3972 (February, 1971), p. 701.

580

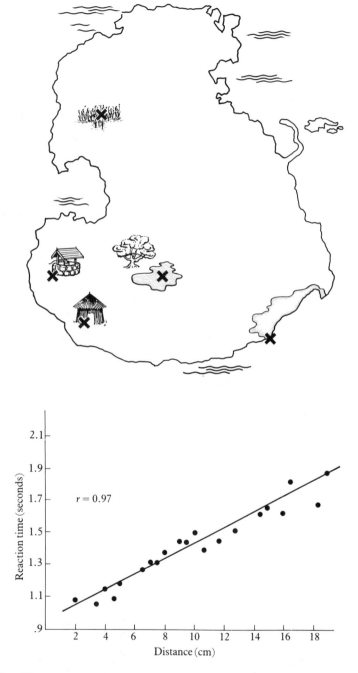

Figure 2 The map scanned, and the time to scan different distances across an image of it. (This figure was reprinted with the permission of Stephen M. Kosslyn from S. Kosslyn, S. Pinker, S. Schwartz and G. Smith, "On the demystification of mental imagery," p. 137 of Ned Block, (ed.), *Imagery*, Cambridge: MIT Press, 1981.)

object that might or might not be on the map. They were instructed to "see" the named object (if it was in fact on the map), pressing a button when they had done so. All pairs of the seven objects were used. Result: time taken to "see" the second object was directly related to the distance on the map between the two objects (correlation = 0.97). This result is taken to indicate that mental images can be *scanned*. Further, this experiment is used to support the idea that parts of mental images can be *unconscious*. For when subjects "zoomed in" on an object on the map, they were not aware of imaging the *other* objects on the map. Yet their scanning times were far faster than would be expected if they were generating images of the other objects anew – based on independent measurements of how long it takes to produce images.

In another scanning experiment, Finke and Pinker showed subjects patterns made up of dots. They turned off the dot pattern, asked the subject to form an image of the pattern, and then flashed an arrow, which, in half the trials, pointed to where a dot had been. Subjects were asked to indicate if the arrow did point at one of the imagined dots. If the arrow did point towards a dot on the original pattern, time taken to answer was directly related to the distance between the tip of the arrowhead and the dot (mistakes were rare).[5]

How do these experiments support the picture-in-the-head view? If it were an intelligent *robot* that exhibited this sort of phenomenon, we would surely be tempted by the hypothesis that the robot was constructing, manipulating and examining pictorial representations somewhere inside its body. Many of us are less tempted to postulate internal pictures in *us*, partly because we have tentative competing hypotheses about what is happening in the experiments and partly because we know no pictures have been found in our brains (more about these matters later).

Experiments such as the ones mentioned above have given rise to considerable controversy. One side, *pictorialism*, supposes that the mental representations of imagery represent in the manner of pictures, for example, of President Reagan being shot. The rival, *descriptionalism* (a popular view, especially in the artificial intelligence community), says that the representations of imagery (and all other internal representations as well) represent in the manner of familiar symbol structures such as those in a computer or those in English (the sentence 'President Reagan was shot'.)[6]

Now that the reader has caught a glimpse of the pictorialism/descriptionalism controversy, I can better explain the plan of this paper. The paper has two quite different argumentative strands. The first, which begins after ground-clearing remarks (on perception, the vagueness of 'mental image', and introspection), is a defense of pictorialism from three rather flat-footed objections:

1 *The No Seeum objection.* When we look in the brain, we don't see any pictures.
2 *The Leibniz's Law objection.* Mental images can be orange- and pink-striped, but bits of the brain never have such properties.
3 *The Paraphernalia objection.* Rotating and scanning pictures in the head would require an internal eye, hands, and other things that are not in fact to be found in the head.

My strategy is to argue that the sort of problem indicated by these objections is one to which descriptionalism is just as vulnerable as is pictorialism, and, more importantly, that there are defenses available to the descriptionalist which are also available to the pictorialist. In short, pictorialist and descriptionalist cognitive science must stand or fall together against such objections. This mode of defense of pictorialist and descriptionalist cognitive science brings in my second and more important argumentative strand. I argue that the common defense of pictorialist and descriptionalist cognitive science reveals a potentially serious limitation on the explanatory power of theories in cognitive science. The key concept in this argument is the concept of a primitive process, a process whose input–output function is appealed to by cognitive science explanations, but whose mode of operation is not itself within the domain of cognitive science. The mode of operation of a primitive process is rather in the domain of a "lower level" science: neurophysiology, in the case of humans. The potentially serious limitation comes in with the possibility that primitive processes may bear most of the burden in explaining human thought. If so, cognitive science "bottoms out" in primitive processors much sooner than expected.

In the course of presenting this point, I shall point out that cognitive science has a ready defense against Wittgensteinian criticisms about representations and rules, but that the employment of this defense leads once again to the potentially serious limitation just mentioned.

The meaning of 'mental image'

The term 'mental image' is too vague to allow a determinate answer to the question of what the nature of mental images is. In the controversy over what the mental imagery experiments show, 'mental image' is *usually* used to denote the internal representations involved in mental imagery, but even in this literature, 'mental image' sometimes denotes the *experiences* we have in imagery, sometimes mental states that *include* these experiences plus more, and sometimes even abstract "imaginary" objects. This sort of vagueness is pretty common in the history of science. Seventeenth-century Europeans did not distinguish among heat, temperature, and even perceived temperature. Often, a single word was used for all three in situations in which context did not disambiguate. I think construing 'mental image' as denoting the internal representations involved in imagery helps to make sense of the controversy over whether mental images are pictures in the head.

To avoid confusion, it may be useful to distinguish mental images in my sense (the internal representations of imagery) from what might be called *phenomenal* images, the "seeming objects of image experiences," the things, if such there be, which are more or less vivid, sometimes orange-and-pink-striped, etc. (even though they reflect no light).[7] Much of the discussion in philosophy over whether mental images *exist* or are objects is usefully construed as concerning phenomenal images, and perhaps not mental images in my sense. I happen to think that phenomenal images are identical to mental images in my sense, though I shall not assume this is so (except to rebut an objection that assumes it) or argue for it here. If phenomenal images are not identical to mental images, then I don't know (or care) what phenomenal images are. If phenomenal images *are* identical to mental images, then according to both pictorialist and descriptionalist cognitive scientists, they are symbols or symbol-structures in the head.

Imagery and perception

The experiments that motivate the pictorialist perspective are often taken to support a different hypothesis: that the representations and processes of imagery are like the representations and processes of *perception*. This hypothesis is often confused with pictorialism, in part because many people seem to find it difficult to understand the possibility that the representations of perception *might not be pictorial* (more on this later). There are many experimental results that support the similarity of imagery and perception without supporting pictorialism. For example, it is known that visual acuity for vertical stripes is better than for oblique stripes. This is called the oblique effect. If the experimenter holds up a grating and slowly moves it away, asking subjects to indicate when the stripes blur, subjects report the vertical stripes beginning to blur further away than the oblique stripes. Amazingly, the oblique effect occurs when the subjects are asked to *imagine* a grating moved slowly away from them. If the imagined grating is vertical, blurring occurs at a greater subjective distance than if it is oblique.[8]

Many perceptual phenomena such as the oblique effect have been found to occur with imagery.[9] While the experimental literature does not distinguish as clearly as one would like between the effects of representations and the effects of the processes that manipulate representations, the evidence is now strong that the representations of imagery and perception are of the same kind.

But – and here is the point – the claim that the representations of imagery and perception are of the same kind is irrelevant to the controversy over pictorialist vs. descriptionalist interpretation of experiments like the image scanning and rotation experiments mentioned earlier. The representations of imaging and of perceiving should be lumped together as either *both* pictorial or both descriptional. But we still want to know *which!* The descriptionalist in committed to regarding the representations of perception as descriptional (given the evidence just mentioned).[10] By lumping the representations of imagery and perception together, we reduce two problems to one problem, but we have not thereby solved the one problem.

Imagery and introspection

The picture-in-the-head theory of images profits from an apparent *convergence* of experiment and introspection. As we look inward, our mental images often seem to us to be pictures in the head, and by golly, when the experimental results come in, they back up this introspective judgment. Part of the basis of the introspective judgment could be put like this: "Of *course*, my mental image of my daughter is pictorial; it looks just like this photograph of my daughter. I carry one around in my wallet and the other in my head." I want to reject firmly this line of reasoning; introspective judgment in this case is a cover for fallacious reasoning.

When someone says his mental image looks like a picture, he must be appealing to the fact that his image experience is like the experience he gets on looking at the picture. But this is a poor reason to suppose that his image *is* a picture. After all, the image experience is *also* like the experience he gets on looking at his daughter *herself*. And one could as well-argue from this fact that his image is a *person*.

If I experience *x* and *y* as similar, this could be due to a similarity in *x* and *y*, but it could be due instead to something about me and my relation to *x* and *y*. I experience my psychiatrist and my father in the same way, but the explanation is not any similarity between my father and my psychiatrist. I would have experienced the psychiatrist as like my father even if either of them had been quite different along almost any dimension you choose. I experience the two as similar because of a neurosis having to do with my father, and the familiar transference of the psychiatric interaction.

Returning to the similarity between the way I experience my mental image of my daughter and a photo (or a wax dummy) of her, we *have* a readily available explanation in terms of something about me, so we don't have to postulate a similarity between the image and the photo or wax dummy. The available explanation appeals first to the fact that the representations of imagery and perception can be experientially similar. Second, a glimpse of a good wax dummy of my daughter can give rise to the same retinal stimulation as a glimpse of my daughter herself, and hence the same visual representations. So we can have a similarity between imaging and perceiving my daughter, and a similarity between perceiving my daughter and perceiving a 3-D or a 2-D picture of her. So the similarity between imaging my daughter and perceiving a picture of her should be no surprise.

Perhaps what I've just said is not quite enough to quiet the claims of introspection. Consider the following reply:

> Your account of the basis for our intuitive judgment that mental images are pictorial just sets up a straw man. Here is the real story:
>
> 1   My mental image of my daughter resembles my daughter, as is typical of pictorial representations of my daughter. Further, there is a detailed point by point correspondence, for example, the top of the image resembles the top of my daughter, the bottom of the image resembles the bottom of my daughter, etc. This is typical of *good* pictorial representations of my daughter.
>
> 2   My mental image of my daughter resembles good pictures of my daughter (again, in a point by point fashion) just as each picture typically resembles the others.
>
> 3   My image does not resemble either words, phrases or sentences about my daughter, nor do any of the other types of pictorial representations of her (movies, wax dummies) resemble language about her.

4 Assuming that my mental image is a representation, and that we are deciding whether to categorize it as pictorial (along with photos and wax dummies) or as descriptional (along with words and phrases) it would therefore be idiotic to choose the latter.

Rejoinder: if we were shown a new form of representation (such as a hologram, when they were first invented) which we see in the manner in which we see objects, including pictures, sentences, and my daughter herself, and if the new representation looked like my daughter and pictures of her, but unlike language about her, we might well be reasonably persuaded to classify the new form of representation as pictorial. The trouble with this reasoning as applied to mental images is that we don't *see* them. My daughter, a photo of her, and the phrase 'my daughter' are things we see; mental images, by contrast, are things we *have*. The argument depends on a false parallel between our relation to our mental images on the one hand, and our relation to pictures, people, and printed words on the other. Perhaps the representations we have when we perceive – the representations that mediate perception – are themselves descriptional; this is the crucial possibility that the introspectionist argument fails to take account of.

In sum, the fact to start with is that we have both introspective and experimental evidence for similarity of representations of imagery and perception: imaging my daughter and seeing her can yield functionally and experientially similar representations. Now a good picture of my daughter is designed to produce a representation experientially like that produced by seeing my daughter. *That* is why my image "looks like" the picture. The important point is that this explanation of why my image "looks like" the picture assumes nothing about whether the internal representations are pictorial or descriptional.

The No Seeum objection

Perhaps the most straightforward objection to the view that mental images are pictures in the head is simply that when one *looks* in the head, one doesn't see any pictures. This is the no seeum objection. In locating what is wrong with this objection, it is useful to note that it is *not* so tempting to make this sort of objection against the chief cognitive science rival to the picture-in-the-head view, descriptionism.

Now it is clear enough why descriptionalism is immune from the argument that we don't *see* descriptional representations when we look in the brain. Before you can recognize a descriptional message, two conditions must be satisfied. First, you must know the representational system, and second, there must be a visible message in that representational system. The hairs on the spy's head are arranged so as to spell out a 500-word message for his barber, his link to the KGB. But *you* don't see any message when you look at his hair.

Here is my point: the reply that protects descriptionalism from the no seeum objection equally protects pictorialism. What *any* representation represents, and *how* it represents – pictorially or descriptionally – depends on the system of representation within which it functions. Ink marks that your tribe uses as a picture could be a letter in *my* tribe's descriptional alphabet. Perhaps some of the inscriptions that archeologists treat as pictures that give insight into long-dead civilizations really functioned originally as symbols in a language. Conversely, imagine an ancient symbol system that archeologists think is a language, one that they have successfully decoded. They write each other letters in this language, and even form a club where only this language is spoken. But actually the language is their own creation; the original symbols they found were really pictures.[11]

This relativity to system of representation also holds *within* the category of descriptional representations and also to some extent within the category of pictorial representations. In the descriptional case, it is illustrated by Davidson's example: the sound we make in saying "Empedocles leaped" means one thing in English and another in German. In the pictorial case, cross-cultural study of picture perception reveals some cultural relativity, though of course nothing like the degree of conventionality found in language. For example, a picture which we see as having an elephant in the background was seen in another culture as having a very small elephant suspended in air in the foreground.[12]

My point is not just that what represents what is relative to a system of representation. Rather, my point is that you can't tell for sure whether you are looking at a representation at all *just* by looking. Whether a thing is a representation at all, and if so, whether it is a pictorial representation or a descriptional representation, cannot be determined if one limits one's attention to the thing itself. One has to determine how the thing functions. Since we know next to nothing about how representations in the brain function, we can hardly expect to tell, just by looking, *which* structures in the brain are representations, much less how brain representations represent.

Now that I have allowed that the pictorialist's pictures in the head can't just be *seen* to be pictures, and the descriptionalist's sentences in the head cannot just be *seen* to be sentences, surely I must say something about what the difference between pictures and sentences in the head is supposed to be. What I would like to do here is introduce an adequate account of the pictorial/descriptional distinction. Unfortunately, though many accounts are in the literature, none that I know of is very satisfactory.

One condition on pictorial representation that has something going for it is this: if a picture represents something, S, then at least one part of the picture must represent part of S; further, typically some of the relations among the parts of the picture represent relations among the parts of S, and some relations between parts of the picture and the whole picture represent relations between the parts of S and S itself.[13] Obviously, such a condition need not apply to descriptional representations. "The first son of Elizabeth II' refers to Charles, but no part of it refers to part of Charles. Though this condition has some appeal, I do not want to place a lot of weight upon it. For one thing, it is doubtful as a sufficient condition. (Part of 'Britain's empire' refers to part of the empire.) Secondly, in the cases in dispute, there is generally as much of a problem about the application of the condition itself as there is about the application of 'picture'. Finally, this account is particularly unrevealing with respect to the very issue I've just been talking about: the dependence of a thing's representational properties on the system of representation in which it functions. The condition takes for granted 'represents' and 'part', concepts which are themselves functional.

I do not know how to characterize what it is about function within a system of representation that makes a representation pictorial or descriptional. The best I can do is to try to evoke a feeling for the difference by means of examples.

Consider what goes into a computer by way of storing a picture of, say, a vertical line. Consider a matrix n squares wide. Each of the squares can be light or dark. A vertical line would be represented if each lighted square is n squares distant from the first lighted square (counting by row, as on a calendar). The descriptionalist sees the line representation as a set of sentences. If $n = 7$, the set of sentences could be: '1 is dark', '2 is light', '3 is dark', . . . '9 is light', '10 is dark', and so on. The descriptionalist sees a representation of a line in the *brain* along the same lines as a set of descriptional representations, akin to a set of sentences. The pictorialist, on the other hand, sees the representation of a line in the brain as like the *matrix itself*, not the corresponding set of sentences.

But what does the distinction come to between the set of sentences and the matrix itself? Aren't they just *different ways* of inscribing the same representation with the same semantic properties?

I say "No." The key is the way the representations *function*. Consider how the descriptionalist would *rotate* his line. A small counterclockwise rotation could be accomplished if the first lighted square stayed lit, the next number of a lighted square was increased by 1, the next by 2, the next by 3, and so on. In terms of the example, 2 would stay lit, 10 would be lit instead of 9, 18 instead of 16, 26 instead of 23, etc. So the descriptionalist's new set of sentences would be '1 is dark', '2 is light', . . . '10 is light', . . . '18 is light', . . '26 is light', and so on. The important point is that the computer's "rotation" calculation just involves the *numbers*, not the arrangement of the numbered squares. The matrix display is *for us* and plays no role in what the computer does. From the point of view of the computer's calculations, the squares *could as well be arranged in a line or a circle rather than a matrix*. Real live computer graphics works this way. The machine manipulates numbers. The programmers think of the numbers as numbers of cells in matrices, and they put in numbers that correspond to matrices of visual interest. They program the computer to operate on the numbers in ways that correspond to visually interesting or useful matrix changes. These correspondences are what makes the computer's number crunching *graphical*, but the correspondences play no role at all in the number crunching itself.

Once we see what the computer *does*, we realize that the representation of the line is descriptional. But what sort of process would show that a representation is pictorial? I don't have a ready answer, since we have no machines that manipulate pictorial representations in the systematic ways that computers manipulate descriptional representations. But I can try to give the flavor with an example, albeit a physiologically absurd one.

Imagine that a space is to be represented by electrical potential and current at points in the visual cortex. The system of representation is polar coordinates, and current represents angle while potential represents distance from the origin. (For those who have forgotten all they learned in high school, in polar coordinates a point is specified by a pair of numbers, one of which gives the distance from the origin, while the other gives the angle (measured counterclockwise) of the arrow pointing from the origin to the specified point.) Suppose there is a region of the visual cortex in which all points have the same current (and thus fall on a line) but differ in potential, being distributed between 0 and 10 units (so we have a line 10 units long). Suppose also that in its present mode, all the points in this region are linked by circuits that cause current to flow from regions of high current to regions of low current. Result: the linkage keeps the region homogeneous in current value and the points represented stay on a line. Now if the current value is smoothly increased, we would have a smooth counterclockwise rotation. Imagine that the current of all the points is increased as a result of increasing the current of a few points (the linkage among currents causing the other currents to increase). This would be like turning a whole stick by applying torque to a small part of it.

I am emphatically not claiming that it is a *sure thing* that there is a legitimate distinction to be made between pictorial and descriptional representations in the brain. I do think, however, that the possibility of a genuine difference here deserves to be taken seriously. Such a difference, if it obtains, is certainly easier to recognize than to characterize.

Leibniz's Law objection

The claim that mental images are physical particulars in the head – let alone pictorial particulars – is widely held to be absurd. In the context of an early defense of a general mind–body identity claim, J. J. C. Smart considered the objection that if an image is orange and identical to a brain state, then the brain state must be orange too.[14] For Leibniz's Law reminds us that if *x is y*, then any property of *x* is a property of *y*. Smart did not want to be committed to orange neurological entities, so he countered by saying that the identity theorist does not suppose that there are orange mental images, but rather only *experiences* of orange images. The experiences are not orange, so there is no Leibniz's Law problem for materialism here. Materialists who have discussed the matter have been nearly unanimous in supporting one or another variant of a Smart-style "disappearance theory" of mental images. If these materialists are right in supposing mental images aren't physical particulars, then mental images certainly aren't pictures in the head either.

Now the pictorialist can agree with the disappearance theory that if there is a sense of 'mental image' in which it is of the essence of mental images to be, for example, orange or striped or vivid, then no mental images in *that* sense of the term exist. But the pictorialist can go on to disagree strongly with the disappearance theorist, insisting on the existence of mental images in *his* sense of the term (the internal representations of imagery). He can avoid the Leibniz's Law problem by allowing that mental images in his sense are *not* orange, vivid, etc., explaining away our temptation to ascribe colors, shapes, etc., to our mental images by noting that when we say a mental image is orange, what is really the case is that it *represents* something as orange. Having the mental image is phenomenally similar to seeing an orange thing. And this is presumably because the neural entity (with which the materialist pictorialist identifies the mental image) has physiological properties of the sort typically produced by seeing an orange thing.

On this view, it is no surprise that we describe the mental image as orange even though, strictly speaking, it is not. For it is easy to slip into ascribing to representations the properties of what they represent. People who work routinely with graphical representations of sounds (such as oscilloscope readings) often speak of them as if they had the properties of the sounds they represent – for example, being loud or high pitched.

This line of response to the Leibniz's Law problem meshes with the illustration given earlier of a pictorial representation in the brain, a representation of a rotating straight line. This pictorial representation was not itself literally straight, nor did it literally rotate. Rather, the homogeneity in current value represented straightness, and the smooth change in current value represented rotation.

Though this response to the Leibniz's Law problem is adequate, I want to go on to mention another pictorialist option, one that does *not* take it to be literally false that mental images can be orange.

There is some reason to think that there is a systematic difference in meaning between certain predicates applied to physical objects and the same predicates applied to mental particulars. Consider a nonimagery example: the predicate '———— is in ————'. This predicate appears in each premise and the conclusion of this argument:

> The pain is in my fingertip.
> The fingertip is in my mouth.
> Therefore, the pain is in my mouth.

This argument is valid for the "in" of spatial enclosure (for example, the sense of 'x is in y') which means that every point of x is surrounded by points of y (though not conversely), since "in" in this sense is transitive. But suppose that the two premises are true in their *ordinary* meanings: my fingertip hurts and I've thrust the finger deep into my mouth. The conclusion obviously does not follow, so we must conclude that "in" is not used in the spatial enclosure sense in all three statements. It certainly seems plausible that "in" as applied in locating pains differs in meaning systematically from the standard spatial enclosure sense.[15] My suggestion is that the same sort of systematic difference in meaning applies with respect to 'orange' and other terms applied to mental images. 'Orange' has one meaning applied to mental images, and another applied to fruit.

Call the sense of 'orange', etc., in which such terms apply to mental images the *phenomenal* sense. Phenomenal orange represents real orange, just as the orange pigment on a painting represents real orange. Of course, orange representing pigment is orange in the nonphenomenal sense too. Imagine a system of pictorial representation for the blind in which texture represents color. Squishiness, say, represents orange. Squishiness, like phenomenal orange, represents real-world orange without *being* real-world orange.

Objection: "But the orange of orange juice *looks just like* the orange of my orange mental images. So how can you deny that my mental images are orange in the very same sense as orange juice?"

Reply: this is the very fallacy scouted earlier in the section on introspection. Recall that you cannot argue from a similarity in the way I experience x and y to a similarity between x and y. (As I noted, I experience my father and my psychiatrist similarly, but not because they are similar.) I experience orange juice and orange images similarly because both *experiences* involve the same quality (what I call phenomenal orange), not because orange images and orange juice are both orange in the same sense.

This color term ambiguity fits into patterns of less controversial systematic ambiguities. "Nude" (for example, in 'looking at nudes') is ambiguous between *representation of an unclothed body* and *unclothed body*. 'Painting trees' is ambiguous between *making representations of trees, using paint,* and *putting paint on actual trees*. Similarly, 'orange image' can be viewed as ambiguous between *image that is colored real-orange* (that is, the color of real orange juice), and *real-orange-representing image,* where the latter is what normally would be meant.

This "ambiguity" line of response to the Leibniz's Law problem differs in one simple respect from the line of response with which this section began. The first line takes talk of orange mental images to be a literally false way of talking of orange-representing images. The present line takes talk of orange mental images to be (sometimes) literally true in one sense of 'orange' (the phenomenal sense), and cashable in terms of orange representing images in another (real world) sense of 'orange'. Both lines fit together with the idea that if two of my images represent real-world orange, then there is some shared neurological property in virtue of which they so represent, and that there are two correspondences (at least in a given person at a given time): one between imageable properties of objects and neurological properties of their brain representations, and another between the relations among imageable properties of objects and the relations among corresponding neurological properties.[16]

Thus far I have been concered more with pictorialism than with cognitive science. Now I shall shift the emphasis to the presuppositions of cognitive science about internal representations and the processes that operate on them. Then I shall return to pictorialism, bringing to bear my conclusions about representation and processing in cognitive science, arguing that pictorialism may carry the seeds of the destruction of cognitive science as it is currently conceived.

The Paraphernalia objection

Suppose that neurophysiologists discover that the reason that they hadn't seen pictures in the brain is that they hadn't thought of flattening out its highly convoluted surface or of looking at it under ultraviolet light. When they do this, they find the long sought-after pictures: red and white cane-shaped pictures of candy canes, and so forth. Such a discovery would get around the no seeum and the Leibniz's Law objection, but would it really *explain* the phenomena illustrated by the experiments described earlier? Obviously not. In one of the experiments, images seemed to be *scanned*. But the presence of pictures in the brain wouldn't explain how images can be scanned without an internal *eye* to do the scanning. And if one acknowledges images of perception, one may need *another* eye in the internal eye's brain. In another experiment, images seemed to be rotated, and in different dimensions. In other experiments, images are expanded and contracted. Pictures in the brain wouldn't explain this unless there were also something to do the rotating and expanding and contracting: for example, internal hands. And since it is dark inside the skull, the eye would require an internal flashlight.

In sum, the presence of pictures in the brain wouldn't explain anything without an internal eye, hands, and other paraphernalia that in fact do not exist. Further, the internal eye claim is not only empirically false, but may lead to a vicious regress as well.

This objection is defused by points already made in connection with the Leibniz's Law objction. Recall that when we speak of mental images being rotated, scanned, and the like, 'rotate' and 'scan' must not be understood in the senses of the terms in which we speak of sticks being rotated and maps being scanned (both lines of reply discussed in the Leibniz's Law section agreed on this). This reply is not entirely satisfactory, however, for a version of the paraphernalia objection applies equally well to descriptionalist cognitive science as to pictorialist cognitive science, and the line of reply just mentioned does not extend to descriptionalism. The descriptionalist postulates internal sentences that are transformed in various ways. How can the sentences be transformed without an internal eye to read them and internal scissors and glue to change the parts? Here it would not do to say that internal sentences are not transformed in the same sense of 'transform' as external sentences.

I shall argue that a deeper reply to the paraphernalia objection protects pictorialism and descriptionalism equally well. The reply depends on two basic presuppositions of contemporary cognitive science which I will sketch below. Of course I don't expect you to accept these presuppositions on faith. Rather, my point is that if the reply works for descriptionalist cognitive science, it also works for pictorialist cognitive science, and further, it is needed for both, so the objection is irrelevant to the pictorialism/descriptionalism controversy. I also have an ulterior motive, for in explaining the cognitive science reply to the paraphernalia objection, I intend to uncover a deeper problem for cognitive science.[17]

The first presupposition of cognitive science is that our thoughts are coded in a system (or perhaps a number of systems) of structures (neurologically instantiated in us, but instantiable in different ways in different beings), at least some of which have syntax and semantics roughly akin to those of familiar natural and artificial languages. Computers use on–off states of binary elements to do this, but no one has any idea how it is done in the brain. *However* the brain does it, there is a finite alphabet of elementary structures. Complex structures – "words" and "sentences" are built up out of elementary structures. The word and sentence structures have meaning, and the meanings of sentences are determined by the meanings of words plus syntax. Cognitive science is committed to these descriptional internal representations, but it need not deny that there are nonlinguistic, pictorial representations as well. The pictorial/descriptional controversy is, of course, a controversy *within* cognitive science.

The second presupposition is that there are (neurally instantiated) processors that operate on the symbolic structures on the basis of the physical properties of the structures. Thus, though the structures have meanings, the processors can take account of these meanings only to the extent that these meanings are reflected in their physical properties.[18] It is important to note that while both the representations and the processors discussed by cognitive scientists are assumed to be neurological entities, and the processors are assumed to operate on neurological properties, the *descriptive machinery* of cognitive science nowhere takes account of this assumption of its practitioners. The descriptive machinery of cognitive science assumes only that the processors have no direct access to the meanings of representations. Cognitive science presupposes *mechanism*, not *materialism*. The talk of representations and processing in cognitive science is compatible with electronic or hydraulic realization. Indeed, it is compatible with nonphysical realization. If the representations were drawn in ectoplasm and the processors were souls, so long as the souls fitted the right regularities, the explanations of cognitive science would remain the same.

Some processors search lists of representations, others compare representations, checking for matching, and others transform representations in various ways. The processors are sometimes described as black boxes, sometimes, more imaginatively, as homunculi. The task of cognitive science is seen as one of modeling human thought by constructing networks of homunculi that examine and change representations, and send messages to one another. Each homunculus is decomposed into further networks of intercommunicating homunculi and their representations until the whole system is grounded in processors whose operation is to be explained neurophysiologically rather than in terms of operations on representations.[19]

The ultimate aim is to "discharge" the homunculi, in Dennett's apt phrase. The first step is to give an account of an homunculus in terms of another network of homunculi and *their* representations, if this can be done. But in the end, discharging depends on finding homunculi that cannot be explained in this way, but only in a different way, nomologically; that is, in terms of laws of nature or their consequences.

The bottom level processors, the ones whose operation can only be explained nomologically, can be called *primitive* processors (this is a definition).[20] For example, a current cognitive science theory of language understanding takes the form of a flowchart which contains a box labeled "Decide if input is a word." This processor can send a "yes" to another box (or rather, the processor symbolized by the box) or a "no" to still another box. But determining whether a given form is a word is not a good candidate for a primitive operation. So a deeper level theory is called for in which the "Decide if input is a word" box is replaced by a network of other boxes, with their own representations; that is, the processor that decides whether something is a word is "decomposed" into other processors. According to one current theory, one more elementary processor fetches words from lists of representations ("dictionaries" in this case), one at a time; another checks whether a fetched word matches the target form, etc. The job is done when all the postulated processors can be reduced to primitive processors.[21]

Now that I have sketched the presuppositions of cognitive science's computation-representation explanations, let us return to the paraphernalia objection. Note to begin with how cognitive science's playmate, the computer, manages to manipulate descriptional representations without internal hands or eyes. Commands given to a computer in a "higher level" language are, in effect, translated into the machine's machine language, a language it *just uses* (in a sense to be explicated). Consider a computer in which addition (but not multiplication) is accomplished by a single machine language instruction. The answer to "How does it multiply n times m?" is: "It adds n to itself m times." The answer to "How does it add x to *y ?*", however, is given not by an algorithm (or by a description of how an algorithm is computed) as with multiplication, but rather by an electronic or mechanical or hydraulic mechanism that is explainable only nomologically.

Suppose the string of zeroes and ones (this is a way of talking about binary elements – literally on–off switches operated by electromagnets in some old machines) that stands for addition, say '1000', appears in the control register. '1000' in this register simply causes the zeroes and ones in two other registers to interact so as to produce a series of zeroes and ones in yet another register that represents the sum.

The answer to "How does it multiply?" has a computational-representational answer in terms of an algorithm (or its implementation); the answer to "How does it add?" is given via a mechanism; that is why addition, in this machine, is where computational-representational explanation bottoms out. Addition is explainable only nomologically. But the border between computational-representational explanation and nomological explanation cannot always be drawn sharply. The line between cognitive science accounts and neurophysiological accounts, like most disciplinary borders, is often fuzzy. The important point for the idea of a primitive processor is that *eventually* the cognitive science "decomposition" strategy leads to processors that *clearly* can only be explained nomologically, even if, on the way, there are mechanisms that cannot be easily classified as computational-representational or as nomological.

For example, one way of constructing an "adder" is by connecting gates together. An "and" gate is a device with two inputs and one output; the output fires if and only if impulses reach both imputs. One can build the adder out of "and" gates and "or" gates. Now an "and" gate *can* be viewed as a representation manipulating device – one that emits a '1' just in case it sees two '1's. So one may wish to regard the gates rather than the adder as the primitive processors. Further, even the gates can be constructed out of processors that can be viewed as representation manipulators; for example, one could make them out of people. One rather old-fashioned way of making gates is constructing them from electromagnetic switches ("relays"). Once one has gotten to the level of these switches, however, one has definitely hit bottom. The only way to explain the operation of such a switch is nomological: electrical pulses in the switch's coil produce a magnetic field (in a way explainable only by laws of physics) which attracts a piece of metal at one end of the coil, closing a circuit.[22]

The application to cognitive science is straightforward, and that is no accident, since cognitive science derives from the metaphor of the mind as a computer. We can explain how the computer accomplishes complex operations, such as multiplication, in terms of decomposition into operations such as addition, operations which cannot be explained in terms of further commands and representations, but whose only explanation is in nomological terms; for example, in terms of electronics. Call these bottom level operations here, as before, the primitive operations.

Similarly, cognitive science postulates complex processors whose operation can be explained in terms of a decomposition into interacting primitive processors whose operation in turn can be explained only nomologically, in terms of physiology. The explanatory "buck" in cognitive science stops at the primitive processors, just as the explanatory buck in the multiplication example stopped at the hard-wired circuitry that allowed the command register to affect the other registers in the appropriate way.

Cognitive science can propose to handle pictorial representations mechanistically in the same way that it handles descriptional representations. Both are to be processed ultimately by mechanisms whose only account is nomological. This answers the paraphernalia objection, as it applies both to pictorial and descriptional representations. We don't need hands, scissors, flashlights or eyes if we have mechanical processes that do the job.

This being said, it is worth noting that descriptionalism is in a better position *vis-à-vis* the paraphernalia objection than is pictorialism. Existing computer models do give us a glimmer of how perception and imagery might be modeled descriptionally, but we have something less than a glimmer of what a pictorial story would be like.

The Background objection

Hubert Dreyfus has argued that cognitive science is doomed to failure because of its assumptions about internal representations.[23] The basic idea (applied to language understanding) has recently been amplified by John Searle. Dreyfus and Searle claim that to understand language, we require a *common sense background* that cannot iself be fully captured by a set of representations. Searle considers the suggestion that the common sense background required to understand language could be spelled out explicitly as a set of representations. He says:

> But this suggestion is unfillable for three reasons. First we would never know when to stop in spelling out the background. Even if, for example, we described the practices of our culture, those practices themselves depend on certain very general facts about what nature is like and what human beings are like, e.g. that grass grows, that it doesn't eat human beings, that grass is softer than steel, that grass growing and cutting goes on at the surface of the earth – and so on indefinitely (though not infinitely). And secondly, for each of our attempts to spell out the "assumptions" we will have to use words in sentences, and those words in sentences determine their own truth conditions only relative to yet other sets of assumptions, which in turn we would have to spell out. And third, it is not at all clear that "assumptions" is even the right word to describe what it is that makes meaning and understanding possible at all, since the expression implies that these assumptions all have propositional content, that they are all representations. But from the fact that any element of the background can be formulated as a representation, it does not follow that prior to that formulation it existed and functioned as a representation. Have we, for example, always believed unconsciously that grass does not eat humans? Well, if I ever saw a strand of grass eating somebody I would certainly be astonished, and that is at least evidnce that one of my intentional states is unsatisfied; but it is at best misleading to assimilate that case to the case where, for example, I expect that it is going to keep on raining and find myself surprised to see the sun come out. The conditions which make representations possible need not themselves all be representations, even though each of them is representable or formulatable as a representation.[24]

The Dreyfus–Searle objection could be summed up as follows:

1 Cognitive science assumes that all of our knowledge is coded in representations in our brains.
2 Our common sense background knowledge cannot be so coded.[25]
3 So cognitive science is committed to an assumption that cannot be true.

Premise (2) obviously needs more backing up than the passage quoted gives it. For example, Searle argues that each represented background assumption will determine truth conditions only relative to others which will also have to be spelled out. But there is no *obvious* difficulty here. Nothing Searle says counts against the possibility of spelling out the *whole* background via a set of representations *each* of which has its truth conditions determined by others. Perhaps attempting to fill this gap in the argument, Dreyfus has recently argued in support of (2) that the satisfaction conditions of mental representations depend on *skills* that are not codable as representations.[26]

Tempting as it is to enter the fray on premise (2), I won't since my real target is premise (1). Cognitive science simply does not assume that all of our knowledge is explicitly coded as representations in our brains. Indeed, cognitive science is more nearly committed to denying this claim.[27]

To make this clear (if it isn't already), I want to introduce the notion of syntactic twins. Syntactic twins can be any devices that fit with the cognitive science ideology. They have internal representations and processors, ultimately grounded in primitive processors. Syntactic twins are defined as pairs of such devices that are *molecule for molecule the same, except inside the primitive processors*. The syntactic form of the representations and the network of primitive processors are the same for syntactic twins, but the input–output function of the primitive processors need not be.[28] For example, two identical digital computers with identical programs could be syntactic twins – and they could *remain* syntactic twins with identical arrays of 0s and 1s, and in that syntactic sense, identical representations, even if we changed the input–output functions of the primitive processors of one (or both) of them, and even though they no longer responded in a similar manner to inputs.

Suppose that the enterprise of cognitive science succeeds, and allows us to build intelligent machines – not necessarily digital computers, since they are only *one* type of device that fits the cognitive science model. Suppose we have two molecule for molecule identical intelligent machines, and once again we change the input–output functions of the primitive processors of one of them. Again, after we have fiddled we still have syntactic twins, since the two machines are the same down to the level of primitive processors – including having the same representations, at least syntactically speaking.[29] Furthermore, the device that we did *not* fiddle with is *ex hypothesi* intelligent. But its syntactic twin may turn out not to be at all intelligent, or it may have a different "style" of intelligence and possess different information. Since the two machines have the same representations, cognitive science cannot hold that possession of information or intelligence or "styles" of intelligence must be entirely a matter of representations; rather, these matters depend on the primitive processors as well. So the Dreyfus objection sticks cognitive science with an assumption that it ought not to accept.

Wittgensteinians sometimes suppose that cognitive science must miss the insight that thinking cannot be just a matter of representations and explicitly represented rules for manipulating the representations. They argue that instructions for using rules would require still further instructions for *their* interpretation, and so on. So we would have an infinite regress.[31] The Wittgensteinian way out is to say that there comes a point at which we have enough instructions for using the rule and we just go on in a certain way. Martians might go on differently, but we go on *this* way. However, the Wittgensteinian appeal to the way we go on has a parallel in the picture I just sketched – the cognitive scientist's appeal to how the primitive processors manipulate representations.

Consider an "add 1" primitive processor, such as the mechanism of a car's odometer. Compare it to a "Wittgensteinian add 1" device, a similar mechanical device that adds 1 to numbers from 1 to 100, adds 2 to numbers from 101 to 200, etc. These devices could be placed respectively in syntactic twins, and cause them to go on in response to "Add one!" in different ways.

This difference between the two "add 1" devices (or perhaps the twins in which they are placed) *can* be seen as an informational difference. And where there is an informational difference there is information. Clearer cases of information implicit in primitive processors require an appreciation of the processor's function in a knowledge possessing system. For example, some birds navigate via internal mechanisms that contain pieces of magnetic material – biological compasses. To the extent that one is willing to think of birds as having navigational knowledge, one can locate directional information in the compass + reading mechanism.

One example illustrating how information can be implicit in the primitive machinery (the primitive processors and their interconnections) derives from the famous Lewis Carroll/W. V. Quine point about *modus ponens*. Imagine a logic machine that has an explicit representation of *modus ponens*, viz.:
Given premises of the form:

(1) Such and such is an A,
(2) All As are Bs,
conclude: (3) Such and such is a B.

Still, not all cases of *modus ponens* reasoning in this machine can be controlled by this explicitly represented rule, since the application of the explicitly represented rule *itself* requires *modus ponens* type reasoning. To see this, imagine a sample argument to which the explicit rule is to be applied, say: All men are mortal; Socrates is a man; conclusion: Socrates is mortal. In order for the machine to apply the explicitly represented version of *modus ponens* to the premises of the Socrates argument to draw the conclusion, it would first have to check that the argument *does have* the specified form (a (1)-style step). Then it would have to take account of the fact that whenever the premises are of the right form, the conclusion of the corresponding form can be drawn (a (2)-style step). Then it could draw the conclusion (which is of the form of (3)). Clearly, this reasoning involves *modus ponens* itself. Conclusion: even in a logic system that has *modus ponens* explicitly represented, the primitive machinery must have the effect of implicitly representing *modus ponens*.[32]

The computer metaphor

I have been arguing that cognitive science can regard some of the information available to an information processing system as implicit in its primitive machinery. The concession avoids the Wittgensteinian and background objections, but it is not without cost for cognitive science. To the extent that our knowledge is to be explained by appeal to the nature of primitive operations, to that extent the kind of computational explanations at the heart of cognitive science explain less.

Let us return to an example used earlier: psycholinguists have made considerable progress in characterizing how we understand language. One current theory has it that an initial stage of this process determines whether an input is a word. This is held to be done for functor words such as 'and', 'in', 'the', and 'all' via a different mechanism than for content words. The two types of words are held to reside in different lexicons which are accessed differently. But suppose pycholinguists find new evidence showing that the processor that determines whether one's current input is a word is actually primitive. Then "How do we determine whether our current input is a word?" would not have a cognitive science answer (such as the one in terms of accessing the lexicons), but rather it would only be explainable in terms of physiology. That is, cognitive science explanations would "bottom out" sooner than expected. The primitive operations of cognitive science are not themselves explainable by cognitive science, so to the extent that the explanation of psychological phenomena requires appeal to primitive processes – to that extent, the psychological phenomena do not have cognitive science explanations.

According to my definition of "primitive processor," primitive processors have only nomological explanations (and not explanations in terms of manipulation of representations). In one of the many senses of the unfortunate term 'analog', this comes to the claim that primitive processors are analog devices.[33] The distinction between analog in roughly this sense, and digital (in the sense of: explainable in terms of manipulation of representations) has loomed large in the writings of some opponents of cognitive science. Their arguments turn on the implicit claim that cognitive science only *postulates digital processes*.[34] But, as we have seen, *cognitive science cannot get along without appeal to analog processes*, for they are the ones that *ground* the digital processes.

Once we see that cognitive science must postulate *both* analog and digital processes, it becomes natural to ask just *how important the analog processes are*. Proponents of the computer metaphor (Pylyshyn, for example – see note 6) often talk as if the burden of proof is on the pictorialist to demonstrate the existence of analog processes in us. But the *existence* of analog processes is presupposed by the computer metaphor itself; the real issue about the adequacy of the computer metaphor is how much of an explanatory role the analog processes play. And here there is neither a burden of proof nor a clear thrust of the evidence.

The computer metaphor has directed attention to models in which everything is accomplished by elaborate combinations of extremely simple primitive operations such as "check for a match," or "move the element in the nth place to the mth place." The explanatory guts of these models are in the lists of representations and the ways the primitive operations are combined. In this respect, cognitive science is very like its predecessor, associationism, which attempted to build intelligence out of a few simple mechanisms of association of ideas. In my view, this is where the computer metaphor may have done real harm. We should consider the possibility that the primitive operations are more complex and have to shoulder more of an explanatory burden.

For example, suppose that cognitive scientists investigate dolphins and find that they are able to take advantage of what by our standards are sophisticated aspects of the hydrodynamics of their environment. Psychologists dominated by the computer metaphor might investigate models which contain explicit representations of the differential equations of hydrodynamics and digital computing machinery for solving these equations. But they might be wrong. The right approach might be to look for neural mechanisms that themselves obey differential equations of the same form as those of hydrodynamics. Models of this sort would cast the dolphin's navigational equipment as analogous to a model airplane in a wind tunnel.

The relevance of the pictorial/descriptional controversy to the viability of the computer metaphor in cognitive science should be becoming visible. The computer metaphor goes naturally with descriptional representations, but it is not at all clear how it can work when the representations are nondescriptional. This is easy to see, but hard to prove. One can imagine computer-type operations such as list searching and movement from one list to another with pictorial representations, but such operations depend on "matching" processes (the way an item on a list is identified is via matching it with a target item). And there is good reason to think that such "match" operations will be useless with nondescriptional representations. The utility of match operations depends on an "alphabet" of symbols. Of course, one can attempt to get "overlap" measures in order to match pictures, but the history of such attempts strongly suggests this is a blind alley. The trouble is that a picture of a horse and a couch can "overlap" more than the couch does with another couch (or even with the same couch pictured from another angle). "Template matching" approaches in artificial intelligence and psychology have failed miserably, even for letters of the alphabet. Success comes only with restriction to specified type fonts.[35]

The hypothetical dolphin example gives a better idea of the sort of processes that go most naturally with nondescriptional representation. The dolphin has a respresentation of itself and the currents in its environment, and they interact in a way explainable only nomologically.

Note that I am not *denying* that cognitive scientists may well come up with primitive (analog) processors appropriate for pictorial representations. Rather, my point is that such processors would probably carry much more of the load of explaining how the mind works than is envisioned by current proponents of the computer metaphor. For example, suppose an analog device is developed that can do about as well as a person in recognizing handwritten letters of the alphabet or in saying whether two pictures from different angles are pictures of the same object. Such an analog device would be *far* smarter than any digital device anyone knows how to make today. Indeed, it is commonly believed by cognitive scientists that "cracking" this sort of pattern recognition problem is the key to understanding the mind. My point is that this "key" may be an analog one.

One of the reasons that the artificial intelligence community has been hostile towards pictorialism is that computers don't have primitive operations appropriate to pictorial representations, for example, "rotate." Of course, one could couple an analog computer containing a "rotator" to a digital computer. But the real danger for artificial intelligence is that the model might soon become an unimportant digital computer coupled to an important analog computer. Rosch's work supports the idea that in some kinds of thought about, say, birds, people employ a representation of a prototypical bird such as a sparrow. There is some evidence for the claim that these representations of prototypical objects are the same sort of entities as mental images. There is also evidence for the role of imagery in reasoning; for example, in inference based on the transitivity of a term such as 'taller than'.[36] Note that I am not saying that these items of evidence are conclusive, or even compelling, but only that they raise a difficulty for standard cognitive science that must be taken seriously.

Where are we? I have been arguing that cognitive science explanations may "bottom out" in analog processes too soon for the comfort of cognitive scientists. My argument depends on taking two possibilities seriously: first, that mental images are pictorial, and second that cognitive processes involving images or image-like representations (such as prototypes) are important in cognition. Even if these possibilities are actualities, I should concede that cognitive science may none the less have substantial explanatory power. Just *how much* explanatory power depends on the "depth" of the layer of "digital" processes that employ imagistic primitives. At one extreme, we can imagine that the brain is a single analog processor – in which case cognitive science is a flat-out dead end. At the other extreme, we can imagine that imagistic primitives are involved in a few peripheral realms of cognitive activity, and that connections among different types of imagistic processes are handled by a central descriptional system. In this case, cognitive science is unscathed.

Dreyfus and Haugeland have long advocated the view that much of what cognitive science seeks to explain digitally can only be explained by appeal to analog processes. However, they don't offer the type of argument presented here.[37] Haugeland does discuss imagery in his critique of cognitive science, "The nature and plausibility of cognitivism," (ibid.), but he gives it short shrift, supposing that it doesn't matter much to cognitivism if it cannot handle imagery. He says:

Since any Cognitivist theory must include some mechanism for getting from retinal images to cognitive descriptions of what is seen, I don't see why that same mechanism couldn't also take inputs from some precognitive visual "tape recorder" (perhaps one with "adjustments" for orientation, size and location). Then playbacks from the recorder would have whatever nondiscursive, "image-y" quality perception has, and Cognitivism would be unruffled.[38]

But Haugeland does not take account of the possibility that our thought processes are *importantly* imagistic. To the extent that imagistic representations play a role in thought, if cognitivists follow Haugeland's advice of sticking imagery phenomena into "precognitive" machine, they will be throwing out the baby with the bathwater.

Epilog on the 'meaning' of picture

Objection: "When you started this paper, I thought you meant by 'picture' what people normally mean by the word. But it soon turned out that in your sense of 'picture', something could be a picture without *looking* like one; indeed, your pictures in the head aren't even perceived at all (except, perhaps, accidentally by the odd brain surgeon, who, as it happens, doesn't even know he is seeing pictures). Then it turned out that a picture that represents something as striped need not itself be striped (in the sense in which tigers are striped). Isn't your sense of 'picture' rather a peculiar one?"

I have been saying that the way a thing functions in a system of representation is what makes it a pictorial representation. Something which is a picture relative to a Martian system of representation may not be a picture relative to a human system. Certainly the system within which our *ordinary* pictures function involves their being perceived. Perhaps conceptual analysis would reveal that nothing could be a picture unless its function involved being perceived. I take no stand on this, and thus no stand on the issue of whether the sense of 'picture' in which mental images could be pictures in the head is an *extended* sense of the word. My point required only that mental images be *like* pictures in respects that make it plausible that primitive operations on them would not be of the sort suggested by the computer metaphor. In short, the objection may be right, but it doesn't matter to my point.

Authors on both sides of the pictorial/descriptional controversy that I've been talking about often implicitly accept the objector's point. Some think of pictorialism as the view.that mental images are "quasi-pictorial" (Kosslyn's term). Others say that mental images are *analog* representations. I've not introduced the term 'analog' as applied to representations until now because 'analog' is no clearer than 'picture', and just raises a different set of problems and confusions.[39]

'Analog' would also have done as well as 'pictorial' for my point against cognitive science, though the concepts of analog and pictorial are clearly different. To see the difference between analog and pictorial, recall the condition on pictorial representation given earlier; if a picture represents something, S, then at least one part of the picture must represent part of S. But values of charge density can represent distance in an analog computer, even though it is wrong to think of part of the charge density as representing part of the distance.[40]

As far as this paper is concerned, there is no problem if a defense of pictorialism must use 'picture' in an extended sense; a problem arises only if the notion of pictorial (or analog) deployed on behalf of pictorialism is totally *obscure*.

I hope I have clarified the doctrine at least a little here, though, as I have conceded, I have no real characterization of 'pictorial' to offer. With respect to obscurity, the descriptionalist is in a better position than the pictorialist, because he can anchor his idea of 'descriptional' in a mechanical device that genuinely uses descriptional representations in a way we can understand: the digital computer. We have a conception of mechanistic models of imagery using descriptional representations, and no corresponding conception for pictorial representation.

The core of pictorialism is a striking analogy: experiments suggest that the internal representations of imagery are analogous to pictures in their mode of representation. What this claim amounts to is perhaps no more than that the internal representations of imagery are like pictures in *unspecified* respects. Indeed, it would be surprising if the internal representations of imagery are pictorial in *all* respects. Wouldn't it be a remarkable coincidence if we developed external representations that represented in exactly the same way as the ones nature designed for use by our cognitive subsystem?

Though the thesis of pictorialism is vague, it would be a mistake to write it off on that account. For it may none the less be importantly true, and the truth in it may challenge the computer metaphor in cognitive science.[41]

NOTES

1 Work by Roger Shepard and his colleagues is the basis for the claim about rotation; the others stem from Stephen Kosslyn's work. See R. N. Shepard and L. Cooper, *Mental Images and their Transformations* (Cambridge: MIT Press, 1982). See also the works mentioned in the next three notes. Kosslyn's work is summarized in his *Image and Mind* (Cambridge: Harvard University Press, 1980).

2 J. Metzler and R. N. Shepard, "Mental rotation of three-dimensional objects," *Science*, 171 (1971), pp. 701–3.

3 J. Metzler, unpublished Stanford University Ph.D. thesis, 1973. Described in Shepard and Cooper, ibid., pp. 59–62.

4 S. Kosslyn, T. Ball and B. Reiser, "Visual images preserve metric spatial information: Evidence from studies of image scanning," *Journal of Experimental Psychology: Human Perception and Performance* 4 (1978), pp. 47–60. Figure 2 was also reprinted with the permission of the American Psychological Association, Copyright, 1978.

5 R. Finke and S. Pinker, "Spontaneous imagery scanning in mental extrapolation," *Journal of Experimental Psychology: Learning, Memory and Cognition* 8, 2 (1982), pp. 142–7 and R. Finke and S. Pinker, "Directional scanning of remembered visual patterns," *Journal of Experimental Psychology: Learning, Memory and Cognition*, 9, 3 (1983), 398–410. Zenon Pylyshyn has objected to Kosslyn's map scanning experiments on the ground that subjects merely mimic features of perceptual interactions of which they have tacit knowledge. They know it takes longer to move their gaze a longer distance, so when they recreate the experience, they make the longer image scan take longer. However, Finke and Pinker in the latter of the two papers just mentioned show that subjects exhibit patterns of *errors* in their dot scanning experiment of a rather surprising sort: there are more errors closer to the point of the arrow. This can be predicted, given the instruction set (and it happens in actual visual scanning), but it is doubtful that it can be explained via tacit knowledge.

6 I shall use 'picture' as short for 'pictorial representation', thus speaking of pictorialism as postulating internal pictures. No commitment to paper or canvas is intended. For a look at the pictorial/descriptional debate, see Zenon Pylyshyn's "Imagery and Artificial Intelligence," and Stephen Kosslyn's and James Pomerantz's "Imagery, propositions and the form of internal representations," in my *Readings in Philosophy of Psychology*. vol. 2 (Cambridge: Harvard University Press, 1981). Pylyshyn is a descriptionalist; Kosslyn and Pomerantz are pictorialists. For a second Pylyshyn vs. Kosslyn faceoff, see Pylyshyn's "The imagery debate: Analog media versus tacit knowledge," and Kosslyn's reply, "The medium and the message in mental imagery: A theory," in my *Imagery* (Cambridge: Bradford/MIT Press, 1981). See also my "The photographic fallacy in the debate about mental imagery," *Noûs* 17, 4 (1983).

An interesting pictorialist theory of imagery is presented in R. N. Shepard, "Psychophysical complementarity," in M. Kubovy and J. Pomerantz (eds), *Perceptual Organization* (Hillsdale, NJ: Erlbaum Associates, 1981), pp. 279–341. A good recent review of descriptionalist and pictorialist theories is given by S. Pinker and S. M. Kosslyn in "Theories of mental imagery," in A. Sheikh (ed.), *Imagery: Current Theory, Research and Application* (New York: Wiley, 1983).

7 The distinction and the quoted phrase are from Georges Rey's "What are mental images?" which appears in my *Readings in Philosophy of Psychology*, vol. 11, ibid. A closely related distinction between metaphysical and scientific iconophobia appears in Dan Dennett's "Two approaches to mental images," *Brainstorms* (Montgomery, VT: Bradford Books, 1978), reprinted in my *Imagery*, ibid.

8 Pennington and Kosslyn did this experiment. See Kosslyn's "The medium and the message in mental imagery," ibid.

9 See R. A. Finke, "Levels of equivalence in imagery and perception," *Psychological Review* 187, 12 (1980); and R. M. Shepard, "The mental image," *American Psychologist* 133 (1978). I should add that there are considerable differences among people in their susceptibility to these phenomena – and these differences correlate with independent measures of the vividness of their images and with ability to reparse images. See Finke, ibid., and J. A. Slee, "Individual differences in visual imagery ability and the retrieval of visual appearances," *Journal of Mental Imagery* 4 (1980), pp. 93–113.

10 It is not at all unusual for descriptionalists to recognize this. See Pylyshyn's "Imagery and Artificial Intelligence" ibid., for example. Descriptionalist views of perception are common in artificial intelligence approaches to vision.

11 I had planned a more detailed exposition of this point, but dropped it when Robert Schwartz sent me his "Imagery – there is more to it than meets the eye," which contains an excellent treatment. Schwartz's article is in *Imagery*, ibid., and is forthcoming in Asquith and Giere (eds), *Philosophy of Science Association 1980*, vol. 2, East Lansing, MI.

12 Cultural relativity of picture perception is discussed in R. J. Miller, "Cross-cultural research in the perception of pictorial materials," *Psychology Bulletin* 80 (1973). Gombrich has long stressed a limited cultural relativity of systems of pictorial representation. See, for example, his "Standards of Truth: The arrested image and the moving eye," in W. J.T. Mitchell (ed.), *The Language of Images* (Chicago: University of Chicago Press, 1980).

13 Such a criterion figures prominently in S. Kosslyn, S. Pinker, S. Schwartz and G. Smith, "The demystification of mental imagery," *The Behavioral and Brain Sciences* 2 (1979); in Kosslyn's *Image and Mind*, ibid.; and in Aaron Sloman's *The Computer Revolution in Philosophy* (Sussex: Harvester, 1978).

14 "Sensations and Brain Processes," *Philosophical Review* 68 (1969), pp. 141–56.

15 This point derives from a draft of a paper on Leibniz's Law objections to materialism that Jerry Fodor and I wrote jointly long ago but never finished.

16 These correspondences are what Shepard had in mind by "second-order isomorphism." See Shepard's review of Neisser's *Cognitive Psychology* in *The American Journal of Psychology* 81 (1968), pp. 285–9, where he first states this idea. See also R. N. Shepard and S. Chipman, "Second-order isomorphism of internal representation: Shapes of states," *Cognitive Psychology* 1, pp. 1–17. Shepard later shifted his focus from this pictorialist view to the claim that mental imagery representations are similar to perceptual representations, but he has recently returned to second-order isomorphism in his original sense in "Psychophysical complementarity," in Kubovy and Pomerantz (eds), *Perceptual Organization*, ibid.

17 When I speak of cognitive science, I have in mind an ideology – stated later in this paper – presupposed by a significant line of work in cognitive psychology and artificial intelligence, and to some extent linguistics and philosophy. Many – and perhaps most – cognitive psychologists do not subscribe explicitly to such a point of view, though most do work that implicitly involves it. Many writers on this topic prefer to use 'cognitivism' to refer to the ideology I have in mind, treating 'cognitive science' as a neutral disciplinary term. I see 'cognitive science' as an ideologically loaded term (as is 'sociobiology'), since the research

programs which parade under the banner of cognitive science would not form a field at all without the ideology.

18 Jerry Fodor speaks of the class of physical properties that processors can attend to as in the category of "shape" or "form." See Fodor's "Methodological solipsism considered as a research strategy in cognitive psychology," *Behavioral and Brain Sciences* 3 (1980), pp. 63–72. Of course, the 3-volt/1-volt difference that codes 1 and 0 in some computers isn't naturally described as a shape or form difference. This is really a terminological matter, but there is a *substantive* dispute about this class of physical properties as well. Fodor seems to hold that the class of physical properties is restricted to monadic properties (as "shape" and "form" suggest), while others suggest that relational properties that contribute to causal role (such as location) may be important too. See the criticism of Fodor by Sylvain Bromberger and me, "States' Rights," in the same issue, and Fodor's response, also in that issue. Fodor's mistake, according to me, is missing the possibility that primitive processors can respond to relational properties.

19 This picture was first sketched as far as I know in Fodor's "The appeal to tacit knowledge in psychological explanation," *Journal of Philosophy* 65, 20, 1968. See also Dan Dennett's "Why the law of effect won't go away," *Journal for the Theory of Social Behavior* (1975), and reprinted in *Brainstorms* (Montgomery, VT: Bradford Books, 1978). Cummins's "Functional analysis" puts the same idea in a wider context of explanation outside psychology. The relevant part is reprinted in my anthology, *Readings in Philosophy of Psychology*, vol. 1, ibid. These articles, however, tend to scant the representationalist presupposition. This presupposition is given more weight in Fodor's *The Language of Thought* (New York: Crowell 1975); John Haugeland's "The nature and plausibility of cognitivism," *The Behavioral and Brain Sciences* 2, (1978), pp. 215–25; and Zenon Pylyshyn's "Computation and cognition: Issues in the foundations of cognitive science," *The Behavioral and Brain Sciences* 3, no. 1 (1980), pp. 111–32. Though Haugeland's article attends to the representationalist presupposition, he rules out pictorialism by assuming that the representations must be descriptional; so what he characterizes is a descriptionalist *school* within cognitive science (one that is more representative of AI than of cognitive psychology) and not cognitive science proper.

20 Terminological question: should *parts* of primitive processors also be counted as primitive? The definition I'm using (primitive processors can be explained only nomologically) would say yes, though one could say instead that primitive processors can be explained only nomologically *and* are not parts of larger systems that can be explained only nomologically. The latter definition captures the idea better, but the former one is simpler, and so I will continue to use it instead.

Approximately this conception of primitive processor appears in Fodor's tacit knowledge paper ("The appeal to tacit knowledge," ibid.). Unfortunately, this idea of primitive processor coexists in Fodor's paper with a quite different idea: ". . . an elementary operation is one which the normal nervous system can perform but of which it cannot perform a proper part." But this latter idea is shown to be defective in Thomas Nagel's comment. "The boundaries of inner space," *Journal of Philosophy* 66, 14, 1969. The main problem is this: consider a process, P, that is primitive by Fodor's first criterion. Biofeedback (and other kinds of intervention) can often allow the subject to perform any of a number of minute parts of P in isolation. But it won't do to regard these minute parts of P as the *real* primitives, since in general when P is performed by itself, it is performed as a whole, just as each minute part is performed as a whole when it is performed by itself.

21 A "machine language" for one machine can be a "higher level language" for a second machine, implemented by the second machine's own machine language. From the point of view of the programmer, the two machines may appear to have the very same primitives. Indeed, the real primitives of the second machine may be inaccessible to the programmer. (To take an extreme case, each primitive processor of the first machine may be simulated by

a separate digital computer with its own primitives in the second machine.) In computer science, the set of primitives that a machine appears to the user to have are often taken to define a "virtual machine," and one speaks of the virtual primitives and their interrelations as specifying the "functional architecture" of the virtual machine. Two machines can have the same functional architecture, even though their *real* primitives are quite different. These ideas are explained lucidly in Pylyshyn's "Computation and cognition" ibid.

I am ignoring the notion of functional architecture (as distinct from real architecture), first, because I doubt that the distinction between functional architecture and real architecture has any application to human mentality. (The point is that it seems unlikely that computer scientists' clever ways of simulating one machine using another machine reflect anything mother nature had any need to do.) Secondly, even if the distinction between functional and real architecture does apply to people, it is the real architecture (with the corresponding real primitives) that play a role in my argument.

22 Another way of defining the level of primitive processors (though one appropriate to functional architecture, not real architecture) would be to regard the "decomposition" process described in the text as having reached the level of primitive processors when in ascribing representations one requires a change of subject matter (cf. Haugeland, "Nature and plausibility of cognitivism," ibid.). In the computer example just mentioned, the add mechanism would be primitive because the gates' representations should be regarded as having a different subject matter, or so I would argue. The key fact is that the algorithm involved in decomposing multiplication into addition (multiply n by m via adding n to itself m times) is independent of notation (e.g., it works as well in decimal as in binary notation). By contrast, if one views the network of "and" gates, "or" gates, etc., which make up the adder as computing an algorithm, the algorithm is one that works only in binary notation. The multiplier's symbols refer to numbers, but if the gates' symbols refer at all, they are better taken as referring to numerals.

The detail of how the network of gates works brings more conviction on this point. One example: the basic idea of one common binary adder is that when two binary digits to be added are the same, the sum digit in their column is a '0', while if they are different, the sum digit is a '1'. The reason is: $1 + 0 = 1$, $0 + 1 = 1$, $0 + 0 = 0$, since 1 and 0 are designated in binary as in decimal, but in binary, $1 + 1 = 10$, since decimal 2 = binary 10. The rightmost digit of the result of $1 + 1$ and $0 + 0$ is the same, viz., '0'. So the rightmost column can be added by an "exclusive or" gate that writes '0' when the input digits are the same and '1' when they are different. When the gate's inputs are two '1's, what it writes is not the sum of 1 and 1, but rather the rightmost numeral of a particular notation for expressing this sum, and that is why it is more natural to regard the gate as a numeral cruncher than as a number cruncher.

23 H. L. Dreyfus, *What Computers Can't Do* (New York: Harper, 1972). The argument I refer to is summarized on pp. 203–4 of the revised edition.

24 The background of meaning," in J. Searle, F. Kiefer and M. Bierwisch (eds), *Speech Act Theory and Pragmatics* (Dordrecht: D. Reidel Publishing Co., 1980), p. 228.

25 In the last of Searle's three arguments (just quoted) for this premise, he appears to be denying only that our common sense background *need* be coded as representations. Of course, proponents of the position that Searle and Dreyfus are arguing against (which is not the cognitive science position, as I shall point out) could say, "We only insist that in fact the common sense background *is* so coded, not that it must be."

26 "Dasein's revenge: Methodological solipsism as an unsuccessful escape strategy in psychology," *The Behavioral and Brain Sciences* 3 (1980), pp. 78–9.

27 One type of nonrepresentational containment of information has been discussed explicitly in connection with David Marr's theory of vision. As Shimon Ullman points out in "The rigidity assumption in the interpretation of structure from motion," *The Proceedings of the Royal Society of London* B, 203 (1979), pp. 405–26, computation in the visual system takes

transformations to be motions of a rigid body if there is a unique rigid body interpretation. We think of the rigidity assumption as being "in" the system because it is presupposed by what the system does, not because it is explicitly represented in the system. I don't discuss this matter in the text, since my focus here is on another type of implicit representation of information: viz., information that is implicit in primitive processors.

28   Since the input–output function of primitive processors (though not their internal operation) is within the domain of cognitive science, these syntactic twins should not be thought of as *cognitive science* twins.

29   The primitive processors of two syntactic twins could be so different that given the relativity of *syntactic* category to process (much discussed in the beginning of this paper), we would not want to regard the two as having even syntactically identical representations. For example, the processors of both twins might skip every other symbol (i.e., treat every other symbol as a "space"), but in one twin the symbols in odd-numbered positions might be so ignored, while in the other twin the even-numbered ones might be ignored. The result: 'CDAOTG' would be regarded as 'DOG' by one twin and 'CAT' by the other. Think of the twins in the examples in the text as having sufficiently similar processors to ensure *syntactically* identical representations.

30   John Searle tells me that he agrees with this objection (and indeed thought of it himself), so he now thinks that the cognitivists can escape the problem posed by the common sense background. However, I think Searle gives in too quickly. As I shall point out below, the background objection *does* pose an obstacle to the program of cognitive science – at least to the extent that this program is tied to the computer metaphor.

31   See, for example, Dreyfus, *What Computers Can't Do*, ibid., p. 203.

32   This point is spelled out in more detail in my "Philosophy of psychology," in P. Asquith and H. Kyburg (eds), *Current Research in Philosophy of Science* (East Lansing, MI: Philosophy of Science Association, 1979). (The same passage is reprinted in the introduction to my *Readings in the Philosophy of Psychology*, both volumes, p. 4) Barry Stroud makes essentially the same point from a Wittgensteinian point of view in "Inference, belief and understanding," *Mind* 88, 35 (1979), pp. 179–96. Dan Dennett makes a similar point in *Brainstorms*, ibid. Note that the implicit information can be "embedded" in the interactions among primitive processors, rather than in any single primitive processor. A Turing machine, for example, can execute *modus ponens* reasoning even when its primitive processors are all just "and" neurons plus peripheral transducers. Any computer with information embedded in a primitive processor (e.g., a computer with a primitive "adder") can be simulated by a Turing machine whose primitives are simple "and" neurons. Of course, this does not show that the original machine does not really have adding information in its primitive adder. A machine which lacks property X can often simulate a machine which has property X.

33   I fear that the introduction of 'analog' into this discussion may be counterproductive. Please note that 'analog' in the sense in which I have just introduced it applies to processes, not representations. So it is to be distinguished from (for example) Goodman's sense of the term. Note that in this sense of 'analog', whether a device "creeps" like a UHF television tuner or "clicks" like a VHF one is irrelevant to whether it is analog. Jerry Fodor and I advocated a sense of 'analog' defined in terms of nomologicity in "Cognitivism and the analog/digital distinction," a paper circulated in 1971, but never published. Similar notions of analogicity have been used by S. Palmer ("Fundamental aspects of cognitive representation," in E. Rosch and B. Lloyd (eds), *Cognition and Categorization* (Hillsdale: Erlbaum, 1973), and Zenon Pylyshyn, "Computation and cognition," ibid. Fodor and Pylyshyn have recently applied this idea ("How direct is visual perception?: Some reflections on Gibson's 'Ecological approach'," *Cognition* 9, 2 (1981)) in defining the concept of a detector (a detector is a primitive peripheral perceptual mechanism). Fodor and Pylyshyn think of an analog device as one "whose output is lawfully dependent on the character of the input." Such proposals make the mistake of trying to characterize analogicity *directly* in

terms of nomologicity.

The trouble is that if one uses a narrow notion of law (say something of the sort one might expect to find in a science textbook), then the primitive devices of some computers (or perhaps the human brain) will fail to be analog. For example, one could design primitive mechanisms for a digital computer whose input–output relations are counterfactual–supporting but not covered by textbook-type laws or chains of them. I have an old-fashioned Swingline stapler whose staples will point in or out depending on the position of the anvil (the metal plate upon which the staples are bent when the top is pressed). The following counterfactual-supporting input–output generalization applies: anvil in – staple points out; anvil out – staple points in. Thus the stapler is a binary device which, together with the appropriate interfaces, could be a "flip-flop" in a rather pitiful digital computer. Of course, the input–output relations of such a device will follow from a collection of textbook-type laws *plus descriptions of the parts of the device* at the appropriate level of detail. But in *this* sense of nomological (i.e., the input–output relation follows from textbook-type laws plus descriptions of the particular mechanisms), the input–output relation of *every* input–output device is nomological.

My strategy in this paper was to define analogicity more obliquely as having *only* a nomological explanation. The defect of this type of definition is vagueness: other types of explanation lurk in the background, but are not explicitly characterized.

34 I would ascribe this claim to Dreyfus and Haugeland, though neither it nor the specific analog/digital distinction I am using is explicitly endorsed by them. See Dreyfus, *What Computers Can't Do*, ibid., and Dreyfus and Haugeland, "The computer as a mistaken model of the mind," in S. C. Brown (ed.), *Philosophy of Psychology* (London: Macmillan, 1974).

35 The *locus classicus* for this point is Ulric Neisser's *Cognitive Psychology* (Meredith, NY: Newpsychology, 1967), pp. 61ff. More recent evidence along the same lines is presented in E. Smith and D. Medin, *Concepts and Categories* (Cambridge, MA: Harvard University Press, 1981).

36 For a recent review of Rosch's work, see C. B. Mervis and E. Rosch, "Categorization of natural objects," in M. R. Rosenzweig and L. W. Porter (eds), *Annual Review of Psychology* 32, 1981. For some evidence on the imagistic nature of prototypes, see Rosch's "Cognitive representations of semantic categories," *Journal of Experimental Psychology: General* 104, 3 (1975), pp. 192–233.

For evidence on the use of imagery in reasoning, see J. Huttenlocher, "Constructing spatial images: A strategy in reasoning," *Psychological Review* 75 (1968), pp. 550–60. A more recent review is R. J. Sternberg, "Representation and process in linear syllogistic reasoning," *Journal of Experimental Psychology: General* 109 (1980), pp. 119–59.

37 Dreyfus briefly mentions Rosch's claim that categories may be coded in the mind as images in the introduction to the revised edition of his book *What computers can't do*, ibid., (p. 24). But his purpose there is only to "highlight the fact that there is no empirical evidence at all" for P. H. Winston's supposition that categories are represented in the mind as sets of necessary and sufficient conditions.

38 p. 271 in Haugeland's anthology *Mind Design* (Cambridge, MA: Bradford, 1981).

39 There are a number of somewhat different quite precise characterizations of 'analog' in the literature. See Nelson Goodman's *Language of Art* (Indianapolis: Bobbs Merrill, 1968). An improved version of Goodman can be found in John Haugeland's "Analog and analog," *Philosophical Topics* 12, 1 (1981). See also David Lewis, "Analog and digital." *Noûs* 5 (1971). 'Analog' is even vaguer than 'pictorial', being a vague *technical* term with no home in everyday thought. Since there is less for a definition of 'analog' to be responsible to, adequate precise characterizations are easier to come by. Unfortunately, *incompatible* precise characterizations are equally justified. Note that 'analog' in the sense in which it applies to representations is to be distinguished from 'analog' in the sense in which it applies to *processes*. This latter sense is the one mentioned in connection with primitive processes

earlier. I shall now indicate how it is that the two kinds of analogicity need not go together. *A digital processor can use analog representations.* Consider a wheel whose rim is divided into 1000 segments; one has negligible electrical resistance, the next segment has a resistance of 1 ohm, the next one 2 ohms, and so on up to 999 ohms. These are analog representations of numbers (being represented by values of a fundamental physical magnitude). The wheel is the main part of an adding machine which works as follows. The starting state is one in which an ohmmeter's stationary prongs span the zero segment of the wheel. If n is to be added to m, the wheel is turned m segments, then n segments more; to get the sum, the resistance of the segment touching the ohmmeter's prongs (the m-plus-nth segment) is measured. The converse point also holds: *an analog processor can use digital representations.* See the article by David Lewis for an example of a hydraulic analog computing device in which numbers are represented by amounts of water. The device can function equally well with BBs as the fluid, the number of BBs doing the representing. This is an analog processor with digital representation. Lewis's discussion and Haugeland's critique (in "Analog and analog," ibid.) fail to distinguish analog processing from analog representation. (The italicized points were made in Fodor's and my "Cognitivism and the analog/digital distinction" mentioned in an earlier note.)

40 Holographic film contains unintelligible "swirls" recording the interference patterns produced by laser beams bouncing off a to-be-pictured object. A holographic image of the object is produced by sending a laser beam through the film and splitting the beam with mirrors, reversing the process by which the pattern was produced. The holographic film has the property that small parts of the film generate a degraded version of the same image as the whole film. Parts of the film do not generate parts of the image (in any usual sense of 'part'). One can perhaps conceive of a processor that changes the image in meaningful ways by processing the "swirls" on the holographic film directly. If this is possible, then holographic film representations would be analog, though not pictorial by the "part" criterion.

41 I am grateful for comments on an earlier draft to Richard Boyd, Sylvain Bromberger, Susan Carey, Hubert Dreyfus, Kathy Emmett, Paul Horwich, Patricia Kitcher, Bob Mathews, Steven Pinker, Georges Rey, Lance Rips, and the editors of the *Philosophical Review*. Earlier drafts were read at UCLA, at a conference sponsored by Bryn Mawr and Temple, at Yale, Northern Illlinois, University of Chicago, and Johns Hopkins. The writing of this paper was supported by the Cognitive Science Program of the University of California at Berkeley, and the Cognitive Science Center at MIT; in both cases from funds supplied by the Alfred P. Sloan Foundation.

The Imagery Debate

KIM STERELNY

I Introduction

In other papers I have defended representationalist accounts of cognition (Sterelny 1981, 1983, 1984; also Fodor 1975, 1978; and Lycan 1981). That is, I have

"The Imagery Debate" by K. Sterelny first appeared in *Philosophy of Science* 53 (4), pp. 560–83 and is reprinted here by kind permission. Copyright © 1986 by the Philosophy of Science Association.

defended the claim that our propositional attitudes are relations to internal representation tokens. Different attitudes are distinguished by the different functional roles an internal representation plays: a representation in the belief-store plays a different causal role in the political economy of the mind than a representation in the desire-store.

What is the nature of these representations? Within cognitive science there is a lively debate on this issue. Zenon Pylyshyn has suggested that representation is propositional.[1] Others have argued for a more pluralist account. Stephen Kosslyn in particular has developed theories finding room for a variety of sentential codes together with a pictorial mode of representation (see, for example, Kosslyn and Pomerantz 1978; Kosslyn 1980; Kosslyn et al. 1979; and Kosslyn 1981).

It's not just difficult to see who is right in this debate; that's to be expected. It's a difficult debate to understand, for this requires disentangling a complex of theoretical, empirical, and conceptual issues. I will attempt to disentangle some of these in this paper.

Kosslyn's view has great initial plausibility. For we seem to be aware of *images* – pictures in the mind – playing an important role in thought. Moreover, the appeal of mental pictures is not based on introspection alone. I will briefly survey some other sources of the appeal of *pictorialism*.

1   *Format.* Pictures are a convenient format for various cognitive tasks. Information can be "read off" visual displays – information that could be extracted only laboriously from sentential coding. For instance, it is much easier to see if three cities lie on a straight line by looking at a map than by consulting a list of cities filed with their locations. So (the idea runs) if you want to know if three cities *are* on a straight line, your natural recourse is to construct a mental map, and read off the result. Pictorial inner representations would be *functional.*

2   *Imagery and visual perception.* No one denies our capacity to imagine objects and scenes. The problem is to explain that capacity. A central feature of our pictorial *imagination* is its link with visual perception. We cannot image what we cannot see. This connection supports pictorialism, for on other accounts of imagery, the restriction is prima facie mysterious. If an image is a network of propositions brought to short-term memory (as Pylyshyn suggests), then there need be no restriction on the *kinds of predicates* that are used in the network. But if imagination involves the same mechanisms as visual perception, this restriction emerges automatically.

3   *The process of imagination.* The attractions of pictorialism have also been boosted by a range of experimental results. Two paradigms concern rotation and scanning imagined objects. I will return to these experimental programs, but I will briefly sketch the main themes here.

Rotation. In his 1970 paper, Shepard announced a suggestive experimental result. Subjects were presented with two complex forms. In some of the presentations, the forms were identical in shape but in different orientations. Subjects were asked whether the forms were identical. Interestingly, the time taken to respond increased linearly with angular distance between the forms; that is, with the degree through which one form would have to be rotated to bring it into congruence with the other. This prototypical rotation experiment has been taken to imply that images, like physical objects, are rotatable.

Scanning. Kosslyn (and others) have required subjects to memorize pictures; for example, maps. Once memorized, the subject calls the map to consciousness as an image. They are then instructed to focus on a particular point, then are asked to confirm or deny the presence of features on the map. The key result: the further the feature from the focused point, the longer it takes to respond. It is, therefore, natural to suppose that images are spatial displays that can be scanned.

In the opinion of many, results like this suggest that visual imagination *represents* spatial relations by in some way *manifesting* spatial relations. For these results would be readily understood if images were photographic slides in our heads. Thus, if a slide needed to be rotated in order for some matching process to take place, then the further a slide needed to be rotated, the longer rotation would take. Similarly, if a scanner were like a reader under which the slide passed, the further a point from the initial focus, the longer it would take to reach the scanner.

While no one believes images are slides, it seems as though these results fit naturally into a pictorial account of imagery. But they can be accommodated by a propositional account only with the help of *ad hoc* stipulations.

The view that we have some pictorial system of representation does therefore have initial plausibility. But it is a view that obviously raises problems as difficult as its solves.

(i) We might have sentences in our heads. For sentences are *not* restricted to any particular medium. Sentences can come as sound waves, marks on paper, electrical pulses, punched cards, and so on. Why not then as patterns of neural firings as well. But pictures *seem* to be medium-specific. Not just anything can be a picture of my big toe. So we might, literally, have sentences encoded in our brains, but we do not have pictures in our brains. So the pictorialist thesis is initially diffuse; we have an internal system of representation that in *some* way(s) is similar to some pictorial system of representation. But in *which* way(s) and to *what* system? Consider, for example, the differences between photographs, stick figures, diagrams, maps.

(ii) This problem leads to a second. Pictorialism moves from the thesis that we have pictures in the head to the thesis that we have something like pictures in the head. But this weakening may not preserve the explanatory power of pictorialism. That power may depend covertly on the naive thesis: the view that we have *real* pictures in the head.

In this paper I concentrate on Kosslyn's pictorialism, since his account is the most developed. In the next section, I outline his position. I then discuss the intelligibility and explanatory power of the pictorialist position. The basic message of this paper is that Kosslyn's model rescues the intelligibility of pictorialism at the cost of its explanatory power.

II Kosslyn's model of imagery

Kosslyn's basic idea is to develop an illuminating initial metaphor of imagery: a spatial display generated on cathode ray tube.

Visual images might be like spatial displays provided on a cathode ray tube by a computer programme operating on stored data. That is we hypothesized that images are temporary spatial displays in active memory that are generated from more abstract representations in long term memory. (Kosslyn et al. 1979, p. 536)

Nothing literally like a display is activated in the mind of course. That would involve commitment to real though evanescent pictures. But images are *like* displays.

1   Mental images are *semantically* like displays, in that they depict situations rather than describing them. Depiction is *not* explained by appeal to similarity. Rather, Kosslyn gives a cluster of criteria that will be discussed in the next section.
2   A display is generated from information in long-term store that is in a quite different form. Similarly, images are generated from information in long-term memory that is coded discursively.
3   A visual display on a CRT is transformable in various ways. Similarly, a mental image is transformable in various ways. A series of experiments by Shepard, Kosslyn, and others have shown, or seem to have shown, that images can be rotated, scanned, scaled up and down in size, in something rather like the ways in which real pictures, especially those on a display, can be.
4   Finally, we can *use* CRT displays. Information can be "read off" displays. Similarly, we can read information off images: in virtue of their explicit representation of various properties and relations only implicitly represented in propositional format. Of course, this "reading-off" is not a primitive function of the mind's eye: for that would introduce a fully fledged homunculus. The interpretation of images will have to be broken into a series of subfunctions until we reach a level that is plausibly primitive.

How can this metaphor be transformed into an explicit theory of imagery? This transformation is not complete, but Kosslyn and his co-workers have constructed a running simulation of human imagery. A simulation is *theory-like* in proceeding at a suitable level of abstraction. A psychologist need not be concerned with how psychological functions are realized in brainwaves though he must ensure that the functions he posits can be so realized. Similarly, the programmer need not be concerned with the hardware implementation of his program. A simulation is *theory-unlike* in having various *theory neutral* characteristics, characteristics it may or may not share with the modeled domain.

The model has three elements. One is the image itself, the surface display. The second is long-term memory store, the information from which the display is generated. The third is the set of processes through which the image is generated and transformed. I will sketch all three, for the general shape of this model is important to the argument of the rest of this paper.

(a)   *Long-term storage.* The crucial feature of long-term storage is that it is divided into two components. One encodes the "literal appearances" of objects or scenes. This information specifies which points in a matrix are filled if a given image is to be activated. The other component consists of lists of factual, discursive information. They play an important part in Kosslyn's model, for instance in determining how the parts of an image are fitted into an image skeleton, and in the generation of composite images not corresponding to a single remembered scene.

(b) *The surface display.* The *medium* of the surface display is a visual buffer implemented in the model as an array of points: an image is a configuration of points on this display. This display has a number of important features.

1 The buffer *functions* as a coordinate space though it is not literally spatial: spatial notions like "adjacent," "distance," "between" will be defined functionally, in terms of accessing procedures.
2 The medium imposes certain constraints on the information that can be accessed. Because the visual buffer has grain, each image has limited resolution. Moreover, the resolution is not uniform: it is highest at the center and decreases towards the periphery. Further, representations in the buffer are transient, and begin to decay as soon as they are activated.
3 There are certain *semantic constraints* on these displays in virtue of their role as images. Their informational content is the depiction of scenes and objects.

(c) *Image generation and transformation.* How are images generated and transformed in this model? In sketch, the functional interrelations between long-term memory, the visual buffer and visual perception look like figure 1.

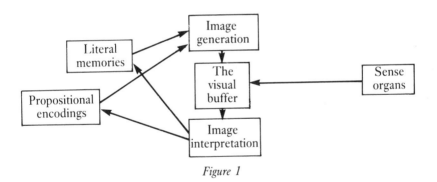

Figure 1

The heart of this system is a visual buffer, common to visual perception and visual imagination. Representations may arise on this buffer through perception, in which case interpretive processes make perceptual information available to the organism, and may filter some through to the two long-term memory stores. Alternatively, representations may be memory generated for cognitive use.

In addition to the image generation processes, Kosslyn includes in his model various transformations. These are designed to account for a variety of experimental findings and introspective reports about the way images can be used and transformed. These processes allow the size of images to be changed (Zoom and Pan); they allow various parts of the image to be centered for maximum resolution (scan) and for the orientation of the images to be changed (Rotate).

Let's now turn to the intelligibility of the pictorialist position and, in particular, the notion of depiction, on which so much of Kosslyn's model turns.

III   What is pictorial representation?

What is it for representation to be pictorial rather than discursive? There is not just one system of pictorial representation; nor can we assume that the different systems have a single defining property. So it is not surprising that different pictorialists center on different properties. But, broadly speaking, three strategies seem to be available. These strategies are compatible, and, partly I suspect for that reason, rarely appear in their pure form.

(i)   *Access strategies.* One idea (see Rey 1981, pp. 122–3) is that we *use* pictorial representation in a characteristic way. I have already mentioned a stock example – using a map to estimate intercity distances. So one might suggest that neural representations are pictorial if they are *used* in the same way that maps and pictures are used. Since there may be no one structural or semantic property in virtue of which a representation is usable mapwise, commonalities between representations might emerge only at the level of their use.

Characterizing representations in terms of their use may seem unpromising. For our whole system of visual information processing is deployed in our use of maps and diagrams. So characterizing *inner* representation in terms of the systems that access it may seem to posit an inner eye. Still, the strategy may apply: it's possible that part of our perceptual mechanisms are used in visual imagination as well.

(ii)   *Semantic strategies.* A more obvious idea, and one that has been tried in various forms, is to argue that neural representations may have the same semantic properties as pictorial representation (see, for instance, Fodor 1975; Block 1981; Rey 1981). These code spatial properties of the *represented* by spatial properties of the *representation.* Neural representations can share this feature, for they can have their spatial properties defined by accessing procedures. For example, two locations on a representation will for example *be* close and hence represent *closeness* just in case the procedures that access the representation can track from one location to the other through only a few intermediate locations. As we shall see, Kosslyn's strategy is a refinement of this approach.

(iii)   *Syntactic strategies.* There may be important syntactic differences between linguistic and pictorial representational systems.

It is sometimes suggested that pictorial systems in general, and images in particular, are *analog* representations.[2] Exactly what this amounts to is not clear. But at least two ideas are involved. Firstly, analog systems are continuous or dense (see Goodman). Every difference in the symbol (on some dimension) is semantically significant. For instance, if the luminosity of a blip on a radar screen represents distance, any variation, however minute, in luminosity represents a difference in distance. Secondly, it is sometimes suggested (for example, by Pylyshyn) that analog systems are intrinsic, or nonconventional, representational systems. More accurately, the respects in which a system is analog are respects in which it is nonconventional. Thus, a mercury thermometer represents temperature intrinsically, since it is so constructed that there is a direct and nomic relationship between its reading and the temperature of the environment. It is because it represents temperature intrinsically that it is a continuous representational system.

Now, perhaps the central feature of pictorial representation is this. Pictorial representation involves analog representation of the spatial properties of the situation presented. Since analog representation of spatial relations need not be restricted to any particular format, neural representation could be pictorial in this sense.

An alternative line has been defended by Shepard. He has suggested that a system of representation is pictorial if the representation shares structural properties of features of the object represented. A map is so-called because relations between map-parts are (or perhaps, weaker, correspond to) relations between parts of the mapped. Though this suggestion has some initial plausibility, it gives no sufficiently strong account of how neural representation could be pictorial.

With these preliminaries in mind, let's now turn to Kosslyn's account of depiction. He suggests five criteria for pictorial representation.

1 Each part of the representation corresponds to part of the referent.
2 There are constraints on corepresentation. For instance, if shape is represented, so too is orientation; if two objects are represented, so too the direction of one to the other, and so on. Kosslyn particularly emphasizes under this heading the constraints on the corepresentation of distance intervals (for example, 1980, p. 33, 1981, p. 215). Indeed, he sometimes writes as though the constraints on distance representation are so strong that only pictures *drawn to scale* count as depictions:

Once patterns in two local regions of the space are used to depict two portions of an object, the regions where patterns can be placed to depict the rest of the object are then determined. That is, mapping two portions into the medium establishes how distance on the object is mapped into distance in the internal medium, and provides anchor points that constrain the possible regions at which patterns can be used to depict other portions of the object. (Kosslyn 1980, pp. 33–4.)

3 Information that is typically implicit in propositional coding is explicit in depictions.
4 Depictions have a point of view (for example, see Kosslyn 1981, p. 216). Of course, there is a problem here. Depictions that have a point of view do not have a constant scale: perspective distorts scale.
5 Images depict pictorial properties: that is, relations between objects (or within objects) in a scene, and the surface properties of those objects – color, texture, and the like (1980, pp. 33–4).

These conditions impose strong restrictions on systems of representation. None the less, I do not think it a completely satisfactory account of the depictive. Let me sketch a few problems.

(i) If the displays on the visual buffer are depictions, the first criterion needs to be understood in a restricted way. For Kosslyn's model is not analog. The resolution on a display is determined by the number of points on the grid, and the first condition must be relativized to these points. Each point is a small patch, and while each patch represents part of the object or scene depicted, no *part* of the patch does.

(ii) Depictions are explicit whereas linguistic encoding is implicit. But the distinction between explicit and implicit representation is not a distinction between *representations themselves* but between representations and the way they are used; in other words, representation–interpretation pairs. Consider a list of sentences. What the list represents explicitly is just what is recoverable from the list by some computationally primitive operation. So even if the list contains (say) Fa, perhaps in conjunction, if extraction of a conjunct from a conjunction is not a primitive (or perhaps near primitive), Fa is *not* explicitly represented. What is explicit depends on access routes. For instance: is the relation "attacks" explicitly represented in an image of a chess position? It is clear that this question has no general answer: it will depend on whether an attack-recognizer is a primitive in the interpretation function. Nothing is explicitly/implicitly represented in itself.

(iii) The conditions are in some respects *too* strong. They rule out pictorial systems. Neither stick figures nor maps obey the fourth constraint: a map does not represent a continent from a point of view. Maps are *not* like aerial photographs, for their scale is constant. They lack the viewer centric features of a photo. Of course, if we take seriously Kosslyn's apparent requirement that images are to scale,[3] only maps and diagrams are depictions. Photographs are nondepictive, except where perspectival effects are negligible.

Moreover, stick figures do not obey the first constraint. A stick figure might have arms, but bits of the stick-arms do not represent bits of real arms, for they typically are entirely silent about the kinds of arms the represented had. This will often be true of sketches and caricatures too. This silence results from their extreme stylization. The exclusion of stick figures is not without importance. For it has long been difficult to see how images could be used in more general or abstract cognitive activities. One suggestion (see Block 1981) is to departicularize images, to strip them of particular reference to particular things. But if I interpret Kosslyn correctly, on his view this would deimage the representation as well. They would cease to be depictions.

(iv) The criteria may be of the wrong kind. It is unlikely that semantic characterizations are the appropriate way of describing our inner representational systems. The processes operating on these representations are sensitive only to the syntactic features of those systems. For computational processes are directly sensitive only to the formal properties of the representation. So, in considering the functional organization of the mind, the causally relevant taxonomy of systems of internal representation are syntactic, *not* semantic (see, for example, Fodor 1980; Dennett 1981). So it must be shown that the semantic features of displays in the visual buffer play a crucial role, via their syntactic correlates, in cognition. Else the imageness of our representations will be epiphenomenal.

(v) Finally, the criteria seem in some respects too weak. A discursive system can be *stipulated* to meet most of them. Perhaps all, granted that condition one applies only to *non*-atomic symbols. Pylyshyn does exactly this in his account of imagery (1978). Stipulated systems meet Kosslyn's conditions in a very jury-rigged way, but none the less this possibility shows that something has been left out. It's not *just* that a system must meet these conditions to be depictive, it must meet them necessarily. It must meet them in virtue of the structure of the system itself.[4] But how can we make sense of this notion?

Perhaps we can explain how a system necessarily meets Kosslyn's conditions by borrowing an idea from Palmer (1978). He introduces the notion of an intrinsic representational system. In a system in which (for example) mass is represented by luminosity, the structure of the *representing medium* ensures that certain relations in the represented domain are preserved. Because, for example, *both* "more massive" and "more luminous" are transitive, irreflexive, and antisymmetric, we need no conventions in our scheme of representation to ensure that our model represents the fact that if *A* is more massive than *B* and *B* is more massive than *C*, *A* is more massive than *C*. Applying this distinction to the case in hand, one might claim that depiction (but not description) of a scene requires that at least spatial relations are intrinsically represented. Paradigm depictions seem to satisfy this condition – for example, maps and photos do.

Kosslyn's suggestions throw no light on some important features of depictive representation. They throw no light, for instance, on *color*. The capacity to employ imagery shows considerable individual variation, but many report colored images. How could color be *depicted* in a mental image? Purple is normally represented, in a picture, by itself; but that's not so for mental images. Some neural feature must code purple without being purple; why would that be a depiction of purple rather than a *reference* to it?

So Kosslyn's account of depiction will need patching up in various ways. But it looks promising. There is nothing unintelligible about the suggestion that neural representation is importantly alike diagrams, photos or maps. But though we *can* say this, should we? To this issue I now turn.

IV Imagery and explanation

In the first section, I described three psychological phenomena that underwrite the appeal to images. These were: the apparent manipulability of representations in visual imagination; the parallels between visual imagination and visual perception; the cognitive uses of visual imagination. In fact, the final two cases can be grouped together. The fact that we seem to use representations in our head in the same way that we use maps and diagrams is a special case of the similarity between perception and imagination. Just as we perceive the relative locations of two cities on a real map without apparent effort or inference, so too we seem to be able to employ the inner eye to perceive these locations on an inner, memory-generated, representation.

In this section, I scrutinize these ideas. I argue that the explanatory power of the appeal to inner depictions is largely illusory. I start with the relationship between imagination and perception.

Imagery and perception. There are important links between visual perception and the mechanisms that underlie the experience of imagery. For imagery has important similarities to perception, similarities of two kinds.

(a)   There are similar constraints on content. Thus in an image, if the size and shape of an object is represented, its orientation is; so too in perception. We cannot image a four-dimensional space (though we can image a projection of that space on to fewer dimensions); nor can we see one.

Obviously the perceptible/nonperceptible distinction is not sharp. But wherever it is made, the equation between perceptible properties and imageable properties remains valid.

(b)   Perception is at least partly an automatic and autonomous process. In some of the same ways, imagery equally seems to be automatic and autonomous (as Pylyshyn notes in his 1981). Thus he writes:

> Imagine dropping an object and watching it fall to the ground or throwing a ball and watching it bounce off away. Does it not naturally obey physical laws. Imagine rotating the letter C counter clockwise through 90°. Does it not suddenly appear to have the shape of a U without you're having to deduce this? Imagine a square with a dot inside it. Now imagine the width of the square elongating until it becomes a wide rectangle. Is the dot not still inside the figure? (Pylyshyn 1981, p. 166).

Perception has these features. But how are these similarities to be explained? Do we need to appeal to shared structures and processes? Pylyshyn thinks not.

According to Pylyshyn images are just networks of discursive quasi-linguistic representations in a computational workspace. What resources has he available that would allow him to capture the similarities between imagery and perception? There are two.

(i)   These networks are drawn from long-term memory. So the content of long-term memory constrains the content of short-term networks. If long-term memory contains no information about the appearance of four-dimensional space, no descriptions of that space can be constructed. If there is a functionally distinct storage for visual memory, then these networks can contain only visual predicates. Some constraints are natural given the source of these short-term networks. But not all. For instance, if images represent shape they must represent orientation as well. We have no easy solution here: the best that can be done is to suggest (as Pylyshyn did in his 1978 article) that short-term networks have special access features: the store is filled by accessing long-term memory by means of spatial properties. But this move is *ad hoc*: it simply *stipulates* that short-store networks are specified for a range of spatial properties. In other words, on Pylyshyn's account of images, it is not an intrinsic feature of images that they are (for example) specified for orientation if specified for shape. If we wish to suggest that it *is* universal, it must simply be an added feature of the model.

(ii)   But perhaps this connection is not universal, but only habitual. This suggestion brings us to Pylyshyn's second resource: the idea of *tacit knowledge*. We know, if only tacitly, a lot about the world and how we perceive it. On Pylyshyn's view, this knowledge is crucially involved in imagery. For, *typically but not universally* when an individual imagines a situation X, he attempts to construct in his workspace a representation as similar as possible to the representation he would have formed if he had seen X. Imagining X is typically the construction of the subject's *prediction* of an X-perception representation. On this view it is not surprising that imagining is importantly like perception for:

a   the representations will be formally alike: both networks in a short-term workspace.

b   the subject is *trying to construct* a representation with many of the same features as a perception.

c   the subject is likely to succeed, for the subject knows a lot about Xs and a lot about how they look when observed.

Hence it is not surprising that images of Xs obey both natural laws and topological constraints. They obey the laws because the observers have knowledge; they seem to do this automatically because this knowledge is tacit. We cannot follow this natural strategy when we have no idea what the observation of Xs would be like, as in the four-dimensional case. Finally, we have an account of why shape and size go together in an image: they go together in an image because they go together in representations resulting from perception. Those perceptual representations in turn have this feature because of the nature of the world: all objects which have shape have size, and our perceptual mechanisms are sensitive to both properties. Of course, since tacit knowledge plays a decisive role here, it would follow that these features of imagery are cognitively penetrable: alterable by altering the subject's cognitive states. We should be able to learn to image four-dimensional scenes, to image the size of some object without imaging its shape, and so on.

There are serious problems for this account.

(i)   It's not a theory, but at best an idea. How does "tacit knowledge" play the role it does in shaping our short-term representations and how does it do so unobtrusively? This story introduces a homunculus at least as powerful as the "mind's eye."

(ii) Kosslyn points out (1981, p. 236) that perception and imagery have a number of surprising similarities: similarities that it is *most* implausible to suppose are known by the subject. For instance, for *both* images and percepts a vertical grating blurs at a greater apparent distance than an oblique grating. But this is a feature hardly known to the masses.

(iii) This account is predictively empty. For it suggests that imagery will bear similarities to, but will also have differences with, perception. But it fails to give any hint of what similarities and differences to expect.

In their 1979 paper, Kosslyn et al. sketch their best guess at the relationship between imagination and perception. They suggest that both the visual buffer, with its fixed spatial properties, and at least some pattern detection processes (p. 547) are shared. But generation and transformation processes are not: we cannot at will rotate a percept.

What light do these suggestions throw on the parallels between perception and imagery?

1   *Restrictions on content.* If both the visual buffer and its interpretative processes are common to both imagery and perception, Kosslyn nicely accounts for the fact that visible properties are also imageable properties. But it is important to note that more than a common buffer is required. For the properties of the buffer are

defined functionally not physically; that is, in terms of the processes that access them. If perception and imagery had distinct interpretative processes a given neural buffer feature could represent quite different properties when the buffer was memory activated from when it was perception generated. Much the same story can be made about restrictions on co-occurrence. If both the buffer and the interpretation processes are shared, we have a joint explanation of why in both perception and imagery, we cannot represent shape without representing orientation. But again: a shared visual buffer is not sufficient, and for the same reason.

So the first point to be made is that it is not just parsimony considerations that demand a common interpretive component. Rather, *only a shared buffer and a shared mind's eye allow pictorialists to explain certain commonalities between perception and imagery*.

2 *The autonomy of perception and imagery*. It is no surprise that perception represents objects as obeying the laws of nature and topology. For this to be so, perception needs only to be reliable. We need make no assumptions about the structure or the syntax of the percepts themselves: their fidelity is all we need.

But how do we explain the fact that imagery, typically *without* conscious monitoring, obeys the same constraints? There are two alternatives open to the defender of spatial images. Firstly, he can give the same account as Pylyshyn: tacit knowledge of laws of nature and topological principles. An explanation of this kind does not turn on the nature of the representational system, so it gives no reason to accept a pictorial account of imagery. But it does not undercut such an account either. Secondly, one might suppose that the processes by which images are transformed on the buffer are constrained. Only sequences that represent nomologically (or logically) possible situations could be generated. This suggestion is obviously more plausible for some constraints than for others. It is implausible for the bouncing tennis ball; plausible for the dot in the distorting square. It is important to note that constraints of these kinds would only help underwrite spatial images if they are built into the model. Thus it is unsatisfactory for Pylyshyn to handle the necessary correspondence of shape and orientation by simply *requiring* or *stipulating* that the network of propositions in the workspace represent both properties or neither. Similarly, a theory of spatial imagery is not advanced by simply *stipulating* that successive images obey certain nomological or topological laws. Instead, one would have to show that any pictorial representational system of a certain kind must constrain image sequences in this way. I do not see much prospect of this in Kosslyn's model. For Kosslyn's model includes a "blink" transformation in which image elements shift from place A on an image to place B without being at any intervening points. So Kosslyn's account of imagery allows successive images to violate natural or topological laws. Both Kosslyn and Pylyshyn must, in explaining the autonomy of imagery, rely on some version of the "tacit knowledge" hypothesis.

It follows that any explanatory advantage pictorialism has over propositional approaches depends on its superiority in explaining restrictions on content, for example, the. constraints on the co-specification of visual properties. This advantage in turn depends on the processes of imagination and perception sharing the visual buffer and interpretation functions.

So Kosslyn is committed to something like the following. A display on the visual buffer can be generated either by autonomous perceptual processes[5] (transducers) or by an image generation and transformation process operating on long-term memory. However the display is produced, it is inspected by a mind's eye: a set of cognitive processes.

I doubt whether this model is tenable.

1   I think that there are some reasons for doubting whether the visual buffer could be shared between perception and imagery. Firstly, the grain and resolution seem to differ. Perceptual resolution is much more fine-grained than that for imagery (hence the need for the Zoom transformation), and shows much less individual variation than visual imagination. Nor does perception exhibit in such a sharp form the decay of resolution as one moves from the center.

Further, though percepts are much *richer* than images, they also fade much more quickly. It is known that a percept has a very short life span once the stimulus is gone (see Dretske 1978; Brown and Hernstein 1981).

2   More importantly, there are strong arguments against the identification of the interpretive mechanisms of imagery with those for perception.

(a)   Kosslyn's account of the interpretation of imagery depends on part–whole relations already coded in long-term memory (1980, pp. 160–2). In other words, the only relations the imager can detect are those already coded in memory. Hence new parsings, new ways of discerning shapes in a grid, will be difficult to find. Now this conclusion seems right about images: it has often been noted that if one images an ambiguous display, it is *very hard* to see the display under the alternate parsing. This is *not* so for perception.

(b)   As Pylyshyn has repeatedly argued, images do not require interpretation to the same extent as percepts: they come pre-interpreted. Pylyshyn has made the point in terms of examples like the "attack" relationship in chess. Typically, an image of a chess position will not *need* interpretation about: where is the white king, what pieces are in the center, etc. For, it is at least partly generated *from* such information: information to which the system has at least some independent access. So the system already knows where and how the image contains this information. But a buffer display resulting from *perception* will require interpretation for just such information, for the buffer display is generated early in perceptual processing. A similar point can be made within the structure of Kosslyn's model: since images are partly constructed from propositional memory and not just from a set of coordinate points, all sorts of information need not be extracted from the display: for example, some part–whole information, and a general classification of the image. If you construct an image of a horse, you do not need to extract from the image the information that a horse is represented, you have *stipulated* that a horse is represented. But if your display is the result of seeing a horse, you do need to extract from the display the information that a horse is being perceived.

3   A central feature of Kosslyn's model is the divisions of long-term memory into two distinct but interrelated systems. Nor is this an accidental feature

of the model; Kosslyn's choice of this mechanism of image generation is not arbitrary. For one thing, the idea of a file of coordinate points is one way of making intuitive sense of the *functional* point of imagery. Files would contain information that could only be accessed by converting that information into (the functional equivalent of) a visual display. Secondly, storing information as a set of coordinate points is computationally convenient for a group of transformations that Kosslyn wants to model: rotation, size change, scanning. Finally, this division is central to his rebuttal of an early inconophobe paper of Pylyshyn. In his 1973 paper, Pylyshyn argued that pictorialists could not account for some central features of visual imagination. Two such features were our effortless access to visual memory, and the *character* of that access. In remembering a scene we can remember significant subparts of an episode rather than recalling the whole. Moreover, *memory failures* are semantically significant; failure of visual memory is never like having a piece torn from a photograph; what is missing is a well-defined unit of some kind. Pylyshyn took these facts to suggest that the contents of memory are *interpreted* rather than stored, uninterpreted appearances.

Kosslyn defuses Pylyshyn's problem through the device of double coding, together with the division of "appearance" memory into a main file plus subfiles. Thus, for instance, the fact that memory loss is loss of significant rather than arbitrary elements is explicable. Memory failure is the loss, or loss of access to, subfiles.

A central feature of this account of long-term memory is open to question. For it is possible to extract from Pylyshyn (1978) an argument *against* the existence of an appearance code. For in this paper Pylyshyn discusses a nice set of examples illustrating the cognitive penetrability of short- and long-term storage. They are examples that fit neatly into place on the assumption that storage is propositional; that is, abstract, discursive, semantically sentence-like. But they are difficult to explain on the basis of functionally relevant appearance storage, as in, for example, sets of matrix points.

I will discuss just one of these examples. Strong players have an extremely good recall for "natural" chess positions: positions that might have arisen from actual play. But when board positions are randomized, the recall of the strong is not better than the recall of the weak.

Pylyshyn's account of representation leads to a straightforward account of this case (and others he discusses). The weak player has a relatively impoverished vocabulary, with respect to chess, of internal representation. This impoverished vocabulary leads to broader equivalence classes: to neutralizing distinctions the cognitively more sophisticated make. It will be expensive to code an exact board position. Strong players have a *rich* internal vocabulary for chess positions: one leading to compact and efficient storage. However, since that vocabulary is adapted to game-like positions, it's inapplicable to randomized distribution of pieces on a board.

We would expect to use depictive representations (if we have them) for this task. After all, even strong players prefer to look at a board (or diagram) rather than a description while thinking about a position. But the example poses a problem for Kosslyn's model. We cannot just take strong players to have efficient appearance memories, for that fails to predict their inability to recall randomized positions. Presumably, it must be allowed that chess memory is propositional.

The same sort of point can be made about the other cases. If, for instance, children are shown a colored liquid in an inclined container, and then asked to draw what they have seen, they typically show the liquid surface parallel to the container bottom, not perpendicular to the direction of gravity. The natural hypothesis is that these children have no equivalent of "geocentric level," and hence cannot reconstruct what they see accurately. But if they were to have a functionally salient appearance memory, their performance becomes inexplicable: the appearance coding of the level of the liquid is independent of their conceptual sophistication.[6]

These and other cases throw doubt on the existence of unconceptualized memory, even as *one* of the memory codes. So: in my view, depictive accounts of the similarities between imagery and perception depend on a particular model of the generation and interpretation of displays on a visual buffer. That model has serious problems. So there is little explanatory point in positing a depictive system to account for these commonalities.

The mental manipulation of images. The special features of depiction ought to be detectable in cognition. In particular, images *represent* spatial relationships by in some way *manifesting* spatial relationships. This feature of imagery should have detectable consequences in the transformation images in the performance of various cognitive tasks. The detection of such consequences has been a central concern of Shepard, Kosslyn and others.

I have outlined the two most characteristic examples of mental manipulation: rotation and scanning. Both take time in proportion to distance rotated or scanned. This is to be expected if we had hard copy pictures in our head. The further you rotate, or scan across, such a picture, the longer it takes. But we don't have hard copies in our head. The most we have are depictions: representations semantically similar to pictures. But depictive representation need not conform to the rotation and scanning data. For suppose that images were like CRT displays. That supposition fails to show why distance rotated is propositional to time. For if the orientation of an object on a display is changed, there is no need for the display to move through the intermediate orientations. One display fades as its cells are deactivated; the new display lights up as it is reactivated. It may change to its new orientation in one jump.

The same point applies to scanning. There is no need for intermediate positions to be the object of focus. Indeed, there are some experimental data that require Kosslyn to add a "blink" transformation to his model that have exactly this feature (see, for example, Kosslyn 1981, pp. 222–3).

So our central concern will be: does positing depictive representation yield a better account of mental manipulations than can be given positing only discursive representation? There is no doubt that Kosslyn's model is predictively successful. If an image is to be scanned from point A on the map to point B all the intermediate locations are also scanned. Similarly, rotation proceeds by small steps. But does this model provide an *explanation* of image manipulation? Pylyshyn argues, correctly in my view, that it does not. Unfortunately, in his various writings on this issue he conflates a number of issues. I will try to sort them out.

Pylyshyn's strategy is double pronged: he argues *against* a pictorialist account of the phenomena while arguing for his own account of image manipulation. I will sketch Pylyshyn's account before turning to his criticism of Kosslyn.

Pylyshyn suggests that the implicit task demands of the experimental setup, plus the nature of the tasks themselves, lead the subjects to attempt to recreate the perceptual events that would occur in real perception. In this recreation process, subjects draw on their tacit knowledge of the world and of human perception (see especially, Pylyshyn 1981). Part of this recreation includes temporal as well as spatial relations. Subjects know that when they scan sections of their environment it takes them longer to scan larger sections. So when they imagine themselves scanning maps, they reproduce, deliberately if not consciously, this relationship. In other words, Kosslyn, Shepard and others interpret reaction-time data as evidence *about* a certain cognitive process; in particular, about its complexity. Pylyshyn, in contrast, suggests that we can take reaction time to be one of the variables being *calculated* by that cognitive process: to be part of the output, rather than a symptom of its complexity.

Should we explain rotation, scanning, et alia, in terms of *analog representations:* representations whose properties are *not* sensitive to the beliefs, goals, etc., of the agent? Pylyshyn suggests that the analog component in Kosslyn's model does little explanatory work. For, though there is considerable debate on its extent, crucial aspects of both scanning and rotation are *cognitively penetrable.*[7] For instance, rotation speed is sensitive to the complexity of the figure rotated (Pylyshyn 1978, pp. 50–2); a slide is not. Similarly, aspects of the scanning process are penetrable. The rate of scanning is sensitive to the beliefs of the subject about the object represented (Richman et al. 1979, p. 564). So too must be the direction of scanning: for time to increase linearly with distance, the subject must know approximately *where* the feature would be found so it can scan in that direction. This underscores the difference between image interpretation and perception: in perception we have no such advance knowledge. Indeed, Kosslyn agrees that a range of strategic aspects of transformation processes are penetrable (for example, 1980, p. 460). But if the rotation and scanning results depend on processes that are cognitively penetrated, the visual buffer's intrinsic properties seem to play a minor role in the prediction explanation of the data.[8]

I think this line of argument is basically right, but in putting it, Pylyshyn conflates three distinct notions, and hence muddies the waters.

1   *Primitiveness.* Analog representation is psychologically primitive; that is, analog representations are hard-wired into the head of the cognizer:

> an analog process is one whose behaviour must be characterised in terms of the intrinsic lawful relations among properties of a particular physical instantiation of a process, rather than in terms of rules and representations. (Pylyshyn 1981, p. 157)

Systems of this kind "are not alterable in nomologically arbitrary ways of tacit knowledge" (p. 153). Analog systems are theoretically crucial for a number of reasons (see especially Pylyshyn 1980 and Block 1983b), but especially because they are regress-blocking. Appeals to inner representational states appear to invoke a homunculus to understand those states and hence appear to involve a regress. Fodor (1975) showed how this regress was broken by appealing to a primitive, hard-wired representational system. A device used a hard-wired system *not* in virtue of explicit rules and representations *about* the system, but because of its internal structure. No homunculus is invoked, hence the regress is stopped. So Pylyshyn is *right* to insist on the importance of this level, and right to insist that the cognitive penetrability of manipulations like rotation and scanning show them not to be psychological primitives. Hard-wired systems are invariant. Thus any account leaving rotation/scanning as primitive appeals to an undischarged homunculus.

Kosslyn does not do this, but his account makes little appeal to the only primitive theory relevant feature of his model, the properties of the visual buffer.[9]

2 *Intrinsic representation.* Pylyshyn seems to conflate primitive with intrinsic representation (for example, 1981, pp. 155–6). Intrinsic representational systems are those in which some relations in the represented domain hold in the representing domain not as a matter of stipulation or convention but as a matter of nomological law. For example, in a system where the length of objects in the represented domain is modeled by the mass of objects in the representing domain we need no convention to ensure that the transitivity of "is longer than" is captured in the representing system. It obviously does *not* follow from the fact that a representational system is primitive that it is intrinsic: English could be hard-wired into my brain, but it is a paradigm of a non-intrinsic system. The converse seems to hold: an intrinsic system is primitive. For only primitive systems do not require the organism to represent to itself instructions about using the system.

All this has a point. Photographic representation *is* an intrinsic representation of spatial relations: hence the explanatory power, though sadly the empirical falsity, of supposing that we had photos in the head. It is *because* the representation of distance is intrinsic that we can *explain*, not just stipulate, why it takes longer to scan longer distances.

It's nomic: it takes more time to traverse more space. But in the shift from real pictorial display to functional displays we *shift* from intrinsic to non-intrinsic representation. For the functional properties of the visual buffer do not reduce 1–1 to physical properties. So the functional relations in the buffer are not expressions of any particular law, though they presumably hold in particular cases because of some law or other. The functional display might still be hard-wired, but that is *insufficient* for its being intrinsic.

3 *Formality.* The question of intrinsic representational systems is in turn run together with Pylyshyn's claim that pictorialists do not respect the formality constraint in cognitive theory. He argues that a number of claims pictorialists make about image processing make sense only if interpreted as remarks about the domain represented, rather than the representations themselves.

> to principles that are expressed in terms of the properties of the represented object rather than in terms of the structure or form of the representation itself. But expressing a principle in terms of the properties of the represented domain begs the question of why processing occurs this way. The mechanism has no access to the

properties of the represented domain except insofar as they are encoded in the form of the representation itself. (Pylyshyn 1981, p. 171)

Pylyshyn instances in this connection a principle that Kosslyn needs for the predictive success of the model: namely "mental images are transformed in small steps, so that images pass through intermediate steps of transformation" (Kosslyn et al. 1979, p. 542). Now, Pylyshyn points out that this principle must be given a *semantic interpretation*: images are transformed in such a way that successive images correspond to small changes in the scene depicted. Consider scanning. Why does it take longer to scan from A to B than from A to C. Because, in the scene represented, B is twice C's distance from A. So what? Scanning from A to B requires constructing *intermediate* representations. Since B is the further from A, there are more intermediate locations, hence more intermediate representations need to be constructed. In other words, intermediate representations are *representations of intermediate positions* in the scene; that is, Kosslyn's principle must be interpreted semantically. But small semantic changes need not correspond to small syntactic changes.

Conflating semantic readings with syntactic readings would be venal *if* the representation scheme were intrinsic. But we have been given no reason to believe that representation in functional space is intrinsic; indeed, there is good reason to believe that it is not. For:

(i)   The properties of functional space depend on the procedures that access that space.
(ii) Accessing procedures are cognitive penetrable, as Kosslyn et al. allow,[10] and hence they are not primitive.
(iii) Only primitive representational schemes are intrinsic.

Once the distinct lines of thought in Pylyshyn's critique are disentangled, I think it can be seen that Kosslyn's reply to this line of criticism (see especially Kosslyn et al. 1979 and Kosslyn 1981) is not adequate.

In reply he urges two main theses:

(i) *Primitive processes.* I think Kosslyn misses the force of Pylyshyn's demand for computational primitives. Kosslyn identifies this demand as a species of reductionism (Kosslyn et al. 1979, p. 546) and as such dismisses it. But the point of this demand is only partially reductionist; it is, more importantly, to show that no regress of understanding is invoked, because only hard-wired representation can be intrinsic.

(ii) *Cognitive penetrability.* Kosslyn argues that the criterion of cognitive penetrability of an overall process like rotation scanning shows only that some components of this process are penetrable, not that there are no fixed, hard-wired processes (Kosslyn 1981, pp. 227f). Kosslyn is undoubtedly right in this claim, but it seems to me *not* to be to the point. For the predictive accuracy and power of Kosslyn's account of mental rotation and scanning do *not* depend on fixed and intrinsic properties of the model – properties the model must have if it is to have a visual buffer – but on cognitively penetrable and/or contingent features of the model. Thus there is nothing that *ensures* that scanning is incremental; indeed, Kosslyn includes a blink transformation in which it is not. Nothing in the model fixes the rate of rotation, nor ensures that it is incremental (rather than, say, a salvo of "blinks" zeroing in on the target representation).

So, though Kosslyn's model is predictively and heuristically valuable, I agree with Pylyshyn's claim that it has little explanatory power. For the predictions are *not* a consequence of the theory's "hardcore"; a visual buffer with fixed properties common to perception. Rather, they are derived from a protective belt of parameters that are unconstrained by this hardcore, and (Kosslyn's claim to the contrary) not much constrained by each other.

Indeed, I think this conclusion is true more generally. Kosslyn's system is very impressive; so impressive that it is hard to believe that he is not on to something important and right. But *what* it is that is important and right does not emerge clearly from his work; at least, not clearly to me. I see little explanatory advantage in positing a distinct system of spatial representation.

NOTES

Thanks to David Armstrong, Ned Block, Michael Devitt, and Bill Lycan for their comments on earlier versions of this paper.

1 Roughly, a system of representation is propositional or sentential if its formulae share the distinctive syntactic and semantic features of natural language: a generative syntax; syntactically structured formulae; semantic properties like truth and reference.

2 The analog–digital distinction is decidedly inchoate, but some light is cast on it by Goodman (1968) and Haugeland (1981).

3 This requirement is not arbitrary; his explanation of scanning data works only if images are depictions to scale.

4 Kosslyn does see this problem. But his response is cryptic. Thus, for instance, in his 1981 article he appears to suggest that the semantics of imagery are innate (p. 214). But that can hardly be right.

5 This model depends on the propriety of dividing perceptual processing into components: a cognitively impenetrable, hard-wired visual component that is relatively independent of the higher cognitive centers, and a component that is sensitive to the beliefs, goals, intentions, etc., of the cognitive system. Pylyshyn (1978 and 1980) defends this division. If it cannot be made, the model above is incoherent, for not all of the perceptual process can be shared with imagination. Similarly, if Fodor's modularity hypothesis is correct Kosslyn's model cannot be. For that hypothesis places perceptual interpretation within a module; these then will *not* be available to central cognitive processing, the presumed locus of imagination.

6 Except its organization into file and subfile. Block (1983) is unimpressed by this argument. He thinks a pictorialist need only allow that there is a *conceptual component* to depictive representation. But I don't see then that pictorialism does any explanatory work: this move is tantamount to admitting that – in this range of tasks – the depictive elements of inner representation are epiphenomenal.

7 See Pylyshyn 1980 on this issue, especially pp. 117–19.

8 See especially Pylyshyn 1978, and 1981, especially pp. 168–81; and Kosslyn 1981, esp. pp. 227–36.

9 It appeals to other primitive elements: for example, the form in which coordinate points in literal files are specified. But I read Kosslyn as not claiming that these details of his model are theory relevant.

10 For they depend partly on the contents of the propositional files, and this is to build penetrability explicitly into the model. Further, FIND and IMAGE are manifestly non-primitive (see Kosslyn 1980, p. 151).

REFERENCES

Block, N. (ed.) (1981) *Imagery*. Cambridge and London: MIT Press.
Block, N. (1983a) "The photographic fallacy in the debate about mental imagery," *Noûs* 17, 651–62.
Block, N. (1983b) "Mental pictures and cognitive science," *Philosophical Review* 92, 499–541.
Brown, R. and Herrnstein, R. J. (1981) "Icons and images," in Block 1981, pp. 19–49.
Dennett, D. C. (1978) *Brainstorms*. Cambridge: The MIT Press/A Bradford Book.
Dennett, D. C. (1981) "Three kinds of intentional psychology," in *Reduction, Time and Reality*, R. Healey (ed.). New York and London: Cambridge University Press.
Dretske, F. (1978) "The role of the percept in visual cognition," in *Perception and Cognition*, C. W. Savage (ed.). Minneapolis: University of Minnesota Press.
Fodor, J. A. (1975) *The Language of Thought*, London: Thomas Y. Crowell.
Fodor, J. A. (1978) "Propositional attitudes," *The Monist* 61, 501–23.
Fodor, J. A. (1980) "Methodological solipsism considered as a research strategy for cognitive psychology," *The Behavioral and Brain Sciences* 3, 63–110.
Goodman, N. (1968) *Languages of Art*. New York: Bobbs-Merrill.
Haugeland, J. (1981) "Analog and analog," *Philosophical Topics* 12, 213–26.
Kosslyn, S. M. (1980) *Image and Mind*. Cambridge: Harvard University Press.
Kosslyn, S. M. (1981) "The medium and the message in mental imagery: A theory," in Block 1981, pp. 207–44.
Kosslyn, S. M., Pinker, S., Smith, G. E. and Schwartz, S. P. (1979) "On the demystification of mental imagery," *The Behavioral and Brain Sciences* 2, 535–81.
Kosslyn, S. M. and Pomerantz, J. R. (1978) "Imagery, propositions and the form of internal representations," in *Readings in Philosophy of Psychology*, vol. 2, N. Block (ed.). Cambridge: Harvard University Press.
Lycan, W. G. (1981) "Towards a homuncular theory of believing," *Cognition and Brain Theory* 4, 139–59.
Palmer, S. E. (1978) "Fundamental aspects of cognitive representation," *Cognition and Categorization*, E. Rosch and B. B. Lloyd (eds). Hillsdale, NJ: Erlbaum Associates.
Pylyshyn, Z. W. (1973) "What the mind's eye tells the mind's brain," *Psychological Bulletin* 80, 1–24.
Pylyshyn, Z. W. (1978) "Imagery and artificial intelligence," in *Perception and Cognition*, Minnesota Studies in the Philosophy of Science, vol. 9, C. Wade Savage (ed.). Minneapolis: University of Minnesota Press.
Pylyshyn, Z. W. (1980) "Computation and cognition," *The Behavioral and Brain Sciences* 3, 111–69.
Pylyshyn Z. W. (1981) "The imagery debate: Analog media versus tacit knowledge," in Block 1981, pp. 151–206.
Rey, G. (1981) "What are mental images?" in *Readings in the Philosophy of Psychology*, vol. 2, N. Block (ed.). Cambridge: Harvard University Press.
Richman, C. L., Mitchell, D. B. and Reznick, S. (1979) "The demands of mental travel," *Behavioral and Brain Sciences* 2, 564–5.
Sterelny, K. (1981) Critical Notice of D. C. Dennett's *Brainstorms*. *Australasian Journal of Philosophy* 58, 442–53.
Sterelny, K. (1983) "Mental representation: What language is brainese?" *Philosophical Studies* 43, 365–82.
Sterelny, K. (1984) Critical Notice of A. Woodfield (ed.), *Thought and Object*. *Journal of Semantics* 3, 277–94.
Shepard, Roger N. (1975) "Form, formation and transformation of internal representations", in *Information Processes and Cognition*, R. L. Solso (ed.). The Loyola Symposium. Washington DC: V. H. Winston.

20

Language and Innateness

On the Nature, Use and Acquisition of Language
NOAM CHOMSKY

For about thirty years, the study of language – or more accurately, one substantial component of it – has been conducted within a framework that understands linguistics to be a part of psychology, ultimately human biology. This approach attempts to reintroduce into the study of language several concerns that have been central to Western thought for thousands of years, and that have deep roots in other traditions as well: questions about the nature and origin of knowledge in particular. This approach has also been concerned to assimilate the study of language to the main body of the natural sciences. This meant, in the first place, abandoning dogmas that are entirely foreign to the natural sciences and that have no place in rational inquiry, the dogmas of the several varieties of behaviorism, for example, which seek to impose a priori limits on possible theory construction, a conception that would properly be dismissed as entirely irrational in the natural sciences. It means a frank adherence to mentalism, where we understand talk about the mind to be talk about the brain at an abstract level at which, so we try to demonstrate, principles can be formulated that enter into successful and insightful explanation of linguistic (and other) phenomena that are provided by observation and experiment. Mentalism, in this sense, has no taint of mysticism and carries no dubious ontological burden. Rather, mentalism falls strictly within the standard practice of the natural sciences and, in fact, is nothing other than the approach of the natural sciences applied to this particular domain. This conclusion, which is the opposite of what is often assumed, becomes understandable and clear if we consider specific topics in the natural sciences; for example, nineteenth-century chemistry, which sought to explain phenomena in terms of such abstract notions as elements, the periodic table, valence, benzene rings, and so on – that

"On the Nature, Use and Acquisition of Language" by N. Chomsky is the text of a lecture delivered in Kyoto in January, 1987. It appears in N. Chomsky, *Generative Grammar: Its Basis, Development and Prospects* (Kyoto University of Foreign Studies, 1987), and N. Chomsky, *Language in a Psychological Setting, Sophia Linguistica XII* (Sophia University, Tokyo, 1987). Reprinted by kind permission of the author.

is, in terms of abstract properties of then-unknown, perhaps still unknown, physical mechanisms. This abstract inquiry served as an essential preliminary and guide for the subsequent inquiry into physical mechanisms. Mentalistic inquiry in the brain sciences is quite similar in approach and character to the abstract inquiry into properties of the chemical elements, and we may expect that this abstract inquiry too will serve as an essential preliminary and guide for the emerging brain sciences today; the logic is quite similar.

This work proceeds from the empirical assumption – which is well-supported – that there is a specific faculty of the mind/brain that is responsible for the use and acquisition of language, a faculty with distinctive characteristics that is apparently unique to the species in essentials and a common endowment of its members, hence a true species property.

These ideas have developed in the context of what some have called "the cognitive revolution" in psychology, and in fact constituted one major factor contributing to these developments. It is important, I think, to understand clearly just what this "revolution" sought to accomplish, why it was undertaken, and how it relates to earlier thinking about these topics. The so-called "cognitive revolution" is concerned with the states of the mind/brain that enter into thought, planning, perception, learning and action. The mind/brain is considered to be an information-processing system, which forms abstract representations and carries out computations that use and modify them. This approach stands in sharp contrast to the study of the shaping and control of behavior that systematically avoided consideration of the states of the mind/brain that enter into behavior, and sought to establish direct relations between stimulus situations, contingencies of reinforcement, and behavior. This behaviorist approach has proven almost entirely barren, in my view, a fact that is not at all surprising since it refuses in principle to consider the major and essential component of all behavior, namely, the states of the mind/brain.

Consider the problem of learning. We have an organism with a mind/brain that is in a certain state or configuration. The organism is presented with certain sensory inputs, leading to a change in the state of the mind/brain. This process is the process of learning, or perhaps more accurately, mental and cognitive growth. Having attained a new state as a result of this process, the organism now carries out certain actions, in part influenced by the state of the mind/brain that has been attained. There is no direct relation between the sensory inputs that led to the change of state of the mind/brain and the actions carried out by the organism, except under highly artificial, uninformative and very marginal conditions.

There is of course a relation of some kind between sensory inputs and behavior; a child who has not been presented with data of Japanese will not be able to carry out the behavior of speaking Japanese. Presented with appropriate data from Japanese, the child's mind/brain undergoes a significant change; the mind/brain comes to incorporate within itself knowledge of Japanese, which then enables the child to speak and understand Japanese. But there is no direct relation between the data presented to the child and what the child says, and it is hopeless to try to predict what the child will say, even in probabilistic terms, on the basis of the sensory data that led to acquisition of knowledge of Japanese. We can study the process by which the sensory data lead to the change of state of the mind/brain, and we may study at least certain aspects of how this attained knowledge is used. But an effort to study the relation between the sensory data and the actual behavior, avoiding the crucial matter of the nature of the mind/brain and the changes it undergoes, is doomed to triviality and failure, as the history of psychology demonstrates very well. The cognitive revolution was based in part on the recognition of such facts as these, drawing conclusions that really should not be controversial, though they are – a sign of the immaturity of the field, in my view. This change of perspective in the study of psychology, linguistics included, was surely a proper one in essence, and in fact was long overdue.

Not only was this change of perspective overdue, but it also was much less of a revolution than many believed. In fact, without awareness, the new perspective revived ideas that had been developed quite extensively centuries earlier. In particular, seventeenth-century science developed a form of cognitive psychology that was quite rich, and basically, I think, on the right track. Descartes's major scientific contribution, perhaps, was his rejection of the neoscholastic idea that perception is a process in which the form of an object imprints itself somehow on the brain, so that if you see a cube, for example, your brain has the form of a cube imprinted in it in some fashion. In place of this fallacious conception, Descartes proposed a representational theory of mind. He considered the example of a blind man with a stick, who uses the stick to touch in sequence various parts of a physical object before him, let us say a cube. This sequence of tactile inputs leads the blind man construct, in his mind, the image of a cube, but the form of the cube is not imprinted in the mind. Rather, the sequence of tactile inputs leads the mind to construct a mental representation of a cube, using its own resources and its own structural principles. Descartes argued that much the same is true of normal vision. A series of stimuli strike the retina, and the mind then forms ideas that provide a conception of the objects of the external world. The mind then carries out various computational processes, as the person thinks about these objects, including processes that enable the person to carry out certain actions involving them: for example, picking up the cube, rotating it, and so on. This is surely the right general approach. It has been revived in recent psychology and physiology, and by now something is known about how the process takes place, including even some understanding of the physical mechanisms involved in the coding and representation of stimuli.

Descartes also observed that if a certain figure, say a triangle, is presented to a person, then what the person will perceive is a triangle, though the presented image is certainly not a Euclidean triangle, but rather some far more complex figure. This will be true, he argued, even if the person is a child who has had no previous acquaintance with geometrical figures. In a certain sense the point is obvious, since true geometrical figures do not exist in the natural environment in which we grow and live, but we nevertheless perceive figures as distorted geometrical figures, not as exact instances of whatever they may happen to be. Why does the child perceive the object as a distorted triangle, rather than as the very complex figure that it actually is: with one of the lines slightly curved, with two sides not quite touching, and so on? Descartes' answer was that the Euclidean triangle is produced by the mind on the occasion of this stimulation, because the mechanisms of the mind are based on principles of Euclidean geometry and produce these geometrical figures as exemplars or models for the organization of perception, and for learning, drawing them from its own resources and structural principles.

In contrast, empiricists such as David Hume argued that we simply have no idea of a triangle, or a straight line, since we could not distinguish "perfect images" of such objects from the "defective ones" of the real world. Hume correctly drew the consequences of the empiricist principles that he adopted and developed: in particular, the principle that the mind receives impressions from the outside world and forms associations based upon them, and that this is all there is to the story (apart from the animal instinct underlying induction). But the consequences that Hume correctly drew from these assumptions are certainly false. Contrary to what he asserted, we do, indeed, have a clear concept of a triangle and a straight line, and we perceive objects of the world in terms of these concepts, just as Descartes argued. The conclusion, then, is that the empiricist assumptions are fundamentally wrong, as a matter of empirical fact; the properties of the mind/brain that are involved in determining how we perceive and what we perceive are crucially different from what was postulated in empirical speculation. It seems reasonable to resort to a representational theory of mind of the Cartesian sort, including the concept of the mind as an information-processing system that computes, forms and modifies representations; and we should also adopt something like the Cartesian concept of innate ideas as tendencies and dispositions, biologically determined properties of the mind/brain that provide a framework for the construction of mental representations, a framework that then enters into our perception and action. Ideas of this sort have been revived in the context of the cognitive revolution of the past generation.

Seventeenth-century psychologists, who we call "philosophers," went far beyond these observations. They developed a form of what much later came to be called "Gestalt psychology" as similar ideas were rediscovered during this century. These seventeenth-century thinkers speculated rather plausibly on how we perceive objects around us in terms of structural properties, in terms of our concepts of object and relation, cause and effect, whole and part, symmetry, proportion, the functions served by objects and the characteristic uses to which they are put. We perceive the world around us in this manner, they argued, as a consequence of the organizing activity of the mind, based on its innate structure and the experience that has caused it to assume new and richer forms. "The book of nature is legible only to an intellectual eye," as Ralph Cudworth argued, developing such ideas as these. Again, these speculations seem to be very much on the right track, and the ideas have been rediscovered and developed in contemporary psychology, in part within the context of the cognitive revolution.

The contemporary cognitive revolution has been considerably influenced by modern . science, mathematics and technology. The mathematical theory of computation, which developed in the 1920s and 1930s particularly, provided conceptual tools that make it possible to address certain classical problems of representational psychology in a serious way, problems of language in particular. Wilhelm von Humboldt understood, a century and a half ago, that language is a system that makes infinite use of finite means, in his phrase. But he was unable to give a clear account of this correct idea, or to use it as the basis for substantive research into language. The conceptual tools developed in more recent years make it possible for us to study the infinite use of finite means with considerable clarity and understanding. Modern generative grammar, in fact, can be regarded in part as the result of the confluence of the conceptual tools of modern logic and mathematics and the traditional Humboldtian conception, inevitably left vague and unformed. A generative grammar of a language is a formal system that states explicitly what are these finite means available to the mind/brain, which can then make infinite, unbounded use of these means. Unfortunately, the classical ideas concerning language and representational psychology had long been forgotten when the cognitive revolution took place in the 1950s, and the connections I am now discussing were discovered only much later, and are still not widely known.

The development of electronic computers has also influenced the cognitive revolution considerably, primarily in providing useful concepts such as internal representation, modular structure, the software–hardware distinction and the like, and also, in areas such as vision at least, in making it possible to develop explicit models of cognitive processes that can be tested for accuracy and refined. It is worthy of note that much the same was true of the seventeenth-century cognitive revolution. The Cartesians were much impressed with the mechanical automata then being constructed by skilled craftsmen, which seemed to mimic certain aspects of the behavior of organisms. These automata were a stimulus to their scientific imagination much in the way that modern electronic computers have contributed to the contemporary cognitive revolution.

Some of these seventeenth-century ideas, which are now being rediscovered and developed in quite new ways, have much earlier origins. What is probably the world's first psychological experiment is described in the Platonic dialogues, when Socrates undertakes to demonstrate that a slave boy, who has had no instruction in geometry, nevertheless knows the truths of geometry. Socrates demonstrates this by asking the slave boy a series of questions, providing him with no information but drawing from the inner resources of the slave boy's mind, and in this way Socrates leads the slave boy to the point where he recognizes the truth of theorems of geometry. This experiment was understood, quite plausibly, to show that the slave boy knew geometry without any experience. Indeed, it is difficult to see what other interpretation can be given. The experiment was, presumably, a kind of "thought experiment," but if it were carried out rigorously, as has never been done, the results would probably be more or less as Plato presented them in this literary version of a psychological experiment.

The human mind, in short, somehow incorporates the princples of geometry, and experience only serves to bring them to the point where this innate knowledge can be used. This demonstration also poses a very crucial problem: the problem is to explain how the slave boy can have the knowledge he does have, when he has had no relevant experience from which he could derive this knowledge. Let us refer to this problem as "Plato's problem," returning to it directly.

The rise of generative grammar in the 1950s, a major factor in the cognitive revolution, also resurrected traditional ideas. The Cartesians, in particular, had applied their ideas on the nature of the mind to the study of language, which was comonly viewed as a kind of "mirror of mind." Subsequent study enriched these investigations in quite impressive ways, which we are now only beginning to understand. The cognitive revolution of the 1950s, then, should be understood, I believe, as having recovered independently the insights of earlier years, abandoning the barren dogmas that had impeded understanding of these questions for a very long period; and then applying these classical ideas, now reconstructed in a new framework, in new ways, and developing them along lines that would not have been possible in an earlier period, thanks to new understanding in the sciences, technology and mathematics.

From the point of view adopted in this "second cognitive revolution," the central problems of the study of language are essentially the following four:

The first question, a preliminary to any further inquiry, is this: What is the system of knowledge incorporated in the mind/brain of a person who speaks and understands a particular language? What constitutes the language that the person has mastered and knows? A theory concerned with this topic for a particular language is called "a grammar of that language," or in technical terms, "a generative grammar of the language," where the term "generative grammar" means nothing more than a theory of the language that is fully explicit, so that empirical consequences can be derived in it. Traditional grammars, in contrast, relied crucially on the knowledge of language of the reader of the grammar to fill in the enormous gaps that were left unstudied, and were not even recognized to be gaps; it is surprising, in retrospect, to see how difficult it was to recognize that even the simplest of phenomena pose rather serious problems of explanation. A traditional grammar, then, is not a theory of the language, but is rather a guide that can be followed by a person who already knows the language. Similarly, a pedagogic grammar of Spanish written in English is not a theory of Spanish but rather a guide to Spanish that can be used by a speaker of English who already knows the basic principles of language, though unconsciously, and can therefore make use of the hints and examples in the grammar to draw conclusions about Spanish. A generative grammar, in contrast, seeks to make explicit just what this knowledge is that enables the intelligent reader to make use of a grammar.

To the extent that we can provide at least a partial answer to the first problem, we can turn to a second problem: How is this knowledge of language used in thought or expression of thought, in understanding, in organizing behavior, or in such special uses of language as communication, and so on? Here we have to make a crucial conceptual distinction between (1) the language, a certain cognitive system, a system of knowledge incorporated in the mind/brain and described by the linguist's generative grammar; and (2) various processing systems of the mind/brain that access this knowledge in one or another way, and put it to use.

Still assuming some kind of answer to the problem of characterizing the knowledge attained, we can turn to a third problem: what are the physical mechanisms that exhibit the properties that we discover in the abstract investigation of language and its use; that is, the physical mechanisms of the brain that are involved in the representation of knowledge and in accessing and processing this knowledge? These are pretty much tasks for the future, and they are very difficult ones, primarily, because for very good ethical reasons, we do not permit direct experimentation that might enable scientists to investigate these mechanisms directly. In the case of other systems of the mind/brain, such as the visual system, the investigation of mechanisms has proceeded quite far. The reason is that we allow ourselves, rightly or wrong, to carry out direct experimentation with cats, monkeys, and so on. Their visual systems are in many ways like our own, so a good deal can be learned about the physical mechanisms of the human visual system in this way. But it appears that the language faculty is a unique human possession in its essentials, and if we were to discover some other organism that shared this faculty in part, we would probably regard it as quasi-human and refrain from direct experimentation. Consequently, the study of physical mechanisms of the language faculty must be studied in much more indirect ways, either by non-intrusive experiments, or by "nature's experiments," such as injury and pathology. Part of the intellectual fascination of the study of language is that it must proceed in such indirect ways, relying very heavily on the abstract level of inquiry – a difficult and challenging task, but one that can be addressed and has much promise.

The fourth problem is to explain how the knowledge of language and ability to use it are acquired. This problem of acquisition arises both for the language – the cognitive system itself – and for the various processing systems that access the language. I will focus attention here on the first of these questions: on acquisition of language. Plainly, the question can be formulated only to the extent that we have some understanding of what is acquired – of what is a language – though as always, inquiry into the acquisition or use or physical basis of some abstract system can and should provide insight into its nature.

The fourth question is a special case of Plato's problem: How do we come to have such rich and specific knowledge, or such intricate systems of belief and understanding, when the evidence available to us is so meager? That was the problem that rightly troubled Plato, and it should trouble us as well. It is a question that for a long period did not trouble psychologists, linguists, philosophers, and others who thought about the matter, except for a few, who were rather marginal to the main intellectual tradition. This is a sign of the serious intellectual failings of the thought of this era, an interesting topic that I will not pursue here. If a rational Martian scientist were to observe what takes place in a single language community on earth, he would conclude that knowledge of the language that is used is almost entirely inborn. The fact that this is not true, or at least not entirely true, is extremely puzzling, and raises many quite serious problems for psychology and biology, including evolutionary biology.

Recall that Plato had an answer to the problem he posed: we remember the knowledge we have from an earlier existence. This is not a proposal that we would nowadays be inclined to accept in exactly these terms, though we should, in all honesty, be prepared to recognize that it is a far more satisfactory and rational answer than the ones that have been offered in the dominant intellectual traditions of recent centuries, including the Anglo-American empiricist tradition, which simply evaded the problems. To render Plato's answer intelligible, we have to provide a mechanism by which our knowledge is remembered from an earlier existence. If we are disinclined to accept the immortal soul as the mechanism, we will follow Leibniz in assuming that Plato's answer is on the right track, but must be, in his words, "purged of the error of preexistence." In modern terms, that means reconstructing Platonic "remembrance" in terms of the genetic endowment, which specifies the initial state of the language faculty, much as it determines that we will grow arms not wings, undergo sexual maturation at a certain stage of growth if external conditions such as nutritional level permit this internally directed maturational process to take place, and so on. Nothing is known in detail about the mechanisms in any of these cases, but it is now widely and plausibly assumed that this is the place to look. At least, it is widely assumed for physical growth. The fact that similar evidence does not lead to similar rational conclusions in the case of the mind/brain again reflects the serious intellectual inadequacies of recent thought, which has simply refused to approach problems of the mind/brain by the methods of rational inquiry taken for granted in the physical sciences. This is strikingly true, particularly, of those who falsely believe themselves to be scientific naturalists, and who see themselves as defending science against the obscurantists. Exactly the opposite is true, in my opinion, for the reasons that I have briefly indicated.

Putting aside various dogmas, let us approach questions of mind/brain, including questions of language, in the spirit of the natural sciences. Abstracting away from unknown mechanisms, we assume that the language faculty has an initial state, genetically determined, common to the species apart from gross pathology, and apparently unique to the human species. We know that this initial state can mature to a number of different steady states – the various attainable languages – as conditions of exposure vary. The process of maturation from the initial state to the steady state of mature knowledge is, to some extent, data-driven; exposed to data of English, the mind/brain will incorporate knowledge of English, not Japanese. Furthermore, this process of growth of the language faculty begins remarkably early in life. Recent work indicates that four-day-old infants can already distinguish somehow between the language spoken in their community and other languages, so that the mechanisms of the language faculty begin to operate and to be "tuned" to the external environment very early in life.

It is fairly clear that the process of maturation to the steady state is deterministic. Language learning is not really something that the child does; it is something that happens to the child placed in an appropriate environment, much as the child's body grows and matures in a predetermined way when provided with appropriate nutrition and environmental stimulation. This is not to say that the nature of the environment is irrelevant. The environment determines how the options left unspecified by the initial state of the language faculty are fixed, yielding different languages. In a somewhat similar way, the early visual environment determines the density of receptors for horizontal and vertical lines. Furthermore, the difference between a rich and stimulating environment and an impoverished environment may be substantial, in language acquisition as in physical growth – or more accurately, as in other aspects of physical growth, the acquisition of language being simply one of these aspects. Capacities that are part of our common human endowment can flourish, or can be restricted and suppressed, depending on the conditions provided for their growth.

The point is probably more general. It is a traditional insight, which merits more attention than it receives, that teaching should not be compared to filling a bottle with water, but rather to helping a flower to grow in its own way. As any good teacher knows, the methods of instruction and the range of material covered are matters of small importance as compared with the success achieved in arousing the natural curiosity of the students and stimulating their interest in exploring on their own. What the student learns passively will be quickly forgotten. What students discover for themselves, when their natural curiosity and creative impulses are aroused, will not only be remembered, but will be the basis for further exploration and inquiry, and perhaps significant intellectual contributions. The same is true in other domains as well. A truly democratic community is one in which the general public has the opportunity for meaningful and constructive participation in the formation of social policy: in their own immediate community, in the workplace, and in the society at large. A society that excludes large areas of crucial decision-making from public control, or a system of governance that merely grants the general public the opportunity to ratify decisions taken by the elite groups that dominate the private society and the state, hardly merits the term "democracy." These too are insights that were alive and vital during the eighteenth century, and have in recent years been largely forgotten or suppressed. The point was made, in another context, by Kant, defending the French Revolution during the period of the Terror against those who argued that the masses of the population "are not ripe for freedom." "If one accepts this proposition," he wrote, "freedom will never be achieved, for one can not arrive at the maturity for freedom without have already acquired it; one must be free to learn how to make use of one's powers freely and usefully . . . one can achieve reason only through one's own experience and one must be free to be able to undertake them . . . To accept the principle that freedom is worthless for those under one's control and that one has the right to refuse it to them for ever, is an infringement of the rights of God himself, who has created man to be free." Reason, the ability to make use of one's powers freely and usefully, and other human qualities can be achieved only in an environment in which they can flourish. They cannot be taught by coercive means. What is true of physical growth holds quite generally of human maturation and learning.

Returning to the language faculty, learning of language, as noted, is something that happens to the child, without awareness for the most part, just as other processes such as sexual maturation happen to the child. A child does not decide to undergo sexual maturation because it sees others doing so and thinks this would be a good idea, or because it is trained or reinforced. Rather, the process happens in its own inner-directed way. The course of the process, its timing, and its detailed nature are in part influenced by the environment, by nutritional level for example, but the process itself is inner-directed in its essentials. The same appears to be true of language learning, and of other aspects of cognitive growth as well. The term "learning" is, in fact, a very misleading one, and one that is probably best abandoned as a relic of an earlier age, and earlier misunderstandings. Knowledge of language grows in the mind/brain of a child placed in a certain speech community.

Knowledge of language within a speech community is shared to remarkably fine detail, in every aspect of language from pronunciation to interpretation. In each of these aspects, the knowledge attained vastly transcends the evidence available in richness and complexity, and in each of these aspects, the fineness of detail and the precision of knowledge goes well beyond anything that can be explained on any imaginable functional grounds, such as the exigencies of communication. For example, children mimic the sounds of the language around them to a level of precision that is well beyond the capacity of adults to perceive, and in other domains as well, the precision of knowledge and understanding, as well as its scope and richness, are far beyond anything that could be detected in normal human interchange. These properties of normal language can often only be discovered by careful experiment. These are the basic and simplest elements of the problem we face.

We therefore conclude that the initial stage of the language faculty can be regarded as in effect a deterministic input–output system that takes presented data as its input and produces a highly structured cognitive system of a very specific form as its "output" – here the output is internalized, represented in the mind/brain; it is the steady state of knowledge of some particular language. The initial state of the language faculty can be regarded, in essence, as a language-acquisition device; in formal terms, a function that maps presented data into a steady state of knowledge attained. This general conclusion allows many specific variants, to some of which I will briefly return, but it is virtually inconceivable that it is wrong in any fundamental way. There has been much debate over this issue in the literature – more accurately, a one-sided debate in which critics argue that the idea has been refuted, with little response from its defenders. The reason for the lack of response is that the criticism must be based on profound confusion, and inspection of the arguments quickly reveals that this is the case, as it must be, given the nature of the problem.

The theory of the initial state – of the language acquisition device – is sometimes called "universal grammar," adapting a traditional term to a somewhat different conceptual framework. It is commonly assumed that universal grammar, so conceived, determines the class of attainable languages. Let me quote from a recent paper by the two leading researchers in the important new field of mathematical learning theory, a paper on models of language acquisition. They write that universal grammar

> imposes restrictions on a [particular] grammar in such a way that the class of [particular] grammars admissible by the theory includes grammars of all and only natural languages, [where] the natural languages are identified with the languages that can be acquired by normal human infants under casual conditions of access to linguistic data.

The first of these propositions is a definition, and a proper and useful one, so it is not open to challenge: we may define a "natural language" as one that accords with the principles of universal grammar. But the second of these propositions need not be correct. The languages attainable under normal conditions of access are those that fall in the intersection of two sets: (1) the set of natural languages made available by the initial state of the language faculty as characterized by universal grammar, and (2) the set of learnable systems. If universal grammar permits unlearnable languages, as it might, then they simply will not be learned. Learnability, then, is not a requirement that must be met by the language faculty.

Similarly, parsability – that is, the ability of the mind/brain to assign a structural analysis to a sentence – is not a requirement that must be met by a language, contrary to what is often claimed. In fact, we know that the claim is false: every language permits many different categories of expressions that cannot be used or understood readily (or at all), though they are perfectly well-formed, a fact that in no way impedes communication. Furthermore, deviant expressions may be readily parsable, and are often quite properly used. In brief, it is a mistake to think that languages are "designed" for ease of use. In so far as their structure does not conform to functional requirements, their elements are not used.

In the case of learnability, the proposition that the natural languages are learnable may very well be true, but if so, that is not a matter of principle, but rather a surprising empirical discovery about natural language. Recent work in linguistics suggests that it probably is true, again, a surprising and important empirical discovery, to which I will briefly return.

There has been a fair amount of confusion about these matters, in part resulting from misinterpretation of properties of formal systems: for example, the well-known observation that unconstrained transformational grammars can generate all sets that can be specified by finite means, and results on efficient parsability of context-free languages. In both cases, entirely unwarranted conclusions have been drawn about the nature of language. In fact, no conclusions at all can be drawn with regard to language, language learning, or language use, on the basis of such considerations as these, though other directions of formal inquiry perhaps show more promise of potential empirical significance; for example, some recent work in complexity theory.

When the study of language is approached in the manner I have just outlined, one would expect a close and fruitful interaction between linguistics proper and the investigation of such topics as language processing and acquisition. To some extent this has happened, but less so than might have been hoped. It is useful to reflect a little about why this has been the case. One reason, I think, is the one just mentioned: misinterpretation of results about formal systems has caused considerable confusion. Other problems have arisen from a failure to consider carefully the conceptual relations between language and learnability, and between language and processing. One instructive example is the history of what was called "the derivational theory of complexity," the major paradigm of psycholinguistic research in the early days of the "cognitive revolution." This theory led to an experimental program. The experiments carried out were tests of a theory with two components: (1) assumptions about the rule systems of natural language; (2) assumptions about processing. Some of the experimental results confirmed this combination of theories, others disconfirmed it. But care must be taken to determine just which elements of the combination of theories were confirmed or disconfirmed. In practice, where predictions were disconfirmed, it was concluded that the linguistic component of the amalgam was at fault. While this might be true, and sometimes was as other evidence showed, it was a curious inference, since there was independent evidence supporting the assumptions about language but none whatsoever supporting the assumptions about processing, assumptions that were, furthermore, not particularly plausible except as rough first approximations. Failure to appreciate these facts undermined much subsequent discussion. Similar questions arise with language acquisition, and confirming evidence too, in both areas, is unclear in its import unless the various factors entering into the predictions are properly sorted out.

The history of the derivational theory of complexity illustrates other problems that have impeded useful interaction between linguistics and experimental psychology. Early experimental work was designed to test certain ideas about rule systems on the assumption that processing satisfies the conditions of the derivational theory of complexity. By the time the experimental program had been carried out, with mixed results, the theories of rule systems had changed. Many experimental psychologists found this disconcerting. How can we carry out experimental tests of a theory if it is not stable and is subject to change? These reactions led to a noticeable shift in focus to work in areas that are better insulated from theoretical modification elsewhere.

There are a number of problems with such reactions. One problem is a point of logic: to insulate one's work from theoretical modifications elsewhere is to keep to topics of limited significance, close to the surface of phenomena. If one's work is important enough to have consequences beyond its immediate scope, then it cannot be immune to new understanding outside of this scope. For example, it is likely that results on order of acquisition of function words or on turn-taking in conversation will be immune to discoveries and new understanding elsewhere; the reason is that the implications are very slight. Relevance, after all, is a two-way street. This reaction to the inevitable changes in theoretical assumptions in a discipline that is alive also reflects a far too limited conception of the work of the experimental psychologist, who is perceived as someone who tests ideas developed elsewhere but does not contribute otherwise to their proper formulation. But research into language should obviously be a cooperative enterprise, which can be informed and advanced by use of evidence of many different kinds. There is no privileged sector of this discipline that provides theories, which are tested by others. One sign that the discipline is approaching a higher level of maturity will be that research into language processing and language acquisition will yield conclusions about the structure of language that can be tested by linguists, using the tools of their specific approach to a common network of problems and concerns. The idea that linguistics should be related to psychology as theoretical physics is related to experimental physics is senseless and untenable, and has, I think, been harmful.

Theories of language have indeed undergone significant changes during the period we are now considering – which is to say that the discipline is alive. I think we can identify two major changes of perspective during this period, each with considerable ramifications for the study of language use and acquisition. Let me review these changes briefly, focusing on the three central questions that I mentioned earlier: (1) what is knowledge of language?; (2) how is it acquired?; and (3) how is it used?

Some thirty years ago the standard answers to these questions would have been something like this.

1 What is knowledge of language? Answer: it is a system of habits, dispositions and abilities. This answer, incidentally, is still widely held, notably by philosophers influenced by Wittgenstein and Quine.

2 How is language acquired? Answer: by conditioning, training, habit-formation or "general learning mechanisms" such as induction.

3 How is language used? Answer: language use is the exercise of an ability, like any skill; say, bicycle-riding. New forms are produced or understood "by analogy" to old ones. In fact, the problem posed by production of new forms, the normal situation in language use, was barely noticed. This is quite a remarkable fact, first, because the point is obvious, and second, because it was a major preoccupation of the linguistics of the first cognitive revolution of the seventeenth century. Here we have a striking example of how ideology displaced the most obvious of phenomena from inquiry.

Attention to the simplest phenomena suffices to show that these ideas cannot be even close to the truth of the matter, and must simply be abandoned. Let me illustrate with a very simple example. Imagine a child learning English who comes to understand the sentence *John ate an apple*. The child then knows that the word *eat* takes two semantic roles, that of the subject (the agent of the action) and that of object (the recipient of the action); it is a typical transitive verb. Suppose that the child now hears the reduced sentence *John ate*, in which the object is missing. Since the verb is transitive, requiring an object, the child will understand the sentence to mean, roughly, "John ate something or other." So far everything is fairly straightforward if we assume the simple principle that when a semantically required element is missing, the mind interprets it to be a kind of "empty pronoun" meaning: something or other. Perhaps an empiricist linguist might be willing to suppose that this principle is available as an innate element of the language faculty.

Consider now a very simple but slightly more complex sentence. Suppose the child comes to understand such sentences as *John is too clever to catch Bill*. Here the verb *catch* also requires a subject and an object, but the subject is missing in this sentence. It therefore has to be supplied by the mind, in the matter of the object of *ate* in *John ate*. By the principle just assumed to account for *John ate*, the sentence should mean: John is so clever that someone or other will not catch Bill. That is a fine meaning, but it is not the meaning of *John is too clever to catch Bill*. Rather, the sentence means: John is so clever that he, John, will not catch Bill. The mind does not use the empty pronoun principle, but rather takes the subject of *catch* to be the same as the subject of *is clever*. Since this is known without instruction or evidence, we must attribute to the mind still a second principle, let us call it the principle of subject control: the missing subject of the embedded clause is understood to be the same as the subject of the main clause. Our assumptions about the innate resources of the mind must therefore be enriched.

Let us carry the discussion a step further. Suppose we delete *Bill* from the sentence *John is too clever to catch Bill*, so that we have *John is too clever to catch*. By the empty pronoun principle and the subject control principle, the sentence should mean: John is so clever that he, John, will not catch someone or other. But the child knows that it does not mean that at all; rather, it means that John is so clever that someone or other will not catch him, John. The child interprets the sentence by some other principle, call it the inversion principle, which tells us that the object of the embedded sentence is understood to be the same as the subject of the main verb, and the subject of the embedded sentence is an empty pronoun referring to someone or other.

We now have to attribute to the mind/brain three principles: the empty pronoun principle, the subject principle, and the inversion principle. Furthermore, some overarching principle of the mind/brain determines when these principles of interpretation are applied.

Turning to slightly more complicated examples, the mysteries deepen. Consider the sentence *John is too clever to expect anyone to catch*. English speakers at first may find this sentence a bit puzzling, but "on reflection" (whatever that involves), they understand it to mean that John is so clever that someone doesn't expect anyone to catch John; that is, it is interpreted by means of the empty pronoun principle and the inversion principle. But now compare this sentence with another that is roughly comparable in complexity: *John is too clever to meet anyone who caught.* Here all principles fail; the sentence is complete gibberish. We can parse the sentence with no difficulty; it just doesn't mean anything sensible. In particular, it is not understood "by analogy" to mean that John is so clever that no one met anyone who caught him, John.

Notice that none of this is the result of training, or even experience. These facts are known without training, without correction of error, without relevant experience, and are known the same way by every speaker of English – and in analogous constructions, other languages. Hence all of this must somehow derive from the inner resources of the mind/brain, from the genetically determined constitution of the language faculty. Clearly the answer cannot be that these resources include the empty pronoun principle, the subject principle, the inversion principle, some principle that determines how they operate, and a principle blocking the "analogy" in the last example. Rather, we would like to show that the observed facts follow from some deeper principles of the language faculty. This is a typical problem of science, and one that has, in fact, been rather successfully addressed in recent work. But the point here is that the facts show rather clearly that the standard answers to our questions that I have just mentioned cannot be on the right track.

Notice again that the concept of "analogy" does no work at all. By analogy to *John ate*, the sentence *John is too clever to catch* should mean "John is too clever to catch someone or other," but it does not. Notice also that such examples refute the conception of knowledge of language as a skill or ability. The child does not fail to provide the analogous interpretation because of a failure of ability – because it is too weak, or needs more practice. Rather, the computational system of the mind/brain is designed to force certain interpretations for linguistic expressions. To put the matter in the context of the theory of knowledge, our knowledge that expression such-and-such means so-and-so is not justified or grounded in experience in any useful sense of these terms, is not based on good reasons or reliable procedures, is not derived by induction or any other general method. Since these are examples of ordinary propositional knowledge, knowledge that so-and-so, the standard paradigms of epistemology and fixation of belief cannot be correct, and investigation of further examples and other cognitive systems reveals exactly the same thing, so I believe.

I think that these are all important facts, insufficiently appreciated, with quite considerable import. We discover facts of this sort wherever we look, if we are not blinded or misled by dogma.

One notable feature of the widely held conceptions of knowledge and language in terms of ability, skill, habit, general learning mechanisms and analogy, is that they were entirely unproductive and without empirical consequences. One can hardly point to a single empirical result of the slightest significance that derived from these conceptions. The psychology of language of the time was almost completely barren. There was an empirical discipline, namely structural linguistics, which did profess these doctrines and did achieve empirical results and some theoretical understanding. But a closer look will show that in practice, research departed from the professed ideology at every crucial point. The general conceptual framework limited and impoverished the discipline, barring natural lines of inquiry, but otherwise was simply professed and abandoned in practice, though it did, I believe, have a serious and generally harmful impact on applied disciplines such as language teaching.

Recognition of the complete inadequacy of these conceptions led to the first major conceptual change, which was, in many respects, a return to traditional ideas and concerns that had been dismissed or forgotten during the long period when empiricist and behaviorist doctrines prevailed. This shift of focus provided a new set of answers to the central questions:

1 What is knowledge of language? Answer: language is a computational system, a rule system of some sort. Knowledge of language is knowledge of this rule system.

2 How is language acquired? Answer: the initial state of the language faculty determines possible rules and modes of interaction. Language is acquired by a process of selection of a rule system of an appropriate sort on the basis of direct evidence. Experience yields an inventory of rules, through the language-acquisition device of the language faculty.

3 How is language used? Answer: the use of language is rule-governed behavior. Rules form mental representations, which enter into our speaking and understanding. A sentence is parsed and understood by a systematic search through the rule system of the language in question.

The new set of answers constitutes a major component of the "cognitive revolution."

This was a significant shift of point of view: from behavior and its products to the system of knowledge represented in the mind/brain that underlies behavior. Behavior is not the focus of inquiry; rather, it simply provides one source of evidence for the internal systems of the mind/brain that are what we are trying to discover – the system that constitutes a particular language and that determines the form, structural properties and meaning of expressions, and more deeply, the innate structure of the language faculty. As I mentioned earlier, this shift towards an avowed mentalism is also a shift towards assimilating the study of language to the natural sciences, and opens up the possibility of a serious investigation of physical mechanisms.

This shift of focus was extremely productive. It led to a rapid decrease in the range of empirical phenomena that were brought under investigation, with many new empirical discoveries, such as those just illustrated, including very simple facts that had never been noticed. It also led to some degree of success in providing explanations for these facts. But serious difficulties arise at once. Basically, these relate to Plato's problem, the problem of acquisition of language. In essence, the problem is that there are too many possible rule systems. Therefore it is hard to explain how children unerringly select one such system rather than another. Furthermore, children seem to select very complex rule systems and systematically to avoid much simpler ones, a conclusion that makes no sense.

These problems set the research agenda since about 1960, within the framework I am considering here. I will not review the steps that were taken, but rather will turn to the result. In the past several years, a new and very different conception of language has emerged, which yields new answers to our three questions. The initial state of the language faculty consists of a collection of subsystems, or *modules* as they are sometimes called, each of which is based on certain general principles. Many of these principles admit of a certain limited possibility of variation. We may think of the system as a complex network associated with a switch box that contains a finite number of switches. The network is invariant, but each switch can be in one of several positions, perhaps two: on or off. Unless the switches are set, nothing happens. But when the switches are set in one of the permissible ways, the system functions, yielding the entire infinite array of interpretations for linguistic expressions. A slight change in switch settings can yield complex and varied phenomenal consequences as its effects filter through the network. There are no rules at all, hence no necessity to learn rules. For example, the possible phrase structures of a language are fixed by general principles and are invariant among languages, but there are some switches to be set. One has to do with order of elements. In English, for example, nouns, verbs, adjectives and prepositions precede their objects: in Japanese, the comparable elements follow their objects. English is what is called a "head-first" language, Japanese a "head-last" language. These facts can be determined from very simple sentences; for example, the sentences "John ate an apple" (in English) or "John an apple ate" (in Japanese). To acquire a language, the child's mind must determine how the switches are set, and simple data must suffice to determine the switch settings, as in this case. The theory of language use also undergoes corresponding modifications, which I cannot explore here.

This second conceptual change gives a very different conception of language and knowledge. To mention one example, notice that from the point of view of rule systems, there are an infinite number of languages, since there are infinitely many rule systems of the permissible form. But from the network-switch point of view, there are only finitely many languages, one for each arrangement of switch settings. Since each of the switch settings can be determined from simple data, each of these finitely many languages is learnable. Hence the general principle of learnability theory discussed earlier is in fact true: each natural language is learnable – though it is far from true that the learnable systems are all natural languages. As I mentioned, this is an empirical result, and a very surprising one, not a matter of principle. There is, incidentally, some intriguing work in mathematical learning theory which suggests that language acquisition is possible in principle under plausible conditions only if the set of natural languages is indeed "finite" (in a special sense).

This second conceptual change has, once again, led to a great increase in the range of empirical materials discovered and subjected to serious inquiry within generative grammar, now from a much wider range of languages.

Assuming that this change is pointing in the right direction, what are the consequences for the study of language acquisition? The problem will be to determine how the switches are set and to discover the principles of learning, or maturation, or whatever is responsible for carrying out the transition from the initial state of the language faculty to the steady state of adult competence; that is, for setting the switches of the language faculty. Recall that two factors enter into language acquisition: the nature of the language faculty, and the principles of learning theory or more properly growth theory, and any evidence about language acquisition must be assessed carefully to determine how it bears on one or the other of these two interacting factors. How can we proceed in studying this question?

Notice that the problems of assessment of evidence and explanation would plainly be simplified if one or the other of these two components – universal grammar or growth theory – does not exist. Each of these positions has been maintained, the first one quite vigorously, the second as a tentative working hypothesis.

Denial of the existence of universal grammar – that is, of the language faculty as an identifiable system of the human mind/brain – is implicit in the empiricist program and in some recent claims about mechanisms of "general intelligence" or "connectionism" or theory formation, mechanisms that are allegedly applied to yield our linguistic abilities and other intellectual achievements in an undifferentiated way. There has been no attempt to formulate these alleged mechanisms that seems to offer any real promise. The clearer formulations have been quickly refuted, in some cases refuted in principle, and for reasons that should be familiar, the prospects for this program seem very dim. Since there is nothing susbtantive to discuss, I will disregard this possibility and proceed to the second possibility: that growth theory is negligible or non-existent, so that language-acquisition simply involves switch setting on the basis of presented data, such as the sentences "John ate an apple" and "John an apple ate." Let us call this the "no-growth theory" of language acquisition.

Obviously, this cannot be literally true. During the first few months or perhaps weeks of life, an infant probably is exposed to enough linguistic data to set most switches, but plainly it has not done so. In fact, the process extends over quite a few years. So to maintain the no-growth theory we would have to argue that some independent and extrinsic change in cognitive capacities, say in memory or attention, accounts for the observed stages of growth.

Such ideas have been advanced with regard to stages of cognitive development in the sense of Jean Piaget, and also with respect to the stages of language growth. For example, it has been observed that the transition from so-called "telegraphic speech," lacking function words, to normal speech is quite rapid, and includes a number of different systems: questions, negations, tag questions, etc. Furthermore, in the telegraphic speech stage, children understand normal speech better than their own telegraphic speech, and if function words are introduced randomly, the results are unintelligible. This suggests that the children knew the facts of normal speech all along, and were using telegraphic speech because of some limitation of attention and memory. When this limitation is overcome in the course of normal growth and maturation, their already acquired knowledge of language can be manifested. But there are some serious problems in assuming this idea in other cases of regular stages of development: for example, the shift from semantic to syntactic categories, the use of color words, the appearance of a true verbal passive construction and other more complex structures, the emergence of semantic properties of control, and so on. Prima facie, it seems hard to explain these transitions without appeal to maturational processes that bring principles of universal grammar into operation on some regular schedule in a manner to be described and accounted for in a genetic theory. Of course, what is prima facie plausible is not necessarily correct, but the questions that arise are clear enough, and it is an important task to address them, as many investigators are now doing in important recent work.

There is, on the one hand, work by Yukio Otsu, Stephen Crain and others that seems to show that principles of universal grammar are available as soon as constructions are used in which they would be manifested, and the delay in use of these constructions might be explained in terms of inherent complexity, hence extrinsic factors such as memory.

To take one complex example of much general interest, consider recent work of Nina Hyams on the null subject property that distinguishes languages like French and English, in which subjects must be overtly expressed, from languages such as Italian and Spanish, in which the subject may be suppressed in the phonetic output. Hyam's work indicates that at an early stage, all children treat their language as if it were a null subject language. The switch, she suggests, has what is called an "unmarked setting," or in the more usual terminology, the null subject parameter has an "unmarked value," a value selected in the absence of data, and this value provides a null subject language. Italian-speaking children maintain the unmarked value, while English-speaking children later change to the marked value of the parameter, setting the switch differently. The question then is: What triggers the change? There is good evidence that positive evidence suffices for language acquisition; that is, correction of error is unnecessary and probably largely irrelevant when it occurs. Assuming so, the answer to the question cannot be that the English-speaking children are explicitly corrected. Nor can the answer be that they never hear sentences without subjects, since they hear no evidence for most of what they know. Assuming a no-growth theory, Hyams suggests that the change is triggered by the presence of overt expletives in English, such elements as *there* in "there is a man in the room," elements that are semantically empty but must be present to satisfy some syntactic principle. The assumption is that universal grammar contains a principle implying that if a language has overt expletives, then it is not a null subject language. This is, incidentally, an example of a hypothesis about universal grammar deriving from language acquisition studies that might be tested by linguists, rather than the converse, as in the usual practice. It cannot be quite correct as it stands, but something similar might be true.

But now we have to ask why the English-speaking children delay in using this evidence. A possible answer (though not the one Hyams proposes) might be that extrinsic conditions of memory and attention render these expletives inaccessible at an early stage.

Pursuing a similar idea, Luigi Rizzi suggests that contrary to Hyams's initial conclusion, the unmarked value for the parameter is: overt subject. English-speaking children appear to violate this principle at an early stage, but only because extrinsic considerations suppress the production of such elements as unstressed subject pronouns. Italian-speaking children then select the marked value of the parameter on the basis of direct evidence of subjectless sentences.

A third approach is to reject the no-growth theory and to suppose that the null subject parameter only becomes available at a certain stage of maturation, and is set at the marked null subject value only if direct evidence of subjectless sentences is presented. At the moment, the question remains open, and these possibilities do not exhaust the options (for example, the null subject parameter might be further differentiated, or cast in different terms).

Notice that further clarification of these issues might well contribute to our knowledge of the principles and parameters of universal grammar – of the nature of the network and the switches – on the basis of evidence from language acquisition, as we should anticipate as the discipline progresses.

Consider a second example. Sascha Felix argues against the no-growth theory on the basis of evidence about use of negatives in several languages. Apparently, at the earliest stage, children use sentence-external negation, as in "not John likes milk." This fact (which, not surprisingly, is itself controversial) already raises problems for a no-growth theory, since natural languages rarely if ever exhibit sentence-external negation. At a later stage, the child shifts to sentence-internal negation, as in "John no likes milk," which is also inconsistent with the evidence from the adult language. Later, the correct form "John doesn't like milk" emerges. Felix points out that stage I, with sentence-external negation, is consistent with Dan Slobin's principle that the learner avoids interruption of linguistic units, and hence might be taken to support this principle. But he notes that that leaves unresolved the question why this principle becomes inoperative at stage II, and is even more radically abandoned at stage III. A maturational theory seems a possible candidate for an explanation. Again, further research should contribute to clarifying both the principles of language growth, if they exist, and the actual principles and parameters of universal grammar.

Consider finally a more complex example studied in some detail by Hagit Borer and Kenneth Wexler. They argue that the results in many languages on acquisition of passives can be explained by a maturational theory, which provides a more sophisticated version of the idea that transformations are acquired step-by-step during language acquisition. Their theory postulates that until a certain stage of development, phrases can only be interpreted in a canonical position in which semantic roles are assigned by principles of universal grammar, thus the position of abstract underlying deep structures, in effect. At this stage, a sentence such as "John was killed" is simply uninterpretable, since *John* is displaced from its canonical position as object of *kill*. Apparent passive forms at this stage, they argue, are in fact adjectives, as in "the door is closed." Later, a device becomes available, through maturation, by which displaced elements can be interpreted through a so-called *chain* formed by a transformation, which links the displaced element to an empty *trace* in the canonical position. Such chains must then meet various conditions of universal grammar, which account for the possibilities of displacement. They argue that the range of available evidence about acquisition of passives can be largely explained on the basis of this assumption: that chains become available at a certain stage of maturation. Again, there are numerous empirical problems and consequences to be explored, and the results should bear directly on the principles of universal grammar as well as growth theory.

If Borer and Wexler are right, one might be tempted to explore a famous suggestion by Roman Jakobson that language acquisition and language loss in aphasia are mirror images: the earlier some items and structures are acquired in language learning, the later they are lost under brain injury. It would then follow that in some kinds of aphasia, we should find that chains are lost while other aspects of phrase structure remain. Evidence to this effect has in fact been presented by Yosef Grodzinsky. This again suggests what might prove to be an intriguing line of inquiry.

These examples barely scratch the surface. A wide range of intriguing questions arise at once if we think through the implications of the principles-and-parameters conception of universal grammar in terms of an invariant network and an associated set of switches, and if we ask how this conception might relate to possible principles of maturation involved in language growth, along with extrinsic factors in cognitive development. I have not had time to consider the question of language processing, but here too the questions look quite different when approached in these terms. And within the study of language proper, many new and exciting questions enter into the research agenda. If the principles-and-parameters approach is correct, it should be possible literally to deduce the properties of each natural language by setting the switches in one or another way and computing the consequences. Typological difference should be a matter of differences in switch-settings. Language change should be the result of a change in such a setting; note that a small change might yield a substantial phenomenal difference as its effects filter through the fixed network of modular principles. These are all questions that are now being addressed, in some cases with some success, in other cases with failures that are highly suggestive in opening up new lines of inquiry. Furthermore, the class of typologically different languages that have come under investigation, and that seem to be amenable to a coherent and uniform approach, has vastly extended, again, a promising sign.

There are, it seems, real grounds for considerable optimism about the prospects that lie ahead, not only for the study of language proper, but also for the study of cognitive systems of the mind/brain of which language is a fundamental and essential component, in the human species.

Modeling Language Development

DAVID LIGHTFOOT

For several years generative grammarians have been developing a selective theory of language acquisition. We have sought to specify relevant information which must be available to children independently of any linguistic experience, in order for a particular child's eventual mature capacity to emerge on exposure to some typical triggering experience. Cutting some corners, we have assumed that that information is genetically encoded in some fashion and we have adopted the explanatory model of (1). The goal is to specify relevant aspects of a child's

"Modeling Language Development" by D. Lightfoot is excerpted from "Modeling Language Change: Ontogenetic and Phylogenetic," in *From Aristotle to Newton*, edited by J. Casti and A. Karlqvist (Birkhauser, 1988), by kind permission of the author and publisher.

genotype such that a particular mature state will emerge when the child is raised in, say, a Japanese or Navaho linguistic environment. (1.b) reflects the usual terminology, where "universal grammar" (UG) contains those aspects of the genotype directly relevant for language growth, and a "grammar" is taken to be that part of a person's mental make-up which characterizes his or her mature linguistic capacity.

(1) a.   trigger (genotype → phenotype)
    b.   primary linguistic data (universal grammar → grammar)

The theory is *selective* in the same sense that current theories of immunology and vision are selective and not instructive. Under an instructive theory, an outside signal imparts its character to the system that receives it, instructing a plastic nervous system; under a selective theory, a stimulus may change a system by identifying and amplifying some component of already available circuitry. Put differently, a selective theory holds that an organism experiences the surrounding environment (and selects relevant stimuli) according to criteria which are already present. Jerne (1967) depicts antibody formation as a selective process whereby the antigen selects and amplifies specific antibodies which already exist. Similarly Hubel and Wiesel showed that particular neurons were pre-set to react only to specific visual stimuli, for example to a horizontal line; there follows a radical increase in the number of horizontal line receptors and a horizontal line can be said to elicit and select specific responses within the organism. Changeux (1980, 1983) argues along similar lines for a theory of "selective stabilization of synapses" whereby "the genetic program directs the proper interaction between main categories of neurons . . . However, during development within a given category, several contacts with the same specificity may form" and other elements, which are not selected, may atrophy (1980, p. 193). Thus to learn is to amplify certain connections and to eliminate other possibilities. Jerne argues that "Looking back into the history of biology, it appears that wherever a phenomenon resembles learning, an instructive theory was first proposed to account for the underlying mechanisms. In every case, this was later replaced by a selective theory". For more discussion, see Piattelli-Palmarini (1986) and Jerne's Nobel Prize address (1985).

Under current formulations, the linguistic genotype, UG, consists of a set of invariant principles and a set of parameters that are set by some linguistic environment, just as certain receptors are "set" on exposure to a horizontal line. So the environment may be said to "select" particular values for the parameters of UG. UG must be able to support the acquisition of any human grammar, given the appropriate triggering experience. Of course, UG need not be seen as homogeneous, and may emerge piecemeal, parts of it being available maturationally only at certain stages of a child's development. Grammars must not only be attainable under usual childhood conditions, but also usable for such purposes as speech production and comprehension, appropriately vulnerable for the kinds of aphasias that one finds, and they should provide part of the basis for understanding the developmental stages that children go through. There is no shortage of empirical constraints on hypotheses about (1).

The "logical problem of language acquisition" has provided much of the empirical refinement of (1). Apparent *poverty of stimulus* problems have led grammarians to postulate particular principles and parameters at the level of UG. The stimulus or trigger experience that children have appears to be too poor to determine all aspects of the mature capacities that they typically attain. It is too poor in three distinct ways: (a) the child's experience is finite but the capacity eventually attained ranges over an infinite domain; (b) the experience consists partly of degenerate data which have no effect on the emerging capacity; and, most important, (c) it fails to provide evidence for many principles and generalizations which hold of the mature capacity. Of these three, (a) and (b) have been discussed much more frequently than (c), although (c) is by far the most significant aspect and provides a means of elaborating theories of UG. For discussion, see Chomsky (1965, ch. 1), Hornstein and Lightfoot (1981, pp. 9–31), Lightfoot (1982, ch. 2).

Any argument from the poverty of the stimulus makes crucial assumptions about the nature of the triggering experience. To illustrate, I shall briefly rehearse one argument, discussing some material from Baker 1978, which was refined in Hornstein and Lightfoot 1981, and then further in Lightfoot 1982. It has been generally agreed for a long time that linguistic expressions are made up of sub-units and have an internal hierarchy. It is also generally agreed that a grammar (in the sense defined) is not just a list of expressions but is a finite algebraic system which can "generate" an infinite range of expressions. One might imagine, in that case, that English noun phrases have the structure of either (2a) or (2b). If the phrase structure rules generating noun phrases are those of (2a), a phrase like *the old man from New York* will have the internal structure of (3a); if the rules are those of (2b), the structure will be (3b). In (3a) *the old man*, for example, is not a single unit, but in (3b) it is. The crucial difference is that the rules of (2a) refer to N′, an element intermediate between the nucleus noun and the maximal noun phrase (NP).

(2) a. NP → Spec N′   b. NP → NP   YP
         N′ → (Adj) $\begin{Bmatrix} N' \\ N \end{Bmatrix}$ YP   NP → Spec (Adj) N

(3) a.

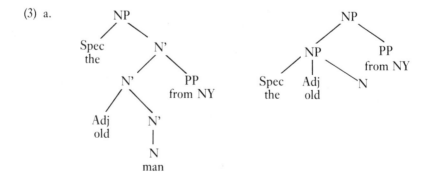

Now, it can be shown that any noun phrase that occurs in English, and thus any noun phrase that an English-speaking child will hear, can be generated by both sets of rules. However, linguists believe that something along the lines of (2a) must be correct, or at least preferred to (2b), because (2b) is consistent with certain phenomena which do *not* occur in English and because (2b) fails to account naturally for certain ambiguities. (2b) has no N' node, and therefore provides no straightforward way to distinguish between (4a and 4b), and no ready means to capture the ambiguity of (5a), which may have the meaning of (5b) or (5c). The details of the analysis need not concern us here.[1]

(4) a. *the student of physics is older than the one of chemistry.
   b. the student from NY is older than the one from LA
(5) a. he wants an old suit but he already has the only one I own
   b. he wants an old suit but he already has the only suit I own
   c. he wants an old suit but he already has the only old suit I own

Here is the problem. It is reasonable to suppose that children might be exposed to any noun phrase that might occur in English, but it is not the case that they are systematically informed that sentences like (4a) are not uttered by most speakers and that (5a) has two possible meanings. In fact, perception of ambiguity is a sophisticated skill which develops late and not uniformly; most ambiguities pass unnoticed and people take the most appropriate of the available meanings. To be sure, children come to know these things and this knowledge is part of the output of the language acquisition process, but it is not part of the input, not part of the "evidence" for the emerging system, and thus not part of the triggering experience. Consequently, if linguists prefer hypothesis (2a) over (2b) on the basis of phenomena like (4) and (5), children have no analogous basis for such a choice if such data are not available to them. In that case they must arrive at (2a) on some other, presumably non-experiential, basis. So linguists have postulated genotypical information that phrasal categories have the structure of (6). By (6a) any noun phrase (NP) consists of a Specifier and a N' in some order to be determined by the child's particular linguistic experience, the "trigger" of (1a); similarly, a verb phrase, VP, consists of a Specifier and a V' in some order, and likewise the other phrasal categories. By (6b) the N' consists of a nucleus (N or N') and some satellite material in some order (the comma indicates an unordered set).

(6) a. XP → Spec, X'
   b. X' → [X' or X], Adj, YP
(7) a. the house
   b. crazy people, students of linguistics

(6a) and (6b) are parameters that are set on exposure to some trigger. The English-speaking child hears phrases like (7a) and after some development, analyzes them as consisting of two words, one of a closed class and the other of an open class; in the light of this prior knowledge and in the light of the parameter (6a), the child adopts the first rule of (2a). Likewise, exposure to phrases like (7b) suffices to set parameter (6b), such that the second rule of (2a) is adopted. Given the parameters of (6), rules like those of (2b) are never available to children and therefore do not have to be "unlearned" in any sense.

Although no "evidence" for the existence of a N' node seems to be available in a child's experience, it is provided by the genotype and therefore occurs in mature grammars (I shall consider an alternative account later).

There is much more to be said about this argument and about its consequences. I have sketched it briefly here in order to demonstrate that any poverty of stimulus argument is based on certain assumptions about the triggering experience. The assumption so far has been that the non-occurrence for many people of (4a) and the ambiguity of (5a) are not part of the trigger, but that data like (7) are. It should be clear that there is a close relationship between the three entities of (1), and a claim made about any one of them usually has consequences for hypotheses about the other two. If the primary linguistic data (PLD) were rich and well-organized, correspondingly less information would be needed in UG, and vice versa. These are not aesthetic swings and roundabouts, and there are clear facts of the matter which limit viable hypotheses.

I shall argue that the trigger consists of a haphazard set of utterances made in an appropriate context and of a type that any child hears frequently. In other words, it consists of robust data and includes no "negative data," information that certain expressions do not occur. I shall flesh this out, making it more precise and more controversial, but first I shall contrast it with some other ideas in the literature.

It is clear that the PLD which trigger the growth of a child's grammar do not include much of what linguists use to choose between hypotheses. To this extent the child is not a "little linguist," constructing her grammar in the way that linguists construct their hypotheses. For example, the PLD do not include well organized paradigms nor comparable data from other languages. Nor do the PLD include rich information about what does not occur, that is, negative data.[2] It is true that some zealous parents correct certain aspects of their child's speech and so provide negative data, but this is not the general basis for language development. First, such correction is not provided to all children and there is no reason to suppose that it is an indispensable ingredient for language growth to take place. Second, even when it is provided, it is typically resisted, as many parents will readily attest. McNeill (1966, p. 69) recorded a celebrated illustration of this resistance.

> *Child*: Nobody don't like me
> *Mother*: No, say "nobody likes me."
> *Child*: Nobody don't like me
> (eight repetitions of this dialogue)
> *Mother*: No, now listen carefully; say "nobody likes me."
> *Child*: Oh, nobody don't likes me.

Third, correction is provided only for a narrow range of errors, usually relating to morphological forms. So, the occasional *taked*, *goed*, *the man what we saw*, etc. might be corrected, and McNeill's child on the eighth try perceived only a morphological correction, changing *like* to *likes*. However, not even the most conscientious parents correct deviant uses of the contracted form of verbs like *is* and *will* (8), and in this case they do not occur in children's speech.

(8) a. *Jay's taller than Kay's (sc. . . . than Kay is)

   b. *Jay'll be happier than Kay'll (sc. . . . than Kay will)

They also do not correct errors in which anaphors are misused. Matthei (1981) reports that children sometimes interpret sentences like *the pigs said the chickens tickled each other* with *each other* referring to *the pigs.* This misinterpretation is unlikely to be perceived by many adults. Similarly with many other features of children's language. For good discussion, see Baker 1979.

It is sometimes argued that while children are not supplied with negative data directly, they may have access to them indirectly. So Chomsky (1981, p. 9) speculates along these lines:

> if certain structures or rules fail to be exemplified in relatively simple expressions, *where they would be expected to be found* [my emphasis – DWL], then a (possibly marked) option is selected excluding them in the grammar, so that a kind of "negative evidence" can be available even without corrections, adverse reactions, etc.

This is illustrated by the so-called null-subject parameter, whereby expressions like (9), with a phonetically null subject, occur in Italian, Spanish and many other languages, but not in English, French, etc.

(9) a. ho trovato il libro
     b. chi credi che partirá?
     c. *found the book
     d. *who do you think that will leave?

Chomsky, following Rizzi (1982), suggests that if the English speaking child picks the wrong setting for this parameter, then failure to hear sentences like (9c) might be taken as indirect evidence that such sentences are ungrammatical and thus do not occur for some principled reason. Consequently the child will pick the setting which bars (9c) and (9d).

Two comments on this. First, if children do have indirect access to negative data, it will have to be specified under what circumstances. That is, in Chomsky's formulation above, the phrase 'in relatively simple expressions, where they would be expected to be found' will need to be fleshed out in such a way that it distinguishes cases like (9) from those like (4) and (8) etc. While one might argue that children may have indirect access to data like (9c), it is hardly plausible to say that they have indirect access to (8). For this distinction to be made, UG would have to be enriched to include analogical notions which have not yet been hinted at.

Second, so far there are no strong arguments for indirect access to negative data. Certainly there are plausible alternatives for the null-subject parameter. One possibility is to claim that the English setting for this parameter is *unmarked*, that is the default case. Thus Italian and Spanish children need specific evidence to adopt the other setting, and (9a) is the required evidence.[3] The fact that the Italian setting of the null-subject parameter seems to be much more common across languages than the English setting does not entail that it is less marked, since markedness values do not reflect statistical frequency. In fact, Berwick's Subset Principle (1985) predicts that the Italian setting should be marked. The Subset Principle requires children to 'pick the narrowest possible language consistent with evidence seen so far' (p. 237). The Italian setting of the parameter entails a language which is broader than one with the English setting, and therefore the English setting needs to be unmarked (p. 290).

A second possibility is to make the null-subject parameter dependent on some other parameter. It has often been suggested that null subjects occur only in grammars with rich verbal inflection. However, rich inflection seems to be a necessary condition for null subjects, but not sufficient. So German does not have null subjects, although its verbal inflection seems to be as rich as that of Spanish, which does allow null subjects. Consequently, the learning problem remains constant and is unaffected by the richness of inflections. As an alternative, Hyams (1983) related the impossibility of null subjects to the occurrence of expletive pronouns (*it's cold, there's no more*) and she marshalled some interesting evidence in favor of something along these lines by considering the developmental stages that children go through.

Indirect access to negative data may prove to be needed but so far no very plausible case has been made.[4] The notion raises non-trivial problems in defining the contexts in which indirect access is available. Meanwhile, plausible solutions for problems which seem to call for indirect access to negative data are suggested by viewing the phenomena in relationship to other parameters and not in isolation. I have mentioned two such parameters here, but there are other suggestions in the literature.

Putting aside further discussion of the possibility of indirect access to certain negative data, one can plausibly argue that the triggering experience, then, is less than what a "little linguist" might encounter and does not include information about starred sentences and much more that occurs in a typical issue of the technical journals. Such things are simply not part of a typical child's linguistic experience. Consequently, we may persist with the idea that the trigger consists of nothing more than a haphazard set of utterances in an appropriate context. However, we can restrict things further: the trigger is something less than the total linguistic experience. The occasional degenerate data that a child hears and idiosyncratic forms do not necessarily trigger some device in the emergent grammar which has the effect of generating those forms. So, for example, a form like (10a) might occur in a child's experience without triggering an unusual form of subject–verb agreement. Similarly a New York child might hear (10b) without having *y'all* triggered as a word in his or her grammar.

(10) a. the person who runs the stores never treat people well
      b. y'all have a good time in South Carolina

A child might even be exposed to significant quantities of linguistic material which do not act as a trigger. So, if a house-guest speaks an unusual form of English, perhaps with different regional forms or the forms of somebody who has learned English imperfectly as a second language, this normally has no noticeable effect on a child's linguistic development. Even children of heavily accented immigrant parents perpetuate few non-standard aspects of their parents' speech.

I take it that this is intuitively fairly obvious, and shows that there is little to be learned about the trigger experience from simply tape-recording everything uttered within a child's hearing (cf. Wells 1981). More can be learned from the historical changes that languages undergo. It is well-known that certain kinds of syntactic patterns become obsolete in certain speech communities at certain times.

What this means is that sometimes speakers hear a form which does not trigger some grammatical device which permits it to be generated and thus to occur in their mature speech. The conditions under which this happens cast some light on the nature of the trigger.

So then, we may now claim that the trigger experience is some subset of a child's total linguistic experience. But where exactly are the limits? This is often a crucial question in grammatical analyses, but it is rare to see alternatives discussed. Consider again the example of the structure of noun phrases. I argued above that any noun phrase that an English-speaking child could hear would be consistent with both the rules of (2a) and (2b). I also claimed that the data which led grammarians to prefer (2a) to (2b) are generally not available to children and therefore that the information which eliminates (2b) must come from some other, presumably genetic source. However, one could look at things somewhat differently. The real difference between (2a) and (2b) is the existence of a N' node in the rules of (2a). The existence of this node is required by the UG parameter of (6b) and, on that account, does not have to be derived from relevant experience. In that case, we might ask if there is anything in a child's experience which would require postulating a N' node, and one can indeed imagine evidence which would force the child to establish such a node.

English speakers use the indefinite pronoun *one* to refer back to a N', as noted earlier, and the fact that it refers to a N', something intermediate between a NP and an N, might in fact be learnable. A sentence like (11a) would not be a sufficient basis for learning this because, regardless of whether Heidi actually has a big or small cup, the sentence could always be interpreted as specifying only that Heidi had some cup regardless of size (with *one* referring only to the N *cup*). Sentence (11b), however, would suffice if uttered in a situation where Heidi has a cup that is some color other than blue; only the interpretation with *one* representing *blue cup* would be consistent with the facts. In that case a child might *learn* correctly that *one* must refer to something larger than a N, namely a N'.[5]

(11) a. Kirsten has a big cup, and Heidi has one too
     b. Kirsten has a blue cup, but Heidi doesn't have one

We now have two alternative accounts: the existence of N' might be derived from a property of UG or it might be triggered by the scenario just sketched. My hunch was and remains that this scenario is too exotic and contrived to be part of every child's experience, and therefore that postulating (6) at UG is more plausible. But this hunch may be wrong. It is certainly falsifiable. If parameters like (6) exist at UG, then strong claims are made about the possible degree of variability that will be found in the languages of the world: in languages where this kind of structural configuration is relevant (which may or may not be *all* languages), there will be essentially four NP types (12). Type (12a) is represented by English, French, etc. and type (12b) seems to be manifested in Basque, Burmese, Burushaski, Chibcha, Japanese, Kannada, and Turkish (see Greenberg 1966, n. 20). Types (12c) and (12d) are more problematic because I know of no carefully studied grammar which manifests them. Greenberg (1966) and Hawkins (1979) discuss several languages in which demonstratives follow the head noun and which therefore might be of type (12c) or (12d), but they do not distinguish between demonstratives which have the syntax of adjectives (as in Latin) and

those which manifest Spec (as in English). If it should turn out that types (12c)
and (12d) do not occur, then parameter (6a) will be tightened to allow only the
Spec-N'order.

(12) a. $_{NP}$[Spec $_{N'}$[nucleus satellite]]
      b. $_{NP}$[Spec $_{N'}$[satellite nucleus]]
      c. $_{NP}$[$_{N'}$[nucleus satellite] Spec]
      d. $_{NP}$[$_{N'}$[satellite nucleus] Spec]

Also, parameters like (6) suggest that one will find developmental stages
corresponding to the fixing by a child of the two parameters. Lightfoot (1982,
pp. 179f), building on work by Klima and Bellugi (1966) and Roeper (1979),
argues that this is indeed the case. Children seem to acquire noun phrase
structures in four identifiable stages. Examples (13a) and (13b) list some noun
phrases occurring in the first two stages.

(13) a.   car   b.   a coat   that Adam
          baby   a celery   more coffee
          wa-wa (water)   a Becky   two socks
          mama   a hands   big foot
          hands   my mommy

All children go through the four stages at some point, although the ages may vary.
Most children utter the stage 2 forms between one and two years. At stage 3
there is more sophistication.

(14)   mama   my doll   a blue flower
       cracker   your cracker   a nice cap
       doll   a your horse
       spoon   that a horse
                                        that a blue horse
                                        your blue cap

At stage 4 the mature system emerges, which normally remains more or less
constant for the rest of the child's lifetime. But consider (15), some forms that
never occur in children's speech.

(15)   *blue a flower   *a that blue flower   *flower a
          *nice a cup   *blue a that   *house that a
          *my a pencil   *that a
          *a that house   *a my
                               *my a

   Recall the parameters for noun phrases developed earlier. These were
hypotheses about how NP structure could vary from grammar to grammar. At
stage 1 these principles are irrelevant, because the child has only one-word
structures. Other cognitive capacities are relevant, such as the conceptual system
that involves properties and conditions of reference, knowledge and belief about
the world, conditions of appropriate use, and so on. These play a role in
explaining why *mama* and *cup* are more likely than *photosynthesis*, *quark* or *grammar*
to be among the earliest words in a child's speech.
   At stage 2 the child seems to have fixed the first parameter and determined that

the order is Spec N': all specifiers appear at the front of the noun phrase. The occurrence of phrases like *a Becky*, *a hands* suggests that children cannot distinguish at this stage definite and indefinite articles, and that they do not know that *a* is singular. There is no evidence that the child can distinguish subtypes of specifiers (articles, possessives, numerals, demonstratives), but they all occur one at a time in front of a noun.

By stage 3, children discriminate some kinds of specifiers and establish some more of the relative orders. In fact, the child knows that all specifiers precede adjectives, which in turn precede nouns, and that specifiers are optional, while the noun is obligatory. The stage 3 grammar differs from the mature system in that the child does not yet know that an article may not co-occur with a demonstrative or with a possessive like *your*. This suggests that the child now has the PS rules NP → Spec N', N' → (Adj) N, but that it takes a little longer to determine the status of a demonstrative and whether a form like *your* is a specifier or an adjective. After all, in other languages demonstratives and possessives are often adjectives instead of specifiers (for example, Italian *la sua machina*, 'his bicycle').

Consequently, there is reason to believe that postulating the parameters of (6) at UG is more plausible than claiming that the existence of N' is *learned* on the basis of exposure to sentences like (11b) uttered in the relevant context. But the important point is that alternatives like this need to be sketched and evaluated, and that grammarians should be paying more attention to their assumptions about the nature of the triggering experience required to set the parameters they hypothesize.

So I persist with the idea that the trigger is a subset of a child's experience, and that it probably does not include exotic events like the one sketched above in the context of (11b). The trigger consists only of robust data which can be analyzed consistent with genotypical principles and already fixed parameters of the child's grammar. The question remains of how small the subset is.

There is a theory, advanced by Snow (1977, etc.) and others, that the crucial input for language growth to take place is very small, a specially structured form of speech transmitted through mothers and caretakers. This "motherese" is supposed to provide a set of patterns which are generalized by children on an inductive basis. This view was held fairly widely for a while.

There are at least four reasons why this kind of pattern generalization is not the answer to how children acquire speech. First, although children no doubt register only part of their linguistic environment, there is no way of knowing quite what any individual child registers. Therefore factual basis is lacking for the claim that children register only what is filtered for them through parents' deliberately simplified speech. Children have access to more than this, including defective utterances. Second, even supposing that they register only perfectly well-formed expressions, that would not be enough to show that the child has a sufficient inductive base for language acquisition. Recall that the child's stimulus is "deficient" in three distinct ways (above); the motherese hypothesis would circumvent only the degeneracy problem (b) but leaves untouched problems (a) and the far more important (c), the absence of evidence in PLD for certain partial generalizations. The poverty of stimulus problems still hold and the child would need to know that the contractability of the first *is* in (8) could not be extended to the second *is*. One wants to know why quite ordinary inductive generalizations like this are in fact not made; the so-called motherese does not show where inductive generalizations must stop. Third, if the child registered only the simplified and well-formed sentences of motherese, the problem of language learning would be *more* difficult because the child's information would be more limited. Fourth, careful studies of parents' speech to children (like Newport et al. 1977) show that an unusually high proportion consists of questions and imperatives; simple declarative sentences are much rarer than in ordinary speech. This suggests that there is very little correlation between the way the child's language emerges and what parents do in their speech directed at children. Thus, the existence of motherese in no way eliminates the need for a genetic basis to language acquisition. The child is primarily responsible for the acquisition process, not parents or older playmates. (For good discussion of this topic, see Wexler and Culicover 1980, pp. 66–78).

Furthermore, while it is by no means clear exactly what this motherese consists of, the general phenomenon is not uniform and does not occur in all households or cultures. Even where motherese is not practised, children none the less attain a normal linguistic capacity. This suggests that the child's trigger experience does not need to be limited artificially along the lines of motherese.

Since the early 1970s grammarians have been seeking to develop locality restrictions, such that grammatical processes only affect elements which are not too far apart. This work suggests that in general grammatical processes affect only items which are clause-mates or where the item in a lower clause is, loosely, at the front of that clause. Locality restrictions are formulated somewhat differently at different stages of the development of UG and by different authors. The details of various locality restrictions need not concern us immediately, but they do raise the following question: if grammatical processes are generally limited to clause-mates or at most to items of which one is at the front of an embedded clause, why should children need to hear more than a single clause (plus the front of a lower clause) in order to hear the effects of all possible grammatical processes in their language? In fact, a good case can be made that everything can be learned essentially from unembedded material (degree-0 learnability); see Lightfoot 1989.

These are some of the issues which arise in the context of the development of language in an individual. The mature linguistic capacity emerges in a child as the environment sets the parameters which are prescribed genetically. For a normal capacity to emerge, the child needs access only to simple, robust expressions. There are several good reasons to view the growth of a child's linguistic capacity as a process whereby exposure to some linguistic environment sets certain parameters which are already available to the child independently of experience, presumably prescribed genetically in some fashion. This yields a system which enables the child to use and understand an infinite range of novel utterances, as is usual.

Taking this general perspective and adopting some specific ideas about the types of genetically prescribed parameters enables us to understand several aspects of the way in which languages tend to change over the course of time. They do not change in arbitrary ways. There are certain kinds of changes which occur frequently: so, languages often adopt new word orders and main clauses are the initial locus of such innovations; morphological endings are formed and erode, often with syntactic consequences. There are also very specialized changes, like a change in the meaning of *like* from "cause pleasure for" to "derive pleasure from". I discuss this in Lightfoot 1988, where I show how this parameter-setting view of language acquisition explains the fact that languages are constantly changing gradually and in piecemeal fashion and that they may also undergo a more radical restructuring from time to time. A process of gradual, piecemeal change punctuated by periodic radical changes is reminiscent of "punctuated equilibrium" models of evolutionary change (see Gould 1978, etc.) and of discussions in the context of Catastrophe Theory. What is interesting about linguistic change of this type is that it requires a particular kind of explanatory model and the model of language development outlined here proves to be appropriate to describe what is observed in historical change.

NOTES

This paper is excerpted from a longer paper, Lightfoot 1988, and is based largely on material in my *The Language Lottery: Toward a Biology of Grammars* (Lightfoot 1982).

1 (2b) provides only one possible structure for a noun phrase consisting of a nucleus noun followed by a preposition phrase, whereas (2a) provides more than one structure: *student from NY* can (and must) have the structure $_{N'}[_{N'}[_{N}[student]]\ _{PP}[from NY]]$, while *student of physics* is $_{N'}[_{N}[student]\ _{PP}[of physics]]$. The process of interpreting the pronoun *one* refers to a preceding N'. *Student* is a N' in (4b), hence a referent for *one*, but not in (4a). In (5a) both *suit* and *old suit* are instances of N' and thus possible referents for *one*, hence the ambiguity. For details and the reasons why *student from NY* and *student of physics* must have different structures, see Lightfoot 1982.

2 Young children are known to have great difficulty in detecting for themselves the absence of forms, even when confronted with carefully prepared paradigmatic sets of patterns (Sainsbury 1971, 1973).

3 The notion of "markedness" has led to much confused discussion. UG includes a theory of markedness which leads one parameter setting to be preferred over another and permits "core grammar" to be extended to a marked periphery (Chomsky 1981, p. 8). So the unmarked parameter setting is adopted in the absence of contrary evidence, but specific evidence will be required for a marked setting.

4 Baker (1979) discusses a transformational movement rule relating *John gave the book to Alice* and *John gave Alice the book*, which does not generalize to *report* and *say*. The fact that the rule is not entirely general suggests that negative data are needed to establish the limits to the generalization. He went on to show that a lexical relationship is preferable to a movement analysis and circumvents the apparent learnability problem if children are conservative in establishing the lexical properties of verbs, generalizing only within narrowly prescribed limits. For further discussion, see Mazurkewich and White 1984, and Randall 1986.

5 Sentences like *Kirsten has* $_{NP}[a\ blue\ cup]$ and *Heidi has a red one* show that *one* must also refer to something smaller than an NP.

REFERENCES

Baker, C. L. (1978) *Introduction to Generative–Transformational Syntax*. Prentice Hall.

Baker, C. L. (1979) "Syntactic theory and the projection problem," *Linguistic Inquiry*, 10 (4): 533–81.

Berwick, R. C. (1985) *The Acquisition of Syntactic Knowledge*. MIT Press.

Changeux, J.-P. (1980) "Genetic determinism and epigenesis of the neuronal network: Is there a biological compromise between Chomsky and Piaget?" in M. Piatelli-Palmarini (ed.), *Language and Learning*. Routledge & Kegan Paul.

Changeux, J.-P. (1983) *L'homme neuronal*. Fayard.

Chomsky, N. (1965) *Aspects of the Theory of Syntax*. MIT Press.

Chomsky, N. (1981) *Lectures on Government and Binding*. Foris.

Gould, S. J. (1978) *Ever Since Darwin: Reflections in Natural History*. Deutsch.

Greenberg, J. H. (1966) "Some universals of grammar with particular reference to the order of meaningful elements," in J. H. Greenberg (ed.), *Universals of Language*, MIT Press.

Hawkins, J. A. (1979) "Implicational universals as predictors of word order change," *Language* 55 (3), 618–48.

Hornstein, N. and Lightfoot, D. W. (eds) (1981) *Explanation in Linguistics: The Logical Problem of Language Acquisition*. Longman.

Hyams, N. (1983) "The Pro-drop parameter in child grammars." *Proceedings of the West Coast Conference on Formal Linguistics*.

Jerne, N. K. (1967) "Antibodies and learning: Selection versus instruction," in G. C. Quarton, T. Melnechuk and F. O. Schmitt (eds), *The Neurosciences: A Study Program*. Rockefeller University Press.

Jerne, N. K. (1985) "The generative grammar of the immune system," *Science*, 229, 13 September: 1057–9.

Klima, E. and Bellugi, U. (1966) "Syntactic regularities in the speech of children," in J. Lyons and R. Wales (eds), *Psycholinguistic Papers*. Edinburgh University Press.

Lightfoot, D. W. (1982) *The Language Lottery: Toward a Biology of Grammars*. MIT Press.

Lightfoot, D. W. (1988) "Modelling language change: Ontogenetic and phylogenetic," in J. Casti and A. Karlqvist (eds), *From Aristotle to Newton*, Birkhauser.

Lightfoot, D. W. (1989) "The child's trigger experience: Degree-0 learnability." *Behavioral and Brain Sciences* 12(2), 321–34.

McNeill, D. (1966) "Developmental linguistics," in F. Smith and G. A. Miller (eds), *The Genesis of Language: A Psycholinguistic Approach*. MIT Press.

Matthei, E. (1981) "Children's interpretation of sentences containing reciprocals," in S. L. Tavakolian (ed.), *Language Acquisition and Linguistic Theory*. MIT Press.

Mazurkewich, I. and White, L. (1984) "The acquisition of the dative alternation: Unlearning overgeneralizations," *Cognition*, 16 (3): 261–83.

Monod, J. (1972) *Chance and Necessity*. Collins.

Newport, E. C., Gleitman, H. and Gleitman, L. (1977) "'Mother, I'd rather do it myself': Some effects and non-effects of maternal speech style," in Snow and Ferguson 1977.

Piattelli-Palmarini, M. (1986) "The rise of selective theories: A case study and some lessons from immunology," in W. Demopoulos and A. Marras (eds), *Language Learning and Concept Acquisition*. Ablex.

Randall, J. (1986) "Retreat routes." Paper presented to the Boston University Conference on Language Development.

Rizzi, L. (1982) "Comments on Chomsky's 'On the representation of form and function'." in J. Mehler, E. C. T. Walker and M. Garrett (eds), *Perspectives on Mental Representation*. Lawrence Erlbaum.

Roeper, T. (1979) "Children's syntax." University of Massachusetts, Amherst.

Sainsbury, R. (1971) "The 'Feature Positive Effect' and simultaneous discrimination learning," *Journal of Experimental Child Psychology* 11: 347–56.

Sainsbury, R. (1973) "Discrimination learning utilizing positive or negative cues," *Canadian Journal of Psychology* 27 (1): 46–57.

Snow, C. (1977) "Mothers' speech research: From input to interaction," in C. E. Snow and C. A. Ferguson (eds) 1977.

Snow, C. and Ferguson C. A. (eds) (1977) *Talking to Children: Language Input and Acquisition.* Cambridge University Press.

Wells, G. (1981) *Learning through Interaction: The Study of Language Development.* Cambridge University Press.

Wexler, K. and Culicover, P. W. (1980) *Formal Principles of Language Acquisition.* MIT Press.

21

The Prospects for Artificial Intelligence

Understanding Natural Language

JOHN HAUGELAND

The trouble with Artificial Intelligence is that computers don't give a damn – or so I will argue by considering the special case of understanding natural language. Linguistic facility is an appropriate trial for AI because input and output can be handled conveniently with a teletype, because understanding a text requires understanding its topic (which is unrestricted), and because there is the following test for success: does the text enable the candidate to answer those questions it would enable competent people to answer? The thesis will not be that (human-like) intelligence cannot be achieved artificially, but that there are identifiable conditions on achieving it. The point is as much about language and understanding as about Artificial Intelligence. I will express it by distinguishing four *different* phenomena that can be called "holism": that is, four ways in which brief segments of text cannot be understood "in isolation" or "on a one-by-one basis."

I Holism of intentional interpretation

Consider how one might *empirically* defend the claim that a given (strange) object plays chess. Clearly, it is neither necessary nor sufficient that the object use any familiar chess notation (or pieces); for it might play brilliant chess in some alien notation, or it might produce "chess salad" in what appeared to be standard notation. Rather, what the defense must do is, roughly:

1 give systematic criteria for (physically) identifying the object's inputs and outputs;
2 provide a systematic way of interpreting them as various moves (such as a

"Understanding Natural Language" by J. Haugeland first appeared in *Journal of Philosophy* 76 (1979), pp. 619–32 and is reprinted here by kind permission.

manual for translating them into standard notation); and then
3　let some skeptics play chess with it.

The third condition bears all the empirical weight, for satisfying it amounts to public *observation* that the object really does play chess. More specifically, the skeptics see that, as interpreted, it makes a sensible (legal and plausible) move in each position it faces. And eventually, induction convinces them that it would do so in any position. Notice that, *de facto*, the object is also being construed as "remembering" (or "knowing") the current position, "trying" to make good moves, "realizing" that rooks outrank pawns, and even "wanting" to win. All these interpretations and construals constitute collectively an *intentional interpretation*.

Intentional interpretation is intrinsically holistic. It is supported empirically only by observing that its object makes generally "sensible" outputs, given the circumstances. But the relevant circumstances are fixed by the object's prior inputs and other outputs, *as interpreted*. Thus, each observation distributes its support over a whole range of specific interpretations, no one of which is supported apart from the others. For example, a chess move is legal and plausible only relative to the board position, which is itself just the result of the previous moves. So one output can be construed sensibly as a certain queen move, only if that other was a certain knight move, still another a certain bishop move, and so on.[1]

This is the *holism of intentional interpretation*; and it is all too familiar to philosophers. Intentional interpretation is tantamount to Quine's "radical translation" – including, as Davidson emphasizes, the attribution of beliefs and desires. The condition that outputs be "sensible" (in the light of prior inputs and other outputs) is just whatever the ill-named "principle of charity" is supposed to capture. I have reviewed it here only to distinguish it from what follows.

II　Common-sense holism

Years ago, Yehoshua Bar-Hillel pointed out that disambiguating "The box was in the pen" requires common-sense knowledge about boxes and pens. He had in mind knowledge of typical sizes, which would ordinarily decide between the alternatives 'playpen' and 'fountain pen'.[2] In a similar vein, it takes common sense to determine the antecedent of the pronoun in: "I left my raincoat in the bathtub, because it was still wet." More subtly, common sense informs our appreciation of the final verb of: "Though her blouse draped stylishly, her pants seemed painted on."

Straightforward questioning immediately exposes any misunderstanding: Was the bathtub wet? Was there paint on her pants? And the issue isn't just academic; a system designed to translate natural languages must be able to answer such questions. For instance, the correct and incorrect readings of our three examples have different translations in both French and German – so the system has to choose. What's so daunting about this, from the designer's point of view, is that one never knows which little fact is going to be relevant next – which common-sense tidbit will make the next disambiguation "obvious." In effect, the whole of common sense is potentially relevant at any point. This feature of natural-language understanding I call *common-sense holism*; its scope and importance was first fully demonstrated in Artificial Intelligence work.

The difference between common-sense holism and the holism of intentional interpretation is easily obscured by vague formulas like: the meaning of an utterance is determinate only relative to *all* the utterer's beliefs, desires, and speech dispositions. This covers both holisms, but only at the price of covering up a crucial distinction. The holism of intentional interpretation is *prior* holism, in the sense that it's already accommodated *before* the interpretation of ongoing discourse. An interpreter *first* finds an overall scheme that "works" and *then* can interpret each new utterance separately as it comes. For example, once a holistic chess-player interpretation has been worked out, its holism can be ignored – moves can perfectly well be translated "in isolation."[3] By contrast, common-sense holism is *real-time* holism – it is freshly relevant to each new sentence, and it can never be ignored. Even if a perfect dictionary and grammar were available, sentences like our three examples would still have to be disambiguated "in real time," by some appeal to common sense.

The point can be put another way. Prior holism is compatible with the (Fregean) ideal of semantic atomism: the meaning of a sentence is determined by the meanings of its meaningful components, plus their mode of composition. This ideal is (nearly) achieved by chess notations, formal logics, and most programming languages; but it is only grossly approximated by English – assuming that "meaning" is what one "grasps" in understanding a sentence, and that words and idioms are the meaningful components.[4] Real-time holism is precisely *in*compatible with semantic atomism: understanding a sentence requires *more* than a grammar and a dictionary – namely, common sense.[5]

The nature of common-sense holism is brought into sharper relief by current efforts to deal with it – those in Artificial Intelligence being the most concentrated and sophisticated. The hard problem, it turns out, is not simply the enormous volume of common knowledge, but rather storing it so that it can be efficiently accessed and used. Obviously, it is quite impractical to check every available fact for possible relevance, every time some question comes up. So the task to design a system that will quickly home in on genuinely relevant considerations, while ignoring nearly everything else. This is the "memory organization" or "knowledge representation" problem; what makes it hard is the quixotic way that odd little "facts" turn up as germane.

Most contemporary systems employ some variant of the following idea: facts pertaining to the same subject are stored together ("linked") in structured clusters, which are themselves linked in larger structures, according as their subjects are related.[6]

We can think of these clusters as "concepts," so long as we remember that they are much more elaborate and rich than traditional definitions – even "contextual" definitions. For example, the concept for 'monkey' would include not only that they are primates of a certain sort, but also a lot of "incidental" information like where they come from, what they eat, how organ grinders used them, and what the big one at the zoo throws at spectators. It's more like an encyclopedia than a dictionary entry.

Three points will clarify how this is supposed to work. First, much of the specification of each concept lies in its explicit links or "cross references" to other concepts, in an overall conceptual superstructure. For instance, part of the monkey concept would be an "is-a" link to the primate concept, which has in turn an "is-a" link to the mammal concept, and so on. So, the monkey, rat, and cow concepts can effectively "share" generic information about mammals. Second, entries in a concept can have modalities, like "necessarily," "typically," "occasionally," or even "only when . . ." The "typically" mode is particularly useful, because it supplies many common-sense "assumptions" or "default assignments." Thus, if monkeys typically like bananas, the system can "assume" that any given monkey will like bananas (pending information to the contrary). Third, concepts often have "spaces" or "open slots" waiting (or demanding) to be "filled up" in stipulated ways. For example, the concept of eating would have spaces for the eater and the eaten, it being stipulated that the eater be animate, and the eaten (typically) be food.

A system based on such concepts copes with common-sense holism as follows. First, a dictionary routine calls the various concepts associated with the words in a given sentence, subject to constraints provided by a syntactical analyzer. Hence, only the information coded in (or closely linked to) these concepts is actually accessed – passing over the presumably irrelevant bulk. Then the system applies this information to any ambiguities by looking for a combination of concepts (from the supplied pool) which fit each other's open spaces in all the stipulated ways. So, for Bar-Hillel's example, the system might call four concepts: one each for 'box' and 'is in', and two for 'pen'. The "is in" concept would have two spaces, with the stipulation that what fills the first be smaller than what fills the second. Alerted by this requirement, the system promptly checks the "typical size" information under the other concepts, and correctly eliminates 'fountain pen'. An essentially similar procedure will disambiguate the pronouns in sentences like: "The monkeys ate the bananas because they were hungry" or " . . . because they were ripe" (cf. Wilks, ibid., p. 19).

The other two example, however, are tougher. Both raincoats and bathtubs typically get wet, so *that* won't decide which was wet when I left my coat in the tub. People opt for the coat, because being wet is an understandable (if eccentric) reason for leaving a coat in a tub, whereas the tub's being wet would be no (sane) reason to leave a coat in it. But where is *this* information to be coded? It hardly seems that concepts for 'raincoat', 'bathtub', or 'is wet', no matter how "encyclopedic," would indicate when it's sensible to put a raincoat in a bathtub. This suggests that common sense can be organized only partially according to subject matter. Much of what we recognize as "making sense" is not "about" some topic for which we have a word or idiom, but rather about some (possibly unique) circumstance or episode, which a longer fragment leads us to "visualize." Introspectively, it seems that we imagine ourselves into the case, and then decide from within it what's plausible. Of course, *how* this is done is just the problem.

The ambiguity of 'painted-on pants' is both similar and different. Again, we "imagine" the sort of attire being described; but the correct reading is obviously a metaphor – for 'skin tight', which is both coordinated and appropriately contrasted with the stylishly draped blouse. Most approaches to metaphor, however, assume that metaphorical readings aren't attempted unless there is something "anomalous" about the "literal" reading (as in "He is the cream on my peaches," or ". . . faster than greased lightning"). But, in this case there is nothing anomalous about pants with paint on them – they would even clash with "stylish," explaining the conjunction "Though . . ." On that reading, however, the sentence would be silly, whereas the metaphor is so apt that most people don't even notice the alternative.

These examples are meant only to illustrate the subtlety of common sense. They show that no obvious or crude representation will capture it, and suggest that a sophisticated, cross-referenced "encyclopedia" may not suffice either. On the other hand, they don't reveal much about what's "left out," nor (by the same token) whether that will be programmable when we know what it is. The real nature of common sense is still a wide-open question.

III Situation holism

Correct understanding of a sentence depends not only on general common sense, but also on understanding the specific situation(s) to which it pertains. I don't have in mind the familiar point about descriptions and indexicals, that only the "context" determines *which* table is "the table . . ." or "this table . . .," and so on. Much more interesting is the situation-dependence of examples like Bar-Hillel's; Dreyfus (ibid.) points out

> in spite of our *general* knowledge about the relative sizes of pens and boxes, we might interpret "The box is in the pen," when whispered in a James Bond movie, as meaning just the opposite of what it means at home or on the farm. (p. 216)

This is not just a problem about "exotic" contexts, where normal expectations might fail; both of the following are "normal":

> When Daddy came home, the boys stopped their cowboy game. They put away their guns and ran out back to the car.

> When the police drove up, the boys called off their robbery attempt. They put away their guns and ran out back to the car.

The second sentence is not exactly ambiguous, but it means different things in the two situations. Did they, for instance, put their guns "away" in a toy chest or in their pockets? (It makes a difference in German: *einräumen* or *einstecken*.) Could 'ran' be paraphrased by 'fled'?

So far, the role of "situation sense" seems comparable to that of common sense, though more local and specific. A fundamental difference appears, however, as soon as the stories get interesting enough to involve an interplay of several situations. A Middle-Eastern folk tale gives a brief example:

> One evening, Khoja looked down into a well, and was startled to find the moon shining up at him. It won't help anyone down there, he thought, and he quickly fetched a hook on a rope. But when he threw it in, the hook snagged on a hidden rock. Khoja pulled and pulled and pulled. Then suddenly it broke loose, and he went right on his back with a thump. From where he lay, however, he could see the moon, finally back where it belonged – and he was proud of the good job he had done.

The heart of this story is a trade-off between two situations: the real one and the one in Khoja's imagination. The narrative jumps back and forth between them; and it is up to the reader to keep them straight, and also to keep track of their interaction and development.

In the first sentence, for example, the embedded clauses "Khoja found the moon" and "it shined up at him," are clearly about the epistemic situation, despite their grammar. One must understand this at the outset, to appreciate Khoja's progressive misperceptions, and thus his eventual pride. A trickier shift occurs in the clause "It won't help anyone down there . . .,' which must mean "*if it stays* down there" (not: "anyone *who is* down there"). In other words, it's an implicit hypothetical which refers us to yet another situation: a counterfactual one in which people are left in darkness while the moon is still in the well. This too is essential to understanding the pride.[7]

The important point is how little of this is explicit in the text: the clauses as written exhibit what can be called "situational ambiguity." It's as if situations were "modalizers" for the expressed clauses, generating "mini-possible-worlds" and implicit propositional operators. I'm not seriously proposing a model theory (though, of course, this has been done for counterfactuals, deontic modalities, and epistemic states) but only suggesting what may be a helpful analogy. Thus the clause "Khoja found the moon" would have not only the modality "Khoja thought that . . ." but also the modality "while looking into the well . . ." The latter is a crucial modalization, for it (along with common sense) is what forces the former.

Given this way of putting it, two things stand out. First, rather than a fixed, lexically specified set of possible modalities, there are indefinitely many of them, more or less like sentences (or indeed, whole passages). Second, many of these have to be supplied (or inferred) by the reader – often, as in the last example, on the basis of others already supplied. That is, to understand the text, the reader must provide for each clause a number of these generalized or "situational" modalities, and must do so largely on the basis of some overall situational or modal coherence. This demand for overall coherence – that all the various "situations" (with respect to which clauses are understood) should fit together in an intelligible way – is what I call *situation holism*. It is a general feature of natural-language text, and coping with it is prerequisite to reading.

Situation holism is especially characteristic of longer texts. We had a brief sample in our folk tale; but it really comes into its own in the forms of dialectic, characterization, and plot. Mystery novels, for example, are built around the challenge of situation holism when pivotal cues are deliberately scattered and ambiguous. Translators (who read the book first, naturally) must be very sensitive to such matters – to use 'ran' or 'flew' instead of 'fled', for instance – on pain of spoiling the suspense. But only the overall plot determines just which words need to be handled carefully, not to mention how to handle them. Engrossed readers, of course, are alert to the same issues in a complementary way. This is situation holism, full-fledged.[8]

IV   Digression: Hermeneutics

Hermeneutics, in the classical (nineteenth-century) sense, is the "science" of textual interpretation – that is, exegesis. It is often described as "holistic," on something like the following grounds: the meanings of particular passages, doctrines, and specialized ("technical") terms, are only apparent in the context of the whole; yet the whole (treatise, life's work, or genre) is composed entirely of particular passages, containing the various doctrines and special terms. So the interpreter must work back and forth among part, subpart, and whole, bootstrapping each insight on one level into new insights on the others, until a satisfactory overall understanding is achieved.

Hermeneutics is like intentional interpretation, in so far as the point is to translate baffling expressions into others more familiar or more intelligible. And the constraint on adequacy is again that the text, as construed, make a maximum of sense, But in exegesis, "sensibleness" is not so easy to determine as it is, say, in translating chess notations. For each sentence will have various presuppositions or "facts" taken for granted and will make sense only in the light of these. Part of the interpreter's task, in determining what the text means, is to ferret such assumptions out and make them explicit. So hermeneutic interpretation must deal explicitly with common-sense holism (though it may be "common" only to the initiated few). But the paramount concern in formal exegesis is exposing the overall structure and purport of the original. A construal cannot stand unless it renders sensible the progression and development of arguments, examples, incidents, and the like. But this is just situation holism, made more articulate. Thus, I don't think the holism of classical hermeneutics is different from the three kinds so far discussed, but is instead a sophisticated combination of them all.[9]

V Existential holism

In the section on intentional interpretation, we noticed how naturally we construe chess-playing computers as "trying" to make good moves, and "wanting" to win. At the same time, however, I think we *also* all feel that the machines don't "really care" whether they win, or how they play – that somehow the game doesn't "matter" to them. What's behind these conflicting intuitions? It may seem at first that what machines lack is a "reason" to win: some larger goal that winning would subserve. But this only puts off the problem; for we then ask whether they "really care" about the larger goal. And until this question is answered, nothing has been; just as we now don't suppose pawns "matter" to computers, even though they subserve the larger goal of winning.

Apparently something else must be involved to make the whole hierarchy of goals worth while – something that itself doesn't need a reason, but, so to speak, "matters for its own sake." We get a hint of what this might be, by asking why chess games matter to people (when they do). There are many variations, of course, but here are some typical reasons:

1   public recognition and esteem, which generates and supports self-esteem (compare the loser's embarrassment or loss of face);
2   pride and self-respect at some difficult achievement – like finally earning a

"master" rating (compare the loser's frustration and self-disappointment); or

3 proving one's prowess or (as it were) "masculinity" (compare the loser's self-doubt and fear of inadequacy).

What these have in common is that the player's self-image or sense of identity is at stake. This concern with "who one is" constitutes at least one issue that "matters for its own sake." Machines (at present) lack any personality and, hence, any possibility of personal involvement; so (on these grounds) nothing can really matter to them.[10]

The point is more consequential for language understanding than for formal activities like chess playing, which are largely separable from the rest of life. A friend of mine tells a story about the time she kept a white rat as a pet. It was usually tame enough to follow at her heels around the campus; but one day, frightened by a dog, it ran so far up her pantleg that any movement might have crushed it. So, very sheepishly, she let down her jeans, pulled out her quivering rodent, and won a round of applause from delighted passers-by. Now, most people find this anecdote amusing, and the relevant question is: Why? Much of it, surely, is that we identify with the young heroine and share in her embarrassment – being relieved, at the same time, that it didn't happen to us.

Embarrassment, however, (and relief) can be experienced only by a being that has some sense of itself – a sense that is important to it and can be awkwardly compromised on occasion. Hence, only such a being could, as we do, find this story amusing. It might be argued, however, that "emotional" reactions, like embarrassment and bemusement, should be sharply distinguished from purely "cognitive" understanding. Nobody, after all, expects a mechanical chess player to *like* the game or to be thrilled by it. But that distinction cannot be maintained for users of natural language. Translators, for instance, must choose words carefully to retain the character of an amusing original. To take just one example from the preceding story. German has several "equivalents" for 'sheepish', with connotations, respectively, of being simple, stupid, or bashful. Only by appreciating the embarrassing nature of the incident, could a translator make the right choice.

A different perspective is illustrated by the time Ralph asked his new friend, Lucifer: "Why, when you're so brilliant, beautiful, and everything, did you ever get kicked out of heaven?" Rather than answer right away, Lucifer suggested a little game: "I'll sit up here on this rock," he said, "and you just carry on with all that wonderful praise you were giving me." Well, Ralph went along, but as the hours passed, it began to get boring; so, finally, he said: "Look, why don't we add some variety to this game, say, by taking turns?" "Ahh," Lucifer sighed, "that's all I said, that's all I said."

Here, even more than Ralph's embarrassment, we enjoy the adroit way that Lucifer turns the crime of the ages into a little *faux pas*, blown out of proportion by God's infinite vanity. But why is that funny? Part of it has to be that we all know what guilt and shame are like, and how we try to escape them with impossible rationalizations – this being a grand case on both counts. It's not the *psychology* of guilt that we "know," but the tension of actually *facing* it and (sometimes) trying not to face it. And actually "feeling" guilty is certainly not just a cognitive state, like believing you did wrong, and disapproving; nor is it that, with some unpleasant sensation added on. It is at least to sense oneself as diminished by one's act – to be reduced in worth or exposed as less worthy than had seemed.

Crime and Punishment, too, is "about" guilt, but it isn't especially funny. The novel is powerful and didactic: the reader's experience of guilt is not simply drawn upon, but engaged and challenged. We enter into Raskolnikov's (and Dostoyevsky's) struggle with the very natures of guilt, personal responsibility, and freedom – and in so doing, we grow as persons. This response, too, is a kind of understanding, and asking questions is a fairly effective test for it. Moreover, at least some of those questions will have to be answered in the course of producing an adequate translation.

One final example will demonstrate the range of the phenomenon I'm pointing at, and also illustrate a different way in which the reader's personal involvement can be essential. It is a fable of Aesop's.

> One day, a farmer's son accidentally stepped on a snake, and was fatally bitten. Enraged, the father chased the snake with an axe, and managed to cut off its tail. Whereupon, the snake nearly ruined the farm by biting all the animals. Well, the farmer thought it over, and finally took the snake some sweetmeats, and said: "I can understand your anger, and surely you can understand mine. But now that we are even, let's forget and be friends again." "No, no," said the snake, "take away your gifts. You can never forget your dead son, nor I my missing tail."

Obviously, this story has a "moral," which a reader must "get" in order to understand it.

The problem is not simply to make the moral explicit, for then it would be more direct and effective to substitute a non-allegorical paraphrase:

> A child is like a part of oneself, such as a limb. The similarities include:
> (i) losing one is very bad;
> (ii) if you lose one, you can never get it back;
> (iii) they have no adequate substitutes; and thus
> (iv) they are literally priceless.
>   Therefore, to regard trading losses of them as a "fair exchange," or "getting even," is to be a fool.

But this is just a list of platitudes. It's not that it misrepresents the moral, but that it lacks it altogether – it is utterly flat and lifeless. By comparison, Aesop's version "lives," because we as readers identify with the farmer. Hence, we too are brought up short by the serpent's rebuke, and that makes us look at ourselves.

The terrifying thing about losing, say, one's legs is not the event itself, or the pain, but rather the thought of *being* a legless cripple for all the rest of one's life. It's the same with losing a son, right? Wrong! Many a parent indeed would joyously give both legs to have back a little girl or boy who is gone. Children can well mean more to who one is than even one's own limbs. So who are you, and what is your life? The folly – what the fable is really "about" – is not knowing.[11]

A single event cannot be embarrassing, shameful, irresponsible, or foolish in isolation, but only as an act in the biography of a whole, historical individual – a person whose personality it reflects and whose self-image it threatens. Only a being that cares about who it is, as some sort of enduring whole, can care about guilt or folly, self-respect or achievement, life or death. And only such a being can read. This holism, now not even apparently in the text, but manifestly in the reader, I call (with all due trepidation) *existential holism*. It is essential, I submit, to understanding the meaning of any text that (in a familiar sense) *has* any meaning. If situation holism is the foundation of plot, existential holism is the foundation of literature.

In the context of Artificial Intelligence, however, there remains an important question of whether this sets the standard too high – whether it falls into what Papert somewhere calls "the human/superhuman fallacy," or Dennett "the Einstein–Shakespeare gambit." Wouldn't it be impressive enough, the reasoning goes, if a machine could understand everyday English, even if it couldn't appreciate literature? Sure, it would be impressive; but beyond that there are three replies. First, if we could articulate some ceiling of "ordinariness" beyond which machines can't pass or can't pass unless they meet some further special condition, that would be very interesting and valuable indeed. Second, millions of people can read – really read – and for most of the others it's presumably a socio-historical tragedy that they can't. Existential holism is not a condition just on creative genius. Finally, and *most important*, there is no reason whatsoever to believe there is a difference in kind between understanding "everyday English" and appreciating literature. Apart from a few highly restricted domains, like playing chess, analyzing mass spectra, or making airline reservations, the most ordinary conversations are fraught with life and all its meanings.

VI

Considering the progress and prospects of Artificial Intelligence can be a peculiarly concrete and powerful way of thinking about our own spiritual nature. As such, it is a comrade of the philosophy of mind (some authors see AI as allied to epistemology, which strikes me as perverse). Here, we have distinguished four phenomena, each with a claim to the title 'holism' – not to trade on or enhance any mystery in the term, but rather, I would hope, the opposite. The aim has not been to show that Artificial Intelligence is impossible (though it is, you know) but to clarify some of what its achievement would involve, in the specific area of language understanding. This area is not so limited as it seems, since – as each of the four holisms testifies – understanding a text involves understanding what the text is "about." The holisms, as presented, increase in difficulty relative to current AI techniques; and my own inclination (it's hardly more than that) is to regard the last, existential holism, as the most fundamental of the four. Hence my opening remark: the trouble with Artificial Intelligence is that computers don't give a damn.

NOTES

1   A different argument for a similar conclusion depends on assuming that the inputs and outputs are semantically compound. Then, since each compound will in general share components with many others, their respective interpretations (in terms of their compositions) will be interdependent. Thus the (semantic) role of 'P' in 'P–K4' must be systematically

related to its role in 'P–R3', and so on. The argument in the text, however, is more fundamental. There are fewer than two thousand possible chess moves. (Martin Gardner, in his June 1979 *Scientific American* column, gives the figure 1840; but he neglects castling and pawn promotion (see pp. 25–6.) These could be represented unambiguously by arbitrary numbers, or even simple symbols; yet interpreting an object using such a system would still be holistic, for the earlier reasons.

2 "The present status of automatic translation of languages," in F. L. Alt (ed.), *Advances in Computers* (New York: Academic Press, 1964), vol. I, pp. 158–9. Quoted in H. L. Dreyfus, *What Computers Can't Do*, 2nd edn (New York: Harper & Row, 1979), p. 215.

3 Cryptography is comparable: code cracking is holistic, but once it succeeds, deciphering goes along on a message-by-message basis.

4 Hilary Putnam argues that there is more to meaning than what competent speakers understand, but his point is orthogonal to ours ("The meaning of 'meaning'," in *Mind, Language and Reality* (New York: Cambridge, 1975)).

5 It is difficult to say what significance this has (if any) for formal semantics. The most common tactic is to relegate matters of real-time holism to "pragmatics," and apply the semantic theory itself only to idealized "deep structures" (in which ambiguities of sense, pronoun binding, case, mood, scope, etc. are not allowed – thus saving atomism (perhaps)). A protective quarantine for semantics may or may not work out, but earlier experience with syntax hardly bodes well.

6 See, for example, Marvin Minsky, "A framework for representing knowledge," in Patrick Winston (ed.), *The Psychology of Computer Vision* (New York: McGraw-Hill, 1975); Yorick Wilks, "Natural language understanding systems within the AI paradigm," Stanford AI Memo-237, 1974; Roger Schank and Robert Abelson, "Scripts, plans, and knowledge," *International Joint Conference on Artificial Intelligence*, IV (1975); Daniel Bobrow and Terry Winograd, "An overview of KRL, a Knowledge Representation Language," *Cognitive Science*, 1 (1) (1977).

7 There are also a number of "background counterfactuals" involved in understanding what happens. Thus, a reader should be able to say what would have happened if the hook hadn't caught on the rock, or if it hadn't broken loose. Anyone who couldn't answer, wouldn't really "have" it.

8 In AI, work on this problem has only just begun. See, e.g., David Rumelhart, "Notes on a schema for stories," in Bobrow and Allan Collins (eds), *Representation and Understanding* (New York: Academic Press, 1975); Bob Wilensky, "Why John married Mary: Understanding stories involving recurring goals," *Cognitive Science*, 2 (1978): 235–66; and Robert de Beaugrande and Benjamin Colby, "Narrative models of action and interaction," *Cognitive Science*, 3 (1979): 43–66. Compare also David Lewis, "Scorekeeping in a language game," *Journal of Philosophical Logic* 8 (1979), 339–59.

9 It can be argued (though not here) that genuine radical translation is less like the interpretation of a chess player than like a hermeneutic investigation of a whole culture – including (so far as possible) an "interpretation" of its practices, institutions, and artifacts. For a good account of what hermeneutics has become in the twentieth century (very roughly, it adds my fourth holism), see Charles Taylor, "Interpretation and the sciences of Man," *Review of Metaphysics*, 25 (1) (September 1971): 3–51.

10 There are many problems in this vicinity. For instance, people (but not machines) play chess for *fun*; and, within limits, winning is more fun. It's very hard, however, to say what fun is, or get any grip on what it would be for a machine actually to *have* fun. One might try to connect it with the foregoing, and say (in a tired European tone of voice) that fun is merely a temporary diversion from the ever-oppressive burden of self-understanding. But that isn't very persuasive.

11 Rumelhart ("Notes on a schema for stories," ibid.) analyzes a different version of this story in terms of an interesting "story grammar," loosely analogous to sentential grammar. Significantly, however, he addresses only the continuity of the story and never touches on its moral or meaning.

Index

Index compiled by Meg Davies (Society of Indexers)